D0075918

IMPORTANT

HERE IS YOUR REGISTRATION CODE TO ACCESS MCGRAW-HILL PREMIUM CONTENT AND MCGRAW-HILL ONLINE RESOURCES

For key premium online resources you need THIS CODE to gain access. Once the code is entered, you will be able to use the web resources for the length of your course.

Access is provided only if you have purchased a new book.

If the registration code is missing from this book, the registration screen on our website, and within your WebCT or Blackboard course will tell you how to obtain your new code. Your registration code can be used only once to establish access. It is not transferable.

To gain access to these online resources

1. **USE** your web browser to go to: **www.mhhe.com/inciardi**

2. **CLICK** on "First Time User"

3. **ENTER** the Registration Code printed on the tear-off bookmark on the right

4. After you have entered your registration code, click on "Register"

5. **FOLLOW** the instructions to setup your personal UserID and Password

6. **WRITE** your UserID and Password down for future reference. Keep it in a safe place.

If your course is using WebCT or Blackboard, you'll be able to use this code to access the McGraw-Hill content within your instructor's online course.

To gain access to the McGraw-Hill content in your instructor's WebCT or Blackboard course simply log into the course with the user ID and Password provided by your instructor. Enter the registration code exactly as it appears to the right when prompted by the system. You will only need to use this code the first time you click on McGraw-Hill content.

These instructions are specifically for student access. Instructors are not required to register via the above instructions.

Thank you, and welcome to your McGraw-Hill Online Resources.

978-0-07-323083-2
0-07-323083-9 t/a
Inciardi
Criminal Justice, 8/e

CRIMINAL JUSTICE

CRIMINAL JUSTICE | Eighth Edition

James A. Inciardi
University of Delaware

Boston   Burr Ridge, IL   Dubuque, IA   Madison, WI   New York   San Francisco   St. Louis
Bangkok   Bogotá   Caracas   Kuala Lumpur   Lisbon   London   Madrid   Mexico City
Milan   Montreal   New Delhi   Santiago   Seoul   Singapore   Sydney   Taipei   Toronto

The McGraw·Hill Companies

Mc Graw Hill **Higher Education**

CRIMINAL JUSTICE
Published by McGraw-Hill, a business unit of The McGraw-Hill Companies, Inc., 1221 Avenue
of the Americas, New York, NY, 10020. Copyright © 2007, 2005, 2002 by The McGraw-Hill
Companies, Inc. All rights reserved. No part of this publication may be reproduced or distributed
in any form or by any means, or stored in a database or retrieval system, without the prior written
consent of The McGraw-Hill Companies, Inc., including, but not limited to, in any network or
other electronic storage or transmission, or broadcast for distance learning.

Some ancillaries, including electronic and print components, may not be available to customers
outside the United States.

This book is printed on acid-free paper.

2 3 4 5 6 7 8 9 0 DOW/DOW 0 9 8 7 6

ISBN: 0-07-312820-1
EAN: 9780073128207

Publisher: *Phillip A. Butcher*
Senior Sponsoring Editor: *Kevin Witt*
Development Editor: *Kate Scheinman*
Senior Marketing Manager: *Daniel M. Loch*
Senior Project Manager: *Christina Thornton-Villagomez*
Art Manager: *Robin Mouat*
Manager, Photo Research: *Brian J. Pecko*
Senior and Cover Designer: *Preston Thomas*
Media Project Manager: *Michele Borrelli*
Associate Media Producer: *Christie Ling*
Lead Production Supervisor: *Randy L. Hurst*
Permissions Coordinator: *Karyn Morrison*
Composition: *10/12 Adobe Caslon, by G&S Typesetters, Inc.*
Printing: *45 # New Mead Pub Plus, R. R. Donnelley/Willard, OH.*
Cover credit: Cover and top right photo: © *James Doberman/Getty Images/Iconica; man in handcuffs,*
   © *Royalty-Free/Corbis; gavel,* © *Thom Lang/Corbis; prison cell,* © *Royalty-Free/Corbis*

Credits: The credits section for this book begins on page 643 and is considered an extension of the
copyright page.

Library of Congress Cataloging-in-Publication Data
Inciardi, James A.
      Criminal justice / James A. Inciardi. — 8th ed.
         p.   cm.
      Includes bibliographical references and index.
      ISBN 0-07-312820-1 (alk. paper)
      EAN: 978-0-07-312820-7
      1. Criminal justice, Administration of—United States.   I. Title.
   HV9950.I52 2007
   364.973—dc22

                                        2005052229

The Internet addresses listed in the text were accurate at the time of publication. The inclusion of a
Web site does not indicate an endorsement by the authors of McGraw-Hill, and McGraw-Hill does
not guarantee the accuracy of the information presented at these sites.
www.mhhe.com

For Hilary

ABOUT THE AUTHOR

JAMES A. INCIARDI is the director of the Center for Drug and Alcohol Studies at the University of Delaware; a professor in the Department of Sociology and Criminal Justice at the University of Delaware; an adjunct professor in the Department of Epidemiology and Public Health at the University of Miami School of Medicine; a guest professor in the Department of Psychiatry at the Federal University of Rio Grande do Sul in Porto Alegre, Brazil; and a member of the Internal Advisory Committee of the White House Office of National Drug Control Policy.

Dr. Inciardi received his PhD in sociology at New York University and has a background in law enforcement, corrections, drug abuse treatment, and research. He began his career as a parole officer with the New York State Division of Parole, first as an institutional parole officer at New York's Green Haven Prison, followed by investigative and undercover work with New York State Parole's Bureau of Special Services, and finally as a field parole officer in a special narcotics project. After leaving the New York parole authority, he conducted street research in many cities across the United States. Although he joined the criminal justice faculty at the University of Delaware during the late 1970s, he has continued conducting research and lecturing in many parts of the world.

In addition to his role as a professor of criminal justice at the University of Delaware, Dr. Inciardi is the director of his university's Center for Drug and Alcohol Studies, a multinational research center with field offices in Delaware, Florida, the United States Virgin Islands, and Porto Alegre, Brazil. His current work includes developing and evaluating drug abuse treatment initiatives for drug-involved offenders; street-based drug studies in Miami, Florida; and HIV prevention research in South Florida, Latin America, and the Caribbean Basin. Finally, Dr. Inciardi is the author of more than 400 articles, chapters, and books in the areas of criminal justice, criminology, substance abuse, history, folklore, public policy, AIDS, medicine, and law.

CONTENTS IN BRIEF

CONTENTS

FEATURES

INTERNATIONAL PERSPECTIVES ON CRIME AND JUSTICE

GENDER PERSPECTIVES ON CRIME AND JUSTICE

VICTIMS AND JUSTICE

CAREERS IN CRIMINAL JUSTICE

LAW AND CRIMINAL JUSTICE

HISTORICAL PERSPECTIVES ON CRIMINAL JUSTICE

RESEARCH ON CRIME AND JUSTICE

DRUGS, CRIME, AND JUSTICE

SIDELIGHTS ON CRIMINAL MATTERS

PREFACE

Crime and justice are concepts and curiosities that have been a part of human history for so many millennia that their roots are buried in antiquity. Cicero spoke of crime and justice during the first century B.C., as did Aristotle and numerous others many years earlier. As such, "criminal justice" is likely as old as civilization. Yet, while the early Greek and Roman scholars studied the philosophy of justice and its application, criminal justice currently refers to the structure, functions, and decision-making processes of agencies that deal with the management and control of crime and criminal offenders—the police, the courts, and correctional systems.

As an independent academic activity, the study of criminal justice is comparatively new in the United States. The first degree-granting program appeared just over half a century ago, and in the 1950s fewer than 5,000 college students were focusing on the study of crime and justice. During the past few decades, however, this situation has changed dramatically. In the 1960s, interest in criminal justice education was spurred by the "war on crime" and the resulting massive federal funding for the upgrading of criminal justice personnel, agencies, technology, and programming. During the 1970s, 1980s, and 1990s, academic programs in criminal justice increased significantly in colleges and universities throughout the nation. Currently, criminal justice courses enroll well over 200,000 students annually, and the upward trend is expected to continue.

Although criminal justice is a relatively new course, the topics have been studied for centuries, making it an interdisciplinary branch of knowledge. From the perspective of legal studies, it examines aspects of criminal law and procedure; from political science, it takes elements of constitutional law and appellate court practice; and from the viewpoint of sociology, it examines the structures of certain social institutions and how they affect the administration of justice. Criminal justice also uses research from psychology, criminology, history, public administration, anthropology, economics, and many other disciplines. Yet, at the same time, criminal justice is often confused with the disciplines of criminology and police science. Criminology, however, focuses on the role of crime in organized society, the nature and causes of crime and criminal behavior, and the relationships between crime and social behavior. Police science concentrates on the pragmatic aspects of law enforcement and peacekeeping operations—the prevention and detection of crime, the apprehension of criminal offenders, the location of suspects and the preservation of evidence, the application of police resources, and the development of police–community relations.

As criminal justice education has evolved and expanded in recent decades, so too has research on the various processes of justice. This growth has resulted in a dramatic proliferation in the criminal justice literature as scholars, researchers, and administrators seek to disseminate their work. So great has been the demand for classroom materials that since the late 1970s publishers have responded with thousands of new textbooks, supplementary readings, manuals, anthologies, monographs, and reports. Several dozen new introductory criminal justice textbooks and revised editions appear every year.

It was within this context of rapid change that the first edition of *Criminal Justice* was published over two decades ago. For much of that time, *Criminal Justice* had a highly successful career, first with Academic Press and then with Harcourt Brace College Publishers. But with the demise of that branch of Harcourt, the seventh edition of *Criminal Justice* found itself in somewhat of a limbo position, until it finally found a home with McGraw-Hill, which published the seventh-edition update of the text in 2005.

This eighth edition of *Criminal Justice* is designed to keep instructors and students up to date with new statistics and major court decisions and, most importantly, with the many changes in the criminal justice system that have occurred in this post-9/11 period in American history. In addition, much of the new material and a number of the boxed exhibits from the seventh-edition update have been retained, while other exhibits have been updated and new ones have been added. For example:

- **Law and Criminal Justice** exhibits appear in 13 chapters and use a combination of current events and case law to shed light on the legal aspects of criminal justice. They highlight particular court decisions, criminal codes, and other legal and legislative matters related to the text material. Pertinent examples include the Bill of Rights, religion in prison, and the importance of the recent *Roper* v. *Simmons* decision by the United States Supreme Court.

- **Historical Perspectives on Criminal Justice** exhibits appear in 13 chapters and highlight some of the historical roots of contemporary procedures, as well as help students to understand how modern notions of criminal justice have evolved over time. Some examples include discussions of homicide rates in the late 19th century, Italy's elite Carabinieri, and the supermax prison known as the "Hellhole" of the Rockies.

- **Research on Crime and Justice** exhibits appear in seven chapters and explore how historical, legal, and behavioral research impacts the field of criminal justice. Topics include such things as the different types of killers, pharmaceutical diversion squads, and therapeutic communities in prisons. A number of these exhibits are based on my own research.

- **Victims and Justice** exhibits appear in eight chapters and address the importance of victims in criminal justice issues and procedures. Some examples include victim advocacy, the AMBER Alert, and the defense of necessity and the right to escape from prison.

- **Careers in Criminal Justice** exhibits appear in 17 chapters and describe the various professional roles available to students interested in criminal justice. They include discussions of the job requirements and duties of such traditional positions as police officers, FBI special agents, and probation and parole officers, as well as some of the less conventional, but equally important, positions in the criminal justice field including forensic psychologists and fingerprint and document examiners. Furthermore, the Chapter 1 exhibit sets the tone for all the rest by explaining what it means to study criminal justice and why students choose this major, and by sharing the diverse career paths my former students have taken.

A major new feature in this eighth edition of *Criminal Justice* is the nine exhibits called **A View from the Field.** The essays were written by me and some of my colleagues, who have direct experience working in the field, in order to share with students "the unexpected" (a meeting I had with cocaine kingpin Pablo Escober), the bizarre (my many visits to the Brooklyn, New York, Gothic horror, the Raymond Street Jail), and the perils (the time I got arrested in a Miami crack house) of the fascinating world of criminal justice.

Another new feature in this edition is the **Famous Criminals** sidebars that appear in the margins of each chapter. These brief biographical sketches and accompanying photos profile a range of eccentric characters, from the "Birdman of Alcatraz" and "Son of Sam" to the "Night Stalker" and LSD guru Timothy Leary.

Other new features include an extended section on some of the better-known theories of crime causation, incorporation of terrorism and white-collar crime discusssions into the text, and the Chapter 5 exhibit "An Overview of the Justice Process," redesigned as a pullout study aid.

Returning to this edition is **Critical Thinking in Criminal Justice.** The purpose of this feature, which appears at the end of every chapter, is to have students analyze the material presented, look for possible biases, and think about whether some of the things they see in media reports make sense or are contrary to logic. In Chapter 1 some suggestions for thinking critically are presented, and in later chapters a variety of areas for critical thinking are examined.

Also returning is the extensive marginalia program that augments the text. These items include charts, graphs, quotes, and anecdotes that present current data and issues and will provoke different ways of seeing the topics. Also returning are the exhibits focusing on gender issues and criminal justice, drugs and the criminal justice system, and international perspectives. These boxed items have been especially popular among students, primarily because of their relevance and content. For example:

- **International Perspectives on Crime and Justice** exhibits, which appear in 10 chapters, offer compelling examples of crime trends and criminal justice concepts and procedures as they are applied in other nations and cultures. These provocative essays and photographs invite students to think critically about our own culture and its approach to the management of crime and the administration of justice. Some examples include marital rights in the Muslim world, honor killings as a cultural tradition, HIV/AIDS among prisoners around the world, and the growing population of Russian street children.
- **Gender Perspectives on Crime and Justice** exhibits, which appear in nine chapters, discuss issues related to both women and men in various roles throughout the criminal justice system. Some examples include warrantless vaginal cavity searches, rape shield laws, and the use of postpartum depression as the basis of a legal defense.
- **Drugs, Crime, and Justice** exhibits, which appear in seven chapters, examine the changing fads and fashions in the American drug scene and how the "war on drugs" has had major impacts on criminal justice processing. Some examples include the "Supreme Court, Bostick, and the War on Drugs"; the drug courts movement; and the answer to the question everyone wants to know: "How long for a clean urine?"

The end-of-chapter materials offer opportunities for study and review. The *Op-Ed* feature revisits the chapter opening story and asks the reader to reflect on this current issue in light of the chapter information. The chapter *Summary* gives students a quick review of the basic principles of the chapter and allows them to focus on understanding one point at a time. *Key Terms* help with the study of vocabulary and concepts presented in the chapter. These terms are shown in **boldface** where they are defined in the chapter. *Issues for Discussion* encourage students to think critically about the chapter and will help them study for exams. *Media Resources* include listings of Web sites, articles, and/or books where students can find additional information on the subject matter covered in the text.

| Supplements for Students and Instructors |
For the Student

- *Online Learning Center Web Site*—This innovative, text-specific Web site features a free comprehensive Interactive Study Guide including chapter outlines, chapter sumaries, chapter quizzes with feedback and instructor reporting, plus Power-Web—password-protected online access to articles from the popular and scholarly press, weekly updates, daily newsfeeds, and a search engine. This Web site also includes critical-thinking exercises, media observations, links to criminal justice sites, and much more. Visit our Web site at **www.mhhe.com/inciardi8**.
- *Reel Justice CD-ROM*—Available on request at nominal cost in a special, optional package with the Inciardi text, this unique, interactive movie takes the concept of active learning to a new level. Students take on the role of a police officer investigating a domestic violence incident that takes place in a college town and influence key plot turns by making choices for the police officer. Text screens explain key criminal justice concepts and guide student decision making. Movie segments are augmented by a robust array of review and assessment features. With this breakthrough learning tool, students can explore a wide variety of criminal justice issues firsthand—criminal responsibility, theories of crime causation, civil versus crimi-

nal law, police roles, functions, and ethics, the courts, and more—and master course concepts more completely than they could by just reading any text.

For the Instructor

- *Instructor's Resource CD-ROM*—a single CD with an easy-to-use interface provides access to a wide array of important instructor tools including the Instructor's Manual, Testbank, Computerized Testbank, and PowerPoint lecture slides.
- *Online Learning Center Web site*—password-protected access to important instructor support materials such as the Instructor's Manual and PowerPoint lecture slides, plus all the student resources listed above.
- *Classroom Management Systems*—Online content for the eighth edition of the Inciardi text is supported by Blackboard, WebCT, eCollege.com, and other course management systems. Additionally, McGraw-Hill's PageOut service is available to help instructors get their course up and running in a matter of hours at no cost. No programming knowledge is required. To find out more about PageOut, ask your McGraw-Hill sales representative for details, or go to **www.mhhe.com/pageout**.
- *Lecture Launcher Video*—This 58-minute VHS videotape features brief clips (3–8 minutes each) from NBC News that dramatize Criminal Justice concepts, serve as lecture launchers, and generate class discussion.
- *Additional Videos*—Please contact your McGraw-Hill sales representative to learn more about videos that are available to adopters of McGraw-Hill introduction to Criminal Justice textbooks.

| Acknowledgments |

As is the case with all textbook revisions, putting together the eighth edition of *Criminal Justice* was a daunting task, and as such, there are a number of people to whom I must give special thanks: University of Delaware research associate Jennifer Syvertsen, who played a major role in finding new materials and making sense out of my scribblings; research associates Christine Spadola, Jason Weaver, and Yamilka Lugo, who contributed their skills and time to assist in the research; and my wife Hilary L. Surratt, a researcher and scholar in her own right, who took on the burden of some of my other work so that I could focus on the revision.

I would also like to thank the following reviewers for their useful and insightful comments during the revision process:

Jerry J. Adams, San Joaqin Delta College

John Brook, Houston Community College–Southwest

Mark R. Davids, Midwestern State University

David N. Falcone, Illinois State University

Florence S. Ferguson, American InterContinental University

Michael Grabowski, Santa Rosa Junior College

Darren Marhanka, Lindenwood University

Kenneth L. Mullen, Appalachian State University

Lastly, I would like to thank Kevin Witt, Kate Scheinman, Christina Thornton-Villagomez, Preston Thomas, Jeanne Calabrese, Susan Gottfried, and the rest of the team at McGraw-Hill for getting this book out in a timely manner.

James A. Inciardi
Coral Gables, Florida

GUIDED TOUR

Latest Developments in Criminal Justice

Developments in the criminal justice system that have occurred post-9/11 in American history include complete coverage of the war on terrorism, analysis of both domestic and international terrorism, the Department of Homeland Security, the USA Patriot Act, harbor policing, Camp Delta (Guantanamo Bay, Cuba), military tribunals, and more.

High-profile faces and cases are placed in the context of key issues in the field, giving students both timely coverage and the background needed to understand the importance of recent events.

Personal Views and Personalities

A View from the Field, new essays written by James Inciardi and others with direct experience working in the field, shares "the unexpected" (a meeting with cocaine kingpin Pablo Escobar), the bizarre (the author's many visits to Brooklyn, New York's Raymond Street Jail), and the perils (the time the author got arrested in a Miami crack house) of the fascinating world of criminal justice.

Famous Criminals offer brief biographical sketches and accompanying photos of the "Birdman of Alcatraz," "Son of Sam," "the Night Stalker," LSD guru Timothy Leary, and others.

Careers and Exhibits

Careers in Criminal Justice boxes describe various professional roles available to students interested in criminal justice.

Victims and Justice exhibits address the role of victims in criminal justice issues and procedures.

Law and Criminal Justice exhibits use a combination of current events and case law to shed light on the legal aspects of criminal justice.

Research on Crime and Justice exhibits explore how historical, legal, and behavioral research impacts the field of criminal justice.

Drugs, Crime, and Justice exhibits examine the American drug scene and how the "war on drugs" has impacted criminal justice processing.

Intriguing Perspectives

Perspective boxes detail investigations of domestic and international issues in criminal justice.

Aids for Understanding

Pull-out Study Guide provides an overview of the criminal justice process from A to Z.

Critical Thinking in Criminal Justice sections encourage students to analyze the material presented, look for possible biases, and think about whether some of the things they see in media reports make sense or are contrary to logic.

End-of-chapter features offer opportunities for study and review. The Op-Ed revisits the chapter opening story and asks the reader to reflect on this current issue in light of the chapter information. The chapter Summary gives students a quick review of the basic principles of the chapter and allows them to focus on understanding one point at a time. Issues for Discussion encourage students to think critically about the chapter and will help them study for exams. Media Resources include listings of Web sites, articles, and/or books where students can find additional information on the subject matter covered in the text, and references to *Reel Justice Interactive Movie CD-ROM,* available at nominal cost in an optional package with the text

Supplements for Students and Instructors

Reel Justice Interactive Movie CD-ROM

Available at nominal cost in a special package with the text, *Reel Justice Interactive Movie* on CD-ROM combines the text with a breakthrough learning tool. Students take on the role of a police officer and influence key plot turns by making choices as they investigate a domestic violence incident in a college town.

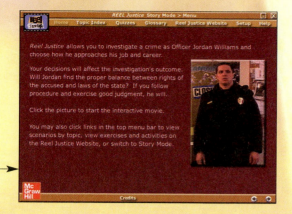

Online Learning Center Web site

Visit our book-specific Web site (http://www.mhhe.com/inciardi8), which features an integrated study guide, chapter quizzes, online access to a wealth of popular press and scholarly articles, interactive video clips, flashcards that can be used to master vocabulary, and many other chapter review tools.

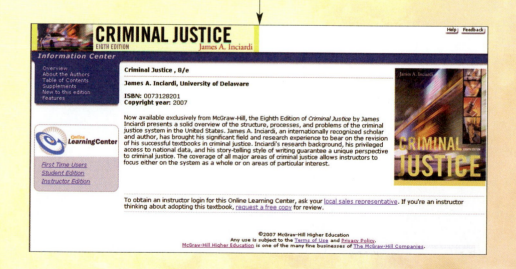

CRIMINAL JUSTICE

PART ONE

THE FOUNDATIONS OF CRIME AND JUSTICE

Morality cannot be legislated but behavior can be regulated.—MARTIN LUTHER KING, JR. Crime may be said to be injury inflicted in defiance of law.—ARISTOTLE Nobody ever commits a crime without doing something stupid. —OSCAR WILDE A thief believes that everybody steals. —E. W. HOWE A burglar who respects his art always takes his time before taking anything else.—O. HENRY People's fear of crime doesn't come from looking over their shoulders. It comes from looking at their television screens. —ROBERT LICHTER, CENTER FOR MEDIA AND PUBLIC AFFAIRS Our new Constitution . . . promises permanency, but in this world nothing can be said to be certain, except death and taxes.—BENJAMIN FRANKLIN

1

"CRIMINAL JUSTICE" IN AMERICA

LEARNING OBJECTIVES

After reading this chapter, you should be able to answer the following questions:

1. To what extent can the mass media have an impact on the criminal justice process?

2. What are the differences among criminal justice, criminology, criminal law, and criminal procedure?

3. In what ways is the study of criminal justice at the beginning of the 21st century an outgrowth of the 1960s "war on crime"?

4. What is the importance of, and the difference between, the "due process" and "crime control" models of criminal justice?

5. What are some of the key issues affecting contemporary criminal justice policy and procedures?

6. What is terrorism?

7. What is "critical thinking" in criminal justice?

8. What is the general content of an undergraduate degree program in criminal justice?

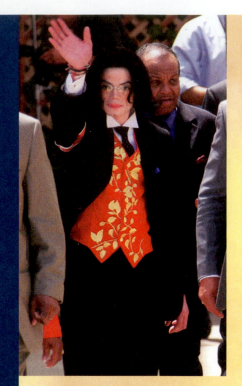

Michael Jackson leaving the Santa Barbara County courthouse.

SANTA MARIA, CA—Setting the stage for a contentious legal battle that would be played out in the world media spotlight, superstar Michael Jackson was put on trial in early 2005, charged with 10 criminal counts including child molestation, attempted child molestation, administering alcohol to a minor to aid in the commission of a felony, and conspiracy to kidnap, extort, and falsely imprison the teenage accuser's family. Thousands of stories were published detailing every minute aspect of the circuslike proceedings, including the day Jackson arrived late to court wearing pajamas and complaining of a serious back injury. Jackson believed he was the victim of a conspiracy and maintained his innocence throughout. Moreover, the list of possible witnesses to testify on his behalf read like a Los Angeles premiere, including the likes of Jay Leno, Elizabeth Taylor, Kobe Bryant, and Diana Ross.[1]

Michael Jackson is certainly not the first major celebrity to be charged with criminal activity and to receive widespread media attention. Sex scandals involving the rich and famous have always attracted readers. Perhaps the first celebrity sex case dates back to when Roscoe "Fatty" Arbuckle, a slapstick silent-film star whose girth begat his nickname, was charged with the rape and death of an aspiring young actress in 1921. Arbuckle was finally acquitted after three trials, but not before starring in the flurry of scandalous headlines touting "the case of the century" that

American comic actor Roscoe "Fatty" Arbuckle.

ultimately ruined his reputation and career.[2] The sensationalistic media attention surrounding Jackson's trial was reminiscent of Arbuckle's debacle, and so too was Jackson's case labeled the "case of the century," even though there were 95 more years to go.

What is it about crimes and trials that fascinates people generation after generation, and why do some cases attract so much public attention?

During the first few years of the 21st century, there were other celebrated criminal cases—basketball star Kobe Bryant, home decorating executive Martha Stewart, and film star Winona Ryder. All exposed many of the details behind our criminal justice system to millions of Americans. The rules of evidence, jury selection methods, DNA testing reliability, media interference, and police investigation techniques suddenly "mattered" to tens of millions of Americans.

Yet such high-profile cases can also lead to an inaccurate and unbalanced view of our criminal justice system. Criminal justice isn't just the police or the courts. Perhaps most important, the overwhelming majority of criminal cases are handled nothing like the cases seen on TV. Media-fed images and preconceptions—whether from the nightly news, amateur footage of "real cops," or the latest Hollywood crime thriller—are more drama-based than focused on understanding how our society handles crime. The details of sensational cases often obscure why the system has evolved into its current form and where criminal justice might be headed in the years ahead.

This book carries you beyond these preconceptions and limitations. Whether you become a criminal justice professional, enter a field that interacts with some part of the criminal justice system, or simply remain a private citizen, it is important that you develop an accurate understanding of how our system works—and how it can fail. This book helps you to analyze the issues that drive the system today and into the future.

The Emergence of "Criminal Justice"

Criminal justice refers to the structure, functions, and processes of those agencies that deal with the management of crime—the police, the courts, and corrections. The content of criminal justice studies comes from a variety of disciplines, including criminology, criminal law, criminal procedure, and constitutional law.

Criminology is the scientific study of the causes of crime, rates of crime, the punishment and rehabilitation of offenders, and the prevention of crime. The great majority of courses and textbooks in criminology provide an overview of the criminal justice system, but its structure and processes are not the major focus.

Criminal law is the branch of modern jurisprudence that deals with offenses committed against the safety and order of the state. Many aspects of criminal law are addressed in criminal justice studies, including definitions of crime, criminal intent, and defenses against crime.

Criminal procedure encompasses the series of orderly steps and actions, authorized by law or the courts, used to determine whether a person accused of a crime is guilty or not guilty. Although much of the field of criminal procedure is addressed in law courses, many of its basic components are studied by criminal justice students.

Constitutional law focuses on the legal rules and principles that define the nature and limits of governmental power and the duties and rights of individuals in relation to the state. The parts of constitutional law that are examined in criminal justice courses are those associated with criminal procedure and the behavior of criminal justice agency personnel. Although criminology is more than a century old, and legal studies have been in existence for millennia, it was not until the end of the 1960s that the foundations of criminal justice as an academic discipline were established. They were an outgrowth of the many calls for "law and order" during the presidency of Lyndon B. Johnson.

"Law and Order" and the "War on Crime"

The 1960s were a violent decade. Crime rates had increased in both urban and rural areas. There were mass protests and political murders associated with the civil rights movement. There were riots in many of the nation's minority communities, brought on by racism and the deterioration of inner-city neighborhoods. There were turbulent campus demonstrations and street revolts in opposition to the war in Vietnam. And there were numerous political assassinations—President John F. Kennedy in 1963, Black Muslim leader Malcolm X in 1965, and both civil rights leader Dr. Martin Luther King, Jr., and Senator Robert F. Kennedy in 1968.[3]

Emotionally charged appeals for **"law and order"** began circulating early in the decade. Those appeals were, in part, a reflection of the temperament of grassroots America, which was seeking a return to the morality of previous decades. They came as well from citizens who despised not only crime in general but also the anarchy that appeared to prevail in the streets.[4]

Also visible at this time was a trend toward the "nationalization" of the Bill of Rights. Its authors' intent was that the Bill of Rights be applicable at the national level—that is, at the level of the federal government—not at the state level. Thus, defendants in state criminal trials were not accorded many of the constitutional protections that were routinely given to those tried in the federal courts. However, in the 1930s the U.S. Supreme Court began extending these rights to state defendants. It was not until the 1960s, however, that significant gains were made. By 1969, nearly all the

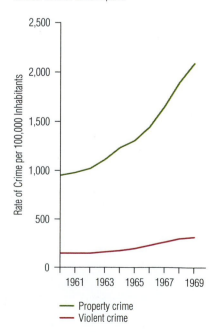

U.S. Crime Rates, 1960–1969
Source: *Uniform Crime Reports.*

— Property crime
— Violent crime

More than 50,000 people formed the funeral cortege for assassinated civil rights leader Dr. Martin Luther King, Jr., in 1968. As violence escalated during the decade, so did emotionally charged appeals for "law and order."

provisions of the Bill of Rights relating to criminal violations were binding on the states, including the prohibitions against compulsory self-incrimination, illegal search and seizure, and cruel and unusual punishment, as well as the rights to counsel, speedy trial, and confrontation of hostile witnesses.[5] Several of these decisions came early in the 1960s, and many people interpreted them as attempts to "handcuff" police and "coddle" criminals.

On July 25, 1965, in response to growing fears of crime and disorder, President Lyndon Johnson's "war on crime" was officially launched with the establishment of the **President's Commission on Law Enforcement and Administration of Justice.** Unknown to Americans at the time, and even to Johnson himself, the commission would initiate a new era for criminal justice in the United States.

The President's Crime Commission

The President's Commission on Law Enforcement and Administration of Justice, commonly referred to as the President's Crime Commission, appointed several task forces to study the crime problem and the structure of criminal justice administration and make recommendations for action. The commission, made up of 19 commissioners, 63 staff members, 175 consultants, and hundreds of advisers, studied most aspects of the crime problem and the machinery of criminal justice. Even before its findings appeared, however, President Johnson announced to the nation that new approaches to old problems must be sought:

> The problems of crime bring us together. Even as we join in common action, we know that there can be no instant victory. Ancient evils do not yield to easy conquest. We cannot limit our efforts to enemies we can see. We must, with equal resolve, seek out new knowledge, new techniques, and new understanding.[6]

Key Recommendations After hundreds of meetings, tens of thousands of interviews, and numerous national surveys, the President's Crime Commission released a series of reports on the police, courts, corrections, juvenile delinquency, organized crime, science and technology, drunkenness, narcotics and drugs, and the assessment of crime—all of which were summarized in its general report, *The Challenge of Crime in a Free Society.*[7] This summary report targeted seven specific objectives, which in many ways would shape the direction of criminal justice for years to come:

1. Society must seek to prevent crime before it happens by assuring all Americans a stake in the benefits and responsibilities of American life, by strengthening law enforcement, and by reducing criminal opportunities.
2. The aim of reducing crime would be better served if the system of criminal justice developed a far broader range of techniques with which to deal with individual offenders.
3. The system of criminal justice must eliminate existing injustices if it is to achieve its ideals and win the respect and cooperation of all citizens.
4. The system of criminal justice must attract more and better people—police, prosecutors, judges, defense attorneys, probation and parole officers, and corrections officials with more knowledge, expertise, initiative, and integrity.
5. There must be much more operational and basic research on the problems of crime and criminal administration by researchers both within and outside the system of criminal justice.
6. The police, courts, and correctional agencies must be given substantially greater amounts of money if they are to improve their ability to control crime.
7. Individual citizens, civic and business organizations, religious institutions, and all levels of government must take responsibility for planning and implementing the changes that must be made in the criminal justice system if crime is to be reduced.[8]

In addition to these major objectives, the commission's reports made more than 200 specific recommendations. The commission, however, as well as the president himself, had been naive in suggesting, for example, that "warring on poverty, inade-

Jeff Stahler reprinted by permission of Newspaper Enterprise Association, Inc.

quate housing, and unemployment is warring on crime"; that "a civil rights law is a law against crime"; and that "money for schools is money against crime." The relationship between crime and poverty had been studied at length for many generations, with the inescapable conclusion that the root causes of crime could not be found in any simplistic equation involving only the disadvantaged segments of society.

Poverty and segregation clearly serve to perpetuate crime, the noted criminologist Edwin H. Sutherland had argued, but "poverty as such is not an important cause of crime."[9] Also, the peculiarity of the poverty-crime nexus was well targeted by political scientist James Q. Wilson in his phrase "Crime amidst plenty: the paradox of the sixties."[10] Wilson was referring to the fact that at the beginning of the 1960s, the United States entered its longest sustained period of prosperity since World War II. During this time, the economy as a whole was strengthened, many people's incomes increased, and the educational attainments of the young rose sharply. Yet, at the same time, crime increased at an alarming rate, along with youth unemployment, drug abuse, and welfare. Thus the suggestion of the President's Commission that the war on crime should

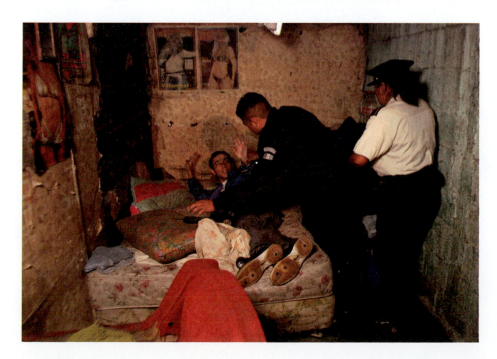

An arrest in an inner-city apartment.

Jeff Stahler (brahlerprincypost.com). *The Cincinnati Post* for *USA Today.*

focus on poverty alone caused acute disappointment among those who had spent their lives studying the problem.

Criminal Justice as a "System" In contrast, the commission's analyses of the *processes* of criminal justice were to have a great impact. They awakened a consciousness of criminal justice as an integrated "system"—an orderly flow of managerial decision making that begins with the investigation of a criminal offense and ends with the offender's reintegration into the free community:

> The criminal justice system has three separately organized parts—the police, the courts, and corrections—and each has distinct tasks. However, these parts are by no means independent of each other. What each one does and how it does it has a direct effect on the work of the others. The courts must deal, and can only deal, with those whom the police arrest; the business of corrections is with those delivered to it by the courts. How successfully corrections reforms convicts determines whether they will once again become police business and influences the sentences the judges pass; police activities are subject to court scrutiny and are often determined by court decisions.[11]

The President's Crime Commission, however, was not altogether unaware of the shortcomings of what it called the "system" of criminal justice, and it called for extensive research and an upgrading of criminal justice personnel and practices. In these areas, the commission had its most visible impact on criminal justice in America.

The Omnibus Crime Control and Safe Streets Act of 1968

The year 1968 occupies a unique place in our images of crime in America. It was a year of riots, protests, and assassinations. It was also a year of increasingly visible street crime. Among the 4.5 million known major crimes that occurred in that year, there were almost 13,000 homicides, 31,000 forcible rapes, 262,000 robberies, 283,000 serious assaults, 778,000 auto thefts, 1.3 million larcenies, and 1.8 million burglaries. At least 1 out of every 45 Americans was the victim of a serious crime.[12]

The use of heroin and other illegal drugs had also reached significant proportions by 1968 (see Exhibit 1.1), having expanded from inner-city areas to suburbia during the early part of the decade.[13] Associated with drug abuse was street crime—burglaries, robberies, and muggings. It was in this setting of street crime, drug abuse, political protest, and violence that fear of crime emerged as an even more important concern than it had been when the President's Crime Commission was established. Noting this growing fear, the commission wrote that the purpose of its report was to reduce the fear

drugs, crime, and justice | EXHIBIT 1.1

The Drug Revolution of the 1960s

The late 1960s marked the beginning of a new epoch of drug use among American youth. Changes in the technology of producing drugs offered a wide array of substances to the eager, drug-taking, disaffected youth cultures. Primary among these substances were newer varieties of amphetamine stimulants, sedatives, and hallucinogens, some of which could be produced in high school chemistry labs and fraternity house bathtubs. They were called "speed," "goofballs," "reds," "yellows," "blues," "black beauties," and other more colorful names. However, few drugs captured the attention and concern of the public as did marijuana and LSD.

Marijuana is a mild hallucinogenic substance derived from the crushed leaves and stems of the hemp plant and has been used for thousands of years. Before the late 1920s, few in the United States had heard of the drug, but by the close of the 1930s it was being called the "weed of madness" and the "assassin of youth" that led users "along a path of destruction and death." These images persisted into the 1960s and beyond.

LSD (lysergic acid diethylamide) was first isolated in 1938 by Dr. Albert Hoffman of Sandoz Research Laboratories, but its hallucinogenic properties were not discovered until years later. In the early 1960s, when it was still relatively unknown, two Harvard University psychologists, Timothy Leary and Richard Alpert, began experimenting with the drug on themselves and their colleagues, as well as on artists, writers, students, prison inmates, and others, to determine its effects. Although the two professors were eventually dismissed from Harvard,

LSD had already gained a reputation. "Taking a trip" or "turning on" became a status symbol on college campuses. By the late 1960s, LSD had become a household word, and chilling stories were told to scare potential users away from the drug.

By 1968, use of marijuana and LSD was believed to have reached epidemic proportions—and even the parents of young children had reason to be frightened when their sons and daughters came home from elementary school chanting the following little melody, to the tune of "Frère Jacques":

Furthermore, an epidemic of narcotics use was also under way. Thus, the use of drugs and the escalating rates of crime that began in the late 1960s initiated a series of "wars on drugs" that have continued into the 21st century.

Source: James A. Inciardi, *The War on Drugs III: The Continuing Saga of the Mysteries and Miseries of Intoxication, Addiction, Crime, and Public Policy* (Boston, MA: Allyn & Bacon, 2002).

---

of crime through its recommendations for a broad and comprehensive attack on the "root causes" of crime.[14]

However, the recommendations of the commission did not and could not culminate in the type of war on crime that was envisioned. To launch a comprehensive attack on the "root causes" of crime was unrealistic, for as noted earlier, those causes have never been fully understood. The search for the causes of crime has been going on for generations with only minimal results. In fact, numerous researchers have concluded that a search for causes is a "lost cause" in criminology.[15]

President Johnson's proposals for the war on crime resulted in the passage of the **Omnibus Crime Control and Safe Streets Act** of 1968, a piece of legislation that generated heated controversy. The act was not directly designed to bring about major reforms in the criminal justice system. Rather, it appeared to be more of a political maneuver aimed at allaying current fears about crime and calming agitation over inner-city riots and anger over Supreme Court decisions that allegedly tied the hands of the police. One provision of the act (Title II) attempted to overturn numerous Supreme Court decisions by stating that all voluntary confessions and eyewitness identifications—regardless of whether a defendant had been informed of his or her rights—could be admitted in federal trials.[16] Title III of the act empowered state and local law enforcement agencies to tap telephones and engage in other forms of eavesdropping for brief periods even without a court order. Primarily because of these two provisions, the Omnibus Crime Control and Safe Streets Act was looked upon as a bad law, one that constituted a significant move toward the establishment of a police state. This concern was forcefully voiced by liberal opponents of the law.

The Law Enforcement Assistance Administration

The primary provision of the Omnibus Crime Control and Safe Streets Act was Title I, which created the **Law Enforcement Assistance Administration.** More commonly known as LEAA, it was organized within the Department of Justice to develop new devices, techniques, and approaches in law enforcement; to award discretionary grants for special programs in the field of criminal justice; and to supply states and municipalities with funds for improving their criminal justice systems and for training and educating criminal justice personnel.[17]

During its early years, the LEAA was criticized for overemphasizing the funding of a "technological" war on crime and for providing grants for purposes beyond its original mission.[18] However, not all LEAA funds were misdirected or misused, nor were all funds channeled for the development of technological tools for a war on crime. A significant proportion of LEAA expenditures was also targeted for social programming and research, court reform, and correctional programs. Moreover, throughout the 1970s LEAA provided more than $40 million per year for the education of some 100,000 persons employed in or preparing for a career in criminal justice. Known as the Law Enforcement Education Program (LEEP) the report of the Twentieth Century Fund Task Force, which examined the operation of LEAA, maintained that the education program was among the agency's most constructive and successful efforts. As such, it was LEAA's Law Enforcement Education Program that initiated the first academic programs in criminal justice. Since then, criminal justice education has become a dominant field in community colleges and universities throughout the United States.

| Models of Criminal Justice |

The procedures for crime control, the processing of criminal defendants, and the sentencing, punishment, and management of convicted offenders are closely linked to the guarantees and prohibitions found in the Bill of Rights and interpretations of those provisions by the Supreme Court. Interestingly, however, the major criminology and criminal justice textbooks used during the first half of the 20th century make no mention of either the Bill of Rights or the United States Supreme Court.[19] Not until the 1960 publication of *Crime, Justice, and Correction* by lawyer-sociologist Paul W. Tappan did Supreme Court decisions begin to creep into discussions of criminal justice processing.[20] Actually, this should *not* be surprising. As will become apparent throughout this book, concerted Supreme Court activity in matters of criminal justice did not begin until the early 1960s. Since then the Court has been extremely active. The Court's decisions and subsequent impact on the American justice system is best understood within the context of two competing models: the *due process model* and the *crime control model*. Since these models underlie much of the discussion in later chapters, it is important to look at them more closely here. Although no single model can possibly describe the reality of the criminal justice system in a completely satisfactory manner, each concept lends important insight into the philosophies on which the American criminal justice system is based.

The Due Process Model

Herbert Packer's classic book *The Limits of the Criminal Sanction* elaborates on the fundamental ideas of the **due process model**.[21] This model stresses the possibility of error in the stages leading to trial. It therefore emphasizes the need to protect procedural rights even if this prevents the legal system from operating with maximum efficiency. Essentially, the model assumes that justice is better served if everyone gets his or her fair day in court; while it is unfortunate if a few guilty people go free, this outweighs the risk of locking up any innocents.

In the 1960s, the **Warren Court**—the Supreme Court under the leadership of Chief Justice Earl Warren—announced a large number of decisions that were in accordance with the due process model. The Warren Court's decisions in the area of criminal law applied a relatively strict version of the due process model to criminal justice. As mentioned earlier, one provision after another of the Bill of Rights was incorporated into the due process clause of the Fourteenth Amendment, thereby obliging the states to grant criminal defendants many of the constitutional safeguards that were already routinely accorded to those accused of federal crimes.

The American Civil Liberties Union, or ACLU, is an advocacy organization dedicated to defending every individual's rights as guaranteed under the Constitution and

Citizens arming themselves continues to be a response to the generalized fear of crime in society. Here, two armed Christmas shoppers take a break to eat lunch in Vermilion, Ohio.

The Supreme Court under the leadership of Chief Justice Earl Warren; (seated, from left) John M. Harlan, Hugo L. Black, Earl Warren, William O. Douglas, and William J. Brennan, Jr.; (standing, from left) Abe Fortas, Potter Stewart, Byron R. White, and Thurgood Marshall.

the Bill of Rights. The ACLU's fundamental philosophy also follows the due process model of justice.

The Crime Control Model

In contrast to the due process model, the **crime control model** emphasizes efficiency and is based on the view that the most important function of the criminal justice process is repression of criminal conduct. Proponents of this model put a premium on speed and finality, and cannot understand why obviously guilty defendants should go free simply because of errors by police or court personnel. The model assumes that it is acceptable to suspend individual rights or perhaps overlook technicalities in procedure in the interest of protecting society from criminal behavior.

The **Burger Court**—the Supreme Court under the leadership of Chief Justice Warren Burger—appeared attuned to the crime control model in its decisions. A legislative enactment of this model includes the "three-strikes" laws, a concept that parallels the sport of baseball. In baseball, it's three strikes and you're out, while under the legislation, it's three crimes and you're imprisoned; in both examples, it's futile to argue your way out of the system no matter how controversial the call. Further discussion of the three-strikes laws is featured in Chapter 13, and other legislative examples and major Supreme Court rulings based on both the due process and the crime control models are examined throughout the remaining chapters of the text.

| Key Factors in Criminal Justice Today |

In addition to being familiar with the major models of criminal justice, students of crime and justice in America need to be familiar with the impact of five important trends on contemporary criminal justice procedures and policies. Those trends are the continuing escalation of the war on drugs, the increasing rate of criminality among women, the significance of crime victims in the process of justice, the ways in which the so-called system of criminal justice can sometimes be, in effect, a "nonsystem," and, most recently, the impact of terrorism on all aspects of the criminal justice system.

The War on Drugs

As noted in Exhibit 1.1, since the late 1960s the nation's "war on drugs" has shaped various aspects of public and criminal justice policy. In fact, because of the linkages between drug use and crime, the policy agenda of almost every U.S. president during the past four decades has addressed the drug problem in one way or another.

In recent years the war on drugs has intensified and has engendered a criminal justice process that appears to be "drug driven" in almost every respect. New laws have been passed to deter drug involvement and increase penalties for drug-related crime. Street-level drug enforcement initiatives have been expanded, and these, in turn, have increased the number of drug-related arrests. In the judicial sector, the increased flow of drug cases has resulted in overcrowded dockets and courtrooms, as well as the creation of new drug courts, special dispositional alternatives for drug-involved offenders, and higher conviction and incarceration rates. In the correctional sector, the results include further crowding of already overpopulated jails and penitentiaries, the establishment of liberal release policies, and experimentation with new prison-based drug treatment programs.

The focus on drugs has also impacted state finances. In a report released by the National Center on Addiction and Substance Abuse at Columbia University, it was estimated that 13% of state budgets were dedicated to dealing with drug abuse but that out of every one dollar spent, only 4 cents were allocated for treatment and prevention.[22] At the same time, however, both federal and state court systems rely heavily on the substance abuse treatment system. In 2002, for example, the criminal justice system was the principal referral source for 36% of all substance abuse treatment admissions.[23] (For a perspective on the author's interaction with a well-known cocaine trafficker, see Exhibit 1.2.)

Many states are devising innovative initiatives in an attempt to more effectively manage their budgets as well as to control and sanction drug-related crime. For example, California's Substance Abuse and Crime Prevention Act, better known as Proposition 36, diverts drug offenders from the traditional channels of the criminal justice system into drug treatment programs. The majority of California voters (61%) supported the ballot measure, which was promoted and funded mostly by George Soros (president of Soros Fund Management), Peter Lewis (philanthropist and CEO of Progressive Insurance), and John Sperling (CEO of Apollo Group, Inc.)—billionaire financiers who view American drug policy as a complete failure and wish to change its focus, including a liberalization of many of the nation's drug laws.[24]

While most Californians seem to support the reformist drug enforcement policies, it remains unclear at this point how effectively the community-based drug treatment system is absorbing and successfully treating the massive influx of Proposition 36 clients. A recent study found that offenders treated under the program were actually more likely to be rearrested for drug offenses than were other groups studied.[25] A more detailed discussion of Proposition 36 (see Chapter 17), as well as other effects of the war on drugs on the criminal justice system, are illustrated in subsequent chapters.

Women, Crime, and Criminal Justice

Another important aspect of criminal justice in the United States today is the increasing visibility of women. The criminal justice system has traditionally been male-dominated, and there are a variety of reasons for this. Historically, the great majority of offenders have been men, and correctional institutions and programs have been designed for men, by men. Moreover, many of the female offenders who have come to the attention of police, courts, and prisons have received some degree of leniency and lighter sentences than men. This situation did not occur because police officers and judges were chivalrous. Rather, it appears that women were typically no more liberated in the world of crime than in other areas, and thus were usually relegated to minor roles in criminal activity.

Recently all of this has been changing. Since the early 1970s, the number of female offenders has increased, and their roles in criminal activity have increasingly

EXHIBIT 1.2 | A View from the Field

Meeting Pablo by James A. Inciardi

On several occasions during the 1980s, at a time when the violence associated with cocaine trafficking was escalating, I journeyed throughout South America at the behest of the United States Information Agency (USIA). My purpose was to tour the university and media lecture circuits in Bolivia, Colombia, Ecuador, and Peru to address the political, social, and economic implications of trafficking for countries producing, refining, and transporting cocaine. The experiences were both exciting and informative, and I was exposed to a variety of new cultures and peoples. But there were times when I never knew who I was really working for. Maybe it was the USIA, but more likely it was the State Department, the Drug Enforcement Administration (DEA), or even the CIA. Perhaps it was all of them, because representatives of each agency seemed to be present everywhere I went.

On one particular visit to Bogota, Colombia, in early 1982, I spent several hours talking to the editor of *El Colombiano*, the city's largest newspaper.* I was accompanied by two interpreters—one from the DEA and one from the CIA. One of the questions asked by the editor was, "We have a growing cocaine problem here, but do you think we'll ever see heroin addicts in Colombia, like in the United States?" My answer was, "Yes, because the traffickers are already growing opium poppies in the Orinoco Llanos region of the country." The DEA and CIA representatives seemed upset by my answer, and later they asked me how I knew about the poppy growing—because it was a high-security topic and they had heard about it from confidential sources only a few days earlier. I told them that I had read it in *High Times,* which was my way of telling them that I would not divulge my source. Actually, I didn't know; it was just a good guess. Before visiting Colombia for the first time, I had learned as much as I could about the country. I came across a discussion of the Colombian *llanos.* The term refers to prairies, specifically those of the Orinoco River basin in eastern Colombia. The *llanos* of the Orinoco is a vast, hot region of rolling savanna broken by low-lying mesas, scrub forest, and scattered palms. It is sparsely populated, and it seemed a likely place for growing poppies. In the more than 20 years since that interview at *El Colombiano,* Colombia has become a major producer and exporter of heroin, with much of the current cultivation in the mountains, but some still in the *llanos.*

Later in the same week I traveled to Medellín, Colombia, escorted by an interpreter and bodyguard from the U.S. Embassy. Travel guides at the time said little about Medellín, only that it was a city of 1.5 million located 345 miles northwest of Bogota; that it was Colombia's industrial hub, manufacturing everything from cigarettes and soft drinks to cement, textiles, and foodstuffs; and that it was not much of a tourist city. What was not spelled out was that Medellín was a city where street crime, brutal violence, terrorism, and cocaine trafficking were prevalent and where bodyguards and armed soldiers were always present, but hardly noticed. Somehow I managed to notice them all.

During lunch on the second day of my visit, my interpreter asked me if I wished to meet a local congressman, who also happened to be an up-and-coming cocaine trafficker. His name was Pablo Emilio Escobar Gaviria. We exchanged greetings, talked about my visit through the interpreter, and then went our separate ways. At the time, I had not

Colombian Drug Lord Pablo Escobar.

heard of Pablo Escobar. Little did I know that he would become one of the most ruthless and powerful drug traffickers Colombia ever had; that he would become head of *El Cartel De Medellín* (the Medellín cartel), which played a pivotal role in the network of international cocaine trafficking; that he would be suspected of ordering more than 100 murders; and that he would be the prime suspect in the killing of three Colombian presidential candidates and scores of newspaper reporters who would write against him. Interesting fellow.

Pablo Escobar ultimately became one of the most feared people in the Americas, and at the height of his success he was listed in *Forbes* magazine as one of the wealthiest men in the world. In the final analysis, however, he was little more than a street thug who had become successful by trafficking in cocaine. In 1993, at the age of 44, he was killed during a shoot-out with the Colombian police.[†]

* *El Colombiano,* June 17, 1982, 2.
† For an in-depth discussion on the history and prominence of Pablo Escobar and the Medellín cartel, see Mark Bowden, *Killing Pablo: The Hunt for the World's Greatest Outlaw* (New York: Atlantic Monthly Press, 2001), and Guy Gugliotta and Jeff Leen, *Kings of Cocaine: Inside the Medellín Cartel—An Astonishing True Story of Murder, Money, and International Corruption* (New York: Simon & Schuster, 1989).

An agent from the Drug Enforcement Administration takes possession of cocaine seized by U.S. Navy personnel off the coast of San Diego.

paralleled those of men. This has become most evident in prison statistics. In 1970, only 2.9 percent of state and federal prisoners were women, yet by 2004 this proportion had increased to 6.9 percent.[26] Moreover, since 1995, the total number of male prisoners has grown by 27 percent, whereas the number of women prisoners has increased by 42 percent.

At the same time, the proportions of female police officers, judges, attorneys, corrections officers, and other criminal justice personnel have also increased. Given these changes, later chapters of this book include a focus on crime and criminal justice issues that relate specifically to women.

The Criminal Justice "Nonsystem"

The notion of criminal justice operating as a "system" may not be entirely accurate. In this sense, there are two competing perspectives of the organization of the criminal justice system: the *consensus model* and the *conflict model*. Likely more of an ideal than a reality, the consensus or *systems* perspective argues that the organizations of the criminal justice system work cooperatively to produce justice. Agencies should share information and coordinate their efforts, thereby moving offenders seamlessly through the justice process.

In contrast, the conflict model, also known as the *nonsystem* perspective, posits that the branches of justice work competitively as individual entities rather than as part of an integrated whole. The interrelationships among police, the courts, and corrections are often beset with both inefficiency and failure. Because of this lack of coordination and failure of purpose, as long ago as the 1960s the American Bar Association referred to criminal justice as a "nonsystem."[27]

In most jurisdictions, the courts appear to be dumping grounds for offenders; correctional systems serve as holding pens for convicted offenders; and the free community—under the protection and patrol of the police—is the reentry point for those released from jails and prisons. Rarely does each segment of the criminal justice process operate with full awareness of the long-term cyclical implications of its activities. Moreover, the conflict theory argues that the characters in the justice process are tainted by personal interests such as fame, promotions, wages, and notoriety, which create conflicts with the larger system. Criminologist Jerome Skolnick argues that clearance rates (the rate of solving crimes) serve as an example of conflict in the system, as police can be more focused on *appearing* to solve crimes than on *actually solving* crimes.

Proportion of Female Inmates in State and Federal Correctional Institutions

Source: Bureau of Justice Statistics.

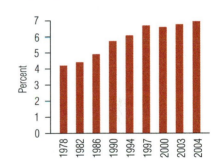

Criminal Justice System Referrals, by Type

Source: SAMHSA Treatment Episode Data Set.

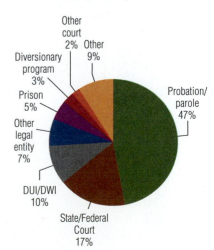

CAREERS IN CRIMINAL JUSTICE

Studying Criminal Justice by James A. Inciardi

Criminal justice, the study of the agencies and procedures set up to manage both crime and the persons accused of violating the criminal law, has become one of the most popular undergraduate majors in the United States. Programs offer students the opportunity to pursue studies leading to law school, graduate school, or careers in the administration of justice. Degree programs are generally structured around a core of criminal justice courses on such topics as law enforcement, the judicial process, juvenile justice, corrections, criminology, and criminal law and procedure. Other courses provide in-depth examinations of such areas as juvenile delinquency, criminal violence, the jury, alcohol and drug abuse, criminal evidence, criminal justice policy and administration, and prisoners' rights. Since the criminal justice process in any jurisdiction does not exist in isolation but naturally reflects the structure, ideas, and concerns of the community and society in which it operates, criminal justice programs draw from a wide variety of academic disciplines—political science, psychology, history, sociology, and even anthropology.

An integral component of degree programs in criminal justice is field experience—a directed practicum with a criminal justice agency that gives students the opportunity to bridge the gap between the theory and applications learned in the classroom and the actual practice of criminal justice in the real world. In field-experience courses, students are provided the opportunity to work on a first-hand basis in actual agency situations—with police, in law offices, and in correctional settings. Such hands-on experience prepares students for the sometimes unorthodox nature of work in the justice system. Throughout this text, exhibits titled "A View from the Field" share some of the more colorful experiences of my more than 40-year career in the field of criminal justice, including the time I found myself on the wrong side of the law (see, in Chapter 5, the exhibit "The Dangers of Street Research").

I have taught courses in criminal justice at the University of Delaware for more years than I would like to admit; in fact, since 1976 I have had the satisfaction of teaching the introductory course in criminal justice to well over 10,000 students. Because of my curiosity as to why my students selected this course, I always asked: "Why are you here?" I have kept a tally of the answers over the years, and they turn out to be quite interesting.

First of all, a little over a third of the students have been nonmajors or undeclared. They have chosen the course as an elective because they heard it was interesting and had a number of "real-world applications," as they put it. The remaining were criminal justice majors, half of whom wanted to pursue traditional career goals including law enforcement, corrections, and the legal profession, while the other half had not yet made any definitive career decisions but simply felt that criminal justice was a "good," "safe," and "practical" choice.

For 15 of my years at the University of Delaware, I was director of its undergraduate criminal justice program, and on more than one occasion I conducted follow-up studies of the program's graduates. The findings were quite fascinating. Most of those who had specific career plans at the outset of their undergraduate studies ultimately secured those positions. Many of them had begun to move up in the ranks in their chosen occupations or had shifted into other aspects of criminal justice work. Of those who had no specific career plans when they entered college, about a third were working in the criminal justice field, while the balance seemed to be everywhere from business to hotel management to advertising and sales.

One of the things that the former students who pursued work in the criminal justice field repeatedly emphasized was that after they had begun at entry-level positions in policing, the courts, or corrections, they began to hear about the many less visible occupations in the field. Scores of graduates shifted into these areas. In fact, in addition to working in the more traditional roles, former majors were employed in well over 100 different types of criminal justice professions, including such jobs as crime lab technician, polygraph operator, police photographer, youth gang street worker, school safety officer, and witness protection agent. Most chapters of this text contain a "Careers In Criminal Justice" exhibit like this one, some of which detail traditional and highly recognizable professions, others of which explore some of these less visible but equally vital occupations within the criminal justice system. While the career exhibits are certainly not an exhaustive list of jobs in criminal justice, they nevertheless demonstrate that the opportunities available to graduates with criminal justice degrees are wide open.

He cites an incident in which police coerced a man into confessing to over 400 burglaries just so that they would appear to have a high clearance rate.[28]

In subsequent chapters, a number of the dysfunctional aspects of the American system of criminal justice are highlighted and illustrated.

Victims and Justice

Historically, the victims of crime and their family members have typically been forgotten in the processing of criminal offenders. Although police generally contact victims when they can offer information that might initiate an arrest, victims have generally had little say in the judicial and correctional processes. This has occurred for at least three reasons:

- The legal tradition in many cultures has been that it is the *state,* not the *individual,* that is officially the victim of crime.
- There has been the belief that most victims might "get in the way" during police investigations and judicial proceedings.
- There has been the concern that victims are both partial and impatient, and hence are incapable of making an objective contribution to the process of justice.

A recognition of the importance of crime victims began during the latter part of the 1960s, with the most significant advances occurring since the 1980s. The wider roles of victims are discussed in later chapters as they relate to specific areas of criminal processing.

Estrella Jail complex in Phoenix, Arizona.

Terrorism, Criminal Justice, and the Constitution

As discussed in Exhibit 1.3 (see next page), **terrorism** is the systematic use or threat of extreme violence directed against symbolic victims, typically performed for psychological rather than material effects, for the purpose of coercing individuals, groups, communities, or governments into making political or tactical concessions. Keeping this definition in mind, the terrorist attacks on September 11, 2001, had a chilling effect across the United States and elsewhere in the world, and they marked a quantum leap in the deadliness and audacity of terror. In addition, they revealed a vulnerability that many Americans had never before realized or appreciated, sparking a fundamental debate about the tension between liberty and security in the United States.[29] The attacks by al-Qaeda raised the question: How can the government keep Americans secure within the confines of the Constitution, without sacrificing due process of law and other hard-won freedoms?

The question is not easily answered, and airline security is an especially sensitive target of debate. While the need for heightened surveillance of airline passengers is obvious, some say that the newly implemented and controversial measures have not made us any more secure. For example, in 2004 Yusuf Islam, better known as folk singer Cat Stevens before his conversion to Islam, was forced off a trans-Atlantic flight after it was discovered by customs officials—while the flight was already en route—that his name

Yusuf Islam, the singer formerly known as Cat Stevens, shortly after his arrest for being on a no-fly list.

EXHIBIT 1.3 | International Perspectives on Crime & Justice

What Is Terrorism?

At the close of the Attorney General's Commission on Pornography in 1986, and after hearing testimony from hundreds of witnesses and reviewing 2,375 magazines, 725 books, and 2,370 films, commission members confessed that they had no better definition of pornography than the one offered years earlier by the late Supreme Court Justice Potter Stewart: "I know it when I see it." A similar case might be made for terrorism. When analyzing television, press, and wire service reports on terrorism, it is never quite clear exactly what the phenomenon in question really is. And from reading much of the terrorism literature, it would appear that "terrorism," most of the time at any rate, is terrorism when people think it is terrorism—clearly a throwback to Justice Stewart's definition of pornography.

For decades, political scientists and specialists in international affairs have struggled with the problems of defining terrorism, so much so that almost every treatise on the topic begins with the definitional question. One result has been a lack of agreement on exactly what "terrorism" is. In fact, one research guide on the topic listed more than 100 definitions of terrorism offered between 1936 and 1981 alone. The difficulty stems from the fact that there are many forms of political violence that, at one time or another, have been called "terrorism." In the broadest sense, terrorism is the use of violence for political ends, but such a definition has a variety of shortcomings because reality is typically far more complicated than any generalization.

At various times terrorism has included such phenomena as the indiscriminate acts of aggression that seem to be a by-product of all forms of war, violent repression on the part of governments to quell opposition to their rule, acts of protest of all types when violence is involved, and, perhaps most conspicuously, the coordinated activities of revolutionary groups organized to bring about political change, such as those of the Irish Republican Army, Italy's Red Brigades, Peru's Shining Path, and, of course, Hamas and al-Qaeda.

This certainly suggests that what has been called "terrorism" is not a uniquely isolated form of political activity. Rather, it exists on a continuum from aspects of conventional warfare, through assassination, guerrilla warfare and insurgency (aggression by small military units for the purpose of establishing liberated zones in which an alternative government can be established), and sabotage, to state repression, persecution, and torture. But despite these many differences in perspective, there are a few points on which virtually all terrorism specialists seem to agree. First, terrorism is almost exclusively a *political* weapon. Second, it is almost always grounded in ideological politics. Third, it is a technique of psychological warfare, accomplished primarily through violence directed against innocent, civilian victims. Fourth, the victims of terrorist violence are not necessarily the primary targets. And fifth, the effects of relatively small amounts of violence tend to be dispro-

portionate to the number of people terrorized; or, to cite an ancient Chinese proverb, "Kill one, frighten ten thousand."

Such was the intention behind Islamic extremists' recent beheadings of foreigners, including *Wall Street Journal* reporter Daniel Pearl, who was decapitated in Pakistan, and Nick Berg, Eugene Armstrong, and Jack Hensley, who were among the victims of their captors in Iraq. While the act of beheading elicits images of savagery and horror to the average Westerner, beheading is permitted by the Koran in the context of warfare and has been used as a legal punishment for criminal acts in many Muslim countries for centuries. A beheading performed correctly with a sharp blade is supposedly a quick and humane method of execution—that is, as humane as any execution can be. However, when served over the Internet and carried out because the demands of renegade kidnappers are not satisfied, the act becomes a drastic tactic to incite widespread fear and intimidate others into cooperation. The beheadings of Hensley and Armstrong, presumably by Abu Mussab al-Zarqawi, a Jordanian terrorist with al-Qaeda ties, was especially brutal in this regard. In what might be considered a jihadi snuff film, al-Zarqawi personally cut the Americans' throats as they struggled and screamed; he then severed their heads and held them up for a bloody close-up and, in one case, casually gauged out one of the victim's eyes.

Terrorists are not simply murderers and vandals. They always have a purpose. What they do is in the name of "justice," although their conception of "justice" often is wildly at odds with that of much of the rest of the world. From the "Assassins" of 11th- and 12th-century Islam to the 21st-century al-Qaeda, there is always a cause to destroy or kill for. Moreover, the cause need not involve an immediate wrong. It might be revenge for something generations old, as when Armenians murder Turkish diplomats today because thousands of Turks exterminated thousands of Armenians long ago. None of the original killers is still alive, but no matter. Some feuds seem to survive in the blood. Irish Catholics are still revenging themselves on Oliver Cromwell.

Keeping these general guidelines in mind, *terrorism* is likely best defined as the systematic use or threat of extreme violence directed against symbolic victims, typically performed for psychological rather than material effects, for the purpose of coercing individuals, groups, communities or governments into making political or tactical concessions.

Sources: Paul Berman, *Terror and Liberalism* (New York: Norton, 2003); David Cole and James X. Dempsey, *Terrorism and the Constitution: Sacrificing Civil Liberties in the Name of National Security* (New York: New Press, 2002); Bruce Hoffman, "Rethinking Terrorism and Counterterrorism Since 9/11," *Studies in Conflict and Terrorism* 25 (2003): 303–316; Susan Taylor Martin, "Horror Is the Point of Recent Beheadings," *St. Petersburg Times,* September 23, 2004, 1A; Alex Schmid, *Political Terrorism: A Research Guide* (New Brunswick, NJ: Transaction, 1984); Cecilia Remón, "Shining Path Active Again," *Latinamerica Press,* July 30, 2003, 1–2; Rod Nordland, "No Place Is Safe," *Newsweek,* October 4, 2004, 30–31.

was on a government list of individuals barred from flying into the United States. Officials said he appears on the list because of alleged financial contributions to the terrorist organization Hamas and to sheik Omar Abdel-Rahman, convicted in the first World Trade Center bombing in 1993. Islam denies any such links to terrorism, but his flight was diverted to Bangor, Maine, where he was escorted off the plane, questioned, and deported nonetheless.[30]

Undeterred by criticism, the government is currently testing a plan called Secure Flight. The program mandates that airlines provide the names, flight information, addresses, phone numbers, and even meal requests of their passengers to the government to help officials screen for terrorists. This comes after $100 million was squandered on another controversial screening program called CAPPS II that never got off the ground.[31] Critics say that the release of such sensitive information to the government is a violation of individual privacy rights and that money and effort are better invested in technologies that can screen all cargo for explosives and dangerous chemicals.

Unquestionably, the September 11 attacks introduced a new era in criminal justice in the United States. Every sector of the criminal justice system has been affected: New laws have been passed to protect citizens, and new procedures have been implemented for ensuring national security and the processing of those suspected of terrorist activity. These changes are addressed at length in later chapters as they affect law and due process, as well as the operations of the police, the courts, and correctional systems.

International and Cross-Cultural Perspectives

No two cultures, societies, or nations view everything in the same way. A global overview of crime rates, definitions of crime, and criminal justice procedures demonstrates many dramatic differences and a few surprising similarities.

Comparative criminology and *comparative criminal justice* are the branches of social science that study justice issues in a cross-national perspective. Such study is rooted in the comparative methods developed by anthropologists in the late 1800s and adopted by the disciplines of psychology, sociology, and political science during the mid-1950s. By the late 1960s and early 1970s, the new concept of comparative criminology emerged, with comparative criminal justice developing later as an outgrowth of the field. Interest in cross-cultural comparison of criminal justice has particularly intensified since the terrorist attacks of 2001, when it became apparent that **ethnocentrism,** or holding one's own culture and way of doing things as superior to all others, was no longer appropriate for the new millennium.[32]

As an illustration of the relationship between culture and criminal justice, at one time or another there has been strong (and sometimes violent) opposition by conservative Islamic governments to global beauty pageants. In 2004, for example, Miss Indonesia faced condemnation from government officials and religious leaders who wanted her barred from competing in the 2005 Miss Universe pageant, claiming that the swimsuit portion of the competition violated religious doctrine governing women's modesty in dress.[33]

Similarly, the first Afghan woman in three decades to take part in a beauty contest also faced sanctions from the Supreme Court of her country if she dared return to her homeland (she is currently cultivating a television career in Los Angeles). Leaders in Afghanistan charged that the California college student's catwalk in a bikini during the 2003 Miss Earth contest was "against Shariah law, against Islam, and against the culture of the Afghan people."[34] Despite not making the final cut in the pageant, she was awarded the first ever "beauty for a cause" award. And during the 2003 Miss Global Beauty pageant in Montreal, Canada, Muslim contestants contended that the Koran did not specifically forbid participation in such contests, and they opted to cover up their swimsuits with hip-hugging sarongs as a way to show respect for their culture, their religion, and the law while still taking part in the festivities.[35]

Other examples abound. Nigeria played the dubious role as host of perhaps the deadliest beauty pageant on record when in 2002, more than 200 people were killed

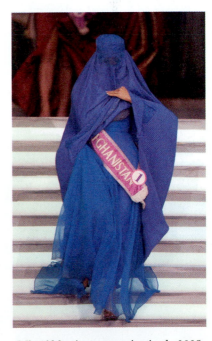

Miss Afghanistan appearing in the 2005 Miss Asia Pacific beauty pageant.

during riots sparked by a journalist's comment that Mohammed would have approved of the event and likely would have chosen (at least) one of the Miss World contestants as his bride. In 2001, Egyptian officials issued a *fatwa*, a legal statement handed down by a religious law official on a specific topic, decrying swimsuit competitions as against Islamic law. A Miss Morality contest was proposed instead to extol the virtues of chaste and proper women. Finally, in 1998 violent demonstrations by Islamic groups caused the cancellation of the Miss Bangladesh pageant.

But legal and religious debate extends beyond the issue of beauty pageants across the Islamic world. For example, many conservative Muslims have been campaigning since the 1998 fall of ex-dictator Suharto, who had banned beauty contests during his 32-year reign, to replace Indonesia's secular government with one ruled by Islamic law. Previously proposed legislation to clamp down on domestic violence against women and permit abortion under certain circumstances has been met with fierce opposition by such groups. In fact, the government has recently considered enacting decrees making kissing in public and erotic dancing crimes that carry jail sentences.[36]

However, it is important to recognize that the influence of cultural and religious values is not absent from our own criminal justice system either. The return of the "culture wars," a phrase first popularized by 1992 presidential hopeful Pat Buchanan, refers to the invigorated right-wing Christian movement that helped propel the Bush administration into office in 2000. In the 2004 presidential election, whether self-proclaimed evangelicals or not, a fifth of all voters said moral values were the most important issue in their consideration, and three out of four of those voters supported President Bush.[37] Many conservative groups have viewed the reelection of Bush to a second term in the White House as a ripe opportunity to advance a morality-based agenda.

While nothing as extreme (in our own ethnocentric view) as barring participation in beauty pageants has been enacted, other new policies are criminalizing women's behavior and choices nonetheless. Within the context of this galvanized conservative movement, for example, the first federal law to criminalize a specific abortion procedure, the Partial-Birth Abortion Ban Act of 2003, was passed. One advocate went so far as to equate politicians who support abortion to individuals who support terrorism, demonstrating once again that everything is relative.[38]

By studying the differences in law, policy, and procedure among different cultures and nations, one can better understand how unique social, economic, political, and cultural factors shape criminal justice and why justice systems around the world operate in the different ways that they do. Perhaps most important, what we learn about law and justice in other cultures and countries may help us better appreciate or improve our own system.

| Organization of This Book |

The content of an introductory course in criminal justice is not simply a collection of definitions and court cases linked together by case studies and anecdotal commentary. Rather, the material is arranged into an organized set of topics presented in a manner that facilitates students' understanding of the basic foundations, structure, and components of the justice process. Thus, the coursework begins with an analysis of the nature and extent of crime, followed by a discussion of the constitutional foundations of law and justice and an overview of the criminal justice process. These introductory topics appear in the balance of Part One—Chapters 2 through 5—of this book. The text is then divided into three parts, each dealing with a major component of the criminal justice process: Part Two (Chapters 6 through 9) examines policing; Part Three (Chapters 10 through 13) provides a detailed look at the court process and sentencing; and Part Four (Chapters 14 through 17) focuses on imprisonment and community-based corrections. Finally, in Part Five, the reader is introduced to juvenile justice, a topic that is generally addressed as a separate course and area in the field of criminal justice.

CRITICAL THINKING IN CRIMINAL JUSTICE

There is the old saying that "things aren't always as they appear." This is certainly the case when it comes to many newspaper and television reports, research studies, and other materials in the area of criminal justice. It is not uncommon in media presentations, for example, to either selectively report information or actually distort the facts to lure readers and viewers for the sake of ratings. And even in scientific research papers, mistakes and biases can be commonplace. As such, it is important to "think critically" about reports on crime and justice issues. Below are some suggested guidelines for thinking critically.[39]

1. *Examine how terms are defined.* Suppose, for example, that a newspaper headline proclaims "Fear of Crime Greater in Southern States." As you read the article, you find that the study compared people from different parts of the country who called in to radio talk shows concerning their fears about crime in their neighborhoods. The first thing to consider is the fact that the story relied on self-reports, rather than on a more objective measure of fear—such as the frequency of crime in a person's community, whether people lock the doors during the day and/or night, the number of locks on their doors, or whether they go out at night alone, or at all. The point here is that conclusions may change when definitions of terms are adjusted.

2. *Inspect the evidence.* Suppose the article noted above reported that the fear of crime was especially high among women, and particularly older women. This conclusion immediately raises a few questions. First, how many younger versus older women called in to the talk show? How many men called in? How large were the differences between older women and younger women? Were tests of statistical significance conducted?

3. *Look for potential biases.* Sticking with the "fear of crime" article for a minute, can you think of anything that may have biased the information? The fact that the conclusions were based on "call-ins" to a talk show is an automatic bias, because it doesn't include people who don't call in to talk shows and all others who do not even listen to such shows. Another bias is the fact that systematic studies have demonstrated that older people view themselves as more vulnerable to crime and, hence, have a greater fear. Moreover, because retired people prefer warm climates, there are higher proportions of older people in some parts of the South than in the North; in addition, because they are retired, they are more likely to be listening to a daytime talk show than younger working people. Importantly, virtually all surveys and polls on the fear of crime, attitudes toward the police, opinions about the death penalty, or any other issues—if they are based on self-reports to talk shows, write-in magazine surveys, Internet polls, or 1-900 call-ins—are biased because of a person's self-selection to participate.

4. *Ask whether the conclusions have been oversimplified.* As you likely suspect already, criminal justice operations are quite complex. As such, you should be very suspicious whenever a report seems to oversimplify a relationship, trying to argue that something very complex can be distilled into a single important answer or catchy slogan. One of my favorites in this regard is the explanation for the police use of deadly force offered some years ago by radical sociologist Paul Takagi, with his statement that "police have one trigger finger for blacks and another for whites" (see Chapter 9).[40]

5. *Ask whether the conclusions have been overgeneralized.* From the latter half of the 1990s through 2001, for example, numerous articles in the national media spoke of how then New York City Mayor Rudolph Giuliani's tough, hands-on approach to the crime problem dramatically reduced the violence rate in the Big Apple. Clearly, by the close of the 20th century, New York had become one of the safest large cities in the world. Could this really be attributed to the policies of one man? Think critically about that one, and check out Chapter 7 for what Giuliani's "spin doctors" left out.

6. *Consider other possible interpretations.* Healthy skepticism is one of the trademarks of critical thinking, and critical thinkers enjoy pursuing alternative explanations to common conclusions. Proponents of California's "three strikes and you're out" law claim that the legisla-

FAMOUS CRIMINALS
Charles Manson

Charles Manson is perhaps one of the best-known criminals of our time. A member of the 1960s counterculture, Manson spent much of his youth as a wandering vagrant who drifted in and out of jails and reformatories. At the age of 35 in 1969, he became visible as the "Christlike" leader of a small "hippie" commune on the edge of Death Valley whose doctrines of "peace, love, and death" became the mantra of his scores of followers. On August 8, 1969, four of Manson's disciples, under his orders, invaded the house of film director Roman Polansky and brutally murdered the five occupants inside, including actress Sharon Tate, Polansky's wife. After writing various slogans on the walls of the home in the victims' blood, Manson's protégés—one man and three women—invaded the home of two additional victims, leaving their bodies mutilated and arranged in grotesque positions. Although Manson did not physically participate in the killings, he was held responsible for their instigation; like the other defendants, he was found guilty of first-degree murder and sentenced to death. However, since the California Supreme Court ruled the death penalty unconstitutional before any of the executions could be carried out, Manson and his followers remain in California prisons to this day (see **www .charliemanson.com**). ∎

"*We find the defendant guilty as charged by the media.*"

Chon Day © 1978 from *The New Yorker Collection.* All rights reserved.

tion is effectively deterring violent crime, citing the more than 42,000 offenders currently in-carcerated under the rule. Looking to California's success, other states and the federal government have followed its lead and enacted similar legislative efforts. But do the sheer numbers of individuals locked up under a particular law demonstrate its success? What types of crimes are people "striking out" on, and are other factors contributing to reduced crime rates? What are the implications of such a policy? (See Chapter 13.)

7. *Consider who is offering the explanation.* It was Mayor Rudolph Giuliani's "spin doctors" who had first released the reports about why New York crime rates were down. They certainly had a vested interest in promoting the policies of their boss. But what were other people saying at the time? Similarly, if a report is released praising the effect of a particular criminal justice approach, be skeptical. Determine who did the evaluation. Was it a self-evaluation or something done by an independent research group? If the latter was the case, did this group have an agenda of its own?

8. *Think through the topic.* In analyzing information, draw upon what you have learned from studying the textbook. Combine that information with what you know from experience and logic. For example, questions are raised in later chapters about the appropriateness of boot camps as a rehabilitative approach, about Internet-based sex offender registries, and about a number of other topics. When thinking critically about these issues, draw upon what you know and think about what kinds of additional information you might need to come up with an educated answer or opinion.

Throughout this text, you will have a number of opportunities to think critically about the material. In addition, examples of issues that require critical thinking are illustrated.

OP-ED

In most cases, few people are aware of the occurrence of the vast majority of crimes—even of violent crimes. Of all the murders, muggings, and rapes reported to the police, less than 5% receive public attention beyond a brief mention from local media. In perhaps 1% of cases, an unusual crime might attract some sustained state or local attention.

On rare occasions, a criminal case galvanizes broad national attention. Among the more recent examples is the case of Scott and Laci Peterson, whose story became the target of obsessive national media coverage from the time of Laci's disappearance in December 2002 until Scott's verdict of guilty and sentence of death in December 2004. The 32-year-old former fertilizer salesman from Modesto, California, was convicted of murdering his pregnant wife Laci and their unborn son Connor and disposing of the remains in San Francisco Bay. There was no murder scene, no proven theory of how she was killed, no weapon, and no tangible evidence to speak of. There was, however, the kind of circumstantial evidence perfect for sensational TV ratings: a pretty, smiling, round-bellied wife whose cheating, lying husband's shady behavior before and after her mysterious disappearance didn't match that of a grieving husband. Perhaps not surprisingly, hundreds of concerned onlookers outside the courtroom cheered and some pumped their fists in the air when his guilty verdict was finally announced, and many felt a sense of justice when the jury later recommended the sentence of death.

As far as celebrity trials are concerned, no matter what the allegations may be—from the rape and murder trial of Roscoe "Fatty" Arbuckle in 1921, the assassination of John F. Kennedy in 1963, the murders of Nicole Brown Simpson and Ronald Goldman in 1994, to the child molestation trial of Michael Jackson in 2005—there will always be intense public interest, continuous investigation, and endless speculation and analysis of these cases. But why? What has driven our fascination? There are several reasons.

One explanation lies in the details of each case. The Michael Jackson accusations, for example, involved the "King of Pop," one of the most celebrated and most talked about entertainers of our time. John F. Kennedy was the president of the United States. The Nicole Brown Simpson and Ronald Goldman murders implicated O.J. Simpson, one of the most widely known and most prominent African Americans on the planet. The sheer visibility of the players in these cases guaranteed attention.

However, there are other, more general approaches to understanding the public's interest in crime. People view the drama of "true crime" as a way of taking them away from boredom of everyday life. Too, they want to know how the unspeakable criminal acts were committed, to convince themselves that they are immune from similar fates, or they may wish to reassure themselves that they are incapable of such wickedness. Most people have a stake in whether justice is being done in America, because almost everyone desires a just society.

As a final note, it is important to recognize that the media coverage of high-profile cases is not an accurate depiction of the norm in the criminal justice system. The circuslike atmosphere of celebrity trials, the tabloid drama of a Scott Peterson case, and even cases linked to terrorism and national security represent the exception rather than the rule in the daily courtroom docket.

Michael Jackson's witnesses: Liz Taylor, Stevie Wonder, Jay Leno, Kobe Bryant, Shirley the psychic, Peter Pan, Easter Bunny, Magdar the magician (not visible), Tinkerbell   ED FISCHER

Reprinted by permission of www.CartoonStock.com

Summary

The news media provide a steady flow of stories about crime and how the justice system attempts to cope with it. Many news reports become "media events," as has been the case with Michael Jackson, Martha Stewart, and Kobe Bryant. However, there is a uniqueness to the majority of criminal cases that achieve national attention, and much of what is seen and read in the media fails to reflect what is typical in the American system of justice. Within this context, the purpose of this book is to analyze the nature of crime and the processes of justice in the United States, to examine the historical and constitutional foundations of the American system of justice, and to consider its strengths as well as its weaknesses.

"Criminal justice" refers to the structure, functions, and processes of those agencies that deal with the management of crime—the police, the courts, and corrections. The study of criminal justice as an undergraduate academic enterprise is relatively new, having emerged as an outgrowth of calls for "law and order" during the 1960s.

The study of criminal justice follows a logical succession of topics—definitions of crime and law, the nature and extent of crime, the constitutional foundations of law and justice, and an examination of policing, the court system, and correctional processes.

A number of major themes appear throughout this book. They are the due process and crime control models of criminal justice, the impact that drug abuse and the "war on drugs" have on crime and criminal justice processing, the growing role of women in criminal justice, cross-cultural and international perspectives in the administration of justice, the significance of victims in processes of justice, the criminal justice "non-system," terrorism and criminal justice, and the importance of critical thinking about criminal justice issues.

| Key Terms |

Burger Court (12)
crime control model (12)
criminal justice (5)
due process model (11)
ethnocentrism (19)

"law and order" (5)
Law Enforcement Assistance Administration (LEAA) (10)
Omnibus Crime Control and Safe Streets Act (9)

President's Commission on Law Enforcement and Administration of Justice (6)
terrorism (17)
Warren Court (11)

| Issues for Discussion |

1. What roles do you think citizens and politicians play in the development of criminal justice policies? How does the existing social climate affect the policies that are implemented?
2. What role do you think the media play in the shaping of criminal justice policy?
3. Why is it important to examine cross-cultural and international issues in criminal justice?
4. Do you feel that criminal justice procedures for women should be the same as those for men?

5. To what extent do you think criminal justice in America is a "system" or "nonsystem"?
6. How does the Omnibus Crime Control and Safe Streets Act of 1968 resemble recent legislative efforts to combat terrorism in the United States?
7. To what extent do you think the terrorist acts of 9/11 have changed American criminal justice practice?

| Media and Literature Resources |

Reel Justice includes scenes that can be used to spark discussion about the following topics from this chapter:

Critical Thinking

Cross-Cultural Perspectives

The Sixties. For students interested in the events of the 1960s that impacted the development of criminal justice, see Todd Gitlin, *The Sixties: Years of Hope, Years of Rage* (New York: Bantam, 1987).

The War on Drugs. For material on the evolution of drug use in the United States, see James A. Inciardi, *The War on Drugs III: The Continuing Saga of the Mysteries and Miseries of Intoxication, Addiction, Crime, and Public Policy* (Boston, MA: Allyn & Bacon, 2002).

Models of Criminal Justice. The major work on this topic is Herbert Packer, *The Limits of Criminal Sanction* (Stanford, CA: Stanford University Press, 1968).

Criminal Justice Abstracts. Criminal Justice Abstracts provide comprehensive coverage of the major journals in criminology and related disciplines, extensive coverage of books, and access to reports from government and nongovernmental agencies. For each document, an informative summary of the findings, methodology, and conclusions is provided. Topics also include crime trends, prevention projects, corrections, juvenile delinquency, police, courts, offenders, victims, and sentencing. To access Criminal Justice Abstracts, go to

http://www2.lib.udel.edu/database/cja.html and click on the yellow button "search database." You can also access this database via the Library Networked Databases Social Sciences Web page or through the National Criminal Justice Reference Service Web site at *http:// abstractsdb.ncjrs.org/content/AbstractsDB_Search.asp*.

Terrorism and Law. Important recent works in this area are David Cole and James X. Dempsey, *Terrorism and the Constitution: Sacrificing Civil Liberties in the Name of National Security* (New York: New Press, 2002), and Bruce Hoffman, "Rethinking Terrorism and Counterterrorism Since 9/11," *Studies in Conflict and Terrorism* 25 (2003): 303-316.

Criminal Justice Education. For an analysis of the evolution of criminal justice education in the United States, see Mittie D. Southerland, "Criminal Justice Curricula in the United States: A Decade of Change," *Justice Quarterly* 19 (December 2002): 589-601. An article of related interest is Willie J. Edwards, Norm White, Ingrid Bennett, and Frank Pezzella, "Who Has Come Out of the Pipeline: African-Americans in Criminology and Criminal Justice," *Journal of Criminal Justice Education* 9 (Fall 1998): 249-265.

Employment Opportunities in Criminal Justice. There are numerous career resources available for students graduating with a degree in criminal justice: Stephen Lambert and Debra Regan, *Great Jobs for Criminal Justice Majors* (New York: McGraw-Hill, 2001); John

Douglas, *John Douglas's Guide to Landing a Career in Law Enforcement* (New York: McGraw-Hill, 2005); Donald B. Hutton and Anna Mydlarz, *Guide to Law Enforcement Careers* (Hauppauge, NY: Barron's Educational Series, 2001); Donald B. Hutton and Anna Myd- larz, *Guide to Homeland Security Careers* (Hauppauge, NY: Barron's Educational Series, 2003); Blythe Camenson, *Opportunities in Foren- sic Science Careers* (New York: McGraw-Hill, 2001).

| Endnotes |

1. *Los Angeles Times,* March 26, 2005, 6B; *The Associated Press State and Local Wire,* March 28, 2005; *USA Today,* February 16, 2005, 3D.
2. Stuart Oderman, *Roscoe "Fatty" Arbuckle: A Biography of the Si- lent Film Comedian, 1887-1933* (Jefferson, NC: McFarland & Company, 1994); Leo Guild, *The Fatty Arbuckle Case* (New York: Paperback Library, 1962).
3. For discussions of the social values and dissent of the 1960s, see Roderick Aya and Norman Miller (eds.), *The New American Revolution* (New York: Free Press, 1971), and Godfrey Hodg- son, *America in Our Time: From WWII to Nixon—What Hap- pened and Why* (New York: Vintage Books, 1995). Many of the violent episodes of the 1960s are described at length in H. D. Graham and T. R. Gurr (eds.), *Violence in America: Historical and Contemporary Perspectives* (New York: Bantam, 1970), and Richard Hofstadter and Michael Wallace (eds.), *American Violence: A Documentary History* (New York: Random House, 1970).
4. See Peter Joseph, *Good Times: An Oral History of America in the Nineteen Sixties* (New York: Morrow, 1974).
5. Henry J. Abraham, *Freedom and the Court: Civil Rights and Lib- erties in the United States* (New York: Oxford, 1977), 33-105.
6. Lyndon B. Johnson, "Message to the Congress," March 9, 1966.
7. President's Commission on Law Enforcement and Administra- tion of Justice, *The Challenge of Crime in a Free Society* (Wash- ington, DC: U.S. Government Printing Office, 1967).
8. President's Commission, *The Challenge of Crime,* vi.
9. Edwin H. Sutherland and Donald R. Cressey, *Principles of Criminology* (Philadelphia: Lippincott, 1966), 95, 241, 265.
10. James Q. Wilson, *Thinking About Crime* (New York: Basic Books, 1975), 3.
11. President's Commission, *The Challenge of Crime,* 7.
12. J. Edgar Hoover, *Crime in the United States: Uniform Crime Re- ports—1968* (Washington, DC: U.S. Government Printing Of- fice, 1969).
13. See Leon Gibson Hunt and Carl D. Chambers, *The Heroin Epi- demics* (New York: Spectrum, 1976).
14. Richard Harris, *The Fear of Crime* (New York: Praeger, 1968), 15–16.
15. Nigel D. Walker, "Lost Causes in Criminology," in *Crime, Criminology, and Public Policy,* edited by Roger Hood (New York: Free Press, 1974), 47-62.
16. The Omnibus Crime Control and Safe Streets Act of 1968, Pub- lic Law 90-351, 90th Congress, June 1968, 18 U.S.C., Sec. 2518.
17. Twentieth Century Fund Task Force on the Law Enforcement Assistance Administration, *Law Enforcement: The Federal Role* (New York: McGraw-Hill, 1976), 4.
18. Jeff Gerth, "The Americanization of 1984," *Sundance Magazine* 1 (April/May 1972): 58-65.
19. See, for example, Philip Parsons, *Crime and the Criminal: An In- troduction to Criminology* (New York: Knopf, 1926); Harry El- mer Barnes, *The Repression of Crime* (New York: Doran, 1926); Marcus Kavanaugh, *The Criminal and His Allies* (Indianapolis:

Bobbs-Merrill, 1928); Fred E. Haynes, *Criminology* (New York: McGraw-Hill, 1930); Harry Best, *Crime and the Criminal Law in the United States* (New York: Macmillan, 1930); Nathaniel F. Cantor, *Crime, Criminals, and Criminal Justice* (New York: Holt, 1932); Edwin H. Sutherland, *Principles of Criminology* (Phila- delphia: Lippincott, 1924, 1939, 1947); Harry Elmer Barnes and Negley K. Teeters, *New Horizons in Criminology* (Engle- wood Cliffs, NJ: Prentice-Hall, 1959).
20. Paul W. Tappan, *Crime, Justice, and Correction* (New York: McGraw-Hill, 1960).
21. Herbert Packer, *The Limits of Criminal Sanction* (Stanford, CA: Stanford University Press, 1968), 154-173.
22. National Center on Addiction and Substance Abuse, *Shoveling Up: The Impact of Substance Abuse on State Budgets* (New York: Columbia University, 2001).
23. Substance Abuse and Mental Health Services Administration and Office of Applied Studies, *The DASIS Report: Substance Abuse Treatment Admissions Referred by the Criminal Justice Sys- tem: 2002,* July 30, 2004.
24. James A. Inciardi, "Proposition 36: What Did You Really Ex- pect?" *Criminology & Public Policy* 3 (November 2004): 593-599.
25. David Farabee, Yih-Ing Hser, M. Douglas Anglin, and David Huang, "Recidivism Among an Early Cohort of California's Propostion 36 Offenders," *Criminology & Public Policy* 3 (No- vember 2004): 563-584.
26. *Prisoners in 2003,* Bureau of Justice Statistics Bulletin (Novem- ber 2004).
27. American Bar Association, *New Perspectives on Urban Crime* (Washington, DC: U.S. Government Printing Office, 1969).
28. Jerome Skolnick, *Justice Without Trial: Law Enforcement in Democratic Society,* 3rd ed., (New York: Macmillan, 1993).
29. David Cole and James X. Dempsey, *Terrorism and the Constitu- tion: Sacrificing Civil Liberties in the Name of National Security* (New York: New Press, 2002); Bruce Hoffman, "Rethinking Terrorism and Counterterrorism Since 9/11," *Studies in Conflict and Terrorism* 25 (2003): 303-316.
30. *USA Today,* September 23, 2004, 3A.
31. *USA Today,* September 22, 2004, 1A.
32. R. Bennett, "Comparative Criminology and Criminal Justice Research: The State of Our Knowledge," *Justice Quarterly* 21,1 (2004): 1-21.
33. *The Miami Herald,* September 19, 2004, 1A.
34. *The Atlanta Journal-Constitution,* November 12, 2003, 2F.
35. *The Montreal Gazette,* November 21, 2003, 6A.
36. *The Miami Herald,* September 19, 2004, 1A.
37. *The Miami Herald,* November 4, 2004, 30A.
38. *The Atlanta Journal-Constitution,* September 25, 2004, 1B.
39. This discussion of critical thinking is based, in part, on Margaret W. Matlin, *Psychology,* 3d ed. (Fort Worth, TX: Harcourt Brace, 1999), 19-25.
40. Paul Takagi, "A Garrison State in a Democratic Society," *Crime and Social Justice* 1 (Spring-Summer 1974): 27-33.

2

CRIME AND THE NATURE OF LAW

LEARNING OBJECTIVES

After reading this chapter, you should be able to answer the following questions:

1. What is crime?

2. What is the meaning of "natural law"?

3. What is the process through which some behaviors come to be defined as criminal?

4. What is the legal definition of crime, and what is the meaning of each element in this definition?

5. What are the differences between the various types of law?

6. What are the various defenses to criminal liability?

7. What is the nature of criminal intent?

8. Where do our criminal laws come from?

9. What are some of the general theories of crime causation?

A streetwalker strikes an alluring pose in Miami Beach.

MIAMI, FL—During the late night and early morning hours along Biscayne Boulevard, Calle Ocho, and the back streets and alleys of Miami, scores of sparsely clad women lean into car windows, prowl on corners, and flag down passing motorists. Most commonly referred to as "streetwalkers," they are commercial "sex workers" looking for "dates"—eager to please the many thousands of tourists and conventioneers that fill the streets of the city. But, as in the days of the Old West in places like Dodge City, Cheyenne, and Tombstone, they have been ordered to "get out of town!" Based on the 2000 ordinance in Miami Beach that created the country's first prostitute-free zone, the city of Miami followed suit in 2003, creating four prostitution-free zones throughout the city.[1] Anyone arrested for soliciting in the designated district will be ordered by the court to stay away from the area. Any streetwalker arrested *again* in the restricted zone goes to jail—and for a longer period than that typically imposed for misdemeanor prostitution.

As with other stories of crime and violence in the greater Miami area, the new offensives against prostitution have been discussed at length in editorials and on local talk shows, picked up by the wire services, and broadcast as "news" in Peoria, Denver, Dallas, and numerous other parts of the United States.

Stories of prostitutes walking the "strolls" of urban America and reports of brutal violence and clever theft are continually offered to the public imagination. Murderers, rapists, and sinister thieves are given prominent attention by the news media; violent crime is the major pursuit of the villains and scoundrels of mystery and detective stories; and homicide, assault, robbery, and prostitution are common themes in the portrayal of crime on television and in movies.

What explains American's fascination with crime?

Many Americans have developed rather distorted and one-sided conceptions of crime. They see crime as something that is intrinsically evil, as something that threatens individual rights, civil liberties, and perhaps the very foundations of society. They seek to protect themselves by locking their doors and windows, insuring their possessions, and avoiding dangerous places and situations. They think of crime as something alien, something that exists outside of organized society.

In actuality, crime goes well beyond the prostitution, street crime, violence, and theft portrayed in the popular media. Moreover, the volume and rates of crime differ considerably from what conventional wisdom suggests. Although violence and theft may appear to be the most typical forms of lawbreaking, crime includes thousands of different types of offenses, and the majority rarely come to our attention unless they are propelled into national consciousness through some media event (see Exhibit 2.1). White-collar crime, for example, is associated with the illegal activities of businesspeople that take place alongside the legitimate day-to-day activities of their businesses or professions. It involves billions of dollars annually in price fixing, embezzlement, restraint of trade, stock manipulation, misrepresentation, bribery, false advertising, and consumer fraud. The economic toll from white-collar crime well exceeds the dollar losses from all known robberies, burglaries, and other thefts—yet it is rarely considered.

Also important is the fact that many activities are considered crimes in some jurisdictions but not in others and in some nations but not in others. There are activities that once were viewed as crimes but are no longer considered as such, and some behaviors that many people consider normal and common are nevertheless defined as criminal under the law.

VICTIMS & JUSTICE | EXHIBIT 2.1

Drag Racing

The belief that violence on TV, in the movies, and in video games spawns copycat violence among young people has long been a concern among parents and the police, and the media are often quick to capitalize on those fears. Now there's a new topic in the debate: Are movies about drag racing to blame for a perceived onslaught of deaths by teenage speed racers?

Illegal street racing has existed for decades and resultant deaths are nothing new, but some critics claim the 2003 release of *2 Fast 2 Furious* has inspired scores of teenagers to mimic the high speeds and risky stunts of the characters in the movie. For example, a 17-year-old Miami teen was killed when he crashed his mother's Corvette into a light pole after consenting to a race challenged by two cars flashing their hazard lights. Though his mother denied her teen was racing, his father said the boy was on his way home from the movie when the incident occurred, and other relatives agreed that the movie was at fault for the teenager's death. Similar tragedies in southern Florida have been blamed on the movie as well, including a woman who lapsed into a coma after being struck by racers and a truck driver who died in a fiery crash instigated by racers. Filmed in the Miami area, *2 Fast 2 Furious* is the sequel to the popular 2001 action flick *The Fast and the Furious.*

But the deaths and destruction caused by drag racing are not confined to Florida. Media outlets across the country have reported on similar incidents. In California, for example, multiple deaths have been linked to *2 Fast 2 Furious,* and in Georgia a teenage girl died on her way to the theater to see the film when the car in which she was riding crashed during a race.

Universal Studios has fended off criticism of *2 Fast 2 Furious,* just as it did during the release of the first *Furious* in 2001, claiming that a cause and effect cannot be proved. The National Highway Traffic Safety Administration admits the difficulty in assessing the impact of the movie on drag-racing deaths, but available statistics reveal that when the first movie came out, at least 135 people died in accidents from alleged drag races, almost twice as many such deaths as in the previous year.

A drag racing scene from 2 Fast 2 Furious.

And thanks to DVDs, the controversy will live longer than the movie's run at the theaters. In 2004, for example, the New Zealand media reported that a young woman was killed and a mother and daughter were left severely injured in a head-on collision during an attempt to drag race after renting the movie. The 20-year-old driver of the other car became the first to face charges under the country's strict new anti-drag-racing laws.

In the United States, penalties for drag racing vary by jurisdiction. Many areas are cracking down hard on the practice in an attempt to avert further tragedies. San Diego and surrounding cities in southern California have gone a step further by making it a crime just to watch a race.

Will the furiously successful movie series turn into a trilogy, drive more young people to wreak havoc on the local highways, and create further uproar in the media and local communities? We'll have to hold on tight and see.

Sources: *The Associated Press,* June 26, 2003; *The Press* (Christchurch, New Zealand), September 1, 2004, 1; *The San Diego Union-Tribune,* August 27, 2003, p. NC3.

What, then, is crime? In this chapter this question is answered through an analysis of crime and its relation to law.

The Nature of Crime

Had I a hundred tongues, a hundred mouths, and a voice of iron, I could not sum up all the types of crime nor all their punishments.

—VIRGIL

Crime has been subject to a variety of definitions and interpretations. For the scholar, crime can be drama, a conflict between good and evil like those portrayed in the Greek tragedies, Shakespeare's *Macbeth,* and Dostoyevsky's *Crime and Punishment.* To the moralist and reformer, crime is a manifestation of spiritual depravity; it is a festering

Proportions of U.S. Population Reporting Crime or Poverty as the Most Important Problem Facing the Nation

Year	Crime	Poverty
1973	17%	17%
1974	3	3
1975	5	5
1976	8	8
1977	6	6
1978	3	*
1979	2	*
1980	2	*
1981	4	*
1982	5	*
1983	2	*
1984	4	3
1985	3	6
1986	3	6
1987	3	6
1988	*	7
1989	6	10
1990	2	11
1991	4	12
1992	5	15
1993	9	15
1994	42	n/a
1995	26	n/a
1996	23	5
1997	22	9
1998	20	4
1999	17	6
2000	13	3
2001	9	4
2002	3	3
2003	2	4
2004	1	1
2005	1	1

* Denotes less than 1%.

Source: The Gallup Organization.

"*Handguns are illegal around here.*"

Reprinted by courtesy of *Playboy* magazine. All rights reserved.

disease of the soul that must be eradicated by the powers of restraint and virtue. Crime has also been equated with sin—with violations of a natural law, the Ten Commandments, or the proscriptions embodied in the Bible, the Talmud, and the Koran.

For others, crime has different meanings: To the reporter it is news, to the detective it means work, to the thief it is a business, and to the victim it suggests fear and loss. But to most individuals, crime is no more than the violation of a generally accepted set of rules that are backed by the power and authority of the state. While these and many other conceptions of crime may be important for particular purposes, they are of little help in arriving at an explicit definition of crime.

Nevertheless, the notion of crime as sin suggests a starting point, for the evolution of criminal definitions is linked to historical images of right and wrong and the precepts of **natural law** (see Exhibit 2.2).

Crime as a Social Construct

A broad definition of crime in England is that it is any lower-class activity which is displeasing to the upper class.

—**BRITISH COMMENTATOR DAVID FROST**

The ideas of natural law and natural crime assume the existence of universal standards as to what constitutes sin or immoral behavior, but a definition of crime framed in these terms lacks both clarity and precision. Conceptions of crime as amoral behavior become even more confusing when one considers that there is no moral code to which all people subscribe, even within a single society or community. A number of social scientists, therefore, have examined crime as a human construction. They suggest that the definition of behavior as "deviant" or "criminal" comes from individuals and social groups and involves a complex social and political process that extends over time. As such, they suggest, people and groups create crime by making rules.

This more sociological view of deviance and crime rejects the notion that the rightness or wrongness of actions is divine in origin. Instead, it begins with an examination of how certain behaviors become deviant and criminal. This perspective focuses specifically on **deviance**—a concept that is considerably broader than crime. It assumes that rules are not created spontaneously but, rather, come about only in response to behavior that is perceived to be harmful to a group. Thus, as sociologist Kai T. Erikson has suggested, "The term *deviance* refers to conduct which the people of a group

LAW & CRIMINAL JUSTICE | EXHIBIT 2.2

Natural Law

Natural law, a concept that has run through human affairs for more than 20 centuries, focuses on perhaps the earliest understanding of crime. Natural law refers to a body of principles and rules, imposed upon individuals by some power higher than man-made law, that are considered to be uniquely fitting for and binding on any community of rational beings. As such, natural law is synonymous with "higher law" and is believed binding even in the absence of man-made law. As stated by Hugo Grotius, the Dutch jurist and statesman whose *De Jure Belli ac Pacis,* published in 1625, is regarded as the first work on international law:

> The law of nature is a dictate of right reason which points out that an act, according as it is or is not in conformity with rational nature, has in it a quality of moral baseness or moral necessity and that, in consequence, such an act is either forbidden or enjoined by the author of nature, God.

Since natural law has generally referred to that which determines what is right and wrong and whose power is made valid by nature, it follows that its precepts should be eternal, universal, and unchangeable. An examination of natural law from the time of the ancient Greeks to the present suggests that there is no single and unchanging view of the concept. To Roman jurists, for example, *jus naturale,* or natural law, meant a body of ideal principles that people could understand rationally and that included the perfect standards of right conduct and justice. Throughout the Middle Ages the law of nature was identified with the Bible, with the laws and traditions of the Catholic church, and with the teachings of the church fathers.

The cogency of natural law would suggest the existence of natural crimes—"Thou shalt not kill" and "Thou shalt not steal"—acts considered criminal by rational persons everywhere. However, research has failed to yield examples of activities that have been universally prohibited. Incest, for example, is believed by some to be a universal crime or taboo, for there are rules forbidding such behavior in one form or another in every known society. However, there is considerable variation among societies and cultures as to what exactly constitutes incest. While it refers in virtually all settings to sexual relations between parents and children and between any sibling pair, in some royal marriages and sacred rituals the incest taboo has been lifted. As another ex-

ample, even the act of murder is not universally viewed as criminal. In Comanche society, for example, for a husband to kill his wife—with or without good cause—was not murder; it was an absolute privilege and right that not even the family of the victim could challenge. In fact, the only crime in the Comanche legal system was excessive sorcery, for it was considered a threat to the tribe as a whole.

Criminologist Hermann Mannheim made a thorough and complex examination of the evolution of natural law throughout Western history, concluding that even the concept of natural law has been subject to widely varying interpretations.

In sum, there has been a persistent conviction throughout history that there exists superior principles of right—some higher law, the violation of which constitutes crime. But the differing conceptions of natural law have served to discredit its importance in the understanding and definition of crime, which has led legal scholars and social scientists to other areas in their search for the meaning and parameters of crime.

Natural law is significant, however, in both the evolution of criminal laws and modern conceptions of natural crimes. Elements of the natural law concept were incorporated into the Code of Hammurabi, the first known written legal document, which dates back to about 1900 B.C. Natural law also played a key role in the formulation of Greco-Roman law, and it is a cornerstone of a portion of contemporary Anglo-American law.

Sources: Heinrich A. Rommen, *The Natural Law: A Study in Legal and Social History and Philosophy* (Indianapolis, IN: Liberty Fund, 1998); Raoul Berger, *Government by Judiciary: The Transformation of the Fourteenth Amendment* (Indianapolis, IN: Liberty Fund, 1997); Arthur R. Hogue, *Origins of the Common Law* (Indianapolis, IN: Liberty Fund, 1986); James McClellan, *Liberty, Order, and Justice: An Introduction to the Constitutional Principles of American Government* (Indianapolis, IN: Liberty Fund, 2000); Hugo Grotius, *De Jure Belli ac Pacis,* cited by Cornelia Geer Le Boutillier, *American Democracy and Natural Law* (New York: Columbia University Press, 1950), 57; Leo Strauss, *Natural Right and History* (Chicago: University of Chicago Press, 1953); Charles Grover Haines, *The Revival of Natural Law Concepts* (Cambridge: Harvard University Press, 1930), 6–11; Benjamin Fletcher Wright, *American Interpretations of Natural Law* (Cambridge: Harvard University Press, 1931), 6; Fernando Henriques, *Love in Action* (New York: Dutton, 1960), 200–201; Margaret Mead, "Incest," in *International Encyclopedia of the Social Sciences,* Vol. 7, edited by David L. Sills (New York: Macmillan, 1968), 115–122; E. Adamson Hoebel, *The Law of Primitive Man: A Study in Comparative Legal Dynamics* (Cambridge: Harvard University Press, 1954), 127–142; Hermann Mannheim, *Comparative Criminology* (Boston: Houghton Mifflin, 1967), 47.

consider so dangerous or embarrassing or irritating that they bring special sanctions to bear against the persons who exhibit it."[2] More specifically, and in contrast to the concept of natural law, it can be described as follows:

> Deviance is *not* a quality of an act the person commits, but rather a consequence of the application by others of rules and sanctions to an "offender." The deviant is one to whom that label has successfully been applied; deviant behavior is behavior that people so label.[3]

Crime and Moral Crusades

The mechanisms through which behavior is viewed as deviant were described by Howard S. Becker as a process of discovery undertaken by "crusading reformers," "rule creators," and "moral entrepreneurs."[4] The reformer or

Members of the WCTU (Women's Christian Temperance Union) sing hymns at the door of the saloon in an effort to call public attention to the "wickedness" of drinking.

Style in crime seems boundless, including what amounts to freelance demolition and theft. In Detroit, scavenger crack addicts steal bricks—which they sell to scrap dealers for $10 per hundred—from the foundations and walls of vacant buildings.

FIGURE 2.1

Alcoholic Beverage Consumption (in Gallons) per Capita of Drinking-Age (15+) Population in Years Prior to National Prohibition

Source: Adapted from W. L. Rorabaugh, *The Alcoholic Republic* (New York: Oxford, 1979), 233.

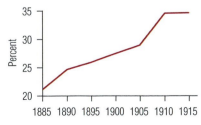

crusader views certain elements in society as truly, totally, and unconditionally evil, and feels that nothing can be right in the society until rules are made to correct and remove the wickedness he or she has perceived. The crusader's mission becomes a holy war, for the wrongs that have been observed are a breach in the stability of the social order and only their eradication can ensure a better way of life for all. The crusader's role, then, involves bringing the evil to the attention of the public at large, to that of the society's opinion makers, and ultimately to that of the designated rule creators and enforcers.

An illustration of this process is the antiliquor crusade that resulted in the ratification in 1919 of the Eighteenth Amendment to the U.S. Constitution, which prohibited the manufacture, sale, and distribution of intoxicating liquors. The Prohibition movement asserted the rural Protestant ethic, which was opposed to the urban culture that was emerging at the close of the 19th century. The earliest colonial settlers designated country and village life as good and deemed only the agrarian way of life to be pure and wholesome; life in the city was seen as wicked. The farmer was viewed as the solid man of the earth, the backbone of American democracy; living in communion with nature, he had an integrity that could never be attained by those who were surrounded by the evil and depravity of the city. This agrarian myth so permeated the ideals and thinking of the frontier people and their descendants that it tended to shape their perceptions of reality and overt behavior. Their activity bias extended to drinking and the liquor trade, which they saw as symbols of urban immorality and of urbanism in general. They viewed urbanism as diametrically opposed to the rural creeds of the Methodists, Baptists, Presbyterians, and Congregationalists, with their emphasis on individual toil and profound faith in the Bible. They also believed that the commercialism of the cities was destroying the self-sufficiency of the farm and village, creating a situation of unwanted dependence. Urbanism, therefore, was the real sin in society, and the reform movement was simply an organization of rural interests striving against the wicked city and its growing dominance.[5]

Note that although the deviance perspective can suggest how some deviance and crime can come into being, it fails to account for all definitions of crime. That is, some crimes may come into being through moral enterprise, and some behavior may become criminal when that label is applied to acts that were previously regarded as noncriminal; but this does not explain how or why many long-standing definitions of crimes against person and property came into being. Murder, for example, is proscribed in both the Old and New Testaments, and its designation as a capital offense appears in an early chapter of the Book of Genesis.

Crime and Deviance   It should further be noted that not all deviant behavior is criminal behavior—and conversely, not all criminal behavior is deviant behavior. Numerous kinds of activities receive social disapproval and may even be deemed blatantly antisocial, but they are not necessarily crimes. While picking one's nose in public, espousing communism or nazism, or being an alcoholic are considered deviant by most Americans, these activities themselves are not criminal and are not treated as such. The behaviors might even be strongly disapproved of, with the deviants being subject to severe ostracism by their peers—but criminal sanctions would not be brought to bear against them.

By contrast, numerous other behaviors are indeed criminal, but the participants are not even called deviant. Wagering money with friends on the outcome of the World Series or the Super Bowl may be a violation of the criminal law in some jurisdictions, yet to the society at large the practice is hardly "deviant." Similarly, many intimate sexual activities may violate state and local criminal laws, but within the context of a consenting adult relationship those activities are considered normal.

Finally, although the labeling perspective fails to offer a basis for a working definition of crime, it does point out how some crime comes into being and, in that sense, how crime can be a social construction. More important, however, it provides a useful

> Rules are made for the obedience of fools and the guidance of wise men.
> — SIR WINSTON CHURCHILL

> The streets are safe in Philadelphia, it's only the people who make them unsafe.
> — FRANK RIZZO

Criminal behavior, or just deviant? Or is it either? The answer depends on the cultural context. While not a criminal act (as long as it is performed in a licensed setting by a professional), tattooing in the United States is often viewed as anomalous behavior. An exposed tattoo is usually considered socially unacceptable in a professional setting. To others, however, tattoos represent freedom of expression. Tattoos can also demarcate allegiance to a particular subculture, though often the affiliation is with a deviant group like a gang. In contrast, the people of the Marquesas Islands in the South Pacific have practiced tattooing as an integral part of their culture since the initial migration and settlement of the islands. Used to express their identity and personality, tattoos are a symbol of social status indicating wealth, strength, and power. Tattoos also symbolize the ability to endure pain among men, who often have their entire bodies (even the tongue!) tattooed. They also represent social maturation among women, who are limited to tattooing their arms, feet, hands, ears, and the border around their lips. Just don't try this before applying for a job in corporate America.

perspective for understanding how people come to be labeled as deviant or criminal, how society may react to them, and how the process of labeling them as outsiders can affect their behavior. Society may react to disapproved behavior in a variety of ways—with disgust, anger, hate, gossip, isolation, physical punishment, incarceration, or even execution. Moreover, there may be significant cultural differences in definitions of what constitutes appropriate conduct, or deviance, or crime. As illustrated in Exhibit 2.3, social and criminal responses tend to vary in different societies and cultures.

Crime as a Legal Construct

I think crime pays. The hours are good and you travel a lot.

—WOODY ALLEN

There's Actually a Law Against That . . . ?

The truth is invariably far more entertaining than fiction, as evidenced by these actual laws on the Florida legal books:

- Unmarried women are prohibited from parachuting on Sunday.
- It is illegal to skateboard without a license.
- It's an offense to shower naked. ∎

If definitions of crime as violations of natural law or as antisocial behavior or deviance lack precision, we may need to look directly at law for a formal definition of crime. This need was best stated nearly seven decades ago by Jerome Michael and Mortimer J. Adler:

> The most precise and least ambiguous definition of crime is that which defines it as behavior which is prohibited by the criminal code. The criminal law describes many kinds of behavior, gives them names such as murder and arson and rape and burglary, and proscribes them. If crime is defined in legal terms, the only source of confusion is such ambiguity as may inhere in the legal definitions of specific crimes. It is sometimes difficult to tell whether specific conduct falls within the legal definition, whether, for example, a specific homicide is murder or what degree of murder, as that offense is defined by law. But even so, *the legal rules are infinitely more precise than moral judgments or judgments with regard to the antisocial character of conduct.* Moreover, there is no surer way of ascertaining what kinds of behavior are generally regarded as immoral or antisocial by the people of a community than by reference to their criminal code, for in theory, at least, the criminal code embodies social judgments with respect to behavior and, perhaps more often than not, fact conforms to theory.[6]

The word *crime* has its roots in the Latin *crimen,* meaning "judgment, accusation, or offense," and its origins are clearly legalistic. Numerous social scientists and legal scholars have offered definitions of crime within this legal perspective. The late Edwin H. Sutherland, perhaps the most renowned American criminologist of the mid-20th century, suggested that "the essential characteristic of crime is that it is behavior which is prohibited by the State and against which the State may react."[7] *Black's Law Dictionary* defines crime as "a positive or negative act in violation of the penal law; an offense against the state."[8] In the field of criminal justice it is defined simply as "an act or omission prohibited by law."[9] Yet these definitions, while correct, fail to offer the kind of precision necessary for a full understanding of the term. We cannot simply call crime a violation of the law, for there are numerous circumstances under which identical behaviors would not be classified as criminal. However, lawyer and sociologist Paul W. Tappan has offered a definition of **crime** that does mark its major boundaries:

> Crime is an intentional act or omission in violation of criminal law (statutory and case law), committed without defense or justification, and sanctioned by the state as a felony or misdemeanor.[10]

Tappan's definition is accepted as the meaning of the term *crime* throughout this text. It is analyzed in detail in the following sections.

Act or Omission   Central to the American system of law is the philosophy that a person cannot be punished for his or her thoughts. Thus, for there to be a crime, there must be an act or the omission of an act that is legally required. A person may wish to commit a crime, or think of committing a crime, but the crime does not occur until the action actually takes place. If one were to consider murdering a relative, there would be no crime until the killing, or an attempt to kill, actually occurred. Moreover, one could conceivably *plan* for a long time to commit a crime, but again the crime would not come into being until the action actually took place.

International Perspectives on Crime & Justice | EXHIBIT 2.3

Men, Women, and Marital Rights in the Muslim World

The Taliban is the militant Islamic group that once controlled most of Afghanistan, prior to its defeat by Afghan rebels and a U.S.-led military coalition in December 2001. Before its downfall the Taliban received considerable international attention, not only because of its extremist interpretation of Islam but also due to its harsh treatment of women. Under the Taliban rule, women were prohibited from going to school or work, earning money, or leaving their homes unless accompanied by a male relative. Furthermore, women ran the risk of being beaten for not wearing the head-to-toe *burqua,* an all-enveloping garment required by the Taliban.

Since the decline of the Taliban, a number of things have changed for the women of Afghanistan. Although some continue to wear the *burqua* out of habit, tradition, or possibly fear, it is no longer required. In addition, women and girls can attend school, and many women have moved back into the workplace. But in the area of marital relations, the situation continues to be an equation of inequity.

Under Islamic law, or *Sharia,* which remains the basis of most Afghan law, a man may take up to four wives, provided he meets a number of conditions. The first wife must consent, or have a contagious disease, or be unable to reproduce. In addition, the man must be able to provide for all of his wives equally. By contrast, a woman may not take a second husband under any circumstances. Moreover, it is difficult for a woman to obtain a divorce.

An Afghan woman, imprisoned for marrying a second time, talks to a visitor through a hole in her cell door, while a guard (at right) looks on.

The outgrowth of this inequity has been the jailing of many women for having married a second time. In one case, a woman had run away with her lover from a marriage arranged by her parents. The parents had married her to an Afghan man living in the Netherlands, who also had a wife there. The woman's father-in-law tracked her down, and she was confined to a jail in Kabul, the capital of Afghanistan. In another case, a woman divorced her husband before a roomful of witnesses. When she later remarried and became pregnant, her former husband had her arrested, claiming that he had never given her a formal document of divorce. She is now serving a sentence of six years.

Afghanistan is undergoing judicial reform, but whether the marriage inequity will change is difficult to predict. Many in Afghanistan, as well as international observers and advisers, hope for a new constitution that will reflect international standards of human rights, including the rights of women. Fundamentalists inside the country want a constitution that reflects the *Sharia.* Because most Afghans are deeply rooted in their traditional culture, in all likelihood the new constitution will be a compromise between international legal norms and strict Islamic principles.

Sources: M. J. Gohan, *The Taliban: Ascent to Power* (New York: Oxford University Press, 2001); Larry P. Goodson, *Afghanistan's Endless War: State Failure, Regional Politics, and the Rise of the Taliban* (Seattle: University of Washington Press, 2001); Amy Waldman, "The 15 Women Awaiting Justice in Kabul Prison," *The New York Times,* March 16, 2003, sec. 4, pp. 1, 14.

By contrast, however, there are circumstances in which "planning" to commit a crime is a criminal act in and of itself. **Conspiracy** is concert (collaboration) in criminal purpose, and it must involve two or more people. Perhaps the best-known case of conspiracy was related to the Leopold and Loeb killing of 14-year-old Robert Franks in 1924. Nathan F. Leopold, Jr., was a graduate of the University of Chicago and the son of a multimillionaire shipping magnate; Richard A. Loeb was a University of Michigan graduate and the son of Sears, Roebuck and Company's vice president, Albert A. Loeb. Leopold and Loeb had structured what they felt would be the perfect crime—the kidnapping, ransoming, and killing of an innocent youth. Their planning extended over many weeks and involved renting a car; opening a bank account for the ransom money; riding trains to the tentative ransom site; purchasing rope, a chisel, and hydrochloric acid with which they would garrote, stab, and mutilate their victim; gathering rags with which they would bind and gag the victim; selecting wading boots to be worn in the swamp where they would leave the victim's body; preparing a ransom note; and discussing potential victims. Because of these actions, Leopold and Loeb were guilty of conspiracy to commit crime. Leopold and Loeb's agreement to murder, combined with their extensive preparations, constituted a criminal act. When they selected Robert Franks as their victim, and then abducted and murdered him, their crimes advanced from a conspiracy stage to include kidnapping and homicide.[11] In a related context, people become *parties to crime* when they assist, aid and abet (help), incite, or otherwise encourage others to commit crimes. More specifically, an **abettor** is one who, with the requisite criminal intent, encourages, promotes, instigates, or stands by to assist the perpetrator of a crime. An **accessory** *before* **the fact** is an individual who abets a crime but is not present when the crime is committed. By contrast, an **accessory** *after* **the fact** is one who, knowing that a felony has been committed, receives, relieves, comforts, or assists the perpetrator to hinder apprehension or conviction.

Failure to act in a particular case can also be a crime if there is some legal duty to act. Consider the case of *People* v. *Beardsley*,[12] which involved a man who spent a weekend with his mistress. After a serious argument, the women took an overdose of narcotics and the man made no attempt to obtain medical help to save her life. His failure to assist her did *not* constitute a crime. Although he may have had a moral obligation to help her, he had no legal duty to do so. There was no contractual relationship such as might exist between parents and a day care center or between a patient and a hospital; there was no status relationship that imposed a legal duty such as that between husband and wife; and there was no legal statute imposing a legal duty on the man.

In contrast to *Beardsley,* in 1988 the California Supreme Court upheld convictions of manslaughter and felony child endangerment for a woman who used prayer in lieu of medical attention in treating her 4-year-old, who was suffering from meningitis and eventually died.[13] The defendant argued that the use of medicine violated her religious beliefs. The court countered that parents may not martyr their children for the sake of their personal religious beliefs.

Less complex instances of failures to act that constitute crime can be found under misprision of felony statutes. **Misprision of felony** refers to the offense of concealing a felony committed by another person, even if the party to the concealment did not take part in the planning or execution of the felony.[14] Thus, if an individual overhears a group discussing their participation in a recent bank robbery, that person would be guilty of misprision of felony if he or she failed to report the conversation to the authorities.

Criminal Intent For an act or omission to be a crime, the law requires the presence of criminal intent, or *mens rea*—from the Latin for "guilty mind." The concept of *mens rea* is based on the assumption that people have the capacity to control their behavior and to choose between alternative courses of conduct. Thus, the notion of criminal intent suggests that the person is aware of what is right and wrong under the law and intends to violate the law, as contrasted with the retarded, the mentally ill, or the young, who may not be capable of full use of reason.

Most legal commentaries divide *mens rea* into two basic types of intent: specific and general. *Specific intent* is present when the circumstances of the crime show that the offender must have consciously desired the prohibited result. Similarly, the crime of burglary reflects the notion of specific intent. Burglary involves two broad elements: entry into the dwelling of another and the intention to commit a crime (usually a theft) therein. The burglar manifests specific intent because he or she consciously desires the prohibited result—theft.

By contrast, consider the case of a man outraged by his neighbor's barking dog. He expresses his disapproval by warning the neighbor that if the dog is not quieted, he will shoot the animal. When the threat is ignored and the dog continues to bark, the angry man fires three shots through his neighbor's window, intending to kill the dog. Instead, one of the bullets kills his neighbor. Although specific intent is not present in this case, general intent is. *General intent* refers to conscious wrongdoing from which a prohibited result follows, even in the absence of a desire for that particular result. Or more specifically, general criminal intent involves the conscious and intentional commission of a crime when the specific result of that crime was not necessarily intended.

Although criminal intent, whether specific or general, is necessary for an act to be considered a crime, there are some exceptions to this rule of law. Under the doctrine of **vicarious liability** (referred to in some jurisdictions as *respondent superior*), liability can be imposed on an employer for certain illegal acts committed by employees during the course and scope of their employment. This doctrine is generally directed at the protection of the public health. For example, the sale of cigarettes to minors by a clerk in a drug or convenience store can result in criminal fines for the store's manager and/or owner.[15]

Violation of Criminal Law

Violation of Criminal Law For an act or its omission to be a crime, not only must there be criminal intent, but the behavior must be in violation of the criminal law. **Criminal law,** as opposed to noncriminal or civil law, is the branch of jurisprudence that deals with offenses committed against the safety and order of the state. As such, criminal law relates to actions that are considered so dangerous, or potentially so, that they threaten the welfare of society as a whole. This is why in criminal cases it is the government that brings the action against the accused. **Civil law,** by contrast, is the body of principles that determine private rights and liabilities. In these cases, one individual or organization brings an action against another—a *plaintiff* versus a *defendant*—as opposed to the government bringing an action against an accused person. More specifically, civil law is structured to regulate the balance of rights between individuals or organizations; it involves such areas as divorce, child support, contracts, and property rights. Civil law also includes *torts,* civil wrongs for which the law provides redress.

There are three basic types of criminal law: statutory law, case law, and common law. **Statutory law** consists of laws or statutes enacted by legislatures. Each state has a statutory criminal code, as does the federal government. The laws that define the boundaries of such offenses as homicide, rape, burglary, robbery, and larceny are generally statutory in nature. By contrast, **case law** is law that results from court interpretations of statutory law or from court decisions in cases in which rules have not been fully codified or have been found to be vague or in error. A classic example of case law is the Supreme Court decision involving ***Robinson v. California,***[16] which overturned Robinson's conviction as a narcotics addict under a section of the California Health and Safety Code. The California law under which Robinson was convicted read as follows:

> No person shall use, or be under the influence, or be addicted to the use of narcotics, except when administered by or under the direction of a person licensed by the State to prescribe and administer narcotics. It shall be the burden of the defense to show that it comes within the exception. Any person convicted of violating any provision of this section is guilty of a misdemeanor and shall be sentenced to serve a term of not less than 90 days nor more than one year in the county jail.

Robinson had been convicted after a jury trial in the Municipal Court of Los Angeles. The arresting officer testified that he had observed scar tissue, discoloration, and what appeared to be needle marks on the inside of the defendant's left arm and that the defendant had admitted to occasional use of narcotics. Under the California law, the use of narcotics was considered a status or condition, not an act; it was a continuing offense that could subject the offender to arrest at any time before he or she "reformed."

Robinson was convicted of the offense charged. He then took his case to the Appellate Department of the Los Angeles County Superior Court, where the conviction was *affirmed* (accepted by the court). Upon appeal to the U.S. Supreme Court, the decision was reversed on the grounds that status offenses such as "being addicted to the use of narcotics" were unconstitutional and that imprisonment for such an offense was cruel and unusual punishment in violation of the Eighth Amendment to the Constitution. Thus, the court's ruling in *Robinson* v. *California* represents case law in that it defined narcotics addiction as a status that was no longer punishable under the law.

Common law refers to customs, traditions, judicial decisions, and other materials that guide courts in decision making but have not been enacted by legislatures or embodied in the Constitution. Among the more familiar aspects of common law are the rights set forth in the Declaration of Independence and other doctrines protecting life, liberty, and property.

Defense or Justification   For an act (or the omission thereof) to be a crime, it must not only be intentional and in violation of the criminal law but also be committed without defense or justification. **Defense** is a broad term that can refer to any number of situations that would serve to mitigate guilt in a criminal offense. The most common defenses are insanity, mistake of fact, mistake of law, duress and consent, consent of the victim, entrapment, and justification.

Insanity is any unsoundness of mind, madness, mental alienation, or want of reason, memory, and intelligence that prevents an individual from comprehending the nature and consequences of his or her acts or from distinguishing between right and wrong conduct. Insanity is a legal concept rather than a medical one. It is also a complex legal issue. A few jurisdictions recognize that some defendants can be partially insane with respect to the circumstances surrounding the commission of a crime but sane as to other matters.

The cornerstone of the insanity defense emerged from the 1843 case of Daniel M'Naghten, who had killed the secretary to Sir Robert Peel. At his trial, heard before the British House of Lords, he claimed that at the time he committed the act he had not been of a sound state of mind. From this came the **M'Naghten Rule**—the "right-or-wrong" test of criminal responsibility—which states:

> If the accused was possessed of sufficient understanding when he committed the criminal act to know what he was doing and to know that it was wrong, he is responsible therefore, but if he did not know the nature and quality of the act or did know what he was doing but did not know that it was wrong, he is not responsible.[17]

The M'Naghten test has been severely criticized on the grounds that it is arbitrary and applies to only a small percentage of people who are actually mentally ill. In 1954 the U.S. Court of Appeals for the District of Columbia broadened the M'Naghten Rule, creating what has become known as the **Durham Rule.** In *Durham* v. *United States,*[18] the court held that an accused person is not criminally responsible if he or she suffers from a diseased or defective mental condition at the time the unlawful act is committed. This rule has also been criticized, but on opposite grounds from M'Naghten. Critics claim that it is far too broad and places too much power in the hands of psychiatrists and juries in determining the presence or absence of insanity.

In actuality, the defense of "not guilty by reason of insanity" has been debated for generations. The verdict finds the defendant incapable of forming the necessary *mens rea* (intent) to commit the crime, resulting in a sentence of psychiatric treatment. Critics argue that time spent in mental institutions by defendants who are acquitted on insanity pleas is generally less than time served by other defendants who are sent to prison for similar crimes. Supporters of the insanity defense claim that it is morally unjust to convict and punish an individual who acted with an unsound mind.

Few students today will remember John W. Hinckley, Jr., who was accused of shooting President Ronald Reagan in 1981. Hinckley's acquittal on grounds of insanity rekindled the controversy over the insanity defense. Many people lost confidence in the criminal justice system because it was unable to punish a man who admitted trying

It's strange that men should take up crime when there are so many legal ways to be dishonest.

—AL CAPONE

Obviously, crime pays or there'd be no crime.

—G. GORDON LIDDY

"I KNOW THE DIFFERENCE BETWEEN RIGHT AND WRONG, BUT SO FAR I'VE NEVER HAD REASON TO ACT ON THAT INFORMATION."

© The New Yorker Collection 2005 Frank Cotham from cartoonbank.com. All Rights Reserved.

to assassinate the president of the United States. There were calls for reform and even for abolition of the insanity defense.[19]

In the aftermath of the Hinckley verdict, four states (Montana, Idaho, Utah, and Kansas) have omitted the insanity defense and instead allow mental conditions to be used as a mitigating factor.[20] Seven other states have opted for verdicts of "guilty but mentally ill" or "guilty but insane."[21] The intent of these rulings is to ensure that the defendant not only undergoes psychiatric treatment but also serves as much time in prison as another person convicted of a similar crime. Moreover, the U.S. Supreme Court's decision in *Jones* v. *United States*[22] (1983) held that persons found not guilty of crimes by reason of insanity may be confined to mental hospitals for a longer time than they would have spent in prison if convicted—a ruling that applied to John W. Hinckley, Jr.

Yet despite the new state statutes and the ruling in *Jones,* the insanity defense has actually been expanded in the post-Hinckley era. A number of Vietnam veterans suffering from the disorientation and flashbacks associated with posttraumatic stress disorder (PTSD) have successfully argued that the intense reliving of their war experiences destroyed their ability to distinguish between right and wrong. The PTSD insanity defense has been used to acquit veterans accused of homicide, armed robberies, and drug law violations.

The problem with the insanity defense is that *insanity* is a legal, not a medical, term. Moreover, there is little agreement on the actual meaning of the word. Conventional wisdom suggests that the use of the insanity defense is widespread and that many clever and willful murderers have avoided death sentences through pleas of guilty by reason of insanity. For a discussion of this issue, see the "Critical Thinking in Criminal Justice" section at the end of this chapter.

"I know how to get out of going to jail. I just tell the judge I hear voices."

—A MIAMI CRACK ADDICT

Mistake of fact is any erroneous understanding of fact or circumstance resulting in some act that would not otherwise have been undertaken. Mistake of fact becomes a defense when an individual commits a prohibited act in good faith and with a reasonable belief that certain facts are correct, which, if they were indeed accurate, would have made the act innocent. Further, the mistake must be an honest one and not the result of negligence or poor deliberation.

For example, if Smith walks away with Jones's suitcase thinking that it is his own, Smith's defense would be that he was operating under a mistake of fact because both parties had identical luggage. Such a mistake precludes Smith from having criminal intent. As a result, he has a defense against a conviction for larceny. Mistake of fact has been used as a defense in cases of statutory rape—that is, sexual intercourse with a person under a certain age (usually 16 or 18) despite his or her consent. Although a defendant may claim that his or her underage sexual partner "looked older," the courts are decidedly mixed in their acceptance of this defense.[23]

Mistake of law is any want of knowledge or acquaintance with the laws of the land insofar as they apply to the act, relation, duty, or matter under consideration. The old cliché that "ignorance of the law is no excuse" suggests that mistake of law is no defense against prosecution for such a crime. Indeed, simple ignorance of forbidden behavior is not usually an acceptable defense; all persons are assumed to have knowledge of the law. This is true for both citizens and foreign nationals. For example, if a British woman were to take a motor tour of the United States and unwittingly drive on the left side of the road, as is the law in her native land, her ignorance would not serve as a defense against a U.S. traffic violation. Similarly, in many jurisdictions it is a crime to fail to come to the aid of a police officer when so ordered and if the request is not hazardous to the citizen. This law is not well known to most citizens. Nevertheless, should an individual fail to comply with such an order on the basis of ignorance, his or her lack of knowledge of the law would not be an adequate defense against the crime. In contrast, however, as the Supreme Court ruled in **Lambert v. California**,[24] ignorance of the law may be a defense against crime if the law has not been made reasonably well known.[25]

Duress and consent refers to any unlawful constraints exercised on an individual forcing him or her to consent to committing some act that would not have been done otherwise. Whereas duress implies that one is not acting out of free will, the American system of law emphasizes both criminal intent and responsibility. A typical example of duress and consent is often portrayed in television and movie themes. The local bank official is forced to aid the thieves in a bank robbery while his family members are held captive by a second group of bandits. If the banker fails to cooperate, his family will be harmed. In this case duress and consent is a legal defense against crime, since there is no criminal intent and since the rule includes injuries, threats, and restraints exercised not only against the individual but against his or her parent, child, or spouse as well. However, such threats or restraints must be against a person (as opposed to property), and they must be immediate (not future). Had the bank official been threatened with the slaying of his family at some future date, there would be no immediate and imposing threat. Similarly, if the threat was to destroy his house, the notion of duress would be a poor defense.

Consent of the victim is any voluntary yielding of the will of the victim causing him or her to agree to the act of the offending party. This defense has several elements. First, the victim must be capable of giving consent. Thus, this rule excludes any consent offered by the mentally ill, the retarded, or persons below the age of reason. Second, the offense must be a "consentable" crime. Murder is considered to be a *nonconsentable* crime, as is statutory rape. Moreover, there are offenses, such as disorderly conduct, for which no consent can generally be given. Third, the consent cannot be obtained by fraud. For example, should an auto mechanic suggest to a customer that the car's transmission must be fully replaced when in fact only a small bolt requires tightening, the victim's consent to have it replaced is not a legal defense. Fourth, the person giving consent must have the authority to do so. Although one party may have the right to give consent to have his or her property taken, such authority cannot be applied to the property of another party.

Entrapment is the inducement of an individual to commit a crime not contemplated by him or her, undertaken for the sole purpose of instituting a criminal prosecution against the offender. Cases of entrapment occur when police officers, or civilians acting at their behest, induce a person to commit a crime that he or she would not have otherwise undertaken.

Inducement is the key word in the entrapment defense. It refers to the fact that the accused had no intention of committing the crime until persuaded to do so by the police officer. Should Officer Jones approach Smith, convince him to rob Brown, and then arrest Smith after the crime has been committed, the defense of police entrapment would be available. Similarly, in some jurisdictions, if a vice squad officer in plain clothes offers a female prostitute money in return for sexual favors and then arrests her after their encounter, entrapment might be an available defense. Even though the accused is a prostitute by profession, the case could be one of entrapment since the particular offense for which she was arrested occurred only because of police inducement.

In recent years, the entrapment defense has been weakened by court decisions that have considered the offender's "predisposition" to commit a crime. In the 1976 case of *Hampton* v. *United States*,[26] the Supreme Court ruled that it was not entrapment for an undercover agent to supply illicit drugs to a suspected dealer and then for another agent to act as a buyer when there was reason to believe that the suspect was inclined, or "predisposed," to commit the crime anyway. What makes this case different from that of the prostitute is the legality of the behavior in question. Sexual intercourse is generally legal, regardless of whether one's partner is a prostitute. What constituted the crime was acceptance of money for the sexual act, and what constituted entrapment was the plainclothes officer's offer of money. In contrast, Hampton's dealing in illicit drugs was illegal; it was not the undercover agent's inducement that made the behavior illegal. Moreover, in contrast to the case of Officer Jones convincing Smith to rob Brown, Hampton was reputedly a drug dealer while Smith was not a robber by trade.

Justification is any just cause or excuse for the commission of an act that would otherwise be a crime. The notion of justification as a defense against crime typically involves the use of force or violence in protecting one's person or property or those of others, in preventing crime, or in apprehending offenders. *Justifiable homicide* includes cases of death resulting from legal demands—the execution of a duly condemned prisoner, the killing of a fleeing inmate by a prison guard, or the shooting of an armed robber by a police officer. *Excusable homicide* includes cases of death from accidents or misfortunes that may occur during some lawful act. Self-defense or the defense of some other individual can be viewed as either a justifiable or an excusable act, depending on the circumstances of the particular case.

Some jurisdictions have particular statutes that may extend the boundaries of justifiable cause or excuse. Until 1974, for example, a Texas law defined as justifiable homicide a husband's shooting and killing of his wife's lover if he found them in the midst of the act of adultery. The law specified, however, that the actual shooting had to occur before the couple separated and that the husband must not have been a party to, or approved of, the adulterous connection. (Interestingly, this statute did not extend to women who found their husbands engaging in adultery.)

There are many kinds of defenses that are not allowed by the courts in most instances. For example, although the First Amendment to the Constitution guarantees religious freedom, *religious practices* that violate criminal law generally cannot be used to justify or excuse criminal conduct. Similarly, if a given law typically is not enforced, this does not justify the violation of that law. *Ethnic custom* is another defense that courts generally do not accept, as in the case of Lee and Neng Vue of South Dakota, who tried to argue that the raw opium they were carrying was customarily used for medicinal purposes.[27] Finally, many people have attempted to use *intoxication* as a defense, claiming that while under the influence of alcohol or drugs they were not in control of their behavior and therefore were not criminally responsible. However, most jurisdictions make a distinction between voluntary and involuntary intoxication. Voluntary intoxication is not a defense under most circumstances. In cases of involuntary intoxication, however, in which liquor or drugs are forced upon an individual, a reasonable

Police Entrapment

If a cop comes up to a prostitute and engages in vague generalities or responses to her leads, this is not entrapment. The scenario might go something like this:

He: Hi.
She: Hi, wanna party?
He: Sure. What's the tariff, and what do you do?
She: Fifty dollars for a blow job.

This is a perfectly legitimate vignette for a legal arrest. The twist on this exchange would be:

He: Hi.
She: Hi.
He: I'm willing to give you $50 for a blow job, how about it?
She: Sure.

Because the officer initiated the action, . . . the arrest, if made, would be illegal.

Source: Former Minneapolis police chief, Anthony Bouza. ∎

I didn't make him buy the damn drugs, I just offered them for sale.

—A SAN FRANCISCO POLICE OFFICER ACCUSED OF ENTRAPMENT

defense can be mounted, depending on the defendant's "degree of intoxication" at the time of the criminal act.

The "little green man" murder case in Texas represents an interesting example of what has been called the *involuntary intoxication defense.* When pulled over by the police, the defendant claimed that his friend had forced him to swallow a letter-size sheet of LSD. Later that night, during a hallucinogenic blackout, he allegedly stabbed his mother's lover to death. The last thing that he remembered when waking up the next morning was a little green man in the freezer taunting him. He was acquitted.[28] In contrast, a defendant was charged with attempting to kill his girlfriend and kidnapping her son. He claimed that PCP had been spilled on his head from the upstairs balcony of his motel room and that his "PCP mind" rendered him unaware of his behavior. In light of his girlfriend's testimony that he spilled PCP on himself while dipping a cigarette in the drug, he was convicted and sentenced to two life terms.[29]

In keeping with drug-related defenses, in 2002 the *duress defense* was used by two illegal Mexican field workers in the case of *United States* v. *Viayra.*[30] The workers had been taken into custody after being found sleeping near guns on an isolated marijuana farm in the Mendocino National Forest. The defense maintained that the workers had been held on the farm under conditions of duress, which should have cleared them of responsibility. A jury rejected the defense and convicted the men, but the decision was later reversed by a U.S. district judge. However, the decision was reversed yet again by a federal appellate court in April 2004. The two men were ultimately sentenced to 10 years in prison, the mandatory minimum for a conviction involving more than 1,000 marijuana plants.[31]

A wide variety of other innovative defenses have been used on behalf of defendants in criminal trials. For example, the *gay panic defense* attempts to win over the emotions of jurors by portraying the victim as a sexual predator. While this defense successfully lessened the severity of charges in several cases during the 1960s and 1970s, recent attempts have yielded mixed results. For example, in 1999 the defense team of Aaron McKinney, one of the accused killers of the University of Wyoming student Matthew Shepard, wanted to use the gay panic defense. The attorneys argued that their client had "snapped" during a drug-induced rage triggered by memories of a childhood sexual assault and by a "confusing" sexual experience with his cousin at age 15. However, the judge barred use of the defense, and McKinney was ultimately convicted of first-degree felony murder.[32]

Cases involving "road rage," acts of harassment or violence that occur while driving, have become more common in the courts in recent years. Charges related to road

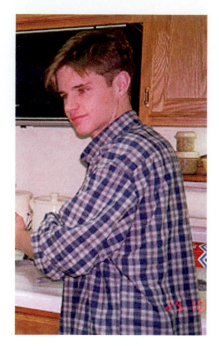

In a case that drew worldwide attention and demands for tougher hate-crime laws, Matthew Shepard was kidnapped, pistol-whipped, robbed, and left tied to a fence in the bitter cold outside of Laramie, Wyoming, in October 1998. The 21-year-old gay college student died 5 days later due to massive head injuries. Russell Henderson and Aaron McKinney, both 21 at the time, are each serving two life sentences for their roles in the crime.

Raeside/Times-Colonist/Victoria, British Columbia; reprinted in *World Press Review,* January 1999, 25.

rage can range from simple assault, to assault with a deadly weapon, to murder. On a few occasions the *road rage defense* has worked to assuage the severity of the charges, although in many others defendants have been sentenced to life in prison.[33] There has also been the recently proposed *bladder defense.* The defense attempts to clear drivers charged with DUI or DWI on the basis of how often they need to urinate. According to the argument, since the consumption of alcohol produces the need to frequently urinate, the defendant should have to use the restroom several times during the course of the arrest and booking process. However, if the defendant never uses the restroom during this time period, this demonstrates that he or she did not consume a large quantity of alcohol. Therefore, any breath test registering above the legal limit should be invalidated.[34]

Most recently, there has been the *grand theft auto defense,* named for a video game that prosecutors claim as the cause for an Alabama teenager's rampage that left two police officers and a dispatcher dead. The extremely violent and popular game, in which players earn points for stealing cars and killing police officers, was illegally sold to the underage youth. The victims' families filed suit against Take 2 Interactive, the maker of the game; the retailers that sold it; and PlayStation, which manufactures the console. Take 2 issued a statement denying any link between its product and the murders, even though the boy reportedly told police after his arrest: "Life is a video game. You've got to die sometime."[35]

On occasion, *medical necessity* has been accepted as a defense in cases of marijuana possession. Advocates of the medical use of marijuana say that the drug is effective in combating the nausea associated with cancer chemotherapy and AIDS wasting syndrome. And in this behalf, in 2001 a California state court acquitted a man who offered the medical necessity defense to a charge of cultivating 850 marijuana plants.[36] In 2001, in *United States* v. *Oakland Cannabis Buyers' Cooperative,*[37] the U.S. Supreme Court ruled against the medical necessity defense. The High Court's ruling was quite narrow, however, and did not overturn state laws in Alaska, Arizona, Colorado, Oregon, California, Nevada, and Maine giving patients access to marijuana.

Other health-related defenses, particularly relating to mental health, have come before the courts as well. For example, an Illinois woman was spared from prison because of the *shopping addict* defense. Her lawyers argued that she suffered from "diminished mental capacity" and used shopping to "self-medicate" her depression. For embezzling $241,061 from her former employer to support her shopping compulsion, she was sentenced to probation and a number of other conditions, a sentence allowing her to continue psychotherapy sessions.[38]

And speaking of therapy, there have been several cases of *blame-the-therapist defense.* For example, there was the case of Alfred Head, who walked out of a psychiatric hospital and drove his car into the front of his mother's home and beat her to death with a baseball bat. Head and his father were unsuccessful in their lawsuit against the doctors who treated him prior to the murder. However, the defense worked for Wendell Williamson, who was found not guilty by reason of insanity for shooting to death two people. He then won a $500,000 claim when a jury agreed that his therapist failed to correctly diagnose his paranoid schizophrenia, did not explain to him the severity of his condition, and did not follow up with him after their sessions ended. These types of cases revolve around the questions of whether or not the individual was adequately evaluated by the mental health professional and whether the crime was foreseeable.[39]

Some health-related defenses are gender-specific, essentially defending a woman's crime on the basis of her mental state during times of hormonal fluctuation. For example, some courts have accepted the *PMS defense* (premenstrual syndrome defense) for generations.[40] Additionally, there has been the *postpartum depression defense,* which made national headlines during the trial of Andrea Yates (see Exhibit 2.4).

Law Sanctioned by the State The maxim *nullum crimen sine poena* (no crime without punishment) dictates that a law must be written, that persons cannot be tried for acts that are not crimes in law, and that persons cannot be punished for acts for

EXHIBIT 2.4 | Gender Perspectives on Crime and Justice

Postpartum Depression and the Insanity Defense: The Trial of Andrea Yates
by Jennifer Syvertsen

Research suggests that women all over the world often experience feelings of unhappiness during the first several days after childbirth. While most of the time these feelings are temporary, about 10% of new mothers develop a more severe condition called *postpartum depression*. Postpartum depression creates intense feelings of sadness, fear, anxiety, and rage, often to the point that the normal course of daily life becomes too much to bear. The most serious form of the syndrome is postpartum psychosis, which affects about 1 in every 1,000 new mothers. Patients suffer from paranoia and mood shifts, or even hallucinations and delusions. Since postpartum depression develops from a combination of hormonal, mental, and cultural factors, the condition manifests differently among women. Some women claim it has driven them to murder their own children.

Legal cases in which postpartum depression is used as the basis of an insanity defense to murder center around childbirth's effects on a woman's mental health and the link between her mental health status and the legal criteria needed to establish "insanity." Many European countries automatically take postpartum depression into account and treat the murder of children by their mothers as the equivalent of manslaughter, a lesser charge than murder. The U.S. criminal justice system, on the other hand, is seldom as consistent or lenient.

Perhaps the most notorious postpartum depression case is that of Andrea Yates, the suburban Houston housewife who in 2001 drowned her five children in a bathtub and then lined up their dead bodies next to each other in bed. Although Andrea suffered a long history of psychotic postpartum depression, her husband insisted on having more children, even against the advice of the first psychiatrist to treat her. The Yates family's lifestyle was guided by a small fundamentalist Christian sect, and Andrea's husband Rusty was in charge of all household decisions. The children were home-schooled, and she rarely had the opportunity to interact with others in public.

In the end, she was convinced that her children were possessed by the devil and that killing them would save their souls. However, the notoriously conservative Harris County jury rejected her insanity defense, instead convicting her of capital murder and sentencing her to life in prison.

Based on the M'Naghten Rule, Texas' insanity defense does not take into consideration illnesses that impair the mental state, like postpartum depression. Therefore, Yates' lawyers needed to prove not only that she suffered from a mental illness (that was not the issue) but also that she did not know her conduct was wrong. Prosecutors instead carefully constructed the image that Yates knew exactly what she was doing based on the methodical execution of her preconceived plan (she often imagined how she would go about drowning her children) and that she knew her actions were wrong, as evidenced by her phone call to police after the murders.

But the First Texas Court of Appeals overturned the convictions in January 2005 after discovering errors in the testimony of a key witness for the prosecution that might have influenced the jury. Specifically, forensic psychiatrist Park Dietz told jurors that Yates might have patterned the murders after an episode of *Law & Order* in which a mother who drowned her children was found not guilty by reason of insanity.

Andrea Yates after her arraignment in a Houston, Texas, court.

As it turns out, the episode never aired, and at least one juror has said that Dietz's testimony helped sway his decision to convict. Prosecutors have appealed, and the request is still pending.

In the meantime, Andrea remains at the Skyview Unit, a psychiatric prison in Rusk, Texas. At times, she has appeared incoherent, shaking, and delusional; her attorney has described her mental state as "blackness," and she was at one point convinced that her children were still alive. Furthermore, Rusty divorced her in 2005, saying that the marriage had become "insupportable." When Andrea stabilized enough to understand what was going on, she made two specific requests in the marriage settlement agreement: a rocking chair that held sentimental value to her and a burial plot in the cemetery next to the graves of her children.

Sources: American College of Obstetricians and Gynecologists, "Postpartum depression," http://www.acog.org/; Paul Burka, "It's Crazy: Andrea Yates and the Insanity of the Insanity Defense," *Texas Monthly*, July 2002, 8; Christopher Caldwell, "Insanity on Trial: Andrea Yates Was Insane and Everybody Knew It," *The Weekly Standard* 7, 27 (2002), 14; V. Dobson, "The Science of Infanticide and Mental Illness," *Psychology of Public Policy and Law* 6, 4 (2000), 1098–1112; M.R. Oates et al., "Postnatal Depression Across Countries and Cultures: A Qualitative Study," *British Journal of Psychiatry* 184, Suppl. 6: S10–S16; *The Independent*, March 14, 2002, 1; *Star Tribune*, August 7, 2003, A1; *The San Francisco Chronicle*, March 17, 2002, A6; *The Houston Chronicle*, July 21, 2004, A1; *The Houston Chronicle*, January 13, 2005; *The Houston Chronicle*, January 22, 2005; *The Houston Chronicle*, March 18, 2005.

which the state provides no penalty. This clearly is necessary for the preservation of social order. If a legal system had no written law, *any* act could potentially be construed as a crime at the whim of the court or the state, resulting in a situation of tyranny. Moreover, if certain types of behavior were defined as crimes but there were no penalties for engaging in them, people would have little respect for the law and the society would be characterized by high levels of *anomie* or normlessness. American law therefore consists of written codes describing the various prohibited forms of behavior and the range of punishments that would occur for their commission.

The law must be specific, however, for there are many acts that, depending on the circumstances, may or may not be crimes. The act of sexual intercourse, for example, describes any number of situations, including adultery, fornication, forcible and statutory rape, seduction, and incest. Sexual intercourse is also a normal, lawful act between mates. However, even as a lawful act it might be called obscenity, pornography, indecent exposure, or disorderly conduct, depending on the place where it occurs. Further, at one time the ethnicity of each partner might have been considered, and it could have been called *miscegenation* (marriage involving people of different races), which was a crime. Thus, the law must be specific as to which sex acts are prohibited and between whom, where, and under what circumstances they may or may not occur.

Also significant in American criminal law is the doctrine that only the offender can be punished. This rule has its roots in the Old Testament doctrine that "every man shall be put to death for his own sin." However, there are a variety of situations in which this rule may not necessarily apply. Recall, for example, the doctrine of vicarious liability, which says that an employer can be held responsible for certain crimes of his employees.

Felonies and Misdemeanors Crimes have been classified in many ways. One distinction is between *mala in se* and *mala prohibita* offenses. Acts are considered to be *mala in se* when they are inherently evil—immoral in their nature and injurious in their consequences. Such acts include murder, rape, and theft. *Mala prohibita* crimes are those that may not necessarily be wrong in themselves but are wrong simply because they have been prohibited by statute. Moral turpitude—that is, depravity or baseness of conduct—is the basis for the distinction between these two types of crime, but since attitudes regarding moral turpitude tend to vary from one jurisdiction to the next, the distinction that is almost universally used instead is that between felonies and misdemeanors.

Historically, under common law, felonies were crimes that were punishable by death or forfeiture of property. They included such offenses as murder, rape, theft, arson, and robbery. Misdemeanors were considered less morally reprehensible than felonies. The current distinction between the two types of offenses is similar. In most jurisdictions, **felonies** are serious crimes that are punishable by death or by imprisonment (usually for 1 year or longer) in a federal or state penitentiary. **Misdemeanors** are minor offenses that are generally punishable by no more than a $1,000 fine and/or 1 year of imprisonment, typically in a local jail. The felony–misdemeanor classification goes beyond the *mala in se–mala prohibita* distinction, since a number of felonies do not reflect moral turpitude. For example, the crimes of wiretapping, carrying a concealed deadly weapon, or possession of forgery instruments are felonies in some jurisdictions in spite of the perpetrator's lack of moral turpitude.

In the legal codes of most jurisdictions, felonies and misdemeanors encompass the boundaries of what is defined as crime. In a few states, however, there is a third category. This category has resulted from the redefinition of certain offenses as less serious than misdemeanors; such offenses are generally referred to as *violations*. In the New York Penal Law, for example, "violation" means an offense for which a sentence to a term of imprisonment in excess of 15 days cannot be imposed.[41] Included in this category are such minor offenses as disorderly conduct, loitering, public intoxication, and patronizing a prostitute.

A misdemeanor is an infraction of the law having less dignity than a felony and constituting no claim to admittance into the best criminal society.

—AMBROSE BIERCE,
THE DEVIL'S DICTIONARY

| Criminal Law |

Law is a statement of the circumstances in which the public force will be brought to bear upon man through the courts.

—JUSTICE OLIVER WENDELL HOLMES, JR.

Sir Frederick Pollock and F. W. Maitland have commented that "law may be taken . . . to be the sum of the rules administered by the courts of justice."[42] Another legal scholar, Sir James Fitzjames Stephen, believes that law is "a system of commands addressed by the sovereign of the state to his subjects, imposing duties and enforced by punishments."[43] There have been numerous attempts to frame philosophical definitions of law, but few have been widely accepted. Efforts to produce pragmatic definitions have been even more numerous. These definitions generally describe law as a body of rules for human conduct that the courts recognize and enforce.

The origins of law likely date from before the beginning of recorded history. It would be safe to assume, however, that even the crudest forms of primitive social organization needed some regulation, and law quickly evolved to fill that need.

Since the beginnings of civilization a number of distinct legal systems have emerged, including the Egyptian, Mesopotamian, Chinese, Hindu, Hebrew, Greek, Roman, Celtic, Germanic, Catholic church (canon), Japanese, Islamic, Slavic, Romanesque, and Anglican systems.[44] The earliest of these was the Egyptian, dating from about 4000 B.C., followed by the Mesopotamian in 3500 B.C. and the Chinese in 3000 B.C. United States law is comparatively recent; it draws from Greek, Roman, and Catholic church law but has its major roots in the Anglican or English common law. Other sources of U.S. law include the state and federal constitutions, statutory law, and the regulations of administrative agencies.

The good of the people shall be the highest law.

—CICERO

Common Law

The history of common law can be traced to 11th-century England, when the existing collection of rules, customs, and traditions were declared the law of the land by King Edward the Confessor. Much of it was unwritten, "preserved mainly in the breasts and closets of the clergy, who, as a rule, were the only persons educated in the law; in the knowledge and recollection of the thanes [barons] and the landowners whose lands and whose persons were governed by it; and in the traditions handed down from fathers to sons."[45] When William the Conqueror seized the English throne in 1066, he found a system of law that was based not on statute but on the customs of the people as reflected in the decisions of judges:

> Common law was judge-made law—molded, refined, examined, and changed in the crucible of actual decision, and handed down from generation to generation in the form of reported cases. In theory, the judges drew their decisions from existing principles of law; ultimately these principles reflected the living values, attitudes, and ethical ideas of the English people. In practice, the judges relied on their own past actions, which they modified under the pressure of changing times and changing patterns of litigation.[46]

As time passed, a process emerged whereby this largely unwritten customary law of the land was translated into specific rules. As judges reached their decisions in judicial proceedings, a body of maxims and principles developed that was derived, in theory, from customs. The result was a set of legal rules in the form of judicial decisions, rather than legislative statutes, that provided precedents for the resolution of future disputes. This body of decisions became the common law,[47] as opposed to law created by statute. Much of common law, moreover, reflected natural law ideas of right and wrong, as well as direct statements from the Holy Scriptures.

The early criminal laws of the American colonies developed within the tradition and structure of English common law and the English charters for the founding of settlements in the New World. As the colonies became more mature, they developed their own legal systems, but these varied little from English common law. For example,

HENRY II ATTEMPTS TO INVENT THE COMMON LAW

Source: http://www.the-orb.net/cartoons/commonlaw.jpg. Reprinted by permission of Stephen Morillo.

the *Original Criminal Code of 1676,* handed down by the Duke of York and applied to the residents of the Pennsylvania colony, was among the early bodies of law in the New World. Much of it was based on common law, combined with a series of rules designed to maintain British dominance over colonial interests. The influence of biblical proscriptions was also apparent in this code, with many capital offenses drawn from the Ten Commandments.[48]

Other Sources of Criminal Law

Although English common law rests at the foundation of American criminal law, contemporary criminal codes also reflect the content of constitutional law, administrative law, and federal and state statutory laws.

Constitutional Law At the apex of the American legal system is **constitutional law,** or law set forth in the Constitution of the United States and in the constitutions of the various states. Constitutional law is the supreme law of the land. As such, it presents the legal rules and principles that define the nature and limits of governmental power as well as the rights and duties of individuals in relation to the state and its governing organs. These are interpreted and extended by courts exercising the power of judicial review.

The U.S. Constitution, which embodies the fundamental principles by which the affairs of the United States are conducted, was drawn up at the Constitutional Convention in Philadelphia in 1787. The Constitution was signed on September 17, 1787, and was ratified by nine states (the number required to put it into effect) by June 21, 1788. It superseded the Articles of Confederation—the original charter of the United States—which had been in force since 1781. It is brief and concise, and includes a preamble, seven articles, and 26 amendments. Although not all of the Constitution relates to criminal law, Supreme Court and lower-court interpretations of its articles and amendments have had a direct impact on criminal law and criminal procedure, as will be evident throughout this book.

Statutory Law Next in order of authority to constitutional law are the federal statutes, which are enacted by Congress, and state statutes, which are passed by state legislatures. Federal statutes must conform to the Constitution, and state statutes must conform to both the U.S. Constitution and the constitution of the state in which they are enacted.

With 50 separate state legislatures creating laws, and an even greater number of separate court systems interpreting them, the application of statutory laws becomes exceedingly complex. Moreover, statutory laws are far from uniform. For this reason criminal laws established by statute tend to vary from one jurisdiction to another, and what may be a violation of the criminal law in one state may not necessarily be a violation in another.

Administrative Law Finally, criminal law can descend from **administrative law,** a branch of public law that deals with the powers and duties of government agencies. More specifically, administrative law refers to the rules and regulations of administrative agencies; the thousands of decisions made by them; their orders, directives, and awards; and the court opinions dealing with appeals from the decisions and with petitions by the agencies to the courts for the law enforcement of their orders and directives.

Much of the content of administrative law is not concerned directly with criminal behavior. Nevertheless, the rules of certain agencies bear directly on violations of behavior that would be dealt with by the criminal courts. The Drug Enforcement Administration, for example, defines substances such as heroin and marijuana as illegal. This is an administrative regulation that has been translated into criminal statutes by Congress as well as many state legislatures.

Selected Capital Offenses From the *Original Criminal Code of 1676*

If any person within this Government shall deny the true God and His attributes, he shall be put to death.

If any person shall commit any willful and premeditated murder he shall be put to death.

If any person slayeth another with a sword or dagger who hath no weapon to defend himself, he shall be put to death.

If any man bear false witness maliciously and on purpose to take away a man's life, he shall be put to death.

If any child or children, above sixteen years of age, and of sufficient understanding, shall smite their natural father or mother, unless thereunto provoked and forced for their self-protection from death or maiming, at the complaint of said father and mother, and not otherwise, there being sufficient witness thereof, that child or those children so offending shall be put to death. ∎

The Rosetta Stone, a basalt slab, dating 196 B.C., found by Napoleon's troops in Egypt in 1799, inscribed in hieroglyphs, demotic script, and ancient Greek.

Theories of Crime Causation

The Rosetta Stone, now in the British Museum, was found in the Nile River delta by an engineer traveling with Napoleon's troops in 1799. It was a slab of volcanic rock erected in 196 B.C. to honor Ptolemy Epiphanes of Syria and was inscribed in three languages—Greek, demotic Egyptian, and hieroglyphic. The significance of the stone was that it furnished Egyptologists with the key by which they could decipher the meaning of Egyptian hieroglyphics, and since that time the Rosetta Stone has served as a symbol for things that may unravel the more elusive mysteries of nature and human behavior. In like manner, it has been suggested that the fervent efforts of students, theorists, and researchers of crime often reflect a belief in some sort of *criminologist's stone*—one monolithic approach or theory that would ultimately account for the entire range of behaviors interpreted by one society or another to be *crime*.

Possession by demons has long since been an explanation for criminal and deviant behavior in many cultures and societies, but the first scientific doctrine of crime causation can be found in the work of the 19th-century Italian criminologist Cesare Lombroso, who once reflected:

> Suddenly, one morning, on a gloomy day in December, I found in the skull of a brigand a very long series of atavistic abnormalities . . . analogous to those that are found in inferior vertebrates. At the sight of these strange abnormalities—as an extensive plain is lit up by a glowing horizon—I realized that the problem of the nature and generation of criminals was resolved for me.[49]

With this "revelation," Lombroso gave substance to the anthropological study of crime and criminals, suggesting that anyone who broke the rules of society was an *atavism*— a throwback to some earlier stage in human evolution. Yet Lombroso's views failed to stand the test of time, and like Sir Walter Raleigh's pursuit of El Dorado and Juan Ponce de Leon's quest for the fountain of youth, the answer to the question "Why do people commit crime?" has continued to challenge the brightest minds in the criminal justice field. For example, over the past hundred or so years:

- A medical approach has sought to study the influence of physical disease on crime.
- A biological approach has attempted to relate crime to heredity.
- Physiological and biomedical approaches have correlated crime with both normal and abnormal physiological functions and types.
- A psychological approach has analyzed motivation and diagnosed personality deviations in relation to crime.
- An IQ approach has characterized low intelligence as morphology of evil.
- A psychoanalytic approach has designated mental disease as the root of crime and traced behavior deviations to the repression of basic drives.
- A geographical approach has tried to demonstrate the influences of climate, topography, natural resources, and geographical location on crime.
- An ecological approach has investigated the impact of the spatial distribution of persons and institutions on behavior patterns.
- An economic approach has looked for relationships between various economic conditions and crime.
- A social approach has considered educational, religious, recreational, occupational, and status factors as they may relate to crime.
- A cultural approach has examined the influence of various institutions, social values, and patterns that characterize groups, and the conflicts among cultures on crime.
- A sociological approach has concerned itself with the nature and effects of social values, attitudes, and relationships on behavior.
- A conflict or "critical" approach has focused on crime as a consequence of the conflicts inherent in law creation.
- A multifactor approach has sought to embrace the combination of any or all of these issues as they may result in the generation of criminal behavior.

RESEARCH ON CRIME & JUSTICE | EXHIBIT 2.5

A Theory of Crime and Rehabilitation for Drug-Involved Offenders

A vast body of research suggests that for the hundreds of thousands of drug-involved offenders who come to the attention of the criminal justice system each year, "drug abuse" and "criminality" are but symptoms of a complex behavioral disorder that cannot be properly addressed through incarceration—either short term or long term. The aspects of this disorder might be referred to as crime-related "impedimenta" to social functioning. The major impedimenta are as follows:

- *Inadequacy,* characterized by a generalized feeling of helplessness; the inability to plan ahead; frequent feelings of despair, negativism, and cynicism; the perception of tasks as likely to lead to failure rather than success; and, a disproportionate fear (and anticipation) of rejection.

- *Immaturity,* characterized by the inability to postpone gratification; a general attitude of irresponsibility; a preoccupation with concrete and immediate objects, wishes, and needs; an orientation of the individual as "receiver" and a tendency to view others as "givers."

- *Dependency,* characterized by a difficulty in coping with unstructured or complex environments; anxiety in situations requiring independent action; and feelings of resentment toward what is believed to be the source of dependency.

- *Limited in social skills,* characterized by a lack of ability to articulate feelings and ideas, and a resulting inability to communicate meaningfully with others except at superficial levels; lack of ability to function in subordinate roles (e.g., inability to take orders from a superior in a work situation); inability to "take the role of the other," (i.e., empathize with others); and inadvertent, socially disapproved behavior (e.g., use of language inappropriate to various social situations, dress inappropriate for job interviews, failure to conform to norms of personal hygiene).

- *Ill-equipped in education,* characterized by functional illiteracy or a conspicuous disproportion between the individual's level of education and his or her potential level, or both.

- *Vocational maladjustment,* characterized by a lack of appropriate technical skills for employment that would be meaningful to the individual.

- *Antisocial attitudes,* consisting of a configuration of values and viewpoints that are defined by society as delinquent, criminal, and antisocial. An individual who possesses antisocial attitudes demonstrates positive attitudes toward trouble, toughness, smartness, excitement, fate, autonomy, and short-run hedonism.

These characteristics may appear singly or in combinations of two, three, four, or more in any individual at any given time. And the drug abuse treatment and psychiatric literatures have documented the presence of impedimenta among substance abusers through literally hundreds of studies.

The criminality of drug-involved offenders is typically but one symptom of a complex of problems that cannot be addressed by any easy solution. Moreover, there is a whole literature that suggests that drug abuse is "overdetermined" behavior. That is, addiction to drugs is secondary to the wide range of influences that instigate and regulate drug-taking and drug-seeking behaviors. Drug abuse is a disorder of the whole person, affecting some or all areas of functioning. In the vast majority of drug offenders, there are cognitive problems, psychological dysfunction is common, thinking may be unrealistic or disorganized, values are misshapen, and frequently there are deficits in educational and employment skills. The research and clinical literature also documents that the great majority of drug abusers were victims of physical abuse, sexual abuse, and/or neglect as children. As such, drug abuse and drug-related criminality are responses to a series of social and psychological disturbances. Thus, the goal of treatment should be "habilitation" rather than "rehabilitation." Whereas *rehabilitation* emphasizes the return to a way of life previously known and perhaps forgotten or rejected, *habilitation* involves the offender's initial socialization into a productive and responsible way of life. What the large drug offender population needs is habilitation in long-term residential treatment.

Sources: James A. Inciardi, "The Irrational Politics of American Drug Policy: Implications for Criminal Law and the Management of Drug-Involved Offenders," *Ohio State Journal of Criminal Law,* 1 (Fall 2003), 273–288; Douglas S. Lipton, *The Theory of Rehabilitation as Applied to Addict Offenders* (New York: Narcotic and Drug Research, Inc., 1989).

The presence of so many theories should not suggest that the explanations proposed have always been without merit. An examination of the major biological theories and classic sociocultural theories of crime can assist in better understanding the nature and causes of crime.

Biological Theories

Biological theories of crime, having achieved initial prominence over a century ago, have persisted in one form or another right up to the present. These theories are grounded in the concept of *biological determinism,* a notion suggesting that the causes of crime are the result of some biological or physical element—that criminals may be "born," not made.

Criminal Anthropology Most closely associated with the biological school of thought are the findings of Cesare Lombroso (1835–1909), an Italian army physician and prize doctor. Often referred to as the "father of modern criminology," Lombroso conducted systematic observations and measurements of the physical attributes of criminals. He believed that he saw in these individuals some of the same characteristics as those found in "savages" or prehuman people. Lombroso maintained that the criminal could be identified by certain "stigmata of degeneration," such as a slanting forehead, excessive dimensions of the jaw and cheekbones, ears of unusual size, peculiarities of the eyes, abnormal teeth, excessively long arms, a sparse beard, a twisted nose, woolly hair, fleshy and swollen lips, or the presence of tattoos. He also noted such nonphysical abnormalities as a lack of morality, excessive vanity, and cruelty.

Having been heavily influenced by Charles Darwin's evolutionary doctrines, Lombroso concluded that the criminal was an atavism, a throwback to a more apelike ancestor.[50] Thus, he maintained, the criminal was *born* a criminal, defective or degenerate in some way. The atavistic features were apparent in both male and female criminals alike. Lombroso added, however, that in the case of prostitutes the typical criminal characteristics might not be immediately evident:

> The art of making up, imposed by their trade on all of these unfortunates, disguises or hides many characteristic features which criminals exhibit openly. If external abnormalities be rare in prostitutes, internal ones, such as overlapping teeth, a divided palate . . . are more common among them.[51]

Heredity A number of biological theorists have suggested that criminal tendencies might be inherited. Among the most frequently cited investigations in this regard is a study of the Jukes family conducted by Richard Dugdale in 1874.[52] Dugdale traced 709 members of the Jukes family back to the year 1790 and found that 20% had been either habitual thieves or prostitutes or had been prosecuted for bastardy. He concluded that their criminality had been caused by "bad" heredity and that the biological transmission of feeblemindedness resulted in degeneracy.[53]

Constitutional Inferiority and Body Types Around the turn of the 20th century, Dr. Charles Goring of Her Majesty's Prisons in Great Britain conducted an exhaustive study of the physical types of 3,000 English convicts.[54] His research revealed no evidence of a "physical criminal type," seemingly repudiating the whole Lombrosian doctrine. Yet in 1939, Harvard University anthropologist Earnest A. Hooton published *Crime and the Man,* a study based on the measurements of almost 14,000 prisoners in 10 states, plus a large sample of noncriminals, which disposed of Goring's work as "scientifically biased" and gave some vindication to Lombroso.[55] Grounded in Lombroso's work, Hooton's ideas were also based on the eugenics doctrine. According to Hooton, criminals belonged to a class of biological degenerates who exhibited a clear pattern of physical inferiority. Therefore, it was necessary to eliminate this "criminal stock" through sterilization, euthanasia, and cutbacks in welfare so as to breed a race disinclined toward criminal behavior.[56]

Shortly after the publication of Hooton's book, William H. Sheldon and his associates at Harvard presented a body-filled thesis for explaining criminal behavior.[57] They contended that all persons could be divided into roughly three basic body types, by which their personalities and their criminal potential could be predicted. Thus, Sheldon was advancing the notion that behavior is a function of the body structure.

Sheldon identified the following basic body types: The *endomorph* was characterized as having a soft and round body with tapering limbs. The *ectomorph* was characterized by a thin and linear body with delicate bones, a small face, a sharp nose, and fine hair. The third type, the *mesomorph,* was a ruggedly muscular individual with a

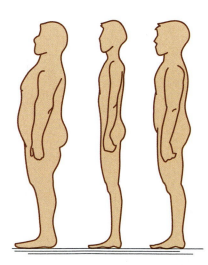

Source: William H. Sheldon, S. S. Stevens, and W. B. Tucker, *The Varieties of Human Physique* (New York: Harper, 1940).

large trunk, heavy chest, and strong limbs. Each of the three body types had its accompanying temperament. Endomorphs were relaxed creatures of comfort who were eternal extroverts. Ectomorphs were introverts—inhibited, secretive, and restrained. Mesomorphs were assertive, aggressive, and action-oriented. Sheldon held that mesomorphs were more inclined toward criminal behavior, a conclusion he stressed again years later, subsequent to his studies of juvenile delinquents.

Sheldon never denied the impact of social variables on deviance, and he held firmly that differences in body type produced differential responses to environmental pressures. In this, at least, there may be some merit to his theory. After all, heavy people (endomorphs) are expected to be jolly and good-natured; weak and skinny people (ectomorphs) are expected to be shy and withdrawn; and the large and physically powerful (mesomorphs) are often expected to be pushy and aggressive. Of course, there are exceptions, but perhaps by anticipating such behaviors, people often encourage them.

Aberrant Chromosomes Advances in the field of molecular biology and micropathology during the second half of the 20th century suggested a link between chromosome abnormality and criminal behavior. Chromosomes are the parts of each living cell nucleus that carry hereditary information in the form of genes. The normal chromosomal pattern that features two similar-size chromosomes is the female XX pattern. The normal male pattern, or the XY pattern, is characterized by two dissimilar chromosomes. But an XYY pattern has also been observed among some men. In the XYY pattern, the particular chromosomes that control the inheritance of sex-linked characteristics are abnormal. Researchers speculate that 1 in every 700 males possesses an XYY chromosomal makeup, resulting in the physical characteristics of tallness, severe acne, long arms, and other skeletal irregularities. The psychological attributes of possible mental retardation or pronounced mental illness, aggressiveness, and perhaps even social isolation, sexual deviation, and criminality are also postulated.[58]

Crime and Human Nature As one might suspect, the biological theories of crime have not received widespread support, and perhaps with some justification. From the "atavistic man" to the "XYY man," the logical base for almost every theoretical posture has been structurally weak. The influences of environmental, cultural, social, and legal factors were continually ignored by proponents of biological explanations. The study samples utilized in biological research included convicted criminals, prison inmates, or certified delinquents; rarely were nondeviant control populations introduced. In addition, many of the samples were so small that the conclusions drawn from them had little meaning. Finally, interpretations were often based on unsound reasoning, contorted logic, or blatant prejudice. Obvious confounding factors were invariably ignored in an effort to support the overall theoretical formulation. Yet, on the other hand, a number of the biological theories have not been disproved by empirical studies. Moreover, the idea that there may be some biological basis for criminality continues to have some research support.

In 1985, the idea that criminals may be born, and not made, received international attention with the publication of *Crime and Human Nature.*[59] Written by prominent Harvard professors James Q. Wilson (a political scientist) and Richard Herrnstein (a psychologist), the book's central thesis was that at least a portion of criminality is innate. Wilson and Herrnstein were influenced heavily by studies of IQ and constitutional inferiority, and while they rejected the idea of a specific criminal gene, they proposed the existence of a particular personality type with features that make a person more likely to value crime. These features, or "constitutional factors" as Wilson and Herrnstein referred to them, either are inborn or emerge early in life and are only minimally influenced by family. Even less influence is credited to cultural and economic factors. The authors argued, for example, that impulsiveness—the inability to contemplate the long-term consequences of one's actions—is a critical element in the criminal personality. Criminals are stunted in their ability to weigh the costs that sanctions will exact or the future benefits of discipline at school, at work, or in a career. Consequently, they opt for the immediate emotional and material gratification that crime provides.

Recent scientific advances in our comprehension of the human genome have reinvigorated the debate over the "born criminal." Some observers have even suggested that political correctness and prejudices have prevented a wider acceptance of the critical influence of genes on criminality.[60] Illustrating this point, a recent conference on the genetic roots of violence had to be canceled in the face of severe opposition and widespread condemnation by the scientific community. Such backlash likely stemmed from fears that supremacist groups could use such theories to support racist ideology and dismiss entire ethnic groups as genetically inferior, similar to the way the Nazis justified their persecution of the Jews.[61]

At the same time, however, many biological theorists admit that although vitally important, genetics alone is insufficient to explain all criminal behavior. Perhaps the best way to encapsulate the modern compromise is that nature endows us with certain innate personality traits and attributes that are then nurtured, for better or for worse, through socialization processes and cultural influences.

Sociocultural Theories

Biological theories of criminal behavior tend to focus on the makeup of the individual. The main concerns of proponents of biological theories are the characteristics of those people already classified as "criminals" and how they may differ from characteristics of the "normals" in the population. Sociocultural theories, on the other hand, examine criminality in terms of how it may be related to society and culture. The core ideas suggest that an individual's place within the social and cultural structure determines his or her behavior and that socialization processes in the family, schools, and peer groups serve to influence and control deviant behaviors. Modern outgrowths of the sociocultural school are organized under two broad categories: social or cultural *structure theories* and social or cultural *process theories*. Structural theories include social disorganization theory, strain theories, (anomie and general strain theory) and cultural deviance theory; process theories include social learning, social control theory, and labeling theory.

From these sociocultural perspectives, the focus shifts from the individual level to a whole range of sociocultural questions: What are the characteristics of situations in which crime tends to occur? Why is crime more common in certain places, within certain groups, and under certain circumstances than in others? What is the process by which some persons become criminal while others do not? Why is it that some behaviors are defined as criminal while others are not?

Social and Cultural Structure Theories
Social and cultural structure theorists believe that crime can be described through social, cultural, and environmental factors. In this school of thought, criminals are not inherently evil people but rather are disadvantaged in terms of their social environment. Disorganized and decaying neighborhoods, weak social support, and a lack of economic opportunity push many individuals to seek alternate means of survival. In this view, the social structure, rather than the individual per se, is the primary cause of crime.

The sociological perspective within the field of criminology in the United States originated with sociologist Robert E. Park and his colleagues at the University of Chicago. The Chicago School of thought, as it was later called, centered on how social forces in specific neighborhoods influenced rates of crime. Park suggested that human communities were divided into "natural areas."[62] He theorized that the anthropological methods of observation and detailed description could lend insight into how neighborhoods developed over time and how areas of destitution formed. Park sent his students out to utilize these methods in studies of the natural areas of Chicago—the

According to Merton, a high premium is placed on social ascent in American society, but for many there is a gap between aspirations and achievable goals.

ghettos and ganglands, skid row, the "gold coast" and the slums, and the underworlds of vice and crime—and the impact of ecological structures on suicide rates, divorce rates, and crime rates.

Among Park's students were Clifford R. Shaw and Henry McKay, who found that delinquency was concentrated in the deteriorated areas of the inner city and that these areas maintained their high rates of delinquency in spite of constant population changes.[63] Through a number of case studies, Shaw and McKay promoted a **social disorganization theory,** directly linking high crime rates to neighborhood ecological characteristics. Their work found that youths from disadvantaged neighborhoods were participants in a subculture in which delinquency was approved behavior and that criminality was acquired in social and cultural settings through a process of interaction.[64]

Anomie Theory. The concept of **anomie** was first introduced during the latter part of the 19th century by the French sociologist Emile Durkheim, who described the phenomenon as a condition of normative confusion or "normlessness," in which the existing rules and values have little impact.[65] Criminologists who have incorporated the concept of anomie into theories of criminal behavior are known as strain theorists. In general terms, strain theorists view crime as a direct result of the "strain"—frustration, anger, and hopelessness—that come from living in disadvantaged, disorganized, and otherwise "normless" communities where legitimate opportunities for prosperity are all but unavailable. To relieve this strain and as an alternate means to reach their goals, it is theorized, people turn to deviant and criminal behavior.

Building on Durkheim's work, Robert K. Merton of Columbia University developed a general theory of criminal behavior, in which two basic complementary concepts are in operation: a culture and a social structure.[66] The culture consists of a set of norms, values, and attitudes that establishes the goals that individuals should pursue and the acceptable means and behavior patterns for achieving those goals. The social structure involves the organized set of social relationships in which the members of a society play their various roles. American society, in both its culture and its social structure, places a high value on wealth, material comforts, status, and power. Too, the society specifies the rules for how to attain these valued goals properly—education, hard work, "smart" business practices, savings, and investments. While a high premium is

FAMOUS CRIMINALS
Osama bin Laden

As the mastermind of the September 11, 2001, attacks on the United States, Osama bin Laden instantly became the world's most notorious terrorist. In reality, bin Laden has fervently crusaded for years against Western "infidels."

Born into a wealthy Saudi family in 1957, bin Laden was the 17th of more than 50 children born to his father Mohammed and his numerous wives. Bin Laden studied engineering and business management at King Abdul Aziz University in Jedda, Saudi Arabia, where he met a radical Palestinian professor who greatly influenced his world outlook.

Covertly backed by the CIA, bin Laden's career began as a mujahideen who fought against the Soviets after their invasion of Afghanistan in 1979. In 1988, he formed the now infamous terrorist network al-Qaeda ("the base") to fight for Islamic causes. He began to set up training camps in Afghanistan, initially for the war there, but eventually to expand the scope of its mission and target other areas in the world. After the Soviet withdrawal in 1989, bin Laden felt empowered and drew his attention to the last superpower remaining: the United States. His anti-Americanism intensified when Saudi Arabia allowed U.S. troops to be stationed on its soil during the 1990 Gulf War. His opposition to the Saudi king stripped him of his Saudi citizenship, and he was subsequently disowned by his family and exiled. He moved to Kartoum, Sudan.

(continued on p. 55)

placed on economic affluence and social ascent for all, however, the possibility for achieving material success is curtailed for many by reason of their position in the social structure. Crime results, Merton explains, from the strain this gap between aspirations and achievable goals creates.

Given these conditions, Merton suggested five modes of adaptation people may employ—conformity, ritualism, innovation, retreatism, and rebellion—to reconcile this conflict between cultural goals and institutionalized means.

Conformity is the term used to describe the acceptance of cultural goals and the approved means for achieving them. Most people conform. Moreover, they do so even when the legitimate means for reaching the valued goals are out of their grasp. They play by the rules and earn a living the best way they can. And they do so because there are other societywide cultural influences that support conformity—religious values, belief in opportunity, public education, and the absence of formal legal restrictions against upward mobility.

Ritualism is the rejection of society's goals but the acceptance of society's means for achieving those goals. Ritualists accept the means for their own sake; the goals become irrelevant and are ignored. Ritualism is thus often "mindless" behavior. The example of a ritualist most often cited is the government bureaucrat, who gets bound up in "red tape" and procedure and insists on strictly enforcing every petty rule.

Merton's other three types of adaptation relate to crime. *Innovation* involves acceptance of cultural goals but rejection of the means a society deems proper for reaching those goals. The innovator selects disapproved means. Students cheating on exams, thieves, con artists, stock manipulators, drug dealers, and CD pirates attain cultural goals, such as wealth or grades, but have rejected conventional routes. Rather, they innovate, choosing new means of achieving these goals. *Innovation,* however, is actually a poor term for this form of adaptation. Most criminals merely copy illegitimate means already known to them. Thus, using disapproved means is hardly the same thing as inventing or creating new ones.

Retreatism describes the rejection of both the goals a society or culture establishes and the means society prescribes for achieving these goals. The retreatists are the alcoholics and derelicts living on skid row; they are the "street people" and "bag ladies" of the central cities; they are the tramps and outcasts in the "hobo jungles" of rural and suburban America; and they are the "junkies," crack addicts, psychotics, vagrants, vagabonds, and other pariahs who live on the fringes of society.

Rebellion is characterized by a rejection of the goals and the means of achieving those goals established by society. Rebels characteristically aim to establish some new social order and to create a new set of goals and norms governing appropriate means. The most visible and expressive examples of rebellion involve the various terrorist organizations throughout the world that resort to kidnappings, bombings, and assassinations in order to draw attention to their cause and to initiate change. Other rebels are the legion of adolescents who revolt in one way or another against the adult value system that has been imposed on them. Many band together into gangs, some turn "punk," while others may live in communes.

Merton's theory of anomie is important to the study of crime and criminal justice, for it not only offers a simple paradigm for understanding the range of criminal behaviors but also suggests how and why such behaviors emerge. Merton's theory does have its limitations, however. First, while it may provide a plausible interpretation of why people commit certain crime (property crimes, for example), it fails to explain other forms of criminality, such as drug abuse, prostitution, and sex crimes, to name but a few. Second, Merton's approach is strongly grounded in the assumption that some sort of value consensus exists in society. The assumption ignores the process through which certain behaviors come to be defined as criminal—a process that often involves a conflict in values between those who have the power to influence public opinion and policy and those who do not. And third, Merton's theory leaves a number of questions unanswered. For example, it does not explain why one mode of adaptation is chosen over another or how norms begin to decay when goals are not achieved. In addition, it is not clear that material success ranks as high among most people as Merton seems to suggest.

General Strain Theory. Further expanding upon the concept of anomie, **general strain theory** was developed in 1992 by sociologist Robert Agnew.[67] While Merton's theory focuses on social class differences in criminality, Agnew examines the reasons why individuals who feel strain are more likely to commit crimes. Moreover, Agnew offers a more general explanation of crime with applicability to all segments of society, rather than restricting his analysis only to those in the lowest socioeconomic classes. General strain theory suggests that criminality is the direct result of negative affective states that are produced by negative social relationships. Specifically, strain creates negative emotions (e.g., anger and anxiety) within the individual, which in turn, can create the inclination toward deviance and criminal behavior. Thus, negative emotions provide a causal link between strain and deviance. Among the range of negative emotions, Agnew emphasizes outer-directed emotions like anger and rage, but inner-directed emotions like depression and anxiety are likely contributory factors as well.

Going further, general strain theory outlines four general types of strain that an individual might encounter: (1) the failure to achieve positively valued goals, (2) the disjunction of expectations and achievements, (3) the removal of previously attained positive achievements, and (4) exposure to negative stimuli.[68] The first general type of strain reflects Merton's theory of anomie, in that strain is created when goals cannot be achieved because educational and financial resources are lacking. A disjunction of expectations and achievements occurs when people compare themselves to others and perceive that others are doing better financially or socially than they are, thus creating feelings of frustration and tension. The removal of positively valued stimuli is the loss of an important person in one's life, whether it occurs through a break up, separation, divorce, or death. The loss of a positive influence can profoundly impact individual's emotions and behavior. Finally, the introduction of negative stimuli can be considered any type of detrimental social relationship, such as an abusive family member or partner, or the occurrence of negative life events which one must cope with. The more sources of strain and the more vigorous the strain that individuals must contend with, the more likely the individual will turn to crime and delinquency.

The major weakness in general strain theory is its inability to account for gender differences in crime rates. While it's true that how individuals deal with these different types of strain depends on a number of internal and external conditioning factors, including the individual's goals, resources, social support, association with delinquent peers, and access to financial and educational attainment, crime rates among females are much lower compared to the crime rates of males, yet females contend with as much, if not more, strain than do males. The theory fails to clarify the reasons that males and females cope with strains in different ways. On the positive side, many in the field of criminology see tremendous potential in general theory because of its interdisciplinary approach that appreciates other social sciences. Because general strain theory is among the most recent additions to criminal theory, more scientific evaluation is needed.

Culture, Conflict, and the Cultural Deviance Theory. Three-quarters of a century ago, Jerome Michael and Mortimer J. Adler argued that crimes were no more than instances of behavior that are prohibited by the criminal law, that "the criminal law is the formal cause of crime."[69] This comment gives direction to an explanation of crime as it emerges from conflicting sets of norms. In other words, if there were no laws and norms, there would be no crimes.

Thorsten Sellin's *Culture Conflict and Crime* similarly regarded the criminal law as a body of rules that prohibits specific forms of conduct and prescribes certain punishments for violations of these rules. Sellin further observed that the types of conduct the rules prohibited and the nature of the sanctions attached to their violation depended directly on the interests of those in the population who influenced legislation. According to Sellin, "In some states, these groups may comprise the majority, in others a minority, but the social values which receive the protection of the criminal law are ultimately those which are treasured by dominant interest groups."[70]

Crime, in this orientation, can emerge from, or be the result of, a conflict between the norms, values, and goal orientations of a social or cultural group and the legal codes

(continued from p. 54)
Under U.S. pressure to leave, he relocated to Afghanistan in 1996.

Known for his voice-recorded and video-taped messages broadcast on Arab media outlets, bin Laden has masterminded, organized, and financed numerous terrorist attacks around the world. His 1998 *fatwa,* or religious edict, directing his followers "to kill the Americans and their allies, civilians, and military" has come to define his life's mission. Al-Qaeda has turned into a worldwide network with thousands of members and an operating budget estimated at $250 million. Bin Laden himself has been linked to the murders of Western tourists in the Middle East and an assassination attempt on the Egyptian president. He has maintained safe houses for those responsible for the 1993 World Trade Center bombing. He has helped bomb targets in France, Yemen, Saudi Arabia and, most notably, in Nairobi, Kenya, and Dar-es-Salaam, Tanzania,—acts that in 1998 killed 224 people—and devised the attack on the USS *Cole* in 2000. His orchestration of the plane highjackings on September 11 was his largest and deadliest mission to date.

Worries of Young Adults, Aged 18 to 29

I'm going to read a list of problems facing the country. For each one, please tell me if you personality worry about this problem a great deal, a fair amount, only a little, or not at all. Source: Gallup Poll, March 2002 and 2003.

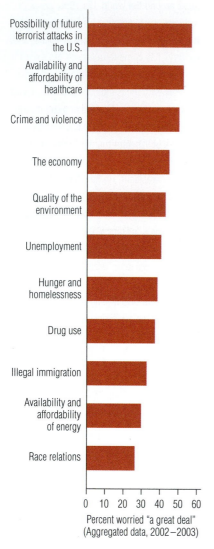

Percent worried "a great deal"
(Aggregated data, 2002–2003)

that have been imposed by an alternative group that has the greater power to shape public policy. Yet, within this framework, the crime that emerges from group conflict can occur when the purposes, interests, and valued goals of groups become competitive with one another in other ways. Albert K. Cohen's concept of the "delinquent subculture" offers an illustration.[71] Cohen suggests that working-class youths are handicapped in attaining social and economic status. Some eventually succeed, but most do not. Therefore, they band together into gangs, which provide them with an arena for striking back at the middle-class values that they oppose and give them status as a subcultural group. These subcultures are "nonutilitarian," "malicious," and "negativistic." They are nonutilitarian in that gang members defy legal codes often simply for the approval given by their peers; they are malicious in that they enjoy the discomfort of their victims because such discomfort is the result of their defiance of norms; and they are negativistic because they repudiate the standards of middle-class culture.

Richard Cloward and Lloyd Ohlin agreed with Cohen that delinquent subcultures are a part of society and that certain delinquent behaviors are required of its members in order to belong. Furthermore, they proposed that the concept of opportunity was important in shaping behaviors. Cloward and Ohlin proposed **differential opportunity theory** in their 1960 book *Delinquency and Opportunity*.[72] The concept suggests that criminals need *access* to illegitimate opportunities and that different groups will have access to different opportunities. Disadvantaged youths with few economic opportunities outside menial, minimum-wage employment may join gangs for the increased prestige and money that drug trafficking promises. On the other hand, persons of middle and high socioeconomic status have the means to commit the less visible and rarely prosecuted white-collar offenses. Such opportunities are not typically available to the inner-city residents, whose only prospects for crime are typically the more visible offenses of burglary and larceny, robbery, and prostitution.

An alternative view that might be interpreted within the culture conflict mode was offered by Walter B. Miller, who contended that certain "focal concerns" within lower-class cultures could often lead to antisocial conduct.[73] He defined *focal concerns* as areas or issues that command widespread and persistent attention and a high degree of emotional involvement. These areas or issues could be found in the middle class but carried higher priorities within lower socioeconomic classes. They included a preoccupation with "toughness," the sensitivity to "smartness," excitement, autonomy, a belief in fate, and a chronic awareness of "trouble." The illegal activity often found in low-income areas represented an adolescent adaptation to the lower-class cultural concerns that were often in conflict with those of the wider society.

Much of what appears in culture conflict theory often seems to reflect on economic concerns. The approach focuses on the political power base occupied by those who have the influence to shape public policy and on how this base and ensuing power and influence serve to extend a criminal status to those of conflicting norms and interests. And a political power base often rests on a strong economic base, or at the very least the two are intricately interwoven. Thus, it is the "underprivileged," the "working class," or the "marginal" that so many theorists are making reference to when they discuss crime in terms of culture conflict. Furthermore, much of what remains unspoken in the theoretical sphere, but which is often nevertheless apparent, is in many ways reminiscent of the early theories of economic determinism. As early as 1516, Thomas More's *Utopia* touched on the issue of crime and its relation to the poor economic status of certain groups. Similar observations were made in 1798 by Thomas Malthus in his *An Essay on the Principle of Population* and by Karl Marx in his *A Contribution to the Critique of Political Economy* in 1859.

Social and Cultural Process Theories Social or cultural process theories posit that criminality is a function of individual socialization. Process theories focus on the interactions that individuals have with various social and cultural institutions and the processes of family socialization, peer relations, education, and employment. If the process of development and the relationships and attachments that individuals form to society are positive, then individuals should be able to succeed and live by legitimate means. On the other hand, if relationships and influences are dysfunctional, individuals may resort to criminal behavior as a way of attaining goals. Process theories suggest that all individuals, regardless of gender, ethnicity, or socioeconomic position in society, have the potential to carry out criminal behavior.

Social and Cultural Learning Theory. Social and cultural learning theorists suggest that crime is learned through the deviant norms, values, and behaviors that are linked with criminal activity. Perhaps the most prominent theory of this nature is that proposed by Edwin H. Sutherland. Sutherland's theory of **differential association** maintains that criminal behavior is learned in the same way that conformity is. His study of professional thieves suggested to him that many criminals learned the knowledge and motivations as well as all the skills necessary for engaging in criminal behavior.[74] Therefore, he extrapolated, criminal behavior and deviance in general are learned within the context of intimate social groups that are criminal. The learning includes the techniques of committing crimes as well as the attitudes and rationalizations that serve to justify such behavior. What distinguishes these attitudes and rationalizations is that they involve a cultural rejection of legal and other social norms. Persons become criminal, Sutherland argued, because they encounter an excess of definitions favorable to violation of the law over definitions favorable to law-abiding behavior. This excess of definitions favorable to law violation, furthermore, is due to a majority of associations with criminals over noncriminals.[75]

In 1966, Robert L. Burgess and Ronald L. Akers reformulated Sutherland's theory by incorporating into it the concept of reinforcement, or an event that strengthens a response. The result is **differential reinforcement theory**.[76] According to Akers, criminal behavior is not only learned but also reinforced by instrumental conditioning. *Instrumental conditioning* refers to learned behaviors that result from the consequences, effects, and outcomes of an individual's social and cultural environment. This theory provided more insight into the learning process and supplied a more refined operating mechanism by which deviant, and for that matter conforming, behavior is produced. In differential reinforcement theory, Akers incorporated four key concepts by which learning operates. The first is *differential association*. The three other mechanisms are differential reinforcement, imitation, and definitions. *Differential reinforcement* incorporates punishments and reinforcers that function to control the frequency, amount, and probability of a behavior. *Imitation* is defined as a behavior that is observed and modeled on the basis of the consequences that behavior renders. Finally, *definitions* are conceptualized as beliefs, attitudes, justifications, and orientations that individuals use to choose between types of behaviors.

With the addition of these learning mechanisms, differential associations could be examined through a causal model. While differential associations may not be a direct cause of deviant acts, they could operate theoretically through the concepts of imitation, reinforcement, and definitions. In other words, an individual may learn different definitions of behaviors through the association with others. In addition, that individual might begin to imitate other's actions within the group and gain rewards through approval by the group that serve to further reinforce the deviant behavior.

These theories represented major breakthroughs for the study of crime. The theoretical conceptions attempted to "normalize" criminal behavior—"normal" in the sense that it was learned through the same processes that other, noncriminal behaviors are learned. Aker's ideas represented an integrated theory. They suggested a chain of interrelationships and correlates in a person's associations and learning experiences that made the commission of crime reasonable and understandable as normal, logical behavior; they advanced a framework within which other theories of crime might be better understood; and they suggested the simpleminded nature of those prior efforts that sought to explain crime in terms of head size and shape, broken homes, feeblemindedness, body structure, and other factors.

Differential association theories, however, also have limitations. First, there is focus on only those kinds of criminality that are systematic in nature, such as professional theft, organized crime, drug selling and trafficking, and certain forms of white-collar

The Wrath of MS 13

Mara Salvatrucha, better known as MS 13, has developed into one of the largest and most ruthless gangs ever known to law enforcement. With some 50,000 members across the United States, Mexico, and Central America, MS 13 is involved in narcotics and gun trafficking, prostitution, murder, and countless other serious crimes. There are even rumors of the gang's collaboration with the terrorist organization al-Qaeda to smuggle individuals into the United States.

MS 13 members are infamous for their particularly brutal and vicious crimes and their calling card of using a machete to hack up their victims. In response, for the first time in its history, the FBI formed a nationwide task force in late 2004 to exclusively target a single gang. The task force comprises local, national, and international law enforcement agencies, as well as the Department of Homeland Security officials. Recently, 103 arrests were made from Los Angeles to Miami. However, hundreds of thousands of MS 13 members remain on the streets, and new recruits, some as young as 13, are joining every day.

Formed in the 1980s in Los Angeles, Mara Salvatrucha roughly translates into "gang of Salvadoran guys." The gang formed to offer protection to Central American immigrants from the already firmly established Mexican gangs in southern California. Many of its U.S. members are illegal immigrants from El Salvador, Guatemala, and Honduras. Even when members are caught and deported, the membership network is so extensive that many find their way back across the border and on to the city streets. ■

Does "Flipping the Bird" Warrant Jail Time?

An American Airlines pilot was arrested in Brazil in January 2004 on charges of "disrespect for authority" when he made an obscene gesture at officials during the fingerprinting and photographing procedures required at customs, a charge carrying a potential 6-month to 1-year jail term. Brazil's new policy—which targets only citizens of the United States—was enacted in retaliation to President Bush's new antiterrorism measures mandating all foreign citizens, save for 27 mostly European countries, to undergo similar screening measures upon entering the United States. Brazilian President Luiz Inacio Lula da Silva personally appealed to Bush for an exemption for Brazilians, telling him that "we have no culture of terrorism" in the nation of almost 180 million.

Ultimately, the pilot averted jail time after agreeing to pay a fine of $12,750 in lieu of facing criminal charges. He was released on his own recognizance.

Sources: *The New York Times,* January 15, 2004, A8; *St. Louis Post Dispatch,* January 15, 2004, A11. ∎

crime, to name but a few. The theories fail, however, to explain certain impulsive and irrational acts that result in crime, such as the majority of homicides, assaults, and forcible rapes. Second, many criminal behaviors are learned through contact with ideas, rather than with people. Furthermore, many of these same behaviors—purse snatching, shoplifting, robbery, assault, and prostitution—require little, if any, training. Third, differential association theory does not address why some persons with extensive contacts with criminals nevertheless resist crime themselves.

Social Control Theory. Travis Hirschi proposed a new theory of criminality in his 1969 work *Causes of Delinquency,* which centered not on individuals' motivations to act deviant but on how individuals are constrained by the social structure.[77] **Social control theory** assumes that people are rational beings in which the motivations behind their behavior are to maximize pleasure and minimize pain. Thus, people are presumed to behave in ways that will maximize their own personal benefits regardless of deviation or conformity. Of interest to social control theory are the mechanisms that keep individuals from acting in deviant ways.

Hirschi proposed four elements of what he called the "social bond," or the measure of an individual's tie to conventional society. The first of these bonds is *attachment,* which indicates how closely attached an individual is to the conventional social world. Examples include attachment to parents, teachers, religious leaders, and peers. *Commitment* is the second bond proposed, as it relates to the time one invests in conforming activities. Common examples are set around the school atmosphere, in which grades and extracurricular activities are measured. *Involvement* is concerned with the time and energy invested in conforming activities. And finally, *beliefs* are suggested to be the moral outlook and standard by which an individual lives. For Hirschi, the bond of belief has to do with the internalization of a common moral system; the measure of "right" and "wrong" in the social world. These four bonds of social control theory are the key factors in a person's rational decision-making process.

However, the theory leaves a few questions unanswered. How do social bonds that change over time affect delinquent behavior? For example, how does the changing relationship between parents and children as they grow up impact behavior? Furthermore, there is speculation that the direction of the proposed social bonds may work both ways, evocative of the age-old "chicken and the egg" argument. Do weakened bonds lead to criminal behavior, as Hirschi contends, or is it that criminal behavior breaks down social bonds?

Labeling Theory. **Labeling theory** attempts to explain why apparently similar acts are treated differently. For example, why is it that the possession of cocaine is illegal, while the possession of alcohol is not? Why is it that sexual intercourse between husband and wife is called "making love," but the same act between sister and brother is called "incest"? Why is an inner-city youth caught stealing a bicycle more apt to be called a criminal than a corporate executive discovered fixing prices? Why is a convicted burglar more likely to end up in prison than a convicted embezzler? Why is it that ex-convicts are more often convicted of crimes than first offenders? And most curiously, why is it that a child who shoots a cat out of a tree on a city street with a BB gun is called "cruel," while his father, who shoots a deer in the woods with a high-powered rifle, is called a "sportsman"?

Somewhat related to these questions is the often repeated anecdote about the colorful playwright George Bernard Shaw. Rather inebriated at a formal British dinner party, Shaw leaned over and whispered to the titled woman seated to his right, "Madam, would you sleep with me for £100,000?" After some mild quivering, the flustered woman answered, "Why possibly I just might." A moment or two later the playwright once again leaned over and asked, "Madam, would you sleep with me for £5?" The suddenly offended noblewoman indignantly replied, "Of course not! What do you think I am?" Shaw regarded her briefly and wryly responded, "Madam, we have already established what you are. All that we are doing now is dickering about the price."

In essence, Shaw's sarcasm gets to the heart of labeling theory. How are definitions of crime formulated by society? How are these definitions or labels applied to individuals? What are the consequences of these labels for those to whom the labels have been applied successfully?

In considering how the labeling process works, consider the discussion of "crime as a social construct" offered earlier in this chapter. The definition of the liquor trades as "evil" and the ratification of the Prohibition amendment in 1919 are clear illustrations of the labeling process.

The impetus for the labeling perspective came in 1951 when sociologist Edwin M. Lemert made an important distinction between *primary* and *secondary* deviations.[78] **Primary deviation** is the violation of some norm, some offensive act or characteristic. **Secondary deviation** results from the societal reaction to the violation—the demeanor and conduct that people cultivate as the result of being labeled deviant or criminal. This distinction between primary and secondary deviation suggests that labeling can indeed have consequences, that the labeling itself adjusts peoples' perceptions of and reactions to criminals, and that these reactions can operationalize the "offender's" criminal role. Most, if not all, people break rules now and then, but they do not necessarily think of themselves as "criminal." However, when circumstances result in their being defined and reacted to as "criminal," they may begin to actively fulfill those roles.

Similarly, many of those labeled as criminal may be forced out of a corner of conventional society into a situation or subculture that further stigmatizes them and makes the continuance of the criminal role inevitable. Persons labeled as "coke heads" may lose their jobs and their friends; they are thus pushed into the drug subculture and the hustling world of the streets for companionship and financial support.

It should be pointed out here that not all primary deviance results in secondary deviance. A number of factors bring about that transformation. First, how important are the norms that are being violated? People view traffic violators, marijuana smokers, and tax cheaters differently than they view child abusers, heroin addicts, and thieves. Second, what is the social identity of the person violating the norm? Certain kinds of rule breaking and nonconformity by the economically powerful are more readily tolerated than are violations of the same norms by socioeconomically disadvantaged ethnic minorities. Third, in what social context is the norm being violated? Marijuana smoking at a rock concert is more likely to be ignored than marijuana smoking at a court hearing.

Labeling theory is an important concept to the study of crime and criminal justice. It explains how certain behaviors come to be defined as criminal, why society will label some individuals and not others, and how the labeling process can produce future lawbreaking. On the other hand, however, the theory does have its weaknesses. Initially, while it suggests how some kinds of crimes "come into being" as a result of moral enterprise (as was the case with the Prohibition amendment), it fails to explain how or why many long-standing forms of crime emerge in the first place. Murder, for example, appears as a prescription in both the Old and the New Testaments, and its designation as an offense punishable by death appears in an early chapter of the Book of Genesis. In addition, and perhaps most important, the labeling perspective fails to explain all of the causes of primary deviance.

As a final note, it should be stressed that it would be unrealistic to expect that any one theory of crime could explain all forms of criminal behavior. Certain aspects of biological theories may hold some scientific merit, while sociocultural theories with bases in both structural and process reasoning also contribute to our understanding of various types of crimes. In fact, it is most likely that each theory or various combinations of theories explain different kinds of lawbreaking (see Exhibits 2.5 and 2.6). It is also important to keep in mind that only a small portion of the existing theories has been discussed in this chapter; the expansive range of theories of crime causation can occupy entire courses in criminology. After all, there are probably as many reasons for engaging in criminal behavior as there are different kinds of crime.

EXHIBIT 2.6 | Gender Perspectives on Crime and Justice

Theoretical Explanations for Violence Against Women

Violence against women has probably gone on since the beginning of time, but only recently has it drawn attention as a serious social problem. Referring to a range of behaviors including emotional, sexual, verbal, and physical abuse; sexual harassment; stalking; murder; and even genital mutilation and prostitution, violence against women takes many forms and cuts across all ethnicities, cultures, and socioeconomic classes.

Theories to explain violence against women vary, but analyses tend to focus on the perpetrator rather than the victim. Such theories can be divided into three broad categories: individual-level, social psychology, and sociocultural theories. The first two theoretical categories can be considered micro theories, in that the focus is on a personal level. The latter category focuses on a macro-oriented approach, or how social and cultural structures can facilitate violence.

Biological theories suggest that violence against women stems from the evolutionary process. For example, some theories suggest an association between hormones and elevated levels of aggression. Another theory attempts to explain rape as the modern-day (albeit extreme) response to the innate pressure that men feel to reproduce; men who have trouble finding a mate with whom to reproduce are more likely to use rape as a way of subconsciously appeasing their evolutionary programming. What this theory fails to explain, however, are the common occurrences of date rape on college campuses that are perpetrated by otherwise healthy, virile males who managed just fine to find a date to victimize.

There are also physiological theories, including research that has looked at the causal relationship of head injuries to violence. One study found that men with head injuries were nearly six times more likely to exhibit violent behavior than men without head injuries; furthermore, more than 90% of the violent men experienced their head injuries prior to their battering behavior. However, this fails to account for violent men who have never experienced physiologic trauma. The problem with biological and physiological theories, however, is that the reasoning eliminates much of the responsibility of the abusers, almost suggesting that they "can't help" their behavior.

Social learning theory applies to violence against women in that it suggests that violence is learned within the context of family. In this sense, it is often referred to as the *intergenerational transmission of violence*. The use of violence as an acceptable means to resolve conflict is passed down within the family from one generation to the next. Similarly, the *family violence perspective* argues that the origin of the violent behavior lies in the family structure. For example, when physical means of punishment are used to control behavior, this creates a sense of confusion among family members by sending the message that love is equated with violence. The weakness in these theories, however, is that not everyone who grows up in a violent family ends up turning to violence.

Theories that focus on the psychological pathology of perpetrators suggest that a personality disorder or some form of mental illness is to blame for their behavior. For example, many theorists posit that violent men really just have a need to exert power and control. This need for power arises out of low self-esteem or the sense that they have little control over events in their lives. Feelings of depression, anger, stress, and narcissism may be culprits as well. Other psychological explanations include the *resource theory,* which also revolves around the concept of power. Since power is the ability to influence others, it may be used as a resource when other resources are lacking. In simple terms, whoever has the most resources in the relationship has the power, and sometimes the only resource is violence.

Sociocultural theories in the context of violence against women include feminist perspectives, the cultural acceptance of violence, and the more specific subculture-of-violence theory. According to the *feminist perspective,* in a patriarchal (or male-dominated) society, the social structure and socialization process proscribe gender-specific roles, of which men's are superior and women's are inferior. Violence is often used to enforce this traditional power structure. Cross-cultural studies appear to lend support to the relationship between male social status and violence, as research has documented lower incidences of violence in more egalitarian societies. On the other hand, other researchers argue that these ideas are too simplistic and do not take into account individual differences in men. Moreover, the feminist perspective fails to explain why only a small proportion of men in patriarchal societies resort to violence.

The *cultural tolerance of violence* likely plays an integral role in the perpetuation of the violence toward women. The more a society glorifies violence and aggression, the more likely these cultural values are to permeate everyday aspects of life and to color the various interactions between people. As such, there is an increased likelihood for violence against women to occur. Gender-based violence has become so normalized within certain cultures that men's dominant and aggressive behavior not only is tolerated but is actually expected because "that's just how men are." Furthermore, cultures particularly tolerant of alcohol and drug use may have high rates of domestic violence perpetuated by substance users, which tend to be men. Finally, the *subculture-of-violence* theory suggests that certain subpopulations may be more likely to experience and accept the use of violence as a normal part of life. (See the discussion "Sex Work in a Subculture of Violence" in Chapter 3).

In all practicality, there is no one specific approach sufficient enough to elucidate such a pervasive and complex issue. A multidimensional framework that draws upon several theories, integrates both micro and macro perspectives, and pays particular attention to cultural context is the most realistic approach from which to try to understand violence against women.

Source: Jana L. Jasinski, "Theoretical Explanations for Violence Against Women," in *Sourcebook on Violence Against Women,* edited by Claire M. Renzetti, Jeffrey L. Edleson, and Raquel Kennedy Bergen (Thousand Oaks, CA: Sage Publications, 2001).

CAREERS IN CRIMINAL JUSTICE

Forensic Psychology

How is insanity determined among defendants who claim it when on trial for a crime? Forensic psychologists are often utilized to establish whether or not a defendant had criminal responsibility—that is, whether the defendant had the mental capacity to distinguish between right and wrong at the time of the alleged offense and could control his or her conduct accordingly.

Forensic psychology is defined by the American Board of Forensic Psychology as "the application of the science and the profession of psychology to questions and issues relating to law and the legal system." In addition to determining criminal responsibility, the expertise of forensic psychologists may also be employed regarding legal matters such as competency to stand trial, eyewitness testimony, sentencing (i.e., death penalty mitigation), waiver of Miranda rights, drug dependence, and sexual disorders, to name but a few. Forensic psychologists may also be called upon to evaluate individuals in civil cases. For example, they may evaluate children and their parents in order to determine custody in guardianship proceedings and evaluate the "psychological pain and suffering" endured by a plaintiff in personal injury cases.

The field of forensic psychology is one of the fastest-growing areas in psychology in the United States today, and the number of graduate programs is increasing rapidly each year. Masters and PhD programs in forensic psychology and programs offering a specialization in forensic psychology are available at about 30 universities across the United States, and many universities are beginning to offer undergraduate coursework in the field as well.

Most forensic psychologists are graduates of general clinical psychology programs who took courses specializing in forensic psychology. As is the case with clinical psychology, a doctoral degree in psychology and licensure as a psychologist is necessary for independent practice. Individuals who obtain masters degrees in clinical psychology typically work under the supervision of a doctoral-level psychologist.

For further information visit the American Psychology-Law Society at http://www.ap-ls.org/ and the American Board of Forensic Psychology at http://www.abfp.com.

Source: E. Englander, "Introduction to Forensic Psychology: Issues and Controversies in Crime and Justice," *Crime, Law and Social Change* 41 (April 2004): 289–292.

CRITICAL THINKING IN CRIMINAL JUSTICE

The Insanity Plea, Texas Style

Conventional wisdom holds that the insanity defense is a loophole in the criminal justice system. Many people believe that it is an easy way to "get away with murder" and other violent crimes and that far too many serious criminals are successfully using it.[79]

But is the insanity defense all that widespread? And what about those who suffer from legitimate mental health conditions? Should defendants found insane be reprimanded or rehabilitated? Is the insanity defense a threat to the safety of our society?

Let's first go back to Texas, where Andrea Yates' insanity defense was rejected for the murder of her children and she was instead sentenced to life in prison (for a review of the case see Exhibit 2.4). In the wake of the Yates case, several other similar cases have gained substantial media coverage in Texas.

Most recently, Dena Schlosser of Plano was charged with capital murder for cutting off her 10-month-old daughter's arms in her crib. Schlosser, who tried to commit suicide by cutting herself after the birth (her third), was diagnosed by a court-appointed expert with bipolar disorder induced by childbirth. However, the judge not only insisted that the case go to trial but reportedly refused to accept any settlements between the two sides. If Schlosser is determined competent to stand trial, an insanity defense would likely be mounted.[80]

Then there's Deanna Laney, an eastern Texas mother, who was found not guilty by reason of insanity for killing two of her sons and seriously injuring the third by bashing in their heads with rocks. She was sentenced to a state mental hospital in 2004. Like Yates, Laney said that God had commanded her to kill her children. In fact, Laney had delusions that she and Yates were chosen by God to survive the end of the world together.[81] Lisa Ann Diaz, another Plano mother, drowned her two daughters during a delusional episode in 2003. Diaz was found not guilty by reason of insanity for one daughter's death, but she still faces a capital murder indictment in the younger daughter's murder.[82] Finally, there is the case of Maria Angela Camacho, who helped her com-

Deanna Laney in a Tyler, Texas, courthouse after pleading not guilty by reason of insanity to the murder of her 6- and 8-year-old children.

mon law husband John Allen Rubio suffocate, stab, and decapitate their three children in their Brownsville apartment in 2003.[83]

Judging by the reports, it might appear that Texas is a state full of mothers about to go off the edge. But think critically: Could that be true? Going further, could the United States have a hidden epidemic on its hands?

According to psychiatrists, the number of cases like these has remained fairly constant throughout the years, and Texas is no exception. However, there are a few unique features that make the state stand out. For one, the media scrutiny and cultlike following of the Yates case detonated a frenzy of coverage of similar cases, making these incidents appear more prevalent than they actually are. Furthermore, the Texas justice system draws attention to itself in the manner that these cases are being prosecuted. Although the insanity defense has worked under some circumstances, in others, including the Yates trial, the prosecution has aggressively sought capital murder charges that potentially carry the death penalty. In fact, the degree of controversy surrounding such cases has in part driven Texas lawmakers to study the insanity defense and its implications in their state. Among the considerations are whether or not to change the plea from "not guilty by reason of insanity" to "guilty but insane," a suggestion that Harris County prosecutors (the county where Yates' trial was held) vehemently oppose. They say they are less concerned with legal discourse than with preventing dangerously ill patients from returning to the community.[84]

But would rewording the language framing the insanity plea make a difference in the course of justice? The jury is still out, so to speak. Experts suspect the problem with the insanity defense lies in the loaded connotations of the word itself. Law professors note that folk concepts of insanity among jurors often override the reality of what an insanity sentence means. Jurors often refuse to consider a sentence of "not guilty by reason of insanity" when the nature of the crime in question is particularly gruesome and hard to comprehend, such as the murder of one's own children. Others equate the phrase "not guilty" with "getting off easy."

Nationally, and contrary to public opinion, statistics reveal that the insanity plea is used in less than 1 percent of all criminal cases. Even though approximately 90 percent of those who use the insanity defense are indeed mentally ill, the claim works in only about a quarter of cases. In about 80 percent of cases in which the plea actually works, it is only because the defense team and the prosecutors agree beforehand on the appropriateness of the defense. Finally, and not without an ironic twist, those found insane actually spend, on average, more time in mental institutions than those found guilty of murder spend locked up and off the streets.[85]

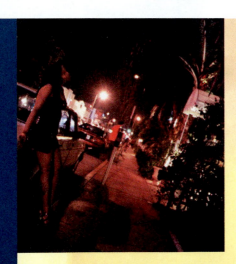

OP-ED

Crime seems to be always in the news. In fact, except for terrorism and the bloodshed in Iraq, of all the news stories featured on the ABC, CBS, and NBC evening newscasts, crime consistently ranks at the top. Although violent crime seems to get the most attention, other types of crime also receive disproportionate attention from the media and in television and films. Organized crime, for example, conjures up images of Eliot Ness and his Untouchables firing machine guns through the open windows of a speeding 1925 Packard; Al Capone and the St. Valentine's Day massacre; films like *The Godfather* and TV shows like *The Sopranos*. Yet, as has been seen in this chapter, these are not the most typical crimes committed in American society, nor do they provide a clear picture of the nature of crime. In reality, crime is a rather complex concept. Crime is not simply a collection of behaviors that are "against the law." Rather, as the chapter has demonstrated, crime has a number of elements and boundaries. It can be an act or a failure to act; it involves violations of one or more aspects of the criminal law. It must be committed without any defense or justification. There must be criminal intent. The behavior in question must be sanctioned by the state as a felony or misdemeanor. And the criminal justice system and the public must choose to enforce and prosecute such crimes.

| Summary |

The concept of crime is not well understood by most people. It goes well beyond the rather imprecise boundaries of "street crime" or the limited issues of violence and theft that are a major focus of mass media news and entertainment.

Drawing on standards of what constitutes "sin" or immoral behavior, people have often defined crime as violations of natural law. However, this definition implies that all individuals define right and wrong the same way. Sociologists argue that people's ideas about appropriate and inappropriate behavior are culturally and historically specific. That is, social scientists choose to focus on the processes through which crime comes into being, and they suggest that crime is a social construction that changes over time and in different contexts. Scholars have argued that not all deviant behavior is criminal behavior and that not all criminal behavior is deviant behavior. Rather, criminal and deviant behavior's are defined by the culture.

The only precise definition of crime, then, is a more legalistic one. As such, crime is an intentional act or omission in violation of criminal law (statutory and case law), committed without defense or justification, and sanctioned by the state as a felony or misdemeanor.

Explanations of why people commit crimes are numerous. Biological theories of crime are grounded in the concept of biological determinism, a notion suggesting that the causes of crime are the result of some biological or physical element—that criminals may be "born," not made. Biological theories tend to be weak, however, because the influences of environmental, cultural, social, and legal factors are generally ignored. Sociocultural theories of crime causation examine criminality in terms of how it may be related to society and culture. From this perspective, the focus shifts . . . from the individual level to a whole range of sociocultural questions: What are the characteristics of situations in which crime tends to occur? Why is crime more common in certain places, within certain groups, and under certain circumstances than in others? What is the process by which some persons become criminal while others do not? Why is it that some behaviors are defined as criminal while others are not?

It would be unrealistic to expect that any one theory of crime could explain all forms of criminal behavior. It is likely that each theory or various combinations of theories explain different kinds of lawbreaking. In all probability, however, there are as many reasons for engaging in criminal behavior as there are different kinds of crime.

| Key Terms |

abettor (36)
accessory after the fact (36)
accessory before the fact (36)
administrative law (47)
anomie (53)
case law (37)
civil law (37)
common law (38)
conspiracy (35)
constitutional law (47)
crime (34)
criminal law (37)

defense (38)
deviance (30)
differential association (57)
differential opportunity theory (56)
differential reinforcement theory (76)
Durham Rule (38)
entrapment (41)
felony (45)
general strain theory (55)
labeling theory (58)
Lambert v. *California* (40)
mens rea (36)

misdemeanor (45)
misprision of felony (36)
M'Naghten Rule (38)
natural law (30)
primary deviation (59)
Robinson v. *California* (37)
secondary deviation (59)
social control theory (58)
social disorganization theory (53)
statutory law (37)
vicarious liability (37)

| Issues for Discussion |

1. How do natural law conceptions of "sin," sociological considerations of deviance, and legalistic definitions of crime differ?
2. In the Leopold and Loeb case, when did the conspiracy actually begin? What elements were present?
3. Under what kinds of circumstances would the consent of the victim be an acceptable defense against crime? What are some examples?
4. What should be done about the insanity plea? Why?
5. What are the differences between *mala in se* and *mala prohibita* crimes? What are some examples of each?
6. Which appear to be the more plausible theories of crime?

| Media and Literature Resources |

Reel Justice includes scenes that can be used to spark discussion about the following topics from this chapter:

Social Control

Crime and Deviance

Natural Law

The Nature of Criminal Intent

Sociological Theories of Crime Causation

Psychological Theories of Crime Causation

Criminal versus Civil Law

Leopold and Loeb. See Gilbert Geis and Leigh B. Bienen, *Crimes of the Century* (Boston: Northeastern University Press, 1998). This volume provides a detailed examination of what the authors consider the five most celebrated crimes of the 20th century, including the Leopold and Loeb murder of Bobby Franks.

Mothers Who Kill Their Children. There are several intriguing resources on this disturbing phenomenon: Margaret G. Spinelli, *Infanticide: Psychosocial and Legal Perspectives on Mothers Who Kill* (Arlington, VA: American Psychiatric Association, 2002); Cheryl L. Meyer et al., *Mothers Who Kill Their Children: Understanding the Acts of Moms from Susan Smith to the "Prom Mom"* (New York: New York University Press, 2001); Suzanne O'Malley, *Are You There Alone? The Unspeakable Crime of Andrea Yates* (New York: Simon & Schuster, 2004); Hanna Putkonen, "Infanticide: Psychological and Legal Perspectives on Mothers Who Kill," *Criminal Behaviour and Mental Health* 14, 4 (2004): 314–315.

Prostitution. For those interested in reading more about the lifestyles of sex workers, a number of excellent resources have been published in the past few years, including:

a. Hilary L. Surratt, James A. Inciardi, Steven P. Kurtz, and Marion C. Kiley, "Sex Work and Drug Use in a Subculture of Violence," *Crime & Delinquency* 50, 1 (2004): 43–59.

b. Matt Bernstein Sycamore (ed.), *Tricks and Treats: Sex Workers Write About Their Clients* (San Francisco: Harrington Park Press, 1999).

c. Frederique Delacoste and Priscilla Alexander (eds.), *Sex Work* (San Francisco: Clies Press, 1998).

d. Kamala Kempadoo and Jo Doezema (eds.), *Global Sex Workers: Rights, Resistance, and Redefinition* (New York: Routledge, 1998).

e. James E. Elia, Vern L. Bullough, Veronica Elias, and Gwen Brewer (eds.), *Prostitution: On Whores, Hustlers, and Johns* (New York: Prometheus Books, 1998).

Theories of Crime. Excellent overviews of the theories of crime causation can be found in J. Robert Lilly's *Criminological Theory: Context and Consequences* (Thousand Oaks, CA: Sage, 2000) and in Ronald Aker's *Criminology Theories: Introduction, Evaluation, and Application* (Los Angeles, CA: Roxbury, 2000).

Criminal Defenses. The following resources investigate some of the less traditional criminal defenses used today: Saundra Davis Westervelt, *Shifting the Blame: How Victimization Became a Criminal Defense* (Piscataway, NJ: Rutgers University Press, 1999); Alison Dundes Renteln, *The Cultural Defense* (Oxford, England: Oxford University Press, 2004); Kenneth J. Weiss, "'Wet' and Wild: PCP and Criminal Responsibility," *Journal of Psychiatry and Law* 32 (Fall 2004): 361–384; Gwen Adshead, "Self-Made Madness: Rethinking Illness and Criminal Responsibility," *British Journal of Psychiatry* 186 (January 2005): 82–83.

American Law. One of the best books on the evolution of law in the United States is Lawrence M. Friedman's *A History of American Law* (New York: Simon & Schuster, 1973).

| Endnotes |

1. *Miami Herald,* July 16, 2003, A1: *Miami Herald* (Keys edition), August 6, 2000, 1B, 6B.
2. Kai T. Erikson, *Wayward Puritans: A Study in the Sociology of Deviance* (New York: Wiley, 1966), 6.
3. Howard S. Becker, *Outsiders: Studies in the Sociology of Deviance* (New York: Free Press, 1963), 9.
4. Becker, *Outsiders,* 147–163.
5. See J. C. Furnas, *The Life and Times of the Late Demon Rum* (New York: Capricorn, 1973).
6. Jerome Michael and Mortimer J. Adler, *Crime, Law and Social Science* (New York: Harcourt Brace, 1933), 2.
7. Edwin H. Sutherland, *White Collar Crime* (New York: Dryden, 1949), 31.
8. Henry Campbell Black, *Black's Law Dictionary,* 4th ed. (St. Paul, MN: West, 1968), 444.
9. Dean J. Champion, *The Roxbury Dictionary of Criminal Justice* (Los Angeles: Roxbury, 1997), 33.
10. Paul W. Tappan, *Crime, Justice, and Correction* (New York: McGraw-Hill, 1960), 10.
11. Nathan F. Leopold, *Life Plus Ninety-Nine Years* (New York: Doubleday, 1958).
12. *People* v. *Beardsley,* 113 N.W. 1128 (1907).
13. *Walker* v. *Superior Court,* 44 CrL 2193 (1988).
14. *United States* v. *Perlstein,* C.C.A.N.J. 126 F.2d 789, 798 (1946).
15. See K. Michael Cummings, Andrew Hyland, Jeanne Perla, and Gary A. Giovino, "Is the Prevalence of Youth Smoking Affected by Efforts to Increase Retailer Compliance with a Minors' Access Law?" *Nicotine & Tobacco Research* 5, 4 (July 2003): 465–47; Elizabeth A. Gilpin, Lora Lee, and John P. Pierce, "Does Adolescent Perception of Difficulty in Getting Cigarettes Deter Experimentation?" *Preventive Medicine* 38, 4 (April 2004): 485–491; Lan Liang, Frank Chaloupka, Mark Nichter, and Richard Clayton, "Prices, Policies and Youth Smoking," *Addiction* 98, Suppl. 1 (2003): 105–122; Joseph R. DiFranza, Judith A. Savageau, and Byron F. Aisquith, "Youth Access to Tobacco: The Effects of Age, Gender, Vending Machine Locks, and 'It's the Law' Programs," *American Journal of Public Health* 86 (February 1996): 221–224.
16. *Robinson* v. *California,* 370 U.S. 660 (1962).
17. Black, *Black's Law Dictionary,* 1101.
18. *Durham* v. *United States,* C.A.D.C. 214 F.2d 862 (1954).
19. Valerie P. Hans and Dan Slater, "John Hinckley, Jr., and the Insanity Defense: The Public's Verdict," *Public Opinion Quarterly* 47 (1983): 202–212.
20. James Hooper and Alix McLearen, "Does the Insanity Defense Have a Legitimate Role?" *Psychiatric Times* 19 (April 2002); *The Associated Press State and Local Wire,* April 18, 2003; *The Associated Press State and Local Wire,* July 8, 2003.
21. "The Defense of Insanity: Standards and Procedures," *State Court Organization, 1998* (Washington, DC: Bureau of Justice Statistics, U.S. Department of Justice, June 2000).
22. *Jones* v. *United States,* 33 CrL 3233 (1983).
23. For contrasting opinions on the matter, see *State* v. *Elton,* Utah SupCt 35 CrL 2071 (1984); *People* v. *Cash,* Mich SupCt 35 CrL 2345 (1984).
24. *Lambert* v. *California,* 355 U.S. 225 (1957).
25. The Supreme Court affirmed the *Lambert* ruling most recently in *Ratzlaf* v. *United States,* 92–1196 (1994).
26. *Hampton* v. *United States,* 425 U.S. 484 (1976).
27. *United States* v. *Vue,* U.S. CtApp 38 F.3d 973 (8th Cir. 1995).
28. *San Antonio Express-News,* December 18, 2003, 2B.
29. *The Associated Press State and Local Wire,* February 24, 2004; *City News Service,* April 6, 2004.
30. *United States* v. *Viayra,* CR S-00-512 (2002).

31. *Sacramento Bee,* September 8, 2004, 1B.

32. *Newsweek,* November 8, 1999, 40–46; *The New York Times,* November 2, 1999, 14A; *The Atlanta Journal Constitution,* February 24, 2005, 6C.

33. *Tampa Tribune,* April 15, 2003, 3B.

34. *National Post,* November 18, 1999, 5A.

35. *The Daily News,* February 16, 2005, p. 42; *The Herald* (Glasgow), February 16, 2005, 2.

36. *The New York Times,* May 15, 2001, 18A.

37. *U.S. v. Oakland Cannabis Buyers' Cooperative,* No. 00–151 (2001).

38. *The New York Times,* May 25, 2001, 14A; *Time,* June 4, 2001, 56.

39. *The New York Times,* October 10, 1998, 1A; *The Washington Post,* October 1, 2000, 2B; *The Washington Post,* May 11, 2001, 2B.

40. L. L. Downs, "PMS, Psychosis and Culpability: Sound or Misguided Defense," *Journal of Forensic Sciences* 47 (2002): 1083–1089.

41. State of New York, Penal Law, 10.00 (3).

42. Sir Frederick Pollock and F. W. Maitland, *The History of English Law Before the Time of Edward I* (Cambridge: University Press, 1911), xxv.

43. Sir James Fitzjames Stephen, *History of the Criminal Law of England,* Vol. 2 (New York: Macmillan, 1883), 75.

44. John H. Wigmore, *A Panorama of the World's Legal Systems* (Washington, DC: Washington Law Book, 1936), 4.

45. F. A. Inderwick, *The King's Peace* (London: Swan Sonnenschein, 1895), 3.

46. Lawrence M. Friedman, *A History of American Law* (New York: Simon & Schuster, 1973), 17.

47. See Richard A. Posner, *Overcoming Law* (Cambridge: Harvard University Press, 1995).

48. Harry Elmer Barnes, *The Repression of Crime: Studies in Historical Penology* (New York: Doran, 1926), 44–45.

49. This quotation from Lombroso's opening speech at the Sixth Congress of Criminal Anthropology at Turin, Italy, in 1906 appears in Leon Radzinowicz, *Ideology of Crime* (New York: Columbia University Press, 1966), 29.

50. Gina Lombroso Ferrero, *Criminal Man According to the Classification of Cesare Lombroso* (New York: Putnam's, 1911), 10–24.

51. Cesare Lombroso and William Ferrero, *The Female Offender* (New York: Appleton, 1895), 101.

52. Richard L. Dugdale, *The Jukes* (New York: Putnam's, 1910).

53. See also Arthur H. Estabrook, *The Jukes in 1915* (Washington, DC: Carnegie Institution, 1916); Arthur H. Estabrook and Charles P. Davenport, *The Nam Family* (Cold Spring Harbor, NY: Eugenics Record Office, 1912); and Henry H. Goddard, *The Kallikaks* (New York: Macmillan, 1912).

54. Charles Goring, *The English Convict* (London: Her Majesty's Stationary Office, 1913).

55. Earnest A. Hooton, *Crime and the Man* (Cambridge: Harvard University Press, 1939).

56. Nicole Rafter, "Earnest A. Hooton and the Biological Tradition in American Criminology," *Criminology* 42 (2004): 735–771.

57. William H. Sheldon, S. S. Stevens, and W. B. Tucker, *The Varieties of Human Physique* (New York: Harper, 1940).

58. R. G. Fox, "The XYY Offender: A Modern Myth?" *Journal of Criminal Law, Criminology, and Police Science* 62 (March 1971): 59–73. See also Donald J. West (ed.), *Criminological Implications of Chromosome Abnormalities* (Cambridge: University of Cambridge, Institute of Criminology, 1969); and "The XYY Chromosome: A Challenge to Our System of Criminal Responsibility," *New York Law Forum* 16 (Spring 1970): 232.

59. James Q. Wilson and Richard J. Herrnstein, *Crime and Human Nature* (New York: Simon & Schuster, 1985).

60. Steven Pinker, *The Blank Slate: The Modern Denial of Human Nature* (New York: Viking, 2002).

61. *Time,* October 28, 2002, 54.

62. Robert E. Park, Ernest W. Burgess, and Roderick D. MacKensie, *The City* (Chicago: University of Chicago Press, 1925).

63. Clifford R. Shaw and Associates, *Delinquency Areas* (Chicago: University of Chicago Press, 1929).

64. Clifford R. Shaw, *Brothers in Crime* (Chicago: University of Chicago Press, 1938); Clifford R. Shaw, *The Jack Roller* (Chicago: University of Chicago Press, 1930).

65. Emile Durkheim, *Suicide: A Study in Sociology* (New York: Free Press, 1951).

66. Robert K. Merton, "Social Structure and Anomie," *American Sociological Review* 3 (1938): 672–682.

67. Robert Agnew, "Foundation for a General Strain Theory," *Criminology* 30 (1992): 47–87.

68. Robert Agnew, "Building on the Foundation of General Strain Theory: Specifying the Types of Strain Most Likely to Lead to Crime and Delinquency," *Journal of Research in Crime and Delinquency* 38 (2001): 319–361; Robert Agnew, "A General Strain Theory of Community Differences in Crime Rates," *Journal of Research in Crime and Delinquency* 36 (1999): 123–155.

69. Jerome Michael and Mortimer J. Adler, *Crime, Law and Social Science* (New York: Harcourt Brace, 1933), 5.

70. Thorsten Sellin, *Culture Conflict and Crime* (New York: Social Science Research Council, 1938), 21.

71. Albert K. Cohen, *Delinquent Boys: The Culture of the Gang* (Glencoe, IL: Free Press, 1955).

72. Richard Cloward and Lloyd Ohlin, *Delinquency and Opportunity* (New York: Free Press, 1960).

73. Walter B. Miller, "Lower Class Culture as a Generating Milieu for Gang Delinquency," *Journal of Social Issues* 14 (1958): 5–19.

74. Edwin H. Sutherland, *The Professional Thief* (Chicago: University of Chicago Press, 1937).

75. Edwin H. Sutherland and Donald Cress, *Principles of Criminology* (Philadelphia: Lippincott, 1947), 6–7.

76. Robert Burgess and Ronald Akers, "A Differential Association-Reinforcement Theory of Criminal Behavior," *Social Problems* 14 (1968): 28–47.

77. Travis Hirschi, *Causes of Delinquency* (Berkeley: University of California Press, 1969).

78. Edwin M. Lemert, *Social Pathology* (New York: McGraw-Hill, 1951), 75–76.

79. James Hooper and Alix McLearen, "Does the Insanity Defense Have a Legitimate Role?" *Psychiatric Times* 19 (April 2002).

80. *The Houston Chronicle,* February 3, 2005, 1B.

81. *San Antonio Express-News,* April 9, 2004, 6B; *The New York Times,* March 31, 2004, 17A.

82. *The Associated Press State and Local Wire,* August 13, 2004.

83. *San Antonio Express-News,* May 13, 2003, 1B.

84. *The Houston Chronicle,* May 7, 2004, 38A.

85. Hooper and McLearen, "Does the Insanity Defense Have a Legitimate Role?"

LEGAL AND BEHAVIORAL ASPECTS OF CRIME

LEARNING OBJECTIVES

After reading this chapter, you should be able to answer the following questions:

1. What are the differences between murder and manslaughter?

2. What is the felony-murder doctrine, and what are its ramifications?

3. What are the legal definitions of the major categories of crime?

4. What does it mean when a crime is referred to as "gender neutral"?

5. What are the subcategories of such major criminal acts as property crimes, sex offenses, and public order crimes?

6. Is rape a gender-specific crime?

7. What is "hate crime," and who are the usual victims of such crimes? What are the arguments for and against hate-crime laws?

8. What is "domestic violence," and who are its typical victims?

NEW ORLEANS, LA—As passengers stroll the decks of sleek ocean liners on cruises to the Caribbean, Hawaii, South America, and other romantic ports of call, few think about such worldly matters as their personal safety. However, a recent lawsuit against Carnival Cruise Lines by a woman claims that her daughter was raped by another passenger as the ship traveled down the Mississippi River. Furthermore, the underage girl was intoxicated at the time of the alleged incident, prompting a spokesperson for the cruise line to comment, "It's very, very rare, within the scope of the millions of passengers that the cruise industry carries on an annual basis, that we have this sort of allegation. It's not unprecedented, but it's extremely rare."[1]

However, numerous other cases against cruise lines over the years have included instances of theft, assault, and sexual battery.[2] Are these just accusations, or is crime rampant aboard cruise ships? If the answer to the latter is yes, what other kinds of crimes typically occur?

FAMOUS CRIMINALS
Butterfingers Moran

When Thomas Bartholomew Moran died in 1971 at the Miami Rescue Mission, he was a vagrant, a derelict, and his pockets were empty—a rather ironic ending to a life spent emptying the pockets of others. Yet, in spite of the dismal circumstances of his death, Moran had been a celebrated criminal whom many considered to be the dean of American pickpockets. His career in crime had been a lengthy one. It began in 1906 when, as a youth of only 14, he would pass through the crowded streets and stores of downtown Kansas City, opening women's purses and removing small change. The practice was called "moll-buzzing" and was looked down on by the more accomplished thieves of his day, since women were considered easy "marks" (victims) and the targets of only rank amateurs.

(continued on p. 69)

This brief description of allegations of crimes aboard cruise ships raises many other questions as well. What are the differences between "sexual assault" and "rape"? What actually constitutes "assault"? Is there really a crime called "battery"? How are all of these things different from one another? What are the specific definitions of other types of crime?

Crime on the high seas illustrates some of the complex issues surrounding the nature and meaning of crime. Although crime may be defined as conduct that is prohibited by criminal law, it has many designations in legal statutes. Moreover, its dynamics go well beyond the sterile classifications, provisions, and subsections that appear in state and federal criminal codes. Crime includes patterns and systems of behavior that occur at one or several points in time. It can involve varying sets of circumstances, social and political environments, and victim–offender relationships. Too, crime can be an isolated event that occurs at only one point in the offender's lifetime; it can reflect the best-developed aspects of a well-established career in illicit enterprise; or it can consist of the activities of an organization structured for the pursuit of illegal behavior.

In any study of crime it is important to understand not only the content of criminal codes but also the wider social context in which crime occurs, for all of these factors influence public images of crime, societal reactions to crime, and the justice system's management of crime and criminals. This chapter therefore begins by discussing the legal aspects of various crimes as they are described in criminal codes, and then it briefly analyzes a few specific patterns of crime that receive widespread attention in the popular media.

Legal Categories of Crime

As noted in Chapter 2, there are literally thousands of acts that are prohibited by law and designated in federal, state, and local criminal codes as felonies, misdemeanors, and violations. There is also administrative law, which lists additional criminal violations. All these laws result in a huge catalog of crimes. Of course, only a few of those crimes can be discussed here, so the focus here is on the ones that appear most often in

The victims of a drive-by shooting in Los Angeles.

local criminal courts and receive the most attention from state-level criminal justice agencies. The crime categories to be covered in this chapter include the following:

- Criminal homicide
- Assault (except sexual assault)
- Robbery
- Arson
- Burglary
- Other property offenses
- Sex offenses
- Drug law violations
- Crimes against public order and safety

This list, although brief, encompasses more than 90 percent of the criminal law violations handled by state and local criminal justice agencies. This is not to say that other crimes are not serious or important, of course. *Treason,* for example, the only crime specifically mentioned in the Constitution of the United States, is clearly an act that can threaten the society as a whole. Yet acts of treason are relatively infrequent, and only rarely do they come to the attention of the criminal justice system. By contrast, *kidnapping*—the forcible taking or detaining of a person against his or her will and without lawful authority—is a serious offense that receives little attention in the media but occurs quite frequently, especially in other parts of the world.

Criminal Homicide

Homicide   **Homicide** is the killing of one human being by another. If it is not excusable or justifiable (see Chapter 2), it is called *criminal homicide.* Criminal homicide is usually divided into the general categories of murder and manslaughter, each of

(continued from p. 68)

By age 17, Moran had graduated to the more complex problems of stealing from men. Under the tutelage of Mary Kelly, a well-known pickpocket in both the United States and Great Britain during the latter part of the 19th century, he polished his approaches to the point where he could remove a diamond pin from a garment, a watch from a vest, and a wallet from a suit coat or pants pocket, all without his victim's knowing that a theft was taking place. Moran quickly achieved the rank of "class cannon," a designation that typified him as a thief with the skill and daring to devote a lifetime to stealing from the pockets of live victims. Moran was also an accomplished shoplifter and forger, although picking pockets was always his prime vocation. He worked the streets and stores of almost every major city in the United States; he followed the circuses and carnivals that traveled across America, lured by the thousands of "rubes" (farmers and hicks) who crowded the midways in search of thrills and excitement; and he visited the resort towns, preying on the wealthy who were careless as they leisured in the sun and at the race tracks. And early in his career, Moran had even been aboard the *Titanic* when it left on its ill-fated maiden voyage. Traveling in steerage under an assumed name, his purpose was to benefit handsomely from the more than 300 first-class passengers whose collective wealth exceeded $250 million. His immediate ambitions were dimmed, however, when the *Titanic* brushed an iceberg in the North Atlantic at 11:40 P.M. on April 15, 1912, and sunk only 2 hours and 40 minutes later. But Moran was among the 705 survivors who managed to find space in one of the ship's 20 lifeboats, and his career in crime continued to flourish for the better part of the 59 remaining years of his life.

Thinking back on his long career, Moran commented shortly before his death: "The *bulls* [detectives] called me 'Butterfingers,' but I was no *rufus* [amateur] or *doormat* [small-time] thief. I'm a *whisker-stif* [charity case] now, but that's just because I'm old." ▪

EXHIBIT 3.1 | RESEARCH ON CRIME & JUSTICE

Not All Murderers Kill Equally

Although those who commit multiple murders are usually lumped together in a single reviled category of criminals, multiple murderers actually have distinct patterns of behavior and motivations that drive their impulse to kill. There are three broad categories of multiple murderers: mass murderers, spree killers, and serial killers.

Mass murderers kill multiple victims in a single location within an uninterrupted period of time, whether it takes place in the span of a few minutes or over a few days. Mass murderers are typically mentally disturbed individuals who take out their aggression on whoever happens to be in the vicinity. Charles Whitman, who shot more than 30 people from a tower on the University of Texas campus in Austin, is a classic example of a mass murderer.

Charles Whitman

Spree killers murder two or more people in more than one location. It is considered a "spree" when the murderer does not take a break in moving from one location to another to continue killing people. Andrew Cunanan is considered a spree killer. Cunanan's cross-country rampage started with he killed his former lover in Minneapolis; he then killed two people for their cars in Chicago and New Jersey before culminating with the murder of fashion designer Giovanni Versace on the steps of his mansion on Miami Beach.

Andrew Cunanan

Serial killers murder three or more people on separate occasions. Unlike the first two types of murderers, who usually select their victims indiscriminately, serial killers carefully choose their victims and methodically plan their crimes. Because they sometimes travel long

---

which is typically subdivided into many "degrees" (e.g., murder in the first or second degree).

All creatures kill—there seems to be no exception. But of the whole list man is the only one that kills for fun; he is the only one that kills in malice; the only one that kills for revenge.

—MARK TWAIN

Homicide is the slaying of one human being by another. There are four kinds of homicide: felonious, excusable, justifiable, and praise-worthy, but it makes no great difference to the person slain whether he fell by one kind or another— the classification is for the advantage of the lawyers.

—AMBROSE BIERCE,
THE DEVIL'S DICTIONARY

Murder Under common law, **murder** was defined as the felonious killing of another human being with malice aforethought. That last phrase implies a definite malicious intent to kill. Common law did not differentiate between murders in the first or second degree, however, and there were varying interpretations of *malice* and *aforethought*. In modern criminal codes the law is more specific, and clear distinctions are made between malice aforethought, deliberation, and premeditation.

Today murder is generally divided into two degrees: first and second. In most jurisdictions, *first-degree murder* includes the notions of malice aforethought, deliberation, and premeditation. **Malice aforethought** refers to the intent to cause death or serious harm or to commit any felony whatsoever. **Deliberation** refers to full and conscious knowledge of the purpose of killing, suggesting that the offender has considered the motives for the act and its consequences. **Premeditation** refers to a design or plan to do something before it is actually done; it is a conscious decision to commit the offense (even though such a decision may occur only moments before the final act).

A good illustration of first-degree murder involving malice aforethought, deliberation, and premeditation is the well-known case of Timothy McVeigh. McVeigh was convicted and sentenced to death in the bombing of the Alfred P. Murrah Federal Building in Oklahoma City. Court testimony and evidence demonstrated that he had planned an act of violence against persons and property, obtained and constructed the components of a truck bomb, parked the truck bomb directly outside the federal building on April 19, 1995, during regular business and day care hours, and caused the truck bomb to explode.[3]

In a number of jurisdictions, statutes also designate murder to be in the first degree when specific circumstances are present. In many states, for example, murder by poisoning automatically carries a first-degree charge, and in some areas a charge of

Dennis Rader, the "BTK" Killer

10 victims in Wichita, Kansas, between 1974 and 1991 and then taunted police with gruesome letters and poems about his crimes. Like many other serial killers, he led a double life: He was part churchgoing Cub Scout leader with deep roots in his community and part sadistic killer who derived sexual pleasure from his crimes.

Ronald Holmes, a criminologist who studies serial killers, contends that serial killers fall into four distinct classes:

- The *visionary* is typically psychotic and driven to kill by the inner voices or personal visions he or she experiences.

- The *power-oriented* killer seeks ultimate control over the victims. These killers are not mentally deranged like the visionaries, but the sense of power and control they exert over their victims becomes an insatiable obsession.

distances between their crimes, kill for idiosyncratic reasons, and frequently wait for periods of time in between killings, serial killers are difficult to apprehend. According to social scientists, serial killers are typically white males, aged 25 to 34, with intelligent and charming personalities. They tend to select vulnerable victims who will fulfill their preoccupation with sadistic and sometimes sexual fantasies involving domination and control of their victims. Moreover, they are inclined to use hands-on methods in their crimes, such as strangulation and stabbing. Many are obsessed with police work and like to associate with the police, such as the BTK killer (bind, torture, and kill), who murdered

- The *mission-oriented* killer specifically targets victims who are deemed unworthy to live; this killer's mission is to cleanse the world of such human misery.

- The *hedonistic* killer murders for the pure thrill of it. Many even become sexually excited by the act itself.

Sources: Ronald M. Holmes and James De Burger, "Serial Murder," in *Studies in Crime, Law and Justice*, Vol. 2, edited by James A. Inciardi (Thousand Oaks, CA: Sage Publications, 1988); Ronald M. Holmes and James De Burger, "Profiles in Terror: The Serial Murderer," *Federal Probation* 49, 3 (1985): 29–34; David Montgomery, "The Mark of a Killer Who Strikes Over and Over Again," *The Washington Post*, October 8, 2002, 1C.

"murder-one" is also mandatory if the homicide involved torture, ambush, the use of destructive devices, the killing of a law enforcement officer, or a murder for hire. (For a discussion of different types of murderers, see Exhibit 3.1.)

Second-degree murder refers to instances of criminal homicide committed with malice aforethought but without deliberation and premeditation. Murders of this type are often impulse killings. They occur among members of a family or lovers, often as the outgrowth of an argument or difference of opinion. The killing is a spur-of-the-moment episode that occurs without planning or full consideration.

Currently, 33 states and the District of Columbia divide murder into at least two degrees. Three states, however—Florida, Minnesota, and Wisconsin—have more than two degrees of murder. The aim is to limit the use of the death penalty without reducing the seriousness of the crime.

The Felony-Murder Doctrine Under common law, the **felony-murder doctrine** maintained that any death resulting from the commission of, or attempt to commit, the crimes of arson, burglary, larceny, rape, or robbery was to be considered murder. In many contemporary legal statutes, the felony-murder doctrine provides that if a death occurs during the commission of a felony, the person committing the primary offense can also be charged with murder in the first degree.[4] Thus, if an individual commits the felonious crime of arson by setting fire to his place of business and one of his employees is killed in that fire, the arsonist would be charged with first-degree murder.

A great deal of confusion surrounds this doctrine. First, the statute is unusual in that although under the law first-degree murder requires malice aforethought, deliberation, and premeditation, the felony-murder rule considers these three essential elements to be implied. The offender is seen to act in a deliberate manner and is therefore responsible for any natural and probable consequences. A second difficult issue is whether the felon must be the agent of the killing. Thus, if a case of arson results in the

EXHIBIT 3.2 | LAW & CRIMINAL JUSTICE

The Felony-Murder Doctrine

In *Enmund* v. *Florida,* decided by the Supreme Court in 1982, a murder had been committed during the course of a robbery. The appellant in the case, who had participated in the robbery but not the killing, was convicted of murder in the first degree and sentenced to death. The Supreme Court held that the Eighth Amendment ban against cruel and unusual punishment does not permit the death penalty on a defendant who aids and abets a felony in the course of which a murder is committed by others, where there was no evidence that the defendant attempted to kill or intended to kill. The Court reasoned that the identical treatment of a robber and his accomplice, and the attribution of culpability of one to the other in these circumstances, is unconstitutional.

The decision in *Enmund* was modified, however, by *Tison* v. *Arizona,* decided in 1987. Specifically, the Tison brothers—Ricky, Raymond, and Donald, along with other members of their family—planned and effected the prison escape of their father Gary. Gary Tison was serving a life sentence for having killed a correctional officer during a previous escape. The three brothers entered the prison with an ice chest filled with guns, armed their father and another convicted murderer, and then effected the escape. Later, the brothers helped to abduct, detain, and rob a family of four and watched their father and the other convict murder the members of that family with shotguns.

Donald Tison was subsequently killed during a shootout at a police roadblock a few days after the prison break. Gary Tison evaded the police and escaped into the desert, but subsequently died of exposure. Ricky and Raymond Tison were arrested, convicted, and sentenced to death.

Although the two surviving brothers stated that they were surprised by the shooting, neither had made any effort to help the victims, and they drove away in the victims' car with the rest of the escape party. After the Arizona Supreme Court affirmed individual convictions for capital murder under the state's felony-murder and accomplice-liability statutes, the Tisons collaterally attacked their death sentences in state postconviction proceedings, alleging that *Enmund* v. *Florida* required a reversal in the court's sentencing decision.

The Arizona Supreme Court determined that the Tison brothers should be executed, holding that *Enmund* requires a finding of "intent to kill" and interpreting that phrase to include situations in which the defendant intended, contemplated, or anticipated that lethal force would or might be taken in accomplishing the underlying felony. Despite a finding that the Tisons did not specifically intend that the victims die, nor did they plan the homicides in advance or actually fire the shots, the court ruled that the requisite intent was established by evidence that they played an active part in planning and executing the breakout and in the events that led to the murders, and that they did nothing to interfere with the killings or to disassociate themselves from the killers afterward. Although only one of the Tison brothers testified that he would have been willing to kill, the court found that both of them could have anticipated the use of lethal force.

The U.S. Supreme Court ruled against Ricky and Raymond Tison, holding that although they neither intended to kill the victims nor inflicted the fatal wounds, the record might support a finding that they had the culpable mental state of reckless indifference to human life. The Court explained that the Eighth Amendment does not prohibit the death penalty as disproportionate in the case of a defendant whose participation in a felony that results in murder is major and whose mental state is one of reckless indifference. A survey of state felony-murder laws and judicial decisions after *Enmund* indicates a societal consensus that this combination of factors may justify the death penalty even without a specific "intent to kill."

Sources: *Enmund* v. *Florida,* 458 U.S. 782 (1982); *Tison* v. *Arizona,* 41 CrL 3023 (1987); James W. Clarke, *Last Rampage: The Escape of Gary Tison* (Boston: Houghton Mifflin, 1988).

---

death of a fire fighter who is fighting the fire, can the arsonist be charged with first-degree murder under the felony-murder doctrine? Exhibit 3.2 summarizes two cases in which the felony-murder doctrine was addressed by the U.S. Supreme Court.

Manslaughter Manslaughter is an alternative category of criminal homicide, typically charged when a killing occurs under circumstances that are not severe enough to constitute murder yet are beyond the defenses of justifiable or excusable homicide. **Manslaughter** is distinguished from murder in that the latter implies malice whereas manslaughter does not. Some jurisdictions divide manslaughter into as many as four degrees, although most differentiate only between voluntary and involuntary manslaughter.

Voluntary manslaughter refers to intentional killings committed in the absence of malice and premeditated design. Its essential elements include a legally adequate provocation resulting in a killing done in the heat of passion. Thus, if two people become involved in a quarrel and one kills the other, the offender can be charged with voluntary manslaughter. In contrast, *involuntary manslaughter* exists when a death results unintentionally as the consequence of some unlawful act or through negligence. For example, if a motorist is driving while intoxicated and loses control of the vehicle, thereby killing a pedestrian, involuntary manslaughter could be charged. In this case, the killing would be unintentional, yet the motorist's intoxicated condition while driving is a violation of the law. In some jurisdictions, however, the charge might be vehicular homicide or driving while intoxicated or second-degree murder. In 1997, a court in Winston-Salem, North Carolina, set a legal precedent with a first-degree murder conviction in a drunk-driving killing. Prosecutors held that the defendant could be convicted without the intent to kill, because he had been acting out of "culpable negligence," as shown by a long history of mixing alcohol with drugs and driving.[5]

A case in De Kalb County, Georgia, demonstrates how broadly the involuntary manslaughter statutes can be interpreted. A dog owner was convicted of involuntary manslaughter and sentenced to 5 years in prison after three of his pit bull terriers killed a 4-year-old boy.[6] His prosecution was based on the *doctrine of implied malice,* in which a person can be convicted of criminal homicide if "wanton disregard for human life" can be proved. In Florida, manslaughter statutes include a *vessel homicide* law aimed at unsafe boat operators—a legislative reaction to the more than 100 boating fatalities that occur there each year.[7]

Note that because voluntary manslaughter can refer to deaths resulting from unlawful acts, it must be differentiated from the felony-murder doctrine. In jurisdictions where all homicides occurring during the commission of a felony are classified as murder, involuntary manslaughter can apply only to misdemeanor cases. Also, in many cases the differences that separate second-degree murder from voluntary manslaughter are not always immediately clear. Both offenses, for example, can relate to crimes of passion, and what differentiates one from another often reflects the degree of passion involved, the court's interpretation of the circumstances of the killing, and the particular legal codes that define the boundaries of the two offenses in a given jurisdiction.

In a few jurisdictions, unfortunately, the criminal codes are so disorganized and vaguely written that they can hardly be called codes at all—thus adding one more element to the already convoluted criminal justice "nonsystem." The problem with poorly drafted criminal codes is that they shift the burden of determining culpability and punishment to the courts and give judges little or no guidance on how to proceed. To cite but one example, North Carolina's criminal code establishes the crimes of voluntary and involuntary manslaughter but provides no definitions to distinguish between the two terms or to differentiate either crime from murder.[8] As a final point here, whether it is classified as murder or manslaughter, homicide can occur in a variety of different contexts. As is illustrated in Exhibit 3.3, murder has sometimes been discussed under the label of "domestic terrorism."

Assault

Contrary to popular notions, **assault** does not refer to the infliction of an injury on another person. In legal terms, it is simply an intentional attempt or threat to physically injure another person. *Battery* is the term for nonlethal culmination of an assault. Thus, **assault and battery** is an assault that inflicts some violence on the victim. Aggravated assault refers to an assault made with the intent to commit murder, rape, or robbery or to inflict serious bodily harm; simple assault is one in which the intended harm fails or no serious harm was ever intended.

Menacing and Mayhem Although aggravated assaults are usually felonies and simple assaults are misdemeanors, many jurisdictions separate the two according to degree of assault rather than by name. Moreover, some states have defined specific kinds of assault as distinct offenses. For example, while assault in the third degree can generally be construed as simple assault and a misdemeanor, other categories of nonfelonious assault might include *menacing* (touching a person with an instrument or part of the body, thereby causing offense or alarm to that person). Similarly, although *may-*

It has long been a well-stated principle that the commission of unlawful sexual intercourse with a female relative is an act obviously calculated to arouse ungovernable passion, and that the killing of the seducer or adulterer under the influence or in the heat of that passion constitutes voluntary manslaughter, and not murder.

— FROM THE OPINION IN *STATE V. THORNTON,* TENNESSEE SUPREME COURT, 41 CRL 2162 (1987), IN WHICH THE DEFENDANT APPEALED HIS FIRST-DEGREE MURDER CONVICTION IN THE SLAYING OF HIS WIFE'S LOVER AFTER DISCOVERING THEM IN FLAGRANTE DELICTO (ENGAGED IN SEXUAL INTERCOURSE)

A police diver investigating the murder of a student bludgeoned to death.

EXHIBIT 3.3 | *historical perspectives on criminal justice*

Domestic Terrorism

Not all terrorism involves Islamic extremists or insurgent groups from distant parts of the world seeking "death to the infidels" or social or political change. There are also "domestic terrorists," homegrown individuals or groups who kill or destroy property here in the United States for vengeance or to bring attention to a person or ideological cause. Not all domestic terrorists have an obvious cause. In fact, many do not even consider themselves as terrorists. Moreover, there are a few who are no more than serial killers but whose actions serve to terrorize entire communities.

An interesting example of a domestic terrorist was George Metesky, a Consolidated Edison employee, also referred to as the "Mad Bomber," who terrorized New York City for 16 years, except for a brief pause during World War II. It all began on November 16, 1940, when Metesky walked into the Con Ed office on the city's Upper West Side, dropped his toolbox, and walked out again. Later in the day workers in the building found a wooden toolbox sitting on a windowsill. Inside was an unexploded pipe bomb with a note wrapped around it: "Con Edison crooks, this is for you." There were no fingerprints or other evidence, and after a brief investigation, the case was left idle. A year later, a second bomb was found in the gutter outside another Con Edison building. This time it was wrapped in an old sock, but there was no note.

In early 1942 Metesky sent a brief note to police proclaiming that he was a patriot and would not make any more bombs until after the war was over. The Mad Bomber then became silent, and most New Yorkers forgot about him. But then, starting in 1950, New York faced

years of terror as bomb after bomb was discovered all over the city. The first was found in Grand Central Station. It was followed by more than 30 other bombs placed in telephone booths, public libraries, transit stations, and movie theaters.

What first galvanized the NYPD into action was an explosion that ripped through the Brooklyn Paramount theater on the evening of December 2, 1956. It had been Metesky's work, and six people were injured, three of them seriously. The bombs were getting more powerful and sophisticated, and it was only a matter of time before people started dying. A criminal profiler was brought into the case, and Metesky was ultimately identified and arrested. And the reason for the bombs? He had had a grudge against Con Edison over a denied workers' compensation case. George Metesky was judged acutely paranoid and committed to an institution. He was eventually released in 1974. Twenty years later he died in his Westbury, New York, home at the age of 90.

There are numerous other cases in the annals of crime, serial murder, and domestic terrorism. Perhaps there are students reading this who are familiar with the films *Badlands, Natural Born Killers,* and *Wild at Heart,* or with Bruce Springsteen's *Nebraska* album. All were inspired by Charles Raymond Starkweather's murderous rampage across the American plains states, which epitomized the 1950s specter of teenage violence. His mass slaughter lasted only 8 days, but it claimed the lives of 10 people and terrorized an untold number of communities. Three of the victims were the parents and baby sister of Starkweather's 14-year-old girlfriend, Caril Ann Fugate, who accompanied

---

hem can be considered a serious and aggravated assault, in some states, such as California, it is classified as a separate felony:

> Every person who unlawfully and maliciously deprives a human being of a member of his or her body, or disables, disfigures, or renders it useless, or cuts or disables the tongue, or puts out an eye, or slits the nose, ear, or lip, is guilty of mayhem.[9]

Jostling Perhaps the most peculiar categories of assault are found in the jostling statutes. *Jostling* refers to the pushing or crowding of an individual. It is generally believed that pickpockets jostle their victims (bump into them and throw them off balance) while stealing their money. New York's jostling statute enables police officers to arrest pickpockets even though they are not caught stealing.[10] In fact, this statute is so widely used in some areas that many career pickpockets have numerous arrests for jostling and few for actually stealing. It might be added, however, that expert pickpockets rarely jostle their victims. As one commented: "No, you never throw them the jostle. All that does is wake up the mark and tell him that something's happening. If a cop knows you and thinks you're going to score, he'll grab you and call it jostling, even though you did nothing."[11]

Robbery

Robbery is the felonious taking of the money or goods of another, from the victim's person or in his or her presence and against the victim's will, through the use or threat of force and violence. As such, it involves aspects of both theft and assault, and since

Robbery distribution by location 2003

Because of rounding, the percentages may not add up to 100.0.

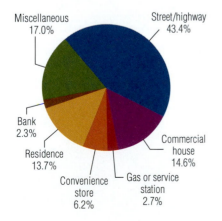

Miscellaneous 17.0%
Street/highway 43.4%
Bank 2.3%
Residence 13.7%
Convenience store 6.2%
Gas or service station 2.7%
Commercial house 14.6%

him on his trail of morbid violence. Yet curiously, while the nation was shocked by the murders, Charlie and Caril quickly became a macabre adornment of 20th-century American folklore. Locals were terrorized, yet others were fascinated with the seemingly matter-of-fact way in which much of the killing had been done. After shooting and stabbing three members of Caril's family, for example, the teenage couple ate sandwiches and watched television only a few yards from where their victims' bodies lay hidden.

Starkweather was finally arrested, convicted, and executed in the Nebraska State Penitentiary electric chair on June 24, 1959. Caril Ann Fugate received a life sentence for her part, but was paroled in 1976. As of early 2004, she was working as a medical assistant in Lansing, Michigan.

There have been scores of other domestic terrorists. More recent events include the Tylenol poisonings of 1982 in a Chicago suburb, which led to tamperproof packaging for many consumer products; there was the 1995 bombing of the federal building in Oklahoma City by Timothy McVeigh. Others include "Unabomber" Theodore Kaczynski, convicted D.C. snipers John Allen Muhammad and John Lee Malvo, and Charles A. McCoy, Jr., arrested in March 2004 as a suspect in the I-270 shootings in Ohio.

As a final point here, domestic terrorism is also undertaken by organized groups. In 1998, for example, an organization known as the Earth Liberation Front admitted responsibility for a series of fires in the

These torched SUVs were the result of domestic terrorism by overzealous environmentalists.

ski village of Vail, Colorado. In an email message to Colorado Public Radio in Denver, the group reported:

On behalf of the lynx, five buildings and four ski lifts at Vail were reduced to ashes on the night of Sunday, October 18. Vail, Inc. is already the largest ski operation in North America and now wants to expand even further. The 12 miles of roads and 885 acres of clearcuts will ruin the last, best lynx habitat in the state. Putting profits ahead of Colorado's wildlife will not be tolerated. This action is just a warning.

the use or threat of violence is present, it is generally classified as a crime against the person. The specific elements necessary for a robbery to take place are clear in its definition: (1) the felonious taking (with the intent to steal) (2) of the money or goods of another (3) from his or her person or in his or her presence (or custody, care, or control) (4) against his or her will (5) through the use or threat of force and violence. Thus, an armed bank holdup, a street mugging, and a purse snatching would all be robberies. If one or more of the five elements just listed were missing, the action would not be a robbery but some other crime, or perhaps no crime at all. If the use or threat of force were absent, for example, the crime would be theft.

Some jurisdictions divide robbery into degrees. Robbery in the first degree is charged when the offender is armed with a deadly weapon or dangerous instrument. Other jurisdictions have specific statutes that recognize unarmed robbery, armed robbery, train robbery, safe and vault robbery, and, most recently, *carjacking* (see Exhibit 3.4).

Arson

Common law conceptions of **arson** referred to the malicious burning of the dwelling of another person, but modern statutes have extended the parameters of arson in a variety of ways. First, while arson originally carried the ideas of fire and burning, most jurisdictions now include the use of explosives in the definition of this crime. Second, contemporary statutes include not only dwellings but also other types of buildings, as well as the property of the arsonist (if, for instance, there is an attempt to defraud an

Greatest Robberies of the 20th Century

- Biggest theft in history: Robbery of Reichsbank after the collapse of Nazi Germany, estimated at $3.75 billion
- No. 1 jewel robbery: $48 million worth of jewels stolen from a shop in Cannes, France, in 1994
- No. 1 cash theft: $22 million stolen at Hong Kong's airport in 1991
- $10.8 million stolen in 1990 from an armored car crew in Rochester, New York, as they stopped to buy lunch ■

EXHIBIT 3.4 | *historical perspectives on criminal justice*

Jack, Hijack, Carjack, and Skyjack

The word *carjack,* referring to auto theft at gunpoint (and sometimes resulting in kidnapping and/or homicide), is heard with considerable frequency. In some locales it has caused such a renewed fear of crime that both public and private police agencies have become highly visible guardians in urban financial and shopping centers as well as in suburban parking garages and lots. Although the term *carjack* was added to the lexicon relatively recently, its roots are quite old—dating back 100 years or so to early American tramp and railroad slang.

Since the closing years of the 19th century, a generic term for a hobo or tramp was *jack,* and the usual greeting between two members of this wandering fraternity was "Hi, Jack." It was a contraction for "How are you, Jack?" If one of the jacks was a "yegg" or "jungle buzzard" (a tramp thief or robber), he would produce a gun after the greeting and demand, "Hands up, Jack!" If this command was not quickly obeyed, the next order would be "High, Jack!" (meaning raise your hands high over your head).

By the second decade of the 20th century, "High, Jack" had entered general American underworld slang, it was contracted to "hijack," and the hijacker was a criminal who robbed other criminals. During the Prohibition era, hijackers were crooks who robbed bootleggers, typically after the liquor had been smuggled past revenue officers. Since this version of hijacking involved the robbery of trucks and their contents, when the robbery of automobiles became a highly visible crime in the early 1990s the term *carjacking* was applied by the media and police.

As for skyjacking—the hijacking of an airplane—it did not begin with 9/11. The first case in the United States occurred on May 1, 1961, when a man forced a commercial airliner enroute from Miami to Key West, Florida, to detour to Cuba. As was the case with 9/11, skyjacking is done almost invariably for terrorist purposes.

A steel beam from Two World Trade Center, indicating the number of people who died at the site during the 9/11 terrorist attacks.

insurer or if the building is occupied). Thus, a person is guilty of arson when he or she intentionally damages a building by starting a fire or causing an explosion.[12]

Arson is a felony in all jurisdictions. Most often it is divided into at least two degrees and sometimes three. In general, if the premises that are set afire are occupied, the charge will be first-degree arson. If they are unoccupied, the case will be one of second-degree arson. A person is guilty of arson in the third degree if the premises burned are his or her own, if they are unoccupied, and if the purpose is to defraud the insurer.

From a legal perspective, the major problem in arson cases is the element of criminal agency, or *intent.* A conviction depends on the state's proving that an accused person had both the intent and the opportunity to commit arson, which is difficult in many cases. Studies have shown that the reasons for arson are numerous and obscure and sometimes hard to detect. There are "revenge firesetters," for example, whose crimes result from anger, hatred, or jealousy in personal relationships; there are "excitement firesetters," who simply enjoy watching fires and the operations of fire equipment; there are "insurance-claim firesetters," who incinerate business property for its insurance value; there are "vandalism firesetters," who set buildings ablaze as part of adolescent peer-group activities; there are "criminal vindication firesetters," who use arson for hiding the evidence of other crimes.[13] To these might be added the "professional torches" who incinerate buildings for a fee, the firebombers of activist and political liberation organizations, the large number of skid row vagrants who are arrested for arson, and the many other types of arsonists for whom intent and motivation are not entirely clear.

Burglary

At one time, burglary was viewed as a crime against the habitation—that is, an invasion of the home—and was defined only in terms of the breaking and entering of a dwelling, at night, with the intent to commit a felony therein. The term comes directly from English common law and has its roots in the Saxon words *burgh,* meaning "house," and *laron,* meaning "theft." In current statutes the definition of burglary has been broadened: It includes structures other than a dwelling; it is applicable whether the illegal entry occurs during the night or day; and it can involve an intended felony or misdemeanor.

The term **breaking and entering** is often used synonymously with *burglary,* but this can be misleading because both breaking and entry need not be formally present for a burglary to occur. "Breaking" suggests forcible entry, but the mere opening of a closed door is sufficient to constitute a breaking. Moreover, simply remaining in a building until after it has closed and then engaging in some criminal activity can also constitute a burglary, even though no actual breaking occurs. *Entry* is the more essential element; it can be limited to the insertion of any part of the body or any instrument or weapon and still be sufficient to constitute a burglary.

Burglary is another offense that appears in a large number of degrees and varieties. A person is typically guilty of burglary in the third degree when he or she knowingly enters or remains unlawfully in a building with the intent to commit a crime therein. The burglary becomes an offense in the second degree if the building happens to be a dwelling, if the offender is armed, or if there is physical injury to any person who is not a participant in the crime. Burglary in the first degree involves unlawful entry or remaining in a dwelling at night, combined with the offender being armed or causing physical injury.[14]

Since burglary involves a criminal intent—that is, unlawful entry for some criminal purpose—two additional points must be stressed. First, even if the purpose of the entry is to commit a minor crime, such as petty theft or some other misdemeanor, the

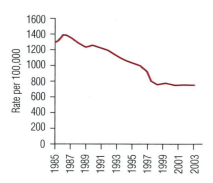

Burglary in the United States, 1983–2003

Source: *Uniform Crime Reports.*

"I understand they have some lovely things."

© The New Yorker Collection 1993 James Stevenson from cartoonbank.com. All Rights Reserved.

burglary has been consummated and a felony has been committed. Further, the offender can be charged not only with burglary but with the other offense as well. Second, the criminal intent aspect has resulted in a number of jurisdictions structuring their laws so that attempted burglary is included in the definition of burglary.

Closely related to burglary are a number of other crimes that are generally defined in separate statutes. For example, in many jurisdictions the very possession of burglar's tools can be prosecuted as a felony:

> A person is guilty of possession of burglar's tools when he possesses any tool, instrument, or other thing adapted, designed, or commonly used for committing or facilitating offenses involving unlawful entry into premises, or offenses involving forcible breaking of safes or other containers or depositories of property, under circumstances evincing an intent to use or knowledge that some other person intends to use the same in the commission of an offense of such character.[15]

Under the law, then, burglar's tools can include any number and type of devices, ranging from sophisticated lock picks and explosives to simple everyday tools such as screwdrivers and chisels.

Also related to burglary are the crimes described as *criminal trespass*. These are generally misdemeanors or violations and are distinguished from burglary when breaking with criminal intent is absent or when the trespass involves property that has been fenced in a manner designed to exclude intruders.

Property Offenses

It is difficult to describe the full range of property offenses because jurisdictions define and categorize them in different ways. In Louisiana, for example, the technical dimensions of the theft statute are quite broad:

> Theft is the misappropriation or taking of anything of value that belongs to another, either without the consent of the other to the misappropriation or taking, or by means of fraudulent conduct, practices, or representations. An intent to deprive the other permanently of whatever may be the subject of the misappropriation or taking is essential.[16]

This definition covers a multitude of property crimes, including what other states may define as larceny, embezzlement, and fraud. Further, while many states may have a broad *larceny* statute, which refers to the taking and carrying away of the personal property of another person with the intent to deprive permanently, other states, such as Delaware, define shoplifting—a clear instance of larceny—as a separate offense.[17] In Ohio and several other jurisdictions, theft statutes include the unlawful use of a person's service.[18] In general, however, **theft** seems to be the broadest of terms relating to property offenses and can be loosely defined as the unlawful taking, possession, or use of another person's property without the use or threat of force and with the intent to deprive permanently. Within the boundaries of this definition, theft would include the following:

- *Larceny:* The taking and carrying away of the personal property of another person with the intent to deprive permanently.
- *Shoplifting:* The theft of goods, wares, or merchandise from a store or shop.
- *Pickpocketing:* The theft of money or articles directly from the garments of the victim.
- *Embezzlement:* The fraudulent appropriation or conversion of money or property by an employee, trustee, or other agent to whom the possession of such money or property was entrusted.
- *Fraud:* Theft by false pretenses; the appropriation of money or property by trick or misrepresentation, or by creating or reinforcing a false impression as to some present or past fact that would adversely affect the victim's judgment of a transaction.
- *Forgery:* The making or altering of any document or instrument with the intent to defraud.

Pump and Run Thefts

As gasoline prices have risen, so too have the number of pump and run thefts from gasoline retailers. Prepayment by cash or credit card would reduce the number of thefts, but many retailers oppose it because it discourages drivers from going inside to shop for more profitable items. Source: Bureau of Transportation Statistics

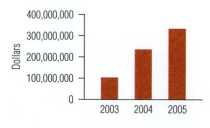

- *Counterfeiting:* The making of imitation money and obligations of the government or corporate body.
- *Confidence games:* The obtaining of money or property by means of deception through the confidence a victim places in the offender.
- *Blackmail:* The taking of money or property through threats of accusation or exposure.
- *Plagiarism:* The copying or adopting of the literary, musical, or artistic work of another and publishing or producing it as one's own original work.
- *Removal of landmarks:* The relocation of monuments or other markings that designate property lines or boundaries for the purpose of fraudulently reducing the owner's interest or holdings in lands and estates.
- *Criminal bankruptcy:* The fraudulent declaration of a person's excessive indebtedness or insolvency in an effort to avoid partial or full payment of one's debts.
- *Usury:* The taking of or contracting to take interest on a loan at a rate that exceeds the level established by law.
- *Ransom:* The demanding of money for the redemption of captured persons or property.
- *Buying, receiving, or possessing stolen goods:* The purchase, receipt, or possession of any property or goods known to be stolen.

This list may be longer or shorter depending on how an offense is interpreted in a particular jurisdiction. *Extortion,* for example, is included in the theft statutes of some states and can be defined to include not only the taking of money or property under threat of physical injury if the property is not delivered (which may also be construed as a form of robbery) but also what has been defined as blackmail. *Theft of services* also appears as a separate offense in some areas. This refers, for example, to a situation in which a homeowner illegally taps into another household's TV cable or electric meter or alters the mechanism in his or her own meter, thus avoiding paying for the service.

Also note that the offenses in the list are not mutually exclusive. What has been defined as counterfeiting may appear under forgery statutes; confidence games are clearly special varieties of fraud; and shoplifting and pickpocketing are forms of larceny. Here we will focus on **larceny,** since this classification includes many types of theft and, at least in terms of official criminal statistics, is the most common of all major crimes.

According to the legal definition provided in the preceding list, the crime of larceny includes five essential elements: (1) the taking and (2) carrying away of the (3) personal property (4) of another (5) with the intent to deprive permanently. The element of *taking* suggests that the offender has no legal right to possession of the property in question. In this sense, taking involves a trespass in that the possession of property has been wrongfully obtained.

This point highlights the difficult distinctions among *possession, custody,* and *control* as they relate to larceny. The renowned **Carrier's Case** of 1473 provided an initial interpretation of this distinction. A mover, entrusted with the task of transporting bales of wool dye and thus having legal custody of them, broke into several bales and took part of the contents. From this case came the time-honored doctrine of "breaking bulk," which maintained that although the mover or carrier had legal custody of the property, his breaking into the bales was a trespass against the possessory interests of the owner and therefore constituted larceny.[19]

Another significant case was the famous **Pear's Case** of 1779. The accused, a man by the name of Pear, had hired a horse from a livery stable, given the owner a false address, and then taken the animal to a local market and sold it as his own. The legal issue was that the stableman had willingly delivered the animal and that Pear had not used force or stealth to obtain custody of it. The court ruled that the act was larceny "by trick." The horse had been hired for a purpose that Pear never intended to execute, and as such his taking of the horse with the intention of selling it was a trespass against the stableman's right of possession.[20] The point, then, is that a taking can occur even when a person has authorized custody or control of an object if his or her use or disposal of that object ultimately deprives someone else of their possessory rights.

He who holds the ladder is as bad as the thief.

—GERMAN PROVERB

Plunder: To take the property of another without observing the decent and customary reticences of theft.

—AMBROSE BIERCE,
THE DEVIL'S DICTIONARY

Thieves respect property; they merely wish the property to become *their* property that they may more perfectly respect it.

—G. K. CHESTERTON

U.S. Larceny-Theft, 2003
Source: *Uniform Crime Reports.*

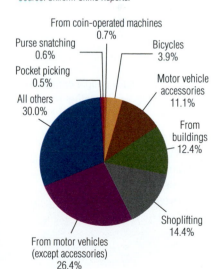

Kidnapping for Ransom

The highest rates of kidnapping for ransom occur in Latin America. As illustrated below, the nation with the highest numbers is Colombia.

Country	2000	2001	2002	2003
Colombia	2,888	3,041	3,896	3,623
Argentina	2	5	165	434
Mexico	300	320	358	340
Venezuela	108	113	201	204
Brazil	455	630	528	607

Source: Brazilian Ministry of Justice, Colombian National Security Advisory, Venezuela Segura, Procurator General of Argentina, media reports. ∎

Is Clucking a Criminal Offense?

In Ballston Lake, New York, in 2000, two men were arrested on a charge of aggravated harassment after a series of "clucking" incidents. After a woman client pulled out of a mortgage deal, for months they called her on the telephone and clucked like a chicken.

Source: *The New York Times,* August 26, 2000, B5. ∎

I don't know of many people who think that two people living together ought to be a crime.

—MASSACHUSETTS GOVERNOR
MICHAEL DUKAKIS, SIGNING
A MEASURE IN 1987 REPEALING
A 200-YEAR-OLD STATE LAW
BANNING COHABITATION

Adultery is the application of democracy to love.

—H. L. MENCKEN

The *carrying away* aspect of larceny, also known as "asportation," involves removal of the property from the place it formerly occupied. The distance of movement, however, need not be significant. The removal of a wallet from a pocket, for example, represents complete asportation.

Personal property, the third element of larceny, refers to anything that can be owned except land or things permanently affixed to it. The property must also be that of *another,* since larceny is a crime against possession and therefore cannot occur with what one already possesses.

The final element of larceny involves *intent*—intent to permanently deprive. If the intent is to deprive only temporarily, there is no larceny, although many states have structured their criminal codes to cover this kind of situation with such lesser offenses as unauthorized use of a vehicle and misappropriation of property. Whether the intent is to deprive permanently or only temporarily, however, is a question of fact on which the court must rule, and the distinction between permanent and temporary can be a matter of interpretation.

In *United States* v. *Sheffield,* the defendant had taken an automobile without consent and by stealth. After driving through several states, he reversed his course but was arrested while in a state other than the one from which he had taken the vehicle. Sheffield was convicted of auto theft in a Maryland court. He appealed on the ground that he had intended to return the auto to the vicinity from which it had been removed. The conviction was upheld, however. The opinion of the court read as follows:

> When an automobile is taken without right of colorable authority and by stealth and to be used by the taker for his own use and benefit for an indefinite period of time, I think there is properly a presumption, or at least sufficient evidence, for an inference of fact that it is being taken to deprive the owner of the rights and benefits of his property; and the mere statement of a defendant who has so feloniously taken a motor car that he intended to abandon it somewhere in the same city . . . is not sufficient to destroy the inference unless well supported by collateral facts.[21]

The distinction between larceny as a felony and as a misdemeanor, or between "grand larceny" and "petty larceny," is statutory in nature. The dividing point ranges from as little as $50 in some jurisdictions to as much as $2,500 in others.[22] At a value below these amounts the larceny is a misdemeanor, while anything valued at or above the statutory figure is a felony.

Sex Offenses

The scope of illegal sexual activity is quite broad in American society. This is due to several factors, including the legacy of the early Puritan codes and the Holy Scriptures, attempts to maintain standards of public decency through the legislation of morality, and efforts to protect those who are too young or are otherwise unable to make decisions as to their own sexual conduct. Although in recent years the codes regulating many sexual activities, such as contraception and miscegenation, have been eliminated or severely limited, the list of sex offenses is still long and includes the following:

- *Forcible rape:* Having sexual intercourse with a person against his or her will and through the use or threat of force or fear.
- *Statutory rape:* Having sexual intercourse with a person under a stated age (usually 16 or 18, but sometimes 14), with or without his or her consent.
- *Seduction:* The act of enticing or luring a woman of chaste character to engage in sexual intercourse by fraudulently promising to marry her or by some other false promise.
- *Fornication:* Sexual intercourse between unmarried persons.
- *Adultery:* Sexual intercourse between a man and woman, at least one of whom is married to someone else.
- *Incest:* Sexual intercourse between parent and child, any pair of siblings, or close blood relatives.

- *Sodomy:* Certain acts of sexual relationship including fellatio (oral intercourse with the male sex organ), cunnilingus (oral intercourse with the female sex organ), buggery (penetration of the anus), homosexuality (sexual relations between members of the same sex), bestiality (sexual intercourse with an animal), pederasty (unnatural intercourse between a man and a boy), and necrophilia (sexual intercourse with a corpse).
- *Indecent exposure (exhibitionism):* Exposure of the sexual organs in a public place.
- *Lewdness:* Degenerate sexual behavior that is so well known that it may result in the corruption of public decency.
- *Obscenity:* That which is offensive to morality or chastity and is calculated to corrupt the mind and morals of those exposed to it.
- *Pornography:* Literature, art, film, pictures, or other articles of a sexual nature that are considered obscene by a community's moral standards.
- *Bigamy:* The act of marrying while a former marriage is still legally in force.
- *Polygamy:* The practice of having several spouses.
- *Prostitution:* The offering of sexual relations for monetary or other gain.
- *Child molesting:* Handling, fondling, or other contact of a sexual nature with a child.
- *Sexual assault:* Any sexual contact with another person that occurs without the consent of the victim or is offensive to the victim.
- *Voyeurism (peeping):* The surreptitious observance of an exposed body or sexual act.

Although the offenses of forcible rape, incest, and child molesting appear in all jurisdictions throughout the United States in one form or another, not all of the sexual behaviors listed here are universally prohibited. Fornication, seduction, and pornography are disappearing from the penal codes of many state and local areas; indecent exposure, in the form of topless dancing and live sex shows, has been decriminalized in several jurisdictions; and prostitution is legal in several parts of Nevada. In some cultures and nations, moreover, definitions of and responses to numerous sexual crimes, including rape, differ greatly from those in the United States. In some cultures, furthermore, the mere "suspicion of immorality" can result in death (see Exhibit 3.5).

For generations, sodomy statutes were a fact of American life. As recently as 1960, every state had an antisodomy law, with many focusing on not only gay men but heterosexual couples. By 2003, in 37 states the statutes had been repealed by lawmakers or blocked by state courts. Of the remaining 13 states with sodomy laws, four—Texas, Kansas, Oklahoma, and Missouri—prohibited oral and anal sex between same-sex couples. The other nine—Alabama, Florida, Idaho, Louisiana, Mississippi, North Carolina, South Carolina, Utah, and Virginia—banned consensual sodomy for everyone. However, the U.S. Supreme Court ruling in **Lawrence v. Texas,**[23] decided in June 2003, held that the Texas statute making it a crime for two persons of the same sex to engage in certain intimate sexual acts violated the due process clause of the Constitution. This ruling has had far-reaching implications. First, it overturned the Supreme Court's 1986 decision in *Bowers* v. *Hardwick,*[24] which held that gay men did not have a constitutional right to engage in sodomy, even if the act was consensual and in private. In addition, it effectively invalidated all sodomy statutes targeting anal and oral sex and also placed in jeopardy statutes that govern fornication and adultery.

Forcible rape is the sex offense about which there is most concern, but rape statutes are often peculiar. In most jurisdictions, **rape** is defined as the unlawful "carnal knowledge" of a female without her consent and against her will.[25] In recent years, however, jurisdictions have been redefining the act of rape, identifying it as a gender-neutral offense in which a wide range of circumstances can characterize each individual crime.[26] The traditional definition of rape suggests that men are the only possible offenders and women the only possible victims. However, one cannot discount the many instances of sexual assault that occur in prisons and jails or the cases of forced oral–genital and other body contacts attempting to simulate heterosexual intercourse that occur in women's institutions.[27]

Historically, *statutory rape* laws included only sexual intercourse with an underage girl. In 1981 the California statutory rape law was challenged before the U.S. Supreme

It'll be a sad day for sexual liberation when the pornography addict has to settle for the real thing.

—**BRENDAN FRANCIS**

The worst that can be said about pornography is that it leads not to "antisocial" acts but the reading of more pornography.

—**GORE VIDAL**

Pornography is the undiluted essence of anti-female propaganda.

—**SUSAN BROWNMILLER**

Bigamy is having one spouse too many. Monogamy has been called the same thing.

—**ANONYMOUS**

Obscenity can be found in every book except the telephone directory.

—**GEORGE BERNARD SHAW**

Bigamy is a big mistake in taste for which the wisdom of the future will adjudge a punishment called trigamy.

—**AMBROSE BIERCE,**
THE DEVIL'S DICTIONARY

EXHIBIT 3.5 | VICTIMS & JUSTICE:

Honor Killings as a Cultural Tradition

A girl in Jordan is raped by her brother, who put sleeping pills in her tea and threatened to kill her if she told the family. When she became pregnant, she had to tell them. She survived her brother's attempt to kill her, but terminated the pregnancy. Later, a marriage to a man 50 years her senior was arranged for her, but the union survived for only 6 months before they divorced. The brother's next attempt to kill her, this time by slashing her throat, was successful.

Her "crime"? She soiled the family name and had to die so that the honor of the family could survive.

Jordan has one of the highest per capita rates of *honor killings* in the world, where each year approximately 25 women are killed for crimes based on "suspicion of immorality," including being too friendly with a brother-in-law, for having "arrogant" body language, for sitting next to a man on a bus, for talking to a man on a telephone, and even for being raped. Elsewhere, the stories are equally as shocking. There's the young Egyptian woman who was on her honeymoon when her father cut off her head and paraded it down a dusty Cairo street—her punishment for marrying a man of whom he did not approve. In Pakistan's Sindh province, a woman was shot dead by her husband because a neighbor had spotted a man who was not a family member near the field where she was working.

The United Nations Population Fund has estimated that as many as 5,000 honor killings occur each year. Exact figures are hard to pinpoint because many crimes go unreported. In some rural areas, girls are not registered at birth and therefore "do not exist" on paper. Moreover, many of these crimes are passed off as suicides. The killings are most visible in Muslim countries, particularly in the Middle East and Central Asia, even though Islamic law does not sanction the practice.

Honor killing is an ancient practice sanctioned by culture, rather than religion, and is rooted in a complex code that allows a man to kill a female relative for actual or even suspected sexual activity. Cultures where the practice exists hold that a woman is a man's possession and a reflection of his honor. According to Madiha El-Safty, a professor of sociology at United States University in Cairo: "It is 100 percent tradition. It's associated with the value of the sexual chastity of the woman." Or more specifically, as the Egyptian feminist author and women's rights advocate Salwa Bakr commented:

A woman in Arab societies is an object for sex and reproduction. As long as she is an object, she is owned by a father, a husband, a brother. The way she uses her body is not her business, but the business of those who own her.

By contrast, a tribal leader in Yemen insisted:

The practice [of honor killings] is because women are weaker than men. If she is immoral, it is the man's duty to kill her. Otherwise, he will be despised by the rest of his tribe.

Honor killings continue to thrive in rural areas where women remain financially dependent on men and justice is administered by village elders. However, honor killings have also been reported in Britain, Norway, Peru, Brazil, Venezuela, and even the United States. In fact, the practice has been increasingly observed in Western countries with large populations of new immigrants from countries that practice the tradition.

Pakistani women protesting a recent honor killing.

Across Europe, the continent's Muslim population has nearly doubled over the past decade. Many immigrants retain the customs from their native countries, but the clash between the culture from the old country and the modern lifestyle of European cities has often created tremendous familial conflict. In Germany, human rights organizations estimate that there have been almost 50 honor killings in that country since 1996. In early 2005, for example, a young Turkish woman was gunned down in the middle of the street by her brothers for divorcing the man to whom her marriage had been arranged and for embracing a Western lifestyle that included wearing jeans, drinking alcohol, and going to discos. Her death incited outrage from most people in her adopted home of Berlin. However, others sympathized with the killers, including a young Turkish schoolboy who said, "She deserved what she got—the whore lived like a German."

Western human rights organizations have initiated movements against honor killings and have put pressure on countries where the practice is more widespread. However, some religious groups and politicians have criticized attempts to condemn the killings or introduce harsh punishments. In Pakistan, the parliament strengthened a law against honor killings in late 2004, in a session at which opposition lawmakers walked out in protest. Human rights activists also criticized the legislation, saying it didn't go far enough to protect the hundreds of victims who are killed in Pakistan each year. A bill that sought to amend and strengthen the new legislation was defeated in 2005.

The heart of the problem remains entrenched in social attitudes. This is reflected in a recent survey of men in Turkey, in which 37 percent agreed that a woman who dishonored her family deserved to be killed. Not until such cultural beliefs about women are altered will any real progress be made.

Sources: Alasdair Soussi, "The First Glimpse of Hope: Each Year 5000 Women Are Victims of Honour Killings, Now Activists in Jordan Want to Stop the Slaughter," *The Herald* (Glasgow), January 11, 2005, 11; Jeffrey Fleishman, "'Honor Killings' Show Clash of Culture in Berlin: The Latest Slaying of a Muslim Woman in the German Capital Has Sharpened the Debate over the Place of Immigrants in Europe," *Los Angeles Times,* March 20, 2005, 10A; Merial Beattie, "Scots Help Turkey to Put an End to 'Honour Killings,'" *The Independent* (London), April 24, 2005, 5; *The New York Times,* March 3, 2005, 8A; Donna Abu-Nasr, "Until Death Do Us Part," *Durban Daily News* (South Africa), July 12, 2000, 9; Zaffer Abbas, "Pakistan Fails to Condemn Honor Killings," *BBC News Online,* August 3, 1999; Khabir Ahmad, "Pakistan Unveils Wide-Ranging Changes to Human Rights Procedures," *The Lancet Interactive,* May 6, 2000.

"We're having a few friends over for dinner, followed by a brainstorming session aimed at helping the Supreme Court define pornography."

The New Yorker Collection 2005 Henry Martin from cartoonbank.com. All Rights Reserved.

Court on the ground that it discriminated on the basis of gender (only men were criminally liable under the statute). The Court upheld the power of the states to enact such statutes, since many were intended to prevent teenage pregnancies.[28] Nevertheless, the statutes in some jurisdictions have become more gender-neutral. A case in point was the 1997 prosecution of Mary Kay LeTourneau, a sixth-grade teacher in Burien, Washington, on several counts of second-degree rape of a child. For more than a year LeTourneau had a sexual relationship with one of her students, eventually becoming pregnant and bearing his child. What was perhaps most interesting about the case was the public's reaction. While some observers called LeTourneau a pedophile, others raised the question, "How can you rape the willing?"[29]

Although rape is considered the most serious of the sex offenses, *prostitution* seems to be the most common. Prostitution is providing sex in return for money or some other desired commodity. It includes not only sexual intercourse but any other form of sexual conduct with another person for a fee. Where prostitution is illegal, it is typically a misdemeanor. (For a discussion of the ways that prostitutes become victims of crime, see Exhibit 3.6.)

Related to prostitution is *procuring*, also referred to as *pandering* or *pimping*. Procuring is promoting prostitution through the operation of a house of prostitution or managing the activities and contacts of one or more prostitutes for a percentage of their earnings. It is most often a felony at the state level, and in some circumstances it can be prosecuted under federal law.

Drug Law Violations

The federal and state statutes that regulate nonmedical use of drugs and control the manufacture, sale, and distribution of "dangerous" drugs are relatively recent, having evolved only during the 20th century. Although a few local ordinances focused on cer-

EXHIBIT 3.6 | VICTIMS & JUSTICE

Sex Work in a Subculture of Violence

The concept of a "culture of violence" has been used to explain high rates of homicide and other violent behaviors in certain cultures and segments of society. The concept expresses the notion that cultural values and social conditions, rather than simply individual biological or psychological factors, are significant causes of violent behavior. For example, the culture of violence thesis has been used to explain the higher rates of violent crime in urban inner-city areas.

In the criminology and delinquency literature, a *subculture-of-violence* thesis has been introduced for the purpose of explaining social-structural causes of violence in urban areas. The general model of such a subculture is one characterized by dense concentrations of socioeconomically disadvantaged persons with few legitimate avenues of social mobility, lucrative illegal markets for forbidden goods and services, a value system that rewards only survival and material success, and private enforcement of the rules of the game. This rendering of the subculture-of-violence concept has been used to analyze juvenile gang violence, as well as generalized violence in urban inner-city neighborhoods. Overall, the subculture-of-violence thesis is a useful analytic approach for understanding the extent to which certain types of violence are socially produced or the result of individual pathology.

Within this context, it has been well documented that women sex workers who walk the boulevards and back streets of urban centers are typically at high risk for assault, rape, and other forms of physical violence—including murder—from a variety of individuals, including muggers, serial predators, drug dealers, pimps, police, "dates" ("johns" or customers), and even passersby. Furthermore, street sex workers are embedded in the same violent social spaces in which other forms of violence, and subcultures of violence, exist. As such, it would appear that to a considerable extent, street sex workers ply their trade in a subculture of violence.

This point of view was examined within the context of a larger research project designed to test the effectiveness of a violence prevention and HIV/AIDS risk reduction initiative targeting women sex workers in Miami, Florida. The data presented in this exhibit were collected during 2002 and 2003, and are based on interviews with 325 drug-involved sex workers.

Participants in this study were located by active sex workers who were trained and paid as outreach workers and were familiar with the many locations where other sex workers could be found—such as specific motels, bars, convenience stores, crack houses and shooting galleries, and secluded empty lots, to name but a few. Interviews were conducted by experienced research interviewers at a field office located near the "stroll" where sex workers solicit their dates. Information was collected on drug use and sexual behaviors, sex work and other criminal activities, and violent crime victimization.

The sex work careers of the clients were quite lengthy, spanning an average of 15.8 years and a mean of 792 sexual partners. Past-month sexual activity included a mean of 35.9 vaginal sexual contacts and

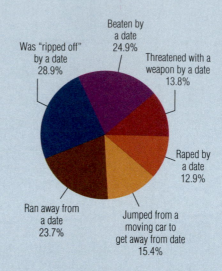

24.4 oral sexual contacts. A substantial proportion (26.8%) also engaged in less traditional forms of sex trading in the past month, including anal sex, bondage, sadism, and "threesomes."

Of interest for the subculture-of-violence thesis, nearly 42 percent of the women had some violent encounter while engaging in sex work in the past year. Most frequently (as illustrated in the chart), they reported that these incidents involved being "ripped off" (the forcible taking back of money paid for sex) by a customer or "date" (28.9%), being beaten by a date (24.9%), being threatened with a weapon by a date (13.8%), and being raped by a date (12.9%). The women themselves often took extreme measures to escape from violent dates, with 15.4 percent indicating that they had jumped from moving cars and 23.7 percent running away from dates.

The survey data collected on this cohort of female sex workers documented that the prevalence of both physical and sexual victimization is extremely elevated by comparison with national estimates. In fact, a recent violence against women survey sponsored by the National Institute of Justice and the Centers for Disease Control and Prevention placed the percentage of women experiencing rape or physical assault in the past 12 months at 0.3 percent and 1.9 percent, respectively. In this analysis of women sex workers, the rates of "date" violence alone are some 43 and 13 times higher, supporting the contention that female sex workers are enmeshed in a social milieu wherein violence is commonplace and victimization is expected.

From a policy point of view, mechanisms need to be established that serve to provide sex workers with alternatives to the street. Virtually all of the women in this project indicated that prostitution was not their chosen career. Rather, for most it was "survival sex" — their only means of support.

Sources: Adapted from: Hilary L. Surratt, James A. Inciardi, Steven P. Kurtz, and Marion C. Kiley, "Sex Work and Drug Use in a Subculture of Violence," *Crime and Delinquency* 50 (January 2004), 43–59.

tain types of drug use and sale during the late 1800s, the *Pure Food and Drug Act of 1906* was the first piece of federal legislation that targeted the distribution of drugs that were considered dangerous. The purpose of the law was to limit the uncontrolled manufacture of patent medicines and over-the-counter drugs containing cocaine and narcotics such as opium, morphine, and heroin. The *Harrison Act of 1914* defined as criminal any manufacture, prescription, transfer, or possession of narcotics by persons who were not authorized to pay a tax on them.[30] In 1937 the *Marijuana Tax Act* prohibited the use or sale of marijuana, and during the 1950s a series of federal statutes were passed to increase the penalties associated with the sale and use of narcotics, marijuana, and cocaine.[31]

The *Comprehensive Drug Abuse and Control Act of 1970,* in effect since May 1, 1971, brought together in a single law most of the drug controls that had been created since the passage of the Harrison Act. Title II of the new law, known as the *Controlled Substances Act,* categorized certain substances into five "schedules" and defined the offenses and penalties associated with the illegal manufacture, distribution, and dispensing of any drug in each schedule.

Before the passage of these laws, federal and state drug laws often varied greatly. The penalties for many drug violations also varied considerably from one jurisdiction to another. Many state marijuana laws, for example, specified that the penalties for marijuana should be the same as those for heroin, and in at least 19 jurisdictions there was no distinction between penalties for the mere possession of one marijuana cigarette or "reefer" and for the sale of large quantities of heroin. By 1972, however, the majority of the states had adopted the provisions of the Controlled Substances Act, thus helping standardize drug laws in most parts of the nation.

In jurisdictions that have not adopted the federal model, drug laws vary considerably. While federal penalties for the possession of even small quantities of marijuana specify probation or a sentence of up to 1 year of imprisonment and/or fines of up to $5,000, penalties in some jurisdictions range from as little as a citation without arrest (New York) to imprisonment for up to 10 years in Georgia, Texas, and Louisiana.[32]

In addition to laws that control the manufacture, transfer, distribution, sale, and possession of drugs, some jurisdictions have laws against the possession of narcotics paraphernalia such as hypodermic syringes and needles. And some states require that controlled substances, such as prescription drugs, be kept in the containers in which they were originally dispensed.

Crimes Against Public Order and Safety

The final category, crimes against public order and safety (public order crimes), tends to be a rather sweeping collection of offenses, mostly misdemeanors, that nevertheless account for a considerable portion of criminal justice activity. The laws in this category vary considerably from one place to another, but the following crimes appear in one form or another in most jurisdictions:

- *Disorderly conduct:* Any act that tends to disturb the public peace, scandalize the community, or shock the public sense of morality.
- *Disturbing the peace:* Any interruption of the peace, quiet, and good order of a neighborhood or community.
- *Breach of the peace:* The breaking of the public peace by any riotous, forcible, or unlawful proceeding.
- *Harassment:* Any act that serves to annoy or alarm another person.
- *Stalking:* The willful, malicious, and repeated following or harassing of another person.
- *Drunkenness:* The condition of being under the influence of alcohol to the extent that it renders one helpless.
- *Public intoxication:* The condition of being severely under the influence of alcohol or drugs in a public place to the degree that one may endanger persons or property.

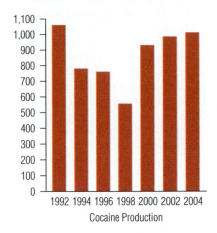

Cocaine Production: Average Estimates in Tons

Source: Bureau for International Narcotics and Law Enforcement Affairs.

Cocaine Production

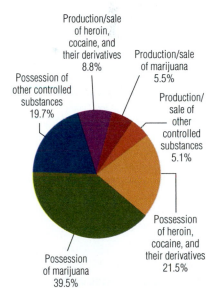

Drug Law Arrests, 2003

Source: *Uniform Crime Reports.*

- Production/sale of heroin, cocaine, and their derivatives 8.8%
- Production/sale of marijuana 5.5%
- Production/sale of other controlled substances 5.1%
- Possession of heroin, cocaine, and their derivatives 21.5%
- Possession of marijuana 39.5%
- Possession of other controlled substances 19.7%

The "New Frontier of Stalking"?

Responding to what the House of Representatives has called the "new frontier of stalking," the Video Voyeurism Prevention Act of 2004 prohibits purposefully capturing improper images of individuals "by video tape, photograph, film, or any means or broadcast" without their consent and under circumstances in which individuals have a reasonable expectation of privacy. Improper images are those that depict "naked or undergarment clad genitals, pubic area, buttocks, or female breasts." The act, which technically legislates violation-of-privacy crimes more so than stalking crimes, makes video voyeurism on federal property punishable by a fine of up to $100,000, or imprisonment up to 1 year, or both. The prohibition does not apply to law enforcement or intelligence activities.

With advances in video and camera phone technologies, law enforcement officials have seen an increase in video voyeurism cases, which commonly involve "up-skirt" or "down-blouse" photos of females taken in public places like shopping malls and movie theaters. Moreover, with the new camera phones that enable the instantaneous transmission of images to the Web, there has also been an increase of voyeurism in cyberspace.

The federal law applies only to acts conducted on federal property, but more than half the states have some form of video voyeurism law as well. In Texas, for example, taking an image of an individual for sexual gratification without his or her consent can tally up to $10,000 in fines and up to 2 years in prison.

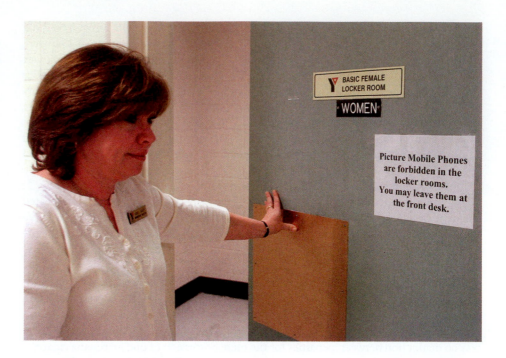

Drunk-Driving Deaths in the United States, 1985–2004

Roughly 41% of the 42,000 traffic fatalities in the United States in 2004 were alcohol-related. While this percentage is a cause for concern, it has not changed dramatically over the past 19 years. Source: National Highway Traffic Safety Administrator.

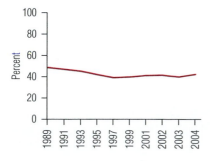

- *Loitering:* Idling or lounging on a street or other public way in a manner that serves to interfere with or annoy passersby.
- *Criminal nuisance:* Any conduct that is unreasonable and that endangers the health and safety of others.
- *Vagrancy:* The condition of being idle and having no visible means of support.
- *Desecration:* The defacing, damaging, or mistreatment of a public structure, monument, or place of worship or burial.
- *Driving while intoxicated (DWI) or driving under the influence (DUI):* Operating a motor vehicle while under the influence of alcohol or illegal drugs.
- *Gambling:* The playing or operation of any game of chance that involves money or property of any value that is prohibited by the criminal code.
- *Violation of privacy:* Any unlawful trespass, interception, observation, eavesdropping, or other surveillance that serves to infringe on the private rights of another.*

In recent years, the constitutionality of many criminal codes designed for the preservation of public order and safety has been challenged. Numerous cases of disorderly conduct, breach of the peace, and vagrancy have come before the U.S. Supreme Court on the ground that they violate First Amendment protections of free speech and assembly or because they are too vague. Moreover, the use of such statutes as mechanisms for penalizing people who are viewed as political and social undesirables has been questioned as a violation of rights of due process. Nevertheless, these statutes remain in the criminal codes of most jurisdictions. Arrests for vagrancy and disorderly conduct alone may total as many as 1 million annually.

| Major Forms of Crime |

The preceding discussion provides a basis for understanding the legal definitions and boundaries of the major categories of crime. However, the criminal codes cannot offer any insight and explanation of the social and behavioral contexts in which certain crimes tend to occur or the relationship of certain criminal acts to the wider social order. Further, the criminal law suggests nothing about the differences in styles and patterns of crime, the offenders, and victim–offender relationships, nor does it tell us how

*Some violations of privacy, such as voyeurism or exhibitionism, may be classified as sex offenses.

CAREERS IN CRIMINAL JUSTICE

Crisis Intervention Counseling

Because of the more than 1 million violent crimes that occur in the United States each year, many police departments, schools, hospitals, and numerous other public and private agencies have crisis intervention counselors available to help victims deal with emotional trauma. Crisis intervention is just one specialization in the broader area of counseling, which provides employment for more than 1 million people in the United States. In addition to crisis work, counseling in the criminal justice field includes work in correctional institutions, drug and alcohol programs, and halfway houses and group homes for both adult and juvenile offenders.

With the spread of AIDS around the world, a new and highly specialized area of counseling has emerged in social service and criminal justice agencies. HIV/AIDS counselors not only provide crisis intervention for those found to be HIV-positive but also function as HIV prevention educators in a variety of settings, including correctional institutions.

The majority of counselors have undergraduate degrees in either criminal justice, psychology, or one of the other social or behavioral sciences, and many have graduate degrees in counselor education. Counseling certification programs are also available in almost every state. Counseling licensure requirements vary from state to state, as do employment opportunities and salaries. In 2004, however, the majority of counselors earned between $25,000 and $50,000 a year, with the top 10 percent earning in excess of $65,000 annually.

For more information on counseling as a career, contact the American Counseling Association in Alexandria, Virginia. For information on national certification requirements for counselors, see the National Board for Certified Counselors homepage (http://www.nbcc.org/).

all of these affect the management of crime. In short, each category of crime has two important aspects: its legal description as stated in the law, and the behavior system that brings it into being.

Literally dozens of different criminal behavior systems have been identified in the literature.[33] However, because domestic violence and hate crime—and, most recently, white-collar crime—are in the public and media spotlight, and because organized crime not only persists but continually re-creates itself, the balance of the chapter is devoted to these four types of criminality.

Domestic Violence

Domestic violence is a form of violent personal crime and can be defined as activities of a physically aggressive nature occurring among members of a family, current or former spouses or lovers, and others in close relationships, as a result of conflicts in personal relations. Domestic violence typically occurs in the home, but it can also take place at the house of another family member or a neighbor, at the victim's place of employment, at a commercial establishment, or even in public. The victim and offender are most often of opposite genders, although they may be of the same gender.

The scope of domestic violence is quite broad and includes a wide range of behavioral patterns and offense categories. There is *battering* by spouses and lovers, which is a consistent pattern of behavior that seeks to establish dominance and control over another through the use or threat of force or violence. There is also *abuse,* which may be psychological or economic in nature, involving ridicule, threats, and harassment. Other forms of domestic violence include marital and date rape, elderly abuse, and child neglect and abuse. These, however, are broad categories. The actual criminal statutes involved include murder and manslaughter, assault, rape, incest, harassment, and stalking, to name just a few.

Domestic violence has occurred throughout human history. In many cultures men were legally and socially permitted to punish their wives and children for disobedience or disloyalty. Moreover, much of what is now referred to as domestic violence was once considered a legitimate means by which men could maintain control over the family.[34]

An important aspect of domestic violence is the relationship between the victim and the offender. This suggests that a large portion of such behavior is well beyond the control of law enforcement. In the case of murder, for example, many offenses occur

Murder Circumstances by Relationship, 2003

Source: *Uniform Crime Reports.*

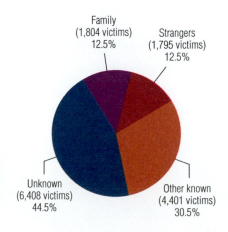

Family (1,804 victims) 12.5%

Strangers (1,795 victims) 12.5%

Unknown (6,408 victims) 44.5%

Other known (4,401 victims) 30.5%

A police officer from the Los Angeles Domestic Violence Unit makes a photographic record of the physical abuse this woman experienced.

Is Swearing a Crime?

In some jurisdictions it is indeed. In Standish, Michigan, for example, a canoeist was convicted in 1999 of cursing in front of children and ordered to pay a $75 fine or spend 3 days in jail. In Sarasota, Florida, two women were jailed in 2000 after they greeted police with a string of profanity.

Sources: *Miami Herald,* August 9, 2000, 5B; *The New York Times* August 24, 1999, A13. ■

between people who know each other. Of the 14,408 murders reported during 2003, 4.8 percent of the victims were spouses, 7.7 percent involved other family members, and 30.5 percent included neighbors or other close acquaintances. In the remaining cases the offender was a stranger or the relationship could not be established. In the case of domestic violence, the majority of killings involved "romantic triangles," quarrels over money or property, or other arguments.

Although official statistics on assault are not as complete as those on criminal homicide, this crime, too, reflects the growing incidence of domestic violence. Random street muggings do indeed occur, but nearly two-thirds of all known aggravated assaults result from domestic quarrels, altercations, jealousies, and arguments over money and property. Further, victim–offender relationships are typically intimate, close, and frequent, primarily involving family members and close acquaintances.

Child abuse, or domestic violence directed against children (also termed *battered child syndrome*), is a form of personal violence that has received widespread attention only during recent years. Studies suggest that the offenders are typically parents or guardians and that the abuse is an enduring pattern provoked by behaviors that are typical of children—persistent crying, failure to use the toilet, aggression toward siblings, breaking toys or household items, or disobedience.[35]

Another form of abuse is child molestation, which is most frequently manifested as parent–child incest, sexual fondling of a child, or persuasion or coercion of a child to engage in other kinds of sexual acts with a parent, sibling, or guardian. Recently the use of cocaine during pregnancy has been defined as child abuse.

Contrary to popular belief, women are not the only victims of domestic violence and men are not the only offenders. Although men are the offenders in most domestic violence situations, studies have found that men are at risk as well and there is indeed a "battered husband syndrome."[36]

Hate Crime

Hate crime can be defined as an offense motivated by hatred against a victim because of his or her race, ethnicity, religion, sexual orientation, handicap, or national origin. Also referred to as "bias-motivated crimes," hate crimes are often difficult to identify, primarily because criminal acts motivated by bias can easily be confused with forms of expression that are protected by the U.S. Constitution.

From the Romans' persecution of the Christians almost two millennia ago and the Nazis' "final solution" for the Jews during World War II to the "ethnic cleansing" in Bosnia and the genocide in Rawanda during the 1990s, hate crimes have shaped and sometimes defined world history. In the United States, most hate crimes have been inspired by racial and religious biases. During the nation's early history Native Americans became the targets of bias-motivated intimidation and violence. Later there were lynchings of African Americans, followed by hate crimes directed against Chinese laborers. More current examples of hate crimes include assaults on gays, the painting of swastikas on Jewish synagogues, and cross burnings intended to drive black families out of predominantly white neighborhoods.[37]

The number of hate crimes that occur in the United States is difficult to calculate and is quite small in official statistics. According to Justice Department estimates, fewer than 1 out of every 2,000 homicides and 1 of every 8,000 reported rapes are bias-motivated. But many hate crimes likely go unreported. Of the nearly 12,000 agencies that report hate crimes to the FBI, only 1,967 reported even a single hate crime in 2003. Over 83 percent of law enforcement agencies did not report any hate crimes. In addition, Hawaii did not participate in the reporting of hate crimes to the FBI, and both Alabama and Mississippi reported just one hate crime each.[38]

The victims of hate crimes in the United States are most often African Americans, followed by Jews, gays, Asian-Americans, and, increasingly, Muslims. Although the Ku Klux Klan and Nazi skinhead groups are the most visible perpetrators of hate crimes, the majority of offenders are individuals rather than groups. During 2003, there were 5,517 hate crimes against persons and 3,139 against property reported to the FBI. Of the suspected offenders, 62 percent were white, 19 percent were black, and the remaining 19 percent were Native American, Asian/Pacific Islander, multiracial, or of unknown race or ethnicity.[39]

Two killings in 1998 brought the problem of hate crime into sharp focus and intensified the lingering national debate about hate crime legislation. On October 8, 1998, just outside of Laramie, Wyoming, a passing bicyclist spotted what he thought was a scarecrow lashed to the fence of a local ranch. A closer look found that it was the burned, battered, and nearly lifeless body of 22-year-old Matthew Shepard, who had been tied to the fence in near-freezing temperatures 18 hours earlier. An openly gay student at the University of Wyoming, Shepard had been the victim of a hate crime, and when he died 5 days later, the outrage became even greater, spawning vigils, demonstrations, and even calls for passage of federal hate-crime legislation by President Clinton. In addition, Shepard's death fueled debates over hate-crime laws in a number of jurisdictions, including Wyoming, one of only a few states that still resisted them.[40]

Also in 1998, 49-year-old James Byrd, Jr., of Jasper County in eastern Texas, was the victim of the most gruesome hate crime in recent memory. On the way home from a family reunion, he had apparently hitched a ride with three white men. They drove him to a wooded area, where he was beaten, chained by his ankles to a pickup truck, and dragged down the road for at least 2 miles. His body literally fell to pieces.

In the aftermath of the Shepard and Byrd murders, there was extensive debate over hate-crime legislation even though Shepard's attackers were arrested on kidnapping, robbery, and murder charges and both received life sentences without parole. Two of Byrd's killers received death sentences, and the third was sentenced to life in prison.

With a lack of subsequent high-profile hate-crime cases over the next several years, interest in the debate waned. However, in the aftermath of the September 11 terrorist attacks and the war in Iraq, hate-crime legislation has once again come into the national spotlight, as Muslims have increasingly come under attack. The Council on American-Islamic Relations reported a 70 percent increase in harassment, violence, and discriminatory treatment toward Muslims in 2003 over the previous year.[41] Adding to the discourse on hate crimes was a 2004 interview with Matthew Shepard's killers in which the men claimed that their crimes were not bias-motivated but, rather, were the result of a robbery while under a methamphetamine-induced rage.[42]

The issue under debate is that hate-crime laws serve to enhance the penalties given to the perpetrators of bias-motivated crimes. But are hate-crime laws really necessary

Hate Crimes by Motivating Factor, 2002–2003

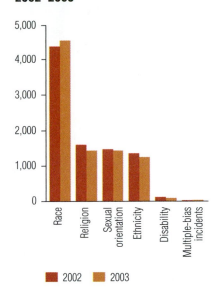

Hate Crimes by Type, 2003

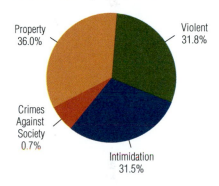

James Byrd, Jr., the victim of a dragging death.

or fair? In light of the ever-changing profile of targets and the ambiguous nature surrounding motivations, is more legislation a sufficient solution to this problem?

The idea behind hate-crime laws is to provide special protection for minorities who are frequently attacked simply because of who they are. Supporters of these laws argue that hate crime does double damage—first to the immediate victim and then to members of his or her minority group in the form of terror and intimidation. They also emphasize that the enhanced penalties have a deterrent effect.

Those opposed to the laws claim that this tenet of special protections violates the principle of equality under the law. Why, they ask, should someone who utters a racial slur while assaulting an African American receive a more severe sentence than another person who says nothing while committing a similar assault? Why should gays get special protections? Why should there be legislation that endorses homosexuality and gay rights in this manner? Opponents also claim that deterrence doesn't work and that in many instances it is not necessary.

Supporters of hate-crime legislation counter these arguments by emphasizing that although established criminal law generally suffices in hate crimes that result in the victim's death—as was the case in the killings of Shepard and Byrd—in other cases justice is not so easily defined. Painting swastika graffiti on a synagogue wall is far more than just petty vandalism, and many feel that the law should acknowledge that. Furthermore, thousands of peaceful, law-abiding Muslims in the United States live in fear of retribution for acts of terrorism that they had nothing to do with. Hate-crime laws have nothing to do with gay rights legislation. A hate-crime law identifies sexual orientation as an "aggravating factor" in an existing criminal act, and has no connection to any imaginary "homosexual," "religious," "feminist," or "racial" agenda.

White-Collar and Corporate Crime

White-collar crime and *corporate crime* can be defined as offenses committed by persons acting in their legitimate occupational roles. Generally, these crimes are committed for financial gain and rely on tactics of deception and fraud instead of physical violence. First introduced by Edwin H. Sutherland in an address to the American Sociological Society Meeting in 1939, the concept of white-collar crime can be analyzed from three broad perspectives: by the type of offender (of a high socioeconomic status or occupation), by the nature of the offense (economic motivation), or in terms of the organizational structure and culture that permit such offenses.

The offenders include businesspeople, members of the professions and government, and other varieties of workers who, in the course of their everyday occupational activities, violate the basic trust placed in them or act in unethical ways. Crime is neither the way of life nor the chosen career of white-collar or corporate offenders but, rather, something that occurs in conjunction with their more legitimate work activities. For example:

- *In the business sector:* financial manipulations, unfair labor practices, rebates, misrepresentation of goods and consumer deception by false labeling, fencing of stolen goods, shortchanging, overcharging, black-marketeering.
- *In the labor sector:* misuse of union funds, failing to enforce laws affecting unions, entering into collusion with employers to the disadvantage of union members, illegal mechanisms for controlling members.
- *In the corporate sector:* restraint of trade, infringement of patents, monopolistic practices, environmental contamination, misuse of trademarks, manufacture of unsafe goods, false advertising, disposal of toxic wastes.
- *In the financial sector:* embezzlement, violation of currency control measures, stock manipulation.
- *In the medical sector:* illegal prescription practices, fee-splitting, illegal abortions, fraudulent reports to insurance companies.
- *In the legal sector:* misappropriation of funds in trusts and receiverships, securing prejudiced testimony, bribery, instituting fraudulent damage claims.

- *In the criminal justice sector:* accepting bribes, illegal arrest and detention practices, illegal correctional practices.
- *In the civil sector:* illegal commissions, issuance of fraudulent licenses and certificates, illegal tax evaluations, misuse of campaign funds, illegal campaign practices.

At all levels of white-collar criminality, the offenders have no criminal self-concept. Rather, they rationalize their behavior as sharp business practice, taking advantage of an "easy rip-off" or maintaining that certain laws are unfair or that whatever they gained "was coming to them."

Currently, losses from white-collar and corporate crime are conservatively estimated to cost the United States in excess of $300 billion annually.[43] But there are also hidden costs associated with white-collar crime. For example, the corruption of corporate officers undermines the public's trust in the business; environmental crimes jeopardize public health; and the faulty manufacturing of products can endanger lives.

Moreover, less visible categories of white-collar crime have recently gained recognition. For example, the trafficking of human organs is a worldwide problem, with many individuals and groups circumventing and violating international laws governing human organ donations and transplants. The sale of human organs is illegal in virtually every country and has been condemned by all of the world's major medical associations. In the United States, the 1984 National Organ Transplant Act makes it a crime to buy or sell organs, punishable by a fine of up to $50,000 and 5 years in prison. However, the laws are not as strict in many developing countries. For example, "medical tourists" from Europe and the Middle East regularly travel to India where organs are legally and illegally bought from living donors. Most controversial are reports that the Chinese government profits from organ trafficking by selling the organs of executed prisoners.[44]

In the United States white-collar crime is generally financial in nature and accounts for approximately 4 percent of reported crime. In 2002, fraud accounted for the majority of all white-collar crime arrests (337,404), followed by embezzlement (18,552). The total number of embezzlement arrests jumped almost 50 percent between 1993 and 2002, the sharpest 10-year trend increase among any crime measured by the FBI's *Uniform Crime Reports*. Overall, however, embezzlement accounts for about 1 percent of the total persons arrested for federal offenses.[45]

While the majority of offenders are white males in their late twenties to early thirties, women are increasingly participating in such crime as well. Currently, women account for nearly one in four federal prisoners incarcerated for white-collar offenses. Between 1993 and 2002 the number of women arrested for forgery and counterfeiting rose 19.3 percent and arrests for embezzlement rose 80.5 percent during the same period.[46]

The massive bankruptcy of Enron was the catalyst that brought white-collar and corporate crime to the forefront of national attention in 2001. Enron, once the seventh

© Grimmy Inc. Reprinted with permission of King Features Syndicate.

most powerful company on the Fortune 500 list, suddenly collapsed into bankruptcy, leaving 10,000 employees without jobs or their $1.2 billion in retirement savings. Meanwhile, company executives walked away from the debacle unscathed. For example, from 1998 until his abrupt resignation in 2001, Enron CEO Jeff Skilling pocketed $70.6 million in profit from the sale of his stock and options and received over $13 million in bonuses. Former chairman Kenneth Lay allegedly cashed in $184 million in company stock between 1996 and the 2001 collapse. Lay, who holds a doctorate in economics, claimed he had no knowledge of the complex accounting ploys used to artificially inflate Enron's profits. Such schemes allegedly produced 96% of the company's profit in 2000 and concealed $12 billion in debt, according to the investigation by the examiner of Enron's Chapter 11 bankruptcy. Even the bankruptcy investigation itself, costing $100 million and producing over 4,000 pages of documents, is the most expensive inquiry ever of its kind.

Thus far, the lengthy investigation has yielded numerous convictions and acquittals of former midlevel employees. Among the high-level company executives, former chief financial officer Andrew Fastow struck a plea deal to serve 10 years in prison in exchange for his cooperation with authorities. Lay, on the other hand, has pleaded not guilty to 11 federal charges that could total up to 175 years in prison and fines of more than $5.7 million; Skilling has pleaded not guilty to 35 felony charges, which could theoretically render him 325 years in prison and $80 million in fines, penalties unlikely to be imposed on either man.[47]

Many argue that white-collar criminals are rarely punished and that if and when penalties are imposed, offenders generally escape criminal sanctions. Recent cases demonstrate a range of outcomes.

For example, former WorldCom founder and CEO Bernard Ebbers was found guilty on charges that he masterminded the biggest accounting fraud in the nation's history. Ebbers was convicted of securities fraud, conspiracy, and seven counts of filing false reports with regulators. Former WorldCom chief financial officer Scott Sullivan, accused of lying, conspiracy, securities fraud, and submitting false SEC filings, had already pleaded guilty and agreed to cooperate with prosecutors.[48] Jurors did not convict the former chairman of Tyco International, Ltd., Dennis Kozlowski, on charges that he pocketed $600 million through unauthorized bonuses and loans from his company. However, he faces a retrial on other charges. Adelphia Communications Corp. founder John Rigas and his sons were accused of plundering $2.3 billion from their company in order to finance personal hobbies, including a golf course, a professional hockey team, and trips on the company jet. A jury found the elder Rigas and one of his sons each guilty of 15 counts of securities fraud, 2 counts of bank fraud, and 1 count of conspiracy; Rigas' other son was acquitted of the charges of conspiracy and wire fraud wrought against him.[49]

But perhaps the biggest media story of all since Enron has been the scandal surrounding ImClone Systems. Founder Sam Waksal was sentenced to prison for insider trading, but it has been Waksal's friend, Martha Stewart, who has garnered the lion share of attention. Stewart was convicted on four counts of making false statements, obstruction of justice, and conspiracy after she sold $230,000 worth of ImClone shares 1 day before the stock price plunged. The "domestic diva," as news reports coined her, was sentenced to 5 months in a minimum-security prison nicknamed "Camp Cupcake" (see sidebar) and 5 months of home detention. To avoid the press, she secretly arrived at prison in the early morning hours of the day of her sentence. While she was there, she received hundreds of supportive letters from fans. Although she was supposed to be an example of how even the rich and famous must suffer the consequences for their crimes, while she was serving the home portion of her sentence, her stock quadrupled in valve, she launched a new line of furniture, a Kmart-Sears merger had the potential to increase sales of her houseware line, and she had two TV shows in the works, one filled with her traditional cooking and homemaking tips and the other modeled after *The Apprentice*.[50]

But such high-profile corporate scandals are not confined to the United States. For example, Mikhail B. Khodorkovsky, a billionaire and former head of the Russian oil

"Camp Cupcake"

Martha Stewart is not the first famous female criminal to serve time in the Federal Prison Camp in Alderson, West Virginia. The minimum-security prison set in the foothills of the picturesque Allegheny Mountains formerly housed blues and jazz legend Billie Holiday, who was convicted of drug charges, and Lynette Fromme, a member of the Charles Manson family, who was convicted of attempting to assassinate then-president Gerald Ford.

Alderson opened as the first federal prison for women in the United States in 1927. It was designed like a college campus, situated on a large parcel of rural property without the typical fences or barbed-wire boundaries. The more than 1,000 current inmates live in large dormitory-style housing or small cottages in cells that do not have traditional bars. Stewart herself said on her Web site to her fans: "The camp is like an old-fashioned college campus—without the freedom, of course." ■

Martha Stewart leaving the courthouse after a meeting with her probation officer.

conglomerate Yukos, and his business partner, Planton Lebedev, have been jailed on fraud and tax evasion charges. They have been accused of conspiring to create an "organized group" to take advantage of a loosely regulated Russian corporate system.[51]

In Italy, dairy empire Parmalat was declared bankrupt after $13 billion in company assets was reported missing. Secret bank accounts, shell entities, and political payoffs, among other tactics, allegedly helped cover the trail of money siphoned out of the company owned by the powerful and well-connected Tanzi family. The case, dubbed the "Enron of Europe," is the continent's worst-ever financial fraud.

Across much of Europe, regulations are tightening to prevent future corporate scandals from taking place. The Italian government, on the other hand, rewrote its bankruptcy laws to accommodate Parmalat's collapse. The nation has also enacted legislation to protect other failed companies from creditors in an attempt to save the country's industry and jobs. Italy is well known for its business culture based on a patriarchal power system; the multilayered ownership structure and lack of checks and balances has long allowed companies to disguise their financial woes. Thus far, 9 of the 27 defendants accused of masterminding the Parmalat deception have agreed to plea bargains. However, the deals that have been reached in the case do not require admissions of guilt from the defendants, do not include fines or financial restitution, and do not necessarily require any prison time either.[52]

Organized Crime

Organized crime consists of business activities directed toward economic gain through unlawful means. At the heart of what is often meant by organized crime are such activities as gambling, loan-sharking, commercialized vice, bootlegging, trafficking in narcotics and other drugs, and disposing of stolen merchandise—enterprises that provide illegal goods and services to anyone who is willing to pay for them. Such activities, however, are not always highly organized. Instead, they range along a continuum from freelance prostitutes and neighborhood bookmakers to regionally organized gambling or drug syndicates. Some forms of organized crime are both national and international in scope.

As a criminal pattern, organized crime is typically pursued as an occupational career. In its most organized aspects, there is a hierarchical structure that includes leaders (or "godfathers" and "dons") at the uppermost levels, followed by a middle level of gangsters and "lieutenants" who carry out the orders of their "bosses" and the *capo di*

Remember, I'm a P.E. graduate, not an economist.

**—BERNARD EBBERS,
FORMER WORLDCOM CEO**

Many good people have gone to prison. Look at Nelson Mandela.

—MARTHA STEWART

Mob boss Tony Soprano.

I know what the Mafia can do to a man who has crossed them. One day you wake up with your head in one room and your legs in another.

—VINCENT "BIG VINNIE" TERESA

Organized crime takes in over $40 billion a year and spends very little on office supplies.

—WOODY ALLEN

tutti capi (the boss of all bosses). At the bottom of the structure are individuals who are only marginally associated with the organization—prostitutes, enforcers, drug sellers, bookies—who typically deal directly with the public and may sometimes operate independently of the power structure.

People who pursue organized crime as an occupational career are recruited on the basis of kinship, friendship, or contacts within lower-class environments, where such activities are sought out as means of gaining economic respectability. Whether individual criminals are part of a highly structured "syndicate" or are low-level independent prostitutes or drug dealers, their commitment to the career is long-term and their entire social organization and lifestyle revolve around crime.

Historically, discussions of organized crime have focused almost exclusively on such activities as prostitution and gambling, groups like the Mafia and *La Cosa Nostra*, and individuals such as Al Capone, Meyer Lansky, Benjamin "Bugsy" Siegal, and Vito Genovese—and more recently John Gotti and Sam "the Bull" Gravano. More recent

"Due to budget cuts, I'm gonna have to let a couple of you boys go."

By Richard Li. From CRIME & JUSTICE INTERNATIONAL, April 2003. Reprinted by permission.

analyses, however, have looked at other criminal groups—not just Italians, but Asians, Jamaicans, Latin Americans, and Russians, to name only a few. In fact, observers of organized crime are familiar with the Jamaican "posses," Mexico's Gulf cartel and Colombia's numerous cocaine cartels, the Chinese "triads" and the Japanese *Yakuza,* and large numbers of African American, Dominican, Korean, Cuban, and Sicilian criminal organizations, many of which are already working together in a complex mosaic of illicit enterprise.[53]

Do you know what the Mafia is?
What?
The Mafia? M-a-f-i-a?
I'm sorry but I don't know what you're talking about.

—AN EXCHANGE BETWEEN
A GOVERNMENT LAWYER AND
RACKETEER SALVATORE MORETTI
DURING THE KEFAUVER COMMITTEE
HEARINGS IN 1950

CRITICAL THINKING IN CRIMINAL JUSTICE

Male Rape

For most Americans, *rape* is a gender-specific term. That is, virtually every time the stand-alone word *rape* is used, it is automatically presumed that the victim is a female and the perpetrator is a male. This would appear to be logical, furthermore, because crime statistics indicate that as many as 90% of all rape victims are women and young girls. Moreover, until only recently, rape laws defined women as the only possible victims and men as the only offenders. Even today, in 12 states—Alabama, Georgia, Idaho, Kansas, Maine, Maryland, Missouri, New York, North Carolina, Oregon, Utah, and Virginia—rape is defined as "the forced penetration of the vagina by the penis," or words to that effect.

Yet some critical thinking about rape seems warranted here. Rape is *not* a gender-specific offense! Nevertheless, like conversations about male nurses, female judges, and women's basketball, discussions of men as victims of rape result in a unique kind of gender designation; that is, "rape" becomes *male* rape. Furthermore, the rape of men by women is likely the least discussed, least reported, and most unaddressed of all violent crimes.

Research suggests that between 5 percent and 10 percent of all reported rapes in any given year involve male victims.[54] The rapes occur most often in all-male institutions, such as prisons, military barracks, college dormitories and fraternities, mental health facilities, nursing homes, boarding schools, and monasteries. The rapists are typically white, heterosexual men in their mid to late twenties, and their victims are generally the same age or younger. Men rape other men for the same reasons that they rape women—out of anger or an attempt to overpower, humiliate, and degrade their victims, rather than out of lust, passion, or sexual desire. Anal penetration is the most common form of assault, followed by oral penetration. Finally, men who rape tend to do so within their own social, cultural, or economic group or to rape those over whom they have power. For these reasons it is not surprising that the incidence of gay men raping heterosexual men is extremely low.

Little is known about female-on-male rape. In fact, in the once widely read textbook *Criminal Law for Policemen,* authors Neil C. Chamelin and Kenneth R. Evans suggested that a female cannot actually rape a male.[55] This assumption, however, is both naive and incorrect. There are many women who can overpower men, and the biology of the male anatomy makes an erection through physical stimulation readily possible, even when sexual interest is totally absent. In fact, in some men and boys, states of pain, anxiety, panic, or fear have been known to cause a spontaneous erection and ejaculation.[56] However, although it is unlikely that a man raped by a woman would bring the crime to the attention of the authorities for fear of ridicule, this does not mean it does not happen. Numerous such cases have indeed been documented.[57]

Although there is no single, typical, emotional response that every man will exhibit after he has been raped, the range of responses is not unlike those seen among female victims of rape. Some may appear calm and rational; others may exhibit anger, depression, or hysteria. Still others may withdraw socially or sexually or appear nonresponsive. Rape trauma syndrome, a form of posttraumatic stress disorder, is also seen. In the majority of cases, furthermore, there is the stigma, shame, embarrassment, and self-blame that male rape victims experience as they begin to cope with what has happened to them. As a final point, the range of symptoms is the same regardless of whether the perpetrator was another man or a woman.

OP-ED

Moving back to the question on the nature and extent of crime aboard cruise ships mentioned at the opening of this chapter, the answer is that it remains a mystery and will likely continue to remain one for some time to come.

What is known, however, is that the cruise industry has long been guilty of violating environmental laws. Royal Caribbean Cruises has continued to be accused of dumping oil and sewage into the ocean, even after paying a record $18 million fine in 1999, on top of paying a $9 million fine a year earlier. In fact, the Environmental Protection Agency has imposed in excess of $50 million in fines since 1997 on not only Royal Caribbean but also numerous other cruise lines for violating waste treatment codes. While a recent report from the General Accounting Office acknowledged that many cruise lines had invested heavily in improvements for their waste management systems, many others continued to pollute and threaten the ecosystems of pristine vacation waters.[58]

Furthermore, drug smuggling into the United States via cruise ships has been a continual issue for authorities. In early 2004, for example, drug agents in Tampa made the second-largest heroin arrest in Florida's history when they found 128 pounds of the drug creatively packed into such items as coats, shoes, CD holders, aerosol perfume bottles, cameras, and hollow plastic hairbrushes and lint removers. Coincidentally, two passengers were arrested on the same voyage for attempting to smuggle over 44 pounds of cocaine in several pairs of pants packed in their suitcases. According to authorities, such arrests are relatively uncommon, however, because they involved passengers. Drug arrests on cruise ships commonly involve small groups of crew members attempting to smuggle 2 to 5 kilograms of cocaine.[59]

As for the most common crimes targeted against passengers, they are sexual assaults and theft by other passengers and crew members alike. When crimes occur, they are rarely reported, for a whole variety of reasons. Primarily, the cruise industry operates largely outside the framework of U.S. laws and regulations, being governed mainly by international maritime treaties and shipping regulations. Under U.S. law, a cruise ship whose hull is not built by an American shipyard cannot fly a U.S. flag. Since American shipyards abandoned passenger shipbuilding in the late 1950s (in favor of more lucrative military shipbuilding contracts), the leading cruise lines operate as foreign corporations registered in such countries as Panama, the Bahamas, and Liberia. Furthermore, many of the alleged crimes take place out at sea, in international waters. So if a crime occurs and is actually reported, who has jurisdiction?

'WE'RE CRUISING IN THE BERMUDA TRIANGLE THIS YEAR.'

Reprinted by permission of www.CartoonStock.com

On the basis of court records, combined with interviews of passengers who report the assaults, their attorneys, and current and former cruise line employees, the FBI has discovered a pattern of cover-ups that often began as soon as the crime was reported at sea, in international waters where the only police are the ship's security officers. Moreover, in cases of sexual allegations, there are almost always denials and countercharges that the sex was consensual.

The cruise line operators claim that the environment on a cruise ship is safe, like a protective gated community, and to some extent that is indeed the situation. But passengers should also remember that ships are floating cities, where the same crimes occur and the same precautions need to be taken as in a city on the mainland.

| Summary |

There are thousands of acts that are prohibited by law and designated as felonies or misdemeanors in federal, state, and local criminal codes across the United States. Such crimes as homicide, assault, robbery, arson, burglary, sex offenses, drug law violations, and offenses against the public order and safety are by no means all that appear in criminal statutes and codes, but they account for some 90 percent of the criminal law violations that are processed by U.S. courts.

However, although crime may be conduct prohibited by the criminal law, its dynamics include certain patterns and systems of behavior. Furthermore, definitions of crime are culturally and historically specific. Some behaviors are tolerated on a wider scale than others, and some have been accepted at different points in history. For example, such sexual activities as sodomy and fornication are prohibited by law in many jurisdictions but are engaged in by otherwise law-abiding citizens on a regular basis and are less likely to be prosecuted. By contrast, the laws against rape are vigorously enforced.

It is important for students of crime and criminal justice to understand not only the content of criminal codes but also the dynamics of several major forms of crime. Domestic violence involves activities of a physically aggressive nature occurring among members of the family, current or former spouses or lovers, live-ins, and others in close relationships, resulting from conflicts in personal relations. Hate crimes are offenses motivated by hatred against a victim because of his or her race, ethnicity, religion, sexual orientation, handicap, or national origin. White-collar crimes are offenses committed by persons acting in their legitimate occupational roles. Organized crime comprises business activities directed toward economic gain through unlawful means.

| Key Terms |

arson (75)
assault (73)
assault and battery (73)
breaking and entering (77)
Carrier's Case (79)
deliberation (70)
domestic violence (87)
felony-murder doctrine (71)

hate crime (88)
homicide (69)
larceny (79)
Lawrence v. *Texas* (81)
malice aforethought (70)
manslaughter (72)
murder (70)
organized crime (93)

Pear's Case (79)
premeditation (70)
rape (81)
robbery (74)
theft (78)
white-collar crime (90)

| Issues for Discussion |

1. In cases where the felony-murder doctrine has been invoked, the intent to commit murder has often been absent. In such circumstances, is conviction of murder in the first degree a just disposition? Why or why not?
2. Which sex offenses, if any, should be abolished from contemporary criminal codes? Why?
3. Are there any types of property offenses other than those listed in this chapter?
4. Should hate-crime legislation be passed throughout the United States?
5. Have you ever been on a cruise? Have you seen situations in which crimes might occur?

| Media and Literature Resources |

Reel Justice includes scenes that can be used to spark discussion about the following topics from this chapter:

Legal Definition of Crime

Social Definition of Crime

Domestic Violence

Violence Against Women. Raquel Kennedy Bergen, Jeffrey L. Edleson, and Claire M. Renzetti, *Violence Against Women: Classic Papers* (Boston: Allyn & Bacon, 2004); Claire M. Renzetti, Jeffrey L. Edleson, and Raquel L. Kennedy Bergen (eds.), *Sourcebook on Violence Against Women* (Thousand Oaks, CA: Sage Publications, 2001). The National Domestic Violence Hot Line (1-800-799-7233) has a Web site (*www.ndvh.org*) with links to related Web sites, including those of the National Organization for Women, Women Leaders Online, and the Center for the Prevention of Sexual and Domestic Violence.

Rape and Sex Crimes. Ronald M. Holmes and Stephen T. Holmes, *Sex Crimes: Patterns and Behavior,* 2d ed. (Thousand Oaks, CA: Sage Publications, 2001); Emilie Buchwald, Pamela R. Fletcher, and Martha Roth, *Transforming a Rape Culture* (Minneapolis, MN: Milkweed Editions, 1995); Ronald M. Holmes and Stephen T. Holmes, *Current Perspectives on Sex Crimes* (Thousand Oaks, CA: Sage Publications, 2002); John Q. La Fond, *Preventing Sexual Violence: How Society Should Cope with Sex Offenders* (Washington, DC: American Psychological Association, 2005).

White-Collar Crime. Lawrence M. Salinger (ed.), *Encyclopedia of White-Collar and Corporate Crime* (Thousand Oaks, CA: Sage Publications, 2004); Stephen M. Rosoff, Henry N. Pontell, and Robert H. Tillman, *Profit Without Honor: White-Collar Crime and the Looting of America,* 3d ed., (Upper Saddle River, NJ: Prentice-Hall, 2003). There is also an interesting Web site that investigates white-collar crime in the corporate sector: *http://www.corporatecrimereporter.com*

| Endnotes |

1. Steve Cannizaro and Aaron Kuriloff, "Cruise Ship Passenger Accused of Rape; 16-Year-Old Girl Was Drunk, Mom Says," *Times Picayune,* July 29, 2003, 1.
2. Ruth Rendon, "Suit Claims Ship's Crew Assaulted Girl on Cruise," *The Houston Chronicle,* July 9, 2004, 26A; *Miami Herald,* July 30, 2000, 1E; *The New York Times,* July 14, 1999, 12A; *U.S. News and World Report,* August 9, 1999, p. 12.
3. *United States* v. *Timothy James McVeigh and Terry Lynn Nichols,* U.S. District Court for the Western District of Oklahoma, CR-95-110-A.
4. Jerome Hall, "Analytic Philosophy and Jurisprudence," *Ethics* 77 (October 1966): 14–28.
5. *The Washington Post,* May 7, 1997, A9.
6. *USA Today,* December 6, 1989, 3A.
7. *Miami Herald,* March 23, 1988, 3B.
8. *Criminal Justice Newsletter,* November 1, 1999, 3.
9. *Penal Code of California,* Section 203.
10. David M. Maurer, *Whiz Mob* (New Haven, CT: College and University Press, 1964), 68.
11. This comment was made to the author by a Miami Beach pickpocket in early 1976. Additional comments on this topic can be found in James A. Inciardi, "The Pickpocket and His Victim," *Victimology: An International Journal* 1 (Fall 1976): 446–453.

12. John F. Boudreau, Quon Y. Kwan, William E. Faragher, and Genevieve C. Denault, *Arson and Arson Investigation: Survey and Assessment* (Washington, DC: U.S. Government Printing Office, 1977), 1.

13. James A. Inciardi, "The Adult Firesetter: A Typology," *Criminology: An Interdisciplinary Journal* 8 (August 1970): 145–155; James A. Inciardi, *Reflections on Crime* (New York: Holt, Rinehart and Winston, 1978), 127–128.

14. See, for example, *Delaware Code,* Title 11, Sections 824, 825, 826.

15. *Delaware Laws,* c. 497, Section 1.

16. *Louisiana Criminal Code,* Section 67.

17. *Delaware Code,* Title 11, Section 840.

18. *Ohio Code,* 2913.02.

19. *Carrier's Case, Yearbook,* 13 Edward IV, 9, pl. 5 (1473).

20. *Pear's Case,* 1 Leach 212, 168 Eng. Rep. 208 (1779).

21. *United States* v. *Sheffield,* 161 F.Supp. 387 (1958, Md.).

22. Wayne Logan, Lindsay S. Stellwagen, and Patrick A. Langan, *Felony Laws of the 50 States and the District of Columbia* (Washington, DC: Bureau of Justice Statistics, 1987).

23. *Lawrence* v. *Texas,* No. 02-102 (2003).

24. *Bowers* v. *Hardwick,* 30 CrL 3261 (1986).

25. Richard A. Posner, *Overcoming Law* (Cambridge: Harvard University Press, 1995).

26. Henry F. Fradella and Kegan Brown, "Withdrawal of Consent Post-Penetration: Redefining the Law of Rape," *Criminal Law Bulletin* 41, 1 (2005): 3–23; Sue Titus Reid, *Criminal Law* (Boston: McGraw-Hill, 1998), 211.

27. See Ian O'Donnell, "Prison Rape in Context," *British Journal of Criminology* 44, 2 (2004): 241–255; Robert W. Dumond, "Confronting America's Most Ignored Crime Problem: The Prison Rape Elimination Act of 2003," *Journal of the American Academy of Psychiatry and the Law* 31, 3 (2003): 356–360; and Christine A. Saum, Hilary L. Surratt, James A. Inciardi, and Rachael E. Bennett, "Sex in Prison: Myths and Realities," *The Prison Journal* 75 (1995): 413–430.

28. *Michael M.* v. *Superior Court of Sonoma County,* 458 U.S. 747 (1981).

29. Erin Van Bronkhorst, "Teacher Has Baby by One of Her Sixth-Grade Pupils," *Associated Press Wire Service,* October 29, 1997.

30. See David F. Musto, *The American Disease: Origins of Narcotic Control* (New Haven, CT: Yale University Press, 1973).

31. For a brief history of drug use in the United States, see James A. Inciardi, *The War on Drugs III: The Continuing Saga of the Mysteries and Miseries of Intoxication, Addiction, Crime, and Public Policy* (Boston, MA: Allyn & Bacon, 2002).

32. *A Guide to State-Controlled Substances Acts* (Washington, DC: Bureau of Justice Assistance and the National Criminal Justice Association, 1988).

33. For some of the classic studies, see Marvin Wolfgang, *Patterns in Criminal Homicide* (Philadelphia: University of Pennsylvania Press, 1958); David J. Pittman and William Handy, "Patterns in Criminal Aggravated Assault," *Journal of Criminal Law, Criminology and Police Science* 55 (December 1964): 462–470; Duncan Chappell, Robley Geis, and Gilbert Geis (eds.), *Forcible Rape: The Crime, the Victim, and the Offender* (New York: Columbia University Press, 1977); Edwin M. Lemert, "An Isolation and Closure Theory of Naive Check Forgery," *Journal of Criminal Law, Criminology, and Police Science* 44 (1953): 296–307; Mary Owen Cameron, *The Booster and the Snitch* (New York: Free Press of Glencoe, 1964); Werner J. Einstadter, "The Social Organization of Armed Robbery," *Social Problems* 17 (Summer 1969): 64–83; Gilbert Reis, "From Deuteronomy to

Deniability: A Historical Perlustration of White-Collar Crime," *Justice Quarterly* 5 (March 1988): 7–32; Joseph L. Albini, *The American Mafia: Genesis of a Legend* (New York: Appleton-Century-Crofts, 1971); Daniel Bell, *The End of Ideology: On the Exhaustion of Political Ideas in the Fifties* (New York: Free Press, 1962), 127–150; Norval Morris and Gordon Hawkins, *The Honest Politician's Guide to Crime Control* (Chicago: University of Chicago Press, 1970), 202–235; Edwin H. Sutherland, *The Professional Thief* (Chicago: University of Chicago Press, 1937); James A. Inciardi, *Careers in Crime* (Chicago: Rand McNally, 1975), 5–82.

34. See Carla Smith Stover, "Domestic Violence Research: What Have We Learned and Where Do We Go from Here?" *Journal of Interpersonal Violence* 20, 4 (2005): 448–454; Rashmi Goel, "Restorative Justice, Domestic Violence, and South Asian Culture," *Violence Against Women* 11, 5 (2005): 639–665; Jeanette Zanipatin, Stacy Shaw Welch, Jean Yi, and Patty Bardina, "Immigrant Women and Domestic Violence," in *Race, Culture, Psychology, and Law,* edited by Kimberly Holt Barrett and William H. George (Thousand Oaks, CA: Sage Publications, 2005), 375–389; and Cliff Mariani, *Domestic Violence Survival Guide* (Flushing, NY: Looseleaf, 1996).

35. See Neil B. Guterman, "Advancing Prevention Research on Child Abuse, Youth Violence, and Domestic Violence: Emerging Strategies and Issues," *Journal of Interpersonal Violence* 19, 3 (2004): 299–321; Gail Erlick Robinson, "Current Concepts in Domestic Violence," *Primary Psychiatry* 10, 12 (2003): 48–52; and Eve S. Buzawa and Carl G. Buzawa, *Domestic Violence: The Criminal Justice Response* (Thousand Oaks, CA: Sage Publications, 1996).

36. See Kris Henning and Lynette Feder, "A Comparison of Men and Women Arrested for Domestic Violence: Who Presents the Greater Threat?" *Journal of Family Violence* 19, 2 (2004): 69–80; Cindy L. Seamans, "A Qualitative Study of Women Perpetrators of Domestic Violence: Comparison with Literature on Men Perpetrators of Domestic Violence," *Dissertation Abstracts International: Section B: The Sciences & Engineering* 64, 3-B (2003): 1506; Coramae Richey Mann, *Women Who Kill* (Albany: SUNY Press, 1996); and Richard B. Felson, "Big People Hit Little People: Sex Differences in Physical Power and Interpersonal Violence," *Criminology* 34, 3 (1996): 433–452.

37. Bureau of Justice Assistance, *A Policymaker's Guide to Hate Crimes* (Washington, DC: Office of Justice Programs, 1997).

38. R. Kelotra, "New FBI Data Reports Increase in Hate Crimes for 2003," *www.civilrights.org,* November 17, 2004 (accessed April 21, 2005).

39. Federal Bureau of Investigation, *Hate Crime Statistics, 2003* (Washington, DC: Department of Justice, November 2004).

40. *The New York Times,* October 10, 1998, A9; *The New York Times,* October 13, 1998, A1.

41. M. B. Sheridan, "Bias Against Muslims Up 70%; Radio Talk Shows, Iraq War Among Reasons, Study Finds," *The Washington Post,* May 3, 2004, 12A.

42. R. Black, "Matthew Shepard's Killers Deny Attack Was Hate Crime in First Interviews Since Gay Student's 1998 Death," *Associated Press,* November 25, 2004.

43. Jacksonville FBI, "White-Collar Crime,". *http://jacksonville.fbi .gov/wcc.htm,* 2004.

44. Rick Weiss, "Trafficking in Body Parts: Where—and How—Do We Draw the Line on What's for Sale?" *The Washington Post,* July 5, 1999, 22–23; Thomas W. Foster, "Trafficking in Human Organs: An Emerging Form of White-Collar Crime?" *International Journal of Offender Therapy and Comparative Criminol-

ogy, 41, 2 (1997): 139–150; Michael Finkel, "This Little Kidney Went to Market," *The New York Times Magazine,* May 27, 2001, 26–33, 40, 52, 59.

45. Federal Bureau of Investigation, *Uniform Crime Reports, 2002* (Washington, DC: Department of Justice, 2003).

46. Sandy Haantz, *Women and White Collar Crime* (Fairmont, WV: National White Collar Crime Center; 2002); *White Collar Crime Statistics* (Fairmont, WV: National White Collar Crime Center, 2004).

47. Marilyn Geewax, "White-Collar Crime: Lay Pleads Not Guilty; Enron's Ex-Chief Faces Long Trial," *The Atlanta Journal-Constitution,* July 9, 2004, 1F; Jeffrey Toobin, "End Run at Enron; Why the Country's Most Notorious Executives May Never Face Criminal Charges," *The New Yorker,* October 27, 2003, 48; Anthony Lin, "Batson Bills Enron $100 Million; Chapter 11 Investigation Seen as Most Expensive in U.S. History," *National Law Journal* 26, 15 (December 8, 2003): 12.

48. Ken Belson, "Ex-Chief of WorldCom Is Found Guilty in $11 Billion Fraud," *The New York Times,* March 16, 2005, 1A.

49. Geewax, "White-Collar Crime"; Gretchen Morgenson, "Trials, Trials, Trials, and Then What?" *The New York Times,* January 8, 2004, 1C.

50. Keith Naughton, "Martha Breaks Out;" *Newsweek,* March 7, 2005, 36; Barry Meier, "Martha Stewart Assigned to Prison in West Virginia," *The New York Times,* September 30, 2004, 1C.

51. Neil Buckley, "Russia's Leading Oligarch Faces Judgment Day in Yukos Affair," *Financial Times,* April 27, 2005, 10.

52. Emily Backus, "Parmalat Plea Bargains Accepted," *Financial Times,* April 7, 2005, 17; John Tagliabue, "Layers of Ownership Conceal Trouble in Italy," *The New York Times,* December 30,

2003, 1C; Richard Owen and Carl Mortished, "Dynasty to Disaster, Parmalat Faults 'la Famiglia,'" *The Weekend Australian,* January 3, 2004, 22.

53. *Organized Crime: World Perspectives* (Upper Saddle River, NJ: Prentice-Hall, 2003); Mike Woodiwiss, Martin Elvins, and James Sheptycki, *Transnational Organized Crime: Perspectives on Global Security* (London: Routledge, 2003); William Kleinknecht, *The New Ethnic Mobs: The Changing Face of Organized Crime in America* (New York: Free Press, 1996).

54. Irina Anderson, "Explaining Negative Rape Victim Perception: Homophobia and the Male Rape Victim," *Current Research in Social Psychology* 10, 4 (November 2004); Kathy Doherty and Irina Anderson, "Making Sense of Male Rape: Constructions of Gender, Sexuality and Experience of Rape Victims," *Journal of Community and Applied Social Psychology* 14, 2 (2004): 85–103; Michael Scarce, *Male on Male Rape: The Hidden Toll of Stigma and Shame* (New York: Plenum, 1997).

55. Neil C. Chamelin and Kenneth R. Evans, *Criminal Law for Policemen* (Englewood Cliffs, NJ: Prentice-Hall, 1976), 109.

56. Scarce, *Male on Male Rape.*

57. See Irina Anderson and Victoria Swainson, "Perceived Motivation for Rape: Gender Differences in Beliefs About Female and Male Rape," *Current Research in Social Psychology* 6, 8 (2001); *Miami Herald,* September 17, 1982, 1B; and *Psychology Today,* September 1983, 74–75.

58. Crystal Bolner, "Cruise Line Is Accused of Dumping; Royal Caribbean Calls Waste Treatment Effective," *Times-Picayune,* July 24, 2003, 1.

59. Elaine Silvestrini, "Drug Bust Provides Training Bonanza," *Tampa Tribune,* February 19, 2004, Metro Section, 1.

NO
PARKING
8 A.M. TO 6 P.M.
EXCEPT SUNDAY

WHP 83   CITY OF LOS ANGELES   2540

DRUG BUYERS
BEWARE!

BUY DRUGS,
LOSE YOUR
CAR!

TOW-AWAY
TEMPORARY
NO PARKING
7 AM TO 10 PM
VEHICLES ENGAGED IN FILM
AND TV PRODUCTION EXEMPT
EXCEPT SAT AND SUN
TO RECOVER IMPOUNDED VEHICLE CALL (818) 756-9419
PROPERTY OF CITY OF LOS ANGELES   IPX

4

CRIMINAL STATISTICS
AND THE EXTENT OF CRIME

LEARNING OBJECTIVES

After reading this chapter, you should be able to answer the following questions:

1. What are the major sources of statistical information about crime?

2. What are the limitations of the *Uniform Crime Reports?*

3. Which kinds of crimes tend to go unreported, and why is there so much nonreporting and concealment of crime?

4. Can you interpret the data in the *Uniform Crime Reports?*

5. How do you compute a crime rate, and what does it mean?

6. What are the strengths and weaknesses of the National Crime Victimization Survey?

7. What are the major sources of statistical data on drug abuse in the United States?

8. Is the United States the most crime-ridden country in the world?

A police officer interviews witnesses near the scene of a dispute among deer hunters over a tree stand in northwestern Wisconsin. The argument erupted into a series of shootings that left 5 people dead and 3 injured on November 21, 2004.

Crime Dominates Airwaves

WASHINGTON, DC—The Center for Media and Public Affairs reported that despite the worldwide acts of terrorism and the wars in Afghanistan and Iraq, crime continued to be among the top stories in the news and that on television, 78 percent of all stories examining rural life looked at crime.[1] Moreover, for the decade of the 1990s, the center reported that crime fully dominated the television news agenda. However, actual crime rates have been steadily falling. In September 2004, the Bureau of Justice Statistics reported that rates of serious crime have been declining for nearly a decade, while overall violent victimization and property crime rates in 2003 were at their lowest levels in 30 years.[2] Why would news coverage of crime be up when actual crime rates are down?

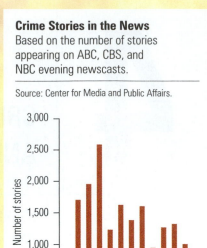

Crime Stories in the News
Based on the number of stories appearing on ABC, CBS, and NBC evening newscasts.

Source: Center for Media and Public Affairs.

The difference between public perceptions and actual crime statistics raises a number of questions. What are the sources of information about the extent of crime in the United States? How are crime data collected, and are the statistics accurate? What is a crime rate, and how does one really know if crime is declining or increasing?

As a first step toward answering these questions, this chapter describes the major sources of information about the magnitude and trends of crime. It explains how the information is compiled, what it includes, how it might best be interpreted, and how it has been misused. The shortcomings and the usefulness of official crime statistics are also discussed. The final section looks at alternate and supplementary sources of crime data.

The *Uniform Crime Reports*

Systematic collection of crime statistics for the nation as a whole began about 75 years ago. Prior to that time, little was known about the extent of crime in the United States (see Exhibit 4.1). At the 1927 annual meeting of the International Association of Chiefs of Police, the Committee on Uniform Crime Reports was appointed to respond to the demand for national crime data. It was commissioned to prepare a manual on standardized crime reporting for use by local police agencies. On the basis of this committee's efforts, Congress authorized the Federal Bureau of Investigation (FBI) to collect and compile nationwide data on crime.[3] The FBI assumed responsibility for directing the voluntary recording of data by police departments on standardized forms provided by the FBI and for compiling and publishing the data received. Known as the ***Uniform Crime Reports (UCR),*** the document was issued monthly at first, quarterly until 1941, semiannually through 1957, and annually since 1958.

Murder Rates in the United States, 1983–2003
Source: *Uniform Crime Reports.*

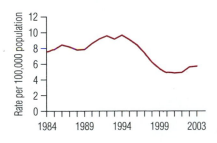

historical perspectives on criminal justice | EXHIBIT 4.1

Late-19th-Century Homicide Rates in the United States

John Billington was among the 102 Pilgrims aboard the *Mayflower* to arrive at Plymouth in 1620. He was described as a rather violent individual, prone toward fighting and feuding with his neighbors. In 1630, only 10 years after the establishment of the Puritan settlement, Billington shot one of his adversaries at close range, was hanged for the killing, and earned the distinction of becoming the country's first known murderer. Since that time, homicide has been a highly visible aspect of American social history.

From the beginning of the 1960s through the closing years of the 1990s, homicide rates in the United States have been quite high, reaching a peak of 10.2 per 100,000 population in 1980. But as indicated in the accompanying table, homicide rates for most of the 1890s were well above those of the 1980s and 1990s.

Why homicide rates were so high during the 1890s would be difficult to unravel. However, it was a period of transition in the United States brought on by the closing of the western frontier, the rapid growth of cities, and social conflicts associated with the high rates of immigration from Europe. One thing that is certain, however, is that homicide rates during this period were likely higher than those in the table. At the time, there was no uniform method for the collection of crime statistics on a national basis, and as such, the underreporting of murders was likely significant.

Sources: James A. Inciardi, *Reflections on Crime* (New York: Holt, Rinehart and Winston, 1978); Arthur Train, *Courts and Criminals* (New York: Scribner's, 1925).

Year	Total Homicides	Rate/100,000 Population
1890	4,290	6.9
1891	5,906	9.2
1892	6,791	10.4
1893	6,615	10.0
1894	9,800	14.5
1895	10,500	15.2
1896	10,652	15.1
1897	9,520	13.3
1898	7,840	10.7
1899	6,225	8.4

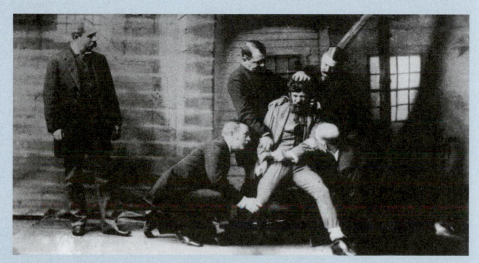

The difficulties of early crime photography. On the left, NYPD chief inspector Thomas Byrnes is watching how bank robber George Mason is being subdued as he resists having his photograph taken for the police album, circa 1870.

As early as 1932, FBI director J. Edgar Hoover was boasting of the value and usefulness of the *UCR*. The purpose, Hoover maintained, was "to determine whether there is or is not a crime wave and whether crime is on the increase or decrease."[4] From that time on, the FBI has charted the degree and nature of the increases and decreases in crime, any geographical variations, and other trends that are deemed significant.

The main publication of the *UCR* is an annual volume, *Crime in the United States,* that has helped establish the FBI's image as the nation's leading authority on crime trends. Administrators, politicians, policy makers and opinion makers, the press, criminal justice agencies, and the public rely on this volume for information about crime trends. Yet the FBI reports have their problems. They are incomplete and structurally biased, resulting in the creation and persistence of many myths about crime in the United States. Moreover, they have been misused and misinterpreted. As a result, inaccurate and distorted representations of crime are continually being offered to both professional and lay audiences, and public pronouncements about "the crime problem"

EXHIBIT 4.2 | VICTIMS & JUSTICE

The Crime Clock, 2003

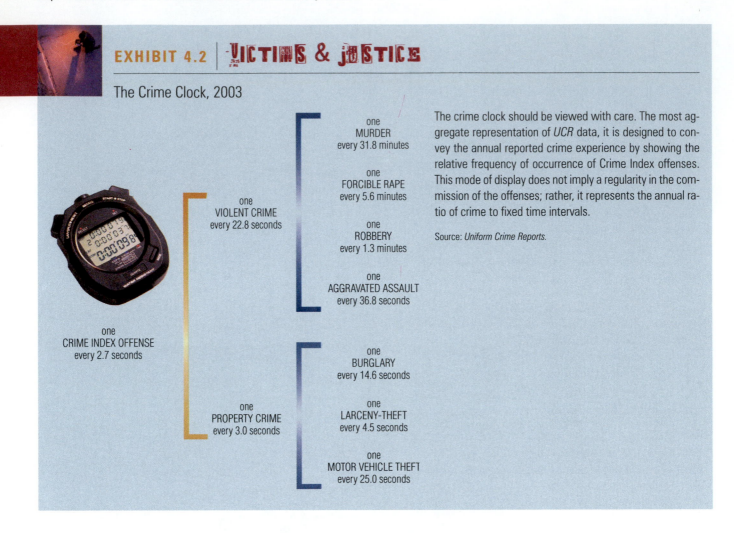

one
CRIME INDEX OFFENSE
every 2.7 seconds

one
VIOLENT CRIME
every 22.8 seconds

one
MURDER
every 31.8 minutes

one
FORCIBLE RAPE
every 5.6 minutes

one
ROBBERY
every 1.3 minutes

one
AGGRAVATED ASSAULT
every 36.8 seconds

one
PROPERTY CRIME
every 3.0 seconds

one
BURGLARY
every 14.6 seconds

one
LARCENY-THEFT
every 4.5 seconds

one
MOTOR VEHICLE THEFT
every 25.0 seconds

The crime clock should be viewed with care. The most aggregate representation of *UCR* data, it is designed to convey the annual reported crime experience by showing the relative frequency of occurrence of Crime Index offenses. This mode of display does not imply a regularity in the commission of the offenses; rather, it represents the annual ratio of crime to fixed time intervals.

Source: *Uniform Crime Reports.*

often have only limited basis in fact. The following commentary includes an explanation of official criminal statistics, an examination of their reliability, and a discussion of how these and other sources of information can be used to understand the nature and extent of crime in America.

Structure and Content

The FBI's *Uniform Crime Reports* presents a nationwide view of crime based on statistics submitted by city, county, and state law enforcement agencies throughout the country.[5] As of 2005, more than 17,000 law enforcement agencies were contributing crime data to this reporting program, representing more than 93% of the national population.

The Crime Clock The *UCR* begins with a rather alarming *crime clock*. As illustrated in Exhibit 4.2, it suggests that in 2003 there was one murder every 32 minutes, one forcible rape every 6 minutes, one robbery every minute, and a property crime every 3 seconds, as well as other crimes in similarly frequent intervals. The reader is cautioned that the crime clock display should not be interpreted to imply some regularity in the commission of crimes; it simply represents the annual ratio of crime to fixed time intervals. Unfortunately, this cautionary comment is easily overlooked, and media reports make frequent reference to the literal meaning of the crime clock.

Part I and Part II Offenses The *UCR* presents statistics in two categories: *crimes known to the police* and *arrests.* "Crimes known to the police" include all events either reported to or observed by the police in those categories of crime that the FBI desig-

VICTIMS & JUSTICE | EXHIBIT 4.3

Index of Crime for the United States, 1990–2003

	Total U.S. Population	Total Crime Index*	Violent Crime	Property Crime
1990	249,464,396	14,475,613	1,820,127	12,655,486
Rate per 100,000 inhabitants	—	5,802.7	729.6	5,073.1
2003	290,809,777	11,816,782	1,381,259	10,435,523
Rate per 100,000 inhabitants	—	4,063.4	475.0	3,588.4
Percentage change, 1990–2003				
By crimes	—	−18.4%	−24.1%	−17.5%
By rate	—	−30.0%	−34.9%	−29.3%

*Arson is not included, due to incomplete reporting.

Source: *Uniform Crime Reports.*

nates as **Part I offenses.** These are the most serious crimes: criminal homicide, forcible rape, robbery, aggravated assault, burglary/breaking and entering, larceny-theft (other than motor vehicle theft), motor vehicle theft, and arson. "Arrests" include compilations of arrest reports for all the Part I offenses *combined with* reports for 21 additional categories that the FBI designates as **Part II offenses.** These are less serious crimes. They include other assaults, forgery and counterfeiting, fraud, embezzlement, stolen property (buying, receiving, possessing), vandalism, weapons (carrying, possessing), prostitution and commercialized vice, sex offenses (except forcible rape, prostitution, and commercialized vice), drug abuse violations, gambling, offenses against the family and children (nonsupport, neglect, desertion), driving under the influence (of alcohol or drugs), liquor law violations, drunkenness, disorderly conduct, vagrancy, violations of curfew and loitering laws, suspicion, runaways, and "all other."

The Crime Index Information on Part I offenses is grouped by city, metropolitan area, state, region, and the nation as a whole to reflect an "Index of Crime" for the given year. First published in 1960, the Crime Index has been under scrutiny for its consistency as a barometer of criminality. Since the Crime Index is a total that does not distinguish the seriousness of different crimes, giving equal weight to larceny or theft as to murder or rape, critics have charged that it creates a biased overall crime rate. Leading criminologists, sociologists, and other advisory groups have urged the development of a more robust index. In June 2004, the Advisory Panel Board of the Criminal Justice Information Service (CJIS), a division of the FBI, approved discontinuing the use of the Crime Index as a true indicator of crime. The FBI will continue publishing a violent crime total and a property crime total until a more viable index is developed.

Nevertheless, it is these **Crime Index** data that are currently relied on for estimating the magnitude and rates of crime. A sample of the *UCR* data appears in Exhibit 4.3, which provides figures for total Index crime, violent crime, and property crime, including their absolute numbers, rates, and percent changes between 1990 and 2003. This table contains several terms that are important for reading and interpreting any crime statistics:

- *Total Crime Index:* The sum of all Part I offenses reported to or observed by the police (that is, "crimes known to the police") during a given period in a particular place (in this example, during 2003 for the total United States).
- *Violent crime:* The sum of all Part I violent offenses (homicide, forcible rape, robbery, and aggravated assault).

- *Property crime:* The sum of all Part I property offenses (burglary, larceny-theft, motor vehicle theft, and arson).
- *Rate per 100,000 inhabitants:* The **crime rate,** or the number of Part I offenses that occurred in a given area for every 100,000 people living in that area, calculated as follows:

$$\frac{\text{Total Crime Index}}{\text{Population}} \times 100{,}000 = \text{rate}$$

- In Exhibit 4.3, the crime rate in the United States for 2003 was 4,063.4 per 100,000 inhabitants. In other words, 4,063.4 Part I offenses were "known to the police" for every 100,000 persons in the nation. And as such,

$$\frac{2003 \text{ Total Crime Index}}{2003 \text{ population}} \times 100{,}000 = \text{rate}$$

$$\frac{11{,}816{,}782}{290{,}809{,}777} \times 100{,}000 = 4{,}063.4$$

- *Percent change:* The percentage of increase or decrease (+ or −) in the Crime Index or crime rate over some prior year, calculated as follows:

$$\frac{\text{Current total Crime Index} - \text{previous total Crime Index}}{\text{Previous total Crime Index}} = \text{percent change}$$

- The total Crime Index was 14,475,613 in 1990. It decreased by 18.4% from 1990 to 2003. This percentage is calculated as follows:

$$\frac{2003 \text{ total Crime Index} - 1990 \text{ total Crime Index}}{1990 \text{ total Crime Index}} = \text{percent change}$$

$$\frac{11{,}816{,}782 - 14{,}475{,}613}{14{,}475{,}613} = \text{percent change}$$

$$\frac{-2{,}658{,}831}{14{,}475{,}613} = -0.1836 = -18.47\%$$

Most of the *UCR* data concern Part I offenses in thousands of cities and towns throughout the nation, but other information is also presented. For example, arrest data are broken down for each offense by age, gender, and race of those arrested and by population area, for both Part I and Part II offenses. In addition, the *UCR* provides data on numbers of law enforcement personnel in communities that contribute to the reporting system, as well as extensive information on the number of law enforcement officers assaulted or killed during the given year.

The Extent of Crime

The data presented in Exhibit 4.3 provide some preliminary indicators of the extent of crime in the United States, at least in terms of those Index crimes that become known to the police. About 11.82 million Part I crimes were reported during 2003, including 16,503 murders, 93,433 rapes, 413,402 robberies, 857,921 aggravated assaults, 2,153,464 burglaries, 7,021,588 larcenies, and 1,260,471 motor vehicle thefts.

It was noted earlier that Part II offenses are reported in the *UCR* only in terms of arrests. Therefore, there is no measure of the relative prevalence of these crimes throughout the nation. However, there were approximately 13,639,479 arrests during 2003, of which nearly 12 million involved Part II–type crimes.

Reliability of Estimates

It must be emphasized at the outset that with the exception of the data on homicide, *UCR* estimates of the volume and rates of crime are considerably lower than the actual frequency of criminal acts. Homicide figures tend to be nearly complete, because most

Drug-Related Arrests, 1980–2003
Source: *Uniform Crime Reports.*

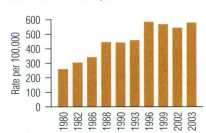

deaths and missing persons are investigated in one way or another. Moreover, comparisons of homicide rates compiled by the FBI and by the Office of Vital Statistics reflect similar figures. But in all other crime categories, *UCR* estimates are severely deficient.

Concealment and Nonreporting   Crime, by its very nature, is not easily measured. It is subject to both concealment and nonreporting—concealment by victims and offenders, and nonreporting by authorities—with the result that official crime statistics fall significantly short of the full volume and range of offenses. There are, for example, wide areas of criminal behavior that rarely find their way into official compilations. When family and other relationships are involved, criminal codes often conflict with emotions and social norms, resulting in the concealment of adultery, sodomy, statutory rape, sexual activity among gay men and women, illegal abortion, desertion, and nonsupport. In the legal and health professions there are unreported white-collar crimes by both practitioners and clients, primarily in the areas of illegal adoption practices, fee-splitting, illegal prescription and drug dispensing practices, falsification of claims, perjury, bribery, and conflicts of interest. Within the business sector there are instances of consumer fraud, purchase and sale of stolen merchandise, shortchanging, price-fixing, and concealment of income. In addition, employees are responsible for countless cases of embezzlement and pilferage, while customers engage in shoplifting, tagswitching, and petty check forgery. Within the public sector there is extensive bribery and corruption, and to these offenses can be added the so-called victimless crimes and syndicate rackets—prostitution, procuring, commercialized vice, drugs, gambling, and liquor violations, which involve another group of nonreporting clientele. Finally, to these might be added the many victims of Part I and Part II offenses who fail to report crimes to the police out of fear of publicity and reprisal, lack of confidence in law enforcement or other authorities, or unwillingness to get involved with crime reporting and control.[6] (For an account of the most notorious instances of "not getting involved," see Exhibit 4.4.)

There are many specific reasons for not wishing to become involved with the police. Consider the case of a liquor store owner whose place of business was held up at gunpoint on three separate occasions. His combined losses were more than $10,000 in money and goods, which could have been reimbursed by his insurance coverage had he reported the robberies to the authorities. He did not, however, because he was hoping

"If the crime rate goes up, we'll know it wasn't you."

EXHIBIT 4.4 | VICTIMS & JUSTICE

Kitty Genovese and the "No Duty to Aid" Rule

The killing of Catherine "Kitty" Genovese is considered to be one of the most infamous and brutal murders of the 20th century. It shocked the nation when it was committed in 1964, and continues to trouble people in the 21st century in its symbolism of urban apathy.

On March 14, 1964, at 3:20 A.M., 28-year-old Kitty Genovese returned home from work and parked her car only 150 feet from her apartment at 8270 Austin Street in Queens County, New York, a residential borough of New York City. Ms. Genovese had walked only a few feet when a man came out of the shadows, stabbed her, and began to sexually assault her. As she began to scream, lights blinked on in the apartment houses along Austin Street. For the next 25 minutes the attacker stalked, assaulted, and stabbed Ms. Genovese until she eventually died just before 3:50 A.M.

Detectives investigating the murder discovered that no fewer than 38 of Ms. Genovese's neighbors had witnessed at least one of the killer's three attacks on the young woman. Although the 38 witnesses heard her cries for help and watched the assault, the first call to the police did not occur until some minutes after her death—almost half an hour after the attack had begun.

Expressions of outrage immediately came not only from public officials and private citizens in the New York area but from across the nation as well. Days later, while the nation was still shocked over the witnesses' behavior during the crime, *The New York Times* published the following editorial comment:

> Seldom has the *Times* published a more horrifying story than its account of how thirty-eight respectable, law-abiding middle-class Queens citizens watched a killer stalk his young woman victim in a parking lot in Kew Gardens over a half-hour period, without one of them making a call to the police department that would have saved her life. They would not have been exposed to any danger themselves: a simple telephone call in the privacy of their own homes was all that was needed. How incredible it is that such motives as "I didn't want to get involved" deterred them from this act of simple humanity. Does residence in a great city destroy all sense of per-

sonal responsibility for one's neighbors? Who can explain such shocking indifference on the part of a cross section of our fellow New Yorkers?

Police officials conceded that there was no law that required someone witnessing a crime to report it to the authorities, but they contended that morality should oblige a witness to do so.

Less than a week after the murder, police arrested a suspect, 29-year-old Winston Moseley, a business-machine operator who lived with his wife and two children in another part of Queens County. Although Moseley had no criminal record, he quickly confessed to the murder of Kitty Genovese and two other women. Moseley told police

Kitty Genovese

to sell his business and felt that if word got out that his establishment was a "target," its potential market value would have dropped significantly.

Crime statistics are also subject to concealment, nonreporting, overreporting, and other manipulations by criminal justice authorities, often for political and public relations purposes. For example, as crime rates were falling in many parts of the United States during the 1990s, police officials in a number of cities were under pressure to show ever-decreasing crime statistics. This occurred during 1997 in Boca Raton, Florida, and police officials systematically downgraded many burglaries to vandalism, trespassing, and missing property. The result was an almost 11 percent decrease in the city's felony crime rate for the year. In Philadelphia, Pennsylvania, furthermore, the city was forced to withdraw its crime figures from the *UCR* for 1996, 1997, and the first half of 1998 because of underreporting and downgrading of crimes to less serious incidents.[7] And in New York City in 2000, several police commanders were

Winston Moseley

held five persons hostage, raping one of them before FBI agents finally recaptured him. Moseley remains in prison to this day.

During the four decades since the murder of Kitty Genovese, scholars and legal reformers have attempted to change the "no duty to aid" rule—which requires no affirmative aid to strangers in peril—in both federal and state statutes. At a University of Chicago Law School conference on the "Good Samaritan and the Bad," a range of questions were raised about the scope of the "no duty to aid" rule:

Is a citizen required, and should he be required, to lend assistance to another who is in danger of severe personal injury or substantial loss of property? Should it make any difference if the potential loss stems from the commission of a crime, or from accident, act of God, or other causes? Must the passerby intervene only when he can do so at no peril to himself? Only when the peril to himself is less than the harm which the victim will suffer?

Despite the continuing debate, legislatures have been reluctant to modify the "no duty to aid" rule. They argue that such a rule would be costly to enforce and would interfere with individual liberty. Only a few states—Vermont, Minnesota, Rhode Island, Colorado, Ohio, Massachusetts, Florida, and Washington—have enacted statutes requiring bystanders to aid someone in peril. Violation of such statutes is generally a petty misdemeanor.

During the 40 years that have passed since the murder of Kitty Genovese, there have been scores of behavioral studies that tried to explain why her neighbors reacted the way they did. The overwhelming conclusion is that they were not apathetic or coldhearted. Rather, they were confused, uncertain, and afraid. As for the 38 neighbors, many were consumed by guilt after the crime. Others got fed up with the negative attention and simply moved out of the neighborhood. And the person hit hardest by Ms. Genovese's death was Mary Ann Zielonko, her roommate and lover—an omission that perhaps was understandable in 1964.

that he had "an uncontrollable urge to kill" and that he prowled the streets looking for victims while his wife was at work. Three months later he went on trial for the murder, pleading not guilty by reason of insanity and testifying in detail about how he stalked and stabbed Ms. Genovese to satisfy his "uncontrollable urge." The jury, however, rejected the insanity defense and rendered a guilty verdict. One month later, Judge J. Irwin Shapiro of the New York State Supreme Court sentenced Moseley to die in the electric chair at Sing Sing Prison. As he gave the sentencing order, Judge Shapiro commented: "When I see this monster, I wouldn't hesitate to pull the switch myself."

In 1967, three years after Moseley's conviction, the New York State Court of Appeals reduced his sentence to life imprisonment on grounds that Judge Shapiro erred in refusing to admit evidence at a sentencing hearing on Moseley's mental condition. The following year, after being taken from prison to a Buffalo hospital for minor surgery, Moseley struck a correctional officer, escaped, obtained a gun, and

Sources: Abraham M. Rosenthal, *Thirty-Eight Witnesses* (New York: McGraw-Hill, 1964); Ervin Staub, "The Psychology of Bystanders, Perpetrators, and Heroic Helpers," *International Journal of Intercultural Relations* 17 (1993): 315–341; James A. Inciardi, "The Murder of Kitty Genovese," in *Encyclopedia of Violence in the United States,* vol. 2, edited by Ronald Gottesman and Richard Maxwell Brown (New York: Scribner's, 1999), 28–30; *The New York Times,* February 8, 2004, sec. 14, p. 1.

either demoted or reassigned because they had manipulated statistics in an effort to "bring down the crime rate" in their precincts.[8]

Problems in Reporting Crime Data
The methods used to record crimes at the local level can affect the reliability of crime statistics. Studies by the National Opinion Research Center (NORC) at the University of Chicago suggest that police may report only three-fourths of the complaints received for certain crimes. Other studies have documented that as many as 20 percent of citizen complaints may not be recorded in police figures, depending on the presence or absence of a suspect; the relationship between the victim and the offender; and the victim's age, race/ethnicity, and behavior toward law enforcement officers.[9]

Clearly, procedures such as these can have a significant impact on the compilation of crime statistics. A study sponsored by the Justice Department, for example, found

A gunman wearing a bullet-proof vest takes a hostage after attempting to rob a motorcycle store.

that the FBI was not informed of approximately one in every five crimes reported by the public. Separately, an independent audit of Atlanta's police department, completed in 2004, unveiled systemic underreporting of crimes and sloppy record keeping. Furthermore, unlike those of most cities, Atlanta's figures did not include all crimes reported by the 15 local law enforcement agencies that operated within the city. Therefore, the city's crime statistics were actually a serious underrepresentation of the true crime rate.[10]

Criminal justice agencies are not the only organizations known for underreporting crime events. Colleges, universities, and other educational institutions, for example, are notorious for failing to report crimes. Since 1990, Congress has required all colleges and universities in the United States to report all crimes in order that prospective students will have some relative indication of campus safety. But for fear of bad publicity, many colleges have regularly understated the number of campus crimes. Many colleges do not count offenses that occur on the city streets that run through their campuses; others omit on-campus rapes that are reported to local police or crisis intervention centers rather than to campus security. Still other institutions ignore incidents that occur in sorority and fraternity houses.[11]

In addition to these problems of concealment and nonreporting, which occur at the victim and agency levels, there are other problems with the statistics that result from the *UCR* process itself. The FBI's *Uniform Crime Reporting Handbook* provides specific definitions of the 29 crime categories in the *UCR*. The FBI also provides standardized reporting forms to police agencies for compiling their data. However, not all law enforcement bureaucracies follow directions and instructions to the letter, resulting in inaccurate statistics.

The *UCR:* An Evaluation

How useful, then, are the *Uniform Crime Reports?* Are the facts reliable enough to provide the researcher, administrator, and observer with baseline data on the phenomenon of crime? As has been pointed out, the *UCR* data do have limitations, including incompleteness and bias, and they fall considerably short in reporting the full extent of crime in the United States.

By examining *UCR* figures from the perspective of rates and proportions, however, as opposed to absolute numbers, some bias can be eliminated. Such analyses can

Fingerprints on File
Since the FBI began collecting fingerprints in 1924, it has received more than 400 million fingerprint cards and has more than 257 million on file. Source: Federal Bureau of Investigation.

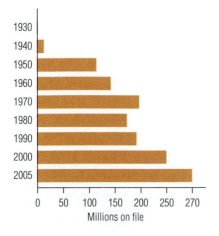

help determine the overall growth, decline, or persistence of particular types of criminal behavior; they can indicate the extent to which the behavior is or is not being brought under control; they can suggest the segments of the population that are most prone to a particular form of criminality; and they can indicate the changing social and economic severity of a given offense.

The most effective use of rate and proportion analysis occurs at the local level. By combining existing *UCR* data with statistical compilations available from local, county, and state criminal justice agencies, planners, administrators, and observers can obtain the specific information they need to identify crime trends in the community.

In 1987, the Department of Justice began testing and implementing a new National Incident-Based Reporting System (NIBRS). When the new program is fully operational, data will be collected and reported in each of 22 crime categories with regard to the following factors:

- *Incident*—date and time.
- *Offense*—whether completed or attempted, type(s) of criminal activity, weapons or force involved, premises involved and method of entry (if applicable), location, whether computer equipment was used, whether the offender used alcohol or drugs during or before the crime.
- *Property*—type of property loss, value, recovery date, type and quantity of drugs involved (if appropriate).
- *Victim*—type (person or business), characteristics (age, sex, race, ethnicity), circumstances if the crime was a homicide or assault (such as lovers' quarrel, killed in line of duty, etc.), relationship between victim and offender.
- *Offender*—characteristics (age, sex, race), date of arrest, arrest offense.[12]

As of 2004, the implementation of NIBRS had been slow, with contributing police agencies representing just 16 percent of the U.S. population.[13] Since conversion to the NIBRS program requires computerization, training, technical assistance, and support at each reporting point, full implementation on a nationwide basis is not expected until well into the first decade of the 21st century.

Victim Survey Research

In 1965, in an effort to determine the parameters of crime that did not appear in official criminal statistics, the President's Commission on Law Enforcement and Administration of Justice initiated the first national survey of crime victimization ever conducted. During that year, the National Opinion Research Center (NORC) surveyed 10,000 households, asking whether the person questioned, or any member of his or her household, had been a victim of crime during the preceding year, whether the crime had been reported to the police, and if not, the reasons for not reporting.[14] The households were selected so that they would be representative of the nation as a whole, and as is the case with political polling and election forecasting, the results were considered to be accurate within a small degree of error. More detailed surveys of medium- and high-crime areas in Washington, D.C., Boston, and Chicago were undertaken by the Bureau of Social Science Research, located in Washington, and by the Survey Research Center of the University of Michigan.

These **victimization surveys** quickly demonstrated that the actual amount of crime in the United States at that time was likely to be several times that reported in the *UCR*. The NORC survey suggested that during 1965, forcible rapes were almost four times the reported rate, larcenies were almost double, and burglaries and robberies were 50 percent greater than the reported rate. Vehicle theft was lower, but by a smaller amount than the differences between other categories of crime, and the homicide figure from the NORC survey was considered too small for an accurate statistical projection. As high as the NORC rates were for violent and property crimes, they were still considered to have understated the actual amounts of crime to some degree, since the victimization rates for every member of each surveyed household were based on the re-

"And finally, would you say your fear of crime had increased?"

Reprinted by permission of *www.CartoonStock.com*

EXHIBIT 4.5 | Gender Perspectives on Crime and Justice

Violence Against Pregnant Women by Jason C. Weaver

Homicide is a leading cause of death among women of reproductive age (15 to 44 years), and the data suggest that homicide accounts for a greater proportion of deaths among pregnant and postpartum women than among nonpregnant women.

Although official records of such homicides are incomplete and inconsistent, a recent study has shed some light on the prevalence of pregnancy-associated homicide. The Pregnancy Mortality Surveillance System (PMSS), initiated in 1987 by the Centers for Disease Control and Prevention (CDC) in collaboration with the American College of Obstetricians and Gynecologists and state health departments, sought to examine the deaths of women during or within 1 year of pregnancy. The data were voluntarily provided by agencies in all 50 states for deaths occurring from 1991 through 1999 and yielded a total sample of 7,342 deaths.

Of the 1,993 women identified as suffering a pregnancy-associated injury death, 31.1 percent died as a result of homicide, ranking homicide second only to motor vehicle death as a leading cause of reported injury death to pregnant and postpartum women. The overall pregnancy-associated homicide rate for the period was 1.7 per 100,000 live births, but the rate was even higher among ethnic minority women. Pregnancy-related homicides of black women were 6.4 per 100,000 live births, seven times the rate of white women. Most of the reported homicides occurred during the postpartum period of women who had delivered live-born infants, while 20.6 percent occurred while the women were still pregnant.

The media have drawn attention to this phenomenon as well. Most recently, Missouri resident Bobbie Jo Stinnett, then 8 months pregnant, was strangled to death and her fetus was cut and stolen from her womb. The woman charged with the murder and kidnapping had presented the baby to her husband and neighbors as her own. Using e-mail records, the police were able to track down the suspect at her home in neighboring Kansas and retrieve the stolen baby.

The tragic murder of Bobbie Jo Stinnett coincided with two other high-profile cases of pregnancy-associated homicides that held media and public attention: Laci Peterson and Lori Hacking. Scott Peterson was accused of killing his wife Laci on Christmas Eve of 2002 in Modesto, California, and Mark Hacking was accused of slaying his wife Lori in Salt Lake City, Utah, in late 2004. Both women were reported missing by their husbands prior to their discovered murders; both were pregnant at the time of their deaths, Laci near full-term and Lori at 5 weeks; and both were believed to have been killed by husbands who later tried to dispose of their bodies. The cases were different, however, in many other respects. Mark Hacking, Lori's husband, had admitted to shooting his wife, yet he was not charged with a capital crime since prosecutors could not accurately determine Lori's said pregnancy. Scott Peterson, on the other hand, denied any involvement in his wife's death, but because of the overwhelming circumstantial evidence against him, was found guilty of the first-degree murder of Laci along with the second-degree murder of their unborn son.

In light of the recent scientific analyses and the high-profile headlines, pregnancy-associated homicides will likely remain in the public view for some time to come.

Sources: CDC, "MMWR Surveillance Summaries: Pregnancy-Related Mortality Surveillance—United States, 1991–1999," http://www.cdc.gov; J. Chang, C. J. Berg, L. E. Saltzman, and J. Herndon, "Homicide: A Leading Cause of Injury Deaths Among Pregnant and Postpartum Women in the United States, 1991–1999," *American Journal of Public Health* 95, 3 (2005): 471–477; *The New York Times*, December 19, 2004, sec. 1, p. 36; *Pittsburgh Post-Gazette*, April 15, 2005, 5A; *The Washington Post*, November 14, 2004, 18A.

Crime Rate (per 100,000) Comparisons Between the First NORC Survey and the *UCR*

Crime	NORC	*UCR*
Homicide	3.0	5.1
Forcible rape	42.5	11.6
Robbery	94.0	61.4
Aggravated assault	218.3	106.6
Burglary	949.1	605.3
Larceny	606.5	393.3
Motor vehicle theft	206.2	251.0
Total violent crimes	357.8	184.7
Total property crimes	1,716.8	1,249.6

Source: President's Commission on Law Enforcement and Administration of Justice, 1967.

sponses of only one family member. For a discussion of the victimization of pregnant women, see Exhibit 4.5.

The National Crime Victimization Survey

The interest and knowledge generated by the initial victim survey research stimulated the Law Enforcement Assistance Administration (LEAA) to continue the effort with surveys of its own. Its first survey, conducted by the U.S. Bureau of the Census in 1972, further documented the disparities between unreported crime and "crimes known to the police." In some cities the ratio between the two was greater than 5 to 1.[15]

Since this study, victim survey research has continued. The National Crime Victimization Survey (NCVS) is conducted by the Bureau of the Census under the direction of the Department of Justice. NCVS data reflect the nature and extent of criminal victimization, characteristics of the victim, victim–offender relationships, the times and places of the crimes, the degree of weapon use, the extent of personal injury, the extent of victim self-protection, the amount of economic and worktime loss due to victimization, the extent to which crimes are reported to police, and the reasons for nonreporting. For example, 2003 survey findings were based on interviews with

VICTIMS & JUSTICE | EXHIBIT 4.6

Crimes of Violence: National Crime Survey and *Uniform Crime Reports,* 2003

Crime	NATIONAL CRIME SURVEY		UNIFORM CRIME REPORTS	
	Number	Rate	Number	Rate
Forcible rape	198,850	83.1	93,433	32.1
Robbery	596,130	249.1	413,402	142.2
Aggravated assault	1,101,110	460.1	857,921	295.0
Total	1,896,090	792.3	1,364,756	469.3

Note: The National Crime Survey rate per 100,000 persons is based on a survey population of all persons age 12 and over. The *Uniform Crime Reports* rate per 100,000 is based on the total U.S. population.

Sources: *Criminal Victimization—2003,* Bureau of Justice Statistics, National Crime Victimization Survey, September 2004; *Uniform Crime Reports—2003.*

149,040 occupants (ages 12 and over) in 83,660 housing units and generalized to the population as a whole.[16]

Although NCVS and *UCR* data are not fully comparable, Exhibit 4.6 suggests that the 1.9 million violent crimes projected by the NCVS go well beyond what appeared in *UCR* for the same year.

The major reason for these large discrepancies is that significant numbers of these crimes were not reported to the police. The NCVS chart in Exhibit 4.7 suggests that the reporting rate for theft was just under a third; for rape, just over a third; and for assault and burglary, just over one-half. The major reason for this high level of nonreporting was the victims' belief that there was nothing the police could do about the

A street mugging in process.

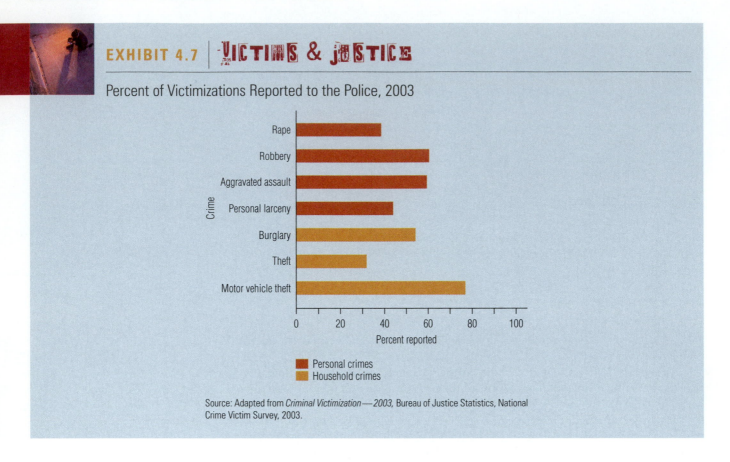

EXHIBIT 4.7 | VICTIMS & JUSTICE

Percent of Victimizations Reported to the Police, 2003

Source: Adapted from *Criminal Victimization—2003,* Bureau of Justice Statistics, National Crime Victim Survey, 2003.

crimes or that the victimizations were simply not important enough to report. Other less frequently mentioned reasons were fear of reprisal, the feeling that reporting was too inconvenient or time-consuming, the assumption that the police would not want to be bothered, and the belief that the crime was a private and personal matter.

Although *UCR* and NCVS data have often been compared, the two are not fully comparable. First, the *UCR* bases its crime rates on the total U.S. population, while the NCVS victimization data relate only to people age 12 and older. Second, the NCVS measures crime by victimization rather than by incident. For crimes against persons, the number of victimizations is normally greater than the number of incidents, since more than one person can be involved in any given incident. Third, NCVS and *UCR* crime classifications are not always uniform. While purse snatching is included with robbery according to *UCR* definitions, it appears as theft in NCVS data. Fourth, NCVS data on homicide are considered unreliable because violence of that type is relatively rare and the few unreported instances that do emerge during a survey are too few to permit accurate projections to the nation as a whole.

Comparisons between NCVS and *UCR* crime figures and rates must therefore be viewed with caution. Neither reporting mechanism alone can offer a fully accurate picture of the extent of specific crimes. Nevertheless, such comparisons do indicate some general weaknesses of the *Uniform Crime Reports* and suggest the relative amounts of crime that go unreported.

Applications and Limitations of Victimization Surveys

The rediscovery of the victim as a more complete source of information on instances of criminal activity has been the chief contribution of victim survey research. The material derived from crime victim surveys helps determine the extent and distribution of crime in a community. In addition, the surveys target not only victimizations but also public conceptions of crime, characteristics of victims and offenders, and conceptions of police effectiveness, as well as other data. Therefore victim-focused studies can also be used for the following purposes:

1. To describe the characteristics of victims and high-crime areas.
2. To evaluate the effectiveness of specific police programs.
3. To develop better insights into certain violent crimes through the analysis of victim–offender relationships.
4. To structure programs for increased reporting of crimes to the police.
5. To sensitize the criminal justice system to the needs of the victim.
6. To develop training programs that stress police–victim and police–community relations.
7. To create and implement meaningful public information and crime prevention programs.

Finally, victimization surveys can also help identify overall crime trends. NCVS data for 2003, for example, indicated that the rate of violent crime had dropped by 55 percent since 1993 and that other types of crime were down as well. These declines were not unlike those reported by the FBI in the *Uniform Crime Reports.*

Despite their usefulness, however, victimization studies do have limitations. For example, a number of weaknesses affect their accuracy. The researchers who conduct these surveys find that those interviewed have trouble remembering exactly when a crime occurred; in property offenses, they forget how great the losses were. But by far the major problem associated with the victimization survey technique is its cost. The greatest advantages come from surveys at the local level that focus on what can be done to upgrade neighborhood crime prevention and police effectiveness programs. However, the cost of conducting annual victimization surveys in most communities would be staggering, and most locales simply cannot afford them.

Self-Reported Criminal Behavior

Since the 1930s, when the FBI began publishing the *Uniform Crime Reports,* criminological research has produced studies that have confirmed the limitations of official crime statistics. Among the earliest of these research efforts was a rudimentary victimization survey, conducted in 1933, that found that of some 5,314 instances of shoplifting that occurred in three Philadelphia department stores, fewer than 5 percent were ever reported to the police.[17]

Violent Crime Rates
Adjusted victimization rate per 1,000 persons age 12 and over

Property Crime Rates
Adjusted victimization rate per 1,000 households

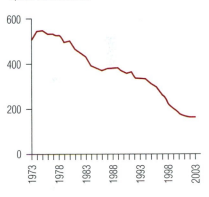

Studies of heroin and cocaine users demonstrate that their self-reported criminal activity can be fairly accurate, provided the inquiries are made by researchers rather than criminal justice personnel, and that confidentiality is assured.

CAREERS IN CRIMINAL JUSTICE

Document Examiners and Fingerprint Analysts

Two positions that operate behind the scenes in the criminal justice field are document examiners and fingerprint analysts. Document examiners establish the genuineness of letters, papers, contracts, and other documents as part of police investigations, as expert witnesses in court, or as consultants to law enforcement agencies. They scrutinize such things as handwriting, watermarks, inks, paper fibers, typeface, and erasures, and they conduct other forms of technical analysis. Minimum qualifications include a community college degree in criminal justice or related field, 3 years experience in law enforcement or other investigative work, and/or 2 years of technical work in examining handwriting. Annual salaries range from $36,000 to $70,000 depending on qualifications, experience, and geographical location.

A related area of expertise is fingerprint analysis. Although the FBI is moving toward computerized fingerprint examinations, the need for human analysts will remain both for the verification of computer results and for routine fingerprint examinations in agencies and jurisdictions where computer technology is unavailable or impractical. Fingerprint analysts compare latent prints to known inked prints, brief court and other criminal justice personnel on findings of fingerprint analyses, construct courtroom exhibits illustrating fingerprint evidence, and maintain

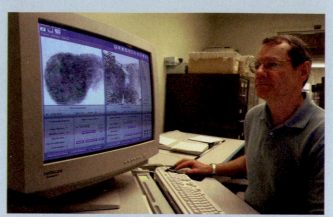

A technician checking fingerprints at the Vermont Crime Information Center.

latent fingerprint files. Minimum qualifications include a community college degree in criminal justice or a related field and completion of the FBI basic fingerprint identification course. Salaries range from $25,000 to $55,000 annually in state and local agencies and higher at the federal level.

	PERCENTAGE ENGAGING IN CRIME	
Crime	Men	Women
Petty theft	89	83
Disorderly conduct	85	76
Malicious mischief	84	81
Assault	49	5
Tax evasion	57	40
Robbery	11	1
Fraud	46	34
Criminal libel	36	29
Concealed weapons	35	3
Auto theft	26	8
Other grand theft	13	11
Burglary	17	4

Another primary mechanism for determining the nature and extent of this "dark figure," or *unknown crime,* is research into **self-reported crime.** The first major study of self-reported crime came in 1947, when two researchers obtained completed questionnaires from 1,020 men and 678 women of diverse ages and a wide range of conventional occupations regarding their involvement in 49 different offenses. Ninety-nine percent of the respondents admitted that they had committed one or more of the offenses listed. The percentages of both men and women who had engaged in many types of crime were significant, as summarized in the table in the margin.[18]

This pioneer effort demonstrated that criminal activity was considerably more widespread than police files even began to suggest. Since then, studies of self-reported criminal involvement have become more common. In addition to their use as a check on the limitations of standard crime-reporting mechanisms, they can also be used to determine the following information:

1. The amount of crime committed by the "normal" (typically noncriminal) population.
2. What kinds of crime typically remain unknown.
3. How the official system of crime control selects cases to pursue.
4. Whether certain categories of offenders are over- or underselected by official control mechanisms.
5. Whether explanations and theories of crime developed for officially known offenders apply to nonregistered offenders as well.[19]

Studies of self-reported crime have provided numerous insights into these issues, but such research has some limitations and problems. First, there are methodological questions of validity and reliability. *Validity* refers to how good an answer the study yields. When the respondents admit to criminal behavior, are their answers true? Do they underreport or exaggerate their offense behavior? Are the respondents' estimates of the frequency of their crimes accurate? *Reliability* refers to the precision or accuracy

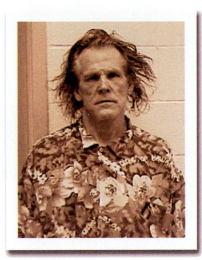

of the instruments used to record and measure self-reported behavior. In other words, does the interview measure what it is intended to measure? Does the respondent interpret the meaning of words such as *burglary*, *robbery*, or some other offense the same way the researcher does?

Besides these potential methodological problems, there are other possible sources of error, such as the following:

- Those who agree to answer questions may be markedly different from those who refuse, which leaves in doubt the representativeness of any sample of people interviewed.
- Those who respond to such inquiries may be truthful in their answers but may choose to conceal large segments of their criminal backgrounds.
- Most studies have focused on groups of students and other juveniles, stressing the incidence of unrecorded delinquency; few studies have targeted populations of adult offenders.

In general, despite sample biases and other methodological limitations, the studies of self-reported crime that have been conducted over the past four decades are important to criminological research. In addition to the advantages mentioned earlier, studies that focus on particular populations (such as drug users) can tell us more about the patterns and styles of criminal careers than any other form of data.

Other Sources of Data on Crime and Justice

For many decades observers have recognized the gaps and abuses in crime data and have stressed the need for a more accurate and comprehensive statistics collection program. One of the earliest suggestions for achieving this appeared in Louis Newton Robinson's *History and Organization of Criminal Statistics in the United States* in 1911. Robinson proposed using a model designed by the Bureau of the Census for collecting mortality statistics, with the responsibility for compilation resting with individual states and cities.[20] In 1931, the National Commission on Law Observance and Enforcement recommended the development of a comprehensive plan for a complete body of statistics covering crime, criminals, criminal justice, and correctional treatment at federal, state, and local levels, with responsibility for the program entrusted to a single federal agency.[21] More than 30 years later, in 1967, the President's Commission on Law Enforcement and Administration of Justice again called for a national crime statistics program.[22] Since then there have been similar pleas for such a program.[23]

To date, the long-awaited national statistics program has yet to emerge. The *Uniform Crime Reports* remains the primary source of data on crime, supplemented to some extent by victimization surveys and to a lesser degree by a smattering of self-report

FAMOUS CRIMINALS
Celebrity Mug Shots

What does this motley crew of offenders have in common? No, it is not their crimes. James Brown was recently arrested for domestic violence; Nick Nolte was nabbed for DUI; and Saddam, well, his offenses are too numerous to mention. Moreover, their professions are different—a singer, an actor, and a tyrant. The only thing left is their "struck-by-lightning" hair, and a common need for a good, strong comb. ∎

EXHIBIT 4.8 | VICTIMS & JUSTICE

The AMBER Alert

The AMBER Alert system (AMBER stands for "America's Missing: Broadcast Emergency Response") is a coordinated and voluntary effort between law enforcement and broadcasters that alerts the public when a child has been abducted and law enforcement has determined him or her to be in imminent danger. The alert contains all available information, including physical descriptions of the child and abductor, a description of the vehicle, and the tag number, and is broadcast on the Internet, television and radio, and electronic highway signs. The immediacy of the information that an AMBER Alert provides is crucial, as 74% of children abducted and murdered are killed within the first 3 hours of captivity.

The AMBER Alert system was developed in 1997 with the notion that the eyes and ears of vigilant citizens are often the best tools to help find abducted children and bring those responsible for the kidnapping to the attention of authorities. While "AMBER" is an acronym, the system is also named for Amber Hagerman, a 9-year-old who was kidnapped and brutally murdered in Arlington, Texas, in January 1996. A neighbor had witnessed a man pull young Amber off of her bicycle and throw her into the front seat of a pickup truck and speed away. The neighbor called the police and gave a description of the suspect and his vehicle. As the police and FBI searched for Amber, local radio and television stations covered the story in their regular newscasts. Although Amber would not be found alive, this cooperation led to the formation of the first alert system in the Dallas–Ft. Worth area to help safely recover missing children.

Since its inception, the program has expanded well beyond the Dallas area. In 2001, a partnership between the Office of Justice Programs, a division of the U.S. Department of Justice, and the National Center for Missing and Exploited Children (NCMEC) facilitated the development of AMBER Alert programs at local, state, and regional levels across the country. In 2003, the AMBER Alert system was further boosted by the PROTECT Act signed into law by President Bush. This act, Prosecutorial Remedies and Other Tools to End the Exploitation of Children Today, provided $25 million in fiscal year 2004 for notifications along highways, improvements to the AMBER Alert broadcast tech-

An electronic sign shows an AMBER Alert over Interstate 80 in Omaha, Nebraska.

nologies, and assistance with regional coordination in closing the geographic coverage gaps.

The AMBER Alert system has demonstrated remarkable success in reuniting parents with abducted children. Currently, there are 112 such AMBER Alert plans, including 50 statewide-, 25 regional-, and 37 local-coverage areas. The NCMEC, which tracks and maintains statistics on AMBER Alert recoveries, reported that as of April 2005 a total of 195 abducted children had been safely returned. Canada and England have already implemented their own versions of the program and other countries are considering the idea as well.

Sources: AMBER Alert Web site: *http://www.amberalert.gov;* National Center for Missing and Exploited Children Web site: *http://www.missingkids.com;* J. Robert Flores, *National Incidence Studies of Missing, Abducted, Runaway, and Throwaway Children (NIS-MART-2),* U.S. DOJ Office of Justice Programs: Office of Juvenile Justice and Delinquency Prevention, 2002; *The New York Times,* December 19, 2004, sec. 1, p. 36; *The Kansas City Star,* February, 20, 2005, B1.

studies. However, these are not the only sources of data on crime, criminals, and criminal justice processing. Many state and federal agencies compile data on their own particular areas of interest; these data are made available to interested students and researchers. They appear in the *Sourcebook of Criminal Justice Statistics,* published annually by the U.S. Department of Justice. In addition, a nationwide alert system designed to apprehend child abductors and collect data associated with these crimes is discussed in Exhibit 4.8.

Given the extent to which the use of illegal drugs has affected crime rates and criminal justice processing, more than two dozen new databases have been developed on drug-use patterns, trends, and correlates. Although most are used regularly by researchers and policy makers, those of particular significance from the standpoint of criminal justice are the *National Survey of Drug Use and Health* and the *Monitoring the Future* survey.

National Survey of Drug Use and Health

Funded by the U.S. Substance Abuse and Mental Health Services Administration and conducted on a regular basis, this survey projects estimates of the use of the major illicit drugs by the general household population of the United States. As such, the estimates tend to be incomplete because they do not include people living in jails or prisons, in other institutions, or on military bases, as well as the homeless and others living "on the streets."

Monitoring the Future Survey

Sponsored by the National Institute on Drug Abuse, this survey is conducted annually with a representative sample of high school students. It explores trends in drug use, attitudes and values about drug and alcohol use, and lifestyle orientations of American youth. However, because it excludes high school dropouts, significant numbers of drug-using adolescents are missing from its estimates.

Of special interest to anyone interested in the drug problem and rates of substance abuse in the United States are the data reports and publications of the National Institute on Drug Abuse (NIDA). This federal agency funds almost 90 percent of the drug abuse research that is undertaken throughout the world, and much of the information collected can be found on the NIDA Web site.[24] Just a few of the topics covered are descriptions and current trends in the drugs of abuse, research on the effects of marijuana use, emerging problems with prescription drug abuse, and approaches for the prevention and treatment of drug abuse, plus a wide spectrum of information on smoking and health, steroids and sports, and the changing nature of club drugs and the club culture.

Illicit Drug Use, by Age, 2003

Source: National Survey of Drug Use and Health.

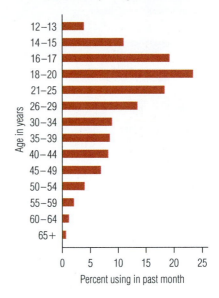

Drug Use Among Violent Offenders

Robbers are the most likely to have used drugs daily, and rapists and other sex offenders the least likely. Of violent offenders, 23% incarcerated for robbery had used drugs daily, compared to 9% of those incarcerated for rape and 6% of those incarcerated for other sex offenses.

Source: Bureau of Justice Statistics. ▪

CRITICAL THINKING IN CRIMINAL JUSTICE

International Crime Statistics and the World's Most Dangerous Places

Citing the Maryland sniper shootings in late 2002 and the mass murder of seven Chicago warehouse workers in August 2003 by a former employee who had been fired 6 months earlier, in September 2003 Madrid's daily newspaper *El País* reported that despite its declining crime rate, the United States was still the most violent industrial nation in the world and one of the most dangerous places on the planet.[25] Just a few months earlier, data published by the British Home Office suggested that the homicide rate in the United States was out of control in comparison to other nations.[26] As such, sectors of the international press seem to thrive on portraying the United States as a vast underworld of drugs, vice, and crime. And from reading the newspaper and listening to television commentators, it is easy to get the impression that the streets of America are indeed dangerous places—at least in terms of murder, robbery, and other street crimes. But is the United States really one of the most dangerous countries on earth? Some critical thinking on the matter, combined with a focused analysis of crime rates in other countries, suggests a vastly different conclusion.

Without question, homicide rates are higher in the United States than in virtually all European nations, and the number of homicides in a community is a good indicator of relative safety, because they are generally the most complete category of criminal statistics. But how do homicide rates in the United States compare with those outside Western Europe? What about places like South Africa, Brazil, and Colombia? Do these countries have higher homicide rates than the United States, and would any of these qualify as the most dangerous places on earth? Some research into crime rates and social conditions in developing nations provide some interesting answers.

An overview of international press and television reports during 2001 through 2005 and studies by the United Nations suggest a number of locations around the world that have dangerously high crime rates. Using less stringent criteria than reported crime figures, the locations include Johannesburg (for muggings, carjackings, assaults, and robberies), Mexico City (for corrupt police and robberies by taxi riders), Tijuana (for an escalating homicide rate), São Paulo and

Homicides per 100,000 Population in Selected Countries

Sources: Interpol; United Nations.

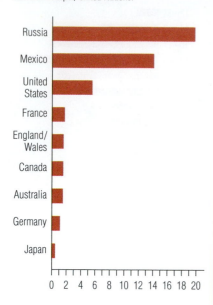

Murders in Greater São Paulo

(rate per 100,000 population) Source: São Paulo Secretariat of Public Security.

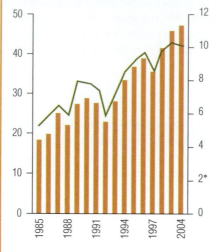

* All numbers on right-hand side are in thousands.

Islands of Death

Murders per 100,000 population
Source: National police forces.

Rio de Janeiro, Brazil (for thefts, muggings, and murders), Lagos, in Nigeria, and Nairobi, in Kenya (for pickpocketing to armed robbery and homicide), and Moscow and Colombia (for a whole host of predatory offenses).[27]

Finding good data to corroborate what is reported in the international media would be difficult, because many countries have only rudimentary mechanisms for the collection of criminal statistics. As a matter of fact, even with all of its imperfections, the FBI's *Uniform Crime Reports* is likely one of the most sophisticated compilations of data on crime anywhere in the world. Nevertheless, some data are available to indicate where a few of the most dangerous places on earth might be.

Beginning with Brazil, the World Bank estimates that the overall homicide rate in Brazil was 33.9 per 100,000 population in 2002—approximately seven times higher than that in the United States.[28] Rio de Janeiro, the country's most popular tourist city, is reported to have a homicide

Even many of the beaches in South Africa are quite dangerous. At the Wild Coast Sun, an upscale resort on the Indian Ocean in the town of Port Edward, hotel guests are warned against venturing on the beach alone.

Kidnapping Rate in Colombia

Per 100,000 population   Sources: Colombian Government; Reuters

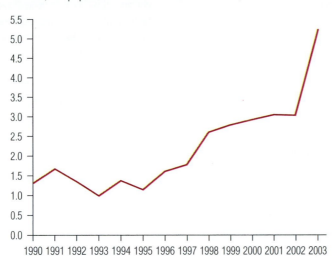

rate of 43.4 per 100,000 population, and São Paulo—Brazil's most populous city and one of the largest cities in the world—has had a dramatically escalating homicide rate for almost two decades. During 2002, furthermore, there were almost 12,000 homicides in the state of São Paulo, reflecting a rate of 46.8 per 100,000 population, and almost 10,000 homicides in the city of São Paulo, reflecting a rate of 52.7 per 100,000 population.[29] And then there is Vitoria, a city of half a million residents some 300 miles northeast of Rio de Janeiro. Because of a recent epidemic of drug trafficking and general lawlessness, the city's murder rate reached 177 per 100,000 population in 2002—the highest in Latin America and perhaps the entire world.[30] Compare that with such places as New York, or Miami, or Chicago. Brazil's high rates of crime in general, and homicide in particular, are an outgrowth of the vast disparities between rich and poor, economic instability, unemployment, lack of confidence in government institutions, widespread cocaine use, and police corruption to name but a few factors.[31]

South Africa's homicide rate is even higher than that of Brazil—47.4 per 100,000 countrywide in 2004 (down from 69.5 in 1994).[32] So high are the rates of violent crime in South Africa that they have affected tourism and foreign investment, two things that the country's struggling economy so desperately needs.[33] In fact, the country's levels of violent crime were seen as a major reason for the selection of Germany over South Africa to host the 2006 World Cup.[34] And crime in South Africa is expected to increase as the result of widening inequalities, growing unemployment, a population that is getting increasingly younger, an escalating number of orphans who have lost their parents to AIDS, and the recent arrival of *crack* cocaine (called "sweets") to South African cities.[35]

Crime rates in the Republic of Colombia seem to be even higher than those in South Africa, so much so that the U.S. Department of State emphasizes the following to travelers:

> The Department of State warns U.S. citizens against travel to Colombia. Violence by narcoterrorist groups and other criminal elements continues to affect all parts of the country, urban and rural. Citizens of the United States and other countries continue to be the victims of threats, kidnappings, and other violence.[36]

The State Department also cites that despite a 20 percent decline in homicides in Colombia between 2002 and 2003, the 23,000 homicides still exceeded U.S. levels by 40 percent. And Colombia continues to have one of the world's highest kidnapping rates, with a reported 1,827 kidnappings in the 12 months prior to April 2004.[37]

Thinking critically, how does crime in the United States compare with that in Colombia, Brazil, and South Africa, and what do you consider the most dangerous place in the world?

OP-ED

Why would news coverage of crime be up when crime rates are down? The answer can be found in a comment by journalist Lincoln Steffens:

> Every now and then there occurs the phenomenon called a crime wave. New York has such things periodically; other cities have them; and they sweep over the public and nearly drown the lawyers, judges, preachers, and other leading citizens who feel that they must explain these extraordinary outbreaks of lawlessness. Their diagnosis and their remedies are always the same. The disease is lawlessness; the cure is more law, more arrests, swifter trials, and harsher penalties.[38]

These curious and rather cynical comments, written by Steffens 75 years ago, remain pertinent today. Radio, television, and newspaper accounts of lawbreaking and scandal, combined with word-of-mouth reports by victims and their families, are the main sources of the public's knowledge and images of crime. Crime stories do have some impact on newspaper circulation and local television news ratings. As such, crime stories in the media affect ratings and sales, and that's probably why there are so many of them.

More important, however, is the question of why crime rates have dropped. The *UCR* and the NCVS documented the decline in violent crime, and this was certainly talked about in the media. Little public notice, however, was given to the sharply falling rates of property crime. FBI data suggested that from 1984 through 2003, burglary rates were down by 41.5 percent. In fact, the drop in property crimes—which outnumber violent crimes by seven to one—was so large through 2003 that the overall crime rate for the United States was no higher than

those for Australia, Canada, New Zealand, and the Netherlands.

Numerous reasons were offered for the falling rates: improved police tactics, a decline in the teenage population (which is the most crime-prone), greater community involvement in crime prevention, a lessening in the crack epidemic, longer prison sentences, and the strong economy. Most likely, all of these factors combined to reduce crime. But consider this: Perhaps none of these things really mattered; perhaps the downswing was just a natural statistical correction. In other words, crime rates had been so high for so long that they were bound to come down sooner or later. And if that's the case, when will they begin to rise again?

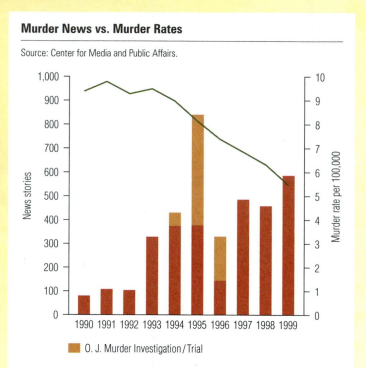

Murder News vs. Murder Rates

Source: Center for Media and Public Affairs.

■ O. J. Murder Investigation/Trial

Note: Murder rate according to the FBI *Uniform Crime Reports*. Number of stories appearing on the ABC, CBS, and NBC evening news casts.

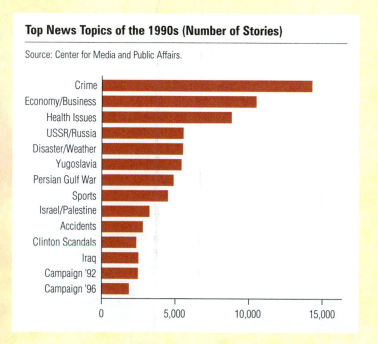

Top News Topics of the 1990s (Number of Stories)

Source: Center for Media and Public Affairs.

Summary

Most of the data on the nature, extent, and trends of crime in the United States come from official crime statistics. Official statistics are collected and compiled by the FBI and published annually as the *Uniform Crime Reports (UCR)*. The *UCR* includes crimes known to the police and arrests. Data are broken down into Part I and Part II offenses, and arrests are subdivided by age, race, and gender. The *UCR* also includes rates of crime, percent changes from year to year, and breakdowns by region, state, and metropolitan area.

Although official statistics are the primary source of crime data, they have numerous shortcomings. Most criminal acts are not reported to the police, and statistical data are subject to concealment, overreporting, nonreporting, and other manipulations. On the other hand, despite these difficulties, *UCR* data are useful for gaining insight into the relative amount of crime and for analyzing crime and arrest trends.

In an effort to determine the parameters of crime that did not appear in official statistics, in 1965 the President's Commission initiated the first national survey of crime victimization ever conducted. Similar surveys have been undertaken since then. These surveys demonstrate that the actual amount of crime is probably several times greater than that estimated in the *UCR*. NCVS and *UCR* data, however, are not fully comparable. The bases of their rates are different, the yardsticks of measurement are different, and crime classifications are not uniform.

Victimization data have numerous useful applications for understanding the characteristics of victims, evaluating the effectiveness of police programs, developing insights into victim−offender relationships, sensitizing the criminal justice system to the needs of the victim, and structuring more focused crime prevention programs. On the other hand, victimization surveys have their shortcomings. They are expensive, and they raise a number of basic methodological issues.

Self-reported data on offenses represent a third source of information on crime. These data reflect the so-called dark figure or unknown crime. The findings of these studies suggest the extent of crime in both "normal" and special populations (such as street drug users), what kinds of crimes are committed that typically remain unknown, and how the official system of crime control may select its cases. Self-report studies, however, have problems of validity and reliability.

Key Terms

Crime Index (105)
crime rate (106)
Part I offenses (105)

Part II offenses (105)
self-reported crime (115)

Uniform Crime Reports (UCR) (102)
victimization surveys (111)

Issues for Discussion

1. What issues of validity and reliability are most apparent with regard to official criminal statistics?
2. Can the *UCR* be improved? How?
3. How might official statistics, victimization data, and self-reported crime data be collected and combined to provide a more accurate picture of crime in the United States?
4. Why is it difficult to use official statistics to make universal claims about crime trends and patterns?
5. Why do you think crime rates are down?
6. Should the media ease up on crime reporting?
7. Is the United States the most violent country in the world?

Media and Literature Resources

Reel Justice includes scenes that can be used to spark discussion about the following topics from this chapter:

The Time Clock

National Crime Victimization Survey

Nonreporting

Uniform Crime Reports. The entire *Uniform Crime Reports* can be found on the Web (*http://www.fbi.gov/ucr/ucr.htm*) and can be either downloaded or printed out.

Self-Reported Crime. Dr. Inciardi, the author of this text-book, has been conducting studies of self-reported crime for more than two decades. A number of these studies have taken place in Miami, Florida, and are summarized in his article "Drug Use and Crime in Miami: An (Almost) Twenty-Year Retrospective," *Substance Use & Misuse* 33 (1998): 1839−1870. For a comprehensive look at the issues in using self-reported data, see J. Junger-Tas and Haen Marshall, "The Self-Report Methodology in Crime Research," *Crime and Justice* 25 (1999): 291−367.

NIBRS and Elderly Victimization. Addressing the limited information available on the elderly and victimization, the authors of the following article developed a model using NIBRS data to show that the elderly have a higher risk of death from assault than do younger people: L. D. Chu and Jess F. Kraus, "Predicting Fatal Assault Among the Elderly Using the National Incident-Based Reporting System Crime Data," *Homicide Studies* 8, 2 (2004): 71–95. See also Kimberly A. McCabe and Sharon S. Gregory, "Elderly Victimization: An Examination Beyond the FBI's Index Crimes," *Research on Aging* 20 (May 1998): 363–373.

National Crime Victimization Survey. The most recent surveys and numerous supplementary analyses are available on the web (*www.ojp .usdoj.gov/bjs/cvict.htm*). See also M. R. Rand and Callie M. Rennison, "True Crime Stories? Accounting for Differences in Our National Crime Indicators," *Chance* 15, 1 (2002): 47–51; this article examines the differences between the UCR and NCVS programs.

Campus Crime. Schools receiving federal funds were required to post tallies of alleged homicides, rapes, assaults, arson, hate crimes, burglaries, liquor law violations, and drug arrests with the U.S. Department of Education. Colleges filing false reports face a $25,000 fine for each misreported figure. Students can view these figures on the Education Department's Web site (*http://ope.ed.gov/security*). For further information regarding the Campus Security Act (later renamed the Jeanne Clery Act) and other campus safety issues, visit *http://www.securityoncampus.org*. This Web site is run by a nonprofit organization started by the parents of Jeanne Clery, for whom the campus safety law is named.

Endnotes

1. "2004 Year in Review," *Media Monitor,* XIX (January/February 2005); "Rural Life Is a Crime Scene on Network News," Center for Media and Public Affairs press release, January 21, 2003; "2000 Year in Review," *Media Monitor,* XV (January/February 2001); "2001 Year in Review," *Media Monitor,* XVI (January/February 2002); "2002 Year in Review," *Media Monitor,* XVII (January/February 2003).
2. Bureau of Justice Statistics, *Criminal Victimization 2003* (Washington, DC: U.S. Department of Justice, 2004).
3. Albert Morris, *What Are the Sources of Knowledge About Crime in the U.S.A.?* United Prison Association of Massachusetts, Bulletin No. 15, November 1965.
4. Sanford J. Ungar, *FBI* (Boston: Little, Brown, 1976), 387.
5. Federal Bureau of Investigation, *Crime in the United States—2003* (Washington, DC: U.S. Government Printing Office, 2004). Throughout this text, these FBI crime reports will be referenced simply as *Uniform Crime Reports* or *UCR.*
6. See James A. Inciardi, "The *Uniform Crime Reports:* Some Considerations on Their Shortcomings and Utility," *Public Data Use* 6 (November 1978): 3–16.
7. *The New York Times,* August 3, 1998, A1, A16.
8. *The New York Times,* January 7, 2000, B1, B3; *The New York Times,* January 8, 2000, B5.
9. D. I. Black, "Production of Crime Rates," *American Sociological Review* 35 (1970): 735–739; *Newsweek,* May 16, 1983, 63.
10. *The Atlanta Journal-Constitution,* February 20, 2004, 1A.
11. *USA Today,* October 4, 2000, 1A.
12. *Structure and Implementation Plan for the Enhanced UCR Program* (Washington, DC: Federal Bureau of Investigation, 1989).
13. Bureau of Justice Statistics, *UCR and NIBRS Participation,* November 17, 2004.
14. President's Commision on Law Enforcement and Administration of Justice, *Crime and Its Impact: An Assessment* (Washington, DC: U.S. Government Printing Office, 1967), 17.
15. Law Enforcement Assistance Administration, *Criminal Victimization in the United States—1977* (Washington, DC: U.S. Government Printing Office, 1979).
16. Bureau of Justice Statistics, *Criminal Victimization—2003* (Washington, DC: Office of Justice Programs, 2004).
17. Thorsten Sellin, *Research Memorandum on Crime in the Depression* (New York: Social Science Research Council, 1937).
18. James S. Wallerstein and Clement J. Wyle, "Our Law-Abiding Law-Breakers," *Probation* 35 (April 1947): 107–118.
19. J. Andenaes, N. Christie, and S. Skirbekk, "A Study in Self-Reported Crime," in *Scandinavian Studies in Criminology,* Scandinavian Research Council on Criminology (Oslo: Universitelsforloget, 1965), 87–88.
20. Louis Newton Robinson, *History and Organization of Criminal Statistics in the United States* (New York: Hart, Schaffner & Marx, 1911).
21. U.S. National Commission on Law Observance and Enforcement, *Report on Criminal Statistics* (Washington, DC: U.S. Government Printing Office, 1931).
22. President's Commission on Law Enforcement and Administration of Justice, *The Challenge of Crime in a Free Society* (Washington, DC: U.S. Government Printing Office, 1967), 123–137.
23. National Advisory Commission on Criminal Justice Standards and Goals, *A National Strategy to Reduce Crime* (Washington, DC: U.S. Government Printing Office, 1973); *The New York Times,* November 19, 1984, B11.
24. See *http://www.drugabuse.gov/NIDAHome.html.*
25. Madrid *El País,* September 15, 2003, 9.
26. Home Office Press Office, "International Homicide Statistics," July 2003.
27. See, for example Institute for Security Studies, *Criminal Justice Monitor,* March 2005; "Taming an Urban Monster—Brazil," *The Economist,* January 27, 2005; United Nations Office of Drugs and Crime, *United Nations Survey on Crime Trends,* April 25, 2005; Marc Lacey, "U.N. Study Says Nairobi Is Inundated with Crime," *The New York Times,* November 29, 2001, p. A13; Ricardo Soca, "Criminal Force," *Latinamerica Press,* December 30, 2002, 4.
28. International Monetary Fund Staff, *Brazil: Selected Issues and Statistical Appendix* (Washington, DC: IMF, 2003).
29. São Paulo State Secretary of Health, *Statistical Reports,* May 2003.
30. *The New York Times,* September 8, 2002, 3.
31. James A. Inciardi, Hilary L. Surratt, and Paulo R. Telles, *Sex, Drugs, and HIV/AIDS in Brazil* (Boulder, CO: Westview Press, 2000).
32. Crime Information Analysis Center, *The Incidence of Serious Crime in South Africa* (Pretoria: South African Police Service, 2003).

33. *Durban Daily News,* July 11, 2000, 5.
34. Capetown *Cape News,* July 7, 2000, 6.
35. *The New York Times,* May 15, 2000, A1; *Minneapolis Star Tribune,* August 19, 2000, 12A; *The New York Times,* August 5, 2000, A3; "South Africa's President Mbeki Faces Huge Crime Challenge," *Reuters News Service,* June 13, 2000.
36. U.S. Department of State, "Travel Warning—Colombia," March 3, 2004.
37. U.S. Department of State, "Colombia—Consular Information Sheet," October 13, 2004.
38. Lincoln Steffens, *The Autobiography of Lincoln Steffens* (New York: Harcourt Brace, 1931), 285.

© The New Yorker Collection 1995 Mike Maslin from CartoonBank.com. All Rights Reserved.

THE PROCESS OF JUSTICE: AN OVERVIEW

LEARNING OBJECTIVES

After reading this chapter, you should be able to answer the following questions:

1. What are the differences between inquisitorial and adversary justice?

2. What are the meanings of "due process of law," and what are the differences between substantive and procedural due process?

3. What is the Bill of Rights?

4. What is meant by the "nationalization" of the Bill of Rights? What were the significant Supreme Court decisions associated with the nationalization process?

5. What was the significance of *Barron* v. *Baltimore?*

6. What are the various stages of the criminal justice process, and what occurs at each stage?

7. Is the criminal justice process a system or a "nonsystem"?

8. What are rape shield statutes?

9. What is the USA Patriot Act?

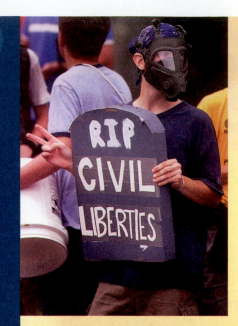

WASHINGTON, DC—The Bush administration, which refers to the USA Patriot Act as one of the most important tools in the war on terrorism, has been using the law in criminal investigations that have little or nothing to do with terrorists. The expanded government authority provided by the law is being used to investigate suspected drug traffickers, white-collar criminals, extortionists, child pornographers, money launderers, and even corrupt foreign leaders. Justice Department officials argue that they are simply using all the means available to them for pursuing crimi-nals—terrorists or otherwise. Critics of the administration counter that such use of the Patriot Act is evidence that the administration is using terrorism as a guise to pursue a broader law enforcement agenda. Others argue heatedly that the Patriot Act was crafted in haste, that it gives the government far too much power, and that it is trampling on the Bill of Rights.[1]

Within the context of this argument, what is the USA Patriot Act, and why is it so controversial? Is it really an infringement on the Bill of Rights?

A Raleigh, North Carolina man demonstrating against the USA Patriot Act.

Given these crucial questions, this chapter examines the Bill of Rights and the concept of due process of law and how it emerged in American jurisprudence. In addition, the chapter introduces the various stages of the criminal justice process. A more complete analysis of the process is presented in later chapters.

Criminal Due Process

No person shall be . . . deprived of life, liberty, or property, without due process of law.
— FROM THE FIFTH AMENDMENT

. . . Nor shall any State deprive any person of life, liberty, or property, without due process of law.
— FROM THE FOURTEENTH AMENDMENT

To this day, no one knows precisely what the words "due process of law" meant to the draftsmen of the Fifth Amendment, and no one knows what these words meant to the draftsmen of the Fourteenth Amendment.
— ARTHUR SUTHERLAND, 1965

Through the ages, justice processes have taken numerous and varied forms. During the early centuries of Christianity, for example, trials were not considered necessary for thieves caught in the act of stealing. If they were poor and could not pay even the smallest fine, they were simply put to death with little formality. In doubtful cases, however, some degree of innocence or guilt had to be determined. One way of accomplishing this was the "ordeal by water," which was carried out by a priest.

Trial by Ordeal

A cauldron of boiling water was placed in the center of the church. Spectators, who were required to be fasting and "abstinent from their wives during the previous night," assembled in two rows on either side of the church and were blessed by the priest.

While they prayed that God would "make clear the whole truth," the priest bandaged the arm of the accused person. Into the bottom of a vat of boiling water the priest dropped a small stone.

If the accused were to undergo only the single ordeal, he had simply to place his hand into the water up to his wrist; but if the more serious triple ordeal had been prescribed, he had to plunge his entire forearm to the bottom of the cauldron and pluck out the stone. After 3 days, the bandages were removed, and evidence of scalding was deemed proof of guilt.[2]

This ordeal by water, which was not formally abolished in England until 1219, could be replaced by similar tests. The accused could be ordered to walk barefoot over red-hot plowshares, place his hand in a glove of near-molten metal, or walk three paces carrying in his bare hands an iron bar reddened with heat. In these cases as well, it was believed that God would make known the truth and that if the accused was innocent he would not be burned.

For those who were not friendless, guilt or innocence could be determined by *compurgation.* Here the accused would assemble a number of his peers who would make an oath with him that he was innocent. Such oaths were accepted, although perjury must have been rampant.

Inquisitorial versus Adversarial Justice

Trials by ordeal, or perhaps by battle, were the cornerstone of the **inquisitorial system** of justice. Under this system the accused person was considered guilty until proven innocent. Inquisitorial justice became manifest when some form of divine intervention spared the accused from pain, suffering, or death, or when the accused readily admitted his or her guilt, usually after torture or other forms of corporal punishment. This system—which now might more properly be called the **inquiry system**—still exists in a modified form in most countries that did not evolve from English or American colonial rule. In the modern inquiry court, all the participants—judge, prosecutor, defense attorney, defendant, and witnesses—are obliged to cooperate with the court in its inquiry into the crime. It is believed that the truth will emerge out of this inquiry (an inquisition, in a value-free sense of the term).

By contrast, American judicial process reflects the **adversary system,** in which the accused person is presumed to be innocent and the burden of proof is placed on the court. In the adversary court, the judge is an impartial arbiter or referee between adversaries—the prosecution and defense. The opposing sides fight within strict rules of procedure, and it is believed that the side with the truth will win. Adversary proceedings are grounded in the right of the defendant to refrain from hurting himself or herself (as opposed to the lack of such a right in an inquiry court) and in the notion of **due process of law,** a concept that asserts fundamental principles of justice and implies the administration of laws that do not violate individual rights.

The Law of the Land

During the Middle Ages—when the championing of the weak was held up as an ideal and when valor, courtesy, generosity, and dexterity in arms were the summit of any man's attainment—inquisitorial justice was dominant. "Due process" meant nothing more than adhering to the *law of the land,* and torture was the most common method of ascertaining guilt. Periods of active torture were usually preceded by imprisonment in a foul dungeon or small cell. Defendants were ill-fed and left in an uncomfortable and half-starved condition to contemplate the infinitely worse treatment that awaited them.

Eventually, the defendant was brought to a torture room to face his or her accusers and those in charge of the gruesome ceremonies. A mechanism called the *strappado* was used in the early phases of torture. The hands of the accused were tied behind his back and then drawn up by a rope and pulley, thus wrenching the shoulders from their sockets without leaving outward marks. Later phases of torture included the application of thumbscrews or "Spanish boots," through which pieces of wood were pressed

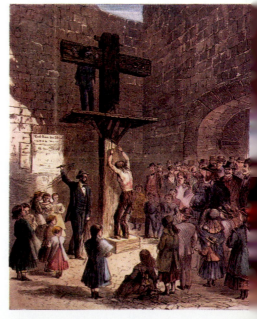

The public whipping post and pillory at New Castle, Delaware, 1868, one of the last states to continue the practice of public punishment.

down on thumbs or shins in such a way as to crush both flesh and bone. Also common was the German *schnure,* in which a piece of rope was sawed back and forth across the limbs of the accused until the flesh was rubbed away, exposing the bone.

If confessions could not be forced by these and numerous other exercises in horror, the final stage of torture, which typically led to death, was initiated. Devices used in this stage included spiked barrels and cradles in which the accused was rocked back and forth, a spiked chair to which the accused was tightly strapped, or the infamous iron maiden. The latter was a hollow statue constructed of wood or iron and braced with metal strips. Long spikes were attached to the inside, and when the accused was placed inside and the vessel closed, the spikes entered the eyes and body, producing certain death. During the Middle Ages this was viewed as "due process," because the use of torture for eliciting confessions was sanctioned by existing law.

The early 19th-century British case of *Ashford* v. *Thornton* illustrates a less gruesome, though equally curious, reflection of early conceptions of due process.[3] Ashford appeared before the king's justices, charging Thornton with murder. He swore that Thornton had raped and drowned Mary Ashford, the accuser's young sister. The sheriff found Thornton and brought him to court, and the justices ordered him to make a plea. "Not guilty," he maintained, "and I am ready to defend the same with my body." He then drew off his glove and threw it onto the floor of the court, a signal that he was demanding trial by battle. It would be his life against Ashford's, and if Thornton won, he would be judged innocent. Ashford argued that the circumstances were so exceptional that Thornton should be denied the right to defend himself in battle, but the justices were not persuaded. They ruled that the established procedure for cases of this kind must be followed—that is, trial by battle. Ashford refused to fight, and due process followed its course: The judgment was that Thornton should go free.

The distinguished attorney and legal writer Charles Rembar points out that the case of *Ashford* v. *Thornton* did not occur during the age of the Norman or Plantagenet kings but less than two centuries ago.[4] The year was 1818, almost 30 years after the United States Constitution and the Bill of Rights had been written.

But even in the United States, the concept of due process was vague at best. The framers of the Constitution had stated in the Fifth Amendment that persons shall not be deprived of life, liberty, or property "without due process of law." The due process guarantee was repeated when the Fourteenth Amendment was added to the Constitution in 1868. But what was intended by these words?

The Bill of Rights

A bill of rights is what people are entitled to against every government on earth.

—THOMAS JEFFERSON, 1787

During the first Congress, in June 1789, 2 years after the signing of the Constitution, James Madison of Virginia, who would later become the fourth president of the United States, proposed a dozen amendments to the Constitution. Congress approved 10 of them in September 1791, and they took effect on December 15 after having been ratified by the required number of states. These first 10 amendments to the Constitution have become known as the **Bill of Rights** (see Exhibit 5.1).*

The significance of the Bill of Rights is that it restricts government, rather than individuals and private groups. It was added to the Constitution at the insistence of those who feared a strong central government. More than a century and a half later, U.S. Supreme Court Chief Justice Earl Warren made this comment:

> The men of our First Congress . . . knew that whatever form it may assume, government is potentially as dangerous a thing as it is a necessary one. They knew that power must be lodged somewhere to prevent anarchy within and conquest from without, but that this power could be abused to the detriment of their liberties.[5]

Within the Bill of Rights, the *First Amendment* prohibits laws and practices that have the effect of establishing an official religion. It also protects freedom of speech, the press, religion, and assembly, and it guarantees the right to petition the government

*Most authorities refer to the first 10 amendments as the Bill of Rights; others include only the first eight or nine.

LAW & CRIMINAL JUSTICE | EXHIBIT 5.1

The Bill of Rights

I

Congress shall make no law respecting an establishment of religion, or prohibiting the free exercise thereof; or abridging the freedom of speech, or of the press; or the right of the people peaceably to assemble, and to petition the government for a redress of grievances.

II

A well regulated militia being necessary to the security of a free state, the right of the people to keep and bear arms shall not be infringed.

III

No soldier shall, in time of peace, be quartered in any house without the consent of the owner, nor in time of war, but in a manner to be prescribed by law.

IV

The right of the people to be secure in their persons, houses, papers, and effects, against unreasonable searches and seizures, shall not be violated, and no warrants shall issue but upon probable cause, supported by oath or affirmation, and particularly describing the place to be searched, and the persons or things to be seized.

V

No person shall be held to answer for a capital or otherwise infamous crime, unless on a presentment or indictment of a grand jury, except in cases arising in the land or naval forces or in the militia when in actual service in time of war or public danger; nor shall any person be subject for the same offense to be twice put in jeopardy of life or limb; nor shall be compelled in any criminal case to be a witness against himself, nor be deprived of life, liberty, or property, without due process

of law; nor shall private property be taken for public use without just compensation.

VI

In all criminal prosecutions the accused shall enjoy the right to a speedy and public trial, by an impartial jury of the State and district wherein the crime shall have been committed, which district shall have been previously ascertained by law, and to be informed of the nature and cause of the accusation; to be confronted with the witnesses against him; to have compulsory process for obtaining witnesses in his favor, and to have the assistance of counsel for his defense.

VII

In suits at common law, where the value in controversy shall exceed twenty dollars, the right of trial by jury shall be preserved, and no fact tried by a jury shall be otherwise reexamined in any court of the United States, than according to the rules of the common law.

VIII

Excessive bail shall not be required, nor excessive fines imposed, nor cruel and unusual punishments inflicted.

IX

The enumeration in the Constitution of certain rights shall not be construed to deny or disparage others retained by the people.

X

The powers not delegated to the United States by the Constitution, nor prohibited by it to the States, are reserved to the States respectively, or to the people.

---

for redress of grievances. The *Second Amendment* guarantees the right to keep and bear arms as part of a well-regulated militia (see Exhibit 5.2); the *Third* forbids the government to quarter soldiers in people's homes; and the *Fourth* protects a person's right to be secure in his or her person, house, papers, and effects against unreasonable searches and seizures.

The *Fifth Amendment* requires indictments for proceedings in serious criminal offenses; it forbids compelling an individual to incriminate him- or herself or trying a person twice for the same offense ("double jeopardy"); it also contains the initial constitutional statement on "due process of law." The *Sixth Amendment* sets out certain requirements for criminal trials, including the defendant's right to counsel, notification of the charges, a speedy and public trial before an impartial jury in the jurisdiction in which the crime was allegedly committed, and the related rights to confront hostile witnesses and to have compulsory processes for obtaining defense witnesses. The *Seventh Amendment* guarantees the right to a jury trial in common law civil suits involving $20 or more; and the *Eighth* forbids excessive bail, excessive fines, and cruel and unusual punishments.

The *Ninth Amendment* has never been cited as the sole basis of a U.S. Supreme Court decision, and there is a long-running debate over what the nation's founders intended it to mean.[6] On its face, it states that the enumeration of specific rights else-

Understanding the First Amendment

When asked rights are guaranteed by the First Amendment, most Americans only think of freedom of speech. Responses of a nationwide sample were:

Source: New England Research Associates

Identifying the Bill of Rights

To coincide with the 200th anniversary of the ratification of the Bill of Rights, the American Bar Association commissioned a nationwide poll to determine what proportion of adults could identify the content and purpose of this historic document. Multiple-choice questions were provided, and the answers given were as follows:

1. What is the Bill of Rights?
   a. The Preamble to the U.S. Constitution — 28%
   b. The Constitution's first 10 amendments — 33%
   c. Any rights bill passed by Congress — 22%
   d. A message of rebellion from the Founding Fathers to the British monarchy — 7%
   e. Don't know — 10%
2. What was the Bill's original purpose?
   a. To limit abuse by the federal government — 9%
   b. To limit abuses by states — 1%
   c. To ensure quality for all citizens — 33%
   d. All of the above — 55%
   e. Don't know — 2%

The proportion of correct answers (1 b and 2 a) suggest that most Americans don't know much about the Constitution. ∎

Constitutions should consist only of general provisions; the reason is that they must necessarily be permanent and they cannot calculate for the possible change of things.

—ALEXANDER HAMILTON, 1788

where in the Constitution should not be taken to deny or disparage other rights, which are not enumerated but are retained by the people. The *Tenth Amendment* clearly was designed to protect states' rights and guard against excessive federal power; but it, too, is subject to a variety of interpretations by judges and legal scholars.

Because no rights are absolute, and because they are subject to reasonable regulation through law, *the original intent of due process was not self-evident.* Madison expected the federal courts to play the major role in implementing them, and he clearly emphasized this point to his fellow members of Congress:

> Independent tribunals of justice will consider themselves . . . the guardians of those rights; they will be an impenetrable bulwark against every assumption of power in the Legislative or Executive; they will naturally be led to resist every encroachment upon rights expressly stipulated . . . by the declaration of rights.[7]

During the decades immediately following the ratification of the Bill of Rights, the Supreme Court had little occasion to apply the guarantees of due process. Slavery, for example, was viewed as a matter of property rights, not human rights; and the constitutional guarantees of civil liberties and due process placed restrictions on government only at the federal level. However, the passage of the Alien and Sedition Acts in 1798 created the potential for constitutional challenge. These four acts were passed by a Congress controlled by the Federalists and were targeted at the Jeffersonians, who were considered to be pro-French. The laws increased the residency requirement for naturalization as a U.S. citizen from 5 years to 14. They also provided for deportation of aliens by the president and for the arrest of editors, writers, and speakers charged with attacking the government. Under the terms of these stringent acts, scores of Jeffersonian leaders and supporters were arrested, convicted, and imprisoned—in direct violation of the First Amendment guarantee of free speech—yet the arrests were never challenged before the Supreme Court.

Nationalization of the Bill of Rights

In 1833, the Supreme Court made it quite clear that the Bill of Rights provided no protection against state or local action, but only against federal authority. In ***Barron v. Baltimore,***[8] the owner of a wharf challenged a local action that seriously impaired the value of his wharf by creating shoals and shallows around it. Barron maintained that this represented a "taking" of his property without just compensation, in violation of the Fifth Amendment. Chief Justice John Marshall ruled, however, that the Bill of Rights had been adopted to secure individual rights only against actions of the federal government.

Barron v. *Baltimore* seemed to have closed the door on the argument that the Bill of Rights should provide protection against abuses of individual rights by state and local governments. However, with the ratification of the Fourteenth Amendment to the Constitution in 1868, it once again became possible to argue that the Bill of Rights should be understood to restrict the powers of the state and local governments as well as the federal government. Section 1 of the amendment includes the following statement:

> No State shall make or enforce any law which shall abridge the privileges or immunities of citizens of the United States; nor shall any State deprive any person of life, liberty, or property, without due process of law; nor deny to any person within its jurisdiction the equal protection of the laws.

Hurtado v. California Legal historians disagree over whether Congress intended the Fourteenth Amendment to make all the provisions of the Bill of Rights binding on the states.[9] In its first decisions after ratification of the Fourteenth Amendment, the Supreme Court rejected the notion that the due process clause ("nor shall any State deprive any person of life, liberty, or property, without due process of law") had "incorporated" the Bill of Rights, thus making each of the provisions of the Bill of Rights applicable to state and local governments. For example, in *Hurtado* v. *California* (1884),[10] the Court declared that the states were under no obligation to follow the Fifth Amendment's requirement that individuals prosecuted for a capital or "otherwise infamous

LAW & CRIMINAL JUSTICE | EXHIBIT 5.2

The Second Amendment

> A well regulated Militia being necessary to the security of a free state, the right of the people to keep and bear arms shall not be infringed.

Otherwise known as the Second Amendment, these may be the most argued and misunderstood 26 words in the history of the United States Constitution. But what do these words really mean? Is there a constitutional right or isn't there? Opinions differ. Pro-gun advocates interpret the amendment phrase by phrase, and quite literally, too, concluding that the right to bear arms is self-evident. Gun control advocates argue the reverse: that the amendment is distorted when split into phrases; that taken as a whole, it restricts the right to activities that the state determines necessary to maintain a militia.

Both historical and legal research, however, suggests something that is relatively clear. It would appear that the Second Amendment was spurred by the early colonists' fear that military forces composed of professional soldiers—such as those used by King George III—were not to be trusted. Federalist James Madison drafted the Bill of Rights for presentation at the first Congress, but his writing of the Second Amendment was ultimately restructured into its present form in order to place greater emphasis on the militia purpose in dealing with the right to keep and bear arms and to diminish the broad individual powers of Madison's original version.

The federal courts, in interpreting the Second Amendment, have created a well-settled principle of law that says the right to bear arms was not extended to each and every individual but, rather, was expressly limited to maintaining effective state militia. During the past half-century, the courts have ruled repeatedly on Second Amendment cases, brought primarily by gun advocates seeking greater ownership rights. In an explicit comment on the amendment, a federal district court ruled as follows in the 1971 case of *Stevens* v. *U.S.*:

> Since the Second Amendment applies only to the right of the State to maintain a militia and not to the individual's right to bear arms, there can be no serious claim to any express constitutional right of an individual to possess a firearm.

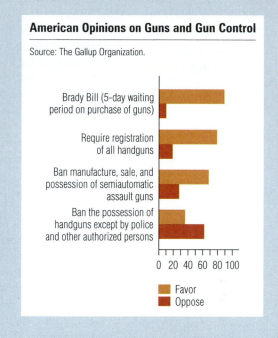

American Opinions on Guns and Gun Control

Source: The Gallup Organization.

Bar chart showing Favor/Oppose percentages (scale 0 to 100) for:
- Brady Bill (5-day waiting period on purchase of guns)
- Require registration of all handguns
- Ban manufacture, sale, and possession of semiautomatic assault guns
- Ban the possession of handguns except by police and other authorized persons

Legend: Favor / Oppose

More recently, the Supreme Court refused to hear a challenge to a 1984 Illinois Supreme Court ruling that upheld the right of an Illinois town to ban the sale and possession of handguns. At the same time, other federal courts consistently have ruled that the Second Amendment is not an entitlement to gun ownership. In 1976, the 6th Circuit Court of Appeals stated in *U.S.* v. *Warin* that the supposition that the Second Amendment is concerned with the rights of individuals rather than those of states was erroneous.

As a final point, most Americans support gun control—even gun owners. In a recent nationwide Harris Poll, 69% of all adults and 57% of gun owners were in favor of some form of stricter gun laws.

Where do you stand?

---

crime" must first be indicted by a grand jury. The practical result of *Hurtado* was that California was permitted to use the practice of "information" (a process in which the prosecutor merely submits the charges in an affidavit of evidence, supported by sworn statements) as a substitute for the more time-consuming and difficult requirement of obtaining an indictment from a grand jury. But the most important aspect of the *Hurtado* decision was the Court's holding that the Fourteenth Amendment's due process clause did not obligate the states or localities to adhere to the specific provisions of the Bill of Rights. (The facts of the *Hurtado* case are presented in Chapter 12.)

Only one Supreme Court justice dissented from the Court's position in *Hurtado* v. *California*. Justice John Marshall Harlan, often referred to as "the great dissenter," insisted that all of the rights in the Bill of Rights are "fundamental" and that there was ample evidence that Congress had intended the Fourteenth Amendment to make each and every provision of the Bill of Rights binding upon the states. In his dissents in *Hur-*

tado and several other notable cases,[11] Justice Harlan unsuccessfully endeavored to convince a majority of his colleagues that "no judicial tribunal has authority to say that [the Bill of Rights] may be abridged by the States."[12]

We need to take a look at it [the Constitution] and maybe from time to time we should curtail some of those rights.

— LEROY MARTIN, CHICAGO
POLICE SUPERINTENDENT

Gitlow* v. *New York Justice Harlan died in 1911, not knowing that arguments for "incorporating" the Bill of Rights would be largely accepted in future Supreme Court decisions. The first step toward incorporating most of the provisions of the Bill of Rights came in 1925 in the famous case of ***Gitlow* v. *New York*.**[13] Benjamin Gitlow, a member of the Socialist party, had been convicted of violating a New York sedition law because he had printed and distributed some 16,000 copies of the "Left Wing Manifesto." This tract called for the overthrow of the United States government by "class action of the proletariat in any form" and urged the proletariat to "organize its own state for the coercion and suppression of the bourgeoisie."

Gitlow appealed his conviction to the Supreme Court, contending that the New York statute unconstitutionally deprived him of his First Amendment right to freedom of speech. The Court sustained the conviction, holding that free speech was not an absolute right and that Gitlow's manifesto fell within the category of speech that could properly be prohibited by law. Over the dissenting votes of Justices Louis Brandeis and Oliver Wendell Holmes, both of whom argued that political speech should be barred only when it created a "clear and present danger" to the security of the nation, the majority of the justices reasoned that Gitlow's tract could properly be suppressed even if it merely contained language that might have the effect of inciting violent attempts to overthrow the government (the so-called bad-tendency test).

Although Benjamin Gitlow lost his effort to overturn his conviction, he won one of his other arguments—a victory that would have an enormous influence on the evolution of the American criminal justice system. To convince the justices to hear his appeal, Gitlow had asserted that the First Amendment rights of free speech and free press were enforceable against the states. If the Court did not accept this proposition, it would lack any legal basis for accepting the case for review and considering the merits of Gitlow's First Amendment arguments. But in a seemingly casual passage in his majority opinion, Justice Edward T. Sanford made judicial history by formally accepting the principle of incorporation of the free speech and free press provisions of the Bill of Rights:

> For present purposes we may and do assume that freedom of speech and of the press— which are protected by the First Amendment from abridgement by Congress—are among the fundamental personal rights and "liberties" protected by the due process clause of the Fourteenth Amendment from impairment by the States.

It soon became apparent that this decision was the first step in a case-by-case process that would significantly expand the Supreme Court's authority to protect individual rights against unconstitutional acts of state and local government officials. In 1927, a unanimous Supreme Court confirmed the incorporation of freedom of speech in the case of *Fiske* v. *Kansas*.[14] Four years later, in *Near* v. *Minnesota*,[15] the Court again declared that freedom of the press was enforceable against the states when it struck down the so-called Minnesota Gag Law as an infringement of the freedom of the press guaranteed by the Fourteenth Amendment.

Powell* v. *Alabama In 1932, the Supreme Court overturned the convictions of seven indigent, illiterate black youths who had been convicted of the rapes of two white women after a raucous trial in an Alabama courtroom without the opportunity to consult with a defense attorney. The case was *Powell* v. *Alabama*,[16] the first of the notorious Scottsboro Boys cases, and the Court's 7-to-2 holding made it obligatory for the states to provide defense counsel in capital cases (that is, cases subject to the death penalty) in which indigent defendants faced such disadvantages as illiteracy, ignorance, and extreme community hostility. Although the *Powell* ruling affected only certain types of capital trials, it represented at least partial incorporation of the Sixth Amend-

The governor of Alabama and New York attorney Samuel Leibowitz conferring with seven of the nine "Scottsboro Boys."

ment's right-to-counsel clause. (See Chapter 11 for a more detailed examination of the Scottsboro Boys cases and the evolution of the right to counsel.)

Palko v. Connecticut

Palko v. Connecticut   The next provisions of the Bill of Rights to be incorporated were the First Amendment's guarantees of freedom of religion,[17] freedom of assembly, and freedom to petition the government for a redress of grievances.[18] By 1937, the process of incorporation was well under way. But many questions remained unanswered. Should all the provisions of the Bill of Rights be made binding upon the states, as Justice Harlan had argued in 1884? Were only certain provisions worthy of incorporation? If so, what principles should the Court apply in deciding which provisions to incorporate? What was needed was an opportunity to explore more fully the legal and philosophical issues involved.

That opportunity came in the historic 1937 case of *Palko* v. *Connecticut*.[19] The state of Connecticut had charged Frank Palko with first-degree murder for the shooting deaths of two policemen. However, the jury chose to convict Palko of second-degree murder—a decision that resulted in a sentence of life imprisonment but spared Palko from the death penalty that surely would have followed a conviction for murder in the first degree. Undaunted, the prosecutor, citing a Connecticut statute that permitted prosecutorial appeals based on an "error of law to the prejudice of the state," sought and won a retrial on the original first-degree charges. At the second trial, the unfortunate Palko was promptly convicted and sentenced to die in Connecticut's electric chair. After losing all of his appeals in the state courts, he and his attorneys appealed to the U.S. Supreme Court on the grounds that his second trial constituted a violation of the Fifth Amendment protection against double jeopardy and that the Fifth Amendment was binding upon the states as a result of the Fourteenth Amendment's due process clause. (See Chapter 12 for more discussion of double jeopardy.)

There was—and is—no question that Frank Palko's retrial and conviction had violated the double jeopardy clause. In a majority opinion written by Justice Benjamin Cardozo, however, the Court ruled against his claims and Palko was subsequently electrocuted. Ironically, it would be reasonable to say that Frank Palko did not die in vain. For Justice Cardozo's majority opinion laid the foundation—a series of guidelines and principles—that would eventually lead to the incorporation not only of the double jeopardy clause but of nearly all the other key provisions of the Bill of Rights.

Whatever is forbidden by the Fifth Amendment is forbidden by the Fourteenth also.

— FROM FRANK PALKO'S APPEAL TO THE U.S. SUPREME COURT IN 1937

What do you want? Blood?

— SUPREME COURT JUSTICE PIERCE
BUTLER DURING ORAL ARGUMENT
IN *PALKO*, TO THE STATE ATTORNEY
REPRESENTING CONNECTICUT

Our recent cases have thoroughly rejected the *Palko* notion that the basic constitutional rights can be denied by the states.

— JUSTICE THURGOOD MARSHALL
IN *BENTON V. MARYLAND*, 32 YEARS
AFTER FRANK PALKO WAS
EXECUTED

A Second Amendment Sisters rally on the grounds of the Washington Monument.

At the heart of Justice Cardozo's opinion was his rejection of the notion of total incorporation and an effort to establish what has been called the "Honor Roll of Superior Rights." Cardozo wrote eloquently of "those fundamental principles of liberty and justice which lie at the base of all our civil and political institutions." He cited freedom of speech as the cardinal example of a "fundamental right," stressing that the right to speak freely "is the matrix, the indispensable condition, of nearly every other form of freedom." Justice Cardozo also cited freedom of the press and the Fifth Amendment's prohibition of governmental seizure of private property without just compensation (the so-called eminent domain clause) as examples of fundamental rights in a democratic society.

At the other end of the continuum of rights were "formal" rights that are admirable and worthy of respect but without which "justice would not perish." As examples, Cardozo cited the Sixth Amendment right to trial by jury and the Fifth Amendment right to be indicted by a grand jury when charged with "a capital or otherwise infamous crime." Such rights, he explained,

> are not of the essence of a scheme of ordered liberty. To abolish them is not to violate a principle of justice so rooted in the traditions and conscience of our people as to be ranked as fundamental.

Justice Cardozo next turned to the Fifth Amendment protection against compulsory self-incrimination. This too was not a "fundamental" right, he asserted, because "justice would not perish if the accused were subject to a duty to respond to orderly inquiry." Having set forth the standards to be applied, Cardozo finally posed the question that would determine the fate of Frank Palko: Did Connecticut's denial of Palko's Fifth Amendment protection against double jeopardy violate those "fundamental principles of liberty and justice which lie at the base of all our civil and political institutions"?

He concluded that the answer was no. The state of Connecticut wasn't trying to harass and wear down Palko by repeatedly charging him with the same crime; the authorities were merely asking that "the case against him . . . go on until there shall be a trial free from the corrosion of substantial legal error." This, Cardozo asserted, was no great affront to fundamental principles of justice. Thus the double jeopardy clause failed to make the Honor Roll of Superior Rights, thereby leaving the states free to pass laws in violation of the Fifth Amendment's command that no person shall "be subject for the same offense to be twice put in the jeopardy of life or limb."

Justice Cardozo's distinctions between "fundamental" rights, on the other hand, are still in effect. The criteria set forth in *Palko* are firmly in place and unlikely ever to be modified or transformed. In fact, Justice Cardozo's Honor Roll itself changed only twice between 1937 and 1961. In 1947, the Court added the First Amendment's requirement of "separation of church and state" to the list of rights that apply to the states as an element of the Fourteenth Amendment's due process clause.[20] One year later, the Sixth Amendment's guarantee of the right to a "public trial" was incorporated, thus barring the states from conducting trials and sentencings in secret.[21]

The Criminal Law "Revolution"   By the early 1960s, the composition of the Supreme Court had changed and so had the beliefs and values of the American people. Under Chief Justice Earl Warren, who was appointed by President Eisenhower in 1953, the Supreme Court made it clear that constitutional rights were not static concepts, frozen in 18th-century notions of justice and fairness. The protections of the Bill of Rights, according to Chief Justice Warren, "must draw [their] meaning from evolving standards of decency that mark the progress of a maturing society."[22]

The year 1961 marks the beginning of what many legal scholars call "the criminal law revolution." Throughout the 1960s, the Supreme Court, applying the guiding principles set forth by Justice Cardozo in *Palko,* greatly expanded the Honor Roll of Superior Rights. By 1969, almost all of the criminal law–related provisions of the Bill of Rights had been made binding upon the states as elements of Fourteenth Amendment due process.

In the historic 1961 case of *Mapp* v. *Ohio,*[23] the Supreme Court declared that both the Fourth Amendment's prohibition of "unreasonable searches and seizures" and the exclusionary rule (prohibiting the use of illegally seized evidence in a criminal trial) are applicable to the states (see Chapter 8). The Eighth Amendment's ban on cruel and unusual punishments was incorporated in 1962,[24] and the Sixth Amendment's right to counsel was imposed on the states 1 year later in the famous case of *Gideon* v. *Wainwright* (see Chapter 11).[25] In 1964, the Fifth Amendment's protection against self-incrimination was incorporated,[26] and in 1965, the Sixth Amendment right to confront hostile witnesses was given the same status.[27] In 1966, *Parker* v. *Gladden* incorporated the Sixth Amendment right to an impartial jury.[28] The year 1967 saw two Sixth Amendment protections added to the Honor Roll: the guarantee of a speedy trial[29] and the right to compulsory processes for obtaining defense witnesses.[30]

The process of nationalizing the Bill of Rights reached its climax in two decisions announced shortly before the end of the Warren Court era. In 1968, the Court declared that the Sixth Amendment's guarantee of trial by jury applies to state criminal trials involving serious offenses.[31] And in the 1969 case of *Benton* v. *Maryland,*[32] the justices finally ruled that the time had come to make the Fifth Amendment ban on double jeopardy binding upon the states. The Court ruled that the provision against double jeopardy is a "fundamental right that was implicit in the concept of ordered liberty." This decision overruled *Palko* v. *Connecticut* (32 years too late for Frank Palko) and completed—for now—the process of nationalizing the Bill of Rights.

Since *Benton,* the Supreme Court has not incorporated any more of the specific provisions of the Bill of Rights. However, it is worth mentioning that in 1965, in **Griswold** v. **Connecticut,** the Court incorporated the right to "privacy"—a right that is not specifically cited in the Bill of Rights (or anywhere else in the U.S. Constitution).[33] This ruling overturned a Connecticut law that made it a crime for any person, married or single, to use any kind of contraceptive. In the majority opinion written by Justice William Douglas, the Court reasoned that a right to privacy is implicit in the Constitution as a result of "zones of privacy" created by the "liberty" safeguards in the due process clauses of the Fifth and Fourteenth Amendments and by the "penumbras" (rights guaranteed by implication) surrounding the First, Third, Fourth, Fifth, and Ninth Amendments.

The question of whether it was proper for the Court to find a right to privacy in the Constitution remains controversial. Certainly, the most famous application of this newly discovered right to privacy came in January 1973 with the announcement of the Court's decision in *Roe* v. *Wade.*[34] In that decision the Supreme Court held that the right of privacy rendered unconstitutional all state laws that made it a crime or otherwise restricted a woman's right to obtain an abortion in the first 3 months of pregnancy. On the other hand, in 1986, in *Bowers* v. *Hardwick,*[35] the Court held that this same right to privacy could not be used to invalidate state laws making it a crime for consenting adults to engage in homosexual sodomy in the privacy of their own homes. In 2003, however, in the case of **Lawrence v. Texas,**[36] the Supreme Court overturned the decision in *Bowers* v. *Hardwick.* Thus, at this point, it seems safe to say that a right to privacy has been found to be implicit in the Constitution and enforceable against the states but that the precise scope of this right will have to be decided on a case-by-case basis.

Due Process of Law in the Early 2000s

Currently, nearly all the provisions of the Bill of Rights as well as the right of privacy are binding upon the states as elements of the Fourteenth Amendment's due process clause. The easiest way to remember what is and is not incorporated is to list the rights that are *not* binding upon the states. Of the first eight amendments (those that refer to the specific rights of individuals), these are the only provisions that have not been incorporated:

1. The Second Amendment right to bear arms as part of a well-regulated militia.
2. The Third Amendment protection against involuntary quartering of soldiers.
3. The Fifth Amendment protection against being prosecuted for "a capital, or otherwise infamous crime, unless on a presentment or indictment of a grand jury".
4. The Seventh Amendment right to a jury trial in cases involving more than $20.
5. The Eighth Amendment protection against excessive bail.
6. The Eighth Amendment protection against excessive fines.

Later chapters of this book trace the process by which incorporation has occurred in greater detail in such areas as self-incrimination and search and seizure (Chapter 8), the right to counsel (Chapter 11), and protection against cruel and unusual punishments (Chapter 13). For now, it is important to understand that although the Supreme Court has not fulfilled Justice Harlan's hope for total incorporation of the Bill of Rights, it has achieved what legal scholars call *selective incorporation*. This means simply that most, but not all, of the provisions of the Bill of Rights are binding upon the states. This accomplishment—the nationalization of the Bill of Rights—has radically altered the practice of criminal justice by state and local governments. None of the major Court-imposed changes in criminal procedure to be discussed in this text (such as the exclusionary rule, the *Miranda* rule, and changes in death penalty laws) could have occurred in the absence of selective incorporation.

The process of selective incorporation also made the phrase *due process of law* more specific. Nevertheless, the concept of due process is still not precise. Whether a particular police practice or court rule is held to violate due process will always depend on the facts and circumstances of each case and upon a court's effort to apply those facts and circumstances in the context of one or more principles of law. Thus, due process should be understood as asserting a fundamental principle of justice rather than a specific rule of law. It implies the administration of laws that do not violate the foundations of civil liberties; it requires in each case an evaluation based on a disinterested inquiry, a set of facts stated fairly and precisely, the consideration of conflicting claims, and a judgment that seeks to reconcile the needs of continuity and change in a complex society. As Daniel Webster maintained, due process suggests "the law which hears before it condemns; which proceeds upon inquiry, and renders judgement only after trial."[37] Yet even these comments fail to explain the due process clause fully. A better understanding might be achieved by considering two aspects of due process: *substantive* due process and *procedural* due process.

Substantive Due Process

Substantive due process refers to the content or subject matter of a law. It protects people against unreasonable, arbitrary, or capricious laws or acts of government. An example is the **void-for-vagueness doctrine.** In accordance with this doctrine, the Supreme Court has struck down criminal statutes and local ordinances that, for example, made it unlawful to wander the streets late at night "without lawful business,"[38] to "treat contemptuously the American flag,"[39] and to willfully "obstruct public passages."[40] In all of these cases, the issue of substantive due process and the void-for-vagueness doctrine came into play because the statutes were neither definite nor certain as to the category of people they referred to or the precise conduct that was forbidden.

A landmark case involving substantive due process occurred in 1927 in the case of ***Buck* v. *Bell.***[41] Carrie Buck was an 18-year-old "feebleminded" white woman who had been committed to the Virginia State Colony for Epileptics and the Feeble Minded. She was the daughter of a feebleminded mother and was the mother of an illegitimate feebleminded baby. At that time a Virginia statute provided that in certain cases the health of the patient and the welfare of society may be promoted by the sterilization of mental defectives. The superintendent of the state colony where Carrie resided could recommend to its board of directors that the sterilization occur. The sterilization was

Norma McCorvey, "Jane Roe" in the famous court case of Roe v. Wade, *during her days as a pro-choice activist. This case was an early application of the Supreme Court's opinion that right to privacy is implicit in the Constitution.*

We justices read the Constitution the only way we can: as 20th-century Americans. The genius of the Constitution rests not in any static meaning it might have had in a world that is dead and gone, but in the adaptability of its great principles to cope with current problems.

— FORMER SUPREME COURT JUSTICE WILLIAM BRENNAN

EXHIBIT 5.5 | Law & Criminal Justice

AN OVERVIEW OF THE CRIMINAL JUSTICE PROCESS

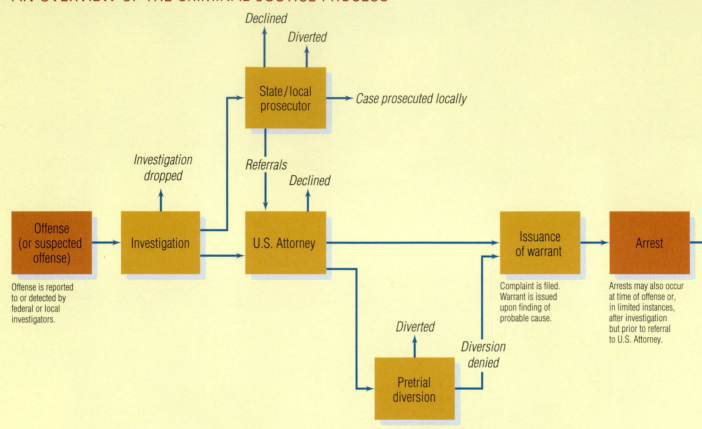

Declined

Diverted

State/local prosecutor → Case prosecuted locally

Investigation dropped

Referrals

Declined

Offense (or suspected offense) → Investigation → U.S. Attorney → Issuance of warrant → Arrest

Offense is reported to or detected by federal or local investigators.

Diverted

Diversion denied

Complaint is filed. Warrant is issued upon finding of probable cause.

Arrests may also occur at time of offense or, in limited instances, after investigation but prior to referral to U.S. Attorney.

Pretrial diversion

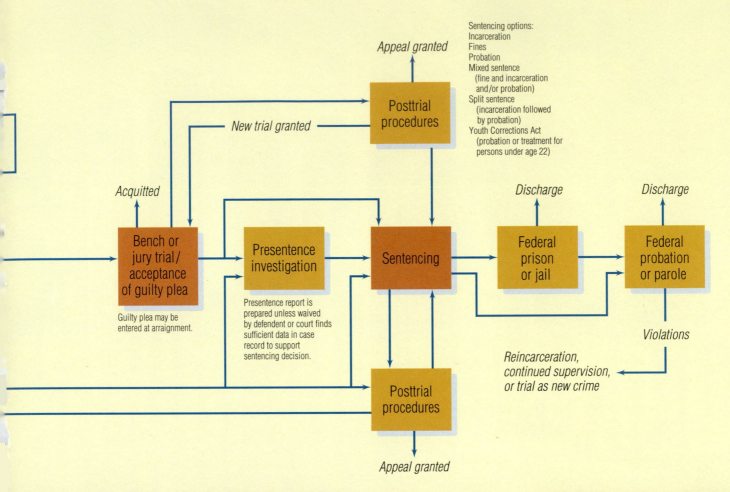

Appeal granted

Sentencing options:
Incarceration
Fines
Probation
Mixed sentence
(fine and incarceration
and/or probation)
Split sentence
(incarceration followed
by probation)
Youth Corrections Act
(probation or treatment for
persons under age 22)

Posttrial
procedures

New trial granted

Acquitted

Discharge

Discharge

Bench or
jury trial /
acceptance
of guilty plea

Presentence
investigation

Sentencing

Federal
prison
or jail

Federal
probation
or parole

Guilty plea may be
entered at arraignment.

Presentence report is
prepared unless waived
by defendent or court finds
sufficient data in case
record to support
sentencing decision.

Violations

Posttrial
procedures

Reincarceration,
continued supervision,
or trial as new crime

Appeal granted

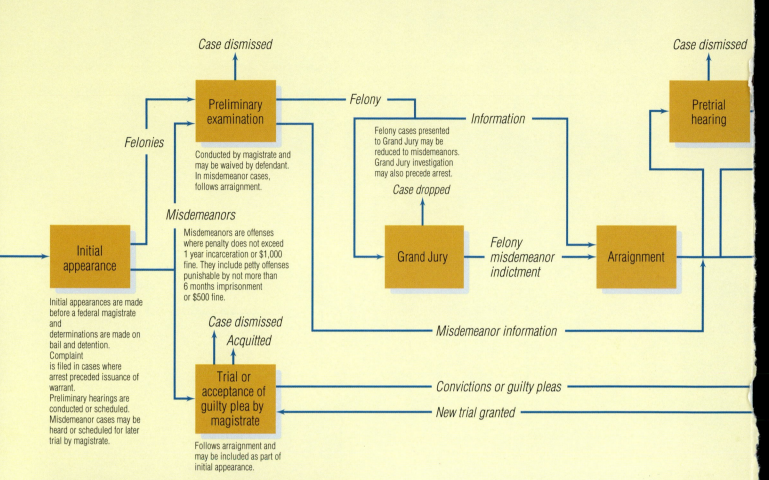

Case dismissed

Preliminary examination

Conducted by magistrate and may be waived by defendant. In misdemeanor cases, follows arraignment.

Felony

Information

Felony cases presented to Grand Jury may be reduced to misdemeanors. Grand Jury investigation may also precede arrest.

Case dropped

Case dismissed

Pretrial hearing

Felonies

Misdemeanors

Misdemeanors are offenses where penalty does not exceed 1 year incarceration or $1,000 fine. They include petty offenses punishable by not more than 6 months imprisonment or $500 fine.

Initial appearance

Initial appearances are made before a federal magistrate and determinations are made on bail and detention. Complaint is filed in cases where arrest preceded issuance of warrant. Preliminary hearings are conducted or scheduled. Misdemeanor cases may be heard or scheduled for later trial by magistrate.

Grand Jury

Felony misdemeanor indictment

Arraignment

Case dismissed

Acquitted

Trial or acceptance of guilty plea by magistrate

Follows arraignment and may be included as part of initial appearance.

Misdemeanor information

Convictions or guilty pleas

New trial granted

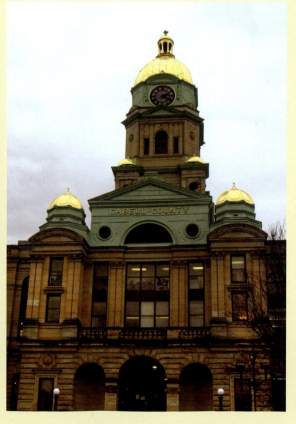

Statutes and ordinances that attempt to make unlawful the "contemptuous" treatment of the American flag have been struck down by the Supreme Court because of vagueness. To be valid, criminal laws must be definite and certain in regard to the categories of people they refer to and the conduct that is forbidden.

ordered, and although Carrie may have been mentally deficient, she understood what was about to happen to her and filed an appeal.

The county circuit court as well as the Virginia Supreme Court of Appeals both affirmed the sterilization decree, stating that the sterilization law was a "blessing" for "feebleminded persons" like Carrie Buck. Her lawyers then appealed to the U.S. Supreme Court on the grounds that the *substance* of the Virginia law represented a denial of due process; that the law was arbitrary, capricious, and unreasonable; and that it was a violation of the Fourteenth Amendment guarantee of equal protection. Chief Justice Oliver Wendell Holmes, Jr., upheld the Virginia statute, making the following comment:

> It is better for all the world, if instead of waiting to execute degenerate offspring for crime, or to let them starve for their imbecility, society can prevent those who are manifestly unfit from continuing their kind. Three generations of imbeciles are enough.[42]

Carrie Buck was ultimately sterilized, but the philosophy of *Buck* v. *Bell* has since been subjected to heavy criticism. Nevertheless, the case illustrates the concept of substantive due process and its inherent problems.

In *Skinner* v. *Oklahoma*,[43] which was a test of the constitutionality of Oklahoma's Habitual Criminal Sterilization Act in 1942, the Supreme Court ruled differently. Arthur Skinner was to be sterilized because he was a three-time habitual offender. (One of the felonies the prosecutor cited was the theft of three chickens.) The Court struck down the sterilization law because it denied both substantive due process and equal protection, since it applied only to felony offenses likely to be committed by poor people, while not considering such felonies as embezzlement, political offenses, and other crimes likely to be committed by more affluent defendants. In retrospect, the fact that Skinner was about to be sterilized partly because he was a chicken thief points to the unfairness and cruelty inherent in the Oklahoma statute.

An interesting area of law that has raised questions of substantive due process involves the rape shield statutes that exist in most jurisdictions in the United States. **Rape shield statutes** are laws that protect alleged rape victims from questioning in

Law and justice are not always the same. When they aren't, destroying the law may be the first step toward changing it.

—**GLORIA STEINEM**

EXHIBIT 5.3 | Gender Perspectives on Crime and Justice

Rape Shield Laws

Rape shield laws are rules of evidence established for the purpose of protecting the privacy of rape victims during trial by restricting the use of evidence relating to a woman's sexual history. As such, they limit evidence of a victim's past sexual behavior. Passed by most states back in the 1970s to keep jury members from blaming the victim of a rape because she was unchaste, rape shield laws helped to keep juries from applying stereotypes about female virtue in their deliberations.

Before the implementation of rape shield laws, the moral character of rape victims was often a main issue at the trials of their rapists. A history of sexual activity with the defendant or others had been used to show a pattern of behavior that implied consent. In fact, during many rape trials it was more likely that the rape victim was on trial instead of her attacker. This situation created reluctance among rape victims to report the sexual attacks on them and is partially responsible for the fact that forcible rape continues to be one of the most under-reported serious crimes, with only 36 percent of victims reporting the crime to law enforcement. In response to this problem, rape shield statutes were enacted in almost every state and by the federal government, although they vary from state to state in how much and under what circumstances evidence of a victim's previous sexual behavior can be admitted.

These laws have recently come under the microscope with the Kobe Bryant case. On June 30, 2003, the Los Angeles Lakers basketball star allegedly sexually assaulted a 19-year-old woman in a Colorado hotel where she worked. Bryant, who formerly maintained a squeaky clean reputation and is married with one child, admitted to consensual sex with his accuser but proclaimed his innocence.

Bryant's attorneys challenged the constitutionality of the state's rape shield laws, arguing that they violate a defendant's right of equal protection. They claimed the laws were unfair because the prior sexual conduct of an alleged sexual assault victim is presumed irrelevant, while the prior sexual conduct of a defendant *is* presumed relevant. They also argued that the woman's sexual conduct is relevant because it could show that injuries found in a rape examination could have been caused by someone other than the defendant.

Rape shield laws are anything but foolproof, and a great deal of judicial discretion exists in deciding how much information about a victim's sexual history is allowed in court. In the case of the *State of Colorado* v. *Kobe Bryant,* the judge decided to allow the defense to question the alleged victim about her sexual past in a closed evidentiary hearing. If the judge had found this information relevant to the case, it would have been admissible at Bryant's trial. However, the charges against Bryant were ultimately dropped, and the case was disposed of through an out-of-court settlement.

Another exception to the rape shield laws and judicial discretion includes federal appellate court case of *People* v. *Santos* (No. 2-00-1301, 2002 WL 1023132). In this case, an alleged victim told personnel at an emergency room that she did not have sex with anyone within 72 hours of the alleged encounter with the defendant. However, her statement was contrary to evidence depicted by the "rape kit." The court ruled that this evidence was permissible since the issue was the defendant's credibility.

As a final point here, it is interesting to note that there is no clear-cut evidence that rape shield laws have had their intended effect. There is evidence that the rate of reporting rape has increased since the early 1970s, when rape shield laws were enacted, but because of the variety of state laws, it is impossible to attribute that increase to the legal reforms. Furthermore, there are no meaningful data on how often a complainant's sexual history had actually been used in cases prior to the enactment of rape shield laws. As can be demonstrated from the aforementioned cases, a great deal of judicial discretion exists in deciding how much evidence about a victim's sexual history is allowed in court.

Sources: "Bryant Case Tests Limits of 'Rape Shield Laws,'" *The Christian Science Monitor* October 22, 2003; "Court: Rape Shield Law Not Absolute," *Chicago Daily Law Bulletin,* July 10, 2002, 6; U.S. Department of Justice, Office of Justice Programs, *Rape and Sexual Assault: Reporting to Police and Medical Attention 1992–2000,* Washington, DC: Bureau of Justice Statistics, August 2002.

court (and depositions) about evidence of past sexual experiences that are not relevant to the case and that might be prejudicial. Some of the due process issues related to these laws are discussed in Exhibit 5.3.

Even more heavily debated is the **USA Patriot Act,** a piece of legislation passed by Congress in the wake of the September 11, 2001, terrorist attacks. The stated purpose of the act is to better enable law enforcement officials to track and punish those responsible for terrorism and to protect U.S. citizens and property against further attacks. The legislation granted federal officials greater powers to trace and intercept terrorists' communications both for law enforcement and intelligence purposes. It reinforced federal anti-money-laundering laws and regulations in an effort to deny terrorists the resources for future attacks. It tightened immigration laws for the purposes of closing U.S. borders to foreign terrorists and expelling those already in the country. And it created a wide variety of new federal crimes. Many observers maintain, however, that the Patriot Act has gone too far (see this chapter's OP-ED), arguing that it gives federal agents virtually unchecked authority to spy on Americans.[44]

Procedural Due Process

Neither *Buck* v. *Bell* nor *Skinner* v. *Oklahoma* had any argument with the procedures through which the decision to sterilize had been made. Rather, they were attacking the *substance* of the laws that demanded sterilization. By contrast, **procedural due process** is concerned with the notice, hearing, and other procedures that are required before the life, liberty, or property of a person may be taken by the government. In general, procedural due process requires the following:

1. Notice of the proceedings
2. A hearing
3. Opportunity to present a defense
4. An impartial tribunal
5. An atmosphere of fairness

United States v. *Valdovinos-Valdovinos* represents a good case example involving violations of procedural due process.[45] In fact, the U.S. District Court for the Northern District of California considered the government's conduct so outrageous that the charges had to be dismissed.

In *Valdovinos-Valdovinos,* the Immigration and Naturalization Service (INS) was attempting to stem the flow of illegal immigrants from Mexico. Its major method of doing so was a "cold line," an undercover telephone operation in which agents posing as U.S. employers offered to reimburse immigrants for their smuggling expenses and give them jobs. The INS used the operation to advise Mexican nationals still within Mexico that it was appropriate to violate U.S. law. The district court ruled that the procedure was a violation of due process; the operation amounted to "the generation by police of new crimes merely for the sake of pressing criminal charges." As such, it constituted entrapment.

Since the 1960s, when questions concerning the procedural rights of criminal defendants came under closer and more frequent scrutiny by the Supreme Court, the due process clauses of the Fifth and Fourteenth Amendments have been clarified and extended. The Court's decisions have had a significant impact on the processing of defendants and offenders through the criminal justice system—from arrest to trial and from sentencing through corrections. These phases of the criminal justice process are outlined and described in the remainder of this chapter. The influence of the Supreme Court's decisions involving questions of due process and other constitutional rights in arrest, trial, and sentencing practices are examined in later chapters.

In retrospect, the Court's interpretations of the content of the Constitution, incorporation of the provisions in the Bill of Rights, and clarifications of what the framers meant by "due process of law" all suggest that the U.S. Constitution has endured well and will continue to do so. As indicated in Exhibit 5.4, however, not all constitutions fare as well.

| The Criminal Justice Process |

Criminal justice exists for the control and prevention of crime. As a "process"—the **criminal justice process**—it involves all the agencies and procedures set up to manage both crime and those accused of violating the criminal law. The agencies of criminal justice include law enforcement agencies charged with the prevention of crime and the apprehension of criminal offenders; the court bureaucracies charged with determining the innocence or guilt of accused offenders and the sentencing of convicted criminals; and the network of correctional institutions charged with the control, custody, supervision, and treatment of individuals convicted of crime.

There are many steps in the criminal justice process. Exhibit 5.5 broadly outlines the process as it occurs at the federal level. Although there are some differences from

Illegal Immigrants Entering the United States, 1970–2004

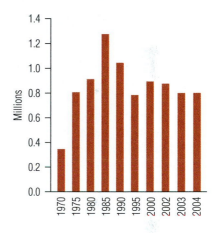

EXHIBIT 5.4 | International Perspectives on Crime & Justice

Constitution and Code Law in Bolivia

The term *constitution* refers to the institutions, practices, and principles that define and structure a system of government, as well as to the written document that establishes or articulates such a system. Every nation has a constitution in the first sense, and since World War II virtually every country—Britain, New Zealand, and Israel are among the few exceptions—has a written constitution as well.

Some constitutions are quite durable. The Constitution of the United States, for example, has lasted for more than two centuries, with additions (the amendments) rather than major changes. At the other end of the spectrum is Bolivia.

Straddling the Andes, Bolivia is a land of gaunt mountains, cold desolate plains, and semitropical lowlands. Its 424,165 square miles occupy an area about the size of Texas and California combined. It is a big country, but with a population of only 7.9 million. Approximately 60 percent of the Bolivian people are members of indigenous ethnic groups (primarily Aymara, Quechua, and Guarani); 15 percent are of European heritage; and the balance are *mestizos* (mixed indigenous and European ancestry). Since gaining its independence from Spain in 1825 under the leadership of Simón Bolívar, three main features have dominated Bolivian history: the importance of mining to the economy; the loss of territory through disputes and wars with neighboring countries; and chronic political instability. Of the three, it would appear that the latter has had the most disruptive impact.

During the past 180 years, Bolivia has had more than 60 revolutions, 79 presidents, and 16 constitutions. The government has changed hands at least 250 times—189 times by coup. From 1978 through the beginning of the 21st century, there have been 21 presidents, with a few having rather colorful politics. In 1980, for example, the presidential election yielded no clear winner. Before the congress could meet to decide between the main contenders, a military junta led by army commander General Luis Garcia Meza staged a coup. Interestingly, Garcia Meza was a major cocaine trafficker, who proceeded to establish alliances between the government and civilian drug enterprises. A year later Garcia Meza was ultimately forced to resign—not because of his involvement with the cocaine trades but for his fiscal mismanagement. Three years later, Bolivian president Hernan Siles Zuazo, the fourth person to hold that office since Garcia Meza's resignation, announced a war on cocaine. In 1984 Zuazo was kidnapped from the presidential palace by a group of cocaine traffickers. Although he was released unharmed and the attempted coup was aborted, the political system was

Bolivian Army troops arrive to take control and custody of the Government Palace in La Paz May 25, 2005.

left in a shambles. Following Zuazo, several other presidents were elected, but each quickly resigned out of frustration with his government's seemingly unsolvable problems.

Currently, Bolivia is a republic, based upon a 1967 constitution (which was interrupted by several coups). The government is headed by a president, who is elected to a 4-year term. There is a two-house legislature consisting of a 130-seat chamber of deputies and a 27-seat senate. The judicial branch is headed by a supreme court, whose justices are appointed to 10-year terms. Bolivia's legal system is based upon Spanish code law, as is common throughout Spanish Latin America. There are two principal differences between code law and common law: (1) Legal decisions are based strictly upon the written code, that is, on statutory rather than case law; (2) in the criminal courts, innocence, rather than guilt, must be proved.

Bolivia's most recent president, Carlos Mesa Gilbert, resigned on June 6, 2005. He was the second president to resign in a 2-year period. Given the country's economic problems, it is difficult to predict how long the next president, the government, and the constitution will endure.

Sources: U.S. Department of State, *Bolivia—Country Profile,* May 2000; Herbert S. Klein, *Bolivia: The Evolution of a Multi-Ethnic Society* (New York: Oxford, 1992); Department of State, Bureau of International Narcotics Matters, *International Narcotics Control Strategy Report* (Washington, DC: Department of State, 1985); *BBC,* March 8, 2005.

one jurisdiction to the next, the federal system is the general model followed by most state and local courts.

Prearrest Investigation

Although one might assume that the first phase of the criminal justice process is arrest, this usually occurs only when a crime is directly observed by a police officer. In other situations, the process begins with some level of investigation. Prearrest investigation

The Prearrest Phase

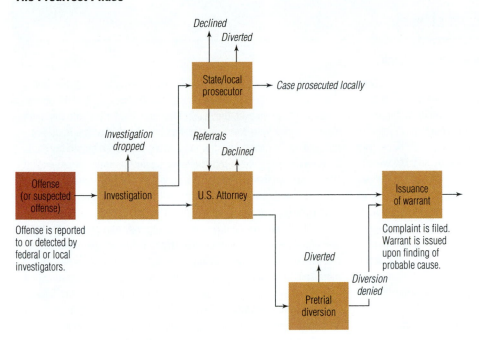

can be initiated when police receive a complaint from a victim or witness or knowledge from informers; ongoing surveillance may also lead to an investigation. Typically, investigative activities include an examination of the scene of the crime, a search for physical evidence, interviews with victims and witnesses, and efforts to locate the offender. Data from informers or general surveillance can suggest that some "suspicious" activity is occurring—perhaps drug sales, prostitution, or systematic theft—at which point an officer's or a detective's "go-out-and-look" investigations take place.

Prearrest investigations can also occur in another manner, sometimes even before a crime has actually been committed. Law enforcement agencies at the local, state, and federal levels become involved in long-term investigations when crime is not necessarily known to have occurred but is strongly suspected or believed to be about to occur. This type of investigation is most typical of federal enforcement agencies, such as the Federal Bureau of Investigation, the Internal Revenue Service, the Customs Service, and the Drug Enforcement Administration. Such investigations, which include the use of informers, undercover agents, surveillance, and perhaps wiretapping and other electronic eavesdropping devices, have been common in recent years in investigations of drug trafficking, international money-laundering operations, and organized crime, to name but a few examples.

It should be noted that in all types of prearrest investigation, it is possible for the investigation activities to continue beyond the point at which the evidence necessary for an arrest has been gathered.

Arrest

When an investigation finds that a crime may have been committed, or when a crime has been directly observed by a police officer, an **arrest** is made. Although the legal definition of "arrest" tends to vary from one jurisdiction to another, in practice an arrest is simply the action of taking a person into custody for the purpose of charging him or her with a crime. In most jurisdictions, an arrest *warrant* is necessary in misdemeanor cases, unless the crime has been observed by a police officer. The warrant is a written order giving authorization to arrest. It is issued by a magistrate or someone with equal authority. Felony arrests can be made without a warrant if the officer is reasonably certain that the person being arrested is indeed the offender. *Reasonable cer-*

EXHIBIT 5.6 | A View from the Field

The Dangers of Street Research by James A. Inciardi

I have been conducting street research with drug-involved populations for more years than I am willing to admit, and when doing this type of work, there is always the possibility that one can end up in the wrong place at the wrong time. For example, during the course of a project in the early 1970s, I was riding in an open convertible with three drug users. Let's call them Manny, Mo, and Jack. Manny and Mo were in the front seat, and Jack was in the back with me. We were on our way to a local "shooting gallery" (a place where drugs are injected). I was getting the $15 tour of the local drug scene, and they were my guides. On the way, they stopped at a convenience store so that Jack could get some cigarettes. So be it. The rest of us sat in the car and waited. Almost immediately, however, Jack came running out of the store. With cash in one hand and a .357 magnum revolver in the other, he jumped back into the car, into the back seat right next to me. The car sped off.

Now, I've always been a pretty laid-back person, but there I was, sitting in an automobile, probably a stolen one at that, speeding away from the scene of a violent crime with the perpetrator at my side. Needless to say, I got a bit irritated. After I threatened Manny (or was it Mo?) and his family and progeny for the next three generations with all manner of ill will, ill fortune, calamity, tribulation, and catastrophe, he pulled over and let me off at the curb. As it turned out, they ended up in a high-speed chase—"hot pursuit," as it is described in Chapter 8 of this textbook. Manny, Mo, and Jack were arrested about 15 minutes after we had gone our separate ways, and the stickup man was identified by a convenience store employee.

In that incident, things fortunately went my way. However, I wasn't quite as lucky late one morning in 1989. I was in a crack house I had visited often, located just off 103d Street in the Hialeah section of Miami. I was doing research on crack use, under a contract from the National Institutes of Health, and access to the crack house had been arranged by a local cocaine dealer whom I had known for many years. As I was entering through the *front* door of the crack house, the police were breaking in through the *rear* door. I was never quite sure of ex-

actly *which* police they were—DEA, state or county police, the "Jump Out Gang" (a special drug task force), "Miami Vice," or all of the above. Whatever and whoever, they burst through the door and into the room like renegades from some warrior-cop hell. *Mad Max,* the *Road Warrior,* and the *Terminator* (just 1 and 2 then) all flashed before my eyes. In seconds, everyone in the place, including me, was spread-eagled (face down) on the floor, searched, cuffed, and put into what was once called a "paddy wagon" (so-named after the early-20th-century Irish police officers who were prominent in the NYPD).

As it turned out, the police were doing a sweep of the area, with warrants to enter certain premises where they had "probable cause" to believe that crack was being manufactured or sold. In all, 100 or more souls were taken into custody that morning and placed in several detention cells. Since our "processing" wasn't all that speedy, I spent the next several hours in jail with a fairly large gathering of paranoid drug users who were beginning to *crash* (that post-drug-euphoria "letdown"). A few fights broke out every so often, and sometimes I didn't get out of the way fast enough.

Eventually, I was taken out of the cell for "processing." Since I had had neither drugs nor weapons in my possession when the police searched me, and since my identification suggested that I was indeed the drug researcher I claimed to be, about the only thing they could have officially charged me with was something like "being in a disorderly place." But the police were interested only in drug arrests, so along with a few others, I *walked* (was let go).

When I was in the area several weeks later, I ran into the cocaine dealer who had arranged my visit to the crack house. He mentioned that the crack house owner had put a price on my head. He was curious as to why the police had come to his place at the same time I did. When I asked how much of a price was on my head, the dealer sheepishly mumbled $200. Although I was both humbled and insulted that that was all I was worth, I nevertheless stayed out of that part of Miami for the rest of the year.

tainty (or probable cause) refers to the arresting officer's "rational grounds of suspicion, supported by circumstances sufficiently strong in themselves to warrant a cautious man in believing the accused to be guilty."[46] (For the arrest story of the author of this textbook, see Exhibit 5.6.)

Arrests can be made not only by police and other law enforcement officers but by private citizens as well. The following is an excerpt from the Idaho Code of Criminal Procedure:

The streets have no sympathy.

—*MIAMI VICE*

A private person may arrest another:

1. For a public offense committed or attempted in his presence.
2. When the person arrested has committed a felony, although not in his presence.
3. When a felony has been in fact committed, and he has reasonable cause for believing the person arrested to have committed it.[47]

In most jurisdictions the statutes governing arrest are quite specific. Criminal codes designate who can make arrests, the circumstances under which arrests can be

Arrest Through Arraignment

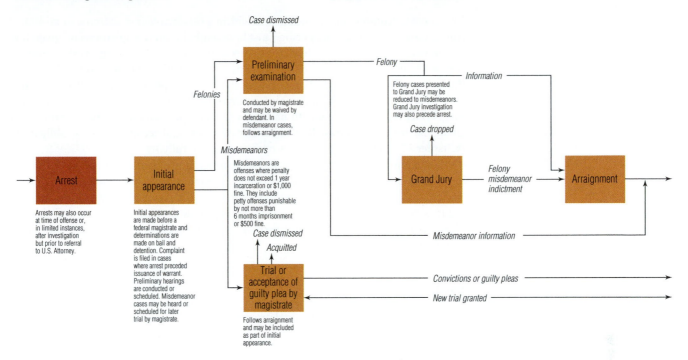

made, and the conditions under which an arrest warrant is and is not mandatory. There are exceptions, however, and these can place law enforcement agencies, private citizens, and others in a tenuous position with regard to the constitutionality of an arrest. For example, the *West Virginia Code*, which designates the laws of criminal procedure for that state, makes no mention of who may make an arrest, when an arrest can be made, and under what circumstances an arrest warrant is not necessary.[48] (Chapter 8 discusses arrests in detail.)

This may come as a surprise to you, but once or twice each year justice does not prevail.

—*NYPD BLUE*

Booking

For some lesser offenses—as in New York State, where prostitution is a minor offense punishable in some circumstances by no more than a fine[49]—the police may be permitted to issue a *citation,* which is an order to appear before a judge at some future date. In all other circumstances, however, a physical arrest occurs when the suspect is present, and the process continues to the booking phase.

Booking refers to the administrative steps and procedures carried out by the police in order to record an arrest properly and officially. At the time of booking, the accused person's name and address, the time and place of arrest, and the arrest charge are entered into the police log. Booking can also include fingerprinting and photographing of the suspect.

The booking phase is the first point at which the accused can drop out of the criminal justice process with no further proceedings. Charges may be dropped if the suspect has been arrested for a minor misdemeanor or if there was a procedural error by the police, such as lack of probable cause for arrest or illegal search and seizure. In the case of a procedural error, the decision to drop the charges can be made by an assistant prosecutor or a high-ranking police officer. Booking is also the first point at which some defendants can be released on bail.

Bail (from the French *baillier,* meaning "to deliver or give") is the most common form of temporary release. It involves the payment of a specified sum by the accused (or by someone else on his or her behalf), guaranteeing that he or she will appear at trial—at which point the money is returned. (Bail is discussed in detail in Chapter 12.)

Initial Appearance

Due process requirements mandate that within a reasonable (not extreme or arbitrary) time after arrest, the accused person must be brought before a magistrate and given formal notice of the charge. Such notice occurs at the initial appearance. At this time the accused is also notified of his or her legal rights, and bail is determined for those who did not receive temporary release during the booking phase. *Release on recognizance (ROR),* a substitute for bail, can also occur, typically at the recommendation of the magistrate, when there seems to be little risk that the accused will fail to appear for trial. The accused is released on his or her own personal recognizance, or obligation. (Chapter 12 discusses release on recognizance more fully.)

For some kinds of minor offenses, such as being drunk and disorderly, or in cases in which a simple citation has been issued, summary trials and sentencing are conducted at this initial appearance, with no further court processing. In other situations, the magistrate presiding at the initial appearance may determine that the available evidence is not sufficient to warrant further criminal processing and consequently may dismiss the case.

Preliminary Hearing

Owing to the complexity of criminal processing and the delays generated by overloaded court calendars, in many jurisdictions defendants have the option to bypass the initial appearance and proceed directly to the preliminary hearing.

The major purpose of the preliminary hearing is to protect defendants from unwarranted prosecutions. Thus, the presiding magistrate seeks to do the following:

- Determine whether a crime has been committed.
- Determine whether the evidence is sufficient to establish probable cause to believe that the defendant committed the crime.
- Determine the existence of a probable cause for which the warrant was issued for the defendant's arrest.
- Inquire into the reasonableness of the arrest and search and the officer's compliance with the requirements of the warrant.
- Set the appropriate bail or temporary release, if this was not already done.

Preliminary hearings are rare. In some jurisdictions, the defense may waive this hearing in order to keep damaging testimony temporarily out of the official records. It is hoped that by the time the trial does occur, witnesses may have forgotten some things, become confused, or disappeared. However, other defense attorneys insist on this hearing as a tactic for gaining insight into the strengths and weaknesses of the prosecution's case.

Determination of Formal Charges

Whether the initial court processing does or does not include an initial appearance or preliminary hearing, the next step in the criminal justice process is the formalization of charges. One mechanism is *indictment* by a grand jury. The indictment is a formal charging document based on the grand jury's determination that there is sufficient cause for a trial. The decision must be supported by a majority of the jurors. When it is reached, the jury issues a *true bill* containing the following information:

- The type and nature of the offense.
- The specific statute alleged to have been violated.
- The nature and elements of the offense charged.
- The time and place of the crime.
- The name and address of the accused or, if not known, a description sufficient to identify the accused with reasonable certainty.
- The signature of the foreman of the grand jury.

Rising Crime and Changes in Lifestyle

People who say they feel less safe due to crime are making the following changes in their lifestyles:

Carrying less cash	55%
Using charge cards more	29%
Carrying a personal protection device	28%
Bought a home security device	23%
Bought a car security device	22%
Bought a gun	17%

Source: Gallup Poll.

- The names of all codefendants, as well as the number of criminal charges against them.

Because the grand jury does not weigh the evidence presented, its finding is by no means equivalent to a conviction. It simply requires that the accused be brought to trial. If the grand jury fails to achieve the required majority vote, the accused is released. This is referred to as a *no bill*.

Grand juries are available in about half the states and in the federal system, but in only a limited number of jurisdictions are they the only mechanism for sending a defendant to trial. The most common method for bringing formal charges is the *information*, a charging document drafted by a prosecutor and tested before a judge. Typically, this testing occurs at the preliminary hearing. The prosecutor presents some, or all, of the evidence in open court—usually just enough to convince the judge that the defendant should be bound over for trial. As indicated earlier, however, the preliminary hearing is sometimes waived, and in those circumstances the information document is not tested before a magistrate.

Arraignment

After the formal determination of charges through the indictment or information, the actual trial process begins. The first phase in this segment of the criminal justice process is the arraignment. The accused person is taken before a judge, the formal charges are read, and the defendant is asked to enter a plea. There are four primary pleas in most jurisdictions:

1. *Not guilty:* If the not-guilty plea is entered, the defendant is notified of his or her rights, a decision is made as to whether the defendant is competent to stand trial, counsel is appointed if the defendant is poor, and in some jurisdictions the defendant can choose between a trial by judge or a trial by jury.
2. *Guilty:* If a plea of guilty is entered, the judge must determine whether the plea was made voluntarily and the defendant understands the full consequences of such a plea. If the judge is satisfied, the defendant is scheduled for sentencing; if not, the judge can refuse the guilty plea and enter "not guilty" into the record.
3. *Nolo contendere:* This plea, not available in all jurisdictions, means "no contest" or "I will not contest it." It has the same legal effect as the guilty plea but is of different legal significance in that an admission of guilt is not present and cannot be introduced in later trials.
4. *Standing mute:* Remaining mute results in the entry of a not-guilty plea. Its advantage is that the accused does not waive his or her right to protest any irregularities that may have occurred in earlier phases of the criminal justice proceedings.

The Trial Process

The complete trial process can be long and complex (see Chapter 12). It may begin with a hearing on *pretrial motions* entered by the defense to *suppress* evidence, *relocate* the place of the trial, *discover* the nature of the state's evidence, or *postpone* the trial itself. After the pretrial motions (if there are any) the jury is selected and the trial proceeds as follows:

1. *Opening statements by prosecution:* The prosecutor outlines the state's case and how the state will introduce witnesses and physical evidence to prove the guilt of the accused.
2. *Opening statements by the defense:* The defense, if it elects to do so, explains how it plans to introduce witnesses and evidence in its own behalf.
3. *Presentation of the state's case:* The state calls its witnesses to establish the elements of the crime and to introduce physical evidence; the prosecutor accomplishes this through direct examination of the witnesses. The witnesses may then be cross-examined by the defense.

FAMOUS CRIMINALS
Willie Sutton

One of the most proficient bank robbers of all time, Willie Sutton stole nearly a million dollars from a hundred different banks in New York and Philadelphia from the late 1920s until his ultimate capture in 1952. Sutton was alternately known as "Slick Willie" for his immaculate dress and politeness, Willie "the Actor" for donning clever disguises during robberies, and Willie "the mole" because he dug his way out of Sing Sing Prison on more than one occasion. His infamous quip that he robbed banks "because that's where the money is" has been quoted countless times in articles, speeches, and even this textbook. Arrested and imprisoned many times throughout his career, he often managed to escape by either sawing, digging, or walking out (dressed in a guard's uniform). He finally landed on the FBI's 10 Most Wanted Fugitives list in 1950. Because of his meticulous attention to fashion detail, his photo was circulated to tailors as well as police departments, a move that led to his recognition by a tailor's son from Brooklyn (who was later found shot dead in the street). Sutton served his final prison term from his capture in 1952 until 1969, when he was released from Attica State Prison as an ailing 68-year-old man. "Slick Willie" had the last laugh when in 1970 he filmed a commercial to promote a Connecticut bank's new photo credit card in which he said, "Now when I say I'm Willie Sutton, people believe me." ∎

The Trial Process

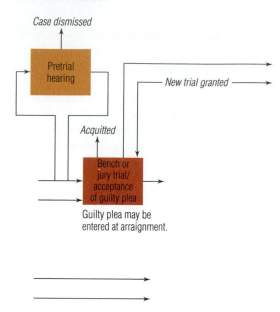

4. *Presentation of the defense's case:* The defense may open with a motion for dismissal on the ground that the state failed to prove the defendant guilty "beyond a reasonable doubt." If the judge concurs, the case is dismissed and the accused is released; if the judge rejects the motion, the defense's case proceeds in the same manner as the state's presentation.

5. *Prosecutor's rebuttal:* The prosecutor may present new witnesses and evidence, following the format of the state's original presentation.

6. *Defense's surrebuttal:* The defense may again make a motion for dismissal; if denied, it too can introduce new evidence and witnesses.

7. *Closing statements:* In most jurisdictions, the defense attorney and then the prosecutor make closing arguments. These statements sum up their cases and the conclusions that can be drawn from the evidence and testimony.

8. *Charging the jury:* In jury trials, the judge instructs the jury as to possible verdicts and orders them to retire to the jury room to consider the facts of the case, deliberate on the testimony, and return a verdict.

9. *Return of the verdict:* After the jury has reached a decision, they return to the courtroom with a verdict, which is read aloud by a member of the court. The jury may be *polled* at the request of either the defense or the prosecution; that is, each member is asked individually whether the verdict announced is his or her individual verdict.

In the case of a trial by judge, the steps involving the jury are eliminated and the judge determines whether the defendant is guilty or not guilty. In the majority of jurisdictions, the victim may have a role in the process, either through active participation or through legislative protection (see Exhibit 5.7).

Posttrial motions can also occur if the defendant is found guilty. The defense is given the opportunity to seek a new trial or have the verdict of the jury *set aside* (revoked).

Sentencing

After conviction or the entry of a guilty plea, the defendant is brought before the judge for the imposition of the sentence. The sentencing process may begin with a presentence investigation, a report that summarizes the offender's family, social, employment, and criminal histories, and serves as a guide for the judge in determining the type of sentence to be imposed. Depending on the nature of the offense and the sentencing guidelines established by law, a simple fine or period of probation in the com-

VICTIMS & JUSTICE | EXHIBIT 5.7

Victim Advocacy

The victims of crime are usually the main source of information about crime and criminals. In fact, the majority of crimes known to the police come from reports by victims, in contrast to the one-third reported by witnesses and the even smaller proportion coming from the police themselves. Victims, not surprisingly, typically suffer the most as a result of crime, yet they are often left in the shadows of the criminal justice system. In the majority of cases, victims are *revictimized* by the justice process. They are frequently shuffled around by law enforcement and court bureaucracies, questioned insensitively by police, subpoenaed by courts, bewildered by procedures for securing restitution, kept ignorant about important court dates, and denied possession of their own property being held as evidence. On the whole, the criminal justice system not only is insensitive to the needs of victims but repeatedly is deliberately intimidating.

To counter the hapless treatment of victims, grassroots movements began to appear at the local level during the early 1970s. More focus was given to the movement in 1982 when the President's Task Force on Victims of Crime recommended a variety of victim assistance programs. Since the beginning of the 1990s, a number of jurisdictions have instituted programs aimed at providing support services for victims, including the following:

- *Victim compensation programs,* which help victims receive reimbursement for their losses.

- *Victim restitution programs,* in which offenders directly compensate victims for their losses.

- *Victim assistance programs,* which aid victims in making social, emotional, and economic adjustments.

- *Victim-witness assistance programs,* which help to explain court procedures to victim-witnesses, make them aware of court dates, and assist them in providing better testimony in court.

A second outgrowth of the victim advocacy movement has been the wider use of *victim impact statements*—written or oral statements by victims or survivors—to assist judges and other criminal justice officials who make sentencing decisions. Currently, all 50 states and the District of Columbia allow some form of victim impact statement either at the time of sentencing or as part of a presentence report. Such statements, however, particularly in death penalty cases, have been controversial. In fact, two such cases have come to the attention of the United States Supreme Court.

Booth v. Maryland (482 U.S. 497)
John Booth was convicted of murder in the first degree in a Baltimore court. During his sentencing, a victim impact statement was read to the jury so that his sentence might be intensified. Booth was sentenced to death, but he appealed, arguing that the victim impact statement was a violation of his Eighth Amendment right against cruel and unusual punishment. The Supreme Court agreed with Booth, hold-

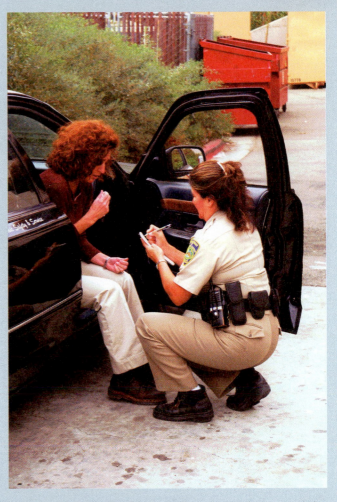

A Laguna Niguel, California police officer interviewing a rape victim.

ing that a victim impact statement creates an unacceptable risk that a jury may impose the death penalty in an arbitrary and capricious manner.

Payne v. Tennessee (501 U.S. 808)
Pervis Payne was convicted of murder in the deaths of a young woman and her 2-year-old daughter. Severely wounded in the incident was the woman's 3-year-old son, who witnessed the murders. At sentencing, the surviving child's grandmother testified that the boy cried daily for his dead mother and sister. Payne was sentenced to death, and appealed to the U.S. Supreme Court. In an about-face from *Booth,* the High Court upheld Payne's death sentence, thus condoning the use of victim impact statements at sentencing hearings.

Sources: Steven R. Donziger (ed.), *The Real War on Crime: Report of the National Criminal Justice Commission* (New York: HarperPerennial, 1996); Robert C. Davis and Barbara E. Smith, "The Effects of Victim Impact Statements on Sentencing Decisions: A Test in an Urban Setting," *Justice Quarterly* 11 (September 1994): 453–469.

Sentencing

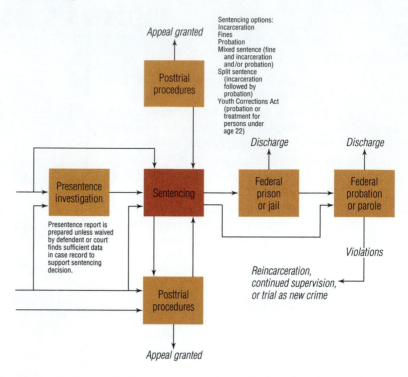

munity might be imposed. Sentences can also include other forms of community-based corrections, imprisonment, or even death.

Appeals and Release

After conviction and sentencing, defendants who have been found guilty may appeal their case to a higher court. Appeals are based on claims that due process was not followed, that new evidence has become available, or that the sentence imposed was "cruel and unusual," in violation of constitutional rights.

"I've always considered the 'Unsolved Mysteries' version the definitive re-enactment of my crime."

© The New Yorker Collection 2005 Mike Twohy from cartoonbank.com. All Rights Reserved.

Release from imprisonment occurs after the time specified in the sentence has been served or if the offender is released on *parole*—a conditional release that occurs after only a portion of the sentence has been served. Release from prison, or any type of sentence, can also occur through *pardon*—a "forgiveness" for the crime committed that bars any further criminal justice processing. Other factors that can affect a sentence are the *reprieve,* which delays the execution of a sentence, and the *commutation,* which reduces a sentence to a less severe one.

Criminal Justice as a "System"

The preceding summary of the various stages in the criminal justice process might suggest that the administration of justice is a *criminal justice "system"*—an orderly flow of managerial decision making that begins with the investigation of a criminal offense and ends with a sentence. This, as noted earlier in Chapter 1, was the ideal fostered by the President's Commission on Law Enforcement and Administration of Justice more than three decades ago in its commentary on criminal justice in America:

> The criminal process, the method by which the system deals with individual cases, is not a hodgepodge of random actions. It is rather a continuum—an orderly progression of events—some of which, like arrest and trial, are highly visible and some of which, though of great importance, occur out of public view. A study of the system must begin by examining it as a whole.[50]

However, the notion of criminal justice operating as an orderly system was and remains a myth. The justice "system" is composed of a series of bureaucracies operating along different and often conflicting paths; also, one segment of the system often serves as a dumping ground for the others.

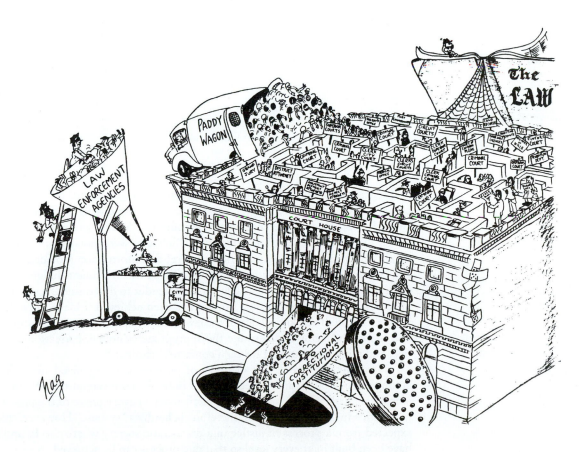

A simplified guide to the criminal justice system

CAREERS IN CRIMINAL JUSTICE

U.S. Marshals Service

The U.S. Marshals Service is the oldest and most versatile federal law enforcement agency in the nation, with deputies serving all three branches of government. Headquartered in Washington, D.C., 95 appointed Marshals direct 94 district offices and personnel in over 350 locations in every state, the U.S. territories, and Puerto Rico. The service employs about 4,200 deputy marshals and other essential personnel.

Since 1789, its mission has evolved to meet the changing needs of the country. At first, the service conducted the census and protected the president. Today, the Marshals Service is responsible for a wide range of law enforcement functions:

Judicial security: The agency's Court Security Officer (CSO) Program deputizes officers with full law enforcement authority to provide protection of federal courtrooms and judicial officials, including judges, attorneys, and jurors. The service protects more than 2,000 sitting judges and court officials at more than 400 court facilities around the country. Furthermore, since 1970, the service has protected, relocated, and granted new identities to more than 7,500 witnesses who have testified in government cases involving major criminal activity.

Fugitive investigations: The men and women of the service pursue and arrest 55 percent of all federal fugitives, more than all other federal agencies combined. In 2004, the agency arrested around 36,000 fugitives and helped arrest 32,000 others in local cases. In April 2005, the Marshals Service made headlines with Operation Falcon, a sweep in collaboration with local law enforcement agencies that led to the arrest of over 10,000 fugitives across the country. Timed to coordinate with National Crime Victims' Rights Week, the arrests included some of the most violent types of offenders, including more than 160 murder suspects, 550 sexual assault suspects, and over 150 gang members.

In addition, the Marshals Service is the primary agency responsible for the apprehension of fugitives that are wanted by foreign nations and are believed to be in the United States. Similarly, the service tracks and extradites fugitives who are apprehended in foreign countries for trial in the United States.

Prison services: The Marshals Service houses more than 47,000 federal unsentenced prisoners in federal, state, and local jails. In 1995, the air fleets of the service and the former Immigration and Naturalization Service merged to form the Justice Prisoner and Alien Transportation System (JPATS). One of the largest transporters of prisoners in the world, the marshals transport, on average, over 270,000 prisoners and aliens each year. Furthermore, the marshals conduct body searches of prisoners and individuals under arrest and maintain custody of prisoners during all court proceedings.

Other operations and programs: The Marshals Service undertakes hundreds of other special missions throughout the course of the year, including matters related to civil and criminal processes. For example, the agency enforces court orders and attorney general orders in cases ranging from civil disturbances to acts of terrorism, as well as manages almost $1 billion worth of seized and forfeited assets from criminal activity. Finally, the Special Operations Group (SOG) is a highly skilled force that responds to emergency situations in which federal law or federal property is threatened.

To qualify for the Marshals Service, an applicant must be a U.S. citizen between the ages of 21 and 36, be in excellent physical condition, and possess a bachelor's degree or equivalent experience. One must also have a valid driver's license and clean driving record; be able to pass a written exam, structured oral interviews, and a background check; and undergo an intense 10-week basic training program.

Every complex problem has a solution that is clear, simple, and wrong.

—H. L. MENCKEN

Questions of definition and interpretation can make criminal procedure even more complex. Police officers interpret situations to determine whether a law has been violated. Prosecutors and defense attorneys interpret the law and the circumstances in which the offense occurred to determine which laws were violated and assess the culpability of the accused person. Juries interpret the information provided by the police and courts to determine the innocence or guilt of the defendant. Judges interpret the evidence presented and the character of the offender to determine the nature and type of sentence and ensure that due process has been achieved. Finally, correctional personnel interpret their knowledge of the law, social science, correctional administration, and human behavior to determine the appropriate custodial, correctional, rehabilitative, and punitive treatment for each convicted criminal.[51]

Not only is there a lack of unity of purpose and organized interrelationships among police, courts, and corrections, but individual interpretations of crime, law, evidence, and culpability create further inefficiency in every phase of the process. Criminal justice in the United States, therefore, is hardly a "system." However, this is to be expected from a process of justice in a democratic society where checks and balances have been built in at every level so that due process can be achieved.

CRITICAL THINKING IN CRIMINAL JUSTICE

"Going Postal"

On August 20, 1986, a U.S. Postal Service employee in Oklahoma shot and killed 14 of his co-workers and then himself. By the mid-1990s, after other incidents of violence and murder by current and former postal workers, the term "going postal" had become part of American slang usage. With the meaning of "losing it" or just becoming maniacally violent, by the close of the 1990s the term was being applied to other incidents of workplace violence.

Thinking critically on this topic, is going postal just a myth, or is there really an epidemic of workplace violence? Has there been evidence in the media that killings, assaults, sexual harassment, or verbal abuse are pervasive throughout the national workforce? Consider the recent highly publicized incidents of workplace homicides:

- *December 2000:* Seven are killed by a software engineer at the Edgewater Technology Center in Wakefield, Massachusetts.

- *February 2001:* Four are slain by a former forklift driver at the Navistar Plant in Chicago.

- *September 2002:* Three are killed by an insurance executive at Empire Blue Cross and Blue Shield in New York City.

- *July 2003:* Six are gunned down at a Lockheed-Martin aircraft plant in Meridian, Mississippi. Later in the month, three are killed at a manufacturing plant in Jefferson City, Missouri.

- *November 2004:* A man opened fire on three individuals in a St. Petersburg, Florida, Radio Shack, killing two.

- *February 2005:* An employee at the Los Angeles Bureau of Street Services opened fire with an AK-47 assault rifle, killing two veteran employees.

Judging by the reports, it would appear that the trend of unstable employees "going postal" has persisted into the new millennium. However, contrary to public opinion, these shocking cases

Police investigators cover the body of a postal worker after he opened fire in a crowded Miami Beach post office, critically wounding his ex–wife and a friend before shooting himself to death.

of multiple murders account for only a fraction of the number of violent incidents. According to the Justice Department, of the average 1.7 million violent victimizations that occur each year, about 95 percent are simple or aggravated assault. Homicides constitute less than 1 percent of crimes in the workplace. And contrary to the popular idea that workplace homicides are carried out by former employees seeking to exact revenge on their coworkers, data indicate that nearly 80 percent of all workplace homicides are committed by individuals not connected to the workplace. Generally, theft is the motive in these cases. Overall, throughout the decade of the 1990s, workplace homicides declined by nearly 40 percent, and the data suggest that the trend may well continue.

Logically, those in the law enforcement field constitute the largest proportion of workplace victimizations (11%). The next most victimized occupational groups include individuals in the mental health field, retail sales, teaching (junior high and high school have the highest rates, college professors have the lowest), transportation, and the medical field. Furthermore, rates of victimization do not differ between private-sector and federal government employees, including postal workers.[52]

As such, a critical thinking examination of the data documents not only that "going postal" is indeed a myth but also that the national workforce is relatively safe on the job.

OP-ED

When the al-Qaeda terrorists hijacked four airplanes on the morning of September 11, 2001, and aimed them at the World Trade Center, the Pentagon, and a third location still unknown, most Americans quickly understood that it was the most brutal act of terrorism ever perpetrated. However, few had any idea of the extent to which it would affect the fabric of American life.

There were many immediate responses to the September 11 attacks, one of which was the USA Patriot Act. It was passed in near record time as far as government operations are concerned, because it was never the subject of a congressional committee debate and was never brought to a vote in the full House of Representatives. By October 26, the president had signed the bill into law.

In many ways, the Patriot Act was a timely piece of legislation. Its measures ensured adequate personnel on our northern borders; it strengthened laws on money laundering; several provisions served to break down many of the barriers between federal law enforcement agencies and the intelligence community; and it expanded the electronic surveillance provisions of many existing laws.

But, in other ways, the Patriot Act was judicial misadventure of magnificent proportions. It imposed guilt by association on many immigrants; it authorized detention on the mere suspicion that an immigrant had at some point engaged in a violent crime or provided humanitarian aid to a proscribed organization; it expanded the government's authority to conduct criminal searches and wiretaps without any probable cause that the individual had engaged in criminal activity; it authorized secret searches in cases having nothing to do with terrorism; and it reduced judicial oversight of intrusive information-gathering powers. There were other problematic measures, and, as such, aspects of the USA Patriot Act threaten a number of First, Fourth, Fifth, Sixth, Eighth, and Fourteenth Amendment rights. However, a number of suits have been filed in the federal courts to have the Patriot Act declared unconstitutional on grounds that it violates privacy, due process, and free-speech rights. Already, in *Doe* v. *Ashcroft*,[53] a U.S. district court declared unconstitutional the provision authorizing the FBI to gather telephone and Internet records on private citizens from Internet service providers. This provision was declared unconstitutional because it allowed the FBI to operate in such instances without judicial oversight.

| Summary |

Interpretations of the meaning of *due process* have varied throughout history. In the Middle Ages, due process merely meant adhering to the *law of the land*. Currently, due process of law—as guaranteed by the Fifth and Fourteenth Amendments—implies and comprehends the administration of laws that do not violate the very foundations of civil liberties. It requires in each case an evaluation based on disinterested inquiry, a balanced order of facts exactly and fairly stated, the detached consideration of conflicting claims, and a judgment mindful of reconciling the needs of continuity and change in a complex society. The concept of due process is anything but precise. It should be understood as asserting a fundamental principle of justice rather than a specific rule of law.

Due process can be better understood by considering it in its two aspects: *substantive* and *procedural*. Substantive due process refers to the content or subject matter of a law, and protects individuals against unreasonable, arbitrary, or capricious acts by the government. Procedural due process, on the other hand, is concerned with the notice, hearing, and other procedures that are required before the life, liberty, or property of a person may be taken by the government. The major distinction between substantive due process and procedural due process is that the former focuses on *what* the government is doing and the latter on *how* the government does it.

The criminal justice process, from investigation and arrest through trial and sentencing, is structured to guarantee due process of law at each of its many stages. Moreover, it is designed to be a system, an orderly flow of managerial decision making that begins with the investigation of a criminal offense and ends with a correctional placement. It can be argued, however, that the criminal justice process is anything but a system, that it lacks unity of purpose and organized interrelationships among its various components. The conflicting paths within the system and the disparate goals among the various players (lawyers, judges, police officers, defendants, members of the jury, and victims) all contribute to a "nonsystem" of criminal justice.

| Key Terms |

adversary system (129)
arrest (143)
Barron v. *Baltimore* (132)
Bill of Rights (130)
booking (145)
Buck v. *Bell* (138)

criminal justice process (141)
due process of law (129)
Gitlow v. *New York* (134)
Griswold v. *Connecticut* (137)
inquiry system (129)
inquisitorial system (129)

Lawrence v. *Texas* (137)
procedural due process (141)
rape shield statutes (138)
substantive due process (138)
USA Patriot Act (140)
void-for-vagueness doctrine (138)

| Issues for Discussion |

1. What do you think the framers of the Constitution meant by due process of law?
2. How does due process of law differ from the law of the land?
3. Have rape shield laws outlived their usefulness?

4. What other rights and liberties do you think should have been incorporated into the Bill of Rights?
5. How do you interpret the Second Amendment?
6. Is the USA Patriot Act in violation of the Bill of Rights?

| Media and Literature Resources |

Reel Justice includes scenes that can be used to spark discussion about the following topics from this chapter:

Prearrest Investigation

Arrest

Booking

The Trial Process

The USA Patriot Act. Amitai Etzioni, *How Patriotic Is the Patriot Act?: Freedom Versus Security in the Age of Terrorism* (New York: Routledge, 2004); Robert P. Abele, *A Users Guide to the USA Patriot Act and Beyond* (Lanham, MD: University Press of America, 2004); Thomas F. Powers, "Can We Be Secure and Free?" *Public Interest,* Spring 2003.

Second Amendment. There are several good books and more than 1,000 Web sites on the Second Amendment and gun control issues. Some recommendations include Michael A. Bellesiles, *Arming America: The Origins of a National Gun Culture* (New York: Knopf, 2000); Robert J. Cottrol (ed.), *Gun Control and the Constitution: Sources and Explorations on the Second Amendment* (New York: Garland Publishing, 1994); Andrew J. McClurg, David B. Kopel, and Brannon P. Denning, *Gun Control and Gun Rights* (New York: New York University Press, 2002); and Abigail Kohn, *Shooters: Myths and Realities of America's Gun Cultures* (Oxford: Oxford University Press,

2004). A comprehensive Web site (*http://www.guncite.com*) also explores these issues in-depth.

Comparative Criminal Justice. For more information on criminal justice in other countries, see "The World Factbook of Criminal Justice Systems" at *http://www.ojp.usdoj.gov/bjs/abstract/wfcj.htm;* U.S. Department of Justice, Office of Justice Programs, *Cross-National Studies in Crime and Justice* (Washington, DC: Author, 2004); Mathieu Deflem and Amanda J. Swygart, "Comparative Criminal Justice," in: *Handbook of Criminal Justice Administration,* edited by Toni DuPont-Morales, Michael Hooper, and Judy Schmidt, (New York: Marcel Dekker, 2001), 51–68; and Gregg Barak (ed.), *Crime and Crime Control: A Global View* (Westport, CT: Greenwood Press, 2000).

U.S. Marshals Service. The Marshals Service has its own Web site that contains historical and contemporary materials, as well as contacts for employment inquiries. See *http://www.usdoj.gov/marshals/*.

The Constitution. For an analysis of the original text of the Constitution, see Leonard W. Levy, *Original Intent and the Framers' Constitution* (New York: Macmillan, 1988). Another useful item is Archibald Cox, *The Court and the Constitution* (Boston: Houghton Mifflin, 1987).

The Bill of Rights. Recent analyses of the Bill of Rights include Nat Hentoff, *The War on the Bill of Rights and the Gathering Resistance*

(New York: Seven Stories Press, 2003), and Akhil Reed Amar, *The Bill of Rights: Creation and Reconstruction* (New Haven: Yale University Press, 1998).

Workplace Violence. There are several resources about the phenomena of workplace violence, including Manon Mireille LeBlanc and Julian Barling, "Understanding the Many Faces of Workplace Violence," in *Counterproductive Work Behavior: Investigations of Actors and Targets,* edited by Suzy Fox and Paul E. Spector (Washington, DC: American Psychological Association, 2005), 41–63; and Lynne F. McClure, "Origins and Incidence of Workplace Violence in North America," in *Violence in Homes and Communities: Prevention, Intervention, and Treatment* edited by Thomas P. Gullotta and Sandra J. McElhaney, *Issues in Children's and Families' Lives,* (Thousand Oaks, CA: Sage Publications, Vol. 11 1999), pp. 71–99.

| Endnotes |

1. Eric Lichtblau, "U.S. Uses Terror Law to Pursue Crimes from Drugs to Swindling," *The New York Times,* September 28, 2003, 1, 21; David Cole and James X. Dempsey, *Terrorism and the Constitution: Sacrificing Civil Liberties in the Name of National Security* (New York: New Press, 2002).
2. Luke Owen Pike, *A History of Crime in England,* Vol. 1 (London: Smith, Elder, 1873–1876), 52–55; Christopher Hibbert, *The Roots of Evil* (Boston: Little, Brown, 1963), 5–8.
3. Cited in Charles Rembar, *The Law of the Land: The Evolution of Our Legal System* (New York: Simon & Schuster, 1980), 18–23.
4. Rembar, *Law of the Land,* 19.
5. Henry M. Christman (ed.), *The Public Papers of Chief Justice Earl Warren* (New York: Simon & Schuster, 1959), 70.
6. See Randy E. Barnett (ed.), *The Rights Retained by the People: The History and Meaning of the Ninth Amendment* (Fairfax, VA: George Mason University Press, 1989).
7. Cited in Irving Brant, *The Bill of Rights* (Indianapolis: Bobbs-Merrill, 1965), 49–50.
8. *Barron* v. *Baltimore,* 7 Pet. 243 (1833).
9. See Richard C. Cortner, *The Supreme Court and the Second Bill of Rights* (Madison: University of Wisconsin Press, 1981), 3–11; Henry J. Abraham, *Freedom and the Court: Civil Rights and Liberties in the United States,* 4th ed. (New York: Oxford University Press, 1982), 30–48.
10. *Hurtado* v. *California,* 110 U.S. 516 (1884).
11. See *Maxwell* v. *Dow,* 176 U.S. 581 (1900); *Twining* v. *New Jersey,* 211 U.S. 78 (1908).
12. *Maxwell* v. *Dow,* 176 U.S. 581, 616 (1900).
13. *Gitlow* v. *New York,* 268 U.S. 652 (1925).
14. *Fiske* v. *Kansas,* 274 U.S. 380 (1927).
15. *Near* v. *Minnesota,* 283 U.S. 697 (1931).
16. *Powell* v. *Alabama,* 287 U.S. 45 (1932).
17. *Hamiltion* v. *Regents of the University of California,* 293 U.S. 245 (1934). Some legal scholars argue that the Court did not make it entirely clear that it intended to incorporate the freedom of religion clause until *Cantwell* v. *Connecticut,* 310 U.S. 296 (1940).
18. These latter two First Amendment rights were incorporated in *DeJonge* v. *Oregon,* 299 U.S. 353 (1937).
19. *Palko* v. *Connecticut,* 302 U.S. 319 (1937).
20. *Everson* v. *Board of Education,* 330 U.S. 1 (1947).
21. *In re Oliver,* 333 U.S. 257 (1948).
22. *Trop* v. *Dulles,* 356 U.S. 86 (1958).
23. *Mapp* v. *Ohio,* 367 U.S. 643 (1961).
24. *Robinson* v. *California,* 370 U.S. 660 (1962).
25. *Gideon* v. *Wainwright,* 392 U.S. 335 (1963).
26. *Malloy* v. *Hogan,* 378 U.S. 1 (1964).
27. *Pointer* v. *Texas,* 380 U.S. 400 (1965).
28. *Parker* v. *Gladden,* 385 U.S. 363 (1966).
29. *Klopfer* v. *North Carolina,* 386 U.S. 213 (1967).
30. *Washington* v. *Texas,* 388 U.S. 14 (1967).
31. *Duncan* v. *Louisiana,* 391 U.S. 145 (1968).
32. *Benton* v. *Maryland,* 395 U.S. 784 (1969).
33. *Griswold* v. *Connecticut,* 381 U.S. 479 (1965).
34. *Roe* v. *Wade,* 410 U.S. 113 (1973).
35. *Bowers* v. *Hardwick,* 106 SupCt 2841 (1986).
36. *Lawrence* v. *Texas,* No. 02-102 (2003).
37. *Dartmouth College* v. *Woodward,* 4 Wheat 519 (1819).
38. *Coates* v. *City of Cincinnati,* 402 U.S. 611 (1971).
39. *Smith* v. *Goguen,* 415 U.S. 566 (1974).
40. *Cox* v. *Louisiana,* 379 U.S. 536 (1965).
41. *Buck* v. *Bell,* 274 U.S. 200 (1927).
42. Cited in *Abraham, Freedom and the Court,* 111–114.
43. *Skinner* v. *Oklahoma,* 316 U.S. 535 (1942).
44. Charles Doyle, *The USA Patriot Act: A Legal Analysis* (Washington DC: Congressional Research Service, 2002).
45. *United States* v. *Valdovinos-Valdovinos,* USDC N Calif 35 CrL 2216 (1984).
46. *Brinegar* v. *United States,* 338 U.S. 161 (1949).
47. *Idaho Code,* 19-604.
48. *West Virginia Code,* 62:1–14.
49. State of New York, *Penal Code,* 40, 80.05.
50. President's Commission on Law Enforcement and Administration of Justice, *The Challenge of Crime in a Free Society* (Washington, DC: U.S. Government Printing Office, 1967), 7.
51. See James A. Inciardi, *Reflections on Crime* (New York: Holt, Rinehart and Winston, 1978), 160.
52. U.S. Department of Justice, Federal Bureau of Investigation, *Workplace Violence: Issues in Response* (Washington, DC: Author, 2004); Detis T. Duhart, *Violence in the Workplace, 1993–99,* Bureau of Justice Statistics Special Report (Washington, DC: U.S. Department of Justice, Office of Justice Programs, 2001).
53. *Doe* v. *Ashcroft,* 334F.Supp.2d 417 (S.D.N.Y. 2004).

PART TWO

THE POLICE

Far more university graduates are becoming criminals than are becoming policemen.—PHILIP GOODHART Very few people ever consider the police as human beings with some of the virtues, failures, and talents common to all.—SIR ROBERT MARK Hey, that sign says "Police," not "Taxi." —A DENVER POLICE OFFICER Cops and taxis have one thing in common. . . . They're never around when you need them most.—A NEW YORK SHOPKEEPER Being a cop today is a stop-and-go nightmare.—*U.S. NEWS AND WORLD REPORT* The .38 service revolver is a police officer's final authority.—FROM *COPS*, BY MARK BAKER Take your hands off me or I'll make your birth certificate a worthless document.—A MIAMI POLICE OFFICER

6

POLICE SYSTEMS IN THE UNITED STATES: HISTORY AND STRUCTURE

LEARNING OBJECTIVES

After reading this chapter, you should be able to answer the following questions:

1. What are the roots of modern policing?

2. What is the meaning of "posse comitatus," and what are its origins?

3. What are the differences among federal, state, and local law enforcement agencies in terms of jurisdiction and authority?

4. How has the role of the Federal Bureau of Investigation changed over the years?

5. What are the functions of private police?

6. What are the functions of auxiliary police?

7. How has policing changed at the federal level since 9/11?

8. What is the Department of Homeland Security?

9. Who are the Federal Air Marshals?

PORTSMOUTH, NH—Heavily armed members of the United States Coast Guard, unmistakably visible and highly menacing, watch over the shoreline of the harbor entrance. In San Francisco, commuters crossing the Golden Gate Bridge cannot help noticing the National Guard troops at the gateway to San Francisco. At the Miami airport, some passengers boarding planes headed to Washington, D.C., become unnerved as they are scrutinized by armed, tough-looking Dade County officers. At power plants, train terminals, and other vulnerable targets throughout the United States, increased police patrols have become evident. What is this all about? Is all of this increased police presence really necessary?

Some observers have suggested that policing has changed dramatically since the catastrophic events of September 11, 2001, while others maintain that only a few departments at a small number of potential terrorist sites have increased their security measures. The most common point of view, furthermore, is that major changes can be seen only at the federal level and that state, county, and municipal policing has not changed much at all. Is this really so? Which police agencies are addressing the realities of homeland security? These questions point to even broader queries about American policing: How did the police emerge, how many kinds of police agencies are there, and what does each do? What are the differences between federal, state, and local police departments? What are the differences between public and private police?

The police are the largest and most visible segment of the criminal justice system. As organized agents of law enforcement and peacekeeping, police officers are charged with the prevention and detection of crime, the apprehension of criminal offenders, the defense of constitutional guarantees, the resolution of community conflicts, the protection of society, and the promotion and preservation of civil order. They have often been referred to as a "thin blue line" between order and anarchy.

Structurally, policing in the United States is decentralized; that is, there is no national police force per se. Rather, there are thousands of independent police agencies throughout the country that developed separately. In spite of this diversity, though, the organization of these enforcement units is remarkably similar. This chapter presents a detailed analysis of the structure of police institutions in the United States. First, however, it traces the origins of policing, which go back to medieval England.

The Emergence of Modern Police

Policing can be traced to the latter part of the 9th century, when England's Alfred the Great was structuring the defenses of his kingdom against an impending Danish invasion. Part of Alfred's strategy depended on internal stability. To gain this, he instituted a system of **mutual pledge** that organized the country at several levels. At the lowest level were *tithings*, 10 families grouped together who assumed mutual responsibility for the acts of their members. At the next level, 10 tithings, or 100 families, were grouped together into a *hundred*; the hundred was under the charge of a *constable*. Hundreds within a specific geographic area were combined to form *shires* (now called counties)—administrative units that were governed by a *shire-reeve*, or *sheriff*.[1]

Magistrates, Constables, Beadles, and Thief-Takers

In the 13th century the *night watch* was established in urban areas to protect city streets; the watch represented the most rudimentary form of metropolitan policing.[2] Modern police forces did not emerge until centuries later, however. Various other approaches were attempted before the need for regular, organized police agencies became widely recognized.

Distribution of Sworn Police Officers in the United States

Source: U.S. Department of Justice.

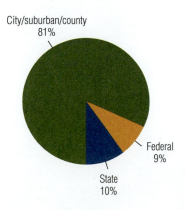

City/suburban/county
81%

Federal
9%

State
10%

Legendary highwayman Dick Turpin terrorized the English countryside in the 17th century.

In 17th-century England there were some officials whose duties included enforcing the law and keeping the peace. There were *magistrates* who not only presided in courts but also ordered arrests, called witnesses, and examined prisoners. There were *parish constables*, carryovers from the days of Alfred the Great, who had limited powers of arrest and whose authority was confined to relatively small districts. And there were *beadles*, constables' assistants, who were paid £20 a year and did little more than clear vagrants from the city streets. But most magistrates and constables were corrupt and had a minimal impact on law enforcement.

To these could be added **thief-takers**—private detectives who were paid by the Crown on a piecework basis.[3] Anyone could be a thief-taker; the thief-takers had no official status as police and no more authority than private citizens. Like the bounty hunters of the American West, thief-takers received a reward for apprehending a criminal.

Thief-takers emerged in response to the problem of highway robbery, which had been flourishing since the time of legendary outlaws such as Robin Hood and Little John. By the 17th century, highway robbery in the grand manner of Jack Sheppard, Dick Turpin, Claude Duval, and Captain Lightfoot had made traveling through the English countryside so perilous that no coach or traveler was safe. As a result, in 1693 an act of Parliament established a reward of £40 for the capture of any highwayman or road agent.[4] The reward was payable upon conviction, and the thief-taker also received the highwayman's horse, arms, money, and property, unless these were proved to have been stolen.

This system was extended during the reigns of Anne and George I to cover offenses other than highway robbery, and soon a sliding scale of parliamentary rewards came into existence. Burglars, housebreakers, and footpads (street robbers), for example, were worth the same amount as a highwayman, but a sheep stealer brought only £10 and an army deserter only £1. In some communities, homeowners joined together and offered supplementary rewards, typically £20, for the apprehension of any highwayman or footpad within their district. During especially serious crime waves, Parliament provided special rewards of £100 for particular felons.

As the system expanded, a class of professional thief-takers developed. Not unexpectedly, many thief-takers were themselves criminals, since the offer of a pardon was an additional incentive. But thief-taking had some drawbacks. Arresting desperate criminals was dangerous, rewards were not paid if the criminal was acquitted, and thief-takers always had to fear the revenge of their victims' friends and associates.

The result was that thief-takers often became *thief-makers*. Many would induce youngsters to commit crimes and then have another thief-taker arrest the youth in the midst of the offense. Others framed innocent people by planting stolen goods on their persons or in their homes. Although some real criminals were apprehended by professional thief-takers, the system generally created more crime than it suppressed.[5]

Henry Fielding and the Bow Street Runners

This picture depicts Sir Henry Fielding, presiding over the examination of a prisoner at Bow Street. Fielding also formed the first organized force against criminals in England, commonly known as the Bow Street Runners.

Although he is probably best known as the author of *Tom Jones,* **Henry Fielding** might also be credited with laying the foundation for the first modern police force. In 1748, Fielding was appointed magistrate in Westminster, a city adjacent to central London. He moved into a house on Bow Street that became both his home and his office, and it was there that the first English police force began to form.

At that time burglaries, street and highway robberies, and other thefts were reaching new heights, and it was Fielding's aim to reduce the profitability of such criminal activities. First he established relationships with local pawnbrokers, provided them with lists and descriptions of recently stolen property, and urged them to notify him if anyone tried to pawn those items. He then placed the following notice in the London and Westminster newspapers:

> All persons who shall for the future suffer by robbers, burglars, etc., are desired immediately to bring or send the best description they can of such robbers, etc., with the time and place and circumstances of the fact, to Henry Fielding Esq., at his house in Bow Street.[6]

What Fielding suggested was original for his time, for few people had ever reported thefts to the authorities. Although Fielding could accomplish little by himself, within a year he had obtained the cooperation of Saunders Welch, the high constable of Holborn, and several other public-spirited constables. Together they formed a small, unofficial investigative division that was the first organized force ever used against criminals in England. Fielding's constables—the **Bow Street Runners**—were not paid as police officers, but they were entitled to the standard thief-takers' rewards.

In time, Fielding's efforts were noticed by the government, which provided funds to support the activities of the Bow Street Runners. Only 4 years after his appointment as magistrate, however, Fielding's health began to deteriorate. He then persuaded the authorities to appoint his half-brother, John Fielding, to share his magistracy. John soon took over the operations of the unofficial Bow Street Police. Because he was blind, he was dubbed the "Blind Beak." (In English cant—the slang of the London underworld—"beak" was a term referring to any judge or magistrate.)[7]

The Bow Street Runners endured, but only on a small scale. Then, in 1763, Fielding was allotted £600 to set up a civilian Horse Patrol of eight men for the direct curtailment of robbers and footpads on the London streets. The patrol seemed to be a success, but after only 9 months it was disbanded because of lack of support from the government. During the next decade, however, a permanent Foot Patrol was established, and in 1804, some 22 years after John Fielding's retirement, a new Horse Patrol was set up. It included two inspectors and 52 men, outfitted in red vests and blue jackets and trousers. This was England's first uniformed police.[8]

Patrick Colquhoun and Sir Robert Peel

The Bow Street Runners had been born and nurtured to some extent in secrecy. If it had been known that even an unofficial band of police was being supported with public funds, it would have been denounced as an instrument of oppression and tyranny. Even the Horse Patrol, as effective as it had been, was disbanded for this reason. The

English people were emphatically opposed to a professional police force because of their love of freedom, faith in private enterprise, respect for tradition, and dislike for spending public money.

In spite of these feelings, which were deeply rooted in English culture, when Glasgow businessman Patrick Colquhoun was appointed as a London magistrate he soon conceived the idea of a "new science of preventive police."[9] His suggestions for a large, organized police force for greater London were quickly rejected, but in 1789 he did form a special river police patterned after Fielding's Bow Street model. Although successful, Colquhoun's efforts met with little support, for throughout that century and decades thereafter the English continued to mistrust any form of enforcement authority.

Although Sir Robert Peel is often credited with the establishment of the first professional police force,[10] it is clear that others came before him. Nevertheless, Peel was a significant figure in this process. In 1828, basing his thoughts on the ideas of Colquhoun, he drew up the first police bill that was ultimately passed by Parliament. London's new Metropolitan Police, established in 1829, was a centralized agency with responsibility for both preventing crime and apprehending offenders. Thus, modern policing finally came into being.

Law and Order in Early America

From the time the first American colonies were founded, the villages and towns in the New World were constantly threatened—on land by Native Americans and from the sea by pirates and foreign enemies. These problems of defense were dealt with by the military. The towns had no protection, however, against disorderly, lawbreaking inhabitants. In the 17th century, village authorities began selecting men to serve as guardians of the peace. The titles and functions of these first police officers were similar to those of the English constable, and the range of their duties can be seen from a 1646 Massachusetts law, reprinted here in the style of its colonial authors:

> Evry cunstable . . . hath, by virtue of his office, full powr to make, signe, & put forth pursuits, or hues & cries, after murthrers, manslayrs, peace breakrs, theeves, robers, burglarers, where no magistrate is at hand; also to apphend without warrant such as those taken with drinke, swearing, breaking ye Saboth, lying, vagrant psons, night walkers, or any other yt shall break our laws; also to make search for all such psons . . . in all houses licensed to sell either beare or wine, or in any othr suspected or disordered places, & those to apphend, & keepe in safe custody.[11]

Constables, or *schouts* in the Dutch settlements, appeared in all the colonies as soon as local governments were organized. They were paid for their services through fines. Nighttime security was provided by "military watches," "rattle watches" composed of paid volunteers, "bellmen," and other forms of night watch. By the 18th century, the daytime peacekeeping of the constables and the nighttime protection of the watches were common everywhere. Unlike the situation in England, where the notion of a paid police force was despised, most colonial peacekeeping activities were supported by municipal authority.

As the colonial towns grew, the number of street riots, drunken brawls, and other types of violent behavior increased considerably. Not only were those charged with keeping the peace incapable of enforcing all of the laws, but often they were lax in their duties, as was noted in Massachusetts's *Bristol Journal* on March 16, 1760:

> *The watch burn Tobacco while Houses are burning,*
> *And the Glass, not the Watch, goes its rounds,*
> *A burning shame this and sad subject of mourning,*
> *That our Guard's such a mute Pack of Hounds.*[12]

Despite these difficulties, however, the constable and the watch were maintained throughout the 1700s and into the early part of the next century as the only sources of urban law enforcement. Some cities did expand the numbers of these paid officers, but

Nighttime security in early America was provided by the night watch.

to little avail. By midcentury, growing levels of lawlessness, combined with corruption within the ranks of the watch, led to the organization of formal police forces.

The Trans-Mississippi West

As settlers moved west, they reached the frontier well before peace officers and courts of law. Violence and crime were inevitable in these sparsely populated regions. Frontiersmen, who used firearms for hunting and self-defense, turned easily to fists, knives, and pistols to settle disputes. Native American tribes, often with cultures that glorified war and acts of revenge, naturally resisted white encroachment. Whites themselves, with European traditions of feuding and revenge, applied these practices both to their neighbors and to the Native Americans. In the absence of any formal mechanisms of frontier justice, the West also served as a sanctuary for a lawless minority of outlaw and criminal migrants.

The Sheriff The *sheriff,* the first of the formal law enforcement agents to appear in the vast territories beyond the Mississippi River, was closely modeled after his British counterpart. But while the powers of the English sheriff had diminished over time, those of the American sheriff expanded to include not only the apprehension of criminals but also the conducting of elections, the collection of taxes, and the custody of public funds. Moreover, American sheriffs were eventually chosen by popular election.

As the West became more populated and more lawless, the sheriff evolved into an active agent of law enforcement. His duties as fiscal administrator and executive arm of the courts were quickly subordinated to the more colorful activities of rounding up cattle thieves, highwaymen, and other bandits, and engaging in gunplay with serious outlaws. Typically, the local sheriff's office did not include a paid staff of trained deputies that could be called on, for example, to track fleeing outlaws. Thus, the *posse* became crucial in frontier law enforcement.

The Posse The origins of the posse go back many hundreds of years. During the time of Alfred the Great, when mutual pledges bound together the members of a tithing, one of the peacekeeping instruments was the *posse comitatus*, Latin for "the power of the county," which consisted of all the able-bodied men in a county. This group was at the absolute disposal of a sheriff, and members were required to respond when called on to do so. The institution of **posse comitatus** was transferred intact to American soil.[13] Here, it became an important component of criminal justice machinery as the frontier moved westward, for it could place the entire power of a community under the leadership of the sheriff.

Territorial Agencies Also among the lawmen of the West were territorial police agencies. The **Texas Rangers** were the first of these organized forces. Equipped by Stephen F. Austin in 1823 to help protect settlers against the Native American tribes, the Rangers were organized as a corps of irregular fighters when the Texas revolution against Mexico broke out in 1835. After 1870, the Rangers evolved into an effective law enforcement agency.[14] Following the lead of the Texas Rangers, the Arizona Rangers were established in 1901 and the New Mexico Mounted Police in 1905—but these were primarily border patrol forces and were abandoned within a few years after their inception.[15]

Federal Marshals Federal marshals were also a part of law enforcement in the American West. When the United States came into being with the ratification of the Constitution, the dual sovereignty of state and republic required the designation of special officers to represent the authority of the federal courts. In 1789, Congress established the position of federal marshal, but these appointed officials did not come to prominence until after the Civil War. The popular image of federal marshals and their

Jailer, San Angelo (Texas) County Jail, 1915.

In the 19th century, the Texas Rangers were a highly romanticized territorial police agency.

FAMOUS CRIMINALS
From an Early Rogues Gallery

(left) Maximilian Shinburn, 1839–1919. Known as the "King of Bank Burglars."

(middle) Sophie Lyons, 1850–1924. Occupation: criminal tendencies since early childhood. Criminal occupations: pickpocket, shoplifter, blackmailer, stall for bank sneaks.

(right) Frederick J. Wittrock, 1858–1921. Occupation: store proprietor. Criminal occupation: express robbery. Distinguishing features: reads dime novels voraciously. ∎

deputies maintaining law and order along the trail and in the violent mining communities has little foundation in fact. Most of the marshals' working time was spent on routine functions related to civil and criminal court activity. Sometimes they conducted criminal investigations and apprehended outlaws, but these activities constituted only a fraction of the duties they performed.[16]

It should be noted that not all marshals were federal marshals. There were also city and town marshals appointed by a mayor or city council. These were community lawmen who served purely as local police. The legendary "Wild Bill" Hickok, for example, was a local marshal in the towns of Hays City and Abilene, Kansas, as was Wyatt Earp in Dodge City, Kansas.

Policing the Metropolis

In 1845, New York City established the first organized metropolitan police force in the United States. But this occurred only because the fear of crime and social disintegration was stronger than the cultural opposition to a standing army.

At the beginning of the 19th century, New York was no longer the homogeneous community with a common culture and a shared system of values and moral standards that it had been in colonial times. In the 55 years before the establishment of the new police force, the population of the city increased by more than 1,000 percent—from 33,131 in 1790 to 371,223 by 1845.[17] A significant proportion of the new arrivals were of foreign ancestry, making the city a mosaic of subcommunities separated by barriers of class, culture, language, attitudes, and behavior derived from vastly different traditions.

The increased population, combined with growing levels of poverty, served to increase the crime rate. The rise in the population brought with it conflicts caused by class and cultural differences. The highly visible and mobile wealthy attracted criminal predators, both foreign and domestic, resulting in sharp increases in crime and vice. In 1840, New York's *Commercial Advisor* commented on how the city's streets had become pathways of danger:

> Destructive rascality stalks at large in our streets and public places, at all times of day and night, with none to make it afraid; mobs assemble deliberately. . . . In a word, lawless violence and fury have full dominion over us.[18]

In 1842, a special citizens' committee made melodramatic reference to the constant increase in crime and the inability of the police to deal with it:

> The property of the citizen is pilfered, almost before his eyes. Dwellings and warehouses are entered with an ease and apparent coolness and carelessness of detection which shows that none are safe. Thronged as our city is, men are robbed in the street. Thousands that

are arrested go unpunished, and the defenseless and the beautiful are ravished and murdered in the daytime, and no trace of the criminals is found.[19]

During this period the city was patrolled by a few hundred marshals, constables, and watchmen who were unsalaried but received fees for their services. As in Britain, this system resulted in numerous instances of graft, corruption, laxity, and misdirected effort. Officers concentrated on duties that would earn them money rather than on bringing criminals to justice. For example, since the recovery of stolen property brought a greater fee than the apprehension of an offender, few thieves were deliberately sought out. This situation also led to arrangements between police and criminals before some robberies and burglaries actually took place. An officer would know of a crime in advance, recover the stolen property, and forward a share of the reward to the thief.[20]

From 1841 to 1844, several plans for the organization of a London-style police force were introduced, but none commanded enough support. In 1844, however, the New York State legislature authorized communities to organize police forces and appropriate special funds to be given to cities to provide 24-hour police protection. When the Democrats won the New York City mayoral election in 1845, Mayor William F. Havermeyer called for the adoption of the new state statute. The bill was signed into law on May 23, 1845, and a police force akin to London's was finally created.

By the outbreak of the Civil War, Chicago, New Orleans, Cincinnati, Baltimore, Newark, and a number of other large cities had followed New York's lead. The foundation of today's municipal police departments had been established. At the same time, police systems were developing in other parts of the world, a few of which were quite unusual. (See Exhibit 6.1).

NYPD Salary Schedules, 1845 and 2005

1845

Captains	$700
Assistant captains	600
Sergeants	550
Officers	500

2005

Captains	$83,900–106,756
Assistant captains	73,000–85,400
Sergeants	61,100–72,000
Officers	35,000–63,400

Sources: A. E. Costello, *Our Police Protectors* (New York: Author's Edition, 1885), 103; Office of Labor Relations, City of New York. ∎

EXHIBIT 6.1 | historical perspectives on criminal justice

Policing by Camel

Just over a century ago, the British emissaries who once governed Botswana (known then as the Bechuanaland Protectorate), wondered how they could possibly patrol such a blazing hot and forsaken stretch of land. Much of the country was (and still is) part of Africa's Kalahari desert, and the colonists' police horses regularly dropped dead from thirst and disease. The answer came in a letter dated August 30, 1889, from Cecil Rhodes, the British industrialist and founder of Rhodesia: "I am willing to defray the cost of the purchase of twenty camels and the cost of the engagement of six camel drivers to be employed in the service of the police."

It was not until some 32 years later, in 1920, that the camels finally arrived. No one seems to know why they took so long to reach the police, but when they finally did, the officers sang their praises. Camels, they rhapsodized, live longer than horses, they can carry heavier loads and walk longer distances than horses. The clincher was that camels drank little water and cheerfully ate the prickly shrubs that grew in great abundance throughout the desert. And there was great joy to be had by the police who patrolled the sands of the Kalahari.

Within a few decades, however, the allure and appeal of the camel patrols had begun to fade. The haughty, lofty, dreamy-eyed, smelly, cantankerous and absurd beasts, whose hair had shielded the body of John the Baptist (Mark 1:6) and who were deemed wealth among biblical nomads (Job 1:3), had become passé. In 1959, Botswana's committee on Police Camel Corps began writing memos suggesting that, with the invention of the motor car, camels had become obsolete.

In the years hence, the Botswana police obtained a number of new Land Rovers, but at the close of the 20th century, hundreds of camels were still part of the fabled Police Camel Corps. In the town of Tsabong, a tiny outpost in southern Botswana where goats wander the streets and where junior officers saddle grunting and snorting camels as part of training exercises, the police commander recently pondered the relative merits of sport utility vehicles over camels:

Policing by camel in the Kalahari Desert.

I prefer a vehicle. With a vehicle, you can go on patrol and come back the very same day. With a camel, you have to spend days on patrol. It's a very slow animal. You don't rush it. Otherwise, it gets tired and it doesn't move.

In 1999, 141 of the Corps' camels—39 bulls, 42 cows, 33 weaners, and 27 calves—were put on the auction block. Although by 2000 the use of Land Rovers and other four-by-fours had become commonplace, the Botswana police still use camels now and then for getting around the Kalahari desert.

Sources: *The New York Times,* February 8, 2000, A4, *Capetown Sunday Times,* February 7, 1999, 6; *Botswana Focus,* June 30, 2003, 1.

Police Systems in the United States

In a nation with a population approaching 300 million people—all of whom are under the authority of competing political jurisdictions at federal, state, county, and local levels—law enforcement in the United States today reflects a structure more complex than that found in any other country. There are 23,000 to 25,000 professional police agencies in the public sector alone—each representing the enforcement arm of a specific criminal code or judicial body. To these can be added numerous others in the private sphere. The duties and authority of each are generally quite clear, but in many respects they can also be rather vague and overlapping. Although enforcing the law and keeping the peace may be the responsibilities of a *municipal* police agency within a small suburban village, for example, also active in that same community may be a county sheriff's department, a state police bureaucracy, and numerous federal enforcement bodies. This level of complexity can be further complicated by jurisdictional disputes, agency rivalries, lack of coordination and communication, and failure to share information and other resources.

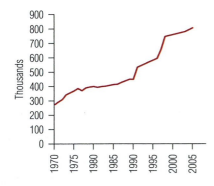

U.S. Police Employees, 1970–2005

Consider, for instance, the jurisdictional and administrative complexities that exist in Dade County, Florida. Located at the southeastern tip of the state of Florida, Dade County has a population of more than 2 million and occupies some 2,109 square miles—a land area larger than the entire state of Delaware. In addition to the cities of Miami and Miami Beach, the county includes 26 other incorporated municipalities. Each of these is an independent political jurisdiction with its own municipal police force. Also included in this essentially urban- suburban county is the Dade County Public Safety Department—whose jurisdiction is countywide—as well as the Florida State Police and the Florida Marine Patrol. At the federal level, numerous agencies also have jurisdiction, including the Federal Bureau of Investigation, the U.S. Citizenship and Immigration Services, the Drug Enforcement Administration, the Internal Revenue Service, the Customs and Border Protection, and the United States Coast Guard. In the private sphere, the railroad industry has its own police force, and thousands of other businesses and industries use private police agencies.

New York City reflects another complex situation. First, there is the well-known NYPD (New York City Police Department), a force of some 39,000 officers whose jurisdiction covers the five boroughs that make up the city as a whole. There are also state police, private police, federal enforcement bodies, and an interstate agency—the New York/New Jersey Port Authority Police—whose jurisdiction and authority cross both county and state lines. Jurisdictional complexities such as these are found outside the United States as well. For example, in addition to a regular police force, some cities also have extremely localized police groups, with specialized, extremely limited jurisdictions (see Exhibit 6.2).

In sum, there are several levels of police authority in most places in the United States, and their jurisdictions often overlap. The result is a highly complex law enforcement system. The rest of this chapter attempts to differentiate among the various levels of law enforcement authority and describe each in detail.

Think back to what New York City was like 100 years ago. The population was less than half of what it is today. Teddy Roosevelt was president, and the Yankees were called the Highlanders.

NEW YORK CITY COMMISSIONER RAYMOND KELLY, ON THE FACT THAT MANHATTAN'S MURDER RATE WAS THE LOWEST THE BOROUGH HAS SEEN IN MORE THAN A CENTURY.

Federal Law Enforcement Agencies

Federal law enforcement agencies have two unique features. First, since their task is to enforce specific statutes—those contained in the U.S. Criminal Code—their units are highly specialized, often with distinctive resources and training. Second, since they are agencies located in the executive branch of the U.S. government, their jurisdictional boundaries, at least in theory, have been limited by congressional authority.

The major federal agencies with enforcement powers are the **Federal Bureau of Investigation** and the newly created **Department of Homeland Security**. There are also the Bureau of Alcohol, Tobacco, and Firearms (ATF), the Drug Enforcement Administration (DEA), the U.S. Marshals Service, Customs and Border Protection, the Secret Service, the U.S. Coast Guard, the Intelligence Division of the Internal Revenue Service (IRS), the Postal Inspection Service, and the Federal Air Marshals, to name but a few.

Department of Justice
Federal Bureau of Investigation (FBI)
The FBI is the chief investigative body of the Justice Department, with legal jurisdiction extending to all federal crimes that are not the specific responsibility of some other federal enforcement agency. The more significant crimes that fall into FBI jurisdiction are kidnapping; crimes against banks; aircraft piracy; violations of the Civil Rights Act; interstate gambling; organized crime; interstate flight to avoid prosecution, custody, or confinement; and terrorism—both domestic and international (see Exhibit 6.3).

Bureau of Alcohol, Tobacco, Firearms and Explosives (ATF)
Originally organized to enforce prohibition, ATF has responsibility for enforcing the tax laws that relate to the manufacture of alcohol and tobacco and for enforcement of the Gun Control Act of 1972.

EXHIBIT 6.2 | A View from the Field

Policing Rio de Janeiro by James A. Inciardi

Rio de Janeiro has been called the *cidade maravilhosa* (wonderful city) and *cidade de Deus* (city of God), and with good reason. Found amid the many cone-shaped mountains near Guanabara Bay, Rio is situated in one of the most beautiful settings in the world. But it is much more than that—it is an exciting and vibrant city, pulsing to a samba beat, alive both day and night. It is the city of Carnival, those days of madness preceding Ash Wednesday that have become the largest street party in the world. Rio also has more than 50 miles of beaches, among them Copacabana and Ipanema, names synonymous with romance and sensual pleasure. There are the internationally famous nightclubs, the wide array of fashionable restaurants, and the legendary beachfront hotels. And towering above it all is the centerpiece of Rio de Janeiro—the 120-foot, 1,200-ton statue of Christ the Redeemer on Corcovado Mountain. Corcovado is surrounded by the lush growth of Floresta da Tijuca, a tropical forest within the city, with urban Rio at its feet.

I directed an HIV prevention project in Rio during the 1990s, and I saw a different side of *Cidade Maravilhosa*. T-shirts sold by curbside vendors read, "I left my heart in Rio, and my watch, and my wallet, and my camera . . ." Crime is a major problem in this festive city. Crime in Rio is a problem because Brazil has one of the greatest wealth disparities in the entire world. And in addition to the significant index of poverty, there are strikingly high rates of urban violence and escalating levels of cocaine use and trafficking.

To deal with what appears to be an out-of-control crime problem, a number of police forces operate in Rio de Janeiro. The most efficient by far are the *Polícia Federal*, the Brazilian equivalent of the American FBI. On almost every street corner in Rio are the *Polícia Militar*. With blue uniforms and military helmets, these military police conduct the day-to-day aspects of patrol and street law enforcement. There is also the plainclothes *Polícia Civil*, who investigate thefts and other forms of criminal activity. And in 1999, the Brazilian government created the Brazilian Intelligence Agency, a civilian-run network of agents set up to combat organized crime.

There was a time when Rio de Janeiro hosted almost 1 million tourists each year. But as the crime rates increased during the 1980s and 1990s, the tourism industry declined. For this reason, on December 21, 1992, the State Secretariat of Civil Police created a specialized bureau, the *Polícia Turística*, to better inform and protect visitors in Rio de Janeiro. Commonly known as the "Rio Tourist Police," it is a contingent of 100 bilingual officers deployed in foot patrols along Rio's popular

The Rio Tourist Police

beaches and neighboring streets, in the tourist sections and "red light" districts, and at the airport and downtown shopping areas.

Although the Tourist Police has had a measurable impact on crime in the few parts of the city where it operates, Rio has yet to shake its image as an unsafe city. Rio's problems of theft and violence continue to receive international media attention; in 2005 Rio de Janeiro was considered by many to be one of the most dangerous cities in the world. The problems are those of widespread poverty combined with open warfare between the military and drug gangs in the city's more than 500 *favelas* (hillside shantytowns).

Sources: *The New York Times,* December 8, 1999, A11; *Rio de Janeiro O Globo,* October 31, 1997, 2; James A. Inciardi, Hilary L. Surratt, and Paulo R. Telles, *Sex, Drugs, and HIV/AIDS in Brazil* (Boulder, CO: Westview Press, 2000); *Economist,* January 25, 2003, 39; *Economist,* March 29, 2003, 36; *The New York Times,* April 16, 2005, 25.

DEA? What does it stand for? It stands for Don't Expect Anything, and for Don't Even Ask!

—AN OHIO POLICE SERGEANT

Drug Enforcement Administration (DEA)   The DEA was formed in 1973 as a consolidation of other drug enforcement agencies. Its major responsibility is control of the use and distribution of narcotics and other dangerous drugs.

U.S. Marshals Service   Under the direct authority of the U.S. attorney general's office, the U.S. Marshals Service is the country's oldest law enforcement agency. It has the power to enforce all federal laws that are not the specific responsibility of some

Sidelights on Criminal Matters | EXHIBIT 6.3

The FBI: In Search of Public Enemies

Although almost all police work is undertaken by county and municipal law enforcement agencies, the Federal Bureau of Investigation also does its share. Somewhat controversial at times, the FBI is considered to be the nation's elite law enforcement body, and it is among the most famous police agencies in the world.

The beginnings of the FBI can be traced to President Theodore Roosevelt's "trust-busting" and his war with the "malefactors of great wealth" and their kept men in Congress. Roosevelt was handicapped in these efforts against industrial combines and graft because, when the need to gather evidence arose, the Department of Justice's lack of an investigative arm forced the president to borrow detectives from other federal agencies. As a result of this problem, Roosevelt's attorney general, Charles J. Bonaparte (who was also the grandnephew of Emperor Napoleon I), appealed to Congress in 1907 and 1908 to create a permanent detective force in the Department of Justice. Bonaparte's requests were denied. The major reason was Congress's expressed fear that a "secret police" would be created—a force so powerful that it might escape all control and turn its investigative energies against even Congress itself.

Congressional response to Bonaparte's appeal went even beyond denial, however. On May 30, 1908, Congress passed a law that specifically forbade the Justice Department from borrowing any investigative agents from other federal organizations. Nevertheless, on July 1, 1908, some 30 days after Congress had adjourned, Bonaparte went ahead and quietly established in the Justice Department the very investigative force that Congress had refused to authorize. He called it the Bureau of Investigation.

During its earliest years, the Bureau occupied itself with small investigations—antitrust prosecutions, bankruptcy and fraud cases, crimes committed on government reservations, and interstate commerce violations. But with the passage of the Mann Act in 1910, sponsored by Congressman James Robert Mann, the Bureau of Investigation stepped into a more national posture.

It was a time when prostitution and commercialized vice had become big business, and there was growing worry over the number of women and young girls who were being imported into the United States "for immoral purposes." Proponents of Victorian morality led an outcry for stern law enforcement action. Under the Mann Act, officially known as the White Slave Traffic Act, it was forbidden to transport women for immoral purposes in interstate or foreign commerce, to assist in procuring transportation for immoral purposes, or to persuade or induce any female to cross state lines for such purposes.

Stanley W. Finch, appointed the first director of the Bureau by Bonaparte, saw the Mann Act as an opportunity to secure funds for the expansion of his agency. He portrayed white slavery as a national menace, suggesting that only his Bureau could save the American people from such a festering horror. He offered grim descriptions of white slave traffic:

Unless a girl was actually confined in a room and guarded, there was no girl, regardless of her station in life, who was altogether safe. . . . There was need that everyone be on his guard, because no one could tell when his daughter or his wife or his mother would be selected as a victim.

Not unexpectedly, with the virtue of every wife, mother, and daughter in the nation at stake, the Bureau got its funding and the full support of Congress. Bureau agents proceeded with zeal, and by 1916 some 2,414 cases had been prosecuted.

During the years that followed, the Bureau began investigating a new "menace" to American society—the radical alien. Among the more onerous statutes passed by Congress during World War I was the Alien Act of 1918, a law designed to exclude and expel from the United States any foreign nationals who were considered to be anarchists. In 1919, as the result of numerous postwar bombings attributed to subversive organizations, William J. Flynn, former head of the Secret Service, was named the new Bureau director and given the mission of a holy war against radicals and dissidents. The General Intelligence Division was organized to concentrate on the alleged alien menace, and the first assistant in charge of the new GID was a 24-year-old up-and-coming Justice Department lawyer named John Edgar Hoover.

continued

Federal Bureau of Investigation Director J. Edgar Hoover is shown in the 1936 FBI documentary "You Can't Get Away With It."

EXHIBIT 6.3 | Sidelights on Criminal Matters continued

In 1922, congressional investigations into rumors of graft and corruption within the Harding administration left the image of the Bureau somewhat tarnished. The attorney general was found to have taken money in lieu of prosecuting Prohibition law violators; the head of the Veterans' Bureau was convicted of fraud, bribery, and conspiracy; and the secretary of the interior was found to have accepted a bribe and leased naval oil reserves at Teapot Dome, Wyoming, to a private oil company. Where, asked congressional critics, had been the watchdog of justice while the naval oil reserves were being looted? Had it been sleeping, or had it simply closed its eyes?

In the aftermath of the implied involvement of the Bureau in the Teapot Dome scandal, President Calvin Coolidge appointed Harlan Fiske Stone as his new attorney general. Stone was ordered to find a new director of the Bureau of Investigation. On May 10, 1924, the position was offered to young J. Edgar Hoover. Hoover set out to clean house and build a new image for his national police force. He established new qualifications for his agents, preferring those with legal or accounting backgrounds; he improved existing training standards; and he created a career service in which the salaries and retirement benefits would be better than in any comparable agency in the federal government or elsewhere. And Hoover did more.

By 1935, when the name of his agency had been changed to the Federal Bureau of Investigation, he had established a vast fingerprint file, a crime laboratory, the Uniform Crime Reporting system, and a training academy. During the same decade, he mounted a campaign to offset the glamorous publicity that was given John Dillinger, Alvin Karpis, Bonnie Parker and Clyde Barrow, and other criminals. For a time his "G-men" were included among the top heroes of American culture. The Bureau's list of "10 most wanted criminals" and "public enemies" provided a continuing scoreboard of Hoover's successes against bank robbers, kidnappers, gangsters, and other lawbreakers, and the entire agency reveled in its image of fearless law enforcement—an image that endured for many decades.

By 1960, Hoover's FBI was considered to be the finest law enforcement agency in the world. It had the respect of the American people. Its 6,000 agents were deployed so efficiently that the Bureau could place one of them at the scene of a federal crime anywhere in the nation within an average of 1 hour or less.

With the revolution in values that occurred in the United States during the 1960s, however, FBI activities became better known, and the image of both Hoover and his empire began to pale. The Bureau had grown into an enormous bureaucracy, with far-reaching power over the life of the nation. It led an autonomous existence and its director had lasted through eight presidencies. Information began to leak out as to the number of files the Bureau had developed on tens of thousands of noncriminals, including presidents and members of the Senate and House.

Disclosures revealed the FBI to have engaged in illegal wiretapping, a mail-opening program aimed at American citizens, the discrediting of its political enemies by attempting to destroy their jobs and credit ratings, accepting kickbacks and bribes, systematically stealing government property, and inciting radicals to commit illegal acts.

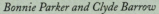

Bonnie Parker and Clyde Barrow

other federal agency, although its major activities involve administering proceedings at the federal courts. U.S. marshals also protect relocated witnesses.

Department of Homeland Security

The creation of the Department of Homeland Security (DHS) represents the most significant transformation of the U.S. government since 1947, when Harry S. Truman merged the various branches of the U.S. armed forces into the Department of Defense to better coordinate the nation's defense against military threats. DHS represents a similar consolidation, both in style and substance.

In the aftermath of the terrorist attacks against America on September 11, 2001, President George W. Bush decided that the United States needed strategic coordination between government agencies in order to better protect against threats to the homeland. President Bush called on former Pennsylvania governor Tom Ridge to be-

Amid the turmoil surrounding his years as director, J. Edgar Hoover died on March 2, 1972, at the age of 77. In the years since, there has been a succession of directors, and the agency has taken on a new image. Agents are chasing fewer bank robbers and car thieves and are focusing more on organized and white-collar crime, public corruption, espionage, drug trafficking, computer crime, and especially counterterrorism. But the "new" FBI has not managed to sidestep all controversy. During the latter part of the 1980s, for example, it became known that the FBI had conducted surveillance of American citizens and groups opposed to the Reagan administration's policies in Latin America. Scandal rocked the agency during the late 1980s and early 1990s when it was charged with widespread harassment of its black and Hispanic agents and with sexual discrimination. And most recently, the FBI received considerable criticism for careless and haphazard work in its forensic laboratories, its mishandling of evidence in the Timothy McVeigh case, its inability to aggressively police itself for spies, and its failure to act upon intelligence about the al-Quaeda 9/11 plot. In fact, in 2001, FBI agents were being compared with the Three Stooges. By 2003, its newest director, Robert S. Mueller was revamping the FBI, with a strong emphasis on restoring its credibility. And by the close of 2003, its reputation as an elite crime fighting

Gary Markstein, Copley News Service. Reprinted by permission.

organization had begun to resurface, with an exerted emphasis on counterterrorism.

Although counterterrorism has always been a priority for the FBI, today it is the Bureau's overriding mission to prevent acts of terrorism before they happen. The FBI's Counterterrorism Division collects, analyzes, and shares critical information and intelligence with the proper authorities to combat terrorism on three fronts: (1) international terrorism operations both within the United States and in support of extraterritorial investigations; (2) domestic terrorism operations; and (3) counterterrorism relating to both international and domestic terrorism.

A 1930's G-man.

Sources: Ronald Kessler, *The Bureau: The Secret History of the FBI* (New York: St. Martin's Press, 2002); David Wise, *Spy: How the FBI's Robert Haansen Betrayed America* (New York: Random House, 2003); Fred J. Cook, *The FBI Nobody Knows* (New York: Macmillan, 1964); Sanford J. Unger, *FBI* (Boston: Little, Brown, 1976); Nancy Gibbs, "Under the Microscope," *Time* (April 28, 1997): 28–35; Bruce Porter, "Running the FBI," *The New York Times* magazine, November 2, 1997, 40–45, 56–57, 72, 77–78; Athan Theoharis, *The FBI: A Comprehensive Reference Guide* (New York: Checkmark Books, 2000); Chitra Ragavan, "Mueller's Mandate," *U.S. News & World Report*, May 26, 2003, 18–29; Chitra Ragovan, "Fixing the FBI," *U.S. News & World Report*, March 28, 2005, 19–30.

come the first secretary of the DHS. In 2005, Judge Michael Chertoff was sworn in as the second secretary in the department's history.

DHS combines 22 previously disparate domestic agencies into one entity whose first priority is to protect the nation against further terrorist attacks. Component agencies analyze threats and intelligence, guard our borders and airports, protect our critical infrastructure, and coordinate the response of our nation for future emergencies. Besides providing a better-coordinated defense of the homeland, the department is also dedicated to protecting the rights of American citizens and enhancing public services, such as natural disaster assistance and citizenship services, by dedicating offices to these important missions.

The 180,000 men and women of the DHS operate under the jurisdiction of one of five major directorates: Border and Transportation Security, Emergency Preparedness and Response, Science and Technology, Information Analysis and Infrastructure Protection, and Management. Besides the directorates, several other agencies are now

A U.S. Border patrol agent drives along the U.S.-Mexico border in Jacumba, California, as men wait on the Mexican side for sunset to attempt an illegal crossing from Jacume, Mexico.

housed in the DHS, including the Office of Private Sector Liaison and the Office of Inspector General. In terms of law enforcement, the major agencies in the DHS include the following.

Customs and Border Protection (CBP) Customs and Border Protection represents a unification of agencies (including the former Customs Service) responsible for administering the laws that regulate the admission, exclusion, naturalization, and deportation of aliens, as well as preventing the illegal entry of aliens and the smuggling of illegal goods.

U.S. Citizenship and Immigration Services (USCIS) Replacing the former Immigration and Naturalization Service, it has inspectors and investigators whose responsibilities include the administration of laws related to the importation of foreign goods; the collection of duties, penalties, and other fees; and the prevention of smuggling.

Secret Service Known primarily for its role in protecting the president of the United States, his family, and other government officials, the Secret Service also has investigative units that focus on the forgery and counterfeiting of U.S. currency, checks, bonds, and federal food stamps. In this post 9/11 era, a special emphasis of the Secret Service has been the tracking of counterfeit money used by terrorists to finance their networks.[21]

Coast Guard The Coast Guard is a special naval force with responsibilities for suppressing contraband trade and aiding vessels in distress. It was formed in 1915 when an act of Congress combined the Revenue Cutter Service (established in 1790 to prevent smuggling) and the Life Saving Service.

Treasury Department
Internal Revenue Service (IRS)
The IRS is the federal agency responsible for the administration and enforcement of the federal tax laws. Its major enforcement activities in the criminal area fall within the Intelligence Division, which investigates possible criminal violations of the tax law.

Alien Apprehensions, 1985–2004

Source: Customs and Border Protection.

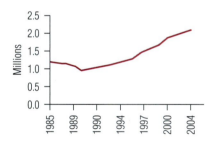

Can anyone break a $20? A Colombian police officer inspecting counterfeit American currency confiscated near Cali. Colombian and American authorities seized $20 million in fake bills in a raid and arrested eight people.

United States Postal Service

Postal Inspection Service As the law enforcement and audit arm of the Postal Service, the Postal Inspection Service has jurisdiction in all criminal matters infringing on the integrity and security of the mail and the safety of all postal valuables, property, and personnel.

Other Federal Law Enforcement Agencies

In addition to these, a variety of other federal agencies have enforcement functions. For example, the departments of Labor, Agriculture, Defense, and Interior have developed enforcement or quasi-enforcement units to deal with operations of a criminal or regulatory nature. Independent regulatory bodies such as the Interstate Commerce Commission (ICC), the Securities and Exchange Commission (SEC), and the Federal

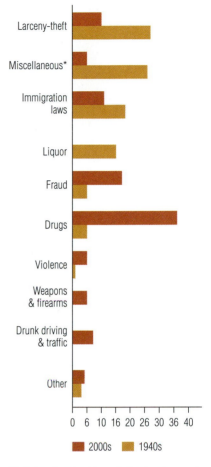

Chasing the Bad Guys, Then and Now
The federal criminal caseload by category in the 1940s and 2000s Source: Administrative Office of U.S. Courts.

- Larceny-theft
- Miscellaneous*
- Immigration laws
- Liquor
- Fraud
- Drugs
- Violence
- Weapons & firearms
- Drunk driving & traffic
- Other

0 6 10 16 20 26 30 36 40

■ 2000s ■ 1940s

*Includes crimes involving agricultural, antitrust, and civil rights issues; food and drug law; postal law; other criminal acts committed by or against federal employees; and terrorism.

Coast Guard rescues Haitians off Key Biscayne, Florida.

Trade Commission (FTC) have enforcement powers. Special investigative and enforcement bodies also appear from time to time, stemming directly from the executive, judicial, or legislative branches of government.[22]

The most secretive of America's law enforcement agents are the **Federal Air Marshals,** a team of armed commandos who travel incognito on planes to watch for hijackers and other terrorists. Most Americans had never heard of the air marshals, but the airborne attacks on the World Trade Center and the Pentagon led to the expansion of the shadowy force, despite questions of whether they would really deter terrorism. Holes in airport security screening continued even after 9/11. In December 2001, the "Shoe Bomber," Richard Reid, boarded a Miami-bound flight with explosives in his shoes. He was subdued by crew and passengers before he could ignite the shoe bomb, but his ability to clear security led to increased talk of placing air marshals on all flights. Started by President Nixon in 1970, the Federal Air Marshals are the Federal Aviation Administration's (FAA) unit of high-tech sharpshooters. Dressed in civilian clothes, they board all flights in and out of Washington, D.C., and others at random, or in response to specific threats, carrying weapons and special ammunition—hollow point, aluminum bullets that can kill without penetrating the skin of airplanes. The FAA has always been secretive about the air marshals, refusing to divulge their number, what they look like, and how they work. Agents in the 1970s were called *sky marshals.* The current force was formed after the hijacking of TWA flight 847 in June 1985.[23]

An international organization, Interpol, also plays a role in the federal law enforcement bureaucracy. Founded in 1923, **Interpol** (International Criminal Police Organization) is the largest crime-fighting organization in the world. With headquarters in Lyon, France, Interpol serves its 178 member countries as a clearinghouse and depository of information about wanted criminals. For example, it keeps data on criminal identification and circulates wanted notices. Although it is neither an investigative nor an enforcement agency, it plays active roles in crime prevention, extradition, and forensic science. In addition, Interpol works with many national police agencies (see Exhibit 6.4).[24]

State Police Agencies

The Texas Rangers were the first state police force on American soil. They were established during the earliest days of the Texas Republic, largely for military service along the Mexican border, and even today they retain some of their frontier flavor. Other state police forces emerged through a slow process of evolution. In 1865, for example, the governor of Massachusetts appointed a small force of "state constables," primarily to suppress commercialized vice. In 1879, the group was reorganized into the Massachusetts District Police and granted more general police powers.[25] In 1920, it was absorbed into a new department of public safety and designated as the Massachusetts State Police.

During the late 1800s and early 1900s, other states began experimenting with similar forces, all because of the basic deficiencies in existing rural police administration and practices. In the decades that followed the Civil War and Reconstruction, population growth and demographic shifts, changing economic conditions, and the complexities of a pluralistic society resulted in increased crime. The office of the sheriff, the only form of law enforcement that existed in many communities, had a variety of weaknesses that limited its effectiveness in preventing and controlling crime.

Weaknesses of the Sheriff System   Most sheriffs were elected by popular vote for terms of only 2 years. This made them vulnerable to political influence. Statutes in many states prohibited incumbent sheriffs from succeeding themselves in office, and in many instances deputies could not even succeed their sheriffs. Moreover, sheriffs were responsible for the conduct of civil processes, the administration of the county jail, and in some cases the collection of taxes as well, leaving little time for law enforcement. Also, the fee system under which they received compensation made civil duties more

Gender and Race or Ethnicity of Full-Time Federal Officers with Arrest and Firearm Authority

Source: Bureau of Justice Statistics.

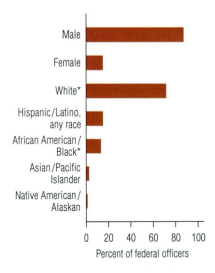

Percent of federal officers

*Non-Hispanic.

International Perspectives on Crime & Justice | EXHIBIT 6.4

Carabinieri Command for the Preservation of Cultural Heritage

It has often been said that 70 percent of the art in the world resides in Italy, and many of the best-known artists—Giotto, Donatello, Botticelli, Raphael, and Leonardo da Vinci, to name but a few—called the Italian peninsula their home. It has also been said that the ceilings of a sampling of the Catholic churches in Rome, Florence, Ravenna, and Verona reflect more artwork than entire countries. The presence of so much artwork, however, has not gone unnoticed by thieves from around the globe.

Current estimates suggest that Italy experiences almost 2,000 art thefts every year, typically involving more than 20,000 individual paintings, sculptures, and antiquities valued at well over $100 million. And art thieves are of many types. Some are amateurs—individuals with an appreciation of fine art but with little sophistication in the world of graft—a Florentine priest with a weakness for stolen religious art; an 83-year-old grandfather who stole two Old Master paintings from a local church; the owners of a villa outside Rome who were found with a marble sarcophagus (which they had converted into a flower box) from a 1st-century Roman temple. At the other end of the spectrum, there are large-scale and well-organized operations that extend beyond Italy's borders and target state museums, unguarded churches, provincial galleries, and private collections. According to insurance estimates, the worldwide trade in stolen art and antiquities ranges from $6 billion to $7 billion every year—a number surpassed on the black market only by drugs and armaments.

One of the more successful operations to recover stolen art is Italy's *Comando Carabinieri Tutela Patrimonio Culturale,* or Carabinieri Command for the Preservation of Cultural Heritage. Established as an 8-person unit in 1969, it is currently recognized worldwide as the most sophisticated art theft squad in existence. Over the years, the squad has recovered more than 185,000 art objects and some 455,000 archaeological pieces. Such success comes from a combination of art market expertise, hi-tech investigative tools, and old-fashioned police know-how.

Van Gogh's The Gardener, *stolen from a Roman museum in 1998 and recovered through high-tech surveillance and an old-fashioned sting.*

To curb the growing trend of art-related thefts in the United States, in 2005 the FBI established the nation's first art crime team. Not surprisingly, it was modeled after its Italian counterpart.

Sources: Hugh Eakin, "The World's Top Art Cop," *ARTNews,* Summer 2002, 158–163; Neil Palmer, "FBI Launches Art-Theft Squad," *ARTNews,* February 2005, 60.

---

attractive than law enforcement. These difficulties also existed in communities where civil and police duties were in the hands of local constables.[26]

There was an additional problem that affected both rural and urban areas. Crime had become more global in nature and was less often localized in a particular community. Improvements in transportation and communication had opened up new vistas for criminals, providing them with convenient access to numerous geographical areas and ready means of escape to others. Yet there was no effective communication or cooperation between the police of one municipality and those of other cities and towns. The formation of state police agencies was a direct response to these issues. They were a law enforcement mechanism that was geographically unconfined, with organization, administration, resources, training, and means of communication that could be applied to an entire state.

The Beginning of Modern State Police Administration   The beginning of modern state police administration dates to 1905, with the creation of the Pennsylvania State Constabulary. This was the first professional statewide force whose super-

The Pennsylvania State Constabulary.

intendent had extensive administrative powers and was responsible only to the governor. From the beginning it operated as a uniformed force, used a system of troop headquarters and widely distributed substations as bases of operations, and patrolled the entire state, including the most remote rural areas.[27] In the years that followed, other states established state police departments based on the Pennsylvania model, and by 1925 formal state police departments existed throughout most of the nation.

Currently, each state has its own police agency, and although the structures and functions of these organizations vary somewhat, they all generally fulfill some of the regulatory and investigative roles of federal enforcement groups as well as some of the uniformed patrol duties of local police. In general, they are organized into one of two models. Some, like the Michigan State Police and the state police forces of New York, Pennsylvania, Delaware, Vermont, and Arkansas, have general police powers and enforce state laws. In addition to performing routine patrol and traffic regulation, they have a full range of support services including specialized units that investigate major crimes, intelligence units that investigate organized criminal activities and drug trafficking, juvenile units, crime laboratories, and statewide computer facilities. Other state police agencies direct most of their attention to enforcing the laws that govern the operation of motor vehicles on public roads and highways. State highway patrols of this type operate in California, Ohio, Georgia, Florida, and the Carolinas. These agencies are not limited to the enforcement of traffic laws, however. In some cases they also investigate crimes that occur in specific locations or under particular circumstances, such as on state highways or state property, or crimes that involve the use of public carriers. State police operations can also include investigative functions relating to alcoholic beverage control, racetrack operations, and environmental pollution.

County and Municipal Policing

Despite the existence of the large federal enforcement bureaucracies and the state police agencies, most law enforcement and peacekeeping in rural, urban, and unincorporated areas is provided by county and municipal authorities.

The office of sheriff has been established by either a state constitution or statutory law in all the states except Alaska. The sheriff serves as the chief law enforcement officer in his or her county and has countywide jurisdiction. In most counties the sheriff is elected. In the past this practice called into question the qualifications of sheriffs as professional police agents as well as the effectiveness of county police organizations in enforcing the law. This issue continues today because, as with most political positions, the ability to get elected is not necessarily related to the ability to do the job.

Currently, the sheriff's office has three primary responsibilities in most jurisdictions. First, it provides law enforcement services to the county. Second, it maintains the county jail and receives prisoners who are in various stages of the criminal justice process or awaiting transportation to a state institution. Third, as an officer of the county courts, the sheriff provides personnel to serve as court bailiffs, to transport defendants and prisoners, and to act in civil matters such as in delivering divorce papers or subpoenas and enforcing court-ordered liens, eviction notices, and forfeitures of property.*

With the establishment of city, town, and other municipal police agencies during the 20th century, a number of jurisdictional disputes emerged between county and municipal police. Many states have given cities and towns statutory authority to provide for their own police protection, thus limiting the sovereignty and jurisdiction of the county police or sheriff's office to rural and unincorporated areas. In other instances, agreements have been reached between county and town police departments whereby sheriffs will not enforce the criminal laws in particular municipalities, except in instances of civil strife, police corruption, or when called on to do so.

Police in the Private Sector

Awareness of and interest in the structure and roles of private policing have increased in recent decades. Among the reasons for this are rising concern over street crime; dramatic increases in industrial thefts, shoplifting, and employee pilferage; incidents of employee violence in the workplace; and the desire of corporate managers to secure their places of business. But private-sector police forces are not new. Before formal public police agencies were organized during the 19th century, *all* policing, with the exception of the military, was private. The constables, shire-reeves, and members of the tithings and hundreds in 9th-century England were essentially a form of private police. Along with those who functioned in the night watches, they were private citizens performing at the request of royal authority or on a fee-for-service basis. The thief-takers of London, as well as the Bow Street Runners, were also private agents of law enforcement, pursuing the cause of law and order in exchange for the bounties, rewards, and other fees offered for the apprehension and conviction of highwaymen and other offenders.

The rudimentary forms of law enforcement that emerged in colonial America were modeled after the British. But during the last 100 or so years, private policing in the United States has taken on new and varied forms, functioning in areas of law enforcement where conventional police are unable, unwilling, ill-equipped, or otherwise prohibited to operate.

The Pinkerton Agency One of the most famous private policing agencies in the world is the Pinkerton National Detective Agency, founded in 1850 in a small Chicago office by a Scottish immigrant, Allan Pinkerton. "The Pinkertons," as they were called, initially gained notoriety just before the Civil War through their thwarting of the alleged "Baltimore Plot" to assassinate president-elect Abraham Lincoln. During the decades that followed, Pinkerton agents played major roles in numerous industrial clashes between workers and management. The best known of these involved the Molly Maguires in 1874 and 1875 and the Homestead strike in Pittsburgh in 1892. Hired to protect the railroads during the era of America's outlaw West, they were responsible for the arrests of John and Simeon Reno, who were credited with having organized the nation's first band of professional bank robbers. They were persistent adversaries of Jesse James, Cole Younger, and other members of the James-Younger gang.

I can see the day when an entrepreneur will come along and say, 'I can police the Bronx for $50 million less and do a better job.'

—**FORMER MINNEAPOLIS POLICE CHIEF ANTHONY V. BOUZA**

We are like a private FBI.

—**WAYNE BLACK, FORMER DIRECTOR OF WACKENHUT'S SPECIAL INVESTIGATIONS SERVICE**

Law enforcement is not a spectator sport.

—**A PINKERTON "PRIVATE EYE"**

*While many sheriffs' offices do all these things, some do not. A number are not full-service police agencies and only serve subpoenas, transport prisoners, and supervise certain civil processes.

In Texas, they were retained by railroad executives to hunt down the legendary Sam Bass and have been credited with the deaths of Jim and Rube Burrows—well known in the 1880s as proficient robbers of both trains and express offices. And they appear in the folklore of the Old West as the group who rid Montana and Wyoming of Robert Leroy Parker (Butch Cassidy), Harry Longbaugh (the Sundance Kid), Blackjack Ketchum, Etta Place, and other members of the now romanticized Wild Bunch from Robbers Roost. Allan Pinkerton himself, with his insistence on detailed descriptions of known criminals—including physical characteristics, background, companions, and hideouts—was the originator of what is now known as the "rogues' gallery."[28] And curiously, the Pinkerton National Detective Agency is responsible for the term *private eye*. The firm's trademark is an open eye above the slogan "We never sleep."

Private Policing Today Today private policing includes a variety of nonpublic organizations and individuals who provide guard, patrol, detection, protection, and alarm services as well as armored car transportation, crowd control, insurance investigation, and retail and industrial security. Pinkerton continues to operate in these areas, but perhaps the best-known agency today is the Wackenhut Corporation, a former mom-and-pop private-eye shop in South Florida that has grown into what some call a free-market army. Wackenhut has some 70,000 employees and annual revenues in excess of $2.5 billion. In addition to carrying out routine private policing chores, Wackenhut guards and monitors public and privately owned nuclear facilities, Department of Energy sites, and the Kennedy Space Center, to name but a few major posts. Then there is Wackenhut Corrections, a subsidiary that designs, builds, staffs, and operates jails and prisons for local and state governments.[29]

In general, the efforts of private police agencies are clearly separate from those of city, county, state, and federal law enforcement. Public police have the primary responsibility of maintaining order, enforcing the law, preventing and investigating crimes, and apprehending criminals. They are also responsible for policing public property. In contrast, policing *private* property is to some extent the responsibility of its owners or managers, and private security and police are often used for this job. In addition, there are areas of criminal and noncriminal activity that conventional law enforcement is either ill-equipped to handle or otherwise prohibited from handling. In cases of sus-

Spending for Private Security and Law Enforcement, 1980–2005

Source: Hallcrest Systems, Inc.

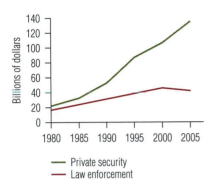

Ocean Reef, a private, high-security enclave on the northern tip of Key Largo, Florida, is said to have the lowest crime rate of any community in the United States. "Serious" crime at Ocean Reef is usually no more than the theft of a golf cart by a local teenager.

pected insurance fraud, for example, most public police agencies have neither the personnel nor the financial resources to undertake intensive investigations. The search for runaway children is also far too large a problem for public agencies, and surveillance of unfaithful spouses is beyond the authority and jurisdiction of any public service agency.

But there are problems with policing in the private sector. Nationally, private police—or "rent-a-cops," as they have come to be called—currently total almost 2 million, far more than the total number of federal, state, and local police. These private agents sometimes go beyond the limits of their authority. There have been occasions, for example, when uniformed and armed private police have fired upon shoplifters and disorderly persons or drew and fired their weapons at people out of anger and frustration. In addition, many private security officers have been found to be convicted felons.

The problem stems from the fact that there are only limited controls over private agencies. In 2003, an investigation of the largest provider of nuclear security in the United States suggested that officers at a Tennessee site may have been cheating on readiness tests at that facility since the mid-1980s. There is also a general lack of training of security personnel. For example, a Chicago police officer typically undergoes 600 to 800 hours of training, while a security officer licensed to carry a gun in Illinois is required to undergo only 40 hours of training.[30]

Although new standards for private policing have been implemented and more stringent legislation governing their activities has been passed, the effects of these changes are difficult to measure. What is clear is that the dramatic growth in the private police industry has had an impact on the quality of public policing. As many budget-conscious communities trim the size of their police forces, the number of private police agents continues to grow.

> It doesn't take a rocket scientist to protect an apartment building—that's pretty much a commodity business.
>
> —HARRY KATICA, ANALYST WITH RAYMOND JAMES AND ASSOCIATES, ON THE PRIVATE SECURITY INDUSTRY

> A quick look around reveals a ragtag army of uniformed security personnel minding property, affording serenity to high-rise dwellers, protecting private functions, bodyguarding dignitaries, and generally affording tranquility, in an uncertain age, to those rich enough to buy their own police forces.
>
> —FORMER MINNEAPOLIS POLICE CHIEF ANTHONY V. BOUZA

Volunteer Police and the Vigilante Tradition

The vigilante tradition refers to the organized activities of individuals who take the law into their own hands. From the 1760s through the beginning of the 20th century, vigilante activity was an almost constant factor in American life. It appeared in numerous forms, ranging from unorganized mobs to quasi-military groups that banded together to establish "law and order" and administer **vigilante justice** in areas where courts and law officers were nonexistent, corrupt, unwilling, or incapable of dealing with the problems at hand. Unlike the frontier lynch mobs, the better known vigilante groups—such as the South Carolina Moderators (1767), the East Texas Regulators (1840–1844), and the California Vigilance Committees (1850–1856)—were highly structured. Historian Richard Maxwell Brown describes their operations in this way:

> The characteristic vigilante movement was organized in command or military fashion and usually had a constitution, articles, or a manifesto to which the members would subscribe. Outlaws or other malefactors taken up by vigilantes were given formal (albeit illegal) trials, in which the accused had counsel or an opportunity to defend himself. An example of a vigilante trial is found in the northern Illinois regulator movement of 1841. Two accused horse thieves and murderers were tried by 120 regulators in the presence of a crowd of 500 or more. A leading regulator served as judge. The defendants were given a chance to challenge objectionable men among the regulators, and, as a result, the number of regulators taking part in the trial was cut by nine men. Two lawyers were provided—one to represent the accused and one to represent the "people." Witnesses were sworn, an arraignment was made, and the trial proceeded. In summation, the prosecuting attorney urged immediate execution of the prisoners. The crowd voted unanimously for the fatal sentence, and, after an hour allotted to the two men for prayer, they were put to death. The accused were almost never acquitted, but the vigilantes' attention to the spirit of law and order caused them to provide, by their lights, a fair but speedy trial.[31]

> The process of law is a little slow. So this is the road you'll have to go. Murderers and thieves Beware!
>
> —A JINGLE FOUND IN 1902 PINNED TO THE BODY OF A MAN HANGED BY THE VIGILANTES OF CASPER, WYOMING

Not all vigilante and regulator groups were this well organized, and not all followed rules of criminal procedure. Like the posse comitatus, in taking the law into their own hands they often seized innocent people and were guilty of depriving all people—whether innocent or guilty—of justice and constitutional rights.

The Minuteman Project

The 370-mile stretch of Arizona-Mexico border is the most porous, and certainly the most popular, piece of real estate chosen by illegal immigrants for crossing into the United States. Intelligence reports also suggest that al-Qaeda operatives may be using the same stretch of land for making their way into the United States. Moreover, a limited number of Border Patrol agents work the area. In response, the Minuteman Project was created as the newest contribution to American vigilantism. In April, 2005, several hundred volunteers patrolled a 25-mile stretch along the Arizona border near Tombstone—the desert town where Wyatt Earp and Doc Holliday exchanged bullets with the Clanton gang in 1881. The "Minutemen" supported the Border Patrol efforts by tracking and reporting smugglers. They have expressed interest in extending their campaign across the entire southern border, as well as expanding their coverage into the northern border states of Maine, Vermont, Michigan, Minnesota, North Dakota, Idaho, and Washington. Is border control by volunteers a useful solution? ■

There was a noticeable decline in the incidence of vigilantism by the close of the 19th century, but it never fully disappeared. During periods of stress, fear, and inter-group tension, it periodically reemerged in rural areas. In the turbulent and crime-ridden decades since the early 1960s, a number of quasi-vigilante groups emerged. Some have quickly come and gone, but others persist. These groups cooperate to some extent with the police. Their main activity is patrolling in radio-equipped vehicles for the purposes of spotting, reporting, and discouraging criminal acts against residents of their communities.

The Guardian Angels In recent years newer types of vigilantes have emerged that have attracted much attention from both law enforcement groups and political officials [32] (see sidebar). One of the first of these groups was New York City's Guardian Angels, founded a quarter of a century ago by Brooklyn-born Curtis Sliwa, whose job required him to ride the No. 4 subway, known as the "mugger's express." To protect riders on the No. 4, Sliwa organized a group of his friends as "The Magnificent Thirteen," and on February 13, 1979, they went on their first subway patrol. They quickly expanded into the Guardian Angels, a group of unarmed but streetwise youths, self-appointed peacekeepers who patrol the city's buses, subways, and streets. Dressed in white T-shirts and red berets, the 700-person force has had a reassuring effect on many New Yorkers. Because they have broken up numerous fights and made hundreds of civilian arrests, city police consider their presence to be significant in the prevention of crime.

The popularity of the Guardian Angels enabled the group to expand, but they have also been controversial. Some city officials view them as untrained and unregulated meddlers out to make police look bad. To others, they are no more than urban vigilantes who take the law into their own hands for the sake of ego fulfillment. [33] But in some cities, their help has been well received. [34] Nevertheless, their less-than-cordial acceptance in some locales is based on several beliefs: that the tasks of enforcing the law and keeping the peace should be entrusted only to well-trained police officers, that the Angels' presence in some situations might provoke trouble, and that they themselves run the risk of serious harm. Yet despite the mixed reactions, the Guardian Angels have endured and continue to branch out, not only in cities but in suburban areas, cyberspace, and around the world as well. [35]

Auxiliary Police Groups In contrast to vigilantes, auxiliary police groups consist of volunteer civilians working *with* local police. They are under the direct supervision of police, are trained and uniformed, and serve as the "eyes and ears" of law enforcement. Also known as "volunteer police," "civilian volunteers," and "reserve officers," the nature of their work and authority vary depending on the jurisdiction. Some auxiliary police units have formal enforcement powers, although most do not. Many are

Reprinted by permission of www.CartoonStock.com

drugs, crime, and justice | EXHIBIT 6.5

Drug Abuse Resistance Education

Not too long after Ronald Reagan moved into the White House in 1981, Nancy Reagan, his wife, began making speeches with an antidrug theme, and it was from her office as First Lady that the "Just Say No" slogan emerged. The most widespread and popular drug education approach that embodies the "Just Say No" principle has been the well-known Drug Abuse Resistance Education (D.A.R.E., or DARE) program.

Implemented both nationally and internationally, DARE was founded in Los Angeles in 1983 and designed to give youths the skills they needed to avoid involvement in drugs, gangs, and violence. Roughly three-fourths of all school districts in the United States have adopted DARE. In most versions it runs for 1 hour a week for 17 weeks, beginning in kindergarten and running through senior high school. Uniformed police officers teach the program, which includes informational messages, group interaction, role-playing, and homework.

DARE programs have been extremely popular because of the image they project—police officers working with kids to reduce the problem of drug abuse. In fact, parents and politicians consider DARE so sacred that approximately $220 million each year (almost all of which is from taxpayer funding) is devoted to it. But numerous studies, including 5- and 10-year follow-ups of students, have demonstrated that DARE is a failure, that it has no sustained effects on adolescent drug use. Although it has shown some short-term positive effects with regard to attitude changes, it has never been shown to have any lasting effects on the likelihood that children will not use drugs in later life.

Sources: Richard R. Clayton, Anne M. Catarello, and Bryan M. Johnstone, "The Effectiveness of Drug Abuse Resistance Education (Project DARE): 5-Year Follow-Up Results," *Preventive Medicine* 25 (1996): 307–318; Donald R. Lynam, Richard Milich, T. K. Logan, Catherine Martin, Carl G. Leukefeld, and Richard Clayton, "Project DARE: No Effects at 10-Year Follow-Up," *Journal of Consulting and Clinical Psychology* 67 (August 1999): 590–593; Ryan H. Sager, "Teach Them Well," *National Review* 52 (May 1, 2000): 30–32.

---

armed, while others are not. In most cases, auxiliary officers have no more authority than ordinary citizens, and they typically do not take direct action against suspects. Job duties vary as well. In some jurisdictions, police reserve officers work side by side with sworn officers. In others, reserve members assist in the care of holding facilities, book and transport prisoners, handle bail transactions, assist in crowd control, provide security during community events and emergencies, or serve as instructors in local DARE programs (see Exhibit 6.5).

Auxiliary police currently exist in most major cities and many smaller ones. In New York, for example, each police precinct has a volunteer auxiliary police unit. Members are not paid, but they are supplied with uniforms and some equipment. Although the volunteers may not issue summonses and are not allowed to carry firearms, they do have the power of arrest and may use physical force when necessary. Applicants must meet certain minimum requirements and, once accepted, are required to attend a 10-week lecture course. Each member of the auxiliary reserve usually patrols 3 nights a week and must put in at least 8 hours per month to remain active. At last count, the New York Auxiliary Police had approximately 4,000 volunteers.[36]

> It beats sitting home and watching the grass grow.
>
> —71-YEAR-OLD ELAINE AVERY, DISCUSSING HER WORK IN THE LOS ANGELES AUXILIARY POLICE FORCE

CRITICAL THINKING IN CRIMINAL JUSTICE

The Lawmen of the American Frontier West

A substantial part of the early writings about law enforcement in the United States is devoted to the exploits of the "lawmen" of America's early frontier West. Some of the major players of that era were James Butler, "Wild Bill" Hickok, Wyatt Earp, and William Barclay "Bat" Masterson, to name but a few. Both history and folklore have described them all as having almost superhuman skill, speed, cunning with weapons, and a concerted devotion to dispensing justice on the lawless frontier. From a critical thinking perspective, however, reason would suggest that these lawmen may not have been the superheros that legend and folklore described them to be. So how did all of this come about? Part of the answer lies in the characteristics of the 19th-century "dime novel," and the rest might be attributed to 20th-century mass media entertainment.[37]

CAREERS IN CRIMINAL JUSTICE

FBI Special Agent

The Federal Bureau of Investigation currently has almost 12,000 "special agents," more than 16,000 support personnel, and an annual budget in the billions.

The general requirements for training as an FBI Special Agent include (1) U.S. citizenship; (2) being at least 23 and not more than 36 years of age and having the ability to pass standard vision tests; (3) availability for assignment anywhere in the FBI's jurisdiction; (4) having a valid driver's license; and (5) having a degree from a 4-year resident program at an accredited college or university.

The FBI has four entry programs: Law, Accounting, Language, and Diversified.

Law: To qualify under the Law Program, the candidate must have a JD degree from an accredited law school.

Accounting: To qualify under the Accounting Program, the candidate must have a BS degree with a major in accounting or a related discipline and be eligible to take the CPA examination. Candidates who have not passed the CPA exam will be required to pass the FBI's accounting test.

Language: To qualify under the Language Program, the candidate must have a BS or BA degree in any discipline, including criminal justice, and be proficient in a language that meets the needs of the FBI. Candidates will be expected to pass a language proficiency test.

Diversified: To qualify under the Diversified Program, the candidate must have a BS or BA degree in any discipline, including criminal justice, plus 3 years of full-time work experience, or an advanced degree accompanied by 2 years of full-time work experience.

For further information, see the FBI Web site listed in the "Media Resources" section at the end of this chapter.

THE DIME NOVEL

On June 7, 1860, the New York *Tribune* printed an advertisement that served to announce the birth of a major publishing phenomenon. "A DOLLAR BOOK FOR A DIME!" it read—"128 pages complete, only Ten Cents!!!"

Such was the birth of the dime novel, a publishing mechanism that ultimately created legends out of any variety of western characters. The first of the novels, *Malaeska: The Indian Wife of the White Hunter,* was not a new work, nor was it particularly sensational. It had first appeared in the *Woman's Companion* magazine in 1839.[38] Furthermore, it was not the first inexpensive book, for low-budget paper ground publications were available in the American colonies as early as 1639. What *was* creative about the dime novel was its marketing, structured in a manner to arouse the interest of a mass audience seeking cheap entertainment. Posters appeared all over the country depicting novels of every variety—classics, romance, adventure, heroes and villains, "true history," and "true crime."

The dime novels that depicted events of the American West were highly sensationalized; few efforts at accurate reporting were undertaken; and many books were totally fictional accounts although accepted as historical and authentic by the reading public. Jesse and Frank James were still alive when their dime novel adventures began to appear, and no other outlaws so fully captured the attention and imagination of the readership.

Other western personalities as well were exploited by the dime novelists, and as the popularity of the novels spread, the lawmen of American's "Wild West" became subjects for consideration. Their exploits, like those of the outlaws, were expanded, energized, sensationalized, and often fully "created." Characteristic in this regard were the writings of Col. Prentiss Ingraham, which significantly contributed to the creation of legends about "Wild Bill" Hickok. In his *Wild Bill, the Pistol Dead Shot* (1882) and other novels in subsequent years, Ingraham portrayed Hickok as a superhuman demigod engaging in exploits that had no basis in fact.[39] Edward Zane Carroll Judson, the author and adventurer more commonly known by his pseudonym Ned Buntline, was also a prolific dime novelist who did much for the legendary careers of both Wild Bill Hickok and Buffalo Bill. While touring Nebraska in 1869, Buntline met William F. Cody, whom he immediately dubbed "Buffalo Bill" and cast as the hero of a long series of dime novels. His stories about Buffalo Bill were so inaccurate and contained so many falsehoods that William F. Cody admitted that many of the deeds had never occurred. Wild Bill Hickok was also a subject for Buntline, but again

Wild Bill Hickok, frontiersman, marksman, and law enforcement officer.

his dime novels about the noted marshal were based on hearsay, rumor, hyperbole, prevarication, and falsehood.[40]

20TH CENTURY MASS MEDIA

Wyatt Earp, a town marshal of somewhat questionable character, was lifted to the status of legend by a variety of mass media. Along with his brothers Morgan and Virgil, and his colleague John H. "Doc" Holliday, Wyatt had been well known in his day for his exploits in Dodge City, Kansas, and Tombstone, Arizona. But never having been a dime novel hero, Earp had yet to enter the annals of American folklore. In 1931, however, this all began to change with the publication of Stuart N. Lake's *Wyatt Earp, Frontier Marshall.* Lake's work claimed to be a "true" biography, written at the insistence of Earp's third wife. But many individuals who knew Earp maintained that he was quite unlike the character portrayed by Lake. The book omitted the many shady incidents in Earp's life, while doing everything to glorify him. In addition, the author described many events that happened to other people as if they had happened to Earp. But the character was presented and the mold created.

In 1939, the Twentieth Century Fox production of *Frontier Marshall,* starring Randolph Scott as Earp, followed the plot created by Lake and placed the marshal's heroics before a wide audience. Producer John Ford's telling of the Wyatt Earp story in the extravagant Fox production *My Darling Clementine,* starring Henry Fonda, served to further solidify Earp's fearless, dauntless, and valiant image. Finally, the John Sturges/Paramount Pictures production of *Gunfight at the OK Corral* in 1957 starring Burt Lancaster as Earp, followed by the television series *The Life and Legend of Wyatt Earp* with actor Hugh O'Brian in the title role, finalized the marshal's elevation to legend and folk hero.

What all of this suggests is that one should question the accuracy of so-called historical facts presented by the entertainment media, particularly those advertised as "based on a true story." In assessing the accuracy of any historical material, whether it be about marshals of the "Wild West," the emergence of law, other aspects of criminal justice, or any other topic for that matter, there are a number of questions that the critical thinker should ask: (1) Who is the author, and what are his or her credentials? (2) What do we know about the author and his or her reliability? (3) What are the author's sources? Are they reliable? (4) What do other sources have to say about the same topic?

OP-ED

Moving back to a question raised in the opening paragraphs of this chapter, did the events of 9/11 really change Ameri-can policing? The answer is a definite yes, and the creation of the Department of Homeland Security and the FBI's increased emphasis on counterterrorism are just small parts of it. Local law enforcement agencies all across the United States have made important changes and have instituted aggressive counterterrorism procedures that were largely the responsibility of federal authorities before September 11. To cite just a few examples, in New York City, police officers with special language skills—from Pashtun and Urdu to Arabic, Farsi, and other dialects—are scanning foreign newspapers and monitoring Internet sites. In Buffalo and Niagara County, New York State troopers and sheriffs' deputies continually maintain the security of border crossings. And in cities and towns across the nation, detectives monitor a wide range of businesses—from heliports, chemical and explosive supply firms, to Army-Navy stores and scuba gear distributors—in a frontline effort to thwart those who might be preparing for a terrorist attack. And finally, police agencies of all sizes have created command centers from which to operate in the event of an attack.

| Summary |

The police represent the largest and most visible segment of the criminal justice system and are charged with enforcing the law and keeping the peace. In the United States, the decentralized organizational structure of police agencies has meant that they operate independently of any national police force. Despite their autonomy, most law enforcement agencies are organized and operated in an essentially similar fashion.

While the rise of organized law enforcement agencies has been a relatively recent phenomenon, modern policing has its roots in the latter part of the 9th century, with the mutual pledge system of England's Alfred the Great. By the 17th century, thief-takers were being used by the Crown as private detectives paid on a piecework basis to apprehend highway robbers, burglars, housebreakers, and footpads. The foundations for the first modern police force were established by Henry Fielding in 1748. His Bow Street Runners comprised an organized investigative division that earned the standard thief-takers' rewards. In the years that followed, Patrick Colquhoun's proposal to establish a "new science of police" and a large, organized police force was ultimately rejected by Londoners suspicious of such centralized enforcement powers—but his work served as a basis for Sir Robert Peel's successful bill that established the London Metropolitan Police and ushered in the era of modern policing.

In the United States, constable and night watch systems were common in most colonial communities. In many cities, these early forms of policing lasted through the early 19th century. They were eventually replaced with more formally organized agencies, following problems with corruption and ever-increasing crime rates. As settlers moved west, sheriffs emerged as active agents of law enforcement. Their duties often included apprehending criminals, conducting popular elections, collecting taxes, and assuming custody of public funds. Because most sheriffs' departments did not employ more than one or two people, they were often forced to rely on the posse comitatus to assist in enforcing the law and capturing wanted criminals. Such posses generally consisted of all able-bodied men in the community. In addition, settlers in various western communities soon established more localized police agencies.

The 19th century also saw the establishment of state police agencies. In general, such agencies were created following the increasingly nomadic character of crime and the inability of local police agencies to coordinate their crime-fighting activities. State police agencies provided an organized means to enforce the law throughout the entire state. In addition, cities set up metropolitan police forces after the London model.

Today there are 23,000 to 25,000 public police agencies across the United States at the federal, state, and local levels. Federal law enforcement agencies enforce specific statutes as contained in the U.S. Criminal Code, and their units are highly specialized. Because these agencies serve as the enforcement branches of the federal court system, their activities are confined to specific jurisdictional boundaries that are defined by congressional mandate. In response to the terrorist attacks of 2001, federal law enforcement agencies have been dramatically reorganized and resources shifted. Specifically, the Department of Homeland Security was created by merging 22 previously disparate domestic agencies into one entity whose first priority is to protect the nation against further terrorist attacks. Component agencies each have unique law enforcement roles to carry out, many of which are now specifically directed at dismantling terrorist networks and preventing future attacks.

State police agencies generally fulfill a number of the regulatory and investigative roles of the federal enforcement groups as well as a portion of the uniformed patrol duties of the local police. However, the majority of modern policing is provided by county and municipal authority.

Police in the private sector became well known in this country during the 19th century, with the efforts of the Pinkerton National Detective Agency. Today, private security companies like the Wackenhut Corporation and Pinkerton have become part of a major growth industry that provides a range of services beyond the mere provision of "rent-a-cops" and private detectives. Private police include a variety of organizations and individuals who provide guard, patrol, detection, and alarm services, as well as armored car transportation, crowd control, insurance investigation, and retail and industrial security.

Other nonpublic police agencies include civilian police auxiliaries and neighborhood watch groups. In general, both types of groups appear to arise from an American tradition of vigilantism. Among the least controversial of modern civilian groups are auxiliary forces that work in conjunction with local police agencies. Their duties are numerous, and some have full enforcement powers and are authorized to carry weapons.

| Key Terms |

Bow Street Runners (162)
Department of Homeland Security (169)
Federal Air Marshals (176)

Federal Bureau of Investigation (169)
Henry Fielding (162)
Interpol (176)
mutual pledge (160)

posse comitatus (165)
Texas Rangers (165)
thief-takers (161)
vigilante justice (181)

| Issues for Discussion |

1. What has been the role of the sheriff down through the ages?
2. To what extent do the functions of federal, state, and local police vary and overlap?
3. Do private police agencies create more problems than their protection is worth? Why or why not?
4. Should quasi-vigilante groups be permitted to patrol the streets?

5. Should auxiliary police have full enforcement powers?
6. Were you ever exposed to the DARE program? What did you think of it?
7. Do you think that the reorganization of a few federal agencies into the Department of Homeland Security will make a difference in the war on terrorism here in the United States?

| Media and Literature Resources |

Reel Justice includes scenes that can be used to spark discussion about the following topics from this chapter:

Roots of Modern Policing

The History of Policing. There are numerous sources on this topic, including Joseph F. King, *The Development of Modern Police History in the United Kingdom and the United States* (Lewiston, NY: Edwin Mellen Press, 2004); Eric H. Monkkonen, "History of Urban Police," in *Modern Policing*, edited by Michael Tonry and Norval Morris (Chicago: University of Chicago Press, 1992), 547–580; Philip Rawlings, *Policing: A Short History* (Devon, UK: Willan Publishing, 2001); James A. Inciardi and Juliet L. Dee, "From the Keystone Cops to Miami Vice: Images of Policing in American Popular Culture," *Journal of Popular Culture* (Fall 1987): 84–102; Wilbur R. Miller, "Cops and Bobbies, 1830–1870," *Journal of Social History* (Winter 1975): 81–101; and Thomas A. Reppetto, *The Blue Parade,* New York: Free Press, 1978.

Violence and Policing in Brazil. Violence in Brazil, as well as police violence and police attempts to control violence in Brazil, has been well documented: Teresa Caldeira, "The Paradox of Police Violence in Democratic Brazil," *Ethnography* 3, 3 (2002): 235–263; Martha K. Huggins, "Urban Violence and Police Privatization in Brazil: Blended Invisibility," *Social Justice* 27, 2 (2000): 113–134; Nancy Scheper-Hughs, *Death Without Weeping: The Violence of Everyday Life in Brazil* (Berkeley: University of California Press, 1992). Moreover, an interesting new work examines police stations run exclusively for women by policewomen with the authority to investigate crimes against women, such as rape, assault, and domestic violence: Cecilia MacDowell Santos, *Women's Police Stations: Gender, Violence, and Justice in Sao Paulo, Brazil* (New York: Palgrave Macmillan, 2005).

Federal Law Enforcement Agencies. Material on the major law enforcement agencies discussed in this chapter can be found at the following Web sites:

Federal Bureau of Investigation (FBI):
http://www.fbi.gov/

Bureau of Alcohol, Tobacco, and Firearms (ATF):
http://www.atf.treas.gov

Drug Enforcement Administration (DEA):
http://www.usdoj.gov/dea/

U.S. Marshals Service:
http://www.usdoj.gov/marshals/

Department of Homeland Security:
http://www.dhs.gov/dhspublic/

U.S. Citizenship & Immigration Services (USCIS):
http://www.uscis.gov

U.S. Secret Service:
http://www.treas.gov/uss

U.S. Coast Guard:
http://www.uscg.mil/

Internal Revenue Service (IRS):
http://www.irs.gov

United States Post Office Postal Inspection Service:
http://www.usps.com/postalinspectors/

International Criminal Police Organization. Material on Interpol can be found at the following Web address: *http://www.usdoj.gov/usncb/*

| Endnotes |

1. Luke Owen Pike, *A History of Crime in England,* Vol. 2 (London: Smith, Elder, 1873–1876), 457–462.

2. Pike, *History of Crime in England,* Vol. 1, 218.

3. See Patrick Pringle, *Hue and Cry: The Story of Henry and John Fielding and Their Bow Street Runners* (New York: Morrow, 1965), 29–58.

4. Arthur L. Hayward, *Lives of the Most Remarkable Criminals* (New York: Dodd, Mead, 1927), 234.

5. See Patrick Pringle, *The Thief-Takers* (London: Museum Press, 1958).

6. Pringle, *Hue and Cry,* 81.

7. For the derivation of the term *beak* and a discussion of underworld cant, see James A. Inciardi, *Careers in Crime* (Chicago: Rand McNally, 1975), 136–139.

8. The complete story of the Bow Street Runners can be found in Patrick Pringle's *Hue and Cry,* as well as in his *Highwaymen* (New York: Roy, 1963).

9. Patrick Colquhoun, *A Treatise on the Police of the Metropolis* (London: Mawman, 1806).

10. Thomas A. Reppetto, *The Blue Parade* (New York: Free Press, 1978), 14.

11. Cited in Carl Bridenbaugh, *Cities in the Wilderness: Urban Life in America, 1625–1742* (New York: Capricorn, 1964), 63–64.

12. Cited in Carl Bridenbaugh, *Cities in the Revolt: Urban Life in America, 1743–1776* (New York: Knopf, 1965), 107.

13. Bruce Smith, *Rural Crime Control* (New York: Columbia University Institute of Public Administration, 1933), 61–63.

14. Walter Prescott Webb, *The Texas Rangers: A Century of Frontier Defense* (Boston: Houghton Mifflin, 1935).

15. Bruce Smith, *Police Systems in the United States* (New York: Harper & Brothers, 1949), 168.

16. Frank R. Prassel, *The Western Peace Officer: A Legacy of Law and Order* (Norman: University of Oklahoma Press, 1972).

17. Ira Rosenwaike, *Population History of New York City* (Syracuse, NY: Syracuse University Press, 1972), 18–36.

18. *Commercial Advisor,* August 20, 1840, cited in James F. Richardson, *The New York Police: Colonial Times to 1901* (New York: Oxford University Press, 1970), 26.

19. Cited in Richardson, *New York Police.*

20. Richardson, *New York Police,* 31.

21. *The New York Times,* September 28, 2003, sec. 4, pp. 1, 4.

22. United States General Accounting Office, *Federal Law Enforcement: Investigative Authority and Personnel at 32 Organizations* (Washington, DC: U.S. Government Printing Office, 1997). Also see the GAO Web site (*http://www.gao.gov/*).

23. Chris Hawley, "Air Marshals Likely to Step Up Presence," *Miami Herald,* September 16, 2001, 18A; Sally B. Donnelly, "My Life as an Air Cop," *Time,* June 28, 2004, 42–43; Samantha Levine, "The Marshals' Cloudy Skies," *U.S. News & World Report,* November 29, 2004, 28–29.

24. Jean-Germain Gros, "Trouble in Paradise: Crime and Collapsed States in the Age of Globalization," *British Journal of Criminology* 43 (2003): 63–80; Michael Fooner, *Interpol: Issues in World Crime and International Criminal Justice (Criminal Justice and Public Safety)* (New York: Plenum, 1989); National Institute of Justice, *A Guide to Interpol: The International Criminal Police Organization in the United States* (Boulder, CO: Paladin Press, 1991).

25. Bruce Smith, *The State Police: Organization and Administration* (New York: Columbia University Institute of Public Administration, 1925), 1–40.

26. See Advisory Commission on Intergovernmental Relations, *State–Local Relations in the Criminal Justice System* (Washington, DC: U.S. Government Printing Office, 1971).

27. Katherine Mayo, *Justice to All: The Story of the Pennsylvania State Police* (New York: Putnam, 1917).

28. James D. Horan and Howard Swiggett, *The Pinkerton Story* (New York: Putnam, 1951); James D. Horan, *The Pinkertons: The Detective Dynasty That Made History* (New York: Crown, 1967).

29. Tim Newburn, "The Commodification of Policing: Security Networks in the Late Modern City," *Urban Studies* 38, 5–6 (2001): 829–848; Deanna Hodgin, "Private Crime Fighting for a Profit," *Insight,* January 21, 1991, 44–45; *Wall Street Journal,* June 24, 1993, A12; see also the Wackenhut Corporation Web site (*http://www.wackenhut.com*).

30. For further information on private policing in the United States, see "Private Security Protects Sensitive Sites," *United Press International,* April 9, 2004; James F. Pastor, *The Privatization of Police in America: An Analysis and Case Study* (Jefferson, NC: McFarland, 2003); and Clifford E. Simonsen, *Private Security in America* (Upper Saddle River, NJ: Prentice-Hall, 1998).

31. Richard Maxwell Brown, "The American Vigilante Tradition," in *Violence in America: Historical and Comparative Perspectives,* edited by Hugh Davis Graham and Ted Robert Gurr (Beverly Hills: Sage, 1979), 162.

32. For example, see Amy Argetsinger, "In Ariz., 'Minutemen' Start Border Patrols; Volunteers Crusade to Stop Illegal Crossings," *The Washington Post,* April 5, 2005; David Kelly, "A Roadblock, Not a Barrier for Migrants," *Los Angeles Times,* April 4, 2005, 12A; and Ted Conover, "Border Vigilantes," *New York Times Magazine,* May 11, 1997, 44–46.

33. "Crime Busters?" *The Washington Times,* November 28, 2003, 24A; "Guardian Angels Back on their Feet," *The San Francisco Chronicle,* December 17, 2004, 1F; "Guardian Angels Now Hunting Terrorists," *Associated Press Online,* June 23, 2003.

34. David Montgomery, "The Halo Squad; Guardian Angels Patrol the Rough Streets, Unpaid but Appreciated," *The Washington Post,* December 10, 2003, 1C; NYC Mayor's Office, Press Release, "Mayor Giuliani Honors the Guardian Angels for Twenty Years of Community Service," February 18, 1999; *Albany Times Union,* May 17, 1999, B2; *The Washington Post,* March 4, 1999, J1.

35. Damien Cave, "In a Divided Town, a Question of Hate, or Cash?" *The New York Times,* October 24, 2004, sec. 1, pp. 1; David A. Fahrenthold, "Guardian Angels Start Anti-Gang Patrols in NW," *The Washington Post,* November 25, 2003, 8B; Mac Daniel, "Vigilante Websites Combat Solicitation of Minors for Sex," *The Boston Globe,* October 11, 2003, 3B; "National Front Plans Security Patrols," *The New Zealand Herald,* September 26, 2004; Stuart Patterson, "Guard-a-Granny Angels Keep the Muggers at Bay," *Scotland on Sunday,* June 8, 2003, 10; Randall Lane, "Virtual Vigilantes," *Forbes,* August 8, 1995, 156(5), 19.

36. See the Auxiliary Police Benevolent Association of New York Web site (*http://www.nycapba.org/*).

37. See Roger D. McGrath, *Gunfighters, Highwaymen, and Vigilantes: Violence on the Frontier* (University of California Press, 1987); and James A. Inciardi, Alan A. Block, and Lyle A. Hallowell, *Historical Approaches to Crime: Research Strategies and Issues* (Beverly Hills: Sage, Publications, 1977).

38. E. F. Bleiler, *Eight Dime Novels* (New York: Dover, 1974).

39. Prentiss Ingraham, *Wild Bill, the Pistol Dead Shot* (New York: Beadle & Adams, 1882); Prentiss Ingraham, *Wild Bill, the Pistol Prince, From Early Boyhood to His Tragic Death* (New York: Beadle & Adams, 1884).

40. R. F. Adams, *Six Guns and Saddle Leather* (Norman: University of Oklahoma Press, 1969).

7

ENFORCING THE LAW AND KEEPING THE PEACE: THE NATURE AND SCOPE OF POLICE WORK

LEARNING OBJECTIVES

After reading this chapter, you should be able to answer the following questions:

1. What are the functions of police?

2. What is the "peacekeeping role" of the police?

3. What is police discretion? Does it refer only to selective law enforcement?

4. In what ways are police agencies paramilitary organizations?

5. What gives police the right to use force?

6. How is the police bureaucracy organized?

7. What are some components of the police subculture?

8. What is the relative importance of patrol units, detective forces, and specialized squads to big-city policing?

9. What is community policing?

10. What is the status of women in American policing?

Jesse L. Martin and Dennis Farina on TV's Law and Order.

TELEVISION CITY, USA—*Law & Order, Cold Case, CSI: Miami,* and similar television dramas present policing as a series of adventures and struggles between good and evil. Good cops (and sometimes bad cops) pursue malevolence and misbehavior relentlessly until decency and morality triumph. But is this what policing is really all about? Are the escapades of Detective Joe Fontana of TV's *Law & Order* or the dangerous edge and blind allegiance to justice of *CSI: Miami*'s Horatio Caine typical in contemporary policing? And then there are *Cops,* the FOX television series *World's Scariest Police Chases,* and a host of others. Are these images of police on the prowl accurate depictions of what happens every day to America's police officers and detectives?

Consider the views of a veteran big-city police sergeant:

> I guess what our job really boils down to is not letting the assholes take over the city. Now I'm not talking about your regular crooks . . . they're bound to wind up in the joint anyway. What I'm talking about are those shitheads out to prove that they can push everybody around. Those are the assholes we gotta deal with and take care of on patrol. They're the ones that make it tough on the decent people out there. You take the majority of what we do and it's nothing more than asshole control.[1]

Is this the basic fabric of American policing?

Within the context of these questions, this chapter examines the character and structure of police work and offers some perspectives on the complexities and frustrations of attempting to enforce the law and maintain order in a democratic society. It seeks to answer questions such as these: What do police do? What do citizens ask them to do? What do they decide to do on their own initiative? And what influences their decisions to do what they do? What is the peacekeeping role of the police?

The Functions of Police

Police work suggests dramatic confrontations between police and lawbreakers, with victory going to those with more strength, power, and resources. It suggests dusting for fingerprints and searching for elusive clues, investigating and pursuing, and ultimately arresting the suspected offender. It might also suggest that the functions of policing are limited to control of crime and protection of society. But police work goes well beyond these tasks.

The Role of Police

Although police work does entail the dangerous task of apprehending criminals, officers assigned to patrol duties, even in large cities, are typically confronted with few serious crimes. In smaller cities and towns such crimes are even less frequent, and in some rural jurisdictions they may be extremely rare. Most police work is a *peacekeeping* operation. It can include intervening in situations that may represent potential threats to the public order—sidewalk agitators exercising their rights of free speech amid hostile crowds, street-corner gatherings whose intentions seem questionable, belligerent drinkers who annoy or intimidate passersby. It can include enforcing civil ordinances—for example, issuing citations for parking and minor traffic offenses, selling merchandise without a license, obstructing sidewalks, failing to post certain certificates of authority to conduct business, or perhaps even littering. Peacekeeping can also include more general areas of public service such as directing traffic, settling disputes, locating missing children, returning lost pets, counseling runaways, giving directions to confused pedestrians, and delivering babies.

Police work encompasses preventive and protective roles as well, for peacekeeping also includes *patrol,* which lessens opportunities to commit crimes. Prevention and protection can also include programs to reduce racial tensions, promote safe driving,

---

I'd love to be a policeman here, but I'm not brave enough.

— **BRITISH CONSTABLE, TRAINING IN NEW YORK CITY**

There's only one Dick Tracy and he's in the funny papers.

— **CHICAGO POLICE OFFICIAL**

He's a collector of suggestions, a clearinghouse for complaints. He listens, weighs options, takes action. Sometimes he attacks the context of crime, the disrepair and disorder that make mayhem possible—drunks on the corner, drug addicts in a lobby, trash on the sidewalk, burned-out cars in the street. And sometimes he moves against the criminals themselves—a burglar preying on a building, a motorcycle gang staking out a block.

— **JOURNALIST MICHAEL NORMAN, DESCRIBING THE DUTIES OF OFFICERS ON PATROL**

reduce opportunities for victimization, and educate the public about home security measures.

Finally, police work involves many other tasks that are often routine, time-consuming, and burdensome. Such activities include maintaining extended surveillances, transporting suspects, protecting witnesses, writing arrest and other reports, and testifying in court.[2] In short, peacekeeping operations generally do not involve criminal activities and often are not even related to law enforcement.[3]

Even the law enforcement aspects of police work do not always involve "dangerous crime." This is reflected in statistics on police *arrest activity*. Of the millions of arrests each year in the United States, only about 20 percent involve the more serious Index crimes—homicide, forcible rape, robbery, aggravated assault, burglary, larceny, vehicle theft, and arson. In contrast, a third of arrests are for lesser crimes such as gambling, driving while intoxicated, liquor law violations, disorderly conduct, prostitution, vagrancy, and drunkenness; and another 10 percent are for drug law violations.

This is not to suggest that arrest activity in areas other than Index crime is either unimportant or not dangerous. On the contrary, of the tens of thousands of assaults on police officers that occur in the United States each year, many are associated with drug-related arrests, and one-third occur when officers are responding to "disturbance" calls. Less than a fourth occur when police are responding to robbery or burglary calls or attempting arrests for other types of crimes.[4]

I'm not against the police, I'm just afraid of them.

— **ALFRED HITCHCOCK**

Police work is 70% common sense. That's what makes a policeman, common sense and the ability to make a quick decision.

— **JOSEPH WAMBAUGH**

EXHIBIT 7.1 | A View from the Field

Terrorism, Peacekeeping, and Police Patrol in Cairo, Egypt:
Some Personal Observations by James A. Inciardi and Hilary L. Surratt

In the years before 9/11, American citizens were aware of the problems of international terrorism, but unless something major occurred that captured the attention of the TV networks, not much thought was given to it on a day-to-day basis. Like other Americans, we were the same way. But something before 9/11 changed that for us.

On May 15, 1997, we flew to Cairo to attend a conference sponsored by the International Council on Alcohol and Addictions. Having never been in Egypt before, we read the tourist books and made a list of the popular attractions that we wanted to visit—the Sphinx and Giza pyramids, Saqqara, the Museum of Egyptian Antiquities, and the like. But as authors and researchers in the criminal justice field, we also inquired into the nature and extent of crime in Cairo. All indications were that in comparison with other major cities in the world, the crime rate in Cairo was quite low. Although incidents of pickpocketing and petty theft in the streets were known to happen on occasion, violence was almost unheard of. The reasons? Well for one thing, Egyptians are a friendly people, with a nonviolent culture. Furthermore, the Egyptian government protects its multibillion-dollar tourism industry by making the streets safe for visitors.

With these assurances, when we arrived at the Cairo airport, we were surprised to see so many members of the military. Not only were they at fixed posts, but they were circulating among the thousands of travelers that were coming and going as well. And all of them were heavily armed—with automatic and semiautomatic weapons.

Another passenger from the same flight immediately explained the situation: "We are in an airport, and this is the Middle East, after all." We didn't give his comment much thought.

As we left by taxi, we observed that the 2 mile stretch of road connecting the airport to the city was lined on both sides, every few feet or so, with armed police officers standing at attention. It seemed unusual, but we assumed that some dignitary was either leaving or arriving and that the police lines were some form of honor guard.

The conference was at the Cairo Marriott, a former palace, and as the taxi approached the hotel gate, we noticed that it was blocked by military police. The driver was briefly questioned, and a mirror attached to a short pole was placed beneath the cab to examine its undercarriage—no bombs were found. After less than a minute, the taxi was waved through. We didn't have time to speculate on that, because almost immediately we had to pass through a metal detector at the hotel lobby entrance. Once inside the Marriott, everything seemed normal, and a desk clerk explained that the security was routine—there was a conference going on and it was important to protect the guests. "From whom?" we asked, but all we got was a shrug.

Other than the fact that all conference attendees had to produce a passport and get a picture ID from the police, who had a substation right in the hotel, the conference was not unlike those in the United States—there were lots of research papers presented (some good but most bad), interesting exhibits by publishers and public health

Police Officers Assaulted, 1974–2004.

Source: *Uniform Crime Reports.*

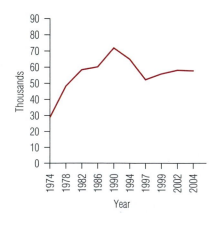

The data from these and other studies testify to the fact that police work involves keeping the peace more than enforcing the law. And the value of police peacekeeping activities should not be underestimated. A large proportion of homicides and assaults occur as an outgrowth of various kinds of disputes, and responding to them takes up a considerable amount of police time. If police no longer intervened in these conflicts, we could expect a significant increase in assaults. (For some interesting insights on police peacekeeping and its relation to terrorism in Cairo, Egypt, see Exhibit 7.1)

The Right to Use Force

The **peacekeeping role** is what mainly separates the functions of police from those of private citizens. This role involves the legitimate right to use force in situations whose urgency requires it. One police observer described it this way:

I share a property line with my neighbor. About one foot to my side of the property line there stands my horticultural pride and joy: a 25-foot apple tree. (Needless to say, a small portion of this gorgeous tree graces my neighbor's yard.) Though the tree is mine and I am willing to share its bounty with my neighbor, he does not like apples. He likes still less the fact that my apples fall off, rot, and litter his yard. One day he gets fed up with my stinking apples and yells to me that he is going to cut down my tree unless I do. "No way," I say. He revs up his chain saw.

Modern democratic society offers me two options in such a situation. First, I can drive to court and file a civil suit against my neighbor and, years hence, recover damages from him. The problem with this remedy is that I love my apple tree and don't want it cut down

organizations, and opportunities to talk with friends and colleagues whom we hadn't seen in a while.

Going to the streets in Cairo was also an experience. Police seemed to be everywhere, and well armed. But in the streets around the city, their demeanor was relaxed. Few stood at attention; most laughed and smoked and talked and joked with each other, and all greeted us and other passersby in English. We don't know how many times we heard, "Welcome to Cairo, welcome to our country," from both police and strangers in the street. At the pyramids and other tourist sites, police patrols were virtually nonexistent. There were many locals selling souvenirs, perfume, guided tours, and camel rides—and although many tended to be pushy at times, they were never offensive. All in all, the trip was a positive experience, and a safe one as well.

A few days after we returned to the United States, there was a fire-bomb and shooting attack on tourist buses outside the Museum of Egyptian Antiquities—the same one that we had visited. Ten people were killed and scores were injured. That was when the reason for the extensive police presence in Cairo was finally reported in the media. It was terrorists! CNN reported that it was the first attack on tourists in 1997. The Egyptian government used the term "Egypt's terrorists groups," but the international media spoke of Islamic militants who had been trying to seize power since 1992. Their intent was, and remains, to cripple Egypt's tourism industry, and they were being quite effective. In 1992 there were four such attacks, followed by dozens more in the years hence.

On the morning of November 16, 1997, in the middle court of the temple of Hatshepsut in Egypt's Valley of the Kings, the ancient burial structures dating to before 1400 B.C. became a late-20th-century slaughterhouse. Militants entered the area and initiated the worst ter-

As an officer stands guard, tourists make their way towards the Temple of Hatshepsut in Luxor, not too long after a band of Islamic militants charged into the temple and gunned down 58 tourists.

rorist attack in Egyptian history. Tourists were systematically shot at close range. The assault lasted for 35 minutes, and in the end 58 were dead and many more seriously wounded.

In the aftermath, those in charge of Egypt's internal security and terrorism control were replaced, and procedures were adjusted to protect tourists and other visitors. No doubt police presence and police patrols in Cairo and other parts of Egypt are far more widespread and diligent than during our visit. Nevertheless, Egypt's internal security system was unable to prevent the terrorist bombings at the Sharm el-Sheikh resort on the Red Sea in July 2005, in which nearly 100 tourists were killed.

even if at some time in the future I am rewarded handsomely for its loss. Hence, modern democratic society offers me another option: call the cops and get them to stop my chain saw–wielding neighbor before his chain bites the bark. What police have that suits them to this task is a right to use coercive force. That is, they can tell my neighbor to stop and if he doesn't, they can use whatever force is necessary to stop him.

This is not true of me, of course. I do not have a general right to use coercive force. Modern democratic society would look very dimly on me if I appeared on the scene with a gun and threatened to blast my neighbor and his revving chain saw into the great orchard in the sky.[5]

The point is simply that modern democratic society severely restricts the right of private citizens to use force and urges them to use legal channels to work out their disputes. This restriction extends to virtually all situations except those involving self-defense; and even in cases of self-defense one must show that all reasonable means of retreat were exhausted. The law does recognize, however, that there are times when something has to be done immediately—when resort to the courts or other mechanisms of dispute settlement would take too long and the damage would already be done. Police forces have been established to handle such situations; the idea is that it is better to have a small group of people (police) with a monopoly on the legitimate right to use force than to allow anyone with a club, gun, knife, or chain saw to use force in such immediately demanding situations. The right to use force in situations that demand it is held by the police in modern democratic society and justifies their role in crime control, peacekeeping, traffic, and everything else they do. In short, this is the essence of the peacekeeping role of the police.

Police Officers Slain on Duty, 1974–2004

Source: *Uniform Crime Reports.*

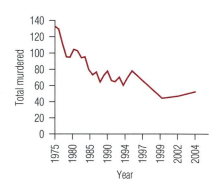

While citizens do not have the right to use coercive force against other citizens, police officers can and do exercise this right when necessary.

The Police Bureaucracy

Today virtually every police organization in the Western world is structured on a military model. Moreover, police departments are bureaucracies. Thus, there are clearly defined roles and responsibilities. Activities are guided by rules and regulations, and there is both a chain of command and an administrative staff charged with maintaining and increasing organizational efficiency. Both the military and bureaucratic characteristics of police organizations are best illustrated by a description of the division of labor, the chain and units of command, and the organizational rules, regulations, and discipline of a typical police department.

Division of Labor

All large police organizations and many smaller ones have a relatively fixed and clearly defined division of labor. As indicated in Exhibit 7.2 in the case of the Los Angeles Police Department, each separate responsibility falls within a specific unit, and the designated tasks of one division are not to be carried out by others. Narcotics, labor relations, air support, detective services, and personnel and training clearly fall within the authority of separate divisions and sections, and only under extraordinary circumstances would the personnel assigned to one division work in the area of another. Moreover, within the detective services group there are numerous separate divisions. The organizational arrangements of smaller police agencies are similar, although scaled down in proportion to their size and workload.

Chain and Units of Command

In theory at least, individual orders, requests, or any other types of information should flow up or down through each level of the organizational hierarchy, and no level of supervision or command should be bypassed. Referring again to Exhibit 7.2, if a detective in the narcotics division has a request that must be acted on by the chief of police, the communication will go up through the chain of command—from the detective to the head of the narcotics division, to the assistant commanding officer of the detective bureau, to the deputy chief heading up the detective bureau, to the office of operations, and finally to the chief of police.

If you aren't in complete control of a situation, anything you do will make it worse.

—HOWARD LEARY, FORMER COMMISSIONER, NEW YORK CITY POLICE DEPARTMENT

Police are social agents that stand ready to employ force upon the citizenry on the basis of situationally defined exigencies.

—PETER K. MANNING

The police can't use clubs or gas or dogs. I suppose they will have to use poison ivy.

—WILLIAM F. BUCKLEY, JR.

Let me explain something to you. When the police PR [public relations] man says that "an arrest is imminent" in some highly visible case, he's usually full of shit. What that line really means is that the police have no leads, no clues, no suspects, no idea of who did it, no nothin'—bupkiss!

—MASSACHUSETTS POLICE OFFICIAL

Within this structure, each employee has only one immediate superior. In addition, supervisors in the chain of command have complete and full authority over their subordinates, and the subordinates, in turn, are fully responsible to their immediate superiors.

Although no uniform terminology has been adopted for ranks, grades of authority, functional units, territorial units, and time units, those that are most common are military-style designations. Ranks and titles include *officers, commanders, sergeants, lieutenants, captains, majors, chiefs,* and sometimes even *colonels.* Functional units include *bureaus,* which are composed of *divisions,* and these, in turn, can include *sections, forces,* or *squads.* Territorial units may be called *posts* (fixed locations to which officers are assigned for duty), *routes* or *beats* (small areas assigned for patrol purposes), *sectors* (areas containing two or more posts, routes, or beats), and *districts* and *areas* (large geographic subdivisions). Finally, time units include *watches* and *shifts,* and the officers assigned to a particular watch or shift are members of a *platoon* or *company.*[6]

Rules, Regulations, and Discipline

Most police organizations have a complex system of rules and regulations designed to control and guide the actions of officers. Operations manuals and handbooks are generally lengthy, containing regulations and procedures to guide conduct in most situations. In New York City, the current rule book is almost a foot thick.[7] Officers are instructed as to when they can legitimately fire weapons (clear and present danger of injury to an officer or citizen, no warning shots, and never from a moving car). If shots are fired, there are detailed rules and procedures for "sweeping the street" (locating spent bullets and determining whether any injury or property damage occurred). Written reports of such matters must follow certain guidelines and be prepared in a specific manner (in blue ink with no erasures).

Elaborate regulations also deal with such varied phases of internal operations as the receipt of complaints from citizens, the keeping of records, the transportation of nonpolice personnel in official vehicles, and the care and replacement of uniforms, ammunition, and other equipment. And there are policies and rules to guide the manner

> Gentlemen, there is a rule for everything.
>
> **— POLICE ACADEMY INSTRUCTOR, NEW JERSEY STATE POLICE**

Brain cancer isn't the only scourge to be blamed on cell phones. They have been accused of threatening aircraft safety, causing rear-end and other automobile collisions, and contributing to the collapse of civilized society. In some jurisdictions, certain types of "multitasking," such as driving while using a cell phone, have been outlawed.

Is Policing the Most Dangerous Profession?

Annual fatality rates per 100,000 workers
Source: Department of Labor

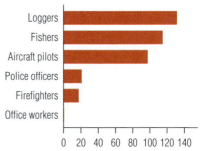

EXHIBIT 7.2 | LAW & CRIMINAL JUSTICE

Organization of the Los Angeles Police Department

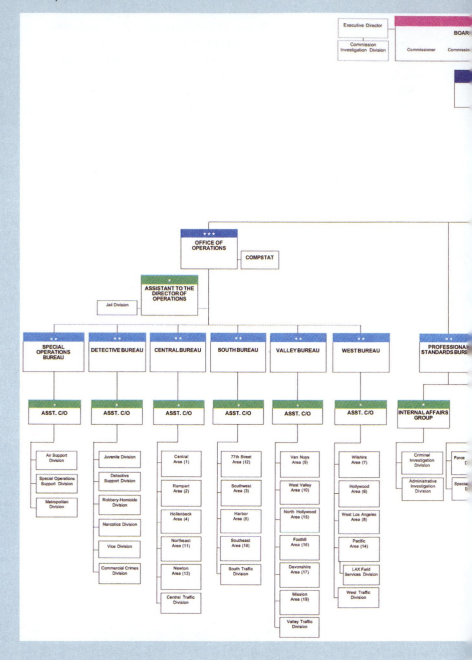

in which an officer makes an arrest, deals with medical emergencies, inspects the residence of a vacationing citizen, or takes a stray dog into custody. In some jurisdictions, there have been rules governing procedures even for mundane activities:

> *Even going to the toilet* . . . the rules dictate the formula by which . . . [an officer] . . . must request permission from a superior officer to leave post for "personal necessity."[8]

While the existence of so many rules may seem absurd at first glance, most were established with good reason. In an organization with such crucial responsibilities, particularly one that can use deadly force, rules must be carefully spelled out. Even the

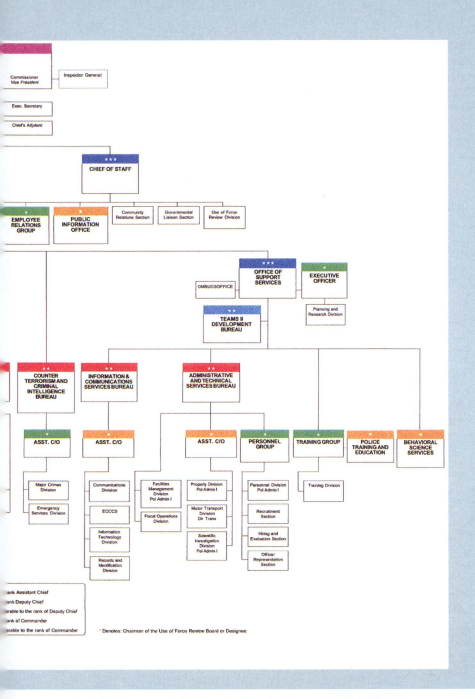

procedure for taking care of "personal necessity" is important, for it involves an officer leaving his or her assigned post. Over time, as circumstances change or become more complex, the number of rules tends to grow.

Most experts agree, however, that many police rules and regulations are essentially useless and for the most part unenforceable. The police process demands compliance with departmental regulations as well as vigorous law enforcement and peacekeeping activities. These demands sometimes conflict, and when they do, proper conduct must often take a backseat to the desirability of good "collars" (arrests). Moreover, although in theory some procedures seem explicit and comprehensive, in practice they are no

CAREERS IN CRIMINAL JUSTICE

Police Officers

Civil service regulations govern the appointment of police officers in practically all state and local jurisdictions. In general, candidates must be U.S. citizens, usually at least 20 years of age, and must meet rigorous physical and personal qualifications. Eligibility for appointment generally depends on performance in competitive written examinations as well as on education and experience. Physical examinations include tests of vision, hearing, strength, and agility. Most police agencies also require background and psychological examinations, as well as polygraph and drug tests.

There was a time when a high school diploma was the only educational requirement for an entry-level position in policing. In recent years, however, this has changed. In most large police departments and many small ones applicants are expected to have college degrees. A degree in criminal justice is preferred.

Salaries in policing vary by both state and city and are generally linked to the cost of living in a community. For this reason, on average, a police officer in New York City earns far more than his or her counterpart in, say, Berrien Springs, Michigan. In 2005, the median salary for nonsupervisory positions in policing ranged from a low of $22,500 to a high of $72,000.

At the beginning of 2005, the availability of positions in policing had reached an unprecedented high throughout the United States because of dwindling numbers of new applications to police academies and a surge in retirements by seasoned officers. The reason for both situations is essentially the same—the strong private-sector economy.

more than vague sermonizing as to what should be done. For example, in the area of police intervention in domestic disputes, no single rule can cover all possible contingencies. Officers are told to deal politely, impartially, and uniformly with citizens—but in a domestic quarrel one or more people may express aggression, fear, or anger. One might be ill, the other drunk and abusive, and there could be children or other parties involved. What the officer must do depends more often on the nuances of the situation than on any regulation or published procedure. As a Monroe County, Florida, deputy sheriff recently explained to the author:

> Got a call about a dispute in a trailer park on Key Largo, and when we get there it's like some kind of chaos. In the front room we had a woman—stoned on who knows what—screaming and crying that her husband was going to kill her. He [the husband] is standing there with a baseball bat posing like he's Babe Ruth, threatening everyone. There's a kid crying in a crib and another screaming not to hurt her parents. And then there are two other guys in there who we thought were armed, who were cousins of the woman and said they were there to "kick the shit out of her husband and no dumb cops were gonna stop them." And all of this is going on in the confines of a house trailer. So what do you do?

Problems of Enforcement Because of the very nature of police work, there are other situations in which rules cannot be enforced. Since most officers are assigned to patrol work on the street or in cars, their superiors have no way of determining what they actually are or are not doing.[9] Patrick V. Murphy, a former police chief in New York City, Detroit, and Washington, D.C., recalled a situation that existed when he was a rookie cop:

> Take the police signal box system. Its official purpose was to maintain a management check on the movement of officers out on patrol. Each precinct had a large number of call boxes that were laid out in the pattern of an electronic grid, more or less in a logical schematic pattern across the territory of the precinct. However, there was a hitch in the scheme's logic which required all officers to phone the precinct switchboard once an hour, the line on which the call was received identifying the caller's location.
>
> The hitch was that there might be two to four boxes on the same line. One learned this beat-the-system fact on the first day. "Kid," one veteran explained, "you can call in on any one of these three boxes, and for all they know at the switchboard, you could be at any one of the three locations. They're all on the same line. You can call up and say, 'This is Murphy on Box Four,' and since Four is connected to Six and Eight, be at either place." What the experienced hand was saying was that Murphy could be playing poker in a

"coop"* near Box Four, but could call in and give the impression that he was blocks away. An hour later, to give the impression that he was on the move, he could call back from the same box and give a different location entirely. Yet the system was designed, and publicized, as a management control measure.[10]

Strategic Leniency Because many rules are unenforceable, police management must practice *strategic leniency*. Administrators routinely ignore minor violations of departmental regulations in exchange for adherence to a few important rules and a modicum of organizational loyalty. Urban ethnographer Jonathan Rubinstein offers the following illustration:

> Although nobody questions a supervisor's right to punish his men . . . he will exhaust every available alternative before exercising his formal authority. For example, the operations room occasionally fills up with men who come in to drop off their reports and hang around to drink a cup of coffee. . . . The supervisors, even when they are annoyed, rarely tell the men in a direct fashion to get back on the street. . . . One day a captain from outside the district was about to enter the operations room when he noticed how many policemen were standing inside. He quickly turned away and walked over to the drinking fountain, where he took a long drink. Their sergeant, who had been urging the men to move . . . said only, "I think he wants to come in here, but he does not want to embarrass anyone so he is waiting for you to leave."[11]

It is important to note that it is not their ranks and uniforms that make the police quasi-military. Even if police officers dressed in jeans and turtleneck sweaters and their job titles were changed to worker, supervisor, and enforcer, police departments would remain quasi-military organizations. What makes them quasi-military is their punitive administrative approach: the specification of numerous rules and regulations and the punishment of deviations as a way of gaining compliance.

Many observers argue that the military model is inappropriate for policing, for several reasons. First, it is based on the assumption that discretion will be broadest at the highest organizational levels. Those at lower levels will simply follow orders. This is not what actually happens: Discretion is actually broadest and most visible at the *lowest* levels. Second, it assumes that people will work in groups, directed and coordinated by an individual who has the big picture. But police officers generally work alone, with no hands-on guidance from the top. Third, the military model treats officers as functionaries, giving them no real input into policy, when, in fact, they are the only members of the agency who are in direct daily contact with its clientele. And fourth, it encourages police to think in terms of "us" versus "them," and to regard segments of the community as "the enemy."[12]

Despite these drawbacks, the military model continues to serve as the basis for police organization. The quasi-military aspects of policing are intertwined with the bureaucratic aspects. For a brief description of one of the earliest quasi-military police organizations, see Exhibit 7.3.

The Organization of Policing

As bureaucratic organizations, most police agencies are broken down into a variety of administrative components—all of which focus either directly or indirectly on the basic police mission. *Line services* include such activities as patrol, criminal investigation, and traffic control. Depending on the size of the agency, line services might also have specific divisions or units that focus on vice, organized crime, intelligence, and juvenile crime. There are also a variety of *administrative services* that back up the efforts of the line staff. These include such activities as training, personnel issues, planning and research, legal matters, community relations, and internal investigation. *Auxiliary services* assist the line staff in carrying out the basic police function, with specialized units assigned to communications, record keeping, data processing, temporary detention, laboratory studies, and supply and maintenance.

*A sleeping or loafing location kept by officers.

EXHIBIT 7.3 | *historical perspectives on criminal justice*

L'Arma dei Carabinieri

L'Arma dei Carabinieri (the Carabinieri Corps) is not only Italy's most elite law enforcement agency but its most respected as well. In fact, it has often been said that if you asked Italian citizens to make a list of all the things that stand for freedom in their lives, the Carabinieri would be at or near the top.

Originally known as *Carabinieri Reali* (the Royal Carabinieri), the agencies was established in 1814 as a corps of both mounted and foot soldiers rigorously selected for their distinguished good conduct and their devotion to protecting the people of Italy. The new corps, created to perform both military and civilian functions, was called "Carabinieri" not only to avoid any comparisons with the former napoleonic *"Gendarmerie"* but primarily because—like all elite forces in the early 19th century—its members were equipped with carbines.

The Carabinieri Corps engaged in armed military actions from its very inception. It was especially active during World War I on numerous battle fronts, and in World War II its members were engaged in Russia, the Balkans, and the African deserts. The modern Carabinieri continues to be a military organization, but much of its work is in the

area of civilian crime fighting, focusing on organized crime, narcotics trafficking, and policing both urban and rural Italy. For visitors to Italy, the Carabinieri's presence is unmistakable—with its colorful uniforms, its high-speed Alfa Romeo sedans, and its mobile police stations in the major city squares.

The Carabinieri, patrolling the canals of 21st-century Venice.

A number of the staff and auxiliary services, such as internal investigations, are discussed elsewhere in this book. However, the basic activities of the line services are examined in greater detail here, because they reflect the primary and most visible aspects of policing.

Patrol

For generations, the "cop on the beat" has been considered the mainstay of policing. In fact, to most people, the omnipresent force of officers dispersed throughout a community, in uniform, armed, and on call 24 hours a day, is policing. Whether officers are on foot or in cars, **patrol** remains basic to police work.

Policing city streets entails a variety of tasks. Some of these are mundane, others are somewhat routine and boring, and a few can be dangerous. Patrol work includes such a wide spectrum of activities that it defies any specific description. It could involve dog catching, administering first aid, breaking up family fights, pursuing a fleeing felon, directing traffic, investigating a crime scene, calming a lost child, or writing a parking ticket. Whatever the tasks might include, the patrol force is the foundation of the police department and its largest operating unit. In cities and towns, along highways and in rural areas, uniformed patrol personnel perform all the major functions of modern law enforcement.

Functions of Police Patrol Police patrols have five specific functions: (1) to protect public safety, (2) to enforce the law, (3) to control traffic, (4) to conduct criminal investigations, and (5) to interpret the law.[13] In their role as *protectors*, patrols promote and preserve the public order, resolve conflicts, and respond to requests for defensive service. Patrol *enforcement* duties include both the preservation of constitutional guarantees and the enforcement of legal statutes. The *traffic control* functions of patrol involve enforcing the motor vehicle and traffic laws and handling accidents and disasters. As *investigators*, police officers on patrol conduct preliminary examinations of complaints of criminal acts, gather physical evidence, and interview witnesses. During such investigations they may also uncover evidence, identify and apprehend suspects, and recover stolen property. Finally, patrol officers have *quasi-judicial functions*, making the first judgment as to whether a law has been violated. It is here that the discretionary aspects of policing begin to surface. In such circumstances police may choose to arrest or take no action, or they may advise, instruct, or warn.

Motorized Versus Foot Patrols Traditionally, prevention and suppression of crime was regarded as the mission of police patrols. For a century or more this interpretation of duties was accepted by the police, public officials, and the general public. As an outgrowth of the early watch system, the first formal police patrols were on foot, and the cop on the beat became the symbol of policing in America. But as early as the 1930s, well before the automobile had fully become part of the American way of life, foot patrols were beginning to vanish.[14] By the 1960s, their efficiency was being called into question. Foot patrols were deemed geographically restrictive and wasteful of personnel. Close supervision of officers had proved difficult, and without immediate transportation, foot patrols could not be deployed quickly to locations where their services might be needed.[15] Moreover, the International Association of Chiefs of Police strongly advocated a conspicuous patrol that would convey a sense of police omnipresence. It believed that this could best be achieved using a highly mobile force of one-person cars:

> The more men and more cars that are visible on the streets, the greater is the potential for preventing a crime. A heavy blanket of conspicuous patrol at all times and in all parts of the city tends to suppress violations of the law. *The most economical manner of providing this heavy blanket of patrol is by using one-man cars when and where they are feasible.*[16]

Thus, beginning in the 1970s, police officers on foot patrol were seen less often, and one-person motor patrols became more common. However, because of the resulting lack of contact between police and citizens, the trend has been toward putting the cop back on the beat.[17] Furthermore, studies have demonstrated that foot patrols reduce citizen fear, increase citizen satisfaction, and improve the attitude and job satisfaction of police officers. In addition, foot patrols show some potential for reducing calls for service.[18] By the beginning of the 21st century, foot patrols had reappeared in Oakland, Los Angeles, Newark, Detroit, New York, Houston, Boston, Minneapolis, Cincinnati, and other locales, and the trend continues to spread.

The Kansas City Experiment Whether police are deployed singly or in teams, in vehicles or on foot, the essential value of police patrol in the prevention and suppression of crime has been called into question. In a study known as the "Kansas City experiment," three different levels of preventive patrol were compared. Fifteen police beats were divided into five matched groups of similar beats. One beat in each group was randomly selected for each of three levels of patrol: normal, proactive, and reactive. *Normal* patrol involved a single car cruising the streets when not responding to calls; the *proactive* patrol strategy involved increasing the level of preventive patrol and police visibility by doubling or tripling the number of cruising cars; and *reactive* patrol was characterized by the virtual elimination of cruising cars, with police entering the designated areas only in response to specific requests. At the conclusion of the study, no significant differences were found in any of the areas—regardless of the level of patrol—in the amount of crime officially reported to the police or in victim surveys, ob-

The "cop on the beat" is the champion of neighborhood policing. A child found wandering alone on the street must be both questioned and comforted.

It works about 90% of the time.

—LANCASTER, SOUTH CAROLINA, POLICE OFFICER, ON FOOLING A DRUG SUSPECT TO GIVE UP BY MIMICKING A FEROCIOUS BARKING DOG

The Kansas City Experiment

Kansas City is a large, rambling city in which police presence per square mile is very low. Would the study have shown the same effect had it been conducted in a place in which police beats were small and police presence per square mile was higher? I'm not sure, but I suspect that people notice more when cops are taken off half-square-mile radio car beats than when they are taken off 20-square-mile beats.

—JAMES J. FYFE

FAMOUS CRIMINALS
Son of Sam

Hello from the gutters . . . I am Son of Sam

— **DAVID BERKOWITZ, 1976**

From July 1976 through most of the following year, David Berkowitz terrorized the more than 12 million residents of the New York metropolitan area. Born on June 1, 1953, Berkowitz was phobic as a child and psychotic as an adult. He lived in a world of fantasy, and boasted of strength and sexual conquests that never indeed existed. By age 21, his fantasies evolved into demons that lurked in his mind and told him to kill.

On Christmas Eve 1975, Berkowitz committed his first act of violence with the stabbing of two women. Six months later he struck again, with a .44 caliber revolver, and by July 1977 he had fired his weapon a total of 32 times, killing six of his victims and wounding another seven.

On April 17, 1977, the situation became even more sinister. After killing two more of his victims, he left a note in the street that made him the centerpiece of thousands of headlines around the world: "I am Son of Sam."

Berkowitz was arrested a few months later, convicted of multiple charges, and is currently serving a sentence of 365 years in New York's infamous Attica Prison. ∎

served criminal activity, citizen fear of crime, or citizen satisfaction with police.[19] In effect, the Kansas City experiment suggested that police patrol was not deterring crime.

Detective Work

Although patrol units conduct preliminary investigations of criminal acts, most sustained investigations are assigned to a police department's detective force, which specializes in apprehending offenders. Detective-level policing, or *detective work,* includes the following responsibilities: (1) identification, location, and apprehension of criminal offenders; (2) collection and preservation of physical evidence; (3) location and interviewing of witnesses; and (4) recovery and return of stolen property. In addition, detective duties may occasionally involve some of the law enforcement functions of patrol units, such as responding to the dispatch of a "burglary in progress."

In small police departments, detective functions are often carried out by members of the patrol force, or there may be a single detective generalist who handles all or most of the criminal investigations. In larger departments, however, there are not only detective squads but also special investigative units that focus only on homicides, robberies, burglaries, or rape. Typically, a detective unit will handle the investigation of all crimes that occur in its geographically assigned area; not all homicides or robberies or burglaries would necessarily be assigned to detectives from one of the specialized units. However, if the nature and method of the offense suggest a link to similar crimes in other areas, or if the crime might have political repercussions, the specialized unit would become involved in the case.

In cities and metropolitan areas where crime rates are high, there may be numerous and sometimes exotic-sounding detective units whose concerns are narrowly focused. The Los Angeles Police Department has had its "Bunco-Forgery" squad; Detroit its "Squad Six," which handled only drug-related homicides; and New York its "Safe, Loft, & Truck" squad. So large, in fact, is the detective bureau of the NYPD that it has dozens of divisions, units, sections, and squads. Special detective sections and teams may also be organized for specific crimes or investigations.

Effectiveness   Media portrayals of detectives suggest that they spend much of their time pursuing criminal offenders and that their efforts at detection are quite successful. But in reality this is not the case. As former police administrator Herman Goldstein points out in *Policing a Free Society:*

> Part of the mystique of detective operations is the impression that a detective has difficult-to-come-by qualifications and skills; that investigating crime is a real science; that a detective does much more important work than other police officers; that all detective work is exciting; that a good detective can solve any crime. It borders on heresy to point out that, in fact, much of what detectives do consists of very routine and rather elementary chores, including much paper processing; that a good deal of their work is not only not exciting, it is downright boring; that the situations they confront are often less challenging and less demanding than those handled by patrolling police officers; that it is arguable whether special skills and knowledge are required for detective work; that a considerable amount of detective work is actually undertaken on a hit-or-miss basis; and that the capacity of detectives to solve crimes is greatly exaggerated.[20]

In fact, a relatively low proportion of arrests result from detective work.[21] Detectives generally receive cases in the form of reports written by patrol officers. Although practically all serious offenses are investigated by detectives in one way or another, such crimes are extremely difficult (and often impossible) to solve. In most robberies, burglaries, and thefts—which account for the majority of the FBI Index offenses—physical evidence that can be subjected to any kind of serious analysis is rarely found. Moreover, if witnesses to a crime are available, many are unwilling to cooperate or their descriptions of the offender are so vague that they are of little value to an investigator. Even victims typically are uncertain about the facts of the case. Only in those few instances where positive information can be found at the scene of a crime, or when victims or witnesses can provide substantial information to an investigating detective, are crimes likely to be solved. As a result, detectives engage in a screening process when they make decisions as to which crimes to investigate.[22]

Evaluation of Detectives Detectives are evaluated on a variety of criteria, including their success in solving major cases, their ability to keep up with paperwork, their skill at handling special types of cases, their capacity to reflect a positive and professional image, and, most important, the number of felony arrests they make during the course of a year and the "clearance rate" for specific crimes. A crime is "cleared" when a suspect has been taken into custody; the **clearance rate** refers to the proportion of crimes that result in arrest. Thus, detectives generally choose to investigate seriously and intensively only those crimes that are most likely to be cleared. It is for this reason that clearance rates for homicide, aggravated assault, and forcible rape are relatively high. A large proportion of these offenses occur as the result of personal quarrels, and the victims and offenders often are at least minimally acquainted. Thus, in many cases victims or members of their families can provide detectives with the identity of the offender or with leads and clues that can result in a possible identification. In contrast, clearance rates for robbery and burglary are quite low.

Since detective bureaus are under pressure to solve crimes, they also use a variety of mechanisms, sometimes illegitimate, to increase local clearance rates. Through the *multiple-clearance method,* a single arrest may ultimately clear numerous unsolved crimes. For example, if an individual is arrested for purse snatching, detectives may contact recent purse-snatch victims to see if they can identify the suspect in an effort to clear previous unsolved cases. But the multiple-clearance method can be abused. One Miami detective—a member of the *real* "Miami Vice"—related the following story to the author:

Police on jet ski patrol.

> It was a damn good *collar* [arrest]. The officer catches him climbing ass first out of a kitchen window with a TV set under his arm. . . . He *bags* [arrests] him, and finds a *piece* [gun] in his back pocket, burglar's tools in his raincoat, and three bags of heroin in his sock. . . . Now we know that this junkie burglar has been doing his thing up and down the coast all year, so we offer him a deal: "You help us and we'll help you." In the end, he *cops* [admits] to twenty-odd burglaries so we can get them off the books, and we drop the gun charge and tell the prosecutor that he's just some poor junkie stiff that cooperated and just needs a little help with his drug problem.

Unfounding and reclassification are also reliable, although sometimes illegitimate, methods of increasing clearance rates and getting the crime rate down.[23] *Unfounding* is a formal declaration that certain crimes that were previously thought to have occurred never actually happened. *Reclassification* is the reduction of certain crimes from felonies to misdemeanors. There are also "exceptional clearances," when some element beyond police control precludes taking the offender into custody, such as the death of a known but unapprehended criminal, a deathbed confession, or the refusal of a victim to prosecute after the perpetrator has been identified.

This is not to suggest that clearance rates are routinely manipulated. However, it is clear that different police agencies have different policies and practices in claiming and calculating clearance rates—so much so, in fact, that clearance rates are very poor indicators of the effectiveness of a detective bureau. It is also important to note that detectives, who constitute less than 15 percent of the sworn officers in most well-managed departments, clear far fewer cases than the considerably larger number of officers assigned to patrol. Yet one should not become cynical about the actual value of detective work. The perseverance of many detectives can be impressive. And routine follow-up investigations often produce new information that can lead to the identity of a perpetrator. In addition, the public relations value of detective work is immeasurable. Victims who are treated sympathetically offer greater assistance to the police in the future, and detectives' advice to victims plays an important role in preventing crime.

Solving Crimes

Police agencies clear or solve offenses when at least one person is arrested, charged, and turned over to the court for prosecution. National clearance rates in 2003 are shown below. Source: *Uniform Crime Reports.*

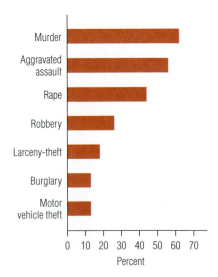

Specialized Police Units

In addition to the patrol and investigative aspects of police work, there are numerous specialized approaches to crime control. For example, many large urban police departments have juvenile or *youth bureaus,* which use proactive strategies to prevent and deter delinquent behavior. These large departments also have specialized units for enforcing vice laws or gathering information about organized crime.

Less conventional is the use of police decoys and "blending"—two related types of undercover work. In *decoy operations,* nonuniformed officers in high-crime areas pose as potential victims—drunks, tourists, young women, the elderly, or the disabled—in order to attract and apprehend street criminals. In *blending,* police officers pose as ordinary citizens, who are strategically placed in high-risk locations to observe and intervene should a crime occur.

How Much Is $1 Trillion?

A trillion dollars ($1,000,000,000,000) in $1 bills placed end to end would stretch 93 million miles—that's all the way from the earth to the sun. A $1 trillion spending spree, at a rate of $1,000 a minute, would take 2,000 years. ■

Web Patrols With the dramatic expansions in computer use and the explosive growth of the World Wide Web, Internet crime has proliferated and new varieties of criminals now stalk their victims in cyberspace. The more common crimes include e-mail fraud, trade-secret hacking, child pornography, pedophilia, and extortion and threats via e-mail. In 2005 the U.S. Department of Justice and the Computer Security Institute estimated that financial losses from computer crime were approaching $100 billion and that by 2010 they could exceed $1 trillion.[24]

To address this growing threat, law enforcement agencies at the federal, state, and local levels have established Internet crime bureaus. Many of the new "cybercops" are the younger officers who grew up with computers in their homes and who were adept at "hacking the Net" even before they began their careers in law enforcement. Others are specialists trained in computer science, and, importantly, still others are civilian volunteers who wish to "hack for a good cause." The activities of the "cyber police" or "cyber sheriffs," as they are often called, include decoy operations attempting to root out pedophiles and purveyors of child pornography, drug smugglers and arms merchants who sell contraband over the Net, and con artists engaging in all manner of fraud. Other cyber detectives specialize in hunting some of the more elite types of Internet criminals—the malicious hackers and virus writers.[25]

SWAT Teams The most controversial of the special approaches to crime control are elite police teams that use aggressive military procedures in exceptionally dangerous or potentially explosive situations. A forerunner of these groups was New York City's Tactical Patrol Force (TPF), a fast-moving battalion made up of the very best police academy recruits and trained in mob control. During the 1960s and early 1970s, the TPF swept into high-crime areas to hunt down muggers and robbers, often using a variety of decoy units.[26]

Even more visible and controversial are commando-style police units known by such names as *SWAT* (Special Weapons and Tactics), *ERT* (Emergency Response Team), or *TNT* (Tactical Neutralization Team). SWAT teams, which are carefully chosen and trained in the use of weapons and strategic invasion tactics, are typically used in situations involving hostages, airplane hijackings, and prison riots. The first of these police guerrilla units was the Philadelphia Police Department's 100-man Special Weapons and Tactics squad, which was organized in 1964 in response to the growing number of bank robberies throughout the city.[27] SWAT teams were also created in other cities during the 1960s, generally in response to riots and similar disturbances. By the mid-1970s, SWAT teams had become popular among police agencies throughout the nation, with squads ranging in size from small two-person teams in suburban and rural areas to large 160-member teams in densely populated metropolitan regions.[28] By the late 1990s, almost every jurisdiction had some type of SWAT team.[29]

The controversy over SWAT teams comes from the fact that a significant number of these specialized tactical forces are regularly engaged in everyday police work. For example, a study by the Criminal Justice Research and Training Center found that 36%

Policing New Orleans in the Wake of Hurricane Katrina

Almost immediately after Hurricane Katrina came ashore on the U.S. Gulf Coast on August 29, 2005, criminal elements exploited the chaos that nature had unleashed. In New Orleans, a wave of looting swept the city; armed criminal gangs roamed what was left of embattled New Orleans; and stranded survivors, Police Chief Eddie Compass, and the media spread stories about rapes, brutal assaults, and murders at shelters, including the Louisiana Superdome. At the height of the looting, there were reports of some police officers refusing to report for duty or resigning from the force. However, reports of mass desertions were overstated. Moreover, given that there were no official reports of rape and no eyewitnesses to sexual assault, the rumors of rape and murder at the Superdome were likely urban myth. Nevertheless, keeping the peace under the rule of law became more than the New Orleans police could do on its own. In addition to the National Guard and police officers from other jurisdictions, the U.S. government sent in thousands of troops to restore calm. Hundreds were arrested, processed, and held at a bus station converted into a temporary jail.

Major contributors to the looting were drug users and dealers. Not surprisingly, supplies of heroin, cocaine, and crack quickly dried up after Katrina made landfall. But prescription drugs like Xanax, morphine, Vicodin, and OxyContin were initially available on the streets, having been looted from local pharmacies. Many users were also trading looted goods for drugs. The going rate for morphine was $40 a tablet, while OxyContin was being traded at $20 a pill.

Within a week after the hurricane, city officials believed that the majority of the gang members and drug users and dealers blamed for the lawlessness had left the city, likely on the countless buses provided for displaced residents. At least a dozen police officers, however, were placed under investigation for alleged participation in the looting.

Chris Britt, Copley News Service. Reprinted by permission.

SWAT police in Seattle firing pepper spray at unruly demonstrators.

of the agencies surveyed used tactical units for routine patrol activities on a frequent basis.[30]

Sting Operations and Drug Enforcement Units

In addition to the specialized police units already discussed, *sting operations* have also become a part of urban law enforcement in recent years. The typical sting involves using undercover methods to control large-scale theft. Police officers pose as purchasers of stolen goods ("fences"), setting up contact points and storefronts wired for sound and videotape. When a crime is observed or recorded, police move in and arrest the suspect.

Finally, almost every urban locale has one or more specialized *drug enforcement units.* These are organized to disrupt street-level drug dealing and/or cooperate with state and federal drug enforcement groups in investigating and apprehending upper-level trafficking organizations. In some jurisdictions, furthermore, there are special squads focusing on the "diversion" of prescription drugs (see Exhibit 7.4).

| Community Policing |

In recent years, American policing has seen the emergence of a new vocabulary and, to some extent, a new approach to policing. Generally referred to as **community policing,** this new approach is more a philosophy than a set of tactics and is best defined as a collaborative effort between the police and the community to identify the problems of crime and disorder and develop solutions within the community. At the heart of community policing is the idea that police should be more responsive and connected to the communities they serve, that policing is a broad problem-solving enterprise that includes much more than reactive law enforcement, and that officers on the street and in the community should have a major role in crime prevention.[31]

Under community policing programs, officers are assigned to particular neighborhoods. Some are encouraged to own a home in or near that neighborhood and work out of a local substation in order to develop a personal stake in the quality of life of their area. The officers patrol their areas, often on foot, "walking the beat" and listening to the concerns of residents. By building trust between police and citizens, community policing makes people feel safer. It also increases the likelihood that officers will receive information to help them enforce the law more effectively.

An important aspect of community policing is the recognition that much crime control is accomplished informally by the people in a neighborhood. When residents report suspicious activity to the police, leave their lights on to deter intruders, watch the houses of neighbors who are away, and make sure the local park has enough lighting, they are helping to prevent crime. Most street criminals avoid neighborhoods where residents look out for one another and take care of their surroundings. As such, an important aspect of community policing is the fostering of cooperation between the crime prevention activities of citizens and those of the police. As noted in the 1996 report of the National Criminal Justice Commission:

> Under community policing, residents must learn to identify and report not only crime but the precursors to crime. If they spot suspicious activity, they should notify the police. If they see vandalism, they should make sure it is repaired as soon as possible. In turn, the police department must relinquish some of its control over crime prevention to the community. Officers must become community advocates and serve as a link between residents and law enforcement agencies.[32]

Community policing also requires police to analyze problems and develop solutions. When a crime occurs, rather than simply disposing of the case, police try to find out *why* it happened and what can be done to avoid it in the future. Central to problem-oriented policing is what political scientist James Q. Wilson referred to as the theory of "broken windows."[33] Wilson argued that if the first broken window in a building is not repaired, people who like breaking windows will assume that nobody cares about the building and will break more windows. Soon, the building will have no windows at all. The sense of decay in the neighborhood will increase and social disorder will flourish, and law-abiding citizens will be afraid and will hide indoors. Thus, a key task is to fix the windows as quickly as possible. This action will have a ripple effect that will influence the quality of life throughout the neighborhood.

Community policing efforts are under way in many jurisdictions, but they face many obstacles. Not all police officers and administrators are ready to accept this new style of policing. Some feel that if it involves working with citizens, it is doomed to fail-

> The bureaucracy adds to the problems by rewarding cops for "turning numbers"—making arrests, not for solving problems. Then there are the dual diseases of brutality and corruption. Beat cops, for the most part, are on their own—historically a risky practice.
>
> —JOURNALIST MICHAEL NORMAN, ON SOME OF THE DILEMMAS ASSOCIATED WITH COMMUNITY POLICING

How Business Travelers Would Make Travel Safer

Source: Carlson Wagonlit Travel Survey, 2005.

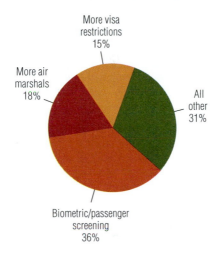

More visa restrictions 15%

More air marshals 18%

All other 31%

Biometric/passenger screening 36%

A new approach on the street: New York City police officers pause during their bicycle patrol in the Bronx to help settle a dispute over a cab fare.

EXHIBIT 7.4 | RESEARCH ON CRIME & JUSTICE

Pharmaceutical Diversion Squads

Diversion is best defined as the unlawful channeling of regulated pharmaceuticals from legal sources to the illicit marketplace, and it can occur along all points in the drug delivery process—from the original manufacturing site to the wholesale distributor, the physician's office, institutions where pharmaceuticals are dispensed, the retail pharmacy, or the patient. Diversion typically occurs in a number of ways, including (1) the illegal sale of prescriptions by physicians and pharmacists; (2) "doctor shopping" by individuals who visit multiple physicians to obtain prescriptions; (3) theft, forgery, or alteration of prescriptions by patients; (4) robberies and thefts from manufacturers, distributors, and pharmacies; (5) thefts of prescription pads and institutional drug supplies; (6) residential burglaries; (7) cross-border smuggling by traffickers and tourists; (8) medicine cabinet thefts by housekeepers, home repair personnel, and family members; and (9) wholesale and retail shipments via the Internet.

Because national studies document that the abuse and diversion of prescription drugs are widespread, more and more police agencies throughout the United States are establishing special task forces to focus on the problem. One of the better-known units is the Pharmaceutical Diversion Squad established by the Cincinnati Police Division in 1990. And because diversion is often associated with the misuse of prescription drugs by health care workers, an important focus of the Cincinnati unit is drug diversion offenses committed by health professionals.

During the period 1992 through 2002, there were 423 documented cases of prescription drug diversion involving health care workers in Cincinnati. With a median age of 40 years, the majority of these offenders were women (73%), and almost all were white (92.4%). As illustrated in Figure 1, the largest single category of diverters was nurses (63.4%), and 74.8 percent of the cases involved the aggregate of nurses, nursing assistants, and medical assistants. There were only single-digit percentages for all other professional groups. As illustrated

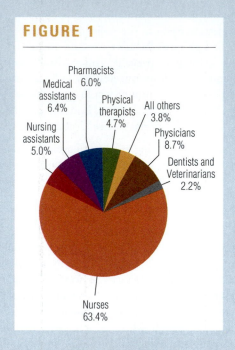

FIGURE 1

(Pie chart) Pharmacists 6.0%, Medical assistants 6.4%, Physical therapists 4.7%, All others 3.8%, Nursing assistants 5.0%, Physicians 8.7%, Dentists and Veterinarians 2.2%, Nurses 63.4%

in Figure 2, the majority of complaints resulting in police intervention were initiated by hospitals and other health care institutions (51.3%), followed by pharmacies (15.8%), with an additional 9.2 percent by law enforcement agencies. Relatively few cases resulted from complaints lodged by physicians (7.6%). However, 9 percent of the complaints came from regulatory agencies, such as the state medical, pharmacy, or nursing board.

As documented in Table 1, narcotics were by far the most widely diverted drugs. In the 423 cases, for example, there was a total of 832 drug "mentions," of which 67.7 percent were prescription narcotics. Hydrocodone (Vicodin) represented the most widely diverted

ure. Others believe that police already have far too many responsibilities, and that adding the community policing dimension will make their tasks even more difficult. Still others feel that most officers are so committed to the traditional roles of fighting crime and keeping the peace that community policing would make them ineffective in performing their basic tasks.[34] Despite these criticisms, however, community policing is increasingly popular in many parts of the nation.

It has been argued that because of the events of September 11, 2001, the threat of terrorism will change the nature of policing. For example, as one police observer recently put it:

> We are at the cusp of a silent, yet fundamental shift that will change the nature of public safety. The new policing model will emphasize tactical methods, technology, and alternative service providers, such as security personnel. It will replace the "community policing" model. . . . With the threat of terrorism, this model will become unsustainable.[35]

Changes are already being observed, in that agencies throughout the United States are shifting scores of resources to the prevention of terrorism.[36] In fact, in most

FIGURE 2

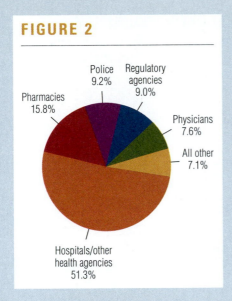

TABLE 1

Drugs Diverted

Narcotics:	
Oxycodone (OxyContin, Percocet)	15.6%
Propoxyphine (Darvon, Darvocet)	4.6
Morphine (MS Contin)	6.5
Hydrocodone (Vicodin)	20.0
Fentanyl (Duragesic, Actiq)	2.8
Codeine (Tylenol 3)	6.9
Meperidine (Demerol)	6.3
Other narcotics	4.8
Benzodiazepines:	
Alprazolam (Xanax)	3.7
Diazepam (Valium)	5.3
Other benzodiazepines	5.5
Barbiturates	3.1
Amphetamines and other stimulants	1.6
All other drugs	13.3

Source: James A. Inciardi, Hilary L. Surratt, Steven P. Kurtz, and John J. Burke, "The Diversion of Prescription Drugs by Health Care Workers in Cincinnati, Ohio," *Substance Use and Misuse,* in press.

drug (20% of all mentions), followed by oxycodone (OxyContin, Percocet) at 15.6 percent. Benzodiazepines were the second most widely diverted drugs, followed by barbiturates and stimulants.

The diversion of prescription drugs by health care workers can occur in many different ways. In the great majority of cases, the diversions occur as a result of the workers' own involvement in prescription drug misuse. For example, the Cincinnati squad was contacted by a local hospice after several AIDS patients complained that they were not getting adequate pain relief, especially when one particular nurse was on duty. An examination of the suspect nurse's curbside garbage uncovered empty vials of Schedule II narcotics, along with needles and syringes. This information, along with the finding that she was injecting her patients with tap water rather than pain medication, led to the nurse's arrest and her confession that she was doing the substitutions to support her drug habit.

Diversions in the health care field can assume numerous forms, such as outright theft of institutional supplies, substitution, forms ma-nipulation, prescription forgery, and intentional underadministration—all of which can affect the overall quality of health care. Diversion might be reduced by better controls over drug supplies and by specialized training for police officers. Most officers are not particularly familiar with prescription drugs, their patterns of misuse, and the laws and regulations that govern them. The best diversion officer is usually a person with a few years of police experience plus on-the-job training with diversion cases, combined with seminars offered regionally by such organizations as the National Association of Drug Diversion Investigators and the National Association of State Controlled Substances Authorities.

jurisdictions, special attention is being given to power plants, bridges, interstate highways, international airports, convention centers, train and bus stations, tall buildings, shopping malls, amusement parks, public transit, and anywhere else that people congregate. And because of the special vulnerability of river ports and sea ports, specialized forms of harbor policing have emerged (see Exhibit 7.5).

| Women in Policing |

In the majority of jurisdictions in the United States, legislation has mandated that male and female police officers have the same professional opportunities. State and local codes require that the hiring of police recruits be based on physical standards and competitive examinations that are designed to be nondiscriminatory; that all recruits receive the same training and that all officers have the same legal authority; that promotions are awarded on merit as decided by competitive procedures to determine professional knowledge and decision-making abilities; and that equal positions rate

EXHIBIT 7.5 | LAW & CRIMINAL JUSTICE

Harbor Policing and Terrorism

Coast to coast, local and federal agencies are teaming up to protect U.S. ports and harbors with the aim of preventing terrorist attacks.

Harbor patrols that used to focus mainly on safety violations now vigilantly focus on suspicious people and activity. Those on harbor duty have been instructed to take extra precaution with individuals taking photos, notes, or sketches or loitering near ships, bridges, and water-side areas. They also watch for vessels circling around pilings or bridges or lurking around commercial passenger vessels. Lights flashing between ships and the shore, crew members throwing or recovering items from the water, and divers near docks and bridges are also red flags to the patrol force.

In Boston, the Coast Guard, along with state, environmental, and police marine units patrol that city's harbor 24 hours a day in 8-hour shifts. A good portion of the 900 ships that dock in Boston every year are now boarded before they enter the harbor, and customs and immigration as well the state police check documents and manifests. Police helicopters skim the rooftops of harborside buildings, patrol cars cruise along the waterfront, and police divers check dock pilings for explosives or other signs of sabotage.

New York City's harbor patrol works in 12-hour shifts, equipped with machine guns and night vision binoculars to scan the approximately 150 square miles of city waterways. The fleet of 27 boats patrols approximately 60 security-sensitive areas around the city. Considering that the city was the site of the deadliest terrorist attack on U.S. soil and that video footage of the Brooklyn Bridge was uncovered in a cave in Afghanistan, harbor law enforcement remains on heightened alert around the clock.

In Miami, the Blue Lightning Strike Force was breathed new life after 9/11 in order to better secure one of the busiest ports in the country. The program, created in 1984 to catch drug smugglers, uses federal money to pay local law enforcement to help out with port security. The force does everything from running background checks on drivers who run cargo from the port to inspecting cargo containers. Likewise, Operation Turbulent Trident involves the divers of several police agencies in southern Florida in its search for narcotics, explosives, and weapons. The unit relies on intelligence gathered by the FBI, Drug Enforcement Administration, and other foreign sources to specifically target high-priority vessels. Further up the Miami River, surveillance cameras equipped with biometric face-recognition software may soon scan the individuals and vessels that come to unload their wares at river docks, providing 24-hour security to the river that flows through the heart of downtown.

New Orleans' harbor police now hold annual terrorism meetings with representatives from the U.S. attorney's office, the FBI, the Coast Guard, and other military branches to brainstorm and share ideas on the logistics of waterfront protection. The city has bolstered efforts to more carefully review foreign freighters before they embark up the Mississippi River, as well as conduct more searches onboard vessels, install new security fences around the shipping terminal, and heighten the screening of individuals visiting the docks. The 60-member Harbor Police Department patrols the docks 24 hours a day, and the city recently launched the Louisiana River Watch Program, the aquatic equivalent of a neighborhood watch program, which encourages people to keep a look out for suspicious activity on the waterways.

On the West Coast, San Diego Bay is monitored by a joint effort between the Coast Guard, the U.S. Navy, and the Harbor Police. Personnel from all agencies staff the Joint Harbor Operations Center and monitor surveillance information from 35 cameras at two cargo terminals, a cruise ship terminal, and several boat launches. In addition, the navy utilizes an underwater swimmer detection system, long-range radar, and heat-sensing technologies. Local police departments are connected to the operations through computer and image monitors.

In San Francisco Bay, obvious machine guns have recently been mounted on new patrol boats to protect the 26 miles of Alameda County coastline. The county sheriff lobbied for the firepower for extra protection of the waterways, which is home to the Port of Oakland, one of the busiest container ports in the country. Even if the machine guns weren't loaded and officers were not yet fully trained on how to fire them when they were first installed, it's yet another example of the innovative strides being made all across the country to keep our waterways safe from acts of terrorism.

Sources: Jules Crittenden, "Vigilance: Holiday Puts Spotlight on Harbor Security," *Boston Herald,* June 30, 2002, 1; Keith Darce, "Port Still Vulnerable, Its Chief Says; New Program Aims to Spot River Terrorists," New Orleans *Times-Picayune,* November 20, 2002, Money: 1; Cassio Furtado, "Ensuring Safe Harbor: Divers Search Ships Arriving in S. Florida," *Miami Herald,* December 14, 2002, B1; Corey Kilgannon, "A Nation at War: Harbor Patrol; On the Water in Wartime, an Eerily Calm View," *The New York Times,* March 21, 2003, B10.

equal pay regardless of the officer's gender. However, this was not always the case, and even now at the beginning of a new millennium, gender bias in policing remains a problem.

The Emergence of Women Police

At the beginning of the 20th century, many women could be found in the ranks of policing. However, they were *not* "police officers." Rather, they were employed in police departments as welfare and social workers; clerks and secretaries; or "police sisters," who helped officers and detectives with their paperwork and other mundane activities. Also common were "police matrons," who had limited authority with duties restricted to such tasks as searching female prisoners and inspecting nightclubs for delinquent girls.[37]

In 1910, a Los Angeles woman by the name of Alice Stebbins Wells became the first woman in the United States to hold the rank of "police officer." She worked as a plainclothes officer with the Los Angeles Police Department, and like her male counterparts she had arrest powers.[38] But despite this breakthrough by Officer Wells, the movement of women in policing was slow. By the end of the 1920s there were fewer than 500 women police officers throughout the country. Furthermore, well into the second half of the 20th century women officers were biased by separate criteria for selection and limited opportunities for advancement. In addition, most were given either menial or gender-biased tasks.

Alice Stebbins Wells of the Los Angeles Police Department (circa 1912), one of the first women police officers in the world.

The Equal Opportunity Movement for Women in Policing

Opportunities for women in policing began to expand with the passage of the Civil Rights Act of 1964 and the Equal Employment Opportunity Act of 1972. Title VII of the Civil Rights Act "prohibits discrimination on the basis of race, religion, creed, color, sex, or national origin with regard to hiring, compensation, terms, conditions, and privileges of employment." Title VII also holds that gender *may* be used as an excuse not to hire if an employer can prove that it is a "bona fide occupational qualification" for the position (such as body cavity searches of male prisoners only by male correctional officers). However, the wording of Title VII does not mean that an employer can refuse to hire a woman because of assumptions about the comparative employment characteristics of women in general (for example, that they are not as strong as men) or because of gender stereotypes (for example, that women are less capable of aggressive tactics than men).

Pursuant to the intent of Title VII, state and federal court decisions helped considerably in the movement for equal employment opportunities, not only for women in general but for women police officers in particular. A leading case in this regard was *Griggs* v. *Duke Power Co.*,[39] decided by the U.S. Supreme Court in 1971. In *Griggs*, the Court held that if job qualifications disproportionately excluded a group or class, the burden falls on the employer to prove that the requirements are "bona fide occupational qualifications" and that no other selection mechanisms can be substituted. As such, a plaintiff was not required to prove that the employer intended to discriminate.

In the wake of *Griggs*, numerous other court decisions during the 1970s and 1980s significantly altered the role of women in policing in five crucial areas: (1) sex-segregated jobs, (2) minimum height and weight requirements, (3) strength or physical fitness tests and requirements, (4) oral interviews and written examinations, and (5) blatant gender discrimination. Perhaps the most important case in this regard was *Blake* v. *Los Angeles*,[40] decided by a U.S. court of appeals in 1979. At the time that Officer Fanchon Blake and several other women officers had filed their class action lawsuit in 1973 against the Los Angeles Police Department, women and men had separate designations: "policewoman" and "policeman," and policewomen could be neither assigned to patrol work nor promoted beyond the rank of sergeant. The court of appeals held that the "Los Angeles Police Department's use of a dual-classification system barring women from police patrol work and from promotions above the rank of

Women and policing in Austin, Texas.

sergeant (1) neither complied with the requirements of Title VII of the Civil Rights Act nor could be justified on grounds of business necessity, and (2) was not substantially related to the achievement of an important governmental objective." Along with the impermissible sex segregation that resulted from this decision, the minimum height requirement of the Los Angeles Police Department was held to be improper because the department could not offer proof that such a requirement was "significantly correlated with minimal use of force so as to justify height as a business necessity."

Griggs, Blake, and numerous other cases brought by women against police departments in the United States resulted in the implementation of affirmative action policies in many police agencies. As a result, by the 1980s, the number of women in policing finally began to expand.[41]

The Current Status of Women in Policing

Studies of women officers have examined their academy performance, capabilities for patrol work, physical training, responses in hazardous situations, and handling of violent confrontations. Virtually all of this research has concluded that women do indeed have such capability.[42] Nevertheless, it would appear that women entering police work continue to encounter numerous difficulties, primarily as a result of the negative attitudes of male officers and supervisory staff. Specifically, male officers expect that women will fail; they doubt that women can equal men in most job skills; they do not consider women as doing "real" police work; and they perpetuate myths about women's emotional fitness for being "on the job."

As such, although women represent a significant number of the police officers in the United States, few have been fully accepted into the police subculture. According to the *Uniform Crime Reports,* across the nation only 11.4 percent of sworn law enforcement officers are women. Breaking down the proportion by jurisdiction type, in urban areas 11.3 percent of officers are women; in metropolitan counties 13.3 percent are women; and in rural jurisdictions only 7.8 percent of officers are women.[43] In addition, a survey by the National Center for Women and Policing (NCWP)[44] found that:

- More than half (55.9%) of large police agencies had no women officers in top-command positions.
- The majority of these large agencies (87.9%) reported that no minority women held high-ranking positions.

Women as Percentage of Sworn Law Enforcement Officers at Largest Agencies, 1990–2005

Source: Bureau of Justice Statistics.

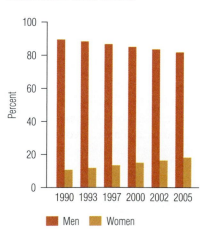

- Among small and rural agencies, 97.4 percent reported no women officers in high-ranking positions and only 1 out of the 235 agencies surveyed reported a minority woman in a high-ranking position.
- Minority women accounted for only 1.2 percent of all law enforcement positions in small and rural agencies.
- Overall, women law enforcement professionals disproportionately represented the lowest ranks in both large and small agencies.

Furthermore, the NCWP study documented that the sexual harassment of women officers was common, as were instances of intimidation and discrimination. Moreover, widespread bias in police hiring, selection practices, and recruitment policies has prevented the number of women officers from expanding. In fact, in many agencies, the pace of increase in hiring women officers has stalled or is in decline. Women's representation in policing has increased so slowly over the years that it may never reach the level of men. The reasons cited for this discrepancy include recruitment policies that favor men, the support for outdated models of policing that reward aggressive behavior, and the large numbers of women officers who are driven from their jobs as the result of unrelenting abuse.

Police Discretion and Selective Law Enforcement

Among the major tasks of police is enforcement of laws that protect people and property. In performing this task, police have the power to make arrests—official accusations of law violation. This requires that they interpret the law. On the basis of their knowledge of the criminal codes, they must make immediate judgments as to whether a law has been broken, whether to make an arrest, and whether to use force in doing so. These decisions tend to be exceedingly complex, especially because laws cannot take into account the specific circumstances surrounding every police confrontation. Moreover, not all laws can be fully enforced, and most police officers, who have minimal if any legal training, are not equipped to deal with the intricacies of law. Therefore, police must exercise a great deal of discretion in deciding what constitutes a violation of the law, which laws to enforce, and how and when to enforce them.

It is difficult to define **police discretion** in a single phrase or sentence, for the term has come to mean different things to different people. In the broadest sense, discretion exists whenever a police officer or agency is free to choose among various alternatives—to enforce the law and to do so selectively, to use force, to deal differently with some citizens than with others, to provide or not provide certain services, to train recruits in certain ways, to discipline officers differently, and to organize and deploy resources in a variety of forms. However, most discussions of police discretion focus on officers' decisions about when and how to enforce the law.

By and large, the idea of "police discretion" is paradoxical, since it appears to flout legal demands. In most jurisdictions police officers are charged with the enforcement of laws—*all* laws! Yet discretion, or selective enforcement, is necessary because of limited police resources, the ambiguity and breadth of criminal statutes, the informal expectations of legislatures, and the often conflicting demands of the public. The potential for discretion exists whenever an officer is free to choose from two or more interpretations of the events reported, inferred, or otherwise observed in any police–civilian encounter.

Situations Requiring Discretion

Studies of actual police practices demonstrate not only that discretion is widespread but also that it occurs in many different kinds of situations. On the basis of extensive field observations of police practices, sociologist Wayne R. LaFave identified many of the reasons for this situation. According to LaFave, police use of discretion most frequently occurs in three specific types of circumstances: (1) those in which the conduct

Law enforcement people are the standard—and the victims—of the unappreciated imperative. Day in, day out, they deal with misfits, liars, drunks, and head bangers. Their only reward is low pay, bad hours, and a firestorm of criticism if they make a mistake. If you're a bureaucrat and screw up, you get a private memo from the department head. If you're a cop and screw up, you get headlines. As a result, law enforcement people are usually a lot more efficient and professional at their jobs than professionals in other fields. But they also develop a myopic under-siege view of the world. They trust no one—why should they?

— MYSTERY WRITER
RANDY WAYNE WHITE

The policeman on post is in all truth the court of first instance; he is a de facto judge just as truly as any ermined magistrate, and a wise patrolman can be guide, philosopher, and friend as he carries on his daily, hourly court.

— ARTHUR WOODS, FORMER
COMMISSIONER, NEW YORK CITY
POLICE DEPARTMENT

in question is clearly illegal but police believe full enforcement was never intended; (2) those in which the act of enforcing the law would place unreasonable constraints on a police agency's time, personnel, and/or financial resources; and (3) those in which an arrest should technically be made but certain aspects of the situation make it impractical to carry out the arrest.[45]

In the first type of situation, the conduct in question is undoubtedly illegal, but there is some speculation about the intentions of legislators regarding its enforcement. This can occur when the laws are ambiguous or vague, as is often the case with statutes aimed at nuisance behavior like vagrancy and loitering. In some cases, criminal statutes are directed at a wide range of activities in order to reduce "loophole" opportunities for criminal entrepreneurs (for example, laws that prohibit not only large-scale organized gambling but friendly poker games as well). Police may also use discretion when the law appears to be intended as an expression of a moral standard and/or when the law appears to be antiquated (as in the case of "blue laws" regulating the sale and consumption of alcoholic beverages).

In the second type of situation, full enforcement of the law would be problematic because it would require too great an investment of personnel, time, and financial resources. This can occur when the offense is trivial, such as puffing on a cigarette in a smoke-free building, or when the illegal activity is an acceptable behavior for members of a particular group, such as the use of peyote in religious ceremonies among some Native American groups. Discretion might also come into play when the victim refuses to bring a complaint or when the victim is party to the offense—for instance, a massage parlor client who complains of being *rolled* (robbed) by a prostitute.

In the third type of situation, an arrest would be technically correct but special circumstances create the potential for discretion. For instance, in some situations an arrest is inappropriate or ineffective (as in the case of skid row drunks) or may damage public support for the police (for example, crackdowns on gambling). Sometimes an arrest might subvert long-range enforcement goals (as when an officer arrests an informant). At other times, an arrest may cause undue harm to the offender. Police often use discretion, for example, when first-time offenders are minors and have good reputations in the community.

Full versus Selective Enforcement

Although police discretion is a controversial issue, the need for selective law enforcement cannot be denied. **Full enforcement** of the law would require an investigation of every disturbing event and every complaint and vigorous enforcement of each and every statute on the books—from homicide, robbery, and assault to spitting on the sidewalk or littering in the street. Full enforcement would mean arresting an elderly couple for gambling at an illegal bingo game, arresting a neighbor for not having his dog licensed, or perhaps even arresting a married couple if it became known that they engage in oral sex.

Full enforcement, of course, is impossible and undesirable. It establishes mandates that exceed the capabilities and resources of police agencies and the criminal justice system as a whole. It places demands on police officers that exceed their conceptions of justice and fairness. And it goes beyond the public's conception of the judicious use of police power. Thus, police departments and officers are forced to be selective, under-enforcing some laws and not enforcing others at all, depending on the situation. However, there are few clear-cut policies to guide these choices, and therein lies the problem. The very nature of police discretion creates situations in which good judgment suggests that enforcement should be initiated, *but it is not,* and others in which enforcement should not occur, *but it does.*

Factors in the Decision to Arrest

Studies of police discretion have demonstrated that the most significant factor in the decision to arrest is the seriousness of the offense committed. This is supplemented by other information such as the offender's mental state, criminal record (when it is known to the arresting officer), whether weapons were involved, the availability of the complainant, and the amount of danger involved.[46] In addition to these seemingly objective criteria, other factors come into play as well. What many police view as "safe" arrests often involve individuals who lack the power, resources, or social position to cause trouble for the officer. The social position of the complainant is also a matter of concern. In addition, a variety of studies have documented that police use their discretionary power of arrest more often when the suspect shows disrespect.

A classic study by Irving Piliavin and Scott Briar, "Police Encounters with Juveniles," provides a particularly useful perspective on these aspects of discretion and differential law enforcement.[47] The researchers found that, with the exception of offenders who had committed serious crimes or were already wanted by the authorities, the disposition of juvenile cases depended largely on how the officer evaluated the youth's character. Such evaluations and decisions were typically limited to the information gathered by police during their actual encounters with juveniles. Piliavin and Briar found that this had serious implications both for the accused and for the justice system as a whole. When police officers believed that a youth's demeanor, race, or style of dress were good indicators of future behavior, arrests became totally discriminatory—the youths who were arrested were those who typically did not fit the officer's idea of normalcy. Demeanor, however, does not always enter into the decision to arrest. In fact, some studies suggest that displays of hostility toward police do not necessarily increase the likelihood of arrest.[48] The 1994 slaying of Nicole Brown Simpson, the former wife of O. J. Simpson, sparked considerable debate among criminal justice scholars, politicians, women's rights organizations, and the general public about the nature and extent of police discretion and its relationship to domestic violence (see Exhibit 7.6). Nicole Simpson had called the police several times—both during her marriage and after her divorce—complaining of abuse, but they had declined to make an arrest.

Command Discretion

A different level of police discretion involves departmental objectives, enforcement policies, the deployment of personnel and resources, budget expenditures, and the organizational structure of police units. Known as *command discretion,* it is implicit in the very structure and organization of a police force. It tends to be less problematic than other types of discretion since it provides at least some uniform guidelines for street-level decision making.[49] Examples of command discretion might involve orders to "clear the streets of all prostitutes" or, conversely, to "look the other way" when observing the smoking of marijuana at rock concerts.

Exactly how police discretion can be controlled is a complex question, for control must be exercised in a manner that does not destroy the basic objectives of law enforcement—effective crime control and protection of the rights of citizens. One scholar, Herman Goldstein, makes the following recommendation:

> As a minimum it would seem desirable that discretion be narrowed to the point that all officers in the same agency are operating on the same wavelength. The limits on discretion should embody and convey the objectives, priorities, and operating philosophy of the agency. They should be sufficiently specific to enable an officer to make judgments in a wide variety of unpredictable circumstances in a manner that will win the approval of top administrators, that will be free of personal prejudices and biases, and that will achieve a reasonable degree of uniformity in handling similar incidents in the community.[50]

| The Police Subculture |

A *subculture* is the normative system of a particular group that is smaller than and essentially different from the dominant culture. It includes learned behavior that is common to members of the group, ways of acting and thinking that, together, constitute a relatively cohesive cultural system. The police are members of a subculture. Their system of shared norms, values, goals, career patterns, style of life, and occupational structure, and thus their social organization, is essentially different from that of the wider

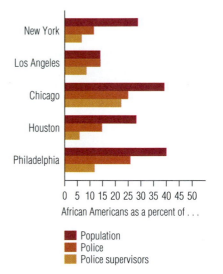

African Americans in U.S. Policing
The racial mix of the population is not reflected in the police forces of the nation's top-five cities.

African Americans as a percent of . . .

■ Population
■ Police
■ Police supervisors

EXHIBIT 7.6 | *Gender Perspectives on Crime and Justice*

Domestic Violence and Police Discretion

Current data indicate that 1,400 women are killed each year by their husbands, ex-husbands, or boyfriends. In addition, some 2 million women annually, or an average of one every 16 seconds, are beaten. In fact, the U.S. surgeon general has listed abuse by husbands and partners as the leading cause of injury to women between the ages of 15 and 44.

Police response to domestic abuse has been ambivalent at best. An Ohio study suggested that 67 percent of domestic abuse incidents reported to police do not result in official action. Of the 25 percent in which criminal complaints were initiated, only 16 percent resulted in arrest. Even in jurisdictions that mandate arrests for domestic abuse, police are hesitant to take an offender into custody. New York City, for example, has had a mandatory arrest law in effect since 1979, but a recent study found that official reports were filed in only 30 percent of the city's 200,000 annual calls and arrests were made in only 7 percent of the cases.

There appear to be a number of factors influencing policy discretion in domestic abuse situations. Most notably are the historic legality of domestic abuse and the often ambiguous character of domestic circumstances. The phrase "rule of thumb," for example, dates back to English common law and held that a man could strike his wife with a stick if it were no wider than his thumb. The legality of wife beating was formally established in an 1824 Mississippi Supreme Court decision that codified a version of the rule of thumb from English common law. Since then, police, legislators, judges, prosecutors, offenders, and even victims have been reluctant to view such behavior as illegal. As a result, many police respond to domestic calls by simply talking to the participants and allowing them to "work it out on their own." A survey of police attitudes toward domestic abuse found that only 28.7 percent of officers surveyed believed that offenders should be criminally charged. The majority—73 percent—suggested that the best course of action should be to refer the case to counseling. In addition, formal police action has often been inhibited by victims, many of whom are unwilling to initiate formal charges against their abusers for a variety of reasons—feelings of shame or humiliation, confusion, or fear of retaliation. Further, police may use discretion to handle domestic violence

A San Francisco police officer interviewing a victim of domestic violence.

calls when they have reason to believe that an arrest will bring further harm to the victim. In these cases, police may refer the victim to a battered-women's shelter so that she may escape the situation without risking additional harm.

Finally, police action in domestic abuse situations is inhibited by risk of physical harm to officers. A number of studies have demonstrated that domestic disturbance calls disproportionately contribute to an officers's risk of being assaulted.

Sources: Anne C. Baird and Obie Clayton, "Domestic Violence and Discretionary Police Action in Urban Areas: Exploring Data Patterns Using Correspondence Analysis," Southern Sociological Society, 2002; "Policing Domestic Violence: An Overview of Emerging Issues," *Police Practice and Research* 2, 4 (2001): 447–459; David Hirschel and Ira W. Hutchison, "The Relative Effects of Offense, Offender and Victim Variables on the Decision to Prosecute Domestic Violence Cases," *Violence Against Women* 7, 1 (January 2001): 46–59; David Hirschel, Charles Dean, and Richard Lumb, "The Relative Contribution of Domestic Violence to Assault and Injury of Police Officers," *Justice Quarterly* 11 (1994): 99–117; Sarah Fenstermaker Berk and Donileen Loseke, "Handling Family Violence: Situational Determinants of Police Arrest in Domestic Disturbances," *Law and Society Review* 15 (1981): 317–346.

society within which they function. Entry into the **police subculture** begins with a process of socialization through which recruits learn the values and behavior patterns characteristic of experienced officers. Ultimately, many develop an occupational or working personality as a response to the danger of their work and their obligation to exercise authority.

The Police Personality

It is widely believed that policing attracts individuals who are predisposed toward authoritarianism and cynicism, and there is some research evidence to support this point of view. Yet the overwhelming majority of the studies done in the past four decades have indicated that policing does *not* attract a distinctive personality type; rather, the nature of police socialization practices creates a distinctive **working personality** among many patrol officers.[51]

Danger and Authority Perhaps the most definitive statement on the development of the police personality comes from Jerome H. Skolnick, who summarized the process as follows:

> The policeman's role contains two principal variables, danger and authority, which should be interpreted in the light of a "constant" pressure to appear efficient. The element of danger seems to make the policeman especially attentive to signs indicating a potential for violence and lawbreaking. As a result, the policeman is generally a "suspicious" person. Furthermore, the character of the policeman's work makes him less desirable as a friend, since norms of friendship implicate others in his work. Accordingly, the element of danger isolates the policeman socially from that segment of the citizenry which he regards as symbolically dangerous and also from the conventional citizenry with whom he identifies.[52]

Skolnick further suggests that the element of authority reinforces the element of danger in isolating the police officer. That is, police are required to enforce unpopular laws, some of which are more morally conservative and others more morally liberal than the values of the community in which they work. Police are also charged with enforcing traffic laws and other codes that regulate the flow of public activity. In these situations police come to be viewed as adversaries. The public denies police authority while stressing the obligation of the police to respond to danger.

Skolnick and others have described other elements that contribute to the development of the police working personality. All officers, for example, undergo academy training followed by a period as a "cop on the beat." Because of this, officers share early experiences in a quasi-military organization that places a high value on similarity, routine, and predictability. Moreover, because they are charged with enforcing the law and keeping the peace, police are required to respond to all assaults against persons and property. Thus, in an occupation characterized by an ever-present potential for violence, many police develop a perceptual shorthand that is used to identify certain kinds of people as "symbolic assailants." As a consequence, police develop conceptions that are shaped by persistent suspicion. In fact, police are specifically *trained* to be suspicious.

Although Skolnick's conceptualization of the police personality was based on his studies of male officers, because of the very nature of all police work a number of the same characteristics are also apparent among women officers. In addition, recent research on the personality of women in policing found them to be independent, self-confident, and idealistic about their role. Moreover, personality tests found that women police score lower than average in terms of anxiety, conformity, social participation, and tolerance—all of which suggests that like male officers, female police officers also have far different personality characteristics than those of the general population.[53]

In sum, the police personality emerges as a result of the very nature of police work and the socialization processes that most police officers experience. To combat the social isolation that stems from their authoritarian role, police develop resources within their own world—other police officers—to combat social rejection. In the end, most police become part of a close-knit subculture that is protective and supportive of its members and that shares similar attitudes, values, understandings, and views of the world.[54] This sense of isolation and the solidarity that grows out of it are typified by the following comment to the author by a Delaware state trooper:

> After only three months on the job I sensed that things were changing. I heard less and less from my high school buddies, old friends didn't call me over to play some poker or have a beer, even my own brother got a little distant. My wife and I didn't get invited to parties any more—maybe they thought I'd arrest them if they pulled out a joint. Enough was enough. We started sticking with the people from Troop 6, and it was better, they were police people.

Police Cynicism An integral part of the police personality is *cynicism*—the notion that all people are motivated by evil and selfishness. **Police cynicism** develops through contact with the police subculture and the very nature of police work. Police officers

O.K., maybe I am too suspicious. But you have to admit that with the kind of work I do, suspicion breeds like bacteria in pus.

—NYPD UNDERCOVER
NARCOTICS DETECTIVE

Criminals are not "criminals," they're perpetrators, and they're not "arrested," they're apprehended.

—NEW CASTLE COUNTY,
DELAWARE, SHERIFF'S DEPUTY,
ON POLICE LANGUAGE

Up With the Cops

Most Americans believe that cops are doing their best to fight the drug war, though a full third disagree. Of those polled, 61% would pay extra taxes to support larger police staffs.

Do you think the police in your community are working as hard as they can to combat drugs?

55% Yes   36% No

If more money is spent to fight crime, what should it go for?

44% More drug treatment programs and social services

28% More police

17% More prisons

4% More judges

Would you be willing to pay extra taxes for a larger police force in your community?

61% Yes   35% No

Note: "Don't Know" answers were omitted.

Source: The Gallup Organization. ∎

are set apart from the rest of society because they have the power to regulate the lives of others, a role symbolized by their distinctive uniform and weapons. Moreover, their constant dealing with crime and the more troublesome aspects of social life serve to diminish their faith in humanity. As the late Arthur Niederhoffer put it:

> Cynicism is an emotional plank deeply entrenched in the ethos of the police world, and it serves equally well for attack or defense. For many reasons police are particularly vulnerable to cynicism. When they succumb, they lose faith in people, society, and eventually in themselves. In their Hobbesian view, the world becomes a jungle in which crime, corruption, and brutality are normal features of the terrain.[55]

Sources of Stress

A final issue here, related both to the police subculture and to the police role in general, is stress. Policing is a stressful occupation, and at least four sources of *police stress* have been identified. First, there is external stress, which results from the real dangers associated with police work—apprehending armed suspects and responding to calls involving potential conflict. Second, there is organizational stress, which is generated by the demands of the police bureaucracy—scheduling, paperwork, rules and regulations, and other requirements. Third, there is operational stress, which results from constant day-to-day exposure to the tragedies that police typically encounter. And fourth, there is personal stress, which is related to interpersonal relations among officers and their families and peers.[56]

In addition to these sources, police stress can also result from the frustrations associated with officers' inability to be effective because of forces beyond their control. For example, as a Canton, Ohio, police officer recently told the author:

> There are times when you just want to explode because the system really works you over. Like when you bust your ass trying to follow the rules to make a clean arrest of some scumbag that is a menace to the streets—and then he "walks" because there's no room in the jail to hold him.

With all these sources of stress acting on the typical officer every day, there is a strong likelihood that the officer will become even more isolated from the rest of society, retreating behind the facade of the police personality.[57]

CRITICAL THINKING IN CRIMINAL JUSTICE

Rudy Giuliani and the "Spin Doctors"

Historically, New York City has had a bad reputation for crime. In fact, for at least two centuries it has been referred to as the "city of sin" and the "crime capital of America," and until recently New York continued to be notorious for its high levels of murder, robbery, and theft. The city's streets and subways were considered extremely unsafe, and New Yorkers were renowned for having multiple locks on their doors and windows. But in the early 1990s crime began to decrease, so much so that by the middle of the decade New York was in the midst of a renaissance, and by the beginning of the new century the "Big Apple" was considered one of the safest large cities in the world. It continues to be so.

But as noted in the preliminary discussion of critical thinking in Chapter 1, numerous articles in the national media spoke of how former New York City mayor Rudolph Giuliani's tough, hands-on approach to the crime problem had reduced the violence rate in the great metropolis. But could this really be attributed to the policies of one man? Or was it the work of Rudy Giuliani's public relations people—the so-called spin doctors?

So why *did* the crime rate in New York City fall so dramatically? Was it part of an overall national trend? Was it the activity of police? Was it Giuliani's policies? Was it just a statistical fluke? Or was it something else?

To some extent, the sliding crime rates were indeed part of the national trend discussed in Chapter 4. The crack epidemic and its related crime wave were in a declining phase as well. In addition, large numbers of immigrants from such places as the Caribbean, Russia, Ukraine, and Uzbekistan—more than 500,000 in all from 1990 through 1994—were taking over the dilapidated and desperate corners of the city and rebuilding them. As a result, neighborhoods that had been "war zones" were vibrant again.

But much of what happened was due to some fundamental changes in policing, many of which were instituted by Mayor Rudolph Giuliani. To begin with, New York's three police departments—the NYPD, the Transit Authority Police, and the Housing Authority Police—were consolidated. Suddenly, some 40,000 officers, along with technical and forensic resources comparable to those of the FBI, were under the control of one police commissioner. This made citywide reform possible.

Next, specific aspects of policing were altered. In the past, for example, local police precincts were evaluated on the basis of how many arrests they made—the more, the better. But arrest rates said nothing about how safe the streets were. Under the new system, all of the city's 76 precincts were judged by the incidence of crime, and some 100 officers were put in charge of monitoring crime rates. Every morning they had to give Mayor Giuliani a report, and if crime rates were up in a particular precinct, an explanation was demanded and strategies and solutions were discussed.

To this was added the CompStat (Computerized Statistics) Unit. This unit was created in 1994 to provide the NYPD with snapshots of preliminary crime statistics, which allow tactical planning and deployment of resources to fight crime. The unit provides critical information to the police commissioner and those compiling and analyzing preliminary crime and homicide statistics and commanding-officer profiles. The unit generates electronic pin maps of crime locations citywide; analyzes geographic locations of shootings, homicides, and other major crimes; monitors crime patterns; develops advanced computerized crime-tracking methods; and provides briefing/presentation materials for the police commissioner. In addition, the CompStat Unit also gauges the crime-fighting effectiveness of field commands by monitoring arrest activity, responses to pattern crimes, bias crimes, and the implementation of crime strategies. CompStat has been so effective in New York that the model has been adopted by police departments throughout the United States.[58]

New York also adopted the "broken windows" philosophy of problem-oriented policing. The focus was on "quality of life" crimes, the minor forms of disorder—subway fare beating, drinking or urinating in the street, graffiti, panhandling, loitering—that were eating away at the informal controls that held neighborhoods together, setting the stage for more serious social decay and major crime. And there were numerous other strategies, such as shortening late-night subway trains from 11 cars to 6, making them easier to patrol. At the same time, police were awakening sleeping passengers, reducing their potential for being targeted by "lush-workers"—thieves who prey on sleeping or intoxicated passengers.

Finally, more stringent requirements for entry into the NYPD were instituted, and police academy training was augmented.

The new strategies began to have an effect. Crime rates started to slide, and people were going out at night as well as during the day—walking, shopping, visiting, riding the subways, seeing the sights. Having many people in the streets at all hours may be the best crime prevention tool of all.[59]

A park police officer on horseback and uniformed Secret Service agents give directions to a tourist outside the White House. A Justice Department survey examining the way the public interacts with police found that one in five Americans makes some kind of contact with law enforcement officers each year, mostly to report a crime, ask for help, or offer assistance.

OP-ED

What is policing? Does it involve enforcing the law or keeping the peace? Or is it both?

The answer is that policing is a peacekeeping operation, because enforcing the law is very much a part of peacekeeping. Police work does entail the dangerous task of apprehending criminals, but for officers assigned to patrol duties, even in large cities, there are few confrontations with serious offenders. Peacekeeping often includes intervening in situations that may represent potential threats to the public order, enforcing civil ordinances, and general areas of public service. Peacekeeping can also include numerous preventive and protective activities, such as patrol, which lessens opportunities to commit crimes, as well as programs to reduce racial tensions, promote safe driving, and reduce opportunities for victimization.

Summary

Police have many functions. In a democratic society like the United States they serve as enforcers, investigators, and traffic controllers. In addition to these roles, police also serve a quasi-judicial function in that officers must determine if a crime has actually been committed and, if so, which response is the most appropriate for the situation. In spite of conventional beliefs, the chief function of the police is not to enforce the law but to keep the peace. As demonstrated consistently in the *Uniform Crime Reports* and other data, serious crimes constitute only a small fraction of all arrests in any given year. By contrast, the daily activity of most officers involves administrative work, answering routine calls, controlling traffic, testifying in court, and providing assistance to citizens.

The peacekeeping role of the police is the key factor that differentiates them from private citizens. Peacekeeping involves the mobilization of the legitimate right to use force in situations where urgency requires it.

Police departments are bureaucratically structured on a military model. All large police organizations and many smaller ones have a fixed division of labor, chains and units of command, and rules, regulations, and discipline. In essence, the militaristic nature of police organization derives from a punitive model of administrative control where deviation from the rules and regulations of the department is met with a variety of punishments designed to ensure compliance within the ranks.

Patrol is the most basic concept and technique of police work. It is through patrol that police protect public safety, enforce the law, control traffic, conduct criminal investigations, and interpret the law. In years past, foot patrols were considered the mainstay of policing. They evolved from earlier traditions of night watch systems but were displaced by motorized patrols because of criticisms characterizing foot patrols as inefficient and ineffective. Currently, they have been replaced almost universally by motor patrols, although several researchers and law enforcement professionals have expressed growing interest in "putting the cop back on the beat." Those interested in reviving foot patrol as an enforcement strategy cite the need to increase and improve contact between citizens and police.

A police department's detective force specializes in the apprehension of offenders. Detective work includes the identification and arrest of criminal offenders, the collection and preservation of physical evidence, the locating and interviewing of witnesses, and the recovery and return of stolen property. In spite of this concentrated activity, however, for their numbers detectives make proportionately few arrests.

Most police departments also have officers assigned to specialized units designed to handle specific types of enforcement situations—surveillance, decoy operations, intelligence gathering, and other enforcement activities. In addition, many departments have highly trained officers assigned to SWAT teams to deal with such high-risk situations as hostage taking and riot control. In recent years, there has been an emphasis on community policing, which involves a variety of linkages between police officers and the communities they patrol.

Police officers, whether detectives or those in uniform, are called on to immediately judge whether a law has been violated, whether to invoke the powers of arrest, and whether to use force in invoking that power. Considerable discretion must be used in making these judgments because departmental rules and guidelines are frequently ambiguous. An outgrowth of this discretionary power is selective law enforcement.

There is the police subculture—a system of shared norms, values, goals, and style of life that is essentially different from that of the wider society within which officers function and which they are charged to protect.

In the majority of jurisdictions in the United States, legislation has mandated that male and female police officers have the same professional opportunities. State and local codes require that the hiring of police recruits be based on physical standards and competitive examinations that are designed to be nondiscriminatory; that all recruits receive the same training and that all officers have the same legal authority; that promotions are awarded on merit as decided by competitive procedures to determine professional knowledge and decision-making abilities; and that equal positions rate equal pay regardless of the officer's gender. However, this was not always the case, and even now at the beginning of a new millennium, gender bias in policing remains a problem.

Finally, in recent years there has been an emphasis on community policing, which involves a variety of linkages between police officers and the communities they patrol. However, because of terrorism, this model is undergoing change.

| Key Terms |

clearance rate (205)
community policing (208)
full enforcement (216)

patrol (202)
peacekeeping role (194)
police cynicism (219)

police discretion (215)
police subculture (218)
working personality (218)

| Issues for Discussion |

1. What is the relative importance of patrol units, detective forces, and specialized squads to big-city policing?
2. In what ways are police agencies similar to military organizations? If you could imagine a police department not organized along military lines, what would it be like?
3. Do the advantages of police discretion outweigh the disadvantages?

4. What might be the most effective combination of foot patrols, motor patrols, and one-person patrols versus team patrols?
5. What kinds of things do you think police and citizens could do as part of the community policing approach?
6. How might community policing be implemented in your community?

| Media and Literature Resources |

Reel Justice includes scenes that can be used to spark discussion about the following topics from this chapter:

The Nature and Scope of Police Work

Police Functions

Procedural Rights

Use of Deadly Force

Role of the Police

Police Discretion

Police Subculture

Patrol Units

Community Policing

Women in Policing

The Status of Women in Policing. An excellent work on gender and policing was recently published: Gwendolyn L. Gerber, *Women and Men Police Officers: Status, Gender, and Personality* (Westport, CT: Praeger, 2001). In addition, the National Center for Women and Policing Web site is a handy resource that includes a link to the publication discussed in this chapter: *http://www.womenandpolicing.org/.*

Community Policing. There are two excellent works on community policing that are readily available: George L. Kelling and Catherine M. Ross, *Fixing Broken Windows* (New York: Free Press, 1996); Susan L. Miller, *Gender and Community Policing: Walking the Talk* (Boston: Northeastern University Press, 1999).

Police Paramilitary Units (PPUs). Type "SWAT" into your Internet search engine, and about *4 million* different Web sites will pop up. Most common are descriptions of individual PPUs or complaints about SWAT activities. Two excellent articles are Peter B. Kraska and Victor E. Kappeler, "Militarizing American Police: The Rise and Normalization of Paramilitary Units," *Social Problems* 44 (1997): 1–18; and David B. Kopel and Paul M. Blackman, "Can Soldiers Be Peace Officers? The Waco Disaster and the Militarization of American Law Enforcement," *Akron Law Review* 30 (1997): 619–659.

NYPD. The New York City Police Department is by far the largest law enforcement agency in the United States, and much has been written about it. Some of the more recent works include William Bratton, *Turnaround: How America's Top Cop Reversed the Crime Epidemic* (New York: Random House, 1998); Eli B. Silverman, *NYPD Battles Crime: Innovative Strategies in Policing* (Boston: Northeastern

University Press, 1999); and James Lardner and Thomas Reppetto, *NYPD: A City and Its Police* (New York: Henry Holt, 2000).

Terrorism and Policing. A number of interesting articles have been published on this topic in *Crime and Justice International:* Willard M. Oliver, "The Era of Homeland Security: September 11, 2001 to . . . ,"

Crime and Justice International, March/April 2005, 9–17; James F. Pastor, "Terrorism and Public Safety Policing," *Crime and Justice International,* March/April 2005, 4–8; William M. Oliver, "The Homeland Security Juggernaut: The End of the Community Policing Era?" *Crime and Justice International,* March/April 2004, 4–10.

Endnotes

1. Quoted in John Van Maanen, "The Asshole," in *Policing: A View from the Street,* edited by Peter K. Manning and John Van Maanen (Santa Monica: Goodyear, 1978), 221.
2. For a more detailed discussion of police tasks, see National Research Council, *Fairness and Effectiveness in Policing* (Washington DC: National Academy Press, 2000); David Weisburd and John E. Eck, "What Can Police Do to Reduce Crime, Disorder, and Fear?" *The Annals* 593 (May 2004): 42–65; Egon Bittner, *The Functions of Police in Modern Society* (New York: Aronson, 1975); Jonathan Rubinstein, *City Police* (New York: Farrar, Straus & Giroux, 1973); and Herman Goldstein, *Policing a Free Society* (Cambridge, MA: Ballinger, 1977).
3. James Q. Wilson, *Varieties of Police Behavior: The Management of Law and Order in Eight Communities* (Cambridge, MA: Harvard University Press, 1968); Albert J. Reiss Jr., *The Police and the Public* (New Haven, CT: Yale University Press, 1971); Richard J. Lundman, "Police Patrol Work: A Comparative Perspective," in *Police Behavior: A Sociological Perspective,* edited by Richard J. Lundman (New York: Oxford University Press, 1980), 52–65.
4. Federal Bureau of Investigation, *Uniform Crime Reports—2003* (Washington, DC: U.S. Government Printing Office, 2004).
5. Carl B. Klockars, *The Idea of Police* (Beverly Hills: Sage Publications, 1985), 15–16.
6. Mark L. Dantzker, *Understanding Today's Police* (Upper Saddle River, NJ: Prentice-Hall, 2000); O. W. Wilson and Ray C. McLaren, *Police Organization* (New York: McGraw-Hill, 1977).
7. NYPD, Office of Public Relations, 2005.
8. Arthur Niederhoffer, *Behind the Shield* (Garden City, NY: Doubleday, 1967), 41–42.
9. Richard J. Lundman, *Police and Policing* (New York: Holt, Rinehart and Winston, 1980), 53; Bittner, *Functions of Police in Modern Society,* 56; President's Commission on Law Enforcement and Administration of Justice, *Task Force Report: The Police* (Washington, DC: U.S. Government Printing Office, 1967), 17.
10. Patrick V. Murphy and Thomas Plate, *Commissioner: A View from the Top of American Law Enforcement* (New York: Simon & Schuster, 1977), 32–33.
11. Rubinstein, *City Police,* 41–42.
12. For an amplification of this issue, see James J. Fyfe and Jerome H. Skolnick, *Above the Law: Police and the Excessive Use of Force* (New York: Free Press, 1993), 113–133.
13. National Advisory Commission on Criminal Justice Standards and Goals, *Police* (Washington, DC: U.S. Government Printing Office, 1973), 192.
14. See Bruce Smith, *Police Systems in the United States* (New York: Harper & Brothers, 1949), 14.
15. President's Commission on Crime in the District of Columbia, *A Report on the President's Commission on Crime in the District of Columbia* (Washington, DC: U.S. Government Printing Office, 1966), 53; Police Department of Kansas City, *1966 Survey of Municipal Police Departments* (Kansas City, MO: Police Department of Kansas City, 1966), 53.
16. International Association of Chiefs of Police, *A Survey of the Police Department of Youngstown, Ohio* (Washington, DC: International Association of Chiefs of Police, 1964), 89.
17. Thomas F. Adams, *Police Field Operations* (Upper Saddle River, NJ: Prentice-Hall, 1997); Robert C. Trojanowicz and Dennis W. Banas, *Perceptions of Safety: A Comparison of Foot Patrol Versus Motor Patrol Officers* (East Lansing: National Neighborhood Foot Patrol Center, School of Criminal Justice, Michigan State University, 1985).
18. George Kelling, *Foot Patrol* (Washington, DC: National Institute of Justice, 1991).
19. George L. Kelling, *The Kansas City Preventive Patrol Experiment: A Summary Report* (Washington, DC: Police Foundation, 1974).
20. Goldstein, *Policing a Free Society,* 55–56.
21. National Research Council, 227–228.
22. See, for example, Donald J. Black, "The Social Organization of Arrest," *Stanford Law Review* 23 (June 1971): 1087–1111; and Jan Chaiken, Peter Greenwood, and Joan Petersilia, "The Criminal Investigation Process: A Summary Report," *Policy Analysis* 3 (1977): 187–217.
23. Lundman, "Police Patrol Work," 64–65.
24. Computer Crime Research Center news release, May 4, 2005.
25. *The New York Times,* May 17, 2000, C1, C5.
26. Charles Whited, *The Decoy Man* (New York: Playboy Press, 1973), 12.
27. *Philadelphia Bulletin,* March 28, 1976, sec. 3, p. 1.
28. See William L. Tafoya, "Special Weapons and Tactics," *Police Chief,* July 1975, 70–74; "The SWAT Squads," *Newsweek,* June 23, 1975, 95; C. Gordon Jenkins, "Countdown to Teamwork," *Security Management,* March 1989, 46–49; and *The Washington Post,* April 1, 1991, A8.
29. Peter B. Kraska and Victor E. Kappeler, "Militarizing the American Police: The Rise and Normalization of Paramilitary Units," *Social Problems* 44 (February 1997): 1–18; *U.S. News & World Report,* June 24, 1996, 58–61; *U.S. News & World Report,* November 17, 1997, 32–33.
30. Kraska and Kappeler, "Militarizing the American Police," *The Nation,* November 1, 1993, 483–484; *FBI Law Enforcement Bulletin,* April 1993, 14; *FBI Law Enforcement Bulletin,* March 1989, 3–9.
31. Ralph A. Weisheit, L. Edward Wells, and David N. Falcone, "Community Policing In Small Town and Rural America," *Crime and Delinquency* 4 (October 1994): 549–567.
32. Steven R. Donziger (ed.), *The Real War on Crime: The Report of the National Criminal Justice Commission* (New York: HarperPerennial, 1996), 171.
33. James Q. Wilson and George Kelling, "The Police and Neighborhood Safety," *Atlantic Monthly,* March 1982, 29–38.

34. See Malcolm K. Sparrow, Mark H. Moore, and David M. Kennedy, *Beyond 911: A New Era for Policing* (New York: Basic Books, 1990).

35. James F. Pastor, "Terrorism and Public Safety Policing," *Crime and Justice International*, March/April 2005, 4–8.

36. Edward R. Maguire and William R. King, "Trends in the Policing Industry," *The Annals* 593 (May 2004): 15–41.

37. Dorothy Moses Schultz, "Invisible No More: A Social History of Women in United States Policing," in *The Criminal Justice System and Women: Offenders, Victims, and Workers*, edited by B. R. Price and N. J. Sokoloff (New York: McGraw-Hill, 1995), 372–382.

38. Dorothy Moses Schultz, "From Policewoman to Police Officer: An Unfinished Revolution," *Police Studies* 16 (1993): 90–99.

39. *Griggs* v. *Duke Power Co.,* 401 U.S. 424 (1979).

40. *Blake* v. *Los Angeles,* 595F.2d 1367 (1979).

41. Susan L. Miller, *Gender and Community Policing: Walking the Talk* (Boston: Northeastern University Press, 1999).

42. Barbara Raffel Price, "Female Police Officers in the United States," National Criminal Justice Reference Service, 1996, on the Web at *http://www.ncjrs.org/policing/fem635.htm.*

43. Federal Bureau of Investigation, *Crime in the United States— 2003* (Washington, DC: U.S. Government Printing Office, 2004).

44. National Center for Women and Policing, *Equality Denied: The Status of Women in Policing* (Arlington, VA: Feminist Majority Foundation, 2002).

45. Wayne R. LaFave, *Arrest: The Decision to Take a Person into Custody* (Boston: Little, Brown, 1965).

46. Stephen D. Mastrofski, "Controlling Street-Level Discretion," *The Annals* 593 (May 2004): 100–118.

47. Irving Piliavin and Scott Briar, "Police Encounters with Juveniles," *American Journal of Sociology* 70 (September 1964): 206–214.

48. See David A. Klinger, "Demeanor or Crime: Why 'Hostile' Citizens Are More Likely to Be Arrested," *Criminology* 32 (1994): 475–493; and Richard J. Lundman, "Demeanor or Crime: The Midwest City Police–Citizen Encounters Study," *Criminology* 32 (1994): 631–656.

49. Paul M. Whisenand and R. Fred Ferguson, *The Managing of Police Organizations* (Upper Saddle River, NJ: Prentice-Hall, 1973), 199–201.

50. Goldstein, *Policing a Free Society,* 112.

51. For example, see Richard Bennett and Theodore Greenstein, "The Police Personality: A Test of the Predispositional Model," *Journal of Police Science and Administration* 3 (1975): 439–445; and Larry L. Tifft, "The 'Cop Personality' Reconsidered," *Journal of Police Science and Administration* 2, 3 (September 1974): 266–278.

52. Jerome H. Skolnick, *Justice Without Trial: Law Enforcement in Democratic Society* (New York: Wiley, 1966).

53. Laura L. Manuel, Paul Retzlaff, and Eugene Sheehan, "Policewomen Personality," *Journal of Social Behavior and Personality* 8 (1993): 149–153.

54. National Research Council, 130–136.

55. Niederhoffer, *Behind the Shield,* 9.

56. Joseph Victor, "Police Stress: Is Anybody Out There Listening?" *New York Law Enforcement Journal,* June 1986, 19–20.

57. For a discussion of the complexity of culture as it relates to policing, see Steve Herbert, "Police Subculture Revisited," *Criminology* 36 (1998): 343–369.

58. David Weisburd, Stephen D. Mastrofski, Anne Marie McNally, Rosann Greenspan, and James J. Willis, "Reforming to Preserve: Compstat and Strategic Problem Solving in American Policing," *Criminology and Public Policy* 2 (July 2003): 421–456.

59. See John Marks, "New York, New York," *U.S. News & World Report,* September 29, 1997, 45–54; James Lardner, "Better Cops, Fewer Robbers," *New York Times Magazine,* February 9, 1997, 45–54, 62; *The New York Times,* September 1, 1997, A12; Eli B. Silverman, *NYPD Battles Crime: Innovative Strategies in Policing* (Boston: Northeastern University Press, 1999); John Marzulli, "City Crime in Decline," *Daily News Express,* October 5, 2000, 5; National Research Council, 185–189.

THE LAW OF ARREST, SEARCH, AND SEIZURE: POLICE AND THE CONSTITUTION

LEARNING OBJECTIVES

After reading this chapter, you should be able to answer the following questions:

1. What is ethnic profiling, and is it constitutionally permissible?

2. What are the differences between police investigative powers and arrest powers?

3. What is probable cause?

4. Under what circumstances may police conduct a search without a warrant?

5. What is meant by search and seizure?

6. What are the issues surrounding hot pursuit?

7. What is the exclusionary rule?

8. What is the significance of *Mapp, Escobedo,* and *Miranda* for both citizens and the police?

9. What are the major U.S. Supreme Court decisions related to police search and arrest?

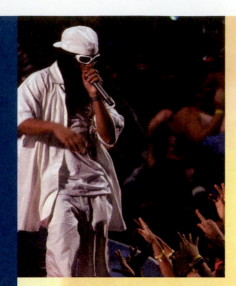

Rapper Lil Jon performs during the MTV Video Music Awards in Miami.

MIAMI, FL—The *Miami Herald* ignited a firestorm with an article headlined "Police Secretly Watching Hip-Hop Artists."[1] The story alleged that ever since South Beach had become a popular spot for rap celebrities and their fans, both the Miami and the Miami Beach police departments were photographing rappers and their entourages as they arrived at the Miami Airport and were also keeping dossiers on their activities. Further reports indicated that officers from the Miami PD and numerous other police departments had attended a "hip-hop training seminar" hosted by the NYPD, at which binders were provided that contained the arrest records and photographs of dozens of rap artists and their companions. Allegations of "ethnic profiling" were made, suggesting that police tactics were targeting citizens for "performing while black."

Within this context, it is well documented that in many places, black and Hispanic drivers are more likely to be pulled over by the police than are white drivers, a phenomenon that has been referred to as "driving while black" and "driving while Hispanic."[2] For example, a report out of Texas found that in addition to being pulled over more often, blacks were 1.6 times more likely to be searched and Hispanics were 1.4 times more likely to be searched than white drivers. And while ethnic profiling is not a new phenomenon, the post-September 11 climate has added a different dimension to the situation: the targeting of Muslim and Arab passengers on airlines. For example, Mohammed Ali Khan filed a lawsuit in federal court after being denied a boarding pass for his domestic flight to Chicago. He had been questioned in front of other passengers and then detained in a back room and interrogated by the FBI. Even after he was cleared, airline officials refused to allow him to board the flight, and he instead had to take another one several hours later.[3]

Ethnic profiling is a practice in which police stop and detain someone on the basis of his or her ethnic identity or skin color. The explanation for ethnic profiling is the belief by some police and law enforcement agencies that blacks are more likely than other groups to be trafficking drugs or other contraband, that Hispanics are more likely to be illegal immigrants, and, in light of the terrorist attacks, that Muslims and Arabs are more likely to commit acts of terrorism or sabotage against American interests. Is ethnic profiling really occurring? Is it legal and constitutional? This question raises a host of others: Under what circumstances can police stop and search drivers or airline passengers? Can they maintain binders of personal information to keep an eye on certain ethnic groups? When can police officers search without a warrant? When can they "seize" property or interrogate suspects? What powers do the police actually have?

Police powers can be divided into two general areas: investigative powers and arrest powers. Police *investigative powers* include, but are not necessarily limited to, the following:

- The power to stop
- The power to frisk
- The power to order someone out of a car
- The power to question
- The power to detain

Police *arrest powers* include the following:

- The power to use force
- The power to search
- The power to exercise seizure and restraint

Because the United States Constitution was designed to protect each citizen's rights, it placed certain restrictions on the exercise of these powers. This chapter discusses the legal constraints on police powers and traces their evolution through Supreme Court decisions, focusing on the Court's impact on law enforcement practice.

Search and Seizure

The right of the people to be secure in their persons, houses, papers, and effects, against un-reasonable searches and seizures, shall not be violated, and no warrants shall issue, but upon probable cause, supported by oath or affirmation, and particularly describing the place to be searched, and the persons or things to be seized.

—FOURTH AMENDMENT, CONSTITUTION OF THE UNITED STATES

The Fourth Amendment is the primary rule guiding the investigative activities of the police. The first objective of investigation is to determine whether a crime has been committed and, if so, what type of crime it was. Police generally analyze available information to find out whether the elements that constitute violation of criminal codes are present. The next objective is to identify the offender through further intelligence-gathering activities. When these activities are successful, an arrest is made—that is, a suspect is taken into custody. Beyond the investigation and apprehension aspects of law enforcement, police are also responsible for gathering additional evidence, if necessary, and for preserving it so that the prosecution phase of the criminal justice process can be effective. Each of these aspects of police investigation and apprehension is subject to procedural rules dictated by law and constitutional rights. It is when these procedures are called into question that law enforcement practice becomes a matter for judicial review.

At the outset, evidence gathering typically depends on *search*—the examination or inspection of premises or persons with a view to discovering stolen or illicit property or evidence of guilt to be used in the prosecution of a criminal action. Associated with search is *seizure*—the taking of a person or property into the custody of the law in consequence of a violation of public law. **Search and seizure,** then, involves means for the detection and accusation of crime. It is the search for and taking of persons and property as evidence of crime.

The very language of the Fourth Amendment, however, prohibits "unreasonable searches and seizures." Unreasonableness, in the constitutional sense, is an ambiguous term that may vary depending on the situation. In general, however, it refers to that which is extreme, arbitrary, and capricious and is not justified by the apparent facts and circumstances.

Search Warrants

Search warrants make search and seizure less problematic, for they reflect the formal authority of the law in sanctioning the use of police search powers. A **search warrant** is a written order, issued by a magistrate and directed to a law enforcement officer, commanding search of a specified premises for stolen or unlawful goods or for suspects or fugitives and the bringing of these, if found, before the magistrate.

The United States Supreme Court has repeatedly ruled that the Fourth Amendment indicates a preference for searches conducted pursuant to a warrant. Most recently, this was emphasized in *Ornelas* v. *United States*,[4] which stressed the importance of maintaining an incentive for police officers to obtain search warrants whenever possible.

Probable Cause

Warrants authorizing a search must pass the constitutional test of reasonableness. In the language of the Fourth Amendment, "no warrants shall issue, but upon probable cause." **Probable cause,** in the constitutional sense, refers to facts or apparent facts that are reliable and generate a reasonable belief that a crime has been committed. In the absence of such "facts," the probable cause element has not been met, and the validity of the warrant can be questioned. And while probable cause "means less than evidence which would justify condemnation,"[5] it does require "belief that the law was being vi-

I recall once in South America that I complained to the police that a camera has been stolen and they ended up arresting me. I hadn't registered or something. In other words, once you get them on the scene they really start nosing around. Once the law starts asking questions, there's no stopping them.

—BEATNIK AUTHOR
WILLIAM BURROUGHS

Call it a ticket, call it a summons, call it a citation, or even call it a mistake. Whatever. But by any name, consider it an affirmation that this is an ordered society that you are visiting.

—A MIAMI POLICE OFFICER TO A BRAZILIAN TOURIST, WHEN CITING HER FOR PARKING HER RENTAL CAR ON THE SIDEWALK IN FRONT OF THE SHOP SHE WAS VISITING

There is no such thing as perfect justice.

—BIRMINGHAM POLICE OFFICER

Kansas City police executing a search warrant.

olated on the premises to be searched; and the facts are such that a reasonably discreet and prudent man would be led to believe that there was a commission of the offense charged."[6]

Establishing probable cause for the issuance of a search warrant is a matter that the Supreme Court has addressed at length in recent years. As a result of *Aguilar* v. *Texas* in 1964 and *Spinelli* v. *United States* in 1969,[7] the general rule was that probable cause for search could not be based solely on hearsay information received by the police. Rather, a valid warrant had to contain a statement that there was a reasonable cause to believe that property of a certain kind might be found "in or upon a designated or described place, vehicle, or person," combined with "allegations of fact" supporting such a statement. The High Court's ruling in ***Illinois* v. *Gates*** in 1983,[8] however, eliminated the *Aguilar-Spinelli* test, replacing it with a "totality of circumstances" analysis. *Gates* required magistrates to simply make a practical, commonsense decision as to whether, given all the circumstances set forth in an affidavit, there was a fair probability that contraband would be found in a particular place (see Exhibit 8.1).

| Warrantless Search |

A civilized system of law is as much concerned with the means employed to bring people to justice as it is with the ends themselves. A first principle of jurisprudence is that the ends do not justify the means.

— JUSTICE WILLIAM O. DOUGLAS, 1956

Although the general rule regarding the application of the Fourth Amendment is that any search or seizure undertaken without a valid search warrant is unlawful, there are exceptions, provided that the arrest, search, and seizure are not unreasonable. The major exceptions include the following situations or circumstances:

- A search incident to a lawful arrest
- Stop-and-frisk procedures
- Probable cause and inventory searches of automobiles
- Fresh pursuit
- Consent searches

LAW & CRIMINAL JUSTICE | EXHIBIT 8.1

Illinois v. *Gates*

On May 3, 1978, the police department of Bloomingdale, Illinois, received an anonymous letter stating that Mr. and Mrs. Gates were engaged in selling drugs; that the wife would drive their car to Florida on May 3 to be loaded with drugs and the husband would fly down in a few days to drive the car back; that the car's trunk would be loaded with drugs; and that Mr. and Mrs. Gates presently had more than $100,000 worth of drugs in their basement.

Acting on the tip, a police officer determined the Gateses' address and learned that the husband had made a reservation on a May 5 flight to Florida. Arrangements for surveillance of the flight were made with an agent of the Drug Enforcement Administration (DEA). The surveillance disclosed that Mr. Gates took the flight, stayed overnight in a motel room registered in his wife's name, and left the following morning with a woman in a car bearing an Illinois license plate issued to Mr. Gates, heading north on an interstate highway used by travelers to the Bloomingdale area.

A search warrant for the defendants' residence and automobile was then obtained from an Illinois state court judge, based on the Bloomingdale police officer's affidavit setting forth the foregoing facts and a copy of the anonymous letter. When Mr. and Mrs. Gates arrived at their home, the police were waiting and discovered marijuana and other contraband in the defendants' car trunk and home.

Prior to their trial on charges of violating state drug laws, the court ordered suppression of all the items seized, and the Illinois Appellate Court affirmed. The Illinois Supreme Court also affirmed, holding that the letter and affidavit were inadequate to sustain a determination of probable cause for issuance of the search warrant under *Aguilar* v. *Texas* and *Spinelli* v. *United States,* because they failed to satisfy the "two-pronged test" of (1) revealing the informant's "basis of knowledge" and (2) providing sufficient facts to establish either the informant's "veracity" or the "reliability" of the informant's report.

The U.S. Supreme Court, however, heard the case and modified the requirements for probable cause. In stating its opinion, the Court held the following:

The question—which this Court requested the parties to address—whether the rule requiring the exclusion at a criminal trial of evidence obtained in violation of the Fourth Amendment should be modified so as, for example, not to require exclusion of evidence obtained in the reasonable belief that the search and seizure at issue was consistent with the Fourth Amendment will not be de-

cided in this case, since it was not presented to or decided by the Illinois courts. . . . Nor does the State's repeated opposition to respondents' substantive Fourth Amendment claims suffice to have raised the separate question whether the exclusionary rule should be modified. The extent of the continued vitality of the rule is an issue of unusual significance, and adhering scrupulously to the customary limitations on this Court's discretion promotes respect for its adjudicatory process and the stability of its decisions.

The Court abandoned the rigid "two-pronged test" under *Aguilar* and *Spinelli* for determining whether an informant's tip established probable cause for issuance of a warrant and substituted in its place the "totality of the circumstances" approach that traditionally has informed probable cause determinations. The elements under the two-pronged test concerning the informant's "veracity," "reliability," and "basis of knowledge," said the Court, should be understood simply as closely intertwined issues that may usefully illuminate the common-sense, practical question whether there is "probable cause" to believe that contraband or evidence is located in a particular place. The task of the issuing magistrate is simply to make a practical, commonsense decision whether, given all the circumstances set forth in the affidavit before him or her, there is a fair probability that contraband or evidence of a crime will be found in a particular place. And the duty of a reviewing court is simply to ensure that the magistrate had a substantial basis for concluding that probable cause existed. The Court stated that this flexible, easily applied standard would better achieve the accommodation of public and private interests that the Fourth Amendment requires than the approach that developed from *Aguilar* and *Spinelli.*

Finally, in its ruling the Court held that the judge issuing the warrant in this case had a substantial basis for concluding that probable cause to search the respondents' home and car existed. Under the "totality of the circumstances" analysis, corroboration of details of an informant's tip by independent police work is of significant value. Here, even standing alone, the facts obtained through the independent investigation of the Bloomingdale police officer and the DEA at least suggested that the respondents were involved in drug trafficking. In addition, the judge could rely on the anonymous letter, which had been corroborated in major part by the police officer's efforts.

Source: *Illinois* v. *Gates,* 462 U.S. 213 (1983).

Search Incident to Arrest

Traditionally, a search without a warrant is allowable if it is associated with a lawful arrest. The Supreme Court explained why in 1973:

It is the fact of the lawful arrest which establishes the authority to search, and we hold that in the case of a lawful custodial arrest a full search of the person is not only an exception to the warrant requirement of the Fourth Amendment, but is also a "reasonable" search under that Amendment.[9]

Public Attitudes Toward Police

How much confidence do you have in the police?

22%	Great deal
30%	Quite a lot
35%	Some
11%	Very little
1%	None
1%	No opinion

In general, do you think police officers are more hard-working and competent than other government employees, less hard-working and competent, or are they about the same?

43%	More hard-working
9%	Less hard-working
46%	Same
2%	No opinion

How much confidence do you have in the ability of the police to protect you from violent crime?

14%	Great deal
31%	Quite a bit
45%	Not very much
9%	None at all
1%	No opinion

Do you favor putting more police on the streets, even if it means paying higher taxes?

43%	Strongly favor
37%	Favor
15%	Oppose
4%	Strongly oppose
1%	No opinion

Source: The Gallup Poll. ∎

But given the language expressed by the Court, what would constitute a lawful arrest? Until recently, it was generally assumed that the Fourth Amendment did not require the issuance of a warrant for an arrest to be lawful. Moreover, in 1976 the Supreme Court ruled that a police officer could make an arrest in a public place without a warrant even if he or she had enough time to obtain one.[10] However, in 1980 the Court ruled that in the absence of "exigent" (urgent) circumstances the home of an accused could not be entered to make an arrest without a warrant.[11]

The foregoing at least suggests that arrests made *with* warrants are lawful, assuming, of course, that the arrest warrants themselves are procedurally correct. Moreover, as indicated in *Gates,* the provisions that determine the validity and legality of search warrants also apply to arrest warrants.

In the absence of a warrant, the legality of an arrest can be more problematic. Under common law, an arrest could not be made without a warrant, but if the felony or breach of the peace occurred within the view of an officer who was authorized to make an arrest, the officer had a duty to arrest without warrant. If a felony had been committed and there was probable cause to believe that a particular person was the offender, he or she could be arrested without a warrant. This common law rule of arrest is not at odds with constitutional guarantees; however, it tends to be vague, leaving much to the interpretation of the individual officer. Even in more definitive statements of this rule in criminal procedure codes, it is the officer's responsibility to determine the probable cause for, and hence the potential legality of, an arrest.

Although a warrantless search incident to a lawful arrest is permissible, the Supreme Court has placed limitations on the *scope* of such a search. The key case in this regard was **Chimel v. California,** decided in 1969.[12]

By way of introduction to this important case, it is safe to say that Ted Steven Chimel was not a particularly astute thief. Prior to the burglary of the coin store for which he was arrested and convicted, Chimel committed several incriminating blunders. He approached the owner of the store, told him that he was planning a big robbery, and questioned him about his alarm system, his insurance coverage, and the location of the most valuable coins. Chimel also carefully cased the store. After the burglary, he called the owner of the shop and accused him of robbing himself. When the victim suggested to Chimel that the crime had been sloppy, Chimel argued that it had been "real professional." On the night of the burglary itself, Chimel declined an invitation for a bicycle ride, commenting that he "was going to knock over a place" and that "a coin shop was all set."

On the afternoon of September 13, 1965, three police officers arrived at Chimel's Santa Ana home with a warrant authorizing his arrest for the burglary of the coin shop. The officers knocked at the door and identified themselves to Chimel's wife, who admitted them. They waited in the house until Chimel returned from work. Upon his arrival, the officers handed him the arrest warrant and asked permission to "look around." He objected, but was advised that although no search warrant had been issued, a search could be conducted on the basis of the lawful arrest.

Accompanied by Chimel's wife, the police officers searched the entire three-bedroom house. During the search they requested that she open drawers in the master bedroom and sewing room and physically move contents of the drawers so that the officers might see any items that would have come from the burglary. When the search was completed, the officers seized a variety of items, including a number of coins.

At Chimel's trial on two counts of burglary, the coins were admitted into evidence against him in spite of his objections that they had been illegally seized. Chimel was convicted, and the judgment was later affirmed by the California Supreme Court.

On appeal to the U.S. Supreme Court, however, Chimel's conviction was reversed. In its majority opinion, the Court analyzed the constitutional principle underlying search incident to arrest:

> When an arrest is made, it is reasonable for the arresting officer to search the person arrested in order to remove any weapons that the latter might seek to use in order to resist arrest or effect his escape. Otherwise, the officer's safety might well be endangered, and the arrest itself frustrated. In addition, it is entirely reasonable for the arresting officer to search

for and seize any evidence on the arrestee's person in order to prevent its concealment or destruction. And the area into which an arrestee might reach in order to grab a weapon or evidentiary items must, of course, be governed by a like rule. A gun on a table or in the drawer in front of one who is arrested can be dangerous to the arresting officer as one concealed in the clothing of the person arrested. There is ample justification, therefore, for a search of the arrestee's person and the area "within his immediate control"—construing that phrase to mean the area from within which he might gain possession of a weapon or destructible evidence. There is no comparable justification, however, for routinely searching rooms other than that in which an arrest occurs—or, for that matter, for searching through all the desk drawers or other closed or concealed areas in that room itself. Such searches, in the absence of well-recognized exceptions, may be made only under the authority of a search warrant. The "adherence to judicial processes" mandated by the Fourth Amendment requires no less.

"Unlawful" or "false" arrest can have several consequences. First, evidence seized as an outgrowth of an unlawful arrest is inadmissible in court. Similarly, any conviction resulting from an illegal arrest may be overturned. Typically, however, if it is clear in the early stages of the criminal justice process that the arrest was indeed unlawful, it is likely that the charges against the suspect will be dropped before adversary proceedings follow their full course. Second, in most jurisdictions a citizen who has been wrongly taken into custody can institute a civil suit against the officer and the police department that initiated or authorized the arrest (although these suits are seldom won).

A number of issues associated with wrongful arrest vary greatly from one state to another. Under Tennessee law, for example, as early as 1860 and in the years hence, numerous court decisions have declared that if "the officer acts at his peril, if he has no right to make an arrest without a warrant, or if his warrant is not valid, he is a trespasser."[13] Under such circumstances, the police officer is liable for money damages. However, where the arrest "would have been proper without a warrant, it is immaterial whether or not the warrant was good or bad."[14]

In Tennessee, Alabama, and numerous other jurisdictions, case law has dictated that every person has a right to resist an unlawful arrest and that "in preventing such illegal restraint of his liberty he may use such force as may be necessary."[15] In Idaho, by contrast, the suspect has no such right.[16] Further, in jurisdictions where resistance to wrongful arrest is lawful, the means or amount of resistance cannot be disproportionate to the effort of the police officer to make the arrest.

Finally, virtually all states place no liability for wrongful arrest on police officers if the arrest was made on the basis of a valid warrant or probable cause but a verdict of not guilty was returned. Thus, an acquittal is not tantamount to a finding of no reasonable grounds for arrest.[17] However, in 1986 the Supreme Court ruled in *Malley* v. *Briggs* that a police officer could be held liable for damages if an arrest was made without probable cause—*even* if he or she had obtained an arrest warrant.[18]

Stop-and-Frisk

Field interrogation or *stop-and-frisk* procedures can be a useful mechanism for police in areas where crime rates or the potential for crime is high. In fact, it is not uncommon for police to stop people whose behavior seems suspicious, to detain them briefly by asking them for identification, and to frisk (conduct a limited search by running the hands over the outer clothing) those whose answers or conduct suggest criminal involvement or threaten police safety.

Before the Supreme Court finally clarified the legal status of stop-and-frisk procedures in **Terry v. Ohio**[19] (see Exhibit 8.2), the authority for those procedures came from individual department directives, state judicial policy, police discretionary practices, and legislative statutes. In *Terry*, which was decided in 1968, the Supreme Court held that police officers are not entitled to seize and search every person they see on the streets and of whom they make inquiries. Before placing a hand on a citizen in search of anything, the officer must have constitutionally adequate, reasonable grounds for doing so.

Excessive Force and Resisting Arrest

In the absence of excessive or unnecessary force by an arresting officer, a person may not use force to resist an arrest by one who he knows or he has good reason to believe is an authorized police officer, engaged in the performance of his duties, regardless of whether the arrest was unlawful in the circumstances. But if an officer uses excessive or unnecessary force to subdue the arrestee, then regardless of whether the arrest is lawful or unlawful, the arrestee may defend himself by employing such force as reasonably appears to be necessary.

— FROM THE OPINION IN *COMMONWEALTH V. MOREIRA*, MASSACHUSETTS SUPREME JUDICIAL COURT, 33 CRL 2078 (1983) ▮

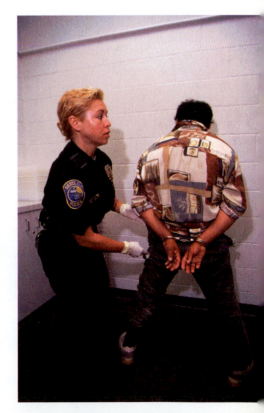

A Santa Ana, California police officer frisking a subject.

EXHIBIT 8.2 | LAW & CRIMINAL JUSTICE

Terry v. Ohio

At 2:30 p.m. on October 31, 1963, the attention of Cleveland police detective Martin McFadden was drawn to the activities of two men, Richard Chilton and John Terry, who were conversing at the intersection of two downtown thoroughfares. Periodically, one of the men would separate from the other, walk southwest along one of the streets, pause for a moment to peer into a particular store window, walk on a short distance, and then turn around and head back to the corner, pausing once again to look into the same window. The two men would then confer briefly before the second man would repeat the identical process of strolling down the street and looking into the very same store window. Detective McFadden observed Chilton and Terry repeat this reconnaissance ritual roughly a dozen times until a third man appeared, spoke with them briefly, and departed down one of the streets. Chilton and Terry resumed their pacing, peering, and conferring for another 10 minutes, after which they departed together, following the path taken earlier by the third man.

At this point, the police detective was thoroughly convinced that Chilton and Terry were "casing a job, a stickup." He followed them, and when they stopped to converse with the third man who had met them earlier on the street corner, he decided to intervene. Detective McFadden approached the three men, identified himself as a police officer, and asked for their names. When the men "mumbled something" in response to his inquiries, McFadden spun Terry around so that he was facing the other two men, patted down the outside of his clothing, and felt what he believed to be a pistol. A more thorough search found that it was a .38-caliber revolver, and a frisk of the other two men revealed a revolver in Chilton's overcoat pocket. All three of the suspects were taken to the police station, where Chilton and Terry were formally charged with carrying concealed weapons.

Terry v. *Ohio* became an interesting case in law, for the prosecution argued that the guns had been "seized" in a "search" incident to a lawful arrest. The defense, however, maintained that Detective McFadden had no probable cause for arrest and the guns ought to be suppressed as evidence obtained through illegal search and seizure.

Not surprisingly, the court recognized that McFadden's search was *not* incident to a lawful arrest, for no arrest had been made prior to the search; rather, it was clearly a case of stop-and-frisk. In fact, it was the court's opinion that it "would be stretching the facts beyond reasonable comprehension" to find that the officer had probable cause to arrest the three men for attempted robbery *before* he patted them down for weapons. Nonetheless, the Ohio trial court did rule that Detective McFadden's method of obtaining the evidence had been lawful: He had a duty to investigate the observed suspicious activity and had an absolute right to protect himself by frisking for weapons.

Chilton and Terry were both convicted of the weapons charge, and Terry was sentenced to a term of 1 to 3 years in the state penitentiary. Two appellate courts in Ohio upheld Terry's conviction, and the U.S. Supreme Court granted *certiorari* (review) in 1967 in order to consider a number of questions concerning the constitutional validity of the stop-and-frisk practice. Showing rare solidarity, the High Court decided by an 8-to-1 margin to uphold a police officer's right to frisk and seize weapons under such circumstances. The Court ruled that Detective McFadden had reasonable grounds to believe that the "suspects" were armed and dangerous, that swift measures were necessary for the protection of himself and others, and that his frisk was appropriately limited to a patting down of the outer clothing until he felt weapons.

But central to the decision in *Terry* was the Court's general concern over police–citizen street encounters. Delivering the opinion of the Court on this issue, Chief Justice Earl Warren stated the following:

> Our first task is to establish at what point in this encounter the Fourth Amendment becomes relevant. That is, we must decide whether and when Officer McFadden "seized" Terry and whether and when he conducted a "search." There is some suggestion in the use of such terms as "stop" and "frisk" that such police conduct is outside the purview of the Fourth Amendment because neither action rises to the level of a "search" or "seizure" within the meaning of the Constitution. We emphatically reject this notion. It is quite plain that the Fourth Amendment governs "seizures" of the person which do not eventuate in a trip to the station house and prosecution for crime—"arrests" in traditional terminology. It must be recognized that whenever a police officer accosts an individual and restrains his freedom to walk away, he has "seized" that person. And it is nothing less than sheer torture of the English language to suggest that a careful exploration of the outer surfaces of a person's clothing all over his or her body in an attempt to find weapons is not a "search." Moreover, it is simply fantastic to urge that such a procedure performed in public by a policeman while the citizen stands helpless, perhaps facing a wall with his hands raised, is a "petty indignity." It is a serious intrusion upon the sanctity of the person, which may inflict great indignity and arouse strong resentment, and it is not to be undertaken lightly.

Chief Justice Warren also emphasized, however, that the frisk was to be a limited search of the outer clothing in an attempt to discover weapons and that the scope of any frisk or search associated with stop-and-frisk procedures was limited by the circumstances of the particular encounter.

Source: *Terry* v. *Ohio*, 392 U.S. 1 (1968).

The *Terry* decision also provided standards for stop-and-frisk encounters, indicating that there had to be specific facts that could justify the police intrusion. According to Chief Justice Warren, there were five conditions—all of which must be met—that justified a stop-and-frisk action:

1. Where a police officer observes unusual conduct that leads him reasonably to conclude, in light of his experience, that criminal activity may be afoot.
2. Where the person with whom he is dealing may be armed and dangerous.
3. Where in the course of investigating this behavior he identifies himself as a police officer.
4. Where he makes reasonable inquiry.
5. Where nothing in the initial stages of the encounter serves to dispel his reasonable fear for his own or others' safety.

Any evidence found during the course of a frisk that is contrary to the *Terry* decision falls under the long-standing **fruit of the poisonous tree** doctrine. Under this rule, evidence that has been seized illegally is considered "tainted" and cannot be used against a suspect. Subsequent evidence derived from the initially tainted evidence must also be suppressed.

Related to both *Terry* and the poisonous tree doctrine is the 1991 case of *California v. Hodari D.,*[20] which was precipitated to a great extent by the "war on drugs." Two officers on a routine drug patrol in a high-crime Oakland neighborhood spotted a group of youths, who fled upon seeing the police approaching. The officers had *not* seen anything illegal happening, yet they knew that drug sales were common in the area. Given this, one of the officers chased Hodari D., a 16-year-old, and saw him toss away a small rock that the officer believed to be crack-cocaine. At that point, the officer tackled and restrained Hodari, and retrieved the "rock" (which was indeed crack-cocaine). The California court of appeals ruled that Hodari had been "seized" when he saw the officer running toward him and that such a seizure was unreasonable under the Fourth Amendment. As such, the crack was the *fruit* of an illegal seizure. The U.S. Supreme Court reversed this decision, however, arguing that the police chase was not a "seizure" but a "show of force" that is not limited by the Constitution. The seizure did not occur until the officer tackled Hodari, but by that time the officer's observance of the discarded rock represented the necessary probable cause.

Situations similar to those in *Hodari D.* are not uncommon in contemporary police work, and there seems to be general agreement in the law enforcement field that there is good reason to be suspicious of a person who runs away from the mere sight of a police officer. The Supreme Court recently addressed this issue in 2000, based on an incident that occurred on a Chicago street in 1995. As four police cars on patrol in a neighborhood where drug sales were known to occur approached the sidewalk where Sam Wardlow was standing, he turned and ran down an alley. Two officers pursued and apprehended Wardlow and, in a pat-down search, felt a gun in a bag he was carrying under his arm. After Wardlow's conviction, the Illinois Supreme Court held that the search was in violation of the Fourth Amendment in that "flight upon the approach of a police officer may simply reflect the exercise—at top speed—of a person's constitutional right to move on." However, the Supreme Court ruled in *Illinois* **v. Wardlow** that flight at the mere sight of a police officer could often, in the context of other factors, be suspicious enough to justify police in conducting a stop-and-frisk.[21] The majority opinion in the case explained that Wardlow's presence in an area known for heavy narcotics trafficking, combined with the unprovoked flight, justified the *Terry* stop and search.

In 1993, the U.S. Supreme Court significantly expanded the power of police to seize property from a suspect undergoing a *Terry*-type frisk. The original purpose of *Terry* was to allow police to conduct pat-down searches for *weapons* when confronting suspicious individuals. In **Minnesota v. Dickerson,**[22] however, the officer conducting the frisk admitted that he did not feel anything resembling a weapon but did feel a "small lump" in the suspect's jacket pocket. He reached into the pocket and pulled out a small packet of cocaine. The Minnesota Supreme Court ruled that the cocaine could not be admitted as evidence, holding that although the stop-and-frisk procedure was permissible under *Terry,* the seizure of the cocaine went beyond the search for a weapon and thus violated the Fourth Amendment.

The U.S. Supreme Court agreed that the cocaine must be suppressed, but it disagreed with the narrow scope of the Minnesota court's decision. The High Court created what is now known as the "plain feel" doctrine. That is, when police officers conduct *Terry*-type searches for weapons, they are free to seize items detected through their sense of touch, as long as the plain feel makes it "immediately apparent" that the item is contraband. Interestingly, however, since the officer in the *Dickerson* case conceded that he did not instantly recognize the lump as drugs, the plain feel did not apply and the cocaine was inadmissible as evidence in Dickerson's trial.

In the 2004 case of *Hiibel v. Nevada,*[23] the Supreme Court decided a logical corollary to *Terry.* Rancher Larry Hiibel had been arrested and convicted in a Nevada state court for failing to identify himself to a police officer who was investigating an assault. Nevada, and many other states, has a law that requires a person to tell an officer his or her name if asked. Hiibel challenged the conviction, claiming it violated his Fifth Amendment right not to incriminate himself and his Fourth Amendment right to be free from unreasonable searches. In a 5-to-4 opinion written by Justice Anthony Kennedy, the Court ruled that the search did not violate the Fourth Amendment because it was based on reasonable suspicion (the police officer was investigating the assault, and Hiibel was nearby) and involved only a minimally intrusive question (his name). It also did not violate the Fifth Amendment because Hiibel never argued that telling the officer his name would actually incriminate him of any crime. Justice Kennedy wrote, "While we recognize petitioner's strong belief that he should not have to disclose his identity, the Fifth Amendment does not override the Nevada Legislature's judgment to the contrary absent a reasonable belief that the disclosure would tend to incriminate him."

Automobile Searches

As early as 1925, the Supreme Court ruled that because of the extreme mobility of motor vehicles, there are situations in which warrantless searches of vehicles can be justified. In *Carroll* v. *United States,*[24] George Carroll was convicted of transporting liquor for sale in violation of the federal prohibition law and the Eighteenth Amendment. The contraband liquor that was used as evidence against him had been taken from his car by government agents acting without a search warrant. The Supreme Court sustained Carroll's conviction, despite his contention that the seizure violated his Fourth Amendment rights. The Court determined that there was probable cause for the search. Chief Justice William Howard Taft explained the decision:

> The guaranty of freedom from unreasonable searches and seizures by the Fourth Amendment has been construed practically since the beginning of the government, as recognizing a necessary difference between a search of a store, dwelling house, or other structure in respect of which a proper official warrant readily may be obtained and a search of a ship, motor boat, wagon, or automobile for contraband goods, where it is not practicable to secure a warrant, because the vehicle can be quickly moved out of the locality or jurisdiction in which the warrant must be sought.

Known as the **Carroll doctrine,** the Court's decision maintained that an automobile or other vehicle may, upon probable cause, be searched without a warrant even though there might be enough time to obtain a warrant. Subsequent rulings clarified the scope of this doctrine. In 1931, the Court upheld the search of a parked car as reasonable, since the police could not know when the suspect might move the car.[25] The Carroll doctrine was reaffirmed in 1970, when the Supreme Court held that a warrantless search of an automobile that resulted in the seizure of weapons and other evidence, but was conducted at a police station many hours after the arrests of the suspects, was lawful.[26]

A sobriety checkpoint in San Francisco, California.

A related issue is how *extensive* the search of an automobile may be in the absence of a warrant. In *United States* v. *Ross,*[27] decided in 1982, the Supreme Court held that when police have probable cause, they may search an entire vehicle, including containers and packages that may conceal the items sought. A year earlier, in *New York* v. *Belton,* the Court examined the scope of a vehicle search incident to an arrest.[28] Two principles were established. First, after making a custodial arrest, police officers may search the entire passenger compartment of the vehicle in conjunction with that arrest. Second, if any containers are found during the course of the search, they may be opened and searched. In effect, this decision seemed to impose no limits on the scope of a search of a vehicle's passenger compartment. And in *California* v. *Acevedo,*[29] decided in 1991, the Court went one step further and permitted police to open and search a closed container found in an automobile, without a warrant, if they have probable cause to believe that the container contains contraband or evidence of a crime. And with regard to the searching of passengers, the courts have addressed the issue of the *intrusiveness* of the search (see Exhibit 8.3).

Related to automobile searches are the random stopping of cars and the searches and arrests that may result. Known as *spot checks,* the random stopping of automobiles for the purpose of checking driver's licenses and vehicle registrations has often been used as a form of proactive police patrol. One New York City police officer made the following comment to the author:

> You try to stop the cars and drivers that look suspicious, but other times you go the pot luck route to break the monotony and start with every 20th car. Some nights we'll stop just blue cars, and other times it'll be big cars or old cars or whatever. Other times we'll pull over just Blacks, or White guys with beards.

Spot checks can aid in the apprehension of criminals, as a Miami Beach police officer related to the author:

> Depending on the time of night and where you are, maybe you'll pick up something. A few weeks back I see this guy stop at a light and I just don't like the looks of him . . . so I pull him over. . . . It ends up that the car is stolen and he's wanted in two other states on forgery charges.

The reflections of these officers point to the dangers of spot checks, for although they can result in the apprehension of some offenders, they also lend themselves to discriminatory enforcement procedures, as in the case of the ethnic profiling incidents described at the beginning of the chapter.

EXHIBIT 8.3 | *Gender Perspectives on Crime and Justice*

Warrantless Vaginal Cavity Searches

As Virginia police were pursuing a suspect who was carrying marked drug money in his vehicle, they saw a brown object come from the passenger-side window, presumably the paper in which the cash had been wrapped. When they stopped the car, they found a passenger, Denise Gilmore, riding with the suspect. They also discovered marijuana, but were unable to locate the marked money. Gilmore was taken into custody and strip-searched, but the police found nothing. A female deputy then inserted the tips of her fingers into Gilmore's vagina and discovered the marked bills. Prior to trial, Gilmore moved to suppress the evidence, arguing that the search violated her Fourth Amendment rights.

When the decision by the trial court supported Gilmore's argument, the case was appealed by the prosecution, and the court of appeals of Virginia agreed that a lawful arrest of a suspect authorizes the police to conduct a "full search" of the arrestee's person. The court asserted, however, that such a search "is only skin deep," citing the U.S. Su-

preme Court's decision in *Schmerber* v. *California,* which ruled that "a search of a body cavity is considered an intrusion into the body that falls outside the permissible scope of a search incident to arrest." The Virginia appellate court held that:

> A warrantless search involving a bodily intrusion, even conducted incident to a lawful arrest, violates the Fourth Amendment unless (1) the police have a "clear indication" that evidence is located within a suspect's body and (2) the police face exigent circumstances.

> Here, the Virginia court emphasized, the police had no "clear indication" that the money would be found in Gilmore's vaginal cavity, and exigent circumstances did not exist.

Sources: *Commonwealth of Virginia* v. *Gilmore,* No. 2700-97-2, May 6, 1998; *Schmerber* v. *California,* 384 U.S. 757 (1966).

The Supreme Court has taken a strong stand against random spot checks. This was indicated in the case of ***Delaware v. Prouse.***[30] On November 30, 1976, a New Castle County, Delaware, police officer stopped the automobile in which William J. Prouse was riding. The car belonged to Prouse, but he was not the driver. As the officer approached the vehicle, he smelled marijuana smoke, and when he came abreast of the window, he observed marijuana on the floor of the automobile. Prouse was arrested and later indicted for illegal possession of the drug.

At a hearing on Prouse's motion to forbid use of the marijuana as evidence, the police officer characterized the stopping of the car as "routine," explaining that "I saw the car in the area and was not answering any complaints so I decided to pull them off." He further indicated that before stopping the vehicle he had not observed any traffic or equipment violations, nor was he acting in accordance with directives regarding spot checks of automobiles.

After the hearing, the trial court ruled that the stop and detention had been wholly capricious and therefore in violation of Prouse's Fourth Amendment rights. When the prosecution appealed the case, the Delaware Supreme Court ruled in favor of Prouse, and the case went to the U.S. Supreme Court. The Supreme Court agreed to hear the case in an effort to resolve the conflict between the Delaware Supreme Court's decision (along with similar decisions in five other jurisdictions) and decisions in six other jurisdictions holding that the Fourth Amendment does *not* prohibit random spot checks.

Ultimately, the Supreme Court ruled that random spot checks are a violation of constitutional rights. However, it did not preclude states from devising methods for making spot checks of drivers' credentials that do not involve police discretion, such as roadblock inspections in which *all* motorists are stopped. Since *Prouse,* a number of states have established roadblock-type stops, primarily for combating drunk driving. Although several state supreme courts (including Oregon and Louisiana) have held that these "sobriety checkpoints" violate their state constitutions' prohibition of unreasonable search and seizure, the Supreme Court ruling in a 1990 case, *Michigan Department of State Police* v. *Stiz,* upheld the procedure.[31]

In 2000, however, the Supreme Court ruled against the use of roadblocks set up to search for drugs. In ***Indianapolis v. Edmond,***[32] the justices held that police checkpoints designed to catch drug traffickers or others engaged in general criminal activity infringe on the Fourth Amendment protection against illegal search and seizure. The High Court distinguished the antidrug roadblocks from the previously upheld checkpoints for illegal immigrants or drunken drivers, noting that the latter are aimed at protecting U.S. borders and reducing immediate hazards on the road. The ruling in *Edmond* would not affect such checkpoints but would quash new attempts to erect roadblocks aimed wholesale at criminal activity. However, in the 2004 case of *Illinois v. Lidster*,[33] the High Court endorsed the use of police roadblocks as an investigational tool for finding witnesses to recent crimes.

As a final point, it is interesting to note that in 1997 the Supreme Court ruled that the Fourth Amendment does not require police officers to tell motorists who are stopped for routine traffic violations that they are free to go before the officers seek permission to search their vehicles.[34]

Fresh Pursuit

Warrantless arrest and search is permissible in situations of *fresh pursuit* (or "hot" pursuit), which involves chasing an escaping criminal or suspect into a house—and consequently searching that house—or into a neighboring jurisdiction. In common law, fresh pursuit referred to the pursuit of a person for the purpose of arrest—pursuit that continued without substantial delay from the time of the commission or discovery of an offense. Thus, fresh pursuit is the following of a fleeing suspect who is attempting to avoid capture.

In contemporary statutes the notion of fresh pursuit has been broadened considerably. In Tennessee, for example, the law reads as follows:

> The term "fresh pursuit" shall include fresh pursuit as defined by the common law, and also the pursuit of a person who has committed a felony or who is reasonably suspected of having committed a supposed felony, though no felony has actually been committed. Fresh pursuit as used herein shall not necessarily imply instant pursuit, but pursuit without unreasonable delay.[35]

Although most state statutes permit hot pursuit, the practice of high-speed automobile chases has been controversial in recent years. The National Highway Safety Administration has estimated that police officers initiate more than 100,000 high-speed chases each year, 20% of which end in accidents, with hundreds of deaths.[36] The vast majority of those who die are fleeing the police, but many are innocent bystanders

> At any time the hazards of the pursuit outweigh the necessity of apprehension, the pursuit will be discontinued.
> **— FLORIDA HIGHWAY PATROL** *POLICY MANUAL*

The charred remains of three cars involved in a crash after a high speed chase sit on the elevated highway in Oklahoma city during the early rush hour.

who simply get in the way. Police departments have responded with new regulations and training initiatives, and the courts are also examining the matter. Ultimately, the issue is a matter of police discretion, with individual officers having to balance the demands of law enforcement with the risks to public safety.[37]

As a final point here, in 1998 the Supreme Court put a major restriction on police traffic-stop searches. In *Knowles* v. *Iowa*,[38] the High Court unanimously held that issuing a speeding ticket does not automatically give the police the authority to search the car. "For simple speeding," the justices emphasized, "the justifications for the Court's doctrine permitting a search incident to an arrest do not apply."

Consent Searches

Bag Inspectors on New York Subways

In the aftermath of the terrorist bombings in the London transit system in July 2005, the NYPD immediately began random searches of backpacks and packages being carried into the subway and commuter trains.

Are these searches a violation of the Fourth Amendment? ■

Warrantless searches may be carried out when the person in control of the area or object consents to the search. But consent searches often give rise to problematic legal issues, since consent waives the person's right to the Fourth Amendment protection against unreasonable search and seizure. Thus, in a consent search, neither probable cause nor a search warrant is required, but when evidence obtained through such a search is used, the burden of proving consent becomes the responsibility of the prosecution. The issues involved are (1) *who* can give consent to search what, (2) *what* constitutes free and voluntary consent, and (3) whether there is a principle of *limited* consent.

Ordinarily, courts are unwilling to accept the simple waiver of a defendant's Fourth Amendment right and require the state to prove that the consent was given voluntarily. In *Wren* v. *United States*,[39] the U.S. court of appeals ruled that a consent is indeed "voluntary" when the search is expressly agreed on or invented by the person whose right is involved. The case of *United States* v. *Matlock* expanded the range of voluntary consent to third parties who possess joint authority with the defendant over the property or premises to be searched.[40] In another case, *Bumper* v. *North Carolina*,[41] the issue of coercion by law enforcement officers was addressed. The police had obtained the consent of the defendant's grandmother to search her house in connection with a crime he was suspected of committing. But the officers had incorrectly informed her that they had a lawful search warrant, and it was on that basis that she had consented to the search. The Court ruled that her consent was not constitutionally valid. Finally, in *Schneckloth* v. *Bustamonte*,[42] the Supreme Court ruled that police officers are not required to inform those whose consent they are seeking that they are not obliged to give consent.

Although the rulings in *Wren, Matlock,* and *Schneckloth* give police wide discretion in carrying out consent searches, the Supreme Court has also ruled that voluntary consents are to some degree limited consents. A search based on voluntary consent must be limited to those items connected to the crime that triggered the desire to search and to other items clearly connected to that crime.[43] By contrast, in 1991 the Supreme Court expanded the scope of consent in two cases. In *Florida* v. *Jimeno*,[44] the Court held that a consent to search an automobile automatically includes a consent to search any closed containers found therein. In **Florida v. Bostick**,[45] the Court cleared away all doubts about the constitutionality of the drug interdiction technique known as "working the buses" (see Exhibit 8.4).

> This court is not empowered to forbid law enforcement practices simply because it considers them distasteful.
>
> — FROM THE MAJORITY OPINION IN *FLORIDA V. BOSTICK*

Other Warrantless Searches

In addition to lawful arrest, stop-and-frisk, automobile searches, fresh pursuit, and consent, there are numerous other types of situations in which the search warrant requirement has been waived. These include the following situations:

1. *Private searches:* As early as 1921, the Supreme Court ruled in *Burdeau* v. *McDowell* that the Fourth Amendment protects individuals only against searches and seizures by government agents, not against such actions carried out by private individuals not acting in concert with law enforcement authorities.[46]
2. *Border searches:* Although a series of rulings in the mid-1970s made it clear that warrantless searches of persons entering the United States at its borders violate the

drugs, crime, and justice | EXHIBIT 8.4

The Supreme Court, Bostick, and the War on Drugs

Drug interdiction efforts have led to the wider use of police surveillance at airports, train stations, and bus depots. Officers approach individuals, either randomly or because they suspect illegal activity, and ask them potentially incriminating questions. The Broward County, Florida, Sheriff's Department uses such a technique, in which officers board buses at scheduled stops and ask passengers for permission to search their luggage.

When officers boarded a Miami-to-Atlanta bus during a stopover in Fort Lauderdale during 1985, without any particular suspicion they conversed with passenger Terrance Bostick. After telling him that he could refuse, they requested his consent to search his luggage. He agreed, and the officers found cocaine in his bag. Bostick was arrested and charged with drug trafficking, but he argued that the seizure of the cocaine was in violation of the Fourth Amendment.

After the case moved through the Florida courts, the U.S. Supreme Court ultimately ruled against Bostick, holding that "bus sweeps" for drugs do not inevitably result in "seizures" requiring reasonable suspicion. The Court explained that it was only applying the same constitutional rules it had developed for police encounters on the street and in other public places to sweeps on buses, trains, and commercial aircraft. The ruling "follows logically," the Court argued, from prior decisions permitting police to approach individuals for questioning even when the officers have no "reasonable suspicion" that crime was afoot. The Court did emphasize, however, that in such cases: (1) consent prior to search is required; (2) officers may not convey a message that passenger compliance with their request is required; and (3) police may not use intimidating gestures or actions to coerce a consent to a search.

Source: *Florida* v. *Bostick*, 49 CrL 2270 (1991).

Fourth Amendment guarantee, *United States* v. *Martinez-Fuerte*[47] in 1976 established that Border Patrol officers need not have probable cause or a warrant before stopping cars for brief questioning at fixed checkpoints.

3. *Inventory searches:* In 1976 the Supreme Court established an inventory search exception to the warrant rule. It held that when police have custody of a lawfully impounded automobile, they do not need a warrant or the owner's consent before routinely inventorying items left in plain view or in the glove compartment.[48] Also of importance is *Illinois* v. *Lafayette*,[49] which was decided by the Supreme Court in 1983. In this decision the Court upheld a police inventory search of an arrestee's shoulder bag, which revealed illicit drugs. The Court stated that such searches serve important goals—protecting the suspect's property, deterring false claims of theft, and the like—and do not require a warrant or probable cause so long as the inventory search is part of a regular and routine police procedure.

4. *Electronic eavesdropping:* In response to the 1967 case of *Katz* v. *United States*,[50] in which the Supreme Court ruled that conversations intercepted through warrantless electronic eavesdropping were in violation of the Fourth Amendment, Congress passed the Omnibus Crime Control and Safe Streets Act of 1968, which included a provision involving electronic surveillance. The new act authorized the federal use of wiretaps and other eavesdropping devices through the issuance of warrants that can be approved only by the attorney general of the United States or his designated assistant.

5. *Abandoned property:* In the 1960 case of *Abel* v. *United States*,[51] the Supreme Court spelled out an "abandoned property exception" to the warrant rule. A hotel manager gave an FBI agent permission to search a room that had been occupied by Abel. During the search, incriminating evidence was found in a wastepaper basket. The Court held that once Abel vacated the room, the hotel had exclusive right to its possession and could freely consent to a search.

6. *Expectation of privacy:* The case of *California* v. *Greenwood*,[52] decided in 1988, illustrates the expectation-of-privacy doctrine. After learning from an informant that Billy Greenwood of Laguna Beach might be dealing in drugs, and after observing a parade of cars making brief nocturnal stops at Greenwood's home, the police asked the local refuse collector to give them the trash bags from Greenwood's house. A search of the garbage uncovered a large amount of drug para-

"Sniffer dogs" are used by police to check for drugs being smuggled across borders, and for explosives at major airports.

The worst peril of garbage searching is dirty diapers.

—ANONYMOUS FBI AGENT

Looking through garbage really calls for care. Let's face it, nobody wants to be poked by an AIDS-infected needle.

—ANONYMOUS DEA AGENT

Why is it that so many drug users seem to suffer from an allergy which causes them to drop things in the presence of a police officer?

—STEVEN M. GREENBERG

Crack has been a real boon to both buyer and seller. It's cheap, real cheap. Anybody can come up with $5 or $10 for a trip to the stars. But most important, it's easy to get rid of in a pinch. Drop it on the ground and it's almost impossible to find; step on it and the damn thing is history. All of a sudden your evidence ceases to exist.

—A MIAMI NARCOTICS DETECTIVE

phernalia, including razor blades, straws containing cocaine residue, and phone bills listing calls to people with records of drug law variations. The police obtained a warrant to search the house, found hashish and cocaine inside, and arrested Greenwood. Two California courts ruled that the search of Greenwood's garbage violated the Fourth Amendment ban against unreasonable search and seizure. The Supreme Court ruled against Greenwood, however, stating that in this instance Greenwood could have no expectation of privacy, thus giving the police broad power to search trash. Justice Byron White commented as follows:

> It is common knowledge that garbage bags left on or at the side of a public street are readily accessible to animals, children, scavengers, snoops, and other members of the public. Requiring police to seek warrants before searching such refuse would therefore be inappropriate.

7. *Open fields:* As early as 1924, in *Hester* v. *United States*,[53] the Supreme Court established the "open fields" exception, declaring that police officers may enter and search a field without a warrant. In *Oliver* v. *United States* (and the companion case of *Maine* v. *Thornton*),[54] decided in 1984, the Court went further, holding that fences and "No Trespassing" signs provide no reasonable expectation of privacy to owners of properties large enough to include areas that extend beyond the curtilage of houses or other buildings. As such, the decision in *Oliver* assured police that even if they enter such property by going over fences and ignoring "No Trespassing" signs in violation of state law, any evidence they discover on the property is nevertheless admissible at trial.

The "Plain View" Doctrine

Pertinent to this discussion of warrantless search and seizure is the **"plain view" doctrine.** In *Harris* v. *United States*[55] (1968), the Supreme Court ruled that anything a police officer sees in plain view, when the officer has a right to be where he or she is, is not the product of a search and is therefore admissible as evidence. James E. Harris's automobile had been observed leaving the scene of a robbery in Washington, D.C. The vehicle was traced, and Harris was later arrested near his home as he was getting into his car. The arresting officer made a quick inspection of the car and then took the suspect to the police station. After some discussion, a decision was made to impound the car as evidence. Harris's vehicle was towed to the station house about 90 minutes after the arrest, arriving there with its doors unlocked and its windows open. Then it began to rain.

According to police procedures in the District of Columbia, the arresting officer is required to thoroughly search an impounded vehicle, remove any valuables, prepare a written inventory, and submit a report on the impounding. The officer conducted the search and tied a property tag to the steering wheel. He then began to close up and lock the auto. When he opened the front door on the passenger side for the purpose of rolling up the window, he saw a registration card lying face up on the metal stripping over which the door closes. The card, which was in "plain view," belonged to the victim of the robbery.

Harris claimed that the registration card could not be used as evidence because it had not been seized at the time of his arrest. In the Supreme Court's opinion, however, the observation of the card was not the outcome of a search; rather, it stemmed from efforts to protect the vehicle while in police custody. The seizure was therefore lawful.

Although the Court made the nature of "plain view" relatively clear in this case, a few police officers have apparently perjured themselves in using the doctrine as a mechanism for justifying illegal searches. If one were to sit in a courtroom in any large urban area where drug dealing is common, one would very quickly get the impression than some drug users suffer from "dropsy." Miami attorney Steven M. Greenberg explained the phenomenon:

> Dropsy is claimed by the police in situations where they have searched a suspect without probable cause or consent and found contraband. To insure the admission of the illegally

seized evidence the police will "improvise" a story similar to the following: As I drove past
_____ School, I noticed two or three suspicious-looking suspects standing in the school-
yard, who glanced apprehensively at me as I passed. I drove on down the street, parked my
vehicle, and walked toward them. As I approached, one of the suspects reached into his
pocket and dropped a clear plastic bag at his feet. I bent down to pick it up and noticed that
it contained a substance which resembled marijuana.[56]

Greenberg goes on to suggest that this clumsiness is extraordinary, since both the
officer and the suspect know that a search would not be lawful under these circumstances. But given the fact that the alleged marijuana suddenly comes into plain view,
the seizure can be explained.

Under the **protective sweep doctrine,** which has been the subject of numerous
court cases in recent years, the scope of plain view has been expanded considerably. The
protective sweep doctrine suggests that when law enforcement officers make an arrest
on or outside private premises, they may, despite the absence of a search warrant, examine the entire premises for other persons whose presence would pose a threat, either
to their safety or to evidence that could be removed or destroyed. Moreover, protective
sweep procedures may be initiated even if there is only a suspicion that other such persons are present on the premises, and any evidence that is in plain view during the
search, or sweep, may be lawfully seized.[57]

As can be seen from the extent and complexity of the principles governing search
and seizure, the legality of police actions when conducting a search is central to the decision as to whether particular items can be used at trial. Since this is often the key to
the outcome of the case, the next section focuses more specifically on the rules of evidence, particularly the exclusionary rule.

| The Exclusionary Rule |

In 1914, the U.S. Supreme Court announced its well-known and highly controversial
exclusionary rule, prohibiting the use of evidence seized by federal agents in violation
of the Fourth Amendment protection against unreasonable search and seizure. The
rule was an outgrowth of *Weeks v. United States,*[58] and during the almost nine decades
since that case there has been a continuing debate over whether the decision is an effective remedy or an expensive constitutional right.

Weeks v. United States

In common law proceedings, the admissibility of evidence in criminal cases (that is,
whether evidence may be used at trial) was unrelated to any illegal actions the police
may have engaged in when securing such evidence. An attorney might argue that a certain piece of evidence was immaterial, inappropriate, irrelevant, or even incompetent,
but if it passed these tests it was clearly admissible. The courts, even at the appellate
and supreme levels, were not concerned with the legality of the methods used to obtain evidence. If the evidence had been stolen, common law provided for prosecution
of the thief, or a civil action for trespass and return of the property, but the illegally obtained evidence could still be used in court proceedings.

Yet it had long been argued that any evidence that was obtained illegally should
not be admissible and that such a rule would provide the only effective deterrent to illegal searches and seizures. Even the Supreme Court adhered to the common law principle, as in *Adams v. New York* (1904),[59] when it ruled that the admissibility of evidence
was not affected by the illegality of the means by which it was obtained.

In *Weeks,* the defendant was arrested at his place of business. The police officer
then searched Weeks's house and turned over the articles and papers found there to
a United States marshal. Thereupon, the marshal, accompanied by police officers,
repeated the search of Weeks's room and confiscated other documents and letters.
No warrants had been obtained for the arrest or the search. Before his trial, Weeks
petitioned the federal district court for the confiscated articles and papers, but the

Reprinted by permission of *www.CartoonStock.com*

court refused and allowed the materials to be used against him at trial, resulting in his conviction.

On appeal, the Supreme Court ruled in Weeks's favor, thus initiating the exclusionary rule. Speaking for the Court, Justice William R. Day explained:

> If letters and private documents can thus be seized and held and used in evidence against a citizen accused of an offense, the protection of the Fourth Amendment, declaring his right to be secure against such searches and seizures, is of no value, and, so far as those thus placed are concerned, might as well be stricken from the Constitution. The efforts of the courts and their officials to bring the guilty to punishment, praiseworthy as they are, are not to be aided by the sacrifice of these great principles established by years of endeavor and suffering which have resulted in their embodiment in the fundamental law of the land.

The decision in *Weeks* quickly became the subject of much legal controversy. By denying prosecutors the use of certain evidence, the rule sometimes caused the collapse of the government's case and the freeing of a defendant against whom there was strong evidence of guilt. In 1931, George W. Wickersham, chairman of the National Commission on Law Observance and Enforcement, commented that the "guarantees as to searches and seizures are often in the way of effective detection."[60] And Benjamin Cardozo (who would later become a Supreme Court justice) wrote, "The criminal is to go free because the constable has blundered."[61]

But *Weeks* was only a partial victory for the Fourth Amendment. The exclusionary rule applied only to material obtained in an unconstitutional search and seizure by a *federal* agent in a *federal* case; it did not apply to *state* actions. In addition, Weeks made possible the "*silver platter*" *doctrine,* which permitted federal prosecutors to use evidence obtained by state agents through unreasonable search and seizure (handed to them on a "silver platter")—provided that the evidence was obtained without federal participation and was turned over to federal officials.[62]

Wolf v. *Colorado*

In *Wolf,* the Supreme Court created a right without a remedy.

—**KENNETH C. HAAS**

In 1949, the Supreme Court made a tentative movement toward applying *Weeks* to state court actions. The case was *Wolf* v. *Colorado,*[63] in which a deputy sheriff seized a physician's appointment book without a warrant, interrogated patients whose names appeared in the book, and thereby obtained the evidence needed to charge Wolf with performing illegal abortions. Wolf was convicted.

On appeal to the Supreme Court, Wolf challenged the use of the evidence, arguing that it had been seized illegally. But the Court upheld Wolf's conviction. At the same time, the Court held that the Fourth Amendment guarantee protected individuals against state as well as federal action. It did not, however, extend the exclusionary rule to the states. In effect, it announced the application of the Fourth Amendment's guarantees to the states but immediately neutralized them by continuing to sanction the admission of evidence that had been illegally obtained by the states. *Wolf* prohibited unreasonable searches and seizures by the states, but if the evidence was trustworthy (that is, if it was "material, relevant, and competent" as required by common law), it was admissible regardless of how it was obtained.

Despite its refusal in *Wolf* to apply the exclusionary rule to illegally seized evidence at the state level, in 1952 the Supreme Court ruled in **Rochin v. California** that evidence acquired in a manner that "shocks the conscience" would be invalid.[64]

In the decade after the *Rochin* decision, two loopholes in the exclusionary rule as it applied to the federal system were closed. In *Rea* v. *United States*,[65] federal law enforcement officials were prohibited from turning over to state prosecutors evidence that had been seized by them in an unconstitutional manner. And in 1960 the "silver platter" doctrine was put to rest by the Court's decision in *Elkins* v. *United States*,[66] which stated that any evidence seized in an unconstitutional fashion by state officials and handed over to a federal prosecutor was inadmissible in federal courts.

Mapp v. *Ohio*

It was not until almost a half-century after the Supreme Court first announced the exclusionary rule that it fully extended the principle to the states. The case was **Mapp v. Ohio**,[67] decided in 1961.

The *Mapp* case began on May 23, 1957, when three Cleveland police officers arrived at the residence of Dollree ("Dolly") Mapp. They had been informed that a suspect in a recent bombing was hiding out in her home and also that a large amount of gambling paraphernalia was being concealed at the residence. Mapp and her daughter lived on the top floor of the two-family dwelling. Upon arriving, the police knocked at the door and demanded entry. After telephoning her attorney, Mapp refused to admit them without a search warrant. The officers advised their headquarters of the situation and began a surveillance of the house.

When at least four additional officers arrived on the scene some 3 hours later, the police again sought entry to the residence. When Mapp did not come to the door immediately, they forced their way into the dwelling. Meanwhile, Mapp's attorney arrived, but the police barred him from either seeing his client or entering the house. From the testimony, Mapp was apparently about halfway down the stairs from the second floor when the police broke into the lower hall. She demanded to see the search warrant. Thereupon one of the officers held up a paper that he claimed to be a warrant.

Mapp grabbed the alleged warrant and stuffed it into her bra. A struggle ensued during which the officers removed the paper and at the same time handcuffed her because she was "belligerent" in resisting their official rescue of the warrant paper from her person. They then took her forcibly to her bedroom, where they searched a dresser, a chest of drawers, a closet, and some suitcases. They also looked through a photo album and some of Mapp's personal papers. The search then spread to the remainder of the second floor, including the daughter's bedroom, the living room, the kitchen, and the dining area. The basement of the building and a trunk found there were also searched. Neither the bombing suspect nor the gambling paraphernalia were found, but the search did turn up an unspecified amount of pornographic literature.

After the search, Mapp was arrested on a charge of possessing "lewd and lascivious books, pictures, and photographs." She was convicted in an Ohio court on possession of obscene materials. At the trial, no search warrant was produced by the prosecution, nor was the failure to produce one ever explained or accounted for.

The issue in *Mapp*, of course, was the legality of the arrest, search, and seizure. There was no search warrant and no consent to search, but one could argue, as the prosecution did, that at the time that the police applied force and searched her apartment, Dolly Mapp was indeed under arrest; hence, it was a search incident to arrest. Yet, as the defense pointed out and the facts of the case confirmed, there was no prob-

Rochin v. California

On the morning of July 1, 1949, three Los Angeles County deputy sheriffs entered Rochin's home without the benefit of a warrant, on the basis of "some information" that he was selling narcotics. Upon locating Rochin in his bedroom, the officers observed "two capsules" on his bedside table and inquired about them. Rochin "seized the capsules and put them in his mouth," and after he swallowed them, the officers forcibly took him to a hospital where they had his stomach pumped to recover the drugs, which were used as evidence at trial.

The Supreme Court ruled Rochin's conviction invalid—but the reversal was based not on the warrantless search by police on less than probable grounds but, rather, on the seizure, which was a blatant violation of the concept of due process of law as found in the Fifth and Fourteenth Amendments. ∎

Scent Identification Lineups

Juries just love dog testimony. As a witness, nothing beats a canine for sincerity and trustworthiness. And everybody knows that dogs have an incredible sense of smell. But is dog scent evidence reliable? Can Rover properly identify a suspect by a scent that he or she left behind? Since 1923, dog scent evidence has played a role in more than 1,000 criminal cases in the United States. However, a scientific basis for the process has yet to be established. Prosecutors skirt that issue by arguing that scent lineups are no more than a logical continuation of the use of dogs for tracking fugitives or sniffing out drugs—uses that have long since passed legal muster. Some judges buy that idea, but many don't. ∎

able cause for arrest. The only background the police had was "information that a fugitive was hiding in her home."

It was on the basis of these facts, or rather the lack of them, that the Supreme Court reversed the decision of the Ohio court and extended the exclusionary rule to all the states. The Court ruled that the Fourth Amendment is incorporated, by inference, in the due process clause of the Fourteenth Amendment. From then on, any evidence that was illegally obtained by the police would be inadmissible in any and every courtroom in the country. The Court's opinion, written by Justice Tom C. Clark, stated as follows:

> The ignoble shortcut to conviction left open to the State tends to destroy the entire system of constitutional restraints on which the liberties of the people rest. Having once recognized that the right to privacy embodied in the Fourth Amendment is enforceable against the States, and that the right to be secure against rude invasions of privacy by state officers is, therefore, constitutional in origin, we can no longer permit that right to remain an empty promise. Because it is enforceable in the same manner and to like effect as other basic rights secured by the Due Process Clause, we can no longer permit it to be revocable at the whim of any police officer who, in the name of law enforcement itself, chooses to suspend its environment. Our decision, founded on reason and truth, gives to the individual no more than that which the Constitution guarantees him, to the police officer no less than that to which honest law enforcement is entitled, and, to the courts, that judicial integrity so necessary in the true administration of justice.

The *Mapp* decision was a controversial one, both within and outside the Supreme Court. It had been reached by a 5-to-3 majority (with Justice Potter Stewart abstaining). Among those concurring with the Court's opinion was Justice William O. Douglas, who asserted that "once evidence, inadmissible in a federal court, is admissible in a state court a 'double standard' exists which leads to 'working arrangements' that undercut federal policy and reduce some aspects of law enforcement to a shabby business." However, Justice Hugo Black, though also concurring with the majority opinion, commented that he was "still not persuaded that the Fourth Amendment, standing alone, would be enough to bar the introduction into evidence against an accused of papers and effects seized from him in violation of its commands." Among the dissenters, Justice John Marshall Harlan believed that "the *Wolf* rule represents sounder constitutional doctrine than the new rule which now replaces it." And Justice Potter Stewart refused to deal with the constitutional issue that was the basis of the *Mapp* reversal. In a separate memorandum to the Court, he commented that the Ohio obscenity law under which Mapp was convicted in the first place was itself unconstitutional.*

Outside the Supreme Court there were also opposing opinions regarding the *Mapp* decision. The very next day, *The New York Times* referred to *Mapp* as "an historic step," and Harvard Law School dean Ervin Griswold—soon to become solicitor general of the United States—saw the case as requiring "a complete change in the outlook and practices of state and local police."[68] In contrast, the decision produced a frantic torrent of complaints from outraged police across the nation, who felt that they were being deprived of their legal right to search for and obtain evidence.[69] In response to police complaints, University of Michigan law professor Yale Kamisar offered the following argument:

> What law enforcement officers were really bristling about was tighter enforcement of long-standing restrictions. Not *Mapp*, but state and federal constitutional provisions that had been on the books for decades, banned arbitrary arrests and unreasonable searches. The police never had the authority to proceed without "probable cause," only the incentive. And the principal contribution of *Mapp* was to reduce that incentive.[70]

The Impact of *Mapp* In 1965, the Court held in *Linkletter* v. *Walker*[71] that the *Mapp* decision would not be retroactively applied to overturn state criminal convictions that occurred prior to the expansion of the exclusionary rule in 1961. The Court stated

---

*The Supreme Court subsequently invalidated all state laws prohibiting the private possession of pornography in the home. See *Stanley* v. *Georgia*, 394 U.S. 557 (1969).

that the goal of *Mapp* was to deter future unlawful police conduct and thereby carry out the guarantee of the Fourth Amendment against unreasonable searches and seizures. The purpose was to deter, not to redress the injury to former search victims, and making the rule retroactive would not have any deterrent effect. Despite this decision, for the 26 state jurisdictions that had rejected the exclusionary rule prior to *Mapp*, the *Mapp* decision was an explosive one. Not only were police required to suddenly change their search and seizure procedures, but the rule also immediately applied to all cases that were currently under court review.

The Retreat From *Mapp*   Throughout the 1960s and into the following decades, dissatisfaction with the *Mapp* rule continued. There was considerable demand for modification, if not outright abolition, of the rule, not only in Congress but also in the Supreme Court and among a public that was fearful of increased levels of street crime.

The justices who wished to modify *Mapp*—including John Marshall Harlan, Byron Raymond White, Harry Andrew Blackmun, and the new Chief Justice, Warren Earl Burger—thought it had developed into a series of confusing and complicated requirements that puzzled the police more than it restrained them. The Fourth Amendment prohibited "unreasonable" searches, but the term *unreasonable* had never been fully defined by either the Constitution or the Court. Moreover, the Fourth Amendment also required that police obtain a warrant and that a warrant be issued only when "probable cause" was shown. Yet over the years the Court had allowed numerous exceptions to this requirement.

Even before his appointment to the Supreme Court, Chief Justice Burger had been a strong advocate of a change in the exclusionary rule. He argued that society had paid a monstrous price for the rule, that evidence should be excluded only in cases of genuine police misconduct, that it was absurd to free a thief or murderer because a police officer had made a minor error in an application for a search warrant, that the rule had little deterrent effect on police misconduct, and that in place of the rule there should be a remedy such as disciplinary action against police officers who abused constitutional rights.

While Justices Harlan, White, Blackmun, and Burger opposed *Mapp*, Justices Thurgood Marshall, William Joseph Brennan, and William O. Douglas strongly supported it. Justice Potter Stewart, though undecided, had views similar to Harlan's—and Justice Hugo Black, a judge since 1910 and a member of the Supreme Court since 1937, was also in doubt. Black's position was that, rather than overrule *Mapp*, a clear checklist should be created of what was and was not a reasonable search and when evidence could and could not be excluded.

This was the situation in the spring of 1971.[72] Fearing the "death of *Mapp*," and possibly of *Weeks* as well, Justices Brennan and Marshall instructed their clerks not to accept cases involving the Fourth Amendment until the positions of Black and Stewart were fully clear. The message was that there would be no free shots at the Fourth Amendment; the Court would hear only cases involving flagrant police violations, not those intended to "right little wrongs." Awaiting decision at this point was *Coolidge* v. *New Hampshire*,[73] a case that involved numerous Fourth Amendment issues—arrest, probable cause seizure, plain view seizure, arrest search, and consent search. The facts in *Coolidge* were so complicated, however, that it was decided that this case would not be used to determine the future of *Mapp*.

The retreat from *Mapp* began less than 3 years later with *United States* v. *Calandra*,[74] decided on January 8, 1974. In this case, the Court ruled that the exclusionary rule was not applicable to the presentation of illegally obtained evidence at grand jury proceedings.

In 1976, the Court's decision in *Stone* v. *Powell*[75] practically closed federal courtrooms to state prisoners convicted by means of illegal searches and seizures. Under the federal *habeas corpus* statute,[76] state prisoners who had allegedly been convicted and incarcerated on the basis of illegally obtained evidence could appeal to the federal courts. In *Powell*, the Court ruled that federal courts are under no constitutional obligation to

FAMOUS CRIMINALS
The Subway Vigilante

On December 22, 1984, an unidentified white man gunned down four African American youths who had demanded $5 from him on a Manhattan subway car. The gunman quickly fled the scene, and New York City as well, renting a car and driving to New Hampshire. Nine days later, he surrendered himself to New Hampshire police. His name was Bernhard Hugo Goetz, a 37-year-old, self-employed electrical engineer.

Goetz claimed that when the youths approached him, he was within seconds of becoming a mugging victim. The incident occurred at a time when street and subway crime in New York City was seemingly out of control, and when it was learned that the youths had criminal records, for urban dwellers who were fed up with crime Goetz was an immediate hero. Subsequent evidence suggested that Goetz's actions may have been unprovoked, but when one of his victims was arrested 6 months later on rape and robbery charges, New York's "subway vigilante," as he was called, received new support. In a national poll conducted by the Roper organization during September 1985, Goetz ranked sixth (following Lee Iacocca, Dan Rather, Peter Jennings, Mike Wallace, and Tom Brokaw) among the most admired personalities in the nation. Moreover, many observers in New York and across the country likened him to the Charles Bronson character in the 1974 film *Death Wish*, in which a mild-mannered businessman turns into

(continued on p. 248)

(continued from p. 247)

a gun-toting vigilante after his wife and daughter are savagely attacked by street thugs. Although Goetz was considered a hero by some, others called him a racist.

In the years immediately following the shootings, the Goetz case was seized upon by advocates on both sides of such urban issues as crime, race relations, gun control, and vigilantism. Goetz ultimately went to trial in 1987 on charges of attempted murder, assault, and illegal possession of a firearm, but his only conviction was on the gun charge, for which he served 8 months in jail. ∎

use the writ of *habeas corpus** to order release of persons who argue that their convictions in state courts were obtained with illegally seized evidence. So long as the state provides an opportunity for a full and fair hearing of the defendant's challenge to the evidence, the Court held, there is no obligation at the federal level to use the *habeas corpus* statute to enforce the exclusionary rule.

A further setback for the exclusionary rule came in 1984 with the Supreme Court's statement of the "good-faith" exception. This came in **United States v. Leon** and *Massachusetts* v. *Sheppard*,[77] two cases involving defective search warrants. In *Leon,* probable cause to support the warrant was lacking, yet this had not been noticed by the prosecutors who reviewed the application, the magistrate who approved the warrant, or the officers who executed the search in accordance with its authorization (see Exhibit 8.5). In *Sheppard,* an inappropriate warrant form had been used and had been filled out improperly. Trial courts had held that these defects required the exclusion of evidence under the Fourth Amendment's exclusionary rule. Disagreeing with this result, the Court adopted a good-faith exception to the rule in *Leon* and then applied the exception in *Sheppard,* thus allowing the evidence as a result of the warrants to be admitted at trial.

Three years after *Leon,* the Supreme Court added a second good-faith exception to the exclusionary rule. In *Illinois* v. *Krull,*[78] the Court justified the use of evidence obtained by police officers who carry out a search under a state law that is later found to be unconstitutional. In *Murray* v. *United States,*[79] decided in 1988, the Court also added an "independent source" exception to the exclusionary rule. It held that evidence discovered by police during an initial, warrantless entry into a warehouse is admissible if the same evidence is discovered in a second search pursuant to a warrant based on information obtained independently of the initial, illegal search.

Custodial Interrogation

No person . . . shall be compelled in any criminal case to be a witness against himself.

— FROM THE FIFTH AMENDMENT

In all criminal prosecutions the accused shall enjoy the right . . . to have the assistance of counsel for his defense.

— FROM THE SIXTH AMENDMENT

Confessions, the Supreme Court stated more than a century ago in *Hopt* v. *Utah,*[80] are "among the most effectual proofs of the law," but they are admissible as evidence only when made voluntarily. This has long been the rule in the federal courts, where the Fifth Amendment clearly applies. A confession, whether written or oral (but now usually recorded), is simply a statement by a person admitting to the violation of a law. In *Hopt,* the Court stressed that for a confession to be valid it must be *voluntary.* It defined as involuntary or coerced any confession that "appears to have been made, either in consequence of inducements of a temporal nature . . . or because of a threat or promise . . . which, operating upon the fears or hopes of the accused . . . deprive him of that freedom of will or self-control essential to make his confession voluntary within the meaning of the law." In 1896 the Court restated this position, ruling that the circumstances in which a confession is made must be considered in order to determine if it was made voluntarily.[81]

Twining v. New Jersey

These rulings on involuntary confessions did not apply to the states, however. The Court's decision in *Twining* v. *New Jersey* (1908)[82] specifically emphasized this point. The defendants, Albert C. Twining and David C. Cornell, executives of the Monmouth Safe and Trust Company, were indicted by a grand jury for having knowingly

---

*Habeas corpus is explored at length in Chapter 16.

LAW & CRIMINAL JUSTICE | EXHIBIT 8.5

United States v. Leon

In *United States* v. *Leon,* a California district court judge issued a search warrant based on information from a confidential source and a lengthy police investigation. The warrant authorized the search of three houses and several automobiles. The subsequent search produced large quantities of cocaine and methaqualone. Defendants filed a pretrial motion to suppress the evidence seized in the search on the grounds that the affidavit was insufficient to establish probable cause. The district court granted part of the motion, and the U.S. Court of Appeals for the Ninth Circuit affirmed. The government's petition for *certiorari* presented only the question of whether a "good-faith" exception to the exclusionary rule should be adopted.

Justice Byron White, writing for the majority, reversed the decision of the court of appeals and finally announced the long-awaited good-faith exception to the exclusionary rule. The majority based its decision on two independent grounds. First, it said that the Fourth Amendment does not contain any expressed provisions precluding the use of evidence obtained in violation of its commands. Once the illegal search is completed, the wrong prohibited by the Fourth Amendment is "fully accomplished" and "the exclusionary rule is neither intended nor able to cure the invasion of the defendant's rights which he has already suffered." The judicially created rule acts only to safeguard Fourth Amendment rights through its deterrent effect.

Second, the majority said that the question of whether a party's Fourth Amendment rights were violated is a separate issue from the question of whether the exclusionary rule should be imposed. In *Leon,* only the latter question had to be resolved. The Court reasoned that it would be resolved by "weighing the costs and benefits of preventing the use . . . of inherently trustworthy tangible evidence." The Court noted that the costs exacted by the exclusionary rule were "substantial." Excluding relevant, probative evidence impedes the "truthfinding" function of judge and jury, which further results in the objectionable consequence that "some guilty defendants may go free. . . ." Such a benefit to guilty defendants is particularly offensive to the criminal justice system when the illegal acts of law enforcement are minor and were done in good faith. Therefore, the indiscriminate application of the exclusionary rule under such circumstances might result in "disrespect for the law and the administration of justice." Thus, after applying a cost–benefit analysis test, the Court concluded that the exclusionary rule should be modified to allow introduction of unconstitutionally obtained evidence where officers acted in "reasonable good faith belief that such a search or seizure was in accord with the Fourth Amendment."

The majority further supported this new exception in those areas where the deterrent effect of the exclusionary rule would not be achieved. In those situations, the benefits of the rule would not outweigh its costs. "In short . . . the Court has applied, in deciding whether exclusion is appropriate in a particular case, attempts to mark the point at which the detrimental consequences of illegal police action became so attenuated that the deterrent effect of the exclusionary rule no longer justifies its cost." This balancing approach provides strong support for adopting a good-faith modification.

The Court concluded that even if the rule effectively "deters *some* police misconduct . . . it can not be expected and should not be applied, to deter objectively reasonable law enforcement activity." Excluding evidence will not in any appreciable way further the ends of the exclusionary rule where the officer's conduct is objectively reasonable. "This is particularly true when an officer acting with good faith has obtained a search warrant from a . . . magistrate and acted within its scope."

Under this rule, suppression of evidence would be an appropriate remedy when the issuing magistrate was misled by information that the affiant knew was false. This exception would also not apply when the issuing magistrate disregards his or her role in such a manner that "no reasonable well-trained officer should rely on the warrant." Nor would the police be acting in objective good faith if the affidavit was "so lacking of probable cause as to render official belief in its existence unreasonable."

The majority concluded that this good-faith exception was not intended to signal an unwillingness to enforce Fourth Amendment requirements. Nor would it preclude judicial review concerning the constitutionality of searches and seizures.

Source: Adapted from J. Michael Hunter, "Is the Exclusionary Rule a Relic of the Past? *Leon, Sheppard,* and 'Beyond,'" *Ohio Northern Law Review* 12 (November 1985). Reprinted by permission of the author.

displayed a false paper to a bank examiner "with full intent to deceive him" as to the actual condition of their firm. At trial, Twining and Cornell refused to take the stand. Judge Webber A. Heisley addressed the jury as follows:

> Because a man does not go upon the stand you are not necessarily justified in drawing an inference of guilt. But you have a right to consider the fact that he does not go upon the stand where a direct accusation is made against him.[83]

The jury returned a verdict of guilty, at which point Twining and Cornell appealed to the U.S. Supreme Court. They contended that the exemption from self-incrimination was one of the privileges and immunities that the Fourteenth Amendment forbade the states to abridge. They claimed that the judge's statement amounted to compulsory self-incrimination and therefore constituted a denial of due process. In

Victims are often the most common sources of leads. An officer makes sure they have an opportunity to calm down and collect their thoughts before conducting an in-depth interview. In this case, a Des Moines, Iowa, police officer interviews a recent victim of crime.

an 8-to-1 decision, the Court ruled against Twining and Cornell, stating that the privilege against self-incrimination was "not fundamental in due process of law, not an essential part of it."

Twining was not a case of forced confession in the strictest sense of the term, for no confession had actually occurred. But the notion of a potentially involuntary confession was inferred, and the resulting decision was that defendants in state courts do not enjoy the Fifth Amendment privilege against compulsory self-incrimination.

Brown v. *Mississippi*

Although more than half a century would pass before the Supreme Court would specifically apply the Fifth Amendment privilege to the states, the Court, through its unanimous decision in *Brown* v. *Mississippi* (1936),[84] forbade states to use coerced confessions to convict persons of crimes.

The case involved three black men who were arrested for the murder of a white man. At trial, they were convicted solely on the basis of their confessions, and sentenced to death. But the confessions had been coerced. The defendants had been tied to a tree, whipped, twice hanged by a rope from a tree, and told that the process would continue until they confessed. And although there was no doubt that torture had been used to elicit the confessions, the convictions were affirmed by the Mississippi Supreme Court.

On appeal to the U.S. Supreme Court, Mississippi defended its use of the confessions obtained through beatings and torture by citing the earlier *Twining* ruling that state court defendants do not enjoy the Fifth Amendment privilege. The Court agreed with *Twining* but rejected the Mississippi defense, holding that the state's right to withdraw the privilege of self-incrimination was not the issue. Speaking for the Court, Chief Justice Charles Evans Hughes distinguished between "compulsion" as forbidden by the Fifth Amendment and "compulsion" as forbidden by the Fourteenth Amendment's due process clause:

> The compulsion to which the Fifth Amendment refers is that of the processes of justice by which the accused may be called as a witness and required to testify. Compulsion by torture to extort a confession is a different matter. . . .
>
> Because a state may dispense with a jury trial, it does not follow that it may substitute trial by ordeal. The rack and torture chamber may not be substituted for the witness stand.

No state shall make or enforce any law which shall abridge the privileges or immunities of citizens of the United States; nor shall any state deprive any person of life, liberty, or property, without due process of law; nor deny to any person within its jurisdiction the equal protection of the laws.

— FROM THE FOURTEENTH AMENDMENT

It would be difficult to conceive of methods more revolting to the sense of justice than those taken to procure the confessions of these petitioners, and the use of the confessions thus obtained as the basis for conviction and sentence was a clear denial of due process.

In the years that followed, the Supreme Court reversed numerous decisions in which confessions had been compelled, examining in each case the totality of circumstances surrounding the arrest and interrogation. The Court's philosophy made it clear that coercion could be psychological as well as physical. As summarized by Justice Felix Frankfurter in 1961:

> Our decisions . . . have made clear that convictions following the admission into evidence of confessions which are involuntary . . . cannot stand. This is so not because such confessions are unlikely to be true but because the methods used to extract them offend an underlying principle in the enforcement of our criminal law: that ours is an accusatorial and not an inquisitorial system—a system in which the State must establish guilt by evidence independently and freely secured and may not by coercion prove its own charge against an accused out of his own mouth.[85]

The Prompt Arraignment Rule

Just before the turn of the 20th century, the Supreme Court had implied that delay in charging a suspect with a crime might be one of the factors in determining whether a confession was voluntary or not.[86] A number of federal statutes served to clarify the Court's intent. Their purpose was to prevent federal law enforcement agents from using postarrest detention as a way of obtaining confessions through interrogation and from justifying illegal arrests through confessions obtained by means of prolonged questioning.

But the rules had no compelling force until 1943, when the Supreme Court ruled in *McNabb* v. *United States*,[87] that confessions obtained after "unreasonable delay" in arraigning a suspect could not be used as evidence in a *federal* court. Five Tennessee mountaineers were arrested when federal agents closed in on their moonshining operations, and during the course of the raid one of the agents was killed. Two of the defendants were convicted of second-degree murder on the basis of their confessions and sentenced to 45 years imprisonment. Their incriminating statements were made after 3 days of questioning in the absence of any counsel and before they were charged with any crime. The Court overturned the *McNabb* convictions, not on the basis of the Fifth Amendment but on that of existing *prompt arraignment* statutes as well as the Court's general power to supervise the functioning of the federal judicial system. Speaking for the Court, Justice Frankfurter explained the purpose of the ban on unnecessary delay between arrest and arraignment:

> This procedural requirement checks resort to those reprehensible practices known as the "third degree" which though universally rejected as indefensible, still find their way into use. It aims to avoid all the evil implications of street interrogation of persons accused of crime. It reflects not a sentimental but a sturdy view of law enforcement. It outlaws easy but self-defeating ways in which brutality is substituted for brains as an instrument of crime detection.

The Federal Rules of Criminal Procedure subsequently incorporated this rule. In *Mallory* v. *United States*,[88] almost 15 years after *McNabb*, the Supreme Court reaffirmed its prompt arraignment requirement by nullifying the death sentence imposed on a convicted rapist who "confessed" to the crime during a delay of more than 18 hours between arrest and arraignment. The defendant, Andrew Mallory, had been arrested in the District of Columbia, and during his long interrogation no attempt was made to bring official charges against him—even though arraigning magistrates were available in the same building throughout the period of questioning.

In both *McNabb* and *Mallory,* the Supreme Court did not rule on whether or not the confessions had been obtained voluntarily. Rather, the cases were decided on the basis of the Court's authority to police the federal judicial system. But the Court's decision in *Mallory* was fiercely criticized. By reversing the conviction on the basis of the prompt arraignment rule, the Court was saying that any evidence gathered during the delay had been acquired unlawfully and hence was inadmissible—even if it included a confession that was indeed voluntary.

The *McNabb-Mallory* prompt arraignment rule would not stand the test of time. At the state level, the example set by the federal courts was never fully followed. And even the decisions in *McNabb* and *Mallory* were ultimately diluted. Less than a month after the *Mallory* decision, a subcommittee of the House Judiciary Committee began hearings to reverse it. Although no "corrective" legislation was passed, in 1968 Congress included in the Omnibus Crime Control and Safe Streets Act a section that was directly related to *Mallory*. The act modified the *Mallory* decision to provide that a confession made by a person in the custody of law officers was not to be ruled inadmissible as evidence *solely* because of delay in arraigning the defendant, if the confession was found to be voluntary, if the weight to be given the confession was left to the jury, and if the confession was made within 6 hours after arrest. The measure also provided that confessions obtained after this 6-hour limit could be used as evidence if the trial judge found the further delay to be not unreasonable.[89]

Confessions and Counsel

Before the 1960s, the Fifth Amendment privilege against self-incrimination and the Sixth Amendment right to counsel were not linked together. The *Brown* v. *Mississippi* decision in 1936 had ruled on the inadmissibility of confessions obtained by physical compulsion. In stating the Court's opinion in that case, Chief Justice Hughes highlighted the constitutional provision that "the state may not deny to the accused the aid of counsel." But in 1958 the Court held in *Crooker* v. *California*[90] that confessions could be both voluntary and admissible even when obtained from a suspect who was denied the opportunity to consult with legal counsel during interrogation. With *Brown* and *Crooker,* the Court took a firm stand on coerced confessions but nonetheless limited the right to counsel.

In the 1960s, the Supreme Court under Chief Justice Earl Warren issued a series of decisions that served to link together the provisions of the Fifth and Sixth Amendments and at the same time strengthen defendants' rights. In 1964, the Court reversed its position in *Crooker,* declaring in *Massiah* v. *United States*[91] that an indicted person could not be properly questioned or otherwise persuaded to make incriminating statements in the absence of his or her attorney. Shortly thereafter, the Court's decision in *Malloy* v. *Hogan* finally extended the privilege against self-incrimination to state defendants.[92] At the same time, it laid the groundwork for the most important decision of the Court's 1964 term, **Escobedo v. Illinois**[93] (see Exhibit 8.6).

The *Escobedo* decision required that an accused person be permitted to have an attorney present during interrogation. The majority view held that the adversary system of justice had traditionally been restricted to the trial stage but that the same rules should apply to earlier stages of criminal proceedings. It also contended, however, that the *Escobedo* decision need not affect the powers of the police to investigate unsolved crimes. But when "the process shifts from investigatory to accusatory," the Court stated, "when its focus is on the accused and its purpose is to elicit a confession, our adversary system begins to operate, and under the circumstances here, the accused must be permitted to consult with his lawyer."

The four dissenting justices were not convinced; they believed that the decision would hamper law enforcement efforts. Across the country police and prosecutors echoed these feelings. Interrogation of suspects behind closed doors in order to secure a confession was a deeply entrenched police practice based on centuries-old custom and usage. No longer would the "third degree" and "good guy–bad guy" interrogation routines be readily available.

Miranda v. *Arizona*

Escobedo seemed to raise more questions than it answered regarding police conduct during arrest and interrogation. In its discussion of the conditions that existed in Danny Escobedo's interrogation and led to the reversal of his conviction, was the

Ernesto Miranda. Ten years after the landmark Supreme Court decision, Miranda was killed in a barfight in Phoenix.

LAW & CRIMINAL JUSTICE | EXHIBIT 8.6

Escobedo v. Illinois

On the night of January 19, 1960, Manuel Valtierra, the brother-in-law of 22-year-old Danny Escobedo, was fatally shot in the back. Several hours later Escobedo was arrested without a warrant and was interrogated for some 15 hours. During that period, he made no statements to the police and was released after his attorney had obtained a writ of *habeas corpus*. Eleven days after the shooting of Valtierra, Escobedo was arrested for a second time and again taken to a police station for questioning. Shortly after Escobedo was brought to the Chicago police station, his attorney also arrived but the police would not permit him to see his client. Both the attorney and Escobedo repeatedly requested to see each other, but both were continually denied the privilege. Escobedo was told that he could not see his attorney until the police had finished their questioning. It was during this second period of interrogation that Escobedo made certain incriminating statements that would be construed as his voluntary confession to the crime.

Danny Escobedo was convicted of murder and sentenced to a 22-year prison term. On appeal to the state supreme court of Illinois, Escobedo maintained that he was told "he would be permitted to go home if he gave the statement and would be granted an immunity from prosecution." The statement in question referred to the complicity of his four codefendants, who had all been arrested on the murder charge. The Illinois Supreme Court reversed Escobedo's conviction, but the state petitioned for, and the court granted, a rehearing of the case. The decision was again reversed, sustaining the trial court's original conviction, and Escobedo still faced the 22-year prison term. Escobedo's counsel appealed further, and the U.S. Supreme Court granted *certiorari*.

On June 22, 1964, the Court ruled in favor of Danny Escobedo by a 5-to-4 decision. In delivering the opinion of the Court, Justice Arthur Goldberg noted that it was based on five pivotal facts in the interrogation:

We hold, therefore, that where . . .

1. the investigation is no longer a general inquiry into an unsolved crime but has begun to focus on a particular suspect,
2. the suspect has been taken into police custody,
3. the police carry out a process of interrogations that lends itself to eliciting incriminating statements,
4. the suspect has requested and been denied an opportunity to consult with his lawyer, and
5. the police have not effectively warned him of his absolute constitutional right to remain silent,

the accused has been denied "the assistance of counsel" in violation of the Sixth Amendment of the Constitution as "made obligatory upon the states by the Fourteenth Amendment," and that no statement elicited by the police during the interrogation may be used against him in a criminal trial.

Danny Escobedo

Source: *Escobedo v. Illinois*, 378 U.S. 478 (1964).

Court suggesting that *all* of these conditions had to be met for a confession to be admissible as evidence? Were police required to warn suspects of their right to remain silent? If a suspect requested counsel but none was at hand, could a police interrogation continue? If a suspect did not wish counsel, what then? And most important, how were the police to determine when an investigation began to "focus" on a particular suspect?

Given these unsettled issues, by January 1966 two separate U.S. courts of appeals had interpreted *Escobedo* in opposite ways. To resolve the conflict, the U.S. Supreme Court sifted through some 170 confession-related appeals and agreed to hear four cases: *Miranda v. Arizona*, *Vignera* v. *New York*, *Westover* v. *United States*, and *California* v. *Stewart*.[94] Known by the leading case, *Miranda*, this set of cases brought together the appeals of four individuals who had been convicted on the basis of confessions made after extended questioning in which they had not been informed of their right to remain silent. In all four cases, the crimes for which the defendants had been convicted involved major felonies—Miranda had been convicted of kidnapping and rape, Vignera of robbery in the first degree, Westover of bank robbery, and Stewart of robbery and

The idea that the police cannot ask questions of the person that knows most about the crime is an infamous decision.

—ATTORNEY GENERAL EDWIN MEESE, COMMENTING ON *MIRANDA*, SEPTEMBER 1, 1985

You can speak up or you can shut up. Either way, you are under arrest and are going to jail.

— **DETECTIVE ANDY SIPOWITZ**
OF *NYPD BLUE*

first-degree murder. The convictions were reversed by the Supreme Court, and from this decision came the so-called *Miranda* warnings, which a police officer must state to a suspect before any questioning occurs:

1. "You have a right to remain silent."
2. "Anything you say can and will be used against you in a court of law."
3. "You have a right to consult with a lawyer and to have the lawyer present during any questioning."
4. "If you cannot afford a lawyer, one will be obtained for you if you so desire."

The reactions to *Miranda,* even within the Supreme Court, were immediate. Four justices prepared a dissenting opinion, and it was reported that Justice Harlan, his face flushed and his voice occasionally faltering with emotion, denounced the decision from the bench, terming it "dangerous experimentation" at a time of a "high crime rate that is a matter of growing concern" and a "new doctrine" without substantial precedent, reflecting "a balance in favor of the accused."[95]

Outside the Supreme Court, the *Miranda* decision was bitterly attacked for handcuffing the police in their efforts to protect society against criminals. Critics asserted that more than three-fourths of the convictions in major crimes depended on confessions. Police officers and prosecutors echoed the belief of New York City's police commissioner, Patrick V. Murphy, that "if suspects are told of their rights they will not confess."[96]

During his 1968 presidential campaign, Richard M. Nixon promised to appoint Supreme Court justices who would be less receptive to the arguments of criminal defendants and more responsive to the needs and reasoning of law enforcement officers. The first of the Nixon appointees, Warren Burger, came to the Court in 1969. Burger was a conservative appeals court judge, and he replaced the retiring Earl Warren as the Court's chief justice. Burger clearly espoused "law and order," which made him attractive to the Senate Judiciary Committee, and he was known in Washington circles as Nixon's "hatchet man." As the new chief justice, he announced to the other justices exactly which previous decisions the Court had to overrule—*Miranda, Mapp, Chimel,* and others—and he eyed closely the votes that might be marshaled to achieve that result.[97] In 1970, Burger was joined on the bench by another Nixon appointee, Harry A. Blackmun, and in 1971 by Lewis F. Powell and William H. Rehnquist. These four justices quickly became known as the "Nixon Court," and it would appear that *Miranda* would soon be overturned. However, that turned out *not* to be the case (see Exhibit 8.7). Since then there have been other challenges to *Miranda,* but the right to remain silent has managed to survive for now.[98]

Show Ups and Lineups

In addition to interrogation, law enforcement officers employ a variety of investigating techniques to detect and identify criminal offenders. Among these are show ups, lineups, photographs, and other forms of "nontestimonial" material that the Supreme Court has allowed as admissible evidence under certain conditions.

The term *show up* is not consistently used by either the police or the courts; *lineup* is more popular. In general, the show up is a one-on-one procedure that generally takes place shortly after a crime has been committed. The victim or witness is taken to the police station, confronted with a suspect, and asked, "Is he the one?" In a lineup, the suspect is placed together with several other persons and the victim or witness is asked to pick out the suspect from this array of individuals. Here is an example of a show up, described in the 1972 case of *Kirby* v. *Illinois:*[99]

> After Kirby and his alleged accomplice Ralph Bean were arrested, police officers brought Willie Shard, the robbery victim, to a room in a police station where Kirby and Bean were seated at a table with two other police officers. Shard testified at trial that the officers who brought him to the room asked him if Kirby and Bean were the robbers and he indicated they were.

Miranda's Nine Lives by Kenneth C. Haas

Rising to announce the High Court's decision, the chief justice began, "You have the right to remain silent. Anything you say can be used against you in a court of law." Chief Justice Earl Warren made these words famous in 1966 when, writing for a closely divided Court, he announced the majority opinion in *Miranda* v. *Arizona,* arguably the most controversial and widely known criminal-law case ever to be decided by the United States Supreme Court. But when the Supreme Court's 1999–2000 term ended on June 26, 2000, it was Chief Justice William Rehnquist, a long-standing critic of *Miranda,* who spoke those words. And he did so as he announced that *Miranda* had survived the most recent and by far the most serious effort yet mounted to convince the justices to relegate *Miranda* to the history books. More than a few legal observers were surprised when Rehnquist, speaking for a 7-to-2 majority in *Dickerson* v. *United States,* went on to assert that the Constitution itself requires officers to inform suspects held under lawful police custody of their *Miranda* rights before interrogating them and to make it clear that both federal and state officers must continue to follow the *Miranda* rule.

© 2005, Steve Kelley, *The Times-Picayune.*

For three decades, the Burger and Rehnquist Courts had steadily chipped away at the *Miranda* holding. The erosion of *Miranda* began in 1971 with the Court's 5-to-4 decision in *Harris* v. *New York.* Chief Justice Warren Burger's *Harris* opinion declared that statements obtained in violation of *Miranda* would nevertheless be admissible in a criminal trial if the defendant took the witness stand in his own behalf and the prosecutor used the otherwise inadmissible statements in an effort to impeach the defendant's credibility. In dissent, Justice William Brennan warned that the *Harris* majority had undermined *Miranda* by, in effect, telling the police that they could ignore *Miranda* and still know that the evidence they obtained would be introduced "if the defendant has the temerity to testify in his own defense."

Despite Brennan's concerns, the Court's willingness to create exceptions to the *Miranda* rule continued. For example, in *Oregon* v. *Mathiason* (1977) the Court upheld the admissibility of a confession elicited without a *Miranda* warning from a man who had been asked by an officer to come to the police station to answer questions about a burglary. The Court reasoned that the suspect, though interrogated in a police station, had not truly been "in custody" for purposes of *Miranda* because he had not been formally placed under arrest before the interrogation and therefore should have felt free to leave the station without answering any questions.

In the highly publicized case of *Rhode Island* v. *Innis* (1980), the Court adopted a similarly narrow definition of "interrogation." Two officers were driving a suspect in a shooting to the police station. Knowing that the suspect had not been "Mirandized," the two officers began discussing the unrecovered gun used in the shooting and expressed fears that children from a nearby school for the handicapped might find the weapon and hurt themselves. The suspect promptly interrupted the conversation and directed the officers to the gun,

thereby incriminating himself. According to the Supreme Court, the officers' failure to advise the suspect of his *Miranda* rights was permissible because no "interrogation" had occurred. Rejecting the defendant's argument that the conversation between the two officers was a ploy designed to elicit incriminating information, the Court held that for *Miranda* purposes, an interrogation must consist of "express questioning" or the "functional equivalent" of such questioning. Neither had occurred in this instance, the majority concluded. The officers merely happened "to engage in a conversation between themselves" and "we cannot say that the officers should have known that the [suspect] would suddenly be moved to make a self-incriminating response."

The Court's assault on *Miranda* intensified in 1984. In *Nix* v. *Williams,* the Court approved an "inevitable discovery" exception to the *Miranda* rule, holding that evidence obtained in violation of defendants' constitutional rights would still be admissible in a criminal prosecution if the evidence "inevitably" or "ultimately" would have been discovered as the police continued to investigate the case. In *New York* v. *Quarles,* the Court approved a "public safety" exception to the *Miranda* requirements. The *Quarles* majority opinion was authored by Justice Rehnquist, who stressed that *Miranda* should not be applied in situations "in which police officers ask questions reasonably prompted by a concern for the public safety." Most ominously for the supporters of *Miranda,* Justice Rehnquist reiterated an argument he had made in the past and would continue to make in the future. The *Miranda* warnings, he asserted, were merely "procedural safeguards," not constitutional rights in themselves. The *Miranda* holding, he added, was not based squarely on the Fifth Amendment's privilege against self-incrimination; it was simply a "prophylactic" remedy designed as a way to protect defendants' rights in the "inherently coercive" circumstances that typically surround custodial interrogation.

The suggestion that *Miranda* was not truly a constitutional decision and thus could be ignored—or perhaps replaced by videotaping or

continued

EXHIBIT 8.7 | A View from the Field continued

other police procedures that could protect the rights of defendants—would be repeated in numerous decisions that continued to weaken *Miranda* or create new exceptions to it. Thus, in *Duckworth* v. *Eagan* (1989), the Court told police that they need not read the *Miranda* warning in the same words used in the *Miranda* decision itself, and in *Pennsylvania* v. *Muniz* (1990), the Court held that police could ask routine questions of people suspected of driving while intoxicated and videotape their responses without giving them the *Miranda* warnings.

Not surprisingly, when the Court granted *certiorari* in *Dickerson* v. *United States* in late 1999, there was a great deal of speculation that *Miranda* would finally be overruled in its entirety. Earlier in 1999, the U.S. Court of Appeals for the Fourth Circuit had refused to suppress statements made by Charles Dickerson, a man suspected of acting as an accomplice in a Virginia bank robbery. During an interrogation by FBI agents, Dickerson admitted to being the "getaway driver" for the bank robbery, but the agents had not read him his *Miranda* rights at the start of the questioning. The Fourth Circuit panel cited a law passed by Congress in 1968 (18 U.S.C. 3501) that stated that all voluntary confessions are admissible and that the question of whether a suspect had been advised of his *Miranda* rights was but one of several factors for trial judges to consider when deciding the overall issue of voluntariness. Although most federal prosecutors had long ignored the 1968 law, assuming it to be unconstitutional, the prosecutors in Dickerson's case argued that the time had come to recognize that the law had, in effect, overruled *Miranda*. The appeals court, relying heavily upon the Supreme Court's many references to *Miranda* as a "prophylactic" remedy with no constitutional status, agreed and held Dickerson's statements to be voluntary and thus admissible as evidence despite the agents' failure to comply with *Miranda*.

Although not everyone was surprised that the Supreme Court reversed the Fourth Circuit's ruling, nearly everyone *was* surprised that Chief Justice Rehnquist wrote and announced the *Dickerson* majority opinion. Rehnquist conceded that he and many other justices had often suggested that the *Miranda* warnings were intended only as a procedural safeguard and that *Miranda* was not truly a constitutional holding and thus could be countermanded by Congress. But the chief justice, joined by justices Breyer, Ginsburg, Kennedy, O'Connor, Souter, and Stevens, contended that there also were "factors on the other side" to be considered. Most important, he wrote, was the fact that the Court for over 30 years had applied *Miranda* to state and federal cases alike. Moreover, a close reading of the *Miranda* opinion indicates that "the majority thought it was announcing a constitutional rule." *Miranda* therefore was a constitutional decision and Congress "may not legislatively supersede our decisions interpreting and applying the Constitution."

How did the majority explain *Harris* v. *New York*, *Oregon* v. *Mathiason*, *New York* v. *Quarles*, and all of the other decisions that had criticized *Miranda* and created exceptions to it? According to the chief justice, these cases simply illustrated that no constitutional rule is immutable. "No court laying down a general rule can possibly foresee the various circumstances in which counsel will seek to apply it, and the sort of modifications represented by these cases are as much a normal part of constitutional law as the original decision." He added that even though some of the current justices might not have agreed with the *Miranda* holding if they had been members of the Court in 1966, the principles of *stare decisis* now weighed heavily against overruling it. "*Miranda* has become embedded in routine police practice to the point where the warnings have become part of our national culture."

Justice Antonin Scalia, joined by Justice Clarence Thomas, issued a caustic dissenting opinion. He cited many of the cases in which the Court and, in particular, Chief Justice Rehnquist had referred to *Miranda* as a set of "prophylactic" rules that go beyond the Fifth Amendment's right against compelled self-incrimination. How, Scalia asked, could the Court suddenly find *Miranda* worthy of preserving? He reserved his harshest criticism for the *Dickerson* majority's contention that it is too late to overturn a decision that has come to occupy a special place in the "public's consciousness" through police television dramas. "Far from believing that *stare decisis* compels this result, I believe we cannot allow to remain on the books even a celebrated decision—*especially* a celebrated decision—that has come to stand for the proposition that the Supreme Court has power to impose extraconstitutional constraints upon Congress and the States."

How did the *Dickerson* holding affect Charles Dickerson, the man who confessed to being the getaway driver for a bank robbery? Not much, if at all, as it turned out. Dickerson "won." The FBI agents admitted that they had violated his *Miranda* rights, and the Supreme Court's affirmation of *Miranda* meant that his confession ordinarily could not have been used against him in court. It was, however, Charles Dickerson took the witness stand in his own defense and pursuant to *Harris* v. *New York*, federal prosecutors introduced his confession into evidence to impeach his credibility. On October 6, 2000, Charles Dickerson was convicted of conspiracy, bank robbery, and a gun charge. He was sentenced to 12 years and 8 months in prison.

Sources: *Miranda* v. *Arizona*, 384 U.S. 436 (1966); *Dickerson* v. *United States*, 67 CrL 472 (2000); *Harris* v. *New York*, 401 U.S. 222 (1971); *Oregon* v. *Mathiason*, 429 U.S. 492 (1977); *Rhode Island* v. *Innis*, 446 U.S. 291 (1980); *Nix* v. *Williams*, U.S. SupCt 35 CrL 3119 (1984); *New York* v. *Quarles*, U.S. SupCt 35 CrL 3135 (1984); *Duckworth* v. *Eagan*, 45 CrL 3172 (1989); *Pennsylvania* v. *Muniz*, 47 CrL 2167 (1990).

The constitutional issues in the use of lineups and show ups have generally focused on their fairness and on the suspects' and defendants' rights to counsel during these procedures. In *Foster* v. *California*,[100] for example, there was only one witness to a robbery. The suspect, who was 6 feet tall, was first placed in a lineup with two other men who were several inches shorter. He was wearing a leather jacket similar to the one the

CAREERS IN CRIMINAL JUSTICE

Police Scuba Units

Working in police scuba units combines the requirements and abilities of two highly skilled areas: police work and scuba tech (technical) diving. The work of a police department's dive team primarily falls into the areas of search and recovery, such as underwater crime scene investigation, body and vehicle recovery, underwater photography, and removal of hazards to navigation.

Since the terrorist attacks of 9/11, along with their usual responsibilities of searching for bodies or criminal evidence, police dive units have been learning a new skill: identifying underwater explosives. They are learning techniques to search for underwater explosives under large ships and underwater structures including piers and bridges. Police divers are trained to give an assessment of an explosive, not handle it. The U.S. Navy would handle the actual removal of an explosive.

In August 2003, Seattle police divers completed a 5-day course that instructed them on how to locate explosives and other terrorist devices that may be attached to larger ships, barges, and other vessels that come to port. This program, funded by the Department of Homeland Security, is the first of its kind in the nation, but other public safety divers at all 361 U.S. ports are expected to undergo similar training as well.

The need to train police scuba units in explosive devices is evident. United States ports are believed to be the most vulnerable aspect of our transportation industry, as well as the most active (95% of international cargo going into the United States is received through its ports). In addition, captured al-Qaeda operatives have reported plans to use scuba divers to attach explosives to ship hulls, bridge supports, and dams.

From recovering vehicles in swamps to searching a huge cargo ship for bombs, police divers require many skills. In addition to requiring basic recreational scuba skills, search and recovery requires proficient underwater navigational techniques, as well as skills in various search patterns appropriate for a range of weather and sea conditions. Divers

A Seattle police scuba unit preparing to examine the bottom of a ship during anti-terrorism training.

must be adept at drift, swift water, high altitude, and cold-water diving. Police divers must also be knowledgeable in the maintenance and repair of all types of diving equipment. In addition, police scuba units that check ships for underwater explosives definitely need to be extra courageous—various threats to these divers include spinning propellers and enormous openings that suction in seawater.

Most large police departments and many smaller ones situated in coastal areas or located along rivers or bodies of water have scuba teams or officers qualified in search and recovery and crime scene diving. Along with the Seattle Police Department, the Los Angeles Police Department, New York City Police Department, Virginia Beach Police Department, and Chicago Police Department, to name a few, all have dive rescue teams or special scuba teams/units.

witness had seen one of the robbers wearing. The witness thought the suspect was indeed the robber, but was not absolutely sure. Several days later another lineup was held, and the suspect was the only one in the second lineup who had been in the earlier one. At this point the witness positively identified the suspect as the robber. The Supreme Court ruled against this type of identification procedure, stating that "in effect, the police repeatedly said to the witness, '*This* is the man.'"

United States* v. *Wade addressed the issue of a defendant's right to counsel during a lineup.[101] The defendant had been shown to witnesses at a postindictment lineup, without the accused or his attorney being notified beforehand and without the attorney present. The Court ruled that under these conditions the chances of an unfair identification, whether intentionally or otherwise, are so great that a person who is subjected to a pretrial lineup or show up is entitled to be represented by counsel at that time. Note, however, that *Wade* referred only to postindictment lineups and not to those occurring in earlier phases of the criminal justice process.

DNA and Other Nontestimonial Exemplars

DNA is a long double-stranded molecule wound in a spiral called a *helix*. Each strand in the helix contains billions of subunits, and the manner in which these are arranged determines an individual's unique genetic code, DNA profile, or "DNA fingerprint." DNA can be extracted from an individual's blood, saliva, semen or vaginal secretions, or even a spec of skin. When forensic scientists conducting criminal investigations examine DNA, they cannot focus on all of these billions of subunits. However, they can look at certain ministrands of DNA. If three of these ministrands match a suspect's, the chances are 2,000 to one that the police have the right person. Nine matches boost the odds to a billion to one, and FBI procedures require no less than 13 matches. Quite clearly, DNA is a powerful tool in criminal investigation. DNA testing has been especially useful in rape cases, because the predator's semen is generally left behind in the victim's vagina or anus. As such, DNA evidence can serve to either convict or exonerate suspects. In fact, in recent years, scores of death row inmates have had their convictions overturned on the basis of new DNA evidence. But because DNA is still relatively new, the U.S. Supreme Court has yet to define the parameters of its collection and use.

With respect to other nontestimonial exemplars, the Supreme Court has maintained a firm position:

*   In *Schmerber* v. *California*,[102] the Court ruled that the forced extraction of a blood sample from a defendant who was accused of driving while intoxicated was admissible at trial.
*   In *United States* v. *Dionisio*,[103] the Court held that a suspect could be forced to provide voice exemplars.
*   In *United States* v. *Mara*,[104] the Court held that a suspect could be compelled to provide a handwriting exemplar.
*   In *United States* v. *Ash*,[105] the Court held that the Sixth Amendment does not grant the right to counsel at photographic displays conducted for the purpose of allowing a witness to attempt an identification of an offender.

The position of the Supreme Court in these cases has been that the Fifth Amendment privilege protects an accused only from being compelled to testify against himself or herself—that is, from evidence of a communicative nature. On the other hand, in *Winston* v. *Lee*[106] the Court held that a suspect cannot be forced to undergo surgery to remove a bullet from his or her chest, even though probable cause exists that surgery would produce evidence of a crime.

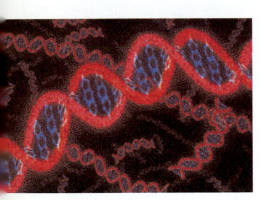

DNA Strands

CRITICAL THINKING IN CRIMINAL JUSTICE

DNA Fingerprinting

In a State of the State message on January 5, 1999, laden with numerous anticrime proposals, New York Governor George E. Pataki called for the collection of DNA fingerprints from all felony offenders and the logging of the DNA prints into state computers. Governor Pataki stressed that "DNA is going to be the fingerprinting of the 21st century."[107] This was the second call for DNA fingerprinting in New York State in so many weeks. Less than a month earlier, the New York City

"Gimme a 'D'! Gimme an 'N'! Gimme an 'A'!!"

© 2005 Mick Stevens from cartoonbank.com. All Rights Reserved.

police commissioner recommended that everyone arrested for a crime—never mind convicted of one—be required to submit a DNA sample to police. Civil rights advocates condemned the idea, arguing that police already have too much power, that once a DNA database is compiled it is unlikely to ever be disassembled, and that it would only be a matter of time before the data would grow to include not just wrongdoers but law-abiding citizens as well.

Thinking critically about these proposals and arguments, should police be permitted to collect DNA? Should there be comprehensive DNA databases? Is this a good law enforcement tool, or are the debates just the result of civil libertarian alarmism? Are there Fourth Amendment issues with DNA databanks?

Over the past decade, anyone who watched such TV journalism broadcasts as *60 Minutes, 20/20, Dateline NBC,* or *48 Hours* might agree that DNA profiling has come to be almost as important to crime fighting as conventional fingerprinting. Although some observers worry about the trend, here is the question to think critically about: What would be the problem with having our DNA prints on file, for after all, don't most of us already have our fingerprints on file for one reason or another?

Opponents of DNA fingerprinting and DNA databases consider the problem to be this: The Fourth Amendment guarantees citizens protection from unreasonable searches and seizures. Although the framers of the Constitution did not contemplate strands of DNA when drafting the Bill of Rights, what search could be more invasive than our very genes? How far will DNA inquiries go? There are indications that by the year 2010, DNA analyses may be able to determine physical characteristics—enough to create a genetic police sketch of a suspect's appearance. The next step might be untangling the genetic hardwiring to uncover DNA strands that influence temperament and behavior, including criminal behavior. And what would be done with that information? Think critically about the ethics of such situations.

OP-ED

Were the Miami and Miami Beach police really watching rappers? As it turned out, a Miami PD spokesperson said that the department had monitored rap artists after an influx of their fans for a Memorial Day Weekend hip-hop festival had overwhelmed police. The police also acknowledged attending the seminar in New York. Pointing to the violent deaths of Tupac Shakur, Notorious B.I.G., Run DMC's Jam Master Jay, and others, the police maintained that the surveillance was for the purpose of protecting the rappers and their fans. Was it ethnic profiling? Most likely. Or at the very least, ethnic harassment.

Was the disproportionate stopping and searching of Blacks and Hispanics by Texas police agencies ethnic profiling? What about the detaining of a Muslim airline passenger? Was it lawful? The answers are more complex than you might think.

First of all, some observers have argued that the disproportionate stopping of members of a particular group is not necessarily ethnic profiling. For example, a federal investigation of the New York City Police Department's Street Crime Unit indicated that its officers engaged in ethnic profiling in recent years as they conducted their aggressive campaign of street searches.[108] Former Mayor Giuliani and police officials immediately attacked the methods and findings of the report as flawed, arguing that they failed to adequately take into account the fact that a disproportionate number of the city's violent crimes take place in minority neighborhoods. Without knowing the methods used in the federal study, it would be difficult to agree with either side of the argument. Nevertheless, it would appear that in many jurisdictions there has been a propensity among some police officers to single out people for criminal justice interventions on the basis of their race, gender, ethnicity, sexual orientation, or social class.

And what about the government's call for heightened vigilance after the September 11 terrorist attacks? In the interest of national security, do law enforcement officials have the right to detain airline passengers on the basis of their nationality or their name? Khan, the detained passenger mentioned in the chapter opener, was never even provided with an explanation for his detainment by airline officials. Later, the FBI told the Associated Press that Khan, the CEO of an investment banking firm and the national treasurer of the American Muslim Council, matched the name and physical description of someone on the federal watch list. Khan has filed a lawsuit challenging the use of ethnic profiling that has made targets out of Muslim and Arab passengers. The American Civil Liberties Union has also filed suit against several airlines, claiming that ethnic profiling has violated the rights of passengers.[109]

As for the constitutionality of ethnic profiling, a number of decisions have already been handed down. The Supreme Court's ruling in *Delaware* v. *Prouse* certainly applies. Further, cases involving "drug courier profiles" are also problematic. The drug courier profile, developed by the Drug Enforcement Administration during the mid-1970s, is a general description of a "typical" drug runner. In *United States* v. *Sokolow*,[110] the Supreme Court upheld the use of such profiles, but in that case there were a number of "suspicious acts" (the defendant had purchased two expensive airline tickets with cash; he was using an assumed name; he did not check any luggage; his itinerary included a short stop in Miami; and he appeared very nervous). Most recently, in *U.S.* v. *Montero-Camargo*,[111] the U.S. Court of Appeals for the Ninth Circuit emphatically stated that "Hispanic appearance" could not be used as a pretext for stopping motorists.

And as the "war on terror" continues, the detentions of Arabs and Muslims are likely to continue as well, and the courts are likely to become further entrenched in the cases challenging the constitutionality of such practices.

On the basis of these examples, do you think that ethnic profiling is a violation of the Fourth Amendment?

Summary

The police have both investigative and arrest powers. Investigative powers include the power to stop and frisk, to order someone out of a vehicle, to question, and to detain. Arrest powers include the power to use force, to search, and to exercise seizure and restraint. The Constitution places restrictions on the exercise of these powers, but determining the specific intent of the Constitution in this behalf has been left to the courts.

Search and seizure refers to the search for and taking of persons and/or property as evidence of crime. The Fourth Amendment prohibits "unreasonable" searches and seizures, although it has been notably ambiguous in defining the parameters of unreasonableness. As a result, the Supreme Court has had to define these limits in a variety of Fourth Amendment challenges. Court decisions have provided guidelines for the issuance of search warrants, searches incident to arrest, and the circumstances involving stop-and-frisk, fresh pursuit, random automobile checks, consent searches, and "plain view" seizure.

In *Terry* v. *Ohio* (1968), the Supreme Court held that police could no longer stop and frisk individuals at will. Instead, the Court ruled that the officer must have constitutionally reasonable grounds for doing so. On the other hand, the Court has tended to be quite liberal in granting police officers access to warrantless searches of automobiles. A number of recent decisions have expanded the circumstances under which officers may search vehicles and their contents. With regard to consent searches, the Court has issued a number of rulings regarding under what conditions and by whom consent can be issued, the nature of free and voluntary consent, and the viability of limited consent as a legal principle. Lastly, in the case of plain view, the Court ruled in *Harris* v. *United States* (1968) that evidence in an officer's plain view is admissible because it was not produced by a search.

The Supreme Court's exclusionary rule prohibits in court the use of any evidence seized in violation of the Fourth Amendment ban against unreasonable search and seizure. In *Weeks* v. *United States* in 1914, the Court established the exclusionary rule for federal prosecutions; *Mapp* v. *Ohio* extended this rule to the states in 1961. Since *Mapp,* however, there has been dissatisfaction with the exclusionary rule. Since the 1960s there has been a general retreat from the guidelines established in *Mapp;* the greatest setback came in 1984 when the Court established the "good-faith" exception, allowing evidence gathered in questionable searches to be admitted into court depending on the circumstances of the search.

In criminal prosecutions, the Constitution prohibits forced confessions and guarantees the assistance of counsel in federal cases. However, these restrictions were applied to the states only recently. The first of these provisions occurred in 1936 as part of the *Brown* v. *Mississippi* decision in which the Court ruled that state courts cannot use coerced confessions as the basis of criminal convictions. During the 1964 term, the Court ruled in *Escobedo* v. *Illinois* that the accused must be allowed to have an attorney present during the police interrogation. In addition, the Court later established in *Miranda* v. *Arizona* (1966) that police officers must issue *Miranda* warnings to all suspects prior to questioning them. As with *Mapp,* there was dissatisfaction with the *Miranda* rule, but over the years it has managed to survive.

Key Terms

Carroll doctrine (236)
Chimel v. *California* (232)
Delaware v. *Prouse* (238)
Escobedo v. *Illinois* (252)
exclusionary rule (243)
Florida v. *Bostick* (240)
fruit of the poisonous tree (235)
Illinois v. *Gates* (230)

Illinois v. *Wardlow* (235)
Indianapolis v. *Edmond* (238)
Mapp v. *Ohio* (245)
Minnesota v. *Dickerson* (235)
Miranda v. *Arizona* (253)
"plain view" doctrine (242)
probable cause (229)
protective sweep doctrine (243)

Rochin v. *California* (245)
search and seizure (229)
search warrant (229)
Terry v. *Ohio* (233)
United States v. *Leon* (248)
United States v. *Wade* (257)
Weeks v. *United States* (243)

Issues for Discussion

1. Given the facts in *Chimel* v. *California,* could the prosecution have applied the doctrines of "plain view" and protective sweep?
2. What are the various rights of the accused during the pretrial phases of the criminal justice process?
3. Applying the concept of probable cause, what specifically was considered "unreasonable" about the search and seizure in *Mapp* v. *Ohio?*

4. What are your opinions of the reasonableness of the Supreme Court decisions in *Escobedo* v. *Illinois* and *Miranda* v. *Arizona?*
5. What are some of the considerations police officers must take into account even when consent has been obtained for a warrantless search?
6. Are DNA databases a good idea? Are there constitutional concerns?

Media And Literature Resources

Reel Justice includes scenes that can be used to spark discussion about the following topics topics from this chapter:

Police Investigative Powers

Search and Seizure

Ethnic Profiling

Ethnic Profiling. For an examination of the research and legal issues pertaining to this topic, see Michael R. Smith and Geoffrey P. Alpert, "Searching for Direction: Courts, Social Science, and the Adjudication of Racial Profiling Claims," *Justice Quarterly* 19 (December 2002): 673–703; Richard J. Lundman and Robert L. Kaufman, "Driving While Black: Effects of Race, Ethnicity, and Gender on Citizen Self-Reports of Traffic Stops and Police Actions," *Criminology* 41 (2003): 195–220; and Roger Dunham and Geoffrey Alpert, "Prejudice in Police Profiling: Assessing an Overlooked Aspect in Prior Research," *American Behavioral Scientist* 47 (March 2004): 896–909.

Miranda v. *Arizona.* For discussions on the changing interpretations and legal implications of the case, see Marvin Zalman, "Reading the Tea Leaves of *Chavez* v. *Martinez:* The Future of *Miranda,*" *Criminal Law Bulletin* 40 (July/August 2004): 299–368, and Marvin Zalman, "The Coming Paradigm Shift on *Miranda:* The Impact of *Chavez* v. *Martinez,*" *Criminal Law Bulletin* 39 (May/June 2003): 334–352.

In 1998, *The New York Times* published two excellent articles describing how police tactics have chipped away at suspects' rights. See *The New York Times,* March 29, 1998, 1, 40; and *The New York Times,* March 30, 1998, A1, B4.

DNA Fingerprinting. For those of you who wish to better understand the intricacies of DNA, genes, and chromosomes, the U.S. Department of Energy has published an excellent report titled *Primer on Molecular Genetics.* It is also on the Web (*http://www.ornl.gov/hgmis*).

Search and Seizure. Two classic works on search and seizure include J. Shane Creamer, *The Law of Arrest, Search, and Seizure* (New York: Holt, Rinehart and Winston, 1980), and Henry J. Abraham, *Freedom and the Court: Civil Rights and Liberties in the United States* (New

York: Oxford University Press, 1977). In addition, issues in search and seizure are continually being examined by state and federal courts. The Bureau of National Affairs in Washington, D.C., publishes summaries of all major state and federal cases on a weekly basis in a document called the *Criminal Law Reporter.* It is available in most law libraries.

The Protective Sweep Doctrine. A comprehensive work on this topic is Gary Kelder and Alan J. Statman, "The Protective Sweep Doctrine: Recurrent Questions Regarding the Propriety of Searches Conducted Contemporaneously with an Arrest on or near Private Premises," *Syracuse Law Review* 30 (1979): 973–1092.

| Endnotes |

1. *Miami Herald,* March 9, 2004, 1A.
2. Richard J. Lundman and Robert L. Kaufman, "Driving While Black: Effects of Race, Ethnicity, and Gender on Citizen Self-Reports of Traffic Stops and Police Actions," *Criminology* 41 (2003): 195–220.
3. *Chicago-SunTimes,* August 1, 2003, 3.
4. *Ornelas* v. *United States,* 116 S.Ct. 1657 (1996).
5. *Locke* v. *United States,* 7 Cr. 339 (1813).
6. *Dumbra* v. *United States,* 268 U.S. 435 (1925).
7. *Aguilar* v. *Texas,* 378 U.S. 108 (1964); *Spinelli* v. *United States,* 393 U.S. 410 (1969).
8. *Illinois* v. *Gates,* 462 U.S. 213 (1983).
9. *United States* v. *Robinson,* 414 U.S. 218 (1973).
10. *United States* v. *Watson,* 423 U.S. 455 (1976).
11. *Payton* v. *New York,* 455 U.S. 573 (1980).
12. *Chimel* v. *California,* 395 U.S. 752 (1969).
13. *McQueen* v. *Heck,* 41 Tenn. 212 (1860); *Shelton* v. *State,* 3 Tenn. Cr. App. 310, 460 S.W. (2d) 869 (1970).
14. *Harris* v. *State,* 206 Tenn. 276 (1960).
15. *Lowery* v. *State,* 39 Ala. 659, 107 So. 2d 366 (1958).
16. *State* v. *Autheman,* 47 Idaho 328, 274 P. 305, 62 A.L.R. 195 (1929); *Appleton* v. *State,* 61 Ark. 590, 33 S.W. 1066 (1896).
17. For example, *Neal* v. *Joyner,* 89 N.C. 287 (1883).
18. *Malley* v. *Briggs,* 38 CrL 3169 (1986).
19. *Terry* v. *Ohio,* 392 U.S. 1 (1968).
20. *California* v. *Hodari D.,* 49 CrL 2050 (1991).
21. *Illinois* v. *Wardlow,* No. 98-1036 (2000).
22. *Minnesota* v. *Dickerson,* 113 S.Ct. 2130 (1993).
23. *Hiibel* v. *Nevada,* 03-5554 (2004).
24. *Carroll* v. *United States,* 267 U.S. 132 (1925).
25. *Husty* v. *United States,* 282 U.S. 694 (1931).
26. *Chambers* v. *Maroney,* 399 U.S. 42 (1970).
27. *United States* v. *Ross,* 456 U.S. 798 (1982).
28. *New York* v. *Belton,* 453 U.S. 454 (1981).
29. *California* v. *Acevedo,* 49 CrL 2210 (1991).
30. *Delaware* v. *Prouse,* 24 CrL 3079 (1979).
31. *Michigan Department of State Police* v. *Stiz,* 47 CrL 2155 (1990).
32. *Indianapolis* v. *Edmond,* N.99-1030 (2000).
33. *Illinois* v. *Lidster,* 02-1060 (2004).
34. *Ohio* v. *Robinette,* 65 U.S.L.W. 4013 (1997).
35. *Tennessee Code,* Title 40, Section 811.
36. John Hill, "High-Speed Police Pursuits: Dangers, Dynamics, and Risk Reduction," *Crime and Justice International* 20 (May/June 2004): 27–34.
37. Geoffrey P. Alpert, Dennis Jay Kenney, and Roger Dunham, "Police Pursuits and the Use of Force: Recognizing and Manag-

ing 'The Pucker Factor'—A Research Note," *Justice Quarterly* 14 (June 1997): 371–385; Geoffrey P. Alpert and Lorie A. Fridell, *Police Vehicles and Firearms* (Prospect Heights, IL: Waveland Press, 1992); Geoffrey P. Alpert, "Analyzing Police Pursuit," *Criminal Law Bulletin* 27 (July–August 1991): 358–367.
38. *Knowles* v. *Iowa,* No. 97-7597 (1998).
39. *Wren* v. *United States,* 352 F 617 (1965).
40. *United States* v. *Matlock,* 415 U.S. 164 (1974).
41. *Bumper* v. *North Carolina,* 391 U.S. 543 (1968).
42. *Schneckloth* v. *Bustamonte,* 412 U.S. 218 (1973).
43. *United States* v. *Dichiarinte,* 445 F 126 (1921).
44. *Florida* v. *Jimeno,* 49 CrL 2175 (1991).
45. *Florida* v. *Bostick,* 49 CrL 2270 (1991).
46. *Burdeau* v. *McDowell,* 256 U.S. 465 (1921).
47. *United States* v. *Martinez-Fuerte,* 428 U.S. 543 (1976).
48. *South Dakota* v. *Opperman,* 428 U.S. 364 (1976).
49. *Illinois* v. *Lafayette,* 462 U.S. 640 (1983).
50. *Katz* v. *United States,* 389 U.S. 347 (1967).
51. *Abel* v. *United States,* 362 U.S. 217 (1960).
52. *California* v. *Greenwood,* 43 CrL 3029 (1988).
53. *Hester* v. *United States,* 265 U.S. 57 (1924).
54. *Oliver* v. *United States,* U.S. SupCt 35 CrL 3011 (1984); *Maine* v. *Thornton,* U.S. SupCt 35 CrL 3011 (1984).
55. *Harris* v. *United States,* 390 U.S. 234 (1968).
56. Steven M. Greenberg, "Compounding a Felony: Drug Abuse and the American Legal System," in *Drugs and the Criminal Justice System,* edited by James A. Inciardi and Carl D. Chambers (Beverly Hills: Sage Publications, 1974), 200.
57. Gary Kelder and Alan J. Statman, "The Protective Sweep Doctrine: Recurrent Questions Regarding the Propriety of Searches Conducted Contemporaneously with an Arrest on or near Private Premises," *Syracuse Law Review* 30 (1979): 973–1092.
58. *Weeks* v. *United States,* 232 U.S. 383 (1914).
59. *Adams* v. *New York,* 192 U.S. 585 (1904).
60. National Commission on Law Observance and Enforcement, *Report on Prosecution* (Washington, DC: U.S. Government Printing Office, 1931), 24.
61. *People* v. *Defore,* 242 N.Y. 13 at 21 (1926).
62. Elder Witt (ed.), *Guide to the U.S. Supreme Court* (Washington, DC: Congressional Quarterly, 1979), 549.
63. *Wolf* v. *Colorado,* 338 U.S. 25 (1949).
64. *Rochin* v. *California,* 342 U.S. 165 (1952).
65. *Rea* v. *United States,* 350 U.S. 214 (1956).
66. *Elkins* v. *United States,* 364 U.S. 206 (1960).
67. *Mapp* v. *Ohio,* 367 U.S. 643 (1961).
68. *The New York Times,* June 20, 1961, 1.

69. Arthur Niederhoffer, *Behind the Shield* (Garden City, NY: Doubleday, 1967), 159.
70. Yale Kamisar, "Criminals, Cops, and the Constitution," *The Nation* 199 (November 9, 1964): 323.
71. *Linkletter* v. *Walker,* 381 U.S. 618 (1965).
72. See Bob Woodward and Scott Armstrong, *The Brethren: Inside the Supreme Court* (New York: Simon & Schuster, 1979), 112–119.
73. *Coolidge* v. *New Hampshire,* 403 U.S. 443 (1971).
74. *United States* v. *Calandra,* 414 U.S. 338 (1974).
75. *Stone* v. *Powell,* 428 U.S. 465 (1976).
76. 28 U.S.C. Sections 2241, 2254a (1976).
77. *United States* v. *Leon,* U.S. SupCt 35 CrL 3273 (1984); *Massachusetts* v. *Sheppard,* U.S. SupCt 35 CrL 3296 (1984).
78. *Illinois* v. *Krull,* 40 CrL 3327 (1987).
79. *Murray* v. *United States,* 43 CrL 3168 (1988).
80. *Hopt* v. *Utah,* 110 U.S. 574 (1884).
81. *Wilson* v. *United States,* 162 U.S. 613 (1896).
82. *Twining* v. *New Jersey,* 211 U.S. 78 (1908).
83. Cited by Henry J. Abraham, *Freedom and the Court: Civil Rights and Liberties in the United States* (New York: Oxford University Press, 1977), 59.
84. *Brown* v. *Mississippi,* 297 U.S. 278 (1936).
85. *Rogers* v. *Richmond,* 365 U.S. 534 (1961).
86. *Bram* v. *United States,* 168 U.S. 532 (1897).
87. *McNabb* v. *United States,* 318 U.S. 332 (1943).
88. *Mallory* v. *United States,* 354 U.S. 449 (1957).
89. Elder Witt, *Guide to the U.S. Supreme Court,* 679. See also Richard Harris, *The Fear of Crime* (New York: Praeger, 1969).
90. *Crooker* v. *California,* 357 U.S. 433 (1958).
91. *Massiah* v. *United States,* 377 U.S. 201 (1964).
92. *Malloy* v. *Hogan,* 378 U.S. 1 (1964).
93. *Escobedo* v. *Illinois,* 378 U.S. 478 (1964).
94. *Miranda* v. *Arizona, Vignera* v. *New York, Westover* v. *United States, California* v. *Stewart*—all 384 U.S. 436 (1966).
95. *The New York Times,* June 14, 1966, 1.
96. Robert F. Cushman, *Cases in Constitutional Law* (Englewood Cliffs, NJ: Prentice-Hall, 1979), 400.
97. William O. Douglas, *The Court Years: 1939–1975* (New York: Random House, 1980), 231.
98. See Marvin Zalman, "Reading the Tea Leaves of *Chavez* v. *Martinez*: The Future of *Miranda*," *Criminal Law Bulletin* 40 (July/August 2004): 299–368; and Marvin Zalman, "The Coming Paradigm Shift on *Miranda*: The Impact of *Chavez* v. *Martinez*," *Criminal Law Bulletin* 39 (May/June 2003): 334–352.
99. *Kirby* v. *Illinois,* 406 U.S. 682 (1972).
100. *Foster* v. *California,* 394 U.S. 440 (1969).
101. *United States* v. *Wade,* 388 U.S. 218 (1967).
102. *Schmerber* v. *California,* 384 U.S. 757 (1966).
103. *United States* v. *Dionisio,* 410 U.S. 1 (1973).
104. *United States* v. *Mara,* 410 U.S. 19 (1973).
105. *United States* v. *Ash,* 413 U.S. 300 (1973).
106. *Winston* v. *Lee,* U.S. SupCt 53 U.S.L.W. 4367 (1985).
107. *The New York Times,* January 6, 1999, B5.
108. *The New York Times,* October 5, 2000, A1, B8.
109. *The Guardian,* June 5, 2002; *Chicago-Sun Times,* August 1, 2003, p. 3.
110. *United States* v. *Sokolow,* 45 CrL 3001 (1989).
111. *United States* v. *Montero-Camargo,* No. 97-50643 (2000).

BEYOND THE LIMITS OF THE LAW: POLICE CRIME, CORRUPTION, AND BRUTALITY

LEARNING OBJECTIVES

After reading this chapter, you should be able to answer the following questions:

1. What is police corruption?

2. What are the main areas in which police corruption manifests itself?

3. What are the primary explanations for why police corruption occurs?

4. What is police brutality?

5. What are the primary explanations for why police brutality occurs?

6. What is the "split-second syndrome"?

7. What are the best ways of controlling police misconduct?

8. What is meant by police professionalism?

9. What are civilian review boards?

ST. THOMAS—The U.S. Department of Justice has begun an extensive investigation of the Virgin Islands Police Depart-

ment. The federal probe has been spurred by a special investigative report by the *Virgin Islands Daily News* which detailed 20 years of questionable and illegal uses of deadly force. The *Daily News* found that over the past two decades, police officers used deadly force 100 times—a considerable number given the Virgin Islands' population of less than 120,000. The officers shot 85 times and killed 15 people; other forms of deadly force were used on 15 people. Only 35 of the people were armed; only 17 of the 72 survivors were charged with a crime; and on only 10 occasions were the officers prosecuted for using deadly force.[1]

No doubt the investigation will call for more citizen oversight of the VIPD, new leadership, better police training, and innovative reforms. It is an old story. It has happened elsewhere—in Los Angeles and New York, in Philadelphia and Chicago, and in other large cities and small towns across the nation. But why do these police abuses occur, over and over again? Why do they persist? And more importantly, what accounts for police misconduct, and how might it best be controlled?

National Comparisons

The Virgin Islands Police Department does not stack up well against other police departments in the United States, according to the most recent study by the Bureau of Justice Statistics, the arm of the U.S. Justice Department that tracks national law enforcement trends. The bureau surveys 3,319 police departments, sheriffs departments and state police agencies for its annual reports.

- **Solved-murders rate**
  VIPD 34%
  National average 62%
- **Shootings by off-duty officers**
  VIPD 40%
  National average 5%
- **Officers per shift per 10,000 residents**
  VIPD 13
  National average 23

These questions focus on two areas of police misconduct: corruption and violence. Police corruption involves illegal activities for economic gain, including payment for services that police are sworn to carry out as part of their peacekeeping role. Police violence, in the forms of brutality and misapplication of deadly force, involves wrongful use of police power.

Police Corruption

Police corruption begins with the notion that policemen by some divine right are entitled to free meals, free movies, and cut-rate prices on virtually everything they buy.

—JOURNALIST DAVID BURNHAM

Research on white-collar crime, combined with government inquiries concerning the internal operations of organized crime, labor unions, and various business enterprises, has demonstrated that work-related lawbreaking can be found in every profession and occupation. Similarly, illegal job-related activities involving graft, corruption, theft, and other practices are evident within the ranks of the police. Yet crime and corruption may be considerably more widespread in policing than in most other occupations. Virtually every urban police department in the United States has experienced both organized corruption and some form of scandal, and similar problems have been uncovered in small towns and rural sheriffs' departments.[2] During the 1970s, for example, the Police Foundation, based in Washington, D.C., arranged to receive newspaper clippings detailing incidents of police corruption across the United States. In a period of only 60 days, the foundation received articles from 30 states. The articles reported on allegations of graft and corruption in major urban centers, small cities, sheriffs' offices, state police forces, and suburban departments. They reflected practices ranging from accepting bribes from traffic offenders to accepting payment to alter testimony at trials.[3]

During approximately the same period, an analysis of police practices in Philadelphia noted that officers saw themselves operating in a world where "notes" (payoffs) are constantly available, "and only the stupid, the naive, and the faint-hearted are unwilling to allow some of them to stick to their fingers."[4] In New York, in the early 1970s the Knapp Commission found that more than half of the city's 29,600 police officers had taken part in corrupt practices;[5] in 1994 the Mollen Commission found a "willful blindness" to corruption throughout the NYPD, which allowed highly organized networks of rogue officers to deal in drugs and prey on citizens in African American and Hispanic neighborhoods.[6] Throughout the 1990s and into the new century, the media reported incidents of all types of corruption in many parts of the nation.[7]

The problem lies in the fact that policing is rich in opportunities for corruption—more so than in most other occupations. The police officer stands at the front lines of the criminal justice system in a nation where crime rates are high and demands for illegal goods and services are widespread. These conditions, combined with a range of other variables, create a situation in which police officers are confronted daily with opportunities for accepting funds in lieu of fully discharging their duties. For a detailed examination of police misconduct in a historical context, see Exhibit 9.1.

Police corruption is best defined as misconduct by police officers in the forms of illegal activities for economic gain and accepting gratuities, favors, or payment for services that police are sworn to carry out as part of their peacekeeping role. It occurs in many forms, but researchers agree that it is most evident in nine specific areas:[8] meals and services, kickbacks, opportunistic theft, planned theft and robbery, shakedowns, protection, case fixing, private security, and patronage. The rest of this section explores each of these areas in detail.

Meals and Services

Free or discount meals are available to police officers in many American cities. A number of restaurant chains have a policy of providing meals to officers on a regular basis, keeping records so that they can demonstrate their goodwill to both the department and the city. Numerous diners, coffee shops, and other small restaurants have a similar policy, but their goal is to encourage **"police presence"** in the establishment. Many restaurant owners feel that attracting police officers will make their places of business more secure. It is true that holdups are much less likely to occur at locations that are regularly visited by police, and if a crime or altercation does occur, police response is typically more rapid. Such deterrent presence is also "purchased" by other types of establishments—hardware stores, dry cleaners, small food shops, clothing outlets, liquor stores, and the like—generally by offering goods and services at discount prices to members of the police force. Or as the owner of a coffee shop New York City recently commented:

> You know, this is the city that never sleeps, and I keep the place open all night. So I feel a little safer when there are a few cops sitting in a booth by the window drinking coffee. [For a discussion of the origins of the term "cop" for police officer, see Exhibit 9.2.]

The free coffee, meals, gifts, and other gratuities—often referred to as "mooching"—that some officers receive from restaurants or small businesses, although a minor form of corruption, are frowned upon by police organizations. Not only are they illegal, but they can lead to major abuses. As a result, many police departments have established "no acceptance" policies, the violation of which can result in formal disciplinary procedures.[9]

Kickbacks

Police officers have numerous opportunities to direct individuals to persons who can assist them—for a profit. Police can also receive fees for referring arrested suspects to bail bond agents and defense attorneys, putting accident victims in contact with physicians and lawyers who specialize in personal injury claims, sending tow trucks and ambulances to accident scenes, and arranging for the delivery of bodies to funeral homes.

Given the very nature of routine police patrol work, opportunities such as these are not uncommon, and the potential for small kickbacks on a regular basis is always present. However, some officers look upon kickbacks as a business enterprise and actively seek out new and more lucrative areas of endeavor. In Tampa, Florida, for example, one police officer made highly profitable use of his access to departmental files. The names of burglary victims were turned over to a dealer in home security systems, who would then use high-pressure salesmanship to demonstrate the advantages of residential burglar alarms. The names of victims who lived in apartments were

No police department can remain free of corruption in a community where bribery flourishes in public office and private enterprise; a corrupt police department in an otherwise corruption-free society is a contradiction in terms.

— **ORLANDO W. WILSON, FORMER CHICAGO SUPERINTENDENT OF POLICE**

Scores of officers told us that they believed the department did not want them to report corruption, that such information was often ignored and that their careers would be ruined if they did so. The evidence shows that this belief was not unfounded.

— **THE MOLLEN COMMISSION**

The practice began at a time when the police were extremely underpaid and overworked, and that is much less the case today.

— **ARTHUR FOLEY, VICE PRESIDENT OF THE RHODE ISLAND–BASED BESS EATON DONUTS CHAIN, ON WHY THE COMPANY STOPPED GIVING FREE COFFEE TO POLICE OFFICERS**

EXHIBIT 9.1 | *historical perspectives on crime and justice*

"Clubber" Williams and the *Tenderloin*

Among the more widely publicized figures in 19th-century American police history was Alexander S. Williams, a Canadian immigrant whose career with the New York City Police Department spanned almost three decades. Born in Nova Scotia in 1839, Williams moved to New York at midcentury in search of work as a ship's carpenter and quickly established himself in the world of shipbuilding. During the Civil War, Williams became the first westerner to construct a ship in Japan, undertook salvage work for the United States government, and ultimately became a partner in a growing shipbuilding firm. Labor problems in that industry, however, quickly put an end to his business aspirations, and as an alternative he joined the NYPD in 1866.

After only 2 years as a patrolman, Williams made the first of a series of moves that would ultimately make him well known among his fellow officers, within the underworld, and to the citizens of New York as well. In 1868, he was assigned to the Broadway Squad in lower Manhattan, where many police officers before him had been either seriously assaulted or murdered by the numerous gang members, street brawlers, and other violent criminals that ranged through the area. On his second day at the new post, Officer Williams positioned himself in front of the Florence Saloon—a notorious resort of local thieves, muggers, and other types of criminals, located at the intersection of Broadway and Houston Street—where he selected two of the neighborhood's toughest characters, picked fights with them, knocked them unconscious with his nightstick, and hurled their bodies through the plate-glass window of their hangout. According to local folklore, 10 of their comrades came to the rescue, but Williams, a large and powerful man, stood his ground and mowed them down one after another with his hardwood club. Thereafter, he averaged a fight a day for almost 4 years. His skill with the nightstick was said to be so extraordinary and the force of his blows so powerful that he was hailed as "Clubber" Williams—a title he retained throughout his life.

Clubber Williams

East St. Louis Police Chief Ronald Matthews is escorted in handcuffs by FBI agents after being arrested in 2005 as part of a federal corruption investigation.

given to other sources in order to generate sales of locks and renter's insurance. Information about robbery, assault, and rape victims was directed to dealers who could provide weapons and instruction in self-defense. The kickbacks from these contacts, which were paid on a commission basis, amounted to many thousands of dollars each year.

Opportunistic Theft

Police have numerous opportunities to pilfer valuable items. Such "opportunistic theft" typically involves jewelry and other goods taken from the scene of a burglary or from a suspect; narcotics confiscated from drug users and dealers; merchandise found at the scene of a fire; funds taken during a gambling raid; money and personal property removed from the bodies of drunks, crime victims, and deceased persons; and confiscated weapons. For example, consider the following:

- During the course of a search incident to an arrest for purse snatching, the police officer found 72 diamond pinky rings in the pockets of the suspect—the proceeds

Following his assignment to the Broadway Squad, Williams's career moved quickly. In July 1871, he was promoted to the rank of sergeant. Only 2 months later he became a captain, and from there he moved on to become a police inspector. His fame grew so rapidly in New York that he once commented, "I am so well known here in New York that car horses nod to me every morning." He was the star feature of police parades and received constant attention from the daily press. He even refereed a major prizefight—in full uniform—at the original Madison Square Garden.

But there was another side to Alexander Williams, for he also epitomized the kinds of brutality and corruption that were characteristic of New York police during the latter part of the 19th century. His use of the nightstick was not limited to warding off thugs and street brawlers but was applied to strikers and sleeping drunks as well. And Williams was also known for clubbing spectators at parades as a means of crowd control. His technique with the nightstick reflected both sadism and brutality. Williams often spoke of how his stick could be used for knocking a man unconscious, for killing him, or for just battering him to pieces. In terms of "art for art's sake," he discussed on many occasions how a tap with the stick on the head, hands, or feet could send a current through the spine to make a prisoner stand up or lie down.

As for graft and corruption within the ranks of policing, Williams was an entrepreneur. It was "Clubber" Williams who reportedly coined the term "tenderloin" as the designation for areas of vice and nightlife. When he was transferred from the not-too-lucrative downtown Broadway precinct to the area bounded by Manhattan's Fourteenth to Forty-second Streets and Fifth and Seventh Avenues, Williams was quite pleased. His new sector was so wide open as a vice resort that New Yorkers called it "Satan's Circus." But Williams gave it the new nickname. As he took over his post, he commented, "I've had nothing but chuck steaks for a long time, and now I'm going to get me a little of the tenderloin."

Williams, of course, was speaking of opportunities for graft, and bountiful it was for him, for by imposing tribute on every kind of illegal activity, he quickly became a wealthy man. Houses of prostitution paid him initiation fees plus monthly charges for protection; saloons paid to stay open after hours; gambling halls paid monthly contributions; and pickpockets, burglars, and other thieves paid him a percentage of their thefts. By the late 1880s, Williams's fortune was said to be worth many hundreds of thousands of dollars. In addition to his considerable cash holdings, he owned a fashionable home in New York City, a mansion in Cos Cob, Connecticut, and a well-equipped yacht. William's fortune also came from graft within the ranks of policing. He had structured an organized fee system for arranging appointments to the force and for promotion within. It cost $300 to become a patrolman, $1,600 to become a sergeant, and as much as $15,000 to become a captain in a profitable district.

During a period of police reform in the 1890s Williams was called before a special committee to explain his large financial holdings, but he denied any wrongdoing, explaining that he had done well speculating on land in Japan. When Theodore Roosevelt was appointed as New York's new police commissioner in 1895, he forced Williams to resign. Undaunted, however, Williams moved into the insurance business. He died a millionaire in 1910 at the age of 71.

The adventures of Alexander "Clubber" Williams were typical, although on a larger scale, of the graft and corruption within the ranks of policing made possible by the politics of city bossism that existed during that period of American history. Although police corruption in this grand and open manner has all but disappeared, Williams's exploits are nevertheless colorful illustrations of the problems that continue to exist in some departments.

Sources: A. E. Costello, *Our Police Protectors* (New York: Author's Edition, 1885), 364–365; Herbert Asbury, *The Gangs of New York* (Garden City, NY: Garden City Publishing Company, 1928), 235; James F. Richardson, *The New York Police: Colonial Times to 1901* (New York: Oxford University Press, 1970), 204; *Report of the Special Committee Appointed to Investigate the Police Department of the City of New York*, Vol. 1 (Albany: State of New York, Senate Documents, 1895), 30–32; Lincoln Steffens, *The Autobiography of Lincoln Steffens* (New York: Harcourt, Brace, 1931), 209; Lloyd Morris, *Incredible New York* (New York: Bonanza, 1951), 112; Edward Robb Ellis, *The Epic of New York City* (New York: Coward-McCann, 1966), 432; M. R. Werner, *Tammany Hall* (Garden City, NY: Doubleday, Doran, 1928), 360–366.

of an earlier theft from a local diamond exchange. Only 70 rings were turned in as evidence.

- When detectives were dusting an apartment for fingerprints after a burglary, one of the investigators removed a man's gold watch that had been left behind. Placing it in his pocket, he commented, "They've got theft insurance."
- The "store" of a local receiver of stolen goods was raided by police and the alleged contraband confiscated. Before a full accounting of the "hot" property had been carried out, three TV sets, a dozen small radios, and several musical instruments were removed and placed in an officer's private automobile. The stolen property was later distributed among the officers involved in the raid.
- In response to a call that a "suspicious and sickening stench" was emanating from a locked room in a skid row rooming house, two police officers discovered the bloated and decomposing body of a well-known neighborhood eccentric. He had apparently died a few days earlier from choking during an epileptic seizure. During a search of the deceased's room in an effort to locate personal papers that might identify his next of kin, the officers found some $18,000 in small bills. The two officers divided the money equally between them.[10]

Drugs corrupt both cops and robbers.

—ANTHONY V. BOUZA

EXHIBIT 9.2 | *historical perspectives on criminal justice*

Cops and Coppers

American slang has a long and curious history, and much of it is traceable to the underworlds of vice and crime of past centuries. Such currently popular slang terms as "beef" (to complain), "fence" (a receiver of stolen goods), "hick" (a farmer), "hump" and "screw" (sexual intercourse), "lush" (a drunk), "snitch" (to inform on someone), and "tail" (a woman, sexual intercourse) have their origins in the *cant,* or slang, of the 16th-century Elizabethan professional thief. Other slang usages date back to 17th-century England.

"Cop" and "copper"—both meaning a police officer—also have their origins in the underworld. Etymological investigation suggests that *cop* is associated with the root of the Latin *capere* (to seize or snatch) or the Gypsy *kap* and *cop* (to take). In the 19th-century cant of both English and American thieves, "to cop" came to mean to snatch, grab, or arrest; hence, the "cop" or "copper" was the police officer who grabbed a thief or made an arrest. From the same root came such slang terms as "copped" (arrested), "cop a plea" (accept a plea of guilty to a lesser crime), "cop a feel" (to surreptitiously touch or grab a woman's breasts), and "cop out" (to offer a plea or excuse). Some ob-

solete terms of this genre include "copper house" (a police station) and "copper-hearted" (at heart a police officer).

The following excerpt, taken from George W. Matsell's *The Rogue's Lexicon,* published in 1859, illustrates some of these usages in 19th-century American underworld slang:

> The knuck was copped to rights, a skin full of honey was found in his kick's poke by the copper when he frisked him.

The translation of this cryptic speech is as follows:

> The pickpocket was arrested, and a purse full of money was found in his pants pocket by the policeman when he searched him.

Sources: Godfrey Irwin (ed.), *American Tramp and Underworld Slang* (New York: Sears, 1931); George W. Matsell, *Vocabulum; or, The Rogue's Lexicon* (New York: Matsell & Co., 1859); J. S. Farmer and W. E. Henley, *Slang and Its Analogues,* 7 vols. (1890–1904; reprint, New York: Arno Press, 1970); Eric Partridge, *Dictionary of Slang and Unconventional English* (New York: Bonanza, 1961); James A. Inciardi, *Careers in Crime* (Chicago: Rand McNally, 1975).

Planned Theft and Robbery

As a type of police corruption, planned theft and robbery refers to the involvement of police in predatory criminal activities, either directly or through complicity with criminals. During the last two decades, such activities have been detected in Denver, Des Moines, Chicago, Nashville, New York, Philadelphia, Buffalo, Birmingham, Cleveland, New Orleans, Miami, and numerous other cities. A typical case involved two New Orleans police officers who were arrested for allegedly robbing six people of some $1,475. Police began investigating after numerous civilian complaints that officers were stopping people while on duty and taking their money.[11] Similarly, a coordinated sting operation engineered by FBI agents and the Los Angeles County Police resulted in the arrest of 31 sheriff's deputies and narcotics officers for money skimming, money laundering, tax evasion, conducting illegal searches and seizures, falsifying evidence, perjury, and conspiracy. A tip to the Los Angeles County Sheriff's Department from a local drug informant indicated that a number of officers had skimmed millions of dollars of the cash proceeds from many big drug busts.[12]

Planned theft and robbery by police officers, unlike some minor forms of corruption, are not tolerated by police departments. Although there might be passive support for free meals and small kickbacks, as soon as police thefts and robbery become known to the public, even corrupt departments generally react in a forceful manner.[13]

> In the old days cops took money to look the other way while others committed street crimes. Now they're competing with the criminals.
>
> — FORMER KNAPP COMMISSION COUNSEL MICHAEL ARMSTRONG

Shakedowns

Shakedowns are forms of extortion in which police officers accept money from citizens in lieu of enforcing the law. The term *shakedown* has its roots in the 19th-century British underworld. A "shakedown" was a temporary substitute for a bed. Since this was common in many an English prostitute's room, her quarters also became known as a shakedown. Also common at the time was an extortion scheme with several variations, usually involving the collective efforts of sneak thieves, prostitutes, and other types of criminals. In a typical situation, an attractively dressed woman would approach a country gentleman, explaining that she was a victim of circumstances and was forced for the first time in her life to accost a man. After agreeing to pay a modest sum for her charms, he would accompany her to her room, bolting the door. While he engaged in sexual relations with the young woman, a wall panel would slide open and a thief would enter, replace the money in the victim's pocket with paper, and silently exit. After the theft had taken place, there would be a sound and the woman would claim that her husband was returning. The gentleman would hastily dress and leave through a rear door, unaware that his money had been taken. It was from rackets such as this that most forms of extortion became known as shakedowns—named after the place where they occurred: the "shakedown," or prostitute's room.[14]

Police have been known to shake down tavern owners by threatening to enforce obscure liquor laws and restaurant owners and shopkeepers by threatening to enforce health regulations and zoning violations. Moreover, as the "war on drugs" has escalated, there have been numerous reports of police shakedowns of drug traffickers and dealers—taking money or drugs in lieu of enforcement of the drug laws.[15]

Protection

The protection of illegal activities by police has been commonplace for well over a century. Such protection usually involves illegal goods and services such as prostitution, gambling, drugs, and pornography, and the resulting corruption is typically well organized.

Case Fixing

As a form of corruption, case fixing appears at all levels of the criminal justice process and involves not only police but bailiffs, court personnel, members of juries, prosecutors, and judges. Fixing a case with a police officer, however, is the most direct method, and often the least complicated and least expensive. The most common form involves a bribe to an officer in exchange for not being arrested—a practice that is typically initiated by pickpockets, prostitutes, gamblers, drug users, the parents of juvenile offenders, members of organized crime, and sometimes burglars. Case fixing can also take the form of perjury on the witness stand, reducing the seriousness of a charge against an offender, or agreeing not to pursue leads that might produce evidence supporting a criminal charge.

Traffic-ticket fixing is likely the most common form of case fixing, and often it does not involve any monetary payment. In some jurisdictions, simply knowing someone on the police force is all that is needed to have a summons discharged, and in other instances a call to a police chief can be effective.

Private Security

Corruption in the form of private security involves providing more police protection or presence than is required by standard operating procedures. Examples might include checking the security of private premises more frequently and intensively than is usual, escorting businesspeople to make bank deposits, or providing a more visible police presence in stores or establishments in order to keep out undesirables. In such instances, payoffs are less likely to be made in cash but typically take the form of goods, services, and favors.

Some officers hire themselves out as bodyguards. A Miami Beach officer who weighed more than 250 pounds and was proficient with weapons, in the martial arts, and in stunt driving often placed himself at the disposal of cocaine dealers carrying large amounts of cash and drugs. He commented to a professional informant: "I'm as big as any fullback on the Dolphins, and they know I hit like one. Besides, they know I'm a cop . . . so they know it's best to stand clear."

This discussion should not suggest, however, that all private policing by public police is corrupt. On the contrary, "extra-duty policing," as it has come to be known, is common in many parts of the nation. In fact, in many jurisdictions there is a great

Here in Bogotá, you can buy your way out of an arrest with a carton of Marlboro.

—AMERICAN DIPLOMAT

Ten or twenty years ago, when you talked about a bribe, it was a $20 bill in a matchbook. Today, you have people in the drug culture saying, "There's ten grand in the bag, and it's yours if you let me go."

—SHELDON GREENBERG,
POLICE EXECUTIVE RESEARCH
FORUM

demand for extra-duty uniformed officers: for traffic control and pedestrian safety at road construction and repair sites; for crowd control at major private events, such as football games and rock concerts; and for private security and protection of life and property.[16] In all of these instances, employers contract directly with police departments for the services of uniformed officers, and the officers, in turn, are paid overtime wages by their departments.

Patronage

Patronage can take a variety of forms, all of which involve the use of one's official position to influence decision making. Historically, patronage has meant making governmental appointments in such a way as to increase one's political strength, and it has always been a part of political life in one form or another.

A comical illustration of political patronage is a note allegedly written by New York political boss William Marcy Tweed to Pennsylvania politician Matthew Quay during the 1870s:

> Dear Tit:
>
> The bearer understands addition, division, and silence. Appoint him!
>
> Your friend,
>
> Bill[17]

Although there may be ethical issues surrounding the practice of political patronage, it is not necessarily illegal in all of its forms. However, patronage clearly becomes corruption when payments are made for political favors. Within the ranks of policing, corruption by patronage can occur through the granting of promotions and transfers for a fee. Arranging access to confidential department records or agreeing to alter such records may also be construed as patronage. In addition, influencing department recommendations regarding the granting of licenses is patronage.

Patronage can occur in other ways as well. Within a police department, for example, people have been paid to falsify attendance records, influence the choice of vacations and days off, report officers as being on duty when they are not, and provide passing grades for training programs and promotion exams.

Many of the areas of police corruption discussed above were uncovered in a single police department during a 4-year federal investigation and trial that concluded during 1999 in Camden, New Jersey.[18] The case, which erupted 2 years earlier with the arrest of 9 officers and 10 residents of West New York, New Jersey, a small town across the Hudson River from Manhattan's Upper West Side, turned out to be the largest police corruption scandal in the history of New Jersey. According to prosecutors and testimony, the West New York Police Department had been on a major crime spree for almost a decade. The police raided illegal gambling dens, stole the proceeds, and then extorted money from the operators. When community residents complained about a house of prostitution in the neighborhood, the police raided the brothel and then took bribes and allowed it to stay in business. In addition, officers were involved in loan sharking, the selling of official accident forms, and even stealing from suspects and corpses. Overall, federal prosecutors described the West New York Police Department as a "bustling organized crime enterprise" that had collected and shared as much as $1.5 million.

Explanations of Police Corruption

A number of hypotheses as to why police corruption occurs have been offered. The three most common interpretations are that police corruption is caused by society at large, by influences within police departments, or by a predisposition toward corruption in some individuals ("rotten apples") who become police officers.[19]

Police monitor demonstrators standing on an overhead walkway in Los Angeles. The demonstrators were protesting the actions of the police in an ongoing police corruption scandal.

The Society-at-Large Explanation

The society-at-large explanation comes from the late O. W. Wilson and is based on his observations and experiences as Chicago's superintendent of police. As Wilson put it:

> This force was corrupted by the citizens of Chicago.... It has been customary to give door-men, chauffeurs, maids, cooks and delivery men little gifts and gratuities.... It is felt that the level of service depends on these gratuities.[20]

Such practices, in turn, led to small bribes, such as accepting money in lieu of enforcing traffic laws or minor city ordinances. Accepting small payoffs from drivers and business operators then extended to more serious crimes. Wilson called this progression the *slippery slope hypothesis*—corruption begins with apparently harmless and well-intentioned practices and eventually leads, in individual officers or in departments as a whole, to all manner of crimes for profit.

The Structural Explanation

In his well-known book *Behind the Shield,* the late Arthur Niederhoffer made the following comment:

> Actual policemen seem to accept graft for other reasons than avarice. Often the first transgression is inadvertent. Or, they may be gradually indoctrinated by older policemen. Step by step they progress from a small peccadillo [trifling sin] to outright shakedown and felony.[21]

Going further, this step-by-step progress results from the contradictory sets of norms that police officers see both in the world at large and in their own departments. Officers, particularly those in large cities, are exposed to a steady diet of wrongdoing. They discover, moreover, that dishonesty and corruption are not limited to those whom the community views as "criminals" but also extend to individuals of "good reputation"—including fellow officers with whom they must establish mutual trust. In time, they develop a cynical attitude in which they view corruption as a game in which every person is out to get a share.[22]

The Rotten-Apple Explanation

The "bad" or "rotten-apple" view is perhaps the most popular explanation of police corruption. It suggests that in an otherwise honest department there are a few bad officers who are operating on their own. Corruption is the result of the moral failure of just a few officers, but it spreads to the others, for after all, as the old proverb suggests, "One rotten apple spoils the rest of the barrel."

The rotten-apple theory is frequently used by police chiefs and commissioners to explain misconduct in their ranks. They suggest this because to do otherwise would condemn the very systems in which they have risen to the top.

In reality, there is probably no *single* explanation that accounts for all police corruption, and unfortunately there are no empirical data supporting any of the explanations. The three discussed here are the principal views, and it is likely that they work in conjunction with one another. The rotten-apple explanation, though the most popular, is also the most criticized, for it fails to explain why individual officers become corrupt. More specifically:

> If corruption is to be explained in terms of a few "bad" people, then some departments attracted a disproportionately high number of rotten apples over long periods of time.[23]

| Police Violence |

Police violence in the form of brutality, unwarranted deadly force, and other mistreatment of citizens is not uncommon in American history. Commentaries documenting the growth and development of both the urban metropolis and the rural frontier give ample testimony to the unwarranted use of force by police. Law enforcement records in the trans-Mississippi West provide numerous examples of the "shoot first and ask questions later" philosophy of many American police officers. Moreover, the brutal and sadistic application of the police officer's nightstick to demonstrate that "might makes right" appears often in the histories of urban police systems.

In 1903, New York City magistrate and former police commissioner Frank Moss made the following comment:

> For three years, there has been through the courts and the streets a dreary procession of citizens with broken hands and bruised bodies against few of whom was violence needed to effect an arrest. Many of them had done nothing to deserve an arrest. In a majority of such cases, no complaint was made. If the victim complains, his charge is generally dismissed. The police are practically above the law.[24]

Moss was expressing his frustrations about a problem that was widespread during his time but received little attention. And the ambivalence toward police violence that he described continued throughout the better part of the 20th century.

It was not until the 1960s that the issue of police misconduct in the forms of brutality and deadly force took on any public and political urgency, and this can be attributed to two phenomena. The first was the "criminal law revolution" (see Chapter 5) carried on by the Supreme Court under the leadership of Chief Justice Earl Warren. The second was the findings of the Kerner Commission—the National Advisory Commission on Civil Disorders.

In 1936, *Brown* v. *Mississippi* (see Chapter 8) established the Court's position on brutality, at least as far as coerced confessions were concerned.[25] It was the first time a state conviction was overturned because it had been obtained by using a confession extracted by torture. But the importance of *Brown* remained unnoticed for 25 years, until the Court finally developed some hard-and-fast rules concerning the methods of interrogation of suspects while in police custody. In *Rogers* v. *Richmond* (1961), *Greenwald* v. *Wisconsin, Georgia* v. *Sims,* and *Florida* v. *Brooks* (1968), the Court asserted that the Fourteenth Amendment bars confessions when "the methods used to extract them offend the underlying principle in the enforcement of our criminal law," especially those which reflect "shocking displays of barbarism."[26]

Every situation I go through I assume right away I'm going to be outgunned.
— CLEVELAND POLICE OFFICER

Houston police tackle a demonstrator protesting against war profiteering.

While the Supreme Court examined police violence in the context of the brutality of squad room interrogations, the Kerner Commission targeted the wider issue of street justice. Known more formally as the National Advisory Commission on Civil Disorders, its purpose was to investigate the causes of the rioting and destruction that occurred in Detroit, Los Angeles, Newark, New York, and 20 other urban areas during the summer of 1967. The commission concluded that there were numerous causes, but it identified police practices in inner-city areas as the primary cause. Aggressive preventive patrol, police brutality, unwarranted use of deadly force, harassment, verbal abuse, and discourtesy were sources of aggravation for African Americans, and complaints of such practices were found in all of the locations studied.[27]

Because police brutality is so central to any discussion for police violence, it is now examined in detail. For a discussion of police "death squads," see Exhibit 9.3.

Police Brutality

Although the Supreme Court and the Kerner Commission brought police violence to public attention during the 1960s, the subject had long been the focus of rigorous study. A half-century ago, for example, sociologist William A. Westley asked police officers in Gary, Indiana, this question: "When do you think a policeman is justified in roughing a man up?"[28] Seventy-four officers responded. The major reasons given covered a variety of areas, including the following:*

Disrespect for police	27%
When it is impossible to avoid	17%
To obtain information	14%
To make an arrest	6%
For the hardened criminal	5%
When you know the person is guilty	2%
For sex criminals	2%

*These percentages must be viewed with some caution. Most of the officers responded "never," and many others gave multiple answers. Thus, although the percentages total to 73%, considerably fewer officers felt that roughing someone up was justified.

EXHIBIT 9.3 | A View from the Field

Police Death Squads in Rio de Janeiro by James A. Inciardi and Hilary L. Surratt

From 1993 through 1998, both of us were affiliated with the State University of Rio de Janeiro and operated an AIDS prevention project designed for the indigent populations living in Rio's hillside shantytowns. Almost immediately after we arrived for our first of some 40 visits to *cidade maravilhosa* (wonderful city), we heard about the death squads.

Police death squads began to operate in Brazil in 1968, principally in Rio de Janeiro, to avenge the terrorist murder of a well-known police officer. Then the killings spread, and the victims were easily recognized. Their hands were always tied behind their backs, their tongues cut out, and a crudely drawn skull and crossbones would be left on the corpse with the initials "E.M."—*Esquadrão de Morte*—appended.

We learned quickly from news reports that many police assassination squads have existed in Latin America. Guatemala had its La Mano Blanca (the White Hand); Argentina, its Anti-Communist Alliance; the Dominican Republic, its La Banda gang; and Paraguay, Honduras, and El Salvador, simply Esquadron de Muerte, or Death Squad. All were organized, but unofficial, police vigilante organizations established with the aim not only of preserving their respective political regimes through selective political murders but also of eliminating those viewed by the police as "undesirables"—trade unionists, street children, drug dealers, and criminals.

The death squads still exist, particularly in Brazil, and especially in Rio de Janeiro. The scores of neglected, abandoned, and homeless children living on the streets of Rio de Janeiro and São Paulo, who survive in part through prostitution and petty theft, are targets of retributive violence by police death squads. Store owners hire off-duty police officers to eliminate the "disposable children," because they consider them to be bad for business. The most notorious of the death squad killings of street children occurred in 1993 in Rio, just before our first visit. At 1 a.m. on July 25, as 50 homeless youths were sleeping on the grounds of the Candelária Cathedral in a downtown section of the city, a group of gunmen drove up and began shooting. Four of the youths died instantly, a fifth was shot and killed as he ran, two more were abducted, beaten, shot, and dumped in the gardens of the nearby Museum of Modern Art, and an eighth died several days later, never waking from a coma. Eight others were also shot but survived their wounds. The shootings were reportedly provoked by an occurrence earlier in the day in which some of the children had allegedly thrown stones at a military police vehicle after one youth had been detained for drug use.

We learned the hard way that transvestites are also a target of police violence in Rio. In fact, one of the populations served by our AIDS prevention research center was male transvestite sex workers. They were reviled by the police, and one of our transvestite clients was found murdered in the project parking lot—allegedly at the hands of police.

Police on patrol in a Rio de Janeiro shantytown.

Police death squads persist in Rio. In 1997, for example, police fired on a group of beggars as they slept under the awning of a Rio furniture store. One of the victims had been a survivor of the 1993 Candelária massacre. It would appear that the killings continue because of tacit support from major segments of the citizenry. Polls suggest that Brazilians have a general disdain for outcasts, whether they be criminals, street children, gays, or transvestites, and have little sympathy when they are killed unlawfully. For example, a recent survey by Rio de Janeiro's Institute for Religious Studies and the Fundação Getúlio Vargas found that almost two-thirds of Brazilians felt that criminals forfeited their rights because they had failed to respect the rights of others. In addition, 40.4% of the population felt that the use of torture by police to extract confessions was acceptable in some cases, and 40.6% of Brazilians considered lynchings of suspected offenders to be wrong but understandable.

The most recent string of killings by police in Rio de Janeiro happened on April 1, 2005. Some 30 people in two working-class neighborhoods were gunned down in drive-by shootings. The gunmen were believed to be military police officers, angered by a recent campaign to curb police violence.

We continue to work in Brazil, but *cidade maravilhosa* has become such a violent metropolis that we avoid it at all costs.

Sources: Stephen Brookes, "Life on Rio's Mean Streets," *Insight,* August 5, 1991, 12–19; "Brazilians Believe Criminals Forfeit Rights," *Reuters News Service,* September 10, 1997; *The New York Times,* December 12, 1997, A6; Andrew Downie, "Public Figures Fear Death Squads," *Miami Herald,* October 25, 2003, 14A; James A. Inciardi, Hilary L. Surratt, and Paulo R. Telles, *Sex, Drugs, and HIV/AIDS in Brazil* (Boulder, CO: Westview Press, 2000); *The New York Times,* April 2, 2005, A3.

Systematic observations in Boston, Chicago, Washington, D.C., and other cities revealed similar patterns.[29] More recently national attention has focused on allegations of police brutality in numerous cities, including the videotaped assault of Rodney King by LAPD officers in 1991, the attack on Abner Louima by NYPD officers in 1997, and the videotaped beating of Thomas Jones by Philadelphia police in 2000, as well as the numerous other incidents reported by CNN, ABC, NBC, and CBS in recent years.

In the past, **police brutality** was believed to be limited to those few sadistic officers who were seen as "bad apples." However, more recent commentaries suggest that police violence is the result of norms shared throughout a police department and that it is best understood as an unfortunate consequence of the police role. Police are given the unrestricted right to use force in situations in which their evaluation of the circumstances demands it. Yet this mandate has never been precisely defined or limited. Moreover, some officers show characteristics of the police "working personality"—the feeling of constant pressure to perform, along with elements of authoritarianism, suspicion, racism, hostility, insecurity, and cynicism. Police norms that emphasize solidarity and secrecy support a structure in which incidents of brutality and other misconduct will not be condemned by fellow officers.

Also contributing to police brutality is the type of policing described by political scientist James Q. Wilson as the "watchman's style."[30] Watchman-style departments tend to be located in older cities with high concentrations of poor and minority citizens. In such cities, police officers act primarily as reluctant maintainers of order. They ignore many minor problems—those involving the poor, gambling, traffic violations, misdemeanors, juvenile rowdiness, and domestic disputes. Officers act tough in serious situations, but in most others they follow the path of least resistance. Moreover, many officers are poorly trained, and the departments rarely meet even minimum standards for planning, research, and community relations. This style of policing often leads to organized corruption, discriminatory arrests, and unnecessary police violence.

Going beyond the working personality and the watchman's style as factors contributing to unnecessary police violence, sociologist Richard J. Lundman has focused on three additional issues:

1. Police perceptions that citizen acceptance of police authority is fundamental to effective policing.
2. Police judgments of the "social value" of certain citizens.
3. The conservative nature of police decision making.[31]

Police Authority Because authority is essential to the police roles of enforcing the law and keeping the peace, those who question or resist that authority represent a challenge to officers, detectives, and the organizations they represent. Often police use intense verbal coercion to establish their authority quickly. Should that fail, some use physical force to elicit compliance from citizens. An officer in Baltimore, Maryland, related the following incident to the author:

> I pulled this kid over one Sunday night for a defective tail light and I asked him for his license and registration. When he started making excuses I told him very clearly: "Look kid, it's late, you're a hazard to other motorists, and I don't want any of your shit!" When he continued to whine about getting a ticket I grabbed him by the jaw and told him that he'd either quit stalling or get his ass kicked from here to kingdom come.

Judgments of Social Value In the view of many police officers, certain citizens—prostitutes, drunks, members of juvenile gangs, gays, sex offenders, drug users, hardened criminals—have little to contribute to society. Many officers do not consider such people worth protecting, or they protect them using norms different from those that guide their protection of other citizens. Some police even single out these people for physical abuse. A Delaware state police officer put it this way: "So what if we knocked him around a little; he was nothing but a dirty junkie."

Police Decision Making Since police work requires officers to make quick decisions, often on the basis of fragmentary information, both officers and their superiors tend to defend the use of violence as a means of rapid problem resolution. As police researcher Richard J. Lundman has pointed out, many members of the criminal justice system and the public at large also hold this view.[32] He cites the example of *Chicago*

If his honor asks how come the suspect has his jaw wired and a few broken teeth, tell him the asshole tripped and fell in a sewer.

—**BOSTON POLICE OFFICER**

There's a great potential for an officer abusing steroids to physically mistreat people.

—**RICHARD WITT, POLICE CHIEF, HOLLYWOOD, FLORIDA**

EXHIBIT 9.4 | Gender Perspectives on Crime and Justice

Women Police Officers and Violence

Police brutality exerts a heavy toll on society, as each year officers and citizens alike are injured or killed during violent confrontations. Such incidents can invite expensive lawsuits against agencies and generate feelings of mistrust among the public, often costing law enforcement the cooperation of those they are under oath to protect and serve.

Research suggests that women officers rely more on verbal rather than physical tactics in diffusing dangerous situations and are therefore less involved in excessive force incidents. For example, a recent study by the National Center for Women and Policing found that although women currently constitute just 11.4 percent of sworn police officers in major metropolitan areas across the United States, female officers are underrepresented in police brutality incidents. Female officers accounted for only 5 percent of citizen complaints for excessive use of force and for just 2 percent of sustained allegations of excessive force. Overall, male officers were found two to three times more likely to be named in a citizen complaint of excessive force and eight and a half times more likely than female officers to have an allegation of excessive force sustained against them. Moreover, male officers cost taxpayers up to five and a half times more money than female officers in terms of excessive-force liability lawsuit payouts.

Research also shows that women are more effective in responding to domestic violence, which accounts for nearly half of all violent crime reported to police. Studies have found that domestic violence is two to four times more common in police families than in the general public, suggesting that a substantial percentage of male officers who respond to such situations are themselves perpetrators of the offense.

Considering the gender differences between female and male officers, both law enforcement agencies and the public would likely benefit from an increase in female police presence.

Sources: Lonsway et al., *Men, Women, and Police Excessive Force: A Tale of Two Genders,* (Arlington, VA: The National Center for Women and Policing, 2002); Lonsway et al, *Equality Denied: The Status of Women in Policing: 2001* (Arlington, VA: The National Center for Women and Policing, 2002).

Arresting suspects can be one of the more dangerous aspects of police work.

Daily News journalist John O. Linstead, who was assaulted by police officers during the 1968 Democratic National Convention. Linstead observed police beating three bystanders and intervened by shouting obscenities at the officers, who then turned on him. The officers were charged with assault, and the evidence against them was overpowering. But the jury returned a verdict of not guilty, and the judge congratulated them with the following comments:

> The language that Mr. Linstead used was vile and degrading to the officers. He charged some of the officers with committing incest with their mothers in the lowest gutter language, which I suggest would be provoking in such a manner that any red-blooded American would flare up.[33]

As a final point here, it has been documented that women police officers have been involved in incidents of brutality and excessive force. However, as illustrated in Exhibit 9.4, there are some significant gender differences with regard to frequency.

Deadly Force

Under common law, police were authorized to use deadly force as a last resort to apprehend a fleeing felon. This rule dates back to the Middle Ages, when all felonies were punishable by death. This "shoot to kill" doctrine persists in one form or another in many jurisdictions throughout the United States, for there are few operational guidelines in the use of deadly force by police. The *Code of Alabama* illustrates this point: "An officer may use reasonable force to arrest, but is without privilege to use more force than is necessary to accomplish the arrest."[34]

The lack of specificity in such codes demonstrates that the decision to use deadly force in making an arrest remains largely a matter of discretion. All jurisdictions permit officers to use lethal force in their own defense, and most allow them to fire on a fleeing felon. Yet before ***Tennessee v. Garner*** in 1985,[35] the conditions under which such force could be applied to a fleeing felon were variable. Some jurisdictions required the suspect to be a "known" felon; others required that the officer be a witness to the felony; and still others permitted deadly force when the officer had a "reasonable belief" that the fleeing individual had committed the felony in question. In *Garner,* the Supreme Court held that deadly force against a fleeing felon is proper only when it is necessary to prevent the escape *and* if there is probable cause to believe that the suspect poses a significant threat of death or serious physical injury to the officer or others (see Exhibit 9.5).

When it comes to explaining the use of force, both lethal and nonlethal, police researcher James J. Fyfe points out that many writers on the topic fail to distinguish between police violence that is clearly extralegal and abusive and violence that is an unnecessary result of police incompetence.[36] He argues that this distinction is important because the causes and motivations for the two types of violence vary greatly. Extralegal violence involves willful and wrongful use of force by officers who knowingly exceed the bounds of their office. By contrast, unnecessary violence, including *deadly force,* occurs when well-meaning officers are unable to deal with the situations they encounter without needlessly or too hastily resorting to force.

Although the number of people killed each year by "police intervention" is relatively small, there is a widespread perception that African Americans are singled out as victims. More important, however, a number of studies have demonstrated that members of minority groups are statistically overrepresented among the victims in police killings.[37] But there is no clear explanation for this phenomenon. Radical sociologist Paul Takagi states that "police have one trigger finger for whites and another for blacks," suggesting that police are engaged in a form of genocide against minority groups.[38] This, however, seems to be a naive oversimplification of a very complex issue, for many factors are operating simultaneously. Another explanation is that communities get the number of police killings they deserve. Richard Kania and Wade

> When police officers fire their guns, the immediate consequences of their decisions are realized at the rate of 750 feet per second.
>
> —JAMES J. FYFE

> Police work on inner-city streets is a domestic Vietnam, a dangerous no-win struggle fought by confused, misdirected and unappreciated troops.
>
> —U.S. NEWS & WORLD REPORT

"Would you mind stepping out of the pumpkin, please?"

© The New Yorker Collection 1999 Michael Maslin from cartoonbank .com. All Rights Reserved.

EXHIBIT 9.5 | LAW & CRIMINAL JUSTICE

Tennessee v. Garner

On the evening of October 2, 1974, Memphis police officers Elton Hymon and Leslie Wright were dispatched to answer a "prowler inside call." Upon arriving at the scene they saw a woman standing on her porch gesturing toward the adjacent house, indicating that she had heard glass breaking and that "someone" was breaking in next door. Officer Hymon went behind the house, heard a door slam, and saw someone run across the backyard. The fleeing suspect, Edward Garner—a 15-year-old eighth-grade student—stopped at a chain-link fence at the edge of the yard. With the aid of a flashlight, Officer Hymon was able to see Garner's face and hands. Hymon saw no sign of a weapon and, although not certain, was "reasonably sure" that the suspect was unarmed. While Garner was still crouched at the base of the fence, Officer Hymon shouted, "Police, halt!" and took a few steps forward. At this point Garner began to climb over the fence. Convinced that if Garner made it over the fence he would elude capture, Officer Hymon shot him. The bullet hit Garner in the back of the neck, causing a wound that proved to be fatal. Ten dollars and a purse taken from the house were found on his body.

In using deadly force to prevent the escape, Officer Hymon was acting under the authority of a Tennessee statute which provided that "if, after notice of intention to arrest the defendant, he either flee(s) or forcibly resist(s), the officer may use all the necessary means to effect the arrest."

The victim's father, Cleamtee Garner, brought an action to the federal district court on the ground that the shooting had violated his son's constitutional rights under Fourth, Fifth, Sixth, Eighth, and Fourteenth Amendments. Seeking damages, Garner named Hymon, the police department and its director, and the mayor and city of Memphis as defendants. The district court dismissed Garner's claims, concluding that the Tennessee statute was constitutional and that Officer Hymon had employed the only reasonable and practicable means of preventing Edward Garner's escape. The court of appeals agreed that Officer Hymon had acted in good-faith reliance on the Tennessee statute, but it ruled in favor of Garner in that the deadly force statute was flawed since it failed to distinguish between felonies of different magnitude. The state of Tennessee, which had intervened in the case to defend the constitutionality of its statute, appealed the decision to the U.S. Supreme Court.

The High Court ruled in favor of Cleamtee Garner, holding the Tennessee statute to be unconstitutional in that it authorized the use of deadly force against an apparently unarmed, nondangerous suspect. The Court emphasized that deadly force may not be used unless it is necessary to prevent the escape of a suspect for whom there is reasonable cause to believe a significant threat of death or serious physical injury to the officer or others exists:

[a] Apprehension by the use of deadly force is a seizure subject to the Fourth Amendment's reasonableness requirement. To determine whether such a seizure is reasonable, the extent of the intrusion on the suspect's rights under that Amendment must be balanced against the governmental interests in effective law enforcement. The balancing process demonstrates that, notwithstanding probable cause to seize a suspect, an officer may not always do so by killing him. The use of deadly force to prevent the escape of all felony suspects, whatever the circumstances, is constitutionally unreasonable.

[b] The Fourth Amendment, for purposes of this case, should not be construed in light of the common-law ruling allowing the use of whatever force is necessary to effect the arrest of a fleeing felon. Changes in the legal and technological context means that the rule is distorted almost beyond recognition when literally applied. Whereas felonies were formerly capital crimes, few are now, or can be, and many crimes classified as misdemeanors, or nonexistent, as common law are now felonies. Also, the common-law rule developed at a time when weapons were rudimentary. And, in light of the varied rules adopted in the States indicating a long-term movement away from the common-law rule, particularly in the police departments themselves, that rule is a dubious indicium of the constitutionality of the Tennessee statute. There is no indication that holding a police practice such as that authorized by the statute unreasonable will severely hamper effective law enforcement.

[c] While burglary is a serious crime, the officer in this case could not reasonably have believed that the suspect posed any threat. Nor does the fact that an unarmed suspect has broken into the dwelling at night automatically mean he is dangerous.

Source: *Tennessee* v. *Garner*, U. S. SupCt 36 CrL 3233 (1985).

Mackey found that there is a statistical correlation between police killings and violent crimes in a community. They argue that "the police officer is reacting to the community as he perceives it."[39] A third view cites the "bad-apple" theory, which puts the blame on a few uncontrollable police officers.[40]

In all likelihood, however, the reasons for the disproportionate number of minority group members killed by police involve all of these explanations. In addition, perhaps the most insightful analysis of police use of deadly force suggests that its frequency is heavily influenced by individual departmental policies, combined with the fact that African Americans and other minorities tend to be overrepresented in the most violent and crime-prone neighborhoods.[41]

Although police shootings are an inevitable part of enforcing the law and keeping the peace, ever since the Supreme Court's decision in *Tennessee* v. *Garner* in 1985, vir-

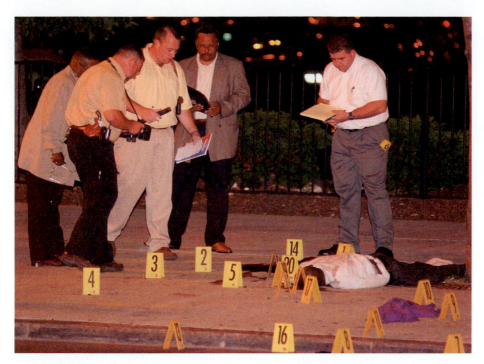

Detectives investigating a fatal police shooting in downtown Cleveland, Ohio.

tually every police department in the United States has reexamined its policies on the use of deadly force. In addition, both new recruits and seasoned officers are exposed to training seminars on the use of restraint and the consequences of an improper shooting. However, some police officials have expressed concern that an overemphasis on restraint has placed some officers in jeopardy. Or as Commander John Burke, head of the Warren County (Ohio) Drug Task Force recently stated:

> I have found that there has been a disturbing trend in law enforcement over the past 10–15 years involving officers faced with shooting decisions.
>
> I taught a class entitled "Shoot or Don't Shoot" for many years. After training virtually everyone at the Cincinnati Police Division in this class, I was much more concerned that an officer would *not* shoot someone he should, than shoot someone that was innocent. Policies and procedures that stress using constraint and consequences of an improper shooting were paramount in most training sessions, but not mine. Officers were reluctant to take their weapon out of the holster to be ready at their side in potentially very dangerous situations.
>
> There's nothing wrong with telling cops when they can't shoot, but we have to temper that with being ready in dangerous times, and that it's okay to defend yourself or someone else. Police administrators, sometimes because of special interest groups and fear of liability, go way too far with hammering home the point of not shooting.[42]

There is also the phenomenon that has become known as "suicide by cop." It has been suggested that of the hundreds of police shootings that occur each year, a significant number are provoked by people seeking to die. The suicides are not usually capricious acts of mania or rage but calculated attempts to force police to act as executioners. A recent analysis of the shootings by police officers that occurred in Los Angeles County from 1987 through 1997 showed that out of the 437 shootings studied, 11 percent were actually "suicide-by-cop" situations.[43] The effects of such suicides on police officers are dramatic, typically resulting in early retirement from policing.

Tasers and Nonlethal Use of Force

In the most recent attempt to reduce the number of fatal shootings by police, law enforcement agencies around the nation have been increasingly arming their officers with Tasers, guns that use an electric current to temporarily immobilize a suspect. Tasers

Citizens and Tasers

Support continued police use of Tasers: 77%

Oppose continued police use of Tasers: 17%

Strongly support police use of nonlethal weapons: 44%

Believe police use of Tasers makes communities safer: 76%

Support private citizens' right to own Tasers: 61%

Source: Zogby International Poll, February 2005. ■

FAMOUS CRIMINALS
Lizzie Borden

*Lizzie Borden took an ax and gave her
    mother forty whacks.
And when she saw what she had done,
she gave her father forty-one . . .*

A group of police officers examined two butchered corpses in Fall River, Massachusetts, on a hot Sunday afternoon late in July 1892. Abbey Borden had been struck at least 20 times with an ax in her bedroom. Her husband Andrew lay downstairs on the sofa with at least 11 wounds from the same weapon. Their deaths had been brutal, agonizing, and grisly. The residents of the town were horrified and shocked. But they were also fascinated and curious. Why had these deaths occurred? Who had killed the Bordens?

Circumstantially, the Bordens' daughter Lizzie was the natural suspect. She hated Abbey, her stepmother, and the death of her well-off but stingy father would guarantee her substantial financial comfort. Lizzie's home life was troubled, uncomfortable, and tense, and there is some evidence that she felt persecuted and wanted to strike back against her family. Indeed, a few days before the murders, Lizzie had tried to buy a powerful poison without a prescription— allegedly to kill vermin. And, other than a maid who was sick in bed, Lizzie was thought to be the only person in the house at the time of the murders. The police reluctantly charged Lizzie with killing her parents.

(continued on p. 283)

utilize compressed nitrogen to project two small probes connected by insulated wire to transmit an electronic signal to a target up to 25 feet away. When the signal makes contact with the suspect's body or through clothing, the 50,000-volt shock renders an immediate loss of neuromuscular control. Some 5,200 of the estimated 23,000 to 25,000 agencies nationwide have adopted the use of Tasers. Hundreds of police departments, including Phoenix, San Diego, Sacramento, Albuquerque, and Reno, have issued Tasers to every patrol officer.

Many police forces, such as Seattle and San Jose, incorporated Tasers into their arsenals after controversial police shootings elicited public outcry. Advocates say Tasers reduce the number of fatal shootings by police while providing an alternative means of subduing rowdy, uncooperative, or dangerous suspects. Statistics indicate a decrease in the number of fatal shootings by several police departments after the acquisition of Tasers. In Phoenix, for example, shootings by police fell by half in the first year of their use. In Houston, civilian shootings plunged to a 25-year low, and in Aventura, Florida, injuries to suspects dropped 60 percent while injuries to police officers were down by 40% after the adoption of Tasers.[44]

Critics, however, maintain that the safety of Tasers has not been sufficiently proved, citing the more than 100 deaths that have occurred nationwide.[45] Although Tasers have been trumpeted as safe and effective in studies sanctioned by the manufacturer, Taser International, skeptics say the company's studies (consisting of tests on a pig in 1996 and five dogs in 1999) have not been thorough or rigorous enough.[46] Since then, however, several other studies have been undertaken, concluding various degrees of safety. Numerous independent studies are listed on the company's Web site.[47] Nevertheless, there is no federal regulation of the devices, nor have there been federal studies of any of the Taser deaths to determine their cause.

There are no uniform guidelines among law enforcement agencies to standardize Tasers use either, prompting critics to charge some agencies with being "trigger happy." In Orange County, Florida, for example, use of pepper spray and batons sharply declined after getting Tasers, but the overall use of force increased 58 percent from 2000 to 2003. Furthermore, human rights groups have voiced concern over who is getting stunned. For example, in San Jose's first year of Taser use, 64 percent of the 174 people tasered were mentally ill or under the influence of drugs or alcohol, and Latinos, who constitute 30 percent of the city's population, accounted for 52 percent of those tasered. In just 4 months with Tasers, officers in Houston tasered 144 suspects, 90 percent of whom were black or Hispanic. And in Miami, the tasering of a 6-year-old boy and 12-year-old girl prompted revisions of the police department's policy on Taser use on minors.[48] But despite the controversies, the public appears to be generally in favor of Tasers. Judging by the popularity among police departments and the company's tremendous financial success, Tasers will likely play an increasing role in modern policing.

Controlling Police Misconduct

Without question, policing is rich in opportunities for corruption, brutality, abuse of discretionary powers, violation of citizens' rights, and other forms of misconduct. Moreover, "policing the police" is difficult, for a variety of reasons. Corruption generally occurs in the most covert of circumstances and involves cooperation by many citizens. In addition, the victims of the misconduct—of the brutality, abuse of discretionary powers, and violations of due process rights—are often reluctant to make the misconduct fully public or are prevented from doing so. Further, police officers operate alone or in small teams—beyond the observation of departmental supervisors. Finally, the internal policing of certain abusive practices, combined with the elements of secrecy and solidarity that are characteristic of all police organizations, inhibit many police agencies from making instances of misconduct a matter of public record.

This is not to say that police abuses cannot be brought under greater control. There are many mechanisms that can affect police behavior for the better, including the legislature, the community, and the police system itself.

Legislative Control

Although the Civil Rights Act of 1964 was an act of Congress, it is actually implemented by the courts; as such, it is not a direct control over police behavior. However, state and local legislative bodies can have a specific impact on the conduct of law enforcement by reevaluating laws that create the potential for police violations and corruption.

Throughout the history of the United States, criminal justice has been faced with the problem of overcriminalization due to the legislation of morality and the overregulation of civilian conduct. Laws that impose restrictions on alcohol consumption, drug use, prostitution, gambling, and other "victimless" crimes, combined with the numerous rules issued by regulatory agencies, are the areas in which most police corruption occurs. Thus, if legislatures are to control police conduct, one could argue that they might begin by decriminalizing these victimless crimes. It seems unlikely that anything will be done in this area, however. The continued existence of many of the victimless crimes that generate the potential for corruption is the result of legislative unwillingness to repeal them for fear of committing political suicide. Nevertheless, a few changes have occurred. Gambling laws have been relaxed through the establishment of state-run lotteries and off-track betting; prostitution has been legalized in at least one jurisdiction and reduced to a minor violation in some others; and a number of restrictions on business owners, landlords, and the building construction industry have been eliminated. However, much police corruption is an outgrowth of the laws controlling the possession of cocaine, crack, heroin, and numerous other drugs, and it is unlikely these will be legalized any time soon, if ever (see Exhibit 9.6).

By contrast, Section 1983 of the Civil Rights Act of 1871 authorizes suits for violations of constitutional rights. Under this provision, an individual can hold a law enforcement agency or municipality liable for an incident of police misconduct.

Civilian Review Boards

The influence of citizens on police behavior is most evident in small communities. There is closer contact between the police and members of the community, officers are typically longtime residents of the locations they patrol, police officials are often dependent on public support for departmental finances and tenure, and police behavior in general is more visible. Further, the opportunities for police abuse are less widespread in small cities, towns, and rural areas. The reverse seems to be true in large urban centers, where community control over policing is almost totally absent. A number of suggestions have been made concerning how to counter this problem, including "putting the cop back on the beat," community policing, sensitivity training for police recruits, and the establishment of civilian review boards to enforce police discipline. More than three decades ago, Arthur I. Waskow offered the following three-part formula for placing control of the police system in the hands of the citizenry:

> *First,* police forces should be restructured along neighborhood lines with control over each force residing in elected officials from the neighborhood; *second,* organizations should be developed to protect those who are policed; and *third,* community control should be established informally by changing the police "profession" so that police are not isolated from the rest of the community.[49]

Waskow's suggestions probably have merit, at least from a technical point of view. But they are based on an idealized concept of police—community relations and may not be unworkable. The paramilitary character of police organizations, the conservative nature of police decision making, and the elements of the police culture that stress secrecy and solidarity combine to create a situation in which police would be highly resistant to outside control. The experience with civilian review boards illustrates this point.

Before 1958, all power to discipline law enforcement personnel was in the hands of police departments, generally in the form of an internal review committee composed of one or more police officials. But concern about this system surfaced during the late

(continued from p. 282)

Fall River was a small, conservative town and the Bordens were not famous in any way, but word of their violent deaths spread rapidly. The *New York Times* featured an article the next day, and across the nation hundreds of newspapers—the most prominent form of media in the 1890s—tracked the investigation for millions of readers.

Lizzie was able to command substantial legal resources for her trial. The prosecution's sensational evidence failed to convince the jury, which rendered a verdict of not guilty after only 90 minutes of deliberation. In the court of public opinion, however, Lizzie Borden was unquestionably, indisputably, and irrefutably guilty, as evidenced by the infamous and gruesome nursery rhyme that millions of children have learned to recite. ∎

Civilian review is no more necessary than jury trials; but both exist to provide citizen input to the system, and to enhance the system's credibility.

— **ORLANDO W. WILSON, FORMER CHICAGO SUPERINTENDENT OF POLICE**

"Nationwide, How Much Police Brutality Do You Think Exists Against Minorities?"

Source: *Newsweek* poll.

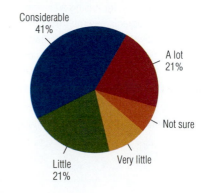

Considerable 41%

A lot 21%

Not sure

Very little

Little 21%

EXHIBIT 9.6 | drugs, crime, and justice

Police Corruption and the Drug Legalization Debate

The Drug Policy Alliance is a New York City–based organization working to broaden the public debate on drug policy, and to promote realistic alternatives to the war on drugs based on science, compassion, health, and human rights. Regarding police corruption, the following comment appears on the alliance's Web site:

> Similar to US alcohol prohibition of the 1920's, current drug prohibition legislation breeds police corruption and abuse. A 1998 report by the General Accounting Office notes that on-duty police officers involved in drug-related corruption engage in serious criminal activities such as (1) conducting unconstitutional searches and seizures; (2) stealing money and/or drugs from drug dealers; (3) selling stolen drugs; (4) protecting drug operations; (5) providing false testimony; and (6) submitting false crime reports. Approximately half of all police officers convicted as a result of FBI-led corruption cases between 1993 and 1997 were convicted for drug-related offenses and nationwide over 100 cases of drug-related corruption are prosecuted each year. Every one of the federal law enforcement agencies with significant drug enforcement responsibilities has seen an agent implicated.

Given this statement, would legalizing drugs reduce police corruption? Here are the arguments *for* and *against.*

Arguing *for* Legalization

The arguments posed by the supporters of legalizing heroin, cocaine, and other illicit drugs are numerous. *First,* the drug laws have created evils far worse than the drugs themselves—police and government corruption, violence, street crime, and disrespect for the law. *Second,* legislation passed to control drugs has failed to reduce demand. *Third,* you cannot declare illegal that which a significant segment of the population in any society is committed to doing. You simply cannot arrest, prosecute, and punish such large numbers of people, particularly in a democracy. And specifically in this behalf, in a liberal democracy the government must not interfere with personal behavior if liberty is to be maintained. *Fourth,* if marijuana, cocaine, crack, heroin, and other drugs were legalized, a number of very positive things would happen:

1. Drug prices would fall.
2. Users could obtain their drugs at low, government-regulated prices and would no longer be forced to engage in prostitution and street crime to support their habits.
3. The fact that the levels of drug-related crime would significantly decline would result in less crowded courts, jails, and prisons and would free law enforcement personnel to focus their energies on the "real criminals" in society.
4. Drug production, distribution, and sale would be removed from the criminal arena; no longer would these activities be within the province of organized crime. Thus, criminal syndicates such as the Colombian drug cartels and the Jamaican posses would be decapitalized, and the violence associated with drug distribution rivalries would be eliminated.
5. Government corruption and intimidation by traffickers as well as drug-based foreign policies would be effectively reduced, if not eliminated entirely.
6. The often draconian measures undertaken by police to enforce the drug laws would be curtailed, thus restoring to the American public many of its hard-won civil liberties.

To these contentions can be added the argument that legalization in any form or structure would have only a minimal impact on current drug use levels. Given the existing levels of access to most illegal drugs, current levels of use closely match demand. Thus, there would be no additional health, safety, behavioral, and/or other problems accompanying legalization. Finally, through government regulation of drugs, the billions of dollars spent annually on drug enforcement could be better utilized. Moreover, through taxation of government-regulated drugs, revenues would be collected that could be used for preventing drug abuse and treating those harmed by drugs.

In sum, the argument *for* legalization boils down to the basic belief that America's prohibitions against marijuana, cocaine, heroin, and other drugs impose far too large a cost in terms of tax dollars, crime, and infringements on civil rights and individual liberties.

The major reason for having a civilian oversight mechanism is mistrust of cops investigating cops. Democratic institutions, such as civilian review or the jury, are instituted not because they are more efficient or able, but because they are trusted.

— **JEROME H. SKOLNICK**

1950s and early 1960s, when the United States Commission on Civil Rights found that many African Americans felt powerless to do anything about police malpractice. These revelations were confirmed by later studies conducted by the American Civil Liberties Union (ACLU), the National Association for the Advancement of Colored People (NAACP), and the University of California. These pointed to a range of dissatisfactions with internal police review boards, including the following:

1. They could not be impartial in judging fellow officers.
2. The procedures for filing complaints were so cumbersome that they discouraged citizen reporting.
3. They made no effort to solicit complaints.
4. They insulated police officers and departments from public accountability.

Arguing *against* Legalization

The arguments posed by those opposing the legalization of drugs are equally as compelling:

1. Although drug prohibition policies have been problematic, it would appear that they have managed to keep drugs away from most people. High school and general population surveys indicate that most Americans don't use drugs, have never even tried them, and don't know where to get them. Thus, the numbers "at risk" are dramatically fewer than is the case with legal drugs. Or, stated differently, there is a rather large population who might be at risk if illicit drugs were suddenly available.

2. Marijuana, heroin, cocaine, crack, amphetamines, PCP, LSD, and the rest are not "benign" substances. Their health consequences, addiction liability, and abuse potential are considerable.

3. There is extensive physiological, neurological, and anthropological evidence to suggest that people are of a species that has been honed for pleasure. Nearly all people want and enjoy pleasure, and the pursuit of drugs—whether caffeine, nicotine, alcohol, opium, heroin, marijuana, or cocaine—seems to be universal and inescapable. It is found across time and across cultures. Moreover, history and research have demonstrated that "availability creates demand."

4. Crack-cocaine is especially problematic because of its pharmacological and sociocultural effects. Because crack makes its users ecstatic and yet is so short-acting, it has an extremely high addiction potential. *Use* rapidly becomes *compulsive use*. Crack acquisition thus becomes enormously more important than family, work, social responsibility, health, values, modesty, morality, or self-respect. Because of its chemistry, crack is easy and inexpensive to produce, and it will likely remain so, regardless of its legal status. A benefit of its current criminalization is that since it *is* against the law, it doesn't have widespread availability and proportionately few people use it. Within the context of reversing the human suffering that crack has helped to exacerbate, what purpose is served by arguing for its legalization? Will legalizing crack make it less available, less attractive, less expensive, less addictive, or less troublesome?

5. The research literature on the criminal careers of people who use cocaine, heroin, and other drugs has convincingly documented that while drug use tends to intensify and perpetuate criminal behavior, it usually does not initiate criminal careers. In fact, the evidence suggests that among the majority of street drug users who are involved in crime, their criminal careers were well established prior to the onset of either narcotics or cocaine use.

6. There is a large body of work suggesting that drug abuse is *overdetermined behavior*. That is, addiction is secondary to the wide range of influences that instigate and regulate drug taking and drug seeking. Drug abuse is a disorder of the whole person, affecting some or all areas of functioning. In the vast majority of drug offenders who come to the attention of the criminal justice system, there are cognitive problems, psychological dysfunction is common, thinking may be unrealistic or disorganized, values are misshapen, and frequently there are deficits in educational and employment skills. As such, drug abuse is a response to a series of social and psychological disturbances. Thus, the goal of treatment should be "habilitation" rather than "rehabilitation." Whereas *rehabilitation* emphasizes the return to a way of life previously known and perhaps forgotten or rejected, *habilitation* involves the client's initial socialization into a productive and responsible way of life.

7. Drug control should remain within the criminal justice sector for some very good reasons. Recent research has demonstrated not only that drug abuse treatment works but also that coerced treatment works best. The key variable most related to success in treatment is "length of stay in treatment," and those who are forced into treatment remain longer than volunteers and, by remaining longer, benefit more. As such, compulsory treatment efforts should be expanded for those who are dependent on drugs and are involved in drug-related crime.

8. Since the "war on drugs" will continue, a more humane use of the criminal justice system should be structured. This is best done through treatment in lieu of incarceration and through corrections-based treatment for those who do end up in jails and prisons.

Sources: Herbert D. Kleber and James A. Inciardi, "Clinical and Societal Implications of Drug Legalization," in *Substance Abuse: A Comprehensive Textbook,* 4th ed., edited by Joyce H. Lowinson (Baltimore: Williams & Wilkins, 2005), 1383–1400; James A. Inciardi, *The Drug Legalization Debate* (Thousand Oaks, CA: Sage Publications, 1999).

5. They rarely disciplined officers, thus giving the impression that they were simply whitewash efforts.[50]

The ACLU also found that in an effort to protect the reputation of their departments, the internal affairs units and other special police squads that were structured for "policing the police" employed a host of tactics to discourage citizens from filing complaints against officers. In New York City, they threatened complainants with criminal libel; in Cleveland, they forced them to take lie detector tests; and in Philadelphia, Washington, D.C., and Los Angeles, they took them into custody on charges of resisting arrest, disorderly conduct, or some other minor offense. Other departments intimidated witnesses, deprived complainants of access to departmental files, or otherwise acted as though the citizens were on trial.[51]

The stronger one's reputation for being tough, mean, and aggressive, the less iron-handed one actually has to be.

—**JEROME H. SKOLNICK**

Kenneth Hall, 14, of the Roxbury neighborhood of Boston, pauses at a memorial for 23-year-old youth basketball coach William "Biggie" Gaines who was killed in front of his team after brandishing a fake gun.

Can Religion Reform Corrupt Cops?

How do you reform a notoriously corrupt, abusive, and undisciplined police force? With a little divine intervention.

At least that's what government officials in the Philippines are hoping to achieve by handing out Bibles and Korans to each of the 115,000 active members of the Philippine National Police (PNP). In addition, pastors and priests accredited by the force conduct weekly Bible lessons at national police headquarters and substations across the country. So far, approximately 90,000 Bibles and several thousand Korans have been distributed, and several thousand more copies of each holy book are ready to be given out in the future.

Notorious for corruption, womanizing, torture, and ties to organized criminal activity, including kidnappings for ransom and drug trafficking, the PNP has very low citizen support. The force's "Movement for Righteous Leadership" seeks to change that by using passages from the spiritual guides to promote positive values among its officers, including respect for authority, the sanctity of marriage, and service for the people. "With divine intervention," said one pastor, "we hope to reduce immorality in the police force."

Do you think this strategy will work? How would this idea be received in the United States? ∎

The ACLU, the NAACP, and other citizen groups urged police authorities to shift the responsibility for handling complaints to citizen-controlled outside review boards. The boards were to serve several purposes:

1. They would restrain officers who engaged in brutality, harassment, and other abusive and even illegal practices.
2. By ensuring a thorough and impartial investigation of all complaints, they would protect other officers against malicious, misguided, and otherwise unfounded accusations.
3. They would offer African Americans and other minority group members an avenue of redress, which would help restore their confidence in the police departments.
4. They would explain police procedures to citizens, review enforcement requirements with police, and initiate a genuine dialogue in place of mutual recrimination.[52]

Proposals for such **civilian review boards** incensed most police officers and were bitterly fought by such organizations as the International Association of Chiefs of Police, the International Conference of Police Associations, and the Fraternal Order of Police. Despite opposition, however, a few cities did establish civilian review boards. The first was set up in Philadelphia on October 1, 1958, but from its inception its potential for objective judgment was severely limited. Philadelphia's five-member Police Advisory Board had no investigatory staff of its own and had to rely on the police department's community relations unit to investigate complaints.

In the ensuing years, civilian review boards have come and gone in a number of places; currently, at least 35 of the nation's largest cities have some form of civilian review. These vary, however, and some are less effective than others. In San Francisco, for example, civilian investigators examine each complaint and present their findings to outside adjudicators. Other cities allow police personnel to investigate a complaint first and then, if it is determined to be unfounded or unresolvable, turn it over to an independent review board for further consideration. In many cases, police managers, not board members, decide how to respond to the board's findings and the type of punishment to be imposed.[53]

Police Control

Control of police misconduct from within police departments is of two types: preventive and punitive.

Preventive control occurs in several areas, all of which involve alterations in the structure and philosophy of a police department. First, the policy of *internal accountability* holds members of a law enforcement agency responsible for their own actions as well as those of other members. It is based on clear communication of standards to which officers and officials will be held accountable and on statements of "who will be responsible for whom." Second, internal accountability becomes workable only under *tight supervision* of police officers by administrators, precinct commanders, and other control staff. Tight supervision involves direct surveillance of officers' work by field commanders, combined with daily logs documenting officer activity. Third, preventive control can affect areas of police misconduct through *abolition of corrupting procedures*. Every large police department and many smaller ones have numerous formal procedures that inadvertently encourage corruption. For example, some policies imply levels of productivity that are all but impossible to achieve by legitimate means; others create pressures for financial contributions by officers that the officers attempt to "earn back" in corrupt ways. Vice investigators and detectives, for instance, often must "purchase" leads from informers, but funds for such purposes may be limited or unavailable in some departments. Similarly, criminal investigation work may require the use of personal autos with no provisions for expense reimbursement.

Sociologist Lawrence W. Sherman has noted that preventive controls along these lines were implemented in Oakland during the 1950s and in New York City as an outgrowth of the Knapp Commission hearings on police corruption in the early 1970s.[54] In both cities, policies of internal accountability were established, aimed at diffusing the responsibility for control of misconduct both vertically and horizontally through-out the police departments. These policies were swiftly enforced. In Oakland, for example, a detective commander lost 5 days' pay for failing to thoroughly investigate a corruption allegation; a sergeant was suspended for failing to investigate a prisoner's complaint that officers had taken money from him; and another sergeant was suspended for letting one of his officers work while intoxicated. Supervision was tightened, primarily by extending decision-making powers to lower levels in the police hierarchy and maintaining a lower ratio of line officers to supervisors.

More recently, the reform administration in New York also focused on potentially corrupting procedures. "Buy money" for purchasing drugs and funds for informers was greatly increased and more rigidly controlled; the cost of using personal autos in surveillance work was reimbursed on a per-mile basis; and the use of arrest quotas to evaluate the productivity of vice investigators was abolished.

Punitive control falls into the area of policing known as internal affairs or *internal policing*—the domain of "headhunters" and "shoo-fly" cops who investigate complaints against police personnel or other actions involving police misconduct. Internal policing may be the responsibility of a single officer or detective, a small police unit, or an entire division or bureau, depending on the size of the department and its commitment to in-house review. Regardless of size, however, internal affairs units are generally responsible for inquiries into the following:

1. Allegations or complaints of misconduct made by a citizen, police officer, or any other person against the department or any of its members.
2. Allegations or suspicions of corruption, breaches of integrity, or cases of moral turpitude from whatever source—whether reported to or developed by internal policing.
3. Situations in which officers are killed or wounded by the deliberate or willful acts of other parties.
4. Situations in which citizens have been killed or injured by police officers either on or off duty.
5. Situations involving the discharging of weapons by officers.[55]

Internal policing began during the latter part of the 19th century, when head-quarters personnel made inspections on a citywide basis and investigated corruption. In New York and a number of other cities they became known as "shoo-flies," a term taken from the language of the professional underworld. The shoo-fly was originally a criminal's spy who watched for police activity in order to warn the thief.[56] By 1900, detectives were also known as shoo-flies, because as nonuniformed investigators they spied on criminals.[57] During Arthur Woods's tenure as commissioner of the New York Police Department, which began in 1914, a confidential squad was organized to spy on the activities of police officers.[58] It was at that point that the term *shoo-fly cop* came into general use.

It was not until the mid-1900s, however, that structured bureaus for internal policing came into being. In the wake of a major scandal during the late 1940s, Los Angeles police chief William A. Worton formed the Bureau of Internal Affairs. Within a decade, Boston, Chicago, and Atlanta followed suit, and at the beginning of the 1960s New York City joined the trend when that city's police commissioner established the Inspection Service Bureau, which brought together several units that had been separately monitoring the integrity and efficiency of the police.

The special internal control units and bureaus, though permanent fixtures in big-city policing, are not without problems. Rank-and-file police officers have always despised the activities of headhunters and shoo-fly cops. Moreover, some internal affairs officers are corrupt themselves, and others are unwilling to tarnish their department's reputation by exposing corruption and incompetence. Finally, citizens have apparently been unwilling to file complaints, and officers have been unwilling to testify against one another. The product of such difficulties is a very low level of efficiency.

Nevertheless, not all aspects of internal policing have been unsuccessful. Even in disorganized and inefficient departments, a certain level of misconduct has been de-

International Corruption

Corruption of some kind likely exists in every country in the world, and much of it involves police corruption. In a recent study by Transparency International, countries were ranked according to their level of corruption. The "corruption index" is a scale from 10 (the least corrupt) to zero (the most corrupt). As indicated below, in 2004, Finland was considered the least corrupt, and Bangladesh and Haiti were the most corrupt. The United States was about one-third of the way down the list. Source: Transparency International.

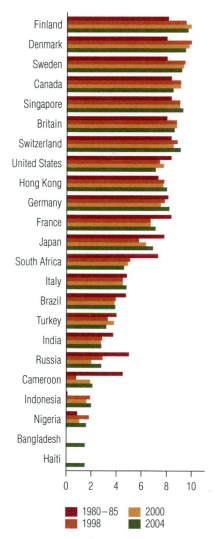

■ 1980–85	■ 2000
■ 1998	■ 2004

IAD [Internal Affairs Division] investigators are considered by many NYPD officers to be scum. To most cops, they are turncoats, known by various epithets, such as "Cheese-eater," "Ben," and "Willard"—all signifying "rat." Mention the three letter IAD and a cop will instinctively sneer.

—FROM *COP HUNTER,*
BY VINCENT MURANO

A field supervisor in Venice Beach, California, gives his officers instructions before they start their shift patrolling the boardwalk.

Trend in Views of Police Ethics

Those rating the honesty and ethical standards of the police as "very high" or "high":

1985	47%
1990	49%
1994	46%
1997	49%
2000	49%
2004	60%

Source: *BJS Sourcebook;* the Gallup Organization. ■

Views of Police Brutality

In some places in the nation, there have been charges of police brutality. Do you think there is any police brutality in your area?

	Yes	No
TOTAL	35%	60%
Whites	33	62
Blacks	45	46
Other	43	56
Large city	59	36
Medium city	40	55
Suburb	33	59
Small town	24	74
Rural	20	74

Note: "No opinion" answers were not listed.
Source: Gallup Poll. ■

tected and ferreted out. Without any internal control mechanisms, police organization would probably become chaotic.

Attempts to reduce police misconduct should not be limited to efforts by legislatures, review boards, and internal policing. These treat only the symptoms of the problem. Greater professionalization of police also seems warranted. However, this too is an area that is problematic, for there are differing conceptions of professionalism in law enforcement. Police understand professionalism to mean more clearly defined rules and regulations, increased central control, strict discipline, and obedience. In every other organization, professionalism means that a large measure of discretion is left to individuals, who respond to situations on the basis of expertise gained from long training and experience, rather than organizational rules and regulations. In law enforcement agencies, such professionalism would come from better trained and educated officers, more sophisticated police resources, closer attention to the needs for community service and police—community relations, and more efficient and detailed policies regarding police behavior in contacts with citizens.

Properly understood, **police professionalism** implies that brutality and corruption are symptoms of incompetent policing. And incompetence may be judged by the following standard: While the right to use force is at the core of the police role, skill in policing is revealed by the ability to avoid its use. With respect to corruption, professionalism gives rise to norms of pride and dignity of occupation that make police intolerant of fellow officers who do not meet these standards.[59]

CRITICAL THINKING IN CRIMINAL JUSTICE

"Zero Tolerance" and Police Shootings

In February 1999, an unarmed street peddler—22-year-old Amadou Diallo—was shot to death by four white NYPD plainclothes police officers. Diallo, an African immigrant with no criminal record, was killed outside his apartment in the Bronx during the officers' investigation of a serial rapist in the area. The officers were part of the NYPD Street Crime Unit, a special task force established as part of New York's "zero-tolerance" crime policy. The killing of Amadou Diallo occurred not too long after Haitian immigrant Abner Louima was assaulted and sodomized by NYPD officer Justin Volpe.

These incidents, it is claimed, are symptomatic of a police force that routinely shoots, or otherwise abuses, suspects who are not white. Moreover, the NYPD has become the focus of a debate of global importance: Is it possible to successfully police a large, modern, democratic city? Think critically about this question, and examine some of the issues. Is the NYPD out of control? Are African American suspects, or suspects in general, the victims of an inordinate number of police shootings? Read the press reports. Look up the figures. Do the math. Analyze the policies. What are your critical thoughts?

Shifting back to the killing of Amadou Diallo, what really happened? Was it a case of police brutality, a racially motivated police execution, or just a tragic accident precipitated by a group of overzealous, trigger-happy officers?

In the months that followed the Diallo killing, the majority of New Yorkers felt that the killing was neither racial nor intentional. Most observers agreed, however, that blacks were far more likely than whites to suffer at the hands of the police. Although the four officers were indicted for second-degree murder, even antipolice activists conceded that it had not been a deliberate killing. In 2000, all four were acquitted of the charges by a multiracial jury. What actually happened, however, may never be fully understood. In all likelihood, the officers said something to Diallo, he moved in a manner that they interpreted as threatening, someone shouted "gun," the officers started firing, and they may have mistaken their own ricocheting bullets as return fire. In all, 41 shots were fired, and 19 hit Diallo. It may have been hysteria, similar to the kind seen in wartime—nervous soldiers are tramping through the jungle, a sound is heard, something moves, and everyone shoots.

What were the underlying causes of the incident? For one thing, there is New York City's zero-tolerance crime policy, which holds that no crime—not the breaking of a window, not the theft of a pack of cigarettes, not the jumping of a subway turnstile, nothing—is too insignificant to capture the swift, decisive attention of the police. But one of the problems is that the policy can trample on individual rights. During 1997 and 1998, before the Diallo killing, officers in the Street Crime Unit frisked more than 45,000 people thought to be carrying guns but arrested just under 10,000. One result was that a lot of guns were taken off the street, but another result was that tens of thousands of citizens were mistakenly detained.

A second problem is the manner in which zero tolerance is applied. Black leaders and civil libertarians point out that when police put emphasis on aggressive prevention strategies, they must rely on intuition and hunches. In doing so, officers invariably lean on broad profiles in stopping and interrogating possible criminals. Those profiles are often based on prejudices, and the people most likely to be stopped are members of minority groups.

A third problem is police training, not only in the areas of police–community relations, the Constitution, and civil rights but on "search and seizure" issues as well.

The claim that the NYPD has become more trigger-happy in recent years does not stand up to serious examination. With a force of 39,000 officers in 2003, 14 people were killed by police. In 1990 the toll was 41, and in 1993 it was 23.[60] By contemporary standards in the United States, 14 police killings is a low figure. More people were killed by the Prince George's County, Maryland, force of 1,400 officers than in all of New York City. In fact, among the largest city and county police departments for the period 1990–2000, Prince George's County ranked first in the number of both fatal shootings per 1,000 sworn officers and fatal shootings per 10,000 arrests.[61]

Although the NYPD has one of the lowest rates of police shootings in the United States, the shooting of even 14 citizens in 2003 suggests that it is still too high and that a good, hard look at zero-tolerance policing initiatives is long overdue.[62]

In the final analysis, there is no conflict between good crime control and respect for people's rights, but maintaining order under the rule of law is difficult to apply in practice.

Most Likely to Shoot

Police in Prince George's County, Maryland, shot and killed more people per sworn officer than police in the other 50 largest local law enforcement agencies in the nation from 1990 through 2000. The chart shows fatal shootings per 1,000 officers.

OP-ED

Policing the police has always been a diffi-cult task. Reforms emerging from police scandals dating back to the late-19th cen-tury have suggested that citizen oversight of police is the answer. But such a rem-edy seems to always run into obstacles. Politicians who build their careers on crime-fighting seldom become champions of police reform legislation. Police unions and administrators often resist the "meddling" of citizen review boards. And the citizen boards, when they manage to get into place, often render themselves ineffective by becoming mired in politics and personality conflicts. Add to this the fact that many citizens want tough policing to keep the crime rate down. But tough policing or not, corrupt and brutal behavior on the part of police can never be tolerated, even if it does result in reducing crime. And as former New York City police commissioner William J. Bratton commented in 2000:

> The common lesson to be learned is that under no circumstances can police be encouraged—by politicians or police leaders or acquiescence from the community—to tolerate lowering of constitu-tional guidelines in order to reduce crime.

Getting back to the Virgin Islands police situation mentioned at the beginning of this chapter, a number of things have happened. Just after the report on police shootings was released, a reporter from the *Virgin Islands Daily News* interviewed the police com-missioner about his views on *Tennessee* v. *Garner.* He said that he could not discuss it because he had not heard of it. A similar an-swer came from the Virgin Islands attorney general.[63] Nevertheless, some solutions are beginning to take shape in the Virgin Islands. The U.S. Justice Department is examining the VIPD's policies and procedures, federal com-munity relations mediators are working with community leaders in easing tensions, and legislation is being drafted for the creation of a civilian review board.[64]

| Summary |

Police misconduct falls primarily into two areas: corruption and the excessive use of violence. Police corruption reflects illegal activities for economic gain, including payment for services that police are sworn to do as part of their law enforcement role. Police violence, in the forms of brutality and the misuse of deadly force, involves the wrongful use of police power.

Police corruption can occur in many ways, but observers and researchers in the field of police behavior agree that it is most manifest in nine specific areas: meals and services, kick-backs, opportunistic theft, planned theft, shakedowns, protec-tion, case fixing, private security, and patronage. Policing is rich in opportunities for corruption—more so than most, if not all, other occupations.

Three major theories that attempt to explain the persis-tence of police corruption have gained considerable atten-tion—the society-at-large explanation, the structural account, and the rotten-apple analogy. The society-at-large theory has attempted to locate the incidence of corruption among offi-cers within a larger frame of relationships with citizens—spe-cifically, those relations that involve the acceptance of gifts and gratuities for service and the waiver of minor traffic fines. The structural explanation can be seen as an extension of the society-at-large hypothesis. In this view, officers develop a cynical attitude when they begin to realize that dishonesty and criminal behaviors are not limited to lawbreaking citizens but are also found among those considered upstanding citizens, including officers in their own departments. Lastly, the rotten-apple theory asserts that corruption occurs among a few bad officers in an otherwise honest department. In this view, crim-inal behavior among officers is the result of a breakdown of morality among certain officers that has the potential to spread like a contagion through the rest of the department.

Police violence has been relatively visible throughout American history but has received much attention in recent years by the U.S. Supreme Court and the Kerner Commission. Studies have shown that police violence occurs most often when people show disrespect for officers, when police encoun-ter certain types of offenders, and when police try to coerce confessions.

In the past, police brutality was considered to be a prac-tice limited to a few sadistic officers. More recent commen-taries suggest that while it is not particularly widespread, it appears to be an unfortunate consequence of departmental norms of conduct and the police role. Specifically, the danger-ous and often controversial role of police officers can contrib-ute to the police "working personality" that involves a variety of performance-related pressures, elements of authoritarian-ism, pervasive suspicion, racism, hostility, insecurity, and cyn-icism. Also related is the "watchman's style" of policing, which tends to be most prevalent in departments that are located within disproportionately poor, minority communities. Police violence also includes the improper use of deadly force—a "shoot-to-kill" doctrine based on common law principles that persist in a few law enforcement agencies.

Attempts to control police misconduct of all varieties have emanated from the legislature, from civilian review boards, and from police agencies themselves. Perhaps the most effec-tive method is police professionalism, which views brutality as incompetent policing and corruption as beneath the dignity of effective law enforcement agents.

| Key Terms |

civilian review boards (286)
police brutality (277)

police corruption (267)
"police presence" (267)

police professionalism (288)
Tennessee v. *Garner* (279)

| Issues for Discussion |

1. In what ways can civilian review boards be improved to increase their effectiveness in controlling and sanctioning police corruption and brutality?
2. Do you think that providing police with "goodwill" services contributes to corruption? Why or why not?
3. How has the war on drugs contributed to police corruption?
4. Is the problem of brutality so much a part of the police role that it can never be routed out? Why or why not?

5. In your community, what do you feel would be the best combination of activities for controlling police corruption?
6. Do you feel that corruption is more or less widespread in the ranks of policing than in other occupations and professions? Why?
7. What kinds of police misconduct have you observed? In each case, were they officer-initiated or citizen-initiated?
8. Do you think that legalizing drugs would reduce police corruption?

| Media and Literature Resources |

The VIPD Scandal. A spread supplement to the *Virgin Islands Daily News* dated December 30, 2003, provides all the details. See Lee Williams, "Deadly Force," *Virgin Islands Daily News,* December 30, 2003, 1–44; and *Virgin Islands Daily News,* January 15, 2004, 1–7. See also the newspaper's Web site at *http:www.virginislandsdailynews.com/index.pl/dforce.*

Human Rights and Police Abuses. See Human Rights Watch, *Shielded from Justice: Police Brutality and Accountability in the United States* (Washington, DC: Human Rights Watch, 1998); this entire report can be found on the Web as *http://www.hrw.org/reports98/police/toc.htm.* See also Ralph Crawshaw, Barry Devlin, and Tom Williamson, *Human Rights and Policing—Standards for Good Behaviour and a Strategy for Change* (The Hague: Kluwer Law International, 1998).

Police Violence. Some of the more interesting items on this topic include Geoffrey P. Alpert, Roger G. Dunham, Alfred Blumstein, and David Farrington, *Understanding Police Use of Force: Officers, Suspects, and Reciprocity* (Cambridge: Cambridge University Press, 2004); Juan Antonio Juarez, *Brotherhood of Corruption: A Cop Breaks the Silence on Police Abuse, Brutality, and Racial Profiling* (Chicago: Chicago Review Press, 2004); Howard Rahtz, *Understanding Police Use of Force* (Monsey, NY: Criminal Justice Press, 2003); Tom Barker and David Carter, "Fluffing Up the Evidence and Covering Your Ass: Some Conceptual Notes on Police Lying," *Deviant Behavior* 11 (1990): 61–73; Jerome Skolnick and James Fyfe, *Above the Law: Police and the Excessive Use of Force* (New York: Free Press, 1993); and Jill Nelson (ed.), *Police Brutality* (New York: Norton, 2000).

Police Corruption. One of the more classic works on corruption is Herman Goldstein's *Police Corruption: A Perspective on Its Nature and Control* (Washington, DC: The Police Foundation, 1975). See also several articles in *Crime and Justice International* 20 (May/June 2004): Ronald K. Noble, "Interpol's Contribution to the World's Anti-Terrorism Fight: Its Role and Activities in a Changing World Environment," 4–6; Stanley E. Morris, "Interpol I-24/7," 7–8, and "Interpol's Global Standards to Combat Police Corruption," 20–22. An excellent collection of essays on the topic of police corruption was recently published as well: Matthew J. Hickman, Alex R. Piquero, and Jack R. Greene (eds.), *Police Integrity and Ethics* (Belmont, CA: Wadsworth Group, 2004).

| Endnotes |

1. Lee Williams, "Deadly Force," *Virgin Islands Daily News,* December 30, 2003, 1–44; *Virgin Islands Daily News,* January 15, 2004, 1–7.
2. Lawrence W. Sherman, *Scandal and Reform* (Berkeley: University of California Press, 1978), xxii.
3. Herman Goldstein, *Police Corruption: A Perspective on Its Nature and Control* (Washington, DC: Police Foundation, 1975), 55.
4. Jonathan Rubinstein, *City Police* (New York: Farrar, Straus & Giroux, 1973), 400.
5. *The Knapp Commission Report on Police Corruption* (New York: Braziller, 1972).
6. Commission to Investigate Allegations of Police Corruption and the Anti-Corruption Procedures of the Police Department, *Commission Report* (New York: City of New York, 1994).
7. *The New York Times,* April 1, 2005, A20; *New York Daily News,* May 5, 2005, 16; *San Antonio Express-News,* September 24, 2004, 1B; Steven R. Donziger (ed.), *The Real War on Crime: The*

Report of the National Criminal Justice Commission (New York: Harper Perennial, 1996), 163–167.
8. See, for example, Kenneth J. Peak, *Policing America,* (Upper Saddle River, NJ: Prentice-Hall, 2000), 254; Richard J. Lundman, *Police and Policing* (New York: Holt, Rinehart and Winston, 1980), 142–148; Herman Goldstein, *Policing a Free Society* (Cambridge, MA: Ballinger, 1977), 194–195; Thomas Barker and Julian Roebuck, *An Empirical Typology of Police Corruption: A Study in Organizational Deviance* (Springfield, IL: Thomas, 1973); and Rubinstein, *City Police;* This discussion is also based on personal observations and contacts with police by the author in New York City, Tampa, Philadelphia, Miami, Key West, Birmingham, San Francisco, Baltimore, and Washington, D.C.
9. Mark L. Dantzker, *Understanding Today's Police* (Upper Saddle River, NJ: Prentice-Hall, 2000), 179–180.
10. The events described were reported to the author by victims, police officers, and detectives in several cities.

11. *Los Angeles Times,* May 15, 1994, A18.
12. *Los Angeles Times,* December 3, 1993, A1.
13. Lundman, *Police and Policing,* 148; Barker and Roebuck, *Empirical Typology of Police Corruption,* 36.
14. James A. Inciardi, *Careers in Crime* (Chicago: Rand McNally, 1975), 29.
15. See James A. Inciardi, *The War on Drugs III: The Continuing Saga of the Mysteries and Miseries of Intoxication, Addiction, Crime, and Public Policy* (Boston: Allyn and Bacon, 2002).
16. Albert J. Reiss, Jr., *Private Employment of Public Police* (Washington, DC: National Institute of Justice, 1988).
17. William Safire, *Safire's Political Dictionary* (New York: Random House, 1978), 517.
18. *The New York Times,* May 22, 1999, B5.
19. Edwin J. Delattre, *Character and Cops: Ethics in Policing* (Washington, DC: American Enterprise Institute for Public Policy Research, 1989), 71–78; National Research Council, *Fairness and Effectiveness in Policing* (Washington, DC: National Academy Press, 2004), 271–275.
20. From Ralph Lee Smith, *The Tarnished Badge* (New York: Arno Press, 1974), 191–192.
21. Arthur Niederhoffer, *Behind the Shield: The Police in Urban Society* (Garden City, NY: Doubleday, 1969), 70.
22. Goldstein, *Policing a Free Society,* 199.
23. Samuel Walker, *The Police in America* (New York: McGraw-Hill, 1983), 180–181.
24. Cited by Albert J. Reiss, Jr., "Police Brutality: Answers to Key Questions," *Trans-Action* 5 (1968): 10.
25. *Brown* v. *Mississippi,* 297 U.S. 278 (1936).
26. *Rogers* v. *Richmond,* 365 U.S. 534 (1961); *Greenwald* v. *Wisconsin,* 390 U.S. 519 (1968); *Georgia* v. *Sims,* 385 U.S. 538 (1968); *Florida* v. *Brooks,* 389 U.S. 413 (1968).
27. *Report of the National Advisory Commission on Civil Disorders* (New York: Dutton, 1968).
28. Cited in William A. Westley, *Violence and the Police* (Cambridge, MA: MIT Press, 1970), 122.
29. Reiss, "Police Brutality," 10.
30. James Q. Wilson, *Varieties of Police Behavior* (New York: Atheneum, 1975), 140–171.
31. Lundman, *Police and Policing,* 161–164.
32. Lundman, *Police and Policing,* 163.
33. *Newsweek,* June 23, 1969, 92.
34. *Livingston* v. *Browder,* 51 Ala. App. 366, 285 So. 2nd 923 (1973).
35. *Tennessee* v. *Garner,* U.S. SupCt 36 CrL 3233 (1985).
36. James J. Fyfe, "The Split-Second Syndrome and Other Determinants of Police Violence," in *Violent Transactions,* edited by Anne Campbell and John Gibbs (New York: Basil Blackwell, 1986).
37. See *U.S. News & World Report* August 27, 1979: 27; *Time,* January 21, 1980, 32; *U.S. News & World Report,* June 2, 1980, 19–22; Arthur L. Kobler, "Police Homicide in a Democracy," *Journal of Social Issues* 31 (Winter 1975): 163–184; Gerald D. Robin, "Justifiable Homicides by Police Officers," *Journal of Criminal Law, Criminology and Police Science,* June 1963, 225–231; Ralph Knoohirizen, Richard P. Fahey, and Deborah J. Palmer, *The Police and Their Use of Fatal Force in Chicago* (Evanston, IL: Chicago Law Enforcement Study Group, 1972); Betty Jenkins and Adrienne Faison, *An Analysis of 248 Persons Killed by New York City Policemen* (New York: New York Metropolitan Applied Research Center, 1974); David Jacobs and David Britt,

"Inequality and Police Use of Deadly Force: An Empirical Assessment of a Conflict Hypothesis," *Social Problems* 26 (April 1979): 403–412; Lennox S. Hinds, "The Police Use of Excessive and Deadly Force: Racial Implications," in *A Community Concern: Police Use of Deadly Force,* edited by Robert N. Brenner and Marjorie Kravitz (Washington, DC: U.S. Department of Justice, 1979), 7–11; and *Miami Herald,* March 27, 1983, 18A.
38. Paul Takagi, "A Garrison State in a Democratic Society," *Crime and Social Justice* 1 (Spring–Summer 1974): 27–33.
39. Richard Kania and Wade Mackey, "Police Violence as a Function of Community Characteristics," *Criminology* 15 (May 1977): 27–48.
40. Kobler, "Police Homicide in a Democracy."
41. James J. Fyfe, "Police Use of Deadly Force: Research and Reform," *Justice Quarterly* 5 (June 1988): 165–205.
42. John Burke, personal communications to the author, August 8, 2000 and October 17, 2000.
43. *Criminal Justice Newsletter,* September 1, 1998, 1–2; *The New York Times,* June 21, 1998, Section 4, 3; HR Hutson et al., "Suicide by Cop," *Annals of Emergency Medicine* 32, 6(1998): 655–669.
44. *Houston Chronicle,* December 26, 2004, A1; Charisse Jones, "Police Say Taser Shocks Are Replacing Deadly Shots," *USA Today,* July 14, 2004, A2; Carli Teproff, "A Stunning Lesson," *The Miami Herald,* March 27, 2005, A3.
45. Alan Gathright, "Police Should Quit Using Stun Guns, Group Says; Officers Seen as Too Quick to Use Tasers—Safety Questioned," *San Francisco Chronicle,* May 10, 2005, B2.
46. Alex Berenson, "As Police Use of Tasers Soars, Questions over Safety Emerge," *The New York Times,* July 18, 2004, 1.
47. See *http://www.taser.com/index.htm.*
48. *Houston Chronicle,* April 1, 2005, B10; *The Miami Herald,* March 27, 2005, A3; *San Francisco Chronicle,* May 10, 2005, B2; *The New York Times,* July 18, 2004, 1; Kris Axtman, "Police Stun Guns Pack Volts—and Debate," *Christian Science Monitor,* July 15, 2004, 3.
49. Arthur I. Waskow, "Community Control of the Police," *Trans-Action* 7 (December 1969): 4–7.
50. Paul Chevigny, *Police Power: Police Abuses in New York City* (New York: Vintage, 1969), 260; David H. Bayley and Harold Mendelsohn, *Minorities and the Police: Confrontation in America* (New York: Free Press, 1971), 127–135.
51. Robert M. Fogelson, *Big City Police* (Cambridge, MA: Harvard University Press, 1977), 283–284.
52. Fogelson, *Big City Police,* 284.
53. See Jerome H. Skolnick and James J. Fyfe, *Above the Law: Police and the Excessive Use of Force* (New York: Free Press, 1993); National Research Council, 288–289; Suzanne Smalley, "O'Toole to Create Police Review Board; Citizen Panel Will Probe Complaints," *The Boston Globe,* January 1, 2005, A1; Jake Wagman, "St. Louis Mayoral Election Ushers in Crucial Time for City; Next Years Are Vital to Turnaround," *St. Louis Post-Dispatch,* March 6, 2005, C1; and Maxine Bernstein, "Portland Police Study Role of Civilian Review," *The Oregonian,* August 15, 2003, C3.
54. Sherman, *Scandal and Reform,* 120–145.
55. George D. Eastman (ed.), *Municipal Police Administration* (Washington, DC: International City Management Association, 1969), 203–204.
56. Langdon W. Moore, *His Own Story of His Eventful Life* (Boston: Moore, 1893), 287–289.

57. Hutchins Hapgood, *The Autobiography of a Thief* (New York: Fox, Duffield, 1903), 265.

58. Thomas A. Reppetto, *The Blue Parade* (New York: Free Press, 1978), 162.

59. Egon Bittner, *The Functions of Police in Modern Society* (New York: Aronson, 1975).

60. *The New York Times,* February 4, 2004, B3.

61. *Washington Post Weekly Edition,* July 16–22, 2001.

62. Wayne A. Logan, "Policing in an Intolerant Society," *Criminal Law Bulletin* 35 (July–August 1999): 334–368.

63. *Virgin Islands Daily News,* July 23, 2004, 2.

64. *Virgin Islands Daily News,* July 29, 2004, 2.

THREE

THE COURTS

Justice is the great interest of man on earth.—DANIEL WEBSTER Injustice is relatively easy to bear; what stings is justice.—H. L. MENCKEN Everyone loves justice in the affairs of others.—ITALIAN PROVERB Felonies worry you to death; misdemeanors work you to death.—LOS ANGELES PUBLIC DEFENDER The task of the trial court is to reconstruct the past from what are at best second-hand reports of the facts.—JEROME FRANK, U.S. COURT OF APPEALS JUDGE I'm not kidding. Capital punishment may not be much of a deterrent against murder, but the sight of a few corpses swinging from a scaffold might work with drug dealers.—*NEWSWEEK* COLUMNIST JAMES J. KILPATRICK

10

THE STRUCTURE OF AMERICAN COURTS

LEARNING OBJECTIVES

After reading this chapter, you should be able to answer the following questions:

1. What is the meaning of "court jurisdiction"?

2. What occurs at each level of the state and federal court systems?

3. What are the problems of the lower courts?

4. How are the federal courts organized?

5. What was the significance of *Marbury* v. *Madison?*

6. How does the U.S. Supreme Court select its cases?

7. What are the functions of the U.S. Supreme Court?

8. What are "drug courts"?

College students on Spring Break gather around a woman drinking beer from a funnel on South Padre Island, Texas.

PANAMA CITY BEACH, FL—Spring break for college students means traveling to a sunny destination for fun, relaxation, and the consumption of copious amounts of alcohol to an extent that often gets out of hand. Panama City Beach is a popular location, but the police in this Florida community quickly became overwhelmed every year with disruptive students—men urinating in the streets, women baring their breasts in public places, and intoxicated members of both genders, often underage, behaving in a disorderly manner. To process the scores of students being arrested every day and night, city officials experimented with the concept of a "spring break court."[1]

The spring break court operated during the 6-week period every year from early March to mid-April when up to half a million college students descended upon the area. Anywhere between 100 and 150 students were being arrested on any given night for infractions ranging from nudity to disorderly conduct, and, not surprisingly, the majority involved excessive drinking. Students were handcuffed, fingerprinted, and photographed on the spot in full public view, after which they were released with a summons to appear in court the following morning. For students who failed to appear, local law enforcement officers immediately tracked them down, armed with a warrant for their arrest. Most made every effort to comply with their court date, evidenced by instances in which many defendants passed out or vomited during the proceedings. Ultimately, students could contest the charges, pay a $215 fine, or suit up in an orange jail work vest for a day of trash detail. Most students chose the latter, and as a result, hundreds of tons of garbage were cleared from the beaches and roadsides (debris usually discarded by students).

How effective is a nontraditional court like this? Do you think students take it seriously? Is it a real court? Are there other kinds of nontraditional courts? What other kinds of courts are there and what types of justice do they serve? How is the court system in the United States organized?

There are many types of courts in the United States. It will soon become clear that the variety is almost endless, as can be seen in the following exchange:

Citizen:	Where's the courthouse?
Police officer:	Which one?
Citizen:	The criminal court, please.
Police officer:	Which one?
Citizen:	Huh?
Police officer:	There's the police court, county court, circuit court, trial court, superior court, and appeals court!
Citizen:	The trial court, I guess.
Police officer:	Which one?

The Evolution of U.S. Courts

As America evolved into a nation, the court emerged as an integral part of life in most communities. It was at the local courthouse that celebrations were held and emergencies brought to the attention of the populace. Courthouses served as mustering places during the War of Independence and the Civil War, and victories and reverses were announced in broadsheets posted on their doors. They also served as meeting places—for religious services, dances, and town council assemblies—as well as fulfilling their

Corn can't expect justice from a court composed of chickens.

—AFRICAN PROVERB

An early American courthouse in Waxahachie, Texas.

primary function, the dispensation of justice. And courthouses were places for exchanging news and meeting old friends.

In matters of law, the procedure was clear and simple. The courthouse stood at the center of town. There, the justice of the peace decided on all aspects of civil disputes and minor criminal transgressions. With the more serious issues of crime, law, and justice, the procedure—at least in its outward aspects—was just as clear. Once each month, on "court day," a judge would visit the community and dispose of these weightier matters.

As towns became cities, the procedures became somewhat less simple. Because there were more people, and hence more problems, there were more courts. For civil matters, there were counterparts of the rural justices of the peace; for less serious criminal affairs, there were police and magistrate's courts; and for serious problems of law and order, there was a more permanent higher court.[2]

As the nation grew more populous and more mature, so too did its system of courts. By the late 19th century, American courts reflected a bewildering mosaic of names, types, structures, and functions. The old courthouse still stood; the rural justices of the peace and the urban magistrates still decided on certain matters of law; and the county courts, night courts, and higher courts still operated. But along with these one could also find mayor's courts, municipal courts, probate courts, chancery courts, superior courts, and various levels of appeals and supreme courts. Some town and county courts were consolidated into circuits and districts; numerous areas had general sessions and special sessions courts; and legal practitioners spoke in terms of appeals courts and trial courts, higher courts and lower courts, superior courts and inferior courts. Over all was a **dual court system** that had evolved throughout America after the signing of the Declaration of Independence—at the state level and at the federal level. Without question, finding "the courthouse," or at least the *right* courthouse, had become a perplexing problem.

Today, the situation is no less knotty, even when one does not include courts that handle only civil matters. In fact, the court system has become even more intricate. The purpose of this chapter is to unravel these complexities of American court configuration and analyze the roles of the various types of courts.

State Courts

Two key characteristics of state court systems are that no two are exactly alike and that the names of the various courts vary widely regardless of their functions. For example, all states have major trial courts devoted to criminal cases. In Ohio and Pennsylvania, these are called courts of common pleas; in California, they are known as superior

I woke up one morning and all of my stuff had been stolen . . . and replaced by exact duplicates.

— COMEDIAN STEVEN WRIGHT

EXHIBIT 10.1 | LAW & CRIMINAL JUSTICE

State and Federal Court Structure

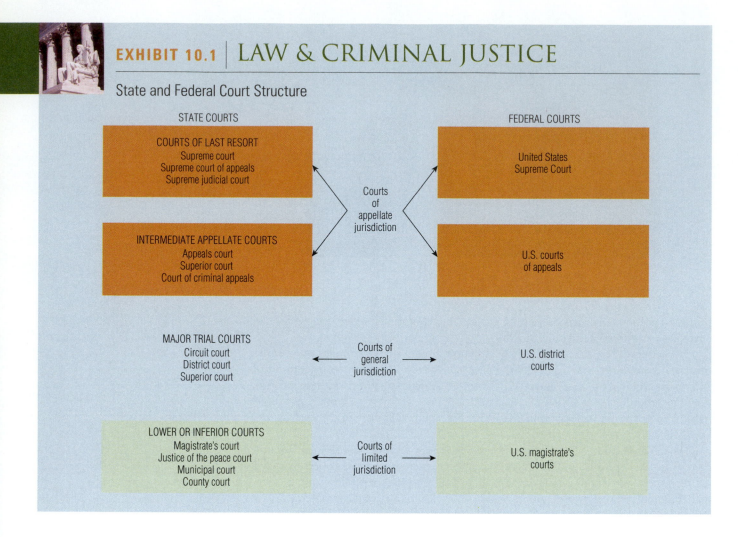

courts; in New York, they are supreme courts—a designation that is typically used elsewhere for appeals courts. Moreover, while Michigan's major trial courts are called circuit courts, within the city of Detroit they are called recorder's courts.

State Court Infrastructure

The many names, functions, and types of state court structures have resulted from the fact that each state is a sovereign government insofar as the enactment of a penal code and the setting up of enforcement machinery are concerned. Thus, in each of the 50 jurisdictions, the court systems developed differently—sometimes in an unplanned, sporadic way—generally guided by different cultural traditions, demographic pressures, legal and political philosophies, and needs for justice administration. Yet, despite this apparent confusion, there is a clear-cut structure within all the state court systems. State judiciaries are divided into three, four, or sometimes five tiers, each with separate functions and jurisdictions.

As outlined in Exhibit 10.1, the courts of last resort are at the uppermost level, occupying the highest rung of the judicial ladder. These are the appeals courts. All states have a court of last resort, but depending on the jurisdiction, the specific name varies—supreme court, supreme court of appeals, or perhaps simply court of appeals. In addition, in some states including Texas and Oklahoma, there are two courts of last resort, one for criminal cases and one for all others.

Immediately below the courts of last resort in more than half the states are the intermediate appellate courts. Located primarily in the more populous states, these courts have been structured to relieve the caseload burden on the highest courts. Like the highest courts, they are known by various names; often the names are similar to

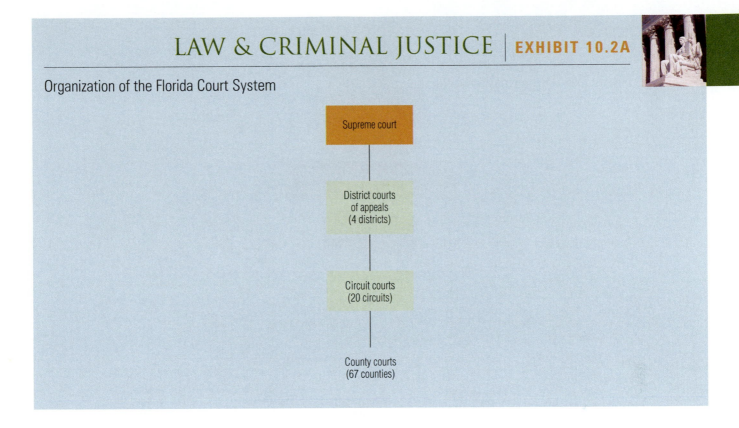

LAW & CRIMINAL JUSTICE | EXHIBIT 10.2A

Organization of the Florida Court System

those of the courts above them in the hierarchy (appeals courts), as well as below them (superior courts).

The major trial courts are the courts of general jurisdiction, where felony cases are heard. All states have various combinations of these, and depending on the locale, they might be called superior, circuit, district, or some other designation.

The lower courts, often referred to as inferior, misdemeanor, minor, or courts of limited jurisdiction, exist in numerous combinations in every state. Variously named county, magistrate, police, municipal, justice of the peace, or justice courts, as well as dozens of other designations, they are the entry point for most defendants and the only level at which infractions and most misdemeanors are processed.

Levels of Jurisdiction in State Courts

The *jurisdiction* of each court varies by geography, subject matter, and hierarchy. Courts are authorized to hear and decide disputes arising within specific political boundaries—a city, borough, township, county, or group of counties. In addition, some courts are limited to specific matters—for example, misdemeanors or civil actions versus all other types of cases. There are family courts that decide on juvenile and domestic relations matters, probate courts whose jurisdiction is limited to the handling of wills and the administration of estates, and many others. Jurisdiction can also be viewed as limited, general, and appellate, as follows:

1. *Courts of limited jurisdiction,* the lower courts, do not have powers that extend to the overall administration of justice; they do not try felony cases; and they do not possess appellate authority.
2. *Courts of general jurisdiction,* the major trial courts, have the power and authority to try and decide any case, including appeals from a lower court.
3. *Courts of appellate jurisdiction,* the appeals courts, are limited in their jurisdiction to matters of appeal from lower courts and trial courts.

Court systems may be simple or complex in their organizational structure. The Florida court system has a simple four-tier structure (see Exhibit 10.2a). The county

EXHIBIT 10.2B | LAW & CRIMINAL JUSTICE

Organization of the New York State Court System

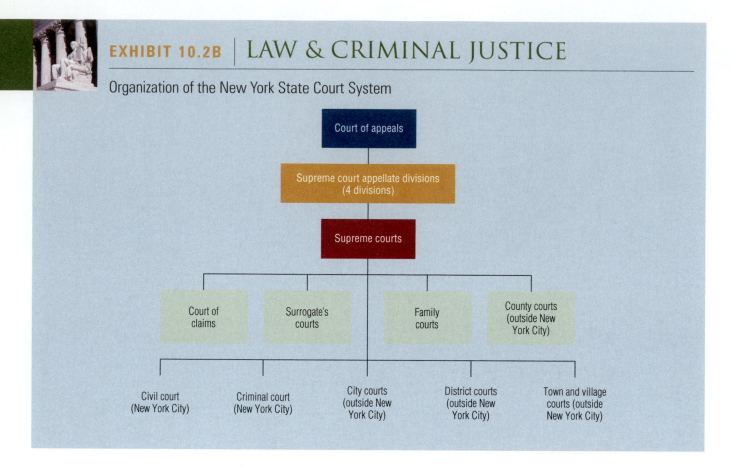

courts are the courts of limited jurisdiction and the circuit courts have general jurisdiction. The supreme court and the district courts of appeal are two levels of appellate jurisdiction. This structure can be contrasted with that of the New York State court system, which also has four tiers (see Exhibit 10.2b). The two lowermost levels are the courts of limited jurisdiction, which are geographically separate and have different functions. The supreme courts are the courts of general jurisdiction, and the upper courts, like those of Florida, are the appellate courts.

In the pages that follow, each level of the state court system is examined in more detail. The greatest amount of discussion will be about the lower courts, for it is there that most defendants begin judicial processing. The chief function of the trial court—the criminal trial—is addressed in Chapter 12.

Courts of Limited Jurisdiction

The lower criminal courts represent a stepchild of the American judicial system.

—H. TED RUBIN

The **courts of limited jurisdiction,** or *lower courts*—more than 13,000 across the nation—are the entry point for criminal judicial processing. They handle minor criminal offenses such as prostitution, drunkenness, petty larceny, disorderly conduct, and violations of traffic laws and city and county ordinances. In addition, courts of limited jurisdiction hear most civil cases and conduct inquests. For defendants charged with felonies, the lower courts have the authority to hold initial appearances and preliminary hearings and to make bail decisions.

In matters involving minor violations, the lower court conducts all aspects of the judicial process, from initial appearance to sentencing. Given the large number of felony cases that are initially processed in this part of the state court structure, the lower courts ultimately deal, in one way or another, with more than 90% of all criminal cases.

© The New Yorker Collection 1987 Arnie Levin from CartoonBank.com. All Rights Reserved.

Historically, the lower courts have been the most significant, yet typically the most neglected, of all the courts. The significance of these courts lies not only in the sheer number of defendants who pass through them but also in their jurisdiction over many of the offenses that represent the initial stage of an individual's criminal career. As pointed out some decades ago by the President's Commission on Law Enforcement and Administration of Justice, most convicted felons have prior misdemeanor convictions, and although the likelihood of diverting an offender from a career in crime is greatest at the time of his or her first brush with the law, the lower courts do not deal effectively with those who come before them.[3] Little has changed the observation made by the President's Commission.

In an address to the members of the New York Bar Association in 1919, Supreme Court Justice Charles Evans Hughes commented on the proper role of the lower courts:

> The Supreme Court of the United States and the Court of Appeals will take care of themselves. Look after the courts of the poor, who stand most in the need of justice. The security of the Republic will be found in the treatment of the poor and the ignorant; in indifference to their misery and helplessness lies disaster.[4]

Although Justice Hughes might have been better advised to make his reference not only to the poor but also to the millions of others who pass through the lower courts each year, his point was well intentioned and unquestionably correct. But in the decades that followed, there were few changes in the lower courts.

In the 1970s, the National Advisory Commission on Criminal Justice Standards and Goals echoed Hughes's impressions and outlined the three major problems that continued to plague the lower courts: (1) neglect by bar associations, higher courts, and government agencies; (2) the volume and nature of their caseloads; and (3) the **trial de novo** system.[5] By the 2000s, little had changed with respect to the operations of the lower courts.[6] However, there are some differences in the nature of these problems as they affect rural and urban courts.

Justice of the Peace Courts Justice of the peace courts, which are similar to alderman's and mayor's courts, developed at a time when a lack of effective transportation and communication tended to isolate small communities. The **justice of the peace** generally was not required to be an attorney and was best known as the person who performed marriages. The justice was either appointed or elected and usually had strong ties to the community. He or she heard cases involving violations of local ordinances, issued search and arrest warrants, set bail, arraigned defendants, and processed civil cases involving limited dollar amounts.[7] For a glimpse at the antics of a justice of the peace in the early American frontier, see Exhibit 10.3.

EXHIBIT 10.3 | *historical perspectives on crime and justice*

Justice of the Peace Roy Bean and the Law West of the Pecos

In history and folklore, Judge Roy Bean of the West Texas frontier is a familiar character. Books have been written about him, and the 1972 Warner Brothers production *The Life and Times of Judge Roy Bean* cast actor Paul Newman as the colorful seat of the rural bench. Although Bean was hardly a Paul Newman look-alike, he was a caricature and exaggeration of everything that could possibly be wrong with a rural magistrate, and his methods of distributing justice were indeed a satirical rendition of the justice of the peace court.

Born in the hills of Mason County, Kentucky, in 1825, Roy Bean's early life hardly reflected the qualities and experiences one would hope to find in a person charged with making decisions in the cause of justice. In 1847 he shot a man in a barroom brawl; several years later, he killed a Mexican army officer in a gun duel over a woman, after which he was hanged (but survived); during the Civil War he operated with Confederate irregulars, and following the war he was a blockade runner in San Antonio.

Bean's career in frontier justice began in 1882 when he drifted across the Pecos River into West Texas, dispensing whiskey from a tent. First at a place called Eagle's Nest on the Rio Grande, and later beside a railroad bed that ran through Dead Man's Canyon just north of the Mexican border, he plied his trade as a saloon keeper. His saloon was called the "Jersey Lilly," and the spot was Langtry, Texas—both named after actress Lily Langtry, whom Bean idolized but had never met.

The records of Pecos County, Texas, document that Roy Bean was appointed justice of the peace on August 2, 1882, by the County Commissioner's Court and that he fully qualified for the position by submitting a $1,000 bond on December 6, 1882.

As a rural magistrate, he dispensed both justice and beer from the same bar, frequently interrupting his court to serve liquor. He knew

Judge Roy Bean holds court in Langtry, Texas. The building functioned as both a courthouse and a saloon.

little of law and criminal procedure, and his methods of handling cases were often bizarre. Once he reportedly fined a dead man $40 for carrying a concealed weapon; on another occasion, he threatened to hang a lawyer for using profanity in the courtroom (the attorney had stated that he planned to *habeas corpus* his client). And in one memorable trial Judge Bean freed a man accused of murdering a Chinese railroad worker because he could not find any law that made it a crime "to kill a Chinaman."

Bean's antics became so widely known that passengers traveling through Langtry often stopped to look at the "Law West of the Pecos," as Judge Bean called himself. These visits sparked more tales, which encouraged Bean to hand down more of his infamous "decisions." In

The problems with this judicial system were, and in some places still are, numerous. First, not only did justices of the peace, referred to as "JPs," have minimal legal training but their "courtrooms" were often located where they worked—in saloons, filling stations, or other unusual settings. Second, methods of compensation were problematic. In some jurisdictions, the JP was compensated with a portion of the court costs paid by convicted defendants. Thus, it was in the justice's interest to convict as many people as possible.

In recent years, justice of the peace courts have been eliminated in some states and downgraded in others. However, some of the original difficulties still persist. For example, in 1927, in *Tumey* v. *Ohio,* the Supreme Court declared that the practice of compensating JPs from court costs paid by defendants only when they were convicted was unconstitutional;[8] nevertheless, this practice has persisted. Moreover, as recently as 1977 the U.S. Supreme Court invalidated a Georgia law that provided JPs with a fee for each search warrant they issued to the police.[9]

Low levels of legal training among magistrates and justices of the peace and the unusual nature of their court settings still endure in several jurisdictions. Indeed, in many areas formal legal training is not considered a prerequisite for dispensing justice. The Louisiana constitution provides that "Justices of the peace shall be of good moral character, freeholders and qualified electors, able to read and write the English language correctly, and shall possess such other qualifications as may be prescribed by

fact, he spent much of his time working on the diffusion of his own legend.

But the "Law West of the Pecos" was anything but just, for Bean was ignorant, biased, racist, and corrupt. He allowed his jurors (when he had them) to drink profusely before considering a verdict; he pocketed most of the fines he collected; he confiscated money and property from bodies brought to him in his role as coroner; he stuffed ballot boxes to ensure his reelection; and although he could hang a horse thief without batting an eye, when his friends were accused of murder, leniency always prevailed.

Besides his involvement—or lack of involvement—with law and order, Roy Bean spent much of his time worshipping Lilly Langtry. As legend tells it, his most precious moment came in the spring of 1888, when the woman whose tattered picture he carried in his pocket played in San Antonio. Free of alcoholic fumes and in a front-row seat, Bean watched the woman who had tortured his mind for years. But no one would introduce him to her, and sadly he returned to Langtry and his "Jersey Lilly," thinking only of a love he could never have.

For the next 8 years he continued his antics in frontier justice, until he finally overstepped his bounds. In 1896, after a count of votes cast for Bean proved their number to be well in excess of the Langtry population, he was removed from the bench. For the next 7 years, until his death in 1903, Bean continued as a saloon keeper, having failed to achieve his lifelong dream of meeting Miss Langtry. Ironically, only months after his death, she visited his saloon while on a tour through Texas. The Langtry townspeople gave Bean's revolver to Lilly, and she kept it until her own death in 1929. Today, Roy Bean's "Jersey Lilly" still stands, and Langtry remains a small town in Texas with a population of some 75 persons.

Actress Lily Langtry

Sources: Horace Bell, *On the Old West Coast* (New York: William Morrow, 1930); C. L. Sonnischen, *Roy Bean: Law West of the Pecos* (Old Greenwich, CN: Devin-Adair, 1943).

law."[10] By contrast, a few jurisdictions have upgraded their systems dramatically. In South Carolina, for example, 25 years ago JPs allegedly had only a high school education, and some had never opened a law book.[11] Currently, although magistrates still are not required to hold college or law degrees, they must pass a qualifying exam, attend a Magistrate Certification Program, and complete 12 hours of judicial legal training each year.[12]

The conditions that led to the development and growth of justice of the peace courts no longer exist. Modern means of transportation and communication have eliminated the total isolation of even the most remote rural outposts. But as long as JPs can convince the electorate and legislature that their closeness to the community and its interests is advantageous, the justice of the peace court will continue to exist. JP courts persist, for example, throughout Delaware, not only in rural areas but also in the densely populated metropolitan county of New Castle.

Alternatives to the JP courts in rural areas are the county courts and their variants, which lack the more negative characteristics of the justice of the peace system. As lower courts, they handle minor offenses, civil issues, and the pretrial aspects of felony processing. County justices usually have at least some legal training; the dispensing of justice occurs in more formal courts of law staffed by judges, clerks, and other personnel on state or county payrolls; and judges are paid salaries rather than fees for service.

Distribution of Cases Filed in Courts of General and Limited Jurisdiction

Source: Bureau of Justice Statistics.

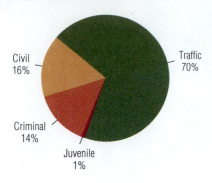

Civil 16%
Traffic 70%
Criminal 14%
Juvenile 1%

Too often, when our citizens seek a dignified place of deliberation in which to resolve their controversies, they find instead aesthetic revulsion. They bear witness—not to dignity, but to deterioration, not to actual justice delivered, but to the perception of justice denied or, worse, justice degraded.

— SOL WACHTLER,
FORMER CHIEF JUDGE,
NEW YORK STATE

Felony Defendants in Urban Areas, by Arrest Charge

Source: Bureau of Justice Statistics.

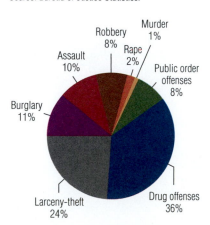

Murder 1%
Robbery 8%
Rape 2%
Assault 10%
Public order offenses 8%
Burglary 11%
Larceny-theft 24%
Drug offenses 36%

Municipal Courts The urban counterpart of the justice of the peace and county courts are municipal courts, also called *magistrate's courts.* In jurisdictions where the judicial system has formally separated the processing of criminal and civil cases, these lower courts may be known as *criminal courts* or *police courts.*

The functions of municipal courts are the same as those of county courts, and many of the problems are similar. But municipal courts have the added problems of large caseloads and assembly-line justice. In the face of heavy workloads, some magistrates exercise wide discretion—for instance, by ordering certain cases dismissed or by abbreviating the law. In addition, in cases involving lesser offenses such as prostitution, drunkenness, and loitering, groups of defendants are sometimes processed en masse.

During the early 1920s, legal scholars Roscoe Pound and Felix Frankfurter participated in an analysis of criminal justice administration in the city of Cleveland, sponsored by The Cleveland Foundation. Their report included a scathing denunciation of that midwestern city's municipal court, noting that it was devoid of any quality and commenting that it was not unlike an early-19th-century police court.[13] Some 50 years later, H. Ted Rubin, a former judge, returned to the Cleveland Municipal Court and described it as follows:

> The courtroom is well worn, crowded, and noisy. Row on row of benches are peopled with defendants out on bail, witnesses, friends and relatives of defendants, attorneys, social service personnel, and others. Most attorneys sit at the several counsel tables at the front of the room. The judge is flanked by a representative of the clerk's office to his right and two police officers. To his left is his bailiff. An assistant police prosecutor is present on one end of the judge's bench, an assistant county prosecutor on the other. A stenotype reporter . . . sits along the bar in front of the judge immediately next to the defendants and counsel who appear. The arraignments, hearings, and conferences which occur at the bench are largely inaudible beyond the second or third row of the spectator gallery. Witnesses generally testify from standing positions off to the side of the judge. There is little dignity to the setting. Jailed defendants are brought in and out from a door behind the judge and off to his right. People leaving the courtroom go out a door in the front of the room and off to the judge's left, where outside noise enters the courtroom as the door opens and closes.[14]

The situation in Cleveland might be considered mild when compared with that in New York City. The criminal court in Brooklyn, for example, is a court of limited jurisdiction that handles minor criminal offenses as well as pretrial processing of all felony cases. Observations by the author in this court from 1980 through 2005 revealed a chaotic system of justice. On one Monday morning in one particular courtroom that dealt almost exclusively with preliminary hearings and arraignments of felony cases, the rows of benches were packed with hundreds of spectators. Presumably, these were the families, friends, and acquaintances of the defendants, together with other interested parties, and possibly sightseers. Although many sat in a dignified manner, attempting to follow the proceedings, others conversed, ate, slept, played cards, read, or attended to other matters. Children played at their mothers' feet; an artist sketched the posture of the magistrate; and a college student studied a physics text.

The rumble of sound made it impossible to pay attention to the proceedings. Only those in the first few rows of the courtroom, which were reserved for attorneys, could hear the words of the judge, defendant, prosecutor, bailiff, and defense. Occasionally the court clerk had to remind the crowd that they were in a court of law and should be quiet.

Along the aisles, sides, and rear walls of the courtroom were dozens of police, as well as parole and probation officers. They complained that the docket was crowded again that day, that their case would not be heard for at least 3 hours: "There goes another day off," said one police officer.

Just beyond the rail that separated the bench from the spectators was a space reserved for the legal aid lawyers. It was a long table piled high with case materials. Court personnel huddled around the table to discuss cases during the proceedings, while defendants, parents, spouses, attorneys, police officers, and probation and parole officers hung over the rail to glance at the materials, plead their cases, or elicit information.

To the left of the magistrate's bench was a door that led to the detention pens where defendants awaited their turn. To the right of the bench, within the courtroom, was another holding area, where the faces of the accused were grim and their hands cuffed.

Actor Robert Blake entering a Los Angeles courthouse prior to his acquittal of murdering his wife.

Justice was swift and to the point. A preliminary hearing in a felony case took only 10 minutes, or 5, or 2. In one hearing, after the charges of robbery, assault, and possession of a deadly weapon had been read, the following exchange took place:

Judge:	Do you understand the charges as they have been read?
Defendant:	Yes, sir.
Judge:	How do you plead?
Defendant:	Not guilty, sir.
Judge:	Is the state's case ready?
Prosecutor:	Yes, your honor.
Judge:	Is the defense's case ready?
Attorney:	Yes, your honor.
Judge:	Bind him over for trial!

The entire proceeding lasted a total of 27 seconds.

Things seem to be no different across the East River in the Manhattan Criminal Court, where one juror recently commented, "The disgraceful physical conditions just fuel the general malevolence of sitting around waiting for something to happen."[15]

Similar styles of criminal processing may be observed in other urban courts around the United States. The basic problem stems from heavy caseloads, and the result is often cursory justice. Defendants may not be granted the full range of procedural safeguards and run the risk of conviction and sentence in situations in which constitutional guidelines may not be fully observed.

Major Trial Courts

The major *trial courts,* or **courts of general jurisdiction,** are authorized to try *all* criminal and civil cases. Such courts, of which there are more than 3,000 across the nation, handle about 10 percent of the defendants originally brought before the lower courts who are charged with felonies and serious misdemeanors (the balance having been disposed of at the lower-court level).

Trial courts may be called *circuit, district,* or *superior* courts or have numerous other titles. But there are some exceptions. For example, Indiana has both circuit courts and superior courts, and in Indianapolis the court is simply called "criminal court." While

Felony Defendants in Urban Areas, by Conviction Offense

Source: Bureau of Justice Statistics.

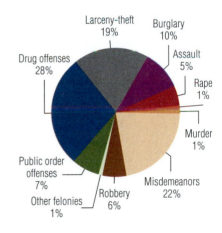

- Larceny-theft 19%
- Burglary 10%
- Assault 5%
- Rape 1%
- Murder 1%
- Misdemeanors 22%
- Robbery 6%
- Other felonies 1%
- Public order offenses 7%
- Drug offenses 28%

EXHIBIT 10.4 | LAW & CRIMINAL JUSTICE

Steps in the Criminal Court Process

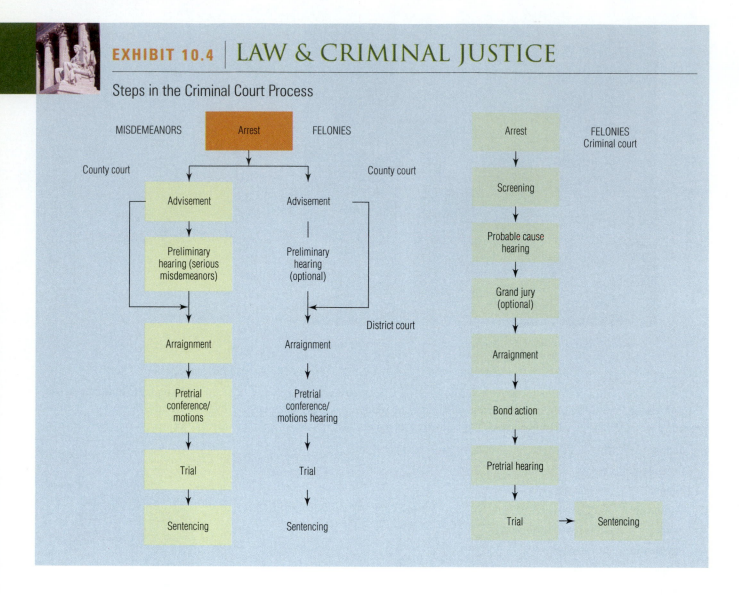

many county courts may be part of a state's lower-court system, as described earlier, other county courts may actually be circuit or district courts and hence are major trial courts. Also, a given county courthouse may often serve as both a lower court and a trial court. For example, when several counties are grouped together in a **judicial circuit,** it is customary for a judge to hold court in each county in turn. The judge moves from county to county within the circuit, and the local county courthouse becomes the circuit court during the judge's term there; the phrase "riding the circuit" is derived from this practice.[16]

The administration of criminal justice in major trial courts tends to be less problematic than it is in courts of limited jurisdiction. Judges are lawyers and members of the bar and hence are better equipped to deal with the complex issues of felony cases; most are salaried, full-time justices and are not tarnished by the fee-for-service payment structure. The adjudication process generally adheres to the principles of procedural criminal law and due process; and as courts of original jurisdiction, the trial courts are **courts of record,** which means that a full transcript of the proceedings is made for all cases. However, this does not mean that the trial courts are without difficulties. As will be seen in later chapters, there are procedural problems involving bail, indictment, plea negotiation, sentencing, and judicial discretion that can affect the fairness of trial court justice.

To understand more fully the separate roles and relationships between the lower and trial courts, consider the criminal case processing in Colorado's First Judicial Circuit (see Exhibit 10.4), which reflects what is typical throughout the nation. *All* cases involving felonies and misdemeanors begin in the lower court, called the county court in that jurisdiction. While the misdemeanor cases remain in the lower court through sentencing, felony processing shifts to the district court (the major trial court) at arraignment. This is in contrast to jurisdictions in which the *entire* felony process occurs in the trial court.

Appellate Courts

In law and criminal justice, the word *appeal* refers to review by a higher court of the judgment of a lower court. Thus, **appellate jurisdiction** is restricted to matters of appeal and review; an appellate court cannot try cases as can courts of general jurisdiction. However, this is not to say that the workload of these courts is light. Filings for appeal emerge not only from criminal cases but from civil matters as well. (In fact, the majority of appeals come out of civil suits. In the area of domestic relations alone, for example, the number of appeals requesting reviews of decisions rendered in matters of child custody rights, dependent support, alimony, and property settlement runs into the tens of thousands.) And if an attorney complies with the court's rules for appealing a case, the court must hear it.*

As a result, there are *intermediate courts of appeal* in more than half the states. These courts serve to relieve the state's highest court from hearing every case. An unfavorable decision from an intermediate appeals court, however, does not automatically guarantee a hearing by the state supreme court, the court of last resort in each state. The state supreme court has the power to choose which cases will be placed on its docket—a characteristic of the highest court in every jurisdiction.

Reform and Unification of State Courts

The state courts have many problems. Prominent among these are problems of organization, structure, and deployment.

For most of the 20th century and into the 21st century, various federal, state, and city commissions and foundations have examined the state courts, and their recommendations for reorganization have remained unchanged through the years:

- Unify felony and misdemeanor courts.
- Create single, unified state court systems.
- Centralize administrative responsibility.
- Abolish the justice of the peace courts.
- Increase the numbers of judicial personnel.
- Improve physical facilities.

Perhaps the most pressing issue in this regard is court unification. A concise description of what is needed was provided by the National Advisory Commission on Criminal Justice Standards and Goals three decades ago:

> State courts should be organized into a unified judicial system financed by the State and administered through a statewide court administrator or administrative judge under the supervision of the chief justice of the State supreme court.
>
> All trial courts should be unified into a single trial court with general criminal as well as civil jurisdiction. Criminal jurisdiction now in courts of limited jurisdiction should be placed in these unified trial courts of general jurisdiction, with the exception of certain traffic violations. The state supreme court should promulgate rules for the conduct of minor as well as major criminal prosecutions.
>
> All judicial functions in the trial courts should be performed by full-time judges. All judges should possess law degrees and be members of the bar.
>
> A transcription or other record of the pretrial court proceedings and the trial should be kept in all criminal cases.
>
> The appeal procedure should be the same for all cases.[17]

These recommendations remain valid today; however, court unification is more easily recommended than implemented. Some unification has occurred in Arizona,

---

*This assumes that the matter is appealable, an issue that is discussed in Chapter 13.

Cabell County courthouse in Huntington, West Virginia.

Illinois, North Carolina, Oklahoma, and Washington, and each year other states consider proposals for a unified system. But because of political, philosophical, and pragmatic obstacles, few such proposals have been adopted. Local governments wish to retain control of their local courts; some judges fear that they would lose their status and discretion; judges who are not lawyers fear that they would lose their jobs; political parties fear a loss of patronage opportunities; local municipalities fear the loss of revenues derived from court fines and fees; and many lawyers, judges, and prosecutors in all jurisdictions are simply resistant to change.[18]

The problem of overloaded court dockets is even more pervasive, for the costs that would be involved in expanding staff and facilities are well beyond the resources of most jurisdictions. Further, it seems that the overload is getting worse, largely as a result of the proliferation of drug abuse and drug-related crime and the increased police activity in drug-ridden neighborhoods. The overall result is greater numbers of drug cases on court dockets across the nation. One response has been the establishment of special "drug courts," which now are operational in more than 900 state and local jurisdictions (see Exhibit 10.5).

The Federal Judiciary

The judicial power of the United States shall be vested in one Supreme Court, and in such inferior courts as the Congress may from time to time ordain and establish.

— THE CONSTITUTION OF THE UNITED STATES

Unlike the state court systems, the federal judiciary has a unified structure with jurisdiction throughout the United States and its territories. But the federal court system is also complex. It has a four-tier structure similar to that found in most of the states (see Exhibit 10.6). Although it handles fewer cases than state court systems do, its scope is considerably greater. It is responsible for the enforcement of the following:

1. All federal codes (criminal, civil, and administrative) in all 50 states, U.S. territories, and the District of Columbia
2. Local codes and ordinances in the territories of Guam, the Virgin Islands, and the Northern Mariana Islands

In addition, the U.S. Supreme Court has ultimate appellate jurisdiction over the federal appeals courts, the state courts of appeal, the District of Columbia court of appeals, and the Supreme Court of Puerto Rico.

U.S. Commissioner's Courts and U.S. Magistrate's Courts

Historically, U.S. commissioners occupied positions comparable to that of justice of the peace in the state court systems. Established by an act of Congress at the beginning of the 20th century, commissioners had the authority to issue search and arrest warrants, arraign defendants, set bail, hold preliminary hearings, and try cases involving petty offenses on certain federal reservations. Many of the criticisms leveled at the justice of the peace system, however, were also applicable to the U.S. commissioner's courts. In 1967, the President's Commission on Law Enforcement and Administration of Justice found that 30 percent of the more than 700 commissioners were not lawyers, that all but seven had outside employment because of the part-time nature of the work, that commissioners' private businesses often took precedence over their official duties, and that the number of commissioners in many districts had no relation to the number that might be needed. The commission concluded by recommending that the system either be abolished or drastically altered.[19]

On the basis of the commission's findings, together with an examination of the situation by the Senate Judiciary Committee, Congress passed the federal Magistrate's Act in 1968. The act provided for a 3-year phasing out of the office of the U.S. commissioner. It also established **U.S. magistrates**—lawyers whose powers are limited to trying lesser misdemeanors, setting bail in more serious cases, and assisting the district

Crimes Referred by the FBI to the Federal Courts

Source: General Accounting Office.

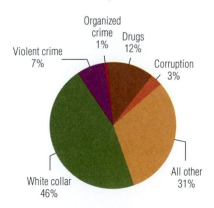

Organized crime 1%
Drugs 12%
Violent crime 7%
Corruption 3%
White collar 46%
All other 31%

drugs, crime, and justice | EXHIBIT 10.5

The Drug Courts Movement

The label "drug court" is actually a generic term for several different kinds of initiatives designed to cope with the growing number of drug cases. These approaches include special courts or judges, distinctive case management systems, and/or pretrial diversion programs. Many of these new entities function as traditional courts by hearing evidence and adjudicating guilt, while others serve as special "plea bargaining" forums. Many handle only first offenders, with others having no such limitations.

Drug courts vary throughout the country, but most fit within three models: dedicated drug treatment, speedy trial and differentiated case management, or a combination of the two.

Dedicated Drug Treatment Courts

Courts that have adopted the dedicated drug treatment model use court-monitored drug treatment under a deferred prosecution or deferred sentencing arrangement. Arrestees are given the opportunity for treatment, and their progress is closely monitored through urinalysis and reports from the treatment program. Negative behavior can result in short periods of jail confinement, but court personnel recognize that relapse to drug use is often part of the recovery process. As such, drug court clients are given several chances to prove themselves. Positive behaviors are rewarded with decreased reporting requirements, and successful completion may result in the charges being dropped or a lesser sentence being imposed. The goals of these courts are (1) to concentrate drug case expertise in one courtroom, (2) to link defendants to community-based drug treatment, (3) to address other defendant needs through effective case management, (4) to reduce drug use and recidivism, (5) to relieve pressures on nondrug caseloads, and (6) to increase overall trial capacity.

Speedy Trial and Differentiated Case Management Courts

Courts set up for speedy trials and differentiated case management bring all felony (and sometimes misdemeanor) drug charges together into one courtroom. Multiple charges against defendants are combined into single hearings, with consistent and firm dates for plea ne-

gotiations, trials, and filing motions set by the judge. Prosecutors, defense attorneys, and judges work together within consistent guidelines to resolve cases quickly through pleas, bypassing jury trials when possible. The goals of these courts are (1) to concentrate drug case expertise in one courtroom, (2) to reduce the time to disposition, without compromising due process or public safety considerations, (3) to reduce the pending drug felony caseload, (4) to relieve pressures on nondrug caseloads by diverting drug felonies out of mixed-calendar courtrooms, and (5) to increase overall trial capacity. In most instances, these courts hear only drug felony cases.

Effectiveness of Drug Courts

Several benefits of drug courts have been identified. First, judges, prosecutors, and public defenders assigned to drug courtrooms become specialists and therefore are able to process cases more quickly and efficiently. Second, new rules for courtrooms—such as early and complete discovery and firm trial dates—encourage early plea negotiation and settlement. Third, segregating drug cases can speed the processing of both drug and nondrug cases. And fourth, the nature of law enforcement results in large numbers of relatively standardized cases—therefore, it reduces the likelihood that defendants will seek a trial and streamlines the case preparation and investigation process for prosecutors.

Data from a number of evaluation studies suggest that drug courts provide an effective alternative to incarceration by reducing recidivism and easing population pressures in overcrowded jails. As a result, the number of drug courts has expanded from one in 1989 to almost 400 by 1997, to over 2000 by the end of 2005.

Sources: James A. Inciardi, Duane C. McBride, and James E. Rivers, *Drug Control and the Courts* (Newbury Park, CA: Sage Publications, 1996); Roger H. Peters and Mary R. Murrin, "Effectiveness of Treatment-Based Drug Courts in Reducing Recidivism," *Criminal Justice and Behavior* 20 (February 2000): 72–96; Barry R. McCaffrey, "Drug Abuse and the Criminal Justice System: Saving Lives and Preventing Crime Through Treatment," *Connection,* Academy for Health Sciences Research and Health Policy, August 2000, 1–2; General Accounting Office, *Adult Drug Courts: Evidence Indicates Recidivism Reductions and Mixed Results for Other Outcomes* (Washington DC: U.S. Government Printing Office, February 28, 2005).

courts in various legal matters. In 1976, their authority was expanded to include the issuance of search and arrest warrants, the review of civil rights and *habeas corpus* petitions, and the conduct of pretrial conferences in both civil and criminal hearings.[20] Magistrates can be either full-time or part-time jurists and all are appointed by the federal district court judges.

U.S. District Courts

The sword of human justice is about to fall upon your guilty head.

—ISAAC C. PARKER, FEDERAL DISTRICT COURT JUDGE, 1876

The U.S. district courts were created by the federal Judiciary Act, which was passed by Congress on September 24, 1789. Originally there were 13 courts, one for each of the original states, but now there are 94—with 89 distributed throughout the 50 states,

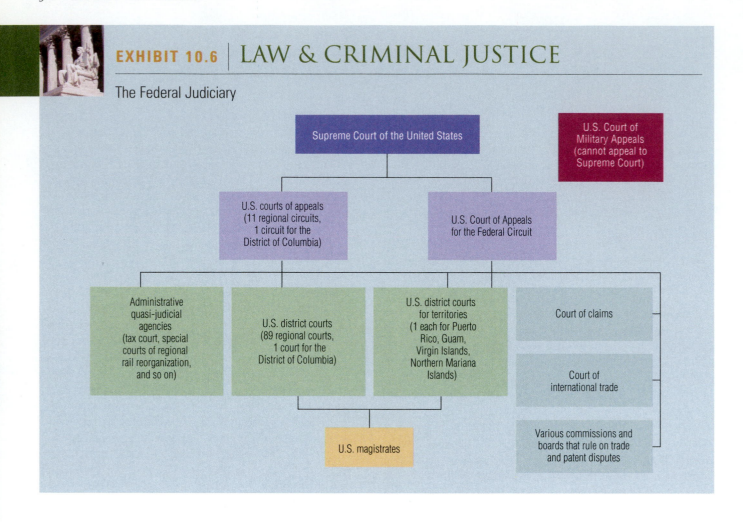

EXHIBIT 10.6 | LAW & CRIMINAL JUSTICE

The Federal Judiciary

U.S. District Courts Criminal Filings, 1980–2004

Source: Administrative Office of the U.S. Courts.

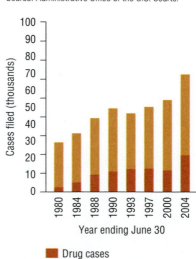

Year ending June 30

- Drug cases
- All other

and 1 each in the District of Columbia, Puerto Rico, Guam, the Virgin Islands, and the Northern Mariana Islands.

The **U.S. district courts** are the trial courts of the federal system and the District of Columbia—the courts of general jurisdiction. They have jurisdiction over cases involving violations of federal laws, including bank robbery, civil rights abuses, mail fraud, counterfeiting, smuggling, kidnapping, and crimes involving transportation across state lines. The district courts try cases that involve compromises of national security, such as treason, sedition, and espionage; selective service violations, copyright infringements, and jurisdictional disputes; and violations of regulatory codes such as the Securities and Exchange Acts, the Endangered Species Acts, the Meat and Poultry Inspection Acts, and the Foreign Agent Registration Act, among many others. In addition, district court caseloads include numerous civil actions and petitions filed by state and federal prisoners.

At present there are 94 district courts. Each has one or more judges, depending on the caseload, with a total of 655 judgeships authorized by law. In most cases, a single judge presides over trials, and a defendant may request that a jury be present. In complex civil matters, a three-judge panel may be convened. In addition to U.S. magistrates, each court has numerous other officers attached to it: a U.S. attorney, who serves as the criminal prosecutor for the federal government; several assistant U.S. attorneys; a U.S. marshal's office; and probation officers, court reporters, clerks, and bankruptcy judges.

Since the 1980s, the district courts have had to function under near-crisis conditions. The workload increased dramatically, from 122,624 cases in 1970 to more than 332,000 by the end of 2004. The level of criminal cases has increased in recent years to over 70,000 in 2004, dealing with everything from traffic offenses to significant vi-

Lincoln County courthouse in Lincoln, Kansas.

olations of the U.S. Criminal Code—the number of district court judges has not been expanded in proportion to the workload. In 1970, there were 649 judgeships, but with an average load of 370 cases. In 2005, there were still 655 judgeships, but with average loads of well over 400 cases. Moreover, more than 10% of these judgeships were vacant.[21]

To keep pace with the workload, hundreds of new judges would have to be hired, and it is unlikely that there are many highly qualified attorneys in the United States who would be willing to work for the salary offered. In 2005, district court judges were earning just under $175,000.[22] Although this is no trifling salary when compared with the average national income, it is well below that of other people in the legal profession with similar credentials and experience. Yet by contrast, district court judges are already among the highest-paid officials in the federal government, and if their salaries were raised significantly, many other federal salaries would have to be raised as well. The public, increasingly disenchanted with high levels of government spending, probably would not stand for it.

In recent years there have been growing jurisdictional conflicts between state trial courts and federal district courts. Since the beginning of the 1990s, moreover, there have been a number of high-profile cases that could have been, and in some instances were, tried in both federal and state courts. The LAPD police officers who brutalized motorist Rodney King were largely exonerated in state court but were tried again in federal court on charges of civil rights violations, where they fared poorly. More generally, the expanding federal role in criminal prosecution (especially in drug cases) means that criminal behavior, which formerly was almost exclusively the province of state courts, is now a concern of federal district courts as well. It is difficult to predict how this jurisdictional dilemma will be resolved. In 2000, however, the U.S. Supreme Court weighed in on the issue when it ruled on the constitutionality of the Violence Against Women Act (see Exhibit 10.7).

U.S. Courts of Appeals

Appeals from the U.S. district courts move up to the next step in the federal judicial hierarchy, the **U.S. courts of appeals.** There are 13 of these courts, with more than 179 authorized judgeships. Each court is located in a *circuit*—described earlier as a specific judicial jurisdiction served by the court, as defined by geographical boundaries. For example, the U.S. Court of Appeals for the First Circuit is located in Boston and serves the district courts located in Maine, Massachusetts, New Hampshire, Rhode Island, and Puerto Rico (see Exhibit 10.8).

**U.S. Courts of Appeals
Filings, 1980–2004**

Source: The Administrative Office of the U.S. Courts.

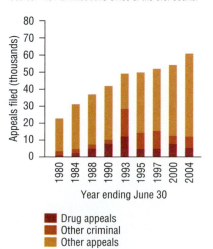

Drug appeals
Other criminal
Other appeals

EXHIBIT 10.7 | VICTIMS & JUSTICE

United States v. *Morrison* and the Violence Against Women Act

The issues in *United States* v. *Morrison* date back to 1994, when in the fall semester of that year, Christy Brzonkala enrolled at Virginia Polytechnic Institute (Virginia Tech). Some weeks later, she met Antonio Morrison and James Crawford, both of whom were students at Virginia Tech and members of the school's varsity football team. Brzonkala claimed that, within 30 minutes of meeting Morrison and Crawford at a party, they assaulted and repeatedly raped her. After the attack, Morrison allegedly told Brzonkala, "You better not have any . . . diseases." During the months that followed, Morrison allegedly announced in his dormitory's dining room that he "liked to get girls drunk and . . ." (Morrison's comments, quoted verbatim in Supreme Court briefs, consisted of boasting, as well as vulgar remarks about what he would do to women.)

Christy Brzonkala alleged that the attack so devastated her that she became severely depressed. She sought assistance from a university psychiatrist, who prescribed antidepressant medication. As a result of the depression, she stopped attending classes and withdrew from the university. She indicated that she was so despondent and humiliated by the crime that she did not go to the authorities until 1995, then filing a complaint against Morrison and Crawford under Virginia Tech's sexual assault policy. During the school's hearing on her complaint, Crawford was exonerated, but Morrison admitted having sexual contact with her despite the fact that she had twice told him "no." Although Morrison was found guilty of sexual assault and was sentenced to immediate suspension for two semesters, he challenged his conviction. A subsequent hearing at Virginia Tech found him guilty only of "using abusive language," and his punishment was set aside. Moreover, a local grand jury refused to indict the two players on any criminal charges.

It was at that point that Brzonkala filed an $8.3 million suit against Morrison and Crawford under the 1994 Violence Against Women Act. The intent of the act was to give women the alternative of filing civil lawsuits against their attackers, regardless of the status of any criminal prosecution. Brzonkala contended that because she subsequently dropped out of college, she had suffered the economic consequence of a lesser education and diminished employment opportunities. Ultimately, the case reached the U.S. Supreme Court.

The legal questions before the Supreme Court were whether the Violence Against Women Act was valid under either the interstate commerce clause of the Constitution or the Fourteenth Amendment. The commerce clause is a provision that gives Congress exclusive powers over interstate commerce. Found in Article I, Section 8, this power is the basis for a considerable amount of federal legislation and regulation. Congress frequently uses the commerce clause to outlaw activities that do social harm. The rationale for the 1964 Civil Rights Act, for example, was that discrimination hurts the economy. Title VII of the Civil Rights Act, which bars employment discrimination, has clear economic consequences because it prevents people from finding work and keeping their jobs. The Violence Against Women Act maintains that violence against women has an adverse impact on interstate commerce by reducing women's capacity to produce goods and services used nationwide, stymieing their travel because of safety concerns. The Fourteenth Amendment issue focused on whether the Violence Against Women Act upheld Americans' right to "equal protection" under the law.

When the High Court delivered its opinion in *United States* v. *Morrison* in 2000, the decision had little to do with rape allegations. At the center of the Court's 5-to-4 ruling was the constitutional justifications Congress employed in passing the Violence Against Women Act. The High Court ruled against Christy Brzonkala's attempt to sue in federal court. The Court concluded that the Violence Against Women Act improperly interfered with the sovereignty of state laws on rape. The link between violence against women, including rape victimization, was not compelling to the justices. The Court also rejected the equal protection argument on grounds that the purpose of the Fourteenth Amendment was to protect against governmental discrimination, not that by individuals.

Source: *United States* v. *Morrison,* 120 S.Ct. 1740 (2000).

The 13 courts of appeals hear almost 90,000 cases each year involving both criminal and civil matters.[23] These cases are appealed from the U.S. district courts—*not* from state supreme courts or appeals courts. Almost all are heard by three-judge panels; a few are heard *en banc,* or "in bank," meaning that the full bench of judges authorized for the court considers the appeal. In only three types of situations can a case appealed from one of the district courts bypass the court of appeals and go directly to the U.S. Supreme Court:

1. When the ruling under appeal was decided by a special three-judge district court hearing.
2. When the case involves a federal statute that was declared unconstitutional by a district court, and the United States is a litigant.
3. When the issue under review is considered so important that it requires immediate settlement.

LAW & CRIMINAL JUSTICE | EXHIBIT 10.8

The 13 Federal Judiciary Circuits

The U.S. Supreme Court

The **U.S. Supreme Court** is the highest court in the nation. It stands at the apex of the federal judiciary and is truly the court of last resort. The Supreme Court is composed of nine justices: one chief justice and eight associate justices, who serve for life. They are nominated by the president of the United States, and their appointments must be confirmed by the Senate. The vast majority of these justices have been white, male, and Protestant.

The Origins of the Supreme Court The Supreme Court was provided for by the Constitution, but only in the briefest of terms. Article III placed the judicial power of the United States in a supreme court and inferior federal courts: Section 1 of the article noted that the justices would retain their posts during "good behavior," and Section 2 outlined the range of judicial power. In contrast to Articles I and II of the Constitution, which spell out in considerable detail the powers and prerogatives of Congress and the executive branch, Article III provides no more than a terse outline of the nature and responsibilities of the nation's highest court. Moreover, the Court had a slow start.

On September 24, 1789, President George Washington signed into law the Judiciary Act, which actually created the Supreme Court, and sent to the Senate for confirmation the names of the first chief justice and five associate justices. However, one of these declined the nomination, another accepted but never attended, and three others either resigned or died before the close of the Court's first decade. John Jay of New York, the first chief justice, spent much of his tenure abroad and resigned in 1795. Two other men followed him as chief justice within 10 years—John Rutledge of South Carolina in 1795 and John Marshall of Virginia in 1801.

Only three of the six justices were present for the Court's opening session on February 1, 1790, but there was no business other than the appointment of a clerk.

EXHIBIT 10.9 | *historical perspectives on crime and justice*

John Marshall, Chief Justice of the U.S. Supreme Court (1801–1835)

The first of 15 children, John Marshall was born on the Virginia frontier on September 24, 1755. His father was surveyor for George Washington and a member of the Virginia House of Burgesses, and his mother was the daughter of an educated Scottish clergyman.

As a youth, Marshall had minimal formal education and saw little of the world beyond his rural countryside.

During the Revolutionary War, young Marshall was first a member of the Virginia Minutemen, and in 1776 he joined the continental Army. He served in the battles of Brandywine, Stony Point, and Valley Forge, leaving the military in 1781 with the rank of captain.

In law, Marshall was primarily self-taught. His father had introduced him to *Blackstone's Commentaries,* but his only formal instruction in this area was a month-long course of law lectures at the College of William and Mary in 1780. While still a member of the Continental Army, he was admitted to the bar at age 25. Over the years he developed a lucrative law practice, specializing in defending his fellow Virginians against their pre-Revolutionary War British creditors.

Marshall's public career began when he was elected to the Virginia House of Delegates in 1782. In 1787, he was instrumental in the ratification of the new U.S. Constitution. At the national level, he was a member of the U.S. House of Representatives for a brief period and was secretary of state under President John Adams.

As chief justice of the United States from 1801 through 1835, John Marshall emerged as the primary founder of the American system of constitutional law. He participated in more than 1,000 Supreme Court decisions and presided over the treason trial of Aaron Burr in the Richmond Circuit Court.

When Marshall died in 1835 at the age of 79, the nation mourned his passing. And as the Liberty Bell tolled at his funeral procession through the streets of Philadelphia, it cracked severely—an event that American folklore has mistakenly attached to Independence Day 1776.

In fact, no judicial decisions were made during the Court's first 3 years, and in 1792 Chief Justice John Jay reportedly described the post of a Supreme Court justice as "intolerable."[24]

Although the early terms of the Court saw few significant decisions, the justices themselves were kept busy. When the Judiciary Act of 1789 created the Supreme Court and the 13 district courts, it also established three judicial circuits, each composed of the geographical areas covered by several of the district courts. Within each of the circuits, circuit court sessions were held twice a year to handle some of the more serious federal cases. But the Judiciary Act had not provided for judges for the federal circuit courts. Thus, the chief justice and the five associate justices were required to travel throughout the country to hold circuit court where and when necessary, a situation that lasted for almost a century.

> The people can change Congress, but only God can change the Supreme Court.
>
> — THE LATE GEORGE NORRIS,
> U.S. SENATOR FROM NEBRASKA

Marbury* v. *Madison   The Supreme Court's power became fully established during the early decades of the 19th century under the leadership of John Marshall, who served as chief justice from 1801 through 1835 (see Exhibit 10.9). In 1803, just 2 years after Marshall assumed his post, the Court announced its decision in ***Marbury* v. *Madison*,**[25] and in so doing it claimed, exercised, and justified its authority to review and nullify acts of Congress that it found to conflict with the Constitution.

Marbury v. *Madison* involved a dispute over presidential patronage that had escalated into a contest for authority between Congress and the Supreme Court. The case emerged from the bitter presidential election of 1800, in which Democratic-Republican Thomas Jefferson defeated Federalist John Adams. Unwilling to relinquish the power they had held since the beginning of the Union, the Federalists sought to entrench themselves in the federal judiciary. John Marshall's appointment to the Supreme Court had been part of that effort. In addition, just before Adams left office, Congress approved legislation creating 16 new district court judgeships. It also authorized Adams to appoint as many justices of the peace for the newly created District of Columbia as he deemed necessary, and it reduced the number of Supreme Court justices from six to five at the next vacancy. This latter move was intended to deprive Jefferson of an opportunity to appoint a new justice.

Adams nominated, and Congress confirmed, the 16 district court judges and 42 justices of the peace. On his last night in office, he signed the commissions for the new justices of the peace and had them taken to Marshall, then secretary of state, who was to affix the Great Seal of the United States and deliver them to the appointees. The Seal was affixed, but not all of the commissions were delivered before Jefferson took office.

William Marbury, an aide to the secretary of the navy, was one of four men who did not receive their commissions. At President Jefferson's request, Secretary of State James Madison refused delivery of the commissions. Marbury asked the Supreme Court to issue a writ of *mandamus* ordering Madison to give the four men their commissions. A **writ of** *mandamus* is simply a command to perform a certain duty, and the Judiciary Act of 1789 had authorized the Supreme Court to issue such writs to officers of the federal government.

Chief Justice Marshall found himself in a dilemma, with the authority of the Supreme Court at stake. If the Court ordered that the commission be delivered, Madison could refuse to obey the order, which seemed likely, and the Court had no means to enforce compliance. If the Court did not issue the writ, it would mean surrendering to President Jefferson's point of view. Either way, the Court would be conceding its power.

In what has been called a "masterwork of indirection, a brilliant example of Marshall's capacity to sidestep danger while seeming to court it, to advance in one direction while his opponents are looking in the other,"[26] the chief justice made a cunning decision. First, he ruled that once the president had signed the commissions and the secretary of state had recorded them, the appointments were complete and valid. Second, he ruled that a writ of *mandamus* was the proper tool to require the new secretary of state to deliver the commissions. These actions served to rebuke Madison, and Jefferson by implication. Marshall then turned to the question of jurisdiction, to whether the Supreme Court had the authority to issue the writ. He concluded that it did not. Marshall stated that Congress could not expand or contract the jurisdiction of the Supreme Court and that Congress had acted unconstitutionally, exceeding its power when, in Section 13 of the Judiciary Act of 1789, it authorized the Court to issue such writs in original cases ordering federal officials to perform particular acts.

Although this matter of jurisdiction served to absolve the Jefferson administration of responsibility for installing several of President Adams's appointees, the real significance of *Marbury* v. *Madison* was the establishment of the Court's power to review acts of Congress. The *Marbury* decision is therefore considered by many to have been the most important ruling in Supreme Court history.

The Jurisdictional Scope of the Supreme Court
In the words of the Constitution, the Supreme Court's jurisdiction is broad but not limitless. As stated in Article III, Section 2:

> The judicial power shall extend to all cases, in law and equity, arising under this Constitution, the laws of the United States, and treaties made, or which shall be made, under their authority; to all cases affecting ambassadors, other public ministers and consuls; to all cases of admiralty and maritime jurisdiction; to controversies to which the United States shall be a party; to controversies between two or more States; between a State and citizens of another State; between citizens of the same State claiming lands under grants of different States, and between a State, or the citizens thereof, and foreign States, citizens or subjects.

Thus, the Constitution outlined eight jurisdictional areas for the Supreme Court, but its main function was to serve as guardian of the Constitution.

As defined by the Constitution and spelled out in the Judiciary Act of 1789, the Supreme Court has two kinds of jurisdiction over cases—general and appellate. The Court's general jurisdiction usually involves suits between two states, issues that test the constitutionality of state laws, and matters relating to ambassadors. In such instances, the Supreme Court can serve as a trial court. In its appellate jurisdiction, the Court resolves conflicts that raise "substantial federal questions," typically questions related to the constitutionality of some lower-court rule, decision, or procedure.

The Supreme Court in session in the 1930s. This photograph, by Dr. Erich Salomon, is believed to be the only one ever taken while the justices were actually hearing a case.

Selection of Cases As the final tribunal beyond which no judicial appeal is possible, the Supreme Court has the discretion to decide which cases it will review. However, the Court *must* review cases in the following instances:

- When a federal court has held an act of Congress to be unconstitutional.
- When a U.S. court of appeals has found a state statute to be unconstitutional.
- When a state's highest court of appeals has ruled a federal law to be invalid.
- When an individual's challenge to a state statute on federal constitutional grounds has been upheld by a state supreme court.

In all other instances, as provided by the Judiciary Act of 1925, the Supreme Court decides whether or not it will review a particular case.

The Supreme Court does not have the authority to review all decisions of state courts in either civil or criminal matters. Its jurisdiction extends only to cases in which a federal statute has been interpreted or a defendant's constitutional right has allegedly been violated. Moreover, a petitioner must exhaust all other remedies before the High Court will consider reviewing his or her case (see Exhibit 10.10). That is, should a matter of "substantial federal question" emerge in a justice of the peace court, for example, the first review would not be in the Supreme Court. Rather, it would be heard as a trial *de novo* in the state trial court. Following that would be an appeal to the intermediate court of appeals (in states where they exist), and then an appeal to the state's highest court. Only then would the case be eligible for review by the Supreme Court. A similar process occurs with respect to the federal court structure.

The Supreme Court's authority to decide which cases it will hear is known as its *certiorari* power and comes from the **writ of *certiorari*,** a writ of review issued by the Court ordering a lower court to "forward up the record" of a case it has tried so that the Supreme Court can review it.

Prior to this granting of *certiorari,* the potential case must pass the **Rule of Four;** that is, a case is accepted for review only if four or more justices feel that it merits consideration by the full Court.

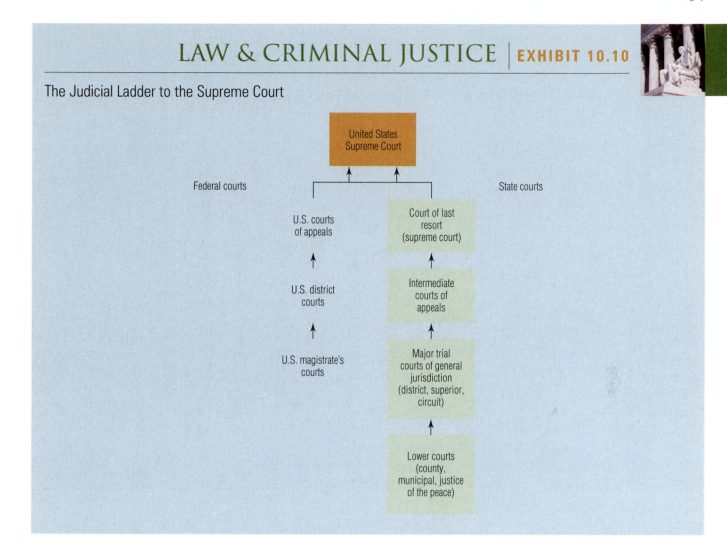

LAW & CRIMINAL JUSTICE | EXHIBIT 10.10

The Judicial Ladder to the Supreme Court

The Supreme Court accepts for review only cases in which its decision might make a difference to the appellant and, as stated earlier, only those involving a "substantial federal question." It does not operate as a court of last resort to correct the endless number of possible errors made by other courts. Rather, it reserves its time and energy for the most pressing matters. Currently, between 8,000 and 9,000 cases are filed annually for review by the Supreme Court. However, the Court limits itself to deciding less than 100 cases with full opinions each term.

Affirming, Reversing, and Remanding When the Supreme Court affirms a case, it has determined that the action or proceeding under review is free from reversible prejudicial or constitutional error and that the judgment appealed from the lower court shall stand. Thus, if a conviction appealed from a lower court is *affirmed*, the conviction remains in force.

A Supreme Court decision that *reverses* or overturns a defendant's conviction or sentence does not necessarily free the appellant or impose a lighter penalty. Rather, it *remands* or returns the case to the court of original jurisdiction for a proper judgment. At that point the trial court has several options, depending on the nature of the case. For instance, many of the criminal cases heard by the Supreme Court revolve around the constitutional issues of illegal search and seizure, illegal confessions, and other matters that might invoke the exclusionary rule. In such instances, the court of original jurisdiction can order a new trial but cannot introduce the "tainted" evidence. In many of these cases, however, the prosecution may decide that without such evidence the state would have a weak case, and so it dismisses the charges. In other circumstances,

"Can you name all nine Supreme Court justices?"

© The New Yorker Collection 1967 Dana Fradon from cartoonbank.com. All Rights Reserved.

EXHIBIT 10.11 | LAW & CRIMINAL JUSTICE

Supreme Court Caseloads, 1930–2004

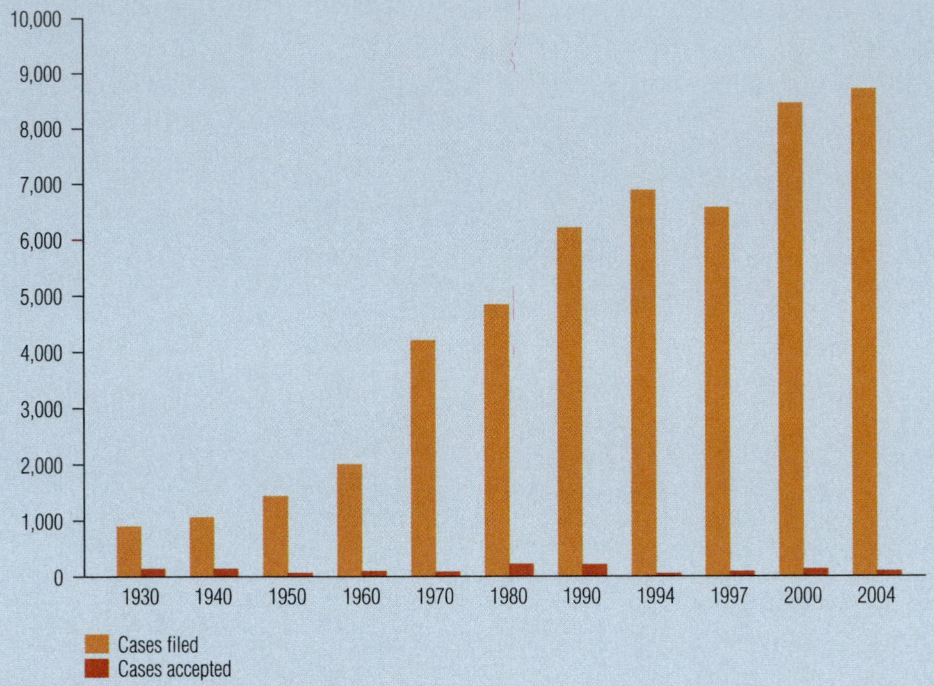

Cases filed
Cases accepted

Source: Supreme Court of the United States, Office of the Clerk.

Not a single law firm in the entire city of New York bid for my employment.

— RUTH BADER GINSBURG,
107TH JUSTICE OF THE
U.S. SUPREME COURT

the Supreme Court's decision may require a *change of venue* because of pretrial publicity or community hostility that resulted in an unfair trial. Any new trial must be held in a different county or judicial district. Other Supreme Court reversals have ordered institutional authorities to remedy unconstitutional conditions of incarceration and have required trial courts to resentence certain defendants on the ground that the original sentences constituted cruel and unusual punishment.

The Supreme Court's Growing Workload When the first Supreme Court convened in 1790, its role as guardian of the Constitution was newly conceived. At the same time, the country itself was new, with 13 states and fewer than 4 million citizens. The work of the Court in those early days was simple. In its first 3 years it decided no cases, and during the next 2 years it ruled on only four matters.

As the United States grew in size, complexity, and maturity, and greater emphasis was placed on due process, human rights, and civil liberties, more and more cases began to work their way up through the appellate system (see Exhibit 10.11). Although the number of justices had increased by 50%, from six to nine, in the more than two centuries since the Court's inception, the population the Court was serving had expanded by some 265 million—an increase of more than 6,000%.

During the term ending in the summer of 2005, the Court received almost 9,000 petitions. With so many appeals, the justices have been forced to rely more and more on their clerks to review cases, and a greater number of cases have been decided without written opinions. Moreover, the Court has had to become more selective in the cases it chooses to hear; or, as Erwin N. Griswold, former dean of Harvard Law School, stated a number of years ago, the justices have been forced into "rationing justice"—ruling in only a smattering of cases, while leaving citizens without guidance on numerous questions.[27]

CAREERS IN CRIMINAL JUSTICE

Legal Studies at the Undergraduate Level

Law is fundamental to many philosophic, social and behavioral science, and public policy issues and inquiries. Many occupations require some understanding of law, and many students whose career objectives do not include the legal professions nevertheless desire some comprehension of what law is all about.

For students majoring in the arts and humanities, the social and behavioral sciences, business, or the natural sciences and engineering, there are numerous opportunities to study law at the undergraduate level. In virtually every college and university, legal studies courses can be found in such departments as accounting, communication, sociology, political science, criminal justice, economics, psychology, history, and philosophy. Although course titles vary from one educational institution to the next, here is a sample of some of the law courses that may be available:

Criminal Justice:	Introduction to Criminal Law
	Criminal Law and Social Policy
	Prisoners' Rights
	Criminal Procedure
	Criminal Evidence
Sociology:	Lawyers and Society
	Gender, Sex, and American Law
	Population, Law, and Society
	Sociology of Law

Accounting:	Business Law
	Law and Social Issues in Business
History:	History of American Law
	American Constitutional History
	English Legal and Constitutional History
Philosophy:	Philosophy of Law
	Justice and Equality
Political Science:	Civil Liberties
	Constitutional Law
	The Judicial Process
	Congress and Public Policy
Economics:	Economics of Regulation
	Issues in Antitrust Law
	Economics of Law

Finally, for undergraduates who are interested in examining the law and legal institutions from an interdisciplinary perspective, there are many colleges and universities that offer legal studies as a minor. The legal studies minor generally involves six to eight courses, some of which are considered mandatory "core" courses, with the remainder to be selected from a specific list of electives.

The Court's increased workload comes not only from the simple mathematics of population growth and the greater emphasis on and awareness of civil liberties but also from the Supreme Court's own performance. For example, in 1961, when it extended the exclusionary rule to the states in *Mapp* v. *Ohio*,[28] the Court opened the door to thousands of appeals involving various aspects of illegal search and seizure. Although the *Mapp* decision was clear enough in its spirit and central holding, it offered lower state and federal courts no guidance as to the specific criteria that cause a search to be in violation of the Fourth Amendment. For example, *Mapp* shed no light on such important questions as whether searches of automobiles following a traffic arrest are valid, whether search warrants issued on the basis of anonymous tips are justifiable, or whether one spouse may waive the Fourth Amendment rights of the other and consent to a search of their home. Indeed, the Court did not even tell the lower courts whether the *Mapp* decision should be regarded as retroactive—that is, applicable to trials that occurred before *Mapp*. In light of the confusion surrounding *Mapp*, then, it is not surprising that no two state supreme courts reacted to *Mapp* in the same way. Some implemented *Mapp* in a very receptive fashion, while others responded in as restrictive a manner as possible.

Studies of the impact of Supreme Court decisions demonstrate that a similar phenomenon has occurred in the aftermath of every major Supreme Court decision affecting the rights of defendants. Like *Mapp*, decisions such as *Escobedo* v. *Illinois* and *Miranda* v. *Arizona* actually created more legal questions than they answered.[29] In the field of criminal law, as in all areas of law, the Court simply cannot hear enough cases to spell out all the principles that may derive from its major decisions. The very nature

FAMOUS CRIMINALS
Richard Speck

"Help me! Help me! Everyone is dead . . .
Oh God . . . he's killed them all!"

The screams from the young girl on a second-story ledge of an apartment building flagged the attention of a Chicago cop on patrol on an early Sunday morning in 1966. The officer entered the apartment to find a horribly gruesome and disturbing crime scene: Near the front door, the nude body of a young female; down the hall, a half-nude woman slashed on her neck and breasts; down the hall in a bedroom, three women with slashed throats; and in the second bedroom, three more young women's bodies slashed and strewn across the room. Corazon Pieza Amurao was the lone survivor of the brutal attack. The man had powered his way inside the apartment of the nine nursing students, forced them into a bedroom, bound and gagged them, and one by one dragged them to other locations throughout the apartment to slash their throats. Amurao managed to escape the attack by hiding under a bed; the killer had apparently lost track of how many women were in the apartment.

Amurao was able to relay a basic description of the man in his early twenties to police, specifically recalling the tattoo on his arm declaring "Born to Raise Hell." Within hours of release of the police artist's sketch, the suspect was identified as Richard Speck, a local merchant seaman. Speck

(continued on p. 323)

of the Court's work permits the justices to do little more than formulate general policy. The pressures generated by heavy caseloads and the necessity to write majority opinions that usually represent a compromise among the viewpoints of individual justices make it highly likely that the Court's decisions will be uncertain and ambiguous.

— CRITICAL THINKING IN CRIMINAL JUSTICE —

The Supreme Court and the Bush Presidency

In June 2000, several months before the election of George W. Bush as 43rd president of the United States, the People for the American Way Foundation issued a dire warning about what could be decided in the November election. The liberal advocacy group declared:

> The United States Supreme Court is just one or two new justices away from curtailing or abolishing fundamental rights that millions of Americans take for granted.[30]

What could People for the American Way have possibly meant with this statement? Think critically about it, and recall what has already been discussed in this textbook about the due pro-

Supreme Court Makeup

Since World War II, 16 Supreme Court justices have been appointed by Republicans and 10 have been appointed by Democrats.

■ Democrat   ■ Republican

Term	President	Appointments
1945–53	Truman (D)	4
1953–61	Eisenhower (R)	5
1961–63	Kennedy (D)	2
1963–69	Johnson (D)	2
1969–74	Nixon (R)	4
1974–77	Ford (R)	1
1977–81	Carter (D)	0
1981–89	Reagan (R)	3
1989–93	Bush (R)	2
1993–00	Clinton (D)	2
2004–08	Bush (R)	1
	By Democrats	10
	By Republicans	16

Of the three justices who are 70 or older, two are generally considered part of a liberal voting bloc, and the one swing vote has announced her retirement.

■ Liberal bloc   ■ Conservative bloc   □ Swing vote

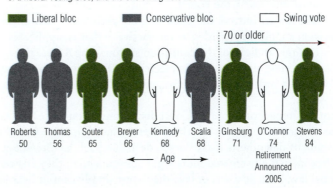

Roberts	Thomas	Souter	Breyer	Kennedy	Scalia	Ginsburg	O'Connor	Stevens
50	56	65	66	68	68	71	74	84

←——— Age ———→

70 or older →

O'Connor: Retirement Announced 2005

The Bush Dream Supreme Court

Left to right (standing) Thomas, Scalia, Scalia, Thomas
(seated) Thomas, Scalia, Scalia, Thomas, Scalia

Jeff Danziger, Los Angeles Times Syndicate

cess and crime control models of criminal justice, the criminal law "revolution," the nationaliza-tion of the Bill of Rights, *Roe* v. *Wade,* and the makeup of the Supreme Court. Any thoughts?

The issue that People for the American Way had in mind was that the next president could ultimately shape the direction of the constitutional and legal framework that will guide the United States for a generation or more. Two factors are significant here. The first is that, as illustrated on the accompanying chart, the High Court has a "liberal bloc" of four justices, a "conservative bloc" of three justices, and a "swing vote" of two justices. As a result, there is no clear majority in the Court, and many recent decisions have been closely divided.

The second point is that Supreme Court justices are appointed for life, and as illustrated, three justices were age 70 or above. As such, the new president, the People for the American Way contended, would have the opportunity to appoint at least one, and perhaps three, new justices during his term.

Had Al Gore been elected, it is likely that he would have appointed justices like Stephen Breyer and Ruth Bader Ginsburg, who interpret the Constitution broadly, relying as much on the principles underlying granted rights as on the intent of the words themselves. Under Gore-appointed justices, abortion would likely remain a constitutional right, and future legislative restric-tions on abortion might have been struck down. Under a Gore-appointed High Court, furthermore, federal power would probably have broadened, permitting laws that would tighten gun control. Gore's nominees would also have supported the rights of the accused.

During his first term, President Bush did not have the opportunity to appoint a Supreme Court Justice. However, during his second term and while this text book was in production, Justice Sandra Day O'Connor announced her resignation, and Chief Justice William Rehnquist passed away. Almost immediately, conservatives and liberals began lobbying the President about his proposed selections. Many felt that they would be similar in ideology to Antonin Scalia and Clarence Thomas, who look to the intent of the Founding Fathers when interpreting the Con-stitution. Under a Court with Bush nominees, abortion rights could be doomed, or at the very least there would be numerous restrictions. The Bush court would also oppose federal licensing of law-abiding gun owners and perhaps erode some of the rights of the accused.

After winning Senate approval by a vote of 78–22, on September 29, 2005 Appellate Court Judge John G. Roberts was sworn in as the 17th Chief Justice of the U.S. Supreme Court. Al-

(continued from p. 322)

was an alcoholic with a long arrest history and two stints in prison already under his belt, and the police investigation began to link Speck to other grisly crimes in which he was a potential suspect: in Monmouth, Illi-nois, to the murder of a barmaid and the rape and murder of a 65-year-old woman in her home; in Indiana, to the murder of three girls who had disappeared near the boat dock where Speck had worked; and in Michigan, to the murders of four females ages 7 to 60 who were murdered near a harbor where Speck's boat was docked.

With all the publicity attached to his case, Speck decided to commit suicide in his sleazy, run-down hotel room by slashing his wrists with the broken shards of a wine bottle. However, he had second thoughts. He was rushed to the local hospital, where the first-year resident attending to his wounds recognized him and notified police.

Speck was arrested, charged, tried, and, only days after the trail began, found guilty of all eight Chicago murders and sentenced to death. However, when the Supreme Court abolished capital punishment in 1972, Speck was spared death and instead sen-tenced to 400 to 1,200 years in prison. He died of a massive heart attack in 1991 at the age of 49 after serving only 19 years of his sentence. He was never charged with any of the other homicides he was sus-pected of involvement in. To this day, those cases remain unsolved. ∎

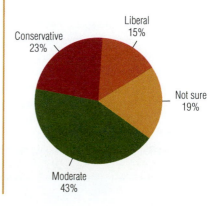

though the Senate hearings leading up to Roberts' confirmation revealed little about how he might vote on the Court, a number of concerns were raised about his stance on women's issues and civil rights.

Which way would you prefer things—under a Bush court or a Gore court?

As a final point here, Bush also has the opportunity to appoint as many as 200 federal district and appellate court judges. These appointments represent another chance to shape federal law for years to come.

OP-ED

Getting back to some of the questions raised in the opening paragraphs of this chapter, it is clear that there are many different types of courts. There are also many non-traditional courts. For example, anyone who has attended a Monday night football game or a European soccer match understands how ill-tempered many sports fans can get. Some people say that Philadelphia sports fans may be among the worst: They have booed injured players as they were carried off the field; they have taunted Santa Claus; police dogs and mounted officers have been needed to control them when Philadelphia teams won world championships; and one fan even fired a flare gun across the playing field. During the opening weeks of

the 1997 football season, some Philadelphia Eagles fans became so rowdy that city officials decided to strike back. On November 23, 1997, a makeshift courtroom was set up in Veterans Stadium to mete out summary justice to disorderly fans.[31]

The majority of Philadelphia Eagles fans welcomed the makeshift court in Veterans Stadium, for they too were fed up with the rowdy behavior that was giving their city a bad name. It is indeed a real court of law, and in the media it quickly became known as "Vet Stadium Court" and the "Eagles Court." And its brand of "stadium justice" seemed to work. On the court's first day of operation, 20 people were arrested and tried on a variety of disorderly conduct charges. In addition to public humiliation, the sentences included fines of up to $600 and loss of the offender's season tickets. Since its first appearance in 1997, the court continues to dispense justice to rowdy fans caught spitting, smoking, stumbling drunk, or starting fights at Eagles games. Now other cities are considering the experiment, so soon there may be a court in a stadium near you.

This brings us back to the spring break courts, and yes, they are indeed real courts. The overwhelming number of rowdy students descending on a resort area can bring frustration to local citizens and police alike. But the students also provide a boost to the local economy. While some Florida cities like Key West and Daytona Beach have overtly discouraged spring breakers from choosing their location, others like Panama City Beach have tried innovative ways to accommodate them. However, although Panama City Beach's spring break court is not currently operational because of a debate over its cost-

effectiveness, city officials may reinstate it due to the negative image that students on break continue to give the community. Key West ran a similar program throughout the 1990s, and that municipality as well is contemplating reviving it.

Proponents of spring break courts say that they avoid clogging the regular court system with minor cases and, at the same time, teach students a lesson, and perhaps a little responsibility as well. Some students appreciate that the program enables them to avoid getting an official arrest record or, worse yet, having their parents find out. One student even declared it "a good way to meet people." Whether or not the students really do learn a lasting lesson is up to the individual, but one thing is for certain: There is a lot less trash on the streets when the court is in session.

Some spring breakers, however, fed up with what they call "police harassment" of their drinking activities, have decided to go "south of the border"—to Acapulco, Mazatlán, Los Cabos, and Cancún—where the laws, and apparently the police, are less vigilant. Cancún, in particular, has become party central. However, fed up with the thousands of drunk and disorderly students, the wet T-shirt contests, and the serial wardrobe malfunctions, combined with the loss of many wealthier visitors—golfers, honeymooners, and ecotourists—the city has launched its Civility Pact, a code of public behavior intended to curb the excesses of spring breakers.[32] The next likely step will be a spring break court. And perhaps the last place a vacationing student would want to visit and spend the night is a Mexican jail.

Summary

The American court system has come to be a bewildering mosaic of names, structures, and functions. There are justice of the peace and municipal courts, county and city courts, superior and inferior courts, trial and appellate courts, plus a host of others. The confusion comes from a variety of sources—no two state court systems are identical, the names of courts vary regardless of function, and there are various levels of jurisdictional authority.

The variability in the structure of state court systems is a result of the constitutional guarantee that all states have sovereignty with regard to penal codes and enforcement mechanisms. Nevertheless, despite the differences among them, state court structures do possess some degree of uniformity. Common to all state court structures are appeals courts, major trial courts, and courts of limited jurisdiction. Court jurisdiction varies by geography, subject matter, and hierarchy. The federal judiciary reflects a structure similar to that of the states.

Appellate state courts ensure that participants in lower-court hearings have access to a higher court's review of the decision and proceedings in the lower court, provided, of course, that petitioners can demonstrate their case is worthy of judicial review. Caseloads in appellate courts are limited to matters of appeal and review in both civil and criminal cases. All states have a high court of appeals in one form or another, and more than half the states have an intermediate court of appeals that staves the flow of cases going directly to higher appeals courts. Major trial courts are also a part of each state's judicial structure. Authorized to try all criminal and civil cases, the major trial courts have different names in different states but are most commonly known as circuit, district, or superior courts. Courts of limited jurisdiction constitute the lower courts in all states and serve as the entry point for criminal judicial processing.

The U.S. Supreme Court stands at the apex of the federal judiciary and is the highest court in the nation. The Constitution provided the Supreme Court with both original and appellate jurisdiction. Its original jurisdiction covers suits between two states, issues that test the constitutionality of state laws, and matters relating to ambassadors. In its appellate jurisdiction, the Court resolves conflicts that raise "substantial federal questions."

The Supreme Court is currently composed of nine justices, although the guidelines established in the Judiciary Act of 1789 allowed for only six justices. Each justice is nominated by the president of the United States and is confirmed by the Senate for a lifetime appointment. Like members of other higher courts, justices of the Supreme Court have discretion over which cases will be considered for review. Nevertheless, there are a number of scenarios under which the Court must grant review to a case. These include cases in which a federal court has determined an act of Congress to be unconstitutional, cases in which a U.S. court of appeals has found a state statute to be unconstitutional, cases in which a federal law was ruled invalid by a state's highest court of appeals, and cases in which an individual's challenge to a state statute on federal constitutional grounds is upheld by a state supreme court.

In recent years the Supreme Court has become overburdened by a crush of appeals. This problem has occurred mostly as a result of the greater emphasis on due process, human rights, and civil liberties. The result has been that a greater number of appeals have been administered in absence of a written opinion and that justices have become increasingly dependent on their clerks to review cases.

Key Terms

appellate jurisdiction (309)
courts of general jurisdiction (307)
courts of limited jurisdiction (302)
courts of record (308)
dual court system (299)
judicial circuit (308)

justice of the peace (303)
Marbury v. *Madison* (316)
Rule of Four (318)
trial *de novo* (303)
U.S. courts of appeals (313)
U.S. district courts (312)

U.S. magistrates (310)
U.S. Supreme Court (315)
writ of *certiorari* (318)
writ of *mandamus* (317)

Issues for Discussion

1. What type of restructuring would be most efficient to unify the state court systems?
2. What are the major problems with the lower courts, and how might these be remedied?
3. Is there any solution to the crush of drug cases in America's courts?

4. What are some of the problems created by the backlog of cases in state and federal courts?
5. What types of cases fall under the jurisdiction of the U.S. Supreme Court?
6. What is the jurisdictional dilemma between state and federal courts in high-profile cases, and how might it be resolved?

Media and Literature Resources

Reel Justice includes scenes that can be used to spark discussion about the following topics from this chapter:

The Court System

Legal Studies

Dual Court System

Courtrooms of the Future. A number of jurisdictions are experimenting with high-technology courtrooms that allow the presentation of evidence by means of video and other multimedia formats and the paperless filing of motions online. Arizona has made substantial efforts in using the Internet to make the courts more accessible to the public. The Maricopa County, Arizona, court Web site, for example, has an online service center where people who are representing themselves can obtain forms to file for court protection orders and other matters (*http://www.superiorcourt.maricopa.gov*).

Drug Courts. See John F. Anderson, "What to Do About "Much Ado" About Drug Courts?" *International Journal of Drug Policy* 12 (2001): 469–475; *The President's National Drug Control Strategy* (Washington DC: Office of National Drug Control Policy, 2005); Denise C. Gottfredson, Stacy S. Najaka, and Brook Kearley, "Effectiveness of Drug Treatment Courts: Evidence from a Randomized Trial," *Criminology and Public Policy* 2 (2003): 171–196; David S. Festinger, Douglas B. Marlowe, Patricia A. Lee, Kimberley C. Kirby, Gregory Bovasso, and A. Thomas McLellan, "Status Hearings in Drug Court: When More Is Less and Less Is More," *Drug and Alcohol Dependence* 68 (2002): 151–157; Douglas B. Marlowe, Effective Strategies for Intervening with Drug Abusing Offenders," *Villanova*

Law Review 47 (2002): 989–1026; James A. Inciardi, Duane C. McBride, and James E. Rivers, *Drug Control and the Courts* (Newbury Park, CA: Sage Publications, 1996); and Roger H. Peters and Mary R. Murrin, "Effectiveness of Treatment-Based Drug Courts in Reducing Recidivism," *Criminal Justice and Behavior* 20 (February 2000): 72–96.

The Supreme Court. Some excellent books on the U.S. Supreme Court are available. See Kermit L. Hall, *The Oxford Guide to United States Supreme Court Decisions* (Oxford: Oxford University Press, 2001); Jethro Koller Lieberman, *A Practical Companion to the Constitution: How the Supreme Court Has Ruled on Issues from Abortion to Zoning* (Los Angeles: University of California Press, 1999); Henry J. Abraham, *Justices, Presidents, and Senators* (Lanham, MD: Rowman & Littlefield, 1999); Peter Irons, *The People's History of the Supreme Court* (New York: Penguin Books, 2000); and David M. O'Brian, *Storm Center: The Supreme Court in American Politics* (New York: Norton, 1990)

The Law of the Western Frontier. For those of you who want to learn more about the history of the "Wild West" as it relates to justice and the law, there are several interesting books available, including Ruel McDaniel, *Vinegarroon: The Saga of Judge Roy Bean, Law West of the Pecos* (Whitefish, MT: Kessinger, 2004); David C. Frederick, *Rugged Justice: The Ninth Circuit Court of Appeals and the American West,* 1891–1941 (Berkeley: University of California Press, 1994); Clare V. McKanna, Jr., *The Trial of "Indian Joe": Race and Justice in the Nineteenth-Century West* (Lincoln, NE: University of Nebraska Press, 2003).

Endnotes

1. *The Atlanta Journal-Constitution,* April 7, 2001, A1; *Miami Herald,* April 7, 2002, 3B.
2. For a retrospective overview of the charm of the early American courthouse, see Richard Pare (ed.), *Court House* (New York: Horizon Press, 1978).
3. President's Commission on Law Enforcement and Administration of Justice, *Task Force Report: The Courts* (Washington, DC: U.S. Government Printing Office, 1967), 29.
4. *Proceedings of the 42nd Annual Meeting of the New York State Bar Association,* 1919, 240–241, as quoted in the President's Commission, *Task Force Report,* 29.
5. National Advisory Commission on Criminal Justice Standards and Goals, *Courts* (Washington, DC: U.S. Government Printing Office, 1973), 161–162.
6. David W. Neubauer, *America's Courts and the Criminal Justice System* (Belmont, CA: Wadsworth, 2004).
7. H. Ted Rubin, *The Courts: Fulcrum of the Justice System* (Pacific Palisades, CA: Goodyear, 1976), 49.
8. *Tumey* v. *Ohio,* 273 U.S. 510 (1927).
9. *Connally* v. *Georgia,* 429 U.S. 245 (1977).
10. Rubin, *The Courts,* 51.
11. *The New York Times,* June 2, 1975, 16.
12. Personal communication, Len Holton, Tri-County Technical College, Pendleton, SC, December 6, 1993.
13. Cleveland Foundation, *Criminal Justice in Cleveland* (Cleveland: Cleveland Foundation, 1922), 627–641.
14. H. Ted Rubin, *The Felony Processing System, Cuyahoga County, Ohio* (Denver: Institute for Court Management, 1971), 16–17.
15. *The New York Times,* August 2, 2000, A24.
16. Murray S. Stedman, *State and Local Governments* (Cambridge, MA: Winthrop, 1979), 156.
17. National Advisory Commission, *Courts,* 164.
18. See Victor Flango, "Court Unification and the Quality of State Courts," *Justice System Journal* 16 (1994): 33–56; Harry Stumpf and John Culver, *The Politics of State Courts* (White Plains, NY: Longman, 1992); and Neubauer, *America's Courts,* 2004.
19. President's Commission, *Task Force Report, America's Courts,* 36.
20. See *United States* v. *Ford,* 41 CrL 2421 (1987).
21. Administrative Office of the United States Courts, 2005.
22. Administrative Office of the United States Courts, 2005.
23. Administrative Office of the United States Courts, 2005.
24. Charles Warren, *The Supreme Court in United States History,* Vol. 1 (Boston: Little, Brown, 1926), 89.
25. *Marbury* v. *Madison,* 1 Cr. 138 (1803).
26. Robert G. McCloskey, *The American Supreme Court* (Chicago: University of Chicago Press, 1960), 40.
27. *U.S. News & World Report,* March 26, 1979, 33.
28. *Mapp* v. *Ohio,* 367 U.S. 643 (1961).

29. *Escobedo* v. *Illinois,* 378 U.S. 478 (1964); *Miranda* v. *Arizona,* 384 U.S. 436 (1966). See Stephen L. Wasby, *The Impact of the United States Supreme Court* (Howard, IL: Dorsey, 1970); and Theodore L. Becker and Malcolm M. Feeley (eds.), *The Impact of Supreme Court Decisions,* 2d ed. (New York: Oxford University Press, 1973).

30. People for the American Way Foundation, *Special Report: Courting Disaster, How a Scalia-Thomas Supreme Court Would Endanger Our Rights and Freedoms,* June 2000.

31. *The New York Times,* November 24, 1997, A18.

32. *The Economist,* March 12, 2005, 42.

11

JUDGES, PROSECUTORS, AND OTHER PERFORMERS AT THE BAR OF JUSTICE

LEARNING OBJECTIVES

After reading this chapter, you should be able to answer the following questions:

1. What are the major roles of judges, prosecutors, and defense attorneys?

2. What is plea bargaining, and what are the roles of the defense attorney, the prosecutor, and the judge in the plea bargaining process?

3. What are the arguments for and against plea bargaining, and what is the Supreme Court's position on it?

4. What are the problems associated with providing legal assistance to indigent defendants?

5. How are judges selected in the state and federal court systems?

6. What are the issues surrounding prosecutorial discretion and the *nolle prosequi?*

7. In addition to judges, prosecutors, and defense attorneys, who are the other members of the courtroom work group and what are their roles?

8. What were the major issues and cases associated with extending the Sixth Amendment right to counsel to state defendants?

Plea Bargains and Withholds of Adjudication Shortcut Courtroom Procedures

COURT STREET, USA—Fred Smith, an 18-year-old white male, stabbed a good samaritan who tried to break up a fight. He pleaded no contest to aggravated battery. Lucky for Smith, a judge called the attack an "isolated incident" and instead of receiving a felony conviction, he received a "withhold of adjudication."

Reginald Wilson, a 16-year-old black male, also stabbed someone during a fight. Wilson, however, wasn't as lucky as Smith and, instead of receiving a withhold, was convicted of a felony and sentenced to 2 years in prison.

Neither Smith nor Wilson had prior records.

Now, 3 years later, Smith is employed as a supervisor at a video store and is attending Florida International University with the intention of becoming a marine biologist. Wilson has dreams of attending school like Smith. However, college appears to be more of a fantasy than reality. He lives alone in a small, run-down apartment. He has applied for about 50 jobs but is having trouble gaining employment because of his status as a convicted felon.

In another community, Jason Frederick struck and killed an elderly woman as she crossed the street; then he drove off. He pleaded "no contest" to leaving the scene of an accident resulting in death. He received a withhold of adjudication and received probation. This means that, in the eyes of the law, he's not a felon and does not lose his civil rights.

A man with prior convictions has been arrested for robbery in the first degree, assault, and possession of a deadly weapon. Robbery in the first degree is a serious offense, carrying a penalty of up to 15 years in prison. The defendant's savvy lawyer, who recognizes that the evidence and testimony point to the defendant without a doubt, suggests the defendant "plea bargain"—that is, plead guilty to robbery 3—and tells him he'll be back on the street in 2 years. His lawyer also informs him that if this goes to trial he will probably be convicted and receive 15 years in prison. The defendant agrees and goes off to prison for 18 to 24 months, and the judge, defense attorney, and assistant DA move on to the next case.

What is a "withhold of adjudication"? In a case where two people are charged with the exact same crime, why is one person granted a withhold and able to move on with his or her life, while the other person, labeled a convicted felon, struggles with unemployment for the rest of his or her life? Is it fair that a guilty man was able to plea-bargain his way out of a 15-year sentence to a sentence that probably lasted less than 2 years? Do withholds of adjudication and plea bargains corrupt our criminal justice system? Has justice been served?

Unquestionably, the processing of criminal cases is not without dramatic moments and characters. There are the many forms of legal magic that combine legislation and judicial interpretation; there are the courtroom wizards who analyze legal axioms and ideals; there are the procedural practitioners who use justice and emotion to influence the outcome of a case; and there is the atmosphere of confusion that sometimes reduces fair-minded legal reasoning to a state of judicial chaos. All of these reflect the melodrama and romanticism of the judicial process. At the same time, there are also the little-known figures who, together with the many other components of the process, represent the backbone of the American court system. This chapter, then, examines the full spectrum of players in the judicial process in order to demonstrate the importance of each to a more unified system of criminal justice.

| The Courtroom Work Group |

The major participants in the criminal judicial process in the United States are the judge, the prosecutor, the defense attorney, and the accused. However, there may be many other participants, depending on the particular phase of the process, the type of case, and the level of the court. For example, there may be police officers and witnesses to contribute evidence of innocence or guilt; there may be grand juries and trial juries to consider the nature and importance of the evidence and render judgment; and there may be officers of the court, such as bailiffs, clerks, and reporters, who attend to administrative matters. Finally, there are others with only quasi-judicial functions, such as coroners and medical examiners, whose testimony and judgment may be required in specific kinds of cases. Each of these participants has a specific role in criminal court processing, and without them various phases in the judicial system would not be fully possible.

Judges

It is upon the judge's wisdom that we must rely.

—JUSTICE CHARLES EVANS HUGHES

Judges are apt to be naive, simple-minded men.

—JUSTICE OLIVER WENDELL HOLMES, JR.

Although there are many high-ranking officials at all levels of the criminal justice process, none have the prominence and the prestige of **judges,** also referred to as *magistrates* or *justices*. They are responsible for the honest, impartial, and equitable administration of justice. To most observers, they are the ultimate arbiters and symbols of law and order. When they enter a courtroom, everyone rises; when they speak, others listen. Although at times their power to decide a case may be assigned to a jury, the judges alone have the authority to interpret the rules that govern court proceedings.

In military tribunals, judges are different in some ways than those seen in other courts—all are military officers (see Exhibit 11.1).

Roles and Responsibilities
The roles and responsibilities of judges are numerous—in fact, in a monograph prepared by the American Bar Association during the 1970s, it took some 100 pages to describe them only briefly.[1] At the most general level, judges are both arbiters and administrators. As arbiters, they are responsible for safeguarding the rights of the accused as well as the interests of the public in the administration of criminal justice. As administrators, they must control the flow of cases through the courts and oversee such ancillary duties as the appointment and evaluation of court personnel, record keeping, and budget requests.

Generally, these roles and responsibilities apply to the justices of urban municipal courts, rural county courts, and state trial courts. Even justices of the peace have similar duties as they preside over minor offenses and civil disputes. However, there are variations depending on the size and complexity of a particular jurisdiction. County judges are more likely to have administrative duties—securing funds to operate the court, hiring personnel, purchasing supplies—than are judges on the higher rungs of the judicial ladder. Conversely, justices in urban municipal courts or state trial courts are likely to devote more of their time to managing the flow of cases through the court than are judges in less populated areas, simply because they have more defendants.

At the appellate level, the responsibilities of judges differ greatly from those of judges in the lower and felony courts. Appeals are dealt with through written briefs or oral arguments, and in the latter case the only participants are the counsels for the defense and the prosecution. The responsibilities of appeals judges are as follows:

1. Determining whether the proper procedures were followed in the presentation of the appeal.
2. Examining the written brief, the trial record, or other materials that may have been filed.
3. Presiding over any oral arguments.
4. Weighing the facts of the case and the nature of the appeal in order to arrive at a decision.
5. Negotiating a decision through vote, persuasion, or compromise in cases in which more than one judge hears the appeal.
6. Preparing a written *opinion* that details the logic and reasons for the decision.

Nobody outside of a baby carriage or a judge's chamber can believe in an unprejudiced point of view.

—LILLIAN HELLMAN

I think a judge should be looked on rather as a sphinx than as a person—you shouldn't be able to imagine a judge having a bath.

—JUDGE H. C. LEON

That judges of important causes should hold office for life is a disputable thing, for the mind grows old as well as the body.

—ARISTOTLE

A trial court must be guided by statutes and the case law.

—JUDGE LANCE ITO

EXHIBIT 11.1 | International Perspectives on Crime & Justice

Terrorism, Faceless Judges, and Military Tribunals

Not too long after American troops were sent to the Middle East in the wake of the 9/11 attacks, the United States declared that persons, captured in connection with the war on terrorism and held at Guantanamo Bay, Cuba, were "enemy combatants." As a result, they would not be entitled to the legal protections espoused by the Geneva Convention. Among the privileges guaranteed by the convention is the right to an individual hearing to determine the status of each prisoner. Because all the prisoners were designated as combatant status, the hundreds of detainees were scheduled to face the first U.S. military tribunals since World War II. By law, only enemy combatants can be tried in military tribunals.

Military tribunals are essentially streamlined court proceedings that operate in secret. The judges are military officers selected by the government, and less stringent rules of evidence apply. For example, defendants have no right to choose their own defense, protect themselves against self-incrimination, or appeal the verdict. Further, the death penalty may be imposed even without the unanimous approval of the judges. Proponents argue that the tribunals can swiftly and effectively dole out punishment for dangerous criminals without getting bogged down in legal technicalities.

Military tribunals in the United States date back to the Civil War. President Abraham Lincoln used them as part of a wider campaign aimed at eradicating public dissent and silencing vocal critics of his administration and the bitterly divisive war. The tribunals were used once again by President Roosevelt in 1942 on eight Germans who plotted terrorist attacks against American interests—eerily similar to those plotted by al-Qaeda. They schemed to destroy railroads, aluminum factories, power plants, bridges, and Jewish-owned and operated places of business. The constitutionality of the military tribunal was challenged and taken to the Supreme Court, whose decision in *Ex parte Quirin* (317 U.S. I), or the "Quirin case," named after one of the defendants, was the basis for the U.S. attorney general's legal argument in favor of using military tribunals. The justices presiding over the World War II-era case unanimously ruled in favor of the legality of the proceedings.

But the secretive nature and harsh form of justice that military tribunals can bequeath has prompted criticism. The problem with military tribunals, critics say, is that they violate the separation-of-powers doctrine. The president oversees the creation of the military commissions and determines who will be tried before them. By circumstance, the military commission acting as the judges cannot be a genuinely independent body since its members answer directly to the secretary of defense and the president, the very same people who ordered them to prosecute the cases.

Other critics have compared the secret military tribunals with Peru's use of "faceless judges," a measure introduced in that country's war against the *Sendero Luminoso,* or "Shining Path," a corps of fanatic guerrilla insurgents seeking to purify Peru by violence. It emerged from a tangled web of Peruvian politics in 1970 in the ancient colonial city of Ayacucho—a community of 70,000 residents located some 200 miles

A Muslim detainee in Camp Delta at the Guantanamo Bay Naval Base in Cuba.

southeast of Lima. The moving force behind Sendero's creation was Abimael Guzman (also known as Chairman Gonzolo), a philosophy professor at the San Cristobal de Huamanga University. Noting the striking class differences in his society, Guzman concluded that as Peru approached the 21st century, it was still a semifeudal and semicolonial society. Moreover, the government embodied a fascist structure masquerading as democracy and engaging in the construction of a corporate state and the development of bureaucratic capitalism. Guzman held that social reform could be had only by making revolutionaries out of Peruvian peasants for the purpose of overthrowing the established government.

Sendero violence against the government began a decade later, in July 1980, and by the end of the year some 240 incidents had been recorded, including the destruction of local tax records, bombings of government offices, and sabotage of electricity pylons. By 1981, the rate of incidents had increased, expanding to such activities as the raiding

Former Peruvian President Alberto Fujimori meeting with leaders of the Shining Path.

of banks, mines, and police posts. Kidnapping was added the following year. The ideological politics of the Sendero Luminoso became most evident in the focus of its terrorist activities during the latter half of the 1980s. In southern Peru, Sendero guerrillas captured plantations and haciendas, sometimes killing their owners and employees, and distributed cattle, sheep, alpacas, and other goods to local peasants.

By the time Guzman and a number of his followers were arrested in 1992, the death toll from the country's guerrilla war had surpassed 30,000 people. Property damage was estimated at nearly $20 billion. A state of emergency, with constitutional guarantees in abeyance, existed in almost two-thirds of Peru, affecting half the population. Moreover, Sendero Luminoso was believed to have fielded some 5,000 guerrillas and 50,000 followers nationwide.

In the wake of Guzman's arrest, Peru established a system of antiterrorism laws and special tribunals to preside over terrorism trials, under which cases were heard by *jueces sin rostro,* or "faceless judges." The system was introduced by President Alberto Fujimori to prevent intimidation by terrorists who could identify the judges at public trials. Under the procedure, suspects were tried in military courts, and judges covered their faces or presided from behind screens or one-way glass to prevent identification and signed their verdicts using code names.

From 1992 through 1997, tribunals of faceless judges convicted and sentenced more than 5,000 accused terrorists—hundreds to terms of life imprisonment—statistics that were intended to demonstrate the efficiency of the system. Among those sentenced was Sendero Luminoso leader Abimael Guzman. But from its very beginning, the system of using faceless judges was seen as a threat to both human rights and the justice it was supposed to administer. In fact, both the press and human rights groups frequently reported instances of doubtful sentences or cases of union leaders, members of opposition parties, municipal authorities, students, and others who spent months in prison waiting for their cases to be heard. Peru's Institute for Legal Defense, a human rights organization, argued that hundreds of innocent people were left defenseless against a system that, at the outset, permitted arrest and accusation based on political persecution and personal revenge and then sanctioned tribunals presided over by faceless judges.

In 1997, Peru abandoned its system of faceless judges. However, other provisions of its antiterrorism legislation remain, including the use of military courts to hear cases of civilians accused of crimes against the government and the shielding of police and military personnel involved in the interrogation and detention of suspects from cross-examination by defense lawyers.

As of 2005, the Sendero Luminoso was still active in several of Peru's rural areas, but its strength had declined dramatically as a result of the Peruvian military's antiterrorism efforts. Membership is unknown; it is estimated to be only 400 to 500 armed militants, but growing again, possibly due to involvement in narcotrafficking.

In retrospect, defendants throughout history whose trials and convictions have been shrouded in secrecy leave the public questioning the true weight of justice served. The practice also sets a precedent for the future suspensions of civil liberties. The U.S. State Department has criticized secret military tribunals in other countries for years, saying that the secrecy can shield corruption and foster distrust among the public.

In an attempt to deflect some of the criticism, but without fully giving up on the idea of military tribunals at Guantanamo, the Bush administration is altering some of the traditional rules of the system. For example, it recently released three juveniles from the prison and also decided to review the status of each prisoner on a yearly basis. The government has also decided to allow a limited media presence at the trials, although it contends that there is not enough room for observers from human rights groups.

At the same time, the federal courts are weighing in on the issue. On January 31, 2005, U.S. district court judge Joyce Green ruled that "enemy combatants' being held at Guantanamo must be allowed to challenge their detention in U.S. courts, holding that the "military commissions" being used are illegal. Specifically, the decision concluded that the Guantanamo military tribunals designed to determine whether the prisoners are members of the Taliban or al-Qaeda were "so stacked against them that their judgments cannot be trusted." However, the ruling directly conflicted with one issued by U.S. district judge Richard Leon, who held in a similar case earlier in the month that the detainees' bid for freedom is supported by "no viable legal theory." No doubt the matter will ultimately be addressed by the United States Supreme Court.

Sources: Mark Weisenmiller, "Military Tribunals in the United States," *History Today,* April 2002, 28–29; "Justice Can't Be Done in Secret," *Nation* 274, 22 (2002), 16–20; Neal Katyal, "Waging War, Deciding Guilt: Trying the Military Tribunals," *Yale Law Journal* 11, 6 (2002), 1259–1310; Sanjuana Martinez, "Montesinos Still Controls Peru," *Proceso,* October 1, 2000, 10; Gustavo Gorriti, *The Shining Path: A History of the Millenarian War in Peru* (Chapel Hill: University of North Carolina Press, 1999); Michael Reid, *Peru: Paths to Poverty* (London: Latin America Bureau, 1985); "'Faceless Judges' Threaten Rights in Peru," *Latinamerica Press,* September 9, 1993, 3; Amnesty International, "End of 'Faceless Judge' System," press release, October 16, 1997; U.S. Department of State, "Sendero Luminoso," *Global Terrorism Report,* November 2000; U.S. Department of State *Country Reports on Terrorism, 2004,* April 2005; Suzanne Goldenberg, "Guantanamo Tribunals Ruled Illegal," *The Guardian,* February 1, 2005, 13.

The Fatal Shooting of Judges: A Trend?

The courtroom is normally the place where justice is served, but on March 11, 2005, in the Fulton County Courthouse in Atlanta, the scales of justice were tipped in the wrong favor.

On that date, Brian Nichols overpowered a sheriff's deputy, stole her gun, and barged into the courtroom of Judge Rowland Barnes, shooting him to death. He also killed a court reporter and deputy sergeant before fleeing the court and killing a U.S. Customs agent outside the courthouse before carjacking a Honda and driving away. Nichols, on trial in Barnes's courtroom for rape, was being led to a holding area to await his trial later that afternoon when the incident occurred. Later, Nichols held a woman hostage in her suburban apartment before finally releasing her to see her daughter, at which point she notified authorities. Prosecutors have charged him with 54 separate counts and plan to seek the death penalty.

The shooting was the second in as many months linked to a courtroom trial. In February, Bart Ross shot to death the husband and mother of Chicago judge Joan Humphrey, who had dismissed his medical malpractice lawsuit. Ross killed himself during a routine traffic stop and left a suicide note claiming responsibility for the deaths.

But these are not the first acts of violence against judicial figures. Consider some of the other more notorious cases:

- In 1989, federal judge Robert Vance was killed and his wife injured when he opened a package containing a bomb outside his home in Birmingham, Alabama. Walter Leroy Moody Jr. sent the bomb because his 1972 conviction of possessing a pipe bomb had not been overturned.

- Federal judge Richard J. Daronco was killed at his home by retired New York City officer Charles L. Koster in 1988. Koster was apparently exacting revenge for the judge's dismissal of a $2.5 million lawsuit filed by his daughter. He later committed suicide.

- In 1979, U.S. district judge John H. Wood Jr. was killed outside his San Antonio home because it was believed the judge (nicknamed "Maximum John") would impose the maximum sentence on the defendants in a drug case. Charles Harrison, the father of actor Woody Harrelson, was convicted and sentenced to two life terms for the first murder of a sitting federal judge in the 20th century. Not even an appeal (continued on p. 335)

Beyond these duties and responsibilities, judges also have influence over other aspects of the criminal justice process that are related directly and sometimes indirectly to the court. In some jurisdictions, for example, service agencies such as probation and release-on-recognizance programs are under the administrative control of the court. In others, where these are separate county or state agencies, their functioning is influenced by the attitudes and judicial policies of the local chief magistrate. Similarly, police and prosecutors are influenced by the judge, whose discretion in the acceptance of evidence and pleas and in sentencing clearly has an impact on the arrest and charging processes.

Selection of Judges

Although judges, justices, and magistrates have the highest authority in the criminal justice process, they are not always the most qualified or best trained. In some lower courts, neither a college degree nor a law degree is required. This situation has evolved from both the manner in which judges are recruited and the methods through which they are trained. Judges are either *elected* or *appointed*, and both mechanisms have a variety of problems.

All federal judges are nominated by the president of the United States and must be confirmed by the Senate. The U.S. Constitution specifies this for Supreme Court justices, and the Judiciary Act of 1789 adopted the same procedure for other federal judgeships.

Because all federal judges hold their offices "during good behavior"—that is, for life—the appointments are extremely important, giving the president great power to shape the direction of federal judicial policy. This is unquestionably true with respect to the United States Supreme Court. Generally, although senatorial confirmation of a presidential nominee to the Court is often little more than a formality, it is a process that the Senate takes seriously and that has resulted in some rugged battles. Nevertheless, on only 28 occasions since the nation's founding (with just 7 of them in the 20th century), has the Senate failed to confirm a presidential choice; the margins of confirmation have been wide, with more than two-thirds of the nominees receiving unanimous Senate approval. The president's power has also been apparent in the partisan nature of most judicial appointments. Of the 108 Supreme Court justices, only 12 were not members of the president's political party.

For recent Supreme Court nominations, however, there has been a good deal of discussion and disagreement about the role of the Senate and about what "advise and consent" means. (The phrase *advise and consent* is taken from Senate Rule 38: "The final question on every nomination shall be, 'Will the Senate advise and consent to this nomination?'") The members of the Judiciary Committee have expressed the view that the Senate must make an independent judgment. Further, the Senate has a role in determining which of a number of choices a president will send forward. For example, consider President Bill Clinton's potential nomination in 1994 of Interior Secretary Bruce Babbitt to replace Justice Harry Blackmun. When key Republicans signaled that they would fight the nomination, Clinton chose someone else.

In the other federal courts, too, the president's nominee is confirmed or rejected by the Senate. In years past, senators used appointments to the U.S. district courts and U.S. courts of appeals as political patronage. Thus, although the president made the nomination, most senators sponsored specific candidates and expected them to receive the appointment, unless it was discovered that a candidate had committed some grave misdeed in the past. Senators enforced their demands in specific ways. They could threaten to withdraw their support for certain bills that were important to the president's legislative program, or they could block the appointment of anyone else to the post by involving the rule of "senatorial courtesy." According to this unwritten rule, if a senator of the president's party declares that an appointee who is to serve in the senator's home state is "personally obnoxious" to him or her, the Senate will not confirm the nomination.[2]

To some extent, the patronage system and senatorial courtesy still persist. However, during the 1980s the Reagan and Bush administrations strengthened the role of the president in federal judicial selection. One tactic, for example, was to have Republican state governors offer two or three names for judicial vacancies rather than only one. This preserved some role for the senator but let the president make the final selection.[3]

During the Clinton administration, however, the process was not quite as simple. Although there were many vacancies in the federal judiciary, the Senate confirmed few district and appellate court judges. With Republicans in control of the Senate, it appeared that efforts were being made to carry out a "conservative revolution" in the federal courts. To this end, many Republican senators abandoned their historic advise-and-consent role. In fact, some in effect declared war on Clinton's choices, claiming that the nominees were "judicial activists" who would use the federal courts to accomplish social goals. As a result of these political maneuvers, many federal judgeships remain vacant and caseloads are creeping out of control. This pattern has continued into the current Bush administration. (For a glimpse at one of the district court appointments made by President Ulysses S. Grant, see Exhibit 11.2.)

In state, county, and municipal jurisdictions where judges are elected, political connections are even more important. To win a judgeship, the candidate must first secure the party nomination and then campaign on the party ticket. Thus, the potential judge becomes embroiled in the same type of partisan politics seen in the election of presidents, governors, legislators, and other government officials. This system generally results in the election of the most politically active, but not necessarily the most qualified, candidates.

In state jurisdictions where judges are appointed, partisan politics still can play a role, but the degree of political influence over specific selections varies by state and by level in the judicial hierarchy. In many systems, governors appear to have more freedom than the president in making selections. Generally, gubernatorial appointments are made to the courts of appeals and sometimes the major trial courts. In both instances, party connections and service in the state legislature play important roles in the nomination process.

At the lower levels of the judicial hierarchy, partisan politics are almost always present in the selection of judges. Appointments of judges in municipal and justice of the peace courts are typically made by mayors, county managers, or town councils, and friendship, kinship, party affiliation, and the political spoils system may play a role in the process.[4]

In an attempt to overcome the shortcomings of judicial selection through appointment or election, the American Bar Association (ABA) has long advocated a hybrid appointment and election system called the **Missouri Plan**.[5] Also known as the *ABA Plan* or "merit selection," it calls for the governor to select a candidate from a list of nominees drafted by a commission of lawyers, members of the public, and an incumbent judge. The appointee serves for 1 or more years, or until the next election, and then must be confirmed by the people in a *plebiscite* (vote of the people). The voters are asked, "Shall Judge _____ be retained in office?" If the voters approve, the judge serves until the next such election. If not, another judge is appointed through the same procedure. The Missouri Plan thus is a mechanism through which the governor, the state bar association, and the public participate in the selection of judges, as well as a means by which the voters can reject a sitting judge.

By the 1990s, the Missouri Plan or comparable forms of merit selection of judges had been established in the majority of states and the District of Columbia.[6] Recently, however, this approach has run into some difficulties. In Missouri, where the plan originated in 1940 as a cure for widespread patronage, there have been allegations that the merit selection process has come under political influence. Moreover, studies comparing the Missouri Plan with partisan election systems suggest that the characteristics of the judges selected under the two processes tend to be similar in both background and legal experience. Currently, the majority of states continue to use merit selection, with the remainder choosing their judges through *partisan* (using political parties) or *nonpartisan* (without party politics) elections.[7]

Judicial Training   Although judges, justices, and magistrates obtain their positions through various political mechanisms, this should not suggest that none are qualified to serve. There are, to be sure, no constitutional or statutory qualifications for serving

(continued from p. 334)
financed by his famous son and representation by well-known Harvard law professor Alan Dershowitz was enough to get the elder Harrelson's conviction overturned. ∎

Judges are the weakest link in our system of justice, and they are also the most protected.

— **ALAN M. DERSHOWITZ**

EXHIBIT 11.2 | *historical perspectives on crime and justice*

The Law West of Fort Smith

During the years immediately following the Civil War, the territory west of Fort Smith, Arkansas, was a virtual no-man's-land. Comprising more than 74,000 square miles of unfriendly Indian country, bounded on the north by Kansas and on the south by Texas, its population seemed to be dominated by frontier predators. Thieves, prostitutes, cattle rustlers, bank robbers, and murderers sought refuge in the territory west of Fort Smith, for there was no court or formal law under which a fugitive could be extradited. The area included the notorious "Robbers Cave" in the San Boise Mountains, celebrated in history and folklore as a junction city of robbers, gamblers, horse thieves, and bounty hunters; just west of the fort were the rugged Cookson Hills, an out-thrust of the Ozark Mountains from which came Frank and Jesse James, the Younger brothers, the Daltons, Belle Starr, and other well-known frontier desperadoes. The territory was one of mountains and hills, crevices with inaccessible canyons, narrow valleys, steep watercourses, natural caves, and segmented deserts that made it an almost impervious outlaw sanctuary where savagery prevailed.

On May 2, 1875, federal judge Isaac C. Parker arrived in Fort Smith to reestablish the federal court in the Western District of Arkansas. The court had originally been created by congressional action in 1851, but from the outset it had been ineffective. During the Civil War the courthouse had been burned to the ground, and in the years that followed it was tended by incompetency and corruption. With Parker's appointment by President Ulysses S. Grant as a federal district judge, law finally came to the territory west of Fort Smith.

Judge Parker was given 200 federal marshals to police the 74,000 square mile area, and only 8 days after his arrival at Fort Smith he opened his first term of court. Eighteen persons were brought before him charged with murder and fifteen were convicted. Eight were sentenced to die on the gallows on September 3, 1875. Before the date arrived, however, one was shot during an escape attempt, and another had his sentence commuted to life imprisonment.

The mass hanging of the remaining six brought international attention to the court and its judge. People from all parts of the country, and even strangers from abroad, began filtering into the town a week before the execution. On the morning of September 3, more than 5,000 people packed the jail yard and clung from the tops of the old fort's stone walls to view the macabre event. The six felons were lined up along a scaffold with their feet across the crack where the planks forming the death trap came together. As the nooses were adjusted about their necks, Judge Parker said: "Farewell forever until the court and you and all here today shall meet together in the general resurrection." The trap door fell, and the six men died at the end of ropes with broken necks.

Press reports of the event shocked people throughout the nation. The deaths on the gallows were considered atrocities, and Parker be-

"Hanging Judge" Isaac Parker.

came known as "the hanging judge"; as one correspondent put it: "None but a heartless judge could be so lacking in compassion as to decree such wholesale killing." But to the locals, it was different. At the time of the hangings crime was so rampant that conditions had given rise to the phrase: "There is no Sunday west of St. Louis—no God west of Fort Smith."

In his 21 years as judge of the federal district court at Fort Smith, Isaac C. Parker sentenced 168 persons to death, of whom 88 were actually hanged. However, Parker was also a civic-minded jurist whose sympathies lay with the victims and their families; he was a supporter of good city government, and an advocate for the many Native American tribes in his jurisdiction.

Parker died in 1896 at the age of 58. His territory "west of Fort Smith" is now the state of Oklahoma, and his restored courtroom and a replica of his hanging gallows are a part of the Fort Smith National Historic Site.

Sources: Glenn Shirley, *Law West of Fort Smith* (New York: Henry Holt, 1957); Clyde B. Davis, *The Arkansas* (New York: Farrar & Rinehart, 1940); Homer Croy, *He Hanged Them High* (New York: Duel, Sloan and Pearch, 1952).

on the U.S. Supreme Court—there is no age limitation, no requirement that the justices be native-born citizens, not even a requirement that appointees have a legal background. However, there are informal criteria for membership on the Court, and *every* nominee has been a lawyer. Curiously, however, it was not until 1957 that the Court was composed entirely of law school graduates.

Current members of the Supreme Court have extensive legal backgrounds, primarily in the federal judicial system. For example, Justice Anthony M. Kennedy, who was nominated by Ronald Reagan in 1988, graduated from Harvard Law School and practiced law for more than two decades, was a part-time professor at the McGeorge School of Law and a member of the United States Tax Court bar, and ultimately served as a U.S. court of appeals judge. U.S. district and appeals court judges have similar backgrounds, and virtually all are law school graduates.

At the state level, the vast majority of trial and appellate judges have legal education and training, but in courts of limited jurisdiction there are some who do not. This problem seems to be more prevalent in county court systems and justice of the peace courts. In larger municipal court systems, however, some changes have been made in recent years. The New York City Criminal Court Act, for example, requires the following:

> Each of the judges of the court shall be a resident of the city. No person, other than one who holds such office on the first day of September, nineteen hundred sixty-two, may assume the office of judge of the court unless he has been admitted to practice law in this state at least ten years.[8]

The New York law, passed in 1962 and adopted by numerous other jurisdictions since then, was designed to prevent the appointment of inexperienced legal practitioners. Although it did not require a law degree, it did mandate admittance to the bar—that is, passing the state bar examination. The wording of the act also implied 10 years' experience in the practice of law, which in effect set the minimum age requirement in the early thirties.

Even with the various changes in judicial selection practices and requirements for legal education, the training of judges remains a problem. Trial judges in the courts of original jurisdiction are the most crucial actors in criminal justice processing, but few have any formal training or apprenticeship in the judicial function. They generally come to the bench with no knowledge of the art of judging other than perhaps some experience as trial lawyers—experiences that *rarely* include extensive criminal practice.

The idea that judges should go back to school for training seminars has never been a popular one, but since the 1960s some programs have been developed through the efforts of the American Bar Association. Currently, the National College of the State Judiciary conducts 2-week and 4-week summer courses for trial judges, and the Federal Judicial Center conducts seminars for newly appointed federal judges as well as continuing education for veteran judges. Yet only a minority of the nation's jurists have exposure to such judgeship training, and the possibility of creating apprenticeships for those who wish to pursue judicial careers—an educational mechanism that exists in most European countries—remains dim.

Prosecutors

In truth, there is a tremendous ambivalence—almost a schizophrenia—that the quasi-judicial role of a prosecutor imposes. On the one hand, he is a trial advocate, expected to do everything in his power to obtain convictions. On the other hand, he is sworn to administer justice dispassionately, to seek humane dispositions rather than to blindly extract every last drop of punishment from every case.

— STEVEN PHILLIPS, FORMER ASSISTANT DISTRICT ATTORNEY,
BRONX COUNTY, NEW YORK

The **prosecutor,** also known as the *district attorney* or DA, the *county attorney,* the *state attorney,* or the *U.S. attorney*—depending on the jurisdiction of his or her office—is a government lawyer and the chief law enforcement authority of a particular community.

FAMOUS CRIMINALS
Richard Ramirez,
"The Night Stalker"

Residents of California were paralyzed by fear for a period of 14 months during the mid-1980s when the killer Los Angeles journalists dubbed as "the Night Stalker" terrorized communities with brutal crimes of rape and murder.

Richard Ramirez was born the youngest of seven children to Mexican-American parents in El Paso, Texas, in 1960. At a young age, he cut school to sniff glue and smoke marijuana, and he gradually got involved in petty crime, including pickpocketing, shoplifting, and burglarizing homes. He spent time in a home for juvenile delinquents and was sentenced to probation for possession of marijuana. He then moved to California, where he became obsessed with knives and guns, developed a cocaine habit, and practiced Satanism. He burglarized homes and warehouses to support his new drug habit, and spent time in jail for car theft. After his release in spring 1984, Ramirez's criminal activity took a wicked turn.

On June 28, 1984, Ramirez made his first strike. When a 79-year-old woman left her apartment window cracked on a humid summer night, Ramirez slipped inside, attacked her while she was sleeping, sexually assaulted her, and stabbed her to death. In the months that followed, heinous crimes of sexual assault and murder were reported throughout the LA area with increasing frequency and intensity. A couple of the

(continued on p. 338)

(*continued from p. 337*)

victims survived, providing police with sketchy details of the attacker's physical description. But there was little to go on other than that he was a tall, thin Hispanic male with rotten teeth who had left an AC/DC baseball hat at one of the crime scenes.

In response to the crime wave, citizens throughout the region formed neighborhood watch programs, vigilantes patrolled the streets, patrol cars and unmarked cars scanned neighborhoods with an increased presence, scores of residents bought guard dogs, and some even created cardboard cutouts of humans to keep in their lit windows so that it would appear that someone was home and awake at night. In August, a special Night Stalker task force was established, with 200 detectives dedicated to the case 24/7.

A break in the case came when alert citizens noticed a man matching the Stalker's description driving slowly back and forth through a neighborhood. Police put out an all-points bulletin on the car, which was later found abandoned in a parking lot. Using what at the time was considered revolutionary technology, crime scene investigators placed a saucer of superglue in the car and locked and sealed all the windows, the idea being that the fumes from the glue would diffuse through the car, react with the moisture, and reveal fingerprints, which could then be enhanced by a laser beam. There was a single print found—matching that of Richard Ramirez, whose prints were on file from his earlier conviction of car theft.

Ramirez's mug shot and the story made front-page headlines. When he arrived back at LA from Phoenix (where he regularly purchased his cocaine), he disembarked from the Greyhound bus, saw a newspaper stand with his photo across the front page of that day's edition, and quickly realized that his cover was blown. He turned and started to run through an eastern LA neighborhood, where he was attacked and beaten to the ground by an angry mob armed with steel bars and tools. The police swooped in and made the arrest.

(*continued on p. 339*)

An attorney arguing her case before the Connecticut Supreme Court.

As an elected or appointed public official, the prosecutor occupies a crucial position in criminal justice processing. It is the prosecutor who decides how cases brought by the police will be disposed of, which cases will be pursued through the courts, and whether the original charges against an accused may be reduced to some lesser offense. In many jurisdictions, the prosecutor prepares and approves arrest and search warrants before they are formally issued by a magistrate.

Roles and Responsibilities   At the most general level, the responsibilities of the prosecutor are threefold: (1) enforcing the law, (2) representing the government in matters of law, and (3) representing the government and the people in matters of legislation and criminal justice reform. As such, the functions of the prosecutor are extremely broad and considerably more diverse than the commonly perceived role of the state's trial lawyer. Moreover, as legal scholar Wayne R. LaFave has pointed out, the specifics of the prosecutorial role are difficult to grasp fully:

> Appraisal of the role of the prosecutor is made difficult because that role is inevitably more ambiguous than that of the police or the trial court. It is clear that the police are concerned with the detection of crime and the identification and apprehension of offenders; it is likewise apparent that courts must decide the issue of guilt or innocence. A prosecutor, however, may conceive of his principal responsibility in a number of different ways. He may serve primarily as trial counsel for the police department, reflecting the views of the department in his court representation. Or, he may serve as a sort of "house counsel" for the police, giving legal advice to the department on how to develop enforcement practices which will withstand challenge in court. On the other hand, the prosecutor may consider himself primarily a representative of the court, with the responsibility of enforcing rules designed to control police practices and perhaps otherwise acting for the benefit of persons who are proceeded against. Another possibility is that the prosecutor, as an elected official . . . will try primarily to reflect community opinion in the making of decisions as to whether to prosecute.[9]

At the very least, the prosecutor is all of these things. Unlike the roles of other players in the administration of justice, those of the prosecutor span the entire criminal justice process, as follows:

1. *Investigation:* During the investigation phase, prosecutors prepare search and arrest warrants and work with police to ensure that investigation reports are complete. In some circumstances, through either citizen complaints or suspicion of al-

leged criminal acts, prosecutors initiate their own investigations, which may be independent of police activity.

2. *Arrest:* After arrests have been made, prosecutors screen cases to determine which should be prosecuted and which should be dropped.

3. *Initial appearance:* During the first court appearance, prosecutors ensure that defendants are notified of the charges against them. In addition, they serve as the government's attorney at summary trials in minor cases and participate in bail decisions. Importantly, prosecutors can also discontinue a prosecution through a **nolle prosequi** (also referred to as *nol. pros.* or simply *nolle*), a formal statement of unwillingness to proceed further in a particular case.

4. *Preliminary hearing:* Prosecutors have two functions at preliminary hearings: to establish probable cause and to *nol. pros.* cases when appropriate. In jurisdictions that have no initial appearance but proceed directly to the preliminary hearing, prosecutors have the additional tasks of giving formal notice of charges and participating in bail decisions.

5. *Information and indictment:* Prosecutors prepare the *information* report that establishes probable cause and binds an accused person over for trial. In jurisdictions that use the indictment rather than the information, prosecutors establish probable cause before the grand jury.

6. *Arraignment:* Prosecutors arraign felony defendants; that is, they bring the accused to the court to answer to matters charged in the information or indictment. Prosecutors also participate in **plea negotiation**—that is, allowing defendants to plead guilty to a reduced charge or charges.

7. *Pretrial motions:* As representatives of the state, prosecutors initiate and participate in the argument of any pretrial motions.

8. *Trial:* Prosecutors are the government trial lawyers, and as such they attempt to prove guilt beyond a reasonable doubt.

9. *Sentencing:* Prosecutors recommend rigid or lenient sentences.

10. *Appeal:* Through written or oral debate, prosecutors argue that convictions were obtained properly and should not be reversed.

11. *Parole:* In some jurisdictions, prosecutors make recommendations for or against parole for all inmates who are up for review. In most instances, however, prosecutors typically limit themselves to opposing early parole release for serious offenders.

Of these many functions and roles, those with the greatest impact on criminal justice processing are the ones involving *prosecutorial discretion*—the decision to prosecute, the *nol. pros.* of cases, and plea bargaining.

The Decision to Prosecute
Prosecutorial discretion typically begins after an arrest has been made, when police reports are forwarded to the county or state attorney for review. At that point, the prosecutor screens and evaluates the evidence and the details of the arrest and decides whether to accept or reject the case for prosecution. In this decision-making process, the prosecutor has, in theory, absolute and unrestricted discretion to choose who is prosecuted and who is not. The prosecutor's decision in this behalf is called "selective prosecution." Its justifications are not unlike those for selective enforcement of the law by police, including ambiguity in the penal codes, the seriousness of the offense, the size of the court's workload, and the need to treat defendants as individuals.

The legitimacy and necessity of the prosecutor's discretion in pressing charges has long been recognized. As the President's Commission on Law Enforcement and Administration of Justice pointed out many years ago:

> There are many cases in which it would be inappropriate to press charges. In some instances, a street fight for example, the police may make lawful arrests that are not intended to be carried forward to prosecution. When the immediate situation requiring police intervention has passed, the defendant is discharged without further action. Often it becomes apparent after arrest that there is insufficient evidence to support a conviction or that a necessary witness will not cooperate or is unavailable; an arrest may be made when there is

(continued from p. 338)

Ramirez was tried and found guilty of 13 murders and 30 other offenses. He reportedly said, "No big deal. Death comes with the territory. I'll see you in Disneyland," after he was handed 19 death sentences. While on death row at San Quentin, he received mail from scores of female fans, and in 1996 he married a 41-year-old magazine editor who believes Ramirez is innocent. "The Night Stalker" remains on death row and continues to appeal his conviction. ▮

Prosecutors' Biggest Complaints
On a scale of 1 to 10, prosecutors rated how seriously various factors hamper their efforts. Source: *National Law Journal.*

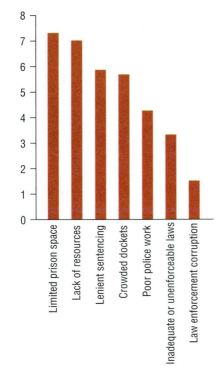

Far more than in any other democracy, American prosecutors have almost unfettered authority to decide whom to charge, what crimes to identify, what penalties to seek, what bail to urge, what evidence to present, what persons to give immunity from prosecution, what plea bargains to make, and what sentences to negotiate.

—*NEW YORK TIMES*
LAW CORRESPONDENT
STUART DIAMOND

Can Two Misdemeanors Equal One Felony?

Remember that old trick with algebra where you could make 2 equal 1? The equations went something like this:

Step 1. If $a = 1$ and $b = 1$, therefore $a = b$.

Step 2. Multiplying both sides by a yields $a^2 = ab$.

Step 3. Subtracting b^2 from both sides yields $a^2 - b^2 = ab - b^2$.

Step 4. Factoring each side of the equation yields $(a + b)(a - b) = b(a - b)$.

Step 5. Dividing both sides by $(a - b)$ yields $a + b = b$, or $2 = 1$.

Although it would appear that 2 might equal 1 here, there is a fallacy. Step 5 called for dividing both sides of the equation by $(a - b)$, which is zero in this case, and you may not divide by zero in any branch of mathematics.

The legal parallel to this example occurred in a Florida courtroom. The case revolved around Ramiro de Jesus Rodriguez and a parent's worst nightmare. When his car hit an oncoming van at a suburban intersection, his 3-year-old daughter pitched from her mother's arms into the windshield, suffering fatal head injuries. Theoretically, it would appear that Rodriguez had committed two crimes: failing to secure his child in a car seat—a misdemeanor punishable in Florida by a $37 fine—and failure to yield the right of way when making a left turn—a traffic infraction. The prosecution interpreted the failure to yield as "reckless driving" and elevated the charge to vehicular homicide.

The case against Rodriguez—a Nicaraguan immigrant who spoke no English and couldn't believe what was happening to him—was so wrenching and so sad that many potential jurors expressed outrage that he was even being put on trial. After the prosecution rested its case, the judge dismissed the charge, ruling that "failure to yield" does not automatically mean "recklessness." In the end, like the mythical $2 = 1$, the prosecutor's legal equation had a fallacy of its own.

Sources: *The New York Times*, May 4, 1991, 1, 8; *Time*, May 13, 1991, 54. ■

probable cause to believe that the person apprehended committed an offense, while conviction after formal charge requires proof of guilt beyond a reasonable doubt. Finally, subsequent investigation sometimes discloses the innocence of the accused.[10]

In addition, there may be tactical matters and law enforcement needs that make it inadvisable to press charges, such as conserving resources for more serious cases or perhaps dropping a charge in exchange for information about more serious crimes. Similarly, invoking the criminal process against marginal offenders may accomplish more harm than good. Attaching a criminal label to a one-time petty offender can conceivably set that person on a course toward a career in serious crime. It should also be noted that a large proportion of arrests are for annoying and offensive behavior—drunkenness, vagrancy, disorderly conduct—rather than dangerous crimes. Prosecuting all these cases would cause undue hardships both for the defendants and for the judicial process.

Other types of cases in which prosecutors are not inclined to seek criminal penalties include minor domestic disturbances; assaults and petty thefts in which the victim and the offender are in the same family or have some social relationship; statutory rape when both parties are young; first-offense car thefts that involve teenagers taking a short joyride; checks drawn on insufficient funds; shoplifting by first offenders, particularly when restitution is made; and criminal acts by offenders suffering from emotional disorders.

In cases in which the accused person poses a serious threat to the welfare of a community—or conversely, when the offense is a minor one—the decision to prosecute or not to prosecute is easy to make. Often, however, the offense and its related elements fall somewhere between these extremes, and the prosecutor must decide whether the benefit to be derived from prosecution would outweigh the costs of such an action.

In practice, the prosecutor's office is the focal point of an exchange system in which numerous marketlike relationships influence the allocation of justice. Political scientist George F. Cole's examination of prosecutorial decision making in Seattle, for example, demonstrated that in actuality, prosecuting attorneys had only a limited degree of discretion when deciding whether to bring formal criminal charges against individuals arrested for violating the law.[11] Cole found that police, court personnel, defense attorneys, and community leaders often managed to affect prosecutorial behavior in circumstances such as the following:

1. Police can apply pressure on a district attorney's office not to prosecute a certain offender because of information the suspect is willing to provide regarding other, more serious criminals. In exchange, the police may offer more investigation resources for a case that the prosecutor is especially interested in.
2. Within courts, pressures from the wardens of overcrowded prison systems affect judges' decisions to convict. Those decisions, in turn, have an impact on the behavior of the prosecutor. The backlog of cases also influences the decision to prosecute.
3. Defense attorneys, too, have exchange relationships with prosecutors. Both prosecutor and defense counsel are interested in a speedy solution to criminal cases. This shared interest results in decisions not to prosecute certain defendants in exchange for the defense's cooperation in prosecuting others.
4. Community leaders, as well, can apply pressure on the prosecutor's office. County, district, and state attorneys are appointed or elected to their posts, and all are vulnerable to public criticism. In an effort to appease the concerns of a community and its influential representatives, prosecutors tend to ignore certain types of offenders and offenses in favor of others. In other instances they may overplay their roles.

In high-profile cases, prosecutors often face special challenges. To cite one example, consider the 1996 case of Amy Grossberg and Brian Peterson, two University of Delaware freshmen who were charged with intentionally killing their newborn son and abandoning him in a dumpster.[12] Initially, the Delaware attorney general's office sought the death penalty because of the age of the victim. This attempt was condemned as too punitive. Later, after Grossberg and Peterson were released on bond and sent home with electronic monitoring pending trial, the attorney general did not contest the pretrial release decision. This decision was also condemned—this time as too lenient. The contradictory reactions to the legal treatment of the young defendants is understandable given the public's ambivalence toward neonaticide and infanticide,[13] yet it also points to the kinds of dilemmas prosecutors face.

Nolle Prosequi   Once prosecution has formally begun and the case is a matter of court record, the prosecutor can terminate any further processing through the *nolle prosequi*. As noted earlier, the *nolle prosequi* or *nol. pros.* is a formal entry in the record by which the prosecutor declares that he or she "will no further prosecute" the case, either (1) as to some of the counts, (2) as to some of the defendants, or (3) altogether.

This right of the prosecutor *not* to prosecute further, even in the face of sufficient evidence, is one of the most powerful examples of discretionary authority in the criminal justice system. There are many reasons for entering a *nol. pros.* The prosecutor may decide, once the judicial process has begun, that the evidence after all is not sufficient for conviction or that it is inadmissible. Alternatively, the decision may rest on aspects of the plea negotiation process or even on leniency.[14] Although this aspect of the prosecutor's discretionary powers has been heavily criticized, it has been repeatedly upheld in the appellate courts. For example, in *United States* v. *Cowen*,[15] a U.S. attorney negotiated a plea agreement whereby the accused would plead guilty to one count of bribery and would cooperate with the Watergate investigation. In exchange, another indictment against the defendant pending in Texas would be dismissed through a *nol. pros.* At trial, the presiding judge denied the U.S. attorney's motion to dismiss, yet on appeal to the Fifth Circuit of the U.S. Court of Appeals the prosecutor's "absolute power" to dismiss proceedings was upheld.

The *nol. pros.* is not without problems, for it can lead to corruption, favoritism, nepotism, and discrimination. Nevertheless, some form of this discretionary process seems necessary, if only to screen out trivial cases, eliminate false accusations, and remove cases in which the accused may indeed be guilty but the prosecution is almost certain to lose—thus wasting the court's time and resources.

Plea Negotiation   In *United States* v. *Cowen*, two aspects of prosecutorial discretion were involved: the *nol. pros.* and plea negotiation. Usually referred to as "plea bargaining," plea negotiation is one of the most commonly accepted practices in criminal justice processing. It is believed that more than 90% of criminal convictions result from negotiated pleas of guilty.[16]

As noted at the beginning of the chapter, plea bargaining takes place between the prosecutor and the defense counsel or the accused. It involves discussions that aim toward an agreement under which the defendant will plead guilty in exchange for some

"How do you plead? Please listen carefully, as the menu has changed."

© The New Yorker Collection 2001 Leo Cullum from cartoonbank.com.
All Rights Reserved.

prosecutorial or judicial concession (see Exhibit 11.3). These concessions are of four types:

1. The initial charges may be reduced, thus ensuring a reduction in the sentence.
2. In instances of multiple charges, the number of counts may be reduced.
3. A recommendation for leniency may be made by the prosecutor, thus reducing the potential sentence from incarceration to probation.
4. In cases in which the charges involve a negative label, such as child molesting, the complaint may be altered to a less repugnant one, such as assault.[17]

The widespread use of negotiated pleas is a result of overcrowded caseloads in criminal courts. Proponents of plea bargaining maintain that it is beneficial to both the accused and the state. For the accused, plea bargaining has three advantages:

1. It reduces the possibility of detention during extensive pretrial and trial processing.
2. It increases the chances of a reduced sentence.
3. It decreases the costs of legal representation.

For the state, plea bargaining also has advantages:

1. It reduces the overall financial costs of criminal prosecution.
2. It improves the efficiency of the courts by having fewer cases go to trial.
3. It enables the prosecution to devote more time and resources to more important and serious cases.

While plea negotiation is common, it is also controversial. First, it encourages the accused person to waive his or her constitutional right to trial. Second, it enables the defendant to receive a sentence that is generally less severe than the one he or she might otherwise have received; in the eyes of the public, the criminal has "beaten the system." Third, it sacrifices legislative policies (embodied in the criminal law) for the sake of tactical accommodations between the prosecution and defense. Fourth, it ignores the correctional needs of the bulk of offenders, for in many instances the accused may ultimately plead guilty to a charge that is far removed from the original crime. Fifth, it raises the danger that an innocent person, fearing a guilty verdict and harsh sentence if the case goes to trial, will plead guilty and accept conviction, hoping for lighter treatment. For example, there is the problematic case of Harry Seigler, a 30-year-old man who was tried in a Virginia court for robbery and murder. Having pleaded not guilty, he was waiting for the jury to return a verdict. With three convictions of robbery already to his credit, he was nervous. His two lawyers had disagreed on his chances of being found not guilty; there was the possibility of his being convicted of capital murder; and another man had just been executed in Virginia's electric chair. The prosecutor offered a deal: Plead guilty to first-degree murder and robbery and receive a 60-year prison term, with 20 years suspended. Seigler accepted the deal, and so did the judge. As Seigler was led away, the judge was informed that the jury had finally reached its verdict: *not guilty.*[18]

Despite its controversial nature, plea bargaining has received the blessing of the U.S. Supreme Court. The Court once commented that although there may be neither a constitutional nor a statutory basis for plea bargaining, the practice can serve the interests of both the accused and the court. However, this formal recognition of the previously unacknowledged custom of plea negotiation did not occur until 1970, in **Brady v. United States.**[19] In later declarations, the Supreme Court built a number of safeguards into the bargaining process. In 1971, it maintained that the promise of a prosecutor made during plea negotiations must be kept;[20] and in 1976, it ruled that to be valid, a guilty plea had to be made *voluntarily* and with full knowledge of its implications.[21]

In defense of the state's position in plea bargaining, the Supreme Court has also made its position clear. In the 1970 case of *North Carolina* v. *Alford,*[22] for example, the Court ruled that a judge may accept a guilty plea from a defendant *who maintains his innocence* if (1) the plea is made voluntarily and understandably and (2) there is strong factual evidence of the defendant's guilt. And in *Bordenkircher* v. *Hayes,*[23] decided in 1978, the Court ruled that due process rights are not violated when a prosecutor threat-

> The typical method of conviction is by the accused's plea of guilty. Mostly, therefore, the system of administering criminal justice in the United States is a system of *justice without trial.*
>
> **—JEROME H. SKOLNICK**

VICTIMS & JUSTICE | EXHIBIT 11.3

Players in the Plea Bargaining Process

Discussions about plea bargaining generally revolve around two issues: (1) the advantages versus disadvantages of the practice and (2) Supreme Court decisions that have attempted to regulate proper conduct of the negotiations. But who are the principal players in the process and what are their roles in the negotiation of a plea? Do crime victims have a say in the negotiations?

The Prosecutor

Without question, it is the prosecutor who plays the major role in plea negotiation. On a case-by-case basis, the prosecutor determines the concessions to be offered. Some jurisdictions have guidelines to provide consistency in plea bargaining cases, but in most there are no procedures to control the discretion of the prosecutor. Thus, such competing alternatives and factors as the seriousness of the crime, the attitude of the victim, the content of the police report, the applicable sentencing provisions, the strength of the state's case, the presiding judge's attitudes toward plea bargaining, the court caseload, and the pressures exerted by the police and the community all represent input to the prosecutor's decision.

The Defense Counsel

The defense, whether a private attorney, assigned counsel, or a public defender, has a very explicit role in the plea bargaining process. First, the counsel for the defense interacts directly with the prosecutor in the negotiation of the plea. Second, once a plea has been initially "bargained," there are well established guidelines—from both the U.S. Supreme Court and the American Bar Association—as to the defense attorney's actions. It is the responsibility of the defense to make certain that his or her client understands both the bargaining process and the plea. That is, the attorney must explain to the accused the facts of the various charges, the sentencing provisions of the alternative charges, and that he or she is waiving certain rights by pleading guilty. Thus, the defense acts in an advisory role and is required to inform the client of all discussions and negotiations throughout the bargaining process.

The Accused

Although it is the accused whose future is at stake, he or she has only a small role in the plea bargaining process. The accused rarely takes part in direct negotiations, the exceptions being defendants who may have some information to offer a prosecutor about other cases in return for further concessions. In general, however, the accused's role is limited to an acceptance or a rejection of the prosecutor's offer.

A plea being negotiated.

The Judge

Participation by federal judges in plea negotiations is prohibited by the federal rules of criminal procedure. At the state level, some jurisdictions formally prohibit the practice while others encourage it. Some argue that judicial participation in plea negotiations would regulate the practice, ensure greater fairness, and make sentencing more uniform. However, opponents claim that such participation lessens the objectivity of the judge in determining the voluntariness of the plea, is inconsistent with the purposes of the presentence investigation report, and suggests to the defendant that he or she may not receive a fair trial.

The Victim

In the majority of states, the victims of crime and/or members of their families are given some level of consultation about a pending negotiated plea agreement. However, the extent of this consultation varies widely from one jurisdiction to the next. In some states, for example, the only requirement under law is that a reasonable effort be made to notify the victim that a plea agreement is being considered. In Arizona, by contrast, the standards are more rigorous. Victims must be given notice of a plea proceeding, their right to be present, and their right to be heard. And in South Dakota, prosecutors are required to disclose the victim's comments and enter them into court records.

While debates continue over the appropriateness, fairness, and efficacy of plea bargaining, the practice persists. Furthermore, because most negotiations take place in judges' chambers, in prosecutors' offices, in courtroom hallways and restrooms, and even in the barrooms adjacent to the courthouse, it remains difficult to fully assess the actual roles played by all of the participants and to more effectively regulate the levels of their conduct and involvement.

ens to reindict a defendant on more serious charges if he or she does not agree to plead guilty to the original charge.

In the final analysis, plea bargaining will necessarily endure. It is a great safety valve, perhaps the only factor that stands between the administration of justice and utter chaos. Without this tool, every defendant charged with an offense, however serious

EXHIBIT 11.4 | International Perspectives on Crime & Justice

Plea Bargaining in France

France enacted sweeping and controversial legislation in early 2004 designed to crack down on crime and expedite the legal process. The Perben II, so named after France's justice minister, Dominique Perben, contains 400 changes to the country's penal system, but among the most controversial is that it, for the first time, introduces American-style plea bargaining to a society traditionally reluctant to wield too much power to prosecutors and the court system. Plea bargaining allows a defendant to plead guilty to a charge in exchange for a lesser sentence, which proponents of the measure say is necessary to expedite the sluggish French courts and to obtain corroborating evidence from defendants.

Vocal critics of plea bargaining are disturbed because it might entice innocent people to plead guilty in order to avoid a harsher sentence later. Hundreds of lawyers, including the presidents of France's 181 bar associations, protested outside the National Assembly after the bill's passage, and most of the country's 40,000 lawyers went on strike to show their distain for the legislation. The socialist opposition in the National Assembly challenges the very constitutionality of the provision, claiming that it may in fact violate the clause guaranteeing a right to a fair trial.

The juxtaposition of the plea bargaining measure lies in the government's claim that it would reduce the backlog of cases in the courts, but at the same time other recent laws have strengthened punishments for crimes, including misdemeanors. France's prisons already exceed their capacity by 25%.

Such dramatic legal changes have come about in France amid an increase in violent crime and evidence of terrorist activity within the country. In 2002, the French elected a center-right government into power in Jacques Chirac's administration, which claims that reforms like the Perben II are necessary in order to fight crime and adapt in accordance with modern times. Those opposed to such restrictive measures say that the police and prosecutorial powers are expanded at the expense of civil liberties and human rights.

Sources: Marc Burleigh, "French Lawyers Strike over Criminal Justice Bill," *Agence France Presse,* February 11, 2004; John Henley, "Lawyers Protest as French MPs Give Police More Powers," *The Guardian,* February 12, 2004, 15; Eric Pape and Adam Piore, "Justice, American Style," *Newsweek,* February 23, 2004, 32; Elaine Sciolino, "Lawyers Protest Across France at Sweeping Anticrime Law," *The New York Times,* February 12, 2004, A11.

or benign, would have to go to trial. As it is, millions of cases are processed in the courts each year. With existing resources, a person arrested today might have to wait a quarter-century for his or her case to come up. Aside from expediency, however, the "virtue" of plea bargaining for both the defense and the prosecution is that it eliminates uncertainty—all sides generally prefer to opt for a "sure thing." For the defendant charged with murder, it can remove the possibility of a life sentence or even death; for the prosecutor, it precludes any possibility of having a serious offender escape justice because of some real or imagined weakness in the case. On the negative side, however, there are innocent individuals who would rather plead guilty to a negotiated offense than face the possible consequences of an adverse verdict; these are people caught in a web of circumstances that have made them appear guilty. There is no way of knowing how many innocent defendants have chosen this course and spent weeks, months, or even years in prison. For a description of the introduction of plea bargaining in France, see Exhibit 11.4.

Defense Attorneys

This case . . . is a loser.[24]

— O. J. SIMPSON'S LEAD DEFENSE ATTORNEY, THE LATE JOHNNIE COCHRAN

Yes, I would defend him. And I would win.

— HARVARD LAW PROFESSOR ALAN DERSHOWITZ, TELLING A GROUP OF YALE LAW STUDENTS THAT, IF HE HAD THE CHANCE, HE WOULD DEFEND ADOLF HITLER

The right of a criminal defendant to be represented by counsel is fundamental to the American system of criminal justice. The reason for this right is the need to protect individual liberties. Defendants facing criminal charges require the assistance of counsel to protect their interests at every phase of the adversarial process and to help them understand the nature and consequences of the proceedings against them. Moreover, courtroom operations are highly technical, and even the best-informed defendants are ill-equipped to represent themselves tactically in the face of the complexities of criminal law and procedure.

"I'm going to concentrate on mergers and takeovers—
with a minor in plea-bargining."

© The New Yorker Collection 2001 Ed Fisher from cartoonbank.com. All Rights Reserved.

Functions of Defense Counsel The defense counsel can perform many functions while representing a defendant in the criminal process. Those functions generally include the following:

1. Representing the accused immediately after arrest to provide advice during interrogation and ensure that constitutional safeguards are not violated during pretrial
   procedures.
2. Reviewing police reports and further investigating the details of the offense.
3. Interviewing the police, the accused, and the witness, and seeking out additional
   evidence and witnesses on behalf of the defendant.
4. Discussing the offense with the prosecutor to gain insight into the strength of the
   state's case.
5. Representing the accused at bail hearings and during plea negotiations.
6. Preparing, filing, and arguing pretrial motions.
7. Preparing the case for trial.
8. Participating in jury selection.
9. Representing the accused at trial.
10. Providing advice and assistance at sentencing.
11. Determining and pursuing the appropriate bases for appeal.
12. Presenting written or oral arguments at appeal.[25]

In actual practice, few defense attorneys participate in all of these activities. As
noted earlier, a number of cases are "screened out" of the justice system through the

Who Has the Lowest Ethics?

Percentage of respondents who say these
people have the lowest ethical standards:

Car salespeople: 17%

Lawyers: 11%

Labor union leaders: 9%

TV reporters and commentators: 8%

Source: Gallup Poll. ∎

prosecutor's decision not to prosecute, and most of the remaining cases are disposed of through guilty pleas. Thus, the defense attorney's activities are usually limited to the pretrial phases of the judicial process. Moreover, studies indicate that most defense lawyers have their initial contacts with their clients only after they have been placed on bail or released on recognizance.

Because more and more government attorneys are selecting for prosecution only cases in which the potential for conviction is high, the defense counsel's most intensive efforts take place at the beginning of the discretionary screening process. During this period, which can last up to 2 weeks in urban areas where arrest rates are high, the defendant's lawyer has the opportunity to gather background material on the client and the case. If this preliminary investigation suggests that the offense was a minor one, that the arrest was weak or questionable, or that there were irregularities in the arresting officer's behavior (such as illegal search and seizure), the defense counsel can put pressure on the prosecutor to dismiss the case or begin plea negotiations.

A second-level activity for the defense counsel involves pretrial motions. A **motion** is an application made to the court or the judge requesting an order or ruling in favor of the applicant. Motions can be of various types, but most common at the pretrial proceedings are those that seek to learn something about the prosecutor's case or to suppress certain types of evidence. Prominent Houston attorney Anthony C. Friloux noted that aggressive use of pretrial motions can have numerous advantages for the defense, including the following:

1. It forces partial disclosure of the prosecutor's evidence at an early date.
2. It puts pressure on the prosecutor to consider plea bargaining early in the proceeding.
3. It forces exposure of primary state witnesses at an inopportune time for the prosecution.
4. It raises before the trial judge, early in the proceedings, matters the defense may want called to his attention.
5. It forces the prosecutor to make decisions prior to his final case preparation.
6. It allows the defendant to see his defense counsel in action, which has a salutary effect on the client–attorney relationship.[26]

The use of motions is in part a bluffing game to determine how the court will react and how many rulings a judge will make. Nevertheless, it tends to wear down many prosecutors. In some heavily populated jurisdictions, it is not unusual for a prosecutor to be carrying 50 to 60 cases at any given time. With this heavy workload it is generally easier for the prosecutor to negotiate a guilty plea or drop the case altogether than to continue in a time-consuming struggle to answer all of an adversary's petitions.

Defending people accused of a crime is the most distasteful function performed by lawyers.

— F. LEE BAILEY

Retained Counsel The idea of a "criminal lawyer" may conjure up images of people such as Alan Dershowitz, F. Lee Bailey, the late Johnnie Cochran, or the fictional Perry Mason. But these are only the most visible defense attorneys. They accept only the most sensational and dramatic cases or the ones that will earn them substantial fees or celebrity. In contrast, the average criminal lawyer deals with more mundane crimes and does not enjoy high prestige—much like the majority of attorneys portrayed in TV's *Law & Order*.

Criminal law is a field that few attorneys actively choose. The greatest financial rewards go to lawyers who devote their professional lives to the litigation of major civil suits and to advising businesses and corporations. Thus the best-trained and most highly skilled attorneys are drawn to the corporate, large-scale, bureaucratic types of practice. The criminal lawyer, on the other hand, exists in an environment characterized by long hours in overcrowded, physically unpleasant courts, generally dealing with people who are educationally, economically, and socially underprivileged. Moreover, studies have demonstrated that criminal work is most often undertaken by lawyers operating as individual practitioners. Many are from working-class families and went to law school on a part-time basis. Known in New York as "Baxter's bar," in the District of Columbia as the "Fifth Streeters," in Chicago as the "State Street bar," and almost

A frontier lawyer awaits clients in his "office" during the Oklahoma land rush of 1889.

everywhere as "the courthouse gang" or the night school "schlocks," these are the attorneys at the lower end of the legal profession. They do the "dirty work" of the bar—not only criminal cases but personal injury, divorce, and collections as well.[27]

The "Court Street lawyers" of Brooklyn, New York, are typical of this group. Referred to locally as "ambulance chasers" and as "shysters," "schlocks," and "schnorrers," many operate from small storefront offices on commercial streets near court buildings. The windows of their premises are filled with notices of the services they perform: real

"He says he wants a lawyer."

© The New Yorker Collection 1999 Tom Chalkley from cartoonbank.com. All Rights Reserved.

On Lawyers

Lawyer: a person learned in the law.

—*BLACK'S LAW DICTIONARY*

To some lawyers all facts are created equal.

—JUSTICE FELIX FRANKFURTER

A lawyer starts life giving five hundred dollars' worth of law for five dollars, and ends giving five dollars' worth for five hundred dollars.

—BENJAMIN H. BREWSTER

If there were no bad people there would be no good lawyers.

—CHARLES DICKENS

I don't want a lawyer to tell me what I cannot do; I hire him to tell me how to do what I want to do.

—J. PIERPONT MORGAN

Accuracy and diligence are much more necessary to a lawyer than comprehension of mind or brillancy of talent.

—DANIEL WEBSTER

99% of lawyers give the rest a bad name.

—COMEDIAN STEVEN WRIGHT

The bad image and reputation lawyers have are earned in part, and part is the nature of the business, which is filled with controversy. It is a business in which, at a minimum, each lawyer makes somebody unhappy either by beating him, embarrassing him, or tying him in knots.

—F. LEE BAILEY

How do you know when a lawyer is lying? When you see his lips moving.

—ELLIS RUBIN,
MIAMI ATTORNEY

estate and insurance sales, tax preparation, and notary work. They are readily found roaming the hallways, galleries, and restrooms of court buildings, searching for clients who can pay them a modest fee.[28]

As to the role of defense counsel in the typical criminal case, lawyer-sociologist Abraham S. Blumberg has referred to it as a "lawyer–client confidence game," in which the mission of the attorney is the fixing and collection of fees.[29] At the outset, attorneys who are members of the local "courthouse gangs" make it clear to their clients that there is a firm connection between fee payment and the zealous exercise of professional expertise, "inside" knowledge, and organizational connections on their behalf. The attorney then manipulates the client and stage-manages the case so that legal service has at least the appearance of being rendered. This is accomplished through a certain amount of sales puff, combined with the implication of access to secret legal knowledge and connections.

For Blumberg, the lawyer–client relationship represents a confidence game in that throughout his or her performance the criminal defense attorney is a "double agent" who works not only for the accused but also for the court organization. Both sides are anxious to terminate the litigation with a minimum of time, expense, and damage. The attorney collects a fee in advance, emphasizes to the client how difficult the case is, speaks of "connections" within the court system, negotiates a lesser plea that is in the interests of the prosecutor, and ultimately "cools out" the client by telling him or her that the lesser sentence on the reduced charge was actually a victory. Moreover, as Blumberg emphasizes, "as in a genuine confidence game, the victim who has participated is loath to do anything that will upset the lesser plea which his or her lawyer has 'conned' him or her into accepting."[30] And the con game is *complete,* since the defendant is separated from any gains he or she may have acquired from illicit activities. Not infrequently, the proceeds from a larceny are sequestered (seized) by a defense lawyer in lieu of a fee.

This lawyer–client confidence game is played not only by many of the "courthouse gang," but also by some of the larger and more prestigious operations:

> The large-scale law firm may not speak as openly of its "contacts" and "fixing" abilities as does the lower-level lawyer. It trades instead upon the facade of thick carpeting, walnut paneling, genteel low pressure, and superficialities of traditional legal professionalism. But even the large firm may be challenged because the services rendered or results obtained do not appear to merit the fee asked. Thus there is a recurrent problem in the legal profession in fixing the fee and justifying it.[31]

Whether the defense counsel is truly representing the interests of the client or is engaging in the lawyer–client confidence game, the general impression given to the public is that the attorney is helping the criminal "beat the rap." To most Americans this seems to be a perversion of justice, especially when evidence suggests that the accused is clearly guilty but, through a lawyer's skillful maneuverings, is set free on a legal technicality.

Many people also question the ethics of an attorney who defends a client that he or she knows is guilty. However, both the code of the legal profession and the principles of American jurisprudence demand such action. The doctrine of fairness in the adversarial system recognizes that individuals accused of criminal offenses are entitled to use every resource at their disposal to defend themselves. The function of the defense attorney is *not* to decide whether the accused is innocent but to give him or her the best possible advice within the limits of the law and the ethics of the legal profession. The rights of the accused are designed to protect the innocent, and if the guilty are freed as the result of some technical issue, then that is the price that must be paid to ensure that the scales of justice remain in balance. Thus, defense attorneys should be seen not as legal technicians who are attempting to "get criminals off" but, rather, as counselors who are protecting the entire system. As one legal commentator put it: "If attorneys refuse to represent defendants who they believe are guilty, the right of a defendant to be represented by counsel is eliminated and with it the entire traditional trial."[32]

This difficulty is often faced by public defenders, who represent a large percentage of the defendants in criminal proceedings. But whether counsel is a private attorney or a public defender, he or she is an advocate whose role is to obtain an acquittal for the client. Of course, under ethical and legal codes a defense lawyer is not permitted to mount a dishonest defense (arranging for witnesses who will lie, for example). Aside from that, the lawyer's only obligation is to the client.

Bailiffs, Clerks, and Other Courtroom Regulars

In addition to the principal actors in the courtroom work group—judges, prosecutors, and defense attorneys—there are other persons who play a role in criminal proceedings. They include bailiffs and sheriffs, the court clerk, court reporters and stenographers, witnesses, coroners and medical examiners, and others.

Bailiffs and Sheriffs   Each courtroom is assigned a *bailiff* or *sheriff,* whose formal duties are to announce the arrival and departure of the judge and maintain order in the courtroom. In addition, depending on local custom, bailiffs and sheriffs serve as messengers for lawyers and other court officials; keep track of prosecutors, attorneys, and witnesses so that they are present when their cases come up; and, in some instances, provide information to defendants—advising them which court they belong in, where their attorney might be found, and, if asked, what the outcome of the case might be.[33]

The Court Clerk   Every court has a clerk, whose responsibilities include "calling the calendar" (calling up the next case before the judge), updating defendants' files, managing the court's files, and ensuring that evidence in the custody of the court is secure. In the small lower courts, there may be only one clerk for the entire courthouse. In larger jurisdictions, each courtroom may have its own *court clerk,* plus several courthouse file clerks who help maintain the court's records, collect any fines and court costs imposed, and prepare the daily calendars.

Although the title may imply otherwise, the court clerk occupies a position of considerable importance. This is especially true of the chief clerk of a large court system. Often the clerk's post is occupied by young attorneys who use it as a stepping-stone to the prosecutor's office. Not only does it provide exposure to the routine of the courthouse, but it also offers experience in some areas of law, since many clerks are empowered to prepare formal writs and process documents issued by the court.

Court Reporters and Court Stenographers   A *court reporter* or *court stenographer* is present at almost every judicial proceeding to report and (perhaps) transcribe matters of record. The mechanics of court reporting have changed considerably over time. In the past most reporters were expert stenographers who used a manual shorthand system to create verbatim accounts (transcripts) of proceedings. Manual shorthand writers are almost extinct, having been replaced by machine writers. Machine writers use a device that resembles a small typewriter to imprint coded letters on a tape. The tape may be translated visually, or it may be optically scanned. Alternatively, the keystrokes may be used to create a cassette from which a computer is instructed to transcribe.

Enormous sums have been spent on electrical equipment for recording judicial proceedings. Although it is cost-effective compared to the use of live reporters—some reporters earn $300 a day or more—this equipment has not lived up to its promise. Objectionable comments of witnesses and counsel, extraneous noises, and privileged communications are regularly recorded—and not easily edited. More important, there is no court reporter present to interrupt proceedings when language is unclear, garbled, or barely audible.

To remedy this situation, computer-assisted reporting and transcription have revolutionized the profession. Not only are transcripts more accurate, but preparation and delivery times have been reduced. Today's court reporter, then, must be a computer-compatible writer.

A man walks into a law office and asks the attorney, "Sir, may I ask you a question?"

"Of course, of course," the attorney replies.

The man then asks, "How much will you charge me to answer 3 questions?"

The lawyer responds: "$3,000! Now what's your third question?" ■

A court reporter records the proceedings of the Alabama Court of the Judiciary.

A "stenographic transcript" fails to reproduce tones of voice and hesitations of speech that often make a sentence mean the reverse of what the mere words signify. The best and most accurate record [of oral testimony] is like a dehydrated peach; it has neither the substance nor the flavor of the peach before it was dried.

—FROM JEROME FRANK,
COURTS OF TRIAL, 1949

Witnesses Almost all criminal proceedings have witnesses, who are of three principal types: the police witness, the lay witness, and the expert witness.

A *police witness* is generally an arresting officer who has some knowledge of the facts of the case, having been at the scene of the crime during or soon after its commission. The police witness would be called to testify if he or she had observed some part of the offense (for example, seeing the accused perpetrating the crime) or pertinent events in its aftermath (for example, observing the accused fleeing from the crime scene). Police also serve as witnesses when they present the results of an investigation that led to the arrest of the defendant.

The *lay witness* is a citizen bystander or victim who has some personal knowledge that is relevant to the case. The lay witness is permitted to testify only on facts that were directly ascertained through sensory perception. Thus, the citizen cannot be a witness if his or her knowledge of the case is based on conjecture or opinion.

The *expert witness* is called into court to provide technical information and opinions about matters of which the judge or jury may have no knowledge. To qualify as an expert, the witness must offer testimony in an area in which the general public has little or no understanding and must have established qualifications and authority in that area. The decision as to whether someone qualifies as an expert witness is made by the trial judge. There are experts on fiber evidence, DNA evidence, eyewitness testimony, and so forth. A psychiatrist, for example, may testify as an expert witness regarding the accused's mental competency; an authority on ballistics may comment on whether a bullet was fired from a certain weapon; or a specialist in earth science may establish whether soil on the accused's clothing matches soil samples from where the murder victim was found.

The expert witness role is a subject of debate, however. There are concerns about "hired guns" and specialists in "junk science" who advertise that they will testify in any court to almost any theory as long as they are well paid. This controversy has intensified since the beginning of the 1990s, perhaps because of wider use of DNA evidence, the battered woman syndrome and "abuse excuse" defenses, and similar issues. Some observers have argued that courts have fallen victim to "junk science" because many judges and juries are unable to separate sound science from fanciful fiction.[34] Although few scholars would agree that jurors are incapable of evaluating scientific evidence, surveys suggest that judges and jurors alike find the task challenging. As a safeguard in this regard, in 1993 the U.S. Supreme Court concluded in *Daubert* v. *Merrell Dow Pharmaceuticals* that trial judges should act as gatekeepers, making preliminary evaluations of the scientific basis of such testimony before allowing the expert to testify in the presence of a jury.[35] Since *Daubert,* a number of court decisions have gone further to establish that judges must now evaluate the proffered expert evidence according to a set of criteria and make a general determination that it is sound science. As a result, the Federal Judicial Center and other judicial education programs now train judges to be "miniscientists" in addition to being judges.

Coroners and Medical Examiners The *coroner* is an appointed or elected county official whose chief function is to investigate the cause of all deaths that have occurred in the absence of witnesses, that show evidence of violence, or that have occurred under suspicious circumstances. The office of coroner is an English invention dating from the 12th century, when the entire realm was considered to be the property of the king. The term derives from *corona,* meaning "crown," and the coroner was second only to the king in power and dignity. He was a man of substance who was considered to be capable of mature judgment; his duties included adjudicating not only on matters of violent and suspicious death but also on questions of property ownership.[36]

The American coroner system is a relic of its early English counterpart. Currently, the office of coroner in most communities is a political position like that of mayor or sheriff, and requires no qualifications other than eligibility to hold political office. The coroner appoints a number of deputies, a forensic pathologist—sometimes with an assistant who specializes in toxicology or ballistics—and a scattering of part-time physicians.

CAREERS IN CRIMINAL JUSTICE

Increasing Numbers of Women in Law School

Although women are increasingly earning law degrees, gender disparities persist in the legal profession. In 2005, females constituted 47.7 percent of the total enrollment in law school, according to the American Bar Association, a dramatic increase over the 3 percent of first-year female students in the class of 1947. In 2004, women earned 20,551 of the 44,121 law degrees awarded for the academic year. And while parity has slowly invaded law school classes, parity after graduation is a different story. Given that women have consistently made up over 40 percent of the graduating law school classes for over two decades now, women continue to be underrepresented in terms of top law positions. Overall, women constitute almost 30 percent of all U.S. lawyers, but of the 250 largest law firms in the country, only 5 percent are run by women. Women constituted just 15 percent of general counsel at Fortune 500 companies in 2005, although that was an improvement over the 9.6 percent in 1999. In addition, the annual median salary of women lawyers averages only about three-quarters that of men.

Perhaps not surprisingly, the attrition rate among women attorneys is higher than that of their male counterparts, which many suggest is due to the demands of work versus family, exclusion from networks, and a lack of adequate mentoring. Studies indicate that 9 percent of women leave their firms within the first year; within 5 years, the rate jumps to 54.9 percent. The attrition rate is even higher among ethnic minorities, as 11 percent leave within the first year and 69.3 percent leave within 5 years.

What are the implications from a dearth of female attorneys? In an increasingly diverse world, a similarly diverse counsel helps re-

Reprinted by permission of www.CartoonStock.com

spond to the varied needs of clients through innovative ways of thinking and responding to situations. For example, one firm that launched a "Women's Initiative" program specifically to help facilitate the success of its female attorneys found that its implementation has improved relations among attorneys, clients, and the community.

If that is the case, then more steps should be taken to ensure that gender parity doesn't end when law school does.

The coroner does not hold a judicial position in the strictest sense, but performs certain quasi-judicial functions. The coroner is authorized, for instance, to conduct *inquests,* which are legal inquiries into deaths in which accident, foul play, or violence is suspected. The inquest is similar to a trial in many ways, although it is not governed by the same precise procedure. The coroner conducts the inquest, subpoenas witnesses and documents, cross-examines witnesses under oath, introduces evidence, and receives testimony—all with a jury present. Should the inquest find "just cause" to arrest a suspect, the coroner issues an arrest warrant or moves for the prosecutor to request a warrant from a magistrate.

The coroner system in the United States has been heavily criticized for both corruption and incompetence. Coroners often gain this position through patronage—either direct appointment or placement on the ballot. Coroners usually have no background in either medicine or law; the physicians who work as adjuncts to the office are not necessarily required to have any medico-legal training; and if a forensic pathologist is appointed as a coroner's deputy, he or she is generally a newly qualified medic with little experience.

As a result, many jurisdictions have abolished the office of coroner and substituted the office of *medical examiner,* thus divorcing the system from political control and influence. The medical examiner is a licensed physician with training in forensic pathology who is appointed by government authority on a nonpartisan basis. He or she carries out only the medical aspects of any investigation, not the quasi-judicial functions, which are handled by the court.[37]

The New York City Medical Examiner's office in July 2004 brings out the body of actor Eric Douglas, the son of Kirk Douglas and brother of Michael Douglas. Eric was found dead earlier in the day by a maid who had come to clean his Manhattan apartment.

The medical examiner system was installed in Massachusetts as early as 1877 and is currently used in more than half the states. It is also found in metropolitan areas of some states where the coroner system still persists. In addition, some jurisdictions have medical examiner–coroner systems, in which the coroner's office is headed by a medical examiner.

Auxiliary Court Personnel Depending on the jurisdiction, the size of the court, and the traditions of a given legal community, a range of additional personnel may provide support services for the criminal judicial process. Both the prosecutor's and public defender's offices may have a number of *secretaries, aides, translators and interpreters,* and *investigators,* who assist in the collection of evidence and the preparation of cases. There are *court officers,* or perhaps *police officers* assigned to the court, or *correctional officers* who maintain custody over detainees who are making court appearances. Also, because many courts have various types of pretrial diversion programs, there may be any number of *pretrial service representatives.* Similarly, because pretrial release often occurs, *bail bond agents* are also part of the court process.

Finally, there are a number of other significant figures who will be discussed in detail in later chapters. These are *probation officers, grand juries,* and *trial juries.*

The Right to Counsel

In all criminal prosecutions, the accused shall enjoy the right . . . to have the assistance of counsel for his defense.

— **FROM THE SIXTH AMENDMENT**

Despite the unambiguous language of the Sixth Amendment, for almost a century and a half after the framing of the Constitution only individuals charged with federal crimes punishable by death were guaranteed the right to counsel. The right of all other defendants—both federal and state—to have the help of an attorney typically depended on their ability to retain their own defense lawyers. In the 1930s, however, this began to change.

Powell v. *Alabama*

On March 25, 1931, a group of nine young African American men, ranging in age from 13 to 21 years, were riding in an open gondola car aboard a freight train as it made its way across the state of Alabama. Also aboard the train were seven other young men and two young women, all of whom were white. At some point during the journey, a fight broke out between the two groups, during which six of the whites were thrown from the train. A message was relayed ahead reporting the incident and requesting that all the blacks be taken from the train. As it pulled into the station at Paint Rock, a small town in northeast Alabama, a sheriff's posse was waiting. The two white women, Victoria Price and Ruby Bates, claimed that they had been raped by a number of the black youths. All nine blacks were immediately taken into custody. Surrounded by a growing and hostile crowd, the youths were taken some 20 miles east and placed under military guard in the local jail at Scottsboro, the seat of Jackson County, Alabama.

The "Scottsboro boys," as they became known to history, were indicted on March 31 and arraigned on the same day, at which point they pleaded not guilty. Until the morning of the trial, no lawyer had been designated by name to represent any of the defendants. On April 6, a visiting lawyer from Tennessee expressed an interest in assisting any counsel the court might designate for the defense, and a local Scottsboro attorney reluctantly offered to represent the defendants. The proceedings began immediately.

The youngest of the nine youths arrested had not been indicted because he was only 13 years old. The remaining eight were divided into three groups for separate trials, each lasting only a single day. Medical and other evidence showed that the two women, who were alleged to be prostitutes, had not been raped. Nevertheless, the eight

The Scottsboro boys in their jail cell in Alabama

Scottsboro boys were convicted of rape. Under the existing Alabama statute, the punishment for rape was to be fixed by the jury—anywhere from 10 years' imprisonment to death. The jury chose death for all eight defendants.[38]

The trial court overruled all motions for new trials and sentenced the defendants in accordance with the jury's recommendation. The supreme court of Alabama subsequently reversed the conviction of one defendant, but affirmed the convictions of the remaining seven. Upon appeal to the U.S. Supreme Court, the Scottsboro defendants, in ***Powell v. Alabama***,[39] alleged a denial of Fourteenth Amendment due process and equal protection of the laws because they had not been given a fair trial, they had been denied the right to counsel, and they had been denied a trial by an impartial jury since blacks were systematically excluded from jury service.

In reversing the rape convictions, the Supreme Court observed that Powell and his codefendants were denied their right to effective assistance of legal counsel, in violation of the due process clause of the Fourteenth Amendment. In the Court's majority opinion, Justice George Sutherland made the following comments:

> It is hardly necessary to say that . . . a defendant should be afforded a fair opportunity to secure counsel of his own choice. Not only was that not done here, but such designation of counsel as was attempted was either so indefinite or so close upon the trial as to amount to a denial of effective and substantial aid in that regard.

And further:

> In the light of the facts outlined—the ignorance and illiteracy of the defendants, their youth, the circumstances of public hostility, the imprisonment and the close surveillance of the defendants by the military forces, the fact that their friends and families were all in other states and communication with them necessarily difficult, and above all that they stood in deadly peril of their lives—we think the failure of the trial court to give them reasonable time and opportunity to secure counsel was a clear denial of due process.

The decision in *Powell* was a very narrow ruling, for it limited its application to defendants who were indigent, accused of a crime for which the death penalty could be imposed, and incapable of defending themselves because of low intelligence, illiteracy, or some similar handicap. Nevertheless, *Powell* was the first in a series of Supreme

Court cases that would extend the Sixth Amendment right to counsel.[40] For more about the Scottsboro defendants and the disposition of their cases, see Exhibit 11.5.

Extending the Right to Counsel

Six years after *Powell*, the High Court's decision in **Johnson v. Zerbst** held that all indigent *federal* defendants facing felony charges were entitled to the assistance of an attorney provided by the government.[41] Johnson, a U.S. Marine charged with passing counterfeit money, had been convicted, but without the aid of a defense attorney. He challenged his conviction and won a reversal from the Supreme Court. But the *Johnson* decision provided no relief for state defendants. Although *Powell* had extended this Sixth Amendment right to individuals charged with capital offenses, and *Townsend* v. *Burke* extended it to defendants in state cases at the time of sentencing,[42] the Court continued to withhold such aid in all other state cases.

In 1942, the Supreme Court reaffirmed its position on the matter in **Betts v. Brady**,[43] ruling that in noncapital crimes, "appointment of counsel is not a fundamental right" for state felony defendants, unless "special" or "exceptional" circumstances such as "mental illness," "youth," or "lack of education" are present. In the ensuing years, the Court slowly expanded the scope of the Sixth Amendment.[44] At the same time, however, there were many cases in which the states failed to appoint counsel in compliance with *Betts*, thus setting the stage for the most important Sixth Amendment ruling in the Supreme Court's history.

Gideon **v.** *Wainwright*   Among the Court's most significant decisions, **Gideon v. Wainwright** (1963)[45] not only extended the right to counsel to all state defendants facing felony trials but also dramatically demonstrated that even the least influential of citizens could persuade those in charge to reexamine the premises of justice in America.

Clarence Earl Gideon was charged with breaking and entering into the Bay Harbor Pool Room in Panama City, Florida, with the intent of committing a crime—a case of petty larceny that is considered a felony under Florida law. The year was 1961, and Gideon was a 51-year-old white man who had been in and out of prisons for much of his life. He was not a violent man, but he had served time for four previous felonies. He was a drifter who never seemed to settle down, making his way by means of gambling and occasional thefts. He also bore the marks of a difficult life: a wrinkled, prematurely aged face, a voice and hands that trembled, a frail body, and white hair. Those who knew him, even the officers who had arrested him, considered Gideon a harmless and rather likable human being but one who had been tossed aside by life.[46]

On August 4, 1961, Gideon was tried on the breaking and entering charge in the Bay County, Florida, Circuit Court before Judge Robert L. McCrary, Jr. The hearing began as follows:

Judge:	The next case on the docket is the case of the state of Florida, plaintiff, versus Clarence Earl Gideon, defendant. What says the state, are you ready to go to trial in this case?
Prosecutor:	The state is ready, your honor.
Judge:	What says the defendant? Are you ready to go to trial?
Gideon:	I am not ready, your honor.
Judge:	Did you plead not guilty to this charge by reason of insanity?
Gideon:	No sir.
Judge:	Why aren't you ready?
Gideon:	I have no counsel.
Judge:	Why do you not have counsel? Did you not know that your case was set for trial today?
Gideon:	Yes sir, I knew that it was set for trial today.
Judge:	Why, then, did you not secure counsel and be prepared to go to trial?

(Gideon answered the court's question, but spoke in such low tones that his answer was not audible.)

Judge: Come closer up, Mr. Gideon, I can't understand you, I don't know what you said, and the reporter didn't understand you either.

(At this point, Gideon arose from the chair in which he was seated at the counsel table and walked up and stood directly in front of the bench, facing Judge McCrary.)

Judge: Now tell me what you said again, so we can understand you, please.

Gideon: Your honor, I said: I request this court to appoint counsel to represent me in this trial.

Judge: Mr. Gideon, I am sorry, but I cannot appoint counsel to represent you in this case. Under the laws of the state of Florida, the only time the court can appoint counsel to represent a defendant is when that person is charged with a capital offense. I am sorry, but I will have to deny your request to appoint counsel to defend you in this case.

Gideon: The United States Supreme Court says I am entitled to be represented by counsel.

Gideon was wrong, of course, for the Supreme Court had *not* said that he was entitled to counsel. In *Betts* v. *Brady,* some 20 years earlier, the Court had stated quite the opposite. The decision in *Betts* had actually *denied* free legal counsel to indigent felony defendants in state courts, unless "special circumstances" were present.

Judge McCrary apologetically informed Gideon of his mistake. Put to trial before a jury, Gideon heroically conducted his own defense as best as he could. He made an opening statement to the jury, cross-examined the state's witnesses, presented witnesses in his own defense, declined to testify on his own behalf, and made a short closing argument emphasizing his innocence of the charge. But Gideon's defense was ineffective; he was found guilty and sentenced to 5 years in state prison.

On January 8, 1962, the U.S. Supreme Court received a large envelope from Clarence Earl Gideon, prisoner number 003826, Florida State Prison, P.O. Box 211, Raiford, Florida. Gideon's petition was *in forma pauperis*—in the form of a poor man. It was prepared in pencil, with carefully formed printing on lined sheets of paper provided by the Florida prison. Printed at the top of each sheet, under the heading Correspondence Regulations, was a set of rules ("Only 2 letters each week . . . written on one side only . . . letters must be written in English . . .") and a warning: "Mail will not be delivered which does not conform to these rules."[47]

Certiorari was ultimately granted to Gideon's petition. The Supreme Court assigned Washington, D.C., attorney Abe Fortas, who was later appointed to the Supreme Court by President Lyndon B. Johnson, to argue Gideon's claim. Fortas contended that counsel in a criminal trial is a fundamental right of due process that is enforced on the states by the Fourteenth Amendment. The Court's decision was unanimous. In overturning *Betts,* Justice Black wrote: "Any person hauled into court, who is too poor to hire a lawyer, cannot be assured a fair trial unless counsel is provided for him. This seems to us an obvious truth."

This ruling, handed down on March 18, 1963, after Gideon had served almost 2 years in prison, entitled Gideon to a new trial. He was immediately retried in the same courtroom and by the same judge as in the initial trial, but this time he was represented by counsel and was acquitted. Gideon was set free, as were thousands of other prisoners in Florida and elsewhere because they had not been represented by an attorney at trial. (For later events in Gideon's life, see Exhibit 11.5).

In extending the right to counsel to all state defendants facing felony trials, *Gideon* also represented the beginning of a trend that would ultimately expand Sixth Amendment rights to cover most phases of criminal justice proceedings. On the same day that it announced its decision in *Gideon,* the Court also delivered its opinion in *Douglas* v. *California,*[48] which stated that indigent felons are entitled to counsel, if requested, at the first appeal proceedings. The ruling in *Douglas* was doubly significant. Most of the Supreme Court decisions dealing with the Sixth Amendment right to counsel had ad-

In forma pauperis means in the character of a poor person—a method by which a litigant without money for lawyers is considerably permitted to lose his case.

—AMBROSE BIERCE,
THE DEVIL'S DICTIONARY

EXHIBIT 11.5 | *historical perspectives on criminal justice*

Whatever Happened to . . . The Scottsboro Boys

For the nine Scottsboro boys—Clarence Norris, Olen Montgomery, Ozie Powell, Haywood Patterson, Willie Roberson, Charlie Weems, Eugene Williams, Roy Wright, and Andrew Wright—the decision in *Powell* v. *Alabama* was but a shallow victory. They were retried in the Alabama courts and reconvicted. At one point, Ruby Bates recanted her earlier testimony, stating that neither she nor Victoria Price had ever been raped but had concocted the charge in an attempt to avoid being arrested for vagrancy. This, combined with the lack of any medical evidence of rape, would suggest that the convictions had been gross miscarriages of justice. Victoria Price, however, did not fully agree with the statements of Bates, but did concede that she had been raped by only six of the defendants. Thus, at least one, *and likely all,* of the Scottsboro boys had to have been innocent of active participation in the alleged crime.

The cases were appealed and retried again, but with little success. In a series of trials held in 1936 and 1937, four of the original nine defendants were, for the third time, convicted of rape by all-white juries. Their sentences ranged from 75 to 99 years to electrocution.

- On July 24, 1937, the rape charges against *Olen Montgomery, Willie Roberson,* and *Eugene Williams* were dropped. A year after their release, the three made a personal appearance at New York's Apollo theater, but they subsequently faded from the public eye.

- *Roy Wright* was released along with Montgomery, Roberson, and Williams in 1937. On August 17, 1959, in a jealous rage, Wright stabbed his wife to death and subsequently took his own life.

- The rape charges against *Ozie Powell* were dropped in 1937. However, on January 24, 1936, Powell attacked a deputy sheriff. He was convicted of assault and sentenced to 20 years' imprisonment. Powell was paroled in 1946 and quickly fell into obscurity.

- *Charlie Weems* was convicted on the rape charges in 1937 and sentenced to 75 years. He was paroled in 1943 and retired to an anonymous existence.

- *Andrew Wright* was convicted on the rape charges in 1937 and drew a sentence of 99 years. He was paroled in 1944 but was returned to prison almost immediately, charged with parole violation for leaving Alabama. He was paroled again in 1947 but returned to prison when his employer learned that he was a Scottsboro boy and fired him. Wright was released for a third time in 1950 and moved to Albany, New York. Since that time, his name surfaced publicly only once. On July 12, 1951, he was arrested for the rape of a 13-year-old girl. He was found innocent and released.

- On January 23, 1936, *Haywood Patterson* was convicted on the rape charges and sentenced to 75 years. In 1948, however, he escaped from prison and fled Alabama. On January 15, 1951, Pat-

---

dressed only the due process clause of the Fourteenth Amendment; *Douglas* was the first case to refer to both the due process and equal protection clauses. In presenting the Court's opinion, Justice William O. Douglas wrote the following:

> There is lacking that equality demanded by the Fourteenth Amendment where the rich man, who appeals as of right, enjoys the benefit of counsel's examination into the record, research of the law, and marshalling of arguments on his behalf, while the indigent, already burdened by a preliminary determination that his case is without merit, is forced to shift for himself. The indigent . . . has only the right to a meaningless ritual, while the rich man has a meaningful appeal.

The Court continued the trend established in *Gideon* and *Douglas* with its decisions in *Massiah* v. *United States, Escobedo* v. *Illinois, Miranda* v. *Arizona,* and *United States* v. *Wade,* which extended the right of access to counsel to indictment, interrogation, and postindictment lineups.[49] In the 1970 decision of *Coleman* v. *Alabama,*[50] the Court ruled that the preliminary hearing is a "critical stage" in a criminal prosecution, during which the "guiding hand of counsel" is essential.

Argersinger v. Hamlin Ever since the Supreme Court's ruling in *Gideon* v. *Wainwright,* there had been some question whether the constitutional right to counsel should apply not only to felony cases but to misdemeanors as well. In 1972, the Court addressed this issue in ***Argersinger v. Hamlin.***[51] The defendant was an indigent who had been charged in Florida with carrying a concealed weapon, for which the potential punishment was up to 6 months' imprisonment and/or a $1,000 fine. At the trial, the defendant was not represented by counsel but was convicted and sentenced to serve 90 days in jail. In a *habeas corpus* petition to the Florida Supreme Court, the defendant

terson was convicted of manslaughter and sentenced to 15 to 20 years by a Michigan court. Less than a year later, however, he died of lung cancer.

- *Clarence Norris* was convicted on the rape charge in 1936 and sentenced to death. In 1938, the death sentence was commuted to life imprisonment, and he was paroled in 1944. Norris immediately left Alabama in violation of his parole, was captured, and returned to prison. He was paroled again in 1946, but left the state just 3 days later and was declared delinquent as a parole violator. Norris remained at large in New York City for many decades. In 1976, Alabama's attorney general recommended Norris's pardon, declaring that studies of the case indicated this last of the Scottsboro boys was innocent of the rape with which he had been charged some 45 years earlier. The pardon was granted by Alabama governor George Wallace. In 1977, a bill to compensate Norris for his wrongful conviction and imprisonment was defeated by an Alabama legislature committee. Regarding the decision, Norris's attorney, Donald Watkins, commented: "The mentality of the 1930s is alive and well in the 1970s." On January 23, 1989, Clarence Norris, the last of the Scottsboro boys, died of natural causes at the age of 76.

Whatever Happened to Clarence Earl Gideon

After the Supreme Court's *Gideon* v. *Wainwright* ruling in 1963, Clarence Earl Gideon was granted a new trial. Represented by counsel, he was found not guilty and set free. Once again he became a drifter, a

Clarence Earl Gideon

style of life he had adopted in 1925 when, at age 14, he left school and ran away from home.

The year 1965 found him in a Louisville courtroom. He had traveled to that part of the country to see the Kentucky Derby—but out of work and having picked a losing horse, he was arrested on a charge of vagrancy. At the trial, the judge recognized Gideon's name and offered to jail him long enough so that he could appeal for the right to counsel in petty trials. That was several years prior to the High Court's decision in *Argersinger*. But Gideon declined, telling the judge he'd just as soon plead guilty and walk away.

On January 18, 1976, Clarence Earl Gideon died at the age of 65 in a Fort Lauderdale medical center. Although he had been the key figure in a Supreme Court decision immortalized in hundreds of legal essays, a major book (*Gideon's Trumpet* by *The New York Times* correspondent Anthony Lewis in 1964), and a Hollywood production (Samuel Goldwyn Studios' *Gideon's Trumpet* in 1979, with actor Henry Fonda in the title role), Gideon died an obscure man—cast aside by life, without money or influence.

argued that because he was poor and had not been provided with counsel, the charge against him could not effectively be defended. The Florida court rejected the claim, and the U.S. Supreme Court granted *certiorari*.

In a unanimous decision, the Court ruled that the right to counsel applies not only to state defendants charged with felonies but in all trials of persons for offenses serious enough to warrant a jail sentence. Speaking for the Court, Justice William O. Douglas recalled both *Powell* v. *Alabama* and *Gideon* v. *Wainwright:*

> Both *Powell* and *Gideon* involved felonies. But their rationale has relevance to any criminal trial, where an accused is deprived of liberty. *Powell* and *Gideon* suggest that there are certain fundamental rights applicable to all such criminal prosecutions.
>
> The requirement of counsel may well be necessary for a fair trial even in a petty offense prosecution. We are by no means convinced that legal and constitutional questions involved in a case that actually leads to imprisonment even for a brief period are any less complex than when a person can be sent off for six months or more. . . .
>
> Under the rule we announce today, every judge will know when the trial of a misdemeanor starts that no imprisonment may be imposed, even though local law permits it, unless the accused is represented by counsel.

Restrictions on the Right to Counsel

While *Powell, Zerbst, Gideon,* and *Argersinger* served to guarantee the right to counsel to all federal and state defendants facing trials on charges for which sentences of death or imprisonment could be imposed, the Court also attempted to avoid overliberalizing the Sixth Amendment right. For example, in *McMann* v. *Richardson,*[52] the Court declared that defendants must assume a certain degree of risk that their attorneys would make some "ordinary error" in assessing the facts of their case and the law that applied and that such error was not a basis for reversing a conviction.

In *Ross* v. *Moffitt*,[53] the Court held that a state's constitutional obligation to provide appointed counsel for indigents appealing their convictions did not extend beyond the first appeal.

In *Scott* v. *Illinois*,[54] the Court decided that a criminal defendant charged with a statutory offense for which imprisonment upon conviction is authorized but not imposed does not have the right to appointed counsel.

In *Pennsylvania* v. *Finley*,[55] the Court ruled that there is no constitutional right to counsel in state postconviction proceedings.

In *Strickland* v. *Washington*,[56] the Court addressed the right to "effective" counsel, holding that in order to prevail on a Sixth Amendment claim of ineffective assistance, the defendant must prove that his or her attorney's performance was deficient, that the deficiency prejudiced the case, and that there was a reasonable probability that if it were not for the unprofessional errors, the result would have been different. It should be noted that this is a difficult standard to meet, as Justice Thurgood Marshall pointed out in his dissenting opinion. The effect of *Strickland* was to uphold a death sentence even though the defense attorney had failed to investigate and present several potentially important mitigating factors during the penalty phase of the trial.

Two cases decided in the 1990s reflect the Supreme Court's confusing view of the Sixth Amendment right to counsel. First, demonstrating a high regard for the provisions of the Sixth Amendment, the Court ruled in the 1994 case of *McFarland* v. *Scott* that federal judges have the authority to postpone an execution until an attorney can be appointed to help prepare a petition for *habeas corpus*.[57] On the other hand, in *Nichols* v. *United States*,[58] also decided in 1994, the Court held that the Sixth Amendment right to counsel is not violated when judges consider a defendant's prior misdemeanor convictions—obtained when the defendant was *not* represented by an attorney—in determining the length of the defendant's prison sentence.

However, despite the numerous restrictions on the Sixth Amendment right to counsel, the High Court's decision in *Alabama v. Shelton*[59] in 2002 represented a shift in the trend. In this case, Lareed Shelton represented himself in an Alabama circuit court criminal trial. The court repeatedly warned him about the problems self-representation entailed but at no time offered him assistance of counsel at state expense. He was convicted of misdemeanor assault and sentenced to a 30-day jail term, which the trial court immediately suspended, placing Shelton on 2 years' unsupervised probation. The U.S. Supreme Court held that a suspended sentence "that may end up in the actual deprivation of a person's liberty" may not be imposed unless the defendant was accorded "the guiding hand of counsel" in the prosecution for the crime charged.

Currently, there remain several areas of criminal processing—from arrest to appeal—in which courts are not required to provide counsel for the accused. These include preindictment lineups, booking procedures, grand jury investigations, and appeals beyond the first review. Decisions that address the right to counsel regarding parole and correctional matters are discussed in Chapter 17. For a discussion of the right *not* to have counsel, see Exhibit 11.6.

Legal Aid, Assigned Counsel, and Public Defenders

Legal services for the indigent (poor) come from three primary sources: voluntary defender programs sponsored by charitable and private organizations; assigned counsel systems, through which a presiding judge can call upon a local practicing attorney to defend a case; and public defenders, who are paid by the courts to represent criminal defendants.

Prior to *Gideon*, the availability of legal counsel for indigent defendants was limited. In 1961, for example, public defender systems existed in only 3% of the nation's

LAW & CRIMINAL JUSTICE | EXHIBIT 11.6

The Right *Not* to Have Counsel and the Concept of "Standby Counsel"

The case of *Faretta* v. *California* (422 U.S. 806), decided by a 6-to-3 majority in 1975, seemed to turn inside out the Supreme Court's series of rulings expanding the Sixth Amendment right to counsel in state proceedings.

The defendant, Anthony Faretta, had been accused of grand theft. At his arraignment the presiding judge assigned a local public defender to represent him. Well in advance of his trial, Faretta requested that he be permitted to represent himself because the public defender's case-load was far too heavy to allow the defender time to prepare an effective defense. The judge approved the request, at least tentatively, but warned the defendant that he was "making a mistake."

Several weeks later, still in advance of the trial date, the judge questioned Faretta about various issues in criminal procedure to determine his ability to conduct his own defense. On the basis of Faretta's answers and demeanor, the judge ruled that the defendant had not made a knowing and intelligent waiver of his right to counsel and that he did not have a constitutional right to conduct his own defense. Over Faretta's objections, a public defender was appointed, and the trial led to a conviction and sentence of imprisonment.

Upon review, the U.S. Supreme Court ruled in Faretta's favor. Writing for the majority, Justice Potter Stewart commented:

> The Sixth Amendment does not provide merely that a defense shall be made for the accused; it grants to the accused personally the right to make his defense. It is the accused, not counsel, who must be "informed of the nature and cause of the accusation," and who must be "confronted with the witnesses against him," and who must be accorded "compulsory process for obtaining witnesses in his favor." Although not stated in the Amendment in so many words, the right to self-representation—to make one's own defense personally—is thus necessarily implied by the structure of the Amendment. The right to defend is given directly to the accused; for it is he who suffers the consequences if the defense fails.

In a dissenting opinion, however, Justice Harry A. Blackmun argued that the decision in *Faretta* left open a host of other procedural issues:

> Must every defendant be advised of his right to proceed *pro se?* If so, when must that notice be given? Since the right to assistance of counsel and the right to self-representation are mutually exclusive, how is the waiver of each right to be measured? If a defendant has elected to exercise his right to proceed *pro se,* does he still have a constitutional right to assistance of standby counsel? How soon in the criminal proceeding must a defendant decide between proceeding by counsel or *pro se?* Must he be allowed to switch in midtrial? May a violation of the right to self-representation ever be harmless error? Must the trial court treat the *pro se* defendant differently than it would professional counsel? . . . Many of these questions . . . such as the standards of waiver and the treatment of the *pro se* defendant, will haunt the trial of every defendant

Sniper John Allen Muhammad, who at one point asserted his right not to have counsel, listens to testimony along with his attorney Christie Leary during his trial in Virginia Beach Circuit Court.

who elects to exercise his right to self-representation. The procedural problems spawned by an absolute right to self-representation will far out-weigh whatever tactical advantage the defendant may feel he gained by electing to represent himself.

Without question, *Faretta* did raise a number of problematic issues. Most critical is the potential catch-22 that could emerge, whereby a judge attempts to carry out the Faretta mandate and at the same time knowingly allows a defendant to make a mockery of his or her own defense or antagonize the court. However, the High Court also held that, consistent with the defendant's right to self-representation, the trial court may appoint "standby" counsel, "to aid the accused if and when the accused requests help, and to be available to represent the accused in the event that termination of the defendant's right of self-representation is necessary."

Nine years later in *McKaskle* v. *Wiggins,* the Supreme Court defined the role of standby counsel. Standby counsel may not speak instead of the accused on any important matters, interfere with witness questioning or any significant tactical decisions, or destroy the jury's perception that the defendant is representing him or herself. But within these broad limitations, standby counsel may advise the defendant, file motions, and bring errors to the court's attention (outside of the jury's presence). And if requested by the defendant and the trial court so permits, standby counsel may also question witnesses, introduce evidence, and make arguments.

Sources: *Faretta* v. *California,* 422 U.S. 806 (1975); *McKaskle* v. *Wiggins,* 465 U.S. 168 (1984); Lisa J. Steele, "Standby Counsel: Coach, Chaperone or Cheerleader?" *Criminal Law Bulletin* 35 (September–October 1999): 505–516.

counties, serving 25 percent of the U.S. population.[60] The balance relied on assigned counsel programs, which were generally rare owing to the organized bar's indifference to the need for defense assistance and to private attorneys' lack of interest in practicing criminal law. Moreover, because the right to counsel was not yet a Supreme Court mandate, most jurisdictions did not make any arrangements for the defense of indigents charged with criminal offenses. However, with *Gideon* in 1963 and *Argersinger* in 1972, the criminal justice system was forced to meet the needs of indigent defendants, who account for some two-thirds of all felony defendants. By 1980, public defender services were available in more than 1,000 counties, serving some 68 percent of the population.[61] Since then, even more public defender programs have been established, assigned counsel systems have been improved, and voluntary defender programs have become more visible. By 2004, in the nation's 75 largest counties more than 80 percent of indigent defendants charged with felonies were represented by either a public defender or an assigned counsel.[62]

Eligibility for these forms of supported defense varies. Some judges apply stringent "indigency standards" before appointing counsel. In some jurisdictions, for example, if the defendant owns a home, is employed full-time, or has the resources to meet the monetary bond that has been established, he or she is not considered indigent. Others require the filing of tax returns or affidavits that document the resources available to the defendant. Some presiding judges simply ask the defendant: "Can you afford a lawyer?" In such cases a simple yes or no determines eligibility.

Voluntary Defender Programs

Many private organizations provide legal assistance to indigents. The most numerous are the legal aid societies, which are financed by state and private contributions and are staffed by full-time attorneys. In addition, there are legal aid bureaus attached to charitable organizations, bar association legal aid offices, and law school clinics that provide legal assistance.

During the mid-1960s, federally supported legal assistance programs were started as part of the Johnson administration's "war on poverty." Originally funded by the Office of Economic Opportunity (OEO) and restructured in 1974 as the Legal Services Corporation when OEO was disbanded, these offices were established in many of the poorest urban neighborhoods and poor rural areas. By 1967, shortly after the program became fully operational, there were 299 legal assistance offices, handling almost 300,000 cases annually.[63] These federally funded service centers endured throughout the 1970s and into the early 1980s, but when the Reagan administration's budget cuts began in 1981, funding for the Legal Services Corporation was sharply reduced, creating a continuing gap in legal services for the poor.[64]

Other voluntary legal services come from individual attorneys and some private agencies that actively seek out specific kinds of court cases. The best known practitioner of this type of service is the *American Civil Liberties Union (ACLU)*. Founded in 1920 as a nonpartisan organization devoted to the preservation and extension of the basic rights set forth in the U.S. Constitution, the ACLU was an outgrowth of earlier groups that had defended the rights of conscientious objectors during World War I. It focuses on three areas of American civil liberties: (1) *inquiry and expression,* including freedom of speech, press, assembly, and religion; (2) *equality before the law* for everyone, regardless of race, nationality, political opinion, or religious belief; and (3) *due process of law* for all.

It should be noted that the various voluntary defender programs have a number of serious weaknesses and shortcomings that have an impact on their usefulness for criminal defendants. For example, the uncertainty of their continuing financial support is a crucial problem and, as with the Legal Services Corporation, can lead to termination of services. More important, however, the voluntary programs accept few criminal cases. With a small number of exceptions, the legal aid societies, federal assistance centers, bar association programs, law school clinics, and other service groups concentrate primarily on family and civil issues. The cases they most readily accept are ones involving divorce and child support, housing problems, conflicts with welfare agencies, and consumer credit disputes. However, organizations such as the Law Center for Constitutional Rights and the ACLU do handle some criminal matters. In recent years, for example, the ACLU has placed considerable emphasis on such due process issues as prisoners' rights, police arrest behavior, and cruel and unusual punishment. More often than not, though, the individuals defended by ACLU lawyers are involved in test cases, and routine criminal trials are handled only rarely.

Assigned Counsel Systems

The assigned counsel system is unquestionably the oldest and most widely used method for representing indigent criminal defendants. Lawyers represent defendants on a case-by-case basis. Appointments are made by a presiding judge from a list that may consist of *all* the practicing attorneys in the jurisdiction or only those who have volunteered to defend indigents. The attorneys, in turn, contribute their time as part of their responsibility to the profession and the community.

The assigned counsel system has some very serious drawbacks, however, including the following:

- In many jurisdictions, assigned counselors are either novices or has-beens; that is, they are either recent law school graduates who seek courtroom experience or older, nonprestigious members of the bar who need numerous appointments to make a living.
- Even when appointments are rotated among all members of the practicing bar, there is no guarantee that the counsel assigned is qualified to handle the complexities of criminal law and procedure. Through the luck of the draw, the defendant's lawyer may be the best tax or probate attorney in the area but have virtually no experience in criminal cases.
- Many jurisdictions neither pay attorneys for representing indigents nor reimburse the assigned counsel for out-of-pocket expenses. Where court-appointed lawyers are paid, compensation is minimal. This not only discourages qualified attorneys who might otherwise serve but also pressures attorneys to dispose of cases quickly in order to devote more time to clients who can afford their fees.
- Assigned counsel systems seldom provide funds to hire investigators or secure the services of expert witnesses, further decreasing the likelihood of a thorough and adequate defense.
- Attorneys who are dependent on the assigned counsel system for a livelihood may be concerned more with pleasing the court than with helping the client. In order not to anger the court, such counselors may avoid arguing for lower bail, filing a greater number of pretrial motions, objecting to court rulings, or using other tactics in the client's defense.[65]

Despite these considerable weaknesses, advocates support the assigned counsel system because it disperses the responsibility for defending indigents among a wide spectrum of practicing lawyers. The assigned counsel system has an additional advantage: Criminal defendants potentially have attorneys with fresh perspectives to represent them. *Not* being a member of the courtroom work group can lead to a more vigorous defense. Moreover, an accused person will often argue that he or she does not like being represented by the public defender, feeling far more confidence in an assigned counsel.

Public Defenders

The public defender is a part-time or full-time county, state, or federal government employee who earns a fixed salary and specializes in representing indigent criminal defendants. The first public defender office was established in Los Angeles County in 1914. Today, public defender systems exist in most urban areas and are increasingly being adopted in many small and medium-sized jurisdictions. The systems vary widely

How Satisfied Are Lawyers with Their Careers?

Source: *National Law Journal.*

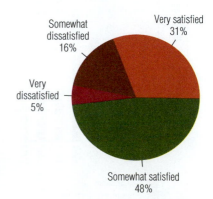

Somewhat dissatisfied 16%

Very satisfied 31%

Very dissatisfied 5%

Somewhat satisfied 48%

in size. In large cities with high crime and arrest rates, for example, there are many hundreds of public defenders to serve the large population of indigent defendants, while in other areas there is only a single such counsel, who may be responsible for the criminal caseload of an entire county.

With few exceptions, defendants who are represented by public defenders are generally more fortunate than those receiving the services of an assigned counsel or a volunteer from a legal aid society. First, defender offices are staffed by attorneys who are as skilled and specialized as those on the prosecutor's staff. Second, the public defender system generally attracts attorneys with greater ability than those in assigned counsel systems, for it provides a regular means of income and the experience necessary for advancement. Third, most defender offices have some funds available for investigations, and the opportunity to conduct an independent investigation makes possible a more vigorous defense. Fourth, since the income of the assigned public defender continues regardless of whether the case goes to trial, the attorney is less likely to force the plea negotiation process in cases in which it may not be appropriate.

On the other hand, the defender system does have problems. The salaries paid to public defenders are not competitive with those paid to other attorneys with similar experience; hence turnover tends to be high. In many jurisdictions, caseloads are extremely heavy, limiting the amount of time available for each case. In fact, a recent report found that one public defender in Griffin, Georgia, handled an average of 900 felony cases a year.[66] Public defender offices lack community support; citizens are often hostile to the system because it uses tax dollars to assist "criminals." Too, although some chief public defenders are elected, most are appointed either by the governor or the court. This creates the potential for patronage and favoritism. Finally, like many attorneys in the assigned counsel system, many public defenders may not wish to anger the court through vigorous use of motions, demands for jury trials, and appeals.

Contract Systems

Relatively new to the spectrum of indigent defense systems is the contract system, in which individual attorneys, bar associations, or private law firms contract to provide services for a specified dollar amount. Contract awards are generally made on the basis of competitive bidding; selection criteria include cost, qualifications of bidders, and their proposed methods of representation. Currently, only a small number of counties use some form of the contract system, and it is the dominant form of indigent representation in only six states. Moreover, while the contract system appears to be growing, it has tended to concentrate in the less populated areas and on cases for which other forms of indigent defense were not available.

Legal, Prosecutorial, and Judicial Misconduct: Aspects of the Criminal Justice Nonsystem

For most of the 20th century, discussions of corruption and other forms of misconduct in criminal justice processing have focused on police behavior. Increasingly, however, problems within the legal and judicial sectors have become more visible. Moreover, a variety of criticisms have been aimed at all members of the courtroom work group. There have been charges of dishonesty—a growing number of judges, lawyers, and prosecutors are being accused of conflicts of interest, defrauding clients, or participating in other misdeeds that reflect contempt for professional ethics. There have been charges of greed—lawyers are being accused of charging fees that go far beyond what is justified by the work involved. And there have been charges of incompetence—various legal practitioners are being cited for costly mistakes and inexcusable errors during trials.[67]

In addition to ineffective representation on the part of attorneys, there are cases of misconduct on the part of prosecutors and judges. Prosecutors can take advantage of defendants and compromise their rights by knowingly admitting false testimony, hid-

Sanctions Imposed on Lawyers by State Courts, 1983–2004

Source: American Bar Association.

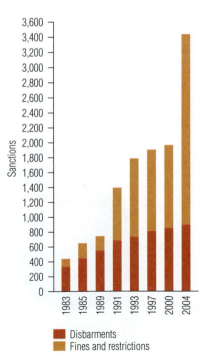

- Disbarments
- Fines and restrictions

ing evidence that may help the defense, and making biased statements to the jury during testimony and closing arguments. A classic example of the latter occurred during the first trial of Mississippi segregationist Byron De La Beckwith, who was accused of the 1963 sniper murder of civil rights leader Medgar Evers. The prosecutor in the trial, Bill Waller, made the following biased and racist statements to the Jackson, Mississippi, jury:

> "Evers was engaged in things that were contrary to what you and I believe in."

> "I'm a little upset right now, with all these nigras in the courtroom—does that bother you?"

> "I like Mr. Beckwith. He has a pleasant way. He's a Mason, you're a Mason; he's a veteran, you're a veteran; you're a father, he's a father."

> "I do not believe you will return a verdict of guilty to satisfy the attorney general of the United States [a reference to Robert F. Kennedy, who was hated by southern racists] and the liberal national media."[68]

Judges, like prosecutors, sometimes exceed the bounds of acceptable behavior. For example, a panel of Kentucky circuit court judges ruled that a Jefferson County (Louisville) district judge had violated the constitutional rights of 18 defendants by setting unreasonably high bail, incarcerating them without hearings, or trying them in absentia.[69] In one case, a 17-year-old youth appeared in court a little late to find that the judge had already convicted him of driving a go-cart across a city street and had sentenced him to 90 days in jail. The judge also had the habit of dismissing drunk-driving cases if police officers or other witnesses failed to come forward as soon as they were called. Although the judge was not formally sanctioned for these judicial indiscretions, he was not expected to do well in his bid for reelection. Similarly, a county circuit court judge in St. Marys, West Virginia, was charged with assaulting a defendant who appeared in his courtroom.[70] Witnesses reported that after the judge refused to lower bail, the defendant cursed at him. The judge then stepped down from the bench, removed his robe, bit the defendant on the nose, and then returned to the bench as if nothing had happened. After being charged with assault, the judge pleaded *nolo contendere* and resigned. And there are numerous other examples.[71]

In an effort to remedy the problems generated by incompetence, corruption, or unethical practices within the courtroom work group, a number of programs have been instituted. Judges and prosecutors are now answerable to judicial discipline commissions in more than two-thirds of the states. The authority of such commissions, which are composed of judges, attorneys, and citizens, extends to investigating complaints against members of the bench, demanding explanations from judges and prosecutors charged with misconduct and recommending disciplinary measures to bar associations and the courts. These court-watching programs have had an impact, for they have led to the resignations and retirements of several judges and prosecutors and to the censure of numerous others.

The disciplining of lawyers is handled by the American Bar Association as well as by local bar associations and the courts; measures range from censure to actual disbarment. Allegations of attorney misconduct and incompetence are investigated by the National Legal Aid and Defender Association. Investigations at the local level, too, aim at protecting the indigent from unfit and unscrupulous attorneys.[72]

CRITICAL THINKING IN CRIMINAL JUSTICE

The International Criminal Court

The International Criminal Court (ICC) is the first ever permanent, treaty-based court designed to prosecute international crimes. The statute establishing the court's jurisdiction and functions was adopted in July 1998, and entered into force in July 2002 upon ratification by 60 participating nations. The seat of the court is presently The Hague, Netherlands, but as a fully independent international organization, the ICC will be permanently based at new premises by 2008. As of March 2005, 98 countries had become parties to the ICC. Shortly after the ICC was officially es-

U.N. Secretary General Kofi Annan addresses the inaugural session of the International Criminal Court in The Hague March 11, 2003.

tablished in 2002, the U.S. State Department gave notice to the United Nations of its intention not to participate in the court.

Given the atrocities of September 11, 2001, does this decision by the State Department make any sense? Wouldn't it be a good idea for the United States to be a part of some sort of international judicial body through which it could file charges against terrorists perpetrating violent acts against American citizens and institutions? Thinking critically on these questions, one must realize that there is more than one international court and that their procedures may not necessarily adhere to adequate principles of justice.

First, there is the International Court of Justice, also known as the World Court, which is the principal judicial organ of the United Nations. Established in 1946 and also located in The Hague, the World Court has a dual role: (1) to settle in accordance with international law the legal disputes submitted by "States" (member countries, including the United States); and (2) to provide advisory opinions on legal questions referred to it by duly authorized international agencies. The World Court is composed of 15 judges elected to 9-year terms by the United Nations General Assembly and Security Council. These judges, or "Members of the Court," act as independent magistrates and do not represent their governments. Since 1946, the World Court has delivered more than 60 judgments on disputes concerning land frontiers and maritime boundaries, territorial sovereignty, noninterference in the internal affairs of member countries, diplomatic relations, the right of asylum, hostage taking, economic rights, and rights of passage. The World Court has also

The United States seat remains empty during a meeting of the newly created International Criminal Court at United Nations headquarters in New York.

issued numerous advisory opinions, with the majority related to admission to the United Nations and U.N. administrative issues.[73]

Then there is the International Criminal Tribunal. Unlike the World Court, the International Criminal Tribunal is not a permanent court but a temporary one, established to deal with specific crimes and human rights violations. The best-known use of an International Criminal Tribunal was the Nuremberg trials, a series of 13 trials held in Nuremberg, Germany, from 1945 to 1949. In these proceedings, leaders of Nazi Germany were charged with causing World War II and waging aggressive war, as well as murder, enslavement, looting, and other atrocities against soldiers and civilians of occupied countries. Some were also tried for the persecution of Jews and other racial and national groups. The Nuremberg trials were a new development in international law. Although trials of war criminals have been carried out for hundreds of years, at Nuremberg, for the first time, the leaders of a government were brought to trial on a charge of starting an aggressive war.

In 1993, an International Criminal Tribunal was established to address the mass murders of Bosnian Muslims. But unlike the situation with the Nuremberg court, enforcement powers are not necessarily provided by all cooperating countries. In addition, the tribunal is dependent on the cooperation of nations in producing and providing access to evidence—which is not always the case. Nevertheless, the tribunal has had numerous successes, the most significant of which was the conviction of Bosnian Croat general Tihomir Blaskic. At his sentencing in 2000, presiding judge Claude Jorda of France stated emphatically:

> You are guilty, General Blaskic, of having ordered the commission of a crime against humanity for persecution of the Muslim civilians in Bosnia. The crimes you committed, General Blaskic, are extremely serious. The acts of war carried out with disregard for international humanitarian law and in hatred of other people, the villages reduced to rubble, the houses and stables set on fire and destroyed, the people forced to abandon their homes, the lost and broken lives, are unacceptable. If armed conflict is unavoidable, those who have the power to make decisions and those who carry them out must ensure that the most basic rules governing the law of nations are respected. General Blaskic, you showed no respect for these rules: Consequently, the Trial Chamber sentences you to a sentence of 45 years imprisonment.[74]

Currently the tribunal is hearing the case of Slobodan Milosevic for alleged crimes in Croatia, Bosnia, and Kosovo. Milosevic has been charged with 66 counts of war crimes, genocide, and crimes against humanity during the Balkan wars in the 1990s. The former Yugoslav president declined to enter a plea in response to the charges, therefore resulting in the judges entering a not-guilty plea to all charges on Milosevic's behalf. Milosevic is the first head of state to have to answer for such actions since World War II. During the opening of the trial, chief prosecutor Carla del Ponte stated that this trial "was the most powerful demonstration that no one is above the law." But there have been many snags along the way. The trial, which began in February 2002, has been delayed on several occasions due to Milosevic's failing health. At the end of February 2004, shortly after the prosecution rested its case, the trial's presiding judge resigned, also due to health problems. A replacement judge was appointed by U.N. secretary-general Kofi Annan in April 2004, and Slobodan Milosevic began the presentation of his defense on August 31. The marathon trial continues to be plagued by delays, as Milosevic's ill health regularly interferes with his ability to participate in his own defense. The most recent setback involved a defense witness who was charged with contempt after refusing to testify while Milosevic was absent from the courtroom.[75]

In contrast to these United Nations–sponsored tribunals, the International Criminal Court is a very different entity, and the State Department cited several reasons for its decision not to participate in this body. The reasons included the purported lack of checks and balances on the authority of the court to investigate and prosecute crimes and the potential for politicized prosecutions of U.S. officials and military personnel by the court. The State Department also refused to recognize the jurisdiction of an independent international organization to detain and try American citizens without the consent of the U.S. government or a mandate from the United Nations Security Council.[76] More specifically, the State Department emphasizes that it fears that rogue nations and anti-American activists could use the court to bring spurious, politically motivated charges against American citizens. And perhaps this fear is real. The world is indeed becoming more anti-American, and the ICC's caseload reflects that. Some 20% of the complaints so far received by the ICC concern Americans, and no one has investigated their validity.

OP-ED

Do withholds of adjudication and plea bargains corrupt the American system of justice? Are guilty offenders simply walking away from their crime or receiving only a slap on the wrist for what should be many years behind bars? Many observers would answer yes to both questions, while others would not.

Withholds of adjudication were developed in 1941 when Florida legislatures passed a law allowing judges to block the convictions of felony offenders. A withhold is intended to be a one-time break to help first offenders and spare them a life of economic hardship and the social stigma attached to being a convicted felon. Plea bargains usually occur when a defendant pleads guilty to a lesser offense than originally charged in return for a lighter sentence than is possible if convicted of the more severe charge.

Critics of withholds of adjudication argue that this "one-time break" appears to be anything but a break in an overburdened state criminal justice system. Rapists, child molesters, child abusers, wife beaters, burglars, drug offenders, and others have all received withholds in the state of Florida. Equally disturbing, it is not uncommon for lawbreakers to avoid convictions multiple times. It has also been found that white criminal offenders are more likely to get withholds than black offenders who were charged with the same crime, as can be demonstrated in the case at the beginning of the chapter.

Critics of plea bargains remark that the great majority of defendants negotiate a plea because they see it as a route to a lesser sentence. Therefore, there are probably more innocent people in prison because of their own guilty pleas than there are inmates who were falsely convicted.

Supporters of these proceedings remark that withholds and plea bargains are both tools to unclog heavily burdened criminal justice systems. Withholds are being handed out in increasing numbers, acting as an incentive to get offenders to cut deals and speed the judicial process. In regard to plea bargains, supporters remark that if every case went to trial, the courts would be hopelessly deadlocked—possibly resulting in the dismissal of large numbers of cases for failure to meet the constitutional demand for a "speedy trial."

So again: Do withholds of adjudication and plea bargains corrupt the American system of justice? If so, is there a viable alternative that won't clog our courts?

| Summary |

The criminal judicial process in the United States has many participants. First, there is a courtroom work group composed of a judge, who serves at the head of the court; a prosecutor, who argues the state's case; and a defense attorney, who argues on behalf of the accused. Second, there are many others who are significant to the process—depending on the nature of the proceeding, the type of case, and the level of the court. These include police officers, witnesses, jury members, and various officers of the court. Third, there are those with quasi-judicial functions, such as coroners and medical examiners. Each of these participants has a specific role in the criminal court process, without which given phases in the judicial system would not be fully possible.

It is generally believed that more than 90 percent of criminal convictions result from negotiated pleas. Plea bargaining takes place between the prosecutor and the defense counsel or the accused and involves discussions looking toward an agreement under which the defendant enters a plea of guilty in exchange for some prosecutorial or judicial concession. Plea bar-

gaining has both advantages and disadvantages, and its abolition has been called for. Advocates for its retraction argue that it encourages defendants to waive their constitutional right to trial and enables them to receive a sentence generally less severe than they might otherwise receive. They further argue that it ignores the correctional needs of the bulk of offenders and raises the danger of an innocent person—fearing a determination of guilt and a harsh sentence if the case goes to trial—pleading guilty to a crime he or she did not commit. Plea bargaining continues to be used, however, for without it the courts would become even more backlogged than they are now.

The prosecutor is a government lawyer acting on behalf of the state. Prosecutors have three basic responsibilities: to enforce the law, to represent the government in matters of law, and to represent the government and the people in matters of legislation and criminal justice reform. Defense attorneys, on the other hand, are advocates for the accused, often receiving harsh criticism from the public for representing "scoundrels," "rogues," and "villains." Their primary role is to ensure that their clients receive both a fair trial and an adequate defense.

The Sixth Amendment holds that "in all criminal prosecutions the accused shall enjoy the right to have assistance of counsel for his defense." Despite this guarantee, until the Scottsboro case in the 1930s, only persons charged with capital federal crimes enjoyed the right to counsel. *Gideon* v. *Wainwright* in 1963 extended the right to virtually all felony defendants, while *Argersinger* v. *Hamlin* in 1972 extended it to misdemeanor cases if imprisonment was a possible penalty. Additional Supreme Court decisions have impacted on the right to counsel as it relates to stages of the criminal justice process other than trial.

Legal services for the indigent come from several sources—legal aid, assigned counsel, and public defenders. All of these suffer from a variety of problems, with the consequence that the poor do not always receive adequate representation.

| Key Terms |

Argersinger v. *Hamlin* (356)
Betts v. *Brady* (354)
Brady v. *United States* (342)
Gideon v. *Wainwright* (354)
in forma pauperis (355)

Johnson v. *Zerbst* (354)
judges (331)
Missouri Plan (335)
motion (346)
nolle prosequi (339)

plea negotiation (339)
Powell v. *Alabama* (353)
prosecutor (337)

| Issues for Discussion |

1. In *McMann* v. *Richardson* and *Strickland* v. *Washington,* the U.S. Supreme Court addressed the issue of incompetent counsel. In *Faretta* v. *California,* the Court tackled the issue of a defendant's right *not* to have counsel. How might these two decisions affect one another?
2. What kinds of problems have the decisions in *Gideon* and *Argersinger* created for the processing of cases in criminal courts?
3. Comparing the roles of police and prosecutors, who has more discretion and who has the greater potential for the abuse of that discretion? Why?
4. Should plea bargaining be abolished? Why or why not?
5. Should the roles of victims in plea bargaining be expanded?
6. Should the United States join the International Criminal Court?

| Media and Literature Resources |

Reel Justice includes scenes that can be used to spark discussion about the following topics from this chapter:

The Role of the Prosecutor

Nolle Prosequi

Witnesses

Plea Bargaining and Crime Victims. The National Center for Victims of Crime has taken a strong stand with regard to plea bargaining. See its Web site: *http://www.nvc.org/ncvc/main.aspx.*

The Scottsboro Boys. There are two excellent books on the Scottsboro case: Dan T. Carter, *Scottsboro: A Tragedy of the American South* (New York: Oxford University Press, 1969); James Goodman, *Stories of Scottsboro* (New York: Pantheon, 1994).

Clarence Earl Gideon. The full story of the Clarence Gideon case was published as *Gideon's Trumpet* in 1964 by *New York Times* correspondent Anthony Lewis. In addition, a 1979 made-for-television production based on the book (Samuel Goldwyn Studios' *Gideon's Trumpet,* with actor Henry Fonda in the leading role) is available on video.

The Judiciary and Human Rights. Amnesty International monitors judicial problems in a number of countries. See its home page on the Web: *http://www.amnesty.org.*

Community Prosecution Programs. Prosecutors, taking a cue from law enforcement agencies' community policing initiatives, are establishing similar programs aimed at involving members of their communities in the justice system. A number of reports on these programs are available from the Center for Court Innovation on the Web: *http://www.courtinnovation.org.*

| Endnotes |

1. Advisory Committee on the Judge's Function, *The Functions of the Trial Judge* (New York: American Bar Association, 1972).
2. For a more detailed discussion of the selection of federal judges, see Nancy Scherer, "Who Drives the Ideological Makeup of the Lower Federal Courts in a Divided Government?" *Law and Society Review* 35, 1 (2001): 191–218; Shelton Goldman, *Picking Federal Judges: Lower Court Selection from Roosevelt Through Reagan* (New Haven: Yale University Press, 1997); Herbert Jacob, *Justice in America: Courts, Lawyers, and the Judicial Process* (Boston: Little, Brown, 1972), 98–107; Richard J. Richardson and Kenneth N. Vines, *The Politics of Federal Courts* (Boston: Little, Brown, 1970).
3. Sheldon Goldman, "Reagan's Judicial Legacy: Completing the Puzzle and the Summing Up," *Judicature* 27 (April–May 1989): 318, 322, 324–325.
4. Elizabeth Ames Jones, "Remove the Partisanship, Money from Judicial Races," *San Antonio Express-News,* November 9, 2003, 5H.

5. See Richard W. Watson and Ronald G. Downing, *The Politics of the Bench and the Bar* (New York: Wiley, 1969).

6. Lyle Warrick, *Judicial Selection in the United States: A Compendium of Provisions* (Chicago: American Judicature Society, 1993).

7. Mark Hansen, "A Run for the Bench," *ABA Journal* 84 (October 1998): 68–72; Robert L. Brown, "From Whence Cometh Our State Appellate Judges: Popular Election Versus the Missouri Plan," *University of Arkansas at Little Rock Law Journal* 20 (1998): 313; D. Y. Joseph, M. D. Zimmerman, C. E. Ares, and K. K. Stuart, "Evaluating the Performance of Judges Standing for Retention," *Judicature* 79 (January–February 1996): 190–197.

8. New York City Criminal Court Act, Laws of 1962, chap. 697, sec. 22 (1).

9. Wayne R. LaFave, *Arrest: The Decision to Take a Suspect into Custody* (Boston: Little, Brown, 1965), 515.

10. President's Commission on Law Enforcement and Administration of Justice, *Task Force Report: The Courts* (Washington, DC: U.S. Government Printing Office, 1967), 5.

11. George F. Cole, "The Decision to Prosecute," *Law and Society Review* 4 (1970): 331–343. See also Eric D. Poole and Robert H. Regoli, "The Decision to Prosecute in Felony Cases," *Journal of Contemporary Criminal Justice* 2 (March 1983): 18–21.

12. See Merle Hoffman, "Fatal Denial? The Tragic Case of Amy Grossberg and Brian Peterson," *OTI Online* 6 (Spring 1997), *http://www.ontheissuesmagazine.com/sp97hoffman.html.*

13. See Michelle Oberman, "Mothers Who Kill," *American Criminal Law Review* 34 (1996): 1–110.

14. See Joan E. Jacoby, *The Prosecutor's Charging Decision: A Policy Perspective* (Washington, DC: U.S. Department of Justice, 1977).

15. *United States* v. *Cowen,* 524 F.2d 785 (1975).

16. U.S. Department of Justice, Bureau of Justice Statistics, *The Prosecution of Felony Arrests* (Washington, DC: U.S. Government Printing Office, 1998).

17. See Candace McCoy, *Politics and Plea Bargaining: Victim's Rights in California* (Philadelphia: University of Pennsylvania Press, 1993); and Arthur Rosett and Donald R. Cressey, *Justice by Consent: Plea Bargains in the American Courthouse* (Philadelphia: Lippincott, 1976).

18. *Miami Herald,* August 22, 1982, 11A; *Time,* August 30, 1982, 22.

19. *Brady* v. *United States,* 397 U.S. 742 (1970).

20. *Santobello* v. *New York,* 404 U.S. 257 (1971).

21. *Henderson* v. *Morgan,* 426 U.S. 637 (1976).

22. *North Carolina* v. *Alford,* 400 U.S. 25 (1970).

23. *Bordenkircher* v. *Hayes,* 434 U.S. 357 (1978).

24. Quoted in Jeffrey Toobin, *The Run of His Life: The People v. O. J. Simpson* (New York: Random House, 1996).

25. Roy Flemming, Peter Nardulli, and James Eisenstein, *The Craft of Justice* (Philadelphia: University of Pennsylvania Press, 1992); Paul W. Wice, *Criminal Lawyers: An Endangered Species* (Beverly Hills: Sage Publications, 1978).

26. Anthony C. Friloux, "Motion Strategy—The Defense Attack" (speech before the National College of Criminal Defense Lawyers, Houston, 1975), cited by Wice, *Criminal Lawyers,* 148.

27. See John Heinz and Edward Laumann, *Chicago Lawyers: The Social Structure of the Bar* (New York: Basic Books, 1982).

28. See Walter Bennett, *The Lawyer's Myth: Reviving Ideals in the Legal Profession* (Chicago: University of Chicago Press, 2002); Richard A. Zitrin and Carol M. Langford, *The Moral Compass of the American Lawyer: Truth, Justice, Power, and Greed* (New York: Ballantine Books, 2000); and Richard L. Abel, *American Lawyers* (New York: Oxford University Press, 1982).

29. Abraham S. Blumberg, *Criminal Justice: Issues and Ironies* (New York: New Viewpoints, 1979), 242–246.

30. Blumberg, *Criminal Justice,* 245.

31. Blumberg, *Criminal Justice,* 243.

32. Murray A. Schwartz, quoted in John Kaplan, *Criminal Justice* (Mineola, NY: Foundation Press, 1973), 261.

33. Malcolm M. Feeley, *The Process Is the Punishment: Handling Cases in a Lower Criminal Court* (New York: Sage Publications, 1979), 121.

34. Peter W. Huber, *Galileo's Revenge: Junk Science in the Courtroom* (New York: Basic Books, 1991).

35. *Daubert* v. *Merrell Dow Pharmaceuticals,* 509 U.S. 579 (1993).

36. Frank Smyth, *Cause of Death* (New York: Van Nostrand Reinhold, 1980), 32–34.

37. William J. Curran, A. Louis McGarry, and Charles S. Petty, *Modern Legal Medicine, Psychiatry, and Forensic Science* (Philadelphia: Davis, 1980), 51–56.

38. The full story of the Scottsboro boys can be found in Dan T. Carter, *Scottsboro: A Tragedy of the American South* (New York: Oxford University Press, 1969). Also see James Goodman, *Stories of Scottsboro* (New York: Pantheon, 1994).

39. *Powell* v. *Alabama,* 287 U.S. 45 (1932).

40. See Howard N. Meyer, *The Amendment That Refused to Die* (Boston: Beacon, 1978).

41. *Johnson* v. *Zerbst,* 304 U.S. 458 (1938).

42. *Townsend* v. *Burke,* 334 U.S. 736 (1948).

43. *Betts* v. *Brady,* 316 U.S. 455 (1942).

44. See *Uveges* v. *Pennsylvania,* 335 U.S. 437 (1948); *Moore* v. *Michigan,* 355 U.S. 155 (1957); *Carnley* v. *Cochran,* 369 U.S. 506 (1962); and *Hamilton* v. *Alabama,* 368 U.S. 52 (1961).

45. *Gideon* v. *Wainwright,* 372 U.S. 335 (1963).

46. Anthony Lewis, *Gideon's Trumpet* (New York: Vintage, 1966), 5–6.

47. Lewis, *Gideon's Trumpet,* 4.

48. *Douglas* v. *California,* 372 U.S. 353 (1963).

49. *Massiah* v. *United States,* 377 U.S. 201 (1964); *Escobedo* v. *Illinois,* 378 U.S. 478 (1964); *Miranda* v. *Arizona,* 384 U.S. 694 (1966); *United States* v. *Wade,* 388 U.S. 218 (1967).

50. *Coleman* v. *Alabama,* 399 U.S. 1 (1970).

51. *Argersinger* v. *Hamlin,* 407 U.S. 25 (1972).

52. *McMann* v. *Richardson,* 397 U.S. 759 (1970).

53. *Ross* v. *Moffitt,* 417 U.S. 600 (1974).

54. *Scott* v. *Illinois,* 440 U.S. 367 (1979).

55. *Pennsylvania* v. *Finley,* 107 S. Ct. 1990 (1987).

56. *Strickland* v. *Washington,* 466 U.S. 668 (1984).

57. *McFarland* v. *Scott,* 114 S. Ct. 2568 (1994).

58. *Nichols* v. *United States,* 114 S. Ct. 1921 (1994).

59. *Alabama* v. *Shelton,* 535 U.S. 654 (2002).

60. Lawrence A. Benner and Beth Lynch Neary, *The Other Face of Justice* (Chicago: National Legal Aid and Defender Association, 1973), 13.

61. Bureau of Justice Statistics, *Criminal Defense Systems,* special report, August 1984.

62. *Statewide Indigent Defense Systems: 2004* (West Newton, MA: Spangenberg Group, 2004).

63. Harry P. Strumpf, "Law and Poverty: A Political Perspective," *Wisconsin Law Review,* 1968, 698–699.

64. Rael Jean Isaac, "War on the Poor—Criticism of the Legal Services Corporation," *National Review,* May 1995, 32–44; Mark Kessler, "Expanding Legal Services Programs to Rural America: A Case Study of Program Creation and Operations," *Judicature* 73 (February–March 1990): 273–280; Kenneth F. Boehm and Peter T. Flaherty, "Legal Disservices Corp: There Are Better

Ways to Provide Legal Aid to the Poor," *Policy Review* 74 (Fall 1995): 17–23.

65. See Michael Moore, "The Right to Counsel for Indigents in Oregon," *Oregon Law Review* 44 (1965): 255–300; Lee Silverstein, *Defense of the Poor* (Chicago: American Bar Association, 1965); H. Richard Uviller, *Virtual Justice: The Flawed Prosecution of Crime in America* (New Haven: Yale University Press, 1996); Burton S. Katz, *Justice Overruled: Unmasking the Criminal Justice System* (New York: Warner, 1997); and *USA Today,* February 3, 1999, A4.

66. Alan Berlow, "Requiem for a Public Defender," *The American Prospect* 11 (June 5, 2000): 28.

67. Uviller, *Virtual Justice,* 132–156.

68. See Maryanne Vollers, *Ghosts of Mississippi* (Boston: Little, Brown, 1995); and Frank McLynn, *Famous Trials: Cases That Made History* (Pleasantville, NY: Reader's Digest Association, 1995), 184–187.

69. *Louisville Courier-Journal,* October 12, 1997, A1, A12.

70. *Miami Herald,* October 26, 1997, 12A.

71. See *The New York Times,* January 30, 2000, 17.

72. A useful source of information on misconduct is the January–February 1997 issue of *Judicature,* which focuses on judicial independence.

73. Jacob Katz Cogan, "The Problem of Obtaining Evidence for International Criminal Trials," *Human Rights Quarterly* 22 (2000): 404–427; *Articles of the International Court of Justice* (New York: United Nations, 1997).

74. Samantha Power, "Mute Justice," *The New Republic,* April 17 and 24, 2000, 20–24.

75. ICT Case Information Sheet, *Milosevic Case* (IT-02-54), "Kosovo, Croatia, Bosnia and Herzegovina," May 12, 2005.

76. Mark Grossman, "American Foreign Policy and the International Criminal Court," U.S. Department of State briefing, May 6, 2002.

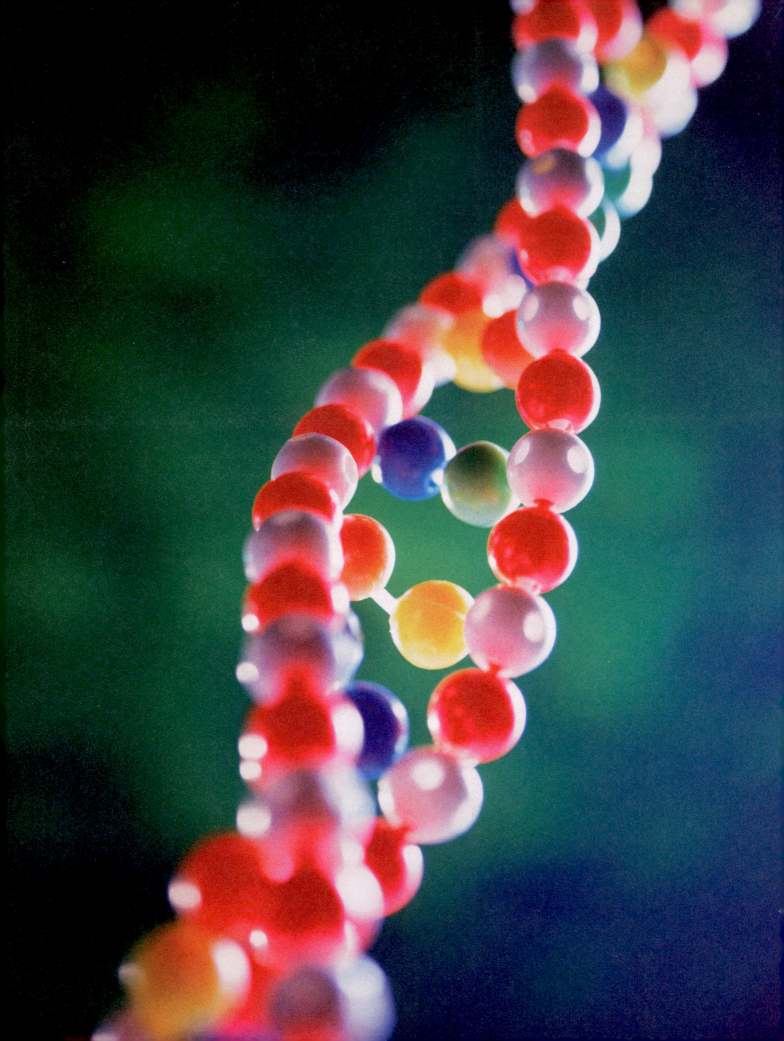

12

THE BUSINESS OF THE COURT: FROM FIRST APPEARANCE THROUGH TRIAL

LEARNING OBJECTIVES

After reading this chapter, you should be able to answer the following questions:

1. What occurs at each stage of the court process?

2. What are the problems with the bail system, and what are the alternatives to bail?

3. What are the main issues related to grand jury proceedings, double jeopardy, and speedy trial?

4. What are the different kinds of pleas?

5. What are *motions?* When are they filed, and for what purposes?

6. What are the steps in jury selection?

7. What are the different types of evidence?

8. What is jury nullification, and why does it occur?

Marg Helgenberger and William Petersen of the hit drama CSI.

LAS VEGAS, NV—Picture this: An elderly couple from Buffalo checks into one of the city's overdone strip hotels, looking forward to a week of relaxation, dining out, and a little gambling. Tired from their long plane flight, they head to the bar to unwind with a few martinis. As they toast their long-awaited vacation, the woman screams with horror. There is an object in her drink, and it is looking back at her—not a stuffed Spanish olive, but a real human eye! Minutes later, the forensic experts arrive. DNA is taken from the eye; fingerprints are found on the glass; the eyeless head of a young woman is found in a dumpster behind the strip club next door; other body parts are located under a car in the hotel parking lot; a bloody paring knife is retrieved from a restaurant potato bin; and fibers, fingerprints, and even more DNA are linked to a suspect. Within just a few hours, an arrest is made and the case is wrapped up and turned over to the county prosecutor's office.

The tangled web of evidence unraveled by the forensic sleuths apparently led to an Iowa beet farmer who had been jilted by the victim a month earlier. She had mistakenly taken a liking to an itinerant vacuum cleaner salesman and ran away with him to Vegas. At trial, the state attorney presents the case—fibers, fingerprints, DNA, a weapon—evidence so complete and convincing that the jury is certain beyond a reasonable doubt. Guilty! The jilted beet farmer is toast! It could be an episode of *CSI: Crime Scene Investigation* or one of the *CSI* spin-offs. But is the evidence presented at criminal trials always this complete? Do jury members always see compelling evidence gleaned from a high-tech crime lab? More importantly, are criminal trials just about evidence? If not, what kinds of things really happen at criminal trials? What is the whole trial process really all about?

Is Criminal Justice Chaotic?

This is the house that justice built,
this is the castle of fair play;
this is the place where wise men sit,
for the law and truth they belay.

The drums of crime, of lust and strife,
these are the souls we see;
in the righteous house that justice built,
here on this star-spangled street.

—ANONYMOUS, C. 1980

You are under arrest for bribery, obstruction of justice, and seven articles of scumbag.

—CAPT. JIM BRASS OF CSI

These few lines of verse, found by the author scribbled on a restroom wall in the basement of the Ross County Courthouse in Chillicothe, Ohio, are expressive of a role that many trial courts play in the administration of justice. Exactly what type of justice the writer of these words had in mind, however, is only open to speculation. The writing is also somewhat curious and paradoxical. Some of the words and even whole lines seem to have been taken from a Milton MacKaye article published in the *New York Evening Post* more than seven decades ago, on January 10, 1930.* The paradox is the fact that MacKaye's commentary was hardly one that praised the "righteous house that justice built." Rather, as a firsthand description of a busy magistrate's court in New York City, it was part of a series entitled "The Magistrate Racket" and addressed only the dismal and frenzied aspects of the American trial system. Or perhaps the anonymous author's poetic celebrations were written in a spirit of sarcasm, for there are literally thousands of tribunals across the United States—small and large, rural and ur-

---

*The MacKaye material is reprinted, in part, in Raymond Moley, *Our Criminal Courts* (New York: Minton, Balch, 1930), 5–9. MacKaye's essay included the following:

This is the house that justice built. This is the castle of fair play. This is the place where wise men shall sit and contemplate our human jealousies, our petty quarrels, our wrong-doings. This, by the grace of God, is a magistrate's court.

Set squarely down in a backwater street, it is not, for some disappointing reason, impressive. But the spangled parade of a city's life passes here, gaudy and gay, drab and mean. The push of ambition, the drums of crime, the blare of pretension, and keen quiet tragedy . . .

This, then, is a magistrate's court set down on the backwater street.

ban—and a number of them are quite chaotic in their approach to the administration of justice.

Going beyond the words of Milton MacKaye and the anonymous poet, many social critics and legal reformers are concerned about the chaotic state of criminal justice in the United States. They often refer to the organization and administration of justice as a "nonsystem," because the police, the courts, and the correctional process have no common goals, cooperative attitudes, or central direction. They claim that America's courts are at the brink of disaster: Backlogs are colossal, workloads are always increasing, and the entire design is misshapen and understaffed. Moreover, it is often argued that the administration of justice has underscored the notions of due process and defendants' rights to such an exaggerated degree that criminals are all too quickly and easily released to continue preying on law-abiding citizens.

Of course, the notion that the legal process is not working is clearly absurd. Each year millions of offenders are arrested and convicted, and a significant number are incarcerated. Others are dismissed or exonerated, presumably because of lack of evidence or because of their innocence—but dismissing and releasing individuals under such circumstances is unquestionably a legitimate function of the court.

When the serious observer takes the time to examine what actually happens in the criminal courts, what is remarkable is not how *badly* they seem to function but how *well*. As inefficient and unjust as it may appear, courthouse justice generally does an effective job of separating the innocent from the guilty. Although most people who are guilty of crimes are never arrested, most of those coming to the courts who should be convicted *are* convicted, and most of those who should be punished *are* punished. Further, there is no evidence to support the contentions that repealing the exclusionary rule, eliminating plea bargaining, legislating mandatory prison terms for serious offenders, or reducing judges' freedom to determine the length of sentences would produce any significant reduction in crime.

This is not to suggest that the administration of justice in the United States, particularly the processing of defendants through the criminal courts, has no problems. The courts *are* overcrowded and understaffed; plea bargaining *does* result in lighter sentences for many offenders and in guilty records for some who are innocent; and rigid adherence to constitutional safeguards *does* allow some dangerous criminals to go free. But it is important to keep in mind that many of these phenomena are the direct result of the U.S. Constitution's protection of individual rights and civil liberties. On the one hand, perfect protection of the accused does mean imperfect protection of society. On the other, a system of justice that automatically checkmates every defendant seeking equity and justice is hardly fair-minded and dispassionate.

Perhaps the greatest difficulties with criminal judicial processing stem from its complexity. There are due process safeguards at every juncture, and it is hardly a speedy process. But its very lack of speed is relevant because it is important to ponder the innocence or guilt of the accused at length. As the distinguished attorney and legal writer Charles Rembar once poignantly remarked: "Speedy justice is not the ultimate aim; just justice is."[1]

> The courts are the final strongholds of feudalism in the United States.
>
> — **HARVEY A. SIEGAL**

> It is as important to keep out of court as it is to keep out of debt.
>
> — **E. W. HOWE**

Bail and Pretrial Release

Excessive bail shall not be required.

— **FROM THE EIGHTH AMENDMENT**

For a defendant, bail is the bottom line of a criminal case.

— **STEVEN PHILLIPS, FORMER ASSISTANT DISTRICT ATTORNEY, BRONX COUNTY, NEW YORK**

Bail is a form of security guaranteeing that a defendant in a criminal proceeding will appear and be present in court at all times as required. Thus, bail is a guarantee: In return for being released from jail, the accused guarantees his or her future appearance by posting funds or some other form of security with the court. When the defendant appears in court as required, the security is returned; if he or she fails to appear, the security is forfeited.

The bail system as we know it today has its roots deep in English history, well before the Norman Conquest in 1066. It emerged at a time when there were few prisons, and the only places secure enough to detain an accused person awaiting trial were the dungeons and strong rooms in the many castles around the countryside. Magistrates often called upon respected local nobles to serve as jailers, trusting them to produce the accused on the day of trial. As the land became more populated and castles fewer in number, magistrates were no longer able to locate jailers known to them. Volunteers were sought, but to ensure that they would be proper custodians, they were required to sign a bond. Known as *private sureties,* these bonds required jailers to forfeit to the king a specified sum of money or property if they failed to live up to their obligations of keeping defendants secure and producing them in court on the day required.[2] When the system was transferred to the New World, it shifted from a procedure of confinement to one of freedom under financial control. In current practice, the accused person posts the bond, or a third party—a **surety**—posts it in his or her behalf.

The Right to Bail

The Eighth Amendment to the U.S. Constitution clearly specifies that "excessive bail shall not be required," but the extent to which accused individuals have any "right" to bail is still a subject of debate. The statutory right of federal defendants to have bail set in all but capital cases was established by the Judiciary Act of 1789. Moreover, the Supreme Court held in *Hudson* v. *Parker* that a presumption in favor of granting bail exists in the Bill of Rights. Justice Horace Gray wrote in 1895:

> The statutes of the United States have been framed upon the theory that a person accused of crime shall not, until he has been fully adjudged guilty in the court of last resort, be absolutely compelled to undergo imprisonment or punishment, but may be admitted to bail, not only after arrest and before trial, but after conviction and pending a writ of error.[3]

But Justice Gray's words carried no firm guarantees for all criminal defendants seeking release on bail. Only a year before, the Court had ruled in *McKane* v. *Durston* that the Eighth Amendment's bail provision places limits only on the federal courts and does not apply to the states.[4] Since that time, the Supreme Court has decided relatively few cases involving bail, mainly because the issue of bail is moot by the time a case reaches the appellate stage of the criminal process. At the state level, the vast majority of state constitutions grant an absolute right to bail in noncapital cases.[5] In practice, however, a constitutional or statutory right to have bail set has never meant an absolute right to freedom before trial. In the past, judges invariably insisted on cash bail or a surety bond from a bail bond agent. If the defendant could not afford it, he or she remained in jail awaiting trial—for days, months, and sometimes even years.

In its principal bail ruling, **Stack v. Boyle** (1951),[6] the Supreme Court left unsettled the constitutional status of a defendant's *right* to bail. But the Court did address the issue of "excessive bail," ruling that the amount must be based on standards relevant to ensuring the presence of the defendant at trial.

Discretionary Bail Setting

In theory, the purpose of bail is to ensure that the accused appears in court for trial. With this in mind, the magistrate is required to set bail at a level calculated to guarantee the defendant's presence at future court hearings. This view has grown out of the historical forms of bail, as well as from the adversarial premise that a person is innocent until proven guilty and therefore should not be confined while awaiting trial. At the same time, however, it is generally believed that the protection of society is more important than bail. Should potentially dangerous defendants who might commit additional crimes be free to roam the streets before trial? Judges often answer this ques-

Spending time in criminal court is like being inside a giant liver. Dark, liver-colored paneling lines the courtrooms. Recessed fluorescent lighting makes jail-pale defendants look that much more like impure particles, there only to be disposed of. Day after day in these courtrooms, the system gets flushed.

Through this huge filtering mechanism pass the accused drug dealers, murderers, home invaders, crack-heads, bad-check passers, and killer drunk drivers. Striving to keep the sludge moving are the judges of the criminal courts.

—LONA O'CONNOR,
IN *SOUTH FLORIDA MAGAZINE*

Statutory Bailing Considerations

1. The principal's character, habits, reputation, and mental condition
2. His or her employment and financial resources
3. His or her family ties and the length of his or her residence, if any, in the community
4. His or her criminal record, if any
5. His or her previous record, if any, in responding to court appearances when required with respect to flight to avoid criminal prosecution
6. The weight of evidence against him or her in the pending criminal action and any other factor indicating probability or improbability of conviction
7. The sentence that may be imposed upon conviction

Source: *New York State Criminal Procedure Law,* Section 510.30. ■

tion by setting bail so high for some defendants that in practice, bail becomes a mechanism for preventive detention.

In many jurisdictions, individuals arrested for minor misdemeanors can gain release almost immediately by posting bail at the police station where they are booked. In these cases, there are established bail amounts, and the size of the bond is relatively small. For serious misdemeanors and felonies, the amount is left to the discretion of the judge. Research has demonstrated, however, that decisions regarding the amount of bail are neither random nor arbitrary.

Under the law, judges in most jurisdictions must consider certain criteria in determining bail. By far the most important factor is the *seriousness of the crime;* it is assumed that the more serious the offense, the greater the likelihood of forfeiture of bail. A second factor is the defendant's *prior criminal record;* the rationale for this is that recidivists (repeat offenders) have a higher probability of forfeiting bond. In conjunction with these two factors is the *strength of the state's case;* the premise is that the greater the chance of conviction, the stronger the accused's interest in fleeing.[7] Thus, if the state has a strong case against an accused person with a prior felony record, and the current offense was a dangerous crime, the amount of bail set will be high.

The Bail Bond Business

Once bail has been set, the requirement can be met in three ways. First, the accused may post the full amount of the bond in cash. Second, many jurisdictions allow a defendant (or family and friends) to put up property as collateral and, thus, post a property bond. In either case, the money or property is returned when all required court appearances have been made, or it is forfeited if the defendant fails to appear.

Neither cash bail nor property bonds are commonly used, however. Most defendants seldom have the necessary cash to post the full bond, and the majority of courts require that the equity in the property held as collateral be at least double the amount of bond. Thus the most common method—the third alternative—is to use the services of a bail bond agent.

Clustered around urban courthouses across the nation are the storefront offices of bail bond agents. Often aglow with bright neon lights, their signs boldly proclaim: BAIL BONDS—24-HOUR SERVICE. And sometimes, during the late-night hours on local television, the viewer is confronted with the most unlikely of commercials: "Are you in trouble? Call us for 24-hour bail bond services!"

A bail bonds agent in the Florida Keys.

Bail Amounts for Felony Defendants

Source: Bureau of Justice Statistics.

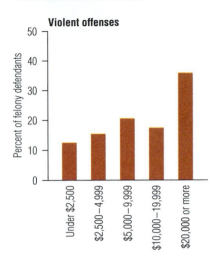

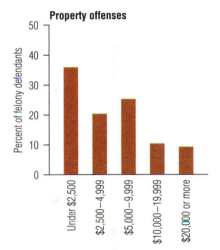

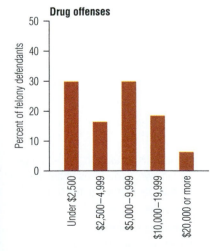

Commercial bond agents are essentially small business entrepreneurs who serve as liaisons with the courts. For a nonrefundable fee, they post a surety bond with the court. If the defendant fails to appear at trial, the bond agent is responsible for the full amount.

Defendants without the funds or property necessary to post the full amount of bail seek out a bond agent, because the fee is usually only 10 percent of the total bail amount. Moreover, in actual practice the bond agent rarely posts a cash surety with the court. Let us assume, for example, that defendant Norman Smith's bail is set at $10,000. His bond agent charges him a nonrefundable fee of $1,000 (10%). The bond agent then purchases a surety bond from an insurance company, which typically costs 30 percent of the fee collected. Smith's cost for pretrial freedom is $1,000, of which $700 becomes the property of the bond agent—whether or not Smith ever appears in court again. If Smith should "jump bail," the insurance company, in theory, pays the forfeiture.

Smith's case, however, would proceed as described only if he was considered a good bail risk. If he was not, it is unlikely that the insurance company would provide a bond or that the bond agent would even accept him as a client. In general, the bond agent views four types of defendants as poor risks:

1. First felony offenders, because they are likely to panic and leave the community.
2. Recidivists, whose new offenses are more serious than their previous ones.
3. Violent offenders, because they can represent a threat to the bond agent.
4. Those whose bail has been set at a high level, because forfeiture would result in large financial losses, as well as damage to the agent's reputation with the insurance company.

In assessing a client's reliability, the bond agent inquires into his or her criminal record, family situation, employment history, roots in the community, and anything else that would suggest whether the defendant has an "investment" in the social system. A client considered to be a bad risk will be rejected; if the client is a marginal risk, the bond agent may require collateral—such as his house, car, or some other resource—in addition to the fee.

Criticisms of the Bail System

For decades, the bail system has been subjected to criticism on many grounds. First, bail tends to discriminate against the poor. When cash bail is set at a high level, it results in pretrial confinement of many low-risk defendants who do not have the funds to either post bond or retain a bond agent. Second, despite the Eighth Amendment safeguard against excessive bail, bail setting is totally discretionary on the part of the judge; many set bail at unreasonably high levels. Third, since bail is generally determined at the initial appearance, the court has little time to investigate the background of the accused and, hence, cannot adequately determine the degree of risk. Fourth, bail is often used as a mechanism for preventive detention. As a means of protecting the community against offenders who are viewed as risks to social welfare and safety, bail is set so high that it can rarely be met.[8]

Bail is forfeited if the defendant fails to appear in court as required. In addition, a *capias*, or **bench warrant**, is issued by the court authorizing the defendant's arrest. Bail jumping itself is an offense that carries criminal penalties and may result in the defendant's pursuit by a modern-day bounty hunter (see Exhibit 12.1). For example, in Maryland, which is typical of most jurisdictions, "failure to surrender after forfeiture of bail" can result in a new felony charge with penalties of 5 years' imprisonment with or without a $5,000 fine.[9]

Pretrial Detention

For defendants, the principal difficulty with the bail system is its relationship to financial well-being. Although most bail premiums paid to bond agents are 5 to 10 percent of the face amount of the bond, rates as high as 20 percent have been reported. When

A bondsman is a fool who, having property of his own, undertakes to become responsible for that entrusted by another to a third.

—AMBROSE BIERCE,
THE DEVIL'S DICTIONARY

LAW & CRIMINAL JUSTICE | EXHIBIT 12.1

Bounty Hunters

An essential yet loosely regulated element to the criminal justice process, the bounty hunter—more typically referred to as a "skip tracer"—is a larger-than-life figure born from tales of the western frontier days. However, this lone wolf of the bail bond business has had to change with the times.

Bounty hunters are private citizens hired by bail bond agents to retrieve defendants who have violated their bail agreement. Broad 19th-century court rulings gave the bounty hunter extensive authority to capture fugitives, but the modern landscape has evolved and the role of a bail enforcer has also changed to reflect this evolution. Armed with pepper spray, steel nerves, and a capture fee of about 10 percent of the bail payment, a typical bounty hunter, male or female, often uses a subdued approach to apprehend the defendant.

In one high-profile instance, though, Wild West *dog*matism made modern news. Earning a national spotlight over his capture of fugitive and "Max Factor" heir Andrew Luster, Duane "Dog" Chapman may have done little to dispel the renegade image of a bounty hunter. Having chased Luster into Mexico, Chapman is accused of entering the country illegally and of kidnapping his target. Most in the business denounce this type of behavior, and Chapman lost his right to the $10,000 reward for Luster's capture. There have been other cases where hunters have overstepped their bounds, having been involved in the use of excessive force, abductions, illegal break-ins, and extortion.

Even though most bounty hunters have some degree of training, tighter restrictions and laws are being enacted to rein in their wide-ranging power. One new twist in the evolution is a proposal to have bounty hunters help catch illegal Internet spammers. Critics of using bounty hunters for any law enforcement purposes, though, point out that there are other, more effective ways to track fugitives, both cyber and actual. Home detention and electronic tagging are just two alternative ways to monitor bailed defendants.

The future role of the bounty hunter is sure to continue to change as the types of crimes being committed and stricter regulatory laws evolve. With bounty hunter video games, television shows, and characters like Duane "Dog" Chapman, the Hollywood "dead or alive" cowboy image is sure to outlast the real thing.

Sources: Bill Hethcock, "Bounty Hunters Rely on Quick Wits to Catch Fugitives," *The Gazette* (Colorado Springs), October 25, 2003; Robert Jablon, "Hunter Got His Man and Colleague's Scorn," *The Miami Herald*, June 21, 2003; David Snyder, "4 Bounty Hunters Charged; Immigrants Abused, Montgomery Says," *The Washington Post*, February 12, 2004; "Pushing the Bounties," *NewsHour* transcript, PBS Organization, September 12, 1997; Bill Draper, "Regulation of Bounty Hunters Clears Senate," *The Associated Press State & Local Wire*, February 27, 2004, retrieved March 25, 2004, from *Lexis Nexis* Academic; "Bounty Hunters: Wanted, Dead or Alive," *The Economist*, September 27, 2003; Marilyn Geewax, "Feds May Turn to Bounty Hunters to Catch Outlaw Spammers," *Cox News Service*, December 12, 2003, retrieved March 25, 2004, from *Lexis Nexis* Academic.

---

bail is set at $1,000 or more, premiums of $100 to $500 are higher than many defendants can afford. In a study of felony defendants in the nation's 75 largest counties, for example, 22 percent failed to post bail at amounts under $2,500, 28 percent failed at amounts of $2,500 to $4,999, and 45 percent failed at amounts of $5,000 to $9,999.[10]

The result of the bail bond system, then, is arbitrary punishment of hundreds of thousands of people, many of whom are innocent. In addition, pretrial detention prevents an accused person from locating evidence and witnesses and having more complete access to counsel. It disrupts employment and family relations. It coerces defendants into plea negotiation in order to settle the case more rapidly. Most important, however, pretrial detainees are confined in city and county jails, which are overcrowded, unsanitary, and poorly equipped. Few jails have enough space for inmates to confer with counsel or visit with families. Defendants awaiting trial are mixed with convicted felons, which, as the late Supreme Court Justice William O. Douglas remarked, is "equivalent to giving a young man an M.A. in crime."[11] Finally, jails are filled with violent offenders, and each year scores of detainees are beaten, raped, and murdered. (For a glimpse at pretrial detention in the People's Republic of China, see Exhibit 12.2.)

Preventive Detention

The Supreme Court's decision in *Stack* v. *Boyle* in 1951 made it clear that the purpose of bail is "to assure the defendant's attendance in court when his presence is required." At the same time, the Court noted that bail is not "a means for punishing defendants nor protecting public safety." Yet the Court has not ruled on whether preventive detention is or is not permissible under the Constitution. As a result, many magistrates

EXHIBIT 12.2 | International Perspectives on Crime & Justice

Pretrial Detention in the People's Republic of China

The violent disruptions of the pro-democracy demonstrations in Beijing's Tiananmen Square by the People's Liberation Army in 1989 have been well documented. Since then, political prisoners and pro-democracy human rights groups have been stifled from speaking out against the government, and many have been subject to long pretrial detentions and criminal prosecutions.

China's Criminal Procedure Law (CPL) of 1979 describes in detail the responsibilities and functions of the criminal justice agencies—the public security bureau (police), procuracy (prosecution), and the judiciary. Under the CPL, the public security authorities may detain anyone suspected of a criminal offense and hold him or her in preventive detention for up to 10 days. The authorities must produce a warrant and, within 24 hours, notify a suspect's family or work unit of the reasons for detention and the place of custody. However, the law allows for discretion in this regard when "notification would hinder the investigation or there is no way to notify." Thus, there is considerable latitude given to authorities to avoid notification.

The public security bureau may formally arrest a suspect if it receives arrest authorization from the procuracy within 10 days after detention. To approve a formal arrest, the procuracy must determine that "the principal facts of [the offender's] crime have already been clarified" and that the offender could be punished with imprisonment. If the arrest authorization is not received within 10 days, the public security bureau is required to release the suspect from custody.

However, the law does not meet international due process standards for pretrial detention. The International Covenant on Civil and Political Rights requires that in criminal cases any person arrested or detained has to be brought "promptly" before a judge—and by "promptly" the United Nations Human Rights Committee means "not in excess of a few days." Some who have experienced China's misuse of the pretrial detention law include literary critic Liu Xiaobo, who was detained on June 6, 1989, but not formally arrested until November 17, 1990; Bao Zunkin, a philosopher and pro-democracy activist who was taken into custody on July 7, 1989, and not notified until November 24, 1990, that he was being charged with "agitating counterrevolutionary propaganda"; and Bao Tong, a senior adviser to dismissed Chinese Communist Party secretary-general Zhao Ziyang, who was detained for 2½ years before being notified of his formal arrest.

The public security authorities give two reasons for not meeting the requirements of the Criminal Procedure Law. First, they argue that 10 days is insufficient to obtain authorization to arrest someone. Second, they contend that it is difficult to meet "approval standards" (that is, to have a completed investigation). Within this context, it would appear that China's public security authorities are able to detain individu-

als in a framework of loopholes that circumvent both local and international law. For example, according to Chinese law, extensions to pretrial detention are permissible, up to a maximum of approximately 6 months. For cases that are "especially major or complex," or where distances involved in investigating cases are "especially large," or when a suspect is under psychological evaluation, these official time limits may be indefinitely extended. Therefore, the authorities enjoy a great deal of discretion when determining detention lengths.

Sources: "No Justice in China," *Human Rights Watch Press Release,* December 21, 1998; *China's Criminal Process and Violations of Human Rights* (Washington, DC: Lawyers for Human Rights, 1993); Rainer Heufers, *The Impact of the Administrative Security Law in the People's Republic of China* (Dallas: Naumann Foundation, 1998); Jim Yardley, "Issue in China: Many in Jails Without Trial," *The New York Times,* May 9, 2005, A1; United States Embassy Bureau of Democracy, Human Rights, and Labor, *China: Country Reports on Human Rights Practices* (Washington DC: Author, 2004); Human Rights in China, *Empty Promises: Human Rights Protections and China's Criminal Procedure Law in Practice* (New York: Author, 2001).

use bail as a mechanism for preventive detention. For those who are considered dangerous offenders or are likely to commit further crimes during the pretrial period, a prohibitively high bail amount is set for the ostensible purpose of ensuring the accused's appearance in court. In fact, despite the implication in *Stack* v. *Boyle,* the District of Columbia, the entire federal system, and the majority of states have laws per-

Women arrestees in an Arizona county jail.

mitting judges to consider an accused's danger to the community in setting pretrial release conditions.[12]

The legal consequences of pretrial detention, preventive or otherwise, can be disastrous. Although there has been no recent research on the issue, civil libertarians argue that detainees are more likely to be indicted and convicted and are likely to be sentenced more harshly than released defendants.

There are some factors, such as strong evidence of guilt or a serious prior criminal record, that necessarily lead to high bail and hence detention. These factors, of course, and not just pretrial detention, can also cause a court to find a defendant guilty and sentence him or her to prison rather than probation. However, one study that took these factors into consideration still found a strong relationship between detention and unfavorable disposition of the case.[13] Moreover, a mock jury study of criminal trial judgments found that "jurors" were more likely to convict "defendants" who had been kept in jail before trial than "defendants" who had been released.[14] In this case, it was theorized that the mock jurors made negative inferences about the guilt of the accused from the fact that he was not granted bail.

Release on Recognizance

At the beginning of the 1960s, increasing dissatisfaction with the bail bond system led to experimentation with alternative forms of pretrial release. For instance, New York industrialist Louis Schweitzer's concern for youths who were detained while awaiting trial led to his establishment of the Vera Foundation (named after Schweitzer's mother). Beginning in 1961 the foundation, later called the Vera Institute of Justice,[15] conducted an experiment with pretrial release based on the notion that "more persons can successfully be released . . . if verified information concerning their character and roots in the community is available to the court at the time of bail determination."[16] Known as the Manhattan Bail Project, the experiment was made possible through the cooperation of the New York criminal courts and law students from New York University. The students interviewed defendants, looking for information that would support a recommendation for pretrial release, including the following factors: (1) present or recent residence at the same address for 6 months or more; (2) current or recent employment for 6 months or more; (3) relatives in New York City with whom the defendant is in contact; (4) no previous conviction for a crime; and (5) residence in New York City for 10 years or more. For those who met the criteria, the students would recommend **release on recognizance (ROR)** to the judge. ROR simply meant that the defendant would be released on his or her own obligation without any requirement of money bail. If the judge agreed with the recommendation, the accused was released, subject to some follow-up contacts to ensure that the defendant knew when he or she was to make a court appearance. Not all defendants were eligible for ROR. Those charged with murder, robbery, rape, or other serious crimes were excluded, as were defendants with long criminal histories.

The experiment was an immediate success in that four times as many defendants were released. Follow-up studies demonstrated that few released defendants defaulted on their obligation, and ROR programs modeled after the Manhattan Bail Project were also successful. Since then, ROR programs have expanded dramatically, and other forms of pretrial release have emerged as well. Under *10 percent cash bond plans,* for example, the court sets bail as it normally would. However, the accused is permitted to deposit 10 percent of the bond directly with the court, eliminating the need for a bond agent. When the accused appears for trial, 90 percent of the deposit is returned, with the remainder held to pay operating costs. For example, if bail is set at $2,000, the defendant deposits a $200 cash bond with the court; when he or she appears for trial, $180 is returned. In this way, the financial incentive to appear at trial is shifted from the bond agent to the accused.

Both the 10 percent cash bond plans and the ROR programs have been successful, and a larger portion of defendants are released who might otherwise have awaited trial in jail. Nevertheless, there have been difficulties. Because of court and jail overcrowding, many suspects in drug-related crimes were failing to appear, and bench warrants were not being served. In effect, the combination of increased drug law enforcement, crowded jails and courts, and widespread use of no-cash bonds has had the effect in some jurisdictions of decriminalizing such offenses as burglary, prostitution, and drug sales.[17]

> Drug defendants now typically have no fear of the criminal justice system. They view the system as ineffective and perceive the possibility of arrest as an acceptable risk since they are reasonably certain of swift release, without even the necessity of posting bail, and because they know that the system lacks the ability to compel their appearance in court.
>
> —PROSECUTING ATTORNEY GALEN CLEMENTS OF PHILADELPHIA'S DANGEROUS DRUG OFFENDER UNIT

The Grand Jury

> It must be remembered that a proceeding before a grand jury is an inquest and not a trial. If defendants are treated as having any right to be heard, the whole affair is likely to cease to be an *ex parte* proceeding resulting in a charge which can be fully met at the trial, but to become a litigation in which each side has the right to offer evidence, and an indictment can only be found if the evidence on the whole case preponderates against the defendants. Such it is believed was never the function of the Grand Inquest.
>
> —JUDGE AUGUSTUS HAND, 1922

Following the initial court proceedings, prosecution is instituted by an information, indictment, or presentment. An **information** is a document filed by the prosecutor that states the formal charges, the statutes that have been violated, and the evidence supporting the charges. The information is generally filed at the preliminary hearing, and the judge then determines whether there is "probable cause" for further processing. An **indictment** is a formal charging document issued by a grand jury on the basis of evidence presented to it by the prosecutor. Slightly different from an indictment is a **presentment,** which is a written notice of accusation issued by a grand jury. The presentment comes not from evidence and testimony provided by the prosecution but, rather, from the initiative of the grand jury, based on its own knowledge and observation. In actual practice, however, the terms *indictment* and *presentment* are largely interchangeable.

The **grand jury** system apparently originated in England in 1166, when King Henry II required knights and other "freemen" from rural neighborhoods to file with the court accusations of murder, robbery, larceny, and harboring of known criminals. In time, as the common law developed, the English grand jury came to consist of not fewer than 12 nor more than 23 men. Not only did they file criminal accusations, but they considered accusations by outsiders as well. The jurors heard witnesses and, if convinced that there were grounds for trial, issued an indictment.[18] Historically, therefore, the purposes of the grand jury were to serve as an investigatory body and to act as

historical perspectives on criminal justice | EXHIBIT 12.3

Hurtado v. California

In the early days of the Republic, due process was construed not as compliance with the fundamental rules for fair and orderly legal proceedings but simply as a limitation on governmental procedure. In terms of criminal procedure, due process was presumed to be spelled out in the Bill of Rights. In the 1878 case of *Davidson* v. *New Orleans* (96 U.S. 97), however, the Supreme Court rejected the notion that due process required adherence to a fixed list of prescribed procedures. Rather, it explained that the meaning of due process would be determined "by the gradual process of judicial inclusion and exclusion." Furthermore, the Court had already decided in 1856 in *Murray's Lessee* v. *Hoboken Land and Improvement Co.* (18 How. 272) that "due" process did not necessarily mean "judicial" process. But if due process procedures were not necessarily "judicial," should they not then be the common law procedures listed in the Bill of Rights? This was the argument in *Hurtado* v. *California.*

In 1882, Joseph Hurtado was accused of killing a man named José Stuardo. In a California court, Hurtado was convicted and sentenced to hang. Some years earlier, in 1879, California's constitution had dropped the grand jury system, substituting the prosecutor's information in its place. Hurtado's attorneys challenged that practice, claiming that their client was forced to trial without having been indicted and thus denied "due process of law."

The Supreme Court upheld Hurtado's conviction and death sentence, stating that the grand jury is merely a form of procedure the states can abolish at will. Furthermore, the Court ruled, the due process clause of the Fourteenth Amendment did not encompass any of the fundamental rights that were enumerated in the first 10 amendments.

Thirteen years later in the 1897 case of *Chicago, Burlington & Quincy Railroad Co.* v. *City of Chicago* (167 U.S. 226), the Court held that it had been narrow-sighted in *Hurtado,* nullifying the justification for its holding in that decision. However, it never overturned *Hurtado,* and states that joined the Union later failed to adopt the grand jury system, doing so without Supreme Court interference.

As if to disregard its belief that grand juries serve a useless purpose in the administration of justice, the Supreme Court has followed a path of almost complete noninterference with grand jury actions.

Source: *Hurtado* v. *California,* 110 U.S. 516 (1884).

---

a buffer between the state and its citizens, to prevent the Crown from unfairly invoking the criminal process against its enemies.

After the American Revolution, the grand jury was incorporated into the Fifth Amendment to the Constitution, which provides that "no person shall be held to answer for a capital or otherwise infamous crime, unless on a presentment or indictment of a grand jury." Despite this guarantee, however, the Supreme Court ruled more than a century ago, in **Hurtado v. California,**[19] that the grand jury was merely a form of procedure that the states could abolish at will (see Exhibit 12.3).

In the American grand jury, the number of jurors under common law—12 to 23—has been retained, and the jury's purposes remain unchanged: to investigate and to protect citizens from unfair accusations. Currently, most of the states and the federal system use grand juries, whose members are generally selected from voting registers. However, many of the territories west of the Mississippi that achieved statehood late in the 19th century did not adopt the grand jury system, choosing instead the prosecutor's information.

Operation of the Grand Jury

There are essentially two types of grand juries: *investigatory* and *accusatory*. The *investigatory grand jury* looks into general allegations of unlawful activity within its jurisdiction in an effort to discover whether there is enough information to justify initiating criminal prosecutions against anyone. An investigatory grand jury may sit for as little as 1 month and as long as 18 months and most often examines suspicions and allegations regarding organized crime and official corruption. More common is the *accusatory grand jury,* a body formed for a set period—generally 3 months—that determines whether there is sufficient evidence against individuals already charged with particular crimes to warrant a criminal trial. The indictment by the accusatory grand jury parallels the prosecutor's filing of an information, and the accusatory grand jury serves as a screening body to decide whether cases already in the early stages of the criminal justice process are worthy of being tried.

Since grand juries are either investigating or accusing bodies, and do not determine guilt or innocence, many of the elements of due process are absent. For example:

- Grand jury sessions are private and secret.
- Witnesses, having been subpoenaed by the prosecutor, are sworn and heard one by one, and excused as soon as they are finished testifying.
- Ordinarily the accused is not present, unless compelled to testify or invited to serve as a witness.
- In most jurisdictions, the defense counsel has no right to be present; if present, the defense counsel has no right to cross-examine witnesses.
- In some jurisdictions, written transcripts are not required.

When the members of a grand jury agree that an accused person should be tried for a crime, they issue a **true bill;** that is, they endorse the validity of the charge or charges specified in the prosecutor's bill, thus issuing an indictment. If they fail to find probable cause, they issue a *no bill* and the accused is released. Since the grand jury proceeding is not a trial, only a majority vote—not a unanimous one—is required for a true bill.

Grand Jury Procedure and the Supreme Court

Prosecutors have wide discretion in the conduct of grand jury proceedings. They may introduce almost any evidence to support their case, for the Supreme Court has generally refused to impose substantive limits on a grand jury's exercise of discretion. One exception occurred in 1906, in *Hale* v. *Henkel.*[20] In this decision, the Court ruled that "a grand jury may not indict upon current rumors or unverified reports." At the same time, however, the justices did agree that indictments could be based on other information, however unreliable, as long as it was not called "rumor." The Court's position on this latter point became more explicit half a century later in the 1956 case of *Costello* v. *United States.*[21]

Frank Costello was well known to the federal judiciary as an associate of such underworld figures as Charles "Lucky" Luciano and Vito Genovese. As a syndicate racketeer who had consolidated gambling interests throughout the United States during the 1930s, he also had the continuous attention of the Internal Revenue Service.

Early in the 1950s, Costello was indicted by a federal investigatory grand jury for willfully attempting to evade payment of federal income taxes for the years 1947 through 1949. The indictments, however, were based on hearsay evidence. Three FBI agents who had no personal knowledge of Costello's finances appeared before the grand jury and "summarized his net worth on the basis of witnesses who were not called to testify." The agents produced "exhibits," which included newspaper stories about Costello's activities. They also made "computations" based on the "exhibits" to demonstrate that Costello and his wife had received a far greater income during those years than they had reported.

After a trial in which 144 witnesses testified and 368 exhibits were introduced, Costello was convicted of tax evasion. The Supreme Court upheld the indictments against Costello, and in so doing established a precedent that grand juries may issue indictments based on hearsay evidence—evidence learned through others and not within the personal knowledge of the witness offering it as testimony.

In **United States v. Calandra,**[22] almost two decades later, the Court addressed the role of the exclusionary rule in grand jury proceedings. The case involved a search of John Calandra's place of business in Cleveland, Ohio. Federal agents, armed with a valid search warrant, were seeking evidence of bookmaking records and gambling paraphernalia. They found none, but they did discover evidence of a loan-sharking operation. Subsequently, a special federal grand jury was convened, and Calandra was subpoenaed to answer questions based on the evidence seized. Calandra refused on Fifth

Grand juries, gentlemen, are in reality, the only censors of this nation.

—HENRY FIELDING, 1749

Amendment grounds, as well as on the basis that the search and seizure exceeded the scope of the warrant and was in violation of the Fourth Amendment. The district court ordered the evidence suppressed, and the U.S. court of appeals affirmed, holding that the exclusionary rule may be invoked by a witness before a grand jury to bar questioning based on illegally obtained evidence.

On an appeal to the U.S. Supreme Court, the lower court ruling was reversed. The High Court held that the exclusionary rule "is a judicially created remedy designed to safeguard Fourth Amendment rights generally through its deterrent effects rather than a personal constitutional right of the party aggrieved."

Grand Juries on Trial

Historically, the grand jury was created to stand between government and the citizen as a protection against unfounded charges and unwarranted prosecutions. Critics maintain, however, that the grand jury process has now become a tool of the prosecutorial misconduct that it was intended to prevent.[23]

One complaint concerns the *ex parte* nature of grand jury proceedings. An *ex parte* is a "one-party" proceeding, meaning that the accused person and his or her attorney are not permitted to be present during the grand jury hearing. Under these circumstances, the accused cannot cross-examine witnesses or object to testimony or evidence.

Critics of grand juries also suggest that they abuse their powers in granting immunity. The Fifth Amendment protects individuals against self-incrimination. Traditionally, the government could compel a witness to testify and still protect his or her Fifth Amendment privilege by providing **transactional immunity.** This meant that the witness was granted immunity against prosecution in return for testifying. Under a federal statute enacted in 1970, however, the government adopted a new form of immunity, **use immunity.** This is a limited immunity that prohibits the government only from using the witness's compelled testimony in a subsequent criminal proceeding. If grand jury witnesses have been granted use immunity, their compelled testimony cannot be used against them as direct evidence or as an "investigatory lead" in a subsequent criminal proceeding. At the same time, the prosecutor has a duty to prove that the evidence he or she proposes to use against a witness who has been granted immunity was derived from a source wholly independent of the compelled testimony. However, as indicated by the Supreme Court's 1972 decision in *Kastigar* v. *United States,*[24] a witness can be indicted on the basis of evidence gathered because of, but "apart" from, his or her testimony. For example, if a grand jury witness has been given use immunity and his compelled testimony reveals that he was a participant in a bank robbery, the witness may be prosecuted for that crime *if* the prosecution is able to produce at trial evidence wholly independent of the witness's grand jury testimony. In the final analysis, then, use immunity is not *total* immunity.

Grand juries also possess *contempt power,* which can be used to compel witnesses to provide testimony needed for criminal investigations. Witnesses who refuse to testify can be jailed for an indefinite period until they "purge" themselves of contempt by providing the requested information. This would seemingly result in the abridgment of certain constitutional guarantees. However, in 1972 the Supreme Court's decision in *Branzburg* v. *Hayes*[25] forced journalists to testify before a grand jury when subpoenaed. Some journalists have gone to jail rather than reveal their confidential sources, because they believe that to do so would erode the freedom of the press protected by the First Amendment. Moreover, some critics maintain that the grand jury's contempt power has been used to intentionally punish political dissidents.

Other criticisms of the grand jury are that it is really an extension of the prosecution, helping to create "plea bargaining chips," and that it is cumbersome, is expensive, and sometimes forces defendants to spend more time in jail awaiting trials. And most recently, members of grand juries have argued that in some jurisdictions, the grand jury system has become so cumbersome and dysfunctional that defendants and grand jury members have become "victimized" by the process.[26]

Torture in Chile is pretty much like what you might see in the movies—metal slivers pushed under your fingernails, a hot match stick or lighted cigarette to an eyeball, or electric shocks to the testicles. But torture in the United States has been refined to a more exquisite level. Here it consists of being surrounded by a roomful of legalists and being remorselessly pecked to death for days on end.

—A CHILEAN REFUGEE SEEKING POLITICAL ASYLUM IN THE UNITED STATES, REFLECTING ON HIS EXPERIENCES WITH GOVERNMENT ATTORNEYS

| The Plea |

After the formal determination of charges through either the information or the indictment, the defendant is arraigned, at which time he or she is asked to make a plea. The four basic pleas, as noted in Chapter 5, are not guilty, guilty, *nolo contendere*, and standing mute. There is also the special plea of not guilty by reason of insanity, as well as other special pleas involving statutes of limitations and double jeopardy.

Not Guilty

The plea of not guilty, the most common type, places the full burden on the state to prove the charges against the defendant beyond a reasonable doubt. Under the principles of American jurisprudence, all accused individuals, regardless of their actual guilt or innocence, are morally and legally entitled to make such a plea. In the adversary system of justice, it is the right of everyone charged with a crime to rely on the presumption of innocence. *Standing mute* at arraignment by failing or refusing to make a plea is presumed to be an entry of not guilty.

Guilty

The guilty plea, whether negotiated or not, has several consequences, as pointed out by the National Advisory Commission on Criminal Justice Standards and Goals:

> Such a plea functions not only as an admission of guilt but also as a surrender of the entire array of constitutional rights designed to protect a criminal defendant against unjustified conviction, including the right to remain silent, the right to confront witnesses against him, the right to a trial by jury, and the right to be proven guilty by proof beyond a reasonable doubt.[27]

As such, a plea of guilty has the effect of surrendering numerous constitutional rights, including those guaranteed under the Fifth and Sixth Amendments.

Nolo Contendere

The **nolo contendere** plea, which means "no contest," or more specifically, "I will not contest it," is essentially a guilty plea. It entails the surrendering of certain constitutional rights, and conviction is immediate. However, there is one important difference between *nolo contendere* and a guilty plea. With *nolo contendere*, there is technically no admission of guilt, which protects the accused in civil court should the victim subsequently sue for damages.

The *nolo contendere* plea is not an automatic option at arraignment. It is acceptable in the federal courts and in about half the states and may be made only at the discretion of the judge and the prosecutor. Generally, this plea is entered for the benefit of the accused, but in at least one instance it carried an unintended consequence for perhaps the whole nation. On August 7, 1973, the *Wall Street Journal* reported that Spiro T. Agnew—at the time vice president of the United States under Richard Nixon—was the target of an investigation by U.S. Attorney George Beall concerning allegations of kickbacks by contractors, architects, and engineers to officials of Baltimore County, Maryland. The alleged violations of conspiracy, extortion, bribery, and tax statutes were supposed to have extended from the time Agnew was a Baltimore County executive in 1962 through his years in the vice presidency. After several sessions of plea negotiation between Agnew's attorneys and the Justice Department, it was agreed that Agnew would resign the vice presidency and plead *nolo contendere* to a single charge of income tax evasion. In return, the Justice Department would not proceed with indictment on the other charges. On October 10, 1973, Agnew announced his resignation and entered his plea. It was accepted by Federal District Judge Walter Hoffman, and Agnew received a $10,000 fine and 3 years' unsupervised probation.

By Richard Li. From CRIME & JUSTICE INTERNATIONAL, March 2003.
Reprinted by permission.

Seven years later, Judge Hoffman recalled the case and remarked that accepting Agnew's plea had been a "wise decision." If he had not accepted the plea, Agnew would have been indicted and tried, and upon conviction he probably would have appealed. This would have meant that the case would still have been pending when President Nixon resigned from the presidency on August 9, 1974. As Hoffman put it, "When Nixon resigned, Agnew would automatically have been President of the United States." [28]

Insanity

The plea of not guilty by reason of insanity is generally not to the advantage of the accused, for it is an admission of guilt accompanied by the claim that the defendant is not culpable in the eyes of the law because of insanity at the time he or she committed the crime. More typically, a dual plea of not guilty *and* not guilty by reason of insanity is made. Such a plea implies that "the burden is on the government to prove that I did the act upon which the charge is based, and, even if the government proves that at trial, I still claim I am not culpable because I was legally insane at the time." [29]

Not all jurisdictions have a separate insanity plea, nor do all have the dual plea of not guilty–not guilty by reason of insanity. In these instances, a plea of not guilty is made and it is up to the defense to raise the issue of insanity. However, even in jurisdictions that allow the insanity plea, the accused and his or her counsel must present an *affirmative defense*. In law, this defense amounts to more than a mere denial of the prosecution's allegations. Thus, while the burden of proving the guilt of the accused is on the state, the responsibility for showing insanity at the time of the commission of the offense generally rests with the defendant.

In recent years there has been considerable opposition to the insanity plea, much of it an outgrowth of the 1980 assassination attempt on President Ronald Reagan by John W. Hinckley, Jr., and his successful plea of guilty by reason of insanity. The Hinckley case led to the enactment of "guilty but mentally ill" statutes in many jurisdictions. Under these regulations, defendants who are found guilty but mentally ill go to prison. If they require psychiatric treatment, they receive it in the penitentiary. [30]

On the other hand, studies suggest that the general public drastically overestimates the incidence of successful insanity pleas, primarily because insanity cases are among the most highly publicized. In reality, comparatively few defendants plead not guilty by reason of insanity. Moreover, as noted earlier in Chapter 2, the insanity defense rarely wins. Of the millions of criminal cases disposed of each year in state and federal courts, fewer than 1 percent involve insanity pleas, only one in four of such pleas lead to acquittals, and the majority of these involve misdemeanor charges. [31]

EXHIBIT 12.4 | *Gender Perspectives on Crime and Justice*

DNA Profiling and Statutes of Limitations

Because of the widespread use of DNA profiling in recent years, statutes of limitations have run into a major complication in a number of jurisdictions. Rape survivors and law enforcement officials, in particular, are finding that with regard to sex crimes, science has outpaced the law.

Through mandatory sampling of prisoners and other known offenders, states and municipalities are developing computerized databases that allow investigators to compare bits of biological evidence left at crime scenes against the DNA profiles of scores of suspects. Because these checks are quite easy and virtually infallible, they offer breakthroughs, particularly in the great backlog of investigations of crimes of violence that have essentially gone cold. DNA profiling is especially useful in rape cases, because in the majority of instances the semen of the rapist is left behind in or on the victim and is collected and preserved, making it possible to identify the perpetrator at some later date.

But a race against time is under way. Most states have statutes of limitations for rape prosecutions—often just 5 years. What that means is that old cases might be solved but not prosecuted, because the statute of limitations has run out. And this would be so even if the names of the rapists were known and the evidence against them were overwhelming.

Florida, Nevada, and New Jersey have already abolished the statutes of limitations on sexual assault, and other jurisdictions have extended their statutes of limitations to 10 and 15 years. Although these changes are not retroactive and old cases still expire, future cases will benefit. Elsewhere, state legislatures are only now beginning to review their statutes in light of DNA profiling. But as the discussions linger, tens of thousands of cold cases are running out of time.

Sources: David H. Kaye and Edward Imwinkelried, *Forensic DNA Typing: Selected Legal Issues* (Phoenix: Arizona State University, 2000); Hans H. Chen, "DNA Indictments Push Law to the Limit," *APB Online,* March 21, 2000; *The New York Times,* February 9, 2000, B1, B4; National District Attorneys Association, "State by State Statutes of Limitations for Sexual Assault Statutes," July 2000.

Statutes of Limitations

Every state has laws, known as "statutes of limitations," that bar prosecution for most crimes after a certain amount of time has passed; that is, the suspect must be accused within a reasonable period after the offense was committed. There are numerous reasons for these statutes. After the passage of time, for example, defendants may be unable to establish their whereabouts at the time of the crime or evidence or witnesses supporting their innocence might be lost. Similarly, after long periods those guilty of crimes may be unable to gather evidence to support their defense or mitigate their conduct. Moreover, during the time since the crime the offender may have become a law-abiding citizen who presents no further threat to the community, and conviction and sentencing would serve little purpose.

Statutes of limitations can be quite complex. Generally, such statutes do not apply to murder prosecutions. In addition, statutes for other offenses may be *tolled* (suspended) owing to circumstances such as the defendant's absence from the state. And finally, in most jurisdictions the plea of statute of limitations must be entered at arraignment; otherwise the accused will be deemed to have waived that particular defense. (For a discussion of the impact of DNA profiling on statutes of limitations, see Exhibit 12.4.)

Double Jeopardy

To restrain the government from repeatedly prosecuting an accused person for one particular offense, the prohibition against **double jeopardy**—two trials for one offense—was included in the Constitution. The Fifth Amendment states, in part: "Nor shall any person be subject for the same offense to be twice put in jeopardy of life or limb."

The Supreme Court has held that this guarantee protects the accused against both multiple prosecutions for the same offense and multiple punishments for the same crime. However, it has taken the Supreme Court almost two centuries to clarify to whom and when the Fifth Amendment guarantee applies.

In 1824, in *United States* v. *Perez,*[32] the Court denied double jeopardy protection in cases in which a jury failed to agree on a verdict. In 1949, the Court ruled in *Wade* v. *Hunter*[33] that the double jeopardy clause does not apply in certain types of mistrials. In the 1922 case of *United States* v. *Lanza,*[34] the Court addressed the issue of double jeopardy and dual sovereignty. The defendant had been convicted of violating Washington State's prohibition law. He had then been indicted on the same grounds for violating the federal prohibition law. In a 6-to-3 vote, the Court ruled that the Fifth Amendment double jeopardy clause protected only against repeated prosecutions by a single sovereign government. The Court's opinion, which viewed the state of Washington and the federal government as separate sovereignties deriving power from different sources, was that the second indictment had been a valid one. The *Lanza* rule was reaffirmed in the 1959 case of *Abbate* v. *United States*,[35] but 11 years later, in *Waller* v. *Florida*,[36] the Court ruled that a city and a state are not separate sovereignties.

As noted in Chapter 5, the application of the double jeopardy clause to state criminal trials was rejected by the Supreme Court in the 1937 case of **Palko v. Connecticut**.[37] Some three decades later, however, in **Benton v. Maryland**[38]—the last announced decision of the Warren Court—the Court declared that the double jeopardy clause applies to the states through the due process clause of the Fourteenth Amendment. Finally, in **Downum v. United States**,[39] the Court declared that double jeopardy begins at the point when the second trial jury is sworn in.

Under state statutes, pleas of not guilty on grounds of double jeopardy are of two types. The accused can plead *autrefois acquit* (formerly acquitted) if he or she was acquitted of the identical charge involving the same set of facts on a previous occasion. Or the accused can plead *autrefois convict* (formerly convicted) if he or she was convicted of the identical charge involving the same set of facts on a previous occasion.

| Pretrial Motions |

All pleas of not guilty (other than those dismissed on statute of limitations or double jeopardy grounds) result in the setting of a trial date. Before the actual commencement of the trial, however, and sometimes before arraignment, both the defense and the prosecution may employ a number of motions. A **motion** is a formal application or request to the court for some action, such as an order or rule. The purpose of motions is to gain some legal advantage, and most are initiated by the defense. The number and type of motions vary according to the nature and complexity of the case. Without question, the court's decisions as to whether to grant or deny motions can have a considerable impact on the outcome of a proceeding.

Motion for Discovery

It is always in the best interests of the defense to know in advance what witnesses and kinds of evidence the prosecution plans to introduce at trial. The *motion for discovery* is a request to examine the physical evidence, evidentiary documents, and lists of witnesses in the possession of the prosecutor. Although some jurisdictions may resist such a motion, discovery is a matter of constitutional law. The Supreme Court's decision in the 1963 case of *Brady* v. *Maryland*[40] held that a prosecutor's failure to disclose evidence favorable to the accused upon request violates due process. However, some years later, in *Moore* v. *Illinois*,[41] the Court ruled that there is no constitutional requirement for the prosecution to fully disclose the entire case file to the defense.

Motion for Change of Venue

Venue, from the Latin meaning "neighborhood," refers to the county or district—not the jurisdiction—within which a case is to be tried. A motion for a change of venue is a request that the trial be moved from the county, district, or circuit in which the crime was committed to some other place. The jurisdiction does not change; the original trial court simply moves if the motion is granted.

Either the defense or the prosecution can introduce such a motion. Typically, however, it is made by the defense in sensational or highly publicized cases when it is felt that the accused cannot obtain a fair trial in the particular locale of the court.

"Most extreme change of venue I've ever seen."

ScienceCartoonsPlus.com. Reprinted by permission.

FAMOUS CRIMINALS
Ira Einhorn, the "Unicorn Killer"

Back in the 1960s, Ira Einhorn was known as the King of the Radicals, the Prince of Flower Power, the Guru of Peace and Love, and the Chief Acquarian in Philadelphia. He called himself "Unicorn," because the name Einhorn (a German-Jewish name) means "one horn." On March 28, 1979, police visited Einhorn on complaints by the neighbors below his apartment who had been detecting a terrible stench coming through the floorboards, accompanied by an occasional oozing of putrid brown matter that stained their ceiling. The Philadelphia police started wondering if the reek had something to do with Holly Maddux, Einhorn's old flame, who had been missing for 18 months. In a small steamer trunk in one of Einhorn's closets, police found the remains of Maddux. Einhorn lit a joint and commented matter of factly, "You found what you found."

Prior to his trial on murder charges, Einhorn jumped bail and left the country. For two decades Einhorn, under the name Eugene Mallon, was living the life of an expatriate gentleman, complete with a Swedish wife, in rural France. In 1993, he was tried in absentia and convicted. When he was finally located, the French government came to see his case as a human rights cause célèbre, with prominent attorneys and others arguing that he'd been unfairly tried in absentia and so should not be extradited. To win his extradition, it took several years, a special law passed by the Pennsylvania

(continued on p. 389)

Motion for Suppression

Mapp v. *Ohio, Escobedo* v. *Illinois,* and *Miranda* v. *Arizona* collectively served to make suppression one of the most common of pretrial motions in criminal cases.[42] The *motion for suppression* is a request to have evidence excluded from consideration. Typically, it is filed by the defense to bar evidence that was obtained as the result of an illegal search and seizure or wiretap or to challenge the validity of a confession.

Motion for a Bill of Particulars

A *bill of particulars* is a written statement that specifies additional facts about the charges contained in the information or indictment. As a motion filed by the defense, it is a request for more details from the prosecution. The motion is not made for the purpose of discovering evidence or of learning exactly how much the prosecution knows, and it is not designed to suggest an insufficient indictment. Rather, the motion for a bill of particulars asks for details about what the prosecution claims in order to give the accused fair notice of what must be defended. For example, if a neighborhood racketeer who operates illegal lotteries and off-track betting schemes is charged with possession of gambling paraphernalia, the defense might wish to know which of the confiscated materials (policy slips, betting cards, and so on) the prosecutor intends to use as the basis of his or her action.

Motion for Severance of Charges or Defendants

Many legal actions involve multiple charges against one defendant. The accused may have been arrested for a number of different crimes resulting from a single incident—for example, an auto theft followed by destruction of property, resisting arrest, and assault upon a police officer. Or the accused may be charged with multiple counts of the same offense—perhaps several sales of dangerous drugs during a given period. In both instances, and for the sake of expediency, the prosecution may consolidate these multiple charges into a single case. The defense, however, may feel that different tactics are required for dealing with each charge. Thus, the *motion for severance of charges* requests that each specific charge be tried as a separate case.

Similarly, often more than one person is charged with participation in the same crime—for example, there may be four codefendants in a bank robbery. There are times when the best interests of one or more of the accused are served by separate trials. Defendant Smith, for example, may wish to have a trial by jury; defendant Jones may wish to place the blame on his codefendants. Thus, the *motion for severance of defendants* requests that one or more of the accused be tried in separate proceedings.

Widely cited research has demonstrated that *joinders* (of charges and/or defendants) may have negative effects. In several mock jury experiments, "jurors" were presented with cases in which "defendants" were charged with individual or multiple charges. When the "defendants" had joined trials, there was a greater tendency to convict. When charges were joined, the "jurors" confused the evidence among the various charges and made more negative inferences about the character of the "defendant."[43]

Motion for Continuance

The *motion for continuance* requests that the trial be postponed to some future date. Such a motion is filed by the defense or the prosecution on the ground that there has not been enough time to prepare the case. There may, for example, have been problems in gathering evidence or locating witnesses. Some defense attorneys use this motion as a stalling tactic to enhance the accused's chances. They feel that if the case is delayed long enough, victims' memories will begin to fail, witnesses will begin to lose interest, and a better plea might be negotiated.

CAREERS IN CRIMINAL JUSTICE

Legal Assistants

Legal assistants, also known as *paralegals,* assist attorneys in the delivery of legal services. Through formal education and training, legal assistants develop expertise in substantive and procedural law, thus qualifying them to do various types of legal work under the supervision of an attorney.

In all 50 states, legal assistants are prohibited from "practicing law." As such, they cannot give legal advice, represent a client in court, set a fee, or accept a case—all of which are generally considered the practice of law. Working under the supervision of an attorney, however, legal assistants perform any function delegated by an attorney, including these:

- Conducting client interviews and maintaining general contact with clients.

- Locating and interviewing witnesses.

- Conducting investigations and statistical and documentary research.

- Conducting legal research.

- Drafting legal documents, correspondence, and pleadings.

- Summarizing depositions, interrogatories, and testimony.

- Attending depositions, court or administrative hearings, and trials with the attorney.

- Authoring and signing correspondence.

In addition to working in private law firms, legal assistants are found in courts, corporations, insurance companies, government offices, and administrative agencies. Some legal assistants establish their own businesses, working for attorneys on a contract basis.

It is estimated that there are more than 750 educational programs in the United States offering paralegal training, including (1) associate's degree programs offered at community colleges and universities; (2) bachelor's degree programs that combine paralegal studies with other disciplines, often criminal justice; and (3) certificate programs offered in schools of continuing education.

Motion for Dismissal

As a matter of common practice at arraignment, defense attorneys make a motion for dismissal of charges on the ground that the prosecution has failed to produce sufficient evidence to warrant further processing. Whether justified or not, most defense attorneys almost automatically file this motion. In practically all instances the motion is denied by the judge. There are situations, however, in which the motion for dismissal is fully warranted and is granted by the presiding magistrate. For example, a previously granted motion for suppression may have weakened the state's case. Here it could be the defense *or* the prosecution who files the motion. Moreover, in jurisdictions where prosecutors do not have full authority to issue a *nolle prosequi,* the dropping of charges must be sought through a judicial dismissal.

Other pretrial motions may include requests to inspect grand jury minutes, determine sanity, or discover statements made by prosecution witnesses. By far the most common, however, are the motions for suppression and dismissal.

It should be emphasized that if a motion by the defense results in the dismissal of a case, the prosecution has the legal authority to reinstate the case. Charges can be filed, dismissed, and refiled, for there is no double jeopardy connected with the pretrial process. As noted in *Downum* v. *United States* and reaffirmed by the Supreme Court in *Serfass* v. *United States,*[44] in a jury trial, jeopardy attaches when the jury is impaneled and sworn; in a bench trial, jeopardy attaches when the court begins to hear evidence.

Speedy and Public Trial

In all criminal prosecutions, the accused shall enjoy the right to a speedy and public trial.

— FROM THE SIXTH AMENDMENT

It is no surprise that the right to a **speedy trial** appears in the Constitution of the United States. Without it, individuals accused of crimes would have no protection against incarceration for an indefinite period prior to trial. Like all other provisions

(continued from p. 388)
legislature, and a promise by the Philadelphia district attorney not to seek the death penalty. In 2002, Einhorn was convicted once again and sentenced to a term of life without parole. As a postscript to the case, jury costs for the 22-day trial came to $95,291. ∎

**Time from Arrest to Disposition
in State Court Cases**

Source: Bureau of Justice Statistics.

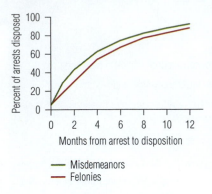

in the Bill of Rights, the guarantee of a speedy trial is to ensure the rights of individual defendants, rather than to protect the state from delays that might be caused by the accused.

Putting the speedy trial clause of the **Sixth Amendment** into practice has been difficult, for several reasons. *First,* in the two centuries since the Constitution was written the criminal justice system has become more complex. Many procedural steps have been added to criminal proceedings in order to guarantee a fair hearing for the accused. *Second,* more people are accused of violations of the law each year, making delays inevitable. In many metropolitan areas where crime rates are high, it is difficult for some defendants to receive any trial at all, least of all a speedy one. *Third,* the criminal law has become more detailed and elaborate. Some state statutes have become so highly specific that the evidence-gathering process has become a time-consuming task. *Fourth,* the requirement of a speedy trial must be balanced against the right of both the defense and the prosecution to have enough time to prepare their cases. *Fifth,* some trials are inexcusably delayed by either the prosecution or the defense for the purpose of achieving their own objectives. A prosecutor, for example, may seek several continuances, hoping to put off a trial until an accused's codefendant is convinced to "strike a deal" and become a witness for the state. A defense attorney may employ the same delaying tactics in the expectation that witnesses will lose interest in the case. *Sixth,* some delays result from little more than prosecutors' apathy or lack of concern for defendants' rights and humanity. And *seventh,* there is no consensus as to the meaning of "speedy trial." Statutory time limits vary by jurisdiction and by the nature of the offense charged. For example:

- In California, the period between arraignment and trial must not exceed 56 days.[45]
- In Alabama, the time limit between arrest and trial is set at 12 months for misdemeanors and at 3 years for all felonies—except capital offenses, for which there is no limit.[46]
- In Maine, there is a flexible standard of "unnecessary delay"—whatever that might mean.[47]

The Supreme Court and Speedy Trial

The Constitution offers no clues to what its framers had in mind when they incorporated the concept of "speedy trial" into the Bill of Rights. As a result, the Supreme Court has attached a standard of *reasonableness.* This is an attempt to achieve a balance between the effects of delays and their causes and justifications. The Court emphasized the need for such a balance as early as 1905, when it ruled in *Beavers* v. *Haubert*[48] that the right to a speedy trial is a "relative" one "consistent with delays and dependent on circumstances."

Many of the Court's subsequent decisions addressed the particulars of individual cases rather than larger policy issues. At the beginning of the 1970s, however, the Court's rulings in a series of cases did provide some guidelines for trial courts. The first of these was *Barker* v. *Wingo,*[49] decided in 1972. Until that time, both federal and state courts operated under the assumption that failure to demand a speedy trial meant that the accused was not opposed to delays. In *Barker,* the Court rejected this assumption, holding that passive compliance does not amount to a waiver of the Sixth Amendment right to a speedy trial. Moreover, although the Court was unwilling to announce any specific time frame for what would constitute delay, it did identify a variety of factors that trial courts should examine in determining whether the right to a speedy trial has been denied: the length of the delay, the reason for the delay, the defendant's assertion of his or her right, and prejudice to the defendant.

The following year, in *Strunk* v. *United States,*[50] the Court unanimously held that if a defendant is denied a speedy trial, "the only possible remedy" is for the charges to be dismissed. Later in the decade, in *United States* v. *Lovasco,*[51] the Court made clear that the Sixth Amendment right does not apply to delays before a person is accused of a crime but, rather, applies only to the interval between arrest and trial.

The interior of the circuit court in the old courthouse at the Jefferson National Expansion Memorial in St. Louis, Missouri.

Speedy Trial and the States

Speedy trial has had a constitutional guarantee at the federal level since the drafting of the Bill of Rights. However, it was not applied to the states until relatively recently. The case was *Klopfer* **v.** *North Carolina,*[52] decided in 1967.

The petitioner in this somewhat unusual case was Peter H. Klopfer, a professor of zoology at Duke University. Klopfer had been indicted by the state of North Carolina for criminal trespass as the result of a sit-in at a segregated motel and restaurant. At trial, however, the jury failed to agree on a verdict. This resulted in a mistrial, thus necessitating a new trial. But after a year had passed and the second trial had not been ordered, Klopfer demanded that his case either be tried immediately or be dismissed. Rather than complying with the petitioner's demands, the presiding judge instead granted the prosecutor's request for a *nolle prosequi.* At the time, this allowed the prosecutor to place the indictment in an inactive status without bringing it to trial—thus retaining it for use at *any* time in the future. On appeal to the North Carolina Supreme Court, Klopfer argued that the trial judge's action denied his Sixth Amendment right, which he regarded as applicable to the states. The court ruled that a defendant's right to a speedy trial did not encompass "the right to compel the state to prosecute him." Thus, still in limbo with his "suspended" trespass indictment, Klopfer petitioned the U.S. Supreme Court.

The Court ruled in favor of Klopfer. It also unanimously struck down the North Carolina law that allowed indefinite postponement of a criminal prosecution without dismissal of an indictment. In addition, Chief Justice Earl Warren explained that the North Carolina procedure denied a defendant the right to a speedy trial, which "is as fundamental as any of the rights secured by the Sixth Amendment"—thus extending the speedy trial clause to the states.

A trial is a formal inquiry designed to prove and put upon record the blameless characters of judges, advocates, and jurors.

— AMBROSE BIERCE,
THE DEVIL'S DICTIONARY

The Speedy Trial Act of 1974

The ruling in *Barker* v. *Wingo* prompted Congress—against the advice of both the Justice Department and the federal judges—to pass the **Speedy Trial Act** of 1974 in an effort to demand a reduction in delays in *federal* trials. The act, sponsored by Senator Sam J. Ervin of North Carolina, established a 100-day deadline between arrest and trial.

The Speedy Trial Act was phased in gradually, not becoming fully effective until June 30, 1980. Currently, failure to bring a case to trial within the 100-day deadline—except in a few rigidly defined situations—results in dismissal of the charges.

The Right to a Public Trial

The Sixth Amendment provides not only for a speedy trial but for a *public trial* as well—a guarantee rooted in the heritage of English common law.

The traditional Anglo-American distrust of secret trials evolved from the notorious use of such trials by the Spanish Inquisition and the English Star Chamber court,* as well as the French monarchy's use of the *lettre de cachet.*† In the hands of despotic groups, these institutions became instruments of political and religious suppression through their ruthless disregard of the accused's right to a fair trial.

Although all jurisdictions have adopted the Sixth Amendment right to a public trial through state constitutions, statutes, or judicial decisions, there have been exceptions in the recent past. *In re Oliver,*[53] decided in 1948, was one of the very few cases in which the Supreme Court addressed the right to a public trial. The issue in *Oliver* stemmed from the actions of a Michigan judge serving in the role of a one-person grand jury. The judge's actions were described in the Court's opinion as follows:

> In the case before us, the petitioner was called as a witness to testify in secret before a one-man grand jury conducting a grand jury investigation. In the midst of petitioner's testimony the proceedings abruptly changed. The investigation became a "trial," the grand jury became a judge, and the witness became an accused charged with contempt of court—all in secret.
>
> Following a charge, conviction, and sentence, the petitioner was led away to prison—still without any break in the secrecy. Even in jail, according to undenied allegations, his lawyer was denied an opportunity to see and confer with him. And that was not the end of the secrecy. His lawyer filed in the state supreme court this *habeas corpus* proceeding. Even there, the mantle of secrecy enveloped the transaction and the state supreme court ordered him sent back to jail without ever having seen a record of his testimony, and without knowing all that took place in the secrecy of the judge's chambers. In view of this nation's historic distrust of secret proceedings, their inherent dangers to freedom, and the universal requirement of our federal and state governments that criminal trials be public, the Fourteenth Amendment's guarantee that no one shall be deprived of his liberty without due process of law means that at least an accused cannot be thus sentenced to prison.

The Court further held that the failure to give the accused a reasonable opportunity to defend himself against the contempt charge was a denial of due process of law. Yet curiously, despite the justices' ruling in behalf of the petitioner, *Oliver* did not expressly incorporate the Sixth Amendment right to a public trial within the meaning of the Fourteenth Amendment. This did not occur until 20 years later in a footnote to *Duncan* v. *Louisiana,*[54] discussed later in the chapter.

| The Jury |

As a criminal prosecution approaches the trial date, a pretrial hearing is held, at which point the pretrial motions are heard and dealt with by the judge. At the same time, the court also asks whether the accused wishes a trial by judge or a trial by jury.

In a trial by judge (or judges), more commonly referred to as a *bench trial,* the decision of innocence or guilt is made by the presiding judge. In some jurisdictions the option of a trial by judge may be dictated by state requirements. Under Tennessee statutes, for example, the accused is not prevented from waiving the right to a trial by jury;[55] in Idaho, however, this waiver is permitted only in nonfelony cases.[56]

---

*In England during the Middle Ages, the Star Chamber was a meeting place of the King's Counselors in the palace of Westminster—so called from the stars painted on the ceiling. The Court of the Star Chamber developed from the proceedings traditionally carried out by the king and his council and typically dealt with equity matters. In the 15th century under the Tudors, the jurisdiction of the court was extended to criminal matters. Faster and less rigid than the common law courts, Star Chamber proceedings tended to be harsh at times, and they were ultimately abolished by Parliament in 1641.

†A part of 17th-century French law, the *lettre de cachet* was a private, sealed document issued as a communication from the king, which could order the imprisonment or exile of an individual without recourse to the courts.

"Your Honor, we're going to go with the prosecution's spin."

© The New Yorker Collection 1997 Mike Twohy from cartoonbank.com.
All Rights Reserved.

When defendants are in a position to make a choice, there are several circumstances under which the bench trial would probably be more desirable. For example, the crime may be so reprehensible or so widely publicized that it could be difficult if not impossible to find a neutral jury. Or the nature of the defense may be too complex or technical for jurors without legal training to fully comprehend. Also, the presiding judge may have a previous record of favorable decisions in similar cases.

The reasons for selecting a trial by jury are perhaps even more compelling. The jury serves as a safeguard against overzealous prosecutors and biased judges, and it gives the accused the benefit of commonsense judgment, as opposed to the perhaps less sympathetic reactions of a single magistrate.

The Right to Trial by Jury

The trial by jury is a distinctive feature of the Anglo-American system of justice, dating back more than seven centuries. The Magna Carta, signed in 1215, contained a special provision that no freeholder would be deprived of life or property except by judgment of his or her peers. This common law principle was incorporated into the U.S. Constitution. Article III contains this simple and straightforward statement: "The trial of all crimes, except in cases of impeachment, shall be by jury." Article III is reaffirmed by the Sixth Amendment, which holds that "in all criminal prosecutions, the accused shall enjoy the right to a speedy and public trial by an impartial jury."

In federal cases, to which Article III applies directly, the Supreme Court has been unrelenting in its view that a jury in criminal cases must have 12 members and reach a unanimous verdict. Curiously, however, for almost two centuries after the framing of the Constitution—despite Article III and the Sixth Amendment—the right to a trial by jury "in all criminal prosecutions" was not fully binding in state trials. This discrepancy ended with the Supreme Court's ruling in ***Duncan v. Louisiana***,[57] decided in 1968.

The setting was Plaquemines Parish, Louisiana, an oil-rich community some 50 miles northwest of New Orleans. At the time, Plaquemines Parish had long been bossed by the skillful political leader Leander H. Perez, a virulent segregationist whose philosophies and opinions seemingly influenced local folkways. Gary Duncan, a 19-year-old African American youth, had been tried in the local court on a charge of simple battery—a misdemeanor punishable by a maximum of 2 years' imprisonment and a $300 fine. His crime had involved no more than slapping the elbow of a white youth. He was convicted, fined $150, and sentenced to 60 days in jail. Duncan had requested a trial by jury, but this was denied on the authority of the Louisiana constitution, which granted jury trials only in cases in which capital punishment or imprisonment at hard labor could be imposed. Duncan appealed to the U.S. Supreme Court, contending that his right to a jury trial was guaranteed by the Sixth and Fourteenth Amendments.

"My client pleads not guilty by reason of still being in denial."

Reprinted by permission of www.CartoonStock.com.

In a 7-to-2 decision, the Court ruled in favor of Duncan, thus incorporating the Sixth Amendment right to a jury into the due process clause of the Fourteenth Amendment. In the words of Justice Byron White:

> Because we believe that trial by jury in criminal cases is fundamental to the American scheme of justice, we hold that the Fourteenth Amendment guarantees a right of jury trial in all criminal cases which—were they to be tried in federal court—would come within the Sixth Amendment's guarantee. Since we consider the appeal before us to be such a case, we hold that the Constitution was violated when appellant's demand for jury trial was refused.

In spite of this holding, the matter was not fully resolved—not for Gary Duncan and not for thousands of defendants who would be requesting jury trials. The Supreme Court's ruling in *Duncan* had reversed the Louisiana trial court's conviction of Duncan. This mandated either a dismissal of the simple battery charge or a new trial. But the Louisiana court refused to comply with either alternative, thus leaving Duncan under a continuing threat of further prosecution. His situation remained unchanged for 3 years, until the federal courts commanded Plaquemines Parish to dispose of the case.[58]

Another unresolved issue related to a segment of Justice White's opinion in *Duncan*. He had pointed out that so-called petty offenses were traditionally tried without a jury. That would continue to be so, but beyond that he offered no distinction between serious and petty offenses in state cases. Two years later the Court brought this matter to rest in *Baldwin* v. *New York*,[59] when it defined a petty offense as one carrying a maximum sentence of 6 months or less.

Jury Selection

Trial juries—sometimes referred to as *petit juries* to differentiate them from grand juries—have historically consisted of 12 jurors. Twelve-member juries are required in all federal prosecutions, but not in all state prosecutions. In *Williams* v. *Florida*,[60] decided in 1970, the Court ruled that it was proper for states to use juries composed of as few as six persons, at least in noncapital cases, and some 8 years later it reaffirmed this decision when it rejected the use of a five-person jury in Georgia.[61]

Jury selection involves a series of procedural steps, beginning with the preparation of a master list of eligible jurors. Eligibility requirements generally include citizenship and literacy. In addition, there are restrictions against minors, individuals with serious felony convictions, and occupational groups such as attorneys, police officers, legislators, physicians, the clergy, and so forth, depending on the jurisdiction. Others, such as the aged, disabled, mothers with young children, and people whose employers will not allow it, may be exempted from jury service on the basis of hardship. Not too many exemptions can be allowed in preparing the master list, however, because in constitutional terms an "impartial" jury means a representative cross section of a community's citizens. This is why in 1975 the Supreme Court struck down a Louisiana law that barred women from juries unless they specifically requested, in writing, to participate.[62]

In current practice, the basis of the master list in many communities is the local voter registration roll. This source is considered to be representative of the population, at least in theory, and it is readily available. However, studies of voting behavior have demonstrated that registration lists are highly biased as sources of jury pools. From 30 to 50 percent of those eligible to vote do not register to vote. Moreover, the registration rates for people with low incomes hover around 60 percent, compared to 85 percent for those with middle incomes or higher.[63] Similarly, members of racial minorities, young people, and the poorly educated more frequently ignore the electoral process or have been excluded from it by legal or extralegal means. To mitigate this difficulty, some communities use multiple-source lists, supplementing voter registration lists with names drawn from rosters of licensed drivers and telephone directories.

The Michael Jackson Jury

Would you have wanted to serve on the Michael Jackson jury? In an early 2005 poll, most people said no. Source: Directions Research, Inc.

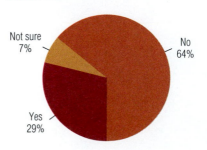

Not sure
7%

No
64%

Yes
29%

The *Venire*

From the master list of eligible jurors, names are randomly selected for the **venire.** The *venire,* or *venire facias,* is the writ that summons jurors. More commonly, however, the term refers to the list of potential jurors who are eligible for a given period of service. These summoned jurors become members of a jury pool, and they are interviewed to confirm their eligibility and availability. Those who remain in the pool are paid for their time; the current rate ranges from $15 to $50 per day.[64]

The procedure through which members of the jury pool become actual trial jurors begins with the selection of a jury *panel.* In a felony prosecution that requires 12 jurors, as many as 30 are selected for the panel (or perhaps hundreds in some high-profile cases). Their names are drawn at random by the clerk of the court, and from there they move on to the *voir dire* examination.

The *Voir Dire*

A **voir dire,** meaning "to speak the truth," is an oath sworn by a prospective juror regarding his or her qualifications. The *voir dire* examination involves questioning by the prosecutor, defense attorney, and sometimes the judge in order to determine a candidate's fitness to serve. The inquiry focuses on the person's background, familiarity with the case, associations with individuals involved in the case, attitudes about certain facts that might arise during the trial, and any other matters that may reflect upon his or her willingness and ability to judge the case fairly and impartially.

A potential juror who is deemed unacceptable to either the prosecutor or the defense is eliminated through either the challenge for cause or the peremptory challenge.

The *challenge for cause* means that there is a sound legal reason to remove a potential juror. Whoever makes such a challenge—either the defense attorney or the prosecutor—must explain to the judge the nature of the concern. Typically, challenges for cause allege that the prospective juror would be incapable of judging the accused fairly. Such challenges are controlled by statute, and the decision to remove a juror is vested with the court. Technically there is no limit on the number of challenges for cause that may be made.

A *peremptory challenge* is an objection to a prospective juror for which no reason must be assigned. It can be made for any reason or no reason at all and is totally within the discretion of the attorney making it. Peremptory challenges generally reflect the biases and strategies of the defense and the prosecution. Clarence Darrow, perhaps the greatest defense attorney of the 20th century, once advised his colleagues to avoid affluent jurors, "because, next to the Board of Trade, the wealthy consider the penitentiary to be the most important of all public buildings."[65] In contrast is an excerpt from a training manual for Texas district attorneys:

> What to Look for in a Juror
>
> 1. You are not looking for a fair juror, but rather a strong biased, and sometimes hypocritical individual who believes that defendants are different from them in kind, rather than degree.
> 2. You are not looking for any member of a minority group that may subject him to oppression—they almost always empathize with the accused.
> 3. You are not looking for the free thinkers and flower children.[66]

In short, many attorneys use these challenges to try to obtain jurors who are sympathetic to their side.

The practice of systematically excluding minorities from juries has a long history in the United States, and was upheld by the Supreme Court in 1965 in its ruling in *Swain* v. *Alabama.*[67] In 1986, however, the Court overruled *Swain* in part, holding that prosecutors may not exclude blacks from juries because of concern that they will favor a defendant of their own race. The case was **Batson v. Kentucky,**[68] in which the prosecutor in the trial of a black man used his peremptory challenges to exclude all four Af-

When you go into court you are putting your fate into the hands of twelve people who weren't smart enough to get out of jury duty.

—NORM CROSBY

The jury consists of twelve persons chosen to decide who has the better lawyer.

—ROBERT FROST

rican Americans on the *venire,* and a jury composed only of whites was selected. The defendant was convicted. On appeal to the U.S. Supreme Court, it was held that the equal protection clause of the Fourteenth Amendment is violated when a defendant is put on trial before a jury from which members of his or her race have been purposely excluded. The Court reasoned that although a defendant has no right under the equal protection clause to a jury composed in whole or part of members of his or her own race, the clause forbids the prosecutor from challenging potential jurors *solely* on account of their race or on the assumption that black jurors as a group will be unable to consider the state's case impartially.

In 1994, the Supreme Court expanded Batson to include gender. The ruling came in a paternity case rather than a criminal case, ***J.E.B. v. Alabama ex rel. T.B.,***[69] which was decided by a 6-to-3 vote. The action was brought by the state on behalf of the mother against the putative father, and the prosecutor used 9 of its 10 peremptory challenges to strike males from the jury panel. The Court held that such an action was in violation of the Fourteenth Amendment's equal protection clause.

Regardless of the number and nature of challenges, the *voir dire* examination continues until the required number of jurors has been selected. In many jurisdictions where a 12-person jury is used, as many as 14 or even more may be accepted. The additional jurors serve as alternates. They sit through the entire trial and are available to take the place of a regular jury member should he or she become ill, be forced to withdraw, or be disqualified while the trial is in progress. Potential jurors who are successfully challenged return to the jury pool, and new ones are drawn from the panel and subjected to *voir dire* (see Exhibit 12.5). Those ultimately selected are sworn in and become the trial jury.

Despite the challenges, a number of studies have indicated that the typical *voir dire* is ineffective in weeding out prejudiced jurors.[70] In one study, for example, a District of Columbia judge conducted the *voir dire* in the usual way, by allowing prospective jurors to come forward if they had a "yes" response to any of the typical questions used to probe for potential bias. Then, the judge questioned every juror who had *not* come up. He discovered a number of clear cases in which jurors had to be struck for cause due to prejudice against both police and defendants. In fact, one of the jurors was the defendant's fiancee.[71]

The *voir dire* can be brief or time-consuming. In prosecutions of misdemeanors and many felonies in which there has been little pretrial publicity and trial proceedings are expected to be fairly routine, there may be few challenges and the *voir dire* may last only a few hours or even less. In other cases, the examination can continue for days, weeks, or even months.

The man that is not prejudiced against a horse thief is not fit to sit on a jury in this town.

— **GEORGE BERNARD SHAW**

LAW & CRIMINAL JUSTICE | EXHIBIT 12.5

The Selection Process for a 12-Person Jury

JURY PANEL
30 persons selected randomly for a specific prosecution

Case settled or dismissed
Return to jury pool

JURY POOL

The *venire* of 100 to 1,000 citizens (or more, depending on the jurisdiction) summoned for a 2- to 4-week period of jury service

Voir dire

16 persons challenged or not used

Return to jury pool

14 persons selected for jury

12-person trial jury

Trial

Verdict

Return to jury pool

It is the challenges for cause that lengthen the *voir dire* proceedings. Any and every potential juror can be challenged for cause. Peremptory challenges, on the other hand, are controlled by statute. In New York, for example, the maximum permitted is 3, except in serious cases such as murder, where as many as 20 are allowed, and in cases where there are multiple defendants.

The *voir dire* can be a crucially important part of a criminal proceeding. Its purpose is to do more than merely choose a fair and impartial jury—as significant as this may be. Its primary functions are to instruct the citizen as to the role of the juror and to develop rapport between jurors and attorneys. Moreover, the *voir dire* gives the defense and the prosecution an opportunity to attempt to influence jurors' attitudes and perhaps their later vote. One prosecutor put it this way:

> There is much more to a *voir dire* than the simple process of questioning and selecting jurors. In addition to the gamesmanship and psychology, a *voir dire* is an opportunity for the attorneys to educate their juries about the theories of their cases. It is also an opportunity to plant seeds of doubt that they hope will produce a favorable verdict. It is a chance to predispose jurors to be receptive to the attorney's case.[72]

Anyone who tries to sell you on the idea that jury selection is a science is jerking your chain. What you're trying to do is match your client, your case, and your lawyer with your juror. At best it's 20% science and 80% art.

—**JURY CONSULTANT ROBERT HIRSCHHORN**

You're not selecting people but eliminating those you find offensive. What you get is what's left over, the people who don't tell you very much.

—**ATTORNEY JERRY GOLDSTEIN, ON JURY SELECTION**

The Criminal Trial

The trial is the climax of the criminal proceeding. It begins as soon as the jury has been sworn in. The only matter that remains in doubt before commentary and testimony can begin is the judge's decision as to whether or not to sequester the jurors for the en-

"The jury will disregard the witness's last remarks."

© The New Yorker Collection 1997 Lee Lorenz from cartoonbank.com. All Rights Reserved.

tire trial. **Sequestration** involves removal of the jurors (and alternates, if any) from all possible outside influence. They are housed in a hotel or motel for the duration of the trial; they are forbidden all visitors; and the newspapers they read, as well as the television programs they watch, are fully censored.

Few juries are sequestered for an entire trial, for most criminal prosecutions fail to generate a line of newspaper copy or even a second of television news time. Only if there is continuing media coverage that has the potential for influencing a juror's decision is sequestration ordered. If the judge does so order, however, sequestration places a tremendous hardship on the jury. One commentator described it as follows:

> Jurors were driven to their homes on January 15, the first evening after they had been selected to serve, so that they could get a week's worth of clothing. They were returned to their homes for clean clothing on January 20 and January 27. . . . Each juror was accompanied by a marshal on each trip . . . and even the windows of the vans [were] covered with paper so a juror [could not] see a newspaper headline at a newsstand. The jurors also were escorted by marshals to two theater productions and to one dinner at a restaurant away from their hotel. . . . The jurors were allowed no visits by relatives and were allowed telephone conversations only after a deputy marshal dialed the number, cautioned the answering party against discussing the case, and listened in on a second telephone that had a cut-off button to be used if either party violated the restrictions.[73]

The procedures used in criminal trials are for the most part the same nationwide. The process consists of the following steps:

- Opening statements
- Presentation of the state's case
- Presentation of the defense's case
- Rebuttal and surrebuttal
- Closing arguments
- Charging the jury
- Deliberation and verdict

In bench trials, this process is altered only minimally. The steps involving the jury are eliminated, and the tactics and strategies of the defense and prosecuting attorneys are simplified, removing much of the dramatic effect.

Opening Statements

The first step in a trial proceeding is the reading of the criminal complaint by the court clerk, followed by opening statements—first by the prosecution and then by the defense.

The prosecutor's statement is an attempt to give the jury an outline of the case and how the state intends to prove, beyond a reasonable doubt, that the defendant did indeed commit the crime or crimes charged in the indictment. This outline generally includes a description of the crime and the defendant's role in it and a discussion of the evidence and witnesses to be presented. In addition, the prosecutor is likely to address the meaning of "beyond a reasonable doubt." Reasonable doubt is fair doubt based on reason and common sense and growing out of the testimony of the case; it is doubt arising from a candid and impartial investigation of all the evidence and testimony presented. The purpose of the prosecutor's analysis here is to distinguish between reasonable doubt and vague apprehension and, at the same time, to emphasize that the state's goal is to prove guilt beyond a *reasonable* doubt—not beyond *all* doubt.

Although the prosecutor has considerable freedom as to what is said in the opening statement, no references may be made to evidence that is known to be inadmissible, and no comment may be made concerning the defendant's prior criminal record (if any exists). To make such a comment would be considered a *prejudicial error*—an error of such significance that it compromises or prejudices the rights of the accused. Prejudicial errors that cannot be corrected by any action of the court are often the bases for appeals. Moreover, they can result in a **mistrial,** a discharging of the jury without a verdict. A mistrial is the equivalent of no trial at all, and it is for this reason that initiating a new trial does not constitute double jeopardy.

The defense attorney's opening statement is an address to the jury that focuses on how the defense will show that the state has a poor case and that proof of guilt beyond a reasonable doubt cannot be demonstrated. It is not uncommon for defense attorneys to stress that the accused is innocent until proven guilty and that the burden of proof rests entirely with the prosecution.

Defense attorneys and prosecutors often vary their strategies for opening statements, depending on the nature of the case, evidence, and witnesses. One approach is to keep opening remarks short and vague, letting the particulars of the case emerge during the course of the trial. Such a tactic makes few promises to the jury, but it allows flexibility. Such flexibility can be important because it enables the attorney, during the final summation, to structure an argument that is not weakened by promises that he or she could not deliver. An alternative is a detailed opening statement, eloquently expressed and forcefully presented, that predisposes the jury to accept the evidence that is ultimately delivered. This technique can be risky, but it is highly rewarding if the promises made are kept during the course of the trial.[74]

In a jury trial, the prosecutor always delivers an opening statement. Without it, the jurors would have no framework within which to consider the evidence and testimony. The defense attorney, however, may choose to make no statement at all—out of necessity perhaps, if the defense strategy cannot be determined until the content of the state's case is revealed, or as part of the strategy, which is not to be revealed until the proper time. Opening statements are infrequently used in bench trials; they are less effective, since the judge has probably handled hundreds of similar cases.

Counsel: Have you any idea of what your defense is going to be?
Defendant: Well, I didn't do it sir.
Counsel: Yes, well, er, I think we can afford to fill that out a little. It's not in itself a cast iron defense.
Defendant: Well I didn't do it sir! I didn't do it! And if I did it, may God strike me dead on the spot, sir!
Counsel: Well, we'll just give him a moment or so, shall we. . . .

—ALAN BENNETT, BBC-TV

Presentation of the State's Case

In order to give the accused an opportunity to provide an informed defense, it is the state that presents its case first in the adversary system of justice. The prosecutor begins by presenting evidence and questioning witnesses.

The Rules of Evidence Generally, **evidence** is any kind of proof, in the form of witnesses, records, documents, concrete objects, and circumstances. Specifically, there are four basic types of evidence:

That's what's wrong with our legal system, ya need evidence!

—ARCHIE BUNKER

1. *Real evidence* is physical details and objects, such as a murder weapon, stolen property, fingerprints, DNA, appearance of the victim's wounds, and appearance of the crime scene. Real evidence may be original objects or facsimile representations, such as photographs, tire tracks, or other duplicates of items that are either unavailable or unusable in their original form.

2. *Testimonial evidence* is the sworn, verbal statements of witnesses. All real evidence is accompanied by testimonial evidence, in that objects presented in evidence are explained by someone who is qualified to discuss them. Conversely, however, not all testimonial evidence is accompanied by real evidence.

3. *Direct evidence* is eyewitness evidence. Testimony from a witness that he or she saw a person painting a fence, for example, is direct evidence that the person painted a fence. But as indicated in Exhibit 12.6, there are some serious problems with eyewitness testimony.

4. *Circumstantial evidence,* or indirect evidence, is evidence from which a fact can be reasonably inferred. Testimony that a person was seen with paint and a paint brush in the vicinity of a newly painted fence is circumstantial evidence that the person painted the fence.

These four types necessarily overlap, since all are ultimately presented through testimony. Moreover, *all* evidence must be *competent,* material, and relevant. Evidence is competent when it is legally fit for admission to court. The testimony of an expert witness on a scientific matter is deemed to be competent, for example, if the court accepts his or her credentials as a reflection of proficiency in the subject area. In contrast, testimonial evidence on ballistics presented by an automobile mechanic would be considered incompetent; or an individual who has been convicted of perjury might be considered incompetent to testify. In common law, a person was considered to be "incompetent" to testify against his or her spouse, on the theory that being compelled or even allowed to do so would undermine the marriage and thus be detrimental to the public welfare. In 1980, however, the Supreme Court ruled in *Trammel* v. *United States* [75] that a criminal defendant could no longer invoke the "privilege against adverse spousal testimony," as long as the testimony is voluntary and does not reveal a confidential marital communication.

Evidence can be deemed incompetent if it is based on hearsay. Under most circumstances the hearsay rule bars a witness from testifying about statements that are not within his or her personal knowledge—that is, about secondhand information. There are two exceptions to this rule. The first is an admission of criminal conduct made by the defendant to the witness. Such hearsay testimony is allowed because the accused is present in court to challenge it. The other exception is the "dying declaration" of a crime victim that has been told to or overheard by the witness; it is based on the assumption that a person who is about to die will not lie. [76]

To be admissible in a court of law, evidence must also be material and relevant. There is only a slight distinction between these two requirements. Evidence is *material* when it has a legitimate bearing on the decision of the case. Evidence is *relevant* when it is applicable to the issue in question. For example, evidence of a defendant's bad character on previous occasions is immaterial (unless the defendant is submitting his or her good character in evidence). By contrast, the fact that an accused person has stolen property in the past is irrelevant to whether or not he or she has murdered someone (assuming, of course, that the accused is not being tried on multiple charges of theft and murder).

There is one way to find out if a man is innocent—ask him. If he says yes, you know he is guilty.

—GROUCHO MARX

Perhaps the most controversial type of evidence is that yielded by the polygraph—commonly known as the lie detector. This machine measures a person's blood pressure, pulse rate, breathing, and perspiration. The premise is that when an individual answers a question deceptively, an involuntary "fight or flight" response is triggered that causes those measures to increase rapidly. Polygraph evidence is inadmissible in the majority of states and the federal system because it is considered unreliable, yet many defense attorneys and prosecutors argue in its favor.*

*In New Mexico, polygraph evidence is admissible in trial and posttrial proceedings; in South Carolina, while polygraph evidence is admissible at the discretion of the trial court, it is generally inadmissible. In

RESEARCH ON CRIME AND JUSTICE | EXHIBIT 12.6

Circumstances Affecting the Accuracy of Eyewitness Testimony by Bianca M. Sullivan

Eyewitness testimony is one of the most powerful tools used in criminal courts when deciding whether a defendant is guilty or not guilty. And this seems to be so due to the belief that memories hold accurate and incommutable accounts of an event. Memories, however, are not errorless remembrances of the factual events. Consequently, hundreds of studies have been conducted that focus on errors in eyewitness testimony. Flawed police procedure and vague memories are commonly cited precursors in cases in which the wrong person is identified. And interestingly, jurors in criminal trials are often more convinced by confident eyewitness testimonials than they are by fingerprints, fiber analyses, DNA matches, and other kinds of *real* evidence.

There are several circumstances that may affect the accuracy of an eyewitness account. As memories accumulate, older ones are pushed back, removed, or replaced by new pieces of information. In order to make sense of an event that has been stored in bits and pieces, details are added, irrelevant information is removed, and a clear and flowing reconstruction of the actual event is created. Each time a memory is recalled, it is reconstructed and likely altered. Memories are subject to other peoples' opinions and suggestions as well as to things that have occurred since the original event. Therefore, rather than being an exact reflection of the event, a memory is instead an interpretation of a past event, and that interpretation may have been influenced by various sources, happenings, opinions, and other developments since the initial incident. For instance, as time passes and pieces of the event are forgotten, exposure to new facts and information of a similar or related nature may merge with the original event memory in order to help fill in gaps and clarify items that were confusing. Additionally, memories can be corrupted by talking with other witnesses or by encountering newspapers and television reports. Also affecting memory distortion are the time interval between viewing and recollecting the event, the verbal form of the postevent information, and the intensity of the violence involved in the event.

Characteristics of the witness, such as age, may have a profound effect on the accuracy of the eyewitness testimony. Very young children and the elderly are especially vulnerable to making errors. In fact, their responses are highly patterned. Young children and the elderly perform nearly as well as young adults when the actual suspect is in the lineup. However, when the suspect is not present, these two groups of eyewitnesses have a higher rate of mistaken identity than the group of young adults.

Similarly, reports have indicated that eyewitness accounts may not be reliable if the accused and the witness are of different races. "Eyewitness testimony is very effective if you're dealing with somebody you know. But if you are dealing with strangers, especially strangers of another race, and if that's the only data you have to go on . . . it could be suspect," commented Jerry Bruce of Sam Houston University.

Often comments made by police officers and prosecutors, which may seem to be harmless and impartial, will influence eyewitness testimony. The eyewitness may be looking for some type of confirmation or feedback regarding the information he or she has given to the police. And since there are few rules regarding what can and cannot be told to the witness after he or she has made, for instance, an identification from a photo spread or lineup, a suggestion may be made that will confirm or deny the witness's identification. By providing feedback, the witness may change his or her testimony in some substantial way or may become more confident in the accuracy of the facts he or she provided—all depending on whether the feedback was consistent with what the police were expecting to hear.

Given the problems encountered while collecting eyewitness evidence, the Department of Justice has prepared a research report that provides recommendations on all aspects of collecting eyewitness testimony, ranging from investigating the scene, to interviewing the witness, and also to composing and conducting lineups. A recurrent theme throughout the Department of Justice report is the importance of eliminating suggestive comments and actions. Asking open-ended, nonsuggestive questions or eliminating influential comments will likely allow for more accurate accounts of situations.

Sources: Elizabeth Loftus and Kathleen Ketcham, *Witness for the Defense: The Accused, the Eyewitness, and the Expert Who Puts Memory on Trial* (New York: St. Martin's Press, 1991); Dan Johnson, "Witnesses: A Weak Link in the Judicial System," *The Futurist* 32 (1998): 14–15; D. W. Miller, "Looking Askance at Eyewitness Testimony," *The Chronicle on Higher Education* 46 (2000): A19–A20; Jeremy Travis and Richard M. Rau, *Eyewitness Testimony: A Guide for Law Enforcement* (Washington, DC: U.S. Department of Justice, National Institute of Justice, 1999); Gary L. Wells and Elizabeth A. Olson, "Eyewitness Testimony," *Annual Review of Psychology* 54 (2003): 277–295.

Examination of Witnesses The state's presentation begins with the *direct examination* of witnesses. This consists only of eliciting facts from the witness in some chronological order. The first witness called is generally one who can establish the elements of the crime. Subsequent witnesses introduce physical, direct, and indirect evidence, and expert testimony.

After the prosecutor has completed his or her interrogation of a witness through direct examination, the defense is permitted (but not required) to cross-examine the

---

18 other states (Delaware, New Jersey, Ohio, Indiana, Kansas, Florida, Georgia, Alabama, Arkansas, Iowa, California, Nevada, Arizona, North Dakota, Idaho, Utah, Wyoming, and Washington) it is permitted if both sides agree. In all others it is prohibited. See the American Polygraph Association's Web site at *http:// www.polygraph.org/index.htm.*

witness. The purpose of *cross-examination* is to discredit the testimony, either by teasing out inconsistencies and contradictions or by attacking the credibility of the witness. The prosecution can ask further questions of the witness through a *redirect examination,* as can the defense with a *recross-examination.* This examination procedure continues until all of the state's witnesses have been called and all the evidence has been presented.

Objections During the examination of any witness, whether by the prosecutor or by the defense counsel, the opposing attorney can *object* to the introduction of evidence or testimony that he or she considers incompetent, immaterial, or irrelevant. Objections can also be made to "leading questions" (ones that inherently instruct or at least suggest to the witness how to answer), to eliciting a witness's opinions and conclusions, to being argumentative, and to "badgering" (abusing) a witness.

If the objection is *sustained* (consented to), the examiner is ordered to withdraw the question or cease the mode of inquiry and the jury is instructed to disregard whatever was deemed inappropriate. If the objection is *overruled* (rejected), the examining attorney may continue with the original line of questioning.

Motion for Directed Verdict

Following the presentation of the state's case, it is not uncommon for the defense attorney to enter a *motion for a directed verdict.* With this, the defense moves that the judge enter a finding of acquittal on the ground that the state failed to establish a *prima facie* case of guilt against the accused. If the judge so moves, he or she directs the jury to acquit the defendant. Even in the absence of a motion by the defense, the trial judge can order a directed verdict. Moreover, the judge can do so not only on the ground that the state failed to prove its case but also because the testimony of the prosecution witnesses was not credible or because the conduct of the prosecutor was not proper. Conversely, *a judge cannot direct the jury to convict the accused.*

Presentation of the Defense's Case

When the U.S. Supreme Court spoke of "the dead hand of the common law rule of 1789" many decades ago,[77] it was referring to a provision of the Judiciary Act of 1789 by which codefendants were not entitled to testify in each other's behalf. The provision seemingly was a remnant of a pre-18th-century English common law principle that denied defendants charged with treason or felonies the right of having witnesses testify in their defense. This restriction, however, seemed to contradict a component of the Sixth Amendment providing that in all criminal prosecutions the accused shall enjoy the right "to have compulsory process for obtaining witnesses in his favor." *Compulsory process* refers to the subpoena power that can force a witness into court to testify. In 1918, the Supreme Court extended the compulsory process clause, without limitation, to federal defendants.[78] In *Washington* v. *Texas,*[79] decided in 1967, the Court extended this right to the states.

This compulsory process clause is at the foundation of the presentation of the defense's case. During this presentation the counsel for the accused calls witnesses to testify in support of the not-guilty plea. Also at this point, the counsel for the accused has the opportunity to offer **evidence in chief**—that is, the first or direct examination of a witness.

At the outset, the defense attorney has the option of presenting many, some, or no witnesses or items of evidence on behalf of the accused. In addition, the defense must decide whether the accused will testify. The Fifth Amendment right against self-incrimination does not require it, but if the defendant chooses to testify, the prosecution has the option of cross-examination.

Once these matters have been decided, the defense's presentation follows the procedures outlined for the state's presentation: direct examination, cross-examination, redirect examination, and recross-examination. In addition, the rules of evidence and the right to make objections apply equally to the defense as to the prosecution.

It is a common misconception that during this stage of the trial the burden of proof shifts to the defense. *This is not so.* The responsibility of proving guilt beyond a reasonable doubt always remains with the prosecution. What shifts to the defense is the "burden of going forward with the evidence." This means that since the prosecution has presented its suit to the jury, the defense is now responsible for offering its own argument for the jury to consider.

Rebuttal and Surrebuttal

When the defense "rests" (concludes its presentation), the prosecutor may introduce new witnesses or evidence in an effort to refute the defense's case. Known as the *prosecutor's rebuttal,* it follows the same format of examination and cross-examination, redirect and recross-examination. In turn, the counsel for the accused may put forth a *surrebuttal,* which is a rebuttal of the prosecutor's rebuttal.

Closing Arguments

The *summation,* or closing argument, gives each side an opportunity to recapitulate all the evidence and testimony offered during the trial. The arguments are made directly to the jury. Closing arguments are often quite eloquent and dramatic.

In most jurisdictions, the summation begins with the defense attorney, who points out any weaknesses or flaws in the prosecutor's theory and evidence. Counsel for the accused argues that proof "beyond a reasonable doubt" has not been established and reminds the jurors that they will have to live with their decision for the rest of their lives. Since the burden of proof rests with the state, the prosecutor is entitled to the final argument. For both the defense and the prosecution, perhaps the most vital element of the closing argument is persuasion. One prosecutor made just this point:

> Summing up in a criminal trial is a throwback to an earlier age. It is one of the few arts left in which time is of no consequence. Standing before twelve people, a lawyer can be brief or lengthy—the choice is his own; there are no interruptions, and a captive audience. All that matters are those twelve people; they must be persuaded, or everything that has gone before is in vain. Summation is the one place where lawyers do make a difference; if an attorney can be said to "win" or "lose" a case, the chances are that he did so in his closing argument to the jury.
>
> The appeal of a summation may be to the heart, the intellect or the belly, or to all of them. There are as many different ways of summing up as there are trial lawyers, and there is no one correct way to deliver a summation, or to learn how to give one. It is largely a matter of instinct and of experience. Either you are able to reach out and move people with your words or you are not, and that is all there is to it.[80]

Charging the Jury

Charging the jury involves an order by the judge that directs the jurors to retire to the jury room, consider the facts of the case and the evidence and testimony presented, and arrive at a just verdict. Regarded by many as the single most important statement made during the trial, it includes instructions regarding the possible verdicts, the rules of evidence, and the legal meaning of "reasonable doubt." The instructions contained in the charge are often arrived at through consultation with the defense and the prosecution and from statutory instructions contained in the jurisdiction's code of criminal procedure.

In some states, judges are permitted to review thoroughly all the evidence that has been presented to the jury. They are free, for example, to summarize the testimony of each witness. This can be useful to jurors, especially if the trial has been long and complex. But it can also be hazardous, for a judge has opinions about innocence and guilt, and these can inadvertently influence the jury.

A Most Unpredictable Jury

Some years ago, a man was tried in a California court for the murder of his wife. The state's case was quite convincing, but one thing was missing—the victim's body. This was the basis of the defense's case, and no evidence of testimony was presented on behalf of the accused.

In a dynamic summation performance, the counsel for the defense soared to eloquent heights of oratory, repeating that with the absence of the body of the alleged victim, it could not be proved that a crime had been committed. "You must find my client innocent for one simple reason," he shouted. And then, dropping to a breathless whisper, he added, "His wife is still alive. In fact—she just walked into the courtroom!"

At once, the heads of all the jurors and spectators turned, only to see that not a soul had entered the chambers. But the attorney had made his point. How could proof beyond a reasonable doubt be concluded if the jurors suspected that the defendant's wife might still be alive?

Everyone agreed that it was a brilliant ploy, and after less than an hour's deliberation, the jury returned with a verdict. Yet, to the amazement and disbelief of all those present, the jury had found the accused guilty of murder.

When the trial was over and the jury dismissed, the bewildered defense counsel confronted the first few jurors he saw. "How," he asked, "could you find a man guilty when you weren't even sure his wife was dead? Hadn't everyone turned to look for her in the back of the courtroom?"

"Yes," answered one of the jurors, "everybody except your client."

Source: Melvyn Bernard Zerman, *Beyond a Reasonable Doubt: Inside the American Jury System* (New York: Crowell, 1981), 10–13. ∎

"*Our jury box exit poll indicates you'll be found guilty.*"

© 2005 Mike Twohy from cartoonbank.com. All Rights Reserved.

A difficult task for judges is to present instructions that juries can understand fully. Because the nuances of the law are so complex, it can take hours to deliver the instructions. And finally, the members of the jury are instructed that they cannot communicate with anyone about the facts of the case. Further sequestration might be ordered, which would place the jurors under the supervision of a court officer until a verdict is reached.

Jury Deliberations

Every jury has a *foreperson* who serves as the nominal leader of the group. He or she is chosen by the jurors during the trial or in the jury room. In some jurisdictions the first juror selected in the *voir dire* becomes the leader. Whether this person becomes the *actual* leader is another matter, depending on personality and the dynamics of group interaction.

Once the jury has retired, it is traditional for the foreperson to sit at the head of the table and call for a vote. Except in Oregon and Louisiana, unanimous verdicts are required by law. If such a verdict is reached, the deliberations are finished. Typically, however, things are not that simple.

Deliberations are important, because they expose jurors to different interpretations of the evidence and thus prevent them from relying too much on their own idiosyncratic views. In addition, jurors often correct one another's factual errors. When their collective memories are pooled, the jury as a whole recalls a substantial amount of the evidence.[81]

Most juries take all the time necessary to reach a fair and honest decision, but some observers hold that a small but increasing number of verdicts are the result of jurors' impatience and individual schedules. In fact, when the verdict in the Oklahoma City bomber Terry Nichols case was reached shortly before Christmas in 1997, a number of judges and jury consultants spoke of the old legal superstition that juries set deadlines for themselves based on approaching weekends and holidays.[82]

When deliberations fail to generate a unanimous decision, the dilemma is referred to as a deadlocked or "hung" jury. The jury is then dismissed in open court; the judge declares a mistrial; and the prosecution can either retry the case or drop the charges. Deadlocked juries result from differences of opinion over the strengths and weaknesses of evidence, varying perceptions of innocence and guilt, and the meaning of "reasonable doubt." The deadlocked jury is not a common occurrence. Reports indicate that only 6% of all criminal trials end with a hung jury.

Verdict and Judgment

When the jury reaches a verdict, it returns to the courtroom to announce its decision: "We, the jury, duly impaneled and sworn, find the defendant guilty [or not guilty] as charged." In cases involving multiple charges, the jury may find the accused guilty of some and not guilty of others.

An enduring issue in criminal trials is the problem of **jury nullification.** It occurs when juries do not follow the court's interpretation of the law in every instance, disregard what they have been told about the law or certain aspects of evidence, consider the application of certain laws to be unjust, refuse to convict because they consider the penalties too severe, or otherwise "nullify" or suspend the force of strict legal procedure. Instances of jury nullification have occurred in cases of battered spouses who kill, political crimes, mercy killings, and, most recently, perceptions of racial injustice.

Jury nullification can occur either inadvertently or by design. If a verdict of guilty is reached and the judge believes that it is erroneous, he or she can refuse to abide by it. The judge can *direct* the jury to acquit, or "arrest" the guilty verdict and enter a judgment of acquittal. However, as mentioned earlier, a trial judge does *not* have the authority to direct a jury to convict or enter a judgment arresting a verdict of not guilty.

Jurors can be *polled* at the request of the defense or the prosecution. The judge (or the bailiff) asks each juror whether the announced verdict is his or her individual verdict. Polling of jurors is done to determine whether any juror has been pressured into voting a particular way.

Many attempts have been made to reform the jury trial so as to reduce problems of comprehension and absorption of complex information, nullification, deadlocking, and related issues.[83] Arizona is in the forefront in this regard. Changes already adopted include raising the jurors' daily payment, allowing them to ask questions and discuss evidence among themselves while the trial is going on, and allowing judges and attorneys to give further information and instruction to deadlocked jurors.[84]

Posttrial Motions

With a judgment of not guilty, the defendant is immediately released—unless other charges are still pending. With a guilty verdict, most jurisdictions allow the defense to file motions to set aside the judgment or file motions for a new trial.

The *motion in arrest of judgment* asks that no judgment be pronounced because of one or more defects in the record of the case. Possible defects might be that the trial court had no jurisdiction over the case; the verdict included conviction on a charge that was not *tested* in the indictment or information; or there was error "on the face of the record." This last term refers to any faults of procedure that may have occurred during the pretrial process.

The *motion for a new trial,* which can be made only by the defense, can be based on numerous grounds. The defense may claim that the jury received evidence outside the courtroom; that the jury was guilty of misconduct during deliberations; that the court erred in overruling an objection or permitting the introduction of certain evidence; that the jury was improperly charged; that the prosecution was guilty of misconduct; that there is a suspicion of *jury tampering* (bribes or threats made to a juror to influence his or her vote); or that newly discovered evidence is available for review.

If either motion is sustained, new proceedings will be initiated. Any new trial that results, however, does not represent double jeopardy because the defendant's motion is an allegation that the proceedings should be declared utterly invalid.

CRITICAL THINKING IN CRIMINAL JUSTICE

Jury Nullification and Race

Does anyone remember the trial of O. J. Simpson? Although it may seem like ancient history to many students, it occurred just over a decade ago, back in 1994 and 1995. Many referred to it as the "trial of the century." It was the center of an unprecedented media frenzy; it was televised and analyzed and reenacted and reanalyzed. And although the jury found Simpson not guilty of the crimes, opinions were split—generally along racial lines—about his culpability in the homicides. True, the Simpson case is old news, but much can still be learned from it.

The chief prosecutors in the Simpson double-murder trial, Marcia Clark and Christopher Darden, have argued that Simpson's acquittal was a racially motivated instance of jury nullification. In fact, Clark, Darden, and numerous other court observers have contended that Simpson's lead attorney, Johnnie Cochran, urged the predominantly African American jury to ignore the trial evidence and deliver a not guilty verdict.[85] During the trial's closing arguments, Cochran stated:

> Your verdict will go far beyond the walls of this courtroom. Your verdict talks about justice in America and it talks about the police and whether they should be above the law. . . . Maybe that's why you were selected. There's someone in your background . . . that helps you understand that this is wrong. . . . Maybe you're the right people, at the right time, at the right place to say, "No more—we're not going to have this."

Thinking critically, what do you think Cochran was trying to say? Was he suggesting that the jury overlook the evidence and deliver a not guilty verdict? And more broadly, is jury nullification illegal? Is it evil? Does it subvert the criminal justice system? Should it be practiced to right the wrongs of bad law or bad policing? What do you think?

Jury nullification is not legal, but it is not necessarily evil—at least not all of the time. It protected fugitive slaves from being sent back to the South during the days just before the Civil War, as northern juries refused to convict. But there are many shameful examples, as well, of how jury nullification has been used to sanction murder, such as the acquittals by all-white juries of Ku Klux Klan members involved in vigilante justice.

The late Johnnie Cochran.

Since the Simpson trial, the debate over jury nullification and race intensified when George Washington University law professor Paul Butler, who is black, wrote in 1995 that black jurors should, in certain nonviolent cases, acquit black defendants as a way of counterbalancing racism in the criminal justice system.[86] In counterpoint, Harvard University law professor Randall Kennedy, who also is black, has attacked Butler's position, arguing that jury nullification, even as an act of civil disobedience, is immoral and self-destructive for African Americans.[87]

Recent research suggests that racially based jury nullification does indeed occur. A recent study in New York State, for example, found a clear relationship between the racial composition of juries and the verdicts they rendered.[88]

In 1997, the U.S. Court of Appeals for the Second Circuit stepped into the controversy, holding that judges have a duty to make sure jurors do not ignore the evidence or law when they decide whether to acquit or convict a defendant. The ruling stemmed from a drug case in Albany, New York, in which the jurors complained to the trial judge that one juror, the only black member of the panel, stated that the defendants (who were African Americans) had a right to deal drugs and that he would not vote to convict no matter what the evidence was. Judge José A. Cabranes wrote for the appellate court:

> We categorically reject the idea that, in a society committed to the rule of law, courts may permit it [jury nullification] to occur when it is in their power to prevent.[89]

OP-ED

Getting back to the questions raised in the opening paragraphs of this chapter, it would appear that *CSI: Crime Scene Investigation*, the *CSI* spin-offs, and similar television dramas foster what court observers say is the mistaken notion that criminal science is fast and infallible and always gets its man (or woman). Defense attorneys complain that shows like *CSI* make jurors rely too heavily on scientific evidence and that forensic data can be compromised by both human and technical errors. Prosecutors, on the other hand, argue that the shows make it more difficult for them to win convictions in a large majority of cases in which scientific evidence is either limited, irrelevant, or absent. Both the defense and the prosecution refer to it as the "*CSI* effect."

Some of what is seen on TV is indeed state of the art. There are such things as DNA sequencers, mass spectrometers, photometric illuminators, and scanning electron microscopes. Moreover, real lab technicians can lift DNA profiles from cigarette butts, candy wrappers, and gobs of saliva. But a lot of what is seen on TV is nevertheless pretty far-fetched. For example, you can't pour caulk into knife wounds to make a cast of a weapon—it just doesn't work with soft tissue; machines that can identify a particular perfume from scents on clothing are still fictional; DNA testing takes weeks, not minutes; and DNA and fingerprints are available in only a small minority of cases, and even in those, the results can be inconclusive. And in many cases, the science is not above reproach—samples are often degraded, the lab work is faulty, and the tests just don't solve the crime.

CSI producers admit that they take a lot of liberties with the facts, for, after all, a 1-hour show, minus the seemingly endless and mindless commercials, is really only 40 minutes long and the story lines have to keep moving.

To counter the *CSI* effect, some members of the courtroom workgroups have introduced a number of novel procedures. In Massachusetts and a number of other states, for ex-

ample, prosecutors are beginning to ask judges if they can question prospective jurors about their TV-watching habits. And in Arizona, Illinois, and California, prosecutors use "negative evidence witnesses" to try to assure jurors that it is not unusual for crime scene investigators to fail to find DNA, fingerprints, and other forms of evidence.

On the upside of all of this, lectures and college courses on forensic science are filled to capacity these days. Perhaps this future generation of forensic scientists will discover ways to make the fantastic science on television crime dramas a reality in the criminal justice system.

Summary

The movement of defendants through the criminal courts is quite complex, characterized by many checks and balances and beset with numerous difficulties. Early in the process is the matter of pretrial release. Bail has been the traditional mechanism of temporary release. The amount of bail set is determined by a number of factors, including the seriousness of the crime, the defendant's prior criminal record, and the strength of the state's case. The bail system has been heavily criticized on the grounds that it discriminates against the poor and that the bail bond industry promotes inequity and corruption. As a result, several states have abolished the bail bond business, and numerous other jurisdictions are debating its future. Nonetheless, the majority of states still view it as a viable and effective means to ensure that defendants appear in court.

Stack v. *Boyle* noted that bail was not a means for punishing defendants or protecting society but, rather, a means of ensuring the accused's attendance in court. Nevertheless, high bail is often set for the purpose of preventive detention. Moreover, for those who cannot make bail, pretrial detention has negative effects on their criminal processing. Release on recognizance has become a popular alternative to bail and has been generally effective.

Following the initial court proceedings, an information or indictment initiates prosecution. An information is filed by a prosecutor, while an indictment is handed down by a grand jury. The purposes of the grand jury are to investigate and to protect citizens from unfair accusations. Since grand juries do not determine guilt or innocence, many of the elements of due process are absent. The Supreme Court has generally refused to impose substantive criteria on the grand jury's exercise of discretion.

After the formal determination of charges, the defendant is arraigned, and he or she is asked to enter a plea. The basic pleas are those of guilty, not guilty, *nolo contendere,* and standing mute. In addition, there are special pleas of insanity, statute of limitations, and the issue of double jeopardy.

Prior to the actual trial a number of motions can be filed by the defense or prosecution: discovery, change of venue, suppression, bill of particulars, severance, continuance, and dismissal. Then there is the matter of a "speedy trial" as guaranteed by the Sixth Amendment. There are many legitimate reasons for delays in formally trying a defendant, but the Supreme Court has held that if a defendant is denied a speedy trial, the remedy is dismissal of the charges.

Criminal defendants have a constitutional right to a trial by jury, a right extended to the states through *Duncan* v. *Louisiana* in 1968. Potential jurors are selected from voter registration rolls or multiple source lists. The *voir dire* examination determines a candidate's fitness to serve, and jurors can be eliminated through challenges by the defense and prosecution. Two recent Supreme Court cases—*Batson* v. *Kentucky* and *J.E.B.* v. *Alabama ex rel. T.B.*—have ensured that neither the prosecution nor the defense may remove a potential juror on the basis of race or gender.

The criminal trial has many steps: opening statements, presentation of the state's and defense's case, rebuttal and surrebuttal, closing arguments, charging the jury, and deliberation and verdict. Furthermore, there may be posttrial motions for arrest of judgment or for a new trial. When deliberations among jurors fail to reach a unanimous decision, the dilemma is referred to as a "hung" jury. When this happens, the jury may be dismissed in open court, the judge may declare a mistrial, and the prosecution must decide whether to retry the case or drop the charges.

Key Terms

bail (373)
Batson v. *Kentucky* (395)
bench warrant (376)
Benton v. *Maryland* (387)
charging the jury (403)
double jeopardy (386)
Downum v. *United States* (387)
Duncan v. *Louisiana* (393)
evidence (399)
evidence in chief (402)
grand jury (380)
Hurtado v. *California* (381)

indictment (380)
information (380)
J.E.B. v. *Alabama ex rel. T.B.* (396)
jury nullification (405)
Klopfer v. *North Carolina* (391)
mistrial (399)
motion (387)
nolo contendere (384)
Palko v. *Connecticut* (387)
presentment (380)
release on recognizance (ROR) (379)
sequestration (398)

Sixth Amendment (390)
speedy trial (389)
Speedy Trial Act (391)
Stack v. *Boyle* (374)
surety (374)
transactional immunity (383)
true bill (382)
United States v. *Calandra* (382)
use immunity (383)
venire (395)
voir dire (359)

Issues for Discussion

1. Should the bail bond business be abolished? Why or why not?
2. Do grand juries play too large a role in criminal justice proceedings? Is their power justified? Why or why not?
3. Given the respective roles of the defense and the prosecution, is the deliberate seeking of biased jurors legal or ethical?
4. Should the concept of "due process of law" be extended to grand jury proceedings?
5. What are the potential consequences of a defendant's waiver of rights?
6. Are there instances when jury nullification would be legal and ethical?

Media and Literature Resources

Reel Justice includes scenes that can be used to spark discussion about the following topics from this chapter:

Bail

Grand Jury Indictment

Jury Nullification. For more information on the topic of jury nullification and its social and cultural impact on the justice system, see John Clark, "The Social Psychology of Jury Nullification," *Law and Psychology Review* 24 (2000): 39–57; and Clay S. Conrad, *Jury Nullification: The Evolution of a Doctrine* (Durham, NC: Carolina Academic Press, 1998). Another good review of the issues appears in Joan Biskupic, "Veto by Jury," *Washington Post National Weekly Edition,* March 29, 1999, 6–8.

Mean Justice. *Mean Justice,* by Edward Humes (Simon and Schuster, 1999) is a Pulitzer Prize–winning story of how an innocent person became a casualty of the "war on crime" in a California community. The book provides an excellent view of the criminal justice system from the point of view of an investigative reporter.

African Americans and the Criminal Justice System. Several recent and noteworthy volumes are available on this topic. See David Cole, *No Equal Justice* (New York: New Press, 1999); Samuel Walker, Cassia Spohn, and Miriam DeLone, *The Color of Justice: Race, Ethnicity and Crime in America* (Belmont, CA: Wadsworth, 2000); and Marvin D. Free (ed.), *Racial Issues in Criminal Justice: The Case of African Americans (Criminal Justice, Delinquency, and Corrections)* (Westport, CT: Praeger Publishers, 2003).

Current Court Cases. Materials on recent trials and court decisions can be found on the *Court TV* Web site, *www.courttv.com/trials/index.html.*

Bail and Bounty Hunters. A thorough treatment of bail and bounty hunters appears in Jonathan Drimmer, "When Man Hunts Man: The Rights and Duties of Bounty Hunters in the American Criminal Justice System," *Houston Law Review* 33 (1996): 731–793. See also Jacqueline Pope, *Bounty Hunters, Marshals, and Sheriffs: Forward to the Past* (Westport, CT: Praeger, 1998); and Joshua Armstrong and Anthony Bruno, *The Seekers: Finding Felons and Guiding Men: A Bounty Hunter's Story* (New York: Avon, 2001).

Endnotes

1. Charles Rembar, *The Law of the Land: The Evolution of Our Legal System* (New York: Simon & Schuster, 1980), 95.
2. See Luke Owen Pike, *A History of Crime in England,* Vol. 1 (London: Smith, Elder, 1873–1876), 57–60; and Ernst W. Puttkammer, *Administration of Criminal Law* (Chicago: University of Chicago Press, 1953), 99–100.
3. *Hudson* v. *Parker,* 156 U.S. 277 (1895).
4. *McKane* v. *Durston,* 153 U.S. 684 (1894).
5. Patricia M. Wald, "The Right to Bail Revisited: A Decade of Promise Without Fulfillment," in *The Rights of the Accused,* edited by Stuart S. Nagel (Beverly Hills, CA: Sage Publications, 1972), 175–205.
6. *Stack* v. *Boyle,* 342 U.S. 1 (1951).
7. See Paul Wice, *Freedom for Sale* (Lexington, MA: Lexington, 1974); and Frederick Suffet, "Bail Setting: A Study of Courtroom Interaction," *Crime and Delinquency,* October 1966, 318–331. See also, John S. Goldkamp and Michael R. Gottfredson, "Bail Decision Making and Pretrial Detentions," *Law and Human Behavior* 3 (1979): 227–249; and Ilene H. Nagal, "The Legal/Extra-Legal Controversy: Judicial Decisions in Pretrial Release," *Law and Society Review* 17 (1983): 481–515.
8. See James G. Carr, "Bailbondsmen and the Federal Courts," *Federal Probation* 57 (March 1993): 9–13. See also K. B. Turner, "The Effect of Legal Representation on Bail Bond Decisions," *Criminal Law Bulletin* 39 (July/August, 2003): 426–444.
9. *Annotated Code of Maryland,* Article 27, Section 12B.
10. *Pretrial Release of Felony Defendants* (Washington, DC: Bureau of Justice Statistics, 1991).
11. *The New York Times,* April 4, 1963, 37.
12. *National Law Journal,* July 8, 1985, 20; Bureau of Justice Statistics, *Pretrial Release and Detention: The Bail Reform Act of 1984* (Washington, DC: U.S. Department of Justice).
13. Brian A. Reaves, *Pretrial Release of Federal Felony Defendants* (Washington, DC: Bureau of Justice Statistics, 1994).
14. P. Koza and A. N. Doob, "The Relationship of Pretrial Custody to the Outcome of a Trial," *Criminal Law Quarterly* 17 (1975): 391–400.

15. For more on the Vera Foundation and the Vera Institute of Justice, see *Programs in Criminal Justice Reform* (New York: Vera Institute, 1972), and *Further Work in Criminal Justice* (New York: Vera Institute, 1977). You can also consult their Web site at *http://www.vera.org/* for more information.

16. Charles E. Ares, Anne Rankin, and Herbert Sturtz, "The Manhattan Bail Project," *New York University Law Review* 38 (January 1963): 68.

17. *Chicago Tribune,* September 2, 1990, 1, 10; *Chicago Tribune,* September 3, 1990, 1, 2; *Chicago Tribune,* September 4, 1990, 1, 10; Paul Nussbaum, "Crime and No Punishment," *Philadelphia Inquirer Magazine,* May 5, 1991, 19–20, 36–38, 40.

18. Marvin E. Frankel and Gary P. Naftalis, *The Grand Jury: An Institution on Trial* (New York: Hill and Wang, 1977), 3–17.

19. *Hurtado* v. *California,* 110 U.S. 516 (1884).

20. *Hale* v. *Henkel,* 201 U.S. 43 (1906).

21. *Costello* v. *United States,* 350 U.S. 359 (1956).

22. *United States* v. *Calandra,* 414 U.S. 338 (1974).

23. Max Bolstad, "The Grand Jury: Eight Centuries of Myth and Reality," *Criminal Law Bulletin* 36 (July/August, 2000): 281–315.

24. *Kastigar* v. *United States,* 406 U.S. 441 (1972).

25. *Branzburg* v. *Hayes,* 408 U.S. 665 (1972).

26. Charlotte Allen, "Grand Illusion," *Insight,* February 17, 1992, 6–11; *The New York Times,* October 9, 1998, B5.

27. National Advisory Commission on Criminal Justice Standards and Goals, *Courts* (Washington, DC: U.S. Government Printing Office, 1973), 13.

28. *The New York Times,* October 5, 1980, 33.

29. Thomas C. Marks and J. Tim Reilly, *Constitutional Criminal Procedure* (North Scituate, MA: Duxbury, 1979), 136.

30. Rita J. Simon and David E. Aaronson, *The Insanity Defense: A Critical Assessment of Law in the Post-Hinckley Era* (Westport, CT: Greenwood, 1988).

31. See Eric Silver, Carmen Cirincione, and Henry J. Steadman, "Demythologizing Inaccurate Perceptions of the Insanity Defense," *Law and Human Behavior* 18 (1994): 63–70; and Henry J. Steadman, Margaret A. McGreevy, Joseph P. Morrissey, Lisa A. Callahan, Pamela Clark Robbins, and Carmen Cirincione, *Before and After Hinckley: Evaluating Insanity Defense Reform* (New York: Guilford, 1993). James Hooper and Alix McLearen, "Does the Insanity Defense Have a Legitimate Role?" *Psychiatric Times* 19 (April 2002).

32. *United States* v. *Perez,* 9 Wheat. 579 (1824).

33. *Wade* v. *Hunter,* 336 U.S. 684 (1949).

34. *United States* v. *Lanza,* 260 U.S. 377 (1922).

35. *Abbate* v. *United States,* 359 U.S. 187 (1959).

36. *Waller* v. *Florida,* 397 U.S. 387 (1970).

37. *Palko* v. *Connecticut,* 302 U.S. 319 (1937).

38. *Benton* v. *Maryland,* 395 U.S. 784 (1969).

39. *Downum* v. *United States,* 372 U.S. 734 (1963).

40. *Brady* v. *Maryland,* 363 U.S. 83 (1963).

41. *Moore* v. *Illinois,* 408 U.S. 786 (1972).

42. *Mapp* v. *Ohio, 367 U.S. 643 (1961);* Escobedo v. *Illinois,* 368 U.S. 478 (1964); *Miranda* v. *Arizona,* 384 U.S. 436 (1966).

43. See Sarah Tanford, Steven Penrod, and Rebecca Collins, "Decision Making in Joined Criminal Trials: The Influence of Charge Similarity, Evidence Similarity, and Limiting Instructions," *Law and Human Behavior* 9 (1985): 319–337; and Kenneth S. Bordens and Irwin A. Horowitz, "Joinder of Criminal Offenses," *Law and Human Behavior* 9 (1985): 339–353.

44. *Serfass* v. *United States,* 420 U.S. 377 (1975).

45. *California Penal Code,* Section 1382 (1).

46. *Code of Alabama,* Title 15, Section 3-1.

47. *State* v. *Brann,* 292 A.2d 173 (Me. 1972).

48. *Beavers* v. *Haubert,* 198 U.S. 77 (1905).

49. *Barker* v. *Wingo,* 407 U.S. 514 (1972).

50. *Strunk* v. *United States,* 412 U.S. 434 (1973).

51. *United States* v. *Lovasco,* 431 U.S. 783 (1977).

52. *Klopfer* v. *North Carolina,* 386 U.S. 213 (1967).

53. *In re Oliver,* 333 U.S. 257 (1948).

54. *Duncan* v. *Louisiana,* 391 U.S. 145 (1968).

55. *Tennessee Code Annotated,* Title 40-2504.

56. *Idaho Code,* Title 19-1902.

57. *Duncan* v. *Louisiana,* 391 U.S. 145 (1968).

58. *Perez* v. *Duncan,* 404 U.S. 1071, *certiorari* denied (1971).

59. *Baldwin* v. *New York,* 399 U.S. 66 (1970).

60. *Williams* v. *Florida,* 399 U.S. 78 (1970).

61. *Ballew* v. *Georgia,* 435 U.S. 223 (1978).

62. *Taylor* v. *Louisiana,* 419 U.S. 522 (1975).

63. See Hiroshi Furakai, Edgar Butter, and Richard Krooth, *Race and the Jury* (New York: Plenum, 1993); and Laura Rose Handman, "Underrepresentation of Economic Groups in Federal Juries," *Boston University Law Review* 57 (January 1977): 198–224. W. C. Smith, "Challenges of Jury Selection," *ABA Journal* 88 (April 2002): 34–39; Hiroshi Fukurai and Richard Krooth, *Race in the Jury Box: Affirmative Action in Jury Selection.* (Albany: State University of New York Press, 2003).

64. Michael Dann and George Logan, "Jury Reform: The Arizona Experience," *Judicature* 79 (March–April 1996): 280–286.

65. In Melvyn B. Zerman, *Beyond a Reasonable Doubt: Inside the American Jury System* (New York: Crowell, 1981), 181.

66. In Zerman, *Beyond a Reasonable Doubt,* 181.

67. *Swain* v. *Alabama,* 380 U.S. 202 (1965).

68. *Batson* v. *Kentucky,* 106 S. Ct. 1712 (1986).

69. *J.E.B.* v. *Alabama ex rel. T.B.,* 55 CrL 2003 (1994).

70. For example, see Cathy Johnson and Craig Haney, "Felony *Voir Dire:* An Exploratory Study of Its Content and Effect," *Law and Human Behavior* 16 (1992): 487–506.

71. Gregory Mize, "On Better Jury Selection," *Court Review,* Spring 1999, 10–15.

72. Steven Phillips, *No Heroes, No Villains: The Story of a Murder Trial* (New York: Vintage, 1978), 136–137.

73. Noted by Zerman, *Beyond a Reasonable Doubt,* 147–148.

74. For example, see Burton S. Katz, *Justice Overruled: Unmasking the Criminal Justice System* (New York: Warner, 1997); Phillips, *No Heroes, No Villains;* and Seymour Wishman, *Confessions of a Criminal Lawyer* (New York: Times Books, 1981).

75. *Trammel* v. *United States,* 445 U.S. 40 (1980).

76. David A. Jones, *The Law of Criminal Procedure* (Boston: Little, Brown, 1981), 475.

77. *Rosen* v. *United States,* 245 U.S. 467 (1918).

78. *Rosen* v. *United States.*

79. *Washington* v. *Texas.* 388 U.S. 14 (1967).

80. Phillips, *No Heroes, No Villains,* 196–197.

81. Phoebe Ellsworth, "Are Twelve Heads Better than One?" *Law and Contemporary Problems* 52 (1989): 205–224.

82. Ian Fisher, "Justice Is Blind, but She Does Wear a Watch," *The New York Times,* December 28, 1997, sec. 4, p. 4.

83. See G. Thomas Munsterman, Paula Hannaford, and Marc G. Whitehead (eds.), *Jury Trial Innovations* (Williamsburg, VA: National Center for State Courts, 1997).

84. B. Michael Dann and George Logan, "Jury Reform: The Arizona Experience," *Judicature* 79 (1996): 280–286; Valerie P. Hans, G. Thomas Munsterman, and Paula Hannaford, "Letting Jurors Talk: An Analysis of the Arizona Jury Reform Permitting Predeliberation Discussion by Civil Jurors," Annual Meeting of the Law and Society Association, St. Louis Missouri, May 30, 1997.

85. Marcia Clark, *Without a Doubt* (New York: Viking, 1997); Christopher Darden, *In Contempt* (New York: Harper, 1996).

86. Paul Butler, "Racially Based Jury Nullification: Black Power and the Criminal Justice System," *Yale Law Journal* 105 (1995): 677–725.

87. Randall Kennedy, *Race, Crime, and the Law* (New York: Pantheon, 1997).

88. James P. Levine, "The Impact of Racial Demography on Jury Verdicts in Routine Adjudication," *Criminal Law Bulletin* 33 (1997): 523–542.

89. *The New York Times,* May 21, 1997, A1, A15.

13

SENTENCING, APPEAL, AND THE JUDGMENT OF DEATH

LEARNING OBJECTIVES

After reading this chapter, you should be able to answer the following questions:

1. What are the different philosophies of sentencing?

2. Under what circumstances are fines typically imposed?

3. What are the different kinds of sentences?

4. What kinds of problems are associated with contemporary sentencing alternatives?

5. What was the significance of the Supreme Court's rulings in *Weems* v. *United States*, *Furman* v. *Georgia*, *Gregg* v. *Georgia*, *Coker* v. *Georgia*, *Lockhart* v. *McCree*, *Tison* v. *Arizona*, and *Witherspoon* v. *Illinois?*

6. What are the arguments surrounding the death penalty debate?

7. How does the Supreme Court interpret the meaning of "cruel and unusual punishment"?

8. For what reasons can a conviction be appealed?

9. What is victim impact evidence?

A prisoner awaiting execution in a Texas "death row" cell.

AUSTIN, TX—To date, 15 inmates have been released from Texas prisons as a result of DNA testing. In 2005, attorneys involved in the exonerations requested that the cases of two other inmates, already put to death, be reexamined to determine whether their executions had been appropriate.[1]

In Louisiana, Ryan Matthews was sentenced to death in 1999 for a crime committed when he was 17 years old. The evidence against him was dubious and his legal representation poor. In April 2004 a judge ordered a new trial after DNA evidence excluded Matthews. In August 2004 prosecutors dropped all charges against him.[2]

In Illinois, Governor George Ryan announced on January 31, 2000, that he was imposing a moratorium on executions in his state. The move by Ryan, a longtime supporter of capital punishment, came after the freeing of 13 wrongly condemned inmates in the state since the late 1980s. Several had been exonerated as the result of DNA testing. One of these was 43-year-old Anthony Porter, released after a group of journalism students from Northwestern University found evidence that cleared him of a double-murder charge for which he had been found guilty. Porter had spent 17 years on death row and was exonerated just moments before he was to be executed. In an even more startling move, only days after pardoning four condemned men who were determined to have been tortured into confessing for crimes they did not commit, Governor Ryan commuted the death sentences of 167 inmates to life without parole. This decision, which Ryan made days before leaving office, emptied the Illinois state death row. Ryan's actions concurred with his pledge to do whatever it took to "prevent another Anthony Porter."[3]

In Baltimore, after serving 9 years in prison, Eastern Shore waterman Kirk Bloodsworth traded his prison cell for freedom, a limousine ride home, and much media attention. He was the first person to be sentenced to death in Maryland and later exonerated by DNA evidence.[4] Nine years earlier, Bloodsworth had been sent to death row for the rape and murder of a 9-year-old girl. The DNA evidence that freed him came from a small stain on the victim's underwear. A lab discovered that Bloodsworth's DNA did not match the genetic profile in the semen stain, clearing him of the crime.

The Texas, Louisiana, Illinois, and Maryland cases, as well as Governor Ryan's announced moratorium and blanket commutation, raise a number of questions. First of all, how has DNA evidence improved our criminal justice system? What about the other innocent people who currently sit behind bars? What is our criminal justice system doing to avoid sending additional innocent people to prison or—more detrimentally—to death? Second, what kind of punishment philosophy fosters execution? Is execution "cruel and unusual punishment," and is it justified at any time? What does the U.S. Supreme Court have to say about the death penalty? What other sentencing alternatives are available for serious offenders?

A fter conviction, the business of the court is not complete. First there is the matter of sentencing, and then there is the potential for appeal.

What makes both sentencing and appeal significant is that in all the earlier phases of the justice process the purpose is to establish, beyond a reasonable doubt, the criminal liability of the defendant. The adversary system of jurisprudence, grounded in due process of law, is structured on the premise that the accused is innocent until proven guilty. Upon conviction, of course, the accused *has* been proved guilty. At sentencing, the court's obligation shifts from impartial and equitable litigation to the imposition of sanctions. In cases of appeal, the court also deals with those who have been found guilty, but who claim that errors were made in procedure or judgment.

In either case, the court's position is challenging. It must mediate among the functions of justice, the statutory authority of law, the assurances of due process, the need for correctional application, the burdens of a congested justice system, the urgency of political realities, the essentials of legal ethics, and demands for community protection.

Without question, sentencing is the most controversial aspect of criminal justice processing. Appellate review, although somewhat less visible, also generates considerable controversy. Perhaps of greatest concern is the judgment of death, a criminal sanction that cuts across both sentencing and appellate decision making.

| Sentencing |

Life for life, eye for eye . . .

— EXODUS 21:23 – 24

What should be done with criminal offenders after they have been convicted? The answer is difficult for a sentencing judge, because the administration of justice has conflicting goals: rehabilitation of offenders, discouragement of potential lawbreakers, isolation of dangerous criminals who pose a threat to community safety, condemnation of extralegal conduct, and reinforcement of accepted social norms. Such varied objectives tend to generate contradictory suggestions such as these:

> "The punishment should fit the crime."
>
> "The public demands a prison sentence."
>
> "The purpose of justice is individualized sentencing."
>
> "The sentence should be a warning to others."
>
> "Rehabilitate the offender so he can be returned to society."
>
> "Lock them up and throw away the key."

The challenge facing the judge, and sometimes the jury, is to choose among one or more of these various goals while subordinating all others.

Sentencing Objectives

Throughout the history of the United States, there has been no single and clearly defined rationale to serve as a guiding principle in sentencing. For more than 200 years, the public has alternated between revulsion at inhumane sentencing practices and prison conditions (denounced as "barbaric" and "uncivilized") on the one hand and dissatisfaction with overly compassionate treatment (seen as "coddling criminals") on the other. The fate of convicted offenders has repeatedly shifted according to prevailing national values and current perceptions of danger and fear of crime. As a result, sentencing objectives are based on at least five competing philosophies: retribution, vengeance, incapacitation, deterrence, and rehabilitation.

Retribution To use a 200-year-old definition once offered by classical scholar Cesare Beccaria, **retribution** is an effort "to make the punishment as analogous as possible to the nature of the crime." In more modern terminology, retribution involves creating an equal or proportionate relationship between the offense and the punishment—an effort to ensure that an offender's punishment is commensurate not only with the crime but also with his or her moral blameworthiness and prior criminal record. Rather than the biblical "eye for eye, tooth for tooth," the philosophy of retribution typically reflects a desire for proportionality—a sentencing structure in which the most heinous offenders receive the harshest punishments and lesser criminals receive lesser punishments.[5]

Vengeance In contrast with retribution, **vengeance** is the desire to punish criminals because society gains some measure of satisfaction from seeing or knowing that they are punished.[6] This philosophy presents an ethical dilemma: Should it be accepted as a valid rationale for punishment? The U.S. Supreme Court's decision in *Payne* v. *Tennessee*[7] suggests that it already has been. In *Payne,* decided in 1991, the Court held that at a capital sentencing proceeding, the Constitution does not forbid the admission

Eye for Eye

Saudia Arabia's strict interpretation of Islamic law calls for cutting off the hands and feet of thieves, and the beheading of murderers, rapists, armed robbers, and drug traffickers. In some cases, victims can either demand retributive punishment or accept money compensation.

Following Islamic law, "an eye for an eye" punishment was imposed in Saudi Arabia in August 2000. For the crime of disfiguring a compatriot by throwing acid in his face, a 37-year-old Egyptian man's left eye was surgically removed in a local hospital. The offender was also fined $68,000 and ordered to serve an undisclosed prison term.

Source: Associated Press, August 14, 2000. ∎

A cellblock at the Men's Central Jail at the Twin Towers Correctional facility in downtown Los Angeles.

of evidence or prosecutorial argument concerning the personal characteristics of the victim or the impact of the crime on the victim's family. In other words, the decision permits *victim impact evidence* at sentencing hearings. **Victim impact evidence** is a statement of the harm suffered by the victim or the victim's family as a result of the offender's actions. As Chief Justice Rehnquist put it: "Victim impact evidence is simply another form or method of informing the sentencing authority about the harm caused by the crime in question." One could reasonably argue that permitting the victim, or members of the victim's family, to testify at sentencing as to the personal harm the offender has caused is tantamount to eliciting requests for vengeance from a sentencing judge or jury.

Incapacitation   **Incapacitation** is simply the removal of dangerous persons from the community.[8] Also referred to as the "restraint" or "isolation" philosophy, its goal is community protection rather than revenge. By removing the offender from society through execution, imprisonment, or exile (as is the case with the *deportation* of foreign nationals upon conviction of certain crimes), the community is protected from further criminal activity.

As a punishment philosophy, incapacitation is problematic. If the goals are crime prevention and community protection, the sanctions would have to be quite severe to be effective. Regardless of the offense, execution is the only form of restraint that can guarantee the elimination of future offenses against the community. Prisoners serving sentences of life-without-parole escape from custody from time to time, and the crimes they commit in prison against institutional staff and other inmates can be considered "crimes against the community" in that prison personnel are clearly part of the community. And for that matter, inmates and their families are also members of the community. Temporary incarceration until the community can be reasonably assured the offender will no longer commit crimes also has unpredictable outcomes. In addition, there is an economic dimension. As the guiding principle of sentencing, incapacitation would require the construction of new prison facilities, combined with higher annual costs of supporting an expanded inmate population and increased expense for new custodial personnel.

Deterrence   The most widely held justification for punishment is reducing crime. Thus, as a sentencing philosophy, **deterrence** refers to the prevention of criminal acts by making examples of individuals convicted of crimes. Deterrence can be both general and specific. *General deterrence* seeks to discourage would-be offenders from committing crimes; *specific deterrence* is designed to prevent a particular convicted offender from engaging in future criminal acts.

The notion of punishment as a deterrent is best illustrated in the words of an 18th-century judge who reportedly told a defendant at sentencing, "You are to be hanged not because you have stolen a sheep but in order that others may not steal sheep."[9] Belief in the efficacy of deterrence, however, is mixed. Although research on general deterrence remains inconclusive, it is clear that some crimes and potential criminals are more easily deterred than others. In addition, a number of studies reinforce the notion that punishment deters crime and, in particular, that the certainty of punishment is more important than the severity of punishment in deterring potential criminals.[10] Nevertheless, more research is needed on the various individual and social factors that may affect the relationship between certainty and severity of punishment on the one hand, and crime rates on the other. By contrast, the philosophy of specific deterrence does seem to have an impact on the behavior of many white-collar criminals and first-time misdemeanor offenders whose arrest and conviction causes them embarrassment and public disgrace and threatens their careers and family life.

General deterrence can be applied to similar populations for certain types of criminal activity. For example, when many jurisdictions made it a misdemeanor to patronize a prostitute, a U.S. Department of Justice employee commented as follows to the author:

> Almost every weekend I'd go to downtown D.C., to Atlantic City, or Times Square and shack up with some sleazy hooker. . . . No more! That's all I need, getting busted for sleeping with a whore. . . . So much for a career in Justice.

Rehabilitation From a humanistic point of view, the most appealing basis for sentencing and justification for punishment is that future crimes can be prevented by changing the offender's behavior. The **rehabilitation** philosophy rests on the premise that people who commit crimes have identifiable reasons for doing so and that these can be discovered, addressed, and altered. Its aim is to modify behavior and reintegrate the lawbreaker into the wider society as a productive citizen.

The goal of rehabilitation has wide support, for in contrast with other sentencing philosophies, it takes a positive approach to eliminating offense behavior. Proponents argue that unlike deterrence or the temporary measures of isolation, rehabilitation is the only humanitarian mechanism for altering criminal careers.

Yet the efficacy of rehabilitation has been seriously questioned. Some suggest that since the causes of crime are not fully understood, efforts to change criminal behavior are of dubious value. Others maintain that since rehabilitative services are either minimal or nonexistent in many institutions and community-based programs, "correction" as such has only limited practical potential. Still a third group espouses a "nothing works" philosophy, arguing that rehabilitation has not demonstrated its ability to prevent or reduce crime.

Statutory Sentencing Structures

Regardless of the sentencing philosophy of the presiding judge, the actual sentence is influenced to some degree by the statutory alternatives in the penal codes, combined with the facilities and programs available in the correctional system. Thus, the competing objectives of retribution, vengeance, incapacitation, deterrence, and rehabilitation may be diluted to some degree, since the judicial sentencing responsibility must be carried out within the guidelines provided by legislative sentencing authority.

Statutory sentencing guidelines, which have generally evolved over long periods and often reflect the changing nature of legislative philosophy, appear in each state's criminal code. No two state codes are quite alike—the punishments they designate for specific crimes vary, and the methods establishing the parameters for sentencing also differ. Moreover, some statutes give judges wide latitude in sentencing, while others do not. In some states—Tennessee, for example—the penal code designates the range of

If you steal from us we take your picture and we beat you.

— SIGN IN A BRONX, NEW YORK, SUPERMARKET WHERE A WOMAN WAS REPORTEDLY LASHED SEVERAL TIMES WITH AN ELECTRICAL CORD AFTER BEING ACCUSED OF STEALING A BOX OF PAMPERS

Two Words That Lengthened a Sentence

Defendant Harold Coleman was facing 35 years in prison after convictions of burglary, theft, and being a habitual criminal. However, following an outburst at his sentencing hearing—during which he called the presiding judge a "prick" and an "asshole"—another 7 years were added to his sentence. The judge remarked that "he called me a few choice names that didn't reflect well on the judiciary, and you can't let them get by with this." Coleman's attorney commented, "I don't think it was worth the satisfaction my client got."

Source: *National Law Journal,* September 3, 1984, 11. ■

"We have one question. Is it 'send him up the river' or 'send him down the river'?"

© 2005 Mike Twohy from cartoonbank.com. All Rights Reserved.

punishments for each specific crime. Other states, such as Idaho, follow the Tennessee model for some crimes but extend almost total discretion to the judge for others. And in other states, such as New York, crimes are first classified according to their severity (for example, rape in the first degree is a class B felony, while incest is a class E felony) and then are assigned punishments according to their felony or misdemeanor class.

Although statutory guidelines provide a range of sentencing alternatives, in many instances judges also have discretion to deviate from the legislative norm, on the premise that sentences should be individualized. Conversely, there are situations in which sentencing discretion is taken away from the judge because of mandatory sentencing statutes (discussed later in the chapter).

In a few jurisdictions, a judge's authority and discretionary power to determine a sentence is delegated by statute to the jury—but only for certain types of crimes. Whatever theory of sanctions ultimately guides the sentencing of the defendant, and depending on the statutory requirements of the jurisdiction, the alternatives for the presiding judge include fines, probation or some other community-based program, imprisonment, or the death penalty.

Fines

Fines are imposed either in lieu of or in addition to incarceration or probation. They are the traditional means of dealing with most traffic law violations and many misdemeanors, and the sentence "$30 or 30 days" is often heard in courtrooms across America. Fines can also be imposed for felonies, instead of or in addition to some other sentence. They can involve many thousands of dollars and sometimes twice the amount of the defendant's gain from the commission of the crime.

However, since *Williams* v. *Illinois* in 1970 and *Tate* v. *Short* the following year,[11] the use of fines has been curtailed. In *Williams,* the Supreme Court ruled that no jurisdiction could hold a person in jail or prison beyond the length of the maximum sentence merely to work off a fine that he or she is unable to pay—a practice that was allowed at that time in 47 states. In *Tate,* the Court held that the historic "$30 or 30 days" sentence was an unconstitutional denial of equal protection. The Court's unanimous

Judge Hampton has a reputation for fairness and impartiality and has never exhibited bias or prejudice toward any group, class, or individual.

— **FROM A REPORT INVESTIGATING MISCONDUCT ACCUSATIONS AGAINST DALLAS DISTRICT COURT JUDGE JACK HAMPTON, WHO CALLED TWO MURDER VICTIMS "QUEERS" AND TOLD REPORTERS THAT THEIR HOMOSEXUALITY WAS A MITIGATING FACTOR IN SENTENCING THEIR KILLER**

I'm not talking to reporters anymore.

— **JUDGE HAMPTON, AFTER THE REPORT WAS RELEASED**

decision maintained that limiting punishment to a fine for those who could pay, but expanding it to imprisonment for those who could not, was a violation of the Fourteenth Amendment. More recently, in *Bearden* v. *Georgia*,[12] decided in 1983, the Supreme Court ruled that a sentencing court may not automatically revoke a defendant's probation solely because he or she could not pay a fine that was a condition of probation.

In 1988, a criminal court in New York City initiated an experiment intended to make fines a more meaningful sentencing option. Judges adjusted fines to account for the financial means of the offender as well as the seriousness of the crime. These fines were referred to as *day fines* because they were figured as multiples of the offender's daily net income.[13] On the basis of the New York experience, other jurisdictions began similar programs of their own. Overall, day fines have been found to be positive sanctions, providing significant deterrence and fostering offender accountability.[14]

Imprisonment

For convicted offenders who receive a prison sentence, there are numerous variations, some of which have elicited considerable controversy. Sentences can be termed *indeterminate*, *determinate*, *definite*, *"flat," "fixed," indefinite*, *intermittent*, or *mandatory*, plus a host of other names, many of which have been confused and mislabeled. In practice, there are three major types: indeterminate, determinate, and definite.

Indeterminate Sentences
The most common type of sentence is the **indeterminate sentence,** which has a fixed minimum and a fixed maximum term for incarceration, rather than a definite period. The actual amount of time served is determined by the paroling authority. Sentences of 1 to 5 years, 7½ to 15 years, 10 to 20 years, or 15 years to life are indeterminate.

The statutory sentencing guidelines for forcible rape in New York are truly indeterminate. For example, the crime of rape in the first degree calls for a period of incarceration of not less than 6 years and not more than 25 years, with the minimum fixed at one-third of the maximum. Within those guidelines, the judge can impose a sentence—for example, 7 to 21 years. Thus, the offender must serve at least 7 years, after which the paroling authority may release him or her at *any* time prior to the completion of the maximum sentence.

The philosophy behind the indeterminate sentence is based on a purely correctional model of punishment, the underlying premise being that the sentence should meet the needs of the defendant. After incarceration begins, the rehabilitation process is initiated, at least in theory, and the inmate should be confined until there is substantial evidence of "correction." At that point, the paroling authority is responsible for assessing the nature and extent of such rehabilitation and releasing the defendant if the evidence warrants it. Thus, the indeterminate sentence rests on the notion that length of imprisonment should be based on progress toward rehabilitation. It makes the following assumptions (all of which are disputable and not widely held in correctional and criminological circles):

1. Criminals are personally or socially disturbed or disadvantaged, and therefore their commission of crime cannot be considered a free choice. If this is the case, then setting prison terms commensurate with the severity of the crime is not logical.
2. Indeterminate sentences allow "effective" treatment to rectify psychosocial problems, which are the root of crime.
3. Readiness for release varies with the individual and can be determined only when the inmate is in the institution, not before.[15]

In its purest form, the indeterminate sentence would involve a term of 1 day to life, but this is rarely found in current statutes. It should also be noted that confusion arises because some refer to this as the "indefinite" sentence while others use the terms *indefinite* and *indeterminate* interchangeably.

In recent years, indeterminate sentencing has received considerable criticism. The following arguments have been made against this form of sentencing:

- Since the causes of crime and criminal behavior are not readily understood, they cannot be dealt with under the premise of indeterminate sentencing.
- Rehabilitation cannot occur within the prison setting, regardless of the nature of the sentencing.
- The indeterminate sentence is used as an instrument of inmate control, put into practice through threats of disciplinary reports and, hence, extended sentences.
- Indeterminate sentences can vary by judge and by jurisdiction, resulting in unfair and disparate terms of imprisonment.
- An offender's uncertainty as to how long his or her prison term may last can lead to frustration, violence, and riot.[16]

Determinate Sentences The concerns over indeterminate sentencing have generated considerable interest in the **determinate sentence.** Known also as the "flat," "fixed," or "straight" sentence, it has no set minimum or maximum but, rather, a fixed period of time. The term of the determinate sentence is established by the legislature, thus removing the sentencing discretion of the judge. However, under determinate sentencing guidelines, the court's discretion to choose either prison, probation, a fine, or some other alternative is not affected. Only the length of the sentence is taken away from judicial discretion, if the judge imposes imprisonment.

In some instances, the determinate sentence can, in effect, become an indeterminate sentence. Under determinate sentencing statutes, inmates are still eligible for parole after a portion of their terms have been served. Thus, in a state where parole eligibility begins after half the term has expired, a determinate sentence of 10 years really ranges from a minimum of 5 years to a maximum of 10.

Definite Sentences The first application of indeterminate sentencing policies in the United States appeared in 1924 at New York's House of Refuge.[17] Before then a regular feature of incarceration was the **definite sentence**—one having a fixed period of time with no reduction by parole. This type of sentence fell out of favor, however, because those interested in rehabilitation found it to be too rigid and insensitive to defendants' individual characteristics and needs.

The diminished appeal of indeterminate sentences, combined with growing concerns in the 1970s over street crime and the "coddling" of criminals, led to renewed interest in definite sentencing guidelines. In 1975, Maine became the first state to abandon the indeterminate sentencing system. At the same time, it also abolished parole. Under its new "flat" sentencing laws, terms of imprisonment are, in effect, definite sentences. Similarly, the new "three strikes and you're out" (or "in") laws calling for life imprisonment without parole upon conviction for a third felony are a form of definite sentence (see Exhibit 13.1).

Other Sentencing Variations

In addition to the three basic types of sentences of imprisonment—indeterminate, determinate, and definite—a number of variations and adaptations have received attention in recent years.

In New York and several other jurisdictions judges may impose a sentence of intermittent imprisonment. Under the New York statute, the **intermittent sentence** is a term to be served on certain days or periods of days specified by the court.[18] For example, a defendant who pleaded guilty to the felonious possession of 74 pounds of marijuana was sentenced to an intermittent term of 60 days, to be served on consecutive weekends, followed by 5 years' probation.[19] This type of sanction is used in cases in which the nature of the offense warrants incarceration, but the defendant's characteristics and habits suggest that full-time imprisonment would be inappropriate. It should be noted that a sentence of intermittent imprisonment is *revocable*. That is, should the offender fail to report to the institution on the days specified, he or she can be returned to court and resentenced to a more traditional term of imprisonment.

State Court Sentences
Percent of felons

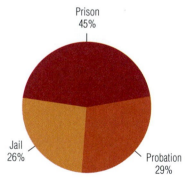

Prison
45%

Probation
29%

Jail
26%

Federal Court Sentences
Percent of felons

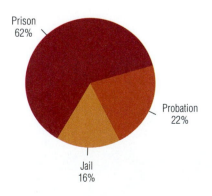

Prison
62%

Probation
22%

Jail
16%

Source: Bureau of Justice Statistics.

RESEARCH ON CRIME & JUSTICE | EXHIBIT 13.1

The Use of the "Three-Strikes" and "Two-Strikes" Laws

Public concern over violent crime has always encouraged the passage of new laws mandating lengthy sentences for repeat felons. California's well-known "Three-Strikes and You're Out" law, which marked its 10-year anniversary on March 7, 2004, mandates that certain (or all) offenders convicted of three felonies face life in prison.

In 1994, California voters approved what has been considered the most sweeping of the three-strikes laws, and the following list reflects some of the felony crimes that qualify as "strikes" under California law:

1. Murder, voluntary manslaughter, or attempted murder.

2. Mayhem (the infliction of serious bodily injury).

3. Rape, sodomy by force, or oral copulation by force.

4. Any felony punishable by death or life imprisonment.

5. Sexual abuse or lewd acts on a child.

6. Kidnapping.

7. Robbery with use of a deadly weapon.

8. Carjacking with use of a deadly weapon.

Although the first two "strikes" must fall under the above serious felony category, the crime that triggers the life sentence (the third "strike") can be *any* felony. Furthermore, once an individual accrues a second "strike," sentences are doubled and these terms must be served in prison rather than on probation. In addition, earned "good time" is limited.

Since its enactment, another 25 states and the federal government have passed similar laws (but with modifications) to the California legislation. Research indicates, however, that only Georgia and California have made much use of the statutes. Most jurisdictions use the three-strikes idea sparingly because of concern with long-term incarceration costs. An additional issue has been the potential for increases in the number of jury trials, because instead of plea bargaining, defendants facing a third conviction are almost certain to request a jury trial.

What has been the California experience? Today, more than 42,000 persons, or over one in four prisoners, are serving a double or 25-years-to-life sentence under California's three-strikes law. But although the law has been promoted as a way to prevent violent crime, interestingly, fewer than half of the second- and third-time strik-

ers are serving time for crimes against people. More than 2,000 of the 7,300 prisoners sentenced to 25-years-to-life are locked up for burglary and theft. In addition, as of September 2003, there were more persons "struck out" for drug possession (672) than there were for second-degree murder (62), assault with a deadly weapon (379), and rape (119) combined.

This very problem has been the subject of recent Supreme Court attention to some California three-strikes sentences that have been perceived by some opponents as "cruel and unusual punishment." Both the cases of *Ewing* v. *California,* in which a parolee, Gary Ewing, was caught shoplifting three golf clubs, and the case of *Lockyer* v. *Andrade,* in which Leandro Andrade was caught stealing nine children's videos from two discount stores, questioned whether the sentences these men received were disproportionate. Both cases were upheld 5-to-4 by the Supreme Court. Ewing will be serving 25-years-to-life under the three-strikes rule for stealing the three golf clubs, priced at $399 per club, and Andrade will spend 50-years-to-life in prison for stealing $150 worth of videotapes.

Georgia has one-upped other states with a two-strikes law. Georgia has enumerated what it calls the "seven deadly sins," which include most of the offenses, listed above, that qualify for a strike in California. A first conviction earns a minimum of 10 years without parole; a second conviction earns life without parole.

Advocates of the two-strikes and three-strikes enhanced sentencing claim that it is an effective deterrent that has reduced crime. The reality, however, is that the decline began 3 years before the law was passed and is due to such factors as a prospering economy, a decline in the population of young men, gun control laws, and the subsiding crack epidemic.

Sources: Scott Ehlers, Vincent Schiraldi, and Jason Ziedenberg, *Still Striking Out: Ten Years of California's Three Strikes* (Washington, DC: Justice Policy Institute), March 2004; Craig Fischer, "Supreme Court Allows Penalties Under California 3-Strikes Law," *Corrections Journal,* March 7, 2003, 1,3; Margot Roosevelt, "Bizarre, Draconian and Disproportionate?" *Time,* November 11, 2002, 65–66; James Austin and John Irwin, *It's About Time: America's Imprisonment Binge* (Belmont, CA: Wadsworth, 2001); Mike Males, Dan Macallair, and Khaled Taqi-Eddin, "Striking Out: The Failure of California's 'Three Strikes and You're Out' Law," *Stanford Law and Policy Review,* Fall 1999; Tomislav V. Kovandzic, John J. Sloan and Lynne M. Vilraitis, "Striking Out as Crime Reduction Policy," *Justice Quarterly* 21 (June 2004): 207–239.

A type of determinate sentence known as the **mandatory sentence** has been a subject of extensive discussion since the middle of the 1970s. Mandatory sentences limit judicial discretion; they are penal code provisions that require the judge to sentence individuals convicted of certain crimes to prison terms of a specified length. Under these statutes, which are intended to guarantee that recidivists, violent offenders, and other serious criminals face the strictness and certainty of punishment, neither probation nor other alternative sentences are permitted.

As part of the nation's "war on drugs," a variation on the mandatory scheme that has appeared in many jurisdictions is the *mandatory minimum sentence.* Numerous other states have mandatory minimum sentences of 3 years or 5 years for possession of

Maricopa County, Arizona, prison inmates participating in what is believed to be the nation's first female chain gang.

even small amounts of illegal drugs. But recent analyses have demonstrated that the mandatory sentences are not working well, for the following reasons:

- They do not achieve certainty and predictability because officials sometimes circumvent them.
- They are redundant with respect to proscribing probation for serious cases because such cases generally are sentenced to imprisonment anyway.
- They are arbitrary for minor cases.
- They may occasionally result in an unduly harsh punishment for a marginal offender.[20]

Judges across the country have imposed unique variations in sentencing—not all of which include imprisonment—in an effort to "let the punishment fit the crime." For example:

- In Rogers, Arkansas, a woman who pleaded guilty to driving without strapping her 3-year-old daughter into a safety seat was ordered to write the toddler's obituary—even though the youngster is alive.[21]
- New York judge Joe B. Brown has become well known for his "maverick" sentencing alternatives. For instance, he has "sentenced" first-time nonviolent offenders to write a book report. In one case he sentenced a young man to stand in front of a gorilla cage for an hour and imagine what it would be like to be behind bars. He sentenced other first-time nonviolent offenders to wash police cars or clear out fields of weeds. If an offender had not finished school, Judge Brown has demanded that he or she return to school to receive a diploma. The judge has also allowed burglary victims to visit the burglar's home and take something of equal value while the burglar watched; the visits were unscheduled, so the burglar could not hide what was most valuable.[22]
- A judge in a Cincinnati suburb ordered a chronic drunk driver to move within walking distance of a liquor store so that he wouldn't have to drive to get his alcohol. He was also sentenced to spend the first week of each of the next 5 years in jail.[23]
- After Peter Rollack of the Latin Kings street gang was convicted of eight murders for ordering several killings while detained in a North Carolina jail, a federal judge sentenced him to a life term. In addition, his prison contacts were to be limited to

his attorney and family members, thus preventing him from ordering the deaths of anyone else.[24]

Finally, sentencing statutes in Montana, California, Florida, Georgia, Iowa, Louisiana, Oregon, Wisconsin, and Alabama permit judges to order "chemical castration" for repeat sex offenders. Chemical castration involves injections of Depo-Provera, a drug that reduces testosterone levels, which in turn reduces the sex drive.[25]

Disparities in Sentencing

Sentencing disparities have long been a major problem in criminal justice processing. The basis of the difficulty is threefold:

1. The structure of indeterminate sentencing guidelines.
2. The discretionary powers of sentencing judges.
3. The mechanics of plea bargaining.

The statutory minimum and maximum terms of imprisonment combined with fines, probation, or other alternatives to incarceration create a number of sentencing possibilities for a specific crime. With judicial discretion in sentencing, sanctions can vary widely according to the jurisdiction, the community, and the punishment philosophy of a particular judge. The dynamics of plea bargaining enable various defendants accused of the same crime to be convicted and sentenced differently. These problems exist, moreover, both within an individual court and across jurisdictions.

Consider, for example, the range of possible sentences for burglary in the first degree (or its equivalent) in the following states:

Idaho: imprisonment for not less than 1 year nor more than 15 years, or probation.[26]

New York: imprisonment for not less than 3 years and not more than 25 years, or probation, or a fine.[27]

West Virginia: imprisonment for not less than 1 year nor more than 10 years, or probation (for a first felony conviction).[28]

Delaware: 2 to 20 years' imprisonment, or a suspended sentence, or probation, or a fine (payable in installments).[29]

Maryland: imprisonment for not more than 20 years, or probation.[30]

Alabama: imprisonment for not less than 10 years, or probation.[31]

Just within these few jurisdictions, the potential for disparate sentences is obvious. In Delaware, for example, the sentence imposed for first-degree burglary can range from a fine to 20 years' imprisonment. Minimum prison terms extend from a low of 1 year in Idaho to a high of 10 years in Alabama. And the maximum term allowable can range from 10 years (West Virginia), to 25 years (New York), to perhaps even life (Alabama).

Statistical comparisons of sentencing tendencies in various jurisdictions demonstrate that disparities are widespread. In West Virginia, for example, a conviction for automobile theft will result in more time in prison than a conviction for rape in 16 other states. In South Carolina, prisoners sentenced for armed robbery end up doing more time in the penitentiary than convicted murderers in six other states.[32]

The consequences of disparities in sentencing can be significant, not only for the convicted person but also for the court and correctional systems and the entire administration of justice. *First,* the wide variations in sentencing make a mockery of the principle of evenhanded administration of the criminal law, thus calling into question the very philosophy of justice in America. *Second,* disparities have a rebound effect on plea bargaining and court scheduling. On the one hand, defendants may opt for a negotiated plea rather than face trial before a judge who is known to be severe. On the other hand, substantial delays often result from the granting of continuances sought by defense attorneys who hope that numerous reschedulings will ultimately bring their case before a lenient judge. Known as "judge-shopping," this practice is so widespread that

EXHIBIT 13.2 | VICTIMS & JUSTICE

A Consequence of Sentencing Disparity?

One of the more celebrated cases of disparate sentencing practices involved the conviction of a 20-year-old youth on charges of conspiracy to commit a felony and assault with the intent to rob. The year was 1924, and the youth, although AWOL from the U.S. Navy, had no prior criminal record. His codefendant, one Edgar Singleton, was a 31-year-old former convict and umpire for a local baseball team.

The two had collaborated to rob a grocery store in Mooresville, Indiana, but the victim resisted, the attempt was thwarted, and both were quickly arrested.

Fearing the strictness and certainty of punishment handed down at the county court in Martinsville, Indiana, Singleton obtained a change of venue, received a term of 2 to 10 years, and was paroled after less than 2 years. The youth, however, threw himself on the mercy of the local court but nevertheless received sentences of 2 to 14 years and 10 to 20 years.

Embittered by unequal justice and the inequitable sentence, the youth rebelled against his wards at the Indiana State Reformatory. He attempted to escape on three occasions, was charged with numerous disciplinary violations, and, as a result, was denied parole when first eligible in 1929. Later that year, he was transferred to Indiana State Prison, where he met a score of experienced criminals who taught him the fine art of bank robbery.

On May 22, 1933, just a few days before his thirtieth birthday, after having spent his entire young-adult life in prison, he was finally paroled. On the basis of the tutelage provided by his inmate associates, he began a professional career in bank robbery. During the next 13 months, he engineered a score of armed holdups at banks and

John Dillinger at age 21.

stores across the Midwest. His efforts netted him many hundreds of thousands of dollars, but in the process he killed at least 15 people. On July 2, 1934, as a young man of only 31 years, FBI agents shot him to death as he exited a theater in Chicago, Illinois. His name was John Dillinger.

Sources: L. L. Edge, *Run the Cat Roads* (New York: Dembner, 1981); J. Edgar Hoover, *Persons in Hiding* (Boston: Little, Brown, 1938); Jay Robert Nash, *Bloodletters and Badmen* (New York: M. Evans, 1973); John Toland, *The Dillinger Days* (New York: Random House, 1963).

---

at one time in the District of Columbia court of general sessions, giving a defendant the judge of his or her choice became part of the plea negotiation arrangements. *Third,* prisoners compare their sentences, and an inmate who believes that he or she received an unfair sentence or was a victim of judicial prejudice often becomes hostile, resistant to correctional treatment and discipline, and even prone to rioting. *Fourth,* the image of the courts and the justice process is even further tarnished. For an interesting perspective on the consequences of sentencing disparities, see Exhibit 13.2.

Sentencing Reform

There have been a number of strong criticisms of sentencing disparities. Decades ago, U.S. attorney general Robert H. Jackson commented:

> It is obviously repugnant to one's sense of justice that the judgment meted out to an offender should be dependent in large part on a purely fortuitous circumstance: namely, the personality of the particular judge before whom the case happens to come for disposition.[33]

More recently, federal judge Marvin E. Frankel of the Southern District of New York commented:

> The sentencing powers of the judges are, in short, so far unconfined that, except for frequently monstrous maximum limits, they are effectively subject to no law at all. Everyone with the least training in law would be prompt to denounce a statute that merely said the

penalty for crimes "shall be any term the judge sees fit to impose." A regime of such arbitrary fiat would be intolerable in a supposedly free society, to say nothing of being invalid under our due-process clause. But the fact is that we have accepted unthinkingly a criminal code creating in effect precisely that degree of unbridled power.[34]

The criticisms of both Attorney General Jackson and Judge Frankel, as well as those of numerous others, are directed not only toward judicial discretion but also toward the penal statutes that make far-reaching discretion possible. Criminal laws that allow jurists to impose terms of "not more than" 5 years, or 10 years, or 30 years proclaim, in effect, that sentencing judges are answerable only to their conscience. The measures that have been proposed or adopted in various jurisdictions to remedy the problem of sentencing disparities remove that key phrase "not more than" from the penal laws, reducing judicial discretion. Mandatory sentencing statutes, with their stipulations of fixed penalties, are in part the result of calls for better community protection, but they also clearly decrease the court's discretion. Mandatory sentence statutes, however, are not a panacea for either crime control or sentencing disparities, for they can easily increase prosecutorial discretion, court delays, and overcrowded prison conditions. In addition, they almost totally eliminate the rehabilitative goals of individualized justice.

A less extreme model for eliminating the abuses of discretion is the *presumptive fixed sentence,* now used in several jurisdictions. The objectives of presumptive sentencing are (1) to reduce disparities by limiting judicial discretion without totally eliminating it and (2) to increase community protection by imposing a sentence that the offender is required to serve. More stringent than the indeterminate sentence but less rigid than the determinate sentence, the presumptive fixed sentence is a good combination of the two. A state legislature sets minimum and maximum terms, with a limited range, for a particular crime. The judge imposes a fixed determinate sentence within that range, basing the decision on mitigating circumstances and the offender's characteristics. This sentencing scheme also eliminates the need for parole.[35]

For example, a presumptive sentence for burglary in the first degree might have a lower legislative limit of 3 years and an upper limit of 10, with a fixed sentence of 5 years as set by the judge. Through this model, imprisonment becomes mandatory, a defined range of terms is established by statute, and a degree of judicial discretion remains. At the same time, such disparity-producing guidelines as Delaware's 2 to 20 years' imprisonment for the same crime, or Alabama's imprisonment "for not less than" 10 years, or other terms "as the judge sees fit to impose" would be eliminated.

Sentencing institutes, councils, and guidelines have also been introduced in the hope of influencing judicial discretion. *Sentencing institutes,* initiated at the federal level in 1958, are designed to generate interest in formulating policies and criteria for uniform sentencing procedures. Periodically convened in the form of 1- and 2-day workshops, they typically involve mock sentencing experiments followed by discussions of any observed disparities. *Sentencing councils* are also intended to reduce disparities. The council consists of three judges, who examine cases awaiting sentence and make recommendations to the sentencing judge. *Sentencing guidelines* are based on the actual sentencing behavior of judges. Statistical tables are constructed that reflect the average sentences imposed by judges in a specific jurisdiction, broken down by the seriousness of the crime and the characteristics of the offender. These tables make it possible for a judge to know what sentences his or her peers have imposed in similar cases. Such tables are intended to curb disparities by basing discretion on the judges' common experience.

None of these approaches has been particularly effective, however.[36] The institutes are poorly attended, the councils have been adopted only rarely, and the guidelines are cumbersome and have appeared only periodically in a few jurisdictions. The reason for the limited attendance and adoption is, for the most part, judicial opposition. Sentencing is the one area of court processing in which judges are in total command and can freely exercise their power and authority—capacities that they are not likely to give up easily. One judge expressed his opposition in this way: "To do away with judicial sentencing is to improperly delegate a responsibility that is rightfully and inherently a part of the judiciary."[37]

Disparate Sentencing

In a study of 41 New York judges from across the state, the judges were asked to review files on actual cases and then indicate the sentences they would impose.

In this case, an elderly man was robbed at gunpoint by a heroin addict. The defendant was convicted of first-degree robbery. He was unemployed, lived with his pregnant wife, and had a minor criminal record. Each bar in the figure represents one judge's hypothetical sentence. (His actual sentence was 0–5 years.) Source: *The New York Times.*

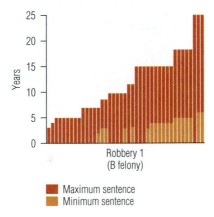

Robbery 1
(B felony)

■ Maximum sentence
■ Minimum sentence

Inmates on Sunday morning at a minimum security honor farm in Riverton, Wyoming.

Federal Sentencing Guidelines In an attempt to reduce disparities at the federal level, in 1985 Congress created the Federal Sentencing Commission, a nine-member committee whose task was to establish sentencing guidelines that would reduce judicial discretion and thereby ensure more equal punishments. After some 2 years of work, the new guidelines went into effect on November 1, 1987. They resulted in greater uniformity and at the same time tended to send more defendants to prison (although for shorter periods).

Although the new federal guidelines held out the promise of sentence reform, they were immediately attacked because of the way the U.S. Sentencing Commission had been formed. The commission was an independent body within the judicial branch of government, but it was argued that the act of writing the guidelines was essentially legislative. As such, this represented an unconstitutional delegation of authority by Congress and a violation of the separation-of-powers doctrine.

The **separation-of-powers doctrine** is a major principle of American government whereby power is distributed among the three branches of government—legislative, executive, and judicial. The officials of each branch are selected by different procedures, have different terms of office, and are independent of one another. The separation is not complete, however, in that each branch participates in the functions of the other through a system of checks and balances. Yet most important, the doctrine serves to ensure that the same person or group will not make the law, interpret it, and apply it.

By early 1988, hundreds of federal judges had faced the question of the guidelines' constitutionality. Slightly more than half had struck them down, for the most part on separation-of-powers grounds. It was at that point that the U.S. Supreme Court agreed to rule on the matter. In 1989, by an 8-to-1 majority, the Court held that the creation of the Federal Sentencing Commission was neither an unconstitutional delegation of legislative discretion nor a violation of the separation-of-powers doctrine.[38]

However, in *United States* v. *Booker*,[39] decided in 2004, the Supreme Court held that the use of the federal sentencing guidelines is no longer mandatory. Judges may still consult them, but they are no longer required to use them.

Truth in Sentencing

The amount of time offenders spend in prison is almost always shorter than the time they are sentenced to serve by the courts. This is the result of "good time" (time off for good behavior) and parole, combined with many correctional systems' efforts to release prisoners early to relieve crowding. A recent Department of Justice study, for example, found that prisoners released in 1996 served on average 30 months in jail or prison—only 44 percent of their actual sentences.[40] In response to this situation, a number of states have passed **truth in sentencing** laws that require offenders to serve a substantial portion of their sentences. Under these laws, parole eligibility and good-time credits are either eliminated or restricted, thus reducing the discrepancy between the sentence imposed and the actual time served.

Although the first truth in sentencing law was passed almost two decades ago, it was not until the second half of the 1990s that the movement was fully under way. By the close of the decade, 40 states and the District of Columbia had truth in sentencing laws in place, and most require inmates to spend 85 percent of their sentences in prison.

The Sentencing Process

Sentencing is generally a collective decision-making process that involves recommendations by the prosecutor, the defense attorney, the judge, and sometimes the presentence investigator. In jurisdictions where sentence bargaining is part of the plea negotiation process, the judge almost invariably imposes what has been agreed on by the prosecution and the defense.

In the federal system and the majority of state jurisdictions, a **presentence investigation** may be conducted prior to actual sentencing. This is undertaken by the court's probation agency or presentence office. The resulting report is a summary of the de-

"MY IDEA OF A VACATION WOULD BE GOING DOWN TO SOME LOWER COURT AND HEARING A NICE, SCANDALOUS DIVORCE CASE."

ScienceCartoonsPlus.com. Reprinted by permission.

fendant's present offense, previous criminal record, family situation, neighborhood environment, school and educational history, employment record, physical and mental health, habits, associates, and group memberships. The report may also contain comments on the defendant's remorse and recommendations for sentencing by the victim, the prosecutor, and the officer who conducted the investigation.

Presentence reports vary in detail and length, depending on the resources and practices of the jurisdiction. Although presentence investigations are not mandatory in all jurisdictions, it is generally agreed that their value goes well beyond their use in determining appropriate sentences. For example:

- They aid probation and parole officers in their supervision of offenders.
- They aid correctional personnel in their classification, treatment, and release programs.
- They give parole boards useful information for release decision-making.

After the presentence report has been submitted to the judge, a sentencing hearing is held. In common law, and in most jurisdictions, a convicted offender has the right to address the court personally prior to the imposition of sentence. Known as **allocution,** this practice is available so that the court can identify the defendant as the person judged guilty and the defendant can be given the opportunity to plead for mercy or a pardon, move for an arrest of judgment, or indicate why judgment ought not be pronounced. The specific matters that a defendant might discuss at the allocution are limited and would not include attempts to reopen the question of guilt. Rather, among the claims that have been included in allocutions are that the defendant is not the person against whom there was a finding of guilt and, in the case of a woman, that the punishment should be adjusted or deferred because of a possible pregnancy (especially in the case of a death sentence).

Allocution is required under Rule 32(a) of the Federal Rules of Criminal Procedure. However, the failure of a federal judge to allow a defendant to address the court

"Which is the bad one, 'concurrent' or 'consecutive'?"

source to come

is not considered an error of constitutional dimension.[41] Such a denial might result only in a remanding of the case for resentencing. Allocution only rarely produces a deferral of punishment.

The presiding judge then imposes the sentence. As noted earlier, the most typical sanctions include fines, imprisonment, probation, some combination thereof, or death. In cases in which the defendant receives multiple sentences for several crimes, the judge may order that terms of imprisonment be served concurrently or consecutively. *Concurrent sentences* are served simultaneously. For example, if the defendant is convicted of both burglary and assault and is given two terms of 5 years' imprisonment to be served concurrently, both terms are satisfied after 5 years. *Consecutive sentences* are successive—one after another.

As noted earlier in the discussions of bail and pretrial detention, it often happens that a defendant comes before a judge for sentencing after having already spent weeks, months, and sometimes even years in a local jail or detention facility awaiting trial. This period of detention, referred to as "jail time," is generally deducted from the length of the prison sentence. When the conviction is for a misdemeanor or minor felony and the period of pretrial detention closely matches the probable term of imprisonment, the judge may impose a sentence of "time served." That is, the accumulated jail time represents the sentence, and the defendant is released. When the jail time spent awaiting trial is not counted as part of the final sentence, it is commonly referred to as "dead time."

The Death Penalty

Death cases are indeed different in kind from all other litigation. The penalty, once imposed, is irrevocable.

—JUSTICE JOHN PAUL STEVENS

For most of the nation's history, the death penalty was used as a punishment for crime, with little thought given to its legitimacy or justification. It was simply accepted as an efficient mechanism for dealing with criminal offenders. When the framers of the Constitution created the Eighth Amendment ban against cruel and unusual punishment, the death penalty itself apparently was not an issue. From the earliest days of the colonial period, capital punishment was considered neither cruel nor unusual. Under the criminal codes for the New Haven colony enacted in 1642 and 1650, for example,

What's one less person on the face of the earth, anyway?

—SERIAL MURDERER TED BUNDY

a total of 11 offenses—some of which do not even appear as misdemeanors in contemporary statutes—called for the death sentence:

1. If any person within this Government shall by direct, express, impious or presumptuous ways, deny the true God and His attributes, he shall be put to death.
2. If any person shall commit any willful and premeditated murder he shall be put to death.
3. If any person slayeth another with a sword or dagger who hath no weapon to defend himself; he shall be put to death.
4. If any man shall slay, or cause another to be slain by lying in wait privily for him or by poisoning or any other such wicked conspiracy; he shall be put to death. . . .
5. If any man or woman shall lie with any beast or brute creature by carnal copulation they shall be put to death, and the beast shall be burned.
6. If any man lieth with mankind as he lieth with a woman, they shall be put to death, unless the one party were forced or be under fourteen years of age, in which case he shall be punished at the discretion of the Court of Assizes.
7. If any person forcibly stealeth or carrieth away any mankind; he shall be put to death.
8. If any man bear false witness maliciously and on purpose to take away a man's life, he shall be put to death.
9. If any man shall traitorously deny his Majesty's right and titles to his Crowns and Dominions, or shall raise armies to resist his authority, he shall be put to death.
10. If any man shall treacherously conspire or publicly attempt to invade or surprise any town or towns, fort or forts, within this Government, he shall be put to death.
11. If any child or children, above sixteen years of age, and of sufficient understanding, shall smite their natural father or mother, unless thereunto provoked and forced for their self-protection from death or maiming, at the complaint of said father and mother, and not otherwise, there being sufficient witnesses thereof, that child or those children so offending shall be put to death.[42]

Within such a context, execution upon conviction for numerous crimes was indeed quite usual. The definition of what was cruel punishment similarly eluded rigid guidelines. Consider, for example, the punishment for treason under the English common law—the very sanction that the leaders of the American Revolution risked by signing the Declaration of Independence:

That you and each of you, be taken to the place from whence you came, and from thence be drawn on a hurdle to the place of execution where you shall be hanged by the neck not till you are dead; that you be severally taken down, while yet alive, and your bowels be taken out and burned before your faces—that your heads be then cut off, and your bodies cut into four quarters, to be at the king's disposal. And God have mercy on your souls.[43]

What the framers of the Constitution probably had in mind when they spoke of "cruel and unusual" punishments were the many more grisly forms of execution that have periodically appeared throughout human history. Through the ages criminals have been burned at the stake, crucified, boiled in flaming oil, impaled, and flayed, to name only a few. Or take the case of Mithridates of ancient Persia:

He was encased in a coffin-like box, from which his head, hands, and feet protruded, through holes made for that purpose; he was fed with milk and honey, which he was forced to take, and his face was smeared with the same mixture; he was exposed to the sun, and in this state he remained for seventeen days, until he had been devoured alive by insects and vermin, which swarmed about him and bred within him.[44]

The Death Sentence, 1864–1967

On January 20, 1864, William Barnet and Sandy Kavanagh were executed in the Vermont State Prison for the crime of murder. During the next 100 or so years, through 1967, a total of 5,707 state-imposed death sentences were carried out across the country.[45] Few of these executions (less than 1%) occurred before 1890, but after that the

Harvesting Body Parts from Death Row Prisoners

According to published reports, China allegedly harvests the organs of executed prisoners without prior consent to use in transplants. "Medical tourists" from the West and Far East, as well as a growing number of Chinese Americans, travel to China, where $10,000 can buy an ailing patient a new kidney or liver. Prisoners are reportedly matched with potential recipients, their sentences are delayed, and they are executed to order once the patient has arrived and is ready for the operation. Executions, which some estimates place at 3,000 each year, are typically carried out by a gunshot to the back of the head, a method that leaves all of the vital organs intact. When prisoners are recruited to donate their corneas, they are instead shot through the heart. The government reportedly profits handsomely from this black market scheme, but the official stance is that the program does not exist.

What do you think about using body parts from death row inmates for transplant operations? ▪

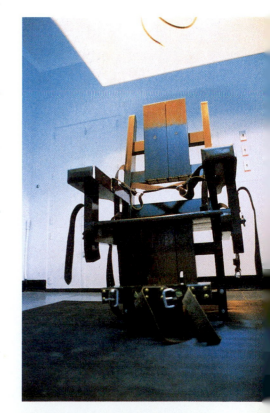

The infamous electric chair, also referred to in underworld lingo as the "hot seat," "hot chair," "hot-shot," "Old Sparky" (in Florida), "Gruesome Gertie" (in Louisiana), or simply the "chair."

Executions Under State Authority, 1850s–1960s

Decade	Number of Executions	Percent of Total
1850s–1860s	12	0.2
1870s	18	0.3
1880s	26	0.5
1890s	154	2.7
1900s	275	4.8
1910s	625	11.0
1920s	1,030	18.0
1930s	1,520	26.6
1940s	1,174	20.6
1950s	682	12.0
1960s	191	3.3
Total	5,707	100.0

number began to grow rapidly. The imposition of the death penalty reached its peak during the 1930s, with more than 1,500 executions during that decade alone. The numbers then began to decline, from 1,174 during the 1940s to fewer than 200 by the 1960s.

This extensive use of the death penalty is explained, at least in part, by the number of states with capital statutes in their penal codes and the proportion of offenses punishable by death. In 1961, for example, of 54 jurisdictions (including the 50 states, the District of Columbia, Puerto Rico, and the federal civil and military authority), 48 carried capital statutes—for homicide in 47 jurisdictions; for kidnapping in 37; for treason in 25; for rape in 20; for carnal knowledge in 16; for robbery in 10; for perjury (in a capital case) in 9; for bombing in 7; for assault (by a life-term prisoner) in 5; for train robbery, burglary, or arson in 4; for train wrecking in 3; and for espionage in 2.[46] In addition, 19 jurisdictions carried a variety of special statutes whereby the death sentence could be imposed for such offenses as aiding a suicide or forcing a woman to marry (in Arkansas), performing an abortion or advising abortion to a woman (in Georgia), lynching (in Kentucky), attempt or conspiracy to assault a chief of state (in New Jersey), use of a machine gun in a crime of violence (in Virginia), and child stealing (in Wyoming). In addition, the death penalty was the mandatory sentence for some offenses (typically homicide and treason) in 27 jurisdictions.

Statutes calling for the death penalty varied widely during these years. In the District of Columbia, Connecticut, Delaware, Massachusetts, and New Hampshire, for example, capital punishment could be imposed only in the case of murder. In Rhode Island the death penalty was restricted even further, being limited to the crime of murder committed by a prisoner serving a life sentence. In contrast, there were 22 capital statutes in the federal criminal codes and a dozen or more in the states of Alabama and Arkansas.

Capital Punishment and Discrimination

In 1967, the President's Commission on Law Enforcement and Administration of Justice commented that the death penalty "is most frequently imposed and carried out on the poor, the Negro, and the members of unpopular groups."[47] This observation was no surprise to those who had watched closely the pattern of capital punishment over the years. Nor was it a surprise to many African Americans, especially in the South. In Virginia during the 1830s, for example, there were 5 capital crimes for whites but at least 70 for blacks.[48] In 1848, the Virginia legislature required the death penalty for any offense committed by a black for which 3 or more years' imprisonment might be imposed as punishment for a white.[49] Pursuant to the South Carolina Black Codes in 1825, burning at the stake was permitted and even carried out—a punishment that had originally been used to execute heretics in medieval Europe.[50] And from 1882 through 1903 at least 1,985 African Americans were hanged or burned alive by the Ku Klux Klan and other southern lynch mobs—often when there was no offense at all or the mere suspicion of one (see Exhibit 13.3).

Even the most superficial analysis of executions under civil authority reveals a clear overrepresentation of blacks. In 1965, for example, sociologist Marvin E. Wolfgang and law professor Anthony Amsterdam began a study to determine the relationship between ethnicity and sentencing for rape in 11 southern and border states where rape was a capital offense. Their findings supported the notion that blacks were treated with undue severity:

> Among the 823 blacks convicted of rape, 110, or 13 percent, were sentenced to death; among the 442 whites convicted of rape, only 9, or 2 percent, were sentenced to death. *The statistical probability that such a disproportionate number of blacks could be sentenced to death by chance alone is less than one out of a thousand.*[51]

From 1930 through 1967, there were 3,859 prisoners executed under civil authority in the United States. When these cases are studied, it becomes even more evident that capital punishment was used in a discriminatory fashion. In this period, some 55%

historical perspectives on criminal justice | **EXHIBIT 13.3**

Squire Birch, Judge Lynch, and the American "Necktie Party"

In both history and folklore, "lynch law" was primarily an American custom. It was the practice of summary judgment and punishment for real or alleged crimes without due process of law, and it seems to have begun in the South Carolina backcountry about a decade before the Revolutionary War.

Well into the 19th century, lynch law generally meant the infliction of corporal punishment. In its most common form, the accused received 39 lashes with a birch rod, a whip, a hickory twig, or any readily available instrument. The man who laid on the lash became known as "Squire Birch," and his tribunal was established under a tree in an open meadow or nearby woods. By the middle of the 19th century, however, lynch law had come to be synonymous with killing—usually by hanging—as a frontier approach to law and order.

The origins of the infamous "Judge Lynch" have been obscured to some degree by legend makers, for a journey through American history and folklore points to several conflicting fables. The court of Judge Lynch is reputed to have derived its name from James Lynch Fitz-Stephen, a 16th-century Irishman who, while engaged as the warden of Galway Jail, was alleged to have hanged his own son for murder. It has also been attributed to a Virginia farmer named Joseph Lynch, who was reported to have executed numerous blacks with reckless abandon during the 1780s.

Upon closer analysis, however, history has documented that there was indeed a *Judge Lynch* and an act of the Virginia legislature known as *Lynch's Law*. The real Judge Lynch, who was to give his name to a form of jurisprudence that he never practiced and would never have tolerated, was the confirmed Quaker Charles Lynch, born in Bedford County, Virginia, in 1736 where the city of Lynchburg now stands. During the Revolutionary War, he was a colonel in the Virginia militia and served as a local judge to deal with the gangs of rustlers that were selling stolen horses to the local militia.

That was the *real* Judge Lynch. In the years that followed, however, the *legendary* Judge Lynch emerged in a sordid American saga. He took over the bench filled by Squire Birch, placing the law in his own hands with promptness and certitude. He gave birth to lynch mob violence, and it is estimated that through January 1938, "lynch law" took the lives of no less than 5,000 victims.

Lynching was practiced most predominantly in the South, with blacks the primary targets. From 1882 through 1903, more than 2,000

A sheriff on horseback finds a stagecoach robber, apparently executed by one of his victims, hanging by the neck from a tree in Boulder, Colorado.

African Americans were either hanged or burned alive—in many instances where there was neither an offense nor even the suspicion of one. In the West, the ephemeral "necktie party" was often gathered for the summary disposal of murderers, robbers, horse thieves, rustlers, and sometimes sheep herders and squatters.

Lynch law executions reached their high point during the early 1890s, with a peak of 235 victims in 1892. With the onset of the 20th century, lynching declined rapidly, but it persisted to some extent in the South and was still directed against blacks. During the 1930s, the number of known lynchings averaged as few as 15 per year, but almost 90 percent of those victimized were southern blacks.

Sources: James Elbert Cutler, *Lynch-Law* (New York: Longman, 1905); Frank Shay, *Judge Lynch: His First Hundred Years* (New York: McKay, 1938); Hugh Davis Graham and Ted Robert Gurr (eds.), *Violence in America* (Beverly Hills, CA: Sage Publications, 1979).

of those executed for all crimes were either black or members of some other minority group. Of the 455 people executed for rape alone, 90 percent were nonwhite.

Cruel and Unusual Punishment

Historically, the Supreme Court's position on the death penalty has been grounded in the broader issue of "cruel and unusual" punishment as prohibited by the Eighth Amendment. It is likely that the framers of the Constitution intended to outlaw punishments that were outside both the mainstream of penalties typically imposed in the

Judicial Candor or Discrimination? A Frontier Judge Imposes Death

"Jose Manuel Miguel Xavier Gonzales, in a few short weeks it will be spring. The snows of winter will flee away. The ice will vanish. And the air will become soft and balmy. In short, Jose Manuel Miguel Xavier Gonzales, the annual miracle of the years will awaken and come to pass, but you won't be there.

"The rivulet will run its soaring course to the sea. The timid desert flowers will put forth their tender shoots. The glorious valleys of this imperial domain will blossom as the rose. Still, you won't be here to see.

"From every tree top some wild woods songster will carol his mating song. Butterflies will sport in the sunshine. The busy bee will hum happily as it pursues its accustomed vocation. The gentle breeze will tease the tissels of the wild grasses, and all nature, Jose Manuel Miguel Xavier Gonzales, will be glad but you. You won't be here to enjoy it because I command the sheriff or some other officers of the county to lead you out to some remote spot, swing you by the neck from a knotting bough of some sturdy oak, and let you hang until you are dead.

"And then, Jose Manuel Miguel Xavier Gonzales, I further command that such officer or officers retire quickly from your dangling corpse, that vultures may descend from the heavens upon your filthy body until nothing shall remain but bare, bleached bones of a cold-bolded, copper-colored, blood-thirsty, throat-cutting, chili-eating, sheep-herding, murdering son-of-a-bitch."

Source: From the judge's decision in *United States* v. *Gonzales* (1881), United States District Court, New Mexico Territory Sessions. ∎

new nation and the moral judgments of the people. Thus, the purpose of the amendment may have been to prevent return to use of the screw and the rack, rather than to outlaw any sanctions that were in common use at the time. But this can be viewed only as conjecture, for the Supreme Court itself, for more than a century, offered little interpretation of the nature and scope of the ban.

The notion that punishment *could* be cruel and unusual was argued by three justices in 1892. The case was *O'Neil* v. *Vermont*,[52] in which the petitioner stood to serve 19,915 days (almost 55 years) in jail for 307 separate illegal sales of liquor. The Court found that since the Eighth Amendment did not limit the states, no federal question was involved, and the sentence imposed by the Vermont court was upheld. However, in a strong dissenting opinion, Justice Stephen J. Field argued that punishment would necessarily be cruel and unusual when it did not fit the crime to which it was attached.

After *O'Neil*, the issue remained dormant for almost two decades until **Weems v. United States**,[53] decided in 1910. The case was significant for the Eighth Amendment ban, for in its ruling the Court struck down a sentence involving a heavy fine, 15 years at hard labor, the wearing of chains, the lifelong loss of certain rights, plus several other sanctions—all for the offense of making false entries in official records. The Supreme Court found the sentence disproportionate to the offense; thus, *Weems* was the first case in which the Court invalidated a criminal punishment on Eighth Amendment grounds.

By 1958, the Court had agreed that the constitutional prohibition could have no fixed and unchanging meaning. Rather, any challenges brought to the Court must necessarily be viewed in terms of "evolving standards of decency."[54]

The Death Penalty and the Supreme Court

On the issue of capital punishment per se, the Supreme Court's interpretation of the Eighth Amendment has remained flexible. As to the method of execution, the Court offered some preliminary guidelines more than a century ago. In *Wilkerson* v. *Utah*,[55] decided in 1878, the justices agreed that public shooting was neither cruel nor unusual. At the same time, however, it noted that the Eighth Amendment would oppose such

The first execution by electrocution took place at Auburn Prison, Auburn, New York on August 6, 1890. The prisoner, William Kemmler, was executed for murder.

punishments as drawing and quartering, burning alive, and other punishments of torturous death. *In re Kemmler,*[56] decided in 1890, held that death by electrocution reflected humane legal intentions and hence did not offend the Eighth Amendment.

After *Kemmler,* the Court remained essentially silent on the constitutionality of capital punishment for almost eight decades. In *Trop* v. *Dulles,*[57] decided in 1958, the Court held that expatriation was a cruel and unusual punishment but noted that this holding did not necessarily apply to the death penalty.

Meanwhile, throughout the 1950s and well into the 1960s the National Association for the Advancement of Colored People (NAACP) Legal Defense and Education Fund combined its efforts with those of the American Civil Liberties Union (ACLU) to wage an all-out legal attack on capital punishment. The two organizations came to the aid of many prisoners who had been sentenced to death. Briefs were prepared, appeals filed, and data on the use of the death penalty for black offenders collected. And the courts showed increasing willingness to review capital cases and to reverse lower court decisions, with the result that many state authorities became reluctant to schedule and perform executions.

In 1963, Justice Arthur J. Goldberg suggested that capital punishment may be a per se violation of the Eighth Amendment. Although he was not speaking for the majority of the justices at the time, his statement, combined with mounting pressure for a decision on the constitutionality of the death penalty, served to advance the NAACP–ACLU effort. The penalty was ultimately challenged on a variety of legal grounds, and on June 3, 1967, the impending execution of more than 500 condemned prisoners throughout the country came to a halt while courts and governors waited to see what the Supreme Court would decide.

Witherspoon v. *Illinois*

The Supreme Court's decision in 1968 in ***Witherspoon* v. *Illinois***[58] was the first indication that the death penalty might be in trouble. An Illinois court had permitted a verdict of guilty and a sentence of death to be handed down by a jury from which the state had systematically excluded all prospective jurors who had any scruples against capital punishment. The Court upheld Witherspoon's challenge, ruling that the "death-qualified jury" was indeed unconstitutional. Coming at almost the same time was the Court's decision in *United States* v. *Jackson,*[59] which invalidated the death penalty provisions of the Federal Kidnapping Act (better known as the Lindbergh Law).

McGautha v. *California*

Witherspoon had not been a total victory for those opposed to capital punishment. They remained firmly optimistic, however, and the moratorium on executions continued as other challenges were prepared for Supreme Court review. The abolition movement eagerly awaited the ruling in *McGautha* v. *California,*[60] which argued that leaving the choice between life imprisonment or death to the total discretion of a jury was a violation of the due process clause of the Fourteenth Amendment. The case was decided in 1971, and the Court held as follows:

> In light of history, experience, and the present limitations of human knowledge, we find it quite impossible to say that committing to the untrammeled discretion of the jury the power to pronounce life or death in capital cases is offensive to anything in the Constitution.

McGautha seemed to be a fatal blow to the movement dedicated to the abolition of capital punishment, and it was widely viewed as the Supreme Court's final word on the death penalty. With no new cases pending before the Court on the issue, and with jury discretion in imposing the death sentence firmly guaranteed, it appeared unlikely that any argument based on the Eighth Amendment could prevail. However, as the states began preparations for executing the more than 600 prisoners who had accumulated on death row, the Court suddenly announced that it would hear a group of cases involving the Eighth Amendment ban on cruel and unusual punishment.

Furman v. *Georgia*

In the fall of 1971, *Furman* v. *Georgia, Jackson* v. *Georgia,* and *Branch* v. *Texas* were brought before the Court on the ground that the death sentences ordered were "cruel and unusual" because of the arbitrary and discriminatory manner

The death penalty is the final resort to truly evil crime.

— TEXAS CORRECTIONAL OFFICER

Whatever can be said about the death penalty, it cannot be said that it causes otherwise unavoidable death.

ERNEST VAN DEN HAAG,
DEATH PENALTY ADVOCATE

in which such sanctions had been imposed in the past for the crimes of murder and rape. The leading case was *Furman* **v.** *Georgia*.[61] William Furman had received the death sentence for a murder that had occurred during the course of a burglary attempt. The decision as to whether Furman's sentence should be life or death had been left to the jury, and his conviction and sentence had been affirmed by all of the Georgia courts.

The Supreme Court's June 29, 1972, decision was complex. It was announced in a nine-opinion *per curium* (unsigned) statement that summarized the narrow argument of the five justices in the majority. In addition, each of the nine justices issued a separate concurring or dissenting opinion. Only Justices Brennan and Marshall were willing to hold that capital punishment was unconstitutional per se. Justices Douglas, Stewart, and White adopted a more narrow view, arguing that the state statutes in question were unconstitutional because they offered judges and juries no standards or guidelines to consider in deciding between life and death. As Justice Stewart put it, the result was that the punishment of death was tantamount to being "struck by lightning." In other words, all state and federal death penalty statutes were deemed to be too arbitrary, capricious, and discriminatory to withstand Eighth Amendment scrutiny. The position taken by Justices Douglas, Stewart, and White represented the common ground of agreement with Justices Brennan and Marshall, thus producing a five-justice majority.

The four dissenting justices were Burger, Blackmun, Powell, and Rehnquist—all appointed to the Court by President Richard Nixon. All four dissenting opinions emphasized the view that in a democracy, issues such as capital punishment should be decided by the legislative branch of government—the people's representatives—and not by the courts. Chief Justice Burger also accused the justices in the majority of "overruling *McGautha* in the guise of an Eighth Amendment adjudication." He also asked rhetorically whether those in the majority would be willing to sanction mandatory death penalty laws on the ground that such laws would eliminate the harmful effects of excessive jury discretion. Although the chief justice may have scored some debating points, the effect of *Furman* was to invalidate every death penalty statute in the United States.

Where the Court had rejected a Fourteenth Amendment due process challenge to jury imposition of the death sentence in *McGautha*, it upheld an Eighth Amendment argument in *Furman*. The *Furman* decision was neither a statement against capital punishment nor an argument against a jury's authority to decide on the death sentence. Rather, it was an attack on state statutes that allowed a jury to find an accused person guilty and then, in the absence of any guidance or direction, decide whether that person should live or die.

Gregg v. *Georgia*

By effectively invalidating all existing state death penalty statutes, *Furman* removed more than 600 persons from death row. At the same time, however, the *Furman* decision provided two avenues by which states could enact new capital punishment laws. First, states could establish a two-stage procedure consisting of a trial at which the question of culpability could be determined, followed by an additional proceeding for those found guilty, during which evidence might be presented to make the death penalty decision better informed and more procedurally sound. Second, states could remove discretion from the jury by making death the mandatory punishment for certain crimes.

In the wake of *Furman*, 35 states passed new capital punishment statutes. Ten chose the mandatory route, while 25 selected the two-stage procedure. By 1976, both approaches were brought before the Supreme Court.

The issue in *Gregg* **v.** *Georgia* was Georgia's new bifurcated trial structure.[62] Following a conviction of guilt in first-degree murder cases, the nature of punishment was decided in a separate proceeding. The Georgia statute required the judge or jury to consider any aggravating or mitigating circumstances, including presence of the following conditions:

- The defendant had a prior conviction for a capital felony or a substantial history of serious assaultive criminal convictions.

Have you noticed that right-to-life people are in favor of capital punishment?

—GORE VIDAL

- The murder was committed during the course of a rape, an armed robbery, a kidnapping, a burglary, or arson.
- The defendant created a grave risk of death to more than one person.
- The defendant killed for profit.
- The victim was a judicial officer or a prosecutor killed during or because of the exercise of official duty.
- The victim was a police officer, correctional employee, or firefighter who was engaged in the performance of his or her duties.
- The defendant directed another person to kill as his or her agent.
- The murder was committed in a wantonly vile, horrible, or inhumane manner because it involved torture, depravity of mind, or aggravated battery.
- The defendant was a prison escapee.
- The murder was committed in an attempt to avoid arrest.[63]

By a 7-to-2 majority, the decision in Gregg upheld the Georgia law, reasoning as follows:

> The new Georgia sentencing procedures, by contrast, focus the jury's attention on the particularized nature of the crime and the particularized nature of the individual defendant. While the jury is permitted to consider any aggravating or mitigating circumstances, it must find and identify at least one statutory aggravating factor before it may impose a penalty of death. In this way is the jury's discretion channeled. No longer can a jury wantonly and freakishly impose the death sentence; it is always circumscribed by the legislative guidelines.

In two companion cases the Court upheld similar procedures adopted by Florida and Texas (and presumably 22 additional states), thus declaring capital punishment laws constitutional as long as they gave judges and juries clear and fair criteria for deciding whether to sentence an offender to death.[64] However, in *Woodson* v. *North Carolina*,[65] which was decided on the same day, the Court struck down state laws that made death the mandatory penalty for first-degree murder. The Court's position was that mandatory death penalty statutes "simply papered over the problem of unguided and unchecked jury discretion" and failed to allow for differences in individual defendants and crimes.

Developments After *Gregg*

During the years after *Gregg*, the Supreme Court continued in its refusal to hold that the death penalty per se constitutes cruel and unusual punishment. However, in a series of rulings from 1977 through 1980, the Court did place limitations on the imposition of capital sentences. In **Coker v. Georgia**,[66] decided in 1977, the Court held that the death sentence could not be imposed for rape because such punishment was grossly disproportionate to the injury caused the victim. Without expressly stating so, it strongly implied that a death sentence was inappropriate except as punishment for murder. And in a series of Ohio cases decided in 1978, the Court ruled against a state statute that required jury consideration of aggravating circumstances, but not mitigating circumstances, in the imposition of capital sentences.[67]

In *Godfrey* v. *Georgia*,[68] decided in 1980, the Supreme Court continued to clarify its holding in *Gregg*. In *Godfrey*, the petitioner had murdered his wife and mother-in-law in the presence of his daughter. The killings had occurred as the result of "heated arguments" that Godfrey felt had been induced by his mother-in-law and stemmed from a host of marital differences. Immediately after the homicides, Godfrey telephoned the local sheriff, confessed to the crimes, led authorities to the slain bodies, and stated that the scene was "hideous." Godfrey was convicted, and under the revised Georgia law as tested in *Gregg*, both murders were found to be accompanied by one of the "aggravating circumstances": The killings had been committed in a "wantonly vile, horrible, or inhumane" manner because they involved "depravity of mind." The jury therefore imposed a death sentence.

Upon review by the Supreme Court, Godfrey's death sentence was overruled on the ground that the jurors had been given too much discretion under the state's statu-

The death penalty is a fact of life, if that isn't an oxymoron.

—GARA LAMARCHE OF THE ACLU

tory guidelines for capital cases. Specifically, the Court held that the Georgia statute had been interpreted too broadly and that the "depravity of mind" clause was a catch-all phrase for cases that did not fit other statutory circumstances. Finally, although Justices Marshall and Brennan concurred with the ruling, they reiterated their minority view that the death penalty was unconstitutional under all circumstances and remarked that *Gregg* was doomed to failure.

The Return of Capital Punishment

On June 2, 1967, Luis José Monge was put to death in Colorado for the crime of murder. He was the last person to be executed in the United States before capital punishment was suspended later that year, and for a full decade capital punishment ceased to exist in the United States. With the decision in *Gregg,* however, made on the eve of the nation's 200th birthday, the Supreme Court upheld the constitutionality of capital punishment. By 1977, more than 400 persons were on death row, with the first execution occurring early in that year.

The prisoner was Gary Mark Gilmore, a convicted murderer who had been sentenced to death by a Utah court. The Gilmore case attracted national headlines, not only because it was the first execution in a decade but also because of the many bizarre events associated with it. The initial sensation came late in 1976 when Gilmore fired his attorneys, abandoned his appeal, and requested that his execution be carried out at the earliest possible date. He even appeared before the U.S. Supreme Court to argue that he had a "right to die."

Attorneys then petitioned the Utah courts, indicating that Gilmore was insane, that he was incapable of representing himself, and that his death wish was "tantamount to suicide." But the state court rejected this argument, and all pending appeals were dismissed. Gilmore's mother then petitioned the U.S. Supreme Court, maintaining that her son was not competent to waive his right to appeal. The stay of execution that she requested was denied, however, on the basis that she had no legal standing to seek relief for her son.

Further sensation came on the morning of November 16, 1976, when Gilmore attempted suicide by taking an overdose of sedatives. At almost the same moment, some 40 miles south of the prison in a small apartment just outside Provo, Utah, 20-year-old Nicole Barrett also took an overdose of drugs. The suicide pact had been arranged as part of a pathetic love affair that Gilmore had been carrying on with the young woman. But Gilmore survived the ordeal, as did Barrett.

Counsel was then appointed to help Gilmore secure an execution date. It was later revealed that this attorney had a financial interest in Gilmore's death, having gained the exclusive right to act as the condemned man's biographer and agent; a six-figure contract had been negotiated for publication and motion picture rights to the story of Gilmore's life and death. "Gary Gilmore" T-shirts also appeared, and media bidding wars for exclusive interviews and stories began.

Independent legal groups challenged the courts, and Gilmore, angered by the new delays, staged another unsuccessful suicide attempt. The Supreme Court elected not to intervene in any further litigation, and an execution date was finally set. As the day approached, the media and pro- and antideath groups held a death watch outside the prison. During his final hours, Gilmore refused any interviews. There was another stay of execution, but it lasted only a few hours. Gilmore was scheduled to die by firing squad, and while he was being led to the execution chamber, mobile television crews attempted to position themselves to record the gunshots. When asked by Warden Samuel W. Smith if he had any last words, Gilmore offered nothing philosophical or dramatic—simply, "Let's do it!" Finally, just after dawn on January 17, 1977, Gilmore was strapped to a wooden chair in a cold and shadowy prison warehouse. At 8:07 A.M., a signal was given to marksmen hidden behind a cubicle 30 feet from the prisoner. Four .30-caliber bullets ripped through his chest, and Gary Mark Gilmore became the first person to be executed in an American prison in almost a decade.[69] (For a discussion of the number of women executed in recent history, see Exhibit 13.4.)

Executions Around the World

What country has the greatest number of executions? The United States? Egypt? Angola? Iran? Italy? China? South Africa? Somewhere else? Where?

During the 1990s, a number of countries abolished the death penalty, but the United States remains as the only Western democracy to retain capital punishment. That includes all of Western Europe, defined as any nation west of Turkey. To gain entry into the Council of Europe, even Russia ended executions in 1999.

The number of executions in many Middle Eastern countries tends to be high, far more than in the United States. But according to Amnesty International, the greatest number of executions occur in China—several thousand every year, although exact figures remain unknown.

Source: Amnesty International. ■

If they are serious about using the death penalty as a deterrent, they should let the people see it. Televise it on the networks.

—JAMES AUTRY, EXECUTED
IN TEXAS IN 1984

It is sweet to dance to violins
When love and life are fair;
To dance to flutes, to dance to lutes
Is delicate and rare;
But it is not so sweet with nimble feet
To dance upon the air.

—OSCAR WILDE

Gender Perspectives on Crime and Justice | EXHIBIT 13.4

Women on Death Row

Throughout U.S. history, the rate at which women have been sentenced to death and actually executed has remained quite small in comparison to men. Women account for only 10 percent of all murder arrests and only 1.6 percent of the death sentences imposed. Actual executions of women offenders in America have been quite rare, totaling only 567 documented instances since the first occurred in 1632 through late 2005. These 567 executions constitute less than 3 percent of the more than 20,000 confirmed executions in the United States since 1608. The only 11 women executed since 1976 have been Frances Newton on September 14, 2005; Aileen Wuornos in Florida on October 9, 2002; Lynda Lyon Block in Alabama on May 10, 2002; Lois Nadean Smith in Oklahoma on December 4, 2001; Marilyn Plantz in Oklahoma on May 1, 2001; Wanda Jean Allen in Oklahoma on January 11, 2001; Christina Marie Riggs in Arkansas on May 2, 2000; Bettie Lou Beets in Texas on February 24, 2000; Judy Buenoano in Florida on March 30, 1998; Karla Faye Tucker in Texas on February 3, 1998; and Velma Barfield in North Carolina on November 2, 1984. Prior to this, the last woman offender executed was Elizabeth Ann Duncan, in California on August 8, 1962.

During the past three decades only 152 death sentences have been imposed on women offenders, and of these only 48 sentences remained in effect as of late 2005. In addition to the 11 that resulted in execution, the rest were either reversed or commuted to life imprisonment. Of the 48 women on death row, a slight majority were there as the result of killings associated with other crimes—robberies, burglaries, drug deals, and the like. Of the others, they had murdered their husbands or boyfriends (or had arranged for the killing) or their children, grandchildren, or relatives. What this suggests is that women are far more likely than men to end up on death row for family-related murders. This should not imply that killings by women are less serious or gruesome. Some of these women murdered their victims by shooting with an AK-47, slicing with a box cutter, injecting with drain cleaner, and beating with a baseball bat. Or consider Kelly O'Donnell, sentenced for killing a Philadelphia man in 1992. With her boyfriend, O'Donnell dismembered the victim, pieces of whom were found in trash bags along the shores of the Delaware River and on the street where she lived. One of the victim's eyes and eyelids, furthermore, was found in a pencil case in O'Donnell's apartment.

With the exception of 38-year-old Karla Faye Tucker, executed in Texas on February 3, 1998, women have rarely made headlines for being put to death. The murder for which Tucker was convicted and sentenced to death had been especially vicious. On June 12, 1983, she killed two people with a pickax, and boasted, just after the killings, that she had experienced a surge of sexual pleasure every time she swung the weapon. But that was not why her case received so much attention. What was troubling to many was that during her years on death row she went from a strung-out killer with a pickax to a penitent, committed Christian. Her supporters, who included Bianca Jagger, Pope John Paul II, and televangelist Pat Robertson, argued that it was a dif-

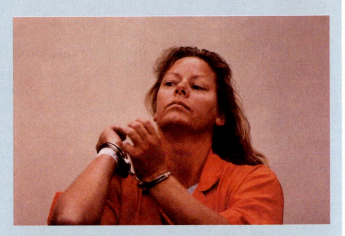

Charlize Theron won an Academy Award for her portrayal of serial killer Aileen Wuornos in the 2003 movie Monster. *Which is the real Aileen Wuornos?*

ferent Karla Faye Tucker who was scheduled to die—she was not the same person who committed the ax murders so many years earlier.

Interestingly, many prosecutors around the country spoke of "equality for women" when Tucker was executed, suggesting that women had indeed achieved equal rights in capital litigation, that they were being held just as accountable for their actions as men are. Given the small percentage of women who are on death row and the even smaller number who are actually executed, one could argue that there may be gender bias at work, that women are screened out of the death penalty track. But on the other hand, it must also be remembered that women commit only a small fraction of the kinds of murders that qualify for capital punishment.

Sources: *The New York Times,* February 8, 1998, sec. 4, pp. 1, 3; Victor L. Streib, "Death Penalty for Female Offenders: January 1, 1973, to June 30, 2003," *http://www.law.onu .edu/faculty/streib/femdeath.htm;* Death Penalty Information Center, "Women and the Death Penalty," May 2005; see also the Center's Web site at *www.deathpenaltyinfo.org.*

Seventeen-year-old Willie Francis, one of the few men ever to have come out of the electric chair alive.

FAMOUS CRIMINALS
Willie Francis

A small note in contemporary American folklore suggests that if the state bungles its attempt to electrocute a convicted killer, it can't try again and the prisoner gets to go free. True or false? The strange case of Willie Francis provides the answer.

On May 3, 1946, 17-year-old Willie Francis, convicted in the murder of a Texas pharmacist, was strapped into the electric chair at the Louisiana State Penitentiary. After the switch was thrown, Francis jumped; he strained against the straps and then groaned. But he didn't die! The switch was thrown again and again. For 2 minutes the procedure was repeated before the panel of horrified spectators.

The electrodes were then removed from Francis's body, and everyone in the jailhouse breathed a sigh of relief. Francis managed to get to his feet and later said that he had felt only a small current of electricity.

The story made headlines across the country, and the governor of Louisiana was engulfed with letters imploring him not to send the youth through the experience again.

Francis appealed to the U.S. Supreme Court, asking it to forbid the state a second execution attempt because that would constitute "cruel and unusual punishment" in violation of the Eighth Amendment.

(continued on p. 439)

Methods of Execution

Paralleling the debate over the constitutionality of the death penalty has been controversy over whether particular methods of execution are constitutional and humane. In a series of decisions spanning the period from 1878 through 1953, the Supreme Court has upheld as constitutional various methods of execution, including hanging, shooting, electrocution, and the use of lethal gas. As of late 2005, there were 35 states with a death penalty in force (see Exhibit 13.5); a number of them allow more than one mode of execution.

While electrocution is generally instantaneous, many consider the use of cyanide gas to be more humane. The well-known "gas chamber," however, also seems to be a grim process. An eyewitness described the 1967 execution of Luis José Monge:

> According to the official execution log unconsciousness came more than five minutes after the cyanide splashed down into the sulfuric acid. Even after unconsciousness is declared officially, the prisoner's body continues to fight for life. He coughs and groans. The lips make little pouting motions resembling the motions made by a goldfish in a bowl. The head strains back and then slowly sinks down to the chest. And in Monge's case, the arms, though tightly bound to the chair, strained through the straps and the hands clawed torturously as if the prisoner were struggling for air.[70]

Interestingly, in 1994 a federal district court declared execution by lethal gas to be in violation of the Eighth Amendment ban against cruel and unusual punishment. In making the decision, presiding Judge Marilyn Hall Patel stated that California's gas chamber at San Quentin Prison, where almost 200 prisoners had been executed since 1938, was a "brutal relic with no place in civilized society and must be immediately shut down."[71] Rejecting the state's assertion that cyanide gas causes virtually instant unconsciousness, Judge Patel cited doctors' reports and witnesses' accounts of numerous past executions as evidence that dying inmates remain conscious for up to a minute or longer. In that time, she said, the inmate is likely to suffer intense physical pain, mainly an "air hunger" similar to that experienced during strangulation or drowning. The ruling prescribed lethal injection for all future executions in California.

Although the Supreme Court has upheld the constitutionality of electrocution, death in the electric chair would appear to be a rather grim process. Almost 80 years ago, Warden Lewis E. Lawes of Sing Sing Prison described it this way:

> The condemned prisoner undergoing electrocution at Sing Sing Prison is given one shock of . . . alternating current at an average starting potential of approximately 2,000 volts. This voltage is immediately reduced at the end of three seconds to the neighborhood of 500 volts where it is held for an additional period of 57 seconds. . . .
>
> This initial force sends a startling current of 8 to 10 amperes through the human body, which causes instantaneous death and unconsciousness by its paralysis and destruction to the brain. The current is then cut down under the lower voltages to from 3 to 4 amperes in order to avoid burning the body and at the same time to hold paralysis of the heart, respiratory organs, and brain at a standstill for the remaining period of execution. This insures complete destruction of all life.
>
> As the switch is thrown into its socket there is a sputtering drone, and the body leaps as if to break the strong leather straps that hold it. Sometimes a thin gray wisp of smoke pushes itself out from under the helmet that holds the head electrode, followed by the faint odor of burning flesh. The hands turn red, then white, and the cords of the neck stand out like steel bands. . . .
>
> If temperatures are taken during and immediately after an application of electricity it will be found that the electrodes making the contact may reach a temperature high enough to melt copper . . . and that the average body temperature will be in the neighborhood of 140 degrees . . . and that the temperature of the brain itself approaches the boiling point of water. . . .
>
> Although it would be absolutely impossible to revive any person after electrocution in Sing Sing's death chair, an autopsy is immediately performed as provided by law. Thus justice grinds out its grist; the hand of the law drops a living man or woman into the death-house hopper, where the chair and the surgeons' knives and saws convert it into the finished product—a grisly corpse.[72]

Gas chamber, Maryland State Penitentiary, Baltimore.

(*continued from p. 438*)

The High Court ruled against his petition, however, and on May 9, 1946, Willie Francis was again strapped into the electric chair. The switch was thrown, and on this occasion his coffin could be used, and the crowd was not disappointed.

Source: See *Louisiana ex rel. Francis* v. *Resweber*, 329 U.S. 459 (1947).

Only three states—Delaware, New Hampshire, and Washington—still offer execution by hanging. Many a defense attorney has vividly described execution via the hangman's noose in an attempt to sway jurors away from imposing a death sentence. This was most effectively done in the case of Mark McKinney, who had been convicted of a 1980 homicide:

> He will walk thirteen steps to the gallows. He will stand, and a hood, black in color, will be placed over his head. A noose with thirteen knots will be dropped over his shoulders and pulled around his neck. There will be an executioner, whom we do not know, who will stand removed, and Mark will stand over a trap door. The executioner will push a button which will cause the trap door to spring open, and Mark will drop between four to six feet. The rope will constrict around his neck, causing him to die.[73]

For inmates sentenced to death under federal statutes, the method of execution is governed by the law of the state in which the punishment is to be carried out.

Lethal Injection Perhaps the most intense arguments regarding the nature of execution emerged in 1977 when a number of states enacted statutes that retired their electric chairs, gas chambers, and gallows. In their place was death by lethal injection, referred to by many death row inmates as "the ultimate high."

Proponents of the new process argued that it would be a more palatable way of killing—it would be instantaneous, and the prisoner would simply fall asleep.[74] Opponents countered that sticking a needle into a vein can be tricky, with the prospect of repeated attempts upon a struggling prisoner posing "a substantial threat of torturous pain."[75] The American Medical Association also took a stand on the matter, instructing its members not to take part in such executions and arguing that the role of the physician is to protect lives, not take them.[76]

Despite the arguments, the new method of execution went forward. On December 7, 1982, Charles Brooks, Jr., was put to death in Huntsville, Texas, becoming the first person to die by a state-sanctioned lethal injection. First a catheter was placed into the vein of his left arm; through it flowed a saline solution—a sterile saltwater rou-

EXHIBIT 13.5 | LAW & CRIMINAL JUSTICE

The Death Penalty, 1976–2005

Inmates on Death Row, Total Executions Since 1976, and Methods of Execution

State	Number of Inmates [a]	Number Executed [b]	Method
Alabama	191	34	Electrocution, injection
Alaska	No death penalty		
Arizona	128	22	Gas, injection
Arkansas	38	26	Injection, electrocution
California	648	11	Gas, injection
Colorado	3	1	Injection
Connecticut	8	1	Injection
Delaware	19	14	Injection
District of Columbia	No death penalty		
Florida	388	60	Electrocution, injection
Georgia	112	39	Injection
Hawaii	No death penalty		
Idaho	21	1	Injection, firing squad
Illinois	10	12	Injection, electrocution
Indiana	30	16	Injection
Iowa	No death penalty		
Kansas [c]	7	0	Injection
Kentucky	37	2	Electrocution, injection
Louisiana	89	27	Injection
Maine	No death penalty		
Maryland	9	4	Gas, injection
Massachusetts	No death penalty		
Michigan	No death penalty		
Minnesota	No death penalty		
Mississippi	70	6	Injection
Missouri	55	66	Injection, gas
Montana	4	2	Injection

tinely used as a medium for drug injections. Brooks was then given intravenous doses of barbiturates and potassium chloride, which paralyzed him, stopped his breathing, and caused his death.[77] Ironically, on Brooks's arm, above the catheter through which the deadly concoction flowed, was a tattoo that read, "I was born to die."

In the middle of the 1980s, the debate over the humanity of lethal injections subsided, while others argued against the brutal nature of electrocution. By the beginning of the 1990s, however, injection had become the primary mechanism, followed by electrocution.

The Death Penalty Debate

Historically the arguments for or against capital punishment have revolved around the issues of economics, retribution, public opinion, community protection, deterrence, irreversibility, discrimination, protection of the criminal justice system, brutalization, and cruel and unusual punishment.

State	Number of Inmates[a]	Number Executed[b]	Method
Nebraska	10	3	Electrocution
Nevada	85	11	Injection
New Hampshire	0	0	Hanging, injection
New Jersey	14	0	Injection
New Mexico	2	1	Injection
New York[d]	2	0	Injection
North Carolina	192	38	Injection
North Dakota	No death penalty		
Ohio	196	18	Injection
Oklahoma	97	79	Injection, electrocution, firing squad
Oregon	32	2	Injection
Pennsylvania	233	3	Injection
Rhode Island	No death penalty		
South Carolina	77	34	Electrocution, injection
South Dakota	4	0	Injection
Tennessee	108	1	Electrocution, injection
Texas	414	355	Injection
Utah	10	6	Injection
Vermont	No death penalty		
Virginia	23	94	Electrocution, injection
Washington	10	4	Hanging, injection
West Virginia	No death penalty		
Wisconsin	No death penalty		
Wyoming	2	1	Injection, gas
Federal jurisdictions	36	3	Injection
Total	**3,415**[e]	**997**	

[a] Number on death row as of late 2005.

[b] Number of inmates executed as of late 2005.

[c] Kansas' death penalty was declared unconstitutional on December 17, 2004.

[d] New York's death penalty was declared unconstitutional on June 24, 2004.

[e] Some inmates are sentenced to death in more than one state.

Sources: Death Penalty Information Center; NAACP Legal Defense and Educational Fund, Inc.

The Economic Argument The economic argument for capital punishment holds that execution is far less expensive than maintaining a prisoner behind bars for the rest of his or her natural life. However, death sentences are invariably appealed, and the appeals can also be costly. In fact, every available quantitative study of this argument demonstrates that because of all of the additional appeals and other procedural safeguards that are constitutionally required in capital cases, the death penalty costs taxpayers substantially more than life imprisonment.[78]

The Retribution Argument The retribution argument asserts that kidnappers, murderers, and rapists are vile and despicable human beings and deserve to die. This is simply a matter of individual opinion, and differences in philosophy appear even within the Supreme Court. In *Furman*, Justice Thurgood Marshall spoke against this position. At the same time, however, the Court stated that while retribution was no longer a dominant objective, "neither is it a forbidden objective nor one inconsistent with our respect for the dignity of men."

A hangman is an officer of the law charged with the duties of the highest dignity and utmost gravity, and held in hereditary disesteem by a populace having a criminal ancestry. In some of the American states his functions are now performed by an electrician, as in New Jersey, where executions by electricity have recently been ordered.

—AMBROSE BIERCE,
THE DEVIL'S DICTIONARY

Hanging someone wasn't really something in our knowledge base.

—VELTRY JOHNSON OF THE WASHINGTON STATE CORRECTIONS DEPARTMENT, ON TRYING TO FIND A COMPETENT HANGMAN IN A STATE WHERE NO ONE HAD BEEN EXECUTED IN ALMOST THREE DECADES

If there were a death penalty, more people would be alive.

—NANCY REAGAN

Capital punishment is our society's recognition of the sanctity of human life.

—SENATOR ORRIN HATCH

The gallows at Washington State Penitentiary, Walla Walla. The noose into which the prisoner's head is placed hangs over a trap door. The prisoner is strapped to the board at the left, and then the trap door is sprung.

The Public Opinion Argument Public opinion has been a motivating factor in the enactment of death penalty statutes. When the California Supreme Court declared the state's death penalty law unconstitutional in February 1972, letters and telegrams opposing the decision poured into the legislature and governor's office. In a referendum held later that year, 5 months after *Furman,* California voters overwhelmingly approved an amendment to the state constitution that made capital punishment mandatory for selected crimes.[79] In the years since, throughout the United States, every poll on the matter has found that the vast majority of Americans favor the death penalty for murder.[80]

The Community Protection Argument The community protection argument made by supporters of the death penalty maintains that such a "final remedy" is necessary to keep the murderer from further ravaging society. Counter to this position is the claim that life imprisonment could achieve the same goal. Yet, as has been pointed out by a number of studies, paroled murderers have lower rates of recidivism than other classes of offenders. For example, in a study of 558 inmates sentenced to death, four were later found to be innocent; of 239 who were eventually released from prison, just 20 percent committed new crimes, and only one of these crimes was a homicide. The conclusion of the study was that these inmates did not pose a "disproportionate danger" to society. In Texas, where "future dangerousness" is used as a determining factor in the death sentencing of a defendant, a recent study of 155 cases concluded that the experts who predicted the defendant's future dangerousness were wrong 95 percent of the time.[81]

The Deterrence Argument Related to community protection is the deterrence argument, which holds that capital punishment not only prevents the offender from committing additional crimes but deters others as well. With respect to deterrence in general, the research of Franklin E. Zimring and Gordon J. Hawkins demonstrated that punishment is an effective deterrent for those who are not predisposed to commit crimes but a questionable deterrent for those who are criminally inclined.[82] A number of studies have also been done specifically on the deterrent effects of capital punishment. One research strategy for such studies has been to compare the homicide rates in states that have death penalty provisions with homicide rates in states that do not. Another has been to examine murder rates in given areas both before and after an execution. And still a third approach has been to analyze crime rates in general as well as murder rates in particular in jurisdictions before and after the abolition of capital punishment. Regardless of the nature and logic of the inquiry applied, the studies have consistently produced no evidence that the death penalty deters homicide.[83]

The Irreversibility Argument The irreversibility argument put forth by those opposed to the death penalty contends that there is always the possibility that an innocent person might be put to death. Those who support the death penalty maintain that although such a risk might exist, there are no documented cases of such an occurrence in recent years. But in reality there are many such cases. Researchers Michael L. Radelet, Hugo Adam Bedau, and Constance E. Putnam documented as of 1992 that during the 20th century there were 416 instances of erroneous convictions in capital cases.[84] Since 1973, 119 people in 25 states have been released from death row with evidence of their innocence, which means that approximately one person has been exonerated for every eight people executed. Some are released because of procedural errors, but for others it is because DNA evidence demonstrates their innocence.[85] Most recently, in one of the most exhaustive studies of capital punishment ever, a team of Columbia University researchers found that of the 5,760 individuals sentenced to death nationwide between 1973 and 1995, only 5 percent were actually executed. And when capital cases were sent back for a new trial, 7 percent of the defendants were found not guilty and less than 20 percent of those who were convicted received another death sentence. Importantly, of the 4,578 cases that were appealed, the researchers found that there were serious legal flaws in more than two-thirds. The most common causes of

CAREERS IN CRIMINAL JUSTICE

Advocacy for the Abolition of the Death Penalty

Although a majority of Americans consider the death penalty to be the appropriate punishment for first-degree murder, there are many who do not. Furthermore, scores of individuals are so opposed to the death penalty that they devote either part of their free time or their entire careers to advocating the abolition of capital statutes and helping death row inmates have their sentences appealed. Some of the most visible organizations are:

Death Penalty Information Center. The DPIC is a nonprofit organization serving the media and the public with analysis and information on capital punishment. Founded in 1990, the center prepares in-depth reports, issues press releases, conducts briefings for journalists, and serves as a resource for those working on the issue (**http://www.deathpenaltyinfo.org**).

Amnesty International. The object of Amnesty International is to foster the observance of human rights throughout the world. One of its mandates is opposition to the death penalty and to the torture or other cruel, inhuman, or degrading treatment or punishment of prisoners or other detained persons (**http://www.amnesty.org**).

American Civil Liberties Union. The ACLU is a 50-state network with 60 staff attorneys and some 2,000 volunteer attorneys who handle almost 6,000 cases annually. The mission of the ACLU is to ensure that the Bill of Rights is preserved, and in this context it maintains that capital punishment is a violation of the Eighth Amendment ban against cruel and unusual punishment (**http://www.aclu.org**).

National Coalition to Abolish the Death Penalty. The NCADP, which has been the only fully staffed national organization solely dedicated to capital punishment, advocates for public policy, provides information, and mobilizes and supports institutions and individuals that share its absolute rejection of capital punishment (**http://www.ncadp.org**).

The Sentencing Project. This nonprofit organization advocates equitable and humane alternatives to incarceration and the death penalty. The project analyzes criminal justice policy and regularly produces reports and publications that are widely used by policy makers, the media, researchers, and the public alike (**www.sentencingproject.org**).

Human Rights Watch. Human Rights Watch is dedicated to defending human rights worldwide. The group champions a number of causes, including opposing the death penalty, by publishing reports and orchestrating political campaigns to promote change in criminal justice policies (**www.hrw.org/campaigns/deathpenalty/**).

---

error were "egregiously incompetent defense attorneys who missed demonstrably important evidence, and police and prosecutors who did discover that kind of evidence but suppressed it." Similarly, a study of 76 inmates released from death row between 1970 and 1998 because of doubts about their guilt concluded that prosecutorial or police misconduct, perjury, and racial discrimination were most often the factors that influenced the wrongful convictions.[86]

One could readily argue that since most of the convictions were ultimately reversed and the defendant's life spared, the moral issue is easily dodged. Yet the very same reasoning can be used to support the irreversibility argument—that wrongful convictions do indeed happen, and only through luck and circumstance have many of the victims managed to escape death. But not everyone has managed to escape death. Research by Radelet and Bedau uncovered compelling evidence that since 1900, at least 23 innocent defendants have gone to their deaths knowing all too well that no system of justice is perfect. However, others have criticized the study's conclusions.[87] In all reality, innocents have indeed been executed over the years, and no one can know for certain just how many.

The Discrimination Argument The discrimination argument against capital punishment contends that the death penalty is a lottery system, with the odds stacked heavily against those who are less capable of defending themselves. As Justice Thurgood Marshall wrote in his concurring opinion in *Furman* v. *Georgia*:

> It also is evident that the burden of capital punishment falls upon the poor, the ignorant, and the underprivileged members of society. It is the poor, and the members of minority groups who are least able to voice their complaints against capital punishment. Their impotence leaves them victims of a sanction which the wealthier, better-represented, just-as-guilty person can escape. So long as the capital sanction is used only against the forlorn, easily forgotten members of society, legislators are content to maintain the status quo, because

We are all sentenced to death—it is part of our life sentence. . . . But execution is probably less painful than most natural ways of dying.

— DEATH PENALTY ADVOCATE ERNEST VAN DEN HAAG

I believe capital punishment to be an appropriate remedy for anyone who does me injury, but under no other circumstances.

— ATTORNEY F. LEE BAILEY

I go to sleep and I dream of me sitting down in that chair. I mean it's such a fearful thought. Me walking down the tier, sitting down in it, them hooking it up and turning it on. . . . I can wake up, my heart's beating fast, I'm sweating like hell, just like I'd rinsed my head in water. . . . I feel I'm gonna have a heart attack.

— ALABAMA DEATH ROW PRISONER

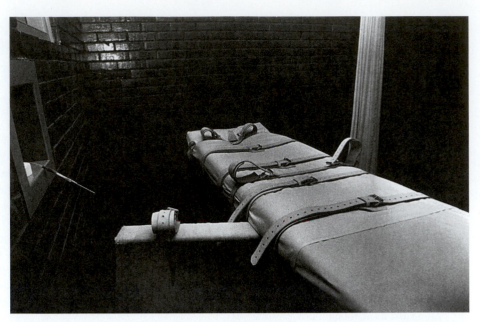

The hospital-type gurney used in Texas executions by injection. Restraints rest on top of the gurney and an intravenous needle is visible in the observation window. Murderer Charles Brooks, Jr., was the first criminal in the United States to be executed by this method, on December 7, 1982. Karla Faye Tucker was also executed here on February 3, 1998.

There is no great difficulty to separate the soul from the body, but it is not so easy to restore life to the dead.

— MUSHARRIF-UDDIN, 1258

I'm pro-death. I believe in the death penalty. Let's get on with it.

— CHICAGO MAYOR RICHARD M. DALEY, ON THE SEPTEMBER 1990 EXECUTION OF CONVICTED MURDERER CHARLES WALKER

change would draw attention to the problem and concern might develop. Ignorance is perpetuated and apathy soon becomes its mate, and we have today's situation.

Analyses of the social characteristics of death row inmates suggest that the death penalty continues to be employed in a selective and discriminatory manner. Studies indicate that a disproportionate number of individuals sentenced to death are members of minority groups, and nearly all inmates on death rows across the United States are indigents—too poor to afford private counsel—who had to rely on a state-supplied attorney.[88] The federal courts have rejected this claim, however, even when arguments have been grounded in precise statistical studies. In *McCleskey* v. *Zant*,[89] a 1984 Georgia case, the U.S. District Court held that statistical data "are incapable of producing evidence on whether racial factors play a part in the imposition of the death penalty in any particular case."

The Protection of the Criminal Justice System Argument

The protection of the criminal justice system argument against capital punishment holds that the very nature of death penalty statutes hinders equity in the administration of justice. As noted by the President's Crime Commission:

> Whatever views one may have about the efficacy of the death penalty as a deterrent, it clearly has an undesirable impact on the administration of justice. The trial of a capital case is a stirring drama, but that is perhaps its most dangerous attribute. Selecting a jury often requires several days; each objection or point of law requires excessive deliberation because of the irreversible consequences of error. The jury's concern with the death penalty may result in unwarranted acquittals and there is increased danger that public sympathy will be aroused for the defendant, regardless of his guilt of the crime charged.[90]

The Brutalization Argument

The brutalization argument holds that executions actually *cause* homicides, rather than deter them. William J. Bowers extensively analyzed numerous studies of both the short-term and long-term effects of executions on homicide rates. He demonstrated that executions cause a slight but discernible increase in the murder rate. This "brutalizing effect," he noted, typically occurs within the first 2 months after an execution and dissipates thereafter. Bowers's explanation is that the effect is most likely to occur among those who have reached a state of "readi-

International Perspectives on Crime & Justice | EXHIBIT 13.6

The Death Penalty in the Caribbean Basin

Although more than half of the world's countries have now abolished the death penalty in law or practice, it retains widespread popularity throughout the English-speaking countries of the eastern Caribbean. Based on British common law, the legal interpretation in many Caribbean countries not only has permitted the death penalty as a means of punishment but actually imposes it as mandatory for all those convicted of murder.

The London-based Judicial Committee of the Privy Council (JCPC) has acted as the final Court of Appeal for many Caribbean nations since gaining their independence from England. But in recent years the council has handed down several decisions on the death penalty that have angered its former possessions. In 2003, for example, the council declared Trinidad and Tobago's mandatory death penalty unconstitutional, ruling that death should be imposed only as the maximum punishment for the most serious killings, rather than a mandatory sentence in every case. The council has blocked 100 executions in Trinidad and Tobago since 1993; this most recent ruling means that the 80 men and 4 women currently on death row can apply to have their sentences reviewed.

In 2002, the JCPC unanimously ruled Belize's mandatory death penalty unconstitutional on the basis that it violates laws prohibiting "inhuman and degrading punishment or treatment." The ruling also extended to other prisoners in the eastern Caribbean, including Antigua, Barbados, Dominica, Grenada, St. Kitts and Nevis, St. Lucia, and St. Vincent and the Grenadines. Also in 2002, the council ruled in three separate cases that the mandatory death sentence was unconstitutional in cases where the defendant was not allowed to present mitigating evidence. The rulings do not forbid the death penalty but allow mitigating evidence to be presented and taken into account prior to sentencing.

Because the independent nations of the Caribbean desire greater autonomy over legal matters, a Caribbean Court of Justice (CCJ) is under formation to take the place of the Privy Council's final jurisdiction. Many throughout the region feel that it is time for policy decisions to be finalized locally, rather than by a foreign judge who may be unfamiliar with local history, culture, and social issues. A former chief justice of Trinidad and Tobago sums up the sentiment shared by many regional leaders in saying that the CCJ will mark the "completion of our independence" from colonial rule.

And while the purpose of the court extends far beyond decisions regarding the death penalty, the court will likely be less opposed to executions as means of punishment.

Caribbean residents say they are fed up with the increase in brutal crime and drug-related violence, and many see death by hanging as an effective deterrent to such behavior. Opinion polls from across the region find strong support for the death penalty; for example, between 77% and 95% of residents in Trinidad and Tobago support it. Politicians capitalize on that, and those who run on get-tough-on-crime platforms and who publicly support the death penalty tend to fare well in elections. On the other hand, those who have worked to abolish the practice in the region have been subjected to threats of physical violence and are vilified by the general public as siding with criminals.

Once the CCJ starts hearing cases, it appears unlikely that the eastern Caribbean will join the ranks of others around the world that have abandoned the notion that death means justice.

Sources: Amnesty International, *http://web.amnesty.org/pages/deathpenalty-index-eng*; The Death Penalty Information Center, *www.deathpenaltyinfo.org*; Amnesty International, *State Killing in the English Speaking Caribbean: A Legacy of Colonial Times*, 2002, AI Index: AMR 05/003/2002; Clare Dyer, "Ruling Brings Hope to Death Row Caribbeans," *The Guardian*, November 21, 2003, 9; Bruce Zagaris, "Privy Council Declares Trinidad & Tobago Mandatory Death Penalty Illegal," *International Enforcement Law Reporter* 20, 1 (2004).

ness to kill"—a small subgroup of the population composed of individuals on the fringe of sanity for whom the suggestive or imitative message of the execution is that it is proper to kill those who betray, disgrace, or dishonor them.[91]

The Cruel and Unusual Punishment Argument Finally, the cruel and unusual punishment argument maintains that the death penalty is a violation of the constitutional right guaranteed by the Eighth Amendment. Supporters and opponents of capital punishment differ, however, in their interpretations of the cruel and unusual punishment clause. The former hold that capital punishment is cruel and unusual *in all circumstances*. The latter insist that a sentence of death is forbidden by the Eighth Amendment only when it is a disproportionate punishment for the crime committed. These conflicting views were the bases for the Supreme Court's rulings in both *Furman* and *Gregg*. (For a discussion of the death penalty in the Caribbean Basin, see Exhibit 13.6.)

Capital Punishment at the Beginning of the 21st Century

By the end of 1980, a total of 714 people were under sentence of death in the United States, and during the following year the death row population increased to more than 900. By mid-2005, this figure had climbed to almost 3,500.[92] And as the growing

Killing human beings is an act so awesome, so destructive, so irremediable that no killer can be looked upon with anything but horror, even when that killer is the state.

—HENRY SCHWARZSCHILD, AMERICAN CIVIL LIBERTIES UNION

Support for the Death Penalty (for Murder) in the United States

Source: The Gallup Organization.

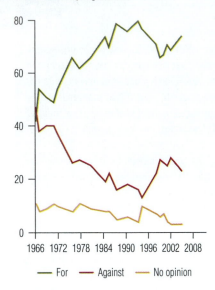

— For   — Against   — No opinion

Number of Persons on Death Row, 1953–2005

Sources: Bureau of Justice Statistics; Death Penalty Information Center.

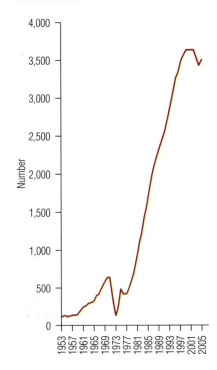

number of offenders awaiting death increased, so too did the number of executions. During the first 6 years after the reinstatement of capital punishment in 1976, there were only 6 executions. After that there were 5 in 1983, 21 in 1984, 18 in 1985, 70 from 1986 to 1989—and a grand total of 997 through late 2005. In fact, the number put to death in 1999 reached a 40-year high of 98 but it has sinced declined over time from 85 in 2000, to 65 in 2003, to 59 in 2004, and 53 through late 2005.

It can be argued that the number of executions may increase, for the next few years, for a variety of reasons. *First,* many death row inmates have exhausted their appeals. *Second,* the Supreme Court ruling in *Pulley* v. *Harris,*[93] decided in 1984, curtailed one avenue of appeal. Specifically, petitioner Robert Alton Harris had claimed that California's capital punishment statute was invalid under the Constitution because it failed to require the California Supreme Court to compare his sentence with others in similar capital cases and thereby determine whether they were proportionate. The U.S. Supreme Court held that Harris's claim was without merit, ruling that the Eighth Amendment prohibition of cruel and unusual punishment does not require, as an invariable rule in every case, a comparative proportionality review of capital sentences by an appellate court. *Third,* in *Barefoot* v. *Estelle,*[94] decided a year before *Pulley,* the Court limited the lengthy appeals process, stating, in effect, that federal appeals courts may compress the time they take to consider appeals as long as all the issues are covered adequately and on their merits. While the ruling in *Barefoot* mandated nothing, it suggested to federal appeals courts the possibility of adopting rules for granting stays of execution; moreover, it noted that stays of execution were not automatic upon the filing of petitions of *certiorari.* And *finally,* since 1986 there have been a number of Supreme Court decisions reaffirming that capital punishment would remain a visible part of American justice. For example:

- In **Lockhart v. McCree,**[95] decided in 1986, the Court asserted that even if juries that support the death penalty are "conviction prone," this in itself does not violate any constitutional provisions (see Exhibit 13.7).
- In *McCleskey* v. *Kemp,*[96] decided in 1987, the Court held that statistical evidence of racial discrimination in death sentencing cannot, in and of itself, establish a violation of the Eighth and/or Fourteenth Amendments. The Court further held that to obtain relief, a defendant must prove either (1) that decision makers in his or her case acted with discriminatory purpose or (2) that the legislature enacted or maintained the death penalty statute *because of* an anticipated racially discriminatory effect.
- In **Tison v. Arizona,**[97] also decided in 1987, the Court held that a defendant who does not intend to commit murder and who does not actually commit murder may be executed when he or she participates in a felony that leads to murder and is found to have exhibited "reckless indifference" for human life.
- In *Penry* v. *Lynaugh,* decided in 1989, the Court ruled, in effect, that the death penalty could be imposed on mentally retarded defendants. However, in the 2002 case of *Atkins* v. *Virginia,* the Court ruled that the execution of mentally retarded defendants constitutes cruel and unusual punishment in violation of the Eighth Amendment.[98]
- In perhaps the most controversial ruling, *Herrera* v. *Collins,*[99] decided in 1993, the Court ruled that death row inmates in all but the most extraordinary cases will not be entitled to bring a federal *habeas corpus* petition claiming "actual innocence" based on newly discovered evidence; the Court *refused to hold that the Eighth Amendment prohibits the execution of innocent persons.*
- In *Delo* v. *Lashley,*[100] decided in 1993, the Court held that a trial judge is not obliged to instruct a jury on a particular mitigating circumstance if the defendant does not proffer any evidence to support the truth of the mitigating circumstance.
- In *Gary* v. *Netherland,*[101] decided in 1996, the Court held that a prisoner who has been sentenced to death is not permitted to bring a federal appeal claiming that prosecutors "ambushed" him by introducing surprise evidence at his sentencing hearing.

LAW & CRIMINAL JUSTICE | EXHIBIT 13.7

Lockhart v. *McCree* and the "Death-Qualified" Jury

In *Witherspoon* v. *Illinois,* decided in 1968, the United States Supreme Court held that in capital cases states cannot exclude from juries *all* persons opposed to the death penalty. To do so, the Court argued, would result in a jury that could not speak for the community. Constituted as such, a jury would be "death-qualified" and thus represent a violation of due process. But the justices held that jurors could be excluded for cause if their scruples against the death penalty were so strong that they would automatically vote against the imposition of capital punishment *regardless of the evidence.* Such jurors have become known as "*Witherspoon* excludables." Moreover, the ruling applied only to juries involved in sentencing decisions, leaving open the question of whether "death-qualification" tainted a guilty or not-guilty verdict. *Lockhart* v. *McCree,* decided by the Court in 1986, addressed this latter issue.

In 1978, Ardia McCree had been charged with capital felony murder. In accordance with Arkansas law, the trial judge at *voir dire* removed for cause, over McCree's objections, prospective jurors who stated that they could never vote for the imposition of the death penalty. McCree was convicted, and although the prosecution had requested a capital sentence, the jury set the punishment at life imprisonment without the possibility of parole.

On appeal before the Eighth Circuit Court of Appeals,* McCree argued two points. First, he claimed that the removal for cause of the *Witherspoon*-excludable prospective jurors violated his right under the Sixth and Fourteenth Amendments to have his guilt or innocence determined by an impartial jury selected from a representative cross section of the community. Second, McCree maintained that the absence of the *Witherspoon* excludables slanted the jury in favor of conviction. He produced the findings of a variety of studies that suggested the juries in question were indeed conviction-prone.

When the court of appeals ruled in favor of McCree, sending the matter to the U.S. Supreme Court, *Lockhart* suddenly became the most important death penalty case in the 1980s. Only days before the Court finally released its opinion on May 5, 1986, there were more than 1,700 inmates housed on death rows nationally, most of whom had been convicted by death-qualified juries. An affirmation of the circuit court decision would have meant new trials for several hundred inmates awaiting execution.

* *Lockhart* v. *McCree,* 39 CrL 3085 (1986).

To the bewilderment of civil libertarians, the Court ruled against McCree by a 6-to-3 majority. It was the opinion of the Court that the death-qualification process does not cast doubt on the impartiality of anyone chosen to be on a jury and that the Constitution does not require that a trial jury hold a balance of viewpoints or attitudes.

At the heart of the Court's decision was the issue of whether the Sixth Amendment required that a jury represent a fair cross section of a community:

> The essence of a "fair cross-section" claim is the systematic exclusion of a "distinctive" group in the community.
>
> In our view groups defined solely in terms of shared attitudes that would prevent or substantially impair members of the group from performing one of their duties as jurors, such as the "*Witherspoon* excludables" at issue here, are not "distinctive groups" for fair cross-section purposes.
>
> "Death-qualification," unlike the wholesale exclusion of blacks, women, or Mexican Americans from jury service, is carefully designed to serve the state's concededly legitimate interest in obtaining a single jury that can properly and impartially apply the law to the facts of the case at both the guilt and sentencing phases of a capital trial.

As to the many studies that addressed the purported conviction-prone nature of death-qualified juries,[†] the Court had examined them closely. But Justice Rehnquist noted:

> We have serious doubts about the value of these studies in predicting the behavior of actual jurors. In addition, two of the three "new" studies did not even attempt to simulate the process of jury deliberation, and none of the "new" studies was able to predict to what extent, if any, the presence of one or more "*Witherspoon* excludables" on a guilt-phase jury would have altered the outcome. . . .
>
> We will assume . . . that "death-qualification" in fact produces juries somewhat more "conviction-prone" than "non-death-qualified" juries. We hold, nonetheless, that the Constitution does not prohibit the States from "death-qualifying" juries in capital cases.

[†] Brief for *Amicus Curiae,* American Psychological Association in Support of Respondent, *Lockhart* v. *McCree,* on Writ of *Certiorari* to the United States Court of Appeals for the Eighth Circuit.

Yet these decisions in no way indicated that the Court had made up its mind on the death penalty. Quite the contrary. Even while public sentiment pushed for more rapid imposition of the death penalty, the justices argued among themselves about the merry-go-round of litigation that had come to characterize capital punishment cases. Thus, as the pace of executions first increased, then ebbed, and then increased once again, the death rows of U.S. prisons were full of convicts preparing briefs. (For an overview of the death penalty in segments of the Islamic world, see Exhibit 13.8.)

EXHIBIT 13.8 | International Perspectives on Crime & Justice

The Death Penalty in the Islamic World

While the death penalty in the United States is presently restricted to the crime of murder, in some cultures capital statutes have a far broader scope. In Nigeria, although it is technically a secular democracy, Shariah, or Islamic law, has recently swept over its largely Muslim northern states. Shariah governs family law in many countries, but it has been directed toward criminal law in a few states including Saudi Arabia, Iran, and Afghanistan while it was under Taliban rule. Shariah rules many everyday issues including prayer and meals, custody battles, and sexual behavior.

This was the situation in a recent case out of northern Nigeria. Eight days after giving birth to her daughter, and 2 years following her divorce from her husband, Amina Lawal was arrested for adultery, a capital crime under Shariah. The man identified as the father of

Amina Lawal, a 31-year-old Nigerian woman, facing judges in an Islamic court. She was later cleared of a sentence that she be stoned to death for committing adultery.

the baby originally said that he didn't want children but later agreed to marry Lawal. However, when he was later questioned by the authorities regarding his paternity of the child, he swore on the Holy Koran that the child was not his. This man was then freed because according to Koranic law, there would have to be testimony of four witnesses to the sexual act itself in order for him to be found guilty of adultery. For Lawal, however, the evidence in the case against her was not as speculative. There was, after all, a newborn child as proof of her actions. Lawal confessed to the crime and was scheduled to be buried in the ground up to her chest and be stoned to death as soon as her daughter was weaned.

During one of Lawal's days in court, the judge said that although death by stoning may seem unkind, such a punishment is necessary to uphold the sanctity of marriage. Radicals have justified stoning through anecdotal information of its use during the time of the Prophet Muhammad and through the text of the Koran, which states that adulterous men and women should be flogged and that women guilty of fornication should be under house arrest until death or until "God ordains for

them another way." The chief prosecutor in Lawal's state has noted that to be stoned to death on earth is to be spared eternal hellfire in the hereafter. And additionally that "if you suffer punishment now, you will not suffer punishment in the hands of God."

In September 2003 an Islamic appeals court overturned the sentence of stoning. The five-judge panel stated that, as in the case of her boyfriend, Lawal was not caught in the act of fornication and that she did not have enough of an opportunity to defend herself. Although prosecutors argued that the child was proof of Lawal's actions, the defense lawyer said that under some interpretations of Shariah, a baby may stay in gestation in the mother's womb for up to 5 years, therefore making it possible that Lawal's ex-husband was in fact the father of the child.

Sources: Todd Pitman, "Nigeria Acquits Woman Sentenced to Death," *AOL News*, September 25, 2003; Somini Sengupta, "As Stoning Case Proceeds, Nigeria Stands Trial," *The New York Times*, January 26, 2003, 3; Simon Robinson, "Casting Stones: The Koran Says Nothing About Stoning, Why Is This Mother Facing Death?" *Time*, September 2, 2002, 36–37; *The Irish Times*, February 3, 2004, 8; *Toronto Star*, April 1, 2005, B4.

| Appellate Review |

An appeal is when you ask one court to show its contempt for another court.

— FINLEY PETER DUNNE

This brief utterance from the essays of the early 20th-century American journalist and humorist Finley Peter Dunne, although cynical and irreverent in tone, is essentially what appeal is all about. More accurately, an **appeal** is a complaint to a superior court of an injustice done or error committed by a lower court, whose judgment or decision the higher court is called upon to correct or reverse.

Despite the fact that appellate procedures exist throughout the federal and state court structures, the right of appeal was unknown in common law, and such a right was not incorporated into the Constitution. Moreover, the constitutionality of a state's denial of appellate review has never been decided by the U.S. Supreme Court, and the Court has often noted, *in dicta,** that such review is not constitutionally required.[102]

The Defendant's Right to Appeal

At the appellate stage, the presumption of innocence has evaporated, and the defendant is obliged to show why a conviction should be overturned. Thus, the nature of the adversary system changes, with the burden of proof shifting from the prosecution to the defense.

All jurisdictions have procedural rules requiring that objections to the admission (or exclusion) of evidence, or to some other procedure, be made by the defense either at a pretrial hearing or at the time that evidence or other procedure becomes an issue at trial. Failure to make a timely objection results in automatic forfeiture of the claim for appeal purposes. This requirement has been instituted so that trial judges can make rules and develop facts that will appear in the record and thus enable the appeals court to conduct an adequate review.

The Plain Error Rule
A notable exception to the timely objection requirement is the *plain error rule,* which is included in the *Federal Rules of Criminal Procedure* and the procedural rules of all state jurisdictions. Under this rule, "plain errors or defects affecting substantial rights" of defendants become subject to appellate review even though they may not have been properly raised at trial or during some prior appeal.[103] Thus, denial of the right to counsel at trial, the admission of an involuntary confession, or the negation of some other constitutional guarantee—even in the absence of a timely objection—are considered "plain errors" and hence appealable.

The Automatic Reversal Rule
On numerous occasions, the Supreme Court has held that certain constitutional errors are of such magnitude that they require automatic reversal of a conviction: hence, the *automatic reversal rule.* The Fourteenth Amendment's due process clause, for example, guarantees a fair trial before an impartial judge. Pursuant to this guarantee, the Court ruled in *Tumey* v. *Ohio,*[104] decided in 1927 by a unanimous vote, that an accused person is denied due process when tried before a judge with a direct, personal, pecuniary interest in ruling against him or her. At issue in *Tumey* was the fact that the petitioner had been tried in a city court whose judge was the mayor and from which fines were deposited in the city treasury. The Supreme Court found the lower court's error to be so significant that it mandated an automatic reversal of Tumey's conviction. Similarly, the Court considers as automatically reversible convictions in cases in which certain plain errors were made, such as the use of an involuntary confession at trial and the denial of counsel at trial in violation of its holding in *Gideon* v. *Wainwright.*[105]

The Harmless Error Rule
In *Chapman* v. *California,*[106] decided in 1967, the Supreme Court established the *harmless error rule,* holding that a denial of a federal constitutional right can at times be of insufficient magnitude to require reversal of a conviction on appeal. Known also as the *Chapman* rule, the "harmless error" doctrine has been applied by the Supreme Court and other appellate courts in numerous areas of constitutional dimension: evidence seized in violation of the Fourth Amendment, denial of counsel at a preliminary hearing, in-court identifications based on invalid pretrial identification procedures, and obtaining a confession from a defendant after indictment without expressly informing the defendant of his right to counsel.[107] When a

Appeal (verb). In law, to put the dice into the box for another throw.

—AMBROSE BIERCE,
THE DEVIL'S DICTIONARY

In dicta are expressions in an opinion of the court that do not necessarily support the decision.

court considers an error to be harmless, it is indicating that the mistake was not prejudicial to the rights of the accused and therefore made no difference in the subsequent conviction or sentence.

The Invited Error Rule Although uncommon, there have been instances when, during the course of a proceeding, the defense requests the court to make a ruling that is actually erroneous and the court does so. Under the *invited error rule,* the defense cannot take advantage of such an error on appeal or review.[108]

The Prosecution's Right to Appeal

Neither the federal government nor the states may appeal the acquittal of a defendant. Nor can the prosecution appeal the conviction on some lesser offense (say, murder in the second degree or manslaughter) when the original indictment was for a greater one (murder in the first degree). Such actions are barred by the double jeopardy clause of the Fifth Amendment.

However, there are two situations in which the prosecution may initiate appellate review. First, if a defendant successfully appeals and his or her conviction is reversed on some matter of law, the prosecution may contest the correctness of that legal ruling to the next higher court or even to the U.S. Supreme Court. Such was the case in *Delaware* v. *Prouse,*[109] which involved a seizure of marijuana following a random "spot check" of the defendant's driver's license and vehicle registration. Upon conviction, the defendant appealed to the Delaware Supreme Court, which overturned the lower court's ruling on the basis of illegal search and seizure. The prosecution then appealed to the U.S. Supreme Court to argue the constitutionality of the state's random license check practices. (See Chapter 8.)

Alternatively, some jurisdictions permit the prosecution to initiate appeals from both convictions *and* acquittals, solely for the purpose of correcting any legal errors that may have occurred during trial.[110]

Appellate Review of Sentences

Although appeals are commonly filed in order to review either real or imagined errors in court procedure, sentences, for the most part, cannot be appealed. This is so because each jurisdiction has statutes that mandate a range of penalties for each specific crime. Although a convicted offender might consider the sentence imposed to be unfair, as long as it falls within statutory guidelines, it is *legal.*

There are, however, a number of circumstances in which sanctions have been appealed and reversed, including the following: (1) if the sentence was not authorized by statute and thus was illegal; (2) if the sentence was based on gender, ethnicity, or socioeconomic status and was, therefore, a violation of due process; (3) if the sentence had no relationship to the purposes of criminal sanctions; or (4) if the sentence was cruel and unusual. Note that in these four potential instances, the bases for appeal are not simply issues of sentencing "excess" but, rather, straightforward matters of constitutional rights.

For many decades it has been argued that all sentences should be subject to some form of appeal. The fact that sentences are discretionary within a jurisdiction's statutory guidelines and, as such, are lawful should not automatically suggest that they cannot be appealed. Discretion, after all, can be abused. Moreover, as Judge Marvin E. Frankel has pointed out:

> The contention that sentencing is not regulated by the rules of "law" subject to appellate review is an argument for, not against, a system of appeals. The "common law" is, after all, a body of rules evolved through the process of reasoned decision of concrete cases, mainly by appellate courts. English appellate courts and some of our states have been evolving general, legal "principles of sentencing" in the course of reviewing particular sentences claimed to be excessive. One way to begin to temper the capricious unruliness of sentencing is to in-

stitute the right of appeal, so that appellate courts may proceed in their accustomed fashion to make law for this grave subject.[111]

Currently, only about 14 states have appellate bodies that review sentences, and state appeals courts are generally reluctant to review sentences. Not wishing to second-guess the sentencing judge, these higher courts feel that the magistrate who presided at the trial and pronounced the sentence had the most information available and was in the best position to determine the penalty.

Finally, although the U.S. Supreme Court has reviewed many sentences when the issue at stake was of constitutional magnitude, only once did it require a sentencing judge to explain the basis of the penalty imposed. The case was *North Carolina* v. *Pearce*,[112] in which the defendant, whose original conviction had been reversed, was then retried by the same judge—only to be reconvicted and sentenced more severely in the second trial. The High Court ruled that in such circumstances, the reasons for the more severe sentence must be placed in the record, the logic being that the due process clause of the Fourteenth Amendment forbids the imposition of a harsher sentence for the purpose of discouraging defendants from exercising their rights of appeal.

The Appeal Process

After conviction, appeals are not automatic. There are specific procedural steps that must be followed. First, within a specified period (from 30 to 90 days) subsequent to conviction, the petitioner must file a notice of appeal with the court. Second, and again within a specified period, the petitioner must submit an "affidavit of errors" setting forth the alleged errors or defects in the trial (or pretrial) proceedings that are the subjects of the appeal. If these requirements are followed, the higher court must review the case.[113] Appeals are argued on the basis of the affidavit of errors and sometimes through oral argument. In either case, the subject matter of the appeal must be limited to the contents of the original proceeding. Thus, no new evidence or testimony can be presented, for an appeal is not a trial. However, if new evidence is discovered that was unknown or unknowable to the defense at the time of the trial, it can be the *basis* of an appeal.*

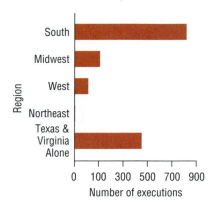

Executions by Region

Source: Death Penalty Information Center.

Note: For executions by region, federal executions are included in the state where the crime occurred.

── **CRITICAL THINKING IN CRIMINAL JUSTICE** ──

Attitudes of College Students Toward the Death Penalty

Throughout this chapter, you have read much about the death penalty—the arguments *for* and *against,* where the U.S. Supreme Court stands on whether a death sentence is "cruel and un-usual punishment," and the problems of discrimination and minority representation on death row. If you didn't have opinions on *all* these issues before, no doubt you thought critically about them as you studied the chapter. How do you think your opinions compare with those of a group of other college students?

On a piece of paper, make a list from 1 to 10, and indicate whether you agree with each of the 10 statements listed below. If you agree strongly, moderately, or even just slightly with each statement, mark "yes." Here they are:

1. Capital punishment is a deterrent to crime.
2. Convicted murderers are given too many appeals.
3. The death penalty helps make society safer.
4. Drug dealers should be executed.
5. Only guilty people should be sentenced to die.

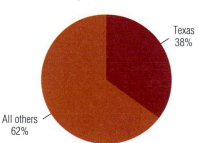

Executions in the United States, 1976–2005

Source: Death Penalty Information Center.

Texas 38%

All others 62%

---

*There are other mechanisms through which cases can be reviewed, such as collateral review proceedings and writs of *habeas corpus.* These are generally initiated after the defendant's sentence has commenced. They are discussed in Chapter 16, under prisoners' rights and postconviction remedies.

6. It costs less to keep someone in prison for life than it does to execute him or her.

7. The death penalty is society's way of getting revenge.

8. Minorities are more likely to be executed than are whites.

9. Mentally retarded murderers shouldn't be executed.

10. The race of the victim plays a major role in whether the accused will be given the death penalty.

Before going further, it should be pointed out that a considerable amount of research has been conducted on attitudes about capital punishment, and one of the general conclusions has been that a person's background has more of an impact on his or her opinion than educational presentations.[114] Having said that, researchers Brian K. Payne and Victoria Coogle conducted a study of college students' attitudes toward the death penalty during the second half of the 1990s.[115] The research was done with a sample of students enrolled at a medium-sized southern university. Aside from the actual attitudes, the most interesting findings were that race and political ideology were important influences on attitudes, while gender, community size, and choice of major (including criminal justice) were not. How do your attitudes compare with those of the students in the study? To find out, see endnote 116 at the end of this chapter.[116] And bear in mind that these figures refer to students in just one study, not the entire U.S. college population.

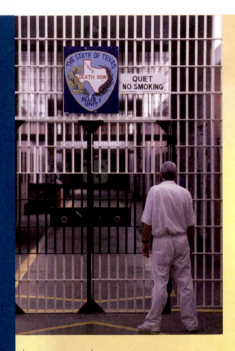

OP-ED

Back to the topic of DNA evidence and the innocent people who were exonerated due to this technology: How has DNA evidence improved our criminal justice system? What about the other innocent people who are still behind bars? What is our criminal justice system doing to avoid convicting more innocent people?

First of all, DNA tests were first used in courts in the late 1980s. In the early 1990s, when the procedure was perfected, many prosecutors began using DNA testing to eliminate suspects before filing charges—proving such testing to be greatly beneficial to our criminal justice system. The examples given at the beginning of the chapter are only a few of the growing number of convicts being exonerated by DNA evidence. There have been many more.

Experts attribute the recent increase in exonerations to improved DNA tests, publicity about successful cases, and a growing number of volunteer lawyers and law students who are working to clear people they believe to be wrongly convicted. One advocacy group formed just for this purpose is The Innocence Project. A nonprofit legal clinic, it was set up in 1992 to help those wrongly prosecuted. The project handles only cases in which postconviction DNA testing of evidence can yield conclusive proof of innocence. The Innocence Project, which relies heavily on volunteer law students and attorneys working pro bono, has set up programs at 18 law schools around the country that use student volunteers to investigate cases.

DNA evidence is a valuable tool in our criminal justice system, proving the inno-

IN THE NATION

TOP 10 EXECUTION STATES SINCE THE SUPREME COURT ALLOWED THE RESTORATION OF CAPITAL PUNISHMENT IN 1976

State	Executions Since 1976	Executions in 2005 *
Texas	355	19
Virginia	94	0
Oklahoma	79	4
Missouri	66	5
Florida	60	1
Georgia	39	3
North Carolina	38	4
South Carolina	34	2
Alabama	34	4
Louisiana	27	0

Source: Death Penalty Information Center.

* As of late 2005

cence of many who have been wrongly convicted while also raising a red flag to a huge problem that exists. The alarming number of DNA exonerations demonstrates how many

continued

OP-ED *continued*

individuals are unjustly prosecuted while many guilty, dangerous people remain at large in our society. We also need to consider that many cases don't involve DNA evidence, leaving little hope of proving the innocence of those unjustly prosecuted in non-DNA cases. Hopefully, our criminal justice system will learn from its mistakes, examining cases in which individuals were wrongly convicted.

With regard to the death penalty, is it "cruel and unusual punishment"? After years of debate, most Americans feel that the death penalty is an appropriate punishment for truly evil crime. A case many supporters of capital punishment point to was the execution of Jimmy Lee Gray in 1983, convicted in a Mississippi court for kidnapping and raping a 3-year-old girl and then murdering her

by suffocation in mud. Even Gray's mother was in favor of her son's execution.

Support for the death penalty is rooted in the underlying assumption that the right person is being executed. However, it would appear that for every seven executions, one other death row prisoner is determined to be wrongfully convicted. There is concern, furthermore, that many mistaken convictions will go unnoticed as record numbers of inmates fill death rows and pressure builds for speedy executions. This certainly is possible in Texas, which ranks first, year after year, in the number of death row residents put to death. Within this context, what should be done with the death penalty?

Jimmy Lee Gray immediately before his execution

Summary

After the verdict, the business of the court is not complete. Next, there is the matter of sentencing. Throughout American history, there has been no single and clearly defined rationale to serve as a guiding principle in sentencing. As a result, even contemporary sentencing objectives are seemingly based on at least four competing philosophies: retribution, incapacitation, deterrence, and rehabilitation. Sentencing alternatives include fines, probation or some other community-based program, imprisonment, or death.

When the framers of the Constitution incorporated the Eighth Amendment ban against cruel and unusual punishment, the death penalty was apparently not at issue. Under colonial philosophy, capital punishment was considered neither cruel nor unusual.

The Supreme Court's interpretation of the Eighth Amendment has been flexible. The Court has ruled on various forms of punishment but has generally been silent regarding the constitutionality of capital punishment. *Furman* v. *Georgia* in 1972 invalidated state death penalty statutes on Eighth Amendment grounds, but it enabled the states to en-

act new capital punishment laws. Executions resumed in 1977, and the number of persons on death rows across the nation began to grow. Meanwhile, the death penalty debate continues, with arguments for and against capital punishment revolving around issues of economics, retribution, public opinion, community protection, deterrence, irreversibility, discrimination, protection of the criminal justice system, brutalization, and cruel and unusual punishment.

At the appellate stage of the criminal justice process, the presumption of innocence has evaporated with the finding of guilt and it becomes the defendant's obligation to show why a conviction should be overturned. There are grounds on which the defense can initiate an appeal, but the prosecution cannot appeal the acquittal of a defendant because of the double jeopardy clause of the Fifth Amendment. However, should an accused successfully appeal and have his or her conviction reversed on some matter of law, the prosecution may contest the correctness of that legal ruling to the next highest court or even to the U.S. Supreme Court.

Key Terms

allocution (427)	deterrence (416)	intermittent sentence (420)
appeal (448)	*Furman* v. *Georgia* (434)	*Lockhart* v. *McCree* (446)
Coker v. *Georgia* (435)	*Gregg* v. *Georgia* (434)	mandatory sentence (421)
definite sentence (420)	incapacitation (416)	presentence investigation (426)
determinate sentence (420)	indeterminate sentence (419)	rehabilitation (417)

retribution (415)
separation-of-powers doctrine (426)
Tison v. *Arizona* (446)

truth in sentencing (426)
Weems v. *United States* (432)
Witherspoon v. *Illinois* (433)

vengeance (415)
victim impact evidence (416)

| Issues for Discussion |

1. Should vengeance be accepted as a rationale for punishment?
2. How might mandatory sentencing statutes lead to increased prosecutorial discretion and court delays?
3. Would mandatory sentencing statutes make the certainty of punishment more realistic? Would such sentences affect the crime problem?
4. Should victim impact evidence be permitted in death penalty cases?
5. Which method of execution is the most humane?
6. What argument in favor of capital punishment seems most valid? Should capital punishment be abolished? Will it be?

| Media and Literature Resources |

The Death Penalty in America. Hugo Adam Bedau, *Killing as Punishment: Reflections on the Death Penalty in America* (Boston: Northeastern University Press, 2004); Hugo Adam Bedau and Paul Cassell, *Debating the Death Penalty: Should America Have Capital Punishment?* (New York: Oxford University Press, 2004); Michael A. Foley, *Arbitrary and Capricious: The Supreme Court, the Constitution, and the Death Penalty* (Westwood, CT: Praeger, 2003); Mark D. Cunningham and Mark P. Vigen, "Death Row Inmate Characteristics, Adjustment, and Confinement: A Critical Review of the Literature," *Behavioral Sciences and the Law* 20 (2002): 191–210.

Beliefs and Attitudes About the Death Penalty. Stacey L. Mallicoat and Michael L. Radelet, "The Growing Significance of Public Opinion for Death Penalty Jurisprudence," *Journal of Crime and Justice* 27, 1 (2004): 119–130; Scott Vollum, Dennis R. Longmire, and Jacqueline Buffington-Vollum, "Confidence in the Death Penalty and Supporting Its Use: Exploring the Value-Expressive Dimension of Death Penalty Attitudes," *Justice Quarterly* 21, 3 (2004): 521–545; Eric Lambert and Alan Clarke, "Crime, Capital Punishment, and Knowledge: Are Criminal Justice Majors Better Informed than Other Majors About Crime and Capital Punishment?" *Social Science Journal* 41, 1 (2004): 53–66. Detailed findings of a recent survey among college students can be found in Brian K. Payne and Victoria Coogle, "Examining Attitudes About the Death Penalty," *Corrections Compendium*, April 1998. This publication can be obtained through the American Correctional Association. Also see the Web site (*http://www.corrections.com/aca*).

Women and the Death Penalty. Victor L. Streib's report, "Death Penalty for Female Offenders," is updated on a regular basis and can be found on the Web (*http://www.law.onu.edu/faculty/streib/femdeath.htm*). The ACLU recently released the first-ever national survey of women currently on death row. The report details the life and experiences of 56 women on death row and documents the cases of 10 women who have been put to death since 1976; see *The Forgotten Population: A Look at Death Row in the United States Through the Experiences of Women* (Washington, DC: The American Civil Liberties Union, December 2004). The report is available to download at *www.aclu.org*.

Minorities and the Death Penalty. Robert L. Young, "Guilty Until Proven Innocent: Conviction Orientation, Racial Attitudes, and Support for Capital Punishment," *Deviant Behavior* 25, 2 (2004): 151–167; Marian R. Williams and Jefferson E. Holcomb, "Racial Disparity and Death Sentences in Ohio," *Journal of Criminal Justice* 29, 3 (2001): 207–218; M. R. Williams and J. E. Holcomb, "The Interactive Effects of Victim Race and Gender on Death Sentence Disparity Findings," *Homicide Studies* 8, 4 (2004): 350–376. The Death Penalty Information Center has prepared an excellent report entitled "The Death Penalty in Black & White: Who Lives, Who Dies, Who Decides," by Richard C. Dieter, June 1998. Contact the Center's Web site for a copy (*http://www.deathpenaltyinfo.org*).

Capital Jury Project. Since 1990, the Capital Jury Project has conducted interviews with more than 1,000 jurors who served in death penalty trials in 14 states. Findings suggest that jurors are subject to a wide range of misconceptions and prejudices that may undermine their ability to render reliable verdicts in capital cases. See William J. Bowers and Benjamin D. Steiner, "Death by Default: An Empirical Demonstration of False and Forced Choices in Capital Sentencing," 77 *Texas Law Review* 605 (1998).

Three-Strikes Laws. Tomislav V. Kovandzic, John J. Sloan, and Lynne M. Vieraitis, "'Striking Out' as Crime Reduction Policy: The Impact of 'Three Strikes' Laws on Crime Rates in U.S. Cities," *Justice Quarterly* 21, 2 (2004): 207–239; John L. Worrall, "The Effect of Three-Strikes Legislation on Serious Crime in California," *Journal of Criminal Justice* 32, 4 (2004): 283–296; Jonathan P. Caulkins, "How Large Should the Strike Zone Be in 'Three Strikes and You're Out' Sentencing Laws?" *Journal of Quantitative Criminology* 17, 3 (2001): 227–246; Franklin E. Zimring, Gordon Hawkins, and Sam Kamin, *Punishment and Democracy: Three Strikes and You're Out in California* (New York: Oxford University Press, 2001). See also John Clark, James Austin, and Alan Henry, "Three Strikes and You're Out: A Review of State Legislation," National Institute of Justice, *Research in Brief,* September 1997.

Fines. For an interesting study on the use of fines, see Michael S. Vigorita, "Fining Practices in Felony Courts," *Corrections Compendium* 27 (November 2002): 1–5, 26–27.

Wrongful Convictions. There are a number of excellent papers published on this topic in the *Criminal Law Bulletin* (March/April 2005), including James E. Robertson, "Symposium: No Longer 'An Unreal Dream': Wrongful Convictions After the DNA Revolution," 109–112; Joy Hadwiger and John R. Cross, "Wrongful Conviction: Evidence from Oklahoma's DNA Exonerations," 113–126; Kathryn M. Campbell, "Policy Responses to Wrongful Conviction in Canada: The Role of Conviction Review, Public Inquiries and Compensation," 145–168; and Marvin Zalman, "Cautionary Notes on Commission Recommendations: A Public Policy Approach to Wrongful Convictions," 169–194.

| Endnotes |

1. *Washington Post,* April 20, 2005, A9.
2. *Times-Picayune,* August 13, 2004, 7.
3. Jeff Flock, "'Blanket Commutation' Empties Illinois Death Row," CNN.com, January 13, 2003; Dirk Johnson and Elizabeth Austin, "A Leap of Faith: A Governor's Controversial Last Hurrah Clears Out Illinois's Crowded Death Row," *Newsweek,* January 20, 2003, 34.
4. *Baltimore Sun,* October 24, 2003, A1.
5. See Andrew von Hirsch, *Doing Justice: The Choice of Punishments* (New York: Hill and Wang, 1976), 45–55, 143–149.
6. Kenneth C. Haas, "The Triumph of Vengeance over Retribution: The United States Supreme Court and the Death Penalty," *Crime, Law and Social Change: An International Journal* 21 (1994): 127–154.
7. *Payne* v. *Tennessee,* 49 CrL 2325 (1991).
8. Paul W. Tappan, *Crime, Justice and Correction* (New York: McGraw-Hill, 1960), 255.
9. Quoted in Sanford H. Kadish and Monrad G. Paulsen, *Criminal Law and Its Processes* (Boston: Little, Brown, 1969), 85.
10. For example, see Henry N. Pontell, *A Capacity to Punish: The Ecology of Crime and Punishment* (Bloomington: Indiana University Press, 1984); and Franklin E. Zimring and Gordon J. Hawkins, *Deterrence* (Chicago: University of Chicago Press, 1973).
11. *Williams* v. *Illinois,* 399 U.S. 235 (1970); *Tate* v. *Short,* 401 U.S. 395 (1971).
12. *Bearden* v. *Georgia,* 33 CrL 3103 (1983).
13. *Criminal Justice Newsletter,* September 1, 1988, 4.
14. Bureau of Justice Assistance, *How to Use Structured Fines (Day Fines) as an Intermediate Sanction* (Washington, DC: Office of Justice Programs, 1996).
15. Michael Tonry, *Fragmentation of Sentencing and Corrections in the United States,* Research in Brief—Sentencing & Corrections: Issues for the 21st Century (Washington, DC: National Institute of Justice, September 1999).
16. See Michael Tonry, *Reconsidering Indeterminate and Structured Sentencing,* Research in Brief—Sentencing & Corrections: Issues for the 21st Century (Washington, DC: National Institute of Justice, September 1999); Marvin E. Frankel, *Criminal Sentences: Law Without Order* (New York: Hill and Wang, 1973); Karl Menninger, *The Crime of Punishment* (New York: Viking, 1968); von Hirsch, *Doing Justice;* and Nigel Walker, *Sentencing in a Rational Society* (London: Penguin, 1972).
17. Harry Elmer Barnes, *The Repression of Crime* (New York: Doran, 1926), 220.
18. State of New York, *Penal Law,* 40–85.
19. *People* v. *Warren,* 79 Misc 2d 777, 360 NYS 2d 961 (1974).
20. See General Accounting Office, *Mandatory Minimum Sentences,* GAO/GGD-94-13, November 1993; Jonathan P. Caulkins, C. Peter Rydell, William L. Schwabe, and James Chiesa, *Mandatory Drug Sentences: Throwing Away the Key or the Taxpayers' Money?* (Santa Monica: Rand, 1997).
21. CNN.com, September 15, 2000.
22. *The New York Times,* February 26, 1993, B16.
23. *The New York Times,* January 3, 1998, A12.
24. *The New York Times,* November 9, 2000, D3.
25. *The New York Times,* April 27, 1997, 17; *Prison Life,* June–July 1997, 13; *Time,* September 9, 1996, 60; *The New York Times on the Web,* March 20, 2000.
26. *Idaho Code,* 18-1403, 19-2601.
27. State of New York, *Penal Law,* 40-70.00, 80.00, 140.30.
28. *West Virginia Code,* Chapter 61, Section 3-11; Chapter 62, Section 12-2.
29. *Delaware Code,* Title 11, Sections 826, 4204-5.
30. *Code of the Public General Laws of Maryland,* Article 27, Sections 29, 641.
31. *Code of Alabama,* 13-2-40, 15-22-50.
32. *The New York Times,* February 15, 1981, 43.
33. President's Commission on Law Enforcement and Administration of Justice, *The Courts* (Washington, DC: U.S. Government Printing Office, 1967), 23–24.
34. Frankel, *Criminal Sentences,* 8.
35. Bureau of Justice Statistics, *National Assessment of Structured Sentencing* (Washington, DC: U.S. Department of Justice, 1996).
36. See, for example, Frankel, *Criminal Sentences.*
37. Joseph Mattina, "Sentencing: A Judge's Inherent Responsibility," *Judicature* 57 (October 1973): 105.
38. *Mistretta* v. *United States,* 44 CrL 3061 (1989).
39. *United States* v. *Booker,* No. 04-104 (2004).
40. Paula M. Ditton and Doris James Wilson, "Truth in Sentencing in State Prisons," Bureau of Justice Statistics Special Report, January 1999.
41. *Hill* v. *California,* 368 U.S. 424 (1962).
42. From Barnes, *Repression of Crime,* 44–45.
43. George Ryley Scott, *The History of Capital Punishment* (London: Torchstream, 1950), 179.
44. Cited by Harry Elmer Barnes, *The Story of Punishment: A Record of Man's Inhumanity to Man* (Montclair, NJ: Patterson Smith, 1972), 232.
45. Negley K. Teeters and Charles J. Zibulka, "Executions Under State Authority: 1864–1967," in *Executions in America,* edited by William J. Bowers (Lexington, MA: Heath, 1974), 200–401.
46. Hugo Adam Bedau, *The Death Penalty in America* (Chicago: Aldine, 1964), 46.
47. President's Commission, *Courts,* 28.
48. C. Spear, *Essays on the Punishment of Death* (London: Green, 1844), 227–231.
49. David A. Jones, *The Law of Criminal Procedure* (Boston: Little, Brown, 1981), 543.
50. Jones, *Law of Criminal Procedure,* 544.
51. Marvin E. Wolfgang and Marc Riedel, "Race, Judicial Discretion, and the Death Penalty," *Annals of the American Academy of Political and Social Science* 407 (May 1973): 129.
52. *O'Neil* v. *Vermont,* 114 U.S. 323 (1892).
53. *Weems* v. *United States,* 217 U.S. 349 (1910).
54. *Trop* v. *Dulles,* 356 U.S. 86 (1958).
55. *Wilkerson* v. *Utah,* 99 U.S. 130 (1878).
56. *In re Kemmler,* 136 U.S. 436 (1890).
57. *Trop* v. *Dulles,* 356 U.S. 86 (1958).
58. *Witherspoon* v. *Illinois,* 391 U.S. 510 (1968).
59. *United States* v. *Jackson,* 390 U.S. 570 (1968).
60. *McGautha* v. *California,* 402 U.S. 183 (1971).
61. *Furman* v. *Georgia, Jackson* v. *Georgia, Branch* v. *Texas,* 408 U.S. 238 (1972).
62. *Gregg* v. *Georgia,* 428 U.S. 153 (1976).
63. *Georgia Code,* 26-1101, 1311, 1902, 2001, 3301 (1972).
64. *Profitt* v. *Florida,* 428 U.S. 325 (1976); *Jurek* v. *Texas,* 428 U.S. 262 (1976).
65. *Woodson* v. *North Carolina,* 428 U.S. 280 (1976).
66. *Coker* v. *Georgia,* 433 U.S. 583 (1977).

67. *Lockett* v. *Ohio,* 438 U.S. 586 (1978); *Bell* v. *Ohio,* 438 U.S. 637 (1978).

68. *Godfrey* v. *Georgia,* 446 U.S. 420 (1980).

69. This account of the Gilmore case is based on Louis R. Katz, *The Justice Imperative* (Cincinnati: Anderson, 1980), 348–349; *The New York Times,* January 18, 1977, 1, 21; *The New York Times,* January 12, 1977, 1, 12; *The New York Times,* January 11, 1976, 1, 14; *The New York Times,* January 16, 1977, 1, 48; *The New York Times,* December 1, 1976, 18; and *The New York Times,* January 17, 1976, 1, 24.

70. Quoted in Austin Sarat and Neil Vidmar, "Public Opinion, The Death Penalty, and the Eighth Amendment: Testing the Marshall Hypothesis," *Wisconsin Law Review* (1976): 206.

71. *Fierro* v. *Gomez,* 56 CrL 1085 (1994).

72. Lewis E. Lawes, *Life and Death in Sing Sing* (Garden City, NY: Garden City Publishing, 1928), 170–171, 188–190.

73. *Wilmington* (Delaware) *News-Journal,* February 17, 1985, A16.

74. *The New York Times,* December 9, 1979, 73.

75. *National Law Journal,* September 14, 1981, 5.

76. *American Medical News,* July 11, 1980, 13.

77. *Time,* December 20, 1982, 28–29. See also *Texas Monthly,* February 1983, 100–105, 170–176, 182.

78. See M. Garey, "The Cost of Taking a Life," *University of California–Davis Law Review* 18 (1985): 1221–1270; Dale O Cloninger and Roberto Marchesini, "Execution and Deterrence: A Quasi-Controlled Group Experiment," *Applied Economics* 33 (2001): 569–576.

79. *National Observer,* November 18, 1972, 2.

80. James O. Finckenauer, "Public Support for the Death Penalty: Retribution as Just Deserts or Retribution as Revenge?" *Justice Quarterly* 5 (March 1988): 81–100; Scott Vollum, Dennis R. Longmire, and Jacqueline Buffington-Vollum, "Confidence in the Death Penalty and Supporting Its Use: Exploring the Value-Expressive Dimension of Death Penalty Attitudes," *Justice Quarterly* 21, 3 (2004): 521–545. See also Jeffrey M. Jones, *Americans' Views of Death Penalty More Positive This Year; Nearly Three in Four Favor It as a Penalty for Convicted Murderers,* May 19, 2005, from *www.gallup.com.*

81. James W. Marquart and Jonathan R. Sorensen, "A National Study of the *Furman*-Committed Inmates," *Loyola of Los Angeles Law Review* 23 (1989): 5–28; *Deadly Speculation: Misleading Texas Capital Juries with False Predictions of Future Dangerousness* (Houston, TX: Texas Defender Service, 2004).

82. Zimring and Hawkins, *Deterrence.*

83. See Thorsten Sellin (ed.), *Capital Punishment* (New York: Harper & Row, 1967); Karl F. Schuessler, "The Deterrent Influence of the Death Penalty," *Annals of the American Academy of Political and Social Science* 284 (November 1952): 54–62; Hugo Adam Bedau and Chester M. Pierce (eds.), *Capital Punishment in the United States* (New York: AMS Press, 1976), 299–416; Hashem Dezhbakhsh, Paul H. Rubin, and Joanna M. Shepherd, "Does Capital Punishment Have a Deterrent Effect? New Evidence from Postmoratorium Panel Data," *American Law and Economics Review* 5, 2 (2003): 344–376; and Helmut Kury, Theodore N. Ferdinand, and Joachim Obergfell-Fuchs, "Does Severe Punishment Mean Less Criminality?" *International Criminal Justice Review,* 13 (2003): 110–148.

84. Michael L. Radelet, Hugo Adam Bedau, and Constance E. Putnam, *In Spite of Innocence: Erroneous Convictions in Capital Cases* (Boston: Northeastern University Press, 1992).

85. *Wilmington* (Delaware) *News-Journal,* July 16, 1997, A3; *Innocence and the Crisis in the American Death Penalty* (Washington DC: The Death Penalty Information Center, 2004).

86. James S. Liebmann, Jeffrey Fagan, and Valerie West, "A Broken System: Error Rates in Capital Cases, 1973–1995," *http://www.thejusticeproject.org;* Talia Roitberg Harmon, "Guilty Until Proven Innocent: An Analysis of Post-*Furman* Capital Errors," *Criminal Justice Policy Review* 12, 2 (2001): 113–139.

87. Michael L. Radelet and Hugo Adam Bedau, "Fallibility and Finality: Type II Errors and Capital Punishment," in *Challenging Capital Punishment: Legal and Social Science Approaches,* edited by Kenneth C. Haas and James A. Inciardi (Newbury Park, CA: Sage Publications, 1988), 91–112; Stephen J. Markman and Paul G. Cassell, "Protecting the Innocent: A Response to the Bedau-Radelet Study," *Stanford Law Review* 41, 1 (1990): 121–160.

88. William J. Bowers and Glenn L. Pierce, "Arbitrariness and Discrimination Under Post-*Furman* Capital Statutes," *Crime and Delinquency* 26 (October 1980): 563–635; Kenneth C. Haas, "Reaffirming the Value of Life: Arguments Against the Death Penalty," *Delaware Lawyer* 3 (Summer 1984): 12–20; Raymond Bonner and Marc Lacey, "Pervasive Disparities Found in the Federal Death Penalty," *The New York Times,* September 12, 2000, A18; Marvin D. Free, "Race and Presentencing Decisions in the United States: A Summary and Critique of the Research," *Criminal Justice Review* 27, 2 (2002): 203–232.

89. *McCleskey* v. *Zant,* 34 CrL 2429 (1984).

90. President's Commission, *Courts.*

91. See William J. Bowers, "The Effect of Executions Is Brutalization, Not Deterrence," in *Challenging Capital Punishment,* edited by Haas and Inciardi, 49–89. See also John K. Cochran and Mitchell B. Chamlin, "Deterrence and Brutalization: The Dual Effects of Executions," *Justice Quarterly,* 17 (December 2000): 685–706.

92. See the Death Penalty Information Center Web site (*http://www.deathpenalty.org*).

93. *Pulley* v. *Harris,* U.S. Sup Ct 34 CrL 3027 (1984).

94. *Barefoot* v. *Estelle,* 103 S.Ct. 3383 (1983).

95. *Lockhart* v. *McCree,* 39 CrL 3085 (1986).

96. *McCleskey* v. *Kemp,* 41 CrL 4107 (1987).

97. *Tison* v. *Arizona,* 41 CrL 3023 (1987).

98. *Penry* v. *Lynaugh,* 45 CrL 3188 (1989); *Atkins* v. *Virginia* 536 U.S. 304 (2002).

99. *Herrera* v. *Collins,* 113 S.Ct. 2222 (1993).

100. *Delo* v. *Lashley,* 113 S.Ct. 1962 (1993).

101. *Gary* v. *Netherland,* 64 U.S.L.W. 4531 (1996).

102. For example, in *McKane* v. *Durston,* 153 U.S. 684 (1894); *Griffin* v. *Illinois,* 351 U.S. 12 (1956).

103. *Federal Rules of Criminal Procedure,* Rule 52 (b).

104. *Tumey* v. *Ohio,* 273 U.S. 510 (1927).

105. *Gideon* v. *Wainwright,* 372 U.S. 335 (1963).

106. *Chapman* v. *California,* 386 U.S. 18 (1967).

107. See Peter W. Lewis and Kenneth D. Peoples, *The Supreme Court and the Criminal Process* (Philadelphia: Saunders, 1978), 515.

108. *Gresham* v. *Harcourt,* 93 Tex. 149, 53 S. W. 1019 (1899).

109. *Delaware* v. *Prouse,* 440 U.S. 648 (1979).

110. Katz, *Justice Imperative,* 315.

111. Frankel, *Criminal Sentences,* 84.

112. *North Carolina* v. *Pearce,* 395 U.S. 711 (1969).

113. *Gilbert Criminal Law and Procedure* (New York: Bender, 1979), 460.10.

114. For example, see R. M. Bohm, L. J. Clark, and A. F. Aveni, "The Influence of Knowledge on Reasons for the Death Penalty Opinions: An Experimental Test," *Justice Quarterly* 7

(1990): 175–188; and R. M. Bohm, R. E. Vogel, and A. A. Maistro, "Knowledge and Death Penalty Opinion: A Panel Study," *Journal of Criminal Justice* 21 (1993): 29–45.

115. Brian K. Payne and Victoria Coogle, "Examining Attitudes About the Death Penalty: Race and Political Affiliation Are Factors Most Likely to Influence Opinion," *Corrections Compendium* 23 (April 1998): 1–5, 24–26.

116. Students agreeing strongly, moderately and slightly:

1) 80%	6) 32%
2) 92%	7) 53%
3) 70%	8) 54%
4) 40%	9) 52%
5) 25%	10) 51%

PART FOUR

CORRECTIONS

Prison of course is the school of crime par excellence. Until one has gone through that school, one is only an amateur. —HENRY MILLER, 1945 We warehouse people, but we don't make persons of the people. We don't really care. —NICHOLAS PASTORE, NEW HAVEN CHIEF OF POLICE, 1994 One learns patience in prison.—FYODOR DOSTOYEVSKY, 1861 The Constitution does not mandate comfortable prisons.—*RHODES V. CHAPMAN*, 1981 Prisoners are not stripped of their constitutional rights, including the right to due process, when the prison gate slams shut behind them. —UNITED STATES EX REL. *GEREAU V. HENDERSON*, 1976 Community-based corrections is the most promising means of accomplishing the changes in offender behavior that the public expects—and now demands—of corrections. —NATIONAL ADVISORY COMMISSION ON CRIMINAL JUSTICE STANDARDS AND GOALS, 1973 Why can't we reform our criminals?—UCLA CRIMINOLOGIST DAVID FARABEE

14

FROM WALNUT STREET TO ALCATRAZ: THE AMERICAN PRISON EXPERIENCE

LEARNING OBJECTIVES

After reading this chapter, you should be able to answer the following questions:

1. What is corporal punishment, and how was it administered in colonial America?

2. What were the contributions of the classical school of criminology?

3. What were the differences between the "separate" and "silent" systems of confinement?

4. What were the types of, and problems with, prison labor during the 19th and early 20th centuries?

5. What were the contributions of the reformatory era in American corrections?

6. What are the problems with jails today, and how might they be alleviated?

7. What is "home incarceration," and is it a useful correctional tool?

8. Are prisons and jails just different names for the same thing?

Sing Sing in the early 1900s. Built in 1825 and located on the banks of the Hudson River some 40 miles north of New York City (and hence the expression "up the river"), Sing Sing is said to have derived its name from the Native American words "sint sinks," meaning "place of many stones." The institution had 100 inmates when it first opened, but now houses more than 3,000.

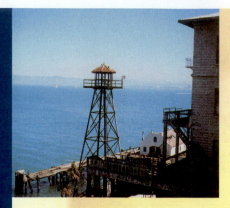

Guard tower at Alcatraz

Alcatraz: Model Prison for "Public Enemies"?

SAN FRANCISCO, CA—In a national radio address on October 12, 1933, U.S. attorney general Homer S. Cummings made the following announcement:

For some time I have desired to obtain a place of confinement to which could be sent our more dangerous, intractable criminals. You can appreciate, therefore, with what pleasure I make public the fact that such a place has been found. By negotiation with the War Department we have obtained the use of Alcatraz Prison, located on a precipitous island in San Francisco Bay, more than a mile from shore. The current is swift and escapes are practically impossible. Here may be isolated the criminals of the vicious and irredeemable type.

The attorney general's interest in an ultra-secure prison was based on the fact that during the early years of the Great Depression, an unusual crime wave had spread across the American Midwest. Banks that had weathered the stock market crash of 1929 were being robbed at the rate of two a day. The outlaws operated with flair and skill. Armed with machine guns, they re-created a frontier pattern of rapid assault followed by elusive retreat. Millions of citizens who were caught in a drab round of idleness and poverty responded to the criminal exploits with admiration. The bandits became folk heroes, and the names of John Dillinger, Frank Nash, Charles "Pretty Boy" Floyd, Bonnie Parker, Clyde Barrow, and George "Baby Face" Nelson quickly found their way into American folklore. But to the Federal Bureau of Investigation they were "public enemies"; to FBI director J. Edgar Hoover they were "public rats," "the lowest dregs of society," "vermin in human form," "slime," "vermin spewed out of prison cells," and "scum from the boiling pot of the underworld." Alcatraz appeared to be the answer.

Was Alcatraz the answer? Was it ever a model prison? Where did it fit in the evolution of American corrections? Are there other kinds of prisons in the United States? What are the differences between jails and prisons?

Historically and cross-culturally, the range of punishments imposed by societies has been vast. Over the centuries, the sanctions for even less serious crimes were exceedingly harsh, and the litany of punishments down through the ages has often been referred to as the story of "man's inhumanity to man."[1]

In early societies the death penalty was a universal form of punishment. It was commonly applied both as a deterrent and as a means of removing an offender from the community. Criminal codes from the ancient East to the modern West included capital statutes for offenses as trivial as adultery and petty theft. As recently as the early 19th century in England there were 200 capital crimes—ranging from murder and rape to larceny and disturbing the peace. The methods of execution went well beyond the diabolical and macabre, and they were often performed in public.

This chapter traces the evolution of corrections in American society, beginning with corporal punishments of various kinds and continuing with the development of the prison system and its operation today.

Varieties of Punishment

Throughout history **corporal punishment,** in the form of mutilation, branding, whipping, and torture, has been commonplace, being used for a variety of punitive purposes. Mutilations were attempts to "let the punishment fit the crime": Thieves and robbers lost their hands, perjurers and blasphemers had their tongues cut out or pierced with hot irons, and rape was punished by castration. Branding and whipping were noncapital sanctions designed to preserve discipline and deter would-be offenders. Torture, a popular means of exacting confessions, included measures of gruesome ingenuity. The torture devices of medieval Europe, for example, were often monstrous. They included

Deportations from the United States

Source: Customs and Border Protection.

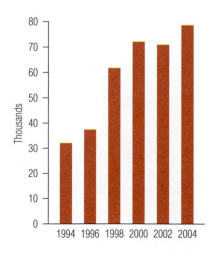

the *rack,* which stretched its victims, and the "Scavenger's Daughter," which rolled them into a ball:

> On the rack the prisoner seemed in danger of having the fingers torn from his hands, the toes from his feet, the hands from the arms, the feet from the legs, the forearms from the upper arms, the legs from the trunk. Every ligament was strained, every joint loosened in its socket; and if the sufferer remained obstinate when released, he was brought back to undergo the same cruelties with the added horror of past experience and with a diminished fortitude and physical power. In the Scavenger's Daughter, on the other hand, the pain was caused by an ingenious process of compression. The legs were forced back to the thighs, the thighs were pressed onto the belly, and the whole body was placed within two iron bands which the torturers drew together with all their strength until the miserable human being lost all form but that of a globe. Blood was forced out of the tips of the fingers and toes, the nostrils and mouth; and the ribs and breastbone were commonly broken in by the pressure.[2]

Banishment and transportation were alternatives to capital punishment. Banishment served to rid the community of undesirables, who would be put to death if they returned. The most systematic form of banishment, in the form of a program of transportation to far-removed lands, occurred in several European countries during the 16th through 19th centuries. England led the world in this practice, which it used to expel convicts as well as to colonize inhospitable territories. Between 1606 and 1775, tens of thousands of vagrants and thieves were shipped to the American colonies in the West Indies. After the American Revolution, convicts were sent to Australia (see Exhibit 14.1).[3] In its most modern form, banishment has taken the form of "deportation" of alien criminals. In 2004, for example, more than 50,000 foreign nationals were deported from the United States, the vast majority to Mexico.[4]

Other punishments have included forced labor, sterilization, excommunication from the Church, loss of property and inheritance rights, disfigurement, and imprisonment. In the American colonial period, however, the most common forms of punishment were corporal in nature.

Origins of American Corrections

With the growth of the American colonies, many of the punishments that had been common throughout medieval Europe found their way to the New World. Capital statutes endured for numerous offenses, as did banishment, and corporal punishments in the form of branding, flogging, and mutilation persisted.

Punishment in the Colonies

The colonies employed a curious variety of sanctions, including the ducking stool, the stocks and pillory, the brank, the scarlet letter, and the bilboes. They were imposed for minor offenses, and although they are generally associated with early American life, most had originated in Western Europe as means to shame and humiliate offenders.[5]

The *ducking stool,* as its name implies, was a chair that was fastened to a long lever and situated at the bank of a river or pond. The victim, generally a village gossip or scold, was repeatedly submerged in the water before a jeering crowd. The *stocks and pillory,* which were common in almost every early New England community, were wooden frames with holes for the head, hands, and feet. They were located in the town square, and the culprit—generally a wife beater, petty thief, vagrant, Sabbath breaker, drunkard, adulterer, or unruly servant—would be subjected to public scorn. Confinement in the stocks and pillory often resulted in much more than simple humiliation. The offenders were often whipped or branded while being detained, and most were pelted by passersby. Some were even stoned to death. Offenders who were condemned to the pillory generally had their ears nailed to the frame and were compelled to tear themselves loose (or have their ears cut off) when their period of detention ended.

The *brank,* also called the "gossip's helm" and the "dame's bridle," was a cage placed about the head. It had a spiked plate or flat dish of iron that was placed in the mouth

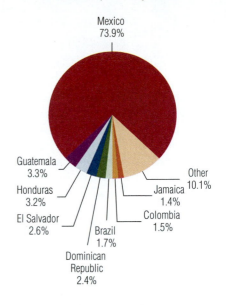

Destination of Deportees
Source: U.S. Citizenship and Immigration Services.

Mexico 73.9%

Guatemala 3.3%

Honduras 3.2%

El Salvador 2.6%

Dominican Republic 2.4%

Brazil 1.7%

Colombia 1.5%

Jamaica 1.4%

Other 10.1%

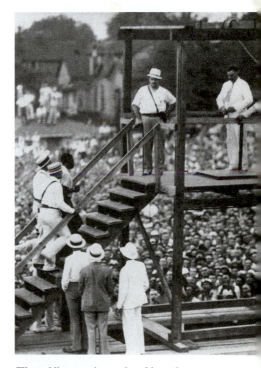

The public execution endured into the 20th century. The last such event in the United States was the hanging of 22-year-old Rainey Bethea in Owensboro, Kentucky, on August 14, 1936. News dispatches stated that some 20,000 spectators witnessed the execution.

The pillory is a mechanical device for inflicting personal distinction.

—AMBROSE BIERCE,
THE DEVIL'S DICTIONARY

EXHIBIT 14.1 | International Perspectives on Crime & Justice

Van Diemen's Land

In 1642, a Dutch navigator by the name of Abel Tasman was the first European known to have sighted a small island some 200 miles or so just south of Australia. In fact, as Tasman swept along the island's west coast, he believed that it was a peninsula jutting out from mainland Australia. He named it Van Diemen's Land, after the governor of the Dutch East Indies.

Tasman's tales of rainy forests, forbidding mountains, dangerous animals, and savages on the beaches didn't do much to kindle any enthusiasm for the place among his masters, and when his subsequent voyage in 1644 turned up pretty much the same things, the Dutch gave up on Australia altogether.

In 1803 the British decided to establish a penal colony on Van Diemen's Land. A year later Hobart Town was established, and soon after convicts began arriving. Van Diemen's Land quickly became a byword for sadism and terror, rum and the lash, and barbaric prison camps. By the time convicts ceased to be transported in 1852, the island's reputation had become so ghastly that its residents decided to change its name to something friendlier-sounding. After navigator Abel Tasman, it is now known as Tasmania.

A Tasmanian rainforest.

---

over the tongue, thus inflicting severe pain if the offender spoke. As this description suggests, this device was designed for gossips, perjurers, liars, and blasphemers, but in colonial New York it was also used for husband beaters and village drunkards.

The *scarlet letter,* made famous by Nathaniel Hawthorne's novel of the same name, was used for a variety of offenses. An adulterous wife wore an *A,* cut from scarlet cloth and sewn to her upper garments. A blasphemer wore a *B,* a pauper a *P,* a thief a *T,* and a drunkard a *D* (see the Critical Thinking section on page 485).

And finally there were the *bilboes,* wherein the citizen convicted of slander and libel was shackled by the feet to a wooden stake.

Punishment versus Reformation

While these punishments were common in colonial times, not everyone was in agreement that these were appropriate responses to lawbreaking. In fact, throughout English and American history, scholars and kings, philosophers and reformers, and legislators and politicians have argued the merits of punishment versus reformation in the management and control of criminal offenders. Their views were shaped by the evolution of criminal law, alternative conceptions of justice, and changing social attitudes.

Before the 18th century, correctional ideas and practices might vary, but they all shared similar goals—the taking of vengeance, the reduction of crime, and the protection of self and society. Criminal sanctions focused on retribution, banishment, isolation, and death and were based on the reasoning that offenders were enemies of society, that they deserved punishment, and that severe approaches would eliminate their potential for future crime. This *punishment ideology* has endured throughout recorded history.

During the 18th century—the Age of Enlightenment—a new ideology began to emerge. It was a reform movement that stressed the dignity and imperfections of the human condition; it recognized the harshness of criminal law and procedure; and it fought against the cruelty of many punishments and conditions of confinement.

> The object of punishment is the reformation of the sufferer, and that of revenge, the gratification of the agent.
>
> —ARISTOTLE

Among the leading European thinkers in the reform movement were Charles Montesquieu, François Voltaire, and Denis Diderot in France; Cesare Beccaria in Italy; and Jeremy Bentham, John Howard, Samuel Romilly, and Sir Robert Peel in England.[6]

The Classical School of Criminology

The principles of Montesquieu, Voltaire, and other Enlightenment philosophers with regard to criminal law and the administration of justice merged during the middle of the 18th century into what has become known as the **classical school of criminal law and criminology.** It has been called "classical" because of its historical significance as the first body of ideas before modern times that was coherently formulated to bring about changes in criminal law and procedure. At the heart of the classical tradition are the ideas that a person is a self-determining being, acting on reason and intelligence, and therefore is responsible for his or her behavior.

The classical school began as an outgrowth of the acquaintanceship between **Cesare Beccaria,** an economist and jurist, and Alessandro Verri, a prison official in Milan. Beccaria's numerous visits to Verri exposed him to existing criminal justice procedures. He observed that judges applied capricious and purely personal justice; he noted that criminal sanctions were almost totally discretionary; he saw many magistrates exercising their power to add to the punishments prescribed by law; and he witnessed tyrannical and brutal punishments in which criminals were branded, mutilated, torn limb from limb, fed to animals, slowly starved, scalded, burned, hanged, enslaved, crucified, and stoned or pressed to death.

Outraged by what he saw, Beccaria began writing what became one of the most significant books of his time. Two years later, in 1764, his *Dei delitti et delle pene (An Essay on Crimes and Punishments)* was published. It outlined a liberal doctrine of criminal law and procedure and highlighted the following points:

1. Because the criminal law places restrictions on individual freedom, the law should be limited in scope. The function of the law is to serve the needs of a given society, not to enforce moral virtue, and as such, to prohibit an action necessarily increases rather than decreases crime.
2. In the administration of justice, the presumption of innocence should be the guiding factor, and at all stages in the criminal justice process the rights of the suspected, the accused, the convicted, and the sentenced should be protected.
3. The criminal law should define in advance both the offenses and their punishments. Thus, there should be a complete written code of criminal law.
4. Punishment should be retributive: "Everyone must suffer punishment so far to invade the province of his own rights as the crime he has committed has penetrated into that of another."
5. The severity of punishment must be limited; it should be proportionate to the crime; it should not go beyond the point that already prevents the offender from further injuring others or beyond the point that already deters others.
6. The nature of the punishment should correspond with the nature of the offense; a fine would be appropriate for simple thefts, but corporal punishment and labor would satisfy crimes of violence.
7. There must be certainty of punishment; penalties must be applied with speed and certainty.
8. Punishment should not be used to make an example of the offender for society, nor should the punishment include reformatory measures, since enforced reformation by its very nature is of little use. Moreover, the punishment should be based on the objective criterion of the crime and not varied to suit the personality of the offender.
9. "It is better to prevent crimes than to punish them"; prevention consists in a clear and limited code of laws, supplemented by the rewarding of virtue.[7]

Beccaria's reformist views were highly praised, for they appeared at a time when European jurists were ready to hear and implement the kinds of changes he proposed.

Care should be taken that the punishment should not be out of proportion to the offenses.

—CICERO

Some young brothers seem like they don't care if they go to prison. They think it's macho, that it gives them more rank out on the street.

—THEODORE RUSSELL, FORMER INMATE

His arguments were incorporated into both English and French criminal codes, and among those inspired by Beccaria's work were the framers of the U.S. Constitution.

The classical school was not limited to the writing and influence of Cesare Beccaria. In England, classicists such as Jeremy Bentham, Samuel Romilly, and John Howard sought to reform the infamous "bloody codes"—a system of laws that permitted execution for such crimes as pickpocketing, cutting down trees on government parklands, setting fire to a cornfield, escaping from jail, and shooting a rabbit.

However, the doctrine of free will, which dominated classical thinking, was problematic in some respects. Classicists argued that all behavior is based on *hedonism,* the *pleasure-pain principle.* People choose the courses of action that give them the most pleasure and avoid those that bring pain. Thus, behavior is purposive—and punishment, they reasoned, should result in more pain than the pleasure received from the forbidden act. This view applied equally to all citizens, with no allowances for aggravating or mitigating circumstances. In spite of these flaws in its perspective, the classical school did make contributions. It was instrumental in making the law impartial, reducing the harshness of penalties, and replacing the arbitrary powers of judges with a specified range of criminal sanctions.

The shift in correctional philosophy stemming from the writings of the classical school led to the use of less severe forms of corporal punishment. There was also growing interest in the use of imprisonment as a form of punishment offering the possibility of reformation of the offender.

American Prisons in Perspective

The American prison system had its beginnings during the second half of the 17th century in Philadelphia. In 1682, William Penn, a religious reformer and the founder of Pennsylvania, made sweeping changes in the administration of justice in the territory under his control. He limited the death penalty to cases of murder, called for fines and imprisonment as penalties for most offenses, and urged flogging for adultery, arson, and rape. These were mild sanctions compared to the executions, brandings, mutilations, and other severe punishments employed in the other colonies. Penn also influenced the construction of county jails, which were designed to be workhouses for convicted felons. The first of these was the High Street Jail in Philadelphia, erected in 1682; others appeared in the decades that followed. But even before Penn's death in 1718, the workhouse idea had failed as a result of overcrowding and inadequate conditions. As one observer described the situation:

> What a spectacle must this abode of guilt and wretchedness have presented, when in one common herd were kept by day and night prisoners of all ages, colors and sexes! No separation was made of the most flagrant offender and convict, from the prisoner who might, perhaps be falsely suspected of some trifling misdemeanor; none of the old and hardened culprits from the youthful, trembling novice in crime; none even of the fraudulent swindler from the unfortunate and possibly the most estimable debtor; and when intermingled with all these, in one corrupt and corrupting assemblage were to be found the disgusting object of popular contempt, besmeared with filth from the pillory—the unhappy victim of the lash, streaming with blood from the whipping post—the half-naked vagrant—the loathsome drunkard—the sick, suffering from various bodily pains, and too often the unanealed [not having received the last rites of the Church] malefactor, whose precious hours of probation had been numbered by his earthly judge.[8]

The Walnut Street Jail

During the 18th century, the Quakers of Pennsylvania were at the forefront of correctional reform. In 1787, they formed the Philadelphia Society for Alleviating the Miseries of Public Prisons and quickly addressed the conditions in local jails. In 1776, a new prison-workhouse opened on Walnut Street in Philadelphia to receive prisoners from the overcrowded High Street Jail. In 1790, influenced by the work of John

Howard, a British prison reformer, the society transformed the new structure on Walnut Street into the first American penitentiary.

The **Walnut Street Jail** was both a prison and a workhouse, and it extended over some 2 acres of land. Those convicted of the most serious crimes were confined without labor in 16 solitary cells, each 6 feet wide and 8 feet long, with an inner iron door, an outer wooden door, and wire across the single window. The prisoners were fed a rather peculiar diet consisting of pudding made of molasses and maize. A large pipe leading from each cell to a sewer served as a toilet, while a stove in the corridor provided heat. Offenders confined for less serious crimes were lodged together in rooms 18 by 20 feet in size. They worked together in a large stone structure at tasks such as shoemaking, carpentry, weaving, tailoring, and nailmaking. Women worked at spinning cotton, preparing hemp and wool, washing, and mending. Vagrants and unskilled prisoners beat hemp or picked moss and oakum (jute fiber used for caulking ships). Male prisoners were credited with the prevailing wage but were charged the costs of their trials, fines, and maintenance. Women were not given wages, nor were they charged for their maintenance. No irons or guard weapons were permitted. Except for women prisoners, silence was enforced in the shops and at meals, but some low-toned conversation was permitted in the night quarters before bedtime. Religious instruction and weekly services were offered.[9]

Throughout the 1790s, the Walnut Street Jail was considered a model prison. Officials from other states and European countries visited to observe its cellular confinement pattern and workhouse program, returning home to praise its design and procedures. By the beginning of the 19th century, however, Philadelphia's acclaimed jail had begun to deteriorate, primarily because of overcrowding. Work activity had been discontinued, discipline had broken down, and riots were common.

The Separate System

The solitary confinement of hardened offenders in the Walnut Street Jail was based on the notion that recidivism could be prevented and offenders reformed if prisoners did not congregate in shared quarters. Confinement in an isolated cell would give the convict an opportunity to contemplate the evils of his past life, thereby leading him to resolve "in the spiritual presence of his Maker" to reform his future conduct.[10] More specifically, supporters of this **separate system** argued that it possessed a number of wholesome virtues, including the following:

* The protection against possible moral contamination through evil association.
* The invitation to self-examination and self-reproach in solitude.
* The impossibility of being visited by anyone (other than an officer, a reformer, or members of the clergy).
* The great ease of administration of discipline.
* The possibility of a great degree of individuality of treatment.
* The minimal need for disciplinary measures.
* The absence of any possibility of mutual recognition of prisoners after discharge.
* The fact that the pressures of loneliness would make convicts eager to engage in productive labor, during which time they could be taught a useful trade.[11]

Such was the basis for the construction of Western Penitentiary near Pittsburgh in 1826 and Eastern Penitentiary near Philadelphia in 1829. Eastern Penitentiary reflected the Pennsylvania correctional philosophy, and its architecture was adapted to the principle of solitary confinement.[12] It had seven wards, housing a total of 844 individual cells, all radiating from a common center like the spokes of a wheel. To each cell on the lower floor of each ward was attached a small exercise yard, which the prisoner could visit twice daily for short periods. In the interim, he washed, ate, and slept in his cell, seeing no one other than prison officials and reformers from the outside community. Massive walls surrounded the entire institution and divided its parts so as to eliminate all contact and make escape impossible.

This community, it grooms you to prepare yourself to go to jail or the penitentiary. A lot of people lose hope. Every day is a struggle. It seems like going to prison is destiny for a lot of young brothers. But we know what time it is. White folks be committing crimes, too. But they get probation, we go to jail.

— ROBERT TAYLOR, CHICAGO PUBLIC HOUSING RESIDENT

The history of correction is a graveyard of abandoned fads.

— ROBERT MARTINSON

It's such an exclusive place, you have to be recommended by a judge to get in.

— DELAWARE INMATE, ON GOING TO PRISON

Eastern Penitentiary, Philadelphia, Pennsylvania, as it appeared in its early years.

Stone walls do not a prison make, nor iron bars a cage.

— RICHARD LOVELACE, 1649

Prison is a place of punishment and rewards. The poet assures us that— "Stone walls do not a prison make," but a combination of the stone wall, the political parasite and the moral instructor is no garden of sweets.

— AMBROSE BIERCE,
THE DEVIL'S DICTIONARY

Visitors from almost every nation in the Western world marveled at the construction and plan of Eastern Penitentiary and recommended that the model be adopted in their home countries. In 1833, the French writers Gustave de Beaumont and Alexis de Tocqueville commented on the reformative effects of the absolute solitude that Pennsylvania's separate system provided for its confined offenders:

> Generally, their hearts are found ready to open themselves, and the facility of being moved renders them also fitter for reformation. They are particularly accessible to religious sentiments, and the remembrance of their family has an uncommon power over their minds. . . . Nothing distracts, in Philadelphia, the mind of the convicts from their meditations; and as they are always isolated, the presence of a person who comes to converse with them is of the greatest benefit. . . . When we visited this penitentiary, one of the prisoners said to us: "It is with joy that I perceive the figure of the keepers, who visit my cell. This summer a cricket came into my yard; it looked like a companion. When a butterfly or any other animal happens to enter my cell, I never do it any harm."[13]

However, the separate system was also a dehumanizing experience. As one commentator described it:

> [The inmate] was given a hot bath, and a prison uniform. Then his eyes were bandaged, and he was led blindfolded into the rotunda, where, still not seeing, he heard the rules of the house explained by the superintendent. And still blindfolded, he was led to his living grave. The bandage was taken from his eyes. He saw a cell less than twelve feet long, less than eight feet wide, and if he was to live on the ground floor, he saw a little courtyard, the same size, highly walled, opening out of it, in which he sometimes might exercise. In that cell, and that courtyard, he stayed, without any change, for three, ten, twenty years or for life. He saw only the guard who brought his food to him, but who was forbidden to speak to him. He got no letters, saw none of his family. He was cut off from the world. When the cholera raged in Philadelphia in 1843, it was months before the prisoners got a hint that an epidemic had visited the city. After the slave had been three days in his cell, he was allowed

to work, if he wished, and the fact that nearly all prisoners asked for something to do proved to the inspectors that reform was beginning. If they did not choose to work they might commune with their corrupt hearts in a perfectly dark and solitary punishment cell.[14]

Despite its attractiveness to European visitors, the Pennsylvania plan never gained widespread popularity in the United States. It was the basis of some experiments in New Jersey and Rhode Island, but by the latter part of the 19th century it had been abandoned, even in Pennsylvania.

The Silent System

The demise of the separate system was due not so much to the destructive effects of long-term solitary confinement as to the emergence of a different pattern of prison administration in New York State. Established at Auburn Prison in 1823, it was known as the **silent system** and was considered to be the most economically sound type of penitentiary program. Rather than having outside cells with individual exercise yards as at Eastern Penitentiary, prisoners at Auburn were confined in banks of inside cells each measuring only 7 feet by 3½ feet. Inmates were employed in shops during the day under a rigid rule of absolute silence at all times. Hard labor was considered essential to the reformation of character and to the economic solvency of the prison. Perpetual silence was seen as mandatory while inmates were together in order to prevent them from corrupting one another and to reduce opportunities for devising plans for insurrection, escape, or riot. All prisoners were totally separated from the outside world; communication with relatives and friends was forbidden.[15]

The attractiveness of the silent system was primarily due to its economic advantages. Small inside cells were cheaper to construct. Also, industrial production in large congregate work areas was far greater and more efficient than the limited output possible under the Pennsylvania plan of handicraft construction in separate confinement. The hard and unremitting labor, perpetual silence, and unquestioning obedience were maintained by means of severe corporal punishments such as flogging, the "douche," and the "water cure." Flogging was considered the most effective method of gaining compliance and was generally done with a rawhide whip or a "cat" made of wire strands. The "douche" involved continuous dumping of frigid water onto the prisoner from a great height. The "water cure" took several forms. At times it consisted of a strong, fine stream of water turned onto sensitive parts of the prisoner's body; on other occasions, water fell a drop at a time onto the prisoner's head, the process sometimes lasting for days. These were common punishments for breaking the silence rule. The technique of talking out of the side of one's mouth—often depicted in gangster movies of the 1930s and 1940s—had its origin in "silent" prisons, where it was a means of getting around the silence rules.

Prison stripes and the *lockstep* also originated at Auburn. Striped uniforms served to degrade convicts and to make them conspicuous if they escaped. The lockstep, which was devised for the purpose of making supervision easier, was a bizarre marching formation. Prisoners were required to line up behind one another with their hands on the shoulders or under the arms of the person in front. The line then moved rapidly toward its destination as the prisoners shuffled their feet in unison, without lifting them from the ground, with their eyes focused on the guard. Another feature of Auburn was the "prison-within-a-prison," or "hole"—an area where prisoners were put into total isolation as a punishment for violations of institutional rules. For a very different view of Auburn, see Exhibit 14.2.

Prison Industries

The Auburn model became the major pattern of prison administration for the rest of the 19th century. Sing Sing Prison in New York adopted the Auburn plan in 1825, and more than 30 other states built similar institutions in the years that followed. However, the rule of absolute silence was soon relaxed, for conditions within most penitentiaries

Once they are jailed they are no longer homeless. Once they are jailed they have balanced meals.

— JESSE JACKSON

EXHIBIT 14.2 | A View from the Field

A Day at Auburn Prison by Lewis Dwight, Boston Prison Discipline Society, 1823

At Auburn we have a more beautiful example still of what may be done by proper discipline, in a prison well constructed. It is not possible to describe the pleasure which we feel in contemplating this noble institution, after wading through the fraud, and the material and moral filth of many prisons. We regard it as a model worthy of the world's imitation. We do not mean that there is nothing in this institution which admits of improvement; for there have been a few cases of unjustifiable severity in punishments; but, upon the whole, the institution is immensely elevated above the old penitentiaries.

The whole establishment, from the gate to the sewer, is a specimen of neatness. The unremitting industry, the entire subordination and subdued feeling of the convicts has probably no parallel among an equal number of criminals. In their solitary cells they spend the night, with no other book but the Bible, and at sunrise they proceed, in military order, under the eye of the turnkeys, in solid columns, with the lock march, to their workshops; thence, in the same order, at the hour of breakfast, to the common hall, where they partake of their wholesome and frugal meal in silence. Not even a whisper is heard; though the silence is such that a whisper might be heard through the whole apartment. The convicts are seated in single file, at narrow tables, with their backs towards the center, so that there can be no interchange of signs. If one has more food than he wants, he raises his left hand; and if another has less, he raises his right hand, and the waiter changes it. When they have done eating, at the ringing of a little bell, of the softest sound, they rise from the table, form the solid columns, and return, under the eye of the turnkeys, to the workshops. From one end of the shops to the other, it is the testimony of many witnesses that they have passed more than three hundred convicts, without seeing one leave his work, or turn his head to gaze at them. There is the most perfect attention to business from morning until night, interrupted only by the time necessary to dine, and never by the fact that the whole body of prisoners have done their tasks, and the time is now their own, and they can do as they please. At the close of the day, a little before sunset, the work is all laid aside at once, and the convicts return, in military order, to the solitary cells, where they partake of the frugal meal, which they were permitted to take from the kitchen where it was furnished for them as they returned from the shops. After supper, they can, if they choose, read Scripture undisturbed and then reflect in silence on the errors of their lives. They must not disturb their fellow prisoners by even a whisper.

Source: From a letter cited by Harry Elmer Barnes, *The Story of Punishment: A Record of Man's Inhumanity to Man* (Montclair, NJ: Patterson Smith, 1972), 136–137.

made it impractical. Not only had most of the institutions become overcrowded, but, more important, the Industrial Revolution had arrived and factory workshop production had been introduced to exploit cheap inmate labor and make penitentiaries self-sustaining. Production became the paramount goal of prisons, and the necessity for communication within the industrial shops served to make the perpetual silence rule counterproductive.[16]

Contract labor and the piece-price system were the earliest forms of prison industry. Under the **contract system,** the labor of inmates was leased to an outside contractor, who furnished the machinery and raw materials and supervised the work. Under such an arrangement the only responsibility of the prison administration was to guard the convicts. The **piece-price system** was a variation on the contract system. The contractor supplied the raw materials and received the finished product, paying the prison a specified amount for each unit produced. Under both plans prisoners were exploited, overworked, and otherwise abused. Contractors often shortchanged convicts in their work tallies, and prison officials forced inmates to work long hours under deplorable conditions for little or no pay. Recalling his experiences at Michigan's Ionia Reformatory in 1889, an inmate at Illinois State Penitentiary wrote some four decades later:

During my stay at this time there was a great deal of fighting, especially in the Cigar Shop, owing to the fact that the boys were continuously stealing cigars from each other to complete the task set them by the Contractors, as it was almost impossible to do what they demanded. In the Shoe Shop things were about the same, and a friend of mine, Tiny Prince, tried to cut off his finger in full view of all of us. Another man on the Shoe Contract took a hatchet and cut off his thumb because he was unable to do his task.

Here I will make a confession I have never made in my life before. The first finger of my left hand is gone. I have always let people think it got cut off accidentally in a machine. Well, it didn't. I cut if off myself like these other men did, in order to cripple myself so I could escape for a little while from the hell of that contract labor at Ionia. I did it by bracing a knife blade against my finger and pounding it with my shoe. That was how bad some of us hated the contract system.[17]

Even more vicious was the **lease system,** under which contractors assumed complete control over prisoners, including their maintenance and discipline. Convicts were taken from the institutions and employed in agriculture, quarrying, bridge and road construction, mining, or in turpentine camps or sugar cane plantations. This forced labor resembled slavery, and prisoners received little, if any, compensation for their work.[18]

Alternatives to the contract labor systems were the **state account** and **state-use systems.** Under the state account plan, inmate production was directed and supervised by prison officials, the manufactured goods were sold on the open market, and the convicts received a small share of the profits. Under the state-use plan, articles produced in prison were used in state-supported institutions and bureaus. Related to these was the public works system of prison labor, under which inmates were employed in the construction and repair of public streets, highways, and structures. Sing Sing Prison, from which came such terms as the "big house" and "up the river" (because it is on the eastern shore of the Hudson River, 30 miles north of New York City), was constructed by a team of 100 inmates from Auburn under the public works system.[19]

Most 19th-century prisons also included farming as a form of prison labor. As a separate form of the state-use philosophy, prison agriculture was viewed as a neces-

An observer in 1893 described the lockstep: "A squad of convicts was passing through the yard. The tallest man was at the head, the shortest at the tail. So close they stood, breast to back, that as each leg was thrown forward it locked its owner in the long striped line, which with a swaying movement and a rhythmical shuffling sound passed on, looking for all the world like a huge striped serpent."

U.S. film actor James Cagney, left (1899–1986) in a scene from "Public Enemy," which established him as the quintessential screen gangster.

Once a penal colony for habitual felons, Norfolk Island is now a South Pacific refuge for world-weary travelers.

sary part of institutional procedure. The raising of crops and vegetables was a means of hard inmate labor, while at the same time it reduced the cost of feeding inmates (see Exhibit 14.3).

The Reformatory Era

During the mid-19th century a *treatment philosophy* of corrections developed. This was an ideology that viewed many forms of offense behavior as manifestations of various social "pathologies," psychological "maladies," and inherited "predispositions" that could be "corrected" through therapeutic or rehabilitative intervention. This new treatment ideology led to the *reformatory era* in American corrections, which endured from 1870 through 1910. The influences that led to the reformatory idea came from numerous theorists and practitioners in many parts of the world, but the movement was affected most directly by the work of Captain Alexander Maconochie in Australia and Sir Walter Crofton in Ireland.

In 1840, Alexander Maconochie, a geographer with England's Royal Navy, was placed in charge of Norfolk Island, a penal colony for habitual felons located 1,000 miles off the coast of Australia. Conditions at Norfolk were so bad that it has been said that "men who were reprieved wept with sorrow that they had to go on living, and those doomed to die fell on their knees and thanked God for the release that was to be theirs."[20] Maconochie eliminated the brutality of the system and implemented a correctional scheme based on five principles:

1. Sentences should be not for a period of time but for the performance of a determined and specified quantity of labor; in brief, time sentences should be abolished, and task sentences substituted.
2. The quantity of labor a prisoner must perform should be expressed in a number of "marks" which he must earn, by improvement of conduct, frugality of living, and habits of industry, before he can be released.
3. While in prison he should earn everything he receives; all sustenance and indulgences should be added to his debt of marks.
4. When qualified by discipline to do so he should work in association with a small number of other prisoners, forming a group of six or seven, and the whole group should be answerable for the conduct and labor of each member of it.
5. In the final stage, a prisoner, while still obliged to earn his daily tally of marks, should be given a proprietary interest in his own labor and be subject to a less rigorous discipline in order to prepare him for release into society.[21]

This "apparatus," as Captain Maconochie called it, abolished the "flat" term of imprisonment and replaced it with a **mark system** in which an inmate could earn early release by hard work and good behavior. But the scheme was not viewed favorably by Maconochie's superiors. He was removed as administrator after only a brief time, his achievements were denied, and the colony quickly returned to its former brutalizing routine.

But what had occurred at Norfolk Island had not gone unnoticed. Drawing on Maconochie's notion that imprisonment could be used to prepare a convict for eventual return to the community, Sir Walter Crofton of Ireland implemented what he called his "indeterminate system." Also known as the *"Irish system,"* it called for four distinct stages of treatment: (1) solitary confinement at monotonous work for 2 years, followed by (2) congregate labor under a marking system that regulated privileges and determined the date of discharge, then by (3) an intermediate stage during which inmates were permitted to work on outside jobs, and finally by (4) conditional release under a **ticket-of-leave.**[22] This ticket, which could be revoked if the convict failed to live up to the conditions of his temporary release, was the first attempt at what has come to be known as *parole.*

Maconochie's mark system and Crofton's Irish system were overwhelmingly endorsed at the American Prison Congress in 1870. The result was the opening of the first reformatory in the United States at Elmira, New York, in 1876. Elmira was an institution for youths and young adults serving their first term of imprisonment.

historical perspectives on criminal justice | **EXHIBIT 14.3**

Contract Prison Labor in the Post-Civil War South

After the Civil War had shattered both the social structure and economy of the South, maintaining adequate prison systems tended to have only minimal priority for state officials. Approaches were sought for making prisons at least self-supporting, and perhaps even profit-making. The obvious solution was to lease prisons and convicts to private contractors, and by 1875 almost every southern state had some sort of contract labor policy.

As in some northern jurisdictions, however, many southern prison lease systems quickly evolved into varieties of penal servitude. Although state inspectors were assigned to monitor such arrangements, inmates typically lived and worked under conditions of poor hygiene and excessive brutality, often spending much of their time shackled to heavy iron balls. A late-19th-century commentary on contract labor conditions in Mississippi reported the following:

> Those on farms and public works have been subjected to indignities without authority of law and contrary to civilized humanity. Often subleasers resort to "pullin" the prisoner until he faints from the lash on his naked back, while the sufferer was held by four strong men holding each a hand or foot stretched out on the frozen ground or over stumps or logs—often over 300 *stripes* [lashes] at a time, which more than once, it is thought, resulted in the death of a convict. Men unable to work have been driven to their death and some have died fettered to the chain gang. . . . When working in the swamps or fields they were refused pure water and were driven to drink out of sloughs or plow furrows in the fields in which they labored. . . . Some were placed in the swamp in water ranging to their bare knees, and in almost nude state they spaded caney and rooty ground, their bare feet chained together by chains that fretted the flesh. They were compelled to attend to the calls of nature in line as they stood day in and day out, their thirst compelling them to drink the water in which they were compelled to deposit their excrement.

The brutal conditions of the lease system received such widespread criticism and legislative focus that contract labor as such became obsolete throughout the South by 1920. In its place emerged public works systems and their well-known *chain gangs.* In South Carolina, Florida, and Georgia, for example, all able-bodied prisoners were sentenced to the county, as an alternative to the state penitentiary, to perform road and bridge work. Although public works systems tended to be less exploitative of inmates than leasing, life on a chain gang was anything but pleasant. "Whipping bosses" maintained discipline through severe punishments, and brutality was not uncommon. The use of the chain gang was so widespread that, with time, its inmates in striped uniforms and chains doing roadwork under the watchful eyes of a gun-toting boss came to symbolize southern corrections.

By contrast, Texas, Louisiana, Arkansas, and Mississippi replaced leasing with the *plantation prison system.* Legislatures in these jurisdictions had stressed self-sufficiency. Too, turning old plantations into productive prison farms appeared to be a solution to the burgeoning black prisoner population of the post-Civil War period. It was the opinion of many whites during these years that former slaves were still fieldhands who could not be reformed.

A hallmark of the southern plantation prisons was the trusty model of inmate control—closely akin to the slave driver system on antebellum plantations. As a mechanism of dealing with limited institutional budgets, select groups of convicts were chosen to watch over their inmate peers. They were housed separately and typically had far more privileges than other prisoners. Convict guards in Arkansas, Louisiana, and Mississippi, generally called "shooters," herded over their quarry with loaded shotguns—an arrangement that endured well into the 20th century. The Texas counterpart to the trusty was the *building tender.* In contrast to trusties, building tenders were unarmed and lived in the same quarters as other inmates but watched them nevertheless. The building tender system survived in Texas until the 1980s, finally crumbling in the aftermath of the *Ruiz* v. *Estelle* prison conditions case (see Chapter 16).

Sources: Edward L. Ayers, *Vengeance and Justice: Crime and Punishment in the 19th Century American South* (New York: Oxford University Press, 1984); Mark T. Carleton, *Politics and Punishment: The History of the Louisiana State Penal System* (Baton Rouge: Louisiana State University Press, 1971); James W. Marquart and Ben M. Crouch, "Co-opting the Kept: Using Inmates for Social Control in a Southern Prison," *Justice Quarterly* 1 (1984): 491–509; *Ruiz* v. *Estelle*, F.2d 115 (5th. Cir. 1982).

An African American chain gang in post-Civil War Arkansas.

Zebulon Brockway, its first superintendent, listed the essentials of a successful reformatory system:

1. The material structure establishment itself. . . . The general plan and arrangements should be those of the Auburn System plan, modified and modernized; and 10% of the cells might well be constructed like those of the Pennsylvania System structures. The whole should be supplied with suitable modern sanitary appliances and with abundance of natural and artificial light.
2. Clothing—not degradingly distinctive but uniform, yet fitly representing the respective grades or standing of the prisoners. . . . Scrupulous cleanliness should be maintained and the prisoners appropriately groomed.
3. A liberal prison dietary designed to promote vigor. Deprivation of food, by a general regulation, is deprecated.
4. All the modern appliances for scientific physical culture; a gymnasium completely equipped with baths and apparatus; and facilities for field athletics.
5. Facilities for manual training sufficient for about one-third of the population. . . . This special manual training covers, in addition to other exercises in other departments, mechanical and freehand drawing; cardboard constructive form work; clay modeling; cabinet making; clipping and filing; and iron molding.
6. Trade instruction based on the needs and capacities of individual prisoners.
7. A regimental military organization with a band of music, swords for officers and dummy guns for the rank and file of prisoners.
8. School of letters with a curriculum that reaches from an adaptation of the kindergarten . . . up to the usual high school course; and, in addition, special classes in college subjects. . . .
9. A well-selected library for circulation, consultation and, for occasional semi-social use.
10. A weekly institutional newspaper, in lieu of all outside newspapers, edited and printed by the prisoners under due censorship.
11. Recreating and diverting entertainments for the mass of the population, provided in the great auditorium; not any vaudeville or minstrel shows, but entertainments of such a class as the middle cultured people of a community would enjoy. . . .
12. Religious opportunities . . . adapted to the hereditary, habitual, and preferable denominational predilection of the individual prisoners.
13. Definitely planned, carefully directed, emotional occasions; not summoned, primarily, for either instruction, diversion, nor, specifically, for a common religious impression, but, figuratively, for a kind of irrigation.[23]

The program established at Elmira quickly spread to other states, but the reformatory movement as a whole proved to be a disappointment for its advocates. Many of Brockway's principles were never put into effect; prison employees were too conditioned to the punishment ideology to support the new concepts; safe and secure custody continued to be regarded as the most important institutional activity; the reformatories quickly became overcrowded, and staff shortages prevented the development of academic programs; and hard-core offenders were housed in the new structures, thus turning them into more typical penal environments.[24]

By 1910, the reformatory experiment had been abandoned. Nevertheless, it left an important legacy for corrections. The indeterminate sentence, conditional release, educational programs, vocational training, and other rehabilitative ideals fostered by the reformatory became part of the correctional ideology of later decades. (For a discussion of reformatory measures in the treatment of women inmates, see Exhibit 14.4.)

The 20th-Century Industrial Prison

By the early years of the 20th century, the American prison system had evolved into a growing number of institutions modeled after those at Sing Sing and Auburn. Reflecting the architecture of medieval dungeons and Gothic castles, they were fortresslike structures operating on the principles of mass incarceration and rigid discipline and security. Their most distinctive feature was the use of inmate labor for the production of industrial goods for sale on the open market. This practice was widely encouraged not only because of the belief in hard labor as a correctional tool but also because of the economics of creating a self-sustaining prison system.

Notice
You are hereby notified that your convict prison camp is violating the law as follows: Garbage cans are not provided with lids; the kitchen is not properly screened; food is exposed to flies and dirt; the beds are very dirty, and need new mattresses and covers; prisoners are not provided with night shirts; sewage disposal is unsanitary; the sleeping tent canvas is rotten and does not prevent rain from entering and thus wetting prisoners and beds.

—NORTH CAROLINA STATE BOARD OF CHARITIES AND PUBLIC WELFARE, 1926

All prisoners who have syphilis, chancroid, or gonorrhea shall be isolated.

—NORTH CAROLINA STATE BOARD OF HEALTH, 1925

Gender Perspectives on Crime and Justice | EXHIBIT 14.4

Sexism and Indeterminate Sentencing

The first separate prison for women opened during 1863 in Indiana. Reformers of the day believed that women who committed crimes suffered from psychological illness, since their participation in crime was indicative of their inability to display "proper" feminine behavior. Indeed, crime was thought to be an unfortunate outgrowth of innate male behavior. The goal of punishment for men during this period was to redirect "natural" male aggression into legitimate economic channels. This goal was accomplished primarily through the requirement that male inmates spend the better portion of their day laboring for the prison. For women, however, the goal of punishment was primarily rehabilitative. This consisted largely of teaching women offenders to behave in a feminine manner and encouraging them to master activities central to the domestic sphere—like cooking, cleaning, and parenting.

Indeterminate sentences played a central role in the effort to rehabilitate women offenders. Indeterminate sentences specify a minimum and maximum amount of time to be served in a correctional facility, and they were systematically applied to women offenders because reformers thought that rehabilitation could be accomplished only on an individual basis. They felt that some women could be rehabilitated in only 2 years, while other women might take considerably longer. Short, fixed sentences, reformers feared, would result in the release of numerous female offenders who were not yet rehabilitated and, therefore, were incapable of properly assuming their feminine duties.

By 1913, Pennsylvania created its first separate correctional facility under the Muncy Act. This act specified that women who were sentenced to more than a year in prison would be sent to the State Industrial Home for Women, where they would be confined for the maximum sentence length under the law. Under the Muncy Act, judges had no discretion when sentencing women; instead, they were forced to rely on the sentence range prescribed for various offenses by state statute. A woman charged with robbery, for example, was sentenced to the 10-year maximum, while a man convicted on robbery charges could receive a sentence of considerably less time. For men, then, judges were allowed to exhibit discretion and depart from state sentencing statutes. Women could receive early release only after correctional personnel deemed them reformed. Generally, decisions to release inmates were based on the discretion of a few influential correctional officers and administrators. Unlike men, neither women inmates nor their counsel were allowed to be present at parole hearings. The net result of indeterminate sentencing policies was that women around the country served unusually long sentences for trivial offenses such

as vagrancy, public drunkenness, prostitution, and petty larceny and served longer sentences than men for all offenses.

The policy of indeterminate sentences for women was not challenged until 1966 when a Pennsylvania judge sentenced Jane Daniels to serve 1 to 4 years for robbery. The sentence was voided because it violated the state's policy of indeterminate sentencing for women. Instead, Daniels was sentenced to 10 years (the maximum sentence for robbery). In *Daniels* v. *Commonwealth,* Daniels took the case to a Pennsylvania Superior Court on the basis that the Muncy Act violated the due process clause of the Fourteenth Amendment. The court rejected Daniels's challenge on the basis that women have inherent physical and psychological differences from men that necessitate differential treatment under the law. The court noted:

> The legislature reasonably could have concluded that indeterminate sentences should be imposed on women as a class . . . in order to provide more effective rehabilitation. Such a conclusion could be based on the physiological and psychological makeup of a woman, the type of crime committed by women, their relation to the criminal world, their role in society, their unique vocational skills, and their reaction as a class to imprisonment.

Daniels later petitioned the state supreme court to hear the case. The court's decision was a bittersweet victory for Daniels, ruling in her favor on the basis that the U.S. Constitution prevents the imposition of longer sentences on women, but it noted that the Constitution does not grant women equal rights under the law. Only recently have courts in most states overturned gender-specific indeterminate sentencing policies. Nevertheless, in some states female inmates continue to be denied access to closed parole board hearings that determine the status of their sentence and the potential for early release.

Sources: Helen Boritch, "Gender and Criminal Court Outcomes: An Historical Analysis," *Criminology* 30 (1992): 293–325; Jill McCorkel, "Justice, Gender, and Incarceration: An Overview and Analysis of the Leniency-Severity Debate," in *Examining the Justice Process,* edited by James A. Inciardi (Fort Worth, TX: Harcourt Brace, 1996); Janice Joseph and Dorothy Taylor, *With Justice for All: Minorities and Women in Criminal Justice* (Upper Saddle River, NJ: Prentice-Hall, 2003); Claire M. Renzetti and Lynne Goodstein, Editors, *Women, Crime, and Criminal Justice: Original Feminist Readings* (Los Angeles, CA: Roxbury, 2001); Melinda E. O'Neil, "The Gender Gap Argument: Exploring the Disparity of Sentencing Women to Death," *New England Journal on Crime and Civil Confinement* 25, 1 (1999): 213–244; Courtney Robison Semisch, *Differential Sentencing Outcomes for Female Federal Drug Traffickers: Gender Disparity or Suitable Sanctions?* (Ann Arbor, MI: University Microfilms International, 2000); Leslie Acoca and James Austin, *The Crisis: The Women Offender Sentencing Study and Alternative Sentencing Recommendations Project: Women in Prison* (Washington, DC: National Council on Crime and Delinquency, 1996).

Yet at the same time that the industrial prison was developing into a prudent financial operation, opposition to inmate labor was growing. Prison industries under the contract, piece-price, lease, and state account systems were seen as threats to free enterprise. After the formation of the American Federation of Labor (AFL) in 1880, the labor movement organized a formal attack on the industrial prison. The culmination of the assault came during the Great Depression with the passage of numerous federal and state statutes.[25]

Don't do the crime if you can't stand the time.

— OLD PRISON SAYING

FAMOUS CRIMINALS
Robert Stroud

In 1962, MGM released the movie *The Bird-man of Alcatraz.* Starring Burt Lancaster in the lead role, it told the story of Robert Stroud, a federal prison inmate who studied the diseases of the sparrows and canaries that he kept in his cell as pets. He excelled at what he did and eventually wrote two books that detailed a variety of cures for many of the diseases that were common to domesticated birds. And he did this in spite of the brutalizing and demeaning prison system and with only minimal formal education. The movie closed with the statement that Robert Stroud was still in prison and had always been denied parole. Almost immediately, theatergoers and celebrities petitioned for the pardon of this kind-hearted gentleman genius. Tables were even set up in theater lobbies soliciting signatures endorsing Stroud's release. Moviegoers even flooded the Justice Department with letters, saying that they had seen the movie and just couldn't believe Stroud hadn't been pardoned. Burt Lancaster even stepped in and offered to have Stroud paroled to him.

What few theatergoers seemed to know was that Stroud was not a particularly nice individual. In 1909 he had brutally murdered a bartender who had allegedly failed to pay a prostitute for whom Stroud was pimping in Alaska. In 1911 Stroud was convicted of manslaughter, and he was sent to serve his sentence at McNeil Island, a federal penitentiary in Washington State. His record at McNeil indicates that he was violent and

(continued on p. 477)

Even before the economic strains of the Depression began to be felt, the *Hawes-Cooper Act* of 1929 disallowed certain prison-made goods from being shipped to other states. Put into force on January 1, 1934, the act, in effect, barred these products from interstate commerce. At the same time, 33 states passed legislation that prohibited the sale of prison goods on the open market. The *Ashurst-Sumners Act* of 1935 banned transportation companies from accepting inmate products for shipment into states where the local laws prohibited their sale. And the *Walsh-Healy Act,* signed into law by President Franklin D. Roosevelt on October 14, 1940, excluded almost all prison-made products from interstate commerce.

Humanitarian concerns also played a role in the demise of the prison industrial complex. Contract labor systems were often no more than exploitation motivated by corruption and greed. Although the philosophy of the time supported the notion that offenders needed discipline and hard labor to teach them the lessons of deterrence and salvation, reformers nevertheless opposed the misuse of convict workers.

The abolition of contract labor was in many ways desirable, but there was little to take the place of free-market prison enterprise. State-use and public works programs survived, but a majority of convicts were left idle. The reduction in institutional self-support and maintenance led to the gradual decay of prison structures and conditions. Eventually many state penitentiaries began shifting back to their original purposes of punishment and custody.

After the Depression years and into the second half of the 20th century, there was great turmoil within state prison systems. Known as the "period of transition" in American corrections, it was a time when clinicians and reformers were introducing new treatment ideas against a backdrop of growing apathy and decaying institutions. Some segments of the public subscribed to the rehabilitative goals of correctional ideology; others felt that prisons should be no more than secure places to house criminal offenders.

The 1960s and 1970s reflected even greater contrasts. Greater emphasis was placed on the needs of individual prisoners, and many of the ideas generated during the reformatory era were put into place. Academic and vocational programs were established; social casework and psychiatric treatment approaches were designed and implemented; many prison facilities were expanded; special institutions were built and equipped for youthful offenders; more concern was demonstrated for the separation of hard-core from amateur criminals; a variety of changes made prison life somewhat more humane and productive; and state and federal judges showed greater awareness of prisoners' rights by providing easier access to the courts for those seeking remedies against cruel and unusual punishment.

At the same time, however, there was growing unrest within the nation's correctional institutions. The majority of state penitentiaries were still walled fortresses—solemn monuments to the ideas of 19th-century penology. Prison administrators were faced with the contradictions of "rehabilitation" within a context of mass overcrowding, personnel shortages, and demands for better security. It was also a time of militancy and violence within prisons. Greater awareness of prisoners' rights under conditions that seemed to be getting worse instead of better led to riots in institutions around the nation.

Throughout the 1980s, 1990s, and into the 21st century, the future of the American prison system remained unclear. Diagnosticians, reformers, social scientists, and civil libertarians continued their efforts to make prisons more humane and geared toward rehabilitation of offenders. Yet the "law and order" approach toward offenders combined with perceptions of inefficiency within the criminal justice system served only to harden public attitudes toward the treatment of criminals.

The Federal Prison System

Many of the reforms and rehabilitative measures introduced in state institutions after the Great Depression were modeled on federal practices. The federal system is the most diversified prison system in the United States. It is also the one that developed most recently, although its roots date back to the signing of the Declaration of Independence.

Beginning in 1776 and for more than a century, all federal offenders were confined in state and territorial institutions. The criminal law of the United States government was not particularly well developed at that time, and the few federal prosecutions that occurred were limited to cases involving counterfeiting, piracy and other crimes on the high seas and to felonies committed on Indian reservations. By the 1880s, however, the number of federal prisoners in state penitentiaries totaled more than 1,000, with an additional 10,000 housed in county jails. This situation put pressure on federal authorities to take a more active role in the field of corrections.[26]

The first federal penitentiaries were authorized by Congress in 1891, and by 1905 institutions had been opened in Atlanta, Georgia, and in Leavenworth, Kansas. In 1919, McNeil Island in Puget Sound off the coast of Washington State was designated as a federal facility; in 1924, a women's reformatory was constructed at Alderson, West Virginia, and during the following year a men's reformatory was authorized at the military reservation at Chillicothe, Ohio.

As a result of the Mann Act of 1910 (which prohibited the transportation of women in foreign and interstate commerce for immoral purposes), the Harrison Act of 1914 (which regulated the distribution and sale of narcotics), the Volstead Act of 1919 (which prohibited the manufacture, transportation, and sale of alcoholic beverages), and the National Motor Vehicle Theft Act of 1919 (which controlled the interstate transportation of stolen vehicles), the number of people convicted of federal crimes grew rapidly during the 1920s. The result was the creation of the *Federal Bureau of Prisons* on May 14, 1930. The legislation creating the bureau called for the "proper classification and segregation of Federal prisoners according to their character, the nature of the crimes they have committed, their mental condition, and such other factors as should be taken into consideration in providing an individualized system of discipline, care, and treatment."[27]

Despite the many negative opinions about its fortresslike Alcatraz Island Penitentiary, the bureau gradually evolved into the acknowledged leader in American correctional practice. The bureau established a graded system of institutions that included maximum-security penitentiaries for the close custody of the most serious felons, medium-security facilities for those who were better prospects for rehabilitation, reformatories for young and inexperienced offenders, minimum-security open camps for offenders requiring little custodial control, detention centers for those awaiting trial and disposition, and a variety of halfway houses, work-release programs, and community treatment centers. By the beginning of 2005, it was operating an integrated system of almost 100 adult and juvenile correctional facilities, housing more than 170,000 inmates.[28]

Although the federal and state prison systems grew dramatically during the 20th century, and although many aspects of correctional practice changed over the years, large numbers of offenders never enter prisons or do so only after a substantial period of detention in jail. Because jails house such large numbers of inmates and conditions in jails are a subject of growing concern, the next section examines jails and detention centers in some detail.

| Jails and Detention Centers |

Jail: An unbelievably filthy institution in which are confined men and women serving sentences for misdemeanors and crimes, and men and women not under sentence who are simply awaiting trial. . . . A melting pot in which the worst elements of the raw material in the criminal world are brought forth, blended and turned out in absolute perfection.

— **JOSEPH F. FISHMAN, INSPECTOR OF PRISONS, UNITED STATES GOVERNMENT, 1923**

The jail is for the poor, the street is for the rich.

— **NOAH POPE, JAIL INMATE**

(continued from p. 476)
difficult to manage. On one occasion, Stroud viciously assaulted a hospital orderly who he insisted had reported him to the administration for attempting to procure narcotics through intimidation and threats. On another occasion he stabbed a fellow inmate. After being transferred to Leavenworth, he stabbed a guard to death. He was convicted of first-degree murder and sentenced to death by hanging, but after his mother petitioned President Woodrow Wilson to spare his life, Stroud's sentence was commuted to life without parole. Stroud never got to see *The Birdman of Alcatraz.* He died of natural causes within a year after the film's release. ∎

Snitches get stitches.

— **OLD PRISON SAYING**

Eric: I'll never forget my mother's words to me when I first went to jail.
Ernie: What did she say?
Eric: Hello, son.

— **ERIC MORCAMBE**
AND ERNIE WISE

Citizenship of U.S. Bureau of Prison Inmates

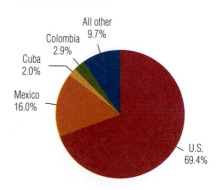

Leavenworth, Kansas, one of the earliest federal penitentiaries.

A jail is not a prison. **Prisons** are correctional institutions maintained by the federal and state governments for the confinement of convicted felons. **Jails** are local facilities for the temporary detention of defendants awaiting trial or disposition on federal or state charges and of convicted offenders who have been sentenced to short-term imprisonment for minor crimes. Historically, however, jails have been somewhat more than this—they have been used for the holding of many types of outcasts, suspects, and offenders.

Origins of American Jails

The jail is the oldest institution for incarcerating offenders, dating as far back as fourth-century England, when Europe was under the rule of the Roman Empire. But little is known of the jails of that period other than that they were places for holding accused individuals and that there were separate quarters for women and men.

Even more wretched were the notorious hulks of 18th- and 19th-century England. In 1776, when transportation of convicts to the American colonies was terminated, a series of acts passed by George III ordered that the excess prison populations be placed in *hulks*, abandoned or unusable sailing vessels, generally of the man-of-war (warship) variety, which were permanently anchored in rivers and harbors throughout the British Isles. Within, they were similar to prisons and other places of detention. For security, inmates were often chained in irons. Hulks were overcrowded and dirty, and they quickly degenerated into human garbage dumps.

The American jail as we know it today is more likely rooted in the 12th century, when places of detention had to be provided for prisoners awaiting trial in the English

CAREERS IN CRIMINAL JUSTICE

Federal Bureau of Prisons

The Federal Bureau of Prisons employs staff in more than 200 job categories at more than 100 locations nationwide and offers excellent benefits and competitive salaries. Qualifications for positions vary in the type of education and work experience required.

Correctional officers are the largest part of the workforce, and all Bureau of Prisons institutions routinely have vacancies for this position. Correctional officers supervise inmates and enforce the rules and regulations of a correctional institution. To qualify for this position at the entry level, you must have successfully completed at least one of the following:

- A bachelor's degree in any field of study.
- At least 3 years of qualifying general work experience such as supervisor, teacher, counselor, parole/probation worker, worker with juvenile delinquents, welfare/social worker, firefighter, clergyman, emergency medical technician, air traffic controller, sales person in commissioned sales, security guard, manager, or day care facility worker.
- A combination of undergraduate education and qualifying general work experience, as previously described, that equals at least 3 full years.

For a higher-level position in this area you must have one of the following:

- At least 6 months of graduate education in criminal justice or a social science.
- At least 1 full year of specialized work experience in correctional work, law enforcement, or mental health facility work.
- A combination of graduate education and specialized work experience, as previously described, that equals at least 1 full year.

Correctional treatment specialists develop, evaluate, and analyze program needs and other data about inmates. The work they perform is similar to that of a social worker. To qualify, you must have successfully completed undergraduate education that includes 24 semester hours of a social science (which would qualify most criminal justice majors) plus 1 year of professional casework experience or 2 years of graduate education in a social science or at least 2 years of a combination of graduate education and professional casework experience.

For more information, contact the Bureau of Prisons Web site (**www.bop.gov**).

---

courts. Known as *gaols* (pronounced "jails"), they often consisted of a single room or two in a castle, a market house, or the gaoler's own dwelling. The inmates were known as *gaolbirds* ("jailbirds"), from the large cagelike cells often used to confine groups of prisoners like "birds in a cage."

By the 17th century, England's gaols housed both accused and convicted criminals. In addition to those awaiting trial, the gaols held minor offenders sentenced to short-term imprisonment; debtors who were detained until they paid their creditors; vagrants, beggars, and other rogues and vagabonds who were considered public nuisances; and prisoners awaiting punishment—branding, mutilation, placement in the stocks or pillory, transportation to the colonies, or execution. Conditions were abominable, and inmates were abused and exploited by their keepers. Moreover:

> Devoid of privacy and restrictions, its contaminated air heavy with the stench of unwashed bodies, human excrement, and the discharges of loathsome sores, the gaol bred the basest thoughts and the foulest deeds. The inmates made their own rules, and the weak and the innocent were exposed to the tyranny of the strong and the vicious. Prostitutes plied their trade with ease, often with the connivance and support of the gaolers, who thus sought to supplement their fees. Even virtuous women sold themselves to obtain food and clothing, and frequently the worst elements of the town used the gaol as they would a brothel. Thus, idleness, vice, perversion, profligacy, shameless exploitation, and ruthless cruelty were compounded in hotbeds of infection and cesspools of corruption. These were the common gaols of England.[29]

The English jail tradition came to the New World with the colonists. Jails first appeared in the Virginia colony in 1626 and were established in Pennsylvania on September 25, 1676, under the *Charter and Laws* of the Duke of York:

> Every town shall provide a pair of stocks for offenders, and a pound for the impounding of cattle; and prisons and pillories are likewise to be provided in these towns where the several courts of sessions are to be holden.

To describe contemporary jails is to give a monotonous repetition of rotten plumbing, horrible overcrowding, damp, dark, and indescribably dirty caverns, and other conditions the description of which are not printable, all bespeaking a callous and brutal disregard of the most elementary rules of hygiene and sanitation.

—J. F. FISHMAN,
CRUCIBLES OF CRIME, 1923

A prison barge of the early 19th century.

Thus, the conventional English detention jail was introduced into America. City and county jails in the colonies, and later in the states, maintained the characteristics of their prototypes. They were overcrowded and poorly maintained, prisoners were exploited by their warders, and suspected and convicted offenders were not separated. It was not until the conversion of Philadelphia's Walnut Street Jail into a prison in 1790 and the development of the penitentiary system during the 19th century that jails and prisons became distinct custodial entities.

Contemporary Jail Systems

A variety of facilities and structures are referred to as jails. Depending on the jurisdiction and locale, they might be also called lockups, workhouses, detention centers, stockades, or town, city, and county jails. Regardless of the terminology, however, all are used for temporary or short-term detention. Some are small and can hold only a few inmates; others can house many hundreds, even thousands, of prisoners.

Jail systems vary widely in organization and jurisdictional authority. There are county jails under the jurisdiction of the local sheriff and city jails under the authority of the chief of police. There are other independent units, not tied to any jail "system" as such. In some large communities, there are complex arrangements involving several segments of local government. In many urban areas, for example, each police precinct has its own *"lockup,"* which holds suspects during the questioning and booking stages of processing. In this phase, the jailing authority is in the hands of the precinct captain and the city police commissioner. Prisoners are then shifted to one of many city or county jails or detention centers. There are also statewide systems, such as those in Alaska, Connecticut, Delaware, Rhode Island, and Vermont, where all jails fall under the authority of a single state agency. Finally, there is the federal system, with its numerous detention centers throughout the United States under the jurisdiction of the Federal Bureau of Prisons.

The Jail Population

The jail is the entrance to the criminal justice system. Except for defendants who post bail while still in initial police custody, most arrestees are placed in jail, even if only for a short period.

In 2004, there were more than 3,500 jails across the nation, holding an estimated total of 714,000 inmates.[30] Of this population, 87 percent were men and over 1 percent were juveniles. Survey data reflect the traditional, twofold function of the jail: (1) as a place for the temporary detention for those awaiting trial and (2) as a confine-

I wasn't too worried about going because my uncle came back all built up. I kind of wanted the experience. He told me it was smooth in there, that doing time was a piece of cake.

— THEODORE RUSSELL,
FORMER INMATE

ment facility where many people who have been convicted of crimes, primarily misdemeanors, serve their sentences. As of 2004, 60 percent of all jail inmates were unconvicted, either not arraigned or arraigned and awaiting trial. The balance were either sentenced offenders or convicted offenders awaiting sentencing.

Noah Pope's contention, noted at the beginning of this section, that "jail is for the poor, the street is for the rich"[31] is borne out by contemporary survey data. The median annual income of jail inmates is below the poverty level; most have less than a high school education and are under age 30. As such, the U.S. jail population consists primarily of poor inmates who are both young and uneducated.[32]

Jail Conditions

For more than two centuries, jails have been described as "cesspools of crime," the "ultimate ghetto," "dumping grounds," and "festering sores in the criminal justice system" (see Exhibit 14.5). And what was said about American jails in the 1780s still applies today.[33] Most jails were, and still are, designed to allow for a minimum of staff while providing secure confinement for inmates. Most cells are large, cagelike rooms that hold significant numbers of prisoners at any given time. Although some structures have separate quarters for violent offenders, "drunk tanks" for the intoxicated, and facilities for youthful offenders, many hold all inmates together in shared quarters. The only exception is the separation of men and women, which is almost universal.

Sanitary facilities are often poor and degrading, especially in older jails. Common open toilets prevent personal privacy; the large percentage of drunks and others who spew vomit and urine on the toilets and floors make for unhealthy and unwholesome circumstances; poor plumbing often results in repeated breakdowns and clogged facilities; and inadequate showers and washrooms inhibit personal cleanliness. To add to these potential health problems, many jails do not provide appropriate medical care or even a physical examination at admission, thus increasing the possibility of disease.

Jails are poorly staffed. Whatever personnel are available are often untrained. This can result in lack of attention to inmate needs and mistreatment by other prisoners or correctional officers. Most jail inmates have little to occupy their time. Some of the

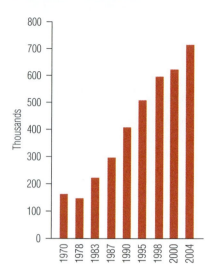

American Jail Population (Average Daily Census), 1970–2004

Source: Bureau of Justice Statistics.

Legend has it that the county jail in Muleshoe, Texas, is haunted by the spirit of an inmate who hanged himself in a cell in 1979. "It's fantastic," says Sheriff Jerry Hicks. "I've never seen so many guys reading Bibles."

EXHIBIT 14.5 | A View from the Field

Brooklyn's Raymond Street Jail by James A. Inciardi

Six o'clock in the morning,
The waiter comes around;
A slice of bread and butter,
That weighs a half a pound.

The coffee's like tobacco java,
The bread is hard and stale,
And that's the way they treat the boys
In Raymond Street's nice jail.

This short chorus, sung to the melody of the Irish patriotic and revolutionary song "The Wearing of the Green," was periodically heard on the streets of Brooklyn, New York, during the early years of the 20th century. But it never fully described the conditions that existed for more than 80 years in the Raymond Street Jail. Officially known as Kings County Jail, this grim "gothic castle" was erected in 1879 and immediately received criticism for the barbaric circumstances within its walls.

My first visit to Raymond Street Jail was in 1962. Having just graduated from college, I was a newly assigned parole officer, directed to interview a parole violator who was being detained there. After I entered the jail's massive doors, my attention was immediately drawn to a series of brown paper bags, carefully hung from a ceiling pipe by long strands of wire. I later learned that the bags contained the guards' lunches, positioned like that to keep them out of reach of vermin.

As I moved to the interior of the facility, being escorted to the cell where the parolee was quartered, I was reminded of the medieval dungeons of the old Robin Hood movies. The jail was like a gloomy cave; the air was stale, thick with the smell of urine, sweat, and excrement; and the walls and floors were damp. The environment seemed more suitable for snakes, bats, and owls than for people, for in competition with the inmates for space was a noticeable population of healthy mice, roaches, and other small creatures.

After being led through the bowels of Raymond Street Jail, I was finally brought to the person I had requested to see. His name was Bernard. "Benny," as the guards called him, was 33 years old. In 1951, not too long after he had arrived from Poland with his parents, he was arrested for opening a garage door and stealing a bicycle. Charged with breaking and entering and grand larceny, he was convicted the following year, sentenced to 7½ to 15 years, and transferred to Sing Sing Prison. It had been not only his first conviction but his first arrest as well.

At Sing Sing, Benny had hardly been a model prisoner. His long record of minor disciplinary reports served to deny him early parole. After 9 years he ultimately earned his release, but within 3 weeks he was cited for parole violation, arrested, and returned to Sing Sing. He was released after 9 more months, again to be cited for violation of parole within only a short period. On this occasion he was arrested for disorderly conduct and resisting arrest—that was what I was there to find out about. As a parolee under the supervision of the state, Benny had had a parole violation warrant lodged against him, so he could not be bailed.

American Jail Inmates and Drugs

Type of Drug	% Who Ever Used Drugs	% Who Used in Month Before Arrest
Any drug	77.7%	43.9%
Major drug		
Cocaine or crack	50.4	23.6
Heroin	18.2	7.0
LSD	18.6	1.6
PCP	13.9	1.7
Methadone	4.8	0.6
Other drug		
Marijuana	70.7	31.3
Amphetamines	22.1	5.4
Barbiturates	17.2	3.3
Methaqualone	14.7	0.8
Other drugs	11.0	2.4

Source: Bureau of Justice Statistics.

larger detention centers have libraries and exercise areas, but for the most part, recreational and academic facilities are not provided. Moreover, "treatment" and "rehabilitation" are not part of the American jail tradition.

Many of these problems can be seen in the jail system of Dade County (Miami), Florida, which houses more than 7,000 inmates on any given day.[34] Similar problems have been identified in New York City's *Rikers Island Penitentiary,* the largest penal colony in the United States. Built in 1895 to house sentenced offenders, some of its cell blocks are the length of a football field. As of 2005, Rikers Island was home to more than 14,000 inmates, most of whom were in detention because they were either denied or unable to make bail. Housing more inmates than the entire prison systems of 40 states, Rikers has 10 buildings, each holding a separate population of offenders. Six are designated for male detainees; one of these is a high-security facility and another is for juveniles. Of the remaining four buildings, one is for detained, convicted, and sentenced women; one for inmates with HIV infection or AIDS; one for inmates with contagious diseases; and one for convicted and sentenced men.[35]

In fairness to sheriffs, police chiefs, wardens, and other jail administrators who have attempted to upgrade personnel and conditions in facilities under their authority, it must be stated that not all detention centers suffer from all of the deficiencies mentioned here. Many jurisdictions have provided funds for the construction of modern, humane jails. Recent court decisions have legislated changes in others. And too, there are individual jailers and wardens who have made an effort to make the best of what otherwise might have been intolerable situations.

Numerous suggestions have been made for improving local jails. They include state inspection; provision of social casework services; development of educational,

Benny's cell looked like a small cave. The door was of strap iron, which ran both up and down and side to side, leaving openings of only about 1 square inch, and providing little fresh air to breathe or light for seeing. We spoke in an adjacent room. He told me his story. I related that the parole board would make a decision after he was tried on the new charges.

Thirty-eight days later he entered a plea of guilty and was sentenced to time served. Then his violation report went to the parole board, and they ordered him to be released. I returned again to Raymond Street to remove the warrant on Benny. As we walked out together, he told me that he would rather die than go back to Raymond Street. He had spent 1,512 hours in that dark, cramped, slimy, smelly, vermin-infested jail with no fresh air, exercise, or recreation, "all for calling a cop a son of a bitch."

In 1963, Raymond Street Jail was ordered closed, bringing an end to what was considered the worst jail in New York's history. The following year the building was razed, and the site is now occupied by Brooklyn Hospital. As for Benny, his fate was no better than that of the Ray-

Brooklyn's Gothic Horror, the Raymond Street Jail

mond Street Jail. In 1966 he was arrested for petty theft. Unable to make bail, he was detained in Manhattan City Prison, better known as the infamous New York Tombs, where he hanged himself.

---

medical, and drug treatment programs; use of volunteers to structure and supervise recreational services; and reorganization and cost sharing by state and local governments. Some of these approaches are beginning to be implemented.

An innovation that is becoming more common in this regard is the *direct supervision jail.* In the traditional jail, the officers come into contact with the inmates only when there is a particular need—meals, transportation, disturbances. Officers are in control rooms behind thick glass or in walkways outside the cells, facilities that are expensive to build and maintain. By contrast, the direct supervision jail attempts to use the physical plant to improve the staff's ability to manage the inmate population. This is accomplished through three architectural concepts—podular design, interaction space, and personal space. Podular units are self-contained living areas, generally for 12 to 24 inmates, composed of single-occupancy rooms in which inmates pursue their own interests and a common, multipurpose dayroom. Daily activities occur within the pod, as do such other jail functions as mail distribution, program activities, commissary, and visitation. The architectural design and facilities associated with the new philosophy create an environment in which normative, civilized behavior is expected of inmates. In addition, each living area is designed to enhance observation of, communication with, and interaction between inmates and the jail staff. One or more jail officers are stationed inside the living area and interact directly throughout the day with those housed within the pod, with the goal of keeping negative behavior in check.[36]

In the final analysis, most of the problems of jails stem from overcrowding. It was once estimated that the daily population of American jails could be reduced by 50%, without endangering the public, by making the following changes:

It reminds me of a television program I once saw with rats running around a large cage, looking happy. When you put them in a smaller cage, they start killing each other.

— **CORRECTIONAL COUNSELOR REFLECTING ON THE SITUATION AT RIKERS ISLAND**

We're literally dealing with the scum of the earth here. They're just not normal human beings like you and me, and it doesn't make sense to treat them that way.

— **RIKERS ISLAND CORRECTIONAL OFFICER**

New York's Suffolk County Jail is a modern direct supervision jail. Inmates and guards mix freely in the multipurpose common area.

1. Wider use of release on recognizance.
2. Preferential trial scheduling for defendants in jail.
3. Use of citations rather than jail terms for more offenses.
4. Creation of installment plans for those who would otherwise go to jail because they cannot pay their fines.
5. Use of work-release for jail inmates.[37]

Although these alternatives have been implemented in many jurisdictions, apparently they have not been enough. The jail population of more than 714,000 inmates in 2004 represented an increase of more than 500,000 inmates since 1985.

Home Incarceration

Although home incarceration, also known as "house arrest," has likely existed in one form or another since the earliest days of parenting, its use as an official sanction for criminal behavior did not begin in the United States until 1984. It quickly became

If invention is born of idleness, it is also born of necessity, and in Rikers, having a weapon of some sort is very much a necessity.

—RIKERS ISLAND INMATE

Martha Stewart in home confinement at her $16 million New York estate.

popular for two reasons: increased crowding of correctional facilities and the development of electronic monitoring equipment. House arrest for many years was not considered a feasible alternative to incarceration because, short of 24-hour surveillance by police or probation officers, there was no way to ensure total compliance with the court's directives, and it was believed that an offender's ability to "beat the system" and leave home undetected would encourage further antisocial behavior. That changed with the advent of electronic monitoring equipment.

A judge in Albuquerque, New Mexico, claims to have invented electronic monitoring after reading a "Spiderman" comic in 1977, but Harvard law professor Ralph Schwitzgebel reported the development of small radio transmitters operating on CB (citizen band) frequencies as early as 1964, and in 1969 he described the results of a field test on 16 offender and nonoffender volunteers. When electronic monitors became sufficiently small in size and reliable enough to be used for home incarceration purposes in the 1980s, both the number of programs and the number of equipment manufacturers increased rapidly.[38] Currently, they exist in all states and the District of Columbia. Recent research has found home incarceration to be a safe and effective community sanction for low-level offenders who might suffer disproportionately from even short-term incarceration, as compared with more serious offenders.[39]

CRITICAL THINKING IN CRIMINAL JUSTICE

The Scarlet Letter Revisited

Nathaniel Hawthorne's *The Scarlet Letter,* published in 1850, is a story of Puritanism and pariahs in 17th-century Boston. Hester Prynne, having given birth to an illegitimate daughter, is scorned by her neighbors and forced by her church to wear a scarlet *A*—signifying "adulteress"—as a token of her terrible sin.

Throughout the 1990s and into the 21st century, a century and a half since Hawthorne's writing and even further removed from the era of Boston Puritanism, courts and legislatures across the United States have been using similar "public" announcements in an effort to deter modern-day crime and "sin."

In New York City, the names of "johns" arrested on charges of soliciting prostitutes are announced on the radio, and in Miami they are posted on local cable TV stations. In Newark, New Jersey, and Washington, D.C., photographs are taken of drivers who pull over to solicit prostitutes, and they are then mailed to the home addresses corresponding to the license plates. In Sarasota, Florida, persons convicted of "driving under the influence" (DUI) of alcohol are required to put red stickers on their cars' rear bumpers that read "CONVICTED DUI."[40]

Among the forms of public ostracism currently receiving considerable attention are those involving sex offenders. All 50 states have either enacted or proposed legislation requiring that communities be informed of the presence of a convicted sex offender. Awareness laws have become more widespread because of the highly publicized cases of Polly Klaas in California, Megan Kanka in New Jersey, and, most recently, Jessica Lundsford in Florida. All three children had been sexually assaulted and murdered by paroled sex offenders. The public outrage created by these incidents prompted both federal and state legislation requiring notification of community residents when a convicted sex offender is living in their neighborhoods.

The most recent mechanism in this regard is the World Wide Web. The majority of states have put lists of sex offender registries on the Web, and the remaining states are considering sex offender registry legislation. The Alaska Department of Public Safety's Web site, for example, maintains an up-to-date list of registered sex offenders, complete with photographs, characteristics, addresses, and employers.[41] Other communities have developed similar notification procedures.

Currently, some 305,000 sex offenders are under the jurisdiction of the criminal justice system, and half of these are on either probation or parole. As such, many community residents argue that they have a right to know when sexual predators are moving into their neighborhoods, so that they can take measures to protect their children and themselves. Wisconsin Governor

A new scarlet letter? A Texas judge has forced numerous "high-risk" sex offenders on probation to post signs outside their homes to notify the public of their crime. Advocates say the signs have a deterring effect on sex offenders who will do whatever it takes to avoid the public humiliation. The signs also hold offenders accountable for their actions and alert neighbors to keep an eye out for suspicious behavior. Critics maintain that the signs violate the right to privacy and constitute cruel and unusual punishment. Furthermore, critics argue, the signs effectively punish the offender's entire family by subjecting those who are innocent to the same public shaming as the offender. The signs have also led to evictions and at least one offender has attempted suicide.

What do you think? Is posting signs outside sex offenders' homes a way to make communities safer, or is it unnecessarily cruel?

Sex Offenders in the U.S. Criminal Justice System, 2005

Source: Department of Justice.

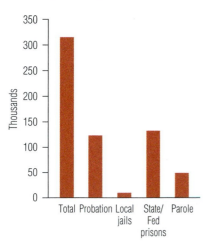

Tommy G. Thompson has stressed in this regard that "registries should make sex offenders think twice before offending again, and they will make this state a safer place." But thinking critically, are Internet registries a good idea? True, they do indeed notify people that sexual deviants are in their midst. But what is the downside to the equation?

Sex offender therapists argue that few people have thought through the consequences of online registries. They worry that the registries have the potential to lead to retributive violence against sex offenders. This, not surprisingly, has already happened. As notification laws have become more widespread, so too have incidents where released sex offenders have been harassed by neighbors, evicted by landlords, fired from new jobs, and even beaten by revenge-minded mobs. In some cases bystanders have become the victims of neighborhood avengers.

There are other issues. Sex offender registries may have the potential for increasing the numbers of sex crimes. Broadcasting sex offenders' names, addresses, telephone numbers, and photographs on unfiltered Web pages could force many of them into isolation—away from counseling and probation/parole supervision. Furthermore, there is the argument that many victims of sex offenders will be less likely to come forward if it means, for example, putting their father's photograph—and the fact that they were victims of sexual abuse—on a Web page that friends and neighbors could readily view. And the potential for this is considerable, given that the majority of sex offenders are known to their victims—brothers and fathers, mothers and uncles, neighbors, teachers, and even members of the clergy.

All of these points were recently summed up by Craig Latham, a child psychologist and president of the Massachusetts Association for the Treatment of Sexual Abusers:

> If you're going to lock him up for life, fine, do that. But if you're going [to] let him out and not let him have a job and burn down his house, if he has one, then you're just making us less safe.[42]

OP-ED

The crime wave, the public enemies, and the vibrant rhetoric of the 1930s ushered in a new phase in 20th-century penology. It was built on the belief that some criminals were so incorrigible that they should be repressed and disciplined with absolute inflexibility. Many thought that Alcatraz might be the answer to the problem.

Named *Isla de los Alcatraces* (Island of Pelicans) by 18th-century Spanish explorers after the birds that roosted there, Alcatraz has an area of 12 acres and rises steeply to 136 feet above San Francisco Bay. In 1859, a U.S. military prison was built on the island, and in March 1934 it was taken over by the Federal Bureau of Prisons.

Alcatraz became the most repressive maximum-security facility in the nation. Its six guard towers, equipped with .30-caliber carbines and high-powered rifles, could observe every square foot of the island. Barbed wire barriers dotted the shorelines, and each entrance to the cell house had a three-door security system.

There were 600 one-man cells, built into three-tiered cell blocks. Measuring 8 feet by 4 feet, each cell contained a fold-up bunk hooked to the wall, a fold-up table and chair, a shelf, a washbasin, a toilet, and a shaded ceiling light. Cell block D provided solitary confinement for more difficult offenders. It included "the Hole," a series of smaller cells with solid steel walls, floors, and doors; there were no furnishings and its inmates were locked into total darkness.

Each day at Alcatraz began at 6:30 A.M. with the clanging of a bell and a burst of electric light. Inmates had 20 minutes in which to dress and make their beds. At 6:50 the bell sounded again and the guard counted the prisoners. A third bell signaled that the count was "right"—all prisoners accounted for. No inmate could wear a watch. Bells told the time: Fourth bell. Breakfast. 7 A.M. Bell. Workshops. Mid-morning. Bell. Recess. Bell. Work. 11:30. Bell. Count. Bell. Noon. Bell. Lunch. 1 P.M. Bell. Work. Midafternoon. Bell. Recess. Bell. Work. 4:30. Bell. Count. Bell. Supper. Bell. Back to cell. Bell. Count. Bell. 6:30. Bell. Lockup. 9:30. Bell. Lights out!

Recreational facilities were limited to an exercise yard and a small library. There was no commissary. Prisoners were allowed three packs of cigarettes per week. Newspapers and radio were denied in order to intensify the sense of isolation. One letter could be written each week and three could be received, but with severe restrictions: Correspondence could not be carried on with non-relatives, and the content was restricted to family matters. One visit per month, from a family member or attorney, was permitted.

A typical maximum security cell at Alcatraz.

Work was limited to cooking, cleaning, maintenance, and laundry. Security was rigid, with one guard for every three inmates.

With its policy of maximum security combined with minimum privileges and total isolation for America's "public enemies," Alcatraz did house a number of underworld aristocrats and spectacular felons, including Arthur "Doc" Barker, the last surviving son of Ma Barker's murderous brood; kidnapper George "Machine Gun" Kelly; Alvin Karpis, the most evasive bank robber of the 1930s; and bootlegger, murderer, and syndicate boss Al "Scarface" Capone. But for the most part, comparatively few big-time gangsters ever went to Alcatraz; many of the island's inmates were actually first offenders.

From its earliest days, the concept behind Alcatraz had generated considerable opposition from social scientists and prison administrators. The prison was closed in 1963 because it was too costly to operate and too typical of the retributive justice that was no longer dominant in the federal prison system. Today, Alcatraz Island Penitentiary is part of the Golden Gate National Recreation Area, having been transformed from a dead-end prison to a tourist attraction.[43]

| Summary |

Throughout history, the range of punishments has been vast. At one time, the death penalty was an almost universal form of punishment. Corporal punishment, particularly in the forms of whippings and torture, was also widespread. During the Age of Enlightenment a new ideology began to emerge in a reform movement that concerned itself with examining the dignity and imperfections of the human condition, in addition to admonishing the harshness of criminal law and the cruelty of various types of punishment. The reform movement also produced the classic school of criminology. Particularly influential was Beccaria's liberal doctrine of criminal law and procedure, which emphasized the principle of free will. This principle sought to establish the pleasure-pain theory, suggesting that individuals choose the course of action that will bring them the most pleasure and avoid the course of action that will bring them the most pain.

The American prison experience began during the 18th century in Philadelphia. The Walnut Street Jail was the nation's first penitentiary. Throughout the 1790s its physical structure and separate system of confinement characterized it as a model prison. The separate system approach was based on the notion that recidivism could be eliminated by obstructing "evil associations" between prisoners through separate living quarters. The decline of the Walnut Street Jail occurred in the beginning of the 19th century, largely due to overcrowding, periodic riots, and inadequate disciplinary control. This correctional approach was subsequently rivaled by New York's silent system as it emerged at Auburn Prison in 1823. The silent system prevailed over the earlier system of separate living quarters for primarily economic reasons. It allowed for smaller cells and large, congregate work areas while attempting to accomplish the same objective: prevention of corruption through obstructing communication among inmates. Ultimately, profits extracted from cheap inmate labor served to weaken the silent system, since perpetual silence on the workfloor was counterproductive.

The work of Alexander Maconochie in Australia and Sir Walter Crofton in Ireland influenced America's reformatory era. Maconochie was responsible for inventing the "mark system" through which an inmate could receive early release if he worked hard and exhibited good behavior. Crofton's "Irish system" built on Maconochie's earlier work, but in addition established a series of stages through which inmates must successfully pass before receiving a conditional release. Based on these systems, the first reformatory was opened at Elmira, New York, in 1876, but by 1910 this correctional experience was abandoned.

As corrections moved from the mid-1800s into the early years of the 20th century, the American prison system had evolved into an expanding hoard of maximum-security insti-

tutions. This period first witnessed active prison industries and then idle convict populations. Following the depression years, new treatment ideas were introduced against a backdrop of growing apathy and decaying institutions. The 1960s through the 1990s saw even greater contrasts—an emphasis on individual prisoners' needs and rights in settings of unrest and massive overcrowding.

The emergence and growth of the federal prison system has been a much more recent phenomenon. From 1776 through 1891, all federal prisoners were housed in state and territorial institutions. Following the passage of the Mann Act (1910), the Harrison Act (1914), the Volstead Act (1919), and the Motor Vehicle Theft Act (1919), the number of federal prisoners in state institutions grew rapidly, ultimately forcing the birth of the first federal penitentiaries in Atlanta, Georgia, and Leavenworth, Kansas. The Federal Bureau of Prisons was created in 1930 and became responsible for the development of a graded system of federal institutions that ranged from maximum- to minimum-security facilities and camps.

The jail is a detention facility quite distinct from a prison. Unlike prisons that are run by state and federal governments, jails are administered by local authorities and house only those individuals who are awaiting trial or who are convicted of relatively minor crimes and receive comparatively short sentences. The jail is one of the oldest known institutions for detaining offenders, dating back to fourth-century England. Jails first appeared in the United States in 1626 and were modeled after the English detention facility. Today, jails vary greatly depending on the area and the demands of the local criminal justice system. One nearly universal similarity, however, is the overcrowded and inadequate living conditions characteristic of most jails today.

| Key Terms |

Cesare Beccaria (465)	corporal punishment (462)	piece-price system (470)	state account system (471)
classical school of criminal	jails (478)	prisons (478)	state-use system (471)
law and criminology (465)	lease system (471)	separate system (467)	ticket-of-leave (472)
contract system (470)	mark system (472)	silent system (469)	Walnut Street Jail (467)

| Issues for Discussion |

1. How did the Industrial Revolution affect the evolution of prisons in the United States?
2. Could the purposes of Alcatraz be achieved by some other penal policies?
3. Which of Beccaria's ideas are reflected in current conceptions of due process?

4. How might the alternative conceptions of bail reform affect the jail problem?
5. Is the "scarlet letter" an appropriate form of punishment? Are sex offender Internet registries a good idea?
6. Is house arrest a rehabilitative option for offenders or a punitive one?

| Media and Literature Resources |

Reel Justice includes scenes that can be used to spark discussion about the following topics from this chapter:

Origins of Criminal Law

History of Prisons. Two of the best recent references on this topic are Eric Monkkonen, *Crime and Justice in American History: Prisons and Jails* (New York: K. G. Saur, 1992), and Lawrence M. Friedman, *Crime and Punishment in American History* (New York: Basic Books,

1993). See also John W. Roberts, *Reform and Retribution: An Illustrated History of American Prisons* (Lanham, MD: American Correctional Association, 1997).

Federal Bureau of Prisons. The Bureau of Prisons has an extensive Web site with information about the entire system's institutions, inmates, and employment (*http://www.bop.gov*).

Rikers Island. The New York City Department of Correction has put together a good Web site with some interesting historical material on the city jail system, including its history, programs, and current statistics (*http://www.ci.nyc.ny.us/html/doc/home.html*).

Human Rights Watch. Human Rights Watch monitors prison conditions around the world and has numerous reports that can be accessed from its Web site (*http://www.hrw.org*).

American Jails. There are two important works that should not be overlooked: Ronald Goldfarb, *Jails: The Ultimate Ghetto of the Criminal Justice System* (Garden City, NY: Doubleday, 1976); John Irwin, *The Jail: Managing the Underclass in American Society* (Berkeley: University of California Press, 1985).

| Endnotes |

1. Harry Elmer Barnes, *The Story of Punishment: A Record of Man's Inhumanity to Man* (Montclair, NJ: Patterson Smith, 1972).
2. Luke Owen Pike, *A History of Crime in England*, Vol. 2 (Montclair, NJ: Patterson Smith, 1968), 87–88.
3. See George Rusche and Otto Kirchheimer, *Punishment and Social Structure* (New York: Columbia University Press, 1939).
4. United States Customs and Border Protection, 2005.
5. See Alice Morse Earle, *Curious Punishments of Bygone Days* (Montclair, NJ: Patterson Smith, 1969).
6. For a discussion of the leading thinkers in the 18th-century reform movement, see Leon Radzinowicz, *Ideology and Crime* (New York: Columbia University Press, 1966).
7. From George B. Vold, *Theoretical Criminology* (New York: Oxford University Press, 1958), 14–18; Radzinowicz, *Ideology and Crime*, 6–14.
8. Cited by Harry Elmer Barnes, *The Evolution of Penology in Pennsylvania* (Indianapolis: Bobbs-Merrill, 1927), 64.
9. Orlando F. Lewis, *The Development of American Prisons and Prison Customs, 1776–1845* (Albany: Prison Association of New York, 1922), 26–28.
10. Harry Elmer Barnes, *The Repression of Crime* (New York: Doran, 1926), 162.
11. Barnes, *Repression of Crime*.
12. See Negley K. Teeters and John D. Shearer, *The Prison at Philadelphia: Cherry Hill* (New York: Columbia University Press, 1957), and William Crawford, *Report on the Penitentiaries of the United States* (Montclair, NJ: Patterson Smith, 1969), 1–2.
13. Gustave de Beaumont and Alexis de Tocqueville, *On the Penitentiary System in the United States and Its Application to France* (Carbondale: Southern Illinois University Press, 1964), 83.
14. Margaret Wilson, *The Crime of Punishment* (New York: Harcourt Brace, 1931), 219–220.
15. Lewis, *Development of American Prisons*, 80–95.
16. See Blake McKelvey, *American Prisons: A History of Good Intentions* (Montclair, NJ: Patterson Smith, 1977), 116–149.
17. Charles L. Clark and Earle Edward Eubank, *Lockstep and Corridor: Thirty-Five Years of Prison Life* (Cincinnati: University of Cincinnati Press, 1927), 30.
18. See J. C. Powell, *The American Siberia* (Chicago: Smith, 1891).
19. McKelvey, *American Prisons*, 14.
20. John V. Barry, "Alexander Maconochie," *Journal of Criminal Law, Criminology, and Police Science* 47 (July–August 1956): 145–161.
21. John V. Barry, "Captain Alexander Maconochie," *Victorian Historical Magazine* 27 (June 1957): 5.
22. McKelvey, *American Prisons*, 37.
23. Zebulon Brockway, *Fifty Years of Prison Service* (Montclair, NJ: Patterson Smith, 1969), 419–423.
24. Harry Elmer Barnes and Negley K. Teeters, *New Horizons in Criminology* (Englewood Cliffs, NJ: Prentice-Hall, 1959), 428.
25. Frank Flynn, "The Federal Government and the Prison Labor Problem in the States," *Social Science Review* 24 (March–June 1950): 19–40, 213–236.
26. Paul W. Tappan, *Crime, Justice, and Correction* (New York: McGraw-Hill, 1960), 619.
27. 18 U.S. Code 907, cited by Tappan, *Crime, Justice and Correction*, 620.
28. Bureau of Prisons, 2005.
29. Robert G. Caldwell, *Criminology* (New York: Ronald, 1965), 495.
30. Bureau of Justice Statistics, *Prison and Jail Inmates at Mid-Year 2004*, April 2005.
31. Cited by Ronald Goldfarb, *Jails: The Ultimate Ghetto of the Criminal Justice System* (Garden City, NY: Anchor, 1976), 3.
32. *Overcrowded Times*, August 1997, 5–7.
33. See Goldfarb, *Jails*; George Ives, *A History of Penal Methods* (Montclair, NJ: Patterson Smith, 1970); Joseph F. Fishman, *Crucibles of Crime: The Shocking Story of the American Jail* (Montclair, NJ: Patterson Smith, 1969); *Newsweek*, August 18, 1980, 74, 76; *The New York Times*, August 14, 1987, B1, B3; *The New York Times*, August 30, 1990, A1, B2; Wayne N. Welsh, Henry N. Pontell, Matthew C. Leone, and Patrick Kinkade, "Jail Overcrowding: An Analysis of Policy Makers' Perceptions," *Justice Quarterly* 7 (June 1990): 341–370; Joel A. Thompson and G. Larry Mays (eds.), *American Jails: Public Policy Issues* (Chicago: Nelson-Hall, 1991); *Washington Post*, April 4, 2005, C8.
34. Caroline Keough, "Critics See Few Improvements in County Jails," *Miami Herald*, October 13, 1997, 1B, 3B.
35. City of New York, Correction Department Web page (*http://www.nyc.gov/html/doc*), 2005.
36. Gerald J. Bayens, Jimmy J. Williams, and John Ortiz Smykla, "Jail Type Makes a Difference: Evaluating the Transition from a Traditional to a Podular, Direct Supervision Jail Across Ten Years," *Corrections Connection Network* (originally published in *American Jails Magazine*), 1997.
37. Richard A. McGee, "Our Sick Jails," *Federal Probation* 35 (March 1971): 4–5.
38. Richard A. Ball and J. Robert Lilly, "A Theoretical Examination of Home Incarceration," *Federal Probation* 50 (March 1986): 17–24; Patricia K. Loveless, "Home Incarceration with Electronic Monitoring: Myths and Realities," *American Jails* (January–February 1994): 2–3.
39. Brian K. Payne and Randy R. Gainey, "The Electronic Monitoring of Offenders Released from Jail or Prisons: Safety, Control, and Comparisons to the Incarceration Experience," *The Prison Journal* 84 (2004), 413–423.
40. *Time*, June 17, 1985, 52; *Newsweek*, February 18, 1991, 75; *The New York Times*, February 20, 1993, 5; *The New York Times*, September 4, 1994, 36.
41. Alaska Department of Public Safety, *http://www.dps.state.ak.us/nSorcr/asp/*.
42. *The New York Times*, May 22, 2000, B1, B6.
43. See E. E. Kirkpatrick, *Voices from Alcatraz* (San Antonio: Naylor, 1947); James A. Johnston, *Alcatraz Island Prison* (New York: Scribner's, 1949); John Kobler, *Capone: The Life and World of Al Capone* (New York: Putnam, 1971); and L. L. Edge, *Run the Cat Roads* (New York: December, 1981).

15

PENITENTIARIES, PRISONS, AND OTHER CORRECTIONAL INSTITUTIONS: A LOOK INSIDE THE INMATE WORLD

LEARNING OBJECTIVES

After reading this chapter, you should be able to answer the following questions:

1. What are total institutions, and what is their purpose?

2. What are the differences between maximum-security, medium-security, and minimum-security prisons? How do institutions for women differ from those for men?

3. What are supermax prisons?

4. What are the roles and functions of wardens and correctional officers?

5. What is classification, what is its purpose, and how is it done?

6. What kinds of programs are available to inmates in American prisons?

7. To what extent is drug abuse treatment available in prison?

8. What are the issues associated with sex in prison and with prison discipline?

9. What is the inmate social system, and how does it function?

10. How effective is correctional treatment?

The exercise yard in California's San Quentin State Prison death row.

Prison Population Increases Despite Decline in Crime

WASHINGTON, DC—The FBI has reported that rates of serious crime have been declining for more than a decade.[1] Government reports also show, however, that the number of inmates in prisons and jails around the nation increased dramatically over the same period. In 1990, there were 774,000 state and federal prisoners; in 1995, that number passed 1 million, with another half-million in jails and detention centers; and by 2004, the number of people incarcerated in the United States exceeded 2.1 million.[2]

What has been happening in communities, in the courts, and elsewhere to cause this incongruity of lower crime rates coupled with expanding incarceration rates? What effect is this having on jails and prisons? Does it appear that the trend will continue? What are the needs of prisoners, and how does the American prison system address them?

Serious crime is down . . .

Reported Crimes

Includes reported murder, forcible rape, robbery, aggravated assault, burglary, and larceny

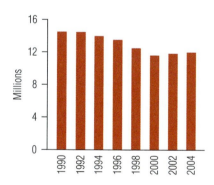

. . . but the number of prison inmates is growing.

Federal and State Prison Inmates

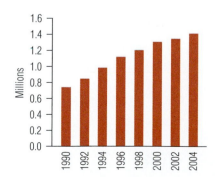

In discussing prisons and what happens within their walls, it is important to be familiar with the concept of a total institution. A **total institution** is a place that erects barriers to social interchange with the world at large.[3] In total institutions, large groups of people live together, day and night, in a fixed area and under a tightly scheduled sequence of activities imposed by a central authority. In total institutions there are "subjects" and "managers." Subjects are the large class of individuals who have restricted contact with the world outside the institution's walls. Managers, who are socially integrated into the outside world, are the small class of individuals who supervise the subjects. The social distance between subjects and managers is great, and communication between them is restricted. Each group conceives of the other in terms of narrow, hostile stereotypes, resulting in the development of different social and cultural worlds that are in continuous conflict with each other. In total institutions, moreover, there is an elaborate system of formal rules intended to achieve the organization's official goals and to maintain the distance between subjects and managers.

Correctional institutions are total institutions organized to protect the community against what are viewed as intentional dangers to it. Correctional institutions include penitentiaries and reformatories, as well as a multitude of training schools, ranches, farms, and camps. Regardless of these designations, however, all are generally referred to as "jails" or "prisons"—two words that have quite distinct meanings for the professional, although probably not for the general public.

Types of Prisons

In the United States correctional institutions have traditionally been divided into three or more categories according to their construction and the measures used to maintain control. This produces three levels of custody or security: maximum, medium, and minimum.

Maximum-Security Prisons

The most famous prisons in the United States are Sing Sing, Attica, San Quentin, Leavenworth, Joliet, and the now-closed Alcatraz Island Penitentiary. These are **maximum-security prisons.** They are walled fortresses of concrete and steel and house the most serious, aggressive, and incorrigible offenders.

Most maximum-security prisons have a similar design. Secure custody and control are the guiding principles. Housing anywhere from many hundreds to several thousands of inmates, they are enclosed by massive concrete walls, sometimes as high as 30 feet, or by a series of double or triple perimeter fences topped with barbed wire or razor ribbon, and often electrically charged. Located along the outer-perimeter walls are well-protected guard towers, strategically placed to provide correctional officers with open fields of fire and easy observation of prison yards and the areas surrounding the prison. New York's Green Haven Correctional Facility (called Green Haven Prison until 1970, when the state legislature decreed that "prisons" henceforth would be "correctional facilities," "guards" would be "correction officers," and "wardens" would be "superintendents") is typical, if not an exaggeration, of this high-control design. Built as a military prison during World War II and acquired by New York in 1949, Green Haven was designed to be an "escape-proof" institution. The mile-long wall of reinforced concrete around the perimeter of the prison is 30 feet high and almost 3 feet thick and is said to go 30 feet below the ground. Twelve towers, reaching 40 feet above the ground, are evenly positioned along it. Tower guards, armed with shotguns, rifles, and tear gas guns, have a sweeping view of both sides of the wall. The towers also provide focused surveillance of "no-man's-land," a 100-foot-wide stretch of open space between the inner and outer walls of the prison across which nothing and no one can pass unobserved. No one has ever managed to escape over the wall at Green Haven.

A characteristic feature of the maximum-security prison is the inside cell block. **Inside cells** are constructed back to back, with corridors running along the outside shell of the cell house. In contrast to *outside cells,* which are affixed to the outside walls of the cell house, inside cells are considered more secure. Whereas escape through the window or wall of an outside cell would place an inmate in the prison yard, escape from an inside cell would leave the prisoner still within the cell block.

The outside wall at the infamous Green Haven Prison in Stormville, New York.

This is the end of the line, the end of the world: Pontiac Correctional Center, one of four maximum-security penitentiaries in Illinois and an archetype of maximum-security prisons across the nation. It is a world of steel bars and stone walls, line-ups and lock-downs, bad food and badder dudes, good time, hard times . . . lots of time. A lifetime.

—JOURNALIST MITCHELL LANDESBURG

Prisons are built with stones of law; brothels with bricks of religion.

—WILLIAM BLAKE

Prison is the only garbage dump we have that is so repulsive we encircle it with barbed wire and a stone wall.

—BRUCE JACKSON

To refer to jail and prison as "unpleasant" . . . is like referring to the Nazi torture of the Jews as "unkind."

—KARL MENNINGER

The Criminal Justice Funnel

1,000,000 Part I crimes

275,000 Arrests

200,000 Available for prosecution

70,000 Formal felony complaints

65,000 Sentences

25,000 Sent to prison

Each tier of cells is called a *cell block,* and the cell house may contain as many as 10 such blocks. The cell blocks are self-contained security enclosures, often partitioned off from one another by a series of gates and pens. This creates a complex of miniature prisons within the penitentiary, increasing overall security. Such a pattern is doubly effective because each cell house is similarly separated from all others.

The emphasis on preventing escape from these institutions also includes tool-proof steel construction, multiple lock devices, frequent *shakedowns* (searches) and counts, infrared sensing devices, and closed-circuit TV. In the construction of modern maximum-security prisons, however, the trend is to move away from the double and triple security patterns—particularly the massive outside walls—because of their prohibitive cost. Instead, prisons are increasing the use of sophisticated technological security devices.

"Supermax" Prisons

The most recent innovation in high-security facilities is the **supermax prison.** Often referred to as secured or special housing unit, maximum-control facility, or just "maxi-maxi," the supermax prison is a highly restrictive, high-custody housing unit within a secure institution (or an entire secure penitentiary) that isolates inmates from the general prison population and from each other due to especially serious crimes, repetitive assaultive or violent institutional behavior, the threat of (or actual) escape from a high-custody facility, or inciting or threatening to incite disturbances in a correctional institution (see Exhibit 15.1).[4]

Medium-Security Prisons

While medium-security facilities reproduce the basic pattern of the maximum-security prison, there is somewhat less emphasis on internal fortification. These prisons are rarely fortresslike structures with high stone walls. Rather, the perimeters are marked by a series of fences and enclosures with fewer guard towers. Outside cells are characteristic, and in the newer structures banks of dormitories and other types of shared living quarters are becoming common.

The inmates placed in medium-security institutions are considered less dangerous and escape-prone than those in the more security-oriented institutions. Their movements within the facility are less controlled, and surveillance is less vigilant. However, these prisons generally do have a maximum-security unit that can be used to house inmates who become custodial problems or threats to the safety of other prisoners.

Minimum-Security Prisons

Minimum-security correctional institutions operate without armed guards, without walls, and sometimes even without perimeter fences. The inmates of these facilities are considered to be low security risks—the most trustworthy and least violent offenders, those with short sentences, and white-collar criminals. A great deal of personal freedom is allowed, dormitory living is common, educational release is encouraged, and the level of surveillance is low.

Some of the newest minimum-security prisons are replacing the stifling nature of the traditional prison compound with a more villagelike atmosphere. A relatively new facility in Vienna, Illinois, for example, does not look like a penal institution. Buildings resembling garden apartments are built around a "town square" complete with churches, school, shops, and library. Paths lead to "neighborhoods" where "homes" provide private rooms in small clusters. Extensive provision has been made for both outdoor and indoor recreation, and academic, commercial, and vocational education facilities equal or surpass those of many technical high schools.

Minimum-security facilities like this one and others that house white-collar criminals—built on what has become known as the "cottage plan"—have often been criti-

historical perspectives on criminal justice | EXHIBIT 15.1

The "Hellhole" of the Rockies

Although Alcatraz was the forerunner of the supermax concept, the first special "high-security" or supermax control unit was established in 1978 at the U.S. Penitentiary in Marion, Illinois, as the result of rising levels of violence directed toward prison staff. In 1983, after the deaths of two officers and one inmate resulting from prison violence, indefinite administrative segregation became the norm and inmates were confined to their cells around the clock and denied exercise, work, and recreation. For years, Marion housed the Bureau of Prisons' most violent and troublesome prisoners, until the opening of the Administrative Maximum Penitentiary in Florence, Colorado, in 1994.

Situated in an arid, remote, high-desert sector of Colorado, the Administrative Maximum Penitentiary is a triangular, two-story, high-tech prison more commonly known as ADX. While a few inmates refer to ADX as the "Alcatraz of the Rockies," most call it the "hellhole of the Rockies." Some observers call it "the end of the line."

The unique mission of ADX is confining "the worst of the worst"— some 400-plus inmates from all over the federal prison system considered so dangerous that no other penitentiary can hold them. Among its more notorious residents are the Shoe-bomber Richard Reid, Unabomber Ted Kaczynski, and terrorist Ramzi Yousef, the mastermind of the first World Trade Center bombing. ADX's other inmates include many who were transferred there because they had assaulted or killed correctional officers or inmates at other prisons.

The cells at ADX look like they were designed for Hannibal Lecter. All furniture is concrete to prevent inmates from making weapons from wooden, metal, or plastic parts. Each cell has a small vestibule where the inmate is shackled, hands behind his back, when he is being taken elsewhere in the prison. And solitary confinement is the norm. Most inmates spend 22 to 23 hours a day in their cells. When they get out to exercise, they do it alone, in a small yard. Planning an escape or a rescue from the outside would appear to be virtually impossible at ADX. The only entry is underground, through a heavily guarded tunnel. Cells have slit windows that show only a sliver of sky, making it impossible for prisoners and visitors to know exactly where they are within the building.

Whether ADX is really necessary is a matter of opinion. Prisoners' rights activists say that it is "cruel and unusual punishment," while others claim that it is the only answer to prison violence. Regardless of one's philosophy, however, it would appear that the supermax concept is here to stay. Following the Bureau of Prisons' example, by 2005 some 40 states had constructed supermax units, with many more expected as we move through the first decade of the 21st century.

Administrative Maximum Penitentiary (ADX) in Colorado.

Sources: Chase Riveland, *Supermax Prisons: Overview and General Considerations* (Washington, DC: National Institute of Corrections, 1999); *From Alcatraz to Marion to Florence* (Chicago: Committee to End the Marion Lockdown, 1996); Leona Kurki and Norval Morris, "Purposes, Practices, and Problems of Supermax Prisons," *Crime and Justice* 28 (2002): 385–434; Jeremy W. Coid, "The Federal Administrative Maximum Penitentiary, Florence, Colorado," *Medicine, Science and the Law* 41, 4 (2001): 287–297.

cized as being more like country clubs than prisons. Yet despite the attractiveness of their physical layout and resources, they are nonetheless "total institutions" and serve as effective barriers to the outside world.

Open Institutions

As a departure from the traditional maximum-, medium-, and minimum-security prisons, which are essentially closed institutions, there are variations in the minimum-security plan that serve as "prisons without walls." These prison farms, camps, ranches, vocational training centers, and forestry settlements are relatively recent innovations. The modern counterparts of the 19th-century reformatories for youthful offenders and young adult felons, they provide instructive work for inmates within an environment conducive to behavioral change.

These **open institutions** have numerous advantages over more traditional correctional facilities. They relieve the problem of overcrowding in other types of institutions; they are less costly to construct and maintain; and they enable various types of prisoners to be separated, thus reducing opportunities for contamination of attitudes. Moreover, they have economic and community service advantages. Prisoners in open camps produce crops and dairy products for use in the state correctional system and other government facilities. Ranches employ inmates in cattle raising and horse breeding. Forestry camps are used to maintain state parks, fight forest fires, and aid in reforestation. Finally, these camps and farms avoid many of the drawbacks of the traditional total institutions. Regulation and regimentation is more relaxed, and greater freedom of movement is possible.

Correctional Organization and Administration

Until the beginning of the 20th century, prisons were administered by state boards of charities, boards of inspectors, state prison commissions, boards of control made up of "prominent citizens," or individual prison keepers.[5] Generally, however, most prisons in most states operated as independent fiefdoms. Few jurisdictions had a state department of corrections. Individual wardens were appointed by governors through the system of political patronage, and institutional staff members held their positions by virtue of their political connections. While governors made hiring and budgetary decisions, the leadership roles and the administrative procedures of individual institutions were under the absolute control of the wardens. Today, every state has some form of centralized department of corrections that establishes policy for all institutions within its jurisdiction.

Prison Administration

The two most common forms of correctional systems are those that are subdivisions of some larger state department, such as justice or welfare, and those that are independent structures. The U.S. Bureau of Prisons, for example, is a division of the Department of Justice; Florida has its Department of Corrections within its Department of Health and Rehabilitative Services; in Vermont and Tennessee, corrections is part of a department of institutions; and in Virginia, corrections is a segment of the Department of Public Welfare. California, Arkansas, Texas, and numerous other states, however, have independent departments of corrections with lines of authority running directly to the governor's office.

At the top of the administrative hierarchy of any department of corrections is the commissioner of corrections. This executive works directly under the governor to establish policy, shape institutional procedures, negotiate annual budgetary allotments for the various institutions, and make major personnel decisions.

The head of each prison, generally appointed by the commissioner of corrections, is a warden, director, principal keeper, or superintendent, depending on the state. In the past, the position of warden was one of great power, but also of questionable reputation because of its association with the political "spoils system." Although such arrangements persist in a few jurisdictions, most wardens and superintendents are civil service employees who have earned their positions on a seniority or merit basis and receive no more fringe benefits than other state employees. One monument to the "old ways" can be found on Spring Street in Ossining, New York: the warden's mansion at Sing Sing Prison. The old mansion now serves as office space for corrections personnel, and recent superintendents of that institution live in their own homes, struggling against rush-hour traffic along with all the other commuters in the area.

Black men born in the U.S. and fortunate enough to live past the age of eighteen are conditioned to accept the inevitability of prison. For most of us, it simply looms as the next phase in a sequence of humiliations.

—BLACK ACTIVIST GEORGE JACKSON

Change is a rare occasion in prison—sameness is the law. The same people with the same crime, the same colored clothes with the same stripe, the same brown-suited guards with the same orders, the same food on the same day, the same disciplinary slips with the same verdicts (guilty), the same bed in the same cell night after night.

—ANONYMOUS PRISON INMATE

The job of the warden or superintendent is to manage the prison. In larger institutions, the warden may be assisted by one or more associates: a deputy warden in charge of discipline, security, inmate movement and control, and prison routine; a second deputy in charge of prison programs, records, library services, mail and visitation, recreation, and release procedures; an industries manager in charge of prison industries, farms, production, and supplies; and a medical supervisor in charge of prison health services and sanitation.

Historically, the majority of prison wardens lacked the educational, managerial, and experiential qualifications appropriate for effective and humanitarian leadership of large institutions. Appointments through political patronage rarely considered the candidate's preparedness for a wardenship. With the establishment of state departments of corrections and the growth of civil service in the 20th century, however, a new recruitment pattern emerged. On the basis of merit and length of service, prison guards worked their way "up through the ranks" to the warden's office. This pattern produced many capable wardens over the years, but it had some serious drawbacks. Many such wardens had minimal education, limited administrative exposure, and a tendency to focus exclusively on custodial issues. These circumstances served to generate attitudes that were not conducive to effective correctional treatment.

Over the last four decades a new pattern of recruitment emerged—one drawing on capable administrators with long careers in corrections, although not necessarily as custodial personnel. In a number of jurisdictions, selection processes favor people with varied and intensive education and experience, who are likely to be sensitive not only to the complexities of prison security and administration but to inmates' needs as well.

Overall, the management of a prison is a major task, rivaling that of many large businesses and industries in its complexity. And interestingly, wardens rank exceptionally high in job satisfaction—well above most other professions.[6]

Prison Personnel

In addition to wardens, their deputies, and other administrators, prison personnel include both professional and custodial staff. The *professional staff* include the physicians, nurses, dentists, chaplains, psychiatrists, psychologists, clerks and secretaries, teachers, counselors, and dietitians who deal with the institutional paperwork and serve the medical, spiritual, and treatment needs of the inmates. The size of the professional staff varies depending on the institution and its particular orientation (custody versus rehabilitation). In larger prisons, professionals constitute about one-third of the workforce. The *custodial staff* is made up of the correctional officers and their supervisors, whose basic functions fall into three areas: inmate security, movement, and discipline. Invariably, however, their roles go considerably further.

Prison *guards*, currently referred to as correction, correctional, or custodial officers, work in a maligned profession. Guarding is considered a tainted occupation because people are repelled by the surveillance and repression that are characteristic of prison life. The media are largely responsible for creating and sustaining this image. Film and television dramas portray the correctional officer as evil and savage. Late-night TV movies like *The Big House* (1930), *White Heat* (1949), *Inside the Walls of Folsom Prison* (1951), *Birdman of Alcatraz* (1962), and *Cool Hand Luke* (1967), to name just a few, have shown prison guards as bigoted, corrupt, brutal, and morally base. Continuing in this vein are the Earle Owensby films of the 1970s, as well as other movies including *Escape From Alcatraz* in 1978, *Brubaker* in 1980, *Bad Boys* in 1983, *The Shawshank Redemption* in 1994, and *Sleepers* in 1996. Literary works, particularly those that contain emotional statements against the prison system—such as Eldridge Cleaver's *Soul on Ice* and George Jackson's *Soledad Brother*—have also portrayed the correctional officer in a negative light.[7]

Without question, there are many corrupt and brutal custodial officers. But to put them all in a common mold would be no more accurate than suggesting that "all convicts are evil," "all police are dishonest," or "all politicians are criminals." In fact, if the

New Commitments to State Prison for Drug and Violent Offenses, 1980–2004

Source: Bureau of Justice Statistics.

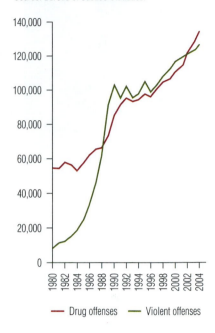

— Drug offenses   — Violent offenses

Assaults on Prison Staff by Inmates, 1986–2004

Sources: *Corrections Compendium;* U.S. General Accounting Office.

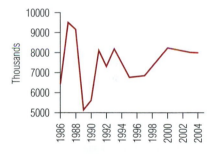

Sometimes referred to as "turnkeys," "hacks," "screws," "hogs," and "bulls," correctional officers are members of a maligned profession.

FAMOUS CRIMINALS

Did Club Fed Get a Martha Makeover?

Martha Stewart, the "Domestic Diva" who made her fortune by dishing out home furnishing, cooking, and decorating advice, was sentenced to 5 months in federal prison and another 5 months of house arrest in March 2004 for lying to federal investigators about a stock sale. Prosecutors said her sale of ImClone Systems shares 1 day before the price plummeted was prompted by inside information. The company was then led by her friend Sam Waksal, who also ended up behind bars for his part in the scandal.

Although she is appealing the verdict, Stewart decided to serve her sentence. She was sent to federal prison in Alderson, West Virginia, a.k.a. "Camp Cupcake," to serve out her short term. Because of the intense media scrutiny surrounding her case, she arrived clandestinely in the early morning hours of October 8, 2004, to trade in her freedom and $900,000 salary for life as federal inmate No. 55170-054 and a pennies-per-hour maintenance position that included scrubbing floors and toilets. She passed the time in prison by cooking, gardening, and making crafts, activities part of her normal repertoire, but modified to prison life: She foraged for dandelions, wild greens, and crab apples on the prison grounds; concocted microwave recipes; and helped create a ceramic Nativity scene for a Christmas decorating contest (her team lost). She also posted several letters on her Web site,

(continued on p. 499)

popular image of the correctional officer were accurate, most prisons would not be able to function.

Correctional officers' duties are difficult, and they must be performed under the most unpleasant circumstances. Their careers unfold while they are locked up in an unattractive and depressing environment. Outnumbered by a legion of hostile, restless, and sometimes desperate and violent inmates, they must always be watchful and always appear vigilant, alert, strong, competent, and self-confident. Moreover, as the eminent criminologist Robert G. Caldwell once put it:

> The guard . . . occupies a pivotal and strategic position in the prison. Upon his competence and loyalty, upon his resourcefulness and skill, depend both the safety of the prison and the spirit of the inmates. He is the first line of attack in case of escapes and the most immediate instrument for the proper handling of the prisoners. He must enforce the rules and regulations. He must be on the alert to detect signs of uprisings and to prevent the introduction of contraband into the prison and its circulation among the inmates. He must count the prisoners under his charge several times a day. He must patrol his gallery and periodically inspect the cells there. He must administer to the inmates' needs and make reports regarding their condition and behavior. During the day he must supervise the prisoners while they are at work and play and as they march from place to place. At night he must lock them in, see that the lights are out, and make certain that all is secure.[8]

Within such a setting—"a closed and timeless world where days, weeks, and months have little to distinguish them"[9]—and faced with few means for carrying out their custodial duties, correctional officers must resort to a number of unconventional mechanisms for maintaining order. Some become brutal and sadistic. A few become indispensable to the inmate black market, providing illegal services and contraband or serving as "mules" who carry drugs into the prison. Still others develop a system of punishments and rewards to encourage compliance with prison rules. Most, however, use the spirit of compromise to accomplish their mission. They overlook a number of infractions. For instance, inmates may be allowed to remain out of their cells without authorization, pass letters back and forth, cook food stolen from the prison kitchen, smoke in unauthorized areas, or possess trivial contraband items. In return, they are expected to refrain from violence, perform their assigned tasks, and be civil to the guards.[10] As one officer from a New Jersey prison related to the author:

> You could write these guys up [prepare a disciplinary report] every day of the week. They're all into something. . . . But you have to bend some if you want to get your job done. . . .
>
> Yesterday I caught this one with a "dropper" [a wire device connected to the light socket, used for boiling water]. It's not allowed because you could electrocute yourself, but he's smart enough not to do that. I could have taken it and cited him, but I just told him to take it down. He'll remember. . . . Next time I tell him to get in line he'll move. . . . It's like the old saying, "grease the floor and you slide easier."

Overall, however, research suggests that there are a number of distinctly different types of correctional officers.[11] For example, almost every institution has its "rule enforcers" and "hard-liners," who are aggressive, sometimes power hungry, and generally inflexible when it comes to rules. They adopt a militaristic approach toward inmates and interpret their official mandate to be custody and control, along with maintaining order and proper conduct. By contrast, institutions also have their "people worker" or "social worker" types of officers, who are among the most dedicated in correctional work. They develop a functional style of working with inmates and tend to be more flexible when it comes to rule enforcement and disciplinary measures. In general, they gain inmate compliance through interpersonal communication and personalized relations. And finally, every correctional institution has a number of officers who reflect characteristics of both the rule enforcers and the social workers. Although they follow institutional rules and regulations very closely, they also attempt to consider the circumstances without deviating too far from official procedure. Other varieties of correctional officers, as well, can be observed in prisons throughout the United States, but the types described above reflect the majority of styles. However, regardless of the different working styles, burnout and stress are common problems for all.[12]

Institutional Routines

When they locked me in my cell that very first day it suddenly hit me all at once. "This is it, asshole," I said to myself, "you're gonna die in this place." I was scared, lonely, and depressed and really feeling sorry for myself. But I didn't die. I became just like all the other shitheads, pissholes, and zombies—playing the games, doing the time, falling into the routine . . . sleep, eat, work, sleep, eat, work, "yes sir," "no sir," "I'm sorry sir," "I must have been mistaken sir."

— **FORMER INMATE, LEAVENWORTH PENITENTIARY**

In 2004, there were some 1.4 million inmates in federal and state correctional institutions in the 50 states, the District of Columbia, and the U.S. territories. The institutions in which these prisoners were being held included the full range of correctional facilities, from maximum-security and supermax walled fortresses to minimum-security cottages and reformatories to "open" forestry camps and ranch settlements. The physical conditions of these institutions also covered a wide spectrum—from the best to the worst that the American prison system has to offer. Although many new correctional facilities have been built over the years, many are old and in varying stages of decay, with conditions that are often appalling.

Prison Facilities

In 1975, studies by the Federal Bureau of Prisons revealed that of the hundreds of state institutions in operation at that time, 47 percent had been built since 1949, about 32 percent dated from the period between 1924 and 1948, and the balance had been put into operation during 1923 or earlier.[13] Twenty-four of the prisons—most of them large maximum-security facilities—had been in continuous use since before 1874. By the beginning of the 21st century, further deterioration had become apparent.

Today, Clinton Prison in New York, Joliet in Illinois, and California's San Quentin are more than 125 years old; Michigan's Jackson Prison and Pennsylvania's Eastern Penitentiary have been housing inmates for over a century and a half; and if current trends in prison use continue, both Auburn and Sing Sing in New York may still be operating 200 years after they were opened. All of these ancient institutions have made improvements over the years: Many of the original cell blocks have been abandoned or modernized, new structures have been added, and sanitary and other facilities have

(continued from p. 498)

www.marthatalks.com, to thank her fans for their support. Most inmates had pleasant things to say about their famous 63-year-old prison mate, although others grumbled that she was spared from the strenuous duty of snow shoveling.

After her release, she served the remainder of her sentence in her sweeping Bedford, New York, estate accessorized with an electronic monitoring ankle bracelet. Her lawyer's request to shorten her home detention sentence, so that Stewart could work 80 hours a week on her new television shows, furniture line, and comeback to her media empire, was denied. As of mid-2005, her appeal continued. ▪

An inside cellblock in Sing Sing Prison in 1935.

been renovated to reflect more humanitarian standards. Nevertheless, in their basic order and design, the more than 100 correctional institutions built during the 19th and early 20th centuries, together with the many more built during the 1920s and 1930s, continue to operate as grim monuments to past penal philosophies.

One of the major reasons that many antiquated prisons remain in use is overcrowding. Put simply, state governments do not have enough funds to build a new prison to completely replace an older one that is already filled beyond capacity. As such, new prisons typically do not replace older ones but, rather, are used to reduce inmate overloads.

Classification

The inmate's prison experience generally begins with classification. In its broadest sense, **classification** is the process through which the educational, vocational, treatment, and custodial needs of the offender are determined. At least theoretically, it is the system by which a correctional agency matches the treatment and security programs of the institution with the requirements of the individual.

In earlier times, as the practice of imprisoning people after conviction developed, the most rudimentary forms of correctional classification consisted merely of separating the guilty from the not-guilty. Only slightly more sophisticated was the separation of debtors from criminals—a type of classification by legal status. Other early forms of classification included the separation of men from women, youth from adults, and first offenders from habitual criminals. The reformatory movements of the late 19th century, the differentiation between maximum-, medium-, and minimum-security prisons, and the designation of Alcatraz as a superpenitentiary for the most incorrigible felons were all examples of rudimentary classification schemes. As correctional systems continued to evolve, the separation of the feebleminded, the tubercular, the venereally diseased, the sexually perverted, the drug addicted, and the aged and crippled from the general prison population or into special institutions was also based on the principle of classification.

Currently, classification goes beyond the mere separation of offenders on the basis of age, gender, custodial risk, or some other factor. It is based on diagnostic evaluation and treatment planning, followed by placement in the recommended institutional program or type of correctional facility.[14] The extent to which classification schemes are used tends to vary, however, not only from state to state but also among institutions within the same jurisdiction. Moreover, there are numerous different organizational structures within which classification may occur. These include reception and orientation units, classification committees, and reception-diagnostic centers.

Reception and Orientation Units   Some jurisdictions have reception units or *classification clinics* staffed by psychologists, social workers, or other professionals. These units carry out a series of diagnostic studies and make recommendations to institutional authorities regarding the custodial, medical, vocational, and treatment needs of each incoming inmate. Classification clinics also provide orientation programs for new prisoners, giving them an overview of institutional life, routine, rules and regulations, and custodial and correctional expectations.

Classification Committees   Whereas the reception unit operates autonomously and its recommendations are not binding on institutional authorities, classification committees have emerged as integrated classification systems. A classification committee may be chaired by the warden or deputy warden and include institutional social workers, psychologists, chaplains, medical officers, teachers, vocational and recreational supervisors, and others. The decisions of the committee are binding on the administration, and any changes in the recommended program must be approved by the committee.[15]

The integrated committee is the most widely used classification system in contemporary institutions. It permits professional and administrative personnel to work

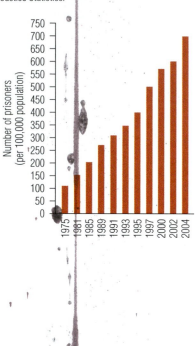

Rate of Imprisonment

Inmates in state and federal prisons, per 100,000 U.S. residents   Source: Bureau of Justice Statistics.

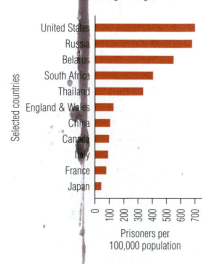

Lands of the Free and Not So Free

Prisoners per 100,000 population, selected countries   Source: International Centre for Prison Studies, King's College, London.

together in determining inmate needs, and at the same time it allows each group of personnel to gain some understanding of the problems the other faces.

Reception Centers The **reception center,** or diagnostic center, is a central receiving institution where all felony offenders sentenced to a term of imprisonment are committed for orientation and classification. These specialized facilities are relatively new in American corrections, dating from the 1940s, when they were established in New York, California, and the federal system.

The purpose of these centers is to make the correctional system, rather than a specific institution, responsible for classification. This standardizes the classification process throughout the state and provides for a facility and staff whose sole functions are classification and orientation. Moreover, the diagnostic recommendations are binding on the institutions to which the classified inmates are ultimately sent. At the reception center, the newly sentenced inmates are studied intensively for 20 to perhaps 90 days. The ensuing recommendations include not only custodial and treatment plans but also a statement as to which correctional facility the inmates should be sent.

Problems with Classification All of these classification schemes have shortcomings. Classification recommendations are not always followed; often there are ineffective linkages between classification units, committees, or centers and institutional programs; and in many systems time and workload pressures tend to make the classification process overly routine. Yet almost a quarter of a century ago the American Correctional Association strongly endorsed the reception-diagnostic center concept, urging that it be established in all 50 states.[16] The association felt that only by using this system could a good diagnosis and treatment plan be developed for each inmate. In its view, the system's pivotal position within a state's correctional structure would ensure that the diagnostic recommendations would be implemented at the receiving institutions.

The Classification Process Three factors generally combine to dictate how intensive the classification process will be: (1) available personnel, (2) the inmate workload, and (3) whether classification occurs in a reception and orientation unit of a prison facility, through an integrated classification committee, or at a separate reception-diagnostic center. The procedure may range from a physical examination and a single interview to an extensive series of psychiatric and psychological tests, academic and vocational evaluations, orientation sessions, medical and dental checkups, and numerous personal interviews. Some classification programs also include analyses of athletic abilities and recreational interests, as well as contacts with religious advisers.

When the testing and interviews have been completed, reports are prepared and placed in the inmate's case file. Summaries of the prisoner's social and family background, work history, criminal record, prior institutionalization (if any), current offense, and any other relevant background data are also included. A classification board or committee then evaluates the case file and makes recommendations. This board can range from a single counselor or social worker to as many as 15 members, including teachers, psychologists, physicians, researchers, members of the administrative and custodial staffs, and experts from numerous other fields. The board discusses the various data and plans the inmate's correctional career. It also takes responsibility for *reclassification* should the inmate's needs or situation change.

Trends in Classification During recent decades, there have been experiments with new approaches to classification. In the *treatment team* approach, a counselor, a teacher, and a custodial officer become a "team" for each individual inmate. The team takes over the duties of classification, coordinates the treatment plan, and handles disciplinary problems. The same team may be assigned to all the inmates in a particular dormitory or cell block. The major benefit of this approach has been to make academic and custodial staff more treatment-oriented and counseling staff more sensitive to custodial issues by virtue of their collective involvement in the correctional and prison management processes.

Nobody wants literate people to go to prison—they have a distressing way of revealing what it's actually like and destroying our illusions about training and rehabilitation with nasty stories about sadism and futility and buckets of stale urine.

— DAVID FROST

States with the Highest and Lowest Incarceration Rates

Rank	State	Rate per 100,000 U.S. Residents
1	Louisiana	794
2	Mississippi	743
.	.	.
.	.	.
.	.	.
49	Maine	141
50	Minnesota	141

Source: Bureau of Justice Statistics.

The U.S. Prison Population

Source: Bureau of Justice Statistics.

Gender

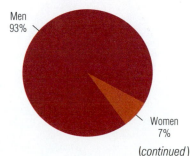

Men 93%

Women 7%

(continued)

The U.S. Prison Population (*cont.*)

Race

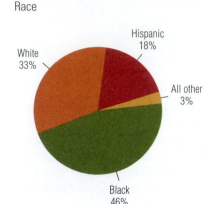

White 33%
Hispanic 18%
All other 3%
Black 46%

Age

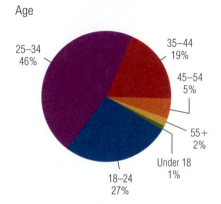

25–34 46%
35–44 19%
45–54 5%
55+ 2%
Under 18 1%
18–24 27%

Commitment offense

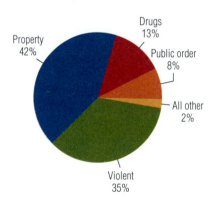

Drugs 13%
Property 42%
Public order 8%
All other 2%
Violent 35%

Education

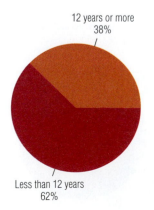

12 years or more 38%
Less than 12 years 62%

Contract classification is similar to other forms of classification, but the recommendations are in the form of a contract signed by the inmate and the chair of the classification committee. Inmate "needs" and requirements are spelled out in the document. When these conditions are met, such benefits as lower security, additional privileges, and recommendation for early parole are awarded.

With the exploding growth of technological literacy across the United States, *computerized classification* has recently been introduced as a diagnostic tool. The process is based on a screening system designed to measure an inmate's potential for aggressive behavior, depression and suicidal tendencies, intellectual status, vocational skills and interests, socialization, criminal sophistication, and physical and mental health.

Closely linked to classification is the increasing use of *protective custody units (PCUs).* They are designed to house inmates who cannot cope with the daily routines of prison life and thus request special placement. PCUs typically house inmates with special medical or psychological conditions or those whose safety is at risk. Child molesters are often placed in protective custody units because of their extremely low status within the inmate social hierarchy.

Finally, in determining placement, classification teams assess and evaluate the security and supervision requirements for each incoming inmate. Indeed, good classification systems can reduce the number of inmate assaults and decrease the potential for prison violence.

Prison Programs

Institutional programs include a variety of activities, all of which can have an impact, either directly or indirectly, on the rehabilitation of offenders and their successful reintegration into the community after release. There are *treatment programs,* for example, that attempt to remove alleged "defects" in an inmate's socialization and psychological development that are responsible for some lawbreaking behaviors. There are *academic and vocational programs,* which attempt to provide inmates with the skills necessary for adequate employment after release. There are *recreational programs,* which have medical, humanitarian, social-psychological, and custodial motives; they are structured to ease the pressures of confinement, making inmates more receptive to rehabilitation and less depressed, hostile, and asocial. There are *work programs,* which serve many of the humanitarian and rehabilitative needs of the offender, yet at the same time are related to the successful economic functioning of the institution. And finally, there are *medical programs* and *religious programs,* which also have implications for institutional management and reintegration of the offender into the community.

Health and Medical Services
The number and types of programs and services available to inmates vary widely by both jurisdiction and institution. Every prison has some form of health and medical program, although some are quite rudimentary. All reception centers have comprehensive medical facilities, with separate hospital units, some of which have well-equipped operating rooms. Similar facilities are also found in the larger prisons and reformatories.

Smaller institutions use a range of medical and health alternatives. Some have small hospital units with a full-time physician or nurse and paraprofessionals who are on hand for the day-to-day care of minor illnesses and injuries. If there is no physician on the institutional staff, a physician from the local community visits on a regular basis. All but the largest prisons and reception centers contract out for the services of dentists and opticians.

The importance of adequate medical care cannot be overstated. Poor diet, alcoholism and drug abuse, and histories of inadequate medical attention are disproportionately evident among prison inmates.[17] There is also the increasing problem of AIDS, not only in U.S prisons but in other parts of the world as well (see Exhibit 15.2). Moreover, the potential for rapid spreading of even the most minor illnesses is high within a population that is confined in such close quarters. The prison medical unit is also responsible for monitoring sanitary conditions and inmate dietary needs, for these too are directly related to the well-being of the institution as a whole.[18]

Religious Programs The availability of spiritual services for prison inmates has a long history in American corrections. Solitary meditation was the theoretical basis of reform in Philadelphia's Walnut Street Jail almost two centuries ago, and penitence was encouraged by frequent visits from missionaries and local clerics. Over the years, various Christian denominations and other religious organizations have devoted their time to the spiritual needs of inmates and have provided ongoing programs of religious instruction.

Contemporary institutions generally retain Protestant, Roman Catholic, and sometimes Jewish chaplains, or at least a nondenominational cleric, on a full-time or part-time basis, for religious counseling and worship services. In some small institutions where there are no educational programs or rehabilitative services, the prison chaplain provides the only available "treatment."

Opinions as to the usefulness of religious programs in prisons are decidedly mixed. Such programs have been praised by wardens as anchors of law and order, by chaplains as powerful treatment forces, and by some inmates as sources of inspiration and cushions against despair. At the same time, however, they have been heavily criticized. Many prison administrators view religious counseling as useless and as a source of trouble and dissension; inasmuch as some jurisdictions prohibit the searching or questioning of clergy, chaplains have also been viewed as potential security risks. Many chaplains look on their own programs as dull and unrealistic, and given the remote locations of many correctional facilities, prison chaplaincies are not highly sought after by ministers. Inmates often consider the programs to be insincere, stale, and platitudinous; as a result, few make use of them. As one inmate expressed it: "If there is a God, he sure as hell was not on my side."

Many of these issues have been further complicated by the current conflicts within organized religion. As more and more members of the clergy drift away from orthodox theology and its uncompromising acceptance of tradition, the role of the prison chaplain has become a frustrating one. Recognizing the inequities of institutional life, many wish to act on behalf of inmates' legitimate interests. Yet the dominance of coercive correctional policies has thwarted their hopes of serving as activist ministers.

Winfield, Kansas, Correctional Facility inmates pray after a "Heart to Heart" session, part of a faith-based prison program called The InnerChange Freedom Initiative.

Causes of Inmate Deaths

Source: Bureau of Justice Statistics.

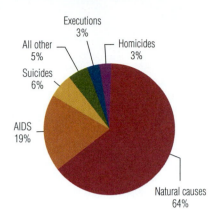

Executions 3%
Homicides 3%
All other 5%
Suicides 6%
AIDS 19%
Natural causes 64%

The Wicked Witch of the Prison?

In an unconventional move to conjure up a sense of spirituality among its inmates, a prison has hired a self-professed witch. Jamyi Witch, a priestess of the Wiccan religion, is a chaplain at the maximum-security Waupun Correctional Institution in southeastern Wisconsin. While her appointment has caused a firestorm of controversy in the Department of Corrections, Witch maintains that people have misconceptions about the Wiccan religion—that it is not all about magic and casting spells but, rather, involves using meditation to focus psychic energy to achieve goals. Working to achieve a positive focus, according to Witch, is exactly the sort of counseling that inmates need.

Even though many in the Corrections Department remain skeptical and legislators' offices have been flooded with angry emails and letters since the hire, lawyers for the state say that it would be illegal to deny her employment on the basis of religion. The only option, therefore, would be to cut the state budget to take away funding for chaplain positions, which total more than 30 statewide. But eliminating prison chaplains because of what many perceive as a bad hiring decision is an unlikely solution. In general, support for chaplains in prisons is strong, and many believe that they play an important role in the rehabilitation of criminals.

What do you think? Does having a Wiccan priestess as a prison chaplain cast the prison in a bad light? ■

EXHIBIT 15.2 | International Perspectives on Crime & Justice

Prisons and HIV/AIDS Around the Globe

AIDS (acquired immunodeficiency syndrome) is likely the most publicized disease of the past century. It is best defined as a severe manifestation of infection with HIV (human immunodeficiency virus), a virus that destroys or incapacitates components of the immune system. The actual causes of death among people with AIDS include a variety of infections and other diseases that an otherwise healthy immune system can effectively cope with.

HIV is transmitted when virus particles or infected cells gain direct access to the bloodstream. This can occur during all forms of sexual intercourse that involve the transmission of body fluids, as well as oral–genital intercourse with an infected partner. Other major routes of transmission include the sharing of injection equipment among injecting drug users, the passing of the virus to unborn or newborn children by infected mothers, and transfusions from an infected blood supply. The World Health Organization estimated in 2004 that 14,000 people are newly infected each day around the world and that the majority of these are in Africa.

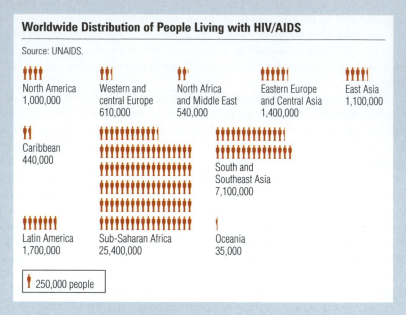

Worldwide Distribution of People Living with HIV/AIDS

Source: UNAIDS.

North America
1,000,000

Western and
central Europe
610,000

North Africa
and Middle East
540,000

Eastern Europe
and Central Asia
1,400,000

East Asia
1,100,000

Caribbean
440,000

South and
Southeast Asia
7,100,000

Latin America
1,700,000

Sub-Saharan Africa
25,400,000

Oceania
35,000

250,000 people

HIV prevalence in many prisons is already high—higher than in the population at large—and still increasing. Many of those who are HIV-positive in prison were already infected before they were incarcerated, having come from those segments of the population with a heavier than average burden of HIV infections. HIV prevalence in prisons ranges from .2 percent in Australia to more than 10 percent in certain European countries. Canadian studies have demonstrated that 2 percent to 3 percent of prisoners are infected with HIV. In the United States, HIV prevalence among federal inmates is higher for women than men, 3.4 percent to 2.1 percent respectively, reflecting the surge in women prisoners with drug and alcohol dependence. Rates of infection in prisons in many developing nations are even higher.

The difficulty is that prisons tend to be ideal breeding grounds for the transmission of HIV. They are frequently overcrowded; sexual strain

Education Programs Most Americans have confidence in education as a mechanism for upgrading skills and understanding, shaping attitudes, and promoting social adjustment. Moreover, it is estimated that the average reading level of adult inmates is at or below the fifth-grade level; that more than half of inmates have not finished high school; and that even those who completed portions of formal education lag two or three grade levels behind what they completed in school.[19] It is not surprising, then, that academic education and vocational training are regarded as the primary programs in correctional institutions.

In *academic education* programs, the emphasis is on basic knowledge and communicative skills. Most institutions have some sort of prison school, and in most state correctional systems education for inmates is mandated by law. Courses of instruction vary from one institution to the next, ranging from literacy programs to high school equivalency studies to college-level curricula.

Prison schools, however, are beset with difficulties. Many institutions are short on classroom facilities and useful teaching aids; there is a lack of qualified instructors, which forces prisons to rely on rejects from the public school system and on inmate teachers, most of whom are undereducated; many inmates lack motivation, which results in teachers being pressured to make classes effortless and complete false reports on inmate progress; and the realities of prison discipline and security often interfere with courses of instruction or curtail enrollments.

is common; and release from tension and the boredom of prison life often occurs through drugs and sex. Drugs are often injected, and the needles—scarce and difficult to hide—are almost always shared. Moreover, prison needles are typically homemade devices, crafted from ballpoint pens and eye droppers. High percentages of prisoners with histories of injection drug use (IDU) have been observed in various countries around the world, including 20 percent in France and 30 percent in the United States. Surveys in European (France, Germany, Italy, the Netherlands, Scotland, and Sweden), Irish, Greek, Russian, and U.S. prisons suggest that around 13 percent of the populations are active injection drug users within the confines of prison. In the largest correctional facility for women in the United States—Chowchilla Prison in California—heroin users were found to be injecting with needles stolen from the prison hospital where HIV-infected and AIDS patients were being treated.

In Thailand, a country where the AIDS epidemic expanded rapidly, the first wave of HIV infections occurred in 1988 among drug injectors. From a negligible percentage at the beginning of that year, the prevalence rate rose to more than 40 percent within 6 months, fueled in part by transmission of the virus as injectors moved in and out of prison.

Sexual contact between men is common in prisons around the world. Published reports have estimated that the percentage of inmates who engage in homosexual activity while incarcerated ranges from as low as 2 percent to as high as 90 percent. A survey in Rio de Janeiro, Brazil, for example, suggested that 73 percent of male prisoners had sex with other men in prison, while a recent study of federal inmates in the United States found that 30 percent engaged in sex with other men while incarcerated. Surveys in Zambia, Australia, England, and Canada reflected rates between 6 percent and 12 percent—figures that are probably quite low because of denial and underreporting. Sex between men in prisons, furthermore, includes unprotected anal sex—an efficient method for transmitting HIV infection. Condoms, as a rule, are not available in prisons.

In women's prisons staffed by male correctional officers, vaginal intercourse does indeed occur. Depending on the country and the prison, these sexual contacts may be through consent, exploitation, and/or rape—any of which create a risk for HIV transmission.

Tattooing is also common in prisons, and the equipment is frequently shared, creating yet another risk of HIV transmission. There are similar risks where skin piercing and "blood brotherhood" rites are practiced.

The potential for the spread of HIV and AIDS is usually increased by a lack of proper medical care. In many institutions, particularly in developing nations, such sexually transmitted diseases as syphilis, hepatitis B and C, and gonorrhea are common. Yet if left untreated, they can greatly increase an individual's vulnerability to HIV through sexual contact. A particularly serious health consideration, furthermore, is tuberculosis (TB), which can easily spread in overcrowded prison conditions. People with HIV are especially vulnerable, and HIV-positive people with TB can transmit this disease to those not infected with HIV.

Correctional administrators have used a number of options for reducing the spread of HIV within their institutions, including education, offering condoms to inmates, providing adequate health care, and reducing crowded conditions. Implementing these changes on a global basis, however, is unlikely.

Sources: James A. Inciardi, Hilary Surratt, and Paulo R. Telles, *Sex, Drugs and HIV/AIDS in Brazil* (Boulder: Westview Press, 2000); UNAIDS, *AIDS Epidemic Update 2004* (Geneva: United Nations, 2004); World Health Organization, *HIV in Prisons*, 2001; M. E. Helland and C. K. Aitken, "HIV in Prison: What Are the Risks and What Can Be Done?" *Sexual Health* 1 (2004): 107–113; WHO, *Policy Brief: Reduction of HIV Transmission in Prisons* (Geneva: Author, 2004).

Vocational training programs focus on preparing inmates for meaningful employment after release. Most of the larger institutions and many small ones have a number of such programs, which provide training in automobile repair and maintenance, welding, sheet metal work, carpentry and cabinetmaking, plumbing and electricity, and radio and television repair. Like the academic programs, these too have some problems. Many prison shops are poorly equipped and lack the appropriate technical staff; in others the machinery and fittings have long since become outmoded; and in some, the training is in fields in which jobs are not available in the outside world. Moreover, inmates who have acquired skills in such areas as plumbing, electrical work, carpentry, and masonry are often barred from joining unions upon release because of their criminal records. Even more frustrating is the fact that some institutional programs continue to train inmates in spheres that have virtually no relevance to the job market.

Although almost one-fourth of inmates in U.S. prisons participate in academic and vocational education programs each year, at least half of all state prisons have made significant cuts in their educational programs. Generally, cutbacks appear to be motivated by shrinking state budgets and the ballooning costs associated with increases in the inmate population. Nevertheless, limiting funds for education programs may prove to be a costly choice in the long run. Studies demonstrate that inmates who participate in academic and vocational programs have lower recidivism rates than those who do not.[20]

Despite the many difficulties, the prospects for academic education and vocational training programs in contemporary corrections are not entirely bleak. Administrators of many institutions have encouraged community volunteers and local school districts to aid in tutoring more motivated inmates; prison routines have been made more flexible for those who wish to attend classes; federal funds have been allocated for upgrading many prison schools; self-taught programmed courses of instruction in elementary and secondary school subjects have become more available; and a growing number of prison systems are introducing programs whereby participants can earn a college degree. Moreover, the need for more relevant vocational education has also been recognized. Numerous correctional facilities are upgrading prison shop equipment; others are implementing new programs in more timely fields such as graphic communications and computer operation and technology.

Public Support for Correctional Treatment

Responses to "What do you think should be the main emphasis in most prisons?"
Source: *Prison Journal.*

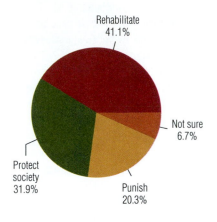

Rehabilitate 41.1%

Not sure 6.7%

Punish 20.3%

Protect society 31.9%

Prison Labor and Industry   Closely related to vocational training in correctional institutions are prison work and industrial programs. These can provide numerous opportunities for inmates to:

• Earn wages while serving their terms.
• Develop regular work habits.
• Gain experience in machine operation, manufacturing, computer technology, and other specialized skills.
• Ease the boredom of institutional confinement.

As recently as the 1990s, prison work programs generally failed to provide these opportunities. The majority of correctional institutions had no such programs, and those that did were open to only a small segment of the inmate population. Moreover, the jobs available to inmates in many jurisdictions were typically dull and irrelevant. The major industries included printing and the production of auto tags, road signs, clothing, and similar articles; many nonindustrial prison jobs were restricted to meaningless tasks such as cleaning, laundry, and other simple maintenance work.[21]

There was a major reason for this. State use was the chief outlet for prison-made products, and as noted in Chapter 14, this situation was the result of state and federal legislation that barred prison industrial production from competing with private enterprise. However, Congress passed legislation in 1979 that lifted the ban on interstate transportation and sale of prison-made goods, with the result that the number of inmates employed in prison industries began to grow.[22] Currently, prison factories are involved in the production of data entry and telephone answering equipment, optical ware, mattresses, flags, furniture, and cleaning equipment and supplies. In addition, inmates are employed in slaughterhouses and meatpacking, vehicle repair, picture framing, Braille translation, silk screening, CD-ROM duplication, fruit and vegetable produce, and many other areas. Moreover, inmates in some jurisdictions participate in all sectors of the computer industry.[23]

One of the more interesting prison industries is the production and mass marketing of *jail-style apparel,* also known as "jailhouse chic" or "incarceration chic." Reflecting the appearances and style of prison and county lockup clothing issued to prisoners, incarceration chic includes orange jumpsuits, blue or green trousers, "one size fits all" low-slung and ill-fitting baggy pants, sneakers without shoe-laces, and sleeveless T-shirts. One of the major manufacturers of jailhouse chic is the Oregon Corrections Department, which produces the clothing in its institutions under the name of "Prison Blues", and sells it through a thriving Web site, **www.prisonblues.com**.

In spite of this progress, however, prison industries in many correctional institutions continue to suffer from the problems of years past. Only a minority of inmates are employed in meaningful jobs because prison industrial plants are costly to construct, equip, maintain, and keep up to date. Moreover, because housing an inmate in a correctional institution is prohibitively expensive—costs range from $10,000 per inmate per year in some jurisdictions to more than $30,000 in others—inmates' wages are kept low, with most of the profits going into state treasuries.

Jailhouse chic? Many correctional institutions have returned to classic prison stripes because so many groups have adopted the orange jumpsuits as a fashion statement.

Female prisoners being searched before going on work detail.

Clinical Treatment Programs Academic education and vocational training are often viewed as the primary rehabilitative tools offered by correctional institutions. It is felt that if inmates can learn the necessary skills and training to obtain and keep a job after release, their need to return to careers in crime will be eliminated or at least reduced. In this sense, academic and vocational programs can also be viewed as treatment programs, for correctional treatment has generally meant explicit activities designed to alter or remove conditions that are deemed to be responsible for offenders' criminal behavior.[24] In a more clinical sense, however, institutional treatment programs are specifically oriented toward helping inmates resolve personal, emotional, and psychological problems that are related to their lawbreaking behavior.

Counseling, social casework, psychological and psychiatric services, and group therapy are at the core of clinical treatment programs in prisons. *Counseling* refers to a relationship between the counselor and the prisoner-client in which the counselor attempts to understand the prisoner-client's problems and help him or her solve them by discussing them together, rather than by giving advice or admonition.[25] *Social casework* is a process that (1) develops the prisoner-client's case history, (2) deals with immediate problems involving personal and familial relationships, (3) explores long-range issues of social adjustment, and (4) provides supportive guidance for any anticipated plans or activities.

Psychological and psychiatric services provide more intensive diagnosis and treatment aimed at (1) discovering the underlying causes of individual maladjustments, (2) applying psychiatric techniques to effect improved behavior, and (3) providing consultation to other staff members. These three modes of treatment involve direct interaction between a clinician and a prisoner-patient on an individual, one-to-one basis. Treatment in a group setting includes one or more clinicians plus several prisoner-patients.

The most common treatment format in the prison setting is group therapy. *Group treatment programs* have been variously referred to as "group psychotherapy," "group therapy," "group guided interaction," "group counseling," and numerous other terms that are often used interchangeably. The underlying approach and philosophy can be expressed as follows:

This treatment stratagem focuses on groups as the "patient." It assumes that specific persons exhibit unfavorable attitudes, self-images, and the like because of the associational net-

I would say there are two basic complaints by prisoners about prison. First: the monotony of prison routine. Second: the numerous ways you are made to feel you are finished as a man.

—**WILLIAM R. COONS**

work in which they are involved. Because the person's interactional associates are extremely meaningful to him, any attempt to change the person without altering those groups with which he associates is likely to fail. Accordingly, group therapy proceeds on the premise that entire groups of persons must be recruited into therapy groups and changed. In addition, it is argued that treatment in which an individual's close associates are participants is likely to have more impact upon a specific person than some other form of treatment. *Group therapy encourages the participants to put pressure on each other for behavioral change and to get the group to define new conduct norms. In a real sense, individual participants in group therapy are at the same time patients and therapists.*[26]

These four models of clinical treatment—counseling, casework, psychological and psychiatric services, and group therapy—are employed to deal with general issues associated with criminality and bring about behavioral change. They are also used to address the problems of specific kinds of offenders, such as sexual deviates and substance abusers. However, these clinical treatment services are not available in most institutions, and only a modest number of prisons have a resident psychiatrist. Moreover, in reception centers, where there are significant numbers of psychologists, social workers, and other clinicians, the primary activities of these professionals are in the area of diagnosis rather than treatment. More common in contemporary correctional facilities are counselors. These, however, generally deal with inmates' confrontations with the day-to-day pressures of institutional life rather than with any long-term treatment goals. Counselors, moreover, rarely have any clinical training or experience. The position of correctional counselor is an entry point to a criminal justice career, and for most counselors it is their first job after graduation from college.

Drug Abuse Treatment   As noted elsewhere in this book, much of the increased activity and backlog in the criminal justice system is an outgrowth of the nation's war on drugs. This is particularly apparent in correctional agencies and facilities. In fact, nationally, it appears that perhaps three-fourths of all inmates have histories of substance abuse.[27]

One approach to the phenomenon has been to increase prison capacity. Another has been to expand drug abuse treatment services. All of the states and the federal system have some sort of drug treatment services for inmates. Most are expanding the capacity of existing programs as well as implementing new ones.

In addition to the four models of clinical treatment described earlier, prison-based drug rehabilitation strategies also include the *therapeutic community*. More commonly referred to as a "TC," the therapeutic community is a total treatment environment established in a separate residential unit of a prison. TC participants are kept separate from other inmates and assigned to separate work, school, and recreational programs as well. The purpose is to create a partnership between prisoner-clients and clinicians. The work supervisors, teachers, counselors, correctional officers, and other staff members involved with TC inmates become part of the treatment regimen and are regarded as agents of behavioral change. Group therapy is the primary treatment method, but the peer pressure characteristic of group therapy sessions appears during other daily routines as well.

The therapeutic community concept was developed during the 1940s by the English psychiatrist Maxwell Jones. He introduced it at a hospital for war veterans who were experiencing difficulties in finding and keeping jobs.[28] In 1958, the approach was adopted in the San Francisco Bay area by ex-alcoholic Charles Dederich for the treatment of narcotics addicts, thus giving birth to the internationally known Synanon drug treatment program.[29] In the ensuing years, other therapeutic communities appeared— Daytop Village, Phoenix House, Odyssey House—and in 1966 the approach was introduced at New York's Clinton Prison and at the Federal Correctional Facility at Danbury, Connecticut.[30]

Currently, the therapeutic community is among the most popular approaches for the treatment of drug abuse. Its application within the prison setting has been primarily for substance abusers, although some non-drug-abusing offenders are also involved. However, few correctional institutions have therapeutic communities, owing to the

Public Confidence in Prison Drug Treatment Programs

Responses to "What effect do prison treatment programs have on the reduction of drug-related crimes?"
Source: University of Maryland, Center for Substance Abuse Research.

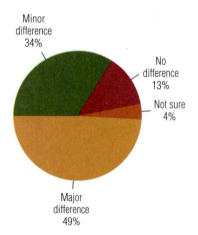

Minor difference 34%

No difference 13%

Not sure 4%

Major difference 49%

lack of special facilities as well as staff shortages and a focus on custodial issues—concerns that tend to limit all varieties of institutional treatment. During the closing years of the 1980s, however, funding from the Bureau of Justice Assistance and other federal agencies rekindled interest in TCs in correctional environments, creating a movement that is expected to continue (see Exhibit 15.3).

Prison Discipline

It was rough doing time, and there was a lot of petty rules, and if the rules all said you can't have your shirttail out, then you would get busted for that, and you would get written up and go to court, and as far as I am concerned this is insanity, and there is no sense to it.

—ANONYMOUS [31]

Upon entering Connecticut State Prison in 1830, inmates were presented with a list of six rules and regulations:

1. Every convict shall be industrious, submissive, and obedient, and shall labor diligently and in silence.
2. No convict shall secrete, hide, or carry about his person any instrument or thing with intent to make his escape.
3. No convict shall write or receive a letter to or from any person whatsoever, nor have intercourse with persons within the prison, except by leave of the warden.
4. No convict shall burn, waste, injure, or destroy any raw materials or article of public property, nor deface or injure the prison building.
5. Convicts shall always conduct themselves toward officers with deference and respect; and cleanliness in their persons, dress, and bedding is required. When they go to their meals or labor, they shall proceed in regular order and in silence, marching in the lockstep.
6. No convict shall converse with another prisoner, or leave his work without permission of an officer. He shall not speak to, or look at visitors, nor leave the hospital when ordered there, nor shall he make any unnecessary noise in his labor, or do any thing either in the shops or cells, which is subversive of the good order of the institution.[32]

Over the years, lists of inmate rules have grown longer, reaching into every aspect of inmate life. Regulations in most prisons number well into the hundreds. Some rules are general in nature, pertaining to the orderly operation and safety of the institution:

Orders shall be obeyed promptly. . . .

Fighting is prohibited. . . .

Locking devices will not be tampered with. . . .

Others are of questionable value:

Long-sleeved sweatshirts will not be worn under a short sleeved shirt. . . .

Only one cribbage board per man. . . .[33]

In New York's Attica Prison, there is even a regulation governing the number of times an inmate may kiss a visitor:

They have locked up guys in the place for felonious kissing in the visiting room. If a guy kisses his wife six times it is felonious kissing.[34]

Although one may consider the rules to be too numerous and many to be trivial, they found their way into inmate handbooks for very specific reasons. Some were designed to prevent disturbances, violence, and escapes; others serve to ensure the health and safety of both inmates and staff; still others were imposed to maintain the orderly movement of prisoners and the flow of institutional life and procedure. Many regulations, however, are punitive in nature or, as in the military, are deemed necessary to provide regimentation, preserve order, and define the boundaries of inmate status. Conversely, a variety of regulations have evolved with the goal of creating a self-respecting prison community and instilling standards that will contribute to successful

I would rather be caught with a knife by a guard than be caught without one by another inmate.

—ANONYMOUS STATE PRISON INMATE

In prison, those things withheld from and denied to the prisoner become precisely what he wants most of all.

—BLACK ACTIVIST ELDRIDGE CLEAVER

EXHIBIT 15.3 | RESEARCH ON CRIME & JUSTICE

Therapeutic Communities in Prisons

There are many phenomena in the prison environment that make reha-bilitation difficult. Not surprisingly, the availability of drugs is a problem. In addition, there is the violence associated with inmate gangs, often formed along racial lines for the purposes of establishing and maintain-ing status, "turf," and unofficial control over certain sectors of the prison for distributing contraband and providing "protection" for other in-mates. And finally, there is the prison subculture—a system of norms and values contending, among other things, that "people in treatment are faggots," as one maximum-security inmate so emphatically put it.

In contrast, the therapeutic community (or simply TC) is a total treatment environment isolated from the rest of the prison popula-tion—separated from the drugs, the violence, and the norms and values that militate against treatment and rehabilitation. The primary clinical staff of the TC are typically former substance abusers who themselves were rehabilitated in therapeutic communities. The treat-ment perspective is that drug abuse is a disorder of the whole per-son—that the problem is the *person* and not the drug, that addiction is a *symptom* and not the essence of the disorder. In the TC's view of recovery, the primary goal is to change the negative patterns of be-havior, thinking, and feeling that predispose drug use. As such, the overall goal is a responsible drug-free lifestyle.

Recovery through the TC process depends on positive and negative pressures to change, and this is brought about through a self-help pro-cess in which relationships of mutual responsibility to every resident in the program are built. Or as TC researcher George De Leon once de-scribed it:

> The essential dynamic in the TC is mutual self-help. Thus, the day-to-day activities are conducted by the residents themselves. In their jobs, groups, meetings, recreation, personal, and social time, it is residents who continually transmit to each other the main mes-sages and expectations of the community.

In addition to individual and group counseling, the TC process has a system of explicit rewards that reinforce the value of earned achieve-ment. As such, privileges are earned. In addition, TCs have their own specific rules and regulations that guide the behavior of residents and the management of their facilities. Their purposes are to maintain the safety and health of the community and to train and teach residents through the use of discipline. TC rules and regulations are numerous, the most conspicuous of which are total prohibitions against violence, theft, and drug use. Violation of these cardinal rules typically results in immediate expulsion from the TC.

Although prison-based TCs are few in number, preliminary evalua-tions have been positive. Moreover, inmates in TCs see them as safe places to finish their time and learn positive values. In addition to see-

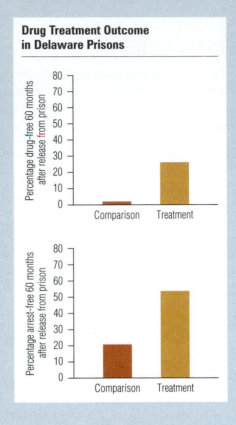

Drug Treatment Outcome in Delaware Prisons

ing their potential for treatment, correctional administrators view TCs as excellent tools for prison management, since they tend to be the cleanest, safest, and most orderly parts of a prison.

Perhaps the most promising corrections-based TC is the one es-tablished within the Delaware Department of Correction by the Center for Drug and Alcohol Studies at the University of Delaware. The pro-gram is a 2-year continuum of therapeutic community treatment for both men and women that begins in the institution and extends to work release and then aftercare. Of those who participated in the en-tire program, 54 percent were arrest-free and 26 percent drug-free 60 months after release from the institution; of those who did not par-ticipate in the program, only 21 percent were arrest-free and 3 percent drug-free over the same period. The program has been so effective that it has become a model that has been replicated in other jurisdic-tions in the United States, as well as in at least 13 countries in Europe, Asia, and Latin America.

Source: James A. Inciardi, Steve S. Martin, and Clifford Butzin, "Five-Year Outcomes of Therapeutic Community Treatment of Drug-Involved Offenders After Release from Prison," *Crime and Delinquency* 50, 1 (January 2004): 88–107.

adjustment after release. Finally, as corrections specialists Harry Allen and Clifford Si-monsen have suggested, many rules have resulted from the *"convict bogey"* syndrome—an exaggerated fear of prisoners requiring unnecessarily severe discipline.[35]

A major issue in inmate regulation is *prison contraband.* Contraband is officially defined as any item that can be used to break a rule of the institution or to assist in es-

Inmates giving hand signals to one another: 911 (or 580 in Texas) is a warning that an officer is coming.

cape. Such articles as drugs, alcohol, knives, guns, bombs, and vaulting poles are contraband. In practice, however, contraband becomes *anything* that the custodial staff designates as undesirable, and the banning power is unrestricted.[36]

Contraband is uncovered by means of periodic searches of prisoners and their cells or dormitories, and rule breaking is either observed or discovered directly by a custodial officer or indirectly through inmate informers. In many instances, the violations are more or less ignored; sometimes the correctional officer will simply give the inmate a warning and, if minor contraband is involved, confiscate it. In more serious cases, there are formal disciplinary proceedings with many due process safeguards.

The major violations in prisons—at least those that result in disciplinary hearings—involve gambling, sex, fighting, stealing, refusing to work, and drugs (see Exhibit 15.4). Most inmates are fairly sophisticated when it comes to hiding serious contraband items such as drugs or weapons. Penalties for violations include solitary confinement, temporary loss of privileges, temporary "keeplock" (being locked in the cell during recreation periods), or loss of "good time" (time off for good behavior). Corporal punishment has also been used, but when it does occur, it is not part of official correctional policy. Numerous disciplinary violations can also affect an inmate's parole date, since institutional conduct is taken into account in parole release decisions.

Weapons confiscated from Florida prison inmates.

EXHIBIT 15.4 | drugs, crime, and justice

How Long for a Clean Urine?

Despite the rigorous security procedures that exist in virtually all correctional systems in the United States, illegal drugs nevertheless have a way of getting into most prisons. To detect drug use, some correctional systems conduct periodic urine tests of all inmates. A positive test results in a disciplinary proceeding. Although the urine testing is "unannounced," word often gets out days or even weeks before the testing, and the advance warning gives inmates a chance to "clean up," so to speak. In this regard, the accompanying list was found in a Florida prison in 2000 indicating how long it would take for various drugs to get out of one's urine.

Pot	1 week (for first-time users)
	66 days (for long-term users)
Cocaine/crack	2–4 days
Heroin	2–4 days
PCP	10–14 days
Anabolic steroids	15–30 days

Interestingly, the people who put the list together had done their homework. The detection times are generally accurate, although they can vary depending on the type of test used, the amount and frequency of drug use, and the user's general health and metabolism, as well as the amount of exercise and fluid intake.

Alcohol	8–12 hours
Speed/crank	2–4 days

Without question, the structure of rules and regulations and their enforcement creates resentment. As one inmate remarked: "I understand why there is riots all of the time, because they treat us like babies, and anything that you do is wrong. . . . It makes you angry inside."[37]

Sex in Prison

I remember the first time I forgot what it was like to fuck a woman. That day, man, was a helluva day. I lay there all night trying to remember. I couldn't remember how it was like. And that was a year and a half ago. That's a helluva experience, man—to forget.

—CALIFORNIA PRISON INMATE[38]

Aside from the loss of liberty itself, perhaps the most obvious area of deprivation associated with prison life is heterosexual activity. Isolation from the opposite sex implies frustration of sexual desires and drives at a time when, for many inmates, those impulses are quite strong. Some prisoners remain abstinent or rely on sexual fantasies and masturbation, while others partake in same-gender sex or even rape. However, the data on these activities are only fragmentary, and any conclusions are at best tentative.

Same-Gender Sex

Several decades ago, lawyer-sociologist Paul W. Tappan commented that homosexual behavior is a universal concomitant of sex-segregated living; that it is a perennial problem in camps, boarding schools, single-sex colleges, training schools, and correctional facilities; and that from a biological point of view homosexuality is normal behavior in prisons.[39] Whether Tappan's argument can be applied equally to all sex-segregated environments is difficult to document. Within the prison setting, however, same-gender sexual contacts indeed occur, although perhaps not to the extent that some popular images suggest.

On the basis of the few studies that have examined the question of sexual behavior among prison inmates, it can be estimated that between 30% and 45% of inmates have experienced same-gender sex. The percentage varies according to the intensity of custodial supervison, the characteristics of the inmate population, and the average length of confinement in a given prison.[40]

A recent study in Delaware suggested that although same-gender sexual contacts might not be widespread, they do occur.[41] Clients in a prison drug treatment program

were interviewed at length regarding their sexual histories and practices and their sexual activities while in prison during the 1-year period prior to entering the program. Although only a small proportion admitted to having sex with other men while in prison, almost all stated that they had "heard" of it occurring, and half reported having observed it.

The nature of sexual practices tends to differ between male and female inmates. Among males, sex seldom involves a close relationship; rather, it is often a response to physical needs. Prostitution is a frequent type of male sexual association. Also, there are cases in which a male who is particularly vulnerable to sexual attacks will enter into a relationship with another male who agrees to "protect" him from the assaults of others.[42]

While there have been only a few studies of sex in women's prisons, most of the sex that takes place there appears to be consensual. Interviews with inmates at the Women's Correctional Institution in New Castle, Delaware, suggest that many inmates form long-standing relationships—friendships rather than pseudo-marriages. Sexual contacts are usually oral-genital and/or involve mutual masturbation. Women have indicated that they wanted to "get a woman" while in prison. Many brag about their sexual conquests of other women, and most talk about their need to "get off." For women who are bound to a heterosexual identity, sexual gratification usually comes by way of masturbation. Nevertheless, same-gender sex does not appear to carry the same stigma among women as it does among male inmates.

Despite the data suggesting that one-third of prison inmates engage in same-gender sexual practices, whether regularly or at least periodically, both inmates and institutional personnel agree that the most frequently observed form of sexual release is solitary masturbation. As one commentator remarked: "Nobody—inmate, staff, or visitor—is in a prison very long before seeing an inmate masturbating in a toilet, shower, or cell."[43]

Sexual Assault

In recent years, considerable attention has been given to the matter of so-called *homosexual rape* in correctional institutions. It is generally believed that sexual attacks are quite common in men's prisons, yet the data on this are fragmentary. Some have argued that the impressions of sexual activity in prison—that behind prison walls the incidence of male-on-male rape is high, and that sexual assault is the most characteristic

A prisoner has no sex. He is God's own private eunuch.

—HENRY MILLER

The best sex I ever had was in here—in Lewisburg.

—LEWISBURG PENITENTIARY INMATE

Freelancing homosexuals, yeah, fags, keep down rapes. It keeps down rapes, and a whole lot of other things too! If there's enough homosexuals, an attractive inmate don't have to worry when he see dudes like us looking at him.

—CALIFORNIA INMATE

form of prison sex—are essentially unfounded assumptions.[44] Rape and coerced sex in women's prisons have received minimal research attention. The few studies that have been done suggest that although rape does indeed occur, it is generally uncommon. By contrast, most sexual coercion incidents committed by women inmates involved fondling, seducing, or somehow pressuring other women inmates into oral sex.[45]

Since the 1960s, women inmates have complained of having been forced into sexual relations with correctional officers and administrators. However with few advocates and limited access to law libraries, they have had few means for filing official complaints. Recently, however, the problem has become more visible. The most notable case centered on the indictments of 14 officials in the Georgia Department of Correction in 1993 on charges brought by more than 150 female inmates claiming that they had been forced to engage in sex.[46] After years of rumors about forced abortions, prostitution rings, and nonconsensual sex in the Georgia women's prisons, federal investigators were finally brought in to investigate the charges. It appears that guards procured sex from inmates by offering them privileges or threatening them with reports of rule violations and changes of classification. Correctional officers and administrative officials were also forcing women who became pregnant to undergo abortions, often by threatening to send them to a harsher prison or take away their accrued good time.

While research on the incidence of rape in prison remains tentative, it is generally agreed that such attacks are more often power plays than sources of sexual release. For example, Leo Carroll's analysis of interracial rape in male prisons suggests that blacks often sexually assault whites in retaliation for 300 years of social oppression and to demonstrate their manhood and dominance. As one of Carroll's informants explained it:

> To the general way of thinking it's 'cause we're confined and we've got hard rocks. But that ain't it at all. It's a way for the black man to get back at the white man. It's one way he can assert his manhood. Anything white, even a defenseless punk, is part of what the black man hates. It's part of what he's had to fight all his life just to survive, just to have a hole to sleep in and some garbage to eat. . . . It's a new ego thing. He can show he's a man by making a white guy into a girl.[47]

Finally, there are many who would argue not only that "homosexual rape" is a misnomer but that referring to prison sex as "homosexuality" is equally incorrect. As a gay man in a Delaware work-release program recently explained to the author:

> It's not having sex with another man—in or out of prison—that makes you gay. It's a matter of identity. I first knew I was different when I was 5 years old, and I finally understood that I was a *homosexual* by the time I was 12. But I didn't have sex with another man until I was almost 18 years old. But even before that, I was still gay. I was a virgin, but I was gay. It's the same in prison. You don't become gay all of a sudden because you got a blow job from a man, or had anal sex. It's an issue of opportunity. If you're gay, you stick with men for sex after you go home. If you're straight, you go back to women.

Conjugal Visitation

Conjugal visitation has been promoted as a means of reducing same-gender sexual contacts in prison, as well as raising inmate morale and maintaining family ties. During a conjugal visit, the inmate and his or her spouse are permitted to spend time together in private quarters on prison grounds, during which they may engage in sexual relations.

Conjugal visitation has been well known in European and Latin American countries for some time, and it has likely always occurred in some American prisons, although on an informal and haphazard basis. As an official correctional program, however, its first appearance in the United States was in 1900 at the Mississippi State Penitentiary at Parchman. In 1968, conjugal visiting began as an experiment at California's Tehachapi facility and was later expanded to other California institutions. New York, New Mexico, Texas, and Washington, to name but a few states, have also introduced conjugal visitation on an experimental basis. Reports on both the Mississippi and California programs have been positive.[48]

A marriage ceremony at the Ware County Correctional Institute, Georgia.

Those who favor conjugal visitation argue that it decreases same-gender sex within the prison, helps preserve marriages, and strengthens family relationships.[49] Yet there is some opposition to conjugal visiting. Opponents argue that such visits can serve only the minority of inmates who have spouses, thus raising the question of fairness; that appropriate visitation facilities are typically lacking; that children may be born to men who cannot support them; and that the situation poses potential security risks.[50]

In recent years, two factors have served to refocus correctional thinking about conjugal visitation. The first issue relates to women. Historically, the majority of programs in the United States have been available only to male inmates; the idea that the same heterosexual opportunities should be extended to women inmates was "shocking" to some.[51] An early exception to this pattern was New York State's Family Reunion Program, begun in 1976 and established at the Bedford Hills Correctional Facility for women in the following year. The program allows overnight visits for selected inmates and members of their immediate families. The "family member" is typically a spouse but can be a parent or child. Other women's institutions throughout the country have similar programs.

The second issue to have an impact on conjugal visitation involves HIV and AIDS. The focus has been on New York, the state with the most AIDS cases not only in the general population but in the prison population as well. In *Doe* v. *Coughlin*,[52] decided in 1987, the New York Court of Appeals held that an inmate with AIDS could not participate in conjugal visitation. Although the inmate and his wife jointly argued that their right to marital privacy had been violated by the ban, the court agreed with state correctional officials that the prohibition was in the interests of halting the spread of AIDS. In 1991, however, New York suddenly reversed its position, making it the first state with a large population of prisoners with AIDS to permit such visits. Under its new policy, inmates who are infected with HIV or have symptoms of AIDS are permitted conjugal visits as long as prison officials can ascertain that their condition has been disclosed and that both partners have received safe-sex counseling.[53] The logic behind the decision was to encourage the state's many thousands of married prisoners to be tested for HIV infection.

Family ties are a major factor in reducing the number of inmates who come back to prison.

—**CHARLOTTE NESBITT, AMERICAN CORRECTIONAL ASSOCIATION**

Coeducational Prisons

Since 1973, prisons housing both men and women have proliferated. Coeducational facilities currently operate in a number of states and the federal system. In these institutions, inmates eat, study, and work together, and associate with each other generally, except with regard to sleeping arrangements.

The philosophy behind the establishment of these institutions was that men tend to behave better in the presence of women, have fewer fights, take more pride in their appearance, and are less likely to engage in same-gender sexual contacts. Moreover, it was felt that for both male and female prisoners, a more normal social environment hastens reintegration into the community upon release.[54] The available evidence suggests that these expectations have been met. Both violence and forced same-gender sex have declined, attendance in work and education programs has increased, and inmates seem to return home with more self-esteem and higher expectations.[55]

When coed prisons were first opened, some feared that they would become X-rated nightmares complete with rape, love fests, and general sexual debauchery. But these fears never came to pass.[56] There are strict sexual codes, pregnancies have been infrequent, and sexual misbehavior generally results in return to a sex-segregated facility. In addition, male candidates are heavily screened—they must be minimum-security risks and near their parole eligibility dates.

Yet not everyone has been thrilled by the coeducational experiments. The coed program at Oklahoma's Jess Dunn Correctional Center, which began in 1986, was ended after only 2 years as the result of jealousies over certain male and female inmates pairing off, as well as the six pregnancies that occurred during that period.[57] For similar reasons, male and female inmates have been separated at the California Youth Authority's Camarillo coeducational compound. Under regulations promulgated in mid-1990, coed activities became limited to school and Sunday worship, with strict separation at all other times.[58]

As for the future of coeducational custody, it is difficult to predict. Expansions are necessarily restricted, however, since women represent such a small proportion of the federal and state correctional populations.

Searching for drugs and other contraband at the Allegheny County Jail in Pittsburgh, Pennsylvania.

The Inmate Social System

The psychological milieu is even more depressing than the physical. What to do with oneself, how to put in the long, dragging hours, becomes a problem. One can sleep only so many hours.

—NATHAN F. LEOPOLD, JR., 1957

The primary task of prisons, despite arguments to the contrary, is custody. The internal order of the prison is maintained by strictly controlling the inmates and regimenting every aspect of their lives. In addition to their loss of freedom and basic liberties, goods and services, heterosexual relationships, and autonomy, inmates are deprived of their personal identities. Upon entering prison, they are stripped of their clothing and most of their personal possessions; and they are examined, inspected, weighed, documented, and given a number. Thus, prison becomes painful both physically and psychologically:

> Unable to escape either physically or psychologically, lacking the cohesion to carry through an insurrection that is bound to fail in any case, and bereft of faith in peaceful innovation, the inmate population might seem to have no recourse but the simple endurance of the pains of imprisonment. *But if the rigors of confinement cannot be completely removed, they can at least be mitigated by the patterns of social interaction established among the inmates themselves.*[59]

The rigors and frustrations of confinement leave only a few alternatives open to inmates. They can bind themselves to their fellow captives in ties of mutual aid and loyalty, in opposition to prison officials. They can wage a war against all, seeking their own

CAREERS IN CRIMINAL JUSTICE

The Corrections Connection

The Corrections Connection Network is an excellent online resource for students studying correctional issues as well as for those interested in working in the corrections field. In addition to weekly updates on correctional matters and news from the front lines in the corrections field, the network has numerous bulletin boards and links to related correctional sites. Among these are postings of available positions in the corrections field in all 50 states.

In most correctional systems, career positions begin with entry-level correctional officers, with starting salaries ranging from $21,000 to $30,000 per year, depending on the jurisdiction. Higher education is generally not required for entry-level correctional officers. Career progressions can include such steps as correctional corporal, sergeant, lieutenant, and captain, with salaries ranging up to $75,000 per year. Administrative positions, such as deputy wardens, wardens, and bureau chiefs, typically require a BA or MA degree. Salaries for these upper-level positions can exceed $100,000 per year.

More information is available on the Internet (**http://www .corrections.com**).

advantage without reference to the needs and claims of others. Or they can simply withdraw into themselves. Ideally these alternatives exist only in an abstract sense, and most inmates combine characteristics of the first two extremes:

> The population of prisoners does not exhibit a perfect solidarity yet neither is the population of prisoners a warring aggregate. Rather, it is a mixture of both and the society of captives lies balanced in an uneasy compromise.[60]

It is within this balance of extremes that the inmate social system functions.

Prisonization

Exposure to the social system of the *prison community* is almost immediate, for all new inmates become quickly aware of the norms and values that are shared by their fellow captives. The internalization of the prison norms and values has been described as **prisonization:**

> Every man who enters the penitentiary undergoes prisonization to some extent. The first and most obvious integrative step concerns his status. He becomes at once an anonymous figure in a subordinate group. A number replaces a name. He wears the clothes of the other members of the subordinate group. He is questioned and admonished. He soon learns that the warden is all-powerful. He soon learns the ranks, titles, and authority of various officials. And whether he uses the prison slang and argot or not, he comes to know its meanings. Even though a new man may hold himself aloof from other inmates and remain a solitary figure, he finds himself within a few months referring to or thinking of keepers as "screws," the physician as the "croaker," and using the local nicknames to designate persons. He follows the examples already set in wearing his cap. He learns to eat in haste and in obtaining food he imitates the tricks of those near him.
>
> After the new arrival recovers from the effects of the swallowing-up process, he assigns a new meaning to conditions he had previously taken for granted. The fact that food, shelter, clothing, and a work activity had been given him originally made no especial impression. It is only after some weeks or months that there comes to him a new interpretation of these necessities of life. This new conception results from mingling with other men and it places emphasis on the fact that the environment should administer to him. This point is intangible and difficult to describe in so far as it is only a subtle and minute change in attitude from the taken-for-granted perception. Exhaustive questioning of hundreds of men reveals that this slight change in attitude is a fundamental step in the process we are calling prisonization.[61]

Thus, prisonization refers to the socialization process through which the inmate learns the rules and regulations of the institution and the informal rules, values, customs, and general culture of the penitentiary.

Entertainment at California's Folsom Prison.

The concept of prisonization comes from Donald Clemmer, who was a staff sociologist at Menard Penitentiary in Chester, Illinois, and is based on his studies of the male prison subculture during the 1930s. He maintains that prisoners share the experience of enforced confinement and that from this come many influences that tend to draw them together in a common cause against their keepers. The close physical proximity in which inmates must live destroys much, if not all, of their privacy; prison regulations and routine push them toward conformity; and their isolation limits their range of experience. Moreover, institutional life fosters a monotonous equalitarianism among inmates. Prisoners occupy similar cells; they wear the same clothes and eat the same food; and they do the same things at the same time and according to the same rules, regulations, and potential for disciplinary punishment. Within such a setting, prison life holds little for inmates, but what it does offer they share in common. And all of this happens under the same structure of authority—one that is direct, immediate, inescapable, and sometimes brutal. Everything that prisoners have, or fail to have, can be traced to that structure. Food and clothing, rules and regulations, pleasures and pains, sorrows and cruelties, indignities and brutalities—all come from the same source. The inmate community, then, has a common hatred—the prison administration—against which it can direct its hostilities.

In presenting this notion of prisonization, Clemmer maintains that prison values can be taken on to a greater or lesser degree. Once they are internalized, however, the prisonized inmate becomes immune, for the most part, to the influences of conventional value systems. This suggests that the process of prisonization transforms the new inmate into a fully accredited convict; it is a *criminalization* process that militates against reform or rehabilitation.

Some people argue against Clemmer's thesis. They point to evidence that inmates are first prisonized and then "deprisonized" just before release; others hold that prisonization itself is a myth.[62] Most observers agree, however, that some form of prisonization does occur but that it is affected by priority, duration, frequency, and intensity of contact with the prison subculture and the values of various segments of the inmate population. This point of view is most likely correct, for circumstances, regulations, population characteristics, and administrative authority structures vary widely from one institution to the next. Socialization into the inmate worlds of the more repressive maximum-security prisons across the nation seems to most closely resemble what Clemmer originally described as "prisonization."

Prison is a place where all sorts of things are not there.

—BRUCE JACKSON, PRISONER ADVOCATE AND AUTHOR

The Inmate Code

Regardless of the degree of prisonization experienced by an inmate, every correctional institution has a subculture. Every prison subculture has its system of norms that influence prisoners' behavior, typically to a greater extent than the institution's formally prescribed rules. These subcultural norms are informal, unwritten rules, but their violation can evoke sanctions from fellow inmates ranging from ostracism to physical violence or even death. The informal rules are referred to as the **inmate code** and generally include at least the following:

1. *Don't interfere with the interests of other inmates.* In concrete terms, this means that inmates never "rat on a con" or betray each other. It also includes the directives "Don't be nosy," "Don't put a guy on the spot," and "Keep off a man's back." There are no justifications for failing to comply with these rules.
2. *Keep out of quarrels or feuds with fellow inmates.* This is expressed in the directives "Play it cool" and "Do your own time."
3. *Don't exploit other inmates.* In concrete terms, this means "Don't break your word," "Don't steal from the cons," "Don't welsh on debts," and "Be right."
4. *Don't weaken; withstand frustration or threat without complaint.* This is expressed in such directives as "Don't cop out," "Don't suck around," "Be tough," and "Be a man."
5. *Don't give respect or prestige to the custodians or to the world for which they stand.* In concrete terms, this is expressed by "Don't be a sucker" and "Be sharp."[63]

If you seek violence, we will put you in jail.

— ED KOCH, FORMER
NEW YORK CITY MAYOR

Although the inmate code is violated regularly, many prisoners adhere to its major directives. They do so, however, not because it represents a "code of honor," but for other, more serious considerations—the same reasons that professional thieves reported following the underworld code:

> Honor among thieves? Well—yes and no. You do have some old pros who might talk about honor, but they're so well heeled and well connected that they can afford to be honorable. But for most people, it's a question of "do unto others"—you play by the rules because you may need a favor someday, or because the guy you skip on, or the guy you rap to the cops about—you never know where he'll turn up. Maybe he's got something on you, or maybe he ends up as your cell-mate, or he says bad things about you—you can't tell how these things could turn out.[64]

Sources and Functions of the Inmate Social System

There is little consensus as to how the inmate subculture evolves behind prison walls. One explanation is the *deprivation model;* that is, upon entering prison, inmates are faced with major social and psychological problems resulting from the loss of freedom, status, possessions, dignity, autonomy, security, and personal and sexual relationships. The inmate subculture emerges through prisoners' attempts to adapt to the deprivations imposed by incarceration. The subculture is a mechanism for reducing the pains of isolation, obtaining and sharing possessions, regaining dignity and status, developing meaningful relationships, and enjoying some personal security.[65]

Another model, the *importation model,* views inmates as doing considerably more than simply responding to immediate, prison-specific problems. Cultural elements are "imported" into the prison from the outside world. Prisoners bring with them their values, norms, and attitudes, and these become the content of the inmate subculture.[66]

Both models seem to be crucial to the inmate subculture. On the one hand, the deprivation thesis serves to explain the emergence and persistence of the subculture. The pains and deprivations of imprisonment represent the stimulus for the formation of a social system that provides status, security, and solidarity. On the other hand, much of the richness of the subculture comes from the norms of the various underworlds and the experiences of inmates within other, outside criminal subcultures.

Whether its sources are deprivation, importation, or both, the inmate social system functions not only for its members but for the prison as a whole. More specifically,

Proportion of Female Inmates in State and Federal Correctional Institutions, 1970–2004

Source: Bureau of Justice Statistics.

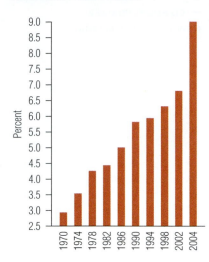

The Increasing Number of Women Behind Bars

Includes state and federal institutions
Source: Bureau of Justice Statistics.

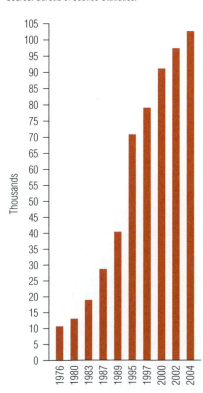

the inmate social system is a mechanism for controlling the behavior of prisoners. Without it, the custodial administration could not fully maintain order. Within most correctional institutions, both officers and inmates play specific roles. Custodial officers provide inmates with illegitimate opportunities for obtaining needed goods and services. In return, inmates exercise control over their peers. Thus, a degree of accommodation develops, and each group becomes captive and captor to the other.[67] This is in stark contrast to prisons in Brazil, where inmate-on-inmate violence dominates the prison social system (see Exhibit 15.5).

Women in Prison

Historically, there have been few women prisoners. Before the 20th century, women accounted for less than 1 percent of the adult felon prison population. This changed somewhat over the years, and from the 1970s through the beginning of the new millennium, the proportion of women in state and federal correctional institutions increased from 2.9 percent to 9 percent.

Women's Institutions

The relatively low percentage of women inmates has resulted in a series of rather disjointed and arbitrary policies for the incarceration of female offenders. Not until 1873, in Indianapolis, Indiana, was the first separate prison for women opened in the United States. Before that time, women were confined with men or held in isolation within small sections of men's penitentiaries and supervised by male warders.[68] During the last 50 years, and especially in the past two decades, the number of correctional facilities for women has increased dramatically. And, in spite of considerable progress, these institutions reflect both the best and the worst elements of the American prison system.

Today, although the institutions may be referred to as reformatories or state farms, women are confined in separate maximum- and medium-security prisons, isolated wings of men's penitentiaries, coeducational facilities, and open institutions. Some states have no correctional facilities for women. Instead, they use the institutions of other jurisdictions under a contract arrangement.

As the general population of prison inmates has grown, so too has the number of women behind bars—in many ways, a reflection of tougher drug laws and mandatory sentencing policies. A recent survey of women inmates found that the majority were serving time for drug or drug-related charges and less than a third were classified as violent offenders.[69]

Despite the growing numbers of incarcerated women, many states have failed to adequately reform their policies and programs for female offenders. Although women's opportunities no longer reflect a complete emphasis on gender-based notions of "women's work," many state institutions for women do not provide the range of opportunities and privileges available at most institutions for men. Recent surveys have found that a disproportionate number of women inmates are still involved in cleaning, kitchen, and manufacturing work while male inmates participate in a far wider range of work initiatives.[70] Vocational training programs at women's prisons continue to offer classes in cosmetology, data processing, food preparation, and nurse's aide training. The gender-typed nature of vocational programming is particularly problematic since these types of jobs are notorious for their lack of benefits and low wages, making it difficult for women inmates (the great majority of whom are single parents) to achieve economic independence after release. Only a few of the nation's correctional institutions for women offer training in areas that meaningfully address the postrelease employment needs of women.[71]

Women and Children in Prison

Historically, each state jurisdiction in the United States had only one prison for women. These institutions were typically staffed by women, isolated from the rest of the correctional system, crowded, and poorly equipped. Yet despite these shortcomings, the

Jails and Prisons in Brazil by James A. Inciardi

I have visited hundreds of prisons and jails during my career, and I have seen both the worst and the best that the United States has to offer. But when I started conducting research in Brazil a little over a decade ago and began field trips to the correctional facilities there, I was suddenly confronted with conditions I had not previously imagined.

Dating back to the Portuguese colonial administration, Brazilian jails and prisons have always had some of the worst conditions in the Western world. Currently, although conditions vary significantly from state to state and from institution to institution, all that I saw were appalling. Many facilities hold two to five times more inmates than they were designed for. In some institutions, the overcrowding has reached inhuman levels. The densely packed cells and dormitories in these places offer such sights as prisoners tied to windows to lessen the demand for floor space and prisoners being forced to sleep on top of hole-in-the-floor toilets.

In most prisons, the distribution of living space is relatively unregulated, so the burden of overcrowding falls disproportionately on certain prisoners. In general, prisoners who are poorer, weaker, and less powerful tend to live in correspondingly less habitable accommodations. Typically, the disciplinary and holding cells—which are as likely to hold prisoners needing protection from other prisoners as they are to hold those being punished—are the most cramped and uncomfortable areas.

While certain prisons are crowded far beyond their capacities, the most overcrowded penal facilities in Brazil are generally the police lockups. Rather than being used as places of short-term detention for newly arrested criminal suspects, as they are supposed to be, police lockups in many states hold inmates for long periods, even years. In states where the prison authorities are able to limit the transfer of additional inmates from lockups to the prisons, the police end up being left in charge of a significant proportion of the inmate population. Indeed, in the most extreme cases, the police have become a de facto prison authority, supplementing or nearly replacing the conventional prison system.

Another serious problem is inmate-on-inmate violence. In the most dangerous prisons, powerful inmates kill others with impunity; and even in relatively secure prisons, extortion and other lesser forms of mistreatment are common. A number of factors combine to cause such abuses, among them, the prisons' harsh conditions, lack of effective supervision, abundance of weapons, lack of activities, and, perhaps most importantly, lack of inmate classification. Indeed, violent recidivists and persons held for first-time petty offenses often share the same cell in Brazil.

On the positive side of the balance, Brazilian penal facilities normally offer generous visiting policies, allowing prisoners regular face-to-face visits with their families and friends, and even conjugal visits. Not all facilities, however, are equally commendable in this regard, and certain systemic abuses can also be identified. The primary obstacle to inmates' visits is the humiliating treatment of visitors, who may be subject to poorly regulated strip searches and even, according to some inmates' allegations, invasive vaginal searches.

A Brazilian inmate smokes a cigarette while dangling from his cell at Carandiru prison in São Paulo.

Women inmates are generally spared some of the worst aspects of the men's prisons—and thus enjoy greater access to work opportunities, suffer less custodial violence, and are provided with greater material support—but they also bear special burdens. Most notably, women in many states face discrimination with regard to conjugal visiting rights. While male prisoners tend to be freely granted such visits, with little or no control exercised by state authorities, women prisoners are sometimes denied them or allowed them only under extremely tight restrictions. In addition, despite the Brazilian constitutional requirement that women prisoners be permitted to keep their nursing babies during the entire lactation period, women confined in some penal facilities lose their infants immediately after delivering them.

According to Brazil's Federal Ministry of Justice, the number of inmates in Brazilian prisons increased from 114,000 in 1992 to over 300,000 in 2005, and efforts are being made to improve conditions. Nevertheless, severe overcrowding and institutionalized violence—such as beatings, torture, and even summary executions—continue. In a recent riot in a Rio de Janeiro prison, inmates killed at least 30 people, beheading half of them.

EXHIBIT 15.6 | RESEARCH ON CRIME & JUSTICE

Parenting Programs for Women Inmates

Of the more than 100,000 incarcerated women in the United States, almost 80% are mothers of an estimated 160,000 minor children. And because the number of incarcerated mothers continues to grow, many correctional institutions have implemented special parenting programs in an attempt to teach women effective parenting skills. The program content, interestingly, is often based on the assumption that because these are women *offenders,* they likely have a punitive approach toward parenting.

In a recent study of a parenting education program for drug-involved women offenders at the Baylor Women's Correctional Institution in New Castle, Delaware, the women's general parenting attitudes were assessed along a variety of dimensions that have been demonstrated to be predictive of abusive parenting practices. A major finding of the research, however, was that the incarcerated women in the study did not have overly controlling or punitive attitudes toward their children. In fact, their scores were similar to those of a national sample of *non*abusive adult parents. Given this, it would appear that the intense focus of prison-based parenting education on disciplinary alternatives to spanking may be misplaced. Parenting program curricula are often guided by implicit assumptions about the needs of the population they serve, without particular attention to research data that may shed light on more appropriate ways to enhance parenting skills.

From a social policy perspective, a reexamination of existing parenting programs for incarcerated women would appear to be warranted. Because this study suggests that the focus of the parenting curriculum was misdirected, scarce correctional resources are likely not being used in the most effective manner. It is conceivable, furthermore, that this situation may also exist in other jurisdictions. One useful approach to solving this problem would be for correctional classification programs to conduct needs assessment surveys on parenting with incoming inmates. This would document the need for different parenting education foci and could lead to the development of more appropriate and matched programming and services for different segments of the correctional population. Moreover, as the number of incarcerated women with children continues to climb, the design and evaluation of appropriate and effective parenting programs must be a priority in correctional institutions across the country.

Source: Hilary L. Surratt, "Parenting Attitudes of Drug-Involved Women Inmates," *The Prison Journal* 83 (2003), 206–220.

leadership in these institutions provided not only humane environments for women but innovative training and educational programs as well. Moreover, since female inmates tended to be less hostile, less aggressive and assaultive, and less destructive than their male counterparts, women's institutions tended to be less repressive in terms of both custodial management and discipline. As trends in corrections changed, so too did women's prisons. Yet regardless of how progressive the correctional philosophy of any given era was, it was generally forgotten that most female inmates were mothers as well, and the separation from their young children tended to exacerbate women's pains of imprisonment.

Fueled by the growing number of incarcerated women over the last two decades, many correctional systems have responded to this difficulty by developing structured arrangements whereby female inmates can have meaningful visits with family members in general and with their children in particular. In Massachusetts, for example, where the majority of female inmates are mothers with young children, a program established in 1985 permits overnight visits with children. At Bedford Hills Correctional Facility in New York, infants may remain with their mothers for up to 18 months, in nursery areas segregated from general housing. At the Nebraska Correctional Center for Women, among the rewards for good behavior are visits of up to 5 days a month by children between 12 months and 9 years of age. Other prisons have similar arrangements.[72] And at the "Key Village," a drug treatment program in a separate housing unit at the Baylor Women's Correctional Institution in New Castle, Delaware, two cells have been decorated as nurseries. Each weekend, two women have the opportunity to care for their infants from Friday afternoon to Sunday evening.[73]

Regardless of the particular arrangement, the female inmates who have these kinds of contacts with their children appear to adjust better not only to prison confinement but to life in the community after release. For a discussion of parenting programs in women's prisons, see Exhibit 15.6.

The Social Order of Women's Prisons

Most studies of prison communities and inmate social systems have been carried out in men's institutions, and the findings are not fully applicable to women's prisons. Fewer women are convicted of crimes, and a greater proportion of those who are found guilty are placed on probation. Those who do receive terms of imprisonment have typically been convicted of aggravated assault, check forgery, shoplifting, and violations of drug laws, with few serving time for burglary and robbery. The numbers of women who have been convicted and sentenced for killing a spouse or male partner are also significant. Many women's prisons have an even greater proportion of minority group members than do institutions for men, but fewer women have had prior prison experiences. Moreover, the cottage system model is typically followed in women's prisons. Although few female inmates are confined in cells, the more "open" nature of the women's institution often requires more frequent security checks and, hence, close custodial supervision. As noted earlier, the great majority of female prisoners are mothers of young children, and in a growing number of institutions children are living with their mothers for varying lengths of time. All of these factors combine to affect the social order of female correctional institutions.

In some ways, the social system in women's prisons is similar to that in the all-male penitentiary. There are social roles, argot, an inmate code, and accommodation between captive and captor. But in other ways the social system of women inmates is not as clearly defined, for it is a microsociety made up of four main groups.[74] There are the "squares" from conventional society, who are having their first experience with custodial life. Many of these are members of the middle class. They see themselves as respectable people and view prisons as places to which only "criminals" go. Most of them have been convicted of embezzlement or situational homicides. A second group comprises the "professionals," career criminals who view incarceration as an occupational hazard. Expert shoplifters fall into this group. They adopt a "cool" approach to prison life that involves taking maximum advantage of institutional amenities without endangering their chances for parole or early release. The third group, and perhaps the largest, is made up of repeat offenders who have had numerous experiences with the criminal justice system since their teenage years. Some are prostitutes who have assaulted and robbed their clients, many are thieves, and others are chronic drug users and sellers. For them, institutional life provides status and familial attachments. Finally, there is the custodial staff, whose values and attributes are the same as those of staff in men's institutions.[75]

Most women inmates are pretty hard when they arrive here. When they leave . . . forget it. Now you're really talkin' tough.

— ANONYMOUS FEMALE CORRECTIONAL COUNSELOR, NEW JERSEY

| The Effectiveness of Correctional Treatment |

What works?

— ROBERT MARTINSON

With few and isolated exceptions, the rehabilitative efforts that have been reported so far have no appreciable effect on recidivism.

— MARTINSON

The treatment approach to the management and control of criminal offenders was used early in the nation's history, and by the middle of the 20th century the idea of "changing the lawbreaker" had become a dominant force in correctional thinking. Most offenders were still "punished," but at the same time classification exercises assigned them to "programs" and "supervision" designed to reintegrate them into law-abiding society.

Yet throughout the history of corrections in America there has also been a tendency among advocates of both the punishment and treatment philosophies to commit themselves to unproven techniques. Correctional and reform approaches were often founded on intuition and sentiment, rather than on awareness of prior successes or failures. This began to change, however, when the rehabilitative ideal emerged as a strong force in correctional thinking. Attempts were made not only to test the efficacy of existing programs but also to design and evaluate experimental and innovative approaches. Research strategies were devised, outcome measures were specified, data were prudently collected and judiciously analyzed, and the findings were publicized.

During the 1950s and 1960s, a body of literature began to accumulate offering testimony on the successes and failures of therapeutic approaches. In the main, however, this literature projected a rather gloomy outlook for the rehabilitative ideal. One of the early disappointments, for example, was the well-known Cambridge-Somerville Youth Study. Begun in 1935 and often described as the most energetic experiment in the prevention of delinquency, it attempted to test the impact of intensive counseling on young male delinquents. The research continued for 10 years, using an experimental group of youths who had access to counseling and a control group who did not; the findings were published in 1951. The researchers found no significant differences between the outcomes of the treatment and the control groups. This led them to conclude that there was no evidence that counseling could make a positive contribution to the rehabilitation of delinquents.[76] In subsequent years, numerous researchers in Europe and the United States evaluated the results of this and similar studies. Their conclusions were overwhelmingly negative—they all found that the treatment of offenders had questionable results.[77] Nevertheless, the focus on treatment continued, and the findings of the studies were largely ignored.

This apparent disregard of negative results could be readily understood. The research had typically been carried out by members of the academic community. The findings were prepared in a technical format, and, perhaps more important, they appeared almost exclusively in professional and scientific journals, government reports, academic symposia, and books published by university presses. For the general public and the nation's legislators and opinion makers, these sources of information were as remote as medieval parchments hidden in the cellars and garrets of some ancient moated castle. But in 1975, all of this suddenly changed.

The Martinson Report

In the late 1960s and early 1970s, researchers in New York carried out a massive evaluation of prior efforts at correctional intervention. The idea for the research went back to early 1966, when the Governor's Special Committee on Criminal Offenders decided to commission a study to determine what methods, if any, held the greatest promise for the rehabilitation of convicted offenders. The findings of the study were to be used to guide program development in the state's criminal justice system. The project was carried out by researchers at the New York State Office of Crime Control Planning. For years they analyzed the literature on hundreds of correctional efforts published between 1945 and 1967.

The findings of the project were put together in a massive volume that was published in 1975.[78] Before the in-depth report appeared, an article by one of the researchers, Robert Martinson, was published in *The Public Interest*. Its title was "What Works?—Questions and Answers About Prison Reform."[79] In it Martinson reviewed the purpose and scope of the New York study and implied that, with few and isolated exceptions, *nothing works!*

There was little that was really new in Martinson's article. In 1966, Walter C. Bailey of the City University of New York had published the findings of a survey of 100 evaluations of correctional treatment programs, concluding that "evidence supporting the efficacy of correctional treatment is slight, inconsistent, and of questionable reliability."[80] The following year, Roger Hood completed a similar review in England, concluding that the different ways of treating offenders lead to results that are not very encouraging.[81] And in 1971, James Robison and Gerald Smith's analysis of

Prisons don't rehabilitate, they don't punish, they don't protect, so what the hell do they do?

—JERRY BROWN

We should not fool ourselves that the "hard rocks" will emerge from the cesspools of American prisons willing or able to conduct law-abiding lives.

—DAVID BAZELON, FEDERAL JUDGE

correctional treatment in California asked, "Will the clients act differently if we lock them up, or keep them locked up longer, or do something with them inside, or watch them more closely afterward, or cut them loose officially?" Their conclusion was a re-sounding "Probably not!"[82]

But the Martinson essay created a sensation, for it appeared in a widely read pub-lication and attracted media attention at a time when politicians and opinion makers were desperately searching for some response to the widespread public fear of street crime. Furthermore, as political scientist James Q. Wilson explained:

> Martinson did not discover that rehabilitation was of little value in dealing with crime so much as he administered a highly visible *coup de grace*. By bringing out into the open the long-standing scholarly skepticism about most rehabilitation programs, he prepared the way for a revival of an interest in the deterrent, incapacitative, and retributive purposes of the criminal justice system.[83]

Martinson also created a sensation—mostly negative—within the research and treatment communities. He was criticized for bias, major distortions of fact, and gross misrepresentation.[84] For the most part, his critics were correct. Martinson had failed to include all types of treatment programs; he tended to ignore the effects of some pro-grams on some individuals; he generally concentrated on whether the particular treat-ment method was effective in *all* the studies in which it was tested; and he neglected to study the new federally funded treatment programs that had begun after 1967.

Despite these criticisms, Martinson's work cannot be overlooked. While he may have been guilty of overgeneralization, most correctional treatment programs were demonstrating little success and, indeed, many were *not* working. Moreover, his essay had an impact in other ways. It pushed researchers and evaluators to sharpen their an-alytical tools for the measurement of success and failure. Yet it also ushered in an "abol-ish treatment" era characterized by a "nothing works" philosophy.

Obstacles to Effective Correctional Treatment

Despite some advances in correctional techniques and program services, there are nu-merous obstacles that prevent most prisons from becoming effective agencies of reha-bilitation, including the following:

1. Many institutions are old and antiquated.
2. Maximum-security prisons are, for the most part, too large or overcrowded.
3. Prison cells and many medium-security dormitories are unsuitable for human habitation.
4. Correctional institutions are typically understaffed, and personnel often lack proper training.
5. The rules for separation of inmates are not widely enforced.
6. Inmate unemployment is common, and too many prisoners are assigned to what has become known as "idle company."
7. Institutional discipline is often too rigid.
8. Prison life tends to be monotonous and oppressive.
9. Parole policies are sometimes unfair or inefficient.
10. Comprehensive classification and program strategies are not universally available.
11. The prisonization and criminalization processes apparent in many correctional fa-cilities prevent many inmates from achieving any motivation for treatment.
12. Effective treatment programs are unavailable for the overwhelming majority of inmates.

By the beginning of 2005, attempts at prison reform had not succeeded in remov-ing these obstacles.[85] Moreover, given the fiscal constraints on state and local govern-ments, combined with sentencing philosophies that serve to further increase prison populations, it would appear that the American penitentiary of the early 21st century will resemble that of the 1970s, 1980s, and 1990s.

Terrifying Statistics
Projections by the Justice Department suggest that 11.3% of boys born in 2001 will go to prison in their lifetime. For black men, it will be one in three. Source: Bureau of Justice Statistics.

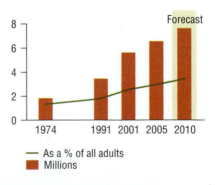

- As a % of all adults
▮ Millions

* State or federal prisons: includes current incarcerations.

─── **CRITICAL THINKING IN CRIMINAL JUSTICE** ───

Shock Incarceration

Imagine that you are a first offender, you have a drug problem, and you have just been convicted of a crime. Your offense was a drug sale, or perhaps a burglary, possession of stolen goods, or auto theft. Whatever the offense, it was nonviolent.

At sentencing, the judge decides to impose one of the more recent innovations in correctional treatment—what some jurisdictions refer to as "shock incarceration" and others call "boot camps." **Shock incarceration** is a 3- to 6-month regimen of military drill, drug treatment, physical exercise, hard labor, and academic work in lieu of a formal prison sentence. Available to young, nonviolent offenders, it attempts to "shock" them out of careers in crime by imposing large amounts of rigor and order in otherwise chaotic lives. Thinking critically for a moment, and considering all that you have learned thus far about crime, criminals, and criminal justice, do you think that shock incarceration would work? Would it work for drug users or thieves in the street culture? Would it work for you? Think critically.

If you need more information before thinking it through, consider this: In the shock incarceration boot camp, inmates live in tents or barracks and usually serve shorter sentences than other prisoners but under conditions designed to "shock" them into changing their behavior. They engage in strenuous work and exercise under the strict guidance of drill instructor–type correctional officers. Many programs also add educational and life-skills-building courses to the regimens. Inmates learn discipline, teamwork, and a respect for authority.

The notion of the boot camp for young or first-time offenders is an appealing concept to many. Correctional authorities like the prospect of diverting nonviolent offenders from overcrowded prisons to the lower costs of camp incarceration; correctional officers appreciate the outdoor time and the opportunities to keep in shape; the public likes the lower cost and the idea of the physical work, rigorous training, military-style discipline, and the "sound bites" of young felons doing shouting cadence calls with calisthenics. For many, boot camps conjure up images of Parris Island Marine training or the scenes from the film *An Officer and a Gentleman,* combined with the public works of the Depression-era Civilian Conservation Corps. As such, boot camps have great curb appeal. So what do you think?

Prisoners in "shock incarceration" boot camp. Although research suggests that this approach is ineffective in reducing recidivism, prison boot camps remain politically popular.

In practice, shock incarceration does have some advantages. Given the opportunity to yell and assign push-ups, officers seem to have less need to "informally" abuse prisoners, and inmates are less likely to be disruptive and fight among themselves. Teamwork and shared experiences create a sense of belonging and group membership. Releasees even report improvement in self-discipline and self-esteem as a result of "surviving" the programs.

Unfortunately, research has not found any reductions in recidivism for boot camp graduates.[86] One study in Louisiana even found that those coming out of boot camps were more likely to be rearrested in their first year out than regular parolees. Similarly, the findings of a recent U.S. Department of Justice study also found boot camps to be somewhat less than successful. Although the camps had lower costs than traditional incarceration, recidivism was worse for the boot camp graduates than for control groups of similar offenders who had been incarcerated or placed on probation. Why such a failure rate for what appears to be such a great idea?

Much of the failure may be due more to an inability to follow up on the program after release than failure of the camps themselves. Almost all programs call for an aftercare program to provide oversight and help reintroduce offenders to street and community life. Short funding often leads to skimping on the community reintegration components of the planned program. Releasees returning to the same neighborhoods and friends that got them involved in crime in the first place find it easy to slip back into old habits and patterns.

OP-ED

Is there some incongruity between the high incarceration rates and declining crime rates noted at the beginning of the chapter, and will there be some fallout in coming years when these large numbers of inmates are eventually returned to the community?

Most observers of the criminal justice system would agree that the declining crime rates are, at least in part, a direct result of the increasing number of offenders being incarcerated. Crime increased during the 1980s, but the rate of imprisonment rose much faster. The result was that there were fewer offenders on the street to commit crimes. But is this necessarily a good thing?

There is no easy answer, because the explosive growth in numbers of inmates and prisons will eventually have some unintended consequences. The first is based on simple mathematics—the larger the number of prisoners, the greater the number of people who will eventually be released. Then, because of their criminal propensities and/or their experiences behind bars, it is highly probable that they will violate parole and be rearrested, or return to drug use and be rearrested, or commit new crimes and be rearrested, or all of the above.

This process is already having a dramatic impact on inner-city communities, particularly African American neighborhoods. Department of Justice projections indicate that if incarceration rates remain unchanged, 1 in every 10 persons will serve a prison term sometime in his or her life; the chances for going to prison are six times higher for black men than for white men. Evidence of this pattern

has already been seen. A recent analysis found that in Washington, D.C., half of the black men between the ages of 18 and 35 were under the control of the criminal justice system on any given day—either in jail, in prison, on probation, or on parole.[87] The result is disruption of families, strong connections between criminal groups in prison and on the street, and, ultimately, higher crime rates.

| Summary |

Total institutions are places that furnish barriers to social interchange with the world at large. Prisons are total institutions, and there are a variety of types of prisons differentiated by their level of security. Maximum-security prisons are best characterized by their massive concrete walls, rows of razor wire, strategically located guard towers, and their overwhelm-ing emphasis on custody and control of inmates. Medium-security facilities tend to be less fortresslike than maximum-security institutions and place fewer restrictions on inmate movement; additionally, inmates housed there are considered less dangerous and less likely to attempt an escape. Minimum-security facilities operate with little emphasis on controlling inmate movement, instead allowing a great deal of personal freedom and low levels of surveillance. Often, minimally secure facilities do not have walls, armed guards, or fences. Open institutions include such correctional facilities as prison farms, work camps, and ranches. Prisons are administratively structured like other large organizations. The physical facilities of correctional institutions vary from one place to another. Many prisons, however, are rather old, and many are deteriorated. As a result, upkeep tends to be difficult.

The prison experience begins with classification, a process through which the educational, vocational, treatment, and custodial needs of offenders are determined. Prison programs focus on health and medical services, religious needs, academic education and vocational training, labor and industry, recreation, and clinical and drug abuse treatment.

Aside from the loss of liberty itself, perhaps the most obvious deprivation associated with prison life is the loss of heterosexual activity. As a result, same-gender sexual relationships and sexual assaults occur behind prison walls. The conjugal visit has been promoted as a means of reducing sexual frustrations in correctional institutions. Furthermore, coeducational facilities are being experimented with for the purpose of reducing both homosexuality and violence.

Every prison has an inmate social system, characterized by a specialized argot, social roles, and an inmate code. Exposure to the social system of the prison community begins almost immediately after the prisoner enters the institution. All new inmates become quickly aware of the norms and values that are shared by their fellow inmates. The internalization of these prison norms and values is known as prisonization. As aspects of the institutional subculture, prevailing norms and informal rules are often referred to as the inmate code. Two models of prison adaptation have been developed by researchers in the field to explain the usefulness of the inmate subculture. Proponents of the deprivation model argue that the inmate social world helps to alleviate the pains of imprisonment through mutual cooperation with other inmates. Advocates of the importation model, on the other hand, suggest that the inmate social world is an outgrowth of the values, norms, and behaviors that inmates engaged in while on the outside. Still a third group of researchers has argued that elements of both models characterize the inmate social world.

Evaluative studies of correctional treatment programs have not been favorable to the notion of rehabilitation. Research findings during the 1960s and early 1970s resulted in a "nothing works" and "abolish treatment" era in corrections. Indeed, many obstacles to treatment are present in the structure of correctional facilities themselves. Many researchers still intent on providing treatment to inmates have been quick to point out that numerous factors compromise even the most effective treatment strategies, citing problems in the following areas: overcrowding; institutional age, physical structure, and size; understaffing; poor staff training; unfair and inefficient parole policies; improper segregation; and institutional rigidity.

| Key Terms |

| Issues for Discussion |

1. In what ways is life in prison similar to that in the military or on the college campus?
2. What are the general characteristics of prison life?
3. Without making prisons into bordellos, what could be done to ease the sexual frustrations of prison life?
4. What steps should be taken to change prison into environments more suitable for rehabilitation and reform?
5. What impact might the changing nature of female crime have on the social order of women's prisons?
6. What kinds of parallels are there between the prison community and certain groups in the outside world?
7. What is your opinion of "shock incarceration" programs?
8. What do you think about letting women keep their children with them while they serve their sentence in prison?
9. Should drug abuse treatment be expanded behind prison walls?

| Media and Literature Resources |

Women in Prison. Concomitant with the increasing numbers of incarcerated women, the literature has also been expanding. Among the more noteworthy books published since the beginning of the 1990s are Joycelyn M. Pollock-Byrne, *Women, Prison & Crime* (Belmont, CA: Wadsworth, 1990); James A. Gondles, *Female Offenders: Meeting the Needs of a Neglected Population* (Lanham, MD: American Correctional Association, 1992); Kathryn Watterson, *Women in Prison: Inside the Concrete Womb* (Boston: Northeastern University Press, 1996); Cynthia Blinn (ed.), *Maternal Ties: A Selection of Programs for Female Offenders* (Lanham, MD: American Correctional Association, 1997); Andi Rierden, *The Farm: Life Inside a Women's Prison* (Amherst: University of Massachusetts Press, 1997); Cristina Rathbone, *A World Apart: Women, Prison, and Life Behind Bars* (New York: Random House, 2005).

The Shawshank Redemption. This is an excellent film about prison life and is available on video. A thorough review of the film by James J. Sobel of the State University of New York at Albany can be found in the *Journal of Criminal Justice and Popular Culture* 4 (1996): 15–17.

The Corrections Connection Network. This is a useful Web site with all types of information and sources in the corrections field, including news and events, bulletin boards, employment and educational opportunities, to name but a few (*http://www.corrections.com*).

Prison Life. There are many interesting books on this topic. Among the more recent are Ted Conover, *Newjack: Guarding Sing Sing* (New York: Random House, 2000); John Irwin and James Austin, *It's About Time: America's Imprisonment Binge* (Belmont, CA: Wadsworth, 1997); Elliott Currie, *Crime and Punishment in America* (New York: Henry Holt, 1998); Mary K. Stohr and Craig K. Hemmens, *The Inmate Prison Experience* (Upper Saddle River, NJ: Prentice-Hall, 2003).

Sex in Prison. For an interesting collection of papers on this topic, see *The Prison Journal,* Volume 80, December 2000. See also Christopher Hensley (ed.), *Prison Sex: Practice and Policy* (Boulder, CO: Lynne Rienner, 2002); and Christopher Hensley, Richard Tewksbury, and Mary Koscheski, "The Characteristics and Motivations Behind Female Prison Sex," *Women and Criminal Justice* 13, 2/3 (2002): 125–139.

Religion in Prison. See Jody L. Sundt and Francis T. Cullen, "The Role of the Contemporary Prison Chaplain," *The Prison Journal* 78 (1998): 271–298; Jody L. Sundt and Francis T. Cullen, "The Correctional Ideology of Prison Chaplains: A National Survey," *Journal of Criminal Justice* 30, 5 (2002): 369–385; Andrew Skotnicki, *Religion and the Development of the American Penal System* (Lanham, MD: University Press of America, 2000); and Todd R. Clear et al., "The Value of Religion in Prison: An Inmate Perspective," *Journal of Contemporary Criminal Justice* 16, 1 (2000): 53–74.

| Endnotes |

1. *Uniform Crime Reports—2004.*
2. U.S. Department of Justice, Bureau of Justice Statistics, *Prison and Jail Inmates at Mid-Year 2004* (Washington, DC: U.S. Government Printing Office, 2005).
3. Erving Goffman, *Asylums* (Garden City, NY: Anchor, 1961), 1–8.
4. Hans Toch, "The Contemporary Relevance of Early Experiments with Supermax Reform," *Prison Journal* 83 (June 2003): 221–228.
5. Blake McKelvey, *American Prisons: A History of Good Intentions* (Montclair, NJ: Patterson Smith, 1977), 150–196.
6. Timothy J. Flanagan, W. Wesley Johnson, and Katherine Bennett, "Job Satisfaction Among Correctional Executives: A Contemporary Portrait of Wardens of State Prisons for Adults," *Prison Journal* 76 (December 1996): 385–397.
7. Eldridge Cleaver, *Soul on Ice* (New York: McGraw-Hill, 1968); George Jackson, *Soledad Brother: The Prison Letters of George Jackson* (New York: Bantam, 1970).
8. Robert G. Caldwell, *Criminology* (New York: Ronald, 1965), 576.
9. James B. Jacobs and Harold G. Retsky, "Prison Guard," *Urban Life* 4 (April 1974): 5–29.
10. Denise L. Jenne and Robert C. Kersting, "Aggression and Women Correctional Officers in Male Prisons," *Prison Journal* 76 (December 1996): 442–460; Jacobs and Retsky, "Prison Guard"; Gresham M. Sykes, *The Society of Captives: A Study of a Maximum Security Prison* (New York: Atheneum, 1965), 40–62; Edgar May, "Prison Guards in America: The Inside Story," *Corrections Magazine* 2 (December 1976): 3–5, 40, 45.
11. Mary Ann Farkas, "A Typology of Correctional Officers," *International Journal of Offender Therapy and Comparative Criminology* 44 (2000): 431–449; Robert Johnson, *Hard Time: Understanding and Reforming the Prison* (Belmont, CA: Wadsworth, 1996); K. Kauffman, *Prison Officers and Their World* (Cambridge, MA: Harvard University Press, 1988).
12. Joseph R. Carlson, Richard H. Anson, and Greg Thomas, "Correctional Officer Burnout and Stress: Does Gender Matter?" *Prison Journal* 83 (September 2003): 277–288.
13. U.S. Department of Justice, *Census of State Correctional Facilities, 1974* (Washington, DC: U.S. Government Printing Office, 1975).
14. Richard A. Berk, Heather Ladd, Heidi Graziano, and Jong-Ho Baek, "A Randomized Experiment Testing Inmate Classification Systems," *Criminology and Public Policy* 2, 2 (2003): 215–242; Kathryn Ann Farr, "Classification for Female Inmates: Moving Forward," *Crime & Delinquency* 46 (January 2000): 3–17.
15. John Hepburn and Celesta A. Albonetti, "Team Classification in State Correctional Institutions: Its Association with Inmate and Staff Attitudes," *Criminal Justice and Behavior* 5 (March 1978): 63–73.
16. American Correctional Association, *Handbook on Correctional Classification* (Cincinnati: Anderson, 1978), 67.
17. Jill A. McCorkel, Clifford A. Butzin, Steven S. Martin, and James A. Inciardi, "Utilization of Health Care Services in a Sample of Drug-Involved Offenders: A Comparison with National Norms," *American Behavioral Scientist* 41 (Spring 1998): 1079–1089.
18. See Barbara A. Nadel, "Correctional Health Care: Challenges and Opportunities for the Future," *Corrections Compendium* (October 1996): 1–5.
19. Gennaro F. Vito and Richard Tewksbury, "Improving the Educational Skills of Inmates," *Corrections Compendium* 24 (October 1999): 1–4, 16–17.
20. *Corrections Compendium* (March 1994): 4–6; Charles B. A. Ubah, "A Grounded Look at the Debate over Prison-Based Education: Optimistic Theory Versus Pessimistic Worldview," *Prison Journal* 83 (June 2003): 115–129; U.S. Department of Justice, Bureau of Justice Statistics, *Education and Correctional Populations* (Washington, DC: U.S. Government Printing Office, 2003); Gail Coulter and Eric Brookens, "Corrective Reading: A Systemwide Program to Improve Reading Performance for Incarcerated Adult Basic Education Students," *Corrections Compendium* 28 (October 2003): 1–4, 28–30.
21. *Corrections Compendium* (June 1997): 10–11.
22. Greg Wees, "Prison Industries," *Corrections Compendium* (June 1997): 1–4.
23. *Corrections Compendium,* March 2000, 8; *Corrections Compendium,* September 2002, 8–9.
24. Don C. Gibbons, *Changing the Lawbreaker: The Treatment of Delinquents and Criminals* (Englewood Cliffs, NJ: Prentice-Hall, 1965), 136.

25. *Manual of Correctional Standards* (Washington, DC: American Correctional Association, 1969), 422.

26. Gibbons, *Changing the Lawbreaker*, 151.

27. *Sourcebook of Criminal Justice Statistics* (Washington, DC: Bureau of Justice Statistics, 2004).

28. Maxwell Jones, *The Therapeutic Community: A New Treatment Method in Psychiatry* (New York: Basic Books, 1953).

29. Lewis Yablonsky, *The Tunnel Back: Synanon* (New York: Macmillan, 1965).

30. For Clinton Prison, see Bruno M. Cormier, *The Watcher and the Watched* (Plattsburgh, NY: Tundra, 1975); for the facility at Danbury, see Louis P. Carney, *Corrections: Treatment and Philosophy* (Englewood Cliffs, NJ: Prentice-Hall, 1980), 203.

31. From Hans Toch, *Living in Prison: The Ecology of Survival* (New York: Free Press, 1977), 99.

32. Gustave de Beaumont and Alexis de Tocqueville, *On the Penitentiary System in the United States and Its Application in France* (Carbondale: Southern Illinois University Press, 1964), 173.

33. Leonard Orland, *Justice, Punishment, Treatment* (New York: Free Press, 1973), 263–269.

34. Toch, *Living in Prison*, 100.

35. Harry E. Allen and Clifford E. Simonsen, *Corrections in America* (Upper Saddle River, NJ: Prentice-Hall, 1998), 46.

36. David Lovell and Ron Jemelka, "When Inmates Misbehave: The Costs of Discipline," *Prison Journal* 76 (June 1996): 165–179.

37. Toch, *Living in Prison*, 104.

38. Cited by Tom Wicker, *A Time to Die* (New York: Ballantine, 1975), 110.

39. Paul W. Tappan, *Crime, Justice and Correction* (New York: McGraw-Hill, 1960), 678–679.

40. Joseph Fishman, *Sex in Prison* (New York: National Library Press, 1934); Donald Clemmer, *The Prison Community* (New York: Rinehart, 1958), 249–273; Sykes, *Society of Captives*; Peter C. Buffum, *Homosexuality in Prisons* (Washington, DC: U.S. Government Printing Office, 1972); John H. Gagnon and William Simon, "The Social Meaning of Prison Homosexuality," *Federal Probation* 32 (March 1968): 23–29; Richard Tewksbury and Angela West, "Research on Sex in Prison During the Late 1980s and Early 1990s," *Prison Journal* 80 (December 2000): 368–378.

41. Christine A. Saum, Hilary L. Surratt, and James A. Inciardi, "Sex in Prison: Exploring the Myth and Realities," *Prison Journal* 75 (1995): 413–430.

42. Sykes, *Society of Captives*, 95–99; Clemmer, *The Prison Community*; Leo Carroll, *Hacks, Blacks, and Cons: Race Relations in a Maximum Security Prison* (Lexington, MA: Heath, 1974); Cindy Struckman-Johnson and David Struckman-Johnson, "Sexual Coercion Rates in Seven Midwestern Prison Facilities for Men," *Prison Journal* 80 (December 2000): 379–390.

43. Gene Kassebaum, "Sex in Prison," *Psychology Today* (January 1972): 39.

44. Michael Scarce, *Male on Male Rape* (New York: Plenum Press, 1997); Michael Braswell, Tyler Fletcher, and Larry S. Miller, *Human Relations and Corrections*, (Prospect Heights, IL: Waveland Press, 1997); Robert W. Drummond, "Inmate Sexual Assault: A Plague That Persists," *The Prison Journal* 80 (December 2000): 407–414.

45. Leanne Fiftal Alarid, "Sexual Assault and Coercion Among Incarcerated Women Prisoners: Excerpts From Prison Letters," *Prison Journal* 80 (December 2000): 391–406; Cindy Struckman-Johnson and David Struckman-Johnson, "Pressured and Forced Sexual Contact Reported by Women in Three Midwest-ern Prisons," Annual Meeting of the Society for the Study of Sexuality and the Association of Sex Educators, Counselors, and Therapists, St. Louis, Missouri, November 1999.

46. *National Law Journal* (September 20, 1993): 8.

47. Leo Carroll, "Humanitarian Reform and Biracial Sexual Assault in a Maximum Security Prison," *Urban Life* 5 (January 1977): 422. See also "From Thief to Cellblock Sex Slave: A Convict's Testimony," *The New York Times*, October 19, 1997, Section 4, 7.

48. Columbus B. Hopper, "The Evolution of Conjugal Visiting in Mississippi," *Prison Journal* 69 (1989): 103–109; Lawrence A. Bennett, "Correctional Administrators' Attitudes Toward Private Family Visiting," *Prison Journal* 69 (1989): 110–114; Bonnie E. Carlson and Neil Cervera, "Inmates and Their Families: Conjugal Visits, Family Contact, and Family Functioning," *Criminal Justice and Behavior* 18 (1991): 318–331; Christopher Hensley, Sandra Rutland, and Phyllis Gray-Ray, "The Effects of Conjugal Visits on Mississippi Inmates," *Corrections Compendium* 25 (April 2000): 1–3, 20.

49. Pauline Morris, *Prisoners and Their Families* (New York: Hart, 1965), 90; Jill Gordon and Elizabeth H. McConnell, "Are Conjugal and Familial Visitations Effective Rehabilitative Concepts?" *Prison Journal* 79 (March 1999): 119–135.

50. Donald Johns, "Alternatives to Conjugal Visits," *Federal Probation* 35 (March 1971): 48; Gordon and McConnell, "Are Conjugal and Familial Visitations Effective Rehabilitative Concepts?"

51. Norman S. Hayner, "Attitudes Toward Conjugal Visits for Prisoners," *Federal Probation* 36 (March 1972): 43.

52. *Doe v. Coughlin*, NY CtApp, No. 219, November 24, 1987; 42 CrL 2227 (1987).

53. *The New York Times*, August 5, 1991, B1, B3.

54. J. G. Ross, E. Heffernan, J. R. Sevick, and F. T. Johnson, *Assessment of Coeducational Corrections* (Washington, DC: U.S. Government Printing Office, 1978); Columbus B. Hopper, "The Evolution of Conjugal Visiting in Mississippi," *Prison Journal*, Spring/Summer 1989, 103–109.

55. *Newsweek*, January 11, 1982, 66.

56. *Newsweek*, January 11, 1982, 66; *Corrections Digest*, September 18, 1974, 2; Sue Mahan, "Co-Corrections: Doing Time Together," *Corrections Today*, August 1986, 134, 136, 138, 164–165; *The New York Times*, June 1, 1987, A12; James R. Davis, "Co-Corrections in the U.S.: Housing Men and Women Together Has Its Advantages and Disadvantages," *Corrections Compendium* 23 (March 1998): 1–3.

57. *The New York Times*, November 15, 1988, A16.

58. *Los Angeles Times*, July 24, 1990, A3; *Los Angeles Times*, July 29, 1990, A29.

59. Sykes, *Society of Captives*, 82.

60. Sykes, *Society of Captives*, 83.

61. Clemmer, *The Prison Community*, 299.

62. For a review and commentary of the various studies and points of view of prisonization, see Gordon Hawkins, *The Prison: Policy and Practice* (Chicago: University of Chicago Press, 1976).

63. Gresham M. Sykes and Sheldon L. Messenger, "The Inmate Social System," in *Theoretical Studies in the Social Organization of the Prison* (New York: Social Science Research Council, 1960), 6–8; Mark Fleisher, *Warehousing Violence* (Beverly Hills: Sage Publications, 1989).

64. From James A. Inciardi, *Careers in Crime* (Chicago: Rand McNally, 1975), 70.

65. Sykes, *Society of Captives*, 81–83.

66. John Irwin and Donald R. Cressey, "Thieves, Convicts, and the Inmate Culture," *Social Problems* 10 (Fall 1962): 143.

67. Richard A. Cloward, "Social Control in the Prison," in *Theoretical Studies in the Social Organization of the Prison* (New York: Social Science Research Council, 1960), 35–48.

68. Paul W. Tappan, *Crime, Justice, and Correction* (New York: McGraw-Hill, 1960), 653.

69. U.S. Department of Justice, Bureau of Justice Statistics, *Women Offenders* (Washington, DC: U.S. Government Printing Office, 2005).

70. Merry Morash, Robin Haar, and Lila Rucker, "A Comparison of Programming for Women and Men in U.S. Prisons in the 1980s," *Crime and Delinquency* 40 (1994): 197–221; Robert Ross and Elizabeth Fabiano, *Female Offenders: Correctional Afterthoughts* (Jefferson, NC: McFarland, 1986); *Corrections Compendium,* March 2000.

71. Barbara A. Nadel, "Designing for Women: Doing Time Differently," *Corrections Compendium,* November 1996, 1–5.

72. George Kiser, "Female Inmates and Their Families," *Federal Probation* 55 (1991): 56–63; Peter Breen, "Bridging the Barriers," *Corrections Today* 57 (1995): 98–99; Sasha Nyary, "When Mom Can't Come Home," *Life* (October 1997): 84–90; Fox Butterfield, "As Inmate Population Grows, So Does a Focus on Children," *The New York Times,* April 7, 1999, A1, A18.

73. Center for Drug and Alcohol Studies, *Annual Report* (Newark: University of Delaware, 2003).

74. Esther Heffernan, *Making It in Prison: The Square, the Cool and the Life* (New York: Wiley, 1972).

75. For descriptive material on women's prisons, see Kathryn W. Burkhart, *Women in Prison* (New York: Doubleday, 1973); Jocelyn Pollock-Bryne, *Women, Prison, and Crime* (Pacific Grove, CA: Brooks/Cole, 1990); Joycelyn M. Pollock-Byrne, *Women, Prison & Crime* (Belmont, CA: Wadsworth, 1990); James A. Gondles, *Female Offenders: Meeting the Needs of a Neglected Population* (Lanham, MD: American Correctional Association, 1992); Kathryn Watterson, *Women in Prison: Inside the Concrete Womb* (Boston: Northeastern University Press, 1996); Cynthia Blinn (ed.), *Maternal Ties: A Selection of Programs for Female Offenders* (Lanham, MD: American Correctional Association, 1997); and Andi Rierden, *The Farm: Life Inside a Women's Prison* (Amherst: University of Massachusetts Press, 1997).

76. Edwin Powers and Helen Witmer, *An Experiment in the Prevention of Delinquency* (New York: Columbia University Press, 1951).

77. See, for example, Walter C. Bailey, "Correctional Outcome: An Evaluation of 100 Reports," *Journal of Criminal Law, Criminology, and Police Science* 57 (June 1966): 153–160; Roger Hood, "Research on the Effectiveness of Punishments and Treatments," in European Committee on Crime Problems, *Collected Studies in Criminological Research* (Strasbourg: Council of Europe, 1967).

78. Douglas Lipton, Robert Martinson, and Judith Wilks, *The Effectiveness of Correctional Treatment: A Survey of Treatment Evaluation Studies* (New York: Praeger, 1975).

79. Robert Martinson, "What Works?—Questions and Answers About Prison Reform," *Public Interest* 35 (Spring 1974): 22–54.

80. Bailey, "Correctional Outcome."

81. Hood, "Research on the Effectiveness of Punishments and Treatments."

82. James Robison, "The Irrelevance of Correctional Programs," *Crime and Delinquency* 17 (January 1971): 67–80.

83. James Q. Wilson, "'What Works?' Revisited: New Findings on Criminal Rehabilitation," *Public Interest* 61 (Fall 1980): 3–17.

84. See, for example, Carl B. Klockars, "The True Limits of the Effectiveness of Correctional Treatment," *Prison Journal* 55 (Spring–Summer 1975): 53–64; Ted Palmer, "Martinson Revisited," *Journal of Research in Crime and Delinquency* 12 (July 1975): 133–152.

85. David Farabee, *Rethinking Rehabilitation* (Washington, DC: American Enterprise Institute, 2005); Dan Richard Beto, "Random Thoughts on the Future of Corrections," *Crime and Justice International* (January/February, 2004): 15–21.

86. Jeanne B. Stinchcomb, "Recovering from the Shocking Reality of Shock Incarceration: What Correctional Administrators Can Learn from Boot Camp Failures," *Corrections Management Quarterly* 3 (1999): 43–52; Doris Layton MacKenzie, "Evidence-Based Corrections: Identifying What Works," *Crime & Delinquency* 46 (October 2000): 457–471; Peter Katel, Melinda Liu, and Bob Cohn, "The Bust in Boot Camps," *Newsweek,* February 21, 1994, 26; Howard W. Polsky and Jonathan Faust, "Boot Camps, Juvenile Offenders, and Culture Shock," *Child and Youth Care Forum* 22 (1993): 403–415; "Boot Camps Not a Panacea, Review of OJJDP Programs Finds," *Criminal Justice Newsletter* (November 17, 1997): 5.

87. *The New York Times,* September 28, 1997, sec. 4, p. 1.

16

PRISON CONDITIONS AND INMATE RIGHTS

LEARNING OBJECTIVES

After reading this chapter, you should be able to answer the following questions:

1. What is the "hands-off" doctrine?

2. What is the writ of *habeas corpus?*

3. What is the significance of Section 1983 of the Civil Rights Act of 1871?

4. From the standpoint of prisoners' rights, what have been the major advances in the areas of legal services, religion, rehabilitative and medical services, and prison labor unions?

5. What was the significance of the Arkansas prison scandal for the prisoners' rights movement?

6. What is the Supreme Court's position on solitary confinement, flogging, and prison disciplinary proceedings?

7. Does an inmate ever have a *right* to escape from prison?

8. How has the prisoners' rights movement been eroded in recent years?

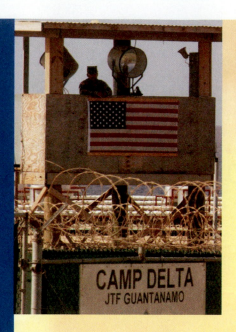

CAMP DELTA
JTF GUANTANAMO

GUANTANAMO BAY, CUBA—Camp Delta, where 520 "enemy combatants" from 42 countries are being held as an outgrowth of the war on terrorism, is isolated on an old gunnery range 100 yards from the Caribbean Sea. Daytime temperatures can reach 100 degrees, but the sea breezes offer some relief to the men living in 8- by 7-foot concrete and metal-gated cells. Detainees are kept in their cells for all but two brief periods a week to bathe and exercise. They get three hot meals each day. Five times a day, the PA system broadcasts the Muslim call to prayer. Each cell contains a Koran, suspended by a surgical mask so as not to touch the ground, and a sign pointing to Mecca, the cultural and religious center of Islamic faith. A green mesh curtain surrounds the compound, so visitors cannot see in and prisoners cannot see out.

Four terror suspects recently released from Camp Delta claim to have been beaten; shackled hand and foot up to 15 hours at a time in wire cages open to rats, snakes, and scorpions; fed yellow water and food dated 10 years past its shelf life; interrogated at gunpoint; sleep deprived; and psychologically tortured; among other claims of inhuman treatment.[1] Is this the typical treatment that prisoners receive? And aside from the prisoners at Guantanamo Bay, do inmates of prisons in the United States have any rights?

To rebuff accusations that the United States government is running a "gulag" at its Guantánamo Bay naval base, the Pentagon last week revealed that it is spending $12.68 per day to feed each of the 520 detainees at the controversial Camp Delta.

The Gitmo diet includes whole wheat bagels, fresh fruit, baklava, yams, veggie patties and nearly 10 pounds of *halal*-certified meat every month to the Muslim inmates.

The $12.68 spent on each detainee's daily meals at Camp Delta is about five times what it costs to feed a prisoner in Florida.

On the other hand, all prisoners in Florida get a few things that the Guantánamo inmates do not. For starters, they get charged with an actual crime.

Then they get a lawyer.

Then they get a day in court, and an opportunity to defend themselves.

In lieu of indictments, the Camp Delta detainees are served bagels and fruit salad. There's reason to believe that many would gladly trade their healthy breakfast for a good old-fashioned American trial.

—CARL HIAASEN,
MYSTERY NOVELIST AND
MIAMI HERALD SOCIAL CRITIC

According to the Supreme Court's ruling in *Ruffin* v. *Commonwealth* in 1871: "A convicted felon has, as a consequence of his crime, not only forfeited his liberty, but all of his personal rights except those which the law in its humanity accords him. He is for the time being a slave of the state."[2]

Until only recently, the opinion expressed in *Ruffin* v. *Commonwealth,* which maintained that prisoners have no legal rights, accurately reflected the judicial attitude toward correctional affairs. The conditions of incarceration and every aspect of institutional life were left to the discretion of the prison administration. Because prisoners were "slaves" of the state, privileges were matters of custodial benevolence, which wardens and turnkeys could "giveth or taketh away" at any time and without explanation. The courts maintained a steadfast hands-off position regarding correctional matters. They unequivocally refused to consider inmate complaints regarding the fitness of prison environments, abuses of administrative authority, the constitutional deprivations of penitentiary life, and the general conditions of incarceration.

Not until the 1960s did the ideology expressed in *United States ex rel. Gereau* v. *Henderson,*[3]—that "prisoners are not stripped of their constitutional rights, including the right to due process"—begin to take noticeable form. The **"hands-off" doctrine** began to lose its vitality, and during that decade and the years that followed, prisoners were given the right to be heard in court regarding such matters as the widespread violence that threatened their lives and security, the problems of overcrowding, the nature of disciplinary proceedings, conditions affecting health and safety, regulations governing visitation and correspondence, and limitations on religious observance, education, work, and recreation.

When the prisoners' rights movement began almost four decades ago, higher courts became the instruments of change in correctional policy. But only a few years after the movement had begun in earnest, there was a major event and human tragedy that served to dramatize the problems associated with prisons and inmate life. That event was the inmate uprising at New York's Attica Correctional Facility on September 9, 1971. Although the riot at Attica occurred more than 30 years ago, it continues to be a case study of the conditions and situations that tend to bring about most prison unrest—even now as American corrections moves through the 21st century.

| Attica, 1971 |

Condemned . . . for its maintenance of Auburn and Sing Sing prisons, New York State will have an answer to charges of inhuman penal conditions when the new . . . State Prison opens at Attica in the next few months with its full quota of 2,000 convicts. Said to be the last word in modern prison construction, the new unit in the State's penal system will do away with such traditions as convict bunks, mess hall lockstep, bull pens, and even locks and keys.

In their places will be beds with springs and mattresses, a cafeteria with food under glass, recreation rooms and an automatic signal system by which convicts will notify guards of their presence in their cells. Doors will be operated by compressed air, sunlight will stream into cells and every prisoner will have an individual radio.

—*THE NEW YORK TIMES*, AUGUST 2, 1931

Perhaps because of the depressed economy, or perhaps for other reasons, when Attica Prison opened during the latter part of 1931 it was hardly the convict's paradise alluded to by *The New York Times*. None of the facilities mentioned in the *Times* article were present. In fact, the style of imprisonment at Attica was no different from that found at Auburn and Sing Sing prisons a hundred years before. Men were locked in their cells, harshly disciplined under a system of rigid rules and regulations; the food was poor, and medical services were lacking; and programs for inmate diversion and rehabilitation were almost nonexistent. Forty years later, however, the *Times* would be given a second opportunity to write about Attica Prison.

Conditions at Attica

For prisoners at Attica in late 1971, "correction" meant little more than daily degradation and humiliation. They were locked in cells for 14 to 16 hours each day; they worked for wages that averaged 30 cents a day, at jobs with little or no vocational value; and they had to abide by hundreds of petty rules for which they could see no justification. In addition, their mail was read, their radio programs were screened in advance, their reading material was restricted, their movements outside their cells were tightly regulated, they were told when to turn lights out and when to wake up, their toilet needs had to be taken care of in the full view of patrolling officers, and their visits from family and friends took place through a mesh screen and were preceded and followed by strip searches in which every opening of their bodies was probed.

In prison, inmates found deprivations worse than any they had encountered on the street: Meals were unappetizing and not up to nutritional standards. Clothing was old, ill-fitting, and inadequate. Most inmates could take showers only once a week. State-issued clothing, toilet articles, and other personal items had to be supplemented by purchases at a commissary whose prices did not reflect the meager wages inmates were paid. To get along in the prison economy, inmates resorted to "hustling."

The sources of inmate frustration and discontent did not end there. Medical care, while adequate to meet acute health needs, was dispensed in a callous, indifferent manner by doctors who feared and despised most of the convicts they treated; inmates were not protected from unwelcome homosexual advances; even the ticket to freedom for most inmates—parole—was handled in an inequitable fashion.

For officers, "correction" meant a steady but monotonous 40-hour-a-week job, with a pension after 25 years' service. It meant maintaining custody and control over an inmate population that included increasing numbers of young blacks and Hispanics from inner-city neighborhoods who were unwilling to conform to the restrictions of prison life and ready to provoke confrontation—men whom the officers could not understand and were not trained to deal with. It meant keeping the inmates in line, seeing that everything ran smoothly, and enforcing the rules. It did not mean, for most officers, helping inmates solve their problems or preparing them to return to society. For the correctional officers, who were always outnumbered by inmates, there was a legitimate concern about security; but that concern was not served by policies that created a level of frustration and tension that was far more dangerous than the security risks they were intended to avert.

Above all, for both inmates and officers, "correction" meant an atmosphere charged with racism. Racism was manifested in job assignments, discipline, self-segregation in the inmate mess halls, and daily interactions between inmates and officers and between inmates and other inmates.

Within the prison there was no escape from the growing mistrust between white middle-class Americans and the residents of the inner-cities. Indeed, at Attica racial polarity and mistrust were magnified by the constant reminder that the "keepers" were white and the "kept" were largely African American or Spanish-speaking. The young black inmate tended to see the white officer as a symbol of a racist, oppressive system that had put him behind bars. The officer, his perspective shaped by his experience on the job, knew blacks only as belligerent, unrepentant criminals. The result was a mutual lack of respect that made communication all but impossible.[4]

The increase in criminality has produced an alarming overpopulation in penitentiaries. The consequence is that no country has been spared in the last few years from prison uprising from the often intolerable conditions.

—FRENCH SOCIAL CRITIC, BERTRAND LE GENDRE

The tower at New York's Attica Prison.

The last day of the revolt at Attica was the bloodiest 1-day encounter between Americans since the Civil War.

The Revolt

The uprising against conditions in Attica was not the result of a planned revolt inspired by a core of inmate revolutionaries. Rather, it was the product of building dissatisfactions and frustrations and was sparked by two incidents that occurred early in September 1971. The first was a confrontation between inmates and correctional officers in the prison yard; the second was the beating of two inmates by several officers. Then on the morning of September 9, the inmates revolted, and because of a defective weld on a gate at a central point in the institution, they quickly spread throughout the prison, attacking officers, taking hostages, and destroying property.

By afternoon, the New York State Police had regained control of part of the prison, but most of the inmates assembled in one of the exercise yards along with their 39 hostages, whom the rioters threatened to kill if their demands were not met.

The Assault

Negotiations went on for days but ultimately failed because of the death of a correctional officer who had sustained serious head injuries during the first day of the riot. Governor Nelson Rockefeller was asked to make a personal appearance at Attica to help with the negotiations and prevent a bloodbath, but he refused. On the morning of September 13, 1971, a local state police troop commander planned and led an assault to retake Attica Prison. Within 15 minutes, the Attica uprising was over. However, the armed state troopers had killed 29 inmates and 10 of the hostages, wounding hundreds more. Ironically, it had been the bloodiest 1-day encounter between Americans since the Civil War.[5]

In Pursuit of Prisoners' Rights

The Attica revolt was a dramatic symbol of a struggle that had been developing for almost a decade. Before the 1960s, convicted felons were deemed to have forfeited virtually all rights except those expressly granted by statute or correctional authority. Thus, inhuman conditions and practices were permitted to develop in many correctional systems, despite the Eighth Amendment's ban on cruel and unusual punishment. The courts generally refused to intervene in correctional matters, for two reasons, as reported by a government commission:

> Judges felt that correctional administration was a technical matter to be left to experts rather than to courts, which were deemed ill-equipped to make appropriate evaluations. And, to the extent that courts believed the offenders' complaints involved privileges rather than rights, there was no special necessity to confront correctional practices, even when they infringed on basic notions of human rights and dignity protected for other groups by constitutional doctrine.[6]

The Writ of *Habeas Corpus*

Whenever an individual is being confined in an institution under state or federal authority, he or she is entitled to seek *habeas corpus* relief. This is guaranteed by Article I, Section 9, of the U.S. Constitution, which states: "The privilege of the writ of *habeas corpus* shall not be suspended." *Habeas corpus* relief also has statutory bases in the Federal Habeas Corpus Act as well as in state *habeas corpus* laws.

By applying for a writ of **habeas corpus,** the person seeking relief is challenging the lawfulness of his or her confinement. *Habeas corpus* is a Latin term meaning "you should have the body." In practice, habeas corpus relief involves a writ issued by a court commanding the person who holds another in captivity to produce the prisoner in court so that the legality of the prisoner's confinement can be adjudicated.[7]

Traditionally, the writ was limited to contesting the legality of confinement itself. However, in *Coffin* v. *Reichard*,[8] decided in 1944, the Sixth Circuit U.S. Court of Appeals held that suits challenging conditions of confinement could be brought under the federal habeas corpus statute. The court reasoned as follows:

> A prisoner is entitled to the writ of *habeas corpus* when, though lawfully in custody, he is deprived of some right to which he is lawfully entitled even in his confinement, the deprivation of which serves to make his imprisonment more burdensome than the law allows or curtails his liberty to a greater extent than the law permits.

Although the U.S. Supreme Court has never fully resolved the question of whether the writ of *habeas corpus* can be applied in seeking relief from allegedly unconstitutional conditions of confinement, most federal courts have elected to follow the logic of *Coffin* v. *Reichard*.[9] From the prisoner's perspective, however, the process of bringing a *habeas* petition to a federal court is unwieldy and time-consuming. This is because existing law requires that inmates of state institutions exhaust all state judicial and administrative remedies before they apply for the federal writ of *habeas corpus.* Moreover, an additional major factor that weighs against attacking prison conditions via *habeas corpus* is that monetary damages are simply not available under the federal *habeas corpus* statute. Victorious *habeas* petitioners can win **injunctive relief**—a court order directing prison officials to improve conditions or to stop enforcing unlawful policies— but no monetary awards are available in a *habeas* action. Thus, most prisoners are effectively barred from the most direct mechanism for challenging the conditions of their confinement.

The privilege of the writ of habeas corpus shall not be suspended, unless when in cases of rebellion or invasion the public safety may require it.

—ARTICLE I, SECTION 9, CONSTITUTION OF THE UNITED STATES

Civil Rights and Prisoners' Rights

The civil rights movement of the late 1950s and early 1960s created a climate that was more conducive to a serious reexamination of the legal rights of prisoners. The specific vehicle that opened federal courts to inmates confined in state institutions was **Section 1983** of the Civil Rights Act of 1871, which provides the following:

> Every person who, under color of any statute, ordinance, regulation, custom, or usage of any State or Territory subjects, or causes to be subjected, any citizen of the United States or other person within the jurisdiction thereof to the deprivation of any rights, privileges, or immunities secured by the Constitution and laws shall be liable to the party injured in an action at law, suit in equity or other proper proceeding for redress.

The long-dormant Section 1983 was resurrected in **Monroe v. Pape,**[10] which was decided by the Supreme Court in 1961. The Court held that citizens could bring Section 1983 suits against state officials in federal courts without first exhausting state judicial remedies.

Three years later, in *Cooper* v. *Pate,*[11] the Court made it clear that the *Pape* holding applied to state prisoners who could articulate cognizable constitutional claims against state prison officials or employees. However, in *Preiser* v. *Rodriguez,*[12] decided in 1973, the Court held that although a Section 1983 suit is a proper vehicle for a constitutional challenge to the *conditions* of prison life, it could not be used to challenge the *fact* or *length* of custody.

In 1997, the Court extended this ruling to apply to a prisoner who brought a Section 1983 suit that did not specifically challenge the fact or length of his custody. In *Edwards* v. *Balisok,*[13] a prisoner's good-time credits had been taken away from him (thereby, in effect, lengthening his prison term) in a disciplinary hearing that allegedly violated constitutional provisions. The prisoner, though, was seeking monetary damages and declaratory relief, not the restoration of his good-time credits. Nevertheless, the Court ruled against the prisoner, reasoning that a finding in favor of the prisoner

Inmate No. 3409, buried in a small cemetery on the grounds of New York's Green Haven Prison in 1962, remains but a number in death as in life. His name was John Baldwin.

would "necessarily imply" that the deprivation of his good-time credits was invalid, and thus his claim was not cognizable under Section 1983. *Balisok* reflects the Supreme Court's continuing efforts to limit the availability of Section 1983 relief for prisoners.

The major advantages of a Section 1983 suit, as opposed to a *habeas corpus* petition, are that a Section 1983 suit does not require that available state remedies be exhausted before the federal district courts will have jurisdiction and that an award of monetary damages is possible. However, the remedy of release from imprisonment is not available under a Section 1983 suit. As the High Court stated in *Preiser* v. *Rodriguez,* only the writ of *habeas corpus* could secure such release.

Despite the importance of Section 1983 of the Civil Rights Act of 1871, actions by the U.S. Supreme Court during the 1980s and 1990s have weakened it as a vehicle by which state prisoners can go to the federal courts to sue prison officials. To cite but one example, in *Will* v. *Michigan Department of State Police,* [14] the High Court ruled that states are not "persons" who can be sued under a Section 1983 suit. As such, prisoners cannot sue a state official for monetary damages for acting in his or her "official capacity" as a state employee. Instead, prisoners must make it clear in their Section 1983 suit that their cause of action identifies a state official who allegedly was acting in his or her *personal capacity.*

Legal Services in Prison

The state and its officers may not abridge or impair petitioner's right to apply to a federal court for a writ of habeas corpus.

—*EX PARTE HULL,* 1941

In *ex parte Hull,* [15] the Supreme Court ruled in a case involving a state prison regulation that required that all legal documents in an inmate's court proceedings be submitted to an institutional official for examination and censorship before being filed with the court. The Court found this and similar prison regulations invalid, holding that whether a petition is properly drawn and what allegations it must contain are issues for the court, not the prison authorities, to decide.

Johnson v. Avery

In spite of the rule established by *Hull,* an inmate's right of access to the courts proved to be more theoretical than actual. In many prison systems, disciplinary actions against inmates pursuing legal remedies, or wholesale confiscation of a prisoner's legal documents, were quite common. Moreover, court access was either curtailed or totally inhibited because most prison officials withheld any services related to inmates' legal needs. In most instances, inmates were provided with a few outdated law books and occasionally the services of a notary public. Since most prisoners were indigent and could not hire an attorney, the courts were essentially closed to them. Many correctional institutions had "jailhouse lawyers": inmates who claimed to have legal expertise and provided advice and counsel to their fellow prisoners, with or without compensation. Yet even this aid was severely restricted by prison officials, thus further denying inmates their basic constitutional right of access.

In 1969, the Supreme Court acknowledged and resolved a number of these problems in **Johnson v. Avery.** [16] The case involved the constitutionality of a Tennessee prison regulation with the following provision:

> No inmate will advise, assist or otherwise contract to aid another, either with or without a fee, to prepare writs or other legal matters. . . . Inmates are forbidden to set themselves up as practitioners for the purpose of promoting a business of writing writs. [17]

The petitioner was a jailhouse lawyer serving a life sentence who had spent almost a year in solitary confinement for repeatedly violating the rule against writ writing.

In its analysis of the Tennessee rule, the Supreme Court addressed the fact that many prisoners are illiterate and frequently are unable to obtain legal help from sources beyond the prison walls. Thus, the justices held that unless the state could provide some reasonable alternative type of legal assistance to inmates, a jailhouse lawyer must be permitted to aid inmates in filing *habeas corpus* petitions.

Although the decision in *Johnson* was a significant one, it did not go into detail on exactly how inmates could obtain legal services. In the years that followed, the U.S. Supreme Court began to address this vagueness:

- *Younger* v. *Gilmore* (1971): The state must maintain an adequate number of law books in prison libraries and other legal materials to inform prisoners of what is legally relevant.[18]
- *Wolff* v. *McDonnell* (1974): Inmates have a right to the legal assistance of a jailhouse lawyer, not only for seeking *habeas corpus* relief but also for filing civil rights actions against prison officials.[19]
- *Procunier* v. *Martinez* (1974): Regulations that prohibit law students and legal paraprofessionals from entering prisons to assist attorneys in case investigations do not satisfy the requirements of *Johnson* v. *Avery*.[20]
- *Bounds* v. *Smith* (1977): Even when prison policy permits mutual legal assistance among inmates, officials are obligated to establish either a legal services program or a law library that will meet the needs of the inmate population.[21]

Jailhouse Lawyers

The prison regulations that forbade inmates from assisting or receiving counsel from fellow inmates in the preparation of legal documents was an outgrowth of several factors. Initially, the rule was a reflection of the general custodial attitude toward prison inmates. That is, the convict was a ward of the state who possessed no civil rights, and the privilege of obtaining legal help from other convicts was simply unthinkable. In addition, a number of security issues were involved. "Writ writers," as they were often called, were seen as potential troublemakers. Officials often felt that the jailhouse lawyer, in advising inmates of their legal rights, might create dissatisfactions within the prison population that could lead to belligerence and revolt. Moreover, the phenomenon of inmates conferring about legal matters was interpreted by some as plotting against administrative authority. Finally, there was the fear that jailhouse lawyers would give their clients inferior representation and false hopes while flooding the courts with spurious claims.

Most of these administrative and custodial concerns had some basis in fact, but in general the problems that jailhouse lawyers caused in correctional institutions were more often ones of inconvenience than of discipline and security. Since *Johnson* v. *Avery* and numerous other state and federal court decisions, the activities of jailhouse lawyers in many jurisdictions have been relatively unrestricted.

In recent years, public and private agencies have awarded grants to law schools for the development of legal aid programs for prisons and jails. But as Justice William O. Douglas pointed out in his concurring opinion in *Johnson*, such programs rest on a shifting law school population and often fail to meet the needs and demands of inmates. As a result, the jailhouse lawyer remains a significant figure in many American prisons. In some states, such as Washington and Massachusetts, jailhouse lawyers are permitted—and even encouraged—to work *with* volunteer law students and paralegals, usually under the supervision of an attorney, in providing legal advice to inmates.[22] Moreover, the courts have continued to recognize the right established by *Johnson* v. *Avery*. In 1984, for example, a Wisconsin prisoner was charged with the unauthorized practice of law for helping two inmates draft postconviction motions. Not only was the charge dismissed on the ground that his activity was constitutionally protected, but in a subsequent proceeding a federal jury assessed $22,000 in damages against his jailers for malicious prosecution.[23]

TV or No TV

Johnson v. *Avery* also held that the Eighth Amendment's prohibition against cruel and unusual punishment could be applied to a variety of prisoner complaints. Shortly after the High Court decision, Georgia correctional officials began providing air conditioning and television to inmates under the threat of having their prisons declared "unconstitutional." A quarter-century later, jurisdictions across the United States began curtailing recreation for prisoners in an effort to make "hard time" harder. The most common activity eliminated was television watching. ∎

Legal Services and Prison Violence

Research has suggested that access to attorneys, law libraries, and formal adjudication mechanisms appears to reduce overall incidence of inmate violence. The work of Matthew Silberman indicates that the availability of "outside" attorneys may prove more helpful than access to jailhouse lawyers, since the latter individuals can often aggravate prison conflicts as frequently as they diffuse them. Silberman's study of federal inmates found that a lack of access to legal resources not only contributed to the use of violent self-help but also heightened feelings of inmate powerlessness and alienation. Regularizing such access appeared to diffuse alienation, as well as provide alternative mechanisms of dispute resolution.

Source: Matthew Silberman, "Dispute Mediation in the American Prison: A New Approach to the Reduction of Violence," *Policy Studies Journal* 16 (1988): 522–532. ∎

Constitutional Rights and Civil Disabilities

Historically, individuals convicted of serious crimes could lose much more than their liberty or their lives. Under early English common law, offenders were "attaint"; that is, they lost all their civil rights and forfeited their property to the Crown. Their families were declared corrupt, which made them unworthy to inherit their property. The U.S. Constitution forbids bills of attainder,[24] and similar provisions against the attainder or its effects are found in the constitutions and statutes of the states. Yet in spite of these, every state has enacted civil disability laws that affect convicted offenders. Depending on the jurisdiction, civil disabilities may include loss of the right to vote, hold public office, sit on a jury, be bonded, collect insurance or pension benefits, sue, hold or inherit property, receive worker's compensation, make a will, marry and have children, or even remain married. The most severe disability is the loss of all civil rights, or **civil death.** Under current Idaho statutes, for example:

> 18-310. A sentence of imprisonment in a state prison for any time less than for life suspends all the civil rights of the person so sentenced, and forfeits all public offices and all private trusts, authority or power during such imprisonment.

> 18-311. A person sentenced to imprisonment in the state prison for life is thereafter deemed civilly dead.

Technically, a civil right is a right that belongs to a person by virtue of his or her citizenship.* Since civil rights include constitutional rights, state statutes and provisions placing civil disabilities on convicted and imprisoned offenders would seem to be in direct conflict with the Constitution. However, the Supreme Court has interpreted these statutes not as complete denials of prisoners' civil rights but as restrictions and conditions of their expression. And in recent years the Court has removed a number of these restrictions.

Religion

The First Amendment to the Constitution provides that "Congress shall make no law respecting an establishment of religion, or prohibiting the free exercise thereof." Historically, freedom of religion was rarely a problem in correctional institutions. In fact, participation in religious instruction and worship services was encouraged. Infringements on this right began only with the rise of minority religions and the demands of their members to have the same rights as members of conventional faiths.

The leading cases involving religious expression occurred with the growing influence of the Black Muslim movement during the 1960s. Issues such as the right to attend services, obtain literature, and wear religious medals were raised by Black Muslim inmates because, unlike Protestant or Catholic inmates, they had been denied the right to engage in such practices. The core question was the recognition of the Black Muslim faith as a religion. This was answered by a federal court in 1962 in *Fulwood* v. *Clemmer*,[25] and in subsequent cases,[26] with the assertion that Black Muslims are entitled to the same constitutional protections that are offered to members of other recognized religions. However, although these cases established the Black Muslims' right to hold religious services, the courts have refused to extend that right in specific circumstances. In some institutions and at certain times, for instance, custodial authorities considered assemblages of Black Muslims to be revolutionary in character and to represent "clear and present dangers" to security. In several decisions, the courts ruled that although Black Muslims had the right to worship, their right to hold religious services could be withheld if they represented potential breaches of security.[27]

In *O'Lone* v. *Estate of Shabazz*,[28] decided in 1987, the Supreme Court ruled that prison policies that had the effect of depriving Muslim inmates of the opportunity to

---

*With the exception of the right to vote and freedom from being subject to deportation, civil rights also apply, generally, to noncitizen residents of the United States.

LAW & CRIMINAL JUSTICE | EXHIBIT 16.1

Religion in Prison

The religious rights of incarcerated men and women have increasingly become a topic for discussion and debate. Where do you draw the line between letting prisoners practice their religion as they please, and when do such practices cause concern for the entire incarcerated community within the facility? Cases regarding an inmate's religious rights are being argued in courts throughout the country.

In Iowa, inmate Benjamin Schreiber filed a case that claimed that the state prison would not dispose of his blood, taken for a test, in a way that was consistent with his religious beliefs. Being a Jehovah's Witness, Schreiber requested that his blood be poured on the ground and covered with dust. The appeals court ruled that the prison official's refusal to do so for the reason of protecting public health was justified. In a time where HIV and hepatitis are of such concern, both of which are transmitted through contact with blood, the court found that the prison official's violation of Schreiber's rights was reasonable and legitimate.

Satanic worship services in Kentucky's Green River Correctional Complex were suspended after prison officials questioned the risk it imposed on the rest of the prison population. U.S. Supreme Court decisions and federal law both state that correctional facilities cannot ban an inmate's religious freedoms as long as the practice of the recognized religion does not threaten the safety of prison staff and other inmates.

A Florida woman is suing her jail because she was disciplined for not participating in a prayer circle. Laurel Clanton, an agnostic, refused to hold hands during a closing message at her jail's drug program. Her actions resulted in her spending several extra weeks in jail. Clanton stated that when she agreed to take part in the program, she was not aware of this aspect of the meeting. This part of the meeting was just a time for the leader to say a quick closing message, but often the leader would close with the Serenity Prayer used in 12-step programs. The jail stated that Clanton was noncompliant but that she was disciplined because she refused to "participate in group closeouts even though she was not required to pray."

A federal appeals court has ruled that the rights of three Pennsylvania inmates were violated when prison officials denied them access to texts by the leaders of the Nation of Islam. The amount of religious literature that was available to these men was limited by their classification in the prison: They were all high-risk inmates in a special unit within the prison. The phase in which they were assigned to within the Special Management Unit determined the amount of religious literature they were entitled to—up to one Bible, Koran, or equivalent, and up to four other religious texts. When the three men requested access to texts by Fard Muhammad, Elijah Muhammad, and Louis Farrakhan, the prison's Muslim chaplain denied the request stating that they were not "religious" documents. The court decided that the writings are "not just the words of Elijah Muhammad and Louis Farrakhan. They are the words of Elijah Muhammad and Louis Farrakhan as inspired by God," and therefore the prison could not deny the men these texts.

Finally, a federal appeals court decided that New Jersey prison officials did not violate the rights of Muslim inmates by serving them vegetarian meals. The lower court found that the state did not have to serve meals containing "halal" meat to Muslim prisoners, a decision that the appeals court upheld. Inmates requested that their meals contain meat that was prepared according with their religious beliefs. Prison officials stated that prisoners could opt for a religious vegetarian meal if their beliefs prevented them from eating food prepared for the general prison population. The prisoners felt that the free exercise clause of the First Amendment was violated because they were required to consume halal meat as a part of their diet and it was not available to them. The Court determined that, among other reasons, because the prison offered the inmates with an alternative means to express their religious beliefs, their rights were not violated.

Sources: "Inmate Loses Religious Claim over Blood Disposal Policy," *Corrections Journal* 5, 19 (2002), 8; "Ex-Inmate Sues over Jail Prayer Circle," *The Miami Herald,* May 4, 2003, 7B; "Kentucky Stops Satan Worship in Prison," *The Miami Herald,* September 1, 2002, 25A; Terry Sullivan, "Prison Erred in Denying Inmates Religious Texts, Court Says," *Corrections Journal,* April 7, 2003, 1–2; Terry Sullivan, "Prisons Do Not Have to Serve Muslim 'Halal' Meat, Court Says," *Corrections Journal,* October 22, 2003, 1, 6.

---

attend *Jumu'ah*—a weekly congregational service—did *not* violate the free exercise clause of the First Amendment. The Court held that (1) the policies were reasonably related to legitimate penological interests and (2) there were other reasonable alternative methods for accommodating the Muslims' religious rights.

Other cases involving religious freedom in prisons dealt with inmate access to clergy, special diets, and the right to wear religious medals. In 1972, the U.S. Supreme Court addressed these issues in *Cruz* v. *Beto.*[29] Cruz, a Buddhist, had been barred from using the chapel in a Texas prison and was placed in solitary confinement for sharing his religious materials with other inmates. The Court ruled that the Texas action was "palpable discrimination" in violation of the equal protection clause of the Fourteenth Amendment. On the other hand, the federal courts have held that placing limits on the practice of "satanism" is not a violation of prisoners' First Amendment rights.[30] For a discussion of other considerations on religion in prison, see Exhibit 16.1.

Mail and Media Interviews

Prison officials in the United States have traditionally placed certain restrictions on inmates' use of the mails. These restrictions generally include limiting the number of people with whom inmates may correspond, opening and reading incoming and outgoing mail, deleting sections from incoming and outgoing mail, and refusing to mail for an inmate or forward to an inmate certain types of correspondence. The reasons for these restrictions have to do with security and budgetary requirements. Contraband must be intercepted, escape plans must be detected, and material that might incite the inmate population in some way must be excluded. Moreover, correctional budgets do not allow for unlimited use of the mails. Prisons have also used the goal of rehabilitation to justify certain restrictions on inmate correspondence. The courts have generally accepted these justifications for mail censorship and limitation, and in the past have rarely intervened in prison mail regulations. More recently, however, a range of situations have been examined by the courts, with major rulings in *Wolff* v. *McDonnell* and *Procunier* v. *Martinez,* both decided by the Supreme Court in 1974.[31]

In *Wolff,* the issue was whether prison officials could justifiably open correspondence from an inmate's attorney. The Court ruled that officials are permitted to open a communication from an attorney to check for contraband, but it must be done in the presence of the inmate, and the contents must not be read. ***Procunier* v. *Martinez*** dealt with the broader issue of censorship of nonlegal correspondence. The Supreme Court held that prison mail censorship is constitutional only when two criteria are met: (1) The practice must promote substantial government interests such as security, order, or rehabilitation; and (2) the restrictions must not be greater than necessary to satisfy the particular government interest involved.

The decision in *Martinez* also confirmed the earlier opinions of other courts on related matters. In the 1970 case of *Carothers* v. *Follette,*[32] a federal district court castigated officials at New York's Green Haven Prison for refusing to mail a letter from an inmate to his parents. The letter contained remarks that were critical of prison conditions. In the 1971 case of *Nolan* v. *Fitzpatrick,*[33] inmates contested the legality of a Massachusetts prison regulation that totally banned letters to the news media. Officials claimed that such communications could inflame the inmates and, hence, endanger prison security. They also maintained that complaint letters would retard rehabilitation and create administrative problems, since they would encourage representatives of the

CLOSE TO HOME © John McPherson. Reprinted with permission of UNIVERSAL PRESS SYNDICATE. All rights reserved.

media to seek interviews with inmates. *Martinez* specifically invalidated prison censorship of statements that "unduly complain" or "magnify grievances"; expressions of "inflammatory political, racial, or religious, or other views;" and matter deemed "defamatory" or "otherwise inappropriate."

Thornburgh v. Abbott,[34] decided by the Supreme Court in 1989, partially overruled the Court's holding in *Martinez.* The mail censorship regulations of the Federal Bureau of Prisons were upheld, but the Court jettisoned the "substantial government interests" test of *Martinez* in favor of a "reasonableness" standard as the proper analysis to be applied when courts evaluate prison restrictions on *incoming* mail or publications. In *Abbott,* the *Martinez* standard was held to apply only to *outgoing* mail, which in the Court's opinion presented a security concern of a "categorically lesser magnitude" than incoming mail. By rejecting the *Martinez* "substantial government interests" test as the foundation for reviewing incoming publications and correspondence, *Abbott* reversed much of the existing case law on prison mail censorship, since most of those cases involved challenges to restrictions on incoming mail. As such, *Thornburgh v. Abbott* has been considered by a number of constitutional scholars to signal a modified hands-off doctrine.

Rehabilitative Services

Many clinicians, legislators, and members of the general public agree that in addition to confinement, one purpose of imprisonment is rehabilitation. Moreover, in the constitutions and statutes of many states, the rehabilitation of prison inmates is implied, if not stated. For example, the New York state correction law indicates that:

> Correctional facilities shall be used for the purpose of providing places of confinement and *programs of treatment* [emphasis added] for persons in the custody of the department. Such use shall be suited, to the greatest extent practicable, to the objective of assisting persons to live as law abiding citizens.[35]

The courts, however, while supporting the rehabilitative ideal, have not defined rehabilitative treatment as a constitutional right. In *O'Connor v. Donaldson,*[36] decided in 1975, the Supreme Court refused to decide on the right of institutionalized mental patients to receive treatment. Other courts have approached the issue more directly:

- *Wilson v. Kelley* (1968) stated that prison officials have a duty "to exercise ordinary care for [the inmate's] protection and to keep him safe and free from harm."[37]
- *Padgett v. Stein* (1976) more specifically ruled that government entities have no constitutional duty to rehabilitate prisoners.[38]

While the courts may not have extended constitutional status to the right to treatment, they have taken a strong stand against several "rehabilitative" practices of questionable moral and legal status. During the early 1970s, for example, a number of behavior modification techniques were imposed on inmates. Several of these techniques seemed to have been taken directly from Anthony Burgess's *A Clockwork Orange,* George Orwell's *1984,* and Aldous Huxley's *Brave New World. A Clockwork Orange* was especially applicable. Burgess's story is set in a semitotalitarian state of the near future in which thugs roam the streets of London engaging in assorted acts of intimidation and violence. Alex, a 15-year-old psychopath, is caught by the police and subjected to "corrective brainwashing." He is bound to a chair and forced to view films of brutal violence for weeks on end until he himself becomes sickened by it. His destructive behavior is destroyed along with his will, and the State succeeds in transforming him into a "good," unthinking, obedient automaton. In a real-life parallel, Connecticut's maximum-security prison at Sommers instituted an electroshock program for habitual child molesters in 1973.[39] The "patient" viewed slides of children and adults, receiving an electric shock every time a picture of a naked child appeared. The purpose of the program was to repress the offender's ability to think of children as sex objects. In a similar case that reached the federal courts in 1973, severely nauseating injections were used to produce an aversion to minor infractions of prison rules.[40] In this case, it was ruled that the procedure was not "treatment" but "punishment," and cruel and unusual as well, in violation of the Eighth Amendment.

However, the courts have supported some prison requirements that mandate enrollment in certain institutional programs (such as class attendance by illiterate convicts) and disciplinary measures for those who refuse to participate.[41] Similarly, in *Washington* v. *Harper,*[42] decided in 1990, the Supreme Court held that the due process clause of the Fourteenth Amendment permits a state to treat a prison inmate who has a serious mental illness with antipsychotic medication against his will if the inmate is dangerous to himself or others and the treatment is in his or her medical interests.

Medical Services

In principle, inmates have a right to "adequate" and "proper" medical care on several grounds. The right is protected by common law and state statutes, the Civil Rights Act of 1964, the due process clauses of the Fifth and Fourteenth Amendments, and the Eighth Amendment ban on cruel and unusual punishment. Prisoners have made claims regarding improper and inadequate medical care and total denial of medical and health services.

In 1976, in **Estelle v. Gamble,**[43] the U.S. Supreme Court enunciated its position on the medical rights of inmates:

> Deliberate indifference to serious medical needs of prisoners constitutes the "unnecessary and wanton infliction of pain" proscribed by the Eighth Amendment. This is true whether the indifference is manifested by prison doctors in their response to the prisoner's needs or by prison guards in intentionally denying or delaying access to medical care or intentionally interfering with the treatment once prescribed.

Beyond this statement, the Court has generally left the specifics of medical rights to the lower courts. The federal judiciary has taken the position that determining what amount of medical aid is "adequate" is largely dependent on the facts of each case.[44] Thus, no uniform definition of "adequate" health care has been specified. Moreover, in *Priest* v. *Cupp,*[45] an Oregon court made it clear that the constitutional prohibition against cruel and unusual punishment does not guarantee that an inmate will be free from or cured of all real or imagined medical problems while in custody. Thus, although prison officials cannot deny medical aid, inmates cannot expect perfect medical services.

The most recent medical issue in the prisoners' rights arena relates to AIDS. In some jurisdictions significant numbers of prison inmates are infected with HIV (human immunodeficiency virus), which causes AIDS (acquired immunodeficiency syndrome). Yet prison management policies for infected inmates vary widely. In this regard, there are two major areas of AIDS litigation involving inmates—segregation and

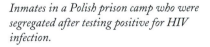
Inmates in a Polish prison camp who were segregated after testing positive for HIV infection.

privacy rights on the one hand, and screening on the other. In general, prisoners' constitutional claims against mandatory HIV testing and segregation have been unsuccessful, on the ground that such practices are rationally related to the legitimate penological goal of reducing the transmission of HIV infection.[46]

Prisoner Labor Unions

Although the courts have recognized the rights of prison inmates to adequate medical care, religious expression, and access to the courts, their opinions on the issue of collective bargaining by inmates are a different matter. In a number of institutions across the nation, inmates have sought to establish what are typically referred to as "labor unions." They have organized for the purposes of advocating increased pay for inmate labor, improving safety and working conditions, increasing inmate participation in the handling of matters affecting their welfare, ending contract labor, expressing dissatisfaction with prison programs, and gaining official recognition for inmate workers as public employees with statutory rights under state labor laws.[47] For prisoners, then, unions could operate as channels for communicating complaints that might otherwise not be brought into the open and to official notice. For prison officials, however, unions represent a foundation for concerted inmate actions that could represent significant threats to institutional safety and control.

Throughout the 1970s, prisoners attempted to organize unions in a number of jurisdictions. However, it was not until 1977, in *Jones* v. *North Carolina Prisoners' Labor Union*,[48] that the U.S. Supreme Court ruled on the matter. The case began when the North Carolina Prisoners' Labor Union (PLU), whose statewide membership included some 2,000 inmates, alleged that correctional regulations violated First and Fourteenth Amendment rights by denying it the opportunity to hold meetings, solicit additional members, and receive organizational materials from the outside and distribute them among inmates.

The Supreme Court disagreed with the PLU's contentions, however, holding that inmates have no constitutional right to organize a labor union and that prison regulations prohibiting the organized activities of an inmate union therefore do not violate the freedom of association clause of the First Amendment. The Court went on to emphasize that prison regulations may constitutionally ban union solicitation, group meetings of members, and bulk mail privileges of the organization as long as such regulations are reasonable and rationally related to such legitimate objectives as maintenance of security, prevention of escapes, safety of inmates and prison personnel, and rehabilitation of inmates.

Although constitutional scholars generally agree that the restrictive conditions of incarceration make the formation of inmate unions a real and distinct threat to prison security, many nevertheless feel that the Court's decision in this case heralded the return of a modified hands-off doctrine.

How do you like that? The next thing you know they're going to demand the right to keep women in their cells, shoot drugs, and take weekend vacation trips to the south of France.

—IDAHO STATE PENITENTIARY OFFICIAL IN 1988, AFTER AN INMATE UPRISING RESULTING FROM PRISONERS' REFUSAL TO LET GUARDS CONFISCATE THEIR HOMEMADE LIQUOR

| Prison Discipline and Constitutional Rights |

Many readers may be familiar with the story of *Papillon*. Written by French novelist Henri Charrière and produced as a motion picture in 1973 starring actors Dustin Hoffman and the late Steve McQueen, it told the story of two convicts confined to camps in French penal colonies. One of the camps was Devil's Island, a patch of rock less than a mile in circumference some 10 miles off the coast of French Guiana. Most striking were the severe disciplinary procedures for escape attempts and other rule violations: slow starvation; confinement for years at a time in small, dark, vermin-infested cells; or even a short interlude with what Frenchmen called "the widow-maker"—the infamous guillotine.[49]

Many may think of such practices as utterly foreign to American soil, or at least far removed in time from contemporary standards. But only a few decades ago, long after the French penal colonies were abolished during World War II, discipline at

FAMOUS CRIMINALS
Timothy Leary

The saga of Timothy Leary began at Harvard University in the early 1960s when he and his colleague, Dr. Richard Alpert, began experimenting with LSD—on themselves, and with colleagues, students, artists, writers, clergymen, and volunteer prisoners. Although their adventures with LSD had earned them dismissals from Harvard by 1963, their comments about the wonders of LSD had been heard. Their messages had been numerous and shocking to the political establishment, not to mention hundreds of thousands of mothers and fathers across the nation. Perhaps most frightening of all to the older generation were Leary's comments to some 15,000 cheering San Francisco youths on the afternoon of March 26, 1967. As a modern-day Pied Piper, Leary told his audience:

> *Turn on* to the scene, *tune in* to what's happening; and *drop out*—of high school, college, grad school . . . and follow me.

Leary's downfall came shortly thereafter, the result of conviction and imprisonment on drug-trafficking charges, followed by a period of time as a fugitive in Algeria and Afghanistan after a prison escape. But his demise was eulogized. At the opening of "Legend of a Mind" on the album *In Search of a Lost Chord,* the Moody Blues sang: "Timothy Leary's dead . . . he's on the outside, looking in."

(continued on p. 549)

Devil's Island is considerably smaller than what was shown in the Hollywood production of Papillon.

least as barbaric as that practiced on Devil's Island could be seen in the heartland of America.

The Arkansas Prison Scandal

Arkansas has the best prison system in the United States.

—**KNOX NELSON, ARKANSAS STATE SENATOR, FEBRUARY 8, 1967**

Ninety-five percent of the complaints of convicts are lies. . . . I don't believe none of that stuff.

—**LLOYD SADLER, ARKANSAS STATE REPRESENTATIVE, JANUARY 17, 1967**

In 1966, Winthrop Rockefeller, grandson of industrialist and philanthropist John D. Rockefeller, was elected governor of Arkansas. As a candidate, he had pledged to eliminate corruption in state government and to hire a professional penologist to reform the state prison system. The following year, the late Thomas O. Murton, a professor of criminology from Southern Illinois University, was put in charge of the Arkansas prisons. (Murton was the real "Warden Brubaker," portrayed by Robert Redford in the 1980 film *Brubaker.*)

What Murton found was a prison system that had been operating on fear for more than a century.[50] The traditional methods of instilling inmate compliance included beatings, needles under the fingernails, starvation, and floggings with the "hide," a leather strap 5 inches wide and 5 feet long. As recently as 1968, custodial officers at Tucker Prison Farm used a contraption known as the "Tucker telephone" to punish inmates and extract information:

> The telephone, designed by prison superintendent Jim Bruton, consisted of an electric generator taken from a crank-type telephone and wired in sequence with two dry-cell batteries. An undressed inmate was strapped to the treatment table at Tucker Hospital while electrodes were attached to his big toe and to his penis. The crank was then turned, sending an electrical charge into his body. In "long distance calls" several charges were inflicted—of a duration designed to stop just short of the inmate's fainting. Sometimes the "telephone" operator's skill was defective, and the sustained current not only caused the inmate to lose consciousness but resulted in irreparable damage to his testicles. Some men were literally driven out of their minds.[51]

Arkansas State Penitentiary in 1968.

For more than 50 years, many boasted that the Arkansas prison system was a symbol of efficiency, for no state appropriations were needed to support the convicts. But Murton found that this was so only because of the exploitation of inmate labor. Moreover, control of inmates, work assignments, promotion, food rations, bed assignments, visiting privileges, commissary privileges, laundry and clothing procedures, and the very survival of the inmate had been delegated to a few powerful convicts, who operated the prison. To make such a system operable, these "trusties" had been granted many privileges, including freedom to sell liquor and narcotics, gamble and loan money, live in squatter shacks outside the prison and spend nights with female companions, and profit from illegal trafficking in prison produce. Thus, there were no traditional custodial officers. Rather, the institutions were run by a powerful structure of convict guards who used bribery and torture to maintain the status quo and profit from inmate slavery. In Arkansas' Cummins Prison Farm, it was alleged that inmates had been routinely murdered as punishment for disciplinary infractions and then buried in a remote cow pasture. The number of these killings was estimated at more than 100.[52]

The barbaric conditions in the Arkansas prisons came to national attention in January 1968 as a result of Murton's discoveries and efforts at reform. However, fearing that Murton was damaging the image of Arkansas, on March 2, 1968, Governor Rockefeller fired him and placed him under house arrest. At a press conference the following day the governor simply explained that Murton had been a "poor prison administrator."

In the years following Murton's departure, the Arkansas prisons were in constant turmoil. On several occasions, inmates protesting prison conditions were shot at by prison officials.[53] Explanations for the continuing difficulties focused on racial conflicts and efforts at integration.

When the courts finally listened to the Arkansas prisoners, the savage discipline and inhumane conditions were more fully acknowledged. In 1970, in **Holt v. Sarver,**[54] a federal court declared the entire Arkansas prison system to be in violation of the Eighth Amendment ban on cruel and unusual punishment. In the written opinion, the court stated:

> For the ordinary convict a sentence to the Arkansas Penitentiary today amounts to a banishment from civilized society to a dark and evil world completely alien to the free world, a world that is administered by criminals under unwritten rules and customs completely foreign to free world culture.
>
> After long and careful consideration the Court has come to the conclusion that the Fourteenth Amendment prohibits confinement under the conditions that have been described and that the Arkansas penitentiary system as it exists today, particularly at Cummins, is unconstitutional.

(continued from p. 548)

Actually, Leary was not quite dead. By 1976 he had straightened out his legal problems and had become a free man and "a cheerleader for scientific optimism," as he once put it. With the onset of the 1980s, Leary joined the ranks of the most highly paid speakers on the college lecture circuit, often debating G. Gordon Liddy of Watergate fame. Quite curiously, Liddy was once his nemesis, having organized a raid in 1966 that led to one of Leary's early drug arrests. During the late 1980s, Leary was heard arguing for the legalization of drugs and suggesting that pharmaceutical firms should be encouraged to develop nonaddicting mood-altering drugs.

On May 31, 1996, at age 75, the man who the late Richard M. Nixon once called "the most dangerous man in America" died of prostate cancer. But as might be expected, he didn't go quietly. A few months prior to his death he was quoted in the *Los Angeles Times* as saying:

> When I found out that I was terminally ill, I was thrilled. Dying is such a taboo topic and I love the topics the establishment says are taboo. ∎

Such confinement is inherently dangerous. A convict, however cooperative and inoffensive he may be, has no assurance whatever that he will not be killed, seriously injured, or sexually abused. Under the present system the state cannot protect him. Apart from physical danger, confinement in the penitentiary involves living under degrading and disgusting conditions. This Court has no patience with those who still say, even when they ought to know better, that to change those conditions will convert the prison into a country club.

The peril and degradation to which Arkansas convicts are subjected to daily are aggravated by the fact that the treatment which a convict may expect to receive depends not at all upon the gravity of his offense or the length of his term. In point of fact, a man sentenced to life imprisonment for first-degree murder and who has a long criminal record may expect to fare better than a country boy with no serious record who is sentenced to two years for stealing a pig.

It is one thing for the State to send a man to the penitentiary as a punishment for crime. It is another thing for the State to delegate the governance of him to other convicts and to do nothing meaningful for his safety, well-being, and possible rehabilitation. It is one thing for the State not to pay a convict for his labor; it is something else to subject him to a situation in which he has to sell his blood to obtain money to pay for his own safety, or for adequate food, or for access to needed medical attention.

However constitutionally tolerable the Arkansas system may have been in former years, it simply will not do today as the twentieth century goes into its eighth decade.

Solitary Confinement

Solitary confinement is variously referred to as "isolation" or "segregation" in "the hole" or in a "strip cell." It is the total separation of an inmate from the general prison population in a small, uncomfortable cell, combined with the revocation of all privileges and constitutional rights, and often with a restricted diet or other physical abuse. Placement in "solitary" generally occurs as punishment for serious violations of prison regulations, such as escape attempts, forced sexual advances, assaulting correctional officers or other inmates, or being excessively troublesome.

The use of solitary confinement in the United States is as old as the nation's prison system, and its application is acknowledged in many state statutes. For example, Title 41 of the current *Tennessee Code* states:

If any convict neglects or refuses to perform the labor assigned him, or willfully injures any of the materials, implements, or tools, or engages in conversation with any other convict, or in any other manner violates any of the regulations of the penitentiary, he may be punished by solitary confinement for a period not exceeding thirty (30) days for each offense, at the discretion of the warden, or person acting in his place.[55]

As with other aspects of prisoners' rights, before the 1960s the courts maintained their hands-off doctrine with respect to inmate complaints concerning isolated confinement. Over the past three decades, however, numerous actions concerning the practice have been brought to the courts by both state and federal inmates. Some suits have argued that the very practice of solitary confinement is unconstitutional. The federal courts, however, have flatly rejected this contention. In *Sostre* v. *McGinnis*,[56] for example, circuit judge Irving R. Kaufman remarked: "For a federal court . . . to place a punishment beyond the power of the state to impose on an inmate is a drastic interference with the state's free political and administrative processes."

Despite their unwillingness to ban solitary confinement on constitutional grounds, the courts have taken a stand on how it can be imposed and administered. Using standards established by the Supreme Court for interpreting what constitutes cruel and unusual punishment,[57] the federal courts have examined the duration of an inmate's confinement, the physical conditions of the cell, the hygienic conditions of the inmate, the exercise allowed, the diet provided, and the nature of the infraction that resulted in punitive isolation.

The courts have been reluctant, however, to establish rigid criteria for deciding on the constitutionality of solitary confinement. In *Jordan* v. *Fitzharris*,[58] for example, the "strip cells" in California's Soledad Prison were deemed "cruel and unusual" because of

As the rights of smokers versus nonsmokers are debated and legislated in the wider community, so too are they argued in prison settings. Calls for smoke-free workplaces and other environments are an outgrowth of the growing body of evidence documenting the harmful effects of both secondhand and sidestream tobacco smoke, particularly the 1986 Report of the Surgeon General. *Several prisoners' rights cases involving lack of nonsmoking areas in correctional institutions reached the federal courts during the late 1980s and early 1990s. Significantly, in* Clemmons v. Bohannon *(48 CrL 1120), decided in 1990, the U.S. Court of Appeals for the 10th Circuit ruled that prison policies that permit the double-celling of smokers with nonsmokers against their expressed will amount to deliberate indifference to the health of nonsmoking inmates in violation of the Eighth Amendment and the due process of the Fourteenth Amendment.*

their poor sanitary conditions. In contrast, in *Bauer* v. *Sielaff*,[59] because the inmate was not denied the minimum necessities of food, water, sleep, exercise, toilet facilities, and human contact, the Federal Court of the Eastern District of Pennsylvania held that depriving an inmate of a comb, pillow, toothbrush, and toothpaste for 7 to 10 days in a cell with continuous lights, a few mice and roaches, and no reading material was not unconstitutional. Moreover, although the stereotypical solitary confinement meal of "bread and water" has been disapproved of by the courts,[60] it has been deemed satisfactory when supplemented by a full meal every third day.[61]

The Lash

Whipping (or flogging) has been a common sanction in most Western cultures. In the United States it was used as a punishment for crimes and for preserving discipline in domestic, military, and academic environments. Curiously, although whipping has been viewed by most as uncivilized brutality, it was not abolished until quite recently. In Delaware, for example, whipping was a constitutionally permissible punishment for specified crimes from the 17th through the 20th centuries.[62]

The end of whipping as an official means of enforcing prison rules and regulations evolved from an Arkansas case, *Jackson* v. *Bishop*,[63] which was decided by a federal circuit court in 1968. In the Arkansas prison system, whipping was the primary disciplinary measure. Facilities for separation and solitary confinement were limited, and inmates had few privileges that could be withheld as punishment. Prison regulations, moreover, allowed whipping for such infractions as sexual contacts between inmates, agitation, insubordination, making or concealing weapons, participating in or inciting a riot, and refusing to work when medically able to do so. Using the criteria of "broad and idealistic concepts of dignity, civilized standards, humanity, and decency," the court declared whipping to be a violation of the Eighth Amendment ban on cruel and unusual punishment, for the following reasons:

1. We are not convinced that any rule or regulation as to the use of the strap, however seriously or sincerely conceived and drawn, will successfully prevent abuse. . . .
2. Rules in this area often seem to go unobserved. . . .
3. Regulations are easily circumvented. . . .
4. Corporal punishment is easily subject to abuse in the hands of the sadistic and the unscrupulous.
5. Where power to punish is granted to persons in lower levels of administrative authority, there is an inherent and natural difficulty in enforcing the limitations of that power.
6. There can be no argument that excessive whipping or an inappropriate manner of whipping or too great frequency of whipping or the use of studded or overlong straps all constitute cruel and unusual punishment. But if whipping were to be authorized, how does one, or any court, ascertain the point that would distinguish the permissible from that which is cruel and unusual?
7. Corporal punishment generates hate toward the keepers who punish and toward the system that permits it. It is degrading to the punisher and to the punished alike. It frustrates correctional and rehabilitative goals. . . .
8. Whipping creates other penological problems and makes adjustment to society more difficult.
9. Public opinion is obviously adverse. Counsel concedes that only two states will permit the use of the strap.

For a discussion of prison "hitching posts," see Exhibit 16.2.

Prison Disciplinary Proceedings

Throughout the history of corrections, disciplinary actions against prison inmates have often been arbitrary administrative operations controlled solely by wardens, their deputies, or other custodial personnel. Without a formal hearing, and at the discretion of an institutional officer, inmates could be placed in solitary confinement, lose some or all of their privileges, or be deprived of good-time credits. Even in correctional settings in which disciplinary hearing committees were convened to review serious infractions of prison regulations, decisions could be made entirely on the basis of a custodial officer's testimony. Evidence was generally not required, prisoners were rarely permitted to speak in their own behalf, and the rules of due process were typically ignored. When the prisoners' rights movement first brought these practices to the attention of the federal courts during the 1960s, the due process clauses of the Fifth and Fourteenth Amendments were applied sparingly and only in specific circumstances. The position of the courts seemed to be that due process should prevent only "capricious" or "arbitrary" actions by prison administrators. In the 1966 case of *Landman* v. *Peyton*,[64] for example, a federal appeals judge made the following statement:

Where the lack of effective supervisory procedures exposes men to the capricious imposition of added punishment, due process and Eighth Amendment questions inevitably arise.

During the 1970s, however, the courts began to focus on the specific procedures used in prison disciplinary proceedings, seeking to resolve the wider issue of due process requirements. The principal case was ***Wolff* v. *McDonnell*,**[65] decided by the U.S. Supreme Court in 1974. The Court held as follows:

1. An inmate must be given advance written notice of the charges at least 24 hours prior to his or her appearance before the prison hearing committee.
2. There must be a written statement by the fact finders as to the evidence and the reasons for the disciplinary action.
3. The prisoner should be allowed to call witnesses and present documentary evidence, provided that such actions would cause no undue hazards to institutional safety or correctional goals.

historical perspectives on criminal justice | EXHIBIT 16.2

Hope v. Pelzer and the Prison "Hitching Post"

On two separate occasions in 1995, Larry Hope, an inmate within the Alabama prison system, was handcuffed to a "hitching post" for disruptive behavior. The first incident resulted from his arguing with a fellow inmate while they were working on a chain gang. Both men were handcuffed to the hitching post, but Hope was released 2 hours later when a correctional officer determined that he had not caused the incident. The second incident, about 1 month later, began when Hope did not move quickly enough when the bus he was riding arrived at the chain gang's worksite.

Vulgar remarks were exchanged between Hope and a guard, and the situation escalated to a wrestling match. Four other guards intervened, leading to Hope's being subdued, handcuffed, put in leg irons, and transported back to the prison where he was ordered to take off his shirt, and thus remain exposed to the sun for 7 hours while handcuffed to the hitching post. While shackled to the post, he was offered water only once or twice, was not given any bathroom breaks, and was taunted by a guard about his thirst. Hope sued three correctional officers who either had ordered that he be handcuffed to the post or had physically restrained him to the hitching post.

The issue that the Supreme Court faced was whether the officers were entitled to qualified immunity, which shields public officials from liability for civil damages if their actions did not clearly violate "established statutory or Constitutional rights of which a reasonable person would have known." The first step was to determine whether or not use of the hitching post was, in fact, a violation of the Eighth Amendment. The court determined that "as the facts are alleged by Hope, the Eighth Amendment violation is obvious." In addition, the court decided to rule against immunity for the officers. The decision was supported by several factors including that at the time of the incidents, federal appeals courts decided that handcuffing inmates to fences or in their cells for long periods of time was in violation of the Eighth Amendment, and that the court of appeals that covered Alabama had warned prisons against denying any inmate drinking water as a form of punishment. In addition, the Alabama Department of Corrections had also come up with regulations regarding the use of the hitching post, including details about drinking water and bathroom breaks. In this case, those rules were not followed by the correctional officers, therefore leading to the decision that they were not entitled to qualified immunity.

Source: Craig Fischer, "Use of Prison 'Hitching Post' Ruled a Constitutional Violation," *Corrections Journal* 5, 24 (2002), 1–2.

4. The inmate must be permitted representation by a counsel substitute (a fellow inmate or staff member) when the prisoner is illiterate or when the complexity of the case goes beyond the capabilities of the person being charged.
5. The hearing committee must be impartial (suggesting that those involved in any of the events leading up to the hearing—such as the charging or investigating parties—may not serve as members of the committee).

In establishing these requirements, the Court made it clear that neither retained or appointed counsel nor the right to confrontation and cross-examination were constitutionally required. The decision stressed some additional points. First, the ruling did not apply retroactively. Second, in writing the Court's opinion, Justice White emphasized that the limitations on due process imposed by the decision were "not graven in stone"; future changes in circumstances could require further "consideration and reflection" by the Court. Third, the due process requirements set forth in the decision applied only to proceedings that could result in solitary confinement and the loss of good-time credits. Left unresolved, however, were the procedures to be followed if other penalties were to be imposed.

In recent years, the Supreme Court has not gone much beyond *Wolff* in protecting inmates' rights in prison disciplinary proceedings. A case in point is *Superintendent, Massachusetts Correctional Institute at Walpole v. Hill,*[66] decided in 1985. As noted earlier, *Wolff* set forth certain safeguards that must be provided when a disciplinary hearing may result in the loss of good-time credits, but that ruling did not require either judicial review or a specific level of evidence to support a disciplinary board's decision. The matter of evidence was addressed in *Hill,* and here the Court ruled that only "some evidence" was necessary. In the *Hill* case, the evidence consisted of a correctional officer's report that he had heard a commotion, discovered an inmate who had apparently been assaulted, observed three other inmates (including those in this case) fleeing

Question: *Exactly how much evidence is* indeed *required by the due process clause to support a prison disciplinary hearing board's finding of guilt? Proof beyond a reasonable doubt? Clear and convincing evidence? Substantial evidence? A preponderance of evidence?*

Answer: In *Superintendent, Massachusetts Correctional Institute at Walpole v. Hill,* the Supreme Court ruled that such a decision will pass constitutional muster if there is "some evidence" to support the board's conclusions. ∎

down an enclosed walkway, and noticed no other inmates in the area. In delivering the Court's opinion, Justice Sandra Day O'Connor emphasized that although the evidence presented in the disciplinary proceeding was "meager," it was sufficient to meet due process requirements. Specifically, she added the following broad guideline: "The relevant question is whether there is *any* evidence in the record that could support the conclusion reached by the disciplinary board."

The Conditions of Incarceration

The Arkansas prison scandal of 1968 pointed to many problems within that state's correctional system. Not only was there corruption and brutality, but as the Court noted, there was also confinement under degrading and disgusting conditions. Although Arkansas during the 1960s may have been unusual in sanctioning the administration of prisons by convicts under a system of unwritten rules, its general prison conditions were not unique. Similar problems of overcrowding and extreme physical danger were commonplace throughout the nation.

In general, the courts have held that most aspects of prison life are dictated by the needs of security and discipline, thus giving custodial authorities wide discretion in the regulation of inmate life. At the same time, however, the federal courts have monitored some conditions of confinement, taking the position that while offenders are sent to prison for punishment, prison should not impose extra punishments of a barbaric and uncivilized nature. For example, prison overcrowding itself has not been declared unconstitutional. Yet, as was pointed out in *Costello* v. *Wainwright* in 1975,[67] overcrowding can be a factor, when combined with other conditions, in declaring the circumstances of incarceration to be in violation of the Constitution. Thus, the federal courts have indicated that it is their duty to protect inmates from conditions of confinement

Overcrowding at a San Diego jail.

A crowded dormitory in Alabama's Tutwiler Women's Prison.

that serve to add punitive measures to those already meted out by a sentencing court. The courts have also ruled, as in the 1974 case of *People* v. *Lovercamp,*[68] that the situations and circumstances some inmates face inside prison walls may serve as a defense for the crime of escape (see Exhibit 16.3).

The Texas Prison Suit

The Texas prison suit, which was in the courts for more than a decade, reflects the kaleidoscope of conditions of confinement and attempts at prison reform that continue to be issues in other jurisdictions even today. At the close of 1980, the penitentiary system in Texas was the largest in the nation, with some 30,000 inmates.* All 19 Texas prisons were maximum-security institutions, designed to foster rigid discipline and inhibit escape. Overcrowding was a major problem. With only 14,000 cells for its tens of thousands of inmates, the system was operating at 230 percent of capacity. That represented a doubling of the prison population since 1974. The reasons for this overcrowding were numerous. In Texas, long sentences had always been the rule. As of 1980, almost 10 percent of the inmates were serving life sentences; an additional 45 percent had terms of 10 years or more. Since 1977, the Texas legislature has passed several laws ordering mandatory sentences for a variety of offenses and requiring inmates convicted of certain crimes to serve at least one-third of their term before becoming eligible for parole.

Overcrowding was not the only problem in the Texas prison system; there was also violence. During 1981, 11 prisoners were murdered by fellow inmates, and during one 7-day period, more than 70 inmates and correctional officers were injured in a series of confrontations. Two factors contributing to this violence were understaffing and the use of prisoners as building tenders, as turnkeys, as counters, and in supervisory roles. A Texas statute specifically prohibited the use of inmates in such administrative and supervisory capacities, but it was generally ignored by institutional officials. Ironically, for a long time these inmate supervisors were *permitted to carry weapons*—weapons that would have been denied them outside the prison walls.[69]

In June 1972, **Ruiz v. Estelle** was instituted as a class action suit in behalf of all past, present, and future Texas Department of Corrections (TDC) inmates.[70] After many years of discovery efforts, a trial finally began on October 2, 1978. At its conclusion, the court had heard 349 witnesses and received 1,565 exhibits into evidence. The

If you're not safe in prison from armed robbery, where are you safe?

— SUPERINTENDENT BARRY AHRINGER OF FLORIDA'S POMPANO BEACH COMMUNITY CORRECTIONAL FACILITY, AFTER A GUNMAN ROBBED TWO CONVICTS IN THEIR CELL

*By 2004, Texas still ranked first, with 169,110 inmates. California was the second largest, with 166,053 inmates.

EXHIBIT 16.3 | VICTIMS & JUSTICE

The Defense of Necessity and the Right to Escape from Prison

Rather early in the legal history of the offense of prison escape, it became clear that all departures from lawful custody were not necessarily escapes. Over two and a half centuries ago it was written that if a prison caught fire and an inmate departed to save his life, then the necessity to save his life "excuseth the felony." * Yet despite this pre-Revolutionary War holding, the courts traditionally have not favored the defense of necessity in escape cases. The principal justification for this hostility has been the frequently expressed fear that the availability of the defense might lead to an increase in prison escapes. This consideration has some courts holding that even the most intolerable of prison conditions will never justify an escape.[†] In *People v. Lovercamp,* however, decided by the California court of appeals in 1974, the conditions under which the defense of escape might be used were established.

In *Lovercamp,* two women inmates had escaped from the California Rehabilitation Center and were promptly captured in a hayfield just a few yards away. They had been in the institution just a few months and during that time they had been threatened by a group of lesbian inmates who told them that they were to perform certain lesbian acts—the exact expression was "fuck or fight." They complained to prison authorities on several occasions, but nothing was done. On the day of the escape, 10 or 15 of the lesbian inmates approached them and again offered the alternative—"fuck or fight." A fight ensued, and the two women were told that they would see the group again. Fearing for their lives, on the basis of what had occurred and the threats that had been made, along with the fact that the prison officials had not done anything for their protection, the two women felt that they had no choice but to leave the institution to save themselves.

In considering these facts, the court ruled as follows:

We conclude that the defense of necessity to an escape charge is a viable defense. However, before *Lovercamp* becomes a household word in prison circles and we are exposed to the spectacle of hordes of prisoners leaping over the walls screaming "rape," we hasten to add that the defense of necessity to an escape charge is extremely limited in its application. . . . We hold that the proper rule is that a limited defense of necessity is available if the following conditions exist:

[1] the prisoner is faced with a specific threat of death, forcible sexual attack, or substantial bodily injury in the immediate future;

[2] there is no time for a complaint to the authorities or there exists a history of futile complaints which make any result from such complaints illusory;

[3] there is no time or opportunity to resort to the courts;

[4] there is no evidence of force or violence used towards prison personnel or other "innocent" persons in the escape; and

[5] the prisoner immediately reports to the proper authorities when he has attained a position of safety from the immediate threat.

In subsequent cases, although the courts have agreed that the *Lovercamp* criteria are generally relevant to the defense of necessity in escape cases, they have disagreed on the role that the criteria should play. As a result, three approaches have emerged.* Under the most restrictive approach, the jury is not permitted to consider the evidence offered in support of the defense if any one of the *Lovercamp* criteria has not been met. The second approach, that taken by the *Lovercamp* court, requires that all five criteria be met before illegal conduct will be excused but allows the jury, rather than the judge, to make this determination. The third approach treats the *Lovercamp* criteria only as factors to be considered by the jury in assessing the credibility of the evidence offered to establish the defense. As such, under this third approach all of the *Lovercamp* criteria need not be met.

---

* 1 Hale P.C. 611 (1736).
[†] Comment, "From Duress to Intent: Shifting the Burden in Prison Escape Prosecutions," *University of Pennsylvania Law Review* 127 (1979): 1142–1173.

* Case Comment, "Intent, Duress, and Necessity in Escape Cases," *Georgetown Law Journal* 68 (1979): 249–266.

The United States Constitution must be enforced within the confines of TDC prison walls by court decree.

—JUDGE WILLIAM WAYNE JUSTICE, 1980

case involved issues of overcrowding, inmate security, and numerous prison services. Presiding over the case was federal judge William Wayne Justice.

In 1980, Judge Justice declared the Texas prison system to be unconstitutional. The court ordered the addition of new facilities to alleviate overcrowding; the abolition of arrangements that placed some prisoners in charge of others; the placement of any new prisons near urban areas with populations of 200,000; changes in the staff-to-inmate ratio; limits on inmate populations; adherence to the due process rights guaranteed by *Wolff;* and improved medical, educational, occupational, and mental health services. The judge made the following statement:

It is impossible for a written opinion to convey the pernicious conditions and the pain and degradation which ordinary inmates suffer within TDC prison walls—the gruesome experiences of youthful first offenders forcibly raped; the cruel and justifiable fears of inmates, wondering when they will be called upon to defend the next violent assault; the sheer misery, the discomfort, the wholesale loss of privacy for prisoners housed with one, two, or three others in a forty-five square foot cell or suffocatingly packed together in a crowded

A cellblock in Huntsville, Texas.

dormitory; the physical suffering and wretched psychological stress which must be endured by those sick or injured who cannot obtain adequate medical care; the sense of abject helplessness felt by inmates arbitrarily sent to solitary confinement or administrative segregation without proper opportunity to defend themselves or to argue their causes; the bitter frustration of inmates prevented from petitioning the courts and other governmental authorities for relief from perceived injustices.

For those who are incarcerated within the parameters of TDC, these conditions and experiences form the content and essence of daily existence.

Despite the ruling in *Ruiz,* many Texas officials maintained that their prison system was the best in the nation, and the Texas Department of Corrections appealed to the United States court of appeals on the ground that the reforms ordered by Judge Justice were beyond the jurisdiction of his court and should not be required. In 1982, the court of appeals upheld the lower-court order,[71] but the reforms were not immediately forthcoming. By 1983, conditions in the Texas system had become worse, and there were allegations of corruption, graft, and mismanagement.

By the 1990s, however, some dramatic changes had become evident in the Texas system. At the end of 1992, Judge Justice approved a settlement between the state and its inmates. As part of the settlement, Texas officials agreed to monitor inmate population levels and take steps to relieve overcrowding by building more prisons and increasing capacity in others.[72] Texas also implemented the Treatment Alternatives to Incarceration Program (TAIP), the Substance Abuse Felony Punishment System (SAFP), and in-prison therapeutic communities. In the TAIP, offenders from the six largest counties are tested for substance abuse and referred to appropriate treatment programs. Under the SAFP system, nonviolent offenders with abuse histories are given indeterminate sentences and substance abuse treatment for 6 to 12 months. In addition, in-prison therapeutic communities were established for thousands of inmates interested in receiving treatment for substance abuse problems.[73]

The New Mexico Inmate Massacre

The vilest deeds, like prison weeds
Bloom well in prison air.
It is only what is good in man
That wastes and withers there.

— OSCAR WILDE

The Attica riot of 1971 was the bloodiest 1-day encounter between Americans since the Civil War. But on February 1, 1980, New Mexico State Penitentiary was the scene of the most gruesome prison riot in U.S. history. Nearly a thousand inmates seized the

An interior of a prison cell with blood covering the floor after the most savage prison uprising in U.S. history by inmates of New Mexico State Penitentiary.

New Mexico's prisons are no different now than they were a decade ago. They are poorly managed, understaffed, and overcrowded with vicious inmate predators.

— **NEW MEXICO CORRECTIONS OFFICIAL**

It's my personal belief that if they're not rehabilitated after 15 years, kill 'em.

— **SENATOR TIM JENNINGS OF NEW MEXICO, ON WHAT TO DO WITH INCORRIGIBLE INMATES AND CRIMINALS**

It's all going to fall on us real soon. A real bloodbath. I think about it every day. And I have nightmares about it every night.

— **CUSTODIAL OFFICER, ATTICA CORRECTIONAL FACILITY**

When you look around, it all looks so safe and calm—TV sets in the cells, an honor block, all kinds of new rights. But you never know where you stand— not the inmates, not the officers—and that's when the trouble comes.

— **CUSTODIAL OFFICER, ATTICA CORRECTIONAL FACILITY**

institution, taking 15 correctional officers as hostages. Prisoners threatened to kill all the captives if state officials refused to meet their demands for improved conditions.[74]

The New Mexico institution, built in 1957 for 850 convicts, had been housing almost 1,200. A 1977 lawsuit by inmates described the prison as unsanitary and lacking medical facilities, and an investigation in 1979 found that the facility was dangerously understaffed and the correctional officers were poorly trained. When the riot broke out, only 18 correctional officers were on duty. Inmates looted the prison hospital for drugs and set fires that gutted all five cell blocks. They had essentially two demands: relief of overcrowded conditions and an end to harassment by officers. The prison was quickly retaken by police and the National Guard, but not before many inmates had died from drug overdoses, burns, and smoke inhalation.

The New Mexico incident was not just another prison riot. It was unmatched in savagery in terms of the nature of inmate violence. Investigators found that during the riot, a seven-man inmate execution squad had been formed to take revenge on convict informers. One prisoner was beheaded; another was found with a metal rod driven through his head; several had their arms and legs cut off or their eyes gouged out; and still others were charred by blowtorches or beaten beyond recognition.[75] In all, 33 prisoners were brutally murdered.

In the wake of the New Mexico holocaust, numerous reforms were proposed, but one commentator reflected as follows:

> Perhaps a disaster such as this can open the windows and allow fresh thinking to enter. But many are not optimistic. Little was learned from Attica. It is hoped more may be learned from Santa Fe.[76]

Future Prospects

There are so many ways that trouble can start—violence over money, drugs, property, territorial rights, and turf, snitching and homosexuality; there's the inmate gangs, "Bloods" and "Crips," unpaid debts, protection racket scams and extortion; then there's the overcrowding, the macho guards who "get-off" by playing "tough-guy," write-ups and disciplinary hearings, the food, and on and on. Just about anything can light the fuse.

— **CALIFORNIA PRISON OFFICIAL**

Despite court intervention and plans for change, throughout the 1990s and into the 21st century conditions in many prisons have remained unconstitutional and in a constant state of chaos.[77] In the aftermath of the 1971 riot at Attica Correctional Facility, a number of reforms were proposed and implemented. But as the years passed, conditions there began to deteriorate again. By the early 1980s, Attica had become overcrowded; it had absorbed inmates from two state hospitals for the criminally insane; most of the inmates were violent offenders; and the number of assaults on correctional officers was increasing steadily. In September 1981, just a few days before the 10th anniversary of the riot, one officer who had been on duty during the 1971 rebellion commented that tensions in Attica once again were reaching the boiling point. "We have all the ingredients for a disaster here," he remarked. Another officer said, "This place could go right now."[78] Throughout the 1990s, the same comments were being heard, not only at Attica but elsewhere as well. While Attica has not exploded again, like other correctional institutions it has undergone a series of what might be called "prison riots in slow motion."

Since 2000, there have been scores of prison disturbances every year in federal and state penitentiaries throughout the nation. At the same time, a number of institutions have experienced lengthy **lockdowns,** situations in which inmates are confined to their cells around the clock—denied exercise, work, recreation, and visits. Lockdown status typically results from inmate violence and is intended to separate prisoners in an effort to prevent further violence.

The reasons for the numerous riots and other disturbances are twofold. First, prisons in almost half the states have been found unfit by the federal courts. The deplorable

Supermax Pelican Bay State Prison in Crescent City, California.

conditions of confinement—combined with the very *fact* of confinement—produces anger, frustration, and emotions that are difficult to control. Secondly, penitentiaries are very dangerous places. Prisoners assault and kill one another. There is sexual assault and racial unrest. The strong prey upon the weak, and rivalries and jealousies are common. Seeking protection and status, many inmates join gangs. But the very presence of gangs within prison walls means additional violence resulting from struggles over power, turf, and contraband.

Reform versus Law and Order

While the 1960s ushered in the era of prisoners' rights and the 1970s witnessed agitation for prison reform, in the 1980s and 1990s calls for "law and order" brought into focus a dilemma that had been evolving for decades. Initially, civil libertarians had agitated for the rights of prison inmates. The federal courts responded by casting aside the "hands-off" doctrine and strengthening the mechanisms available to inmates in their attempts to file lawsuits against their keepers. Prisoners were no longer the complete slaves of the state, and they slowly won significant victories with respect to legal and medical services, religious expression, access to the media, and their general treatment inside penitentiary walls. Moreover, the courts began to take a more balanced look at the conditions of incarceration. The result was that correctional systems in most jurisdictions were declared unconstitutional and ordered to reform.

At the same time, however, a slow erosion of the rights of the accused, combined with calls for strict and certain punishment of criminal offenders, led to an unprecedented escalation in the growth of prison populations. The ultimate consequence was a corrections system that, while in the throes of reform, was still deteriorating rapidly.

Added to this state of affairs were indications of a trend aimed at limiting the rights of prisoners. In 1979, in *Bell* v. *Wolfish*,[79] the Supreme Court upheld the constitutionality of "double bunking," broad room search powers, frequent body cavity searches, and other restrictions imposed on federal pretrial detainees, on the ground that such restrictions are rational responses to legitimate security concerns. Writing for the majority, Justice Rehnquist commented that he did not see "some sort of one man, one cell principle lurking in the Due Process Clause of the Fifth Amendment." The Court upheld the double bunking, in part, on the ground that pretrial detainees rarely remain incarcerated for more than 60 days.

CAREERS IN CRIMINAL JUSTICE

Correctional Counseling

Most correctional systems in the United States have a staff of correctional counselors who work directly with offenders while they are still incarcerated. The major roles of correctional counselors involve assisting inmates in coping with the "pains of imprisonment" and institutional life, as well as helping them to prepare for community reintegration as they approach their release dates. Counselors typically have a caseload of inmates for whom they develop and implement treatment plans. This is typically accomplished by examining an inmate's institutional files and gathering information from family members, associates, former employers, and other counselors and rehabilitation team members. The treatment plan is often developed in conjunction with the classification process and may ultimately include individual counseling sessions, performed by the correctional counselor and/or other members of the treatment team. With the recent growth of substance abuse treatment programs in prison settings, correctional counselors often work exclusively with drug-involved offenders.

The requirements for correctional counselors are a BA or MA in criminal justice or one of the social or behavioral sciences, plus coursework or a background in counseling. Some correctional systems prefer that counselors have master's-level degrees in either psychology or social work. Given the expansion in prison populations, as well as the growth of corrections-based drug abuse treatment programs, the demand for correctional counselors is significant. Starting salaries range from $35,000 to $50,000, depending on education, experience, and jurisdiction.

A dog in a California pound gets more running space than we do

— CALIFORNIA INMATE

Then there was ***Rhodes v. Chapman,***[80] which was decided by the Supreme Court in 1981. The suit was filed in 1975 by Kelly Chapman, an armed robber being held at the Southern Ohio Correctional Facility in Lucasville. Chapman argued that the one-man cell he shared with another prisoner gave him only 32 square feet of personal living space, an area about 4 feet wide and 8 feet long. That was less, he contended, than Ohio law required for 5-week-old calves in feed lots. The district court agreed that double celling violated the Eighth Amendment, and ordered Lucasville to reduce its inmate population. Governor James Rhodes of Ohio filed an appeal for the state, but the lower court's decision was affirmed by the U.S. court of appeals.

In an 8-to-1 decision, the U.S. Supreme Court reversed the lower court's ruling, holding that the double celling was *not* unconstitutional at the Ohio prison. The Court was claiming not that double celling was itself constitutional but, rather, that given the nature of other services and conditions at the institution, the cell overcrowding was neither "cruel or unusual" nor the cause of physical or mental injury. Thus, as Justice Brennan pointed out, the Court had used the "totality of circumstances" test and found the double celling to be constitutional. *Rhodes* v. *Chapman* has resulted in a reduction—but not a drastic reduction—in the number of cases in which prisoners successfully challenge overcrowding on Eighth Amendment grounds.

In 1984, in ***Hudson v. Palmer,***[81] the Supreme Court made clear that prison inmates have few, if any, privacy rights. On September 16, 1981, Ted S. Hudson, an officer at the Bland Correctional Center at Bland, Virginia, along with a fellow officer, conducted a shakedown search of inmate Russel Palmer's prison locker and cell. Looking for contraband, the officers discovered a ripped pillowcase in a trash can near Palmer's cell bunk. Palmer was charged with destroying state property and ordered to reimburse the state for the material destroyed.

In petitioning the U.S. district court, Palmer asserted that Hudson had intentionally destroyed letters from his wife, pictures of his children, legal papers, and other noncontraband items. He also claimed that the search of his cell and the destruction of the noncontraband items were violations of his Fourth Amendment rights. The Supreme Court ruled that a prisoner has no reasonable expectation of privacy in his prison cell entitling him to the protection of the Fourth Amendment against unreasonable searches. The Court noted that it would be impossible to accomplish the prison objectives of preventing the importation of weapons, drugs, and other contraband if inmates retained a right of privacy in their cells. Imprisonment, the Court emphasized, carries with it the loss of many rights as necessary to meet the institutional needs and objec-

"I sentence you to twenty years or until your prison becomes overcrowded, whichever comes first."

Reprinted by permission of Robert Englehart.

tives of prison facilities, particularly internal security and safety. Moreover, the Court held that since the state of Virginia provided an adequate mechanism through which Palmer could bring suit for any losses he suffered from the destruction of his personal property, he was not entitled to bring a civil rights suit against Hudson in federal court.

The erosion of the rights of prisoners continued through the 1990s. A key case was ***Wilson v. Seiter,***[82] decided in 1991. The Supreme Court ruled that prisoners filing lawsuits about inhuman living conditions must show not only that conditions are so deplorable as to violate the Constitution *but also that prison officials have acted with "deliberate indifference" to basic human needs.* This standard of "deliberate indifference" previously applied only in medical care cases, as ordered by *Estelle* v. *Gamble* in 1976. The *Seiter* decision made it considerably more difficult for prisoners to prevail in Eighth Amendment lawsuits.

It is difficult to predict how correctional systems will deal with prison overcrowding and the other problematic conditions of incarceration. Some jurisdictions have instituted procedures for early parole, while others have placed some of their excess prisoners in local jails. But these are only temporary measures. Moreover, early paroling of convicted offenders is unpopular with the public; placement of prison inmates in local facilities further strains the already excessive jail populations; and neither approach addresses the basic need for better institutional conditions. A number of states and the federal system have allocated funds for new prison construction. But correctional facilities are costly to build, equip, and properly staff; the prison population continues to expand; and the funding for new institutions must come from increased taxation. Yet although citizens continue to ask for swifter and more certain punishment for criminal offenders, they tend to be unwilling to bear the financial and social costs of new prison construction. As both taxpayers and the victims of crime, they feel that they would be paying twice for the misdeeds of lawbreakers.

One new approach to the problem is **privatization of corrections**—the construction, staffing, and operation of prisons by private companies *for profit.* Such an approach might be highly cost-effective, but there is strong opposition to privatization. Opponents raise a variety of moral, legal, and ethical questions, including whether it is appropriate for the state to hand over incarceration to a profit-making organization, how liability and disciplinary issues will be handled, and whether private firms will end up lobbying for more and longer prison sentences instead of alternatives to incarceration.[83] Despite the debate, privatization appears to be gaining ground. Privatization, which began in 1982 in Florida, has become a growth industry as states look for more cost-effective ways for housing their increasing numbers of inmates. Private prisons are currently operating in 26 states, with many others moving toward privatization.

The whole system is groaning and wobbling toward collapse. California is headed toward disaster in corrections.

— CALIFORNIA ATTORNEY GENERAL JOHN VAN DE KAMP

CRITICAL THINKING IN CRIMINAL JUSTICE

Inmates and the Web

Most of the students reading this text were likely born during the 1980s and are far too young to remember the "hippies," the "flower children," and the "Summer of Love." It all began on March 26, 1967, when 10,000 youths congregated in New York City's Central Park to honor peace and love. They joined hands in "love circles," flew kites, sang, and took drugs. On the West Coast that Easter Sunday, another 15,000 youths met in San Francisco and participated in a similar happening. The crossroads of the Summer of Love was the Haight-Ashbury section of San Francisco, where the natives were known as "flower children." During the spring and summer of 1967, the word had gone out across the country to come to San Francisco for love and flowers. Yet other things also waited in "the Haight," as it was locally known. There were vicious criminals who grew long hair, bikers who tried to take over the drug market with sadistic tactics, "speed freaks" going through aggressive paranoid delusions, and satanist-rapist death freaks. Among these was a bearded little psychotic who haunted the Grateful Dead concerts at the Avalon Ballroom, curling into a fetal position on the dance floor. He would be well remembered in the Haight—his name was Charles Manson.

Manson was not typical of the middle-class youth who made up the flower children. Born in Cincinnati, Ohio, in 1934, Manson was a wandering vagrant who was in trouble most of his life, spending much of his time in jails and reformatories throughout the country. At age 35, he was the organizer of a commune located on the edge of Death Valley that practiced free love and pseudo-religious ceremonies centering around his role as a Christlike leader. As noted earlier in Chapter 1, on August 8, 1969, Manson directed five of his followers to the Los Angeles mansion of film director Roman Polanski. Spouting Manson's doctrines of "peace, love, and death," the group proceeded to brutally murder the five persons there. The victims were shot and stabbed to death, and various slogans were written on the walls of the house with the blood of those slain. Among the victims was Polanski's pregnant wife, actress Sharon Tate, and coffee heiress Abigail Folger. A few hours later, Manson's protégés—one man and three women—invaded the home of two additional victims, Leno and Rosemary LaBianca, leaving their bodies mutilated and arranged in grotesque positions. Manson and his followers who carried out the homicides were ultimately arrested and convicted and are serving life sentences in California prisons.

Why all of this attention to an aging and apparently psychotic criminal serving out his life behind bars? The issue is one of prisoners' rights, victims' rights, and access to the Internet. Manson has an elaborate Web site, maintained by Lynette Fromme, a devout Manson follower since the 1960s who had not taken part in the 1969 slayings.

The Internet has given Manson and other American prisoners a platform to plead their cases and to seek pen pals and other contacts; others use the Internet to raise funds for inmate litigation. Although no prison in the United States allows inmates direct access to the Internet, prisoners use third-party services, often for a fee, to reach out to the Web's worldwide audience. In Manson's case, his Web site is maintained by a follower. Other inmates use such commercial services as PrisonPenPals.com, writeaprisoner.com, and friendsbeyondthewall.com. Thinking critically about this matter, is there anything wrong with prisoner use of the Web? What are the prisoners' rights issues? And at the same time, are there any victims' rights questions at stake?

In terms of prisoners' rights, it could be argued allowing access to the Internet via third-party services is a humane gesture. It provides inmates with the opportunity to find someone to write to, a way of whiling away the hours in their cells. There is also a First Amendment issue. New York and Arizona have enacted policies forbidding inmates to use third-party Internet services, and other states are debating similar policies. But in the view of prisoner advocate groups and the American Civil Liberties Union, such actions by states impinge on an inmate's First Amendment right to communicate.

By contrast, victims' rights groups contend that it is humiliating for victims and their families to see prisoners on Web sites, arguing their cases, passing themselves off as decent people who were wrongly convicted, and seeking sympathy. There is also the potential for browsing the

Artwork by Charles Manson posted on his Web site www.CharlieManson.com.

Internet and initiating correspondence with violent predators or offering prisoners compassion, empathy, or even money without knowing the real details of their crimes.

Thinking critically, are there other concerns? Is prisoners' access to the Internet really a First Amendment issue? Can the different points of view be negotiated or compromised? Where do you stand on the matter?

OP-ED

Getting back to the allegations about Guantanamo Bay, most of the detainees who have been released have chosen not to speak about their experiences. However, those who have had something to say paint a different picture. Three teenagers recently released say the food was delicious, prison life was good, and they spent their days going to class, playing football, and doing other pleasant activities. These boys were, however, kept in Camp Laguna, an area that reportedly had better conditions than the camps holding adult detainees. The reality of the situation is that prisoners are likely being held under circumstances somewhere in between these two accounts. The Bush administration reports that detainees are being treated "humanely," that they are housed in individual cells, and that they are being given "culturally appropriate" meals and reading material. There is no way of knowing the true situation within the fence since human rights groups have not been allowed in; however, the Red Cross has called the lack of due process for prisoners and the open-ended detentions "unacceptable."

In U.S. prisons, there are many problems that violate constitutional protections and require correction. At the other end, however, there are far too many frivolous suits. Inmates have filed petitions in federal courts over broken cookies, chunky rather than smooth peanut butter, a lack of X-rated films in the prison library, bath towels that were not of a color preferred by the inmate, and quilted rather than flat toilet paper. A California inmate claimed that prison officials had planted an electronic device in his brain, and an Idaho prisoner filed suit after correctional officers refused to "tidy up" his cell after a search. There have been waves of frivolous lawsuits on religious grounds as well—over practices ranging from masturbation to reggae music to serving expensive cuts of beef as part of religious freedom.[84] A potential solution to the problem lies in the Prison Litigation Reform Act of 1996, which restricts inmate lawsuits and discourages "abusive" filers from bringing suits against their keep-

ers.[85] And as Supreme Court Justice Antonin Scalia has pointed out:

> The Constitution does not guarantee inmates the wherewithal to transform themselves into litigating engines capable of filing everything from shareholder derivative actions to slip and fall claims.

Summary

For the better part of U.S. history, prisoners were considered "slaves" of the state. Upon conviction, defendants experienced "civil death." The conditions in prison were generally brutal, and inmates had no recourse. The Supreme Court, furthermore, maintained a "hands-off" doctrine regarding correctional matters, refusing even to consider inmates' complaints.

The Constitution guarantees that all individuals confined to correctional institutions under state or federal authority have the right to file *habeas corpus* petitions with the courts to challenge the lawfulness of their confinement. It was not until 1944 in *Coffin* v. *Reichard*, however, that inmates could use *habeas corpus* petitions to challenge anything other than the legality of their confinement. The prisoners' rights movement began in 1961 when the High Court ruled in *Monroe* v. *Pape* that the long-dormant Section 1983 of the Civil Rights Act of

1871 was an appropriate mechanism for challenging the constitutionality of the conditions of prison life. Through a rush of petitions to the federal courts, convicts secured favorable decisions regarding legal services, the use of jailhouse lawyers, religious expression, media and mail services, medical programs, rehabilitative services, disciplinary proceedings, and the use of solitary confinement and corporal punishment.

During this period of prisoners' rights activity, however, many institutions across the nation continued to maintain archaic conditions. In the late 1960s, the Arkansas prison scandal erupted. It was the event upon which the 1980 film *Brubaker* was based, and it demonstrated, as stated in a federal court's opinion in *Holt* v. *Sarver,* that "a sentence to the Arkansas Penitentiary today amounts to a banishment from civilized society." In 1971, news from New York's Attica Prison reached the press around the world. Attica's inmates revolted because of the conditions of incarceration, and the siege to recover the prison resulted in the deaths of scores of inmates and correctional officers. In 1980, New Mexico State Prison distinguished itself for having the most gruesome riot in U.S. history. A year later, the entire Texas prison system was declared unconstitutional.

Throughout the 1990s, riots continued to erupt throughout the nation's prisons and jails, though none gained the notoriety of Attica or New Mexico. Nevertheless, riots continue to present a major problem to corrections officials—one that is not easily dealt with, as the conditions of overcrowding continue to overwhelm institutional capacities. The persistent problems across the nation continue to be overcrowding, inadequate programming, and a general lack of inmate safety. One solution that has gained considerable popularity among lawmakers in the last decade has been the somewhat controversial privatization of corrections.

Key Terms

civil death (542)
Estelle v. *Gamble* (546)
habeas corpus (538)
"hands-off" doctrine (534)
Holt v. *Sarver* (549)
Hudson v. *Palmer* (560)
injunctive relief (538)

Jackson v. *Bishop* (551)
Johnson v. *Avery* (540)
Jones v. *North Carolina Prisoners' Labor Union* (547)
lockdown (558)
Monroe v. *Pape* (539)
privatization of corrections (561)

Procunier v. *Martinez* (544)
Rhodes v. *Chapman* (560)
Ruiz v. *Estelle* (555)
Section 1983 (539)
Thornburgh v. *Abbott* (545)
Wilson v. *Seiter* (561)
Wolff v. *McDonnell* (552)

Issues For Discussion

1. Why was the Supreme Court's decision in *Cruz* v. *Beto* based on Fourteenth Amendment rather than on First Amendment grounds?
2. How are inmates' rights to proper and adequate medical care protected by the Constitution?
3. By applying the criteria and reasoning of the court in *Jackson* v. *Bishop*, what other penal practices—in addition to whipping—could be considered cruel and unusual punishment? Why?
4. The decision in *Wolff* v. *McDonnell* was not retroactive to disciplinary proceedings that had failed to follow the established due process requirements. In this case, can the loss of good-time credits through prior unconstitutional disciplinary hearings be reconciled? If *Wolff* were retroactive, how might prison authorities deal with sanctions already imposed?
5. Discuss the constitutional debate over smoking in prisons and jails. What is your point of view?
6. To what extent should prison inmates have rights?
7. Should prisoners have access to the Internet?

Media and Literature Resources

Attica. The details of the riot at Attica Prison in 1971 appear in Tom Wicker, *A Time to Die* (New York: Ballantine, 1975).

The Arkansas Prison Scandal. A full examination of the prison conditions that led to the federal court decision in *Holt* v. *Sarver* can be found in Tom Murton and Joe Hyams, *Accomplices to Crime: The Arkansas Prison Scandal* (New York: Grove Press, 1969). The 1980 film *Brubaker*, with Robert Redford, Morgan Freeman, and Yaphet Kotto, is also highly recommended.

Prisoners' Rights. See John A. Fliter, *Prisoners' Rights: The Supreme Court and Evolving Standards of Decency* (Westport, CT: Greenwood Press, 2000). An excellent review article on the topic is Fred Cohen, "The Law of Prisoners' Rights," *Criminal Law Review* 24 (July–August 1988): 321–349. In addition, there are a number of good articles in Peter M. Carlson and Judith Simon Garrett (eds.), *Prison and Jail Administration: Practice and Theory* (Gaithersburg, MD: Aspen Publishers, 1999).

Endnotes

1. *The Economist,* March 20, 2004.
2. *Ruffin* v. *Commonwealth,* 62 Va. (21 Gratt.) 790, 796 (1871).
3. *United States ex rel. Gereau* v. *Henderson,* 526 F. 2d 889 (1976). For a history of the "hands-off" doctrine, see Kenneth C. Haas, "Judicial Politics and Correctional Reform: An Analysis of the Decline of the Hands-Off Doctrine," *Detroit College of Law Review* (Winter 1977–1978): 795–831.
4. *Attica: The Official Report of the New York State Special Commission on Attica* (New York: Bantam, 1972), 3–15.
5. See Tom Wicker, *A Time to Die* (New York: Ballantine, 1975).
6. National Advisory Commission on Criminal Justice Standards and Goals, *Corrections* (Washington, DC: U.S. Government Printing Office, 1973), 18.
7. David A. Jones, *The Law of Criminal Procedure* (Boston: Little, Brown, 1981), 574.
8. *Coffin* v. *Reichard,* 143 F.2d 443 (1944).
9. See Kenneth C. Haas, "The Comparative Study of State and Federal Judicial Behavior Revisited," *Journal of Politics* 44 (August 1982): 729–739.
10. *Monroe* v. *Pape,* 365 U.S. 167 (1961).

11. *Cooper* v. *Pate,* 378 U.S. 546 (1964).

12. *Preiser* v. *Rodriguez,* 411 U.S. 475 (1973).

13. *Edwards* v. *Balisok,* 117 S.Ct. 1584 (1997).

14. *Will* v. *Michigan Department of State Police,* 491 U.S. 58 (1989).

15. *Ex parte Hull,* 312 U.S. 546 (1941).

16. *Johnson* v. *Avery,* 393 U.S. 483 (1969).

17. Cited by Kenneth C. Haas and Anthony Champagne, "The Impact of *Johnson* v. *Avery* on Prison Administration," *Tennessee Law Review* 43 (Winter 1976–1977): 275.

18. *Younger* v. *Gilmore,* 404 U.S. 15 (1971).

19. *Wolff* v. *McDonnell,* 418 U.S. 539 (1974).

20. *Procunier* v. *Martinez,* 416 U.S. 396 (1974).

21. *Bounds* v. *Smith,* 430 U.S. 817 (1977).

22. Kenneth C. Haas and Geoffrey P. Alpert, "American Prisoners and the Right of Access to the Courts," in *The American Prison: Issues in Research and Policy,* edited by Lynne Goodstein and Doris MacKenzie (New York: Plenum, 1989), 68–72.

23. *National Law Journal,* December 24, 1984, 6.

24. See Article I, Section 9.

25. *Fulwood* v. *Clemmer,* 206 F. Supp. 370 (D.C. Cir. 1962).

26. *Howard* v. *Smyth,* 365 F.2d 28 (4th Cir. 1966); *State* v. *Cubbage,* 210 A.2d 555 (Del. Super. Ct. 1965).

27. *Jones* v. *Willingham,* 248 F.Supp. 791 (D. Kan. 1965); *Cooke* v. *Tramburg,* 43 N.J. 514, 205 A.2d 889 (1964).

28. *O'Lone* v. *Estate of Shabazz,* 482 U.S. 342 (1987).

29. *Cruz* v. *Beto,* 405 U.S. 319 (1972).

30. *Childs* v. *Duckworth,* CA 7, 33 CrL 2120 (1983).

31. *Wolff* v. *McDonnell,* 418 U.S. 539 (1974); *Procunier* v. *Martinez,* 416 U.S. 396 (1974).

32. *Carothers* v. *Follette,* 314 F. Supp. 1014 (S.D. N.Y. 1970).

33. *Nolan* v. *Fitzpatrick,* 451 F.2d 545 (1st Cir. 1971).

34. *Thornburgh* v. *Abbott,* 109 S. Ct. 1874 (1989).

35. State of New York, *Correction Law,* Article 4, Section 70 (2).

36. *O'Connor* v. *Donaldson,* 422 U.S. 563 (1975).

37. *Wilson* v. *Kelley,* 294 F. Supp. 1005 (N.D. Ga. 1968).

38. *Padgett* v. *Stein,* 406 F. Supp. 287 (M.D. Pa. 1976).

39. William E. Cockerham, "Behavior Modification for Child Molesters," *Corrections* (January–February 1975): 77.

40. *Knecht* v. *Gillman,* 488 F.2d 1136 (8th Cir. 1973).

41. *Rutherford* v. *Hutto,* 377 F. Supp. 268 (E.D. Ark. 1974); *Jackson* v. *McLemore,* 523 F.2d 838 (8th Cir. 1975).

42. *Washington* v. *Harper,* 110 S. Ct. 1029 (1990).

43. *Estelle* v. *Gamble,* 429 U.S. 97 (1976).

44. For example, see *Gates* v. *Collier,* 390 F. Supp. 482 (N.D. Miss. 1975).

45. *Priest* v. *Cupp,* 545 P.2d 917 (Ore. Ct. App. 1976).

46. See Kenneth C. Haas, "Constitutional Challenges to the Compulsory HIV Testing of Prisoners and the Mandatory Segregation of HIV-Positive Prisoners," *Prison Journal* 73 (1993): 391–422.

47. Barbara B. Knight and Stephen T. Early, *Prisoners' Rights in America* (Chicago: Nelson-Hall, 1986), 113.

48. *Jones* v. *North Carolina Prisoners' Labor Union,* 433 U.S. 119 (1977).

49. For further study of Devil's Island and the other French penal colonies, see George J. Seaton, *Isle of the Damned* (New York: Farrar, 1951); Aage Krarup-Nielson, *Hell Beyond the Seas* (New York: Dutton, 1940); and Blair Niles, *Condemned to Devil's Island* (London: Jonathan Cape, 1928).

50. Tom Murton, "Too Good for Arkansas," *Nation,* January 12, 1970, 12–17.

51. Tom Murton and Joe Hyams, *Accomplices to Crime: The Arkansas Prison Scandal* (New York: Grove, 1969), 7.

52. *Newsweek,* February 12, 1968, 42–43.

53. Thomas O. Murton, *The Dilemma of Prison Reform* (New York: Holt, Rinehart and Winston, 1976), 35–38.

54. *Holt* v. *Sarver,* 309 F. Supp. 362 (E.D. Ark. 1970).

55. *Tennessee Code,* 41-707.

56. *Sostre* v. *McGinnis,* 442 F.2d 178 (2d Cir. 1971).

57. *Wilkerson* v. *Utah,* 99 U.S. 130 (1878); *Weems* v. *United States,* 217 U.S. 349 (1910); *Trop* v. *Dulles,* 356 U.S. 86 (1958); *Robinson* v. *California,* 370 U.S. 660 (1962).

58. *Jordan* v. *Fitzharris,* 257 F. Supp. 674 (N.D. Cal. 1966).

59. *Bauer* v. *Sielaff,* 372 F. Supp. 1104 (E.D. Pa. 1974).

60. *Landman* v. *Royster,* 333 F. Supp. 621 (E.D. Va. 1971).

61. *Novak* v. *Beto,* 453 F.2d 661 (5th Cir. 1972).

62. Robert G. Caldwell, *Red Hannah: Delaware's Whipping Post* (Philadelphia: University of Pennsylvania Press, 1947); *State* v. *Cannon,* 55 Del. 587 (1963).

63. *Jackson* v. *Bishop,* 404 F.2d 571 (8th Cir. 1968).

64. *Landman* v. *Peyton,* 370 F.2d 135 (4th Cir. 1966).

65. *Wolff* v. *McDonnell,* 418 U.S. 539 (1974).

66. *Superintendent, Massachusetts Correctional Institute at Walpole* v. *Hill,* 471 U.S. 491 (1985).

67. *Costello* v. *Wainwright,* 397 F. Supp. 20 (M.D. Fla. 1975).

68. *People* v. *Lovercamp,* 43 Cal. App.3d 823, 118 Cal. Rptr. 110 (1974).

69. Fred Cohen, "The Texas Prison Conditions Case: *Ruiz* v. *Estelle,*" *Criminal Law Bulletin* 17 (May–June 1981): 252–257.

70. *Ruiz* v. *Estelle,* 74-329 (E.D. Tex., Dec. 19, 1980).

71. *Ruiz* v. *Estelle,* F.2d 115 (5th. Cir. 1982).

72. *The New York Times,* December 13, 1992, 42.

73. *Texas Criminal Justice Treatment Initiative,* Texas Department of Criminal Justice, Commission on Alcohol and Drug Abuse, 1993; *Austin American Statesman,* January 16, 1994, A1, A19.

74. *The New York Times,* February 2, 1980, 1; *U.S. News & World Report,* February 18, 1980, 68.

75. Kinesley Hammett, *Holocaust at New Mexico State Penitentiary* (Lubbock, TX: Boone, 1980).

76. *Time,* October 26, 1981, 26; Adolph Saenz, *Politics of a Prison Riot: The 1980 New Mexico Prison Riot: Its Causes and Aftermath* (Corrales, NM: Rhombus, 1986).

77. For example, see *The New York Times,* September 16, 2000, A13.

78. *The New York Times,* September 1, 1991, 34.

79. *Bell* v. *Wolfish,* 441 U.S. 520 (1979).

80. *Rhodes* v. *Chapman,* 452 U.S. 337 (1981).

81. *Hudson* v. *Palmer,* U.S. SupCt 35 CrL 3230 (1984).

82. *Wilson* v. *Seiter,* 49 CrL 2264 (1991).

83. Ira P. Robbins, "Privatization of Corrections: Defining the Issues," *Judicature* 69 (April–May 1986): 325–331; United States General Accounting Office, *Private Prisons: Cost Savings and Bureau of Prisons' Statutory Authority Need to Be Resolved,* February 1991; Christine Bowditch and Ronald S. Everett, "Private Prisons: Problems Within the Solution," *Justice Quarterly* 4 (September 1987): 441; Jeff Gerth and Stephen Labaton, "The Pitfalls of Private Penitentiaries," *The New York Times,* November 24, 1995, A1, B18; and Pam Belluck, "As More Prisons Go Private, States Seek Tighter Controls," *The New York Times,* April 15, 1999, A1, A24.

84. See *USA Today,* September 30, 1996, 1A; *Criminal Justice Newsletter,* October 1, 1997, 2–3; and Carl Reynolds and Trisha Steffek, "Reducing Frivolous Inmate Litigation," *Corrections Compendium,* December 1997, 4–5, 29.

85. "Inmate Litigation and the PLRA," *Corrections Compendium,* December 1996, 1–3.

HM PRISON

ELMLEY

NOTICE TO VISITORS.

Health and Safety at
Work Act 1974
Persons entering these premises
must conform with the safety
regulations under the above act.

17

PROBATION, PAROLE, AND COMMUNITY-BASED CORRECTION

LEARNING OBJECTIVES

After reading this chapter, you should be able to answer the following questions:

1. What is community-based correction, and what kinds of programs does it encompass?

2. What are the purposes of community-based correction?

3. What is criminal justice diversion, and how useful has it been?

4. What is probation, and what kinds of services are associated with it?

5. What is intensive probation supervision? How effective is it?

6. What is parole? Is it effective? Should it be abolished?

7. What are the differences between probation and parole?

8. What are the major Supreme Court decisions associated with probation and parole revocation?

9. What are some of the current trends and issues in community-based correction?

10. What are reentry courts?

11. What is Proposition 36?

Solano County Prison

SACRAMENTO, CA—After spending 4 years behind bars at a cost to the state (and taxpayers) of over $30,000 a year, Francois Williams was released on parole from California's Solano County Prison with no money, no job skills, and not much in terms of prospects. Although on the surface he seems like a nice person, intelligent and polite, he is the person you worry about when you leave town on vacation; he is the reason you lock your doors at night. In fact, Francois Williams is the guy who has made gated communities and home alarm systems so popular. As a habitual criminal with a drug problem who has spent a significant part of his life in and out of courtrooms and institutions, Williams's prospects for recovery were dismal as he left the prison gates in a taxi back to Sacramento. Before too long, he was back on drugs, failed to meet his parole obligations, got himself arrested for a new crime, and ended up being returned to prison.[1] In retrospect, was paroling Francois the right thing to do?

Who makes parole decisions, and on what criteria? And for that matter, what is parole and what happens when someone is on parole? How is it different from probation? Are there other forms of community-based corrections? What purposes do they serve?

The principle of community-based correction rests on the fundamental fact that offenders either are incarcerated or are not. Logically, therefore, the concept refers to all correctional strategies that take place within the community. Accordingly, many types of court-determined sentences could be viewed as community-based correction. Some sanctions of the colonial era—such as the stocks and pillory, the ducking stool, the brank, and the scarlet letter—were certainly community-based. The same might be said of floggings in the public square and the imposition of fines in lieu of imprisonment. But these are oversimplifications of the community-based correctional philosophy, for other factors besides sanction and location are involved. **Community-based correction** includes activities and programs within the community that have effective ties with the local environment. These are generally of a rehabilitative rather than a punitive nature and can include arrangements with employment, educational, social, and clinical service delivery systems. Many also involve supervision by a community or governmental agency.

Within this context, the more typical forms of community-based correctional services include pretrial diversion projects; probation and parole; education and work-release activities; and furlough, restitution, and halfway house programs. Certain types of community-based correctional services, such as diversion programs and probation, are sometimes referred to as **intermediate sanctions**—sanctions falling between the extremes of fines and imprisonment.

The reasons for community-based correctional strategies encompass a range of humanitarian, fiscal, and pragmatic motives. *First,* along with the growth of the humanitarian movement in corrections, the notions of mercy and compassion, combined with considerations of human dignity, began to infiltrate sentencing practices and correctional decision making. For offenders who cannot help themselves, and for others who represent diminished risks to society, it is felt that custodial coercion might be unnecessary. *Second,* for an untold number of lesser and situational offenders, many reformers hold that the unfavorable consequences of imprisonment—loss of liberty and self-esteem, placement in physical jeopardy, and the fact that penitentiaries can be "schools of crime"—impede successful rehabilitation and community reintegration. *Third,* from an economic point of view, it generally costs far less to supervise criminals in the community than to maintain them in institutions. Moreover, the families of inmates often become financial burdens to the state. *Fourth,* many community-based correctional strategies have the practical value of helping offenders play productive roles in their neighborhoods and communities, as opposed to the more negative implications of imprisonment. *Fifth,* given the current trends in prison overcrowding, reducing or altogether eliminating the offender's period of confinement has been viewed as a more pragmatic approach to the management and control of the less seriously involved criminal offenders. And *sixth,* since the beginning of the 1960s, a "last resort" philosophy has developed in corrections. In this view, the traditional avenues of punishment and correction have not been working, and new, innovative approaches must be tested.

Criminal Justice Diversion

Criminal justice **diversion** refers to the removal of offenders from the application of the criminal law at any stage of the police and court processes.[2] It implies the formal halting or suspending of traditional criminal proceedings against individuals who have violated criminal statutes, in favor of processing them through some noncriminal disposition or means. Thus, diversion occurs *before* adjudication.

The Development of Diversion

Diversion is not a new practice. It has probably existed in an informal fashion for thousands of years, ever since the inception of organized law enforcement and social control. In both ancient and modern societies, informal diversion has occurred in many ways: A police officer removes a public drunk from the street to a Salvation Army shelter; a prosecutor decides to *nolle pros.* a petty theft; a magistrate releases with a lecture an individual who assaulted a neighbor during the course of an argument. These are generally discretionary decisions, made at random and off the record, and they tend to be personalized and inconsistent. They are often problematic in that they may reflect individual, class, or social prejudices. Moreover, they serve only to remove offenders from the application of criminal penalties; there is no attempt to provide appropriate alternatives.

Although these haphazard and unsystematic practices will continue, more formal diversion programs place offenders in social-therapeutic programs in lieu of conviction and punishment. These programs began to emerge within the juvenile justice system during the early part of the 20th century. Among the first was the *Chicago Boys' Court,* founded in 1914 as an extralegal form of probation. As explained many years ago by Chicago municipal court judge Jacob Braude, the rationale of the Boys' Court was to process and treat young offenders without branding them as criminals:

> While the facility of probation is available to the court, it is used at a minimum because before one can be admitted to probation he must first be found guilty. Having been found

guilty, he is stamped with a criminal record and then telling him to go out and make good is more likely to be a handicap than an order.[3]

The Boys' Court system of supervision placed a young defendant under the authority of one of four community agencies: the Holy Name Society, the Chicago Church Federation, the Jewish Social Service Bureau, or the Colored Big Brothers. After a time, the court requested a report of the defendant's activities and adjustment, and if it was favorable, he would be officially discharged from the court with no criminal record.

Later developments in youthful diversionary programs included New York City's Youth Counsel Bureau. This agency was established during the early 1950s to handle juveniles who were alleged to be delinquent or criminal but not deemed sufficiently advanced in their misbehavior to be adjudicated and committed by the courts.[4] Referrals came from police, courts, schools, and other sources. The bureau provided counseling services and discharged youths whose adjustment appeared promising. In many instances, defendants avoided not only criminal convictions but arrest records as well.

Other programs in the developing area of juvenile diversion included the District of Columbia's Project Crossroads, aimed at unemployed and underemployed first offenders aged 16 to 25, who were charged with property offenses.[5] Upon agreement to enter the program, a youth's charge was suspended for 90 days, during which time counseling, education, and employment services would be made available. At the end of the 3-month period, project staff would recommend either a *nolle pros.* of the charges, further treatment, or resumption of prosecution.

Patterns of Diversion

As criminal justice diversion continued to evolve, the arguments in its favor increased. It was felt that it would reduce court backlog, provide early intervention before the development of full-fledged criminal careers, ensure some consistency in selective law enforcement, reduce the costs of criminal processing, and enhance an offender's chances for community reintegration. More important, however, many social scientists and penal reformers had concluded that the criminal justice process, which was designed to protect society from criminals, often contributed to the very behavior it was trying to eliminate. This typically came about as a result of the following conditions:

1. Individuals convicted of criminal offenses were forced to interact with other, perhaps more experienced criminals, thus becoming socialized to a variety of criminal roles, learning the required skills and the criminal value system.
2. Convicted felons were denied opportunities to play legitimate roles.
3. The individual's self-concept was changed to that of a criminal. This occurs when individuals are told that they are criminals and placed in an institution where inmates and guards define them as criminals.[6]

Both the President's Commission on Law Enforcement and Administration of Justice in 1967 and the National Advisory Commission on Criminal Justice Standards and Goals in 1973 heavily endorsed the diversion concept, holding that it would not only offer a viable alternative to incarceration but also minimize the potential criminal socialization and labeling of first offenders.

Primarily as a result of massive federal funding for the prevention and reduction of crime, diversion programs of many types emerged during the 1970s and have expanded throughout the nation since the 1980s. Most are designed for youths, for individuals who commit minor crimes (such as assaults, simple thefts, and property damage resulting from neighborhood disputes), or for special offenders whose crimes are deemed to be related to problem drinking or drug use. For example:

1. *Youth service bureaus:* Specifically recommended by the President's Commission and begun in California during 1971, youth service bureaus are similar in concept

to New York's original Youth Council Bureau, but many operate as adjuncts to local police departments. They offer counseling, tutoring, crisis intervention, job assistance, and guidance for truants, runaways, and delinquent youths dealing with school and family problems.

2. *Public inebriate programs:* In municipalities where public intoxication remains a criminal offense, several types of diversionary alternatives to prosecution have been structured for public inebriates. Some are placed in alcohol detoxification centers rather than in jails. Others are referred before trial to community service agencies for more intensive treatment and care.

3. *Civil commitment:* Based on a medical model of rehabilitation, civil commitment programs were founded on the notion that some types of criminality result from symptoms of illness rather than malicious intent. Such offenders as drug users, sexual deviants, and the mentally ill might be diverted either before or after trial to a residential setting for therapeutic treatment. The community is protected by the removal of offenders to a rehabilitation center, while the offenders receive treatment instead of criminal sanctions and stigma. Civil commitment programs are most common in California, New York, and the federal system (for the treatment of drug abusers).

4. *Citizen dispute settlement:* Citizen dispute settlement programs are designed to deflect from the criminal justice system complaints related to family and neighborhood quarrels and evolving from petty crimes, simple assaults, property damage, threats, and bad checks. Cases are mediated by a disinterested third party at the family or neighborhood level. Local community service agencies provide help in addressing problem areas identified through mediation.

5. *Treatment Accountability for Safer Communities:* Better known as TASC, Treatment Accountability for Safer Communities is a program designed to be a liaison between the criminal justice system and community treatment programs. As a program for substance-abusing arrestees, probationers, and parolees, its more than 220 sites in 25 states make it the most widely supported form of court diversion in the United States (see Exhibit 17.1).

The Impact of Diversion

It is difficult to assess the overall value and impact of the national diversion effort. Many programs have never been evaluated, and estimations of their effectiveness have been based on little more than clinical intuition and hunch. Among those that have undergone rigorous assessment, the findings have ranged from promising to bleak. But as jail and prison populations continue to grow well beyond capacity, diversion programs remain popular because they permit judges to impose intermediate sanctions yet still avoid incarcerating offenders.

Community Service Programs

Often linked to diversion are *community service programs.* In many jurisdictions, defendants charged with petty offenses perform community service in lieu of prosecution or instead of incarceration upon conviction. New York City instituted such a program in 1992. Defendants receive a conditional discharge upon conviction and can be sentenced to provide up to 10 days of unpaid labor to the city. Work assignments typically include cleaning subway platforms, picking up debris in Central Park, assisting in homeless shelters, stuffing envelopes, and cleaning courtrooms and holding cells. Offenders placed in community service programs generally have been found guilty of lesser crimes such as shoplifting, soliciting prostitutes, and "fare-beating" (or "turnstile jumping" in the subway system).[7] Through much of the last decade, community service programs have been used in Baltimore, Chicago, New York, and several other cities in conjunction with "problem oriented policing" approaches. Under the "broken windows" theory discussed in Chapter 7, individuals arrested for panhandling, loiter-

"Could you elucidate on this item in your resume: '1992–1993,
500 hours' community service'?"

© 2005 Henry Martin from cartoonbank.com. All Rights Reserved.

ing, and similar "quality of life" crimes are sentenced to community cleanups and other public works initiatives.[8]

Probation

In the month of August, 1841, I was in court one morning, when the door communicating with the lock-room was opened and an officer entered, followed by a ragged and wretched looking man, who took his seat upon the bench allotted to prisoners. I imagined from the man's appearance that his offense was that of yielding to his appetite for intoxicating drinks, and in a few moments I found that my suspicions were correct, for the clerk read the complaint, in which the man was charged with being a common drunkard. The case was clearly made out, but before sentence had been passed, I conversed with him for a few moments, and found that he was not yet past all hope of reformation. . . . He told me that if he could be saved from the House of Correction, he never again would taste intoxicating liquors; there was such an earnestness in that tone, and a look of firm resolve, that I determined to aid him; I bailed him, by permission of the Court. He was ordered to appear for sentence in three weeks from that time. He signed the pledge and became a sober man; at the expiration of this period of probation, I accompanied him into the courtroom. . . . The Judge expressed himself much pleased with the account we gave of the man, and instead of the usual penalty—imprisonment in the House of Corrections—he fined him one cent and costs, amounting in all to $3.76, which was immediately paid. The man continued industrious and sober, and without doubt has been by this treatment, saved from a drunkard's grave.

—JOHN AUGUSTUS, 1852

The foregoing incident, which occurred during the latter part of 1841, gave birth to the concept of probation in the United States. John Augustus was a Boston shoemaker, and his method was to bail an offender after conviction and provide him with friend-

drugs, crime, and justice | EXHIBIT 17.1

Treatment Accountability for Safer Communities

Originally known as "Treatment Alternatives to Street Crime," TASC is a diversion approach that is designed to provide an objective and effective bridge between two separate institutions: the justice system and the drug abuse treatment community. The justice system's legal sanctions reflect community concerns for public safety and punishment, whereas the treatment community emphasizes therapeutic relationships as a means for changing individual behavior and reducing the personal suffering associated with substance abuse and other problems. Under TASC supervision, community-based treatment is made available to drug-dependent individuals who would otherwise burden the justice system with their persistent and associated criminality.

TASC programs were initiated in 1972 in response to recognized links between substance abuse and criminal behavior. The mission of TASC is to participate in justice system processing as early in the continuum as acceptable to participating agencies. TASC identifies, assesses, and refers appropriate drug- and/or alcohol-dependent offenders accused or convicted of nonviolent crimes to community-based substance abuse treatment as an alternative or supplement to existing justice system sanctions and procedures. TASC then monitors the drug-dependent offender's compliance with individually tailored progress expectations for abstinence, employment, and improved social and personal functioning. It then reports treatment results back to the referring justice system component. Clients who violate conditions of their justice mandate, TASC, or treatment agreement are usually sent back to the justice system for continued processing or sanctions.

To motivate treatment cooperation by the substance abuser, TASC combines the influence of legal sanctions for probable or proven crimes with the appeal of such innovative justice system dispositions as deferred prosecution, creative community sentencing, diversion, pretrial intervention, probation, and parole supervision. Through treatment referral and closely supervised community reintegration, TASC aims to permanently interrupt the vicious cycle of addiction, criminality, arrest, prosecution, conviction, incarceration, release, readdiction, criminality, and rearrest.

TASC programs not only offer renewed hope to drug- and alcohol-dependent clients by encouraging them to alter their lifestyles while remaining in their own communities; they also provide important incentives to other justice and treatment system participants. TASC can reduce the costs and relieve many processing burdens related to substance abuse within the justice system through assistance with such duties as addiction-related medical situations, pretrial screening, and posttrial supervision.

The treatment community also benefits from TASC's legal focus, which seems to motivate and prolong client cooperation in treatment programs and ensures clear definition and observation of criteria for treatment dismissal or completion. Public safety is also increased through TASC's careful supervision of criminally involved clients during their community-based treatment.

Although there has not been a national evaluation of the entire TASC effort, a number of studies over the years have found that the TASC initiative is meeting its intended operational goals. In short, the TASC experience has been a positive one. TASC has been demonstrated to be highly productive in (1) identifying populations of drug-involved offenders in great need of treatment; (2) assessing the nature and extent of their drug use patterns and specific treatment needs; (3) effectively referring drug-involved offenders to treatment; (4) serving as a link between criminal justice and treatment systems; and (5) providing constructive client identification and monitoring services for the courts, probation, and other segments of the criminal justice system.

Perhaps most importantly, evaluation data indicate that TASC-referred clients remain in treatment longer than non-TASC clients and, as a result, have better posttreatment success.

Sources: Treatment Accountability for Safer Communities, *Strategic Plan* (Washington, DC: National TASC, 2005); James A. Inciardi, Duane C. McBride, and James E. Rivers, *Drug Control and the Courts* (Thousand Oaks, CA: Sage Publications, 1996); James A. Inciardi and Duane C. McBride, *Treatment Alternatives to Street Crime: History, Experiences, and Issues* (Rockville, MD: National Institute on Drug Abuse, 1991).

ship and support in family matters, as well as job assistance. When the defendant was later brought to court for sentencing, Augustus would report on his progress toward reformation and request that the judge order a small fine and court costs in lieu of a jail sentence.[9] As such, Augustus could be considered the first probation officer. By 1858, he had bailed almost 2,000 defendants. His efforts led to the first probation statute, passed in Massachusetts in 1878. By 1900, four other states had enacted similar legislation, and probation became an established alternative to incarceration.

The Nature of Probation

Probation can be a rather confusing concept, for the term has been used in a variety of ways. First of all, probation is a sentence of conditional release to the community. More specifically, as defined by the American Bar Association, probation is a sentence not involving confinement that imposes conditions and retains authority in the sentencing

Former Olympic skater Tonya Harding performing community service work as part of her sentence after being convicted on a disorderly conduct charge.

court to modify the conditions of sentence or to resentence the offender if he or she violates the conditions.[10]

In addition to being a disposition, the word *probation* has also been used to refer to a status, a system, and a process.[11] As a status, probation reflects the unique character of the probationer: He or she is neither a free citizen nor a confined prisoner. As a system, probation is a component in the administration of justice, as embodied by the agency or organization that administers the probation process. As a process, probation refers to the set of functions, activities, and services that characterize the system's transactions with the courts, the offender, and the community. This process includes preparation of reports for the courts, supervision of probationers, and obtaining and providing services for them.

The Probation Philosophy

The premise behind the use of probation is that many offenders are not dangerous and represent little, if any, menace to society. It has been argued that when defendants are institutionalized, the prison community becomes their new reference point. They are forced into contact with hard-core criminals, the prison experience generates embitterment and hostility, and the "ex-con" label becomes a stigma that impedes social adjustment. Probation provides a more therapeutic alternative. The term comes from the Latin *probare,* meaning "to test or prove"; the probationer is given the opportunity to demonstrate that if given a second chance, he or she will engage in more socially acceptable behavior.

The probation philosophy also includes elements of community protection and offender rehabilitation. Probationers are supervised by agents of the court or probation agency. These are trained personnel with dual roles. They are present to ensure that the conditions of probation are fulfilled and to provide counseling and assistance in community reintegration. Moreover, as with all types of community-based correction, it is generally agreed that rehabilitation of offenders is more realistically possible in the natural environment of the free community than behind prison walls.

While these are the philosophical underpinnings of probation, several more pragmatic issues have entered into its use as an alternative to imprisonment. First, as noted in Chapters 15 and 16, correctional institutions throughout the nation have become painfully overcrowded. In view of the almost prohibitive costs of new prison construction, probation is seen by many as a more economically viable correctional alternative. Second, and also as a matter of simple economics, the probation process is considerably cheaper than the prison process. The cost of maintaining an inmate in prison has been estimated to average some $30,000 per year.[12] Probation costs are less than one-tenth of that amount. Third, within some sectors of the criminal justice community, imprisonment is being viewed more and more as cruel and unusual punishment. Prisons are dangerous places to live. Inmates are physically, sexually, and emotionally victimized on a regular basis. Probation is considered to be a more humane form of correctional intervention.

Suspended Sentences and Conditional Release

A variety of terms are used interchangeably with *probation* but represent quite different concepts. The best known of these is the **suspended sentence,** a disposition that implies supervision of the offender with a set of specified criteria and goals. The suspended sentence is a form of quasi-freedom that can be revoked at the pleasure of the court. Suspended sentences are of two types: *suspension of imposition* of sentence and *suspension of execution* of sentence. In the case of suspension of imposition (which is not common), there may be a verdict or plea, but no sentence is pronounced. The presiding magistrate releases the defendant on the general condition that he or she stay out of trouble and make restitution for the crime. With the suspension of execution, the sentence is prescribed but is postponed or not carried out. In a number of jurisdictions, a sentence can be suspended, and this suspension is followed by an order for probation.

Alternatively, the laws of several states provide for sentences of *conditional discharge* and *unconditional discharge.* The sentence of conditional discharge is similar to a suspended sentence:

> The court may impose a sentence of conditional discharge for an offense if the court, having regard to the nature and circumstances of the offense and to the history, character, and condition of the defendant, is of the opinion that neither the public interest nor the interests of justice would be served by a sentence of imprisonment and that probation supervision is not appropriate.[13]

In the penal codes of New York, for example, the period of conditional discharge is 1 year for a misdemeanor and 3 years for a felony, and the conditions generally involve making restitution or reparation for losses suffered by the victim. The sentence of unconditional discharge goes one step further: The defendant is released without imprisonment, fine, probation, or any conditions whatsoever. Such a sentence is used when it is the opinion of the court that no proper purpose is served by the imposition of conditions. However, it should be stressed that such a discharge is nevertheless a final judgment of conviction.[14]

The Presentence or Probation Investigation

Probation is administered by hundreds of independent government agencies, each jurisdiction operating under different laws and many with widely varying philosophies. In some jurisdictions, such as Hawaii and Delaware, a single state authority provides services for all probationers. In other jurisdictions, probation descends from county or municipal authority, functioning under state laws and guidelines, but is administered by the lower courts. In some areas, such as South Carolina, probation and parole are combined into a single state unit. In the federal system, probation is administered as an arm of the federal district courts.

Probationers in the United States, 1980–2004

Source: Bureau of Justice Statistics.

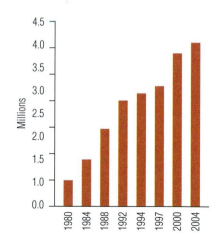

The presentence investigation is one of the basic services provided by the probation agency. As noted in Chapter 13, such reports are generally mandatory if probation appears to be a possible sentence. Almost all presentence reports are conducted by the probation authority. However, some are done privately, commissioned by the accused's defense attorney.[15] The idea is that since probation officers are overworked, a privately commissioned report can be more thorough and comprehensive and can be slanted toward the interests of the defendant. On occasion, in the classified section of *The National Law Journal,* one can find advertisements by attorneys, criminal justice professors, and former probation officers who, for a fee, will conduct a presentence investigation and write a report.

In their examination of the backgrounds and characteristics of defendants, presentence reports can vary widely in depth, content, and usefulness. In some regional offices in South Carolina, for example, selected presentence investigation reports are less than a page long and contain only the basic facts of the defendant's criminal history and current offense, followed by a brief statement of the offender's prognosis and the probation agent's recommendation for sentencing. In contrast, some presentence investigations conducted in Kings County (Brooklyn), New York, take up more than 30 single-spaced legal-size pages and recount numerous aspects of the defendant's life, including whether he or she had a normal birth experience. The norm is somewhere between these two extremes, however, and includes the characteristics of the offender, the circumstances of his or her offense, an evaluative summary, and a recommendation.

Studies have demonstrated that in most sentences involving probation, there is a high correlation between the presentence or probation officer's recommendation and the judge's sentencing decision.[16] This should not suggest, however, that judicial decision making is dictated by the content of a presentence report recommendation or that judges and presentence investigators interpret defendants' life histories and background characteristics in the same way. Rather, there are a number of more logical factors at work. First, because probation is one of the most common sentences, the simple laws of chance are operative. Second, most criminal convictions occur as the result of guilty pleas. The details of the plea negotiation and the prosecutor's sentencing recommendation are generally known to the presentence investigator, and these typically influence his or her recommendation. Third, presentence or probation officers tend to be aware of the sentencing recommendations that will be acceptable to specific judges for given kinds of cases, and they often take the path of least resistance.[17]

The U.S. Supreme Court has upheld the validity of the presentence investigation as meeting the due process requirements of the Constitution. In ***Williams* v. *New York,***[18] decided in 1949, the Court held that, at sentencing, a convicted defendant does not have a Sixth Amendment right to cross-examine individuals who have supplied information to the court (in a presentence report) regarding sentencing. However, the Supreme Court has given defendants some safeguards in this matter. In the 1977 case of *Gardner* v. *Florida,*[19] for example, the Court ruled that a defendant is denied due process when a sentence is based, even in part, on confidential information contained in a presentence report that the defendant is not given the opportunity to deny or explain. Although both *Williams* and *Gardner* dealt with presentence reports in the context of capital cases, subsequent decisions in state courts of appeals served to apply the Court's rulings to noncapital cases as well.

Conditions of Probation

Most states have statutory restrictions on the granting of probation. In some jurisdictions, defendants who have been convicted of such crimes as murder, kidnapping, and rape are ineligible for probation, as are second- and third-felony offenders. Other states tend to be less specific, but structure their penal codes in such a manner as to preclude a sentence of probation for most serious offenders. In Alabama, for example, individuals convicted of crimes that typically call for sentences of death or imprisonment for 10 years or more are ineligible for probation.[20] In North Carolina, "a person who has been convicted of any noncapital criminal offense not punishable by a minimum term of life imprisonment may be placed on probation."[21]

Thus, in most jurisdictions, probation is a statutory alternative to imprisonment for most felony convictions. Judges differ, however, in their approaches to granting it. As noted earlier, both plea bargaining and information contained in the presentence report enter into the decision. Other factors are the prosecutor's recommendation, anticipated community reaction, political considerations, the court's backlog, the availability of space in the prison system, and the judge's own feelings toward the particular offense or the offender. A Delaware judge made the following comment to the author:

> Although the statutes permit it, I find sentences of imprisonment for convictions of marijuana possession to be unreasonable. . . . However, in *my court,* any person found guilty of a felony offense involving the exploitation of a child, sexually or otherwise, will receive the maximum term of imprisonment that the law allows.

Upon the granting of probation and as part of their probation agreement, defendants are required to abide by a variety of regulations and conditions. These are fairly standard from state to state. They exhort the probationer to live a law-abiding and productive life, to work, to support his or her dependents, to maintain contact with the supervising probation officer, and to remain within the jurisdiction of the court.

Special conditions of probation may also be imposed, either by the sentencing judge or by the supervising probation agency. Many of these have been challenged as "improper," but most have been upheld by state appellate courts. Court decisions have affirmed the correctness of special requirements such as undergoing treatment for drug abuse,[22] abstaining from the use of alcohol,[23] serving a short jail sentence prior to release on probation with no credit for prior confinement,[24] refraining from operating a motor vehicle during the period of probation,[25] submitting to a search by the supervising probation officer,[26] and payment of restitution.[27]

Some special conditions are very specific yet at the same time trivial, but these too have been affirmed by the courts. In one New York case, for example, the court found proper a condition of probation that required a person convicted of embezzling from the bank account of a cemetery association to mow the lawn in the local cemetery during the grass-cutting season.[28] More recently, a federal judge in Fort Worth, Texas, ordered a woman and her four children to attend church services every Sunday for a year as part of the conditions of her probation. The woman had been charged with trafficking and possession of drugs, and she faced up to 3 years' imprisonment and a $250,000 fine. The judge did not require her to fulfill her probation agreement specifically in a Christian church; she could attend services of any denomination or faith.[29]

Since the beginning of the 1980s, a new condition of probation has become common: In more than half the states, probation clients are being assessed a fee for services. Supervision services typically range from $10 to $30 per month, with presentence investigation costs running from $100 to $300.[30] Although there are waivers for the indigent, nonpayment must be sanctioned by the court or probation agency. Texas is among the most successful states in collecting fees from probationers. Officials estimate that probation departments in Texas collect fees from at least 90% of all misdemeanor probationers and 65% of all felony offenders on probation. Collected fees have paid for more than 50% of the cost of basic supervision. In one year, for example, Texas spent more than $100 million on the supervision of probationers but collected $57.2 million in fees.[31]

Generally, conditions of probation are considered constitutional and proper unless they bear no reasonable relationship to the crime committed or the defendant's probationary status. Thus, placement in a drug treatment program becomes an appropriate condition of probation only when the offense is considered to be a consequence of a drug abuse problem. Conversely, staying away from places where children congregate would be an improper condition for probationers who had never been convicted of child molesting.

In *Griffin* v. *Wisconsin,*[32] decided in 1987, the Supreme Court ruled that state regulations permitting probation officers to conduct searches of probationers' homes

"Since you're still under house arrest, Dad, can I borrow the car tonight?"

© 2005 Frank Cotham from cartoonbank.com. All Rights Reserved.

Can Reading *Maxim* Magazine Result in Jail Time?

For a 23-year-old sex offender it did because his probation agreement prohibited having "sexually stimulating" material. The probation violation resulted in 6 days in the Dade County Jail.

Source: *Miami Herald,* July 17, 2005, A1. ■

without warrants, upon "reasonable grounds" (rather than probable cause) to believe that contraband might be found, do not violate the Fourth Amendment. However, while warrantless searches of probationers, their automobiles, and premises are permissible if carried out by probation officers with just cause, the courts have ruled that such searches cannot be extended to all law enforcement officers.[33]

Restitution Programs

Among the more widely endorsed conditions of probation in recent years is **restitution:** requiring offenders to compensate their victims for damages or stolen property (monetary restitution) or donate their time to community service (community service restitution).

There are numerous rationales for restitution. First, while fines go into court or government treasuries, monetary restitution goes directly to the victims of crime, compensating them for injuries, time lost from work, and other losses. Second, restitution forces the offender to take personal responsibility for his or her crime. Third, it has the potential for reconciling victims and offenders. Fourth, it can be incorporated into a probation program without the need for additional programs and expenditures. And fifth, it provides a vehicle for including the victim in the administration of justice.[34]

Despite these apparent virtues, restitution has its critics. It has been suggested that restitution can be a punitive sanction rather than a rehabilitative one, since it places an additional burden on offenders that they might not ordinarily have. More important, restitution carries the potential for nullifying any deterrent effects of punishment by allowing criminals to "write a check" and "pay a fee" for their offenses. Finally, it can be argued that restitution serves only the interests of people who can afford it. Although in many ways this latter argument is true, there are a number of alternatives that make restitution available to offenders at all levels of the socioeconomic ladder. There are, for example, community service restitution outlets through which juvenile vandals can work to repair the damage they have caused, drunk drivers can work in alcohol detoxification centers, and other offenders can work in hospitals, nursing homes, or juvenile counseling programs.[35]

In cases of white-collar crime, judges typically attach heavy restitution payments to offenders' sentences—money to compensate victims for their losses. These assessments, often announced with considerable media attention, take on even greater importance given that most prison sentences imposed on white-collar criminals tend to be short, if sentences are imposed at all. However, despite the fanfare, it would appear that many of these restitution orders are never enforced. A study by the General Accounting Office in 2002 found that the amount of criminal debt owed in federal cases, but uncollected, increased from $5.6 billion in 1995 to $13 billion in 1999 and to $16.2 billion by 2002.[36]

Probation Services

At least in theory, probation service incorporates the casework approach. During the probationer's initial interview with the probation officer, an evaluation is made to determine what type of treatment supervision is most appropriate. On the basis of information contained in the presentence investigation and on his or her skills in counseling and problem solving, the officer plans a treatment schedule designed to allow the probationer to make a reasonable community adjustment. He or she examines the probationer's peer relationships, family problems, work skills and history, educational status, and involvement with drug or alcohol abuse. During the course of the probation period, the officer works with the offender in these designated areas as required. The treatment may be limited to one-to-one counseling, or it may involve referral to community service agencies for drug abuse treatment, vocational skill enhancement, or job assistance. Some probation agencies have special supervision units with officers specifically trained in these areas. Others provide psychiatric services or structured group counseling programs.

Unpaid debt

Criminals owe billions in restitution, and the numbers keep soaring. Source: General Accounting Office.

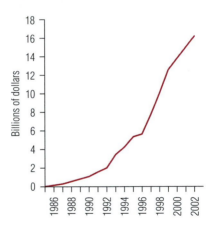

Kansas City, Missouri, police officers entering the residence of a high-risk probation violator.

Because probationers are convicted criminal offenders and one of the officer's roles involves community protection, a second function of the intake interview is to determine what level of community supervision appears necessary. Such supervision can involve regular visits to the probationer's home and place of employment and can require him or her to report to the probation office on a weekly, semimonthly, or monthly basis.

Although many probation agencies do operate in the manner outlined, in practice few probationers receive such individualized treatment and supervision, for many reasons. *First,* the educational backgrounds, skills, and experiences of probation officers vary widely. A number of agencies require graduate education and related experience for a career in probation work, but others have no such prerequisites. This often results in the recruitment of inexperienced college graduates, and probation becomes an entry-level position for employment in the criminal justice field. Moreover, in some states high school graduates with no training in counseling, psychology, social work, or any other behavioral field have managed to obtain jobs in the probation area. *Second,* like members of any occupation or profession, many probation officers have little dedication or interest in their work. This often results in apathy toward their clients' needs and problems, an avoidance of responsibility, and the "stealing of time" during business hours.

A *third* problem is the low level of career mobility in probation work. Combined with moderate to low salaries in many jurisdictions are limited opportunities for advancement. This results in frustration, dissatisfaction, cynicism, and high staff turnover. In addition, there is the issue of caseload size. Workloads range from a dozen probationers per officer in a few agencies to more than many hundreds per officer in others. By law, for example, Arizona probationers can have no more than 60 cases, but in Los Angeles, the county's 44 officers were supervising 33,000 probationers in 2000, and one San Francisco probation officer had a caseload of 3,500 clients.[37] The treatment and supervision aspects of probation become even further diluted by the need to perform presentence investigations. In consequence, treatment sometimes becomes reduced to making a telephone call every other week to determine whether a probationer is managing to hold a job, and supervision amounts to as little as one mail contact each month to determine whether probationers are residing where they say they are.

Finally, as with police work, probation officers can differ dramatically in approaches to their work and attitudes toward their clients. There are probably many who can successfully fulfill their dual role as clinicians and supervisors. However, there are also many who are exclusively "social workers" or "rule enforcers." In addition, there are "legalists," who stress the upholding of law for its own sake; there are "company agents," who focus almost exclusively on rising in the hierarchy of the probation organization; and there are the stereotyped "civil service hacks," who think of little else than the number of years left until retirement and in the meantime work hard at getting the lion's share of days off, sick pay, fringe benefits, lunch hours, and coffee breaks. Each of these types can negatively affect a probationer's potential for readjustment.

Most clinicians would agree that even the most dedicated workers, including probation officers, often limit the impact of the assistance they provide by not giving enough help to those who could benefit most. Throughout the human services network, including offender rehabilitation agencies, the nature of the clients served varies widely. At one end of the spectrum, perhaps 5 percent to 25 percent, are clients with a minimum of problems. Many are highly motivated to fulfill the terms of their probation, and no matter what support and assistance is or is not provided, their chances of success are high. At the opposite end are another 5 percent to 25 percent who are so dysfunctional and committed to an antisocial lifestyle that little can change them. With or without service and treatment, most of these typically fail. Those in the middle, the remaining 50 percent to 90 percent, can go either way, depending on the nature and intensity of the service and supervision provided. These are the ones who could benefit most from rehabilitation programs. Yet there is a tendency to focus the majority of energy and services on those who appear to need them most. As a result, within the probation system it is the most dysfunctional clients—those who will potentially profit the least—who receive most of the treatment and supervision available. In consequence, the middle group, that large percentage whose behavior is most receptive to change, tends to be neglected.

Shock Probation

Shock probation gives an offender a little taste of the bars.

— OHIO PROSECUTOR

In 1965, the Ohio state legislature passed the first **shock probation** law in the United States, allowing judges to incarcerate an offender for a brief part of the sentence, suspend the remainder, and place him or her on probation. Under the Ohio statute, shock probation (also known as a *mixed* or *split* sentence) is not part of the original sentence. Rather, the defendant can file a petition requesting it between 30 to 60 days after sentencing, or the judge can order it in the absence of any petition. Its "shock" value comes from the contention that the staggering effect of exposure to prison or jail can be a significant deterrent to crime. Eligibility for shock probation procedures follows the same statutory guidelines that govern the granting of probation in general.

Opinions regarding the suitability of shock probation as a rehabilitative tool are mixed. From a positive standpoint, it represents a way for the courts to do the following:

• Impress offenders with the seriousness of their actions without imposing a long prison sentence.
• Release offenders found by the institutions to be more amenable to community-based treatment than was realized by the courts at the time of sentence.
• Arrive at a just compromise between punishment and leniency in appropriate cases.
• Provide community-based treatment for offenders who can be rehabilitated, while still imposing deterrent sentences where public policy demands it.[38]

In addition, because the imprisonment is only short-term, the offender is less likely to be absorbed into the "hard rock" inmate culture. At the same time, the costs of shock probation are significantly lower than those of a full period of incarceration.

Opponents of shock probation argue vigorously that it is counterproductive as a rehabilitative tool. First, its deterrent effect is limited or totally negated by the job loss and broken community ties associated with incarceration, however brief. Second, the purpose of probation is to *avoid* incarceration, not supplement it. Third, even a short period of incarceration can expose offenders to hardened criminals and the hostilities and resentment of prison life. Fourth, it stigmatizes offenders for having been in jail or prison and may damage their self-concept. Fifth, and perhaps most important, prison and probation are at opposite ends of the punishment–rehabilitation continuum; they are mutually exclusive and therefore should not be mixed.

Although shock probation may be functional from the perspective of the criminal justice system in terms of the lower costs of probation versus imprisonment and the alleviation of prison overcrowding, there is no evidence demonstrating that it reduces recidivism. Several empirical studies have examined the shock probation experience, but the findings remain inconclusive.[39] In the opinion of the National Institute of Justice, shock probation and "split sentences" *do not* reduce repeat offending.[40]

Intensive Probation Supervision

Intensive probation supervision is a program of closer surveillance and more exhaustive services that place a probationer under tighter control than he or she might experience under regular probation. Although it is not a particularly new concept, it has received considerable attention in recent years because of the dual purposes it serves, given today's overcrowded penitentiaries and escalating criminal justice costs. First, it restrains the growth of prison populations and associated costs by controlling selected offenders in the community. Second, and at the same time, it satisfies at least a part of society's demand that offenders be punished for their crimes.[41]

The degree of surveillance varies considerably from one jurisdiction to another. In general, caseloads are small and there are frequent contacts between the probationer and the probation officer in the home, on the job, and at the probation office. The Georgia program is widely regarded as the most stringent, with standards including these:

- Five face-to-face contacts per week.
- Mandatory community service.
- Mandatory employment.
- Mandatory curfew.
- Weekly checks of local arrest records.
- Routine alcohol and drug testing.[42]

As for the effectiveness of intensive probation supervision, research data suggest somewhat mixed and ambiguous results. For example, in a comprehensive study of 14 intensive probation supervision programs in nine states, no clear relationship was found between frequency of contact and recidivism.[43] Offenders under intensive supervision were just as likely as those on regular probation to commit a crime. Nor was there any indication that probationers under intensive supervision were rearrested for less serious crimes than their counterparts. Intensive supervision programs did, however, succeed in altering offenders' perceptions about crime. Those in intensive programs believed that their chances of getting caught for a crime while on probation were high, particularly if the crime involved drug use. They also believed that, if caught, they would be treated more harshly than offenders on regular probation. Finally, the study found that while intensive supervision programs are not necessarily more cost-effective than regular probation, they are considerably cheaper than housing offenders in prison.

Probation Violation and Revocation

Because probation is a conditional release, it does not guarantee absolute freedom. Arrests for new crimes or violations of the conditions of probation can result in *revocation of probation* and imprisonment of the offender.

As noted earlier, the conditions of probation are established by statute, and special conditions can be imposed by the sentencing court. There has been little argument as to whether a new arrest constitutes a violation of probation. Moreover, the appellate courts have given the lower courts considerable latitude in imposing conditions of probation. Thus, such technical violations as nonpayment of a fine imposed as a condition of probation, failure to pay off civil judgments for fraud though able to pay, failure to make child support payments, failure to report to one's probation officer, and driving

Actor Robert Downey, Jr., jailed on more than one occasion for drug violations

while intoxicated, to name only a few types of violations, have been grounds for revocation. *Absconding* from probation supervision—that is, failing to report and concealing oneself from the probation authorities—represents another serious violation of probation.

The issue of probation violation tends to underscore the tremendous discretionary authority of the probation officer. Technical violations generally come to the attention only of the supervising officer. If the defendant fails to report, reverts to using drugs, consorts with known criminals, refuses to remain gainfully employed, or fails to live up to other conditions of the probation contract, the officer has several options. He or she can cite the probationer for violation, can engage in more intensive counseling and supervision, or can simply "look the other way." Thus, violation proceedings are initiated by the probation officer, and these generally begin only when revocation is the course decided on. It should be emphasized, however, that although the probation officer or department can recommend revocation, *only the court has the authority to revoke probation.*

In the event of a new arrest, a warrant may be lodged against the probationer in order to prevent his or her release on bail. If the violation is only technical, a warrant may also be issued and the violator taken into custody by either the police or probation authorities. Some jurisdictions issue such warrants as a matter of course; others do so only when there is evidence that the probationer would abscond if left in the community pending a revocation hearing.

Once the probation authorities decide to seek revocation, the offender is given notice of the decision, the probation officer prepares a violation report, and a formal court hearing is scheduled. Until recently, revocation hearings included few procedural safeguards. In 1967, however, the U.S. Supreme Court held in **Mempa v. Rhay** that a probationer has a constitutional right to counsel at any revocation proceeding where the imposition of sentence had been suspended but would be enjoined following revocation.[44] In 1972, the Court ruled in **Morrissey v. Brewer** that when the potential for revocation of parole is at issue, an informal inquiry is required to determine whether there is probable cause to believe that the parolee has indeed violated the conditions of parole.[45] The Court added the mandate of a formal revocation hearing as well, within minimum due process requirements.

While *Morrissey* was a parole case, its significance for probationers came the following year with **Gagnon v. Scarpelli.**[46] In this decision the Court extended its holding in *Morrissey* to probationers and also held that both probationers and parolees have a constitutionally limited right to counsel during revocation proceedings. Exhibit 17.2 explores these three cases in more detail.

In the years since *Mempa, Morrissey,* and *Gagnon,* both state and federal courts have made a number of significant decisions regarding revocation proceedings. In *United States* v. *Reed,*[47] a U.S. circuit court of appeals stressed the rehabilitative nature of probation and indicated that the accumulation of a few minor technical violations should not necessarily be grounds for revocation. In *United States* v. *Pattman,*[48] the court ruled that hearsay evidence that is "demonstrably reliable" need not be subject to confrontation and cross-examination in revocation proceedings. In other decisions, courts have held that revocation can be based on conduct occurring prior to the actual granting of probation,[49] that a probationer may not invoke the Fifth Amendment privilege against self-incrimination in revocation proceedings when asked to testify about technical violations of probation,[50] and that evidence to support a revocation of probation need not establish guilt "beyond a reasonable doubt."[51]

The Effectiveness of Probation

Probation is by far the most widely used criminal sanction. At the end of 2004, for example, over 4.1 million offenders were under probation supervision in the United States.[52] Half had been convicted of a misdemeanor (50%), 49 percent had been convicted of a felony, and 1 percent were for other infractions.

There are reasons for this widespread use of probation, most stemming from economic and humanitarian considerations. In addition, some observers believe that probation is the most effective phase of the criminal justice process. This notion has been called into serious question, however, as the vast majority of studies of probation effectiveness are more than three decades old. Moreover, these studies may not be meaningful as indicators of the success of probation. More recent data contradict the findings of the earlier research.

One of the more comprehensive studies of probation effectiveness found that most felony offenders placed on probation were still a considerable threat to the community.[53] Commissioned by the National Institute of Justice and conducted by the Rand Corporation during the 1980s, the study examined 1,672 felony cases from California's Los Angeles and Alameda counties. During the 40-month follow-up period of the study, 65 percent of those placed on probation were rearrested. Almost 80 percent of these, or 51 percent of the entire sample, were convicted of new crimes. Of the sample, 18 percent were reconvicted of serious violent crimes, and 34 percent were reincarcerated. Charges were filed against 53 percent of the felony probationers: 19 percent had only one charge, 12 percent had two charges, and 22 percent had three or more charges against them. Moreover, 51 percent of the entire study population experienced a filing for property crime, 24 percent for violent crime, and 14 percent for a drug law violation. (The percentages were based on 2,608 charges; some of the 1,672 cases had multiple charges.)

The Rand study, however, described only one population. In 1986, researchers at Southeast Missouri State University conducted a similar study for the state of Missouri.[54] A total of 2,083 felons from the most urban population in Missouri were tracked for 40 months, but with very different results. The rearrest rates were considerably lower in Missouri than in California. This suggests that the effectiveness of probation varies from one jurisdiction to the next and that individual studies of probation effectiveness may not be representative of felony probation in general. A recent analysis of probation by the Department of Justice came to the same conclusion.[55] A number of studies suggest that probation can have a positive impact when it occurs in conjunction with treatment for drug abuse.[56]

EXHIBIT 17.2 | LAW & CRIMINAL JUSTICE

Due Process and Revocation Hearings

Mempa v. _Rhay,_ 398 U.S. 128 (1967)

On June 17, 1959, a court in Spokane, Washington, convicted 17-year-old Jerry Douglas Mempa of "joyriding" (riding in a stolen automobile). His conviction was based on a guilty plea entered with the advice of his court-appointed counsel. The court suspended the imposition of his sentence and placed him on probation for a period of 2 years.

Several months later, the county prosecutor moved for the revocation of Mempa's probation on the allegation that he participated in a burglary on September 15, 1959. At the revocation hearing, Mempa was not represented by counsel, nor was he asked if he wished counsel. Mempa admitted participation in the burglary, and the sole testimony connecting him with the crime came from a probation officer. There was no cross-examination of the officer's statement. Without asking Mempa if he had anything to say or any evidence to supply, the court revoked his probation and sentenced him to 10 years in the state penitentiary.

In 1965, Mempa petitioned for a writ of _habeas corpus,_ claiming he had been deprived of his right to counsel at the revocation proceeding at which the sentence was imposed. The Washington Supreme Court denied his petition, however. On appeal, the United States Supreme Court ruled in Mempa's favor. In its opinion, the High Court did not question the authority of the state of Washington to provide for a deferred sentencing procedure coupled with its probation provisions. However, it emphasized that the "appointment of counsel for an indigent is required at every stage of a criminal proceeding where substantial rights of a criminal accused may be affected."

Mempa v. _Rhay_ resulted in a variety of judicial interpretations. The Supreme Court's holding required that counsel be provided only at those revocation proceedings involving deferred sentencing and did not apply to cases when the probationer was sentenced at the time of trial. Many lower courts treated the decision in exactly that way. However, other courts extended _Mempa_ to all revocation proceedings, with the view that any revocation hearing was a "critical stage" that required due process protection. Furthermore, although _Mempa_ applied only to probation revocation hearings, a number of courts interpreted it to apply to parole as well.

Morrissey v. _Brewer,_ 408 U.S. 471 (1972)

The decision in _Morrissey_ v. _Brewer_ related to parole revocation, but since parole and probation revocation are similar in nature, it had potential significance for both types of proceedings.

In 1967, John Morrissey was convicted in an Iowa court of falsely drawing checks, and he was sentenced to a maximum term of 7 years' imprisonment. He was released on parole the following year, but within 7 months Morrissey was cited for violation of his parole. He was arrested, and he admitted to purchasing an automobile without permission, obtaining credit under an assumed name, having become involved in an automobile accident, and failing to report these and other matters to his parole officer. He maintained that he had not contacted his parole officer due to sickness.

One week later, the parole violation report was reviewed, parole was revoked, and Morrissey was returned to prison. On a _habeas corpus_ petition to the U.S. district court, Morrissey claimed that he had been denied due process under the Fourteenth Amendment in that his parole had been revoked without a hearing. The district court denied his petition, the U.S. court of appeals affirmed the lower-court decision, and the U.S. Supreme Court granted _certiorari._

The Court began its opinion stating that the revocation of parole is not part of a criminal prosecution and thus the full panoply of rights due a defendant in such a proceeding would not apply. However, the Court went on to state that parole revocation involves the potential termination of an individual's liberty and, therefore, that certain due process safeguards are necessary to ensure that the finding of a parole violation is based on verified facts to support the revocation.

In establishing procedural safeguards, the Court considered parole revocation to be a two-stage process: (1) the arrest of the parolee and the preliminary hearing and (2) the revocation hearing. In desig-

| Parole |

I believe there are many who might be so trained as to be left on their parole during the last period of their imprisonment with safety.

— DR. SAMUEL G. HOWE, 1846

The granting of parole is an act of grace, comparable to the pardoning power that was once the prerogative of the monarchy. As such, it is infected from the outset with the arbitrariness and unpredictability that is characteristic of penal institutions and other autocracies.

— JESSICA MITFORD, 1974

Parole, a term that comes from the French meaning "word of honor" and was first used in 1846 by the Boston penal reformer Samuel G. Howe,[57] refers to the practice of allowing offenders to serve the final portion of a prison sentence in the community. More specifically:

nating a preliminary hearing for all parole violators, the Court held as follows:

> Such an inquiry should be seen in the nature of a preliminary hearing to determine whether there is probable cause or reasonable grounds to believe that the arrested parolee had committed acts which would constitute a violation of parole condition.

The Court also specified that at this preliminary review, the hearing officer should be someone not involved in the case and that the parolee should be given notice of the hearing and the opportunity to be present during the questioning of persons providing adverse information regarding the alleged violation. Subsequently, a determination should be made to decide if the parolee's continued detention is warranted.

In reference to the revocation hearing, the Court held as follows:

> The parolee must have an opportunity to be heard and to show, if he can, that he did not violate the conditions or if he did, that circumstances in mitigation suggest the violation does not warrant revocation. The revocation hearing must be tendered within a reasonable time after the parolee is taken into custody. A lapse of two months as the state suggests occurs in some cases would not appear to be unreasonable.

And in terms of due process at revocation hearings:

> Our task is limited to deciding the minimum requirements of due process. They include (a) written notice of the claimed violation of parole; (b) disclosure to the parolee of evidence against him; (c) opportunity to be heard in person and to present witnesses and documentary evidence; (d) the right to confront and cross-examine adverse witnesses (unless the hearing officer specifically finds good cause for not allowing confrontation); (e) a "neutral and detached" hearing body such as a traditional parole board, members of which need not be judicial officers or lawyers; and (f) a written statement by the fact finders as to the evidence relied on and reasons for revoking parole.

> However, the Court left open the question of counsel: "We do not reach or decide the question whether the parolee is entitled to the assistance of retained appointed counsel if he is indigent."

Gagnon v. Scarpelli, 411 U.S. 778 (1973)

During the year following *Morrissey,* the issue of right to counsel at revocation proceedings again came before the Court. In July 1965, Gerald Scarpelli pleaded guilty in a Wisconsin court to a charge of armed robbery. He was sentenced to a term of 15 years' imprisonment, but the judge suspended his sentence and placed him on probation for a period of 7 years. The following month, he was arrested on a burglary charge, his probation was revoked without a hearing, and he was incarcerated in the Wisconsin State Reformatory to begin serving his original 15-year sentence.

Some 3 years later, Scarpelli applied for a writ of *habeas corpus.* After the petition had been filed, but before it had been acted on, Scarpelli was released on parole. A U.S. district court judge ruled that the petition was not moot because of Scarpelli's parole status, because the original revocation carried "collateral consequences," namely, the restraints imposed by his parole. The district court then held that the revocation of probation without a hearing and counsel was a denial of due process. The court of appeals affirmed, and the state of Wisconsin appealed to the United States Supreme Court.

In its decision, the Supreme Court made two points. First:

> Probation revocation, like parole revocation, is not a stage of a criminal prosecution, but does result in loss of liberty. Accordingly, we hold that a probationer, like a parolee, is entitled to a preliminary hearing and a final revocation hearing in the conditions specified in *Morrissey* v. *Brewer.*

And furthermore:

> Counsel should be provided in cases where, after being informed of his right to request counsel the probationer or parolee makes such a request based on a timely or colorable claim:
>
> 1. That he has not committed the alleged violation of the conditions upon which he is at liberty; or
> 2. That, even if the violation is a matter of public record or is uncontested, there are substantial reasons that justified or mitigated the violation and made revocation inappropriate, and that the reasons are complex or otherwise difficult to develop or present.

> [Parole is] the status of being released from a penal or reformatory institution in which one has served a part of his maximum sentence, on the condition of maintaining good behavior and remaining in the custody and under the guidance of the institution or some other agency approved by the state until a final discharge is granted.[58]

Thus, parole actually comprises two operations: (1) "parole release," the procedures used to establish the actual periods of confinement that prisoners serve, and (2) "parole supervision," the conditions and provisions that regulate parolees' lives outside of prison until the final discharge from their sentence.

For almost a century, parole has been an established part of American correctional theory and practice. It has had the ostensible purposes of ensuring that imprisonment is tailored to the needs of the inmate, reducing the harshness of long prison sentences, and hastening the offender's reintegration into the community when it appears that he or she is able to function as a law-abiding citizen. In addition, it has had the more subtle goals of alleviating the overcrowded conditions of correctional institutions and assisting in maintaining social control within prisons through the threat of denial of parole as punishment for misbehavior.

The Origins of Parole

As a combination and extension of penal practices, parole has a long history. It seems to have first appeared in a rudimentary form when the British economy declined during the latter part of the 16th century.[59] In the colonies, the need for cheap labor was critical. The British government began granting reprieves and stays of execution to felons who were physically able to work so that they could be transported to the New World. The pardoned convicts became indentured servants whose labor was sold to the highest bidder in the colonies. The newly arrived felons were required to work off their indenture, and the only other condition of their pardon was that they not return to England.

Captain Alexander Maconochie of Norfolk Island, however, was the "father of parole" in its purest form. As noted in Chapter 14, Maconochie established a "mark system" whereby an inmate could earn early release through hard work and good behavior. Sir Walter Crofton's "Irish system" was a refinement of Maconochie's ideas in which inmates could earn a conditional release through a "ticket-of-leave."

The concept of parole continued to evolve in the United States with the principles of *"good-time" laws* and indeterminate sentencing. The notion underlying good-time laws was modest. If, in the opinion of prison authorities, inmates maintained an institutional record of hard work and good conduct, they could be released after a shorter period than that imposed by the sentencing court. The purposes of the laws were somewhat more complex, however. They were attempts to assist in the reformation of criminals, combined with endeavors to mitigate the severity of the penal codes; to solve the problems of prison discipline; and to get good work from inmates, thereby increasing the profits of prison industries and contract labor.[60]

The first good-time law was passed in New York in 1817. It provided that first-term prisoners with sentences of 5 years or less could reduce their sentences by one-fourth for good behavior. Although the New York statute was not immediately put into practice, shortly after midcentury more than half the states had provisions granting time off for good behavior. Then, in 1869 Michigan adopted the first indeterminate sentencing law. In 1876, as a result of the efforts of Elmira Reformatory warden Zebulon Brockway, similar legislation was passed in New York. Under its provisions, an offender could be released when his behavior showed that he could be returned to society. Since the offender was being released before the expiration of sentence, special provisions were made for community supervision, and thus parole became a reality. By the second decade of the 20th century, most states had indeterminate sentencing laws, and the nature of parole as it is understood today had become firmly established.[61]

Parole Administration

The terms *parole* and *probation* have often been mistakenly used interchangeably—but as is already apparent, there are many differences between the two. Probation involves a sentence to community supervision in lieu of imprisonment; parole is a conditional release from a correctional institution after a period of imprisonment has already been served. Beyond this distinction, there are administrative differences. First, the authority to both grant and revoke probation falls within the realm of the lower courts. In contrast, the authority to grant and revoke parole is held by an administrative board that can be (1) an independent state agency, (2) a unit within some larger state department, or (3) the same body that regulates the state's correctional institutions. Second, responsibility for the supervision of probationers can rest with a single court, a county agency, a state department or division, or some combination thereof in any given jurisdiction. Parole supervision services, however, are under the authority of a single state agency in all instances but are not necessarily under the leadership of the parole board.

It used to be that you got ten bucks, a bus ticket, and a new suit when you walked through the prison gate. Now your gate money is $21 and a free van ride, but that's all you get. If you don't have your own clothes, you go home in your prison blues. Real nice!

— A NEVADA INMATE

The advantages and disadvantages of the various models of parole administration have been heavily debated. Which model is actually followed, however, is generally a matter of state politics. In recent years, as both parole and correctional agencies have become more professional, the trend has been to combine administration of the two.

The Parole Board The functions of parole boards are essentially fourfold: (1) to select and place prisoners on parole; (2) to provide continuing control over parolees in the community; (3) to discharge parolees from supervision when they complete their sentences; and (4) to review parole violations and determine whether revocation and return to prison is appropriate. Thus, the overall task of the parole board is the implementation of indeterminate sentencing.

Since parole boards make decisions on parole release and revocation, as well as create policy regarding planning and supervision services, it seems logical that the efficiency and viability of the entire parole system depend on the qualifications, skill, and experiences of the members of the board. The American Correctional Association recommends that parole board members command respect and public confidence; be appointed without reference to creed, color, or political affiliation; possess academic training that would qualify them for their professional practice; and have intimate knowledge of the situations and problems confronting offenders.[62] To these, the National Advisory Commission on Criminal Justice Standards and Goals adds:

> No single professional group or discipline can be recommended as ideal for all parole board members. A variety of goals are to be served by parole board members, and a variety of skills are required. Knowledge of at least three basic fields should be represented on a parole board: the law, the behavioral sciences, and corrections. Furthermore, as a board assumes responsibility for policy articulation, monitoring and review, the tasks involved require persons who are able to use a wide range of decision-making tools, such as statistical materials, reports from professional personnel, and a variety of other technical information. In general, persons with sophisticated training and experience are required.[63]

However, surveys sponsored by the American Correctional Association and the National Council on Crime and Delinquency indicate that qualifications such as these are required in only a minority of jurisdictions.[64] Independent observations have shown that in a number of states some parole board members have had *no* previous exposure to the criminal justice system or offender problems. This was especially true in two selected jurisdictions where decision making was in the hands of part-time boards. Board membership included physicians, ministers, retail sales clerks, and small business operators—most of whom had an interest in correctional issues but few of whom had training or experience in law, social work, corrections, or related skills. This should not suggest, however, that all parole board members are ill-equipped for the responsibilities they share. Quite the contrary: There are many whose career experiences include law, probation, and parole, plus graduate degrees in one or more of the social or behavioral sciences.

Eligibility for Parole

There are numerous statutory restrictions on the granting of parole. As a result, inmates are not automatically paroled as a matter of right. Parole eligibility, then, refers to the earliest date that an inmate can be considered for parole. However, because of the nature of their offenses and sentences, some prisoners can never be paroled.

A key factor in the determination of parole eligibility are the statutes regarding "good time." Good time, as explained earlier, refers to the number of days deducted from a sentence for good behavior, meritorious service, particular kinds of work, or other considerations. Some states have a fixed formula for allocating good time, such as 2 or 3 days for each month served. In others it is left to the discretion of the prison authorities but cannot exceed a certain portion of the term imposed by the court.

Contrary to the opinion of many correctional authorities, however, it would appear that good time is protected by the *ex post facto* clause of the U.S. Constitution.

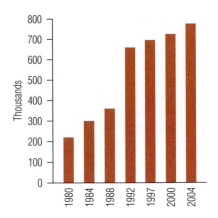

Parolees in the United States, 1980–2004

Source: Bureau of Justice Statistics.

Who Are the Best Parole Risks?

Who, indeed, do the best on parole without repeating the crimes for which they were initially convicted? Rapists? Robbers? Prostitutes? Burglars? Check forgers? Shoplifters? Who?

Actually, it's none of the above. Quite surprisingly, the answer is murderers. There are several explanations. Many murderers tend to be first offenders who have committed crimes of passion and emotion. Another explanation is *age:* Because the majority of convicted murderers serve long prison sentences, they tend to be older when released—well beyond the high-crime-risk years of adolescence and young adulthood. Finally, the so-called felony murderers whom one would expect to be repeaters—the killers for hire, robber-murderers, and serial killers—never really get the chance, at least not on the street. Most of these end up on death row or receive terms of life without parole. ∎

Article I, Section 10 of the Federal Constitution provides that "no State shall . . . pass any . . . *ex post facto* law." In the context of good-time credits, the *ex post facto* clause prevents the increase of punishment after the date of the criminal offense.[65] What this means is that since good-time credits technically are part of the original sentence, states cannot enact new laws for computing good time and apply them retroactively.[66]

At the same time, however, good-time credits must be earned, and as noted in the discussion of prison disciplinary proceedings in Chapter 16, they can be forfeited for poor behavior.

The Parole Hearing Parole hearings are generally private and are attended only by the inmate, the board, a representative of the institution in which the inmate is incarcerated, and a stenographer or stenotypist to record the proceedings. The board reviews the inmate's case as well as any institutional reports that may have been submitted; questions the inmate regarding his or her adjustment, plans if released, and perhaps the circumstances of the offense; and offers the inmate an opportunity to make a statement on his or her own behalf. The inmate is then dismissed, and the board discusses the case and makes its decision.

The specific procedures used by different boards vary. In the past, one board member examined the institutional records and interviewed each inmate under consideration. He or she would then make a recommendation, and the entire board would either ratify or modify the recommendation in an executive session. Currently, several models are used. Some boards meet *en banc* for every case; others break up into groups to hold hearings in different parts of the jurisdiction. Since the mid-1970s, the U.S. Board of Parole and many of the larger states have been using hearing examiners, who make recommendations on which the board acts. Regardless of the particular procedure, parole authorities have been given wide discretion as to how hearings are actually conducted. This discretion has been supported by the courts. In *Menechino* v. *Oswald*,[67] decided by the U.S. Court of Appeals in 1970, the petitioner argued that his due process rights had been violated by the manner in which his parole hearing had been conducted. He claimed that the Constitution required that he be given the following:

1. Notice.
2. Fair hearing with right to counsel, cross-examination, and presentation of witnesses.
3. Specification of the reasons for the parole board's decision.

The court, however, ruled that the due process clause did not apply to parole hearings since inmates, who are already imprisoned, do not have "present private interests" that require protection. The following year, though, the court did hold that written reasons must be given for denial of parole.[68] In 1979, the U.S. Supreme Court in *Greenholtz* v. *Inmates of Nebraska Penal and Correctional Complex* affirmed previous decisions that parole hearings need not have all the elements of due process that are required at criminal trials.[69] And in 1998, in **Pennsylvania Board of Probation and Parole v. Scott**,[70] the United States Supreme Court ruled that the exclusionary rule does not apply in parole revocation hearings, thus giving parole and police agencies a powerful weapon in investigating parole violations and criminal activity (see Exhibit 17.3).

Parole Selection An overview of contemporary parole practice suggests that many release decisions reflect variable, arbitrary, and sometimes whimsical standards. A variety of legislative mandates, for example, express the vague policy that a prisoner should be paroled only when such action is not incompatible with the welfare of the community.[71] More specific criteria have included such factors as the offender's prior criminal record, personality and physical condition, social history, employment record, intelligence, family status, institutional conduct, parole plan, prior probation or parole history, and stated intentions for the future, among others. Yet questions exist as to how these variables should be weighted in determining if or when a prisoner should be released. Factors that are deemed significant may be emphasized even though they may indeed have no significance at all.

LAW & CRIMINAL JUSTICE | EXHIBIT 17.3

Pennsylvania Board of Probation and Parole v. Scott

In granting Keith M. Scott parole, the Pennsylvania Board of Probation and Parole stipulated that he must refrain from owning or possessing weapons of any kind. When officers suspected Scott might be in possession of several weapons, they searched his home and found a bow and arrow and a number of firearms. Although he objected at his parole violation hearing that the search was unconstitutional, the seized weapons were admitted as evidence and Scott was ultimately returned to the institution. On appeal, the Commonwealth Court of Pennsylvania affirmed Scott's challenge to the search and the Pennsylvania Supreme Court sustained the decision.

When the case came before the United States Supreme Court, the question at hand was whether the federal exclusionary rule, which prohibits the introduction of evidence seized in violation of the Fourth Amendment ban against unreasonable search and seizure, applies to parole revocation hearings.

In a 5-to-4 decision, the High Court held that the federal exclusionary rule does not apply to parole revocation hearings. Noting that the exclusionary rule is not constitutionally mandated, the Court explained that the deleterious impact that an application of the exclusionary rule would have on traditionally flexible state parole revocation proceedings is great. State parole authorities must have greater legal latitude since they deal with individuals who, in light of past criminal activities, are more likely than average citizens to offend again.

In a number of settings, the decision to release falls within a political arena. The recommendations of a sentencing judge, a prosecuting attorney, or the news media can invariably affect the paroling process when they have implications for the political power of a member of the parole board. Moreover, in some state jurisdictions and the federal system, crime victims are permitted to testify at the release hearings of inmates who have been convicted of victimizing them—a practice with a probable impact on parole decision making.

The decisions that emerge from such a nexus of policy, autocracy, and whim typically fall within the spectrum of "intuitive prognosis," "common sense," expediency, and hunch. The members of a paroling board *guess,* or follow their instincts, on the basis of the limited information submitted to them; they may observe potential candidates and make predictions based on insight, intuition, and inductive assumption; or they may examine various types of more or less scientific data to arrive at a decision.

A scene from The Shawshank Redemption, *a film which addresses the problems of prison and parole.*

Good-Time Laws in the United States (maximum number of days per inmate) *

MORE THAN 30 DAYS A MONTH

Alabama
North Carolina
Oklahoma
Texas

30 DAYS A MONTH

Arkansas
Florida
Illinois
Indiana
Louisiana
West Virginia

20 DAYS A MONTH

New Jersey

15 DAYS A MONTH

California
Colorado
Connecticut
Minnesota

LESS THAN 15 DAYS A MONTH

Delaware	Nebraska
District of	Nevada
Columbia	New York
Federal Bureau	North Dakota
of Prisons	Oregon
Iowa	Rhode Island
Kentucky	Tennessee
Maine	Vermont
Michigan	Virginia
Mississippi	Washington
Missouri	Wyoming

NO GOOD TIME GIVEN

Georgia
Hawaii
Idaho
Kansas
Massachusetts
Minnesota
Montana
Ohio
Pennsylvania
South Dakota
Utah
Wisconsin

States not responding to the survey: South Carolina, Alaska, Arizona, New Hampshire, New Mexico.

Source: *Corrections Compendium.*

* Includes automatic good time plus earned time.

Further confounding this process is the tendency to base decisions on a majority rule or, in some jurisdictions, a unanimous verdict.

Finally, predictions of human behavior are especially problematic when the individuals under review have already demonstrated a reduced capacity to function in a socially approved manner. Selection decisions may totally bypass *all* inmates who are considered less likely to succeed. Indeed, conservative parole boards have been known to release only prisoners who are seen to be good risks while denying parole to the remainder.[72]

Statistical Prediction Methods   Scientific parole prediction emerged as an attempt to inject some degree of precision into the selection of prospective parolees. The goal was to increase the number of conditional releases of offenders who are likely to succeed and to reduce the number granted to those who are likely to fail.

Essentially, **parole prediction** refers to estimates of the probability of violation or nonviolation of parole on the basis of experience tables that have been developed with regard to groups of offenders possessing similar characteristics.[73] An *experience table* summarizes the postinstitutional experience of a given release group. It classifies offenders by their admission characteristics and uses only characteristics that have been shown to make a difference in postrelease response or adjustment in an aftercare setting. An experience table is similar to an actuarial table, which calculates or estimates insurance risks—but rather than indicating mortality or morbidity rates for each type of person, it points to violation or recidivism rates.[74]

However, *parole prediction tables do not predict,* for several reasons. First, they are often heavily based on factors that were present in the inmate's social situation prior to arrest, and thus generally do not include postsentence variables such as institutional behavior and relationships. Second, they cannot anticipate differences in parole officers' attitudes and willingness to revoke parole. Third, they are based on data from presentence reports, some of which is of questionable accuracy. Fourth, the solely empirical approach of prediction methods is weakened by the lack of any theoretical basis for assuming that particular variables have higher predictive value than others. In the final analysis, statistical prediction methods seem no more accurate at predicting which individuals will successfully complete their parole than are parole systems that do not use such methods.[75]

Mandatory Release   A related issue involves repeated denial of parole in spite of an inmate's eligibility for conditional release. It is not uncommon, for example, for a parole board to request a recommendation from the district attorney or chief prosecutor for the county in which a defendant was convicted. Depending on the nature of the case, the prosecutor's parole recommendation can influence the board's decision. Similarly, an inmate's parole may be opposed by the police, the news media, the victims of the crime, and the general public. Consider the case of Richard Speck, who was convicted and sentenced to life imprisonment for the brutal murder of eight student nurses in Chicago in 1966. Given the sentiment of Illinois residents and the agitation of the victims' families, Speck's bids for parole were repeatedly denied, and he died in prison on December 5, 1991. For similar reasons, it is likely that Sirhan Sirhan (Robert F. Kennedy's assassin) and Charles Manson will never be paroled.

In less notorious cases, in which inmates are serving indeterminate sentences and parole is repeatedly denied, or in certain types of definite ("flat") sentences, another factor comes into play—good-time credits. As noted earlier, **good time** refers to the number of days deducted from a sentence for good behavior, meritorious service, particular kinds of work, or other considerations. There are three kinds of good time. *Statutory good time* is given automatically when inmates serve their time without problems. In addition, there is *earned time* for participation in work, educational, or treatment programs. In a few jurisdictions there is *meritorious time,* which is earned for some exceptional act or service (such as fire fighting or other life-saving efforts).

Almost all jurisdictions provide for some type of automatic good time, ranging from 4.5 days per month in the federal system to 7.5 days per month in Alabama.[76] Although the maximum number of good-time days is fixed by statute, in some jurisdictions "earned time" credits, which can total as many as 30 days per month, are applied beyond this upper limit.

The accumulation of good-time days ultimately results in **mandatory release**—release as a matter of law. In New York and Missouri, inmates on mandatory release are subject to the same conditions as parolees and are under the supervision of a parole officer. In all other jurisdictions, however, mandatory release is *unconditional*.

Conditions of Parole

As with probation, all individuals on parole are released under a series of conditions, whose violation can result in revocation and return to prison. These "dos and don'ts" of parole originated under the ticket-of-leave system.

Parole conditions are fairly uniform from state to state and can be grouped into two general areas: *reform conditions*, which urge parolees toward a noncriminal way of life; and *control conditions*, which enable the parole agency to keep track of them. The most common conditions include the following:

- *Reform conditions:*
  Comply with the laws.
  Maintain employment and support dependents.
  Refrain from use of drugs.
- *Control conditions:*
  Report to parole officer upon release and periodically thereafter.
  Cooperate with the parole officer.
  Get permission (or notify) to change employment or residence.

In addition, as with probationers, there may be special conditions of parole geared to particular treatment and control needs.

In many jurisdictions, the list of parole regulations tends to be long, designed to control almost every aspect of the parolee's life. For instance, until the late 1960s, the conditions of parole in New York included a prohibition against "having sexual relations with anyone other than your lawful spouse." This restriction allegedly crept into the New York rules as a result of the moralistic Irish Catholic influence that dominated that system during its early years. However, such a condition was considered unreasonable and unenforceable, and parolees and parole officers alike tended to ignore it. Since 1970, a number of states, including Alaska, Connecticut, Massachusetts, and Ohio, have abandoned a number of restrictions, including regulations dealing with marriage and divorce, association with undesirables, motor vehicle usage, and alcohol use.

On the other hand, some conditions have been abolished because they were violations of broad constitutional rights. In *Hyland* v. *Procunier*,[77] for example, a condition that required a parolee to secure permission before making a public speech was ruled invalid. Similarly, in *Sobell* v. *Reed*,[78] the court struck down a rule that denied a parolee the right to make an antiwar speech. In both cases, the courts held that conditions that impinged upon First Amendment rights of free speech were beyond the authority of the parole board.

Parole Supervision and Services

Like probation officers, parole officers are responsible for supervising, aiding, and controlling the clients assigned to them. As counselors, officers ease parolees' reentry into society and aid them in overcoming obstacles to adjustment. In addition to providing individual counseling, they may help in the development of employment plans and job readiness, work with families to resolve problems, and refer parolees to community agencies that can help overcome certain persistent difficulties. Some parole agencies have special units that focus on such areas as alcoholism, drug use, and unemployment, or on the needs of mentally ill or retarded offenders.

Call it good time, gain time, earned time, statutory time, meritorious time or commutation time. Identify it as provisional credits, good conduct credits, disciplinary credits. Whatever the term, it's corrections' carrot for good behavior, and a management tool of long standing in the United States prisons.

—SU PARK DAVIS

In addition to serving as counselors, parole officers have the duty to police the behavior of those under their supervision. In many states, parole officers are armed peace officers. As one officer explained to the author:

> It's a rather contradictory bag to be in. We're what you might call "gun-carrying social workers." Or better yet, how about if we refer to it as the discipline of "authoritarian casework"?

Although quasi–law enforcement responsibilities are apparent in probation supervision, they are considerably more pronounced with respect to parole. Parolees tend to be more dangerous and serious offenders. Many have been incarcerated for long periods with intensive exposure to prison violence and the inmate culture. Moreover, the stigma of the ex-con label and former inmate status make it more difficult to adjust to life in the community. All of these factors combine to put stress on the law enforcement role of the parole officer and hinder the pursuit of rehabilitative goals.

Parole Violation and Revocation

The violation and revocation process in parole is very similar to that described earlier for probation. After a new arrest or serious technical violation, a warrant is issued and the parolee is taken into custody. Pursuant to the Supreme Court's decision in *Morrissey* v. *Brewer,* the delinquent parolee is given a measure of due process during his or her preliminary and revocation hearings, and the parole board can make one of two decisions: "restore to supervision" or "return to prison."

If parole is revoked, the next issue is exactly how much time the parolee must serve in prison. This decision is made by the parole board either at the revocation hearing or during the next board meeting at the institution. A bitterly disputed matter in this regard is whether "street time"—the period spent under parole supervision prior to violation—should be credited against the remaining sentence. In some jurisdictions, the parole board establishes the violator's "date of delinquency"—the point at which the violation occurred. From that date on, any time served on the street is considered "dead time." Thus, if an inmate with a 15-year sentence is paroled after 3 years, serves 2 years in the community in good standing but is then declared delinquent, 5 years of his sentence will be considered as having been completed. The parole board may put a 3-year "hold" on the individual, meaning that he or she will be eligible to be considered for parole in 3 years. In other jurisdictions, however, time spent on the street in good standing is not credited in this manner.

This issue has also been addressed with respect to probation violation. In regard to both probation and parole revocation, the denial of street-time credit represents a nonjudicial increase in sentence. Despite this argument, the courts have consistently upheld the right of states to deny street-time credits. They have done so on the theory that since the probationer or parolee was not physically in custody, he or she was not "serving a sentence."

Parole Discharge

Individuals can be discharged from parole in a number of ways. First, they can "max out." That is, they can reach their **maximum expiration date**—the date on which their full sentence formally terminates. Second, in more than half the states and the federal system, parolees can be discharged by the parole board before their maximum expiration date. In this instance, however, a number of jurisdictions require that some minimum parole period be served. In Ohio, for example, discharge can occur after 1 year of satisfactory supervision and after 5 years in the case of a life sentence. Under New York's *executive clemency* statute, if the time remaining on the maximum sentence at the time of parole is more than 5 years, the board can issue a discharge after 5 consecutive years of satisfactory supervision. Third, discharge can occur through commutation of sentence or pardon by the governor. In about half the states, pardon is the chief mechanism through which the civil rights lost upon conviction and imprisonment can be restored. In the remaining states, civil rights are automatically restored upon release from

My job is to trail 'em, nail 'em, and jail 'em.

—A RHODE ISLAND PAROLE OFFICER

the penitentiary, upon discharge from parole, or at the final expiration of the sentence. In Hawaii, Indiana, Massachusetts, Michigan, and New Hampshire, however, a defendant's civil rights are not lost upon conviction for a felony offense.

The State of Parole in the United States

The institution of parole in the United States has undergone significant changes in the past several decades. Each state varies in its approach to parole, with some eliminating or diminishing the authority of parole boards and with others retaining it as a significant function of prisoner reentry.

Three major trends have occurred in parole over time. First, the role of parole boards in determining the release of offenders has declined in favor of mandatory releases. The second major trend lies in the tremendous growth of the parole population. Currently, over 80 percent of offenders released from prison are on parole, an increase from 60 percent in 1960. Finally, the proportion of parole violators as a percentage of the total prison population has increased substantially. However, there are significant variations in these trends among individual states, rendering it difficult to draw any single conclusion about the current state of parole.

The first major component of parole, the decision to release an offender, has shifted over time. As noted earlier, there are two types of prisoner release—discretionary and mandatory. Discretionary decisions have been the traditional function of the parole board, while mandatory release is mandated by law. The criminal justice system has moved away from the practice of indeterminate sentencing by judges that granted parole boards considerable flexibility in deciding the length of an offender's sentence. Increasingly, the legislative branch of government is dictating the release of offenders by establishing mandatory sentencing and release laws. The overall share of mandatory prison releases rose to 52 percent of those entering parole in 2004, up from 45 percent in 1995.

Less than 1 percent of releases are based on parole board decisions in states such as California and Illinois. On the flip side, however, several states continue to heavily rely on the discretion of the parole board for offender release, including Florida, Pennsylvania, and Washington, which release over 95 percent of prisoners on the basis of parole board recommendations. Some states, like Ohio, have an even mix of releases by parole board decisions and mandatory releases.

Overall, the parole population has experienced significant growth. In 1980, 220,000 individuals were released on parole; by 2004, there were almost 800,000 individuals on parole, an all-time record. The number of individuals on parole per 100,000 has increased from 136 in 1981 to almost 360 in 2004. Over the past decade alone, the parole population has grown over 30 percent, but there is significant variation among states: 16 states have experienced a decline in their parole populations during this time, while 11 others more than doubled their parole populations. Over 60 percent of the nation's total parole population is from just five states—California, Texas, Pennsylvania, New York, and Illinois.

The sanctioning of those found in violation of parole has altered the composition of the prison population, creating a distinct and increasingly common pathway back to incarceration for former inmates. Parole failures can be classified as either technical violations—that is, violating one of the terms of condition of release—or new crime violations, in which case a parolee is arrested, charged, and convicted of new and unrelated charges. Between 1980 and 2004, the number of parole violators sent back to prison increased sevenfold from 27,000 to almost 210,000. The number of parole violators sentenced to state prison in 2004 mirrored the *total* number of state prison admissions in 1980.

Currently, more than a third of incoming prisoners are incarcerated for parole violations. In California, those who violate the terms of their parole constitute a whopping 67 percent of the state's prison population. California accounts for 42 percent of all parole violators returned to prison, while the other 49 states account for the remaining 58 percent of offenders imprisoned on parole violations.

FAMOUS CRIMINALS
Willie Horton

Willie Horton hadn't intended to run for the 1988 vice presidency, but the political spin doctors of the day had other ideas.

Born August 12, 1951, in Chesterfield, South Carolina, Horton eventually made his way to Massachusetts, where in October 1974 he and two accomplices robbed and stabbed a 17-year-old gas station attendant 19 times before stuffing him in a trash can and leaving him for dead. Horton was convicted of murder, sentenced to life in prison, and sent to the Concord Correctional Facility to serve out his term. On June 6, 1986, as part of a controversial weekend furlough plan enacted by the state of Massachusetts, Horton was set free for the weekend. He never returned.

On April 3, 1987, Horton resurfaced in Oxon Hill, Maryland, where he broke into a home and assaulted the owner—punching, pistol-whipping, kicking, and stabbing the victim 22 times—and then brutally raping his wife when she unsuspectingly returned home. He then stole their car and drove off, only to be captured by the police after a high-speed pursuit. On October 20, Horton was sentenced to two consecutive life terms, plus 85 years for his crimes. The judge, in refusing to extradite him back to Massachusetts, said: "I'm not prepared to take the chance that Mr. Horton might again be furloughed or otherwise released. This man should never draw a breath of free air again."

(continued on p. 595)

In terms of measuring the success rate of parole, there is no national standard. The Bureau of Justice Statistics defines success as the completion of the terms of supervision without the parolee's returning to prison or jail or absconding. Using this standard, 42 percent of parolees were successful in 1999, a measurement that remained relatively constant throughout the decade of the 1990s, when success rates ranged from 42 percent to 49 percent. However, policies and level of enforcement vary by state and contribute to widespread differences in success rates, which range from just 19 percent in Utah to 83 percent in Massachusetts. And California, which accounts for 18 percent of the national population on parole, has a success rate of just 21 percent. Differences also exist among first-release and re-release parolees, the latter having already returned to prison at least once for violation of parole. Overall, first-release parolees are more successful at avoiding a return to prison (79%) than those re-released (46%).[79]

While examining these trends provides some insight into the current state of parole, continued research into what works and what doesn't among states is needed to better direct future public policy initiatives.

Trends in Community-Based Correction

By 2004, the prison population in the United States had well exceeded 2 million. In addition, there were almost 5 million probationers, parolees, and offenders on mandatory release under the supervision of probation and parole authorities, with an additional 600,000 offenders under the supervision of various community agencies. Given the overcrowding of prisons and the pressures on state correctional systems to remedy the unconstitutional conditions in many of their facilities, combined with the trend toward mandatory prison sentences for violent offenders and drug traffickers, the character of inmate populations across America will probably undergo some change. More and more, prisons and penitentiaries will become places for holding serious criminals, at least for a time, and there will be increased use of community corrections for other types of offenders. Thus probation, diversion, and other forms of community-based supervision and service will become even more significant. However, many issues and alternatives remain problematic, casting doubt on the effectiveness and future use of community supervision.

Furlough and Temporary Release

A **furlough** is an authorized, unescorted absence from a correctional institution for a specified period.[80] It is granted for the purpose of enabling inmates to reestablish community contacts and family ties on a gradual basis. It has emerged in a variety of forms, including the home furlough, work release, and educational release.

Home Furlough   A home furlough is a short leave of absence, often taken on weekends and lasting anywhere from half an hour to as long as 180 days.[81] Under furlough programs, eligible inmates are given the opportunity to leave the institution for such purposes as seeking employment, maintaining family ties, solving family problems, seeking postrelease housing, or attending short-term educational or vocational training courses.

The home furlough serves a number of rehabilitative, humanitarian, and pragmatic purposes. It is a means whereby inmates can begin the process of normalizing family relationships, reestablish contacts with the community, and prepare for eventual release. In addition, prison administrators view the furlough as an instrument of institutional management, feeling that the promise of a home visit for good behavior fosters greater compliance with custodial regulations. In settings where conjugal visitation is either impractical or not permitted, the furlough also has the benefit of reducing sexual frustration.

Virtually unknown before the late 1960s, home furloughs have been adopted by most states as well as the federal system. Eligibility criteria vary, however. In some states, it is a statutory matter and applies only to inmates who are within 1 year of parole eligibility or conditional release and have not been convicted of escape, absconding, or violent offenses. In others, eligibility is a matter of legislative, judicial, or correctional policy, with the criteria ranging from highly specific to hopelessly vague.[82]

Work Release Similar in concept and purpose to the home furlough, work release is an alternative to total incarceration whereby inmates are permitted to work for pay in the community but must spend their nonworking hours in the institution. Work release is not a recent innovation; it was initiated in 1913 under Wisconsin's Huber Law (introduced by Senator Huber). However, the idea has been accepted only slowly, and it was not until the early 1970s that work release became a widespread correctional practice for felony offenders.[83] Eligibility criteria are similar to those for home furloughs, restricting release to inmates nearing parole or conditional release who do not represent a significant risk to the community.

In addition to the advantages of furloughs in general, work release offers the benefit of potentially reshaping an offender's self-image and promoting the process of decarceration. Moreover, offenders can assume some financial responsibilities by paying for transportation to and from the institution, contributing to the costs of their room and board, supplementing any welfare benefits given to their families, and beginning payments on any court-ordered restitution. Thus, work release can also serve the interests of the taxpaying public.

However, there are many obstacles to effective implementation of work release. It has been opposed on the ground that prisoners take jobs away from law-abiding citizens; inmates on work release have been exploited by some employers who feel that "cons" should not be paid at normal wage levels; and prison-based training has not always been usable in the modern employment market. The distance between many correctional institutions and active job centers has also restricted work-release efforts. Many prisons are in isolated rural areas, and it is generally neither feasible nor cost-effective to transport inmates for long distances on a daily basis. This problem has been mitigated, to some extent, by the nightly housing of inmates in jails and detention centers located near their job sites. Some jurisdictions provide residential work-release centers. These offer not only living facilities for working inmates but counseling and supervised recreation during evening and weekend hours.

(continued from p. 594)

As then-Massachusetts governor Michael Dukakis was running for president against George H. W. Bush, the weekend furlough program in the governor's home state became a hot-button issue and the target of many an attack ad by both independent supporters and the official Bush campaign. Dukakis had not actually signed the legislation into action, his predecessor had, but when given the opportunity to exclude murderers from the furlough program, he vetoed the measure. No matter the details, the independent Americans for Bush Political Action Committee ran an ad featuring Horton's intimidating mugshot with the words "every suburban mother's greatest fear." Bush's campaign manager Lee Atwater, intoxicated over the campaign's own set of attack ads, was quoted as saying he was going to "make Willie Horton [Dukakis's] running mate," a remark he later apologized for and denied racist overtones about.

Dukakis likely lost the election over more than just the Willie Horton fiasco, and as for Horton, he languishes in a Maryland maximum security prison to this day. ■

"MAYBE YOU COULD REFER TO YOUR TIME BEHIND BARS AS 'LIVING IN A GATED COMMUNITY.'"

Reprinted by permission of www.CartoonStock.com.

I think it's been a situation where the administrative staff of the prison system has used good time, in a large sense, to flush prisoners out the door to make room for incoming prisoners.

—ALLEN POLUNSKY, BOARD OF TEXAS CRIMINAL JUSTICE, ON THE NUMBER OF VIOLENT OFFENDERS WHO HAVE BEEN GRANTED PAROLE

Study Release   A natural extension of the work-release principle, study release is offered to minimum-security, parole-eligible inmates who seek vocational or academic enrichment. Following the criteria and regulations of a state's work-release project, study release provides opportunities for full-time, on-site participation in vocational school and college programs.

Experiences with Temporary Release   Temporary release programs have their critics, and crimes committed by inmates on work release or home furlough are given major coverage in the news media. During 1988, for example, few Americans were unaware of the name of Willie Horton, who had been sentenced to life without parole in Massachusetts for a homicide in 1974, only to be released on a weekend furlough during which he committed a brutal rape and murder.[84] After that incident, states became conservative in the granting of furloughs, but almost immediately the trend reversed, perhaps as a result of prison crowding. From 1988 to 1990, for example, the number of furloughs increased from 200,000 to 230,960. In 1996, the figure was down to 156,000, a result of the number of inmates serving mandatory minimum sentences. By 2005, furloughs still existed in most states, but with numerous restrictions.[85]

In spite of incidents of bad publicity, however, the concept of temporary release continues to hold promise as a form of partial incarceration, as a bridge between the prison and free society, and as another treatment mechanism in the spectrum of community-based correctional services. Perhaps many of the difficulties in existing programs might be eliminated, or at least minimized, with better screening of candidates and monitoring of releasees. However, the kind of public outrage that is generated when even a few isolated violent crimes are committed by people who are supposed to be behind bars militates against its use as a correctional tool. This, combined with many unresolved questions as to whether temporary release actually reduces recidivism, and the political realities associated with it, cloud the prospects for the implementation of such programs on a continuing basis.

A strong contrast is provided by the *halfway houses* and *prerelease centers* that have developed since the 1960s. Designed for inmates who are just a few months away from their parole dates, these residential facilities in urban locations provide individual counseling, vocational guidance, and job placement. Residents are required to abide by minimum security regulations, attend counseling and therapy sessions, and actively seek employment when ready.[86]

Whether halfway houses are effective in reintegrating offenders into the community is open to question. Studies of their experience found significant levels of escape, recidivism, and returns to prison for disciplinary violations. But since recidivism seemed to be no higher among prerelease center residents than among other newly released inmates, it has been recommended that the halfway house concept be expanded. There seems to be little likelihood that this will occur, however, not only for political reasons but also because of the opposition of many communities to "placing convicts in our backyards."

If you put $2 billion on a table and sat some criminologists around it to solve the crime problem, nobody would talk about building prisons. But when you put some politicians around that table, you see what happens.

—VIRGINIA CONGRESSMAN ROBERT SCOTT

Should Parole Be Abolished?

In 1938, FBI Director J. Edgar Hoover commented that the biggest job of law enforcement was the chasing down of "canny recidivists," "mad dogs," and "predatory animals" who have been "cloaked by the mantle of parole."[87] Arguments about parole still persist. Among the reasons for opposition to parole are the following:

1. Procedures for parole decision-making are not guided by explicit standards or traditional elements of due process;
2. The tasks that parole is supposed to perform—accurate prediction of the offender's likelihood of recidivism and monitoring of rehabilitative progress—are beyond our present capacities; and,
3. Aside from questions of effectiveness, it is unjust to base decisions about severity of punishments on what the offender is expected to do in the future.[88]

The current system is actually a non-system. It defeats the reasonable expectation of the public that a realistic penalty will be imposed at the time of conviction, and that the sentence received will be the sentence served.

—SENATOR EDWARD KENNEDY

To the foregoing reasons, Senator Edward Kennedy adds that sentencing disparities are compounded by parole, since it encourages some judges to impose the kind of harsh

Estimated Time to Be Served in State Prison

	(%) Percent of Time Served	Mean Sentence (months)	Estimated Time Served (months)
All offenses	33	75	25
Violent offenses	38	119	45
Murder	43	243	104
Rape	39	160	62
Robbery	39	115	45
Assault	33	78	26
Other	34	85	29
Property offenses	29	65	19
Burglary	32	80	26
Larceny	27	49	13
Fraud	28	58	16
Drug violations	29	66	19
Possession	27	49	13
Trafficking	31	74	23
Weapons	40	50	20
Other	30	44	13

Source: National Judicial Reporting Program.

sentences that the community expects. He has suggested that if flat or determinate sentencing policies were adopted, parole would not be needed:

> Under this system of judicially fixed sentences, parole release would be abolished and whether or not a prisoner has been "rehabilitated" or has completed a certain prison curriculum would no longer have any bearing on his prison release date.[89]

Recently the noted author and political scientist John J. DiIulio of Princeton University called for the abolition of parole, arguing that it is neither effective in reducing recidivism nor cost-effective as an alternative to prison.[90] For similar reasons, Texas state senator Jane Nelson and former Wisconsin governor Tommy G. Thompson have also called for the abolition of parole. However, the Center for Effective Public Policy argues that states that have abolished parole have jeopardized public safety and wasted tax money:

> Getting rid of parole dismantles an accountable system of releasing prisoners back into the community and replaces it with a system that bases release decisions solely on whether a prison term has been completed.[91]

Former FBI director J. Edgar Hoover.

CAREERS IN CRIMINAL JUSTICE

Probation and Parole Officers

The work of probation and parole officers tends to be similar. Probation officers work with adult offenders ensuring that they comply with the terms of court-imposed probation, whereas the mission of parole officers is to ensure that offenders comply with the conditions of their release from adult correctional facilities. In most jurisdictions, probation officers are employed by a probation department linked to the county court system, while parole officers are state employees. In a few jurisdictions, probation and parole officers are one and the same.

Overall, probation officers provide counseling, agency and employment referrals, and services related to offenders' risks and needs. Extensive field and public relations contacts are required. Officers work extensively with trial judges, prosecutors, police, the parole board, and other criminal justice personnel. Officers also conduct presentence investigations of background investigations of parolees. In addition, because probation and parole officers are armed peace officers in many

jurisdictions, they make arrests, transport probation or parole violators, and testify at violation hearings. While most officers work in the community, some work in correctional institutions preparing preparole summaries for those inmates about to be released.

The minimum qualifications for probation and parole work in most jurisdictions include a bachelor's degree in criminal justice, law enforcement, social service, communications, or a related field from an accredited educational institution and no legal prohibition against carrying a firearm. In lieu of the educational requirement, a few jurisdictions accept 2 years' experience in some area of social service. By contrast, some jurisdictions require a master's degree, or a bachelor's degree and 2 years' experience in social service or law enforcement.

Starting salaries for probation and parole officers vary by jurisdiction, with a range of $28,000 to over $35,000 per year.

Revolving Door

Parole violators returned to custody in California   Source: California Department of Corrections.

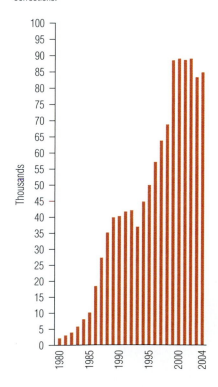

From the perspective of many inmates, parolees, civil libertarians, criminal justice reformers, and informed observers, parole is not without faults. The parolee has often been described as a "walking suspension of the Constitution,"[92] a status that seems to have evolved from the alternative theories upon which the concept of parole is based. First, there is the *grace theory*, which holds that parole is a privilege, a gift from the state and parole board that must be returned if certain conditions are violated. Second, there is the *custody theory*, which states that parolees, though walking the streets, are legally in the custody of the parole board. As a result, they remain in a quasi-prisoner status, they are not fully at liberty, and their constitutional rights remain limited and abridged. Finally, there is the *contract theory*, which argues that since parolees are required to agree to certain terms and conditions in return for their conditional freedom, violation of those conditions represents a "breach of contract," which can result in revocation of parole. As Jessica Mitford points out, parole is "a curious sort of contract, in which one side has all the bargaining powers and in which the contracting parolee, if accused of breaking it, has no redress in the courts."[93]

Discussions about abolishing parole typically surface when violent offenders receive early release as the result of extensive good-time credits. For example, in 1994, Virginia became the ninth state (along with the federal system) to abolish parole.[94] At the same time, state legislators lengthened prison sentences and restricted good time. The "get tough" sentiment in Virginia was directly linked to incidents of violent crime committed by parolees.

What Works and What Does Not with Prisoner Reentry

Prisoner reentry is one of the most pressing issues in the U.S. criminal justice system today. Hundreds of thousands of offenders are released every year, and recidivism rates are high. The challenge lies in developing innovative ways to ensure the successful reintegration of ex-offenders into the community. But how is this best achieved?

It is difficult to provide a definitive answer because there have been virtually no comprehensive research efforts or policy directives aimed at prisoner reentry. Those in the criminal justice field who are involved in reentry initiatives advocate programs that balance treatment and accountability measures for ex-offenders. The combination of treatment and rehabilitation for offenders is more likely to prove successful at reducing recidivism than is surveillance and enforcement alone. For example, a National Institute of Justice analysis of 53,614 individuals found that adding a treatment component to a release program resulted in a 10 percent reduction in recidivism.

Without sufficient preparation in terms of housing, employment, social support, and counseling, ex-offenders are more likely to fail in their attempt to reintegrate into the community. While funding for prison construction and operating costs have been increasing dramatically, funds for rehabilitative programs have not kept pace with the need. Resources including job skills training and counseling for substance abuse and mental health issues are important for individuals coping with reintegration into the community. The Office of National Drug Control Policy has found that more than 70% of state prison inmates need substance abuse treatment but just 13% receive any such services in prison. Given the high relapse rates of addiction and the connection between drug use and criminal activity, treatment options deserve increased attention. Likewise, studies have found that a substantial portion of inmates have serious mental health problems and that their greater involvement in the criminal justice system is partially because their mental health needs go unmet.[95]

The Sentencing Project in Washington, D.C., calls the restrictions and obstacles facing newly released offenders a form of "invisible punishment." For example, ex-offenders' chances of avoiding crime and rearrest can be hindered by a lack of job skills and stigmatization by potential employers who do not want to hire individuals with criminal backgrounds. Moreover, the denial of federal benefits and services because of a criminal record further puts ex-offenders at a disadvantage. Programs that aim to reduce these barriers are essential to the success of prisoner reentry and need to be funded with greater urgency.[96]

The needs of offenders released from prison are varied and many, and ex-offenders require assistance in their transition to the community after they have paid their debt to society. However, in addition to treatment and services, ex-offenders must also develop accountability for their actions in order to achieve long-term results.

The diminishing authority of parole boards in many states in favor of mandatory sentencing, as discussed earlier in the chapter, is one area that experts say must be more closely evaluated. Diminishing the power of the parole board in release decisions may actually be removing a crucial gatekeeping mechanism that keeps offenders incarcerated if they are not deemed fit to reenter society. Integrating offender accountability measures into parole supervision may play an important function in prisoner reintegration as well.

Reentry courts are another initiative that provides services while placing a high value on accountability. Reentry courts are based on the drug court model and use judges to closely monitor released offenders and to sanction or reward for behavior as necessary. Initial results have proved promising (see Exhibit 17.4).

Although the sheer number of ex-offenders released from prison has forced attention on the topic of prisoner reentry, our understanding of what makes the transition successful remains somewhat limited. Continued development of innovative programs, funding of services, and increased research evaluations of the functions of parole are needed to strengthen reentry initiatives.

CRITICAL THINKING IN CRIMINAL JUSTICE

California's Proposition 36

It has been argued for almost two decades that the "get tough" policies of America's "war of drugs" have had far too many casualties.[97] In many jurisdictions, for example, persons arrested for the possession of even small amounts of heroin, cocaine, and other illegal drugs face mandatory prison sentences of 3 or more years.

Vigorous drug control initiatives have led to escalating numbers of people behind bars, overcrowded jails and prisons, and increased taxation for prison construction and management. At the same time, there have been reductions in vocational and rehabilitative programming. This process has been especially visible in California, where the state's prison system is one of the

EXHIBIT 17.4 | RESEARCH ON CRIME & JUSTICE

What Are Reentry Courts?

Over the past several decades, the United States has imprisoned record numbers of offenders. Aside from the 5% who are sentenced to life, all prison terms eventually end, and the release of offenders back into society is inevitable. Currently, 600,000 prisoners are released each year at a rate of about 1,600 per day, quadruple the rate of just two decades ago.

However, current programs of offender reintegration are grossly ineffective, and as many as two-thirds of offenders return to prison within 3 years of release. So prisoner reentry not only is a product of the recent surge in incarceration but is a leading cause of it as well. Therefore, innovative approaches to reentry are under development, including the concept of a reentry court.

Based on the drug court model, the premise of the reentry court centers on the judge's aggressive supervisory role over offenders released from prison. The idea is akin to an intensive parole: The reentry court manages the release of ex-offenders and aims to reduce recidivism by providing ex-offenders with the tools they need to reintegrate into the community.

The concept of the reentry court is rooted in the labeling theory. Labeling theory posits that negative labels such as "criminal" and the negative reactions that people have to such labels actually serve to stigmatize and reinforce the criminal behavior of the individual in question. Reentry courts seek to reverse this labeling by affirming that ex-offenders have paid their debt to society and should be given every opportunity to move forward with their life.

Pilot programs are under way in numerous states across the country. Certain core elements, as advocated by the Department of Justice, are incorporated into the various reentry court initiatives:

Assessment and planning. This should include meetings between the offender, the judiciary, and other key personnel prior to release to identify an inmate's desire to participate in the program, to assess the individual's needs, and to determine the best course of action.

Active oversight. The reentry court requires ex-offenders to meet frequently with the judge and other support personnel, includ-

ing family members and community representatives. It is crucial that the judge is able to effectively track the progress, or lack thereof, of the ex-offender and to either reward or sanction their behavior.

Management and coordination of multiple support services. The reentry court must work closely with substance abuse treatment services, job training programs, private employers, housing services, and other social programs in order for the ex-offender to have access to resources that will facilitate a smooth transition back into society.

Accountability to the community. A jurisdiction may want to implement citizen advisory boards, crime victims' organizations, and community organizations to work with the court on community-wide issues.

The use of sanctions. The reentry court should establish and articulate specific sanctions for breaking the conditions of release. A range of low-level sanctions should be in place that can be handed down summarily and uniformly to anyone found in violation.

Rewards for success. Rewards, particularly early release, should be bestowed upon the ex-offender when established goals have been achieved. The courts should be used to encourage positive behavior and acknowledge the individual's effort in achieving their goals. Graduation ceremonies, as used in drug courts, could be a powerful way to publicly destigmatize the ex-offender. The reward may also involve the expiration of the individual's criminal history, exempting him or her from having to declare it on paperwork and face bias from employers and social agencies.

Sources: Elizabeth Brockett, "Reentry Court Aims to Reduce Recidivism and Help Ex-offenders Transition into the Community," *The Indiana Lawyer,* November 6, 2002, 7; John Buntin, "Mean Streets Revisited," *Governing Magazine,* April 30, 2003; Michael L. Siegfried, "The Promises and Problematics of Reentry Court," *The Justice Professional* 14 (2001): 201–219; Shadd Maruna and Thomas P. LeBel, "Welcome Home? Examining the 'Reentry Court' Concept from a Strengths-Based Perspective," *Western Criminology Review,* 4, 2 (2003): 91–107.

largest in the Western Hemisphere, and where one in every three of the state's more than 163,000 inmates is serving time for a drug-related crime.

In response to this situation, on November 7, 2000, 61 percent of California voters supported the Substance Abuse and Prevention Act of 2000. Better known as Proposition 36, the California initiative sought to focus on treating drug addiction not as a crime but as a health problem. It mandates probation and drug treatment for nonviolent offenders convicted of possession of illegal drugs for personal use. At a cost of some $120 million a year for treatment, Proposition 36 was expected to divert as many as 35,000 drug users from jails and prisons every year. The estimated savings are projected to be $250 million per year in incarceration costs and to save local governments $40 million annually in operating costs, plus a one-time savings of $550 million in reduced expenditures for prison construction. Drug offenders who fail treatment programs twice could be sentenced to terms of incarceration.[98]

The plan sounds positive! Or does it? Think critically for a few moments about its ramifications. What might be the impact of Proposition 36 on California's criminal courts and probation systems? And further, is such a plan even feasible?

With respect to the criminal courts, many offenders arrested for drug crimes might opt for a jury trial rather than accepting a plea bargain. The reason? If convicted by a jury, the worst punishment would be treatment. Just think of the court backlogs if even a small percentage of drug offenders insisted on jury trials.

With respect to probation, most county departments already have more cases than they can handle. An influx of tens of thousands of additional probationers each year would result in a supervision process that would be virtually nonexistent.

So what did happen with Proposition 36? Not surprisingly, it is not doing very well. In the first rigorous scientific study of Proposition 36 clients, rearrest rates were significantly higher than non-Proposition 36 clients.[99] As for why, the answer is a little complicated.

Proposition 36 followed the generic diversion, TASC, and drug court model and philosophy of moving drug-involved offenders into treatment rather than prison, but there was one thing that was quite unique about it. Most importantly, the impetus for, and campaign support behind, the promotion of Proposition 36 came primarily from George Soros (president of Soros Fund Management), Peter Lewis (philanthropist and CEO of Progressive Insurance), and John Sperling (CEO of The Apollo Group, Inc.)—billionaire financiers who view American drug policy as an all-embracing failure and wish to change its focus, including a liberalization (and perhaps elimination) of some or all of the nation's drug laws.

As for the implementation of Proposition 36, it can be argued that diversion programs, TASC, drug courts, and Proposition 36 can be only as good as the treatment programs to which the drug-involved offenders are sent. Given the scores of scientific studies conducted over the years, we know that drug abuse treatment works.[100] However, because the overwhelming majority of existing programs have never been evaluated, little is known as to which ones have demonstrated long-term effectiveness, which ones are only marginally helpful, and which ones should be immediately shut down. Going further, there are simply not enough programs to meet the need—nationwide *and* in California.

Research has documented that a significant majority of the drug-involved offenders coming to the attention of the criminal justice system are in need of long-term residential treatment. As a result, beginning in the mid-1980s there was a movement to increase the number of treatment programs and beds in correctional institutions. This culminated in the passage of the Residential Substance Abuse Treatment for State Prisoners (RSAT) legislation in 1994, which provided tens of millions of dollars each year for residential treatment programs in state and local correctional facilities. However, in the community-based settings to which Proposition 36 and other diversion clients are channeled, residential treatment beds tend to be quite scarce. As such, the great majority of clients end up being "undertreated" in outpatient programs.

It wasn't always this way. In 1990, for example, there were more than 16,000 substance abuse treatment facilities in the United States: About 55 percent were residential or inpatient-hospital, some 30 percent were outpatient, and the balance were methadone maintenance programs.[101] By 2001, there were 2,000 fewer programs, and the overwhelming majority were abstinence-oriented outpatient programs.[102] In the main, the elimination of residential slots evolved from transformations in the management of health care and the preference for lower-cost, short-term, outpatient care.[103]

Perhaps the greatest problem affecting Proposition 36 and other treatment initiatives is that the infrastructure of the nation's community-based drug abuse treatment system is crumbling. This was most vividly demonstrated in a study of the treatment system recently published in the *Journal of Substance Abuse Treatment.*[104] Based on systematic inquiries made with a representative sample of the nation's 13,484 treatment programs, the findings were quite disturbing. Results indicated that during the 16-month period prior to contact, 15 percent of the facilities had closed or had stopped addiction treatment, and an additional 29 percent had been reorganized under a different agency. Moreover, there had been a 53 percent turnover among program directors and a similar rate among counselors within just the previous year. Only about half of the programs had even a part-time physician on staff, and except for methadone maintenance programs, less than 15 percent of the programs had a nurse and very few had a social worker. The predominant form of treatment was abstinence-oriented group counseling. Overall, the study called into question the ability of the national treatment system to meet the complex needs and demands of both the patients who enter the system and the agencies that refer clients to it.

What does this suggest for the California treatment system's ability to meet the demands of Proposition 36? One could speculate that Soros, Lewis, Sperling, and the others who pushed for the passage of Proposition 36 had not done their homework and failed to realize that the system was underfunded, understaffed, and underequipped and had too few residential beds. However, one could also speculate that they had indeed done their homework and had done it very well. Perhaps the intention was to force tens of thousands of new clients into a system that they knew could not handle them properly. In demonstrating that neither incarceration nor treatment was effective in dealing with drug abuse, the ground would then be fertile for a drug policy liberalization initiative.[105]

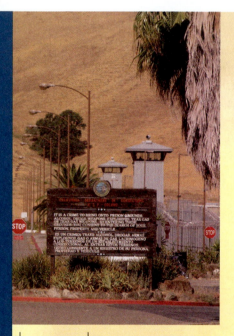

OP-ED

The experience of Francois Williams, discussed in the opening section of this chapter, is not unique. Williams was one of almost 600,000 offenders discharged from U.S. prisons every year, and one of almost 200,000 placed on parole each year.

Given the outcome of Williams's release experience, placing him on parole served little purpose, for he quickly got into trouble again. And his story is a familiar one. But does this suggest that parole be abolished? Should Williams have remained in the institution until his original term had "maxed out"? Should something else have been done with him?

The problem with answering these questions is that all too often it is emotion and politics, and not rational thinking, that drive criminal justice legislation and policy. For example, when the crack epidemic emerged in the 1980s and officials during the Reagan–Bush era pushed their "war on drugs," many states responded with mandatory minimum sentences for crack dealers. It was a "get tough" approach on the part of legislators and other politicians—many of whom were seeking reelection and felt that a hard-line "law and order" strategy might buy more votes. But the structuring and implementation of the laws was done in a very sloppy manner. What the country ended up with were prisons filled beyond capacity with crack "dealers" whose real problem was drug addiction. Most were minor offenders who needed treatment more than anything else, not long-term incarceration. But creating treatment slots doesn't win elec-

tions—tough laws, arrests, convictions, and long prison sentences do. Most politicians haven't figured out yet that you can't legislate your way out of a drug problem (with tough laws) and you can't build your way out of a crime problem (with new prisons).

As for Williams, it is clear that he was not ready for parole. Parole works for some, and not others. What the system needs to do is not abolish parole but figure out the best way of using it. And it might have worked better for Williams if the system had done something to prepare him for release—if it had provided him with some job skills, a job and a place to stay, and somewhere to go for the support he needed to deal with the frustrations of life on the outside.

Francois Williams

| Summary |

Community-based correction involves programs and activities within the community that are generally of a rehabilitative, nonpunitive nature. Such correctional approaches include criminal justice diversion, probation and conditional release, restitution programs, and furlough and temporary release.

Criminal justice diversion refers to the removal of offenders from the application of the criminal law at any stage of the police or court processes. Diversion as such began with the Chicago Boys' Court in 1914. Today its use is widespread for both juvenile and adult offenders, but its impact is difficult to assess. Both researchers and penal reformers have generally agreed that diversion programs are an essential part of correctional programming, since the experience of incarceration for many individuals often contributes to the very behaviors it was designed to eliminate. Diversion typically includes programs like youth service bureaus, public inebriate programs, civil commitment, citizen dispute settlement, and Treatment Accountability for Safer Communities (TASC).

The concept of probation emerged in 1841 with the work of John Augustus. Today probation is a judicial disposition, a status, a system, and a process. As an alternative to imprisonment, it is the most widely used adjudication disposition, encompassing elements of both community protection and offender rehabilitation. Probation was initially developed in recognition of the fact that a large number of offenders pose little, if any, threat to the community. It was later developed with the notion that these offenders could be spared the stigmatizing experience of prison and still be successfully punished for their crimes. Additionally, the appeal of probation has also been economic, since the costs of placing an individual on probation are considerably less than the costs of incarceration. Today, many jurisdictions vary their probation programming to meet the security, punishment, and rehabilitative needs of individual offenders. Such programs include restitution, shock probation, and intensive probation supervision.

Parole, common in the United States for almost a century, refers to the practice of allowing the final portion of a prison sentence to be served in the community. In contrast to probation, which involves community supervision in lieu of imprisonment, parole occurs after some part of the prison term has been completed. Also, the power to grant parole is not held by the courts, as is the case with probation, but is determined by an administrative board that can be an independent state agency, a unit in a larger state department, or part of the body that regulates the state's correctional institutions.

Both probation and parole are subject to conditions, the violation of which may result in incarceration. The U.S. Supreme Court, through a series of decisions during the 1970s, has established guidelines regarding the due process requirements at probation and parole revocation proceedings.

Other forms of community-based corrections include temporary release programs, restitution, and halfway houses. Temporary release programs include furlough, work release, and study release. Furlough involves a short leave of absence from a correctional facility that is intended to ease the transition from institutional to community life. Work release, not unlike home furlough, allows inmates to work in the community for a certain number of hours while they spend their nonworking hours in a correctional institution. Study-release programs, though not as widespread as work release, allow inmates to pursue vocational or academic schooling outside the correctional facility.

| Key Terms |

community-based correction (568)
diversion (569)
furlough (594)
Gagnon v. *Scarpelli* (583)
good time (590)
intensive probation supervision (581)
intermediate sanctions (568)
mandatory release (591)

maximum expiration date (592)
Mempa v. *Rhay* (582)
Morrissey v. *Brewer* (582)
parole (584)
parole prediction (590)
Pennsylvania Board of Probation and Parole v. *Scott* (588)
probation (573)

restitution (578)
shock probation (580)
suspended sentence (575)
Williams v. *New York* (576)

| Issues for Discussion |

1. What are the differences between probation and parole in terms of organization and administration, eligibility and selection, supervision and services, and conditions and revocation?
2. In *Mempa* v. *Rhay*, why did the Supreme Court restrict its ruling on right to counsel to cases involving deferred sentencing?
3. Which would appear to be the more effective form of parole authority structure: an independent parole board or a board housed within the state correctional system? Why?
4. Should parole be abolished? Why?
5. How do you feel about community-based corrections? Is this a helpful way to deal with nonviolent offenders? Why or why not?
6. Can California's Proposition 36 be fixed? How?

| Media and Literature Resources |

What Works. The National Institute of Justice has prepared an interesting summary report on the effectiveness of various types of criminal justice programs. See Lawrence W. Sherman, Denise C. Gottfredson, Doris L. MacKensie, John Eck, Peter Reuter, and Shawn D. Bushway, "Preventing Crime: What Works, What Doesn't, and What's Promising," *National Institute of Justice Research in Brief,* July 1998.

Probation and Parole Data. The Bureau of Justice Statistics has compiled a number of reports on probationers and parolees, which may be obtained through their Web site (*http://www.ojp.usdoj.gov*).

Parole Watch. The American Probation and Parole Association describes itself as "a strong unified voice for probation, parole, and corrections professionals." Its Web site, *http://www.appa-net.org,* pro-

vides additional information, including membership information, publications and resources, and the "Adult Probation and Parole Directory."

Parole Revocation Hearings. The implications of the U.S. Supreme Court decision in *Pennsylvania Board of Probation and Parole* v. *Scott* are examined at length in Craig Hemmens, Katherine Bennett, and Rolando V. del Carmen, "The Exclusionary Rule Does Not Apply to Parole Revocation Hearings: An Analysis of *Pennsylvania Board of Probation and Parole* v. *Scott,*" *Criminal Law Bulletin* 35 (July–August 1999): 388–409.

Prisoner Reentry. For a thorough discussion of current trends, see Jeremy Travis, *But They All Come Back: Facing the Challenges of Prisoner Reentry* (Washington DC: Urban Institute Press, 2005).

| Endnotes |

1. *Sacramento Bee,* November 28, 2004, A1; *Sacramento Bee,* November 29, 2004, A1.
2. Duane C. McBride, "Criminal Justice Diversion," in *Crime and the Criminal Justice Process,* edited by James A. Inciardi and Kenneth C. Haas (Dubuque, IA: Kendall/Hunt, 1978), 246.
3. Jacob M. Braude, "Boys' Court: Individualized Justice for the Youthful Offender," *Federal Probation* 12 (June 1948): 9–14.
4. Daniel Glaser, James A. Inciardi, and Dean V. Babst, "Later Heroin Use by Marijuana-Using, Heroin-Using, and Non-Drug-Using Adolescent Offenders in New York City," *International Journal of the Addictions* 4 (June 1969): 145–155.
5. Leon G. Leiberg, *Project Crossroads: Final Report* (Washington, DC: National Committee for Children and Youth, 1971).
6. McBride, "Criminal Justice Diversion," 250.
7. *The New York Times,* March 8, 1992, 40.
8. See George L. Kelling and Catherine M. Coles, *Fixing Broken Windows: Restoring Order and Reducing Crime in Our Communities* (New York: Free Press, 1996).
9. See John Augustus, *A Report of the Labors of John Augustus, for the Last Ten Years, in Aid of the Unfortunate* (Boston: Wright & Hasty, 1852), reprinted as *John Augustus, First Probation Officer* (New York: National Probation Association, 1939).
10. American Bar Association Project on Standards for Criminal Justice, *Standards Relating to Probation* (New York: Institute for Judicial Administration, 1970), 9.
11. National Advisory Commission on Criminal Justice Standards and Goals, *Corrections* (Washington, DC: U.S. Government Printing Office, 1973), 312.
12. James J. Stephen, *State Prison Expenditures 2001,* US Department of Justice NCJ 202949, June 2004; US Department of Justice, *Budget Trend Data: 1975 Through the President's 2003 Request to the Congress,* Budget Staff, Justice Management Division, Spring 2002.
13. State of New York, *Penal Law,* 65.05.
14. State of New York, *Penal Law,* 65.20.
15. Thomas Gitchoff and George Rush, "The Criminological Case Evaluation and Sentencing Recommendation: An Idea Whose Time Has Come," *International Journal of Offender Therapy and Comparative Criminology* 33 (1989): 77–83.
16. James A. Inciardi, "The Impact of Presentence Investigations on Subsequent Sentencing Practices," paper presented at the

Annual Meeting of the American Sociological Association, New York City, August 1976.
17. Robert M. Carter and Leslie T. Wilkins, "Some Factors in Sentencing Policy," *Journal of Criminal Law, Criminology, and Police Science* 58 (December 1967): 503–514.
18. *Williams* v. *New York,* 347 U.S. 241 (1949).
19. *Gardner* v. *Florida,* 430 U.S. 349 (1977).
20. *Code of Alabama,* 15-22-50.
21. *General Statutes of North Carolina,* 15A-1341 (a).
22. *Cox* v. *States,* 283 S.E. 2d 716 (Ga Ct. App. 1981).
23. *People* v. *Mitchell,* 178 Cal. Rptr. 188 (Cal. Ct. App., 1981).
24. *State* v. *Behrens,* 285 N. W. 2d 513 (Neb. Sup. Ct., 1979).
25. *State* v. *Wilson,* 604 P. 2d 739 (Idaho Sup., 1980).
26. *Wood* v. *State,* 378 So. 2d 111 (Fla. Dist. Ct. App., 1980).
27. *State* v. *Alexander,* 267 S. E. 2d 397 (N.C. Ct. App., 1980).
28. *People* v. *Sprague,* 430 N.Y.S. 2d 260 (N.Y. Sup. Ct. App. Div., 1980).
29. *The New York Times,* February 11, 1994, B3.
30. Denny C. Langston, "Probation and Parole: No More Free Rides," *Corrections Today,* August 1988, 90–93.
31. Peter Finn and Dale Parent, "Texas Collects Substantial Revenues from Probation Fees," *Federal Probation,* June 1993, 17–18.
32. *Griffin* v. *Wisconsin,* 483 U.S. 868 (1987).
33. See *Barber* v. *State,* 387 So. 2d 540 (Fla. Dist. Ct. App., 1980).
34. See Roy Sudipto, "Juvenile Restitution and Recidivism in a Midwestern County," *Federal Probation* 59 (1995): 55–62; Gilbert Geis, "Restitution by Criminal Offenders: A Summary and Overview," in *Restitution in Criminal Justice,* edited by Joe Hudson and Burt Galaway (Lexington, MA: Lexington, 1977), 246–264.
35. Richard Lawrence, "Restitution Programs Pay Back the Victim and Society," *Corrections Today* (February 1990): 96–98; Michael Courlander, "Restitution Programs: Problems and Solutions," *Corrections Today* (July 1988): 165–167; Barbara Sims, "Victim Restitution: A Review of the Literature," *Justice Professional* 13, 3 (2000). 247–269; R. Barry Ruback, Jennifer N. Shaffer and Melissa A. Logue, "The Imposition and Effects of Restitution in Four Pennsylvania Counties: Effects of Size of County and Specialized Collection Units," *Crime & Delinquency* 50, 3 (2004): 168–188; R. Barry Ruback, *Restitution in Pennsylvania: A Multimethod Investigation* (Erie, PA: Pennsylvania

Commission on Crime and Delinquency, 2002); Albert W. Dzur and Alan Wertheimer, "Forgiveness and Public Deliberation: The Practice of Restorative Justice," *Criminal Justice Ethics* 21, 1 (2002): 3–20.

36. *U.S. News & World Report,* December 23, 2002, 26.

37. *San Francisco Chronicle,* November 30, 2000, A23; *Los Angeles Times,* November 9, 2000, A1.

38. Paul C. Friday and David M. Petersen, "Shock of Imprisonment: Comparative Analysis of Short-Term Incarceration as a Treatment Technique," paper presented at the Inter-American Congress of the American Society of Criminology and the Inter-American Association of Criminology, Caracas, Venezuela, November 1972.

39. See David M. Petersen and Paul C. Friday, "Early Release from Incarceration: Race as a Factor in the Use of 'Shock Probation,'" *Journal of Criminal Law and Criminology* 66 (March 1975): 79–87; Joseph A. Waldron and Henry R. Angelino, "Shock Probation: A Natural Experiment on the Effect of a Short Period of Incarceration," *Prison Journal* 57 (Spring–Summer 1977): 52; Gennaro Vito, "Developments in Shock Probation: A Review of Research Findings and Policy Implications," *Federal Probation* 50 (1985): 22–27; Michael S. Vaughn, "Listening to the Experts: A National Study of Correctional Administrators' Responses to Prison Overcrowding," *Criminal Justice Review* 18, 1 (1993): 12–25; *Evaluation of the Omnibus Criminal Justice Improvements Act of 1986, Section 3, 4, and 5, Second Year Report* (Columbia, SC: South Carolina State Reorganization Commission, 1990); David Diroll, *The Use of Community Corrections and the Impact of Prison and Jail Crowding on Sentencing* (Columbus, OH: Governor's Office of Criminal Justice Services, 1989); Susette M. Talarico and Martha A. Myers, "Split Sentencing in Georgia: A Test of Two Empirical Assumptions," *Justice Quarterly* 4, 4 (1987): 611–629.

40. Lawrence W. Sherman, Denise C. Gottfredson, Doris L. MacKensie, John Eck, Peter Reuter, and Shawn D. Bushway, "Preventing Crime: What Works, What Doesn't, and What's Promising," *National Institute of Justice Research in Brief,* July 1998.

41. Billie S. Erwin and Lawrence A. Bennett, "New Dimensions in Probation: Georgia's Experience with Intensive Probation Supervision," *National Institute of Justice Research in Brief,* January 1987.

42. Erwin and Bennett, "New Dimensions in Probation."

43. Joan Petersilia and Susan Turner, "Evaluating Intensive Supervision Probation/Parole: Results of a Nationwide Experiment," *National Institute of Justice Research in Brief,* May 1993, 1–10.

44. *Mempa* v. *Rhay,* 398 U.S. 128 (1967).

45. *Morrissey* v. *Brewer,* 408 U.S. 471 (1972).

46. *Gagnon* v. *Scarpelli,* 411 U.S. 778 (1973).

47. *United States* v. *Reed,* 573 F. 2d 1020 (8th Cir., 1978).

48. *United States* v. *Pattman,* 535 F. 2d 1062 (8th Cir., 1976).

49. *United States* v. *Jurgens,* 626 F. 2d 142 (9th Cir., 1980).

50. *Watson* v. *State,* 388 So. 2d 15 (Fla. Dist. Ct. App., 1980).

51. *United States* v. *Lacey,* 661 F. 2d 1021 (5th Cir., 1981).

52. Lauren E. Glaze and Seri Palla, Probation and Parole in the United States, 2004, Bureau of Justice Statistics Bulletin, NCJ 210676, November 2005

53. Joan Petersilia, Susan Turner, James Kahan, and Joyce Peterson, *Granting Felons Probation: Public Risk and Alternatives* (Santa Monica, CA: Rand, 1985).

54. Johnny McGaha, Michael Fichter, and Peter Hirschburg, "Felony Probation: A Re-Examination of Public Risk," *American Journal of Criminal Justice* 11 (1987): 1–9.

55. Joan Petersilia, "Probation in the United States: Practices and Challenges," *National Institute of Justice Journal,* September 1997, 2–8.

56. For example, see Kirk M. Broome, Kevin Knight, Matthew L. Hiller, and D. Dwayne Simpson, "Drug Treatment Process Indicators for Probationers and Prediction of Recidivism," *Journal of Substance Abuse Treatment* 13 (1996): 487–491.

57. G. I. Giardini, *The Parole Process* (Springfield, IL: Thomas, 1959), 9.

58. Edwin H. Sutherland, *Principles of Criminology* (Philadelphia: Lippincott, 1947), 534.

59. Harry Elmer Barnes, *The Story of Punishment: A Record of Man's Inhumanity to Man* (Montclair, NJ: Patterson Smith, 1972), 68–80.

60. See E. C. Wines, "Commutation Laws in the United States," *Report of the Prison Association of New York,* 1868, 154–170.

61. See David Dressler, *Practice and Theory of Probation and Parole* (New York: Columbia University Press, 1969), 56–76; Marjorie Bell (ed.), *Parole in Principle and Practice* (New York: National Probation and Parole Association, 1957).

62. National Advisory Commission, *Corrections,* 399.

63. National Advisory Commission, *Corrections,* 399.

64. William Parker, *Parole: Origins, Development, Current Practices and Statutes* (College Park, MD: American Correctional Association, 1975); Vincent O'Leary and Kathleen J. Hanrahan, *Parole Systems in the United States* (Hackensack, NJ: National Council on Crime and Delinquency, 1976).

65. James Cjing, "Credits as Personal Property: Beware of the New Ex Post Facto Clause," *Corrections Compendium,* July 1997, 1–2.

66. *Weaver* v. *Graham,* 450 U.S. 24 (1981); *Lynce* v. *Mathis,* 117 S.Ct. 891 (1997).

67. *Menechino* v. *Oswald,* 430 F. 2d 403 (2d Cir., 1970).

68. *Johnson, U.S. ex. rel.* v. *Chairman, New York State Board of Parole,* 363 F. Supp. 416, aff'd, 500 F. 2d 925 (2d Cir., 1971).

69. *Greenholtz* v. *Inmates of Nebraska Penal and Correctional Complex,* 422 U.S. 1 (1979).

70. *Pennsylvania Board of Probation and Parole* v. *Scott,* 524 U.S. 357 (1998).

71. See, for example, *Tennessee Code,* 40-3614.

72. James A. Inciardi and Duane C. McBride, "The Parole Prediction Myth," *International Journal of Criminology and Penology* 5 (August 1977): 235–244.

73. Peter P. Lejins, "Parole Prediction: An Introductory Statement," *Crime & Delinquency* 8 (July 1962): 209–214.

74. James A. Inciardi and Dean V. Babst, "Predicting the Post-Release Adjustment of Institutionalized Narcotic Addicts," *Bulletin on Narcotics* 23 (April–June 1971): 33–39.

75. General Accounting Office, *Federal Offenders: Trends in Community Supervision* (Washington DC: U.S. Government Printing Office, 1997); Peter B. Hoffman, "Twenty Years of Operational Use of a Risk Prediction Instrument," *Journal of Criminal Justice* 22 (1994): 447–494.

76. "Good Time," *Corrections Compendium,* July 1997, 4–15.

77. *Hyland* v. *Procunier,* 311 F. Supp. 749 (N.D. Cal., 1970).

78. *Sobell* v. *Reed,* 327 F. Supp. 1294 (S.D. N.Y., 1971).

79. Jeremy Travis and Sarah Lawrence, *Beyond the Prison Gates: The State of Parole in America* (Washington DC: Urban Institute, 2002); Probation and Parole in the United States, 2004.

80. E. Eugene Miller, "Furloughs as a Technique of Reintegration," in *Corrections in the Community,* edited by E. Eugene Miller and M. Robert Montilla (Reston, VA: Reston, 1977), 201.

81. "Inmate Furloughs in the Wake of Willie Horton," *Corrections Compendium,* April 1997, 10–25.

82. "Inmate Furloughs in the Wake of Willie Horton."

83. Elmer H. Johnson and Kenneth E. Kotch, "Two Factors in Development of Work Release: Size and Location of Prisons," *Journal of Criminal Justice* 1 (March 1973): 44–45.

84. "Inmate Furloughs in the Wake of Willie Horton."

85. *Corrections Compendium,* April 2005.

86. Richard P. Seiter, *Halfway Houses: National Evaluation Program* (Washington, DC: U.S. Government Printing Office, 1977).

87. J. Edgar Hoover, *Persons in Hiding* (Boston: Little, Brown, 1938), 189–190.

88. Andrew von Hirsch and Kathleen J. Hanrahan, *Abolish Parole?* (Washington, DC: U.S. Government Printing Office, 1978), 1.

89. Edward M. Kennedy, "Toward a New System of Criminal Sentencing: Law with Order," *American Criminal Law Review* 16 (Spring 1979): 361.

90. John J. DiIulio, "Reinventing Parole and Probation," *Brookings Review,* Spring 1997, 1–3.

91. Center for Effective Public Policy, *Abolishing Parole: Why the Emperor Has No Clothes* (Philadelphia: Center for Effective Public Policy, 1995).

92. Jessica Mitford, *Kind and Unusual Punishment: The Prison Business* (New York: Vintage, 1974), 238.

93. Mitford, *Kind and Unusual Punishment,* 239.

94. *Baltimore Sun,* October 2, 1994, 20A.

95. Richard P. Seiter and Karen R. Kadela, "Prisoner Reentry: What Works, What Does Not, and What Is Promising," *Crime & Delinquency* 49 (July 2003): 360–388.

96. Joan Petersilia, "Prisoner Reentry: Public Safety and Reintegration Challenges," *Prison Journal* 81 (2001): 360–375.

97. Franklin E. Zimring and Gordon Hawkins, *The Search for Rational Drug Control* (Cambridge: Cambridge University Press, 1992); Eva Bertram, Morris Blachman, Kenneth Sharpe, and Peter Andreas, *Drug War Politics: The Price of Denial* (Berkeley: University of California Press, 1996); Elliot Currie, *Reckoning: Drugs, the Cities, and the American Future* (New York: Hill and Wang, 1993); Arnold S. Trebach, *The Great Drug War* (New York: Macmillan, 1987).

98. *The New York Times,* November 10, 2000, 18.

99. David Farabee, Yih-Ing Hser, M. Douglas Anglin, and David Huang, "Recidivism Among an Early Cohort of California's Proposition 36 Offenders," *Criminology and Public Policy* 3 (November 2004): 563–584.

100. George De Leon, *Community as Method: Therapeutic Communities for Special Populations and Special Settings* (Westport, CT: Praeger, 1997); J. A. Egertson, D. M. Fox, and A. I. Leshner, *Treating Drug Abusers Effectively* (Malden, MA: Blackwell, 1997); Institute of Medicine, *Treating Drug Problems: A Study of the Evolution, Effectiveness, and Financing of Public and Private Drug Treatment Systems* (Washington, DC: National Academy Press, 1990); Carl G. Leukefeld, Frank M. Tims, and David Farabee, *Treatment of Drug Offenders: Policies and Issues* (New York: Springer, 2002).

101. *Uniform Facility Data Set* (Rockville, MD: Substance Abuse and Mental Health Services Administration, 1990).

102. *National Survey of Substance Abuse Treatment Services* (Rockville, MD: Substance Abuse and Mental Health Services Administration, 2001).

103. Institute of Medicine, *Managing Managed Care: Quality Improvement in Behavioral Health* (Washington, DC: National Academy Press, 1997).

104. A. T. McLellan, D. Carise, and H. D. Kleber, "Can the National Addiction Treatment Infrastructure Support the Public's Demand for Quality Care?" *Journal of Substance Abuse Treatment* 25 (2003): 117–121.

105. James A. Inciardi, "Proposition 36: What Did You Really Expect?" *Criminology and Public Policy* 3 (November 2004): 593–598.

PART FIVE

JUVENILE JUSTICE

We drove from Second Avenue to Eleventh Avenue—most of the enemy was inside. They knew there was gonna be a retaliation, but, like idiots, some of 'em were out that night. We pulled the van up to the end of the street, got out real slow . . . then we started shooting. Everyone who was standin' in front of the house got hit. I remember there was one girl, she had on a black bomber jacket with white fur on the collar. She was the first to get hit, and I remember that fur just goin' red—bam—just like that. Looked like red flowers comin' out all over white.—ONE OF THE CRIPS, AS QUOTED IN *DO OR DIE*, BY LÉON BING, 1991 I waited for him across the street. Then he comes out, flashin' his colors to the world. Then I hit him—Pop! Pop! Everybody runs, and there is one less of the Latin Kings in Miami.—A 16-YEAR-OLD MEMBER OF THE NORTHSIDE NATION, 2005

Chapter 18   Juvenile Justice: An Overview

18

JUVENILE JUSTICE: AN OVERVIEW

LEARNING OBJECTIVES

After reading this chapter, you should be able to answer the following questions:

1. In American justice, what are the differences between adults and juveniles?

2. What is the philosophy of the juvenile justice system?

3. What are status offenders? Even though they have not committed crimes, why are they dealt with by the juvenile courts?

4. How is juvenile justice different from the rest of the criminal justice system?

5. What rights do juvenile offenders have when being processed by the juvenile justice system?

6. What is a waiver of jurisdiction?

WASHINGTON, D.C.—The homicide rate has dropped to a 20-year low in the nation's capital, but the number of victims younger that 18 has increased significantly. In 2000, 1 in 20 homicide victims was under 18, but by 2004, the ratio had dropped to 1 in 8.[1] Meanwhile, the Justice Department has estimated that there are more than 30,000 gangs in the United States with over 800,000 members and that every city and town in the country with a population of 250,000 or more has a gang problem.[2] Are the juvenile homicides related to gang activity? Have the activities of gangs changed in recent years? Should gang members and other juveniles be treated differently by the justice system?

To answer these questions, a number of others must be addressed. What, first of all, constitutes a juvenile? Why does the criminal justice system treat juveniles differently from adults? What is the philosophy underlying juvenile justice? And with a special justice system designed for youths, why are so many juvenile cases transferred to adult criminal courts? Indeed, should any juvenile cases be transferred to adult courts? Should there be a death penalty for juvenile murderers?

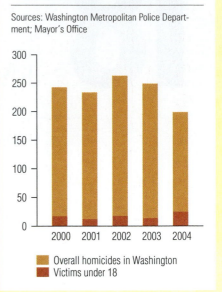

Youth Killings Increase
In Washington, killings of people under 18 have increased in the last 5 years, even as overall homicides have decreased.

Sources: Washington Metropolitan Police Department; Mayor's Office

Legend:
- Overall homicides in Washington
- Victims under 18

Teenagers' Sense of Safety

Based on interviews with teenagers ages 13 to 17 in 1994, 1999, and 2005*

The biggest problem facing teenagers is:	1994	1999	2005
Drugs	37%	31%	40%
Peer pressure	8	21	20
Violence/crime	22	9	19

"How much do you worry about being a crime victim?"	1994	1999	2005
A lot	12%	6%	4%
Some	28	18	20
Hardly ever	39	46	50
Never	22	30	26

Percentage who said they personally knew someone who had been shot:	1994	1999	2005
	40%	34%	40%

* "Don't know" answers are excluded.

Source: Adapted from *The New York Times*/CBS News/CNN Polls.

| The Nature of Juvenile Justice |

An *adult* is a person who has reached the age of majority—some "magic number" (usually 18) that indicates the individual is legally responsible for his or her actions and behavior. An adult has the right to vote, to marry, to hold government office, and to enter into contracts. Moreover, if an adult should violate the criminal law or be accused of a crime, he or she is processed through a justice system that is grounded in the due process of law guaranteed by the U.S. Constitution.

A *juvenile* is a person who has not reached the age of majority—and therefore is deemed to have a special status. Juveniles are held to a standard of behavior that is different from that for adults. Children are required to attend school between the ages of 6 and 16; they are expected to obey their parents; they are forbidden to purchase alcohol or cigarettes or drive motor vehicles; they may not marry without parental permission; they cannot enter into business or financial contracts; and they are not permitted to vote, enter the military, or run away from home. Some jurisdictions place other restrictions on juveniles, such as curfews or laws against "incorrigible" or "immoral" behavior. Like adults, children *can* be charged with violations of the criminal law. But because of their special status, an alternative system has evolved for dealing with juvenile lawbreakers.

The juvenile justice system in the United States is based on the philosophy that the special status of children requires that they be protected and corrected, not necessarily punished. But as the system evolved, it failed to accord juveniles any individual rights. After all, in American society a juvenile is essentially in the "custody" of parents or guardians or of the state.

Beyond the philosophical orientation stemming from the special status of children, there are other differences between adult and juvenile justice systems. For adults to fall within the jurisdiction of the criminal courts, they must be charged with some violation of the criminal law. A young person, however, can come to the attention of the juvenile courts in a variety of ways. First, the juvenile may indeed be found to have violated the criminal law. Second, he or she can be charged with having committed a **status offense**—an act declared by statute to be a crime because it violates the behavior standards expected of children. Because of their status, only juveniles can be charged with the offenses of running away, truancy, or being incorrigible. Third, a child may fall within the jurisdiction of the court because of the behavior of an adult. That is, should a juvenile be the victim of abuse, neglect, or abandonment by a parent or guardian, the courts may intervene.

Perhaps the major difference between the adult and juvenile justice systems involves the purpose and nature of the sanctions imposed. As noted in Chapter 13, there are five competing philosophies that guide sentencing in adult courts—retribution, vengeance, incapacitation, deterrence, and rehabilitation. By contrast, actions taken in juvenile courts are, at least in theory, deemed to be "in the best interests of the child." The juvenile justice system, then, is based on the notions that every child is treatable and that judicial intervention will result in positive behavioral change. One would thus assume that juvenile court sanctions are based on a rehabilitation model and do not include any other sentencing objectives.

The Emergence of Juvenile Justice

From the early colonial period in America through much of the 19th century, juvenile offenders were handled in essentially the same way as adults. Children beyond the age of reason (about 7 years old) were held to adult standards of behavior. For criminal offenses, they were subject to the same sanctions, placed in the same institutions, and hanged from the same gallows.

Reformation in the treatment of juvenile offenders began during the early decades of the 19th century, but it was piecemeal at best and limited to only a few jurisdictions. Especially noteworthy was New York City's *House of Refuge,* established in 1825 as the first systematic attempt to separate juvenile offenders from adult criminals and to provide "correction" rather than punishment (see Exhibit 18.1). In the courts, the separation of juveniles from adults in trial proceedings first occurred in Chicago in 1861. Chicago's lead was followed by Massachusetts in the early 1870s and New York and Rhode Island in the 1890s.[3]

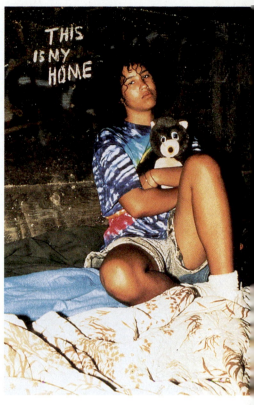

If a juvenile runs away, it is a crime because it violates the behavior standards expected of children. This young runaway lives under a freeway bridge in Hollywood, California.

Parens Patriae

The early changes in the processing and treatment of juvenile offenders in Chicago and several eastern states marked the beginning of widespread reforms. During the latter part of the 19th century there was increasing awareness that the roots of crime and delinquency were not necessarily to be found within individual offenders but, rather, were products of the culture and environment in which they lived. This new awareness, coupled with ongoing concern over the abuse and neglect of children both in and out of institutions, led to the emergence of a new juvenile justice philosophy based on the already established concept of *parens patriae.*

Under the common law in England at the time, the Court of Chancery had the authority to intervene in property matters to protect the rights of children. In the United States this jurisdictional focus was expanded to include the handling of "dependent and neglected" children. Court intervention was justified by the theory that such a child's natural protectors—the parents—were unable or unwilling to provide an appropriate level of care. The court took the place of the parents; hence, ***parens patriae,*** meaning "the state as parent."

Reformers merged the concept of *parens patriae* with the medical model of treatment to establish a system of juvenile justice designed to reform and rehabilitate young offenders. The underlying philosophy was that if a child "went astray," it was the *parents* who had failed. The court could take over the role of the parent, diagnose the problem, and prescribe the appropriate treatment. It did not matter what the child had done. His or her deviant behavior was merely a symptom of the problem. The duty of the court was not to blame the child or determine guilt but to identify and treat the underlying problem. Moreover, the youth's welfare was to be the central concern of the court. This would not only protect the future of the child but also permit an informal

When Laura Bush spoke about gangs recently, by her descriptions of them some people in the audience wondered if the First Lady had watched *West Side Story* once too often.

—*THE ECONOMIST*

EXHIBIT 18.1 | *historical perspectives on crime and justice*

The House of Refuge

The New York City House of Refuge, composed of a bleak set of barracks leased from the federal government, was the first house of correction for juveniles in the United States. It was dedicated on January 1, 1825, to its first nine inmates. Its founder, Reverend John Stanford, stated to his charges:

> You are to look at these walls which surround the building, not so much as a prison, but as a hospitable dwelling, in which you enjoy comfort and safety from those who once led you astray. And, I may venture to say, that in all probability, this is the best home many of you ever enjoyed. You have no need for me to tell you, that the consideration of all these favors should stimulate you to submission, industry, and gratitude. You are not placed here for punishment, but to produce your moral improvement.

The first director of the House of Refuge was Joseph Curtis, an educator whose aims were to develop the individuality of his wards and to enhance their powers of self-expression. Although progressive in philosophy, Curtis could do little to control the behavior of his wards and he quickly became a strict disciplinarian. At the table, children "must be silent, holding up a hand if they want water, a thumb for vinegar, three fingers for bread, and one finger for salt." Violation of these and the many other rules he instituted could result in corporal punishment and solitary confinement. Curtis lasted only 1 year, for the chief characteristic of his tenure was a high rate of escape.

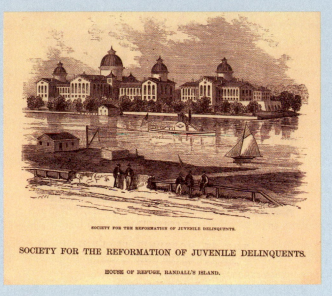

SOCIETY FOR THE REFORMATION OF JUVENILE DELINQUENTS.

SOCIETY FOR THE REFORMATION OF JUVENILE DELINQUENTS.

HOUSE OF REFUGE, RANDALL'S ISLAND.

The House of Refuge

Curtis was succeeded by N. C. Hart, a high school teacher who shifted the focus of the House of Refuge from education to work. The juvenile inmates labored 8 hours each day at weaving and the making of brass nails, shoes, and cane seats for chairs. Children were also sent

---

court process that considered the entire history and background of the child's difficulties, without being hampered by the limitations and requirements of official criminal procedure. Thus, juvenile processing would be a civil rather than a criminal matter.[4]

The early juvenile justice reform efforts were heavily promoted by a number of penologists, philanthropists, and women's organizations, collectively known as the "child savers," (see Exhibit 18.2). The child savers movement crystallized in 1899 with the passage of the **Illinois Juvenile Court Act,** which established the first statewide juvenile court system in the United States.[5]

Modern Juvenile Courts

By 1945, there was a juvenile court system in every state in the United States. Currently, more than 3,000 courts across the nation hear juvenile cases. While they all reflect the same general underlying philosophy, their sophistication and procedures vary. Some systems are highly organized, with extensive and well-trained support staffs and large probation and treatment components. Others rely on the resources of the adult criminal courts and correctional systems.

The jurisdiction of juvenile courts is defined in terms of the offender's age and alleged offense. Typically, the maximum age is 18, although age 16 is the upper limit in some locations. Juvenile courts have authority over delinquency and status offenses. **Delinquency** involves criminal law violations, such as those listed in the FBI's *Uniform Crime Reports,* that would be considered crimes if committed by an adult. As such, a **delinquent** is a juvenile offender who has been **adjudicated** by an officer of a juvenile court. Status offenses, as noted earlier, are specific acts (truancy, running away) and

out to labor on distant farms or were indentured in the service of others. Records indicate that the first child to be so indentured in a foster home was 13-year-old Diana Williams, sent to the House of Refuge for stealing. The agreement signed by Diana charged that she faithfully serve her mistress and obey every lawful command:

> She shall not waste her mistress's goods, nor lend unlawfully to any; she shall not commit fornication, nor contract matrimony within the said term. At cards, dice, or any other unlawful game she shall not play; not haunt alehouses, taverns, nor playhouses, but in all things behave herself as a faithful apprentice ought to.

Although the philosophy that led to the establishment of the New York City House of Refuge may have been praiseworthy at the time, in actual practice the institution was a juvenile prison. Structured to hold children securely, its interior was designed to implant the notions of order and rationality. Rooms were small and windowless and, much like jail cells, their doors were of iron-lattice slab. The treatment also paralleled that of a penitentiary. As children were admitted, they were given identical clothing and haircuts. "Troublemakers" were always punished. The milder sanctions included either a diet of bread and water or the depriving of meals altogether. For more serious cases there was bread and water coupled with solitary confinement, manacling with a ball and chain, or whipping with a cat-o'-nine-tails. The most troublesome offenders were typically shipped off to sea.

The House of Refuge grew rapidly, accepting not only those children who had been adjudicated for delinquent acts but also the poor, the destitute, the orphaned, the incorrigible, and others who were simply in danger of getting into trouble. Rather than a house of "refuge," the institution had become a reformatory for delinquents and a repository for street waifs that New York had nowhere else to put. But to the society at large, the House of Refuge was a model juvenile institution. A "refuge movement" began, and by the late 1840s similar facilities had been established in most eastern cities. By then, however, New York had already begun to phase out the refuge system.

In 1854, a facility large enough to hold more than a thousand juveniles was opened on Randall's Island—a small strip of land in New York's East River northeast of Manhattan. It was the new House of Refuge. Although it had retained its original name, it represented the state's first of many juvenile reformatories yet to come. In practice, youths placed in the Randall's Island facility were in prison at hard labor. In 1901, reformers exposed the Randall's Island refuge as an immense "chamber of horrors." Crusading journalists declared that beyond the waters of the East River and behind the bastions of Randall's Island lay a barbaric prison colony. An investigation was launched, but the refuge somehow endured, at least for a time. Finally, in 1935, the structure on Randall's Island was closed, the inmates were moved to a new juvenile prison recently built by the New York State Department of Corrections some 50 miles north of New York City, and the House of Refuge passed into history, remaining only as a curious anecdote in the annals of juvenile justice.

Sources: B. K. Pierce, *A Half Century with Juvenile Delinquents: The New York House of Refuge and Its Times* (New York: Appleton, 1869); Homer Folks, *The Care of Destitute, Neglected and Delinquent Children* (New York: Macmillan, 1902); Negley K. Teeters and John Otto Reinemann, *The Challenge of Delinquency* (Englewood Cliffs, NJ: Prentice-Hall, 1961), 429–443; David J. Rothman, *The Discovery of the Asylum* (Boston: Little, Brown, 1971); Robert S. Pickett, *House of Refuge: Origins of Juvenile Reform in New York State, 1815–1857* (Syracuse, NY: Syracuse University Press, 1969).

general conditions (incorrigibility, uncontrollable behavior) that are unique to the status of being a juvenile. Although most cases heard by juvenile courts involve delinquents or status offenders, there is a third category: dependent and neglected children, the deprived, and the abused. These juveniles are victims rather than offenders, and the court's intent is to provide assistance "in their best interests."

The Processing of Juvenile Offenders

Each year, more than a million juveniles are arrested in the United States. The offenses cover all categories of crime, from the most serious violent crimes of murder, forcible rape, and robbery, to status offenses such as running away, truancy, and curfew violations. Although perhaps a third of these offenses result in release with no more than a warning, the majority are referred to the courts for official processing. However, given the less formal nature of juvenile justice combined with the dynamics of police discretion, it is likely that for each arrest of a juvenile there are perhaps 500 "probable cause" arrest situations.

A Maryland youth being arrested after a high speed "hot pursuit."

Police Discretion

Police officers who encounter status offenders or juveniles involved in delinquent activities have several alternatives at their disposal. First, the officer may simply release the youth with a reprimand. Second, the officer may take the youth to the police station, where a "juvenile card" is prepared that briefly describes the incident. The parents

EXHIBIT 18.2 | historical perspectives on crime and justice

The "Child Savers"

The civic-minded citizens who became concerned about the problem of juvenile misconduct in the 19th century have become popularly known as the "child savers." As social reformers, they were instrumental in the development of the houses of refuge, the later reform schools, and ultimately, the juvenile courts. Some, such as Charles Loring Brace and his Children's Aid Society, also introduced the idea of placing vagrant and poor children with western frontier farm families. They sought to "drain the city" of its problem "street urchin" children and ship them westward. The pioneer spirit, fresh air and wide open spaces, and hard work were apparently considered desirable for wayward youth.

The child savers advocated not only specialized institutions for children but also stern, regimented discipline, which they considered essential to reform. It was for this reason that the institutions had to be given extensive discretionary authority over children, again in the name parens patriae.

The first of the state reform schools for juveniles was opened in Massachusetts in 1847. These institutions were aimed at teaching children an honest trade and at instilling respect for advancement through hard work, in addition to teaching discipline. The reform schools developed rapidly, and between 1850 and 1890 almost every state had opened one or more of them. These institutions were congregate care facilities that, in addition to institutional jobs and the learning of a trade, also emphasized basic education. Unfortunately, the reform schools were also characterized by race/ethnic and gender segregation, by harsh discipline and corporal punishment, and by poor physical care. Commitments by courts to the reform schools were indeterminate until the legal age of majority, which in most states was age 21.

This period in American juvenile justice history is particularly interesting and controversial. Many scholars have discussed it and written about it, especially about the role of the child savers. The motivations of the reformers in creating and expanding the juvenile justice system have been interpreted generally in one of two ways. The first and more traditional interpretation is that these reformers held a positivistic philosophy that emphasized individual values and judgments in the care of children. Individual treatment was the order of the day. The reformers believed, according to this view, that children's problems should be handled in the best interests of both the state and the child, so as to help the child develop into a law-abiding and productive adult.

A second, what can be termed critical and revisionist, interpretation is much less glowing in recounting the motives of the child savers. According to this view, the reform movement expressed the vested interests of a particular group, namely the middle and upper classes. The concept of parens patriae was exploited in order to continue middle- and upper-class values, to control relevant political systems such as education, and to further the child labor system. The emphasis was on controlling and perhaps resocializing young miscreants.

The reality seems to lie somewhere between these two perspectives, as misguided and as ambivalent as that reality might be. Undoubtedly there were reformers guided only by benevolent and humanitarian concerns for helping the young. But there were also those who sought to control, to repress, and only maybe to resocialize children who were viewed by them as being dangerously deviant. This curious blend resulted in a juvenile justice and corrections system that can best be described as ambivalent or even schizophrenic.

Sources: Jameson W. Doig, "For the Salvation of Children: The Search for Juvenile Justice in the United States," in Crime and Criminal Justice, edited by John A. Gardiner and Michael A. Mulkey (Lexington, MA: Heath, 1975); Alexander W. Pisciotta, "Theoretical Perspectives for Historical Analyses: A Selective Review of the Juvenile Justice Literature," Criminology 19 (May 1981); James O. Finckenauer, Juvenile Delinquency and Corrections (Orlando: Harcourt Brace Jovanovich, 1984).

Gangs have declared war on our nation.

—VIRGINIA CONGRESSMAN
J. RANDY FORBES, 2005*

One-third of individuals under 18 are now members of gangs.

—U.S. DEPARTMENT OF JUSTICE
SPOKESPERSON, 2005†

may then be called in for a discussion, after which the youth is released. A typical "adjustment" of this type was described to the author by a Maryland sheriff's deputy after a homeowner complained that "a group of tough-looking kids" was "drinking, taking drugs, swearing, and raising hell" behind his garage:

> When I got there it wasn't really all that bad. There were these three kids, two boys and a girl, all about thirteen years old, passing around a "joint" and a pint of wine. A little loud, maybe, but none of them were drunk or stoned and they didn't seem to be making any kind of trouble. I made them grind out their joint and pour out the rest of the wine and told them to sit in the patrol car. The complainant said he would be satisfied if the kids promised not to return, so I drove them around for fifteen minutes lecturing them on the virtues of neighborliness, good deeds, and wholesome all-American conduct. They said they'd behave themselves, so I let them go with just a warning.

The working style of the officer, the circumstances of the incident, and the policies of the department typically play a role in the decision to release or to detain juve-

---

*Author's note: Violent crime in the state of Virginia dropped 25% from 1993–2003.
†Author's note: That would mean that 24.2 million youths are gang members. According to the FBI, there are less than 1 million gang members in the United States.

© 2001. By Mike Smith, Las Vegas Sun. Reprinted by permission.

niles. Studies have demonstrated, however, that numerous other factors can come into play. Among these are the attitude of the victim; the juvenile's prior record; the seriousness of the offense; the age, gender, race, and demeanor of the offender; the likelihood of adequate parental handling of the matter; the time and location of the incident; the availability of a service agency for referral; and the officer's perception of how the case will be handled by the court.[6] Consideration of these factors by a police officer, consciously or otherwise, is more likely to result in an "on-the-street disposition," or no action at all.

Beyond these, there is the third option: taking the juvenile into custody. Even in this event, the police still have alternatives. Some law enforcement agencies in large urban areas have their own diversion and delinquency prevention programs to which they may send a juvenile, while status offenders may be brought to social service agencies for counseling and treatment. For felony offenses, and particularly those involving violence, there is the fourth police option: referral to the juvenile court.

How often do students witness one student bullying another?

Source: National Crime Prevention Council.

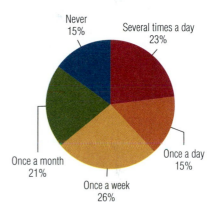

Never 15%
Several times a day 23%
Once a day 15%
Once a week 26%
Once a month 21%

Police officers have many options open to them when dealing with children. This young girl is delinquent from school because she is worried about her ill mother at home.

The Juvenile Justice Funnel

100,000
Juvenile suspects

50,000
Handled
informally

50,000
Handled
formally

25,000
Dismissed

22,000
Not adjudicated

12,500 Dismissed

15,000
Informal probation

9,000
Other dispositions

1,500
Formal probation

10,000
Other dispositions

2,000 Transferred
to criminal court

3,000 Placed in
juvenile institutions

In certain situations, however, it would appear that police officers see themselves as having few, or no, discretionary alternatives. In 1998, for example, a waitress in a Miami, Florida, restaurant observed a 10-year-old boy kick his mother during an argument. After she notified the police of the incident, two officers promptly arrived, arrested the fourth-grader, and took him away in handcuffs. The youth was charged with simple domestic battery, a misdemeanor, and jailed overnight. The police claimed that they had no discretion in the matter because of the way the domestic violence law was written. They had to intervene, before the child's assaultive behavior escalated. Miami circuit court judge Tom Petersen, however, had a different take on the situation: "The tragedy seems to be that we've reached the point in the juvenile justice system where policies and fear of political repercussions completely obliterate common sense."[7]

Petition and Intake

The mechanism for bringing juveniles to the attention of the courts is a **petition** (as opposed to an arrest warrant). This can be filed by the police, a victim, parents, school officials, or a social worker. Like an arrest warrant, the petition specifies the alleged offense or delinquency, the name and address of the child, the names and residences of his or her parents, and a description of the circumstances of the offense. This petition initiates the formal judicial processing of a juvenile (see Exhibit 18.3).

After the petition is filed, an **intake hearing** is held. This is conducted by the court as a preliminary examination of the facts of the case. However, it is not presided over by a judge, nor does it occur in open court. Rather, the hearing officer is usually an attorney, a probation officer, a referee with a background in social work, or someone else assigned by the juvenile court. The purpose of this hearing is to protect the interests of the child and to quickly dispose of cases that do not require the time and expense of formal court processing.

In effect, the intake officer makes a legal judgment of the probable cause of the petition; this may be the only time that the sufficiency of the evidence is evaluated. The officer may also conduct a brief investigation into the background of the juvenile, have an informal hearing with the child and parents, or discuss the case with the police and attorneys. Depending on the hearing officer's judgment of the sufficiency of the evidence, the seriousness of the offense, and the need for court intervention, there are three alternatives:

1. The hearing officer can dismiss the case, in which instance the matter is over—no further court processing is required and the child can go home.
2. The officer can make an informal judgment, such as arbitration, restitution, or referral to some social agency.
3. The officer can authorize an inquiry before the juvenile court judge.

Detention and Bail

When the intake decision recommends a hearing before the juvenile court judge, most state statutes require a **detention hearing** to determine whether the child should be released to a parent or guardian or retained in custody. The issues addressed might include such considerations as whether there is a need to protect the child, whether the child presents a serious threat to the community, or the likelihood that the child will return to court at the scheduled time.

In theory, the temporary detention of juveniles should meet three basic objectives:

1. Secure custody with good physical care that will offset the damaging effects of confinement.
2. A constructive and satisfying program of activities to provide the juvenile with a chance to identify socially acceptable ways of gaining satisfaction.
3. Observation and study to provide screening for undetected mental or emotional illnesses as well as diagnoses that can serve as a basis for treatment plans.[8]

LAW & CRIMINAL JUSTICE | EXHIBIT 18.3

The Juvenile Justice System

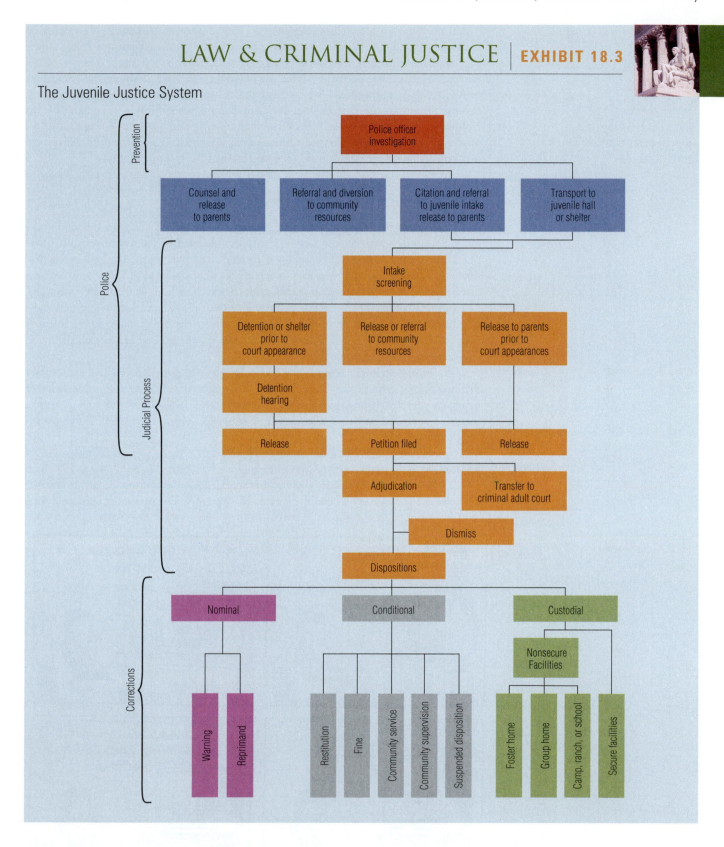

Should these goals be met, the detention experience might actually aid both the child and the court. In practice, however, most children in detention are housed in facilities that provide little more than security. Many are held in police lockups or local jails; even in the 1990s some tens of thousands of juveniles were being temporarily detained in secure state correctional facilities and local jails for adults.[9]

If the decision is to release the juvenile, the question of bail arises. This question is the subject of some debate. On the one hand, there are liberal statutory alternatives for juveniles, including release on recognizance or release to parents. On the other, there is considerable opposition to the use of bail bonds and other financial conditions of release. A bail agreement is a contract that is not binding on a minor. Moreover, most children must rely on parents or others for the needed funds or collateral. This circumstance gives the juvenile little motivation to appear in court as required. And finally, as with adult defendants, bail tends to discriminate against the poor. Nevertheless, some states have established bail procedures in the juvenile courts.

Adjudication and Disposition

At the **adjudication inquiry,** which is generally closed to the public and the media, the judge determines whether the facts of the case and the child's behavior warrant a formal hearing by the court. This inquiry is similar in purpose to the intake hearing, but now it is a magistrate who rules on the need for further processing. The magistrate can dismiss the case, order a formal adjudication hearing, or refer the juvenile elsewhere.

In recent years, the juvenile justice system has employed a variety of alternatives to the official adjudication of youths. The major alternative is diversion to community agencies for counseling and treatment. However, a youth may refuse such diversion and request a formal adjudication hearing.

The **adjudication hearing** is not a trial. It is legally classified as a civil rather than a criminal proceeding. The judge presides *on behalf of* the child to determine whether he or she actually committed the alleged offense and, if so, to determine whether the youth's parents are providing adequate care, supervision, and discipline. The judge relies on any available clinical, social, or diagnostic reports.

Should the judge determine that no misconduct occurred, the case is dismissed. If misconduct is apparent, a disposition hearing is scheduled.

At **disposition hearings,** juvenile court judges have extremely broad discretion. They have the authority to dismiss a case, give the juvenile a warning, impose a fine,

> The gun is your best friend.
>
> —FIFTEEN-YEAR-OLD
> SOUTH-CENTRAL LOS ANGELES
> GANG MEMBER

BY WASSERMAN FOR THE BOSTON GLOBE

Reprinted by permission of Tribune Media Services.

order the payment of restitution, require the performance of community service, refer the offender to a community agency or treatment facility, or place the child on probation under the supervision of a court officer. They may also put the child in a foster home, enter an order against the parents for the protection of the child, or have the youth committed to a juvenile institution. In practice, the most common dispositions are probation, court-sponsored restitution programs, and institutional commitment.

Juveniles and the Constitution

As noted earlier, the juvenile court process is not a criminal proceeding. It is not a matter of *"State v. Child."* There is no prosecutor acting on behalf of the state to prove the youth guilty, and there is no jury. The process is a civil one that is designed, at least in theory, to aid and protect the child. But is a youthful defendant in juvenile court protected by the Bill of Rights? Does the juvenile have the same constitutional rights that are enjoyed by adult defendants in criminal trials? For the most part, the answer to these questions is no—and until the Supreme Court's decision in *Kent* v. *United States* in 1966,[10] juvenile courts seemed to accord few, if any, rights at all. In that case (discussed briefly later), for the first time in its history the Supreme Court evaluated juvenile court proceedings and the constitutional rights of children. The Court noted that youths involved in juvenile proceedings were being deprived of constitutional rights and denied the rehabilitation they were supposed to receive under juvenile court philosophy.

Due Process and Juvenile Proceedings

The *Kent* case did not give the Court the opportunity to render a decision on the content of juvenile delinquency proceedings. The next year, however, the Court was able to do so in the case of ***In re Gault***,[11] an appeal involving the detention of a 15-year-old in a state industrial school for allegedly making an obscene telephone call (see Exhibit 18.4). The *Gault* decision extended to juvenile courts the requirement of notice of charges, the right to counsel, the right to confrontation and cross-examination of witnesses, the privilege against self-incrimination, and the rights to a transcript of proceedings and appellate review.

Before *Gault*, juvenile courts had almost unlimited power, and most youths' constitutional rights were totally denied. In the view of some critics, this situation was unacceptable. As Supreme Court Justice Abe Fortas put it, "Under our Constitution, the condition of being a boy does not justify a kangaroo court."

After *Gault*, additional rights were applied to juvenile proceedings. In a 1970 case, ***In re Winship***,[12] the Supreme Court held that proof "beyond a reasonable doubt" was required for an adjudication of delinquency. Prior to that, in juvenile matters guilt needed to be established only by the lower standard of "preponderance of evidence." In ***Breed*** **v.** ***Jones***,[13] decided in 1975, the Fifth Amendment protection against double jeopardy was extended to juveniles. In the 1971 ruling of ***McKeiver*** **v.** ***Pennsylvania***,[14] on the other hand, the Court held that due process of law does not require a jury in juvenile court hearings. However, the Court was careful to note that there "is nothing to prevent a juvenile court judge in a particular case where he feels the need is demonstrated from using an advisory jury."

Police Encounters and Juvenile Rights

While *Gault* addressed the rights required at the adjudication stage of the juvenile justice process, the Supreme Court left other due process issues to the state and lower federal courts. For the most part, many of these issues remained unresolved, particularly those having to do with juvenile rights and police encounters. The Court has not ruled specifically, for example, on the applicability of the *Miranda* safeguards to the juvenile

There was nothing to do.

—FIFTEEN-YEAR-OLD BOSTON YOUTH ON WHY HE AND A COMPANION ALLEGEDLY RAPED, STABBED, AND MURDERED A WOMAN ON HALLOWEEN NIGHT

EXHIBIT 18.4 | LAW & CRIMINAL JUSTICE

In re Gault

On June 8, 1964, 15-year-old Gerald Francis Gault and a friend, Ronald Lewis, were taken into custody by the sheriff of Gila County, Arizona. Gerald was then still subject to a 6-month probation order as a result of having been in the company of another boy who had stolen a wallet from a woman's purse. Gerald and Ronald's trip to the police station on that day in June was the result of a verbal complaint by Mrs. Cook, a neighbor of the two boys, about a telephone call made to her in which lewd and indecent remarks allegedly had been made.

At the time Gerald was picked up, both his mother and father were at work. No notice that he was being taken into custody was left at the home, and no other steps were taken to advise the Gaults that their son had, in effect, been arrested. Gerald was taken to a children's detention home. When his mother returned home that evening, she learned from the Lewis family that Gerald was in custody. Mrs. Gault went to the detention home and was informed by deputy probation officer Flagg that her son was indeed there and that a hearing would take place at the juvenile court the following day.

Officer Flagg filed a petition with the court on the hearing day, but a copy was not served on Gerald's parents. The petition was formal but very brief. It made no reference to any factual basis for the court action, but merely recited that "said minor is under the age of eighteen years, and is in need of protection of this Honorable Court"; and that "said minor is a delinquent minor."

On June 9, Gerald, his mother, his older brother, and probation officers Flagg and Henderson appeared before the juvenile court judge. Mrs. Cook, the complainant, was not there. No one was sworn at the hearing, no transcript or recording of the proceedings was made, and no record of the substance of the proceedings was maintained. From later testimony it appeared that presiding Judge McGhee had questioned Gerald about the phone call, but there were differences of opinion as to how he answered. Judge McGhee and Officer Flagg stated that Gerald had admitted making one of the obscene statements. Mrs. Gault recalled that her son said he only dialed Mrs. Cook's number and handed the telephone to his friend Ronald. At the conclusion of the hearing the judge said he would "think about it." Gerald was not sent home but was returned to the detention center. Several days later, however, he was driven home with no explanation as to why he had been held in custody for almost a week. Then, at 5 p.m. on the day of Gerald's release, Mrs. Gault received the following note, on a plain piece of paper, signed by Officer Flagg:

Judge McGhee has set Monday, June 15, 1964, at 11 a.m. as the date and time for further hearings on Gerald's delinquency.

s/Flagg

Present at the June 15 meeting were Gerald and his parents, Ronald Lewis and his father, Officers Henderson and Flagg, and Judge McGhee. Again there was conflict about what Gerald actually admitted to, and again Mrs. Cook was not there. In fact, the judge denied Mrs. Gault's request that her son's accuser be present. The only contact the court ever had with Mrs. Cook was a telephone call from Officer Flagg on June 9.

At the June 15 hearing a referral report was filed with the court, yet its contents were not disclosed to the Gaults. This report charged Gerald with "lewd phone calls." At the conclusion of the hearing, the judge committed Gerald Francis Gault as a juvenile delinquent to the State Industrial School until age 21. Since Gerald was only 15 years old, that meant a term of incarceration of almost 6 years for a crime that, if committed by an adult, would have resulted in a fine of $50 or less. Furthermore, no appeal was permitted by Arizona law in juvenile cases.

Under a writ of *habeas corpus,* the Gaults managed to initiate the appeals process, but both the local superior court and the Arizona Supreme Court dismissed the writ. Meanwhile, Gerald Gault remained in detention at the State Industrial School.

In 1967, 3 years after Gault's arrest, the U.S. Supreme Court reviewed the case. The Supreme Court ruled against the Arizona courts, holding that Gerald Gault had been denied the following basic rights:

1. Notice of charges.

2. Right to counsel.

3. Right to confrontation and cross-examination of witnesses.

4. Privilege against self-incrimination.

5. Right to a transcript of the proceedings.

6. Right to appellate review.

The result of the Supreme Court's decision was to extend these constitutional guarantees to every case in every juvenile court in the United States.

Source: *In re Gault,* 38 U.S. 1 (1967).

Is this going to take long? I've got someplace to go tonight.

— EIGHT-YEAR-OLD CHICAGO BOY BEING QUESTIONED BY DETECTIVES AFTER HE SHOT A CLASSMATE IN THE SPINE WITH A SEMIAUTOMATIC HANDGUN

process.[15] Although *Gault* applied the privilege against self-incrimination to juveniles, the Court limited the scope of its ruling:

> We do not in this opinion consider the impact of these constitutional provisions upon the totality of the relationship of the juvenile and the state. We do not even consider the entire process relating to juvenile "delinquents." For example, we are not here concerned with the procedures or constitutional rights applicable to the pre-judicial stages of the juvenile process.

In 1968, the National Conference of Commissioners on Uniform State Laws drafted the *Uniform Juvenile Court Act* and recommended its enactment in all states.[16] The purpose of the act was to encourage uniformity of purpose, scope, and procedures in the juvenile justice system. One of its provisions dealt with the issue of self-incrimination. Jurisdictions that adopted the Uniform Juvenile Court Act, in whole or in part, have similar provisions. Moreover, following *Gault,* other jurisdictions enacted statutes designed to implement the *Miranda* safeguards during the investigatory stage of juvenile proceedings.

New Jersey v. T.L.O.

Another issue that has not been fully resolved is the scope of the principle of *in loco parentis* — literally, "in the place of the parent." This principle emerges in cases involving searches of students and their lockers by school officials. The Supreme Court has held that the Fourth Amendment does not protect individuals from searches conducted by private persons acting on behalf of the government. When searches of students occur, four questions arise:

1. Is the school official acting as a private individual or as a government agent?
2. Is the official authorized to conduct a search on the basis of his or her *in loco parentis* relationship to the student?
3. Does the *in loco parentis* relationship give to a school official a parent's immunity from the Fourth Amendment?
4. Is the search reasonable?

These questions were addressed by the Supreme Court in *New Jersey v. T.L.O.*,[17] decided on January 15, 1985.

In this case, a teacher at a New Jersey high school discovered Ms. T.L.O., a 14-year-old first-year student, and her companion smoking cigarettes in a school lavatory in violation of a school rule. The two girls were taken to an office, where they were questioned by a vice principal. When T.L.O. denied smoking and claimed that she was not a smoker, the vice principal demanded to see her purse. Upon opening it, he observed cigarettes and the rolling papers typically associated with marijuana use. He then searched the purse thoroughly and found marijuana, a pipe, plastic bags, a substantial amount of money, an index card listing students who owed T.L.O. money, and two letters that implicated T.L.O. in marijuana dealing. The police were called, and delinquency charges were brought against Ms. T.L.O. in juvenile court. The court denied T.L.O.'s motion to suppress the evidence found in her purse on Fourth Amendment grounds, declared the search to be a reasonable one, and adjudicated T.L.O. to be delinquent. T.L.O. appealed the decision. Eventually the New Jersey Supreme Court reversed the decision in T.L.O.'s favor and ordered that the evidence be suppressed, holding that the search of the purse was unreasonable. On appeal to the U.S. Supreme Court, entered by the Reagan administration in behalf of the State of New Jersey, the High Court ruled in favor of New Jersey and stated the following:

> 1. The Fourth Amendment's prohibition on unreasonable searches and seizures applies to searches conducted by public school officials and is not limited to searches carried out by law enforcement officers. Nor are school officials exempt from the Amendment's dictates by virtue of the special nature of their authority over schoolchildren. In carrying out searches and other functions pursuant to disciplinary policies mandated by state statutes, school officials act as representatives of the State, not merely as surrogates for the parents of students, and they cannot claim the parent's immunity from the Fourth Amendment strictures.
>
> 2. Schoolchildren have legitimate expectations of privacy. They may find it necessary to carry with them a variety of legitimate, noncontraband items, and there is no reason to conclude that they have necessarily waived all rights to privacy in such items by bringing them onto school grounds. But striking the balance between schoolchildren's legitimate expectations of privacy and the school's equally legitimate need to maintain an environment in which learning can take place requires some easing of the restrictions to which searches by

School lockers are searched at a Travis County, Texas, high school. The Supreme Court has ruled that school officials, "with reasonable grounds to believe that the law or school rules are being violated, may conduct reasonable searches if needed to maintain safety, order, and discipline in school."

public authorities are ordinarily subject. Thus, school officials need not obtain a warrant before searching a student who is under their authority. Moreover, school officials need not be held subject to the requirement that searches be based on probable cause to believe that the subject of the search has violated or is violating the law. Rather, the legality of the search should depend simply on reasonableness, under all the circumstances of the search. Determining the reasonableness of any search involves a determination of whether the search was justified at its inception and whether, as conducted, it was reasonably related in scope to the circumstances that justified the interference in the first place. . . . Such a search will be permissible in its scope when the measures adopted are reasonably related to the objectives of the search and not excessively intrusive in light of the student's age and sex and the nature of the infraction.

The Court's ruling in *T.L.O.* left a number of questions unanswered. There were no views expressed on whether evidence obtained by school authorities through an illegal search could be used in court; whether the standard announced also applied to searches of desks and lockers; what standard would apply to searches undertaken at the request of police; and whether authorities require "individualized suspicion" before searching a particular student.

As for 14-year-old T.L.O.—as she was referred to in court records—when the High Court delivered its opinion in early 1985 she was 18 years old. When the incident originally took place, in 1980 at New Jersey's Piscataway High School, T.L.O. was ordered expelled. That action was postponed, however, given the litigation. Moreover, as the case moved up the judicial ladder, a New Jersey trial court affirmed the juvenile court's original finding that there had been no Fourth Amendment violation. At the same time, however, the trial court also vacated T.L.O.'s adjudication of delinquency. In June 1984, Ms. T.L.O. graduated from Piscataway High School.

One could interpret the decision in *T.L.O.* as signaling a retreat from the trend toward giving juveniles full procedural due process rights. Whatever the trend, state and federal court decisions since the mid-1960s have opened the juvenile courts to defense lawyers and prosecutors and have instilled greater regard for the rights of juvenile defendants. It would appear that the days of the closed, protected, benevolent, and sometimes unfair system based on the philosophy of *parens patriae* are little more than history.

Critical Issues in Juvenile Justice

Much like the wider criminal justice process, juvenile justice in America has often been described as a "system." There are diagrams and flowcharts that depict how the various agencies and components fit together as each case is being processed and what decisions are possible at each stage. In many ways, at least on the surface, juvenile justice seems indeed to function as a system. Juveniles violate laws; police take juveniles into custody; detention facilities admit juveniles; juveniles and their parents or guardians appear at hearings in court; attorneys are present in behalf of juveniles and the state; judges make decisions; and adjudicated youths are placed on probation, assigned to group homes, or committed to institutions. Yet as with criminal justice in general, there is considerable tension and dissonance within the juvenile justice system. Former juvenile court judge H. Ted Rubin once described it this way:

> Below the surface, police get tired and angry when they arrest the same youth time and again, detention centers admit youngsters who don't require being locked up and experience the release of other youngsters who will shortly be reapprehended by the police, youngsters dislike the way someone in the system handled them, parents feel they are on trial when they accompany their youngsters to court, lawyers may fulfill only a limited advocacy role, the judge is unsure whether he made the right dispositional choice, the probation officers and group home and institutional staffs meet their new client and tell him they will help him as much as he will let them.[18]

Juvenile justice thus is an imperfect system suffering from some of the same problems that are apparent within the adult system. Yet beyond this, juvenile justice also has

The Roots of Delinquency

Where judges place the greatest blame for the delinquency of today's youth
Source: *National Law Journal.*

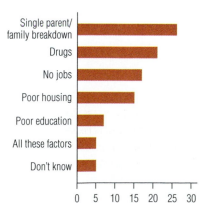

a number of unique problems—problems that raise some serious questions about the efficacy and fairness of a process that is structured to handle children "in their best interests."

Status Offenders

In New York they are "persons in need of supervision" (PINS); in Illinois they are "minors otherwise in need of supervision" (MINS); in Colorado they are "children in need of supervision" (CHINS); in Florida they are also "children in need of supervision," but with a different acronym (CINS); in New Jersey they are "juveniles in need of supervision" (JINS); in Montana they are "youths in need of supervision" (YINS); and elsewhere they are known, however informally, as "ungovernable" or "unruly" or "wayward." Whatever the name or acronym, these are the **status offenders**—the runaways, truants, and other "incorrigibles" who, because of their special status as children, can be brought to the attention of the juvenile courts for certain kinds of noncriminal behavior.

The creation of PINS, CHINS, and other designations was an outgrowth of a movement during the 1960s and 1970s to decriminalize status offense behavior. Before that time, such acts were included under statutory definitions of "delinquency."[19] The need to decriminalize status offenses was obvious. Children who were runaways, curfew violators, truant, or otherwise "incorrigible" were handled in the same manner as juvenile law violators, given the same delinquent status, and housed in the same reform and industrial schools.

While the decriminalization of status offenses in most states was a positive step, it fell short of what many experts consider a necessary reform: total repeal of status offender jurisdiction and shifting of care and management from the juvenile courts to social service agencies. In many jurisdictions, status offenders continue to be detained or incarcerated with hard-core offenders—sometimes including detention in adult jails and state correctional facilities.

Perhaps the most significant problem faced by the juvenile courts is the sheer number of status offenders. Some 40 percent of juvenile court dispositions involve status offenders, and the attention and resources spent on them reduce the ability of the courts to deal effectively with serious criminal offenders.

A move toward repeal of the current process was the passage of the *Juvenile Justice and Juvenile Delinquency Prevention Act* in 1974.[20] This federal legislation specified that states would no longer receive federal funds for delinquency programs unless they reformed their status offender management processes. It required the deinstitutionalization of status offenders, their removal from the justice system, and the detaining and incarceration of delinquents in separate facilities from adults; these steps were to be completed by 1985. Nevertheless, while a few jurisdictions complied with the mandates of the act and most separated status offenses from the former delinquency classifications, tens of thousands of status offenders continue to be incarcerated in the most unfavorable of conditions. For a discussion of status offenders in Russia, see Exhibit 18.5.

Juveniles in Adult Courts

The process of transferring a case from a juvenile court to an adult criminal court has become known as **waiver of jurisdiction.** The effect of such a transfer is to deny the youth the protection and treatment afforded by the juvenile process. Although state and federal statutes specify the age at which the criminal courts gain jurisdiction over young offenders (generally 17 or 18), they also provide for waivers of jurisdiction. The scope of such waivers varies widely, however. In California and Oregon, for example, waivers can be applied to all juveniles age 16 and over, regardless of the offense involved. By contrast, in Alabama, Colorado, and Pennsylvania, waivers can occur for juveniles as young as 14 years but only in the case of felony offenses. And in Florida and Texas there is the equivalent of the "three-strikes-and-you're-out" law, except that it translates into "three strikes and you are an adult."[21]

Lionel Tate at age 13.

FAMOUS CRIMINALS
Lionel Tate

Lionel Tate is likely the "poster child" for the debate over the treatment of juveniles as adults in the criminal court system. At age 14, Tate was convicted of first-degree murder for beating to death 6-year-old playmate Tiffany Eunick while simulating WWF wrestling moves. The evidence was clear that the victim was brutally murdered: She sustained up to 35 injuries, including brain contusions, a fractured skull, fractured ribs, injuries to her pancreas and kidneys, a lacerated liver, and severe bruising all over her body. The controversy surrounding the case centered on Tate's age and mental capacity: Tate was a 12-year-old with the mental capacity of a 9- or 10-year-old at the time of his crime. Tate and his family rejected a plea bargain offer and instead opted for a trial in adult criminal court, where he ended up the youngest person in U.S. history to be sentenced to life in prison without parole. The case garnered international attention and outcry among critics of sending juveniles to adult court.

In early 2004, Tate was released after serving 3 years of his sentence. His murder conviction was overturned on appeal, and this time his family accepted a plea bargain for second-degree murder charges that mandated him a year of house arrest and another 10 years of probation—the same deal he was initially offered.

(continued on p. 624)

(continued from p. 623)

However, Tate has not been a model probationer since his release from prison. In September 2004, he was arrested for being outdoors at 2 a.m. with a knife, but he avoided a trip back to prison by admitting that he broke the conditions of his probation. In May 2005, at age 18, Tate was in trouble again—this time in connection with the armed robbery of a pizza delivery man. He allegedly ordered four pizzas from Domino's, and when the delivery man arrived, Tate "greeted him with a gun," said a Broward County, Florida, Sheriff's Office spokesperson. The delivery man returned to the restaurant and called police. Tate was later arrested on charges of armed burglary with battery, armed robbery, and probation violation. ■

If a kid gets arrested at the age of 11 for murder and gets a sentence of 50 years without possibility of parole, his friends will take note of that. Maximum prison sentences, and prisons with no privileges, no drugs, no television or inmate gangs—that will eliminate the glamour of serving time. Only then will the criminal occupation of our cities be broken.

— STANLEY CROUCH, AUTHOR OF
NOTES OF A HANGING JUDGE

Juveniles and the Death Penalty
Percentage of judges who support letting youths face the death penalty
Source: *National Law Journal.*

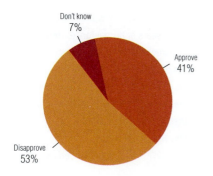

Don't know
7%

Approve
41%

Disapprove
53%

The waiver statutes in a number of other jurisdictions permit extremely young children to be tried in adult courts. In Mississippi and Illinois the age is 13. In Indiana, 10-year-olds charged with murder can be transferred to the criminal courts. In New Hampshire and Wyoming, waivers are permitted but no age is indicated in the statutes; this theoretically means that 7- or 8-year-olds can face official criminal proceedings. Ironically, depending on the jurisdiction, children may commit crimes whose seriousness they do not understand and yet come before the courts as adults. But if they steal from the local convenience store or become involved in the sale and distribution of crack-cocaine, they are still considered "youths," and their understanding of the nature of their crimes is not at issue.

Although the decision to waive jurisdiction is critical in its effect on a juvenile offender's subsequent treatment, for a long time youths had no protection against arbitrariness in the waiver process. Change finally occurred in 1966 with **Kent v. United States**,[22] the first case in which the Supreme Court evaluated the constitutionality of juvenile court proceedings. The Court held that there must be waiver hearings, and although such hearings need not conform to all the requirements of a criminal trial, they must measure up to the essentials of due process and fair treatment (see Exhibit 18.6).

Policy makers have looked on the transfer of juvenile offenders to adult court with increasing favor in recent years. The rationale has been that by "getting tough" with juveniles, they will get the message that their offenses will have "real" consequences, that they will face more severe sanctions, such as longer sentences and "hard time" in more demanding and less forgiving institutions. Hence, transfers to adult criminal courts will have a deterrent effect on future crime. Recent research suggests, however, that this may not necessarily be the case. In a study of all of the Texas youths waived to adult court over a 12-year period and sentenced to prison, their sentences were longer than those typically available in juvenile court. However, when the actual time served was taken into consideration, the youths rarely served sentences longer than those that might have been given to them in the juvenile court. On average, in fact, the youths served only 27 percent of their actual sentences.[23] Going further, in a study of almost 3,000 Florida youths transferred to adult courts, their recidivism was compared with that of a matched sample of delinquents who were retained in juvenile court. Recidivism was examined in terms of rates of reoffending, seriousness of reoffending, and time to reoffending. By every measure of recidivism employed, reoffending was greater among the transfers than among those retained in juvenile court.[24]

Children on Death Row

Although the decision in *Kent v. United States* accorded a measure of constitutional safeguards to waiver proceedings, the question remains as to whether *any* juvenile should be dealt with in the adult criminal courts. On the one hand, there is the pragmatic issue of community protection and the state's right to wage war against its enemies. On the other, there is the more abstract and philosophical consideration of confinement in a penitentiary as an appropriate treatment for what is defined under state statutes as "delinquent" behavior. Of even greater significance is the matter of juveniles and capital punishment. Until 2005, several states still permitted the execution of criminals who committed capital offenses as juveniles. However, the case of *Roper v. Simmons* (discussed later) changed that.

The execution of juveniles in the United States began with Thomas Graunger in 1642 in Plymouth, Massachusetts. Since that time, through the close of 2000, 361 persons have been executed for crimes committed as juveniles. One of these executions was in 1964, when the state of Texas electrocuted James Andrew Echols,[25] convicted of a rape—a crime that is no longer punishable by death as the result of the Supreme Court's decision in *Coker v. Georgia*[26]—committed at age 17. The *youngest* person to be executed during the 20th century was a 13-year-old, electrocuted in Florida in 1927.[27]

Opponents of the death penalty argue that the execution of any juvenile is "cruel and unusual punishment" in violation of the Eighth Amendment. Moreover, they

International Perspectives on Crime & Justice | EXHIBIT 18.5

Street Kids in Russia

There are two very alarming situations facing children in Russia: (1) There are very young children leaving home and living on the streets, using drugs, and trying to make a few dollars any way that they can; (2) there has been a large increase in the population of juvenile prison colonies, and many of those residents do not belong in jail.

The streets of St. Petersburg are not an unfamiliar place for the thousands of children currently occupying the syringe-filled alleyways between buildings. The exact number of children is disputed, with a German humanitarian group putting the number at about 30,000 to 40,000 and Russian social workers estimating the number at around 17,000 out of a population of 4.7 million. Many of these children are runaways, trying to escape family situations that are intolerable. Half of the kids are under 13 years of age. The children live together in groups, earning money stealing, begging, doing odd jobs, and selling their bodies—with an estimated 40% of girls and 1% of boys working as prostitutes or in the porn industry. These young people are constantly hiding and running from the authorities. If they are apprehended, they are returned to their parents or sent to juvenile homes, special school, or, perhaps worst of all, juvenile detention. In the juvenile detention facilities, the youngsters are subject to overcrowding, unsanitary conditions, and military regulations including uniforms, shaved heads, and ritual punishments.

Of course, there are some individuals who belong in these facilities, but as a result of a rise in crime rates during the 1990s, Russia made its laws tougher than they already were. As a result, juvenile prisons are swarming with boys and young men who were found guilty of petty charges, for instance, school fights, petty theft, and joyriding. These boys serve their time mingled in with youthful rapists, murderers, and robbers.

Perhaps surprisingly, the lead advocates for these boys are the juvenile colonies. At the youth facility in Mariinsk, the staff acknowledges that although they truly want to help reform the boys, they are just not equipped to do so. The prison, which houses about 350 inmates, has only one psychologist, who alone cannot keep track of all the boys.

There is a possibility that there will be change in the future for these boys. There has been a bill drafted that would limit the maximum term of pretrial detention, significantly cut the number of crimes that a per-

Homeless street youths in Moscow underground shelter.

son could be jailed for before trial, and expand the number of inmates permitted to live in settlement colonies without guards. And although the bill has much support from prison staff, human rights activists, and former inmates, there is a very strong opposition from two of the most powerful federal agencies in Russia—the Russian Interior Ministry and the prosecutor general's office.

Sources: Wolfgang Müller, "The Street Kids of St. Petersburg," *World Press Review,* September 2003, 42–43; Masha Gessen, "Russia's Boys behind Bars," *U.S. News & World Report,* January 29, 2001, 22–23; Susan Swarbrick, "The Lost Generation," *Glasgow Herald Magazine* (Scotland), January 22, 2005, 8.

---

hold, a child's behavior is different from that of an adult. On the other hand, supporters of the death penalty insist that youthful offenders should not be permitted to wrap themselves in the shield of age in order to escape responsibility for their crimes.

Interestingly, the U.S. Supreme Court remained silent on the matter of juveniles and the death penalty until only recently. In *Thompson* v. *Oklahoma*,[28] decided in 1988, the High Court put forth the somewhat narrow ruling that a state may not execute a person who was less than age 16 at the time of the offense, *unless* the state legislature had spoken clearly on the matter by setting a minimum age for the death penalty. In *Stanford* v. *Kentucky*,[29] decided in 1989, the Court made the more specific ruling that the imposition of the death penalty for a crime committed at 16 or 17 years of age does

EXHIBIT 18.6 | LAW & CRIMINAL JUSTICE

Kent v. United States

Morris A. Kent, Jr., first came under the authority of the District of Columbia juvenile court in 1959. He was age 14 at the time and had been apprehended as a result of several housebreakings and an attempted purse snatching. He was placed on probation, in the custody of his mother, and from time to time he was contacted by the juvenile court officials.

Two years later, on September 2, 1961, an intruder broke into the home of a District of Columbia woman, took her wallet, and raped her. Fingerprints found in the apartment matched those of Kent, having been taken during his juvenile court contact in 1959. At this point 16 years of age and still on juvenile probation, Morris Kent was taken into custody by the police. After almost 2 days of interrogation, he admitted his involvement in this and several other housebreakings, robberies, and rapes.

Following Kent's apprehension, his mother obtained an attorney, who promptly conferred with the social service director of the juvenile court. In a brief meeting, they discussed the possibility that the court might waive its jurisdiction and transfer the case to the district court for trial—a waiver that the attorney indicated he would oppose. Meanwhile, Kent was being held in detention, during which time there was neither an arraignment nor a hearing by a judicial officer to determine probable cause for arrest. Kent's attorney, however, arranged for psychiatric examinations of his client, after which he filed two motions with the juvenile court. The first was for a hearing on the question of the waiver of juvenile court jurisdiction; accompanying it was a psychiatrist's affidavit certifying that Kent "is a victim of severe psychopathology" and recommending hospitalization for psychiatric evaluation.

The second motion, in behalf of effective assistance of counsel, was for access to the social service file that had been compiled by the staff of the juvenile court during Kent's probation period.

The juvenile court judge did not rule on these motions; he held no hearing; and he did not confer with Kent, his mother, or his attorney. Rather, the judge entered an order stating that after "full investigation, I do hereby waive" jurisdiction of Kent and directing that he be "held for trial for the alleged offenses under the regular procedure of the U.S. District Court for the District of Columbia." The judge made no findings;

he did not recite any reason for the waiver; and he made no reference to the motions filed by Kent's attorney.

After the juvenile court waived its jurisdiction, Kent was indicted by the grand jury and received a jury trial in the criminal court. On the rape, he was found not guilty by reason of insanity. Yet he was found guilty on six counts of housebreaking and robbery, for which he was sentenced to a term of 30 to 90 years. On appeal to the U.S. court of appeals, Kent's attorney argued that the detention, interrogation, and fingerprinting were unlawful. As to the proceedings by which the juvenile court waived its jurisdiction, he attacked them on statutory and constitutional grounds: "no hearing occurred, no findings were made, no reasons were stated before the waiver, and counsel was denied access to the social service file." The court of appeals affirmed the lower-court decision, and the United States Supreme Court granted *certiorari*.

By a 5-to-4 majority, the High Court nullified the juvenile court's waiver of jurisdiction, holding that such a waiver is a "critically important" stage in the juvenile process and must be attended by minimum requirements of due process and fair treatment as required by the Fourteenth Amendment. Specifically, the Court set forth four basic safeguards required by due process during waiver proceedings:

1. If the juvenile court is considering waiving jurisdiction, the juvenile is entitled to a hearing on the waiver.

2. The juvenile is entitled to representation by counsel at such hearing.

3. The juvenile's attorney must be given access to the juvenile's social records on request.

4. If jurisdiction is waived, the juvenile is entitled to a statement of reasons in support of the waiver order.

The ruling in *Kent* was initially limited in scope, since it was seemingly based on an interpretation of the waiver requirements under District of Columbia statutes rather than on constitutional principles. However, following the many references to *Kent* in *In re Gault* and subsequent cases, the requirements stated in *Kent* have taken on constitutional dimension and are applicable to *all* juvenile court waiver decisions.

Source: *Kent v. United States,* 383 U.S. 541 (1966).

---

not constitute a violation of the Eighth Amendment ban against cruel and unusual punishment. However, in **Roper v. Simmons**,[30] decided on March 1, 2005, the Supreme Court overturned its ruling in *Stanford,* holding that the imposition of the death penalty on offenders who were under the age of 18 when their crimes were committed violated the Eighth and Fourteenth Amendments (see Exhibit 18.7).

Where does the general public stand on the matter of executing juveniles? Gallup polls suggest that 69 percent of Americans oppose the death penalty for juveniles.[31] Research suggests, moreover, that there is widespread support for alternatives to execution for juveniles. In a statewide study of Tennessee residents, for example, nearly two-thirds favored life imprisonment without parole. Even a majority of those who supported the notion of juvenile executions preferred the "life, without parole," alternative.[32]

LAW & CRIMINAL JUSTICE | EXHIBIT 18.7

Roper v. *Simmons*

Christopher Simmons was convicted and sentenced to death for the first-degree murder of Shirley Cook in 1993. He appealed his sentence on the grounds that he was 17 at the time he committed the murder and that a death sentence constituted cruel and unusual punishment in violation of the Eighth Amendment. The Supreme Court of Missouri overturned Simmons's death sentence, noting that in *Stanford* v. *Kentucky* the United States Supreme Court upheld statutes setting the minimum age for capital punishment at 16. At the time, the Court had held that there was no national consensus on whether the death penalty for crimes committed at the ages of 16 and 17 constituted cruel and unusual punishment. The Supreme Court of Missouri held that a national consensus had developed since *Stanford* was decided and that society's standards of decency would no longer tolerate executions for crimes committed by juveniles.

By a vote of 5 to 4, the U.S. Supreme Court held that the Eighth and Fourteenth Amendments forbid the execution of offenders who were under the age of 18 when their crimes were committed. Writing for the majority, Justice Kennedy stated: "When a juvenile offender commits a heinous crime, the State can exact forfeiture of some of the most basic liberties, but the State cannot extinguish his life and his potential to attain a mature understanding of his own humanity."

The Court reaffirmed the necessity of referring to "the evolving standards of decency that mark the progress of a maturing society" to determine which punishments are so disproportionate as to be cruel and unusual. The Court reasoned that the rejection of the juvenile death penalty in the majority of states, the infrequent use of the punishment even where it remains on the books, and the consistent trend toward abolition of the juvenile death penalty demonstrated a national consensus against the practice. The Court determined that today our society views juveniles as categorically less culpable than the average criminal.

The Court explained that the primary criterion for determining whether a particular punishment violates society's evolving standards of decency is objective evidence of a national consensus as expressed by legislative enactments and jury practices. The majority opinion found significant that 30 states prohibit the juvenile death penalty, including 12 that have rejected the death penalty altogether. The Court counted the states with no death penalty, pointing out that "a State's decision to bar the death penalty altogether of necessity demonstrates a judgment that the death penalty is inappropriate for all offenders, including juveniles." The Court further noted that juries sentenced juvenile offenders to death only in rare cases and that the execution of

juveniles is infrequent. The Court found a consistent trend toward abolition of the practice of executing juveniles and ruled that the impropriety of executing juveniles has gained wide recognition.

In addition to considering evidence of a national consensus as expressed by legislative enactments and jury practices, the Court recognized that it must also apply its own independent judgment in determining whether a particular punishment is disproportionately severe. When ruling that juvenile offenders cannot with reliability be classified as among the worst offenders, the Court found significant that juveniles are vulnerable to influence and susceptible to immature and irresponsible behavior. In light of juveniles' diminished culpability, neither retribution nor deterrence provides adequate justification for imposing the death penalty.

The Court further noted that the execution of juvenile offenders violated several international treaties, including the United Nations Convention on the Rights of the Child and the International Covenant on Civil and Political Rights, and stated that the overwhelming weight of international opinion against the juvenile death penalty provides confirmation for the Court's own conclusion that the death penalty is disproportional punishment for offenders under 18.

Source: *Roper* v. *Simmons,* 543 U.S. ___ (2005).

Juvenile Detention

The temporary detention of youths pending juvenile court action presents significant problems for both juvenile justice officials and youths held in custody. The Supreme Court's ruling in **Schall v. Martin,**[33] decided in 1984, sanctioned the practice of preventive detention for certain juvenile arrestees. On December 13, 1977, 14-year-old

Options Requested

What judges seek as options for dealing with troubled youths　Source: *National Law Journal.*

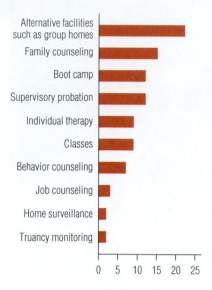

Ghetto boys think having a reputation as someone who blows people away is much more important than having a reputation as someone who is smart in school. These kids need a step-by-step guide to this strange and wonderful thing called middle-class existence. They reject it, not because it is hopelessly square, but because they believe it is unattainable.

—*WASHINGTON POST* COLUMNIST WILLIAM RASPBERRY

The only direction these kids receive is from their peers on the street, the local drug dealers and other role models who engage in criminal conduct.

— LOS ANGELES PROSECUTOR KATIE BUCKLAND

The boys I know think it's fun to be in jail because other boys they know are in jail too.

—FIFTEEN-YEAR-OLD APRIL ALLEN OF BOSTON

Gregory Martin had been arrested along with two other youths on charges of robbery, assault, and weapons violations. Martin had been held in detention for 15 days, after which he was adjudicated a juvenile delinquent and placed on probation. While still in detention, however, Martin instituted a *habeas corpus* class-action suit on behalf of *all* youths being held in preventive detention pursuant to New York's Family Court Act. The U.S. Supreme Court held that preventive detention is permissible with respect to an accused juvenile delinquent when there is evidence that he or she presents a "serious risk" of committing a crime before adjudication of the case. The New York procedure was upheld because it served the legitimate purpose of community protection and because there were numerous procedural requirements in the New York Juvenile Court Act intended to safeguard against erroneous deprivations of liberty.

Schall v. *Martin* is the most significant case addressing the issue of juvenile detention because of the perspective on juvenile justice reflected in the Court's opinion:

> Juveniles, unlike adults, are always in some form of custody. Children, by definition, are not assumed to have the capacity to take care of themselves. They are assumed to be subject to the control of their parents, and if parental control falters, the State must play its part as *parens patriae.* In this respect, the juvenile's liberty interest may, in appropriate circumstance, be subordinated to the State's *parens patriae* interest in preserving and promoting the welfare of the child.

In addition to its contention that preventive detention acts in behalf of the welfare of a child, the Court also noted that such detention is for a limited period, as most youths are released after only a few days. And therein lies the dilemma for both youths "in trouble" and the juvenile justice system as a whole. Jails and detention centers, particularly those that mix juveniles with adults, can be depressing and exceedingly dangerous places. Youthful offenders are often victimized while in detention, but few such incidents are ever reported. What is known, however, is the relative extent to which youths find themselves in contact with jail populations—both juvenile and adult. For well over a decade, for example, close to a million youths were being placed in juvenile detention and correctional facilities annually, with an average commitment period of more than 100 days.[34] Moreover, a fourth of these had not been adjudicated, and literally tens of thousands were status offenders and dependent, neglected, and abused children. And these figures do not include the many thousands more being held in *adult* facilities.

Juvenile Corrections

The juvenile due process requirements derived from the *Kent, Gault,* and *Winship* cases, combined with the rising costs of operating correctional institutions, have resulted in wider use of community-based treatment for adjudicated juveniles. A recent trend is greater use of diversion programs, with many young offenders being placed in remedial education and drug abuse treatment programs, foster homes, and counseling facilities.

Probation is by far the primary form of community treatment in the juvenile justice system, and the probation process for youths is essentially the same as that for adults. At any given time more than 500,000 youths are on probation in the United States.

There are still many juveniles in correctional institutions, however. These institutions are of two main types. *Cottage systems* are similar to facilities for women offenders. They are typically campuslike environments with dormitory rooms rather than cells. For serious juvenile offenders, there are secure training and industrial schools, which generally resemble medium-security penitentiaries for adults.

Nearly all juvenile correctional facilities have a variety of treatment programs—counseling on an individual or group basis, vocational and educational training, recreational and religious programs, and medical and dental facilities. A number of institu-

CAREERS IN CRIMINAL JUSTICE

Juvenile Probation Officers

The duties of juvenile probation officers are not unlike those of other probation officers, as described earlier in Chapter 17. Specifically, juvenile probation officers are responsible for the guidance and supervision of youths under age 18 who have been referred to them by local courts, police departments, and social agencies as a result of having committed a crime or for having been designated as a status offender. Juvenile probation officers ensure that youths who are placed on probation abide by the rules of probation, receive appropriate court-related services, are referred to other community services when necessary, and coordinate with schools, agencies, employment and training programs, substance abuse treatment, and other services within the community. Juvenile probation officers sometimes supervise truancy cases as well.

For those who wish to work in the criminal justice field, probation work (juvenile and adult) is an excellent entry-level position. It provides individuals with (1) broad exposure to most aspects of state and local criminal justice operations and procedures, (2) the requisite experience for higher-level criminal justice positions, and (3) access to employment opportunities in other criminal justice agencies.

In most jurisdictions, the minimum qualifications for juvenile probation work are U.S. citizenship and a bachelor's degree in criminal justice or one of the social or behavioral sciences.

tions also provide legal services for juveniles, and a few have substance abuse treatment programs. But regardless of the settings and available services, juvenile facilities are still places of confinement that militate against rehabilitation in the same ways that adult penitentiaries do. They have been described as "crime schools" offering only an illusion of treatment under conditions that represent "legalized child abuse." A case in point is the South Dakota State Training School at Plankinton. At the close of the 1990s, after the death of a 14-year-old girl from heatstroke during a forced run in the facility's boot camp program, investigations found that status offenders placed there were routinely subjected to harsh treatment that included shackling, isolation, the inappropriate use of psychotropic drugs, and other abuses.[35]

| Is "Child Saving" Dead? |

As noted earlier in this chapter, the original "child savers" included numerous civic-minded and humanitarian citizens who became concerned about the problems of juvenile misconduct during the 19th century. These social reformers were instrumental in the development of the houses of refuge, the later reform schools, and ultimately the juvenile courts. Although a number of the early child savers sought only to control, repress, and perhaps resocialize children whom they viewed as "dangerously deviant," many were guided only by benevolent concerns for helping the young.[36] Throughout the 20th century, the juvenile justice system developed and prospered, but at the same time, there were many who argued that the child savers' promise of rehabilitation never materialized.[37]

At the beginning of the 21st century, just after the 100th anniversary of the birth of the juvenile court, serious concerns remained over the viability of the juvenile justice process. Although rates of juvenile violence have declined in recent years, the steady rise of such violence since the late 1980s led to portrayals of many youthful offenders as "superpredators" who were all but beyond redemption. This notion was further fueled by the mass murders by teenagers in schools in Paducah (Kentucky), Jonesboro (Arkansas), Littleton (Colorado), Santee (California), and Red Lake Indian Reservation (Minnesota).

Amid the increased criticism of the juvenile justice system and its correctional policy of trying to "save" youthful offenders, there are some indications that public support for juvenile rehabilitation persists. Recent studies suggest that rehabilitation is favored as an integral role of juvenile corrections, and that a broad range of commu-

These young boys are confined to a detention center in California. Detention centers can be frightening and extremely dangerous places where victimization of youthful offenders occurs, but is rarely reported.

Major Changes in the System Favored by Juvenile Court Judges (percent in favor)

Source: *National Law Journal.*

Fingerprinting juveniles	
Incarcerating and supervising juveniles past the age of majority	
Opening juvenile records to adult law enforcement agencies	
Opening juvenile court hearings to the public	

0   25   50   75   100

At Curie High School in Chicago, security officers check monitors for student misconduct as well as signs of criminal activity.

nity-based treatment initiatives is favored including early intervention programs rather than imprisonment as a response to juvenile crime.[38]

CRITICAL THINKING IN CRIMINAL JUSTICE

"The Color of Justice"

Shortly after the beginning of the new millennium, the Justice Policy Institute—a San Francisco–based advocacy group—released the findings of a 3-year study of juvenile crime in California. The report, titled *The Color of Justice,* found that juveniles accused of serious crime were less likely to be tried as adults *if they were white.*[39] More specifically, for every 1,000 juvenile crime suspects arrested in each race/ethnic category, 88 Hispanics, 83.7 Asians, and 72 African Americans were deemed to be unsuitable for the juvenile justice system and, instead, transferred to adult court. That compared to a rate of 37 per 1,000 white violent crime suspects arrested who were transferred to adult court. After transfer, furthermore, African American delinquents were found to be 18.4 times more likely to receive adult court sentences—that is, held in a California Youth Authority facility until their 18th birthday and then transferred to adult prison. Hispanics were 7.3 times more likely and Asians 4.5 times more likely than their young, white criminal counterparts to receive adult sentences.

Think critically about these data. Could there be sample bias in the study, or is the bias against minority youth? Is it possible that such disparities could really occur? Perhaps the disproportionate transfer of minority youth to adult court reflects not discrimination but higher arrest rates of minority youths for serious crimes. Could it be that minority youths are more crime-prone? Or might there be other explanations? The study data for Los Angeles County are illustrated below. What do they suggest?

**Proportions of Los Angeles County Youths Arrested
for Serious Crimes and Transferred to Adult Court**

Percent of:	White	Hispanic	Black	Asian/Other	Number
Pop. 10–17	24.7%	51.4%	12.6%	11.3%	998,400
Arrested for:					
Violent crime	10.4%	51.7%	32.3%	5.6%	7,253
Homicide	2.8	53.9	31.5	11.8	178
Rape	7.7	45.4	42.3	4.6	130
Robbery	7.1	51.6	36.6	4.8	3,691
Ag. assault	14.7	52.1	27.1	6.1	3,254
Property crime	12.6	56.3	23.4	7.8	11,481
Drug felonies	12.8	65.6	19.1	2.5	2,672
All felonies	12.2	56.0	25.4	6.4	240,163
Transfers to adult court	5.0	58.8	30.1	6.1	561

Source: Justice Policy Institute, 2000.

Without analyzing the table number by number, what should be examined are the proportions of whites, Hispanics, blacks, and Asian/others in the base population (the top line in the table), as compared to the proportions in each race/ethnic group that are arrested for various crimes. Then compare all of that with the bottom line in the table. Overall, whites account for 24.7 percent of the youth population, 12.2 percent of the juveniles arrested for felonies, 10.4 percent of those arrested for violent crimes, but only 5.0 percent of those transferred to adult court. By contrast, while blacks represent 12.6 percent of the population and account for 25.4 percent of those arrested for felonies as well as 32.3 percent of those arrested for violent crimes, some

Disparities in the Justice System
Source: National Council on Crime and Delinquency.

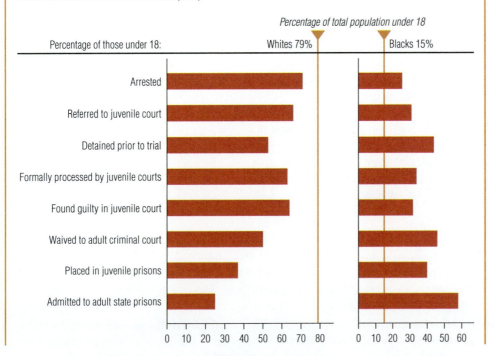

30.1 percent are transferred to adult court. Although there seems to be a correlation between the proportions of each minority group arrested for violent crimes and the proportions transferred to adult courts, that certainly is not the case for whites. There is no conclusive answer here, but the data are indeed suspicious.

Only a few months after *The Color of Justice* report was released, the findings of *And Justice for Some,* a national study of juvenile justice processing sponsored by the U.S. Department of Justice, were made public.[40] From the summary findings presented in the table at the bottom of the previous page, what might be concluded? Think critically.

OP-ED

At the beginning of the 1990s, a number of influential criminal justice researchers and politicians met to discuss future trends in juvenile crime and violence. Many of them saw a "crime storm" on the horizon—a storm teeming with a new breed of "superpredators," as they called them, who would soon be reaching their teens. Even the Federal Bureau of Investigation bought into the idea and predicted that the annual number of juvenile arrests for violent crimes would increase from 125,000 in 1990 to almost 300,000 by 2005.

The predictions had been made on the basis of pieces of information: social trends and simple demographics. The trends included the increasing rates of violence among youths, the rising number of adolescents who were using drugs and alcohol, and the wider availability of guns among juveniles in both urban and rural communities. The demographics were

even more clear-cut. Youths in the 15-to-19 age cohort tend to be more crime-prone than most other age groups, and the number of 15- to 19-year-olds would be increasing by 21 percent by the year 2005.

Had the forecasts been accurate, the storm of youth crime should have hit by now. But the skies are still clear. Although gun-related homicides by youths are up, overall violent crime is down. So what happened?

It would appear that the pessimistic projections about youth crime stemmed from a "historical fact" about youth crime long held to be sacred theory among many academic criminologists and demographers: *Teenagers commit a lot of crimes, and more teenagers would mean more crime.* The problem with this conventional wisdom is that you just can't predict the criminal potential of groups of people who are just toddlers now or not even born at all. Too many things can intervene. For example, few anticipated the fall-offs in the inner-city crack markets, the booming economy and high rates of employment, the effectiveness of community policing programs, and the growth in youth crime prevention initiatives.

But despite everything, perhaps the chaos will still arrive. John J. Dilulio, a professor of politics and public affairs at Princeton University, has commented that the dip in the crime rate may just be the "lull before the crime storm." Let's wait and see.

Troubling Projections
The number of youths aged 15 to 19 increased 21% by the year 2005, leading researchers to speculate that a sharp spike in the crime rate could occur. Crime could rise even faster if recent trends like inner-city drug use and wider availability of guns continue, they argue.

Source: Federal Bureau of Investigation.

— If recent increases in crime continue
— If arrests reflect increases in teen population only

Summary

The juvenile justice system in the United States is based on the philosophy that, as minors, young offenders have a "special status" that requires that they be protected and corrected and not necessarily punished. Given this special status, juveniles can come to the attention of the courts as delinquents, for having violated the criminal law; as status offenders, for having departed from the behavior expected of youths; and as dependent or neglected children, for having been the victims of abuse, neglect, or abandonment.

Juvenile justice processing is grounded in the notion of *parens patriae,* which holds that the state must intervene when a child's natural protectors are either unwilling or unable to provide appropriate care. Until comparatively recently, therefore, juvenile offenders were rarely treated with the "due process of law" accorded to adults by the Bill of Rights.

Much juvenile justice is informal, with a wide degree of discretion permitted at every stage. Police who take juveniles into custody have the options of releasing them with a reprimand, referring them to police-based diversion programs, or detaining them for court processing. Similar discretionary alternatives are apparent in the juvenile courts. The actual court process is viewed as a civil matter. It is not considered a trial, there is no jury, and the judge presides *in behalf of* the child.

It was not until 1966 that the U.S. Supreme Court first evaluated juvenile court proceedings and the constitutional rights of children. *Kent* v. *United States* brought the juvenile justice system within the framework of the Constitution and the Bill of Rights. Subsequently, *In re Gault* (1967), *In re Winship* (1970), and *Breed* v. *Jones* (1975) extended basic due process rights to juvenile court proceedings.

Although juvenile justice philosophy and procedure have attempted to provide fair and beneficial treatment for children, the system as a whole suffers from some major problems. First, status offender laws in many jurisdictions place nondelinquent youths in contact with criminals and reduce the ability of the juvenile courts to deal effectively with youths involved in serious criminal conduct. Second, there are questions about the wisdom of transferring delinquents to the adult courts for formal criminal processing. Third, the widespread practice of confining juveniles in detention facilities has placed the health and welfare of many youths at high risk. Fourth, regardless of the disposition of juvenile delinquents and status offenders, little is known regarding the effectiveness of juvenile correctional approaches. Nevertheless, support for juvenile rehabilitation seems to persist in the United States.

| Key Terms |

adjudication (612)
adjudication hearing (618)
adjudication inquiry (618)
Breed v. *Jones* (619)
delinquency (612)
delinquent (612)
detention hearing (616)
disposition hearing (618)

Illinois Juvenile Court Act (612)
in loco parentis (621)
In re Gault (619)
In re Winship (619)
intake hearing (616)
Kent v. *United States* (624)
McKeiver v. *Pennsylvania* (619)
New Jersey v. *T.L.O.* (621)

parens patriae (611)
petition (616)
Roper v. *Simmons* (626)
Schall v. *Martin* (627)
status offenders (623)
status offense (610)
waiver of jurisdiction (623)

| Issues for Discussion |

1. Given the *parens patriae* philosophy of the juvenile justice system in the United States, would delinquent youths be better off in the adult criminal courts with its strict guarantees of due process of law?
2. Do status offender laws serve any real purpose for today's youths? Should such laws be fully abolished? Why?

3. Should youths who commit murders be given capital sentences, placed on death row, and executed?
4. How might contemporary juvenile correctional programs and procedures be best upgraded or reformed? What ought to be done with juvenile offenders? Should they be treated as children or as adults?

| Media and Literature Resources |

Juvenile Justice Web Sites. The School of Criminology and Criminal Justice at Florida State University has constructed a number of useful Web links (see *http://www.fsu.edu/cjlinks/jd.html*). The U.S. Department of Justice Office of Juvenile Justice and Delinquency Prevention has numerous publications available to download from its Web site, *http://ojidp.ncjrs.org/,* as does the Center on Juvenile and Criminal Justice, *http://www.cjcj.org/index.php.*

The Fourth Amendment and Public Schools. A series of papers on the topic of search and seizure in America's public schools appears in *Criminal Law Bulletin* 36 (September–October 2000).

Youth, Guns, Gangs, and Violence. Several interesting books are available on these topics: Deanna L. Wilkinson, *Guns, Violence, and*

Identity Among African American and Latino Youth (New York: LFB Scholarly Publishing, 2003); Douglas Century, *Street Kingdom: Five Years Inside the Franklin Avenue Posse* (New York: Warner Books, 1999); Susan A. Phillips, *Wallbangin': Graffiti and Gangs in L.A.* (Chicago: University of Chicago Press, 1999); Joseph F. Sheley and James D. Wright, *In the Line of Fire* (New York: Aldine, 1995); Malcolm W. Klein, *The American Street Gang* (New York: Oxford, 1995).

Status Offenders. Gene Kassebaum, Nancy L. Marker, Patricia Glancey, et al., *Youth on the Run from Families and School: The Problem of Status Offenders in Hawaii* (Manoa, HI: Center for Youth Research, University of Hawaii at Manoa, 1997); Gwen A. Holden and Robert A. Kapler, "Deinstitutionalizing Status Offenders: A Record of Progress," *Juvenile Justice* 2, 2 (1995): 3–10; See also Randall G.

Shelden, John A. Horvath, and Sharon Tracy, "Do Status Offenders Get Worse? Some Clarifications on the Question of Escalation," *Crime & Delinquency* 35 (April 1989): 202–216.

Disparities in Juvenile Processing. Both of the reports discussed in the Critical Thinking section of this chapter can be downloaded from the Web. See *The Color of Justice: An Analysis of Juvenile Court Transfers in California* (*www.buildingblocksforyouth.org/colorofjustice/coj.html*) and *And Justice for Some* (*www.buildingblocksforyouth.org/justiceforsome/jfs.html*).

| Endnotes |

1. *The New York Times,* April 2, 2005, A9.
2. *The Economist,* February 26, 2005, 29.
3. President's Commission on Law Enforcement and Administration of Justice, *Task Force Report: Juvenile Delinquency and Youth Crime* (Washington, DC: U.S. Government Printing Office, 1967), 2–3.
4. Evelina Beldon, "Courts in the United States Hearing Children's Cases," *Children's Bureau Publication 65* (Washington, DC: U.S. Department of Labor, 1918), 8.
5. Illinois Juvenile Court Act, *Illinois Statutes,* 1899, Section 131.
6. Irving Piliavin and Scott Briar, "Police Encounters with Juveniles," *American Journal of Sociology* 70 (September 1964): 206–214.
7. *The New York Times,* April 22, 1998, 24.
8. H. Ted Rubin, *Juvenile Justice: Policy, Practice, and Law* (Santa Monica, CA: Goodyear, 1979), 86–108.
9. Stan C. Proband, "Jail and Prison Populations Continued to Grow in 1996," *Overcrowded Times* 8 (August 1997): 5–7.
10. *Kent* v. *United States,* 383 U.S. 541 (1966).
11. *In re Gault,* 38 U.S. 1 (1967).
12. *In re Winship,* 397 U.S. 358 (1970).
13. *Breed* v. *Jones,* 421 U.S. 519 (1975).
14. *McKeiver* v. *Pennsylvania,* 403 U.S. 548 (1971).
15. *Miranda* v. *Arizona,* 384 U.S. 436 (1966).
16. The Uniform Juvenile Court Act has been reprinted in its entirety in Samuel M. Davis, *Rights of Juveniles: The Juvenile Justice System* (New York: Clark Boardman, 1983), A1–A53.
17. *New Jersey* v. *T.L.O.,* 105 S.Ct. 733 (1985).
18. H. Ted Rubin, *Juvenile Justice,* 270.
19. See Herbert A. Bloch and Frank T. Flynn, *Delinquency: The Juvenile Offender in America Today* (New York: Random House, 1956), 471.
20. *Juvenile Justice and Juvenile Delinquency Prevention Act of 1974* (P.L. 93–415).
21. National Conference of State Legislatures, 1997.
22. *Kent* v. *United States,* 383 U.S. 541 (1966).
23. Eric J. Fritsch, Tory J. Caeti, and Craig Hemmens, "Spear the Needle but Not the Punishment: The Incarceration of Waived Youth in Texas Prisons," *Crime & Delinquency* 42 (October 1996): 593–609.
24. Donna M. Bishop, Charles E. Frazer, Lonn Lanza-Kaduce, and Lawrence Winner, "The Transfer of Juveniles to Criminal Court: Does It Make a Difference?" *Crime & Delinquency* 46 (April 1996): 171–191.
25. *Echols* v. *State,* 370 S.W. 2d 892 (1963).
26. *Coker* v. *Georgia,* 433 U.S. 583 (1977).
27. *National Law Journal,* August 8, 1983, 4.
28. *Thompson* v. *Oklahoma,* 43 CrL 4084 (1988).
29. *Stanford* v. *Kentucky,* 45 CrL 3103 (1989).
30. *Roper* v. *Simmons,* 543 U.S. ___ (2005).
31. Gallup News Service, May 20, 2002.
32. Melissa M. Moon, John Paul Wright, Francis T. Cullen, and Jennifer A. Pealer, "Putting Kids to Death: Specifying Public Support for Juvenile Capital Punishment," *Justice Quarterly* 17 (December 2000): 663–684.
33. *Schall* v. *Martin,* 35 CrL 3103 (1984).
34. Office of Juvenile Justice and Delinquency Prevention, *Juvenile Corrections* (Washington, DC: Office of Justice Programs, 2004).
35. *Criminal Justice Newsletter,* February 1, 2000, 1–2.
36. See James O. Finckenauer, *Juvenile Delinquency and Corrections* (Orlando: Academic Press, 1984).
37. Melissa M. Moon, Jody L. Sundt, Francis T. Cullen, and John Paul Wright, "Is Child Saving Dead? Public Support for Juvenile Rehabilitation," *Crime & Delinquency* 46 (January 2000): 38–60.
38. See David C. Anderson, *Sensible Justice: Alternatives to Prison* (New York: New Press, 1998); Brandon K. Applegate, Francis T. Cullen, and Bonnie S. Fisher, "Public Support for Correctional Treatment: The Continuing Appeal of the Rehabilitative Ideal," *Prison Journal* 77 (1997): 237–258; Francis T. Cullen, John Paul Wright, Shayna Brown, Melissa M. Moon, Michael B. Blankenship, and Brandon K. Applegate, "Public Support for Early Intervention Programs: Implications for a Progressive Policy Agenda," *Crime & Delinquency* 44 (1998): 187–204; Fairbank, Maslin, Maullin & Associates, *Mapping California's Opinion* (San Rafael, CA: Resources for Youth, 1998).
39. *The Color of Justice: An Analysis of Juvenile Court Transfers in California* (San Francisco: Justice Policy Institute, January 2000).
40. Eileen Poe-Yamagata and Michael A. Jones, *And Justice for Some* (San Francisco: National Council on Crime and Delinquency, April 2000).

GLOSSARY

abettor A person who, with the requisite criminal intent, encourages, promotes, instigates, or stands ready to assist the perpetrator of a crime.

accessory after the fact A person who, knowing that a felony has been committed, receives, relieves, comforts, or assists the felon to hinder apprehension or conviction.

accessory before the fact A person who abets a crime but is not present when the crime was committed.

adjudication In juvenile proceedings, the court's decision or judgment.

adjudication hearing The stage in juvenile court proceedings in which a judge presides on behalf of the child to determine if he or she actually committed the alleged offense.

adjudication inquiry The stage in juvenile court proceedings in which a judge determines whether the facts of the case warrant a formal hearing by the court.

administrative law A branch of public law that deals with the powers and duties of government agencies.

adversary system A system of justice in which the innocence of the accused is presumed and the burden of proof is placed on the court.

allocution The right of a convicted offender to address the court personally prior to the imposition of sentence.

anomie A condition of normative confusion or "normlessness," in which existing rules and values have little impact.

appeal A complaint to a superior court of an injustice done or an error committed by a lower court, whose judgment or decision the higher tribunal is called upon to correct or reverse.

appellate jurisdiction Jurisdiction restricted to matters of appeal and review.

Argersinger v. *Hamlin* The Supreme Court ruling that a defendant has the right to counsel at trial whenever he or she may be imprisoned for any offense, even for 1 day, whether it is classified as a felony or as a misdemeanor.

arrest The action of taking a person into custody for the purpose of charging him or her with a crime.

arson The willful or malicious burning or attempt to burn, with or without intent to defraud, any dwelling, other building, vehicle, or personal property.

assault An intentional attempt or threat to physically injure another.

assault and battery An assault carried into effect by doing some violence to the victim.

bail Security posted to guarantee that a defendant in a criminal proceeding will appear and be present in court as required.

Barron v. *Baltimore* The Supreme Court ruling that the Bill of Rights was added to the Constitution to protect citizens only against the action of the federal, not state or local, government.

Batson v. *Kentucky* The Supreme Court ruling that a prosecutor's use of peremptory challenges to exclude from a jury members of the defendant's race solely on racial grounds violates the equal protection rights of the defendant.

bench warrant A written order, issued by the court, authorizing a defendant's arrest.

Benton v. *Maryland* The Supreme Court ruling that overruled *Palko* and extended the double jeopardy protection to state actions.

Betts v. *Brady* The Supreme Court ruling that in noncapital crimes the Fourteenth Amendment's due process clause does not require states to supply defense counsel to defendants too poor to employ their own attorneys.

Bill of Rights The first 10 amendments to the Constitution of the United States, which restrict government actions.

booking The police administrative procedures for officially recording an arrest.

Bow Street Runners Henry Fielding's unofficial band of constables who were paid as thief-takers.

Brady v. *United States* The Supreme Court ruling that upheld the use of plea negotiations.

breaking and entering The forcible entry into a building or structure, with the intent to commit a crime therein.

Breed v. *Jones* The Supreme Court ruling that extended the Fifth Amendment protection against double jeopardy to juveniles.

Buck v. *Bell* The Supreme Court ruling that Virginia did not violate the Fourteenth Amendment's due process guarantee when it sterilized, without her consent, a mentally defective mother.

Burger Court The Supreme Court under the leadership of Chief Justice Warren Burger.

Carrier's Case Legal ruling whereby a person in possession of another's packaged goods, who opens the package and misappropriates its contents, is guilty of larceny.

Carroll doctrine The ruling, from the Supreme Court's decision in *Carroll* v. *United States,* that warrantless searches of vehicles are permissible where reasonable suspicion of illegal actions exists.

case law Law that results from court interpretations of statutory law or from court decisions where rules have not been fully codified or have been found to be vague or in error.

Cesare Beccaria The founder of the classical school of criminology and criminal law. Beccaria, an Italian economist and jurist, proposed a whole new concept for the administration of justice. His major work, *An Essay on Crimes and Punishments,* became the manifesto of the liberal approach to criminal law. It condemned capital punishment and torture, suggested that the law should be specific, and advocated the prevention of crime and rigid rules of criminal procedure.

charging the jury An order by the judge directing the jurors to retire to the jury room, consider the facts of the case and the evidence and testimony presented, and from their deliberations return a just verdict.

Chimel v. *California* The Supreme Court ruling that a search incident to a lawful arrest in a home must be limited to the area into which an arrestee might reach in order to grab a weapon or other evidentiary items.

civil death The loss of *all* civil rights.

civil law The body of principles that determine private rights and liabilities.

civilian review boards Citizen-controlled boards empowered to review and handle complaints against police officers.

classical school of criminal law and criminology A body of ideals from Enlightenment philosophers and reformers for transforming criminal law and procedure.

classification The process through which the educational, vocational, treatment, and custodial needs of the offender are determined.

clearance rate The proportion of crimes that result in arrest.

Coker v. *Georgia* The Supreme Court ruling that a sentence of death for the crime of rape is an excessive and disproportionate penalty forbidden by the Eighth Amendment.

common law Customs, traditions, judicial decisions, and other materials that guide courts in decision making but have not been enacted by the legislatures into statues or embodied in the Constitution.

community-based correction Rehabilitative activities and programs within the community that have effective ties with the local government.

community policing A collaborative effort between the police and the community to identify the problems of crime and disorder and to develop solutions from within the community.

conjugal visitation The practice of permitting inmate and spouse to spend time together in private quarters on prison grounds, during which time they may engage in sexual relations.

conspiracy Concert in criminal purpose.

constitutional law The legal rules and principles that define the nature and limits of governmental power and the duties and rights of individuals in relation to the state.

contract system A form of prison industry in which the labor of inmates is leased to an outside contractor, who furnishes the machinery and raw materials and supervises the work.

corporal punishment Punishment applied to the body, such as whipping or branding.

courts of general jurisdiction Courts authorized to try *all* criminal and civil cases.

courts of limited jurisdiction The entry point for judicial processing, with jurisdiction limited to full processing of *all* minor offenses and pretrial processing of felony cases.

courts of record Courts in which a full transcript of the proceedings is made for all cases.

crime An intentional act or omission in violation of criminal law, committed without defense or justification, and sanctioned by the state as a felony or misdemeanor.

crime control model The model of the criminal justice system that views the repression of criminal conduct as its most important function.

crime index The sum of Part I offenses reported in a given place for a given period of time.

crime rate The number of Part I offenses that occur in a given area per 100,000 inhabitants living in that area.

criminal justice The structure, functions, and decision processes of those agencies that deal with the management of crime — the police, the courts, and corrections.

criminal justice process The agencies and procedures set up to manage both crime and the persons accused of violating the criminal law.

criminal law The branch of jurisprudence that deals with offenses committed against the safety and order of the state.

defense Any number of causes and rights of action that serve to excuse or mitigate guilt in a criminal offense.

definite sentence A sentence of incarceration having a fixed period of time with no reduction by parole.

Delaware v. *Prouse* The Supreme Court ruling that police may not randomly stop motorists, without any probable cause to suspect crime or illegal activity, to check their driver's license and auto registration.

deliberation The full and conscious knowledge of the purpose to kill.

delinquency Criminal law violations that would be considered crimes if committed by an adult.

delinquent A juvenile offender who has been adjudicated by an officer of a juvenile court.

Department of Homeland Security A consolidation of 22 domestic agencies into one department to protect the nation against threats to the homeland.

detention hearing The stage in juvenile court proceedings in which it is determined whether a child is to be released to a parent or guardian or retained in custody.

determinate sentence A sentence of incarceration for a fixed period of time but with possible reduction by parole.

deterrence A sentencing philosophy seeking to prevent criminal acts by making an example of persons convicted of crimes.

deviance Conduct that the people of a group consider so dangerous, embarrassing, or irritating that they bring special sanctions to bear against the persons who exhibit it.

differential association The theory of crime that suggests that criminal behavior is learned through the same processes that noncriminal behaviors are learned.

differential reinforcement theory The theory that criminal behavior is not only learned but also reinforced by instrumental conditioning, i.e., the learned behaviors that result from the consequences, effects, and outcomes of an individual's social and cultural environment.

disposition hearing The stage in juvenile court proceedings in which the judge exercises his or her discretionary authority to choose among a variety of alternatives for resolving a case.

diversion The removal of offenders from the application of the criminal law at any stage of the police or court processes.

domestic violence Activities of a physically aggressive nature occurring among members of the family, current or former spouses or lovers, live-ins, and others in close relationships, resulting from conflicts in personal relations.

double jeopardy Multiple prosecutions for the same offense and/or multiple punishments for the same crime; prohibited by the Fifth Amendment.

Downum v. *United States* The Supreme Court ruling that double jeopardy begins at the point where the second trial jury is sworn in.

dual court system Courts at the state and federal levels.

due process model The model of the criminal justice system that stresses the possibility of error in the stages leading to trial and emphasizes the procedural rights over system efficiency.

due process of law A concept that asserts fundamental principles of justice and implies the administration of laws that do not violate the sacredness of private rights.

Duncan v. *Louisiana* The Supreme Court ruling that the Fourteenth Amendment's guarantee of due process requires states to provide trial by jury to persons accused of serious crimes.

Durham Rule Legal standard by which an accused is not held criminally responsible if he or she suffers from a diseased or defective mental condition at the time the unlawful act is committed.

entrapment The inducement of an individual to commit a crime not contemplated by him or her.

Escobedo v. *Illinois* The Supreme Court ruling that when the process shifts from the investigatory to the accusatory and its purpose is to elicit a confession, the accused must be permitted to consult with his or her attorney.

Estelle v. *Gamble* The Supreme Court ruling that the deliberate indifference of prison officials or personnel to the serious medical needs of inmates constitutes cruel and unusual punishment proscribed by the Eighth Amendment.

ethnocentrism The belief that one's own culture or ethnic group is superior to others.

evidence Any species of proof, through the media of witnesses, records, documents, concrete objects, and circumstances.

evidence in chief The first or direct examination of a witness.

exclusionary rule The judicially established rule that prohibits, in court, the use of illegally obtained evidence.

Federal Air Marshals A team of armed commandos who travel incognito on planes to watch for hijackers and other terrorists.

Federal Bureau of Investigation The chief investigative body of the Justice Department, with jurisdiction extending to all federal crimes that are not the specific responsibility of some other federal enforcement agency.

felony A crime punishable by death or imprisonment in a federal or state penitentiary.

felony-murder doctrine Principle maintaining that if a death occurs during commission of a felony, the person committing the primary offense can also be charged with murder in the first degree.

Florida v. *Bostick* The Supreme Court ruling that police officers' conduct in boarding stopped passenger buses and approaching seated passengers to ask them questions and to request consent to search their luggage does not constitute a Fourth Amendment "seizure" in every instance but, instead, must be evaluated in each case.

fruit of the poisonous tree The doctrine that evidence seized illegally is considered "tainted" and cannot be used against a suspect.

full enforcement The tenacious enforcement of every statute in the criminal codes.

furlough An authorized, unescorted absence from a correctional institution for a specified period.

Furman v. *Georgia* The Supreme Court ruling that statutes which leave arbitrary and discriminatory discretion to juries in imposing death sentences are in violation of the Eighth Amendment.

Gagnon v. *Scarpelli* The Supreme Court ruling that the holding in *Morrissey* v. *Brewer* also applies to probationers and that neither probationers nor parolees are entitled to counsel as a matter of right at revocation hearings.

General Strain Theory Robert Agnew's theory through which crime is viewed as a direct result of strain, or the negative feelings that originate from life in disorganized and lower socioeconomic areas where legitimate opportunities to achieve success are restricted. It conceptualizes strain as relationships in which an individual is not treated the way he or she wishes to be treated, proposes three types of strain an individual might encounter, and includes the influence of negative emotions in creating criminal behavior.

Gideon v. *Wainwright* The Supreme Court ruling that an indigent defendant charged in a state court with any noncapital felony has the right to counsel under the due process clause of the Fourteenth Amendment.

Gitlow v. *New York* The Supreme Court ruling that the First Amendment prohibition against government abridgment of the freedom of speech applies to state and local governments as well as to the federal government.

good time The number of days deducted from a sentence for good behavior, meritorious service, particular kinds of work, or other considerations.

grand jury A body of persons who have been selected according to law and sworn to hear evidence against accused persons and to determine whether there is sufficient evidence to bring those persons to trial, to investigate criminal activity generally, and to investigate the conduct of public agencies and officials.

Gregg v. *Georgia* The Supreme Court ruling that (1) the death penalty is not, in itself, cruel and unusual punishment; and (2) a two-part proceeding—one for the determination of innocence or guilt and the other for determining the sentence—is constitutional and meets the objections noted in *Furman* v. *Georgia*.

Griswold v. *Connecticut* The Supreme Court ruling that a right of personal privacy is implicit in the Constitution.

habeas corpus A writ that directs the person holding a prisoner to bring him or her before a judicial officer to determine the lawfulness of imprisonment.

"hands-off" doctrine The refusal of the courts to hear inmate complaints about the conditions of incarceration and the constitutional deprivations of penitentiary life.

hate crime Offenses motivated by hatred against a victim because of his or her race, ethnicity, religion, sexual orientation, handicap, or national origin.

Henry Fielding The 18th-century British novelist and magistrate who laid the foundation for the first modern police force.

Holt v. *Sarver* The federal court decision declaring the Arkansas prison system to be in violation of the Eighth Amendment.

homicide The killing of one human being by another.

Hudson v. *Palmer* The Supreme Court ruling that a prisoner has no reasonable expectation of privacy in his prison cell entitling him to Fourth Amendment protection.

Hurtado v. *California* The Supreme Court ruling that the due process clause of the Fourteenth Amendment does not require states to use grand jury indictments or presentments in capital cases.

Illinois Juvenile Court Act Legislation that established the first statewide juvenile court system in the United States.

Illinois v. *Gates* The Supreme Court ruling that in establishing probable cause for the issuance of a search warrant, magistrates may make a commonsense decision, given all the circumstance set forth in an affidavit, whether there is a fair probability that contraband can be found in a particular place.

Illinois v. *Wardlow* The Supreme Court ruling that flight at the mere sight of a police officer could often, in the context of other factors, be suspicious enough to justify police in conducting a stop-and-frisk.

incapacitation A sentencing philosophy seeking to remove the offender from society.

indeterminate sentence A sentence of incarceration having a fixed minimum and a fixed maximum term of confinement, rather than a definite period.

Indianapolis v. *Edmond* The Supreme Court ruling that police checkpoints aimed at discovering drugs were in violation of the Fourth Amendment.

indictment A formal charging document returned by a grand jury, based on evidence presented to it by the prosecutor.

in forma pauperis The characterization of an appeal by a poor person.

information A formal charging document drafted by a prosecutor and tested before a magistrate.

injunctive relief A court order, emanating from a *habeas corpus* action, directing prison officials to improve conditions or to stop enforcing unlawful policies.

in loco parentis A position in reference to a child of that of lawful guardian or parent.

inmate code The unwritten rules of the prison subculture, which, if violated, can result in sanctions ranging from ostracism to death.

inquiry system A system of justice in which all participants in a proceeding are obliged to cooperate with the court in its inquiry into the crime.

inquisitorial system A system of justice in which the accused is considered guilty until he or she is proved innocent.

In re Gault The Supreme Court ruling that extended some—but not all—due process privileges to juvenile court proceedings.

In re Winship The Supreme Court ruling that required proof "beyond a reasonable doubt" for an adjudication of delinquency.

inside cells Cells constructed back to back, with corridors running along the outside shell of the cell house.

intake hearing An early stage in juvenile court proceedings in which a court officer makes a legal judgment of the probable cause of the petition.

intensive probation supervision A program of closer surveillance and more exhaustive services that serve to place a probationer under tighter control than he or she might experience under regular probation.

intermediate sanctions Sanctions falling between the extremes of fines and imprisonment.

intermittent sentence A sentence to periods of confinement interrupted by periods of freedom.

Interpol An international police organization of 178 member countries that serves as a depository of intelligence information on wanted criminals.

Jackson v. *Bishop* The federal court decision declaring that whipping is in violation of the Eighth Amendment.

jails Local facilities for temporary detention.

J.E.B. v. *Alabama ex rel. T.B.* The Supreme Court ruling that the exercise of peremptory challenges on the basis of gender violates the equal protection clause of the Fourteenth Amendment.

Johnson v. *Avery* The Supreme Court ruling that unless a state provides some reasonable legal assistance to inmates seeking postconviction relief, a jailhouse lawyer must be permitted to aid inmates in filing *habeas corpus* petitions.

Johnson v. *Zerbst* The Supreme Court ruling that the Sixth Amendment right to counsel applies to all felony defendants in federal prosecutions.

Jones v. *North Carolina Prisoners' Labor Union* The Supreme Court ruling that prison regulations prohibiting the organized activities of inmate labor unions are not violative of the freedom of association clause of the First Amendment.

judges Public officers who preside over courts of law.

judicial circuit A specific jurisdiction served by a judge or court, as defined by given geographical boundaries.

jury nullification The refusal or marked reluctance on the part of a jury to convict, because of the severe nature of the sentence involved or other factors or because a jury otherwise "nullifies" the force of strict legal procedure.

justices of the peace The judges in many lower courts in rural areas, who are typically not lawyers and are locally elected.

Kent v. *United States* The Supreme Court ruling that the waiver of jurisdiction is a critically important stage in juvenile proceedings and must be attended by minimum requirements of due process and fair treatment.

Klopfer v. *North Carolina* The Supreme Court ruling that the Sixth Amendment right to a speedy trial applies in state as well as federal proceedings.

labeling theory The theory of crime that focuses on the processes of interaction through which behaviors become defined as criminal and the ways in which the labeling process can bring about more criminality.

Lambert v. *California* Ruling whereby the U.S. Supreme Court held that due process requires that ignorance of a duty must be allowed as a defense when circumstances that inform a person as to the required duty are completely lacking.

larceny The taking and carrying away of the personal property of another, with the intent to deprive permanently.

"law and order" A political ideology and slogan that sought a return to the morality and values of earlier times and rejected the growing permissiveness in government and social affairs.

Law Enforcement Assistance Administration (LEAA) A federal bureaucracy created to involve the national government in local crime control by supplying funds to the states for training and upgrading criminal justice agencies.

Lawrence v. *Texas* The Supreme Court ruling that the Texas statute making it a crime for two persons of the same sex to engage in certain intimate sexual acts violated the due process clause of the Constitution.

lease system A form of prison industry under which contractors assume complete control over prisoners.

lockdown A situation in which inmates are confined to their cells around the clock, denied exercise, work, recreation, and visits.

Lockhart v. *McCree* The Supreme Court ruling that a prosecutor's removal for cause, at the start of the guilt phase of a capital trial, of prospective jurors so opposed to the death penalty as to be unable to perform their duties at sentencing is not a violation of the Fifth Amendment.

malice aforethought The intent to cause death or serious harm or to commit any felony whatsoever.

mandatory release A release from prison required by statute when an inmate has been confined for a time period equal to his or her full prison sentence minus statutory "good time" if any.

mandatory sentence A statutory requirement that a certain penalty shall be set and carried out in all cases upon conviction for a specified offense or series of offenses.

manslaughter The unlawful killing of another, without malice.

Mapp v. *Ohio* The Supreme Court ruling that evidence obtained in violation of the Fourth Amendment must be excluded from use in the state as well as federal trials.

Marbury v. *Madison* The Supreme Court decision that established the High Court's power to review acts of Congress and declare invalid those it found in conflict with the Constitution.

mark system Started by Alexander Maconochie at Norfolk Island, a system by which inmates earn early release by hard work and good behavior.

maximum expiration date The date on which the full sentence ends.

maximum-security prisons Correctional institutions designed to hold the most aggressive and incorrigible offenders.

McKeiver v. *Pennsylvania* The Supreme Court ruling that due process does not require a jury in juvenile court hearings.

Mempa v. *Rhay* The Supreme Court ruling that the right to counsel applies to state probation revocation hearings at which deferred sentence may be imposed.

mens rea (criminal intent) A person's awareness of what is right and wrong under the law with an intention to violate the law.

Minnesota v. *Dickerson* The Supreme Court ruling that established the "plain feel" doctrine: that an object a police officer detects on a suspect's person during the course of a valid protective frisk under *Terry* v. *Ohio* may be seized without a warrant if the officer's sense of touch makes it immediately apparent to the officer that the object, though not threatening in nature, is contraband.

Miranda v. *Arizona* The Supreme Court ruling that the guarantee of due process requires that suspects in police custody be informed that they have the right to remain silent, that anything they say may be used against them, and that they have the right to counsel—before any questioning can permissibly take place.

misdemeanor A crime punishable by no more than a $1,000 fine and/or 1 year of imprisonment, typically in a local institution.

misprision of felony The concealment of a felony committed by another.

Missouri Plan A method of selecting judges in which the governor, the bar association, and the voters all participate in the process.

mistrial A trial that has been terminated without a verdict and declared invalid by the court because of some circumstance that creates a substantial and uncorrectable prejudice to the conduct of a fair trial.

M'Naghten Rule The "right-or-wrong" test of criminal responsibility.

Monroe v. *Pape* The Supreme Court ruling that citizens can bring Section 1983 suits against state officials in federal courts without first exhausting state judicial remedies.

Morrissey v. *Brewer* The Supreme Court ruling that a parolee facing revocation is entitled to both a preliminary hearing to determine whether he or she actually violated parole and a final hearing to consider not only the facts in question but also, if there was a violation, what to do about it.

motion An application made to the court or judge requesting an order or ruling in favor of the applicant.

murder The felonious killing of another human being with malice aforethought.

mutual pledge Alfred the Great's system of internal policing that organized people into tithings, hundreds, and shires.

natural law General principles that determine what is right and wrong according to some higher power.

New Jersey v. *T.L.O.* The Supreme Court ruling that school officials, with reasonable grounds to believe that the law or school rules are being violated, may conduct reasonable searches if needed to maintain safety, order, and discipline in a school.

nolle prosequi A formal entry in the record by which the prosecutor declares that he or she "will no further prosecute" the case.

nolo contendere A plea of "no contest" or "I do not wish to contest," with the same implication as a guilty plea.

Omnibus Crime Control and Safe Streets Act A piece of federal law-and-order legislation that was viewed by many as a political maneuver aimed at allaying fears of crime rather than bringing about criminal justice reform.

open institutions "Prisons without walls," such as correctional camps, farms, and ranches.

organized crime Business activities directed toward economic gain through unlawful means.

Palko v. *Connecticut* The Supreme Court ruling that the due process clause of the Fourteenth Amendment does not require the states to observe the double jeopardy guarantee of the Fifth Amendment.

parens patriae A philosophy under which the state takes over the role of parent.

parole The status of being released from a penal or reformatory institution in which one has served a part of his or her maximum sentence, on the condition of maintaining good behavior and remaining in the custody and under the guidance of the institution or some other agency approved by the state until a final discharge is granted.

parole prediction An estimate of probability of violation or nonviolation of parole, based on experience tables, developed with regard to groups of offenders possessing similar characteristics.

Part I offenses Crimes designated by the FBI as the *most serious* and compiled in terms of the number of reports made to law enforcement agencies and the number of arrests made.

Part II offenses Crimes designated by the FBI as *less serious* than the Part I offenses and compiled in terms of the number of arrests made.

patrol A means of deploying police officers that gives them responsibility for policing activity in a defined area and that usually requires them to make regular circuits of that area.

peacekeeping role The legitimate right of police to use force in situations in which urgency requires it.

Pear's Case Legal ruling whereby a person who has legal control of another's property and converts that property so as to deprive the owner of his possessory rights is guilty of larceny.

Pennsylvania Board of Probation and Parole v. *Scott* The Supreme Court ruling that the exclusionary rule does not apply in parole revocation hearings.

petition In juvenile proceedings, a document alleging that a youth is a delinquent, a status offender, or a dependent child and asking that the court assume jurisdiction over the juvenile.

piece-price system A variation of the contract system of prison industry in which the contractor supplies the raw material and receives the finished product, paying the prison a specified amount for each unit produced.

"plain view" doctrine The rule, from the Supreme Court decision in *Harris* v. *United States,* that anything a police officer sees in plain view, when that officer has a right to be where he or she is, is not the product of a search and is therefore admissible as evidence.

plea negotiation The negotiation of an agreement among the prosecutor, the judge, and the accused's attorney as to the charge(s) and sentence imposed if the accused pleads guilty.

police brutality The unlawful use of physical force by officers in the performance of their duties.

police corruption Misconduct by police officers in the forms of illegal activities for economic gain and accepting gratuities, favors, or payment for services that police are sworn to carry out as part of their peace-keeping role.

police cynicism The notion, developed by many officers, that all people are motivated by evil and selfishness.

police discretion The freedom to choose among a variety of alternatives in conducting police operations.

"police presence" The almost continuous presence of police officers in a place of business for the crime deterrent effects it affords.

police professionalism The notion that brutality and corruption are incompetent policing.

police subculture The values and behavior patterns characteristic of experienced police officers.

posse comitatus The able-bodied men of a county who were at the disposal of a sheriff when called for service.

Powell v. Alabama The Supreme Court ruling that an indigent charged in a state court with a capital offense has the right to the assistance of counsel at trial under the due process clause of the Fourteenth Amendment.

premeditation A design or conscious decision to do something before it is actually done.

presentence investigation An investigation into the background and character of a defendant that assists the court in determining the most appropriate sentence.

presentment A written notice of accusation issued by a grand jury, based on its own knowledge and observation.

President's Commission on Law Enforcement and Administration of Justice A series of task forces appointed by President Lyndon B. Johnson to study crime and justice in the United States and to make recommendations for change.

primary deviation The term used in labeling theory to describe the violation of some norm or law.

prisonization The socializing process by which the inmate learns the rules and regulations of the institution and the informal rules, values, customs, and general culture of the penitentiary.

prisons Correctional institutions maintained by federal and state governments for the confinement of convicted felons.

privatization of corrections The construction, staffing, and operation of prisons by private industry for profit.

probable cause Facts or apparent facts that are reliable and generate a reasonable belief that a crime has been committed.

probation A sentence not involving confinement that imposes conditions and retains authority in the sentencing court to modify the conditions of sentence or to resentence the offender if he or she violates the conditions.

procedural due process Due process protection whereby certain procedures are required before the life, liberty, or property of a person may be taken by the government.

Procunier v. Martinez The Supreme Court ruling that prison mail censorship is constitutional only when the practice furthers government interests in security and rehabilitation and when the restrictions are no greater than necessary to satisfy the particular government interest involved.

prosecutor A government attorney who instigates the prosecution of an accused and represents the state at trial.

protective sweep doctrine The rule that when police officers execute an arrest on or outside private premises, they may conduct a warrantless examination of the entire premises for other persons whose presence would pose a threat, either to their safety or to evidence capable of being removed or destroyed.

rape The unlawful carnal knowledge of a female without her consent and against her will.

rape shield statutes Laws that protect alleged rape victims from questioning about evidence of past sexual experiences that are not relevant to the case and that might be prejudicial.

reception center A central receiving institution where all felony offenders sentenced to a term of imprisonment are committed for orientation and classification.

rehabilitation A sentencing philosophy seeking to reintegrate the offender into society.

release on recognizance (ROR) The release of an accused on his or her own obligation rather than on a monetary bond.

restitution A condition of probation requiring offenders to compensate their victims for damages or to donate their time in service to the community.

retribution A sentencing philosophy seeking to create an equal or proportionate relationship between the offense and the punishment.

Rhodes v. Chapman The Supreme Court ruling that cell overcrowding, in and of itself, is neither cruel nor unusual.

robbery The felonious taking of the money or goods of another, from his or her person or in his or her presence and against the individual's will, through the use or threat of force and violence.

Robinson v. California The 1962 ruling whereby the U.S. Supreme Court declared that sickness may not be made a crime nor may sick people be punished for being sick. In a new approach to the Eighth Amendment's ban on "cruel and unusual punishments," the Court viewed narcotic addiction to be a "sickness" and held that a state cannot make it a punishable offense any more than it could put a person in jail "for the 'crime' of having a common cold."

Rochin v. California The Supreme Court ruling that evidence acquired in a manner that "shocks the conscience" is in violation of the Fourth Amendment.

Roper v. Simmons The 2005 Supreme Court decision holding that the imposition of the death penalty on offenders who were under the age of 18 when their crimes were committed violates the Eighth and Fourteenth Amendments. The decision overturned *Stanford* v. *Kentucky,* in which the Court had upheld statutes setting the minimum age for capital punishment at 16.

Ruiz v. Estelle The federal court decision declaring the Texas prison system to be unconstitutional.

Rule of Four The decision of at least four Supreme Court justices that a case merits consideration by the full court.

Schall v. Martin The Supreme Court ruling that preventive detention is permissible for accused juvenile delinquents when there is evidence that the youth presents a serious risk of committing a crime before adjudication of the case.

search and seizure The search for and taking of persons and property as evidence of crime.

search warrant A written order, issued by a magistrate and directed to a law enforcement officer, commanding a search of a specified premises.

secondary deviation The term used in labeling theory to describe the demeanor and conduct that people cultivate as a result of being labeled deviant or criminal.

Section 1983 The section of the Civil Rights Act of 1871 used by state prisoners as a vehicle for access to the federal courts to litigate inmate rights.

self-reported crime Crime statistics compiled on the basis of self-reports by offenders.

separate system A prison system whereby each inmate is kept in solitary confinement in an isolated cell for the purpose of eliminating evil association in congregate quarters.

separation-of-powers doctrine The principle that power is distributed among three branches of government—the legislative, the executive, and the judicial—for the purpose of ensuring that no one person or group will make the law, interpret the law, and apply the law.

sequestration The removal of the jurors (and alternates, if any) from all possible outside influences.

shock incarceration A 3- to 6-month regimen of military drill, drug treatment, physical exercise, hard labor, and academic work in return for having several years removed from an inmate's sentence.

shock probation Brief incarceration followed by suspension of sentence and probation.

silent system A prison system whereby inmates experience confinement under a rigid rule of absolute silence at all times.

Sixth Amendment Amendment to the Constitution guaranteeing the right to:
- A speedy and public trial, by an impartial jury, in the district where the offense was committed.
- Notice of charges.
- Confrontation with witnesses.
- Compulsory process for obtaining witnesses.
- Assistance of counsel.

Social control theory A theory of crime that centers on how individuals are constrained by the social structure and holds that crimes are committed when an individual's attachments to society are weakened.

speedy trial The Sixth Amendment guarantee that protects an accused from indefinite incarceration prior to coming to trial.

Speedy Trial Act A congressional measure that established a 100-day deadline between arrest and trial in federal cases.

Stack v. *Boyle* The Supreme Court ruling that bail set at a figure higher than an amount reasonably calculated to ensure the presence of the accused at trial and at the time of final submission to sentence is "excessive" under the Eighth Amendment.

state account system A form of prison industry in which inmate production is directed by prison officials, goods are sold on the open market, and inmates receive a share of the profits.

state-use system A form of prison industry in which inmate-produced goods are used in state institutions and bureaus.

status offenders Youths who, because of their special status as children, can be brought to the attention of the juvenile courts for certain kinds of noncriminal behavior.

status offense An act declared by statute to be a crime because it violates the standards of behavior expected of children.

statutory law Law created by statute, handed down by legislatures.

substantive due process Due process protection against unreasonable, arbitrary, or capricious laws or acts.

supermax prisons Highly restrictive, high-custody housing units within a secure facility (or an entire secure facility) that isolate inmates from the general prison population and from each other due to especially serious crimes, violent institutional behavior, the threat of (or actual) escape, or inciting prison disturbances.

surety A third party who posts a bond for an accused.

suspended sentence A court disposition of a convicted person, pronouncing a penalty of a fine or commitment to confinement but unconditionally discharging the defendant or holding execution of the penalty in abeyance upon good behavior.

Tennessee v. *Garner* Supreme Court decision stating that deadly force against a fleeing felon is proper only when it is necessary to prevent the escape *and* when there is probable cause to believe that the suspect poses a significant threat to the officers or others.

terrorism The systematic use or threat of extreme violence directed against actual or symbolic victims, typically performed for psychological rather than material effects, for the purpose of coercing individuals, groups, communities, or governments into making political or tactical concessions.

Terry v. *Ohio* The Supreme Court ruling that when a police officer observes unusual conduct and suspects a crime is about to be committed, he may frisk a suspect's outer clothing for dangerous weapons.

Texas Rangers Founded by Stephen F. Austin in 1823, the first territorial police agency in the United States.

theft The unlawful taking, possession, or use of another's property, without the use or threat of force, and with the intent to deprive permanently.

thief-takers Citizens who received a reward for the apprehension of a criminal.

Thornburgh v. *Abbott* The Supreme Court ruling that federal prison regulations restricting prisoners' receipt of publications from outside prison pass First Amendment muster if they are reasonably related to legitimate penological interests.

ticket-of-leave Started by Sir Walter Crofton of Ireland, a system of conditional release from prison that represented an early form of parole.

Tison v. *Arizona* The Supreme Court ruling that a "nontriggerman" who does not intend to commit murder may be executed when he or she participates in a felony that leads to murder and is found to have exhibited "reckless indifference" for human life.

total institutions Places that furnish barriers to social interchange with the world at large.

transactional immunity Immunity against prosecution given to a grand jury witness in return for testifying.

trial *de novo* A new trial, on appeal from a lower court to a court of general jurisdiction.

true bill A grand jury's endorsement of the charge or charges specified in the prosecutor's bill.

truth in sentencing Laws that require offenders to serve a substantial portion of their sentences.

Uniform Crime Reports (UCR) The annual publication of the FBI, presenting official statistics on the rates and trends in crime in the United States.

United States v. *Calandra* The Supreme Court ruling that refused to extend the exclusionary rule to grand jury questions based on illegally seized evidence.

United States v. *Leon* The Supreme Court ruling that the Fourth Amendment exclusionary rule does not bar the use of evidence obtained by police officers acting in objectively reasonable reliance on a search warrant issued by a magistrate but ultimately found to be unsupported by probable cause.

United States* v. *Wade The Supreme Court ruling that a police lineup identification of a suspect made without the suspect's attorney present is inadmissible as evidence at trial.

USA Patriot Act A federal administrative law passed by Congress in the wake of the September 11, 2001, terrorist attacks to better enable law enforcement officials to track and punish those responsible for terrorism and to protect U.S. citizens and property against further attacks.

U.S. courts of appeals The federal courts of appellate jurisdiction.

U.S. district courts The trial courts of the federal judiciary.

use immunity A limited immunity that prohibits the government only from using a grand jury witness's compelled testimony in a subsequent criminal proceeding.

U.S. magistrates Federal lower-court officials whose powers are limited to trying lesser misdemeanors, setting bail, and assisting district courts in various legal matters.

U.S. Supreme Court The highest court in the nation and the court of last resort.

vengeance A sentencing philosophy seeking satisfaction from knowing or seeing that offenders are punished.

venire A writ that summons jurors.

vicarious liability The doctrine under which liability is imposed upon an employer for the acts of employees that are committed in the course and scope of their employment.

victim impact evidence A statement of the harm suffered by the victim or the victim's family as a result of the offender's action.

victimization surveys Surveys of the victims of crime based on interviews with representative samples of the household population.

vigilante justice Extralegal criminal justice activities by individuals or groups who take the law into their own hands for the sake of establishing "law and order."

void-for-vagueness doctrine The rule that criminal laws that are unclear or uncertain as to *what* or to *whom* they apply violate due process.

voir dire An oath sworn by a juror regarding his or her qualifications.

waiver of jurisdiction The process by which the juvenile court relinquishes its jurisdiction over a child and transfers the case to a court of criminal jurisdiction for prosecution as an adult.

Walnut Street Jail The first American penitentiary.

Warren Court The Supreme Court under the leadership of Chief Justice Earl Warren.

Weeks* v. *United States The Supreme Court ruling that a person whose Fourth Amendment rights of security against unreasonable search and seizure are violated by federal agents has the right to require that evidence obtained in the search be excluded from use against him or her in federal courts.

Weems* v. *United States The Supreme Court ruling that a sentence disproportionate of the offense is in violation of the Eighth Amendment ban against cruel and unusual punishment.

white-collar crime Offenses committed by persons acting in their legitimate occupational roles.

Williams* v. *New York The Supreme Court ruling that at sentencing, the defendant does not have a Sixth Amendment right to cross-examine persons who have supplied information to the court (in a presentence report) regarding sentencing.

Wilson* v. *Seiter The Supreme Court ruling that an inmate alleging that the conditions of his or her confinement violate the Eighth Amendment's prohibition against cruel and unusual punishment must show deliberate indifference on the part of the responsible prison officials.

Witherspoon* v. *Illinois The Supreme Court ruling that states cannot exclude from juries in capital cases *all* persons opposed to the death penalty.

Wolff* v. *McDonnell The Supreme Court ruling that the due process clause of the Fourteenth Amendment protects, in part, state prisoners facing loss of good-time credit or punitive confinement.

working personality A personality characterized by authoritarianism, cynicism, and suspicion, developed by police officers in response to danger and the obligation to exercise authority.

writ of *certiorari* A writ issued by the Supreme Court ordering some lower court to "forward up the record" of a case it has tried so the High Court can review it.

writ of *mandamus* A command issued by a court to perform a certain duty.

PHOTO CREDITS

Chapter 1 p. 2, 4L, © AP/Wide World Photos; p. 4R, ©Hulton Archive/Getty Images; p. 6, © Bettmann/Corbis; p. 7, © Daniel Leclair/Reuters/ Corbis; p. 10, 11, © AP/Wide World Photos; p. 12, © Bettmann/Corbis; p. 14, © Hutchinson Samuel/Corbis Sygma; p. 15, © Earl S. Cryer/ZUMA Press; p. 17T, © 1998 Alon Reininger/Contact Press Images; p. 17M, © Ralph Orlowski/Getty Images; p. 17B, © Jeremiah Trimble; p. 19, © China Photos/Getty Images; p. 21, 23, © AP/Wide World Photos

Chapter 2 p. 26, © AP/Wide World Photos; p. 28, © John Kral/Miami Herald; p. 29, © Universal/Courtest Everett Collection; p. 32L, © 1989 The Detroit News; p. 32R, © Culver Pictures; p. 33L, © Tony Savino/Sipa Press; p. 33R, © Dave G. Houser/Corbis; p. 35, © AP/Wide World Photos; p. 42, © Corbis Sygma; p. 44, © AP/Wide World Photos; p. 48, © Betttmann/Corbis; p. 53, 54, 61, © AP/Wide World Photos; p. 62, © John Kral/Miami Herald

Chapter 3 p. 66, 20th Century Fox/ The Kobal Collection; p. 68, © AP/Wide World Photos; p. 69, © Alon Reininger/ Contact Press Images; p. 70, © AP/Wide World Photos; p. 71, © Handout/Sedgwick County Sheriff's Office/Reuters/ Corbis; p. 73, © Graeme Robertson/ Getty Images; p. 75, 76, 82, 86, © AP/ Wide World Photos; p. 88, © Ted Soqui/ Corbis Sygma; p. 89, © Sipa Press; p. 93, © AP/Wide World Photos; p. 94, © Anthony Neste/HBO/The Kobal Collection; p. 96, © AP/Wide World Photos

Chapter 4 p. 100, © Steve Crise/Corbis; p. 102, © AP/Wide World Photos; p. 103, © Henry Guttmann Collection/ Hulton/Getty Images; p. 104, PhotoDisc/Getty Images; p. 108, © 1999 Daily News, L.P.; p. 109, © AP/Wide World Photos; p. 110, © Reuters/Corbis; p. 113, © Alan Thornton/Getty Images/Stone; p. 115, © Royalty-Free/Corbis; p. 116, 117, 118, © AP/Wide World Photos; p. 120, Courtesy of the author; p. 122, © AP/Wide World Photos

Chapter 5 p. 128, © AP/Wide World Photos; p. 129, © The Granger Collection, New York; p. 135, 136, © AP/Wide World Photos; p. 138, © Mark Perlstein/ New York Times; p. 139, © Juan Carlo

Ulate/Reuters/Corbis; p. 142, © Reuters/ Corbis; p. 148, © AP/Wide World Photos; p. 149, © Spencer Grant/PhotoEdit; p. 153, 154, © AP/Wide World Photos

Chapter 6 p. 158, Everett Collection; p. 160, © Richard E. Beauchesne; p. 161, © Bettmann/Corbis; p. 162, 164, © Culver Pictures; p. 165T, Library of Congress; p. 165B, © Bettmann/Corbis; p. 166, Pinkerton Archives; p. 167, Library of Congress; p. 168, © Bettmann/Corbis; p. 170, Courtesy of the author; p. 171, © AP/Wide World Photos; p. 172L, © Bettmann/Corbis; p. 172R, © Corbis; p. 173, © The New York Times; p. 174, 175T, © AP/Wide World Photos; p. 175B, © Lou Toman/Corbis Sygma; p. 177, © Scala/Art Resource, NY; p. 178, © Bettmann/Corbis; p. 180, Courtesy of the author; p. 185, © Albert Davis Collection/Hulton/Getty Images; p. 186, © Richard E. Beauchesne

Chapter 7 p. 190, © Bob Daemmrich/ Stock Boston; p. 192, © Will Hart/NBC/ Courtesy Everett Collection; p. 193, © Ron Chapple/Getty Images/Taxi; p. 195, © AP/Wide World Photos; p. 196, © Richard Lord/The Image Works; p. 197, © AP/Wide World Photos; p. 202, Courtesy of the author; p. 203, © Rich Meyer/Corbis; p. 204, © AP/ Wide World Photos; p. 205, © Reuters/ Corbis; p. 207, 208, © AP/Wide World Photos; p. 209, © Norman Y. Lono; p. 212, © Reuters/Corbis; p. 213, © Topical Press Agency/Hulton/Getty Images; p. 214, © Bob Daemmrich/The Image Works; p. 218, © Dwayne Newton/ PhotoEdit; p. 222L, © Will Hart/NBC/ Courtesy Everett Collection; p. 222R, © AP/Wide World Photos

Chapter 8 p. 226, © Mike Karlsson/ Arresting Images; p. 228, © AP/Wide World Photos; p. 230, © Mike Karlsson/ Arresting Images; p. 233, © Spencer Grant/PhotoEdit; p. 237, © Justin Sullivan/Getty Images; p. 239, 241, © AP/Wide World Photos; p. 245, © Michael Connor/The Washington Times; p. 247, © AP/Wide World Photos; p. 250, © Mike Karlsson/Arresting Images; p. 252, 253, © AP/Wide World Photos; p. 254, © T. Cenicola/New York Times; p. 257, © AP/Wide World Photos; p. 258, © Paul Morrell/Getty Im-

ages/Stone; p. 260, © AP/Wide World Photos

Chapter 9 p. 264, © AP/Wide World Photos; p. 266T, Photo by Eric Johnson copyright 2003, The Virgin Islands Daily News. Reprinted with permission.; p. 268T, © The Granger Collection, New York; p. 268B, 273, 275, 276, © AP/Wide World Photos, p. 278, © Mark Richards/ PhotoEdit; p. 281, © AP/Wide World Photos; p. 282, © Bettmann/Corbis; p. 286, © AP/Wide World Photos; p. 288, © Jonathan Nourok/PhotoEdit; p. 290, Photo by Eric Johnson copyright 2003, The Virgin Islands Daily News. Reprinted with permission.

Chapter 10 p. 296, © Royalty-Free/Corbis; p. 298, © AP/Wide World Photos; p. 299, © Lindsay Hebberd/Corbis; p. 304, © Corbis; p. 395, © Bettmann/ Corbis; p. 307, 310, 313, © AP/Wide World Photos; p. 318, © Erich Salomon/ Magnum Photos; p. 322, 324, © AP/ Wide World Photos

Chapter 11 p. 328, © NBC/Courtesy Everett Collection; p. 330, © Jose Luis Pelaez/Corbis; p. 332, © AP/Wide World Photos; p. 333, © Jaime Razuri/AFP/Getty Images; p. 336, 337, 338, © AP/Wide World Photos; p. 343, © Michael Newman/PhotoEdit; p. 347, © Western History Collections, University of Oklahoma Library; p. 349, © AP/ Wide World Photos; p. 351, © Nancy Kaszerman/Corbis; p. 353, © Bettmann/ Corbis; p. 357, © Flip Schulke/Getty Images/Time Life Pictures; p. 359, © Tracy Woodward/Corbis; p. 364, © AP/Wide World Photos; p. 366, © Jose Luis Pelaez/Corbis

Chapter 12 p. 370, Nick Koudis/Getty Images; p. 372, © CBS/Courtesy Everett Collection; p. 375, Courtesy of the author; p. 378, © Reuters/Corbis; p. 379, © A. Ramey/PhotoEdit; p. 388, © AP/ Wide World Photos; p. 391, © Richard Cummins/Corbis; p. 396, © Alan Klehr/ Getty Images/Stone; p. 406, © AP/Wide World Photos; p. 407, © CBS/Courtesy Everett Collection

Chapter 13 p. 412, © Warner Brothers/ Courtesy Everett Collection; p. 414 © Greg Smith/Corbis; p. 416, © AP/ Wide World Photos; p. 422, © Tim Zielenbach/AFP/Getty Images; p. 424,

© AP/Wide World Photos; p. 426, © Eastcott/Momatiuk/Woodfin Camp and Associates p. 429, © AP/Wide World Photos; p. 431, © Corbis; p. 432, © The Granger Collection, New York; p. 437T, © Daytona Beach News Journal/Corbis Sygma; p. 437B, © Newmarket/Courtesy Everett Collection; p. 438, © Bettmann/Corbis; p. 439, © Corbis; p. 442, © Eddie Adams/Getty Images/Time Life Pictures; p. 444, © AP/Wide World Photos; p. 448, © AFP/Getty Images; p. 452, © Greg Smith/Corbis; p. 453, © AP/Wide World Photos

Chapter 14 p. 460, © Bettmann/Corbis; p. 462 Courtesy of the author; p. 463, © Bettmann/Corbis; p. 464, © Paul A. Souders/Corbis; p. 468 © H. Armstrong Roberts; p. 471 © Culver Pictures; p. 472T, © Hulton Archive/Getty Images; p. 472B, © Catherine Karnow; p. 473, © Nathan Lazarnick/Getty Images; p. 476, © Bettmann/Corbis; p. 478, © Culver Pictures; p. 480, © Bettmann/Corbis; p. 481, © Special to the Dallas Morning News/Rick White; p. 483, Courtesy Photography Unit, New York City Municipal Archives/Department of Records; p. 484T, © Rick Friedman/Black Star; p. 484B 486, © AP/Wide World Photos; p. 487T, Courtesy of the author; p. 487B, © Nik Wheeler/Corbis

Chapter 15 p. 490, 492, © AP/Wide World Photos; p. 493, © Spencer Ainsley/Poughkeepsie Journal; p. 495, © Chuck Bigger; p. 497, © Shepard Sherbell/Corbis SABA; p. 498, © AP/Wide World Photos; p. 499, © Hulton Archive/Getty Images; p. 503, 506, © AP/Wide World Photos; p. 507, © Joseph Rodriguez/Black Star; p. 511T, © Robert McElroy/Newsweek; p. 511B, © AP/Wide World Photos; p. 513, Courtesy of the author; p. 515, © J. Crawford/The Image Works; p. 516, © AP/Wide World Photos; p. 517, © Bentley/Black Star; p. 521, © Reuters/Corbis; p. 526, © Steve Starr/Corbis; p. 527, © AP/Wide World Photos

Chapter 16 p. 532, © A. Ramey/PhotoEdit; p. 534, 536, © AP/Wide World Photos; p. 537, © Bettmann/Corbis; p. 539, Courtesy of the author; p. 546, 548L, © AP/Wide World Photos; p. 548R, © Reuters/Corbis; p. 549, © JP Laffont/Sygma/Corbis; p. 551, © David R. Frazier/Getty Images/Stone; p. 554, © Alon Reininger/Contact Press Images; p. 555, © AP/Wide World Photos; p. 557T, © Greg Smith/Corbis; p. 557B, © Steve Northup/Time Life Pictures/Getty Images; p. 559, 563, © AP/Wide World Photos

Chapter 17 p. 566, © Fiona Hanson/PA/EMPICS; p. 568, © Bonnie Kamin; p. 574, © AP/Wide World Photos; p. 579, © Mike Karlsson/Arresting Images; p. 582, © AP/Wide World Photos; p. 589, © Sipa Press; p. 594, 597, © AP/Wide World Photos; p. 602L, © Bonnie Kamin; p. 602R, © Sacramento Bee/Renee C. Byer

Chapter 18 p. 608, © A. Ramey/PhotoEdit; p. 610, © Robin Nelson/PhotoEdit; p. 611, © Dorothy Littell/Stock Boston; p. 612, Courtesy New York State Library; p. 613, © Tom Carter/PhotoEdit; p. 615, © Michael Newman/PhotoEdit; p. 622, © Bob Daemmrich/Stock Boston; p. 623, 625, 627, © AP/Wide World Photos; p. 629, © A. Ramey/PhotoEdit; p. 630, © Steve Kagan/New York Times; p. 632, © Robin Nelson/PhotoEdit

Endpapers Front, © Underwood & Underwood/Corbis; Back, © Bettmann/Corbis

CASE INDEX

Abbate v. *United States,* 387, 410n35
Abel v. *United States,* 241, 262n51
Adams v. *New York,* 243, 262n59
Aguilar v. *Texas,* 230, 231, 262n7
Alabama v. *Shelton,* 358, 368n59
Appleton v. *State,* 262n16
Argersinger v. *Hamlin,* 356–357, 368n51
Ashford v. *Thornton,* 130

Baldwin v. *New York,* 394, 410n59
Ballew v. *Georgia,* 410n61
Barber v. *State,* 604n33
Barefoot v. *Estelle,* 446, 456n94
Barker v. *Wingo,* 390, 391, 410n49
Barron v. *Baltimore,* 132, 156n8
Batson v. *Kentucky,* 395, 410n68
Bauer v. *Sielaff,* 551, 565n59
Bearden v. *Georgia,* 419, 455n12
Beavers v. *Haubert,* 390, 410n48
Bell v. *Wolfish,* 556, 565n79
Benton v. *Maryland,* 136, 137, 156n32, 387, 410n38
Betts v. *Brady,* 354, 355, 368n43
Blake v. *Los Angeles,* 213, 225n40
Booth v. *Maryland,* 149
Bordenkircher v. *Hayes,* 342, 368n23
Bounds v. *Smith,* 541, 565n21
Bowers v. *Hardwick,* 81, 97n24, 137, 156n35
Brady v. *Maryland,* 387, 410n40
Brady v. *United States,* 342, 368n19
Bram v. *United States,* 263n86
Branch v. *Texas,* 433, 455n61
Branzburg v. *Hayes,* 383, 410n25
Breed v. *Jones,* 619, 634n13
Brinegar v. *United States,* 156n46
Brown v. *Mississippi,* 250–251, 263n84, 274, 292n25
Buck v. *Bell,* 138–139, 156n41
Bumper v. *North Carolina,* 240, 262n41
Burdeau v. *McDowell,* 240, 262n46

California v. *Acevedo,* 237, 262n29
California v. *Greenwood,* 241, 262n52
California v. *Hodari D.,* 235, 262n20
California v. *Stewart,* 253, 263n94
Cantwell v. *Connecticut,* 156n18
Carnley v. *Cochran,* 368n44
Carothers v. *Follette,* 544, 565n32
Carroll v. *United States,* 236, 262n24
Chambers v. *Maroney,* 262n26
Chapman v. *California,* 449, 456n106
Chicago, Burlington & Quincy Railroad Co. v. *City of Chicago,* 381
Childs v. *Duckworth,* 565n30
Chimel v. *California,* 232, 262n12

Clemmons v. *Bohannon,* 551
Coates v. *City of Cincinnati,* 156n38
Coffin v. *Reichard,* 538, 564n8
Coker v. *Georgia,* 435, 455n66, 624, 634n26
Coleman v. *Alabama,* 356, 368n50
Commonwealth v. *Moreira,* 233
Connally v. *Georgia,* 326n9
Cooke v. *Tramburg,* 565n27
Coolidge v. *New Hampshire,* 247, 263n73
Cooper v. *Pate,* 539, 565n11
Costello v. *United States,* 382, 410n21
Costello v. *Wainwright,* 554, 565n67
Cox v. *Louisiana,* 156n40
Cox v. *States,* 604n22
Crooker v. *California,* 252–254, 263n90
Cruz v. *Beto,* 543, 565n29

Daniels v. *Commonwealth,* 475
Dartmouth College v. *Woodward,* 156n37
Daubert v. *Merrell Dow Pharmaceuticals,* 350, 368n35
Davidson v. *New Orleans,* 381
Delaware v. *Prouse,* 238, 260, 262n30, 450, 456n109
Delo v. *Lashley,* 446, 456n100
Dickerson v. *United States,* 255, 256
Doe v. *Ashcroft,* 154, 156n53
Doe v. *Coughlin,* 475, 530n52
Douglas v. *California,* 355, 368n48
Downum v. *United States,* 387, 389, 410n39
Duckworth v. *Eagan,* 255, 256
Dumbra v. *United States,* 262n6
Duncan v. *Louisiana,* 156n31, 392, 393–394, 410n54, 410n57
Durham v. *United States,* 38, 64n18

Echols v. *State,* 634n25
Edwards v. *Balisok,* 539–540, 565n13
Elkins v. *United States,* 245, 262n66
Enmund v. *Florida,* 72
Escobedo v. *Illinois,* 252, 253, 263n93, 321, 327n29, 356, 368n49, 388, 410n42
Estelle v. *Gamble,* 546, 561, 565n43
Everson v. *Board of Education,* 156n20
Ewing v. *California,* 421

Faretta v. *California,* 359
Fierro v. *Gomez,* 456n71
Fiske v. *Kansas,* 134, 156n14
Florida v. *Bostick,* 240, 241, 262n45
Florida v. *Brooks,* 274, 292n26
Florida v. *Jimeno,* 240, 262n44
Foster v. *California,* 256, 263n100

Fulwood v. *Clemmer,* 542, 565n25
Furman v. *Georgia,* 433–434, 441, 443–444, 445, 455n61

Gagnon v. *Scarpelli,* 583, 585, 604n46
Gardner v. *Florida,* 576, 604n19
Gary v. *Netherland,* 446, 456n101
Gates v. *Collier,* 565n44
Gault, In re, 619, 620, 634n11
Georgia v. *Sims,* 274, 292n26
Gideon v. *Wainwright,* 137, 156n25, 354–356, 357, 368n45, 449, 456n105
Gitlow v. *New York,* 134, 156n13
Godfrey v. *Georgia,* 435, 456n68
Greenholtz v. *Inmates of Nebraska Penal and Correctional Complex,* 588, 604n69
Greenwald v. *Wisconsin,* 274, 292n26
Gregg v. *Georgia,* 434–435, 445, 455n62
Gresham v. *Harcourt,* 456n108
Griffin v. *Illinois,* 456n102
Griffin v. *Wisconsin,* 577, 604n32
Griggs v. *Duke Power Co.,* 213, 225n39
Griswold v. *Connecticut,* 137, 156n33

Hale v. *Henkel,* 382, 410n20
Hamilton v. *Alabama,* 368n44
Hamilton v. *Regents of the University of California,* 156n17
Hampton v. *United States,* 41, 64n26
Harris v. *New York,* 255, 256
Harris v. *State,* 262n14
Harris v. *United States,* 242, 262n55
Henderson v. *Morgan,* 368n21
Herrera v. *Collins,* 446, 456n99
Hester v. *United States,* 242, 262n53
Hiibel v. *Nevada,* 236, 262n23
Hill v. *California,* 455n39
Holt v. *Sarver,* 549, 565n54
Hope v. *Pelzer,* 553
Hopt v. *Utah,* 248, 263n80
Howard v. *Smyth,* 565n26
Hudson v. *Palmer,* 560, 565n81
Hudson v. *Parker,* 374, 409n3
Hull, Ex parte, 540, 565n15
Hurtado v. *California,* 132–134, 156n10, 381, 410n19
Husty v. *United States,* 262n25
Hyland v. *Procunier,* 591, 604n77

Illinois v. *Gates,* 230, 231, 262n8
Illinois v. *Krull,* 248, 263n78
Illinois v. *Lafayette,* 241, 262n49
Illinois v. *Lidster,* 239, 262n33
Illinois v. *Wardlow,* 235, 262n21
Indianapolis v. *Edmond,* 238, 262n32

645

SUBJECT INDEX